InuYasha

Volume 37
Metamorphosis

Volume 38
The Wind

Volume 39
Changing Shard

Story & Art by
Rumiko Takahashi

Shonen Sunday Manga / VIZBIG Edition

CONTENTS

❧

Cast of Characters..............................6

Volume 37: Metamorphosis

Scroll One: Hitokon 11
Scroll Two: Memories of a Father 29
Scroll Three: Hidden Feelings..................47
Scroll Four: Escape 65
Scroll Five: Goryomaru's Identity...............83
Scroll Six: Metamorphosis 103
Scroll Seven: The Vanished Demonic Energy..........121
Scroll Eight: The Vessel..................139
Scroll Nine: The Location of the Infant...............157
Scroll Ten: Kagura's Decision 175

Volume 38: The Wind

Scroll One: Hakudoshi's Scheme 197
Scroll Two: Hakudoshi's End 215
Scroll Three: Kagura's Heart..................233
Scroll Four: Pain Without End.................251
Scroll Five: Siblings 269
Scroll Six: The Wind...............287
Scroll Seven: The Hole in Her Chest................305
Scroll Eight: The Same Soul 325
Scroll Nine: Mission.................343
Scroll Ten: The Orochi's Lair................361

Volume 39: Changing Shard

Scroll One: Changing Shard 383
Scroll Two: The Burial Ground of the Wolves 401
Scroll Three: The Guardian of the Treasure 419
Scroll Four: Goraishi..437
Scroll Five: Mujina 455
Scroll Six: Causes..473
Scroll Seven: Dakki...491
Scroll Eight: Toshu...509
Scroll Nine: Ryujin's Shield...527
Scroll Ten: The Wielder of Dakki 545

Original Cover Art Gallery..565
Coming Next Volume 568

CAST OF CHARACTERS

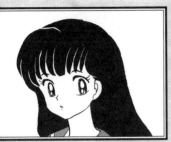

Kagome

A modern-day Japanese schoolgirl who is the reincarnation of Kikyo, the priestess who imprisoned Inuyasha for fifty years with her enchanted arrow. As Kikyo's reincarnation, Kagome has the power to see the Shikon Jewel shards.

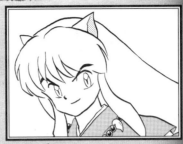

Inuyasha

A half-human, half-demon hybrid, Inuyasha has doglike ears and demonic strength. He assists Kagome in her search for the shards of the Shikon Jewel, mostly because a charmed necklace allows Kagome to restrain him with a single word.

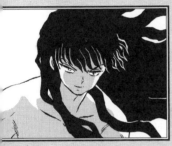

Naraku

This enigmatic demon is responsible for both Miroku's curse and for turning Kikyo and Inuyasha against each other.

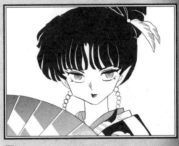

Kagura

Kagura was produced as a doppelganger from part of Naraku's body. Kagura inherited her abilities from a demon that controlled the wind.

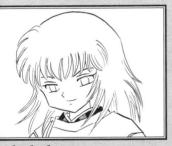

Hakudoshi

Hakudoshi is the eighth incarnation of Naraku, split off from the body of the Infant that houses Naraku's heart.

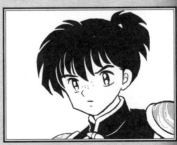

Kohaku

Naraku controlled Kohaku with a Shikon shard, then resurrected him after he was killed and used him as a puppet. Kohaku has regained his memories and is trying to redeem himself.

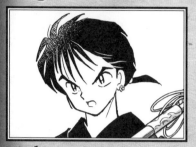

Miroku

An easygoing Buddhist priest of questionable morals. Miroku bears a curse passed down from his grandfather and is searching for the demon Naraku, who first inflicted the curse.

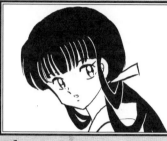

Kikyo

A village priestess who was the original protector the Shikon Jewel. She died fifty years ago.

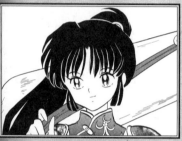

Sango

A proud Demon Slayer from the village where the first Shikon Jewel was born. Her clan and family lost, she fights on against the demonic Naraku along with Inuyasha.

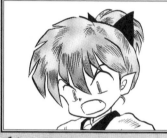

Shippo

A young orphan fox demon. The mischievous Shippo enjoys goading Inuyasha and playing tricks with his shape-shifting abilities.

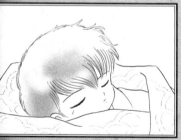

The Infant

Naraku's heart is safely housed inside the body of the Infant that he created. The Infant enables Naraku to avoid being influenced by the heart's feelings and to survive even if his primary body is killed.

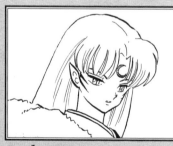

Sesshomaru

Inuyasha's half brother by the same demon father, Sesshomaru is a pureblood demon who covets the sword left to Inuyasha by their father.

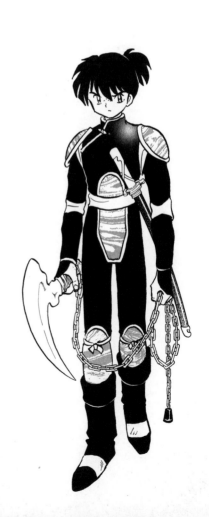

InuYasha

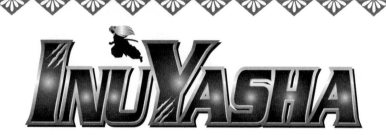

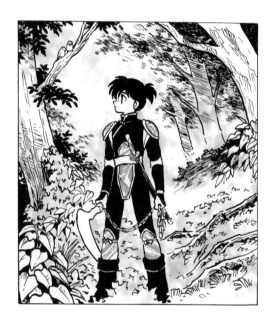

Volume 37
Metamorphosis

SCROLL ONE
HITOKON

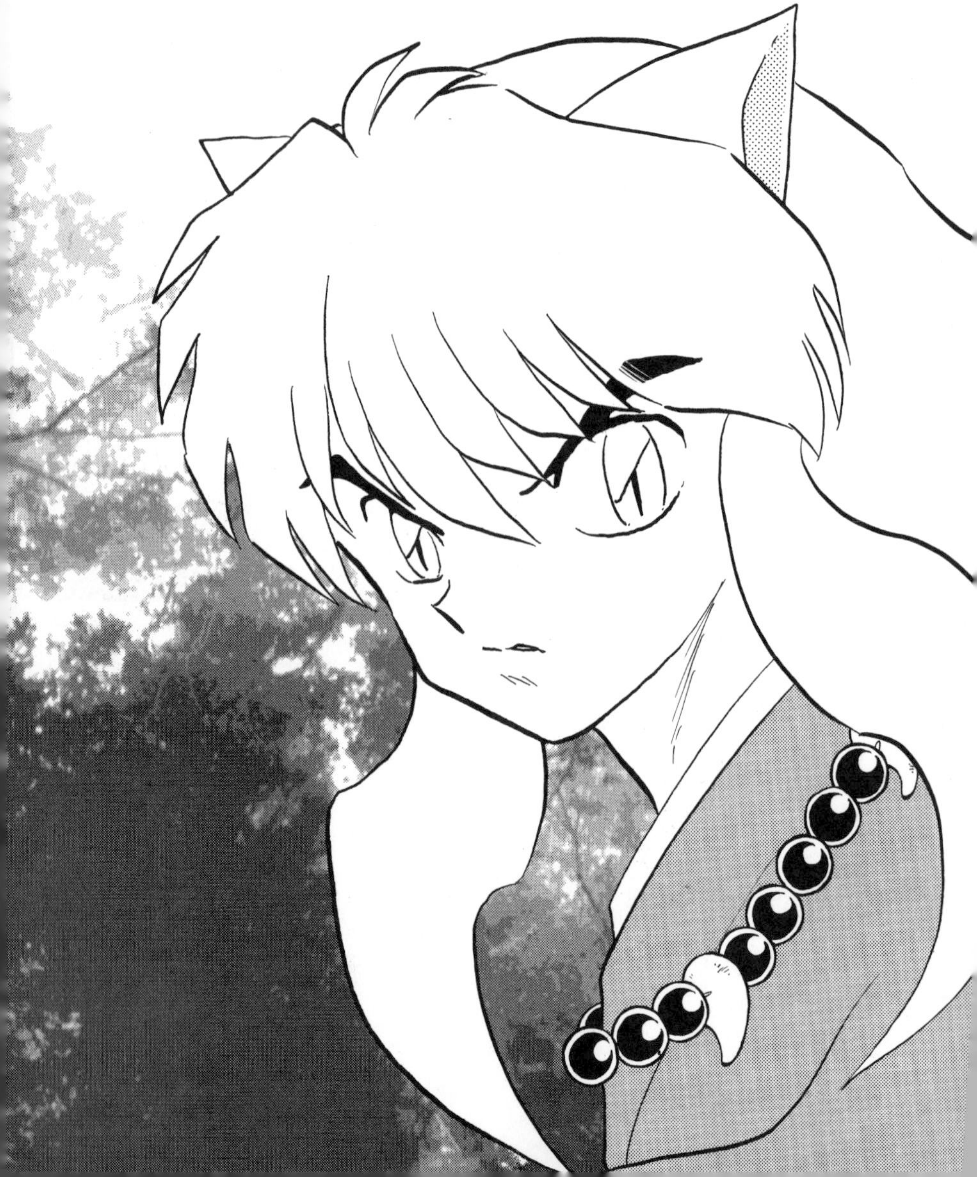

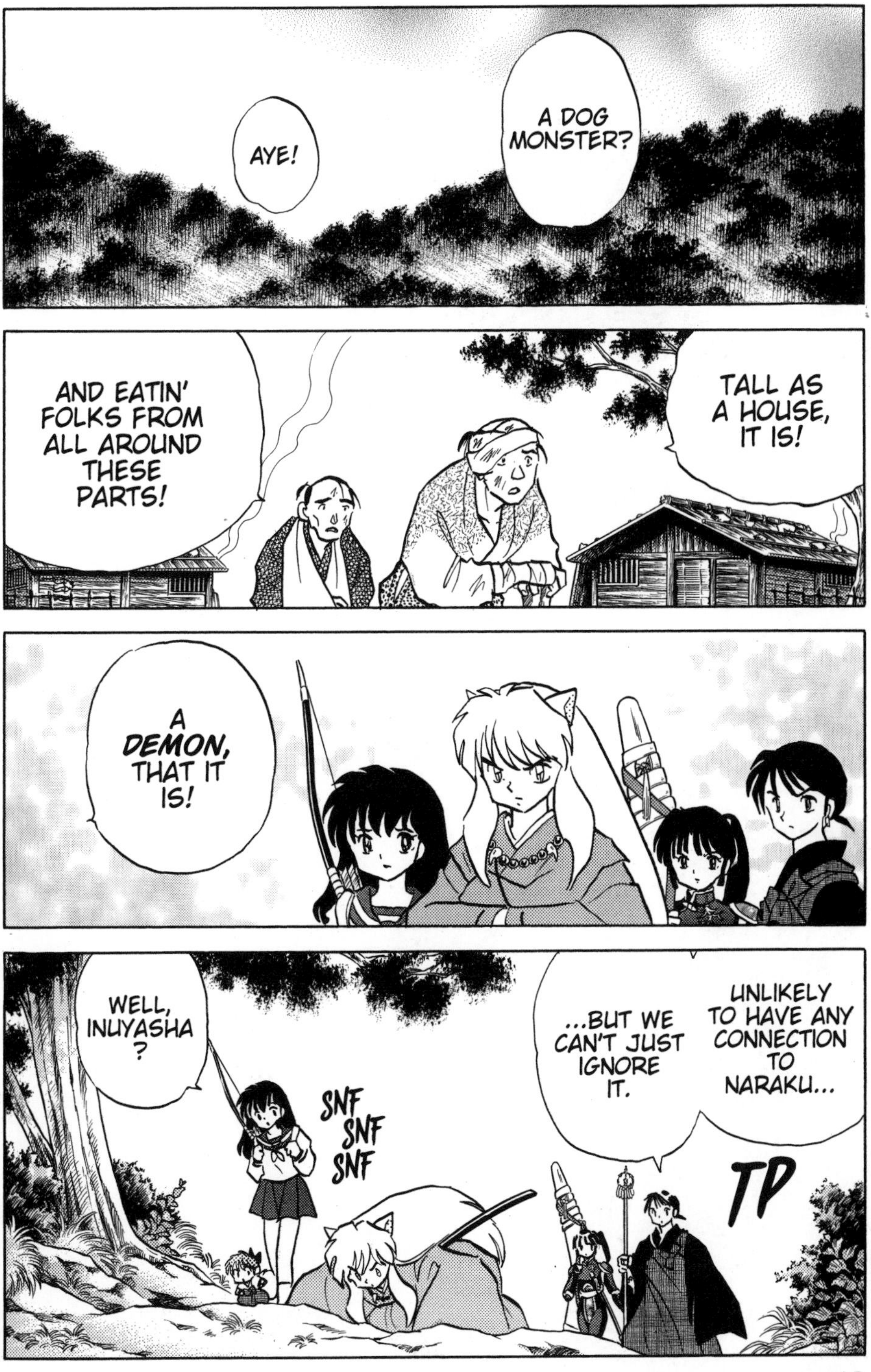
A DOG MONSTER?
AYE!
TALL AS A HOUSE, IT IS!
AND EATIN' FOLKS FROM ALL AROUND THESE PARTS!
A DEMON, THAT IT IS!
UNLIKELY TO HAVE ANY CONNECTION TO NARAKU...
...BUT WE CAN'T JUST IGNORE IT.
TP
SNF SNF SNF
WELL, INUYASHA?

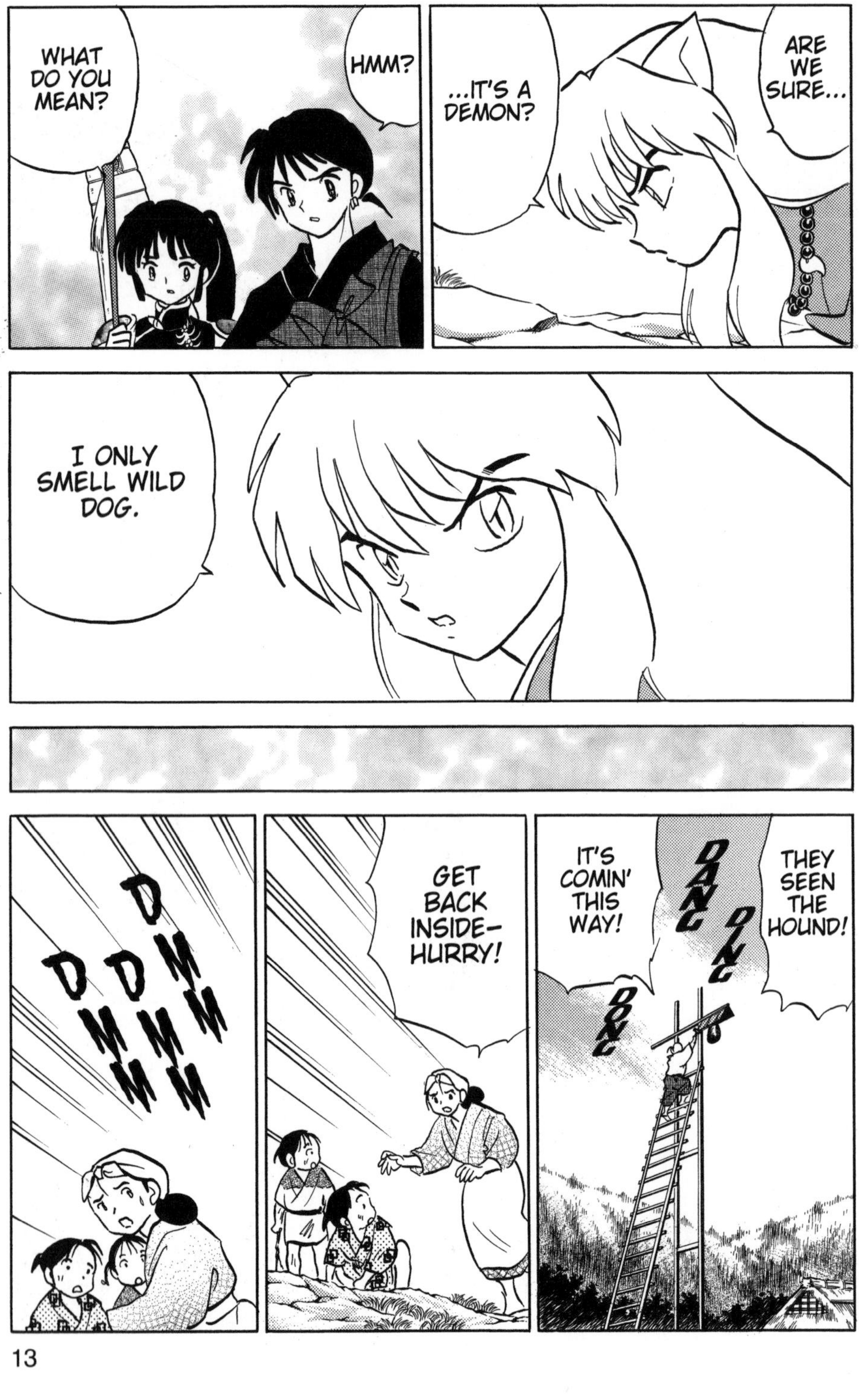
ARE WE SURE...
...IT'S A DEMON?
HMM?
WHAT DO YOU MEAN?
I ONLY SMELL WILD DOG.
THEY SEEN THE HOUND!
DANG
DING
DONG
IT'S COMIN' THIS WAY!
GET BACK INSIDE-HURRY!
DMMM
DMMM
DMMM

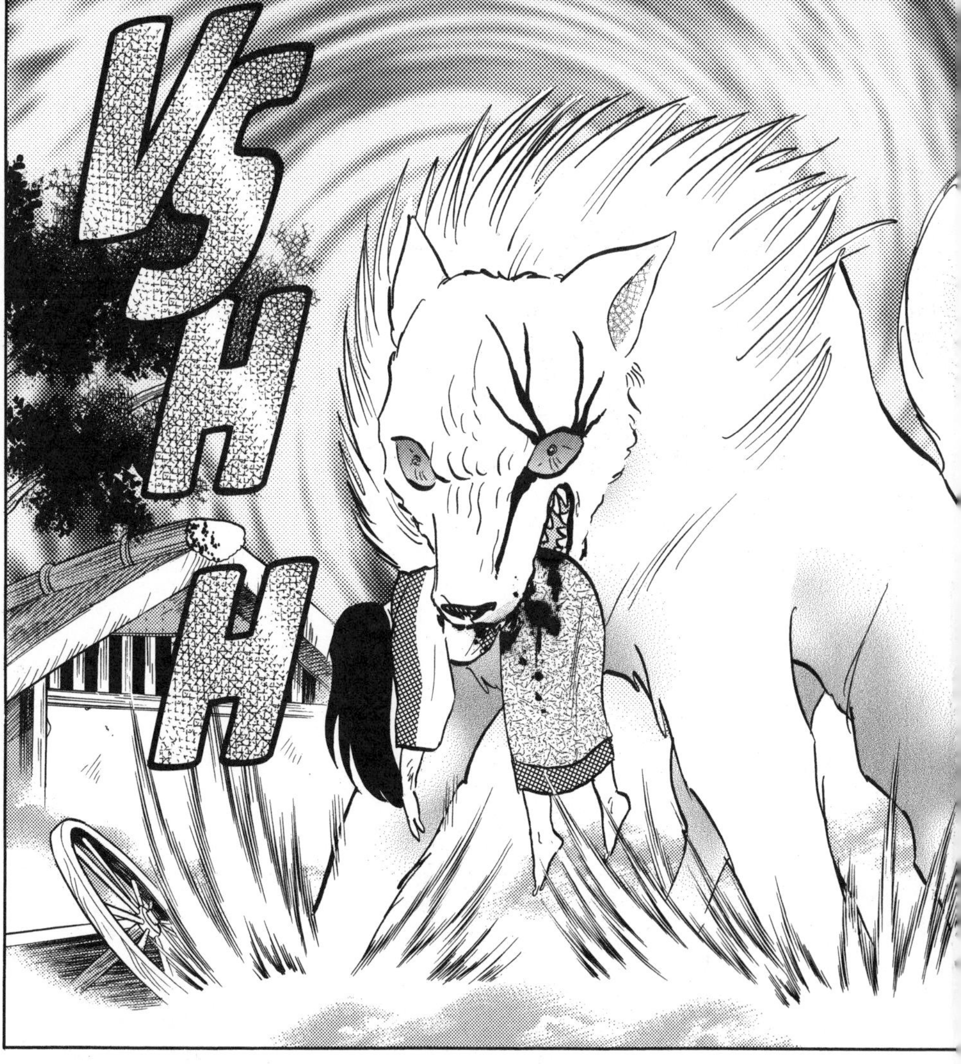
VSHHH
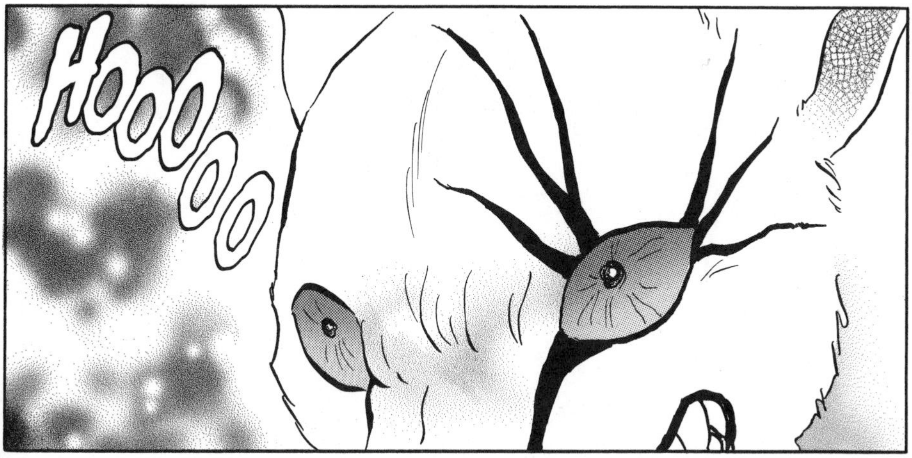
HOOOOO

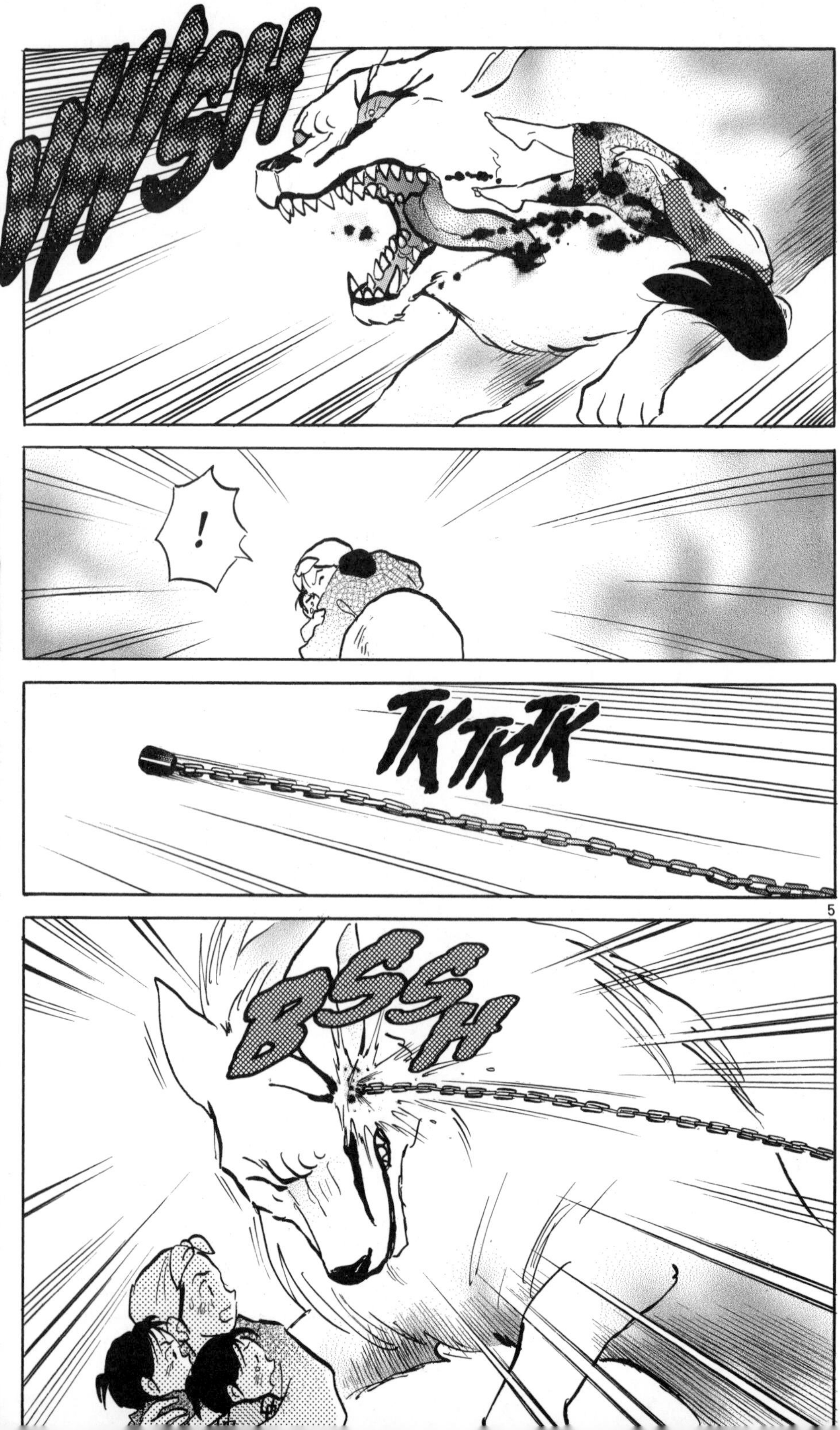
WHSH
!
TKTKTK
BSSH

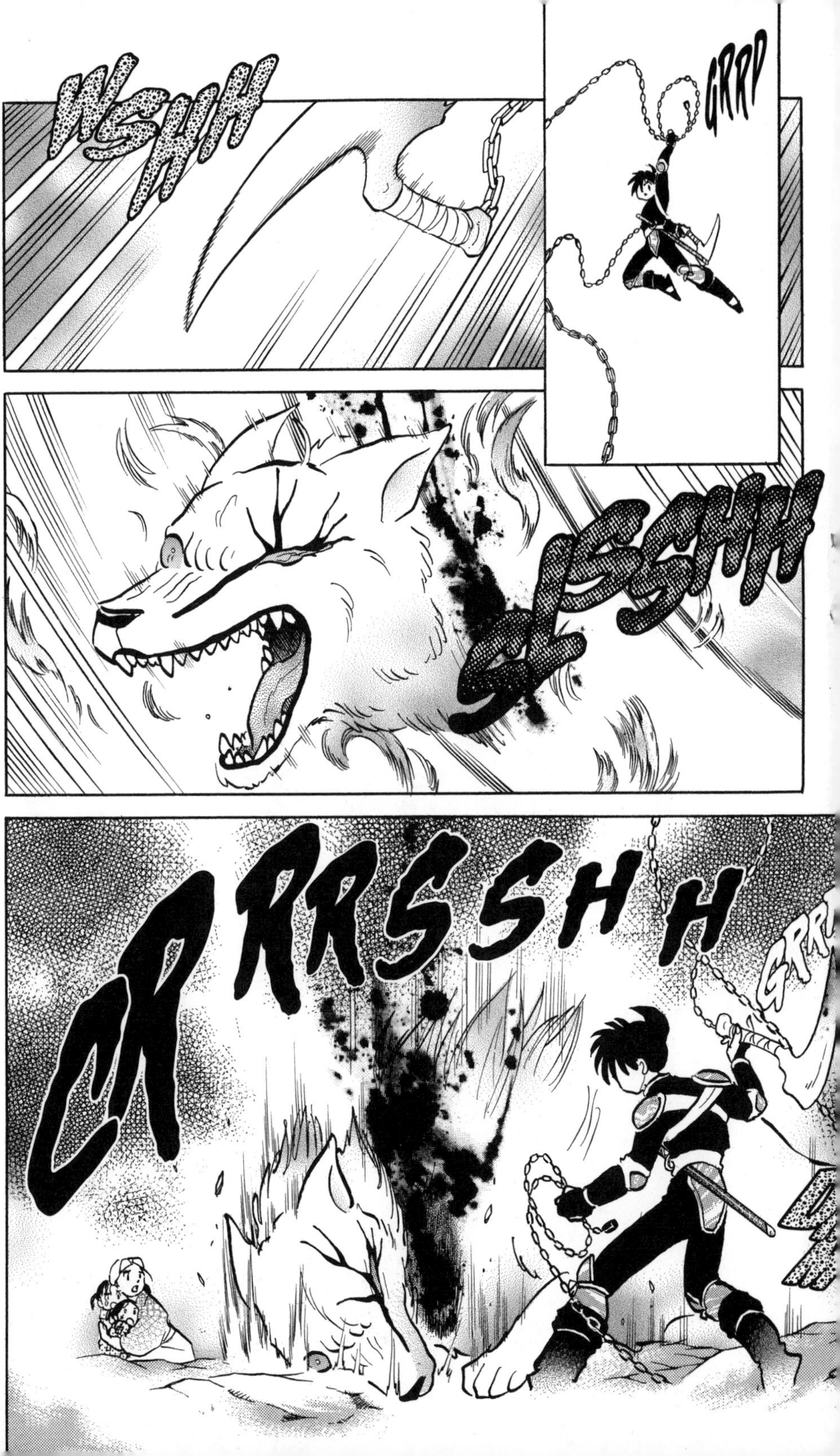
GRRP
WSHH
SLSSHH
CRRRSSHH

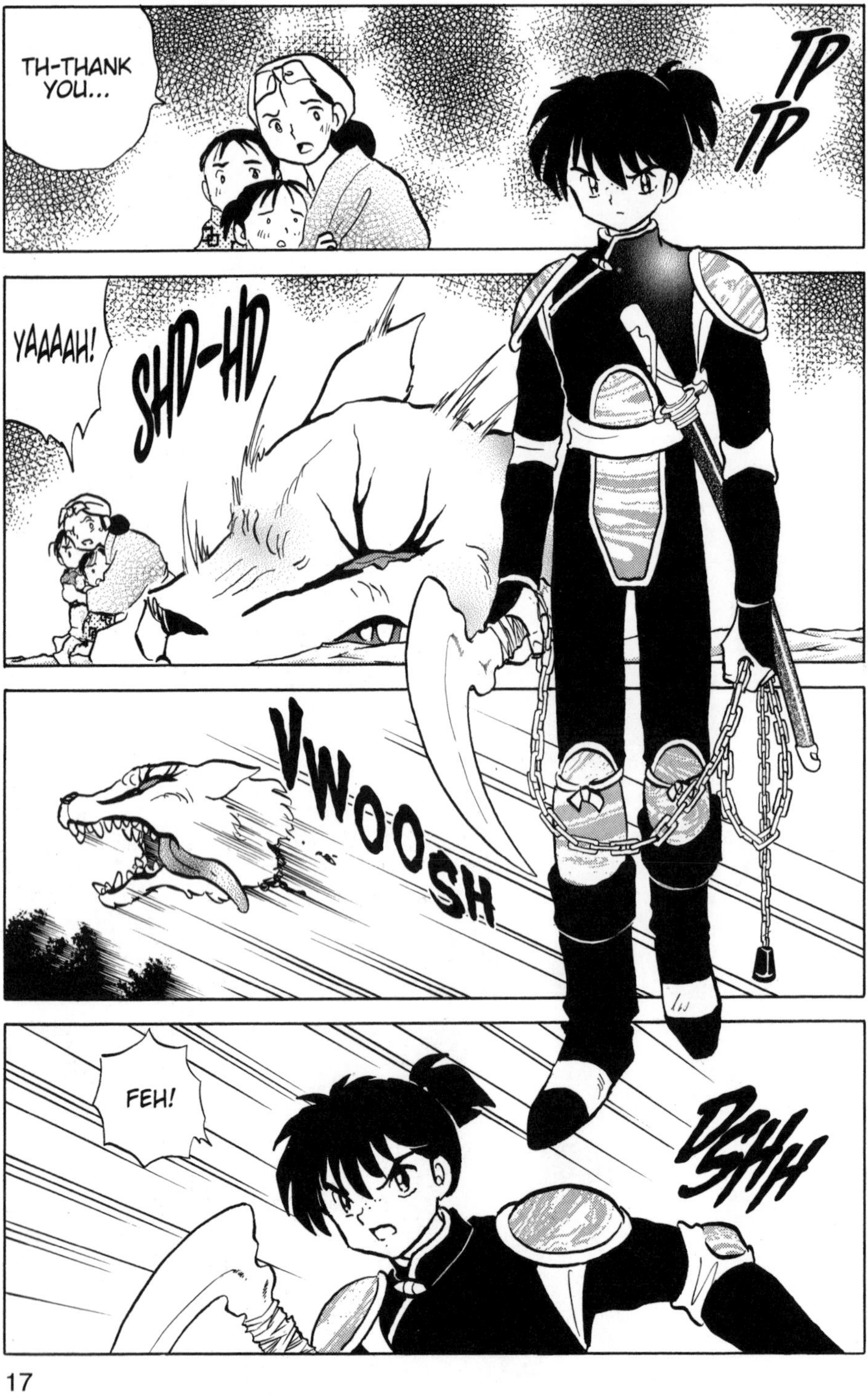
TP TP
TH-THANK YOU...
SHD-HD
YAAAAH!
VWOOSH
DSHH
FEH!

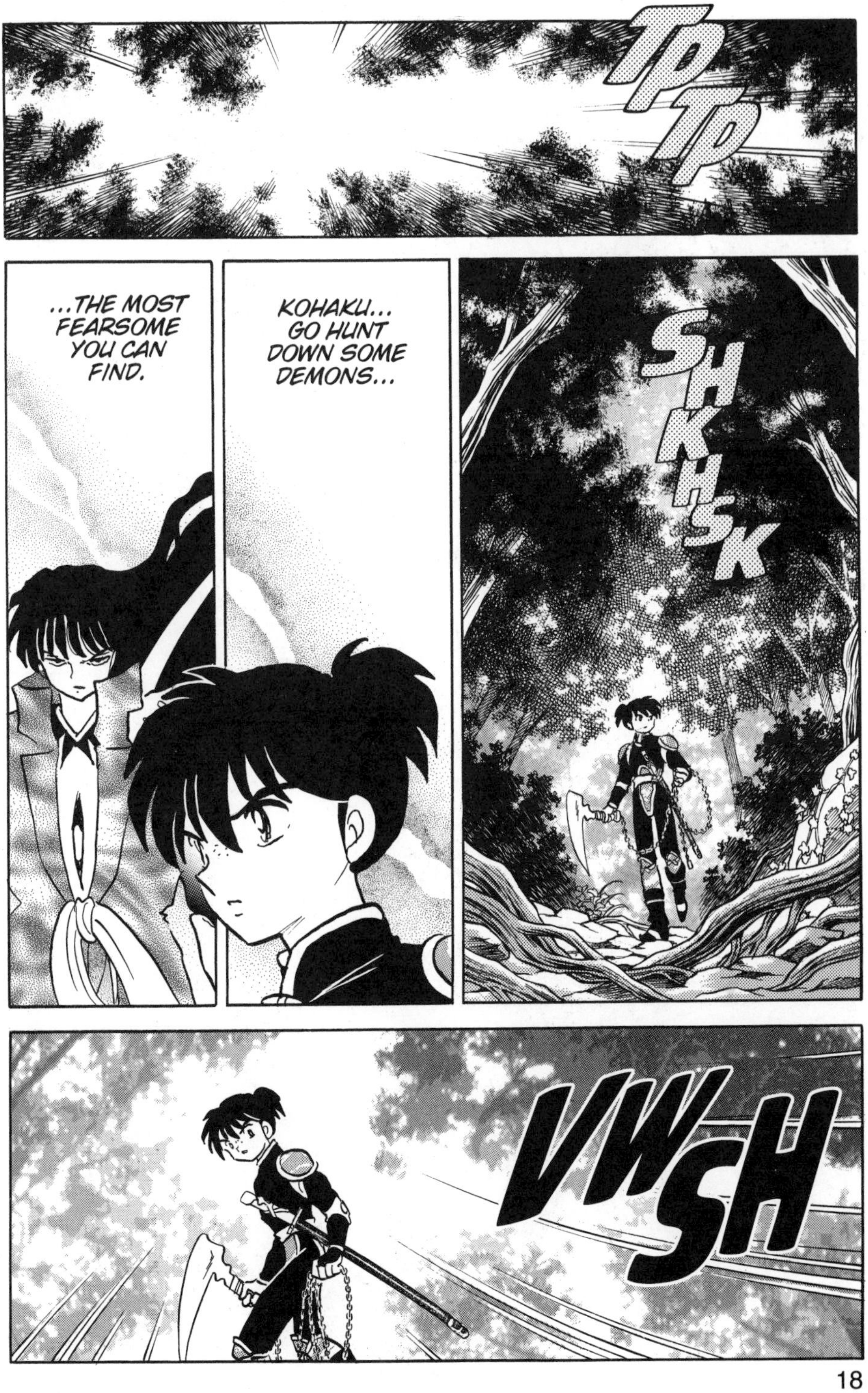
TP TP
SHKHSK
KOHAKU... GO HUNT DOWN SOME DEMONS...
...THE MOST FEARSOME YOU CAN FIND.
VWSH

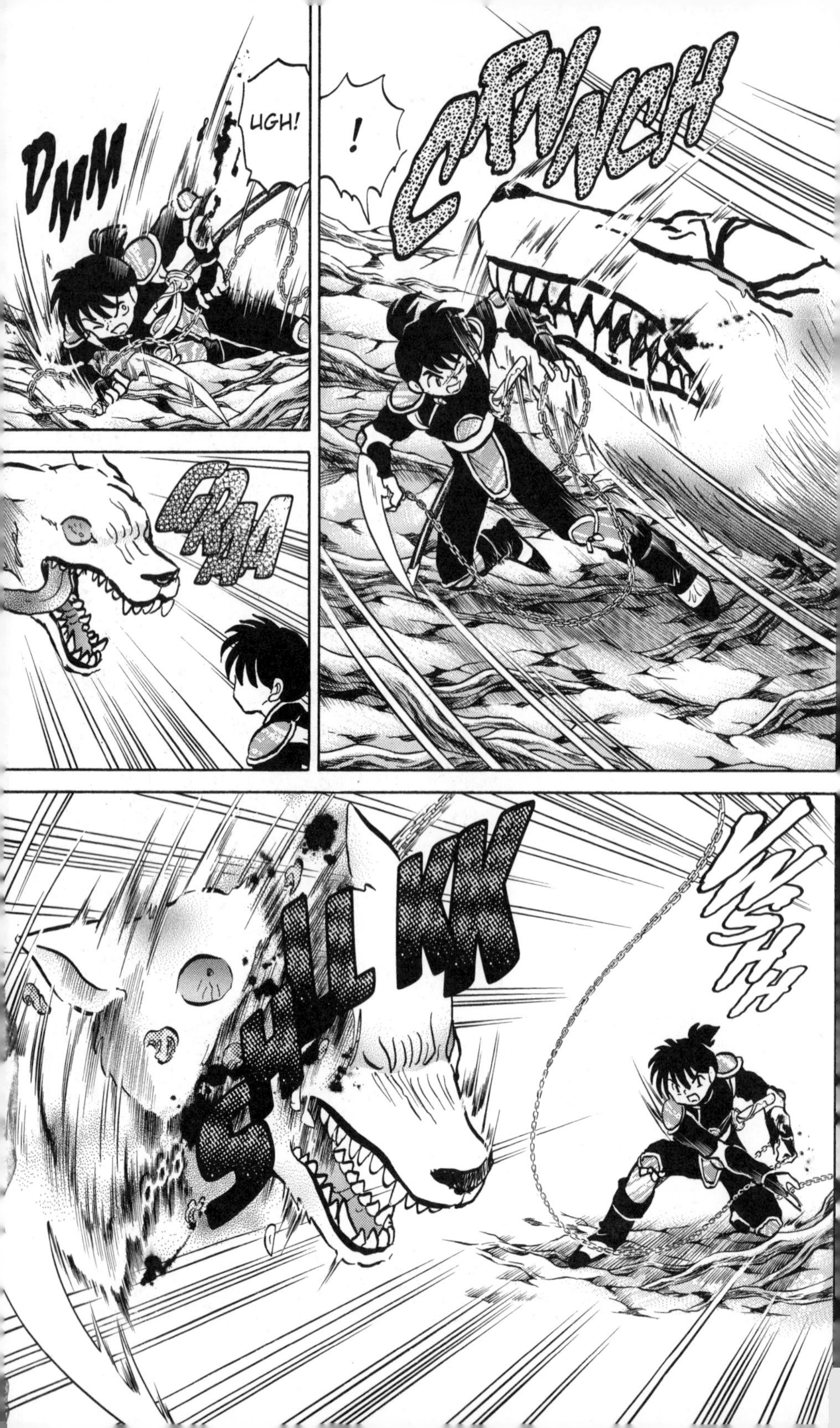
CRNNCH
!
DMM
UGH!
GRAA
SHLLKK
VWSHH

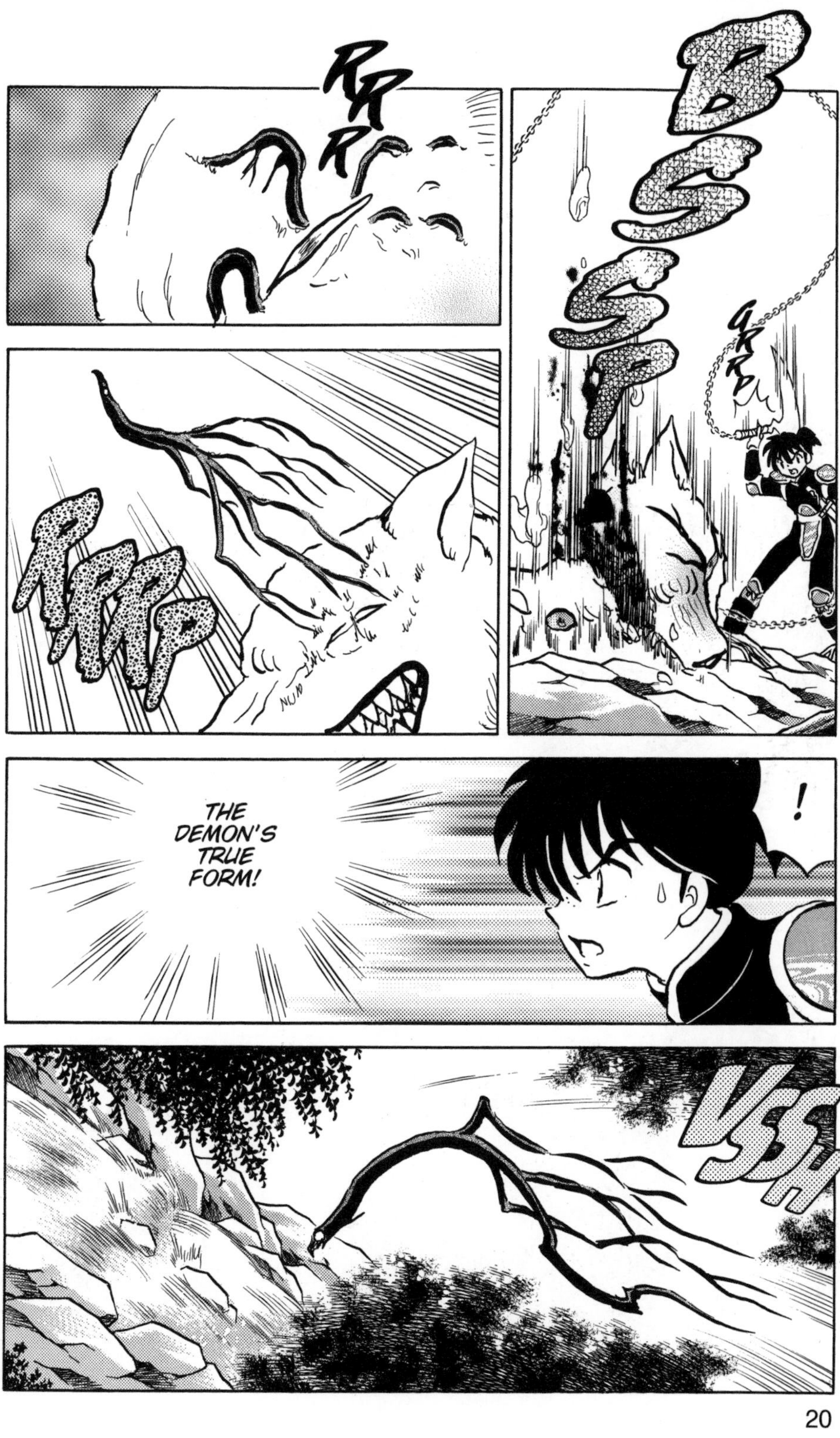
BSSP
GRRR
RRR
RRRP
THE DEMON'S TRUE FORM!
!
VSSH

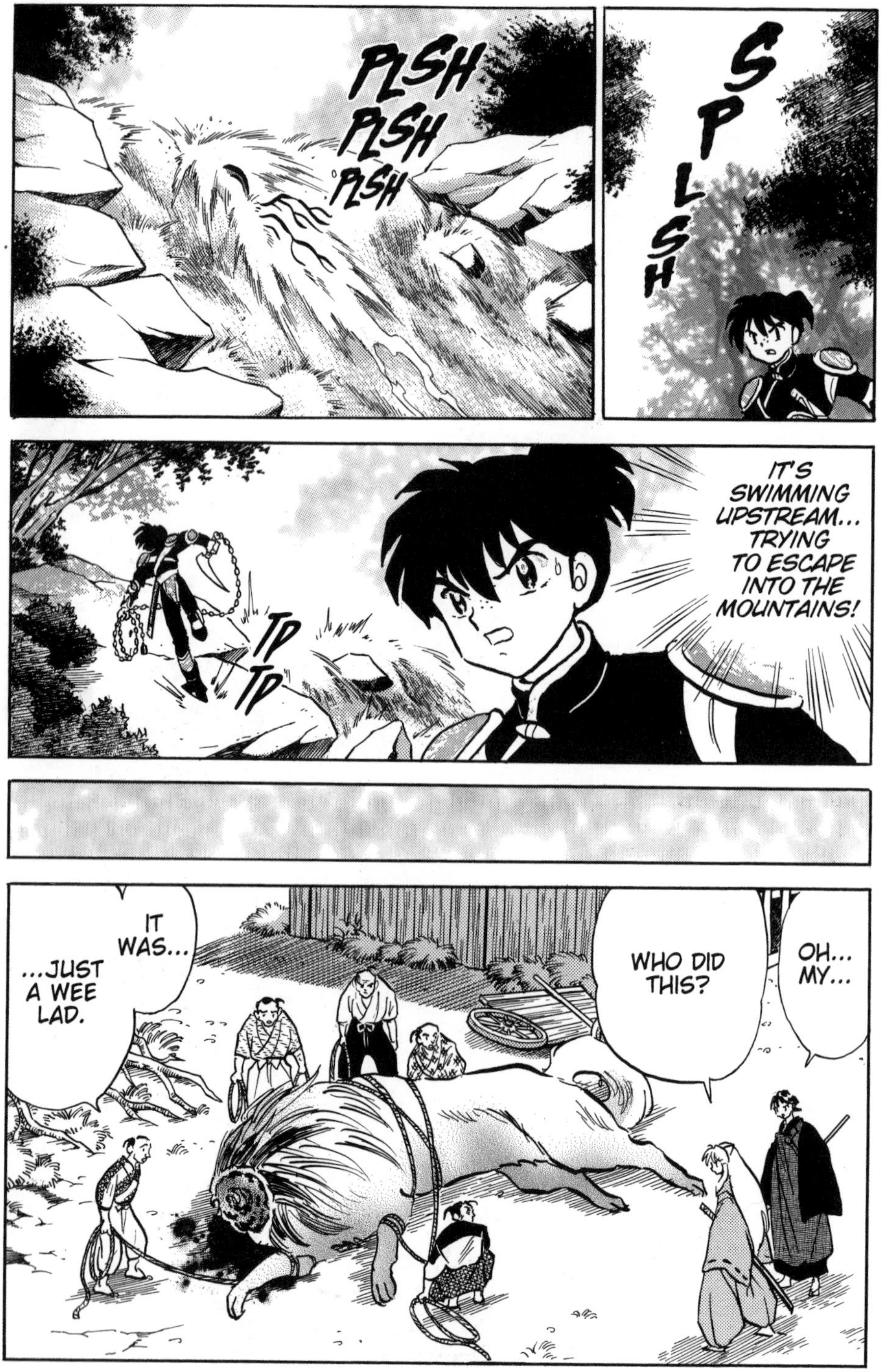
SPLSH
PLSH PLSH PLSH
IT'S SWIMMING UPSTREAM... TRYING TO ESCAPE INTO THE MOUNTAINS!
TP TP
OH... MY...
WHO DID THIS?
IT WAS...
...JUST A WEE LAD.

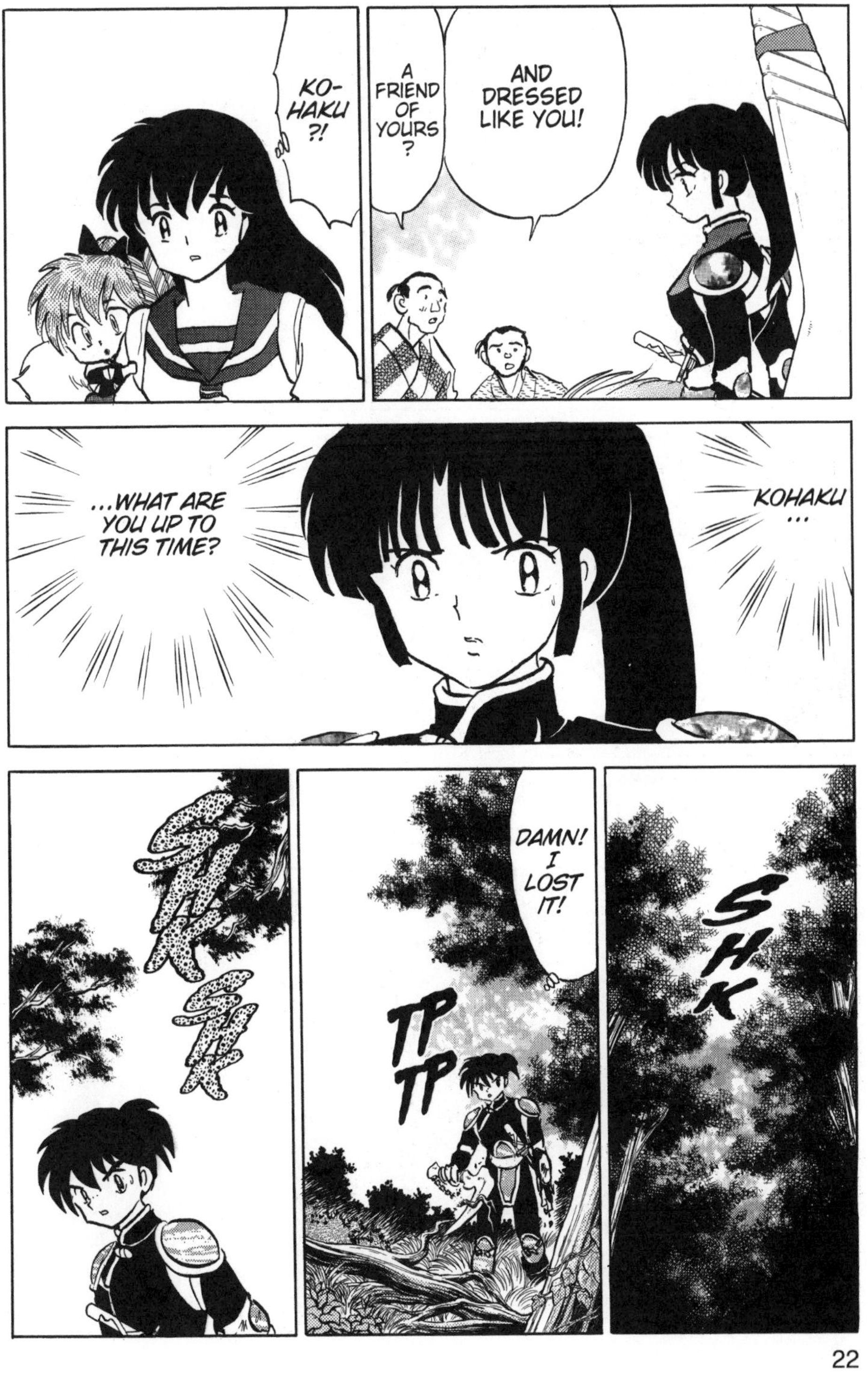
AND DRESSED LIKE YOU!
A FRIEND OF YOURS?
KO-HAKU?!
KOHAKU...
...WHAT ARE YOU UP TO THIS TIME?
SHK
DAMN! I LOST IT!
TP TP

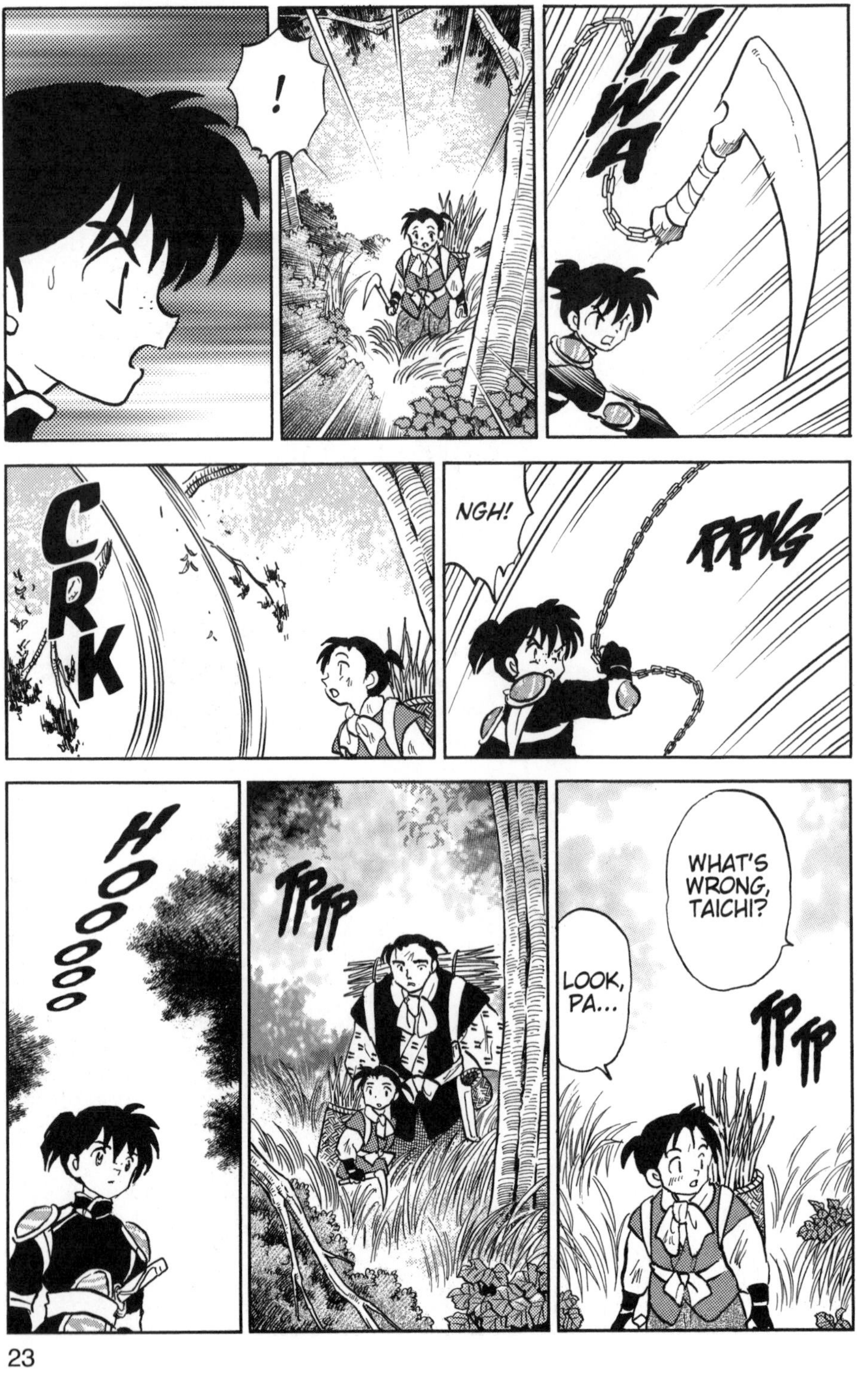
HWA
!
NGH!
CRK
WHAT'S WRONG, TAICHI?
LOOK, PA...
TP TP
TP TP
HOOOOOO

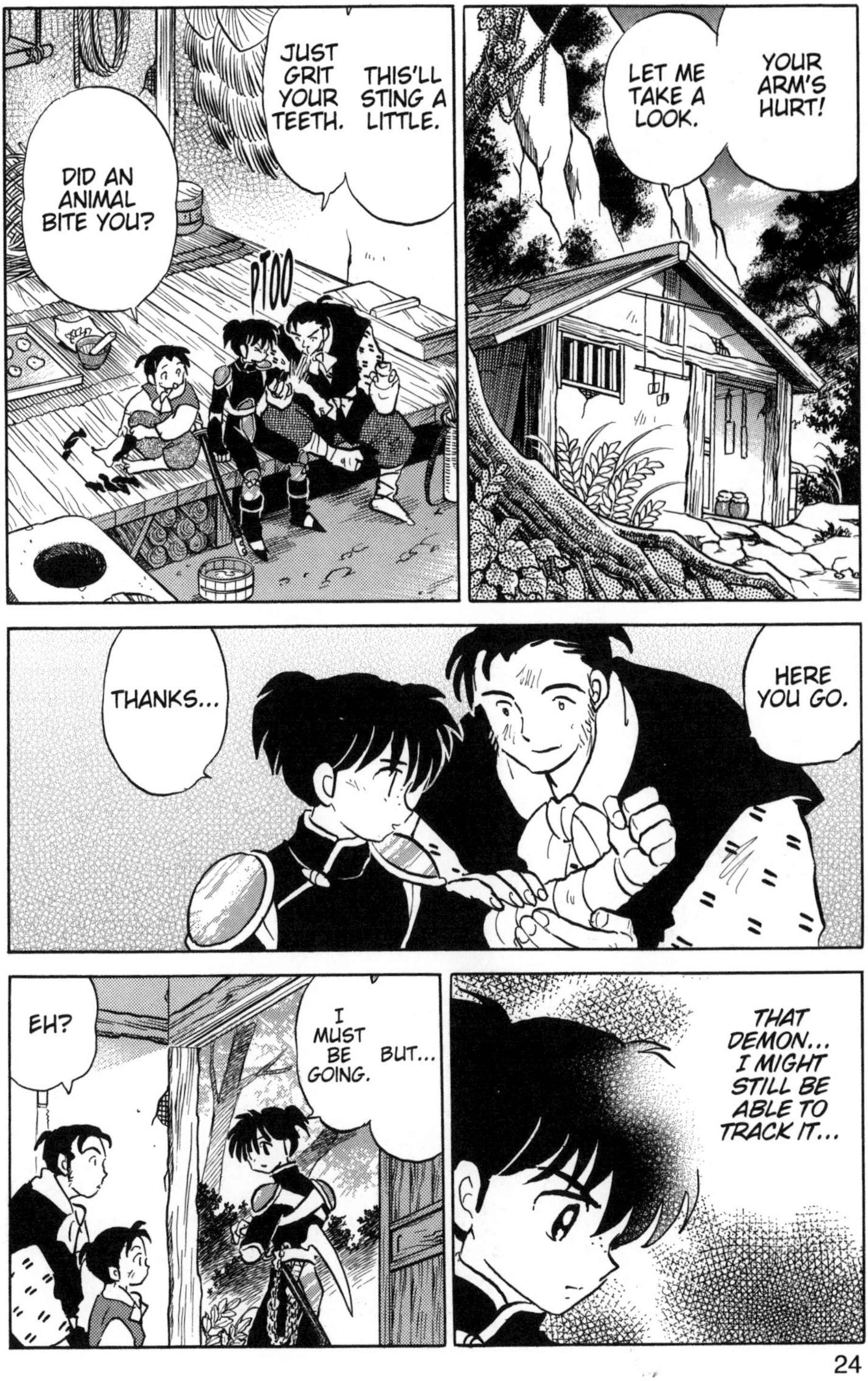
YOUR ARM'S HURT!
LET ME TAKE A LOOK.
THIS'LL STING A LITTLE.
JUST GRIT YOUR TEETH.
PTOO
DID AN ANIMAL BITE YOU?
HERE YOU GO.
THANKS...
THAT DEMON... I MIGHT STILL BE ABLE TO TRACK IT...
BUT...
I MUST BE GOING.
EH?

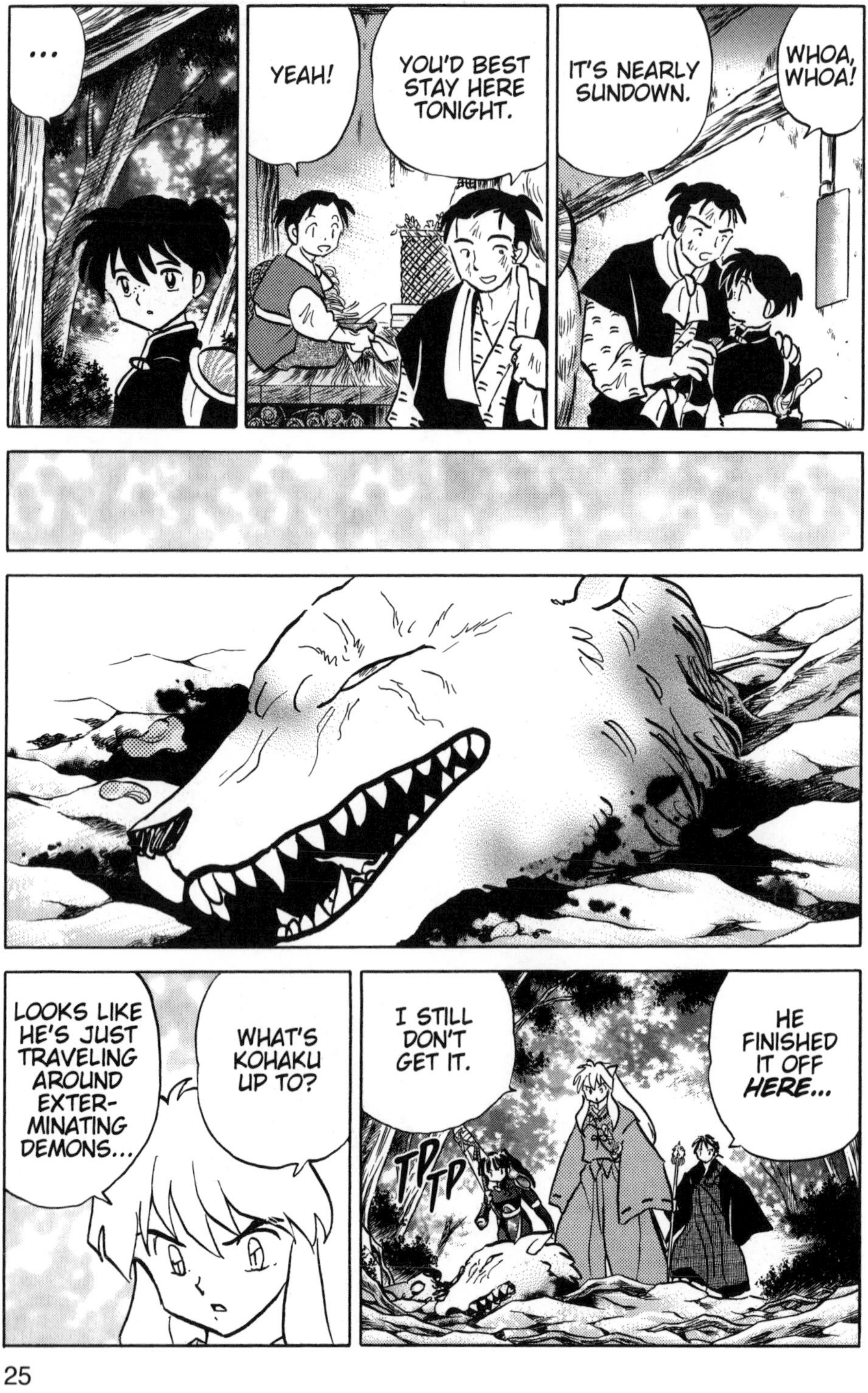
WHOA, WHOA!
IT'S NEARLY SUNDOWN.
YOU'D BEST STAY HERE TONIGHT.
YEAH!
...
HE FINISHED IT OFF *HERE*...
I STILL DON'T GET IT.
TP TP
WHAT'S KOHAKU UP TO?
LOOKS LIKE HE'S JUST TRAVELING AROUND EXTER-MINATING DEMONS...

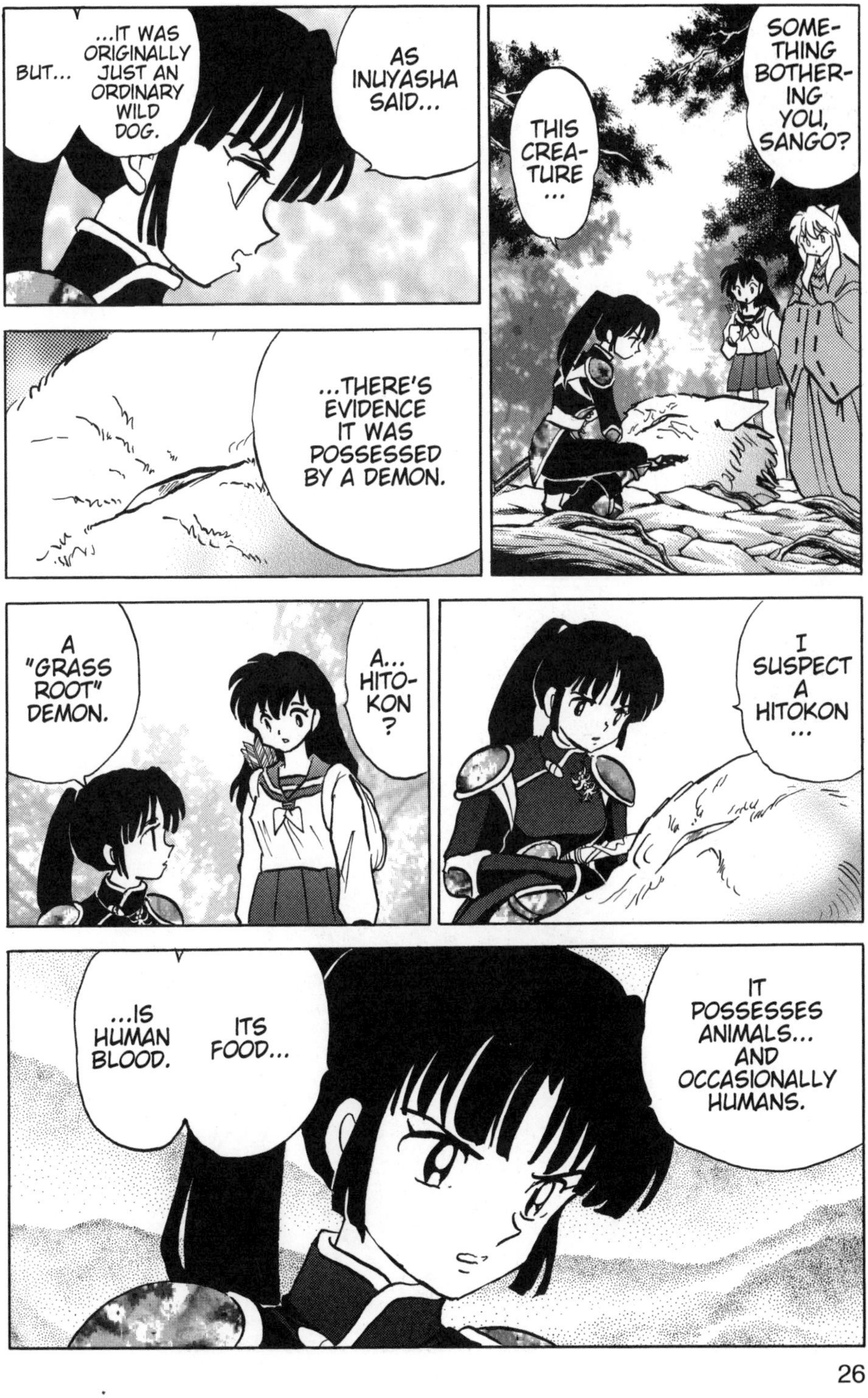
SOME-THING BOTHER-ING YOU, SANGO?
THIS CREA-TURE ...
AS INUYASHA SAID...
...IT WAS ORIGINALLY JUST AN ORDINARY WILD DOG.
BUT...
...THERE'S EVIDENCE IT WAS POSSESSED BY A DEMON.
I SUSPECT A HITOKON ...
A... HITO-KON ?
A "GRASS ROOT" DEMON.
IT POSSESSES ANIMALS... AND OCCASIONALLY HUMANS.
ITS FOOD...
...IS HUMAN BLOOD.

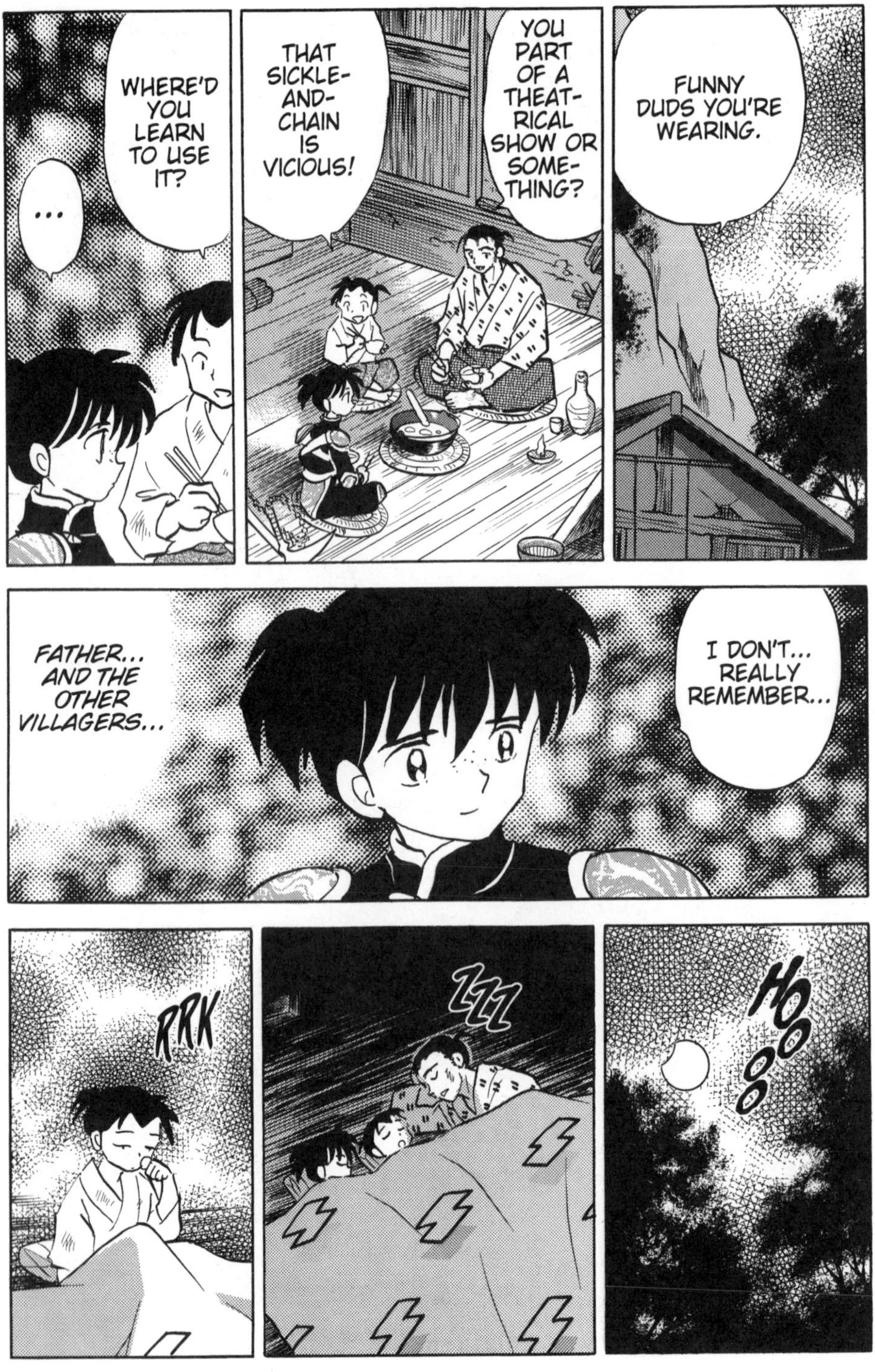
FUNNY DUDS YOU'RE WEARING.
YOU PART OF A THEATRICAL SHOW OR SOMETHING?
THAT SICKLE-AND-CHAIN IS VICIOUS!
WHERE'D YOU LEARN TO USE IT?
...
I DON'T... REALLY REMEMBER...
FATHER... AND THE OTHER VILLAGERS...
HOOOOO
ZZZ
RRK

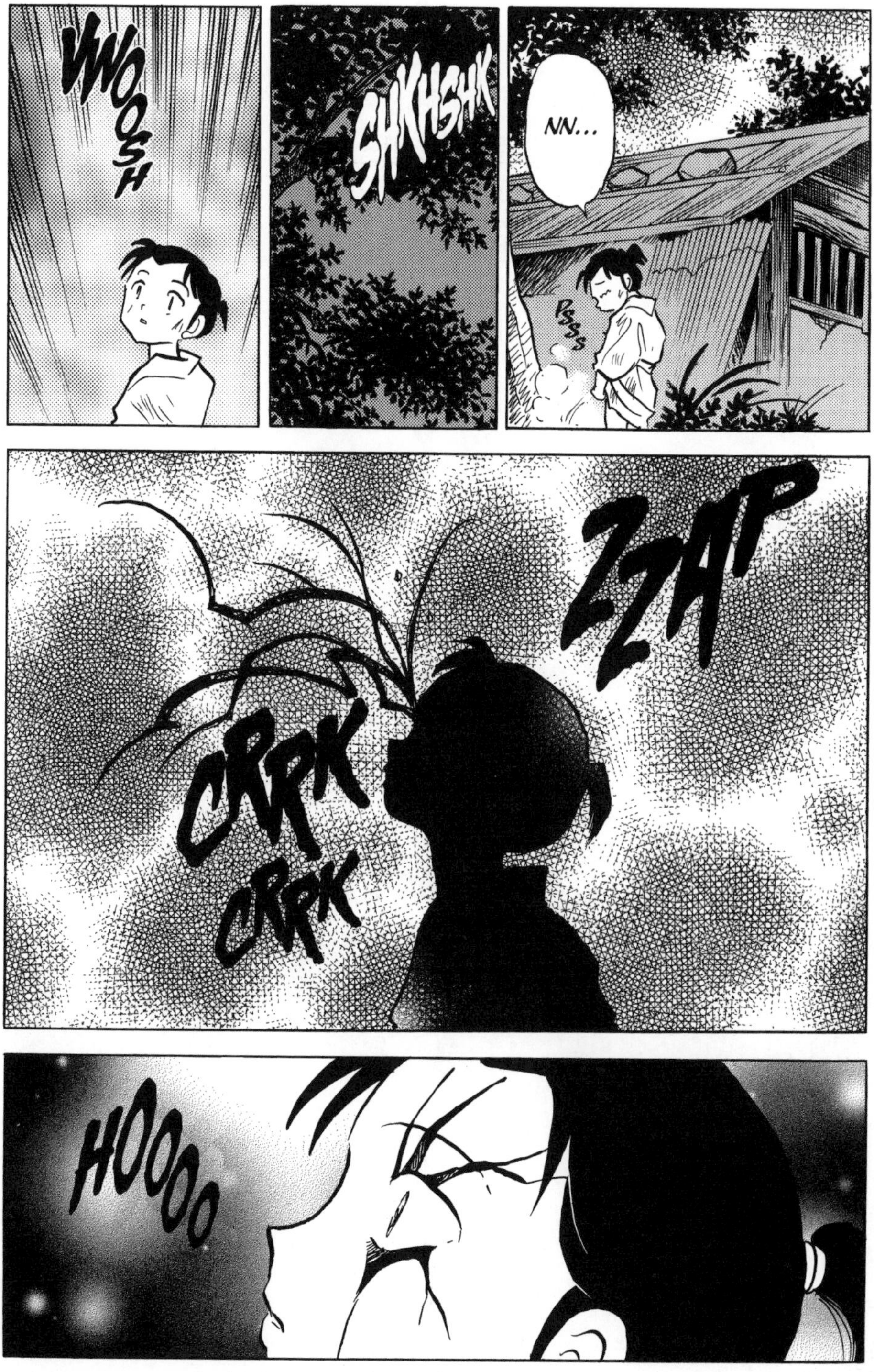
NN...
PSSSS
SHKHSHK
VWOOSH
ZZAP
CRPK
CRPK
HOOOO

SCROLL TWO
MEMORIES OF A FATHER

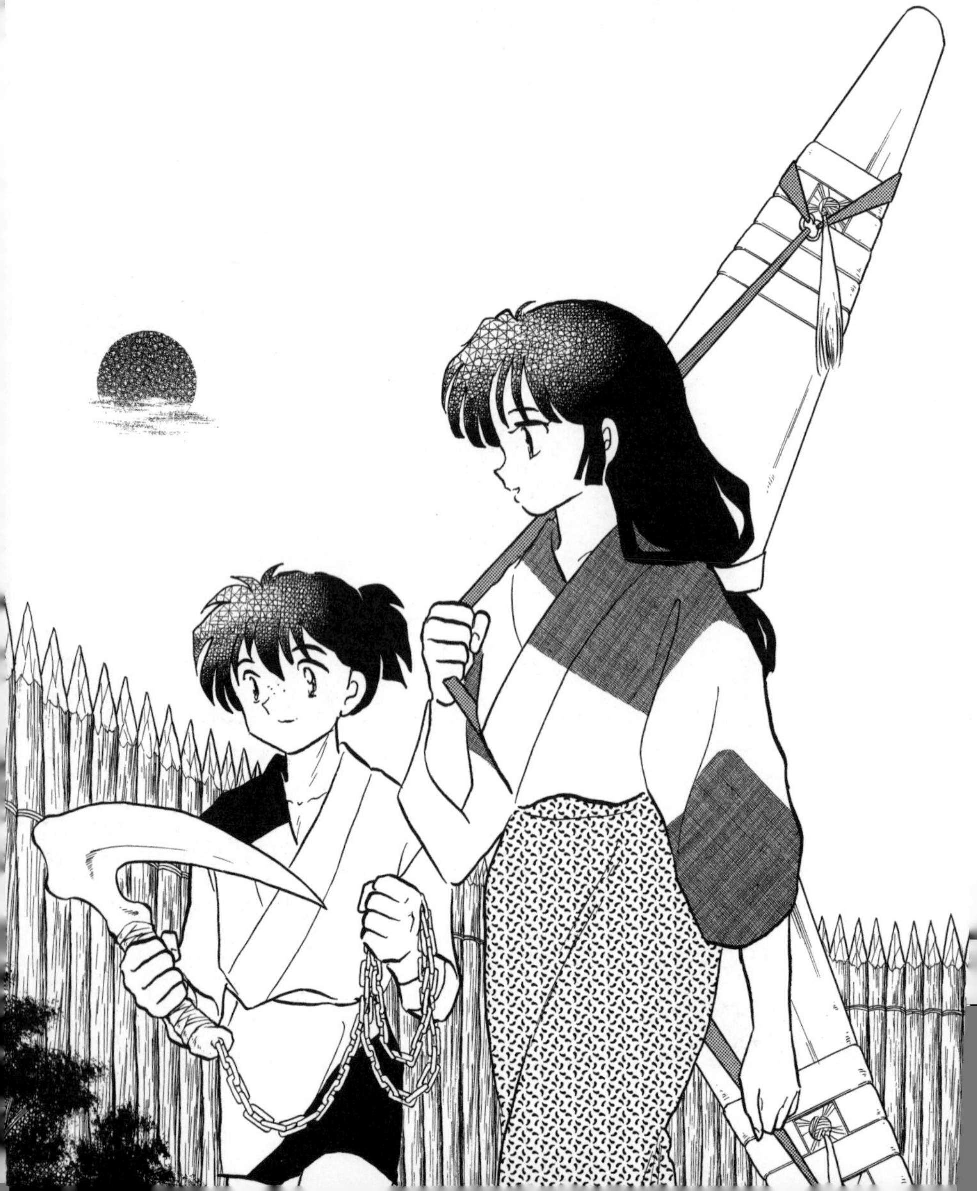

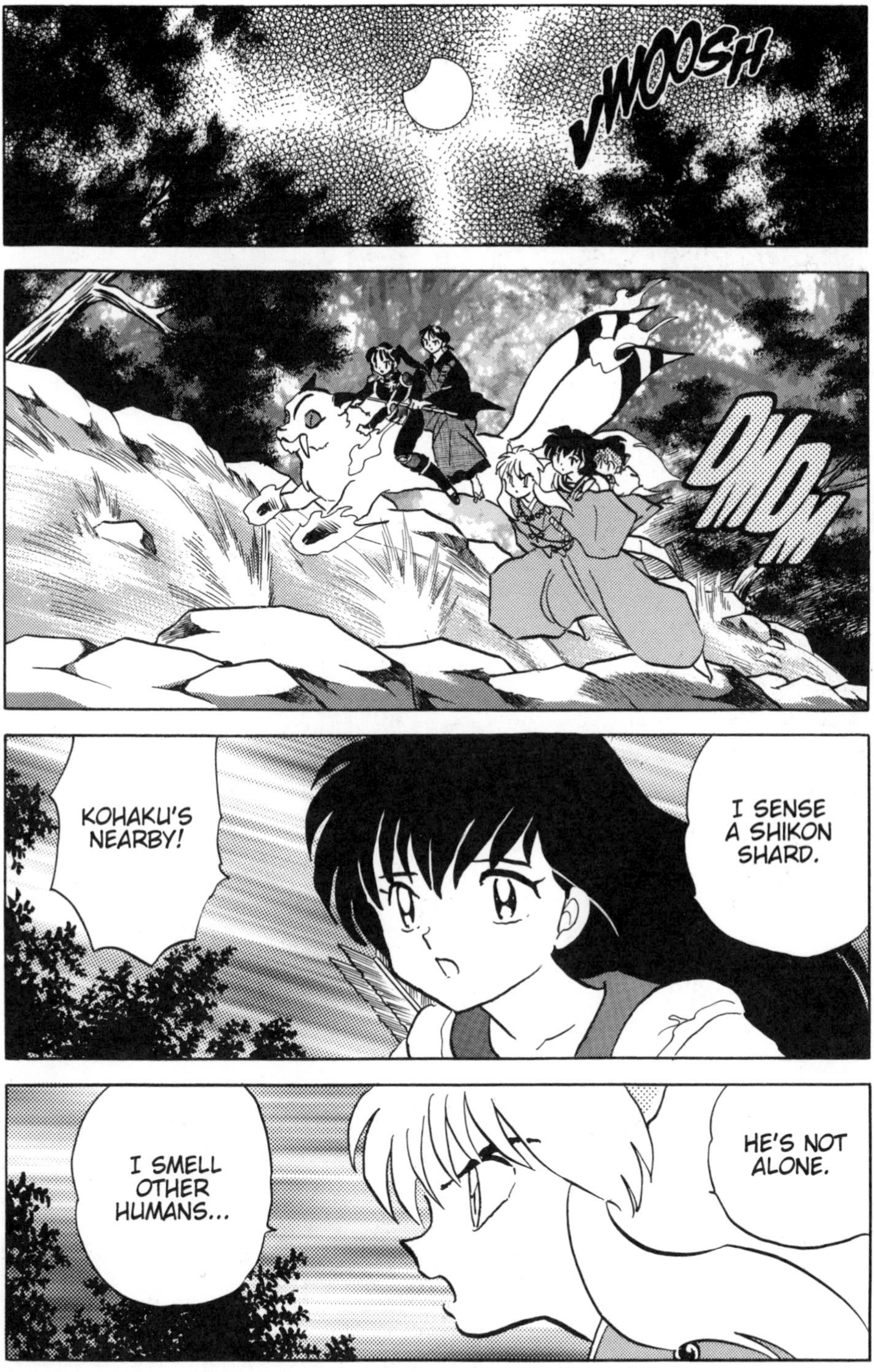
VWOOSH
DMDM
I SENSE A SHIKON SHARD.
KOHAKU'S NEARBY!
HE'S NOT ALONE.
I SMELL OTHER HUMANS...

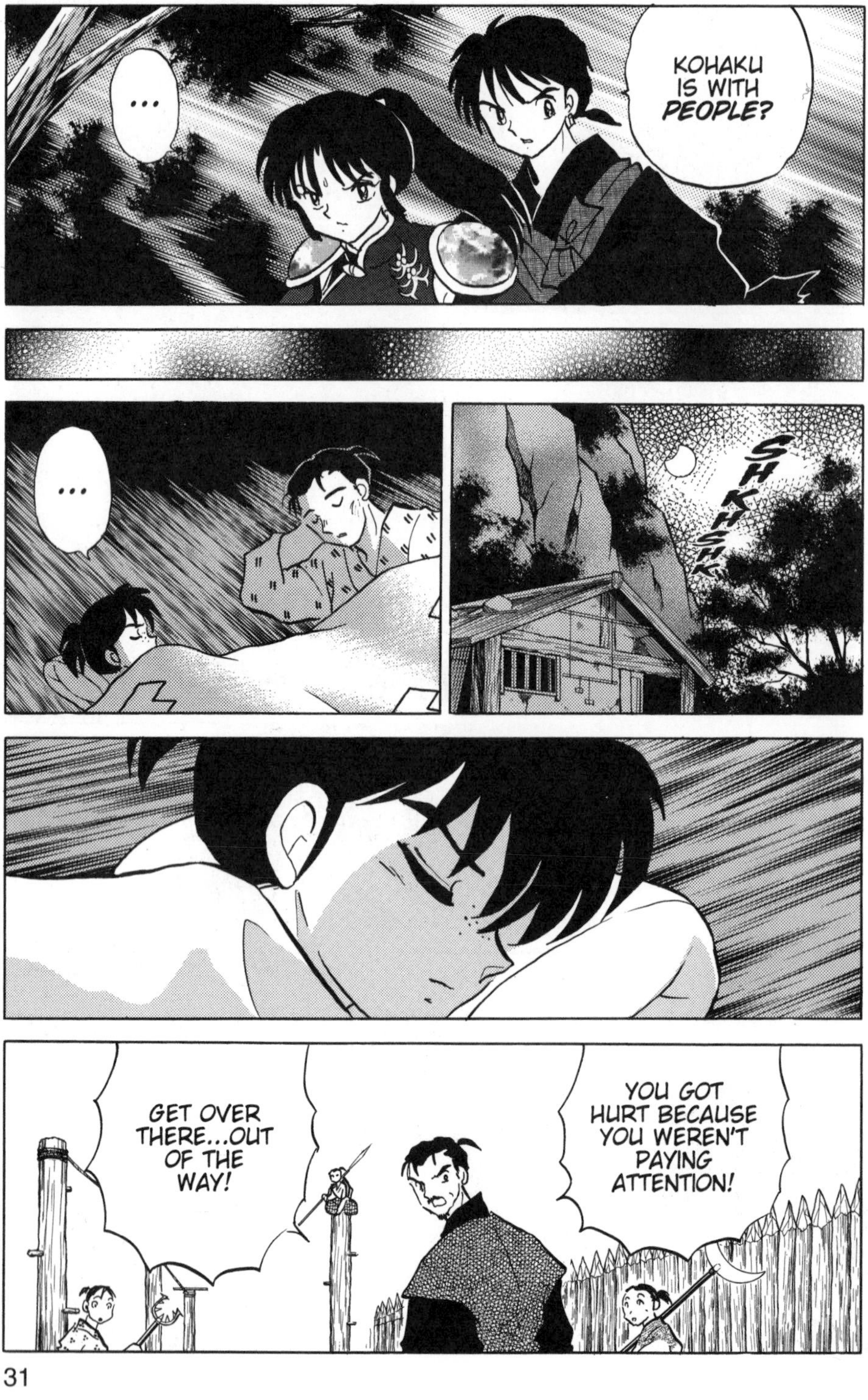
KOHAKU IS WITH PEOPLE?
...
SHKSHK
...
YOU GOT HURT BECAUSE YOU WEREN'T PAYING ATTENTION!
GET OVER THERE...OUT OF THE WAY!

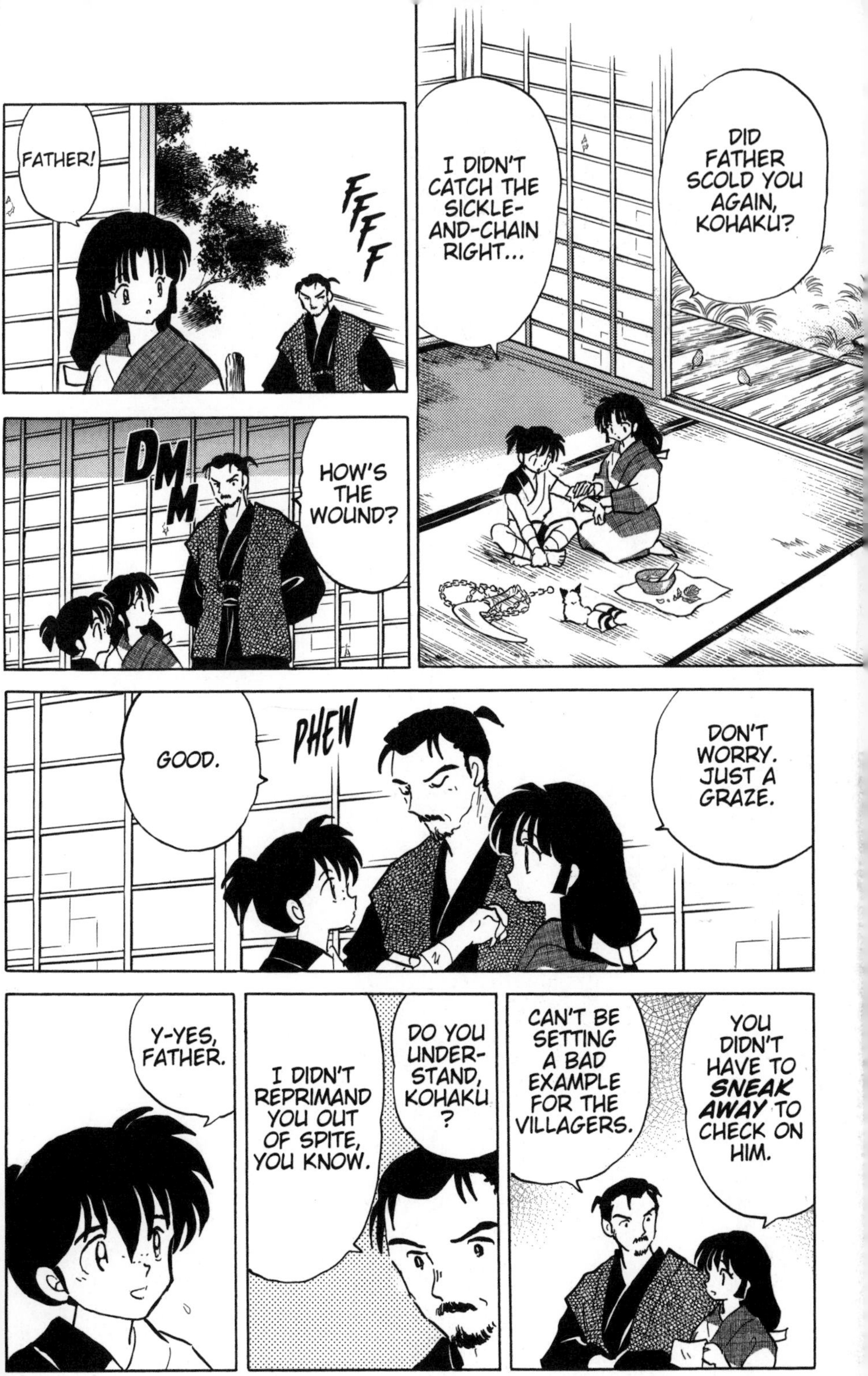
DID FATHER SCOLD YOU AGAIN, KOHAKU?
I DIDN'T CATCH THE SICKLE-AND-CHAIN RIGHT...
FATHER!
FFFF
DMM
HOW'S THE WOUND?
DON'T WORRY. JUST A GRAZE.
PHEW
GOOD.
YOU DIDN'T HAVE TO **SNEAK AWAY** TO CHECK ON HIM.
CAN'T BE SETTING A BAD EXAMPLE FOR THE VILLAGERS.
DO YOU UNDERSTAND, KOHAKU?
I DIDN'T REPRIMAND YOU OUT OF SPITE, YOU KNOW.
Y-YES, FATHER.

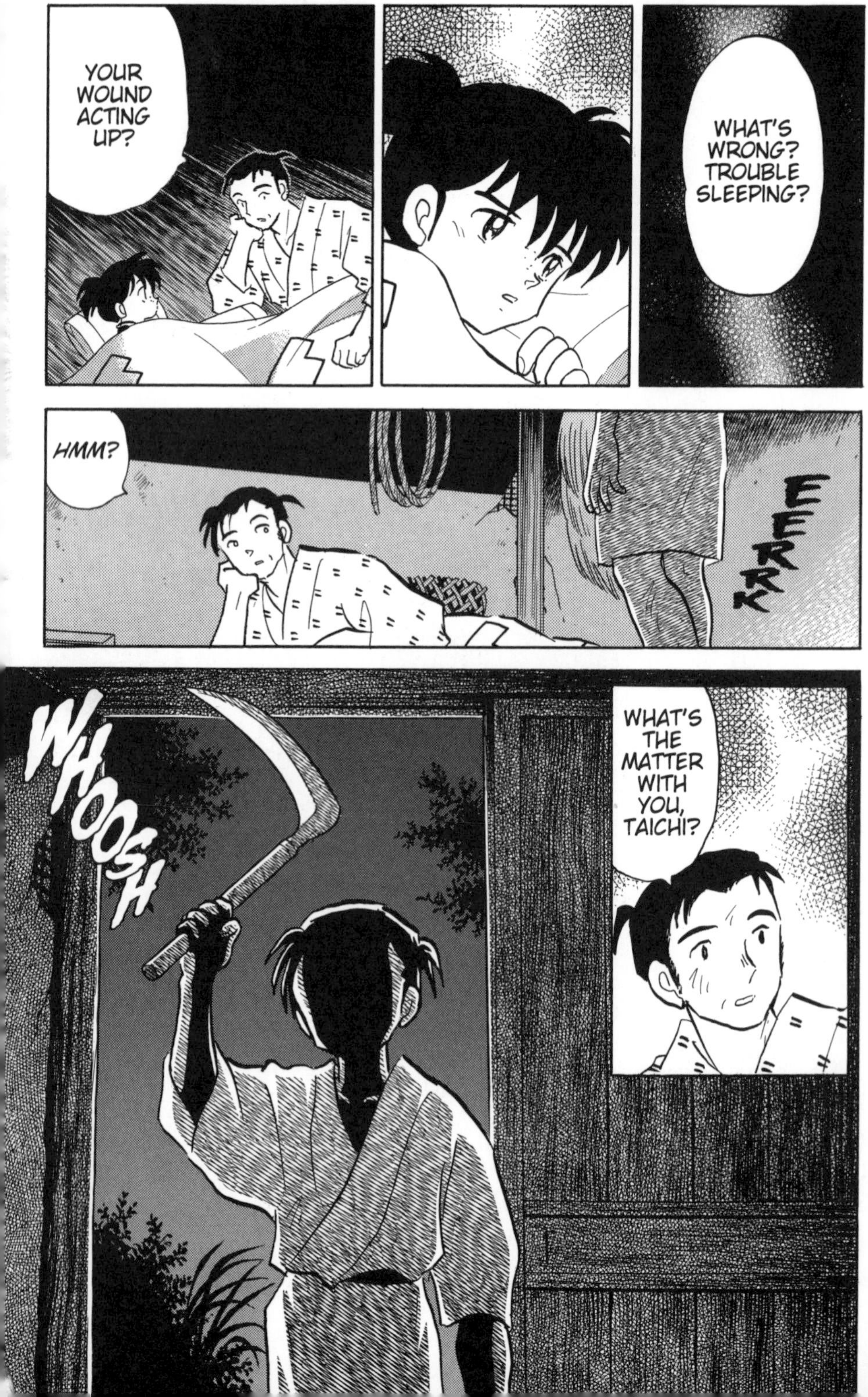
WHAT'S WRONG? TROUBLE SLEEPING?
YOUR WOUND ACTING UP?
EERRK
HMM?
WHAT'S THE MATTER WITH YOU, TAICHI?
WHOOSH

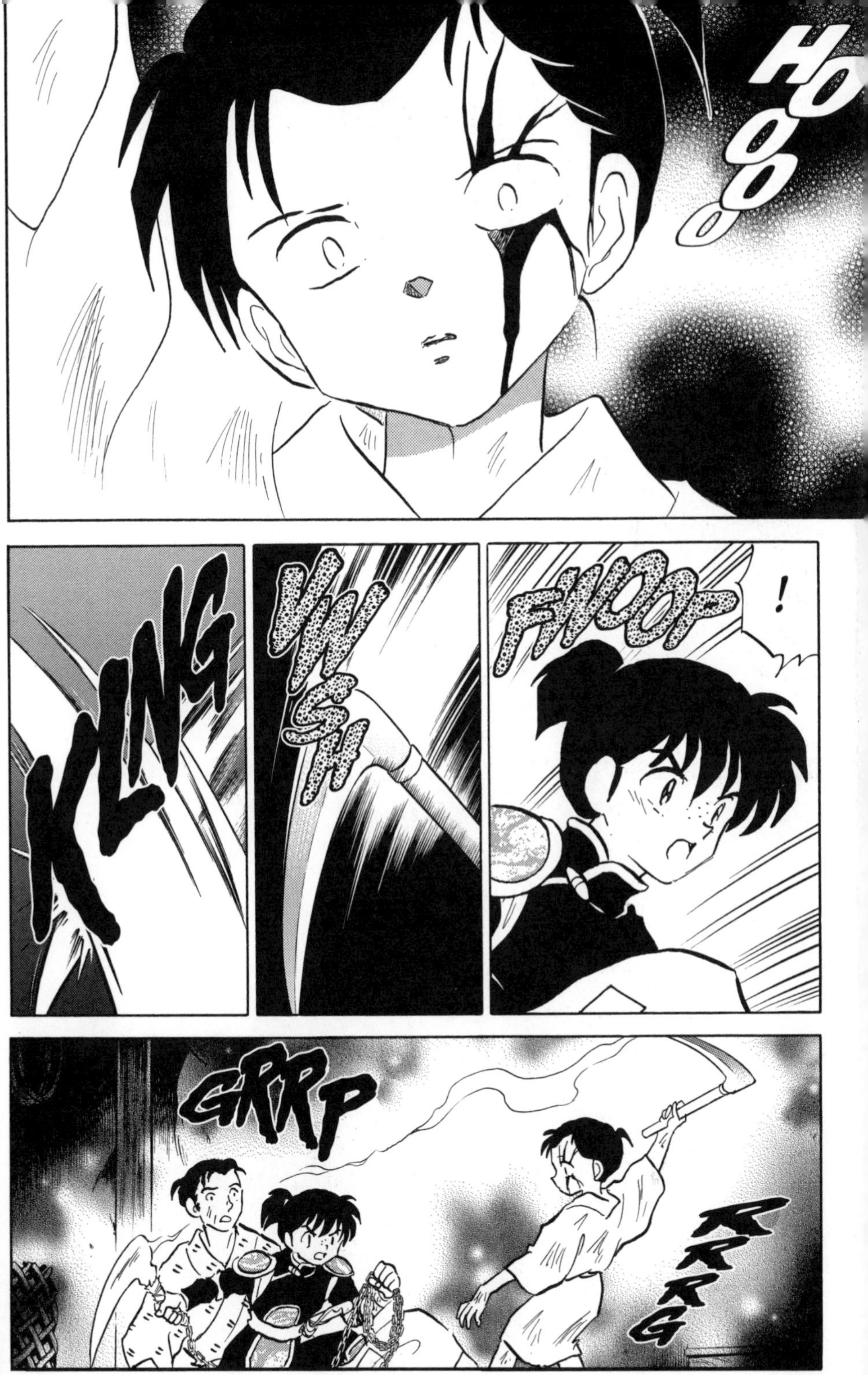
HOOOO
FWOOP
!
VWSH
KLING
GRRP
RRRG

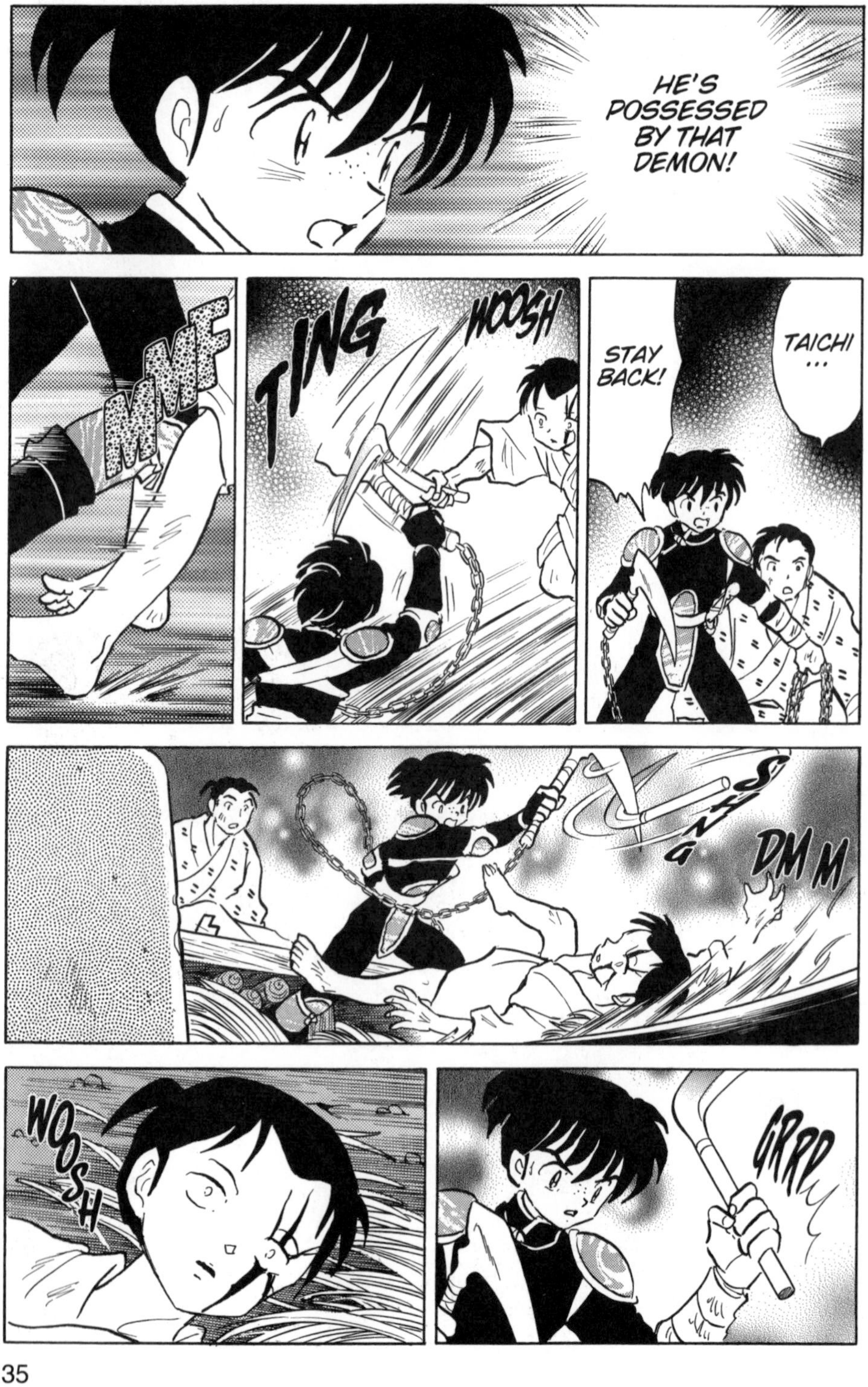
HE'S POSSESSED BY THAT DEMON!
TAICHI ...
STAY BACK!
WOOSH
TING
MMF
SHING
DMM
GRRP
WOOSH

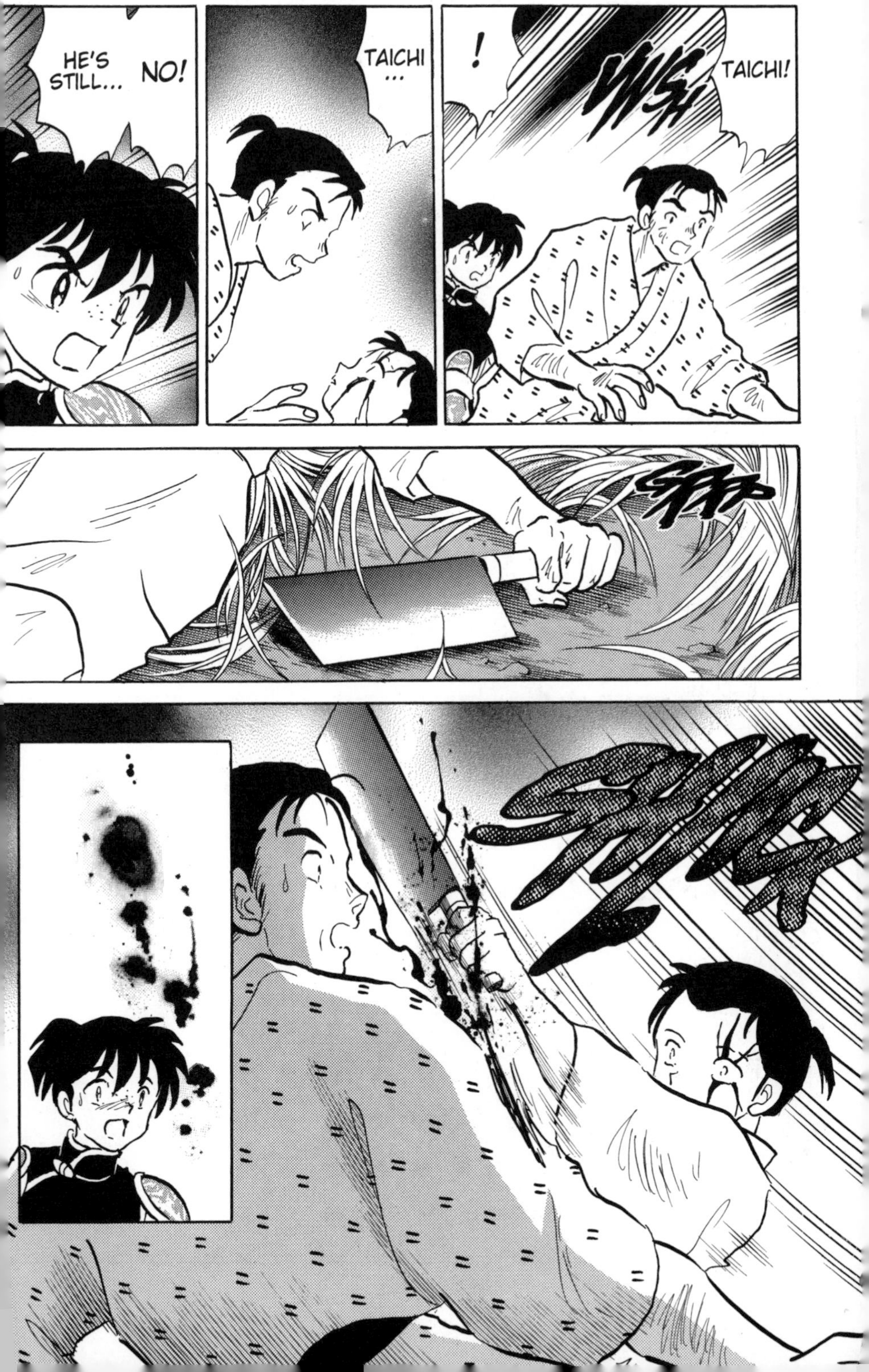
TAICHI!
!
TAICHI ...
NO!
HE'S STILL...

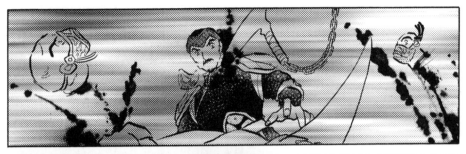

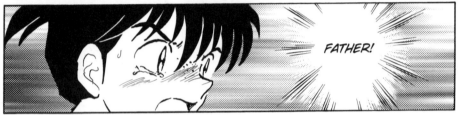

FATHER!

STOP IT!

S...

WOOSH

TAICHI...!

DMMM

KLNG

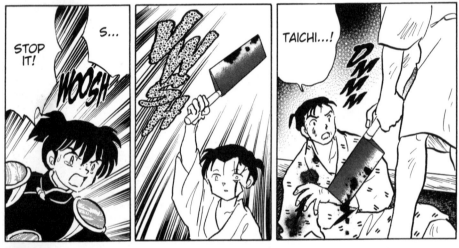

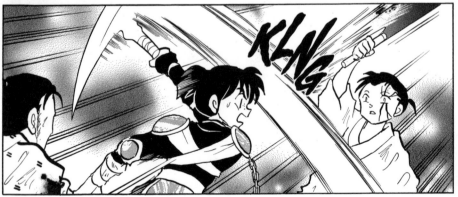

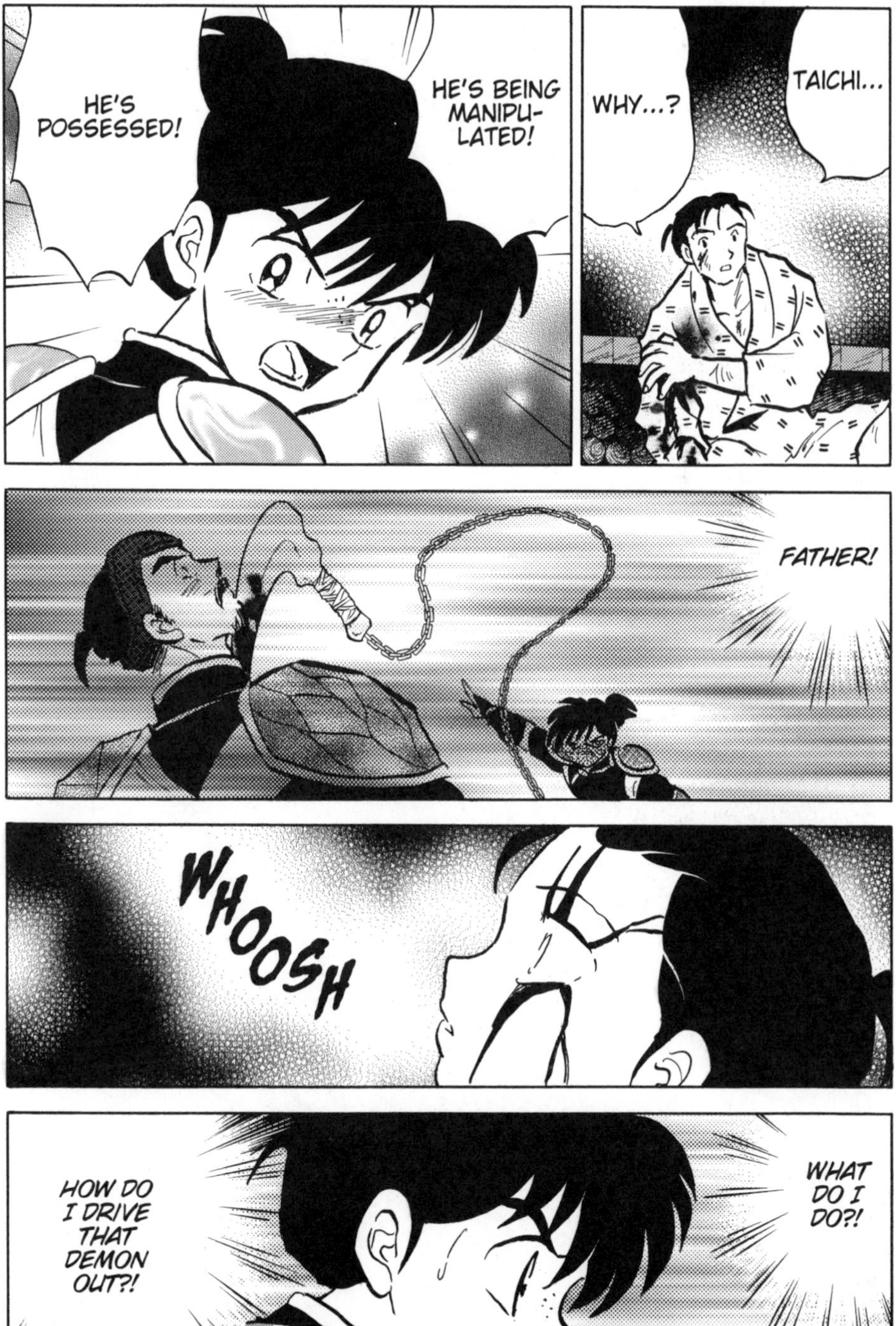
TAICHI...
WHY...?
HE'S BEING MANIPU-LATED!
HE'S POSSESSED!
FATHER!
WHOOSH
WHAT DO I DO?!
HOW DO I DRIVE THAT DEMON OUT?!

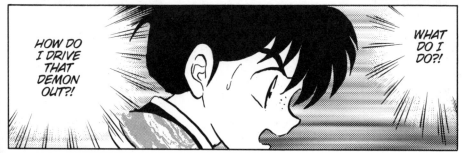

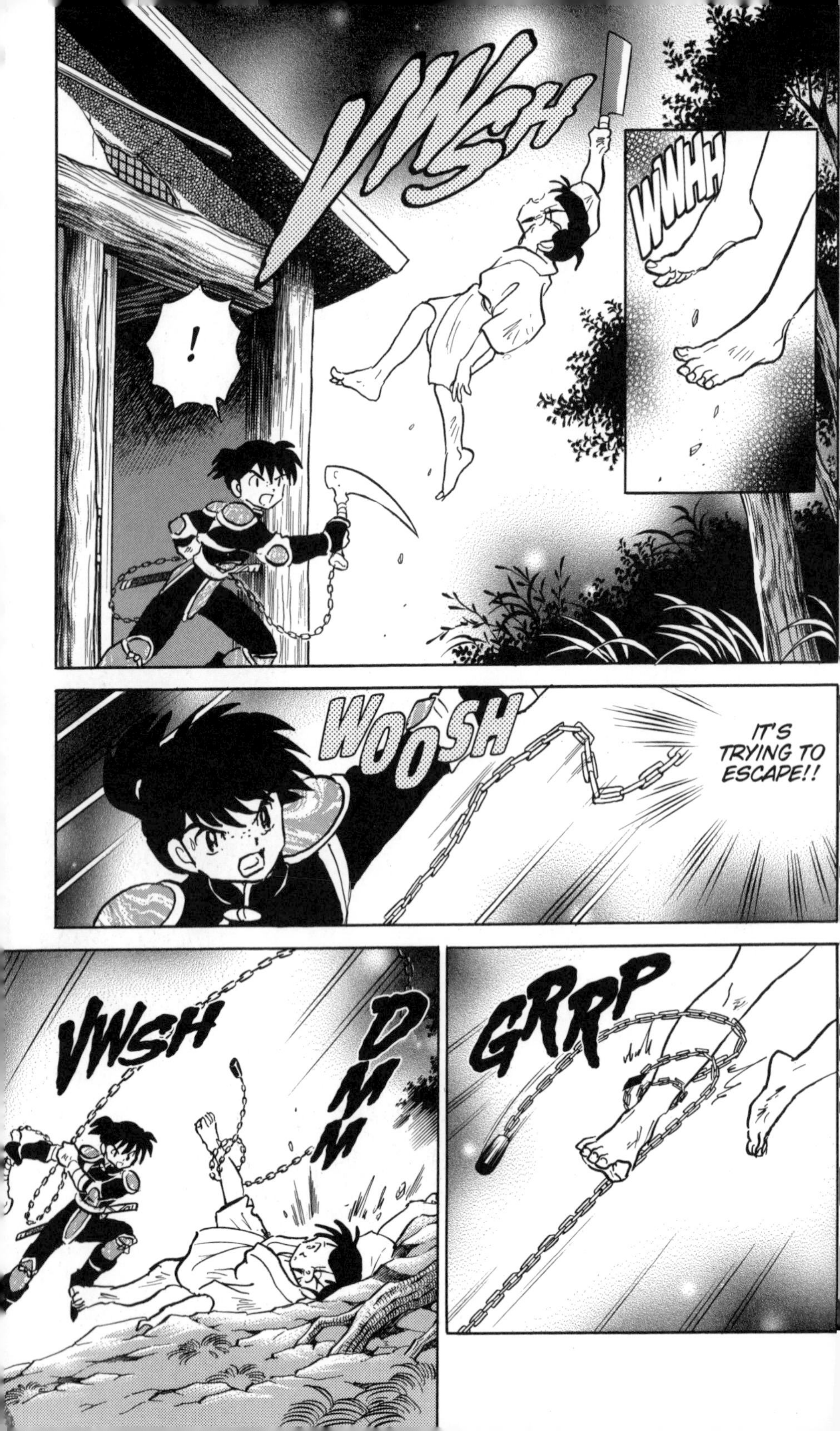

WNHH
VWSH
!
IT'S TRYING TO ESCAPE!!
WOOSH
GRRP
VWSH
DMMM

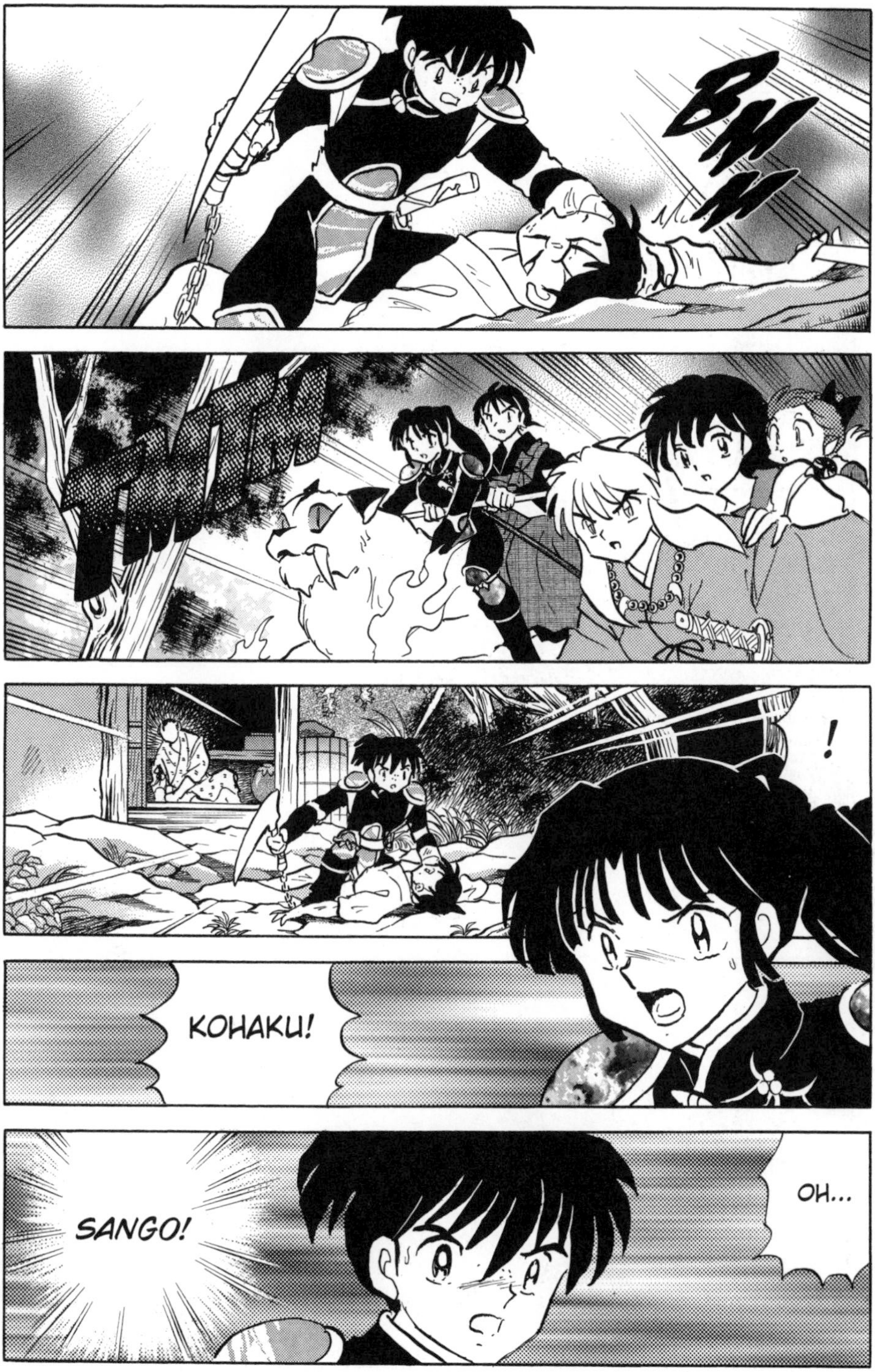
BMM
!
KOHAKU!
OH...
SANGO!

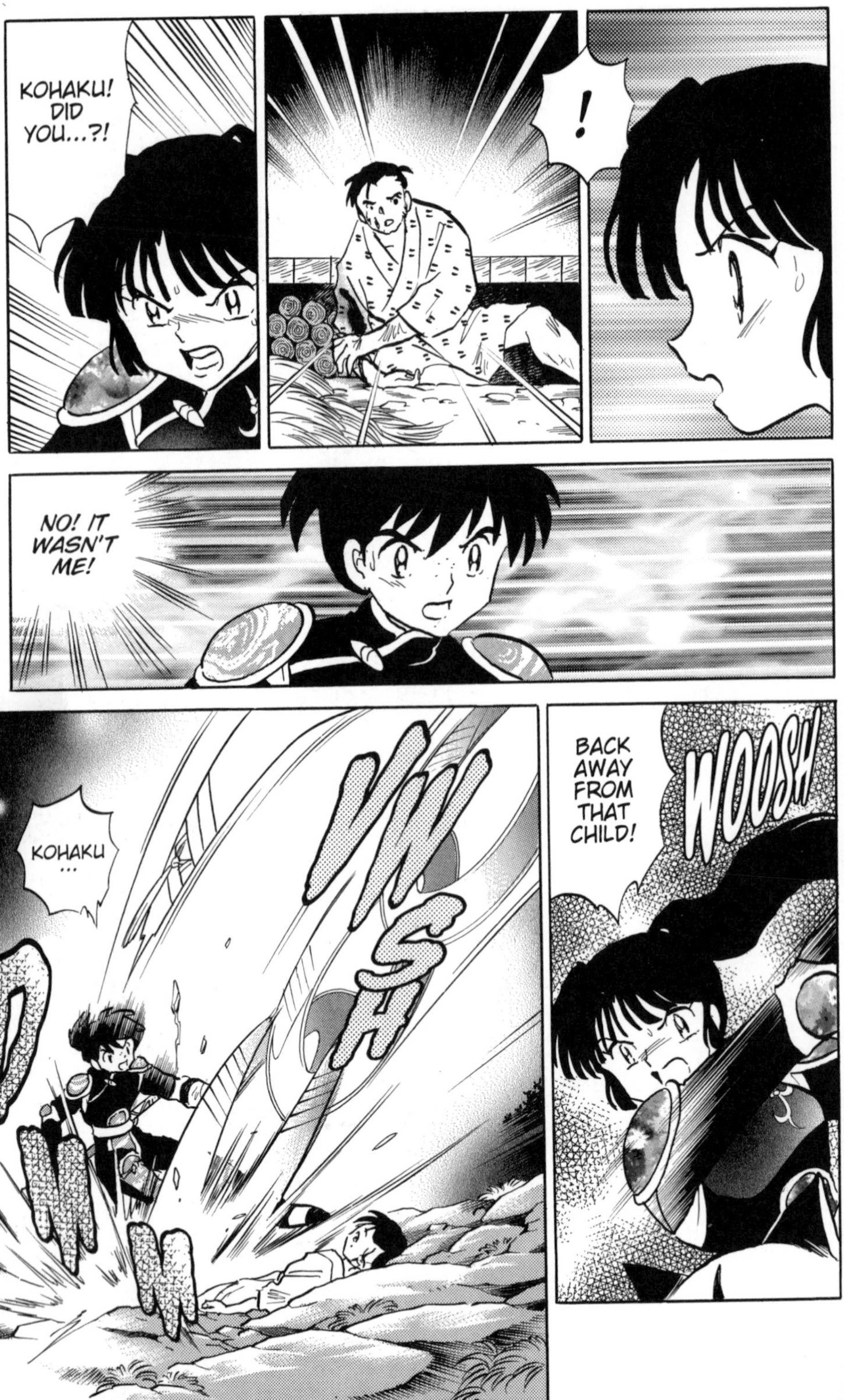
!
KOHAKU! DID YOU...?!
NO! IT WASN'T ME!
BACK AWAY FROM THAT CHILD!
WOOSH
KOHAKU ...
VWSH
DMM

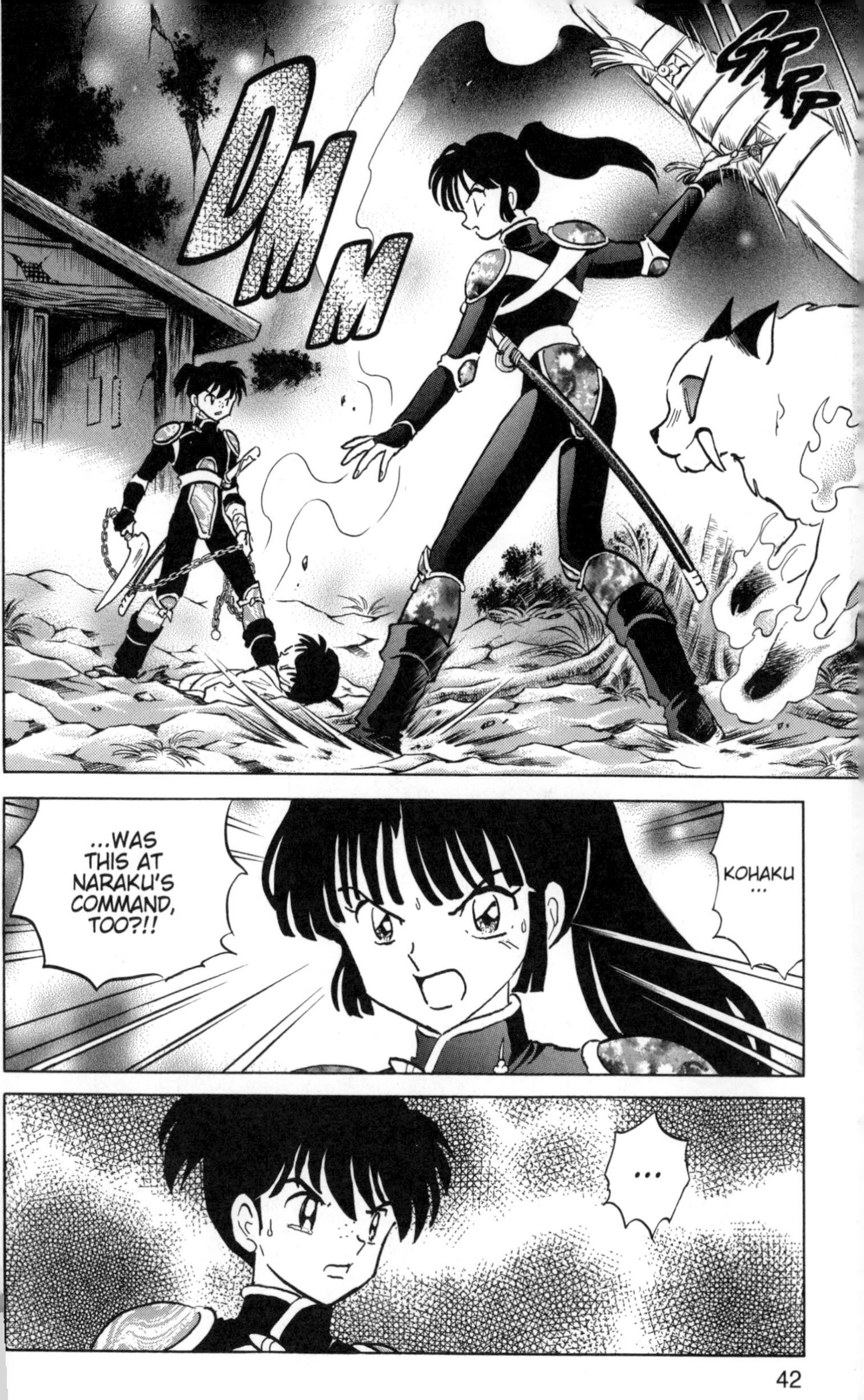
GRRP
DMMM
KOHAKU ...
...WAS THIS AT NARAKU'S COMMAND, TOO?!!
...

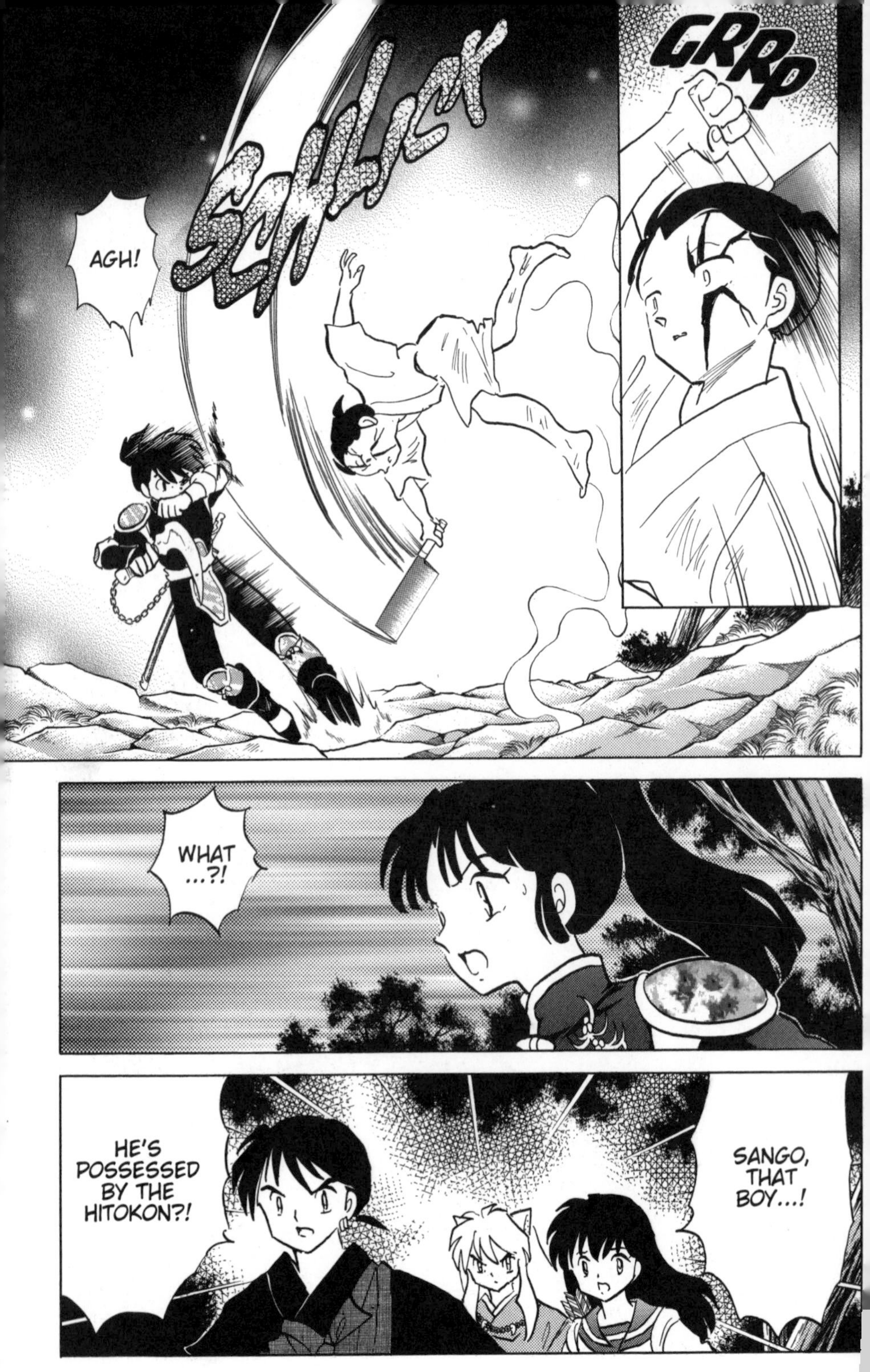
GRRP
SCHLICK
AGH!
WHAT ...?!
SANGO, THAT BOY...!
HE'S POSSESSED BY THE HITOKON?!

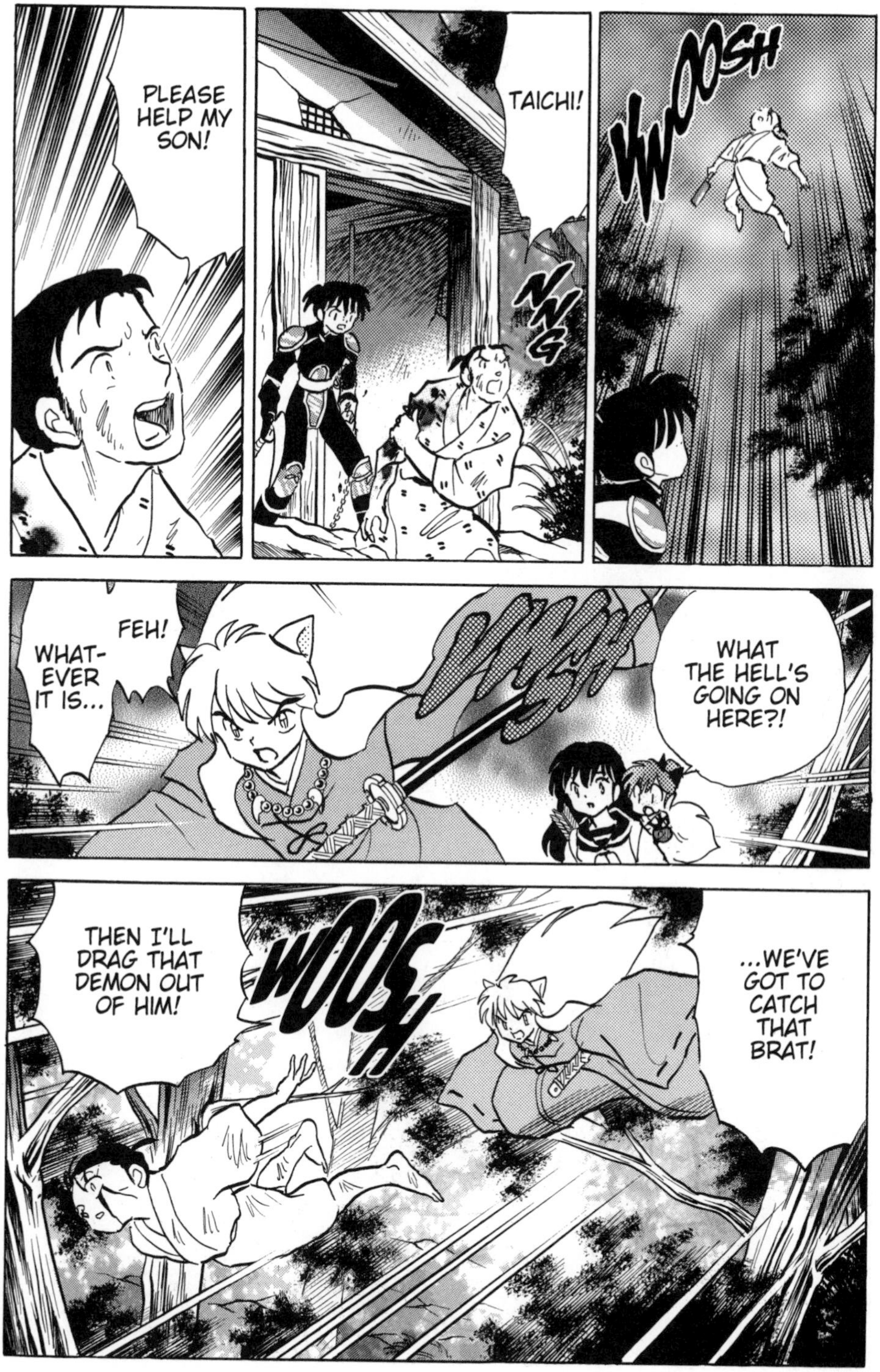
TAICHI!
NNG
PLEASE HELP MY SON!
WHAT THE HELL'S GOING ON HERE?!
FEH!
WHAT-EVER IT IS...
...WE'VE GOT TO CATCH THAT BRAT!
THEN I'LL DRAG THAT DEMON OUT OF HIM!

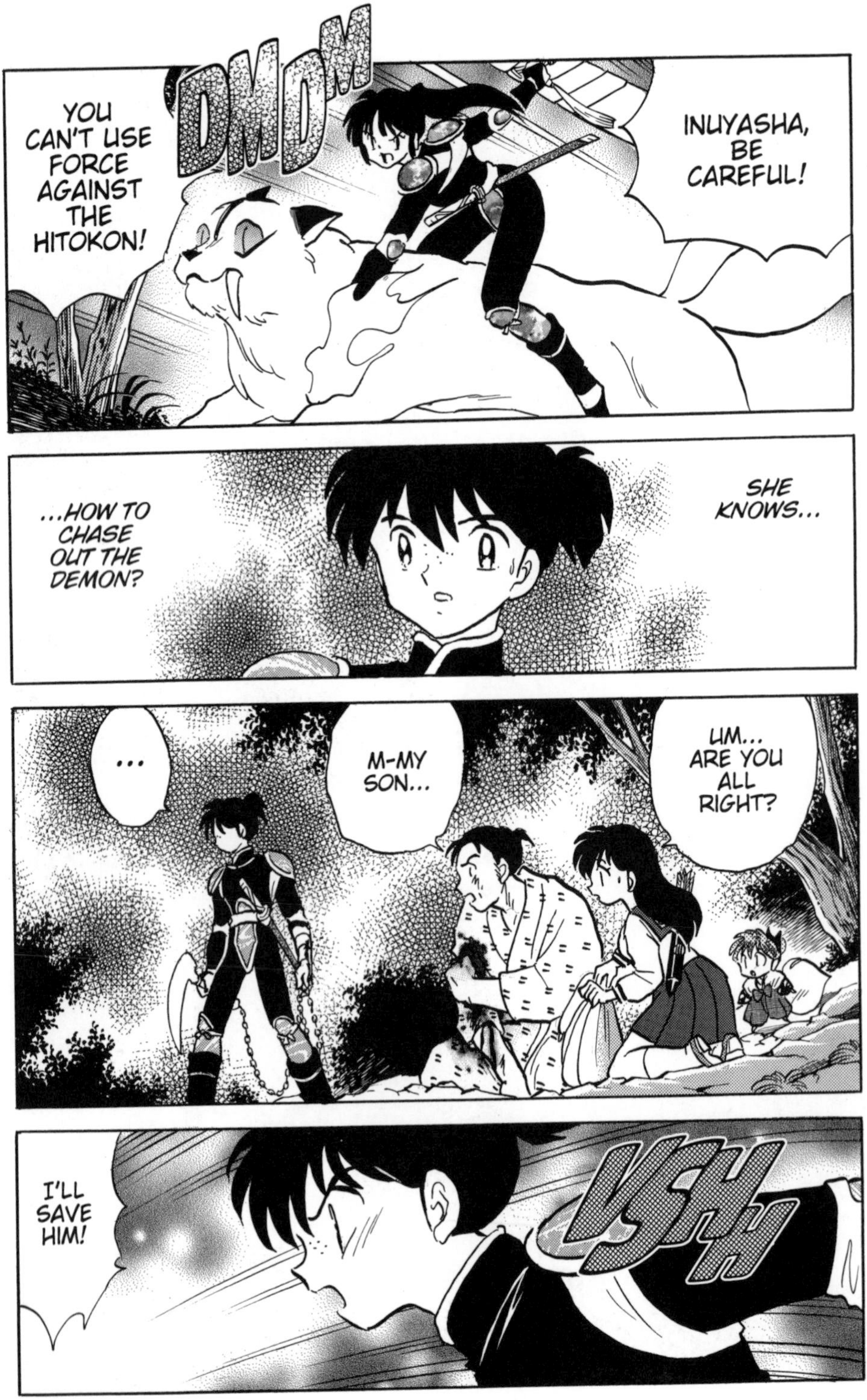

INUYASHA, BE CAREFUL!
DMDM
YOU CAN'T USE FORCE AGAINST THE HITOKON!
SHE KNOWS...
...HOW TO CHASE OUT THE DEMON?
UM... ARE YOU ALL RIGHT?
M-MY SON...
...
VSH
I'LL SAVE HIM!

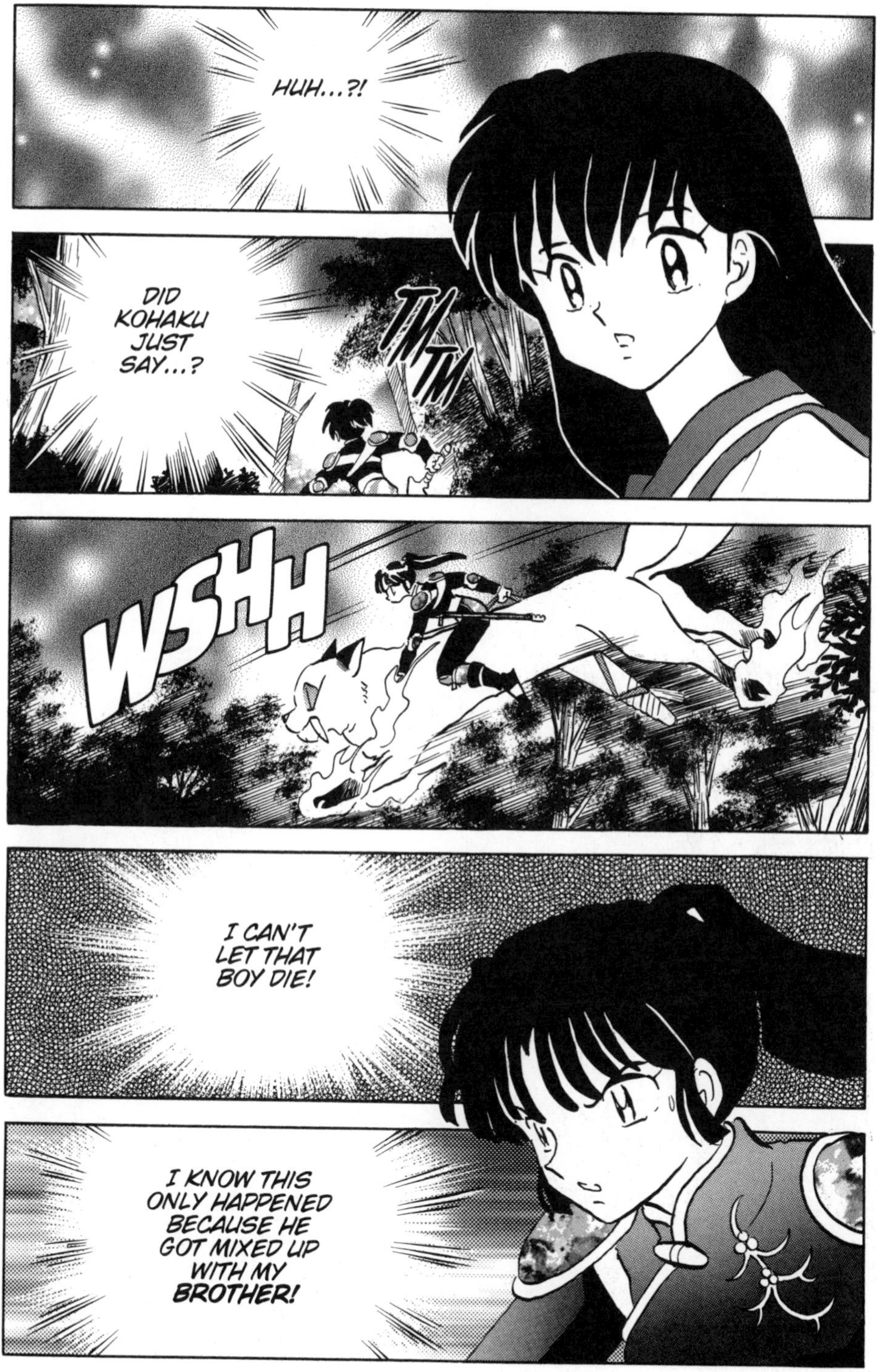
HUH...?!
DID KOHAKU JUST SAY...?
TMTM
WSHH
I CAN'T LET THAT BOY DIE!
I KNOW THIS ONLY HAPPENED BECAUSE HE GOT MIXED UP WITH MY **BROTHER!**

SCROLL THREE
HIDDEN FEELINGS

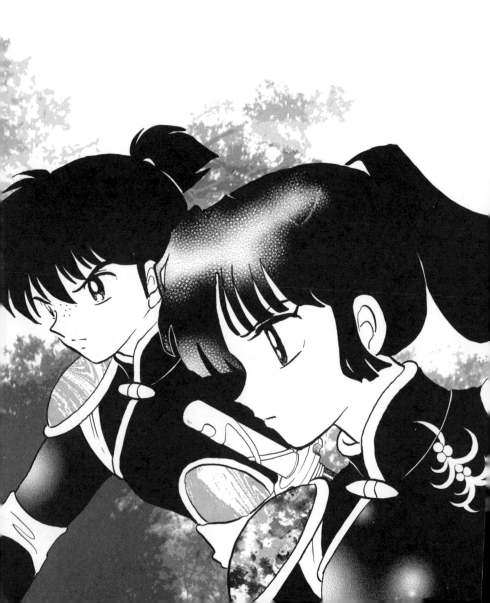

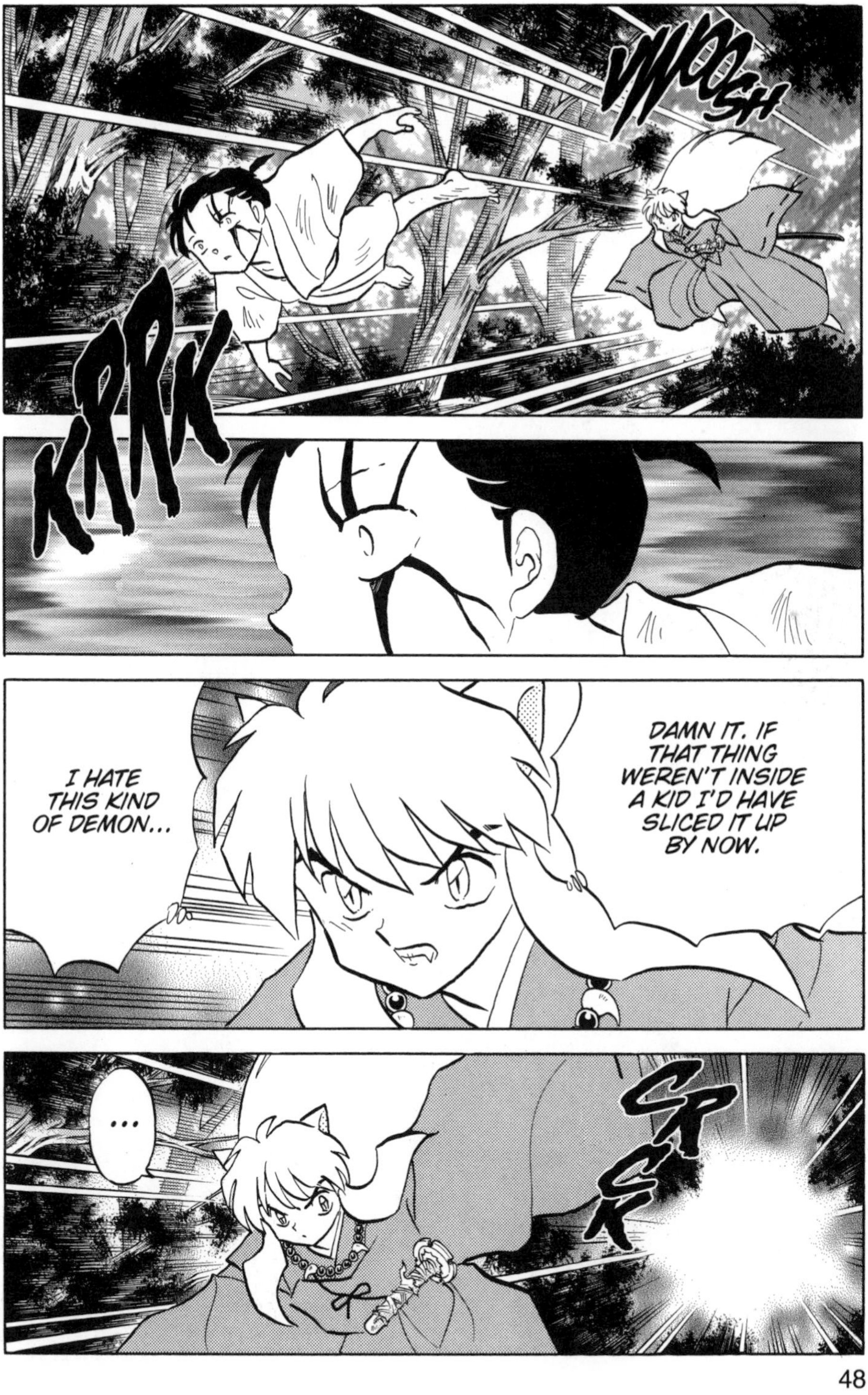
VWOOOSH
KRRK
DAMN IT. IF THAT THING WEREN'T INSIDE A KID I'D HAVE SLICED IT UP BY NOW.
I HATE THIS KIND OF DEMON...
CRSK
...

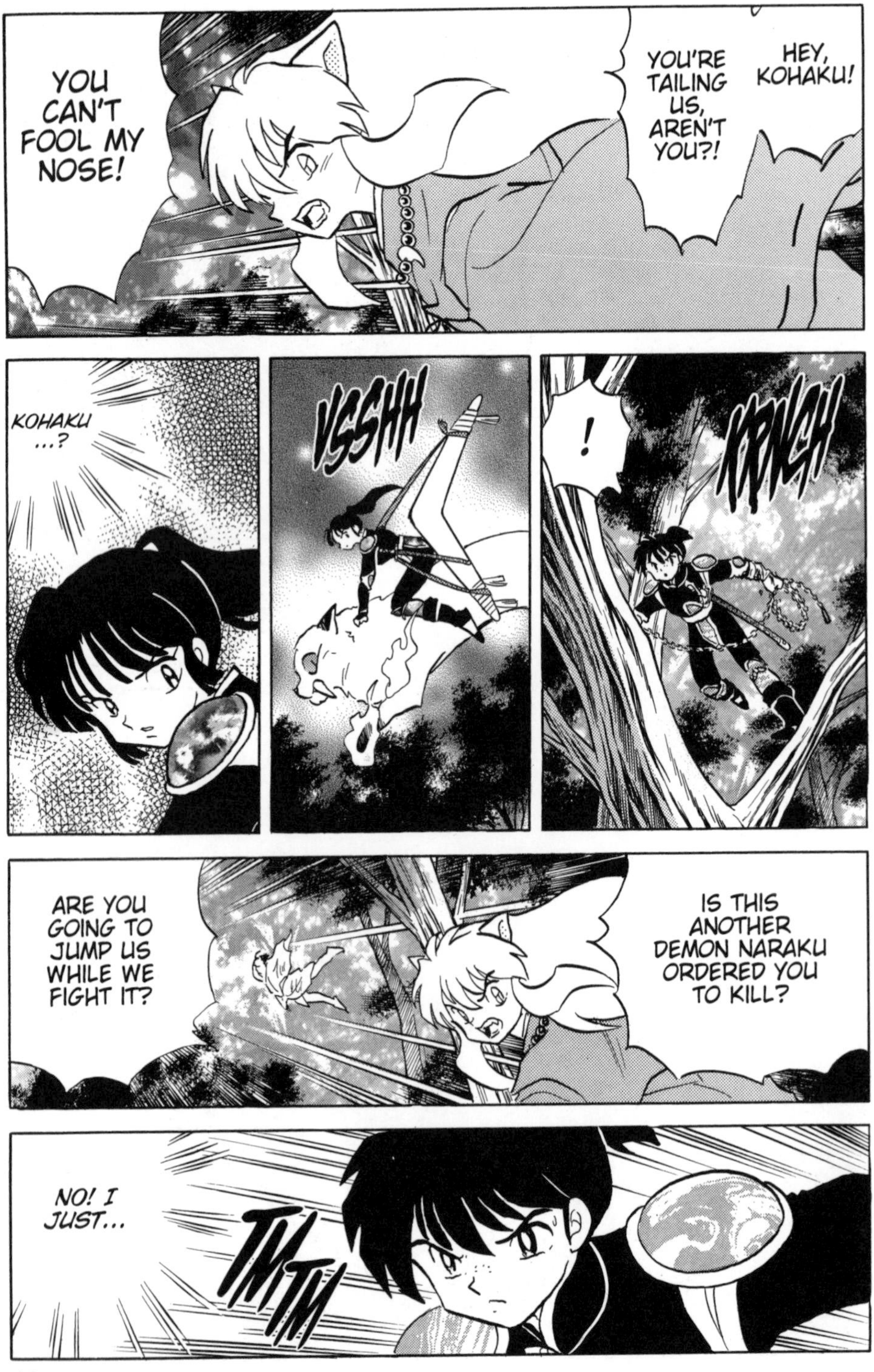
HEY, KOHAKU!
YOU'RE TAILING US, AREN'T YOU?!
YOU CAN'T FOOL MY NOSE!
!
KRNCH
VSSHH
KOHAKU ...?
IS THIS ANOTHER DEMON NARAKU ORDERED YOU TO KILL?
ARE YOU GOING TO JUMP US WHILE WE FIGHT IT?
TMTM
NO! I JUST...

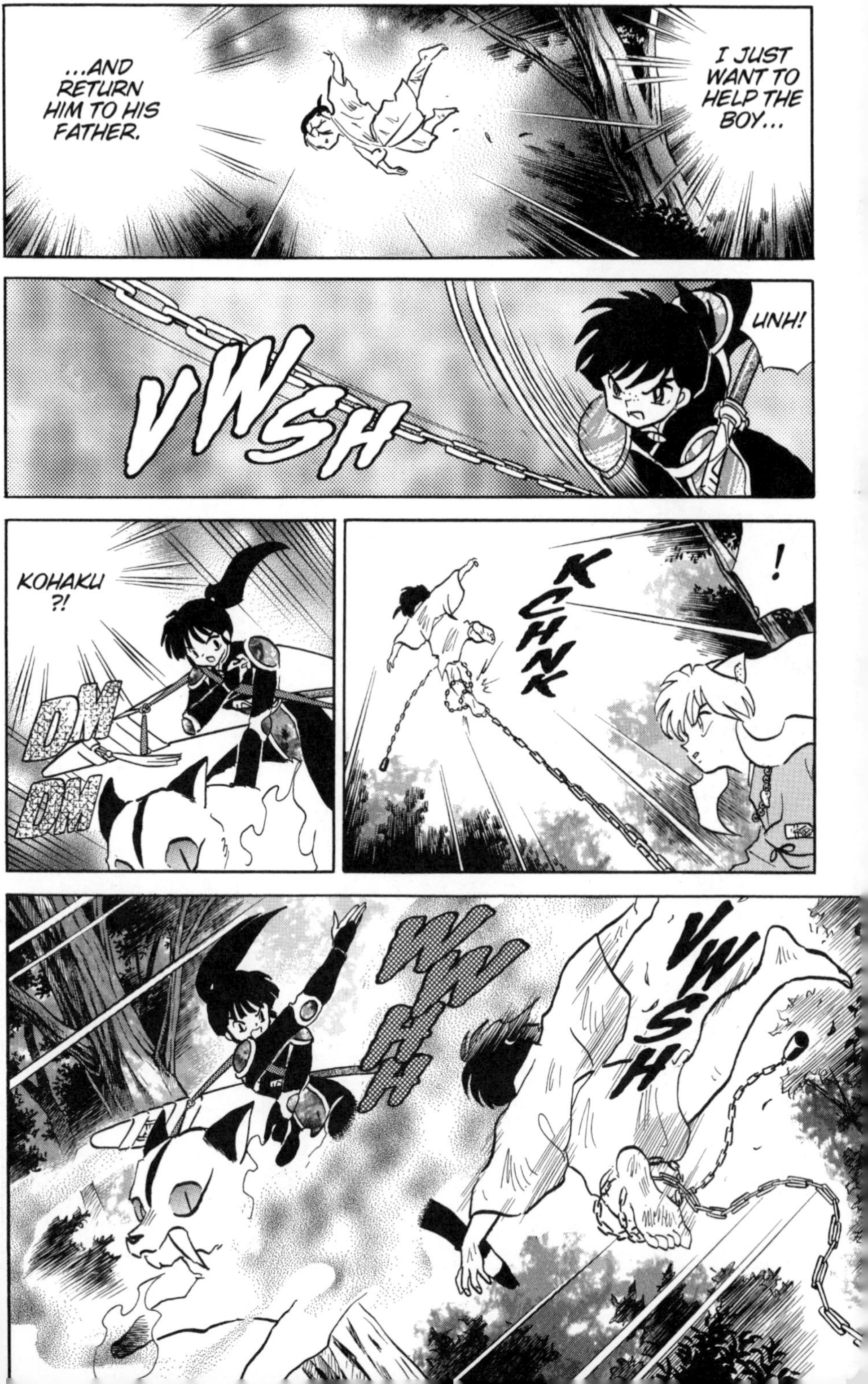
I JUST WANT TO HELP THE BOY...
...AND RETURN HIM TO HIS FATHER.
UNH!
VWSH
!
KCHNK
KOHAKU ?!
DM DM
VWSH

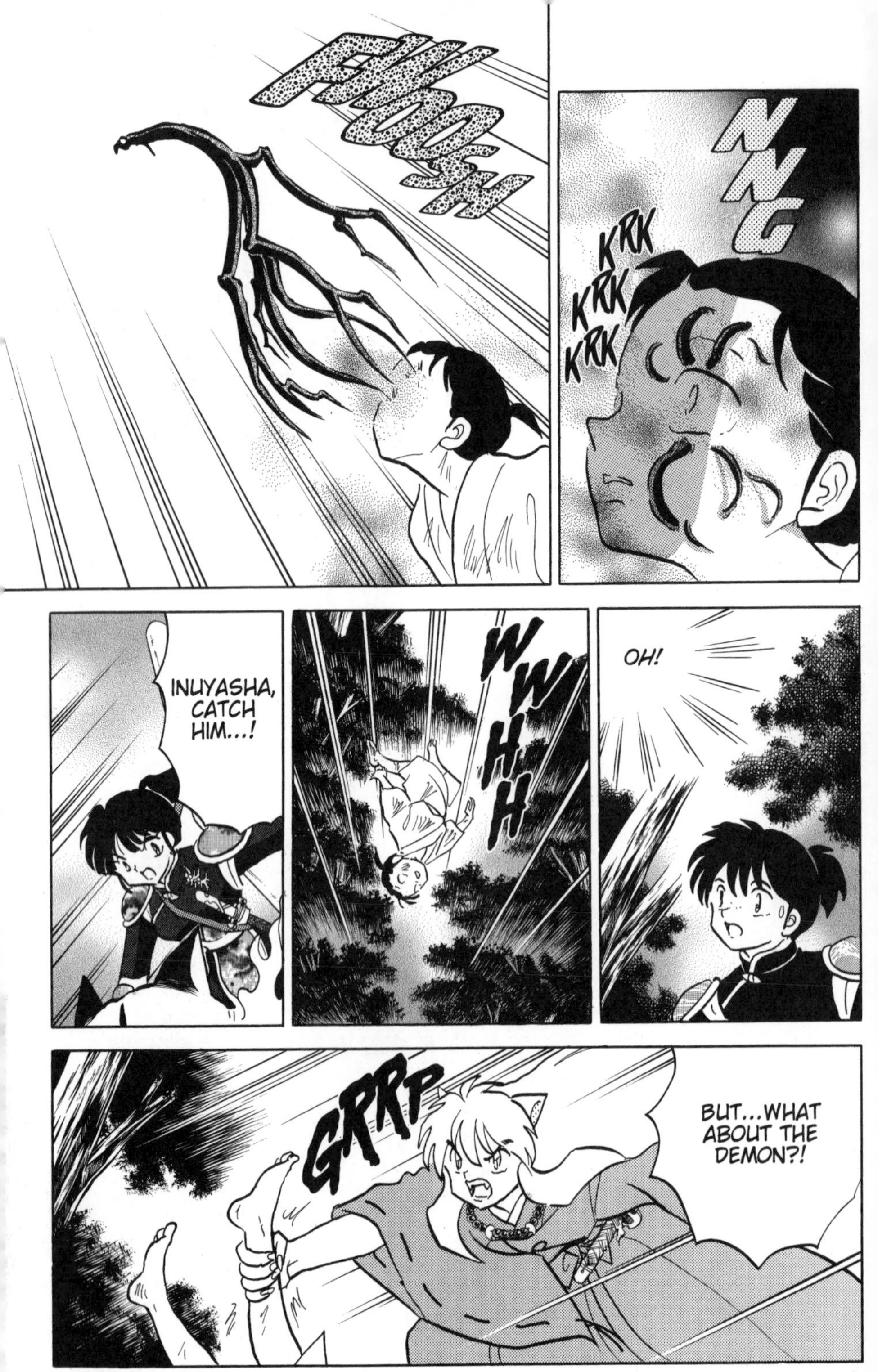
NNG
KRK KRK KRK
FWOOSH
OH!
WWHH
INUYASHA, CATCH HIM...!
BUT...WHAT ABOUT THE DEMON?!
GRRP

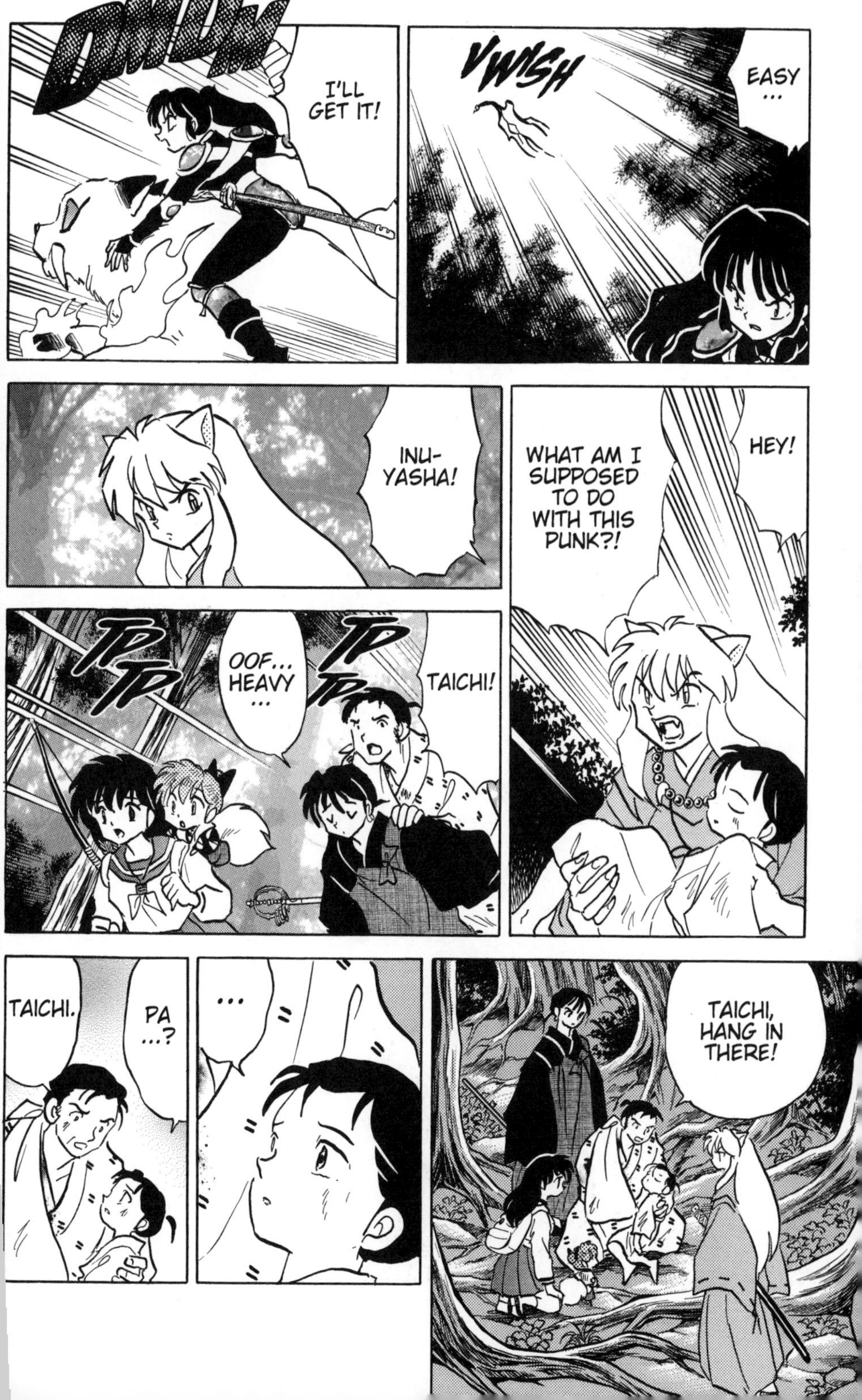
VWISH
EASY...
DMDM
I'LL GET IT!
HEY!
WHAT AM I SUPPOSED TO DO WITH THIS PUNK?!
INU-YASHA!
TP TP
TAICHI!
OOF... HEAVY...
TP TP
TAICHI, HANG IN THERE!
...
PA...?
TAICHI.

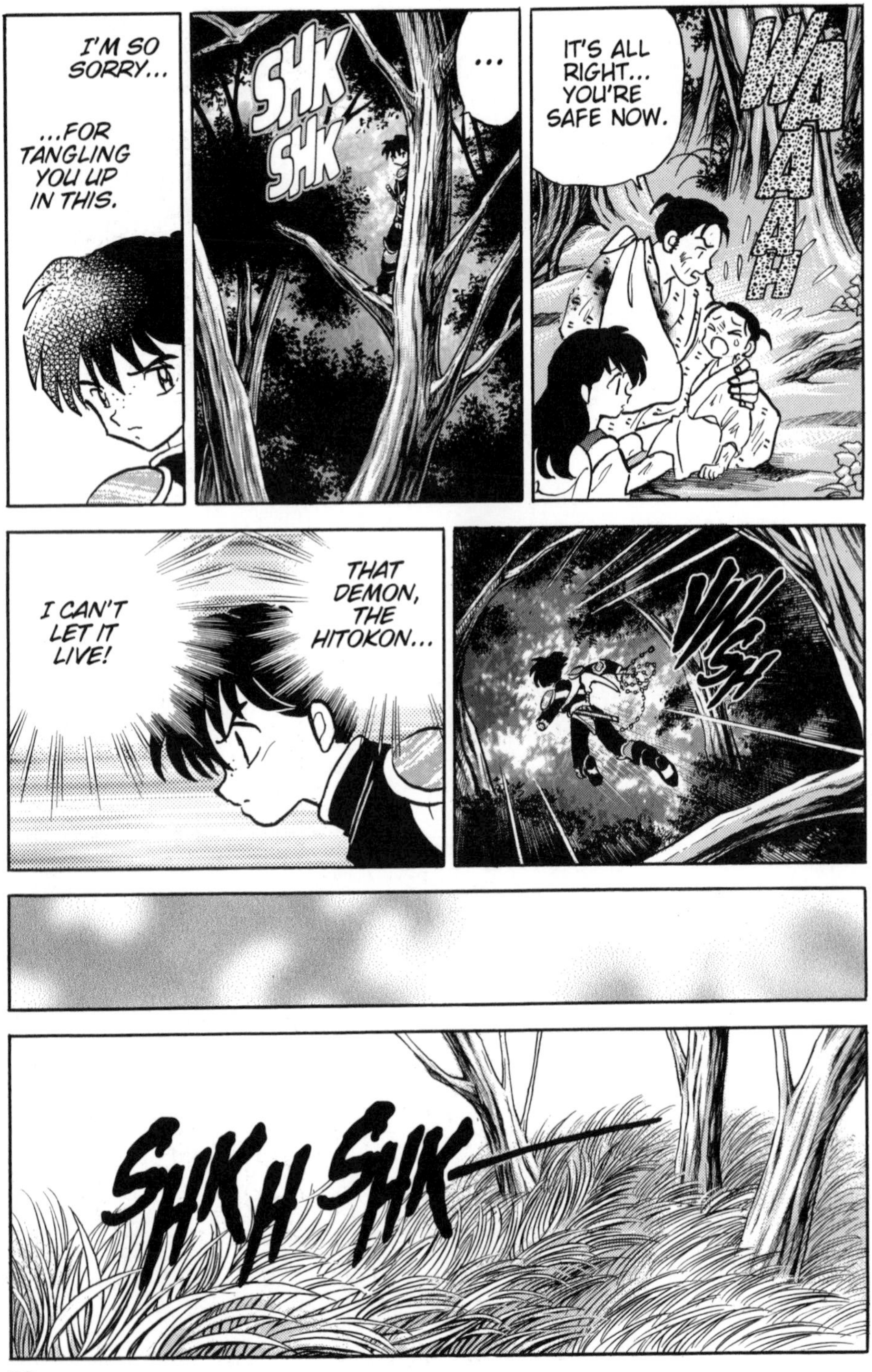

IT'S ALL RIGHT... YOU'RE SAFE NOW.
WAAAAH
...
SHK SHK
I'M SO SORRY...
...FOR TANGLING YOU UP IN THIS.
VWSH
THAT DEMON, THE HITOKON...
I CAN'T LET IT LIVE!
SHK H SHK

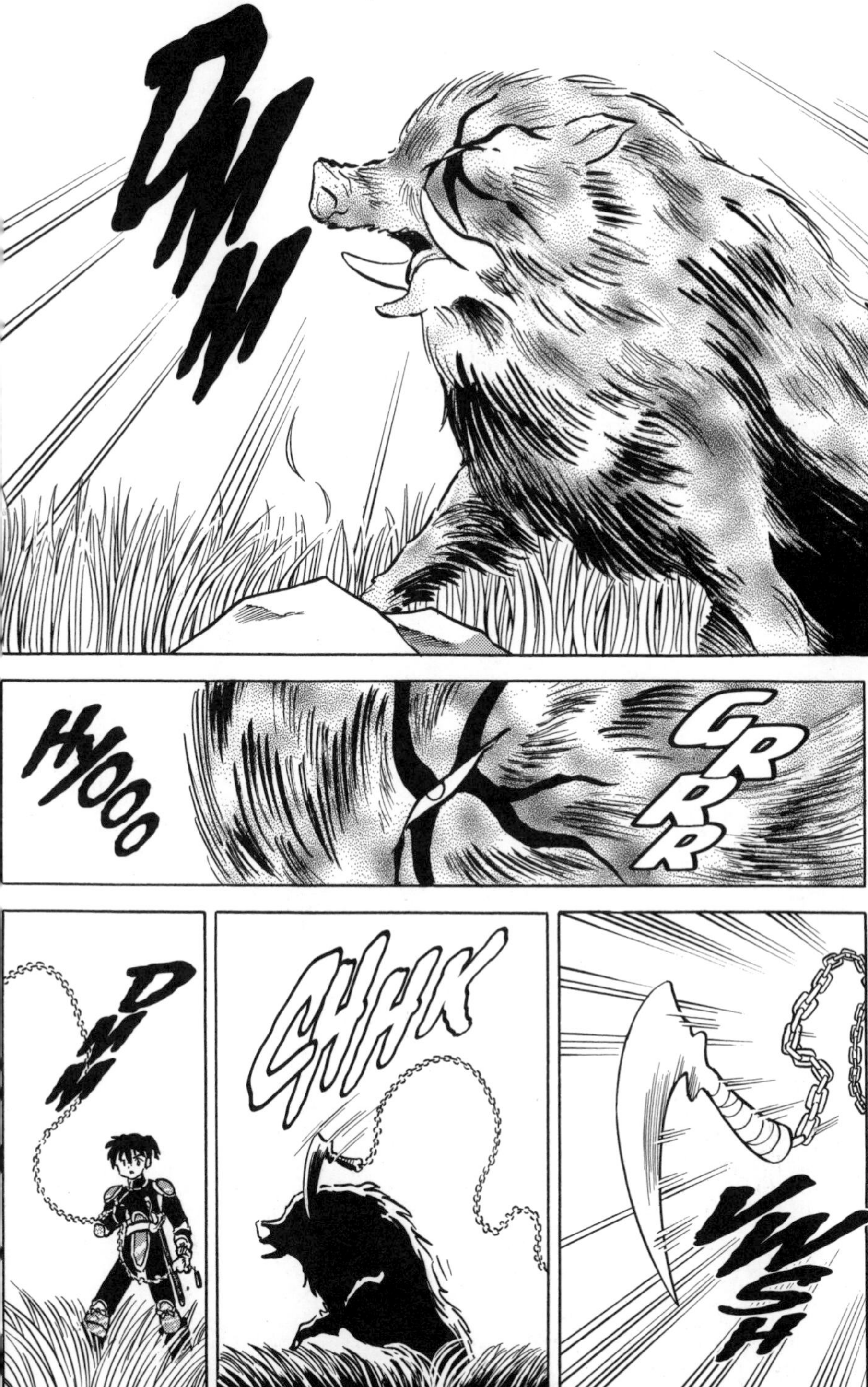
DMM
GRRR
HWOOO
VWSH
CHAK
DMM

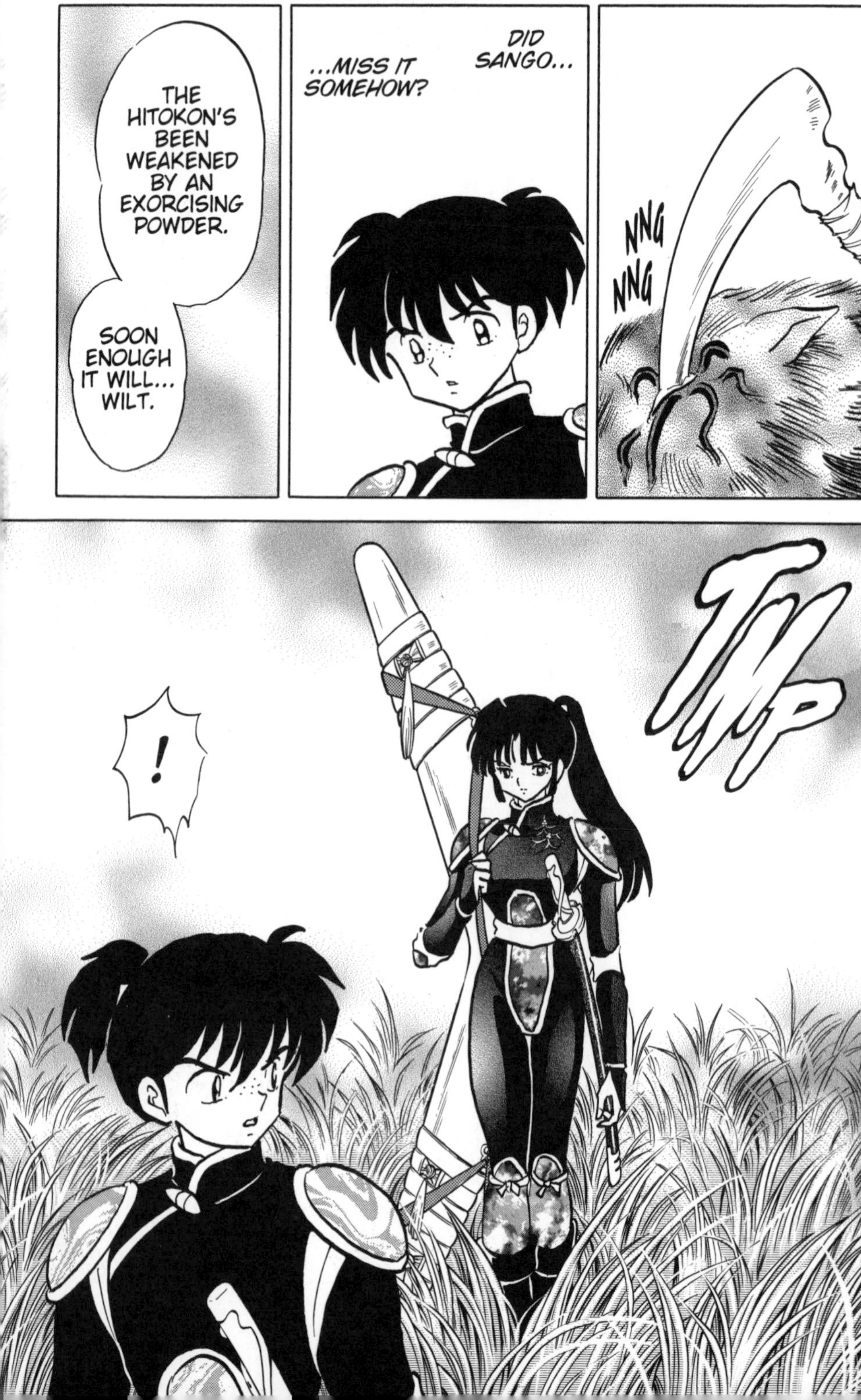
NNG NNG
DID SANGO...
...MISS IT SOMEHOW?
THE HITOKON'S BEEN WEAKENED BY AN EXORCISING POWDER.
SOON ENOUGH IT WILL... WILT.
THMP
!

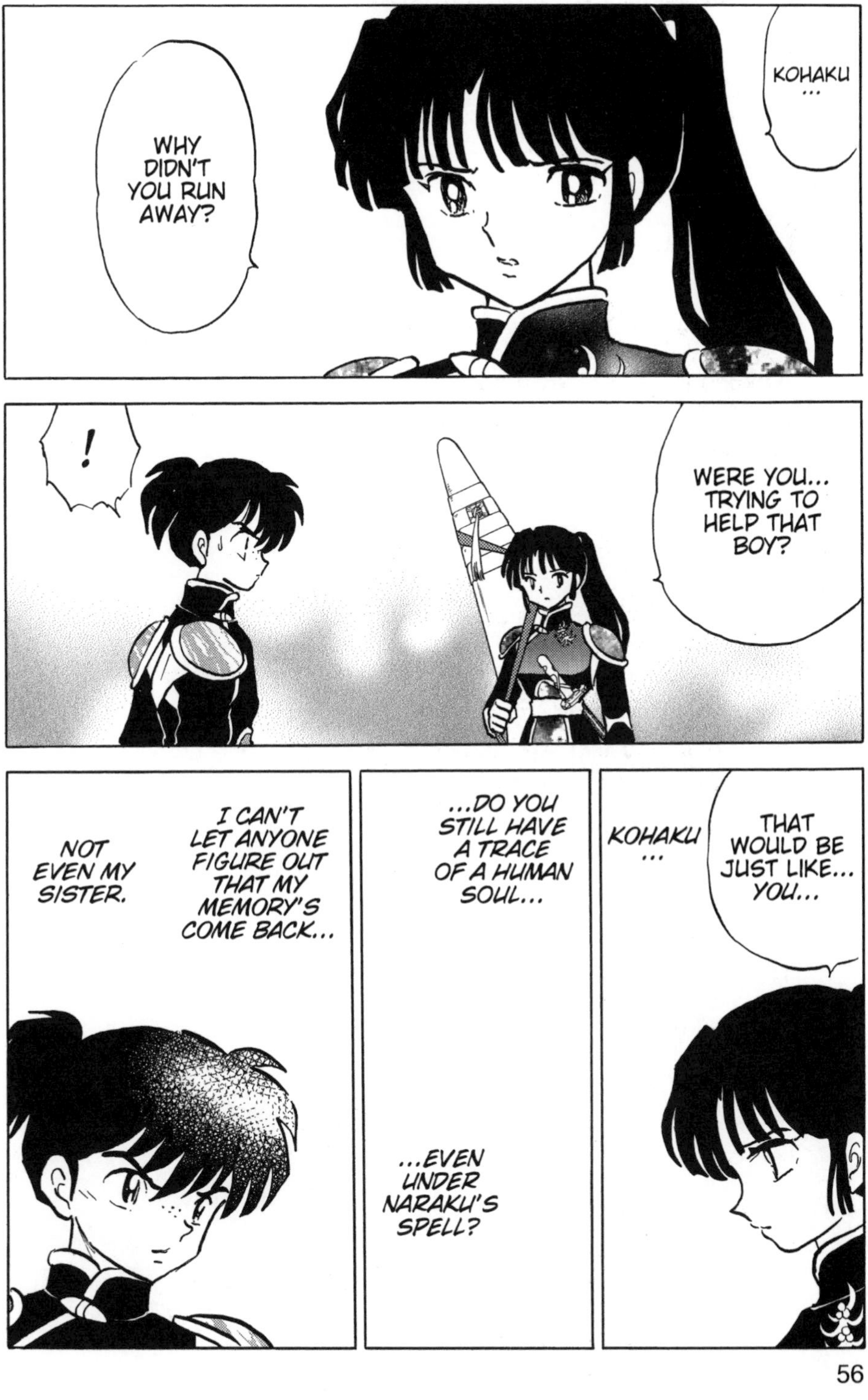
KOHAKU ...
WHY DIDN'T YOU RUN AWAY?
WERE YOU... TRYING TO HELP THAT BOY?
!
THAT WOULD BE JUST LIKE... YOU...
KOHAKU ...
...DO YOU STILL HAVE A TRACE OF A HUMAN SOUL...
...EVEN UNDER NARAKU'S SPELL?
I CAN'T LET ANYONE FIGURE OUT THAT MY MEMORY'S COME BACK...
NOT EVEN MY SISTER.

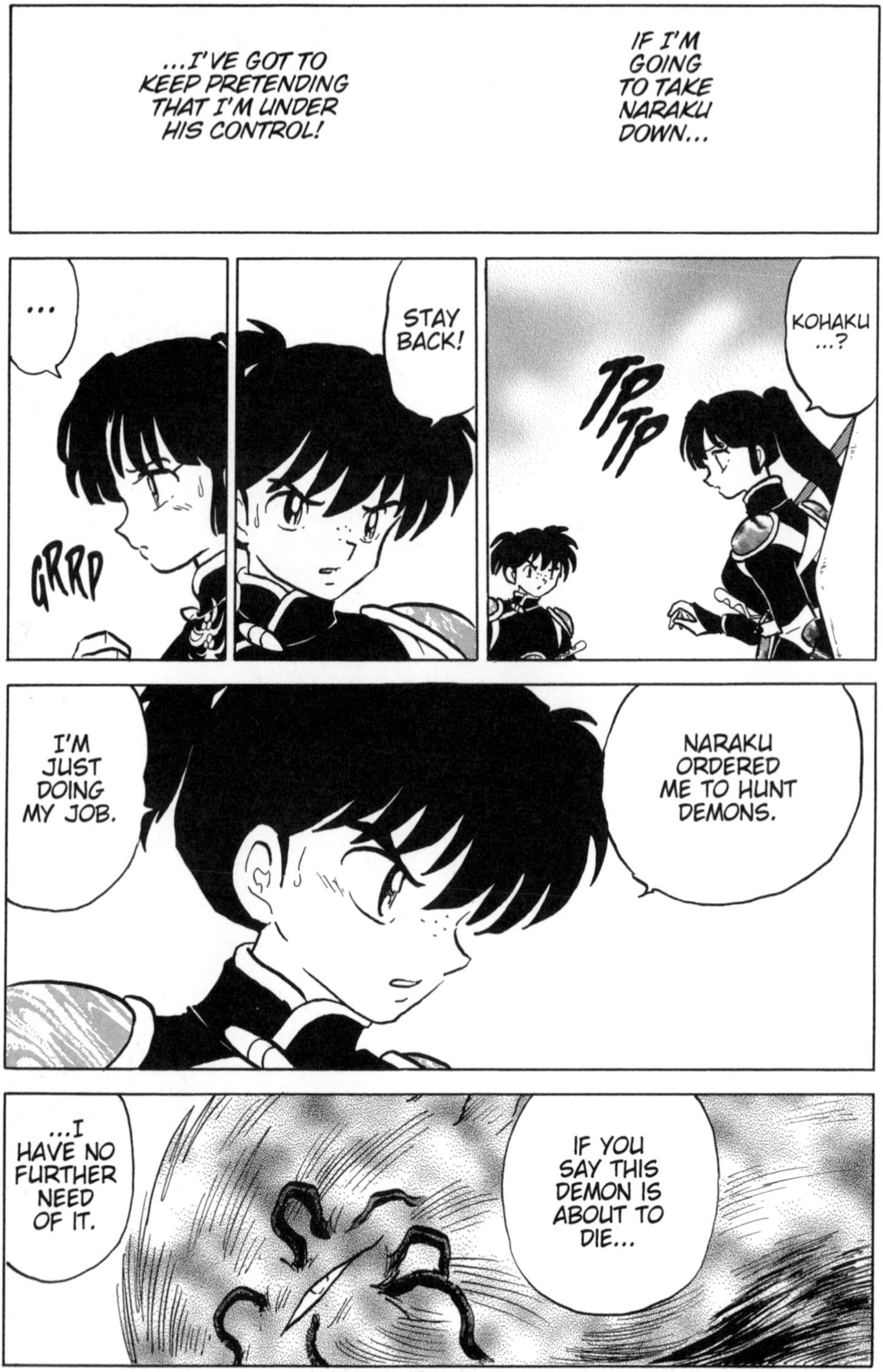

IF I'M GOING TO TAKE NARAKU DOWN...
...I'VE GOT TO KEEP PRETENDING THAT I'M UNDER HIS CONTROL!
KOHAKU ...?
TPTP
STAY BACK!
...
GRRP
NARAKU ORDERED ME TO HUNT DEMONS.
I'M JUST DOING MY JOB.
IF YOU SAY THIS DEMON IS ABOUT TO DIE...
...I HAVE NO FURTHER NEED OF IT.

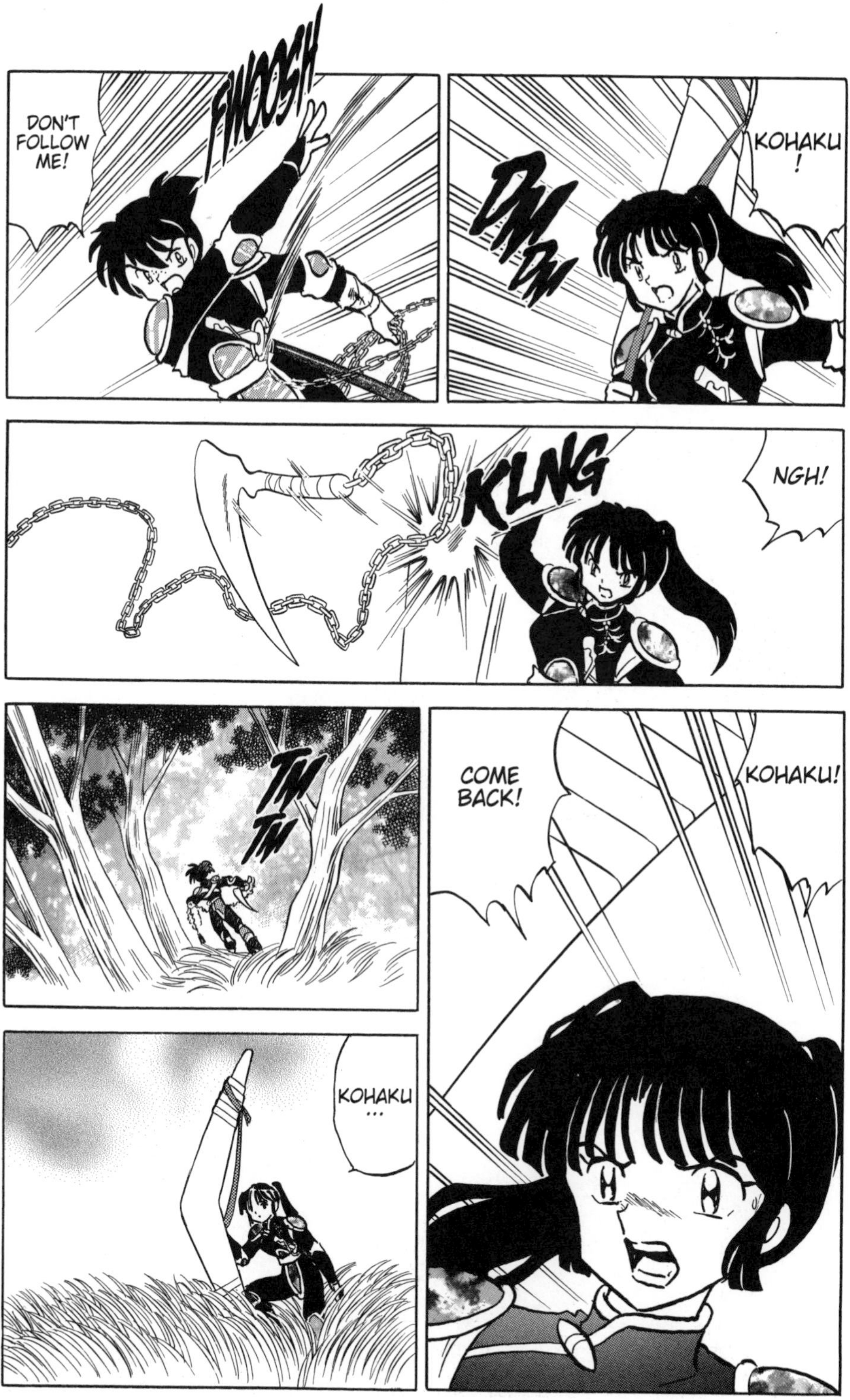
KOHAKU !
DM DM DM
FWOOSH
DON'T FOLLOW ME!
NGH!
KLNG
KOHAKU!
COME BACK!
TM TM TM
KOHAKU ...

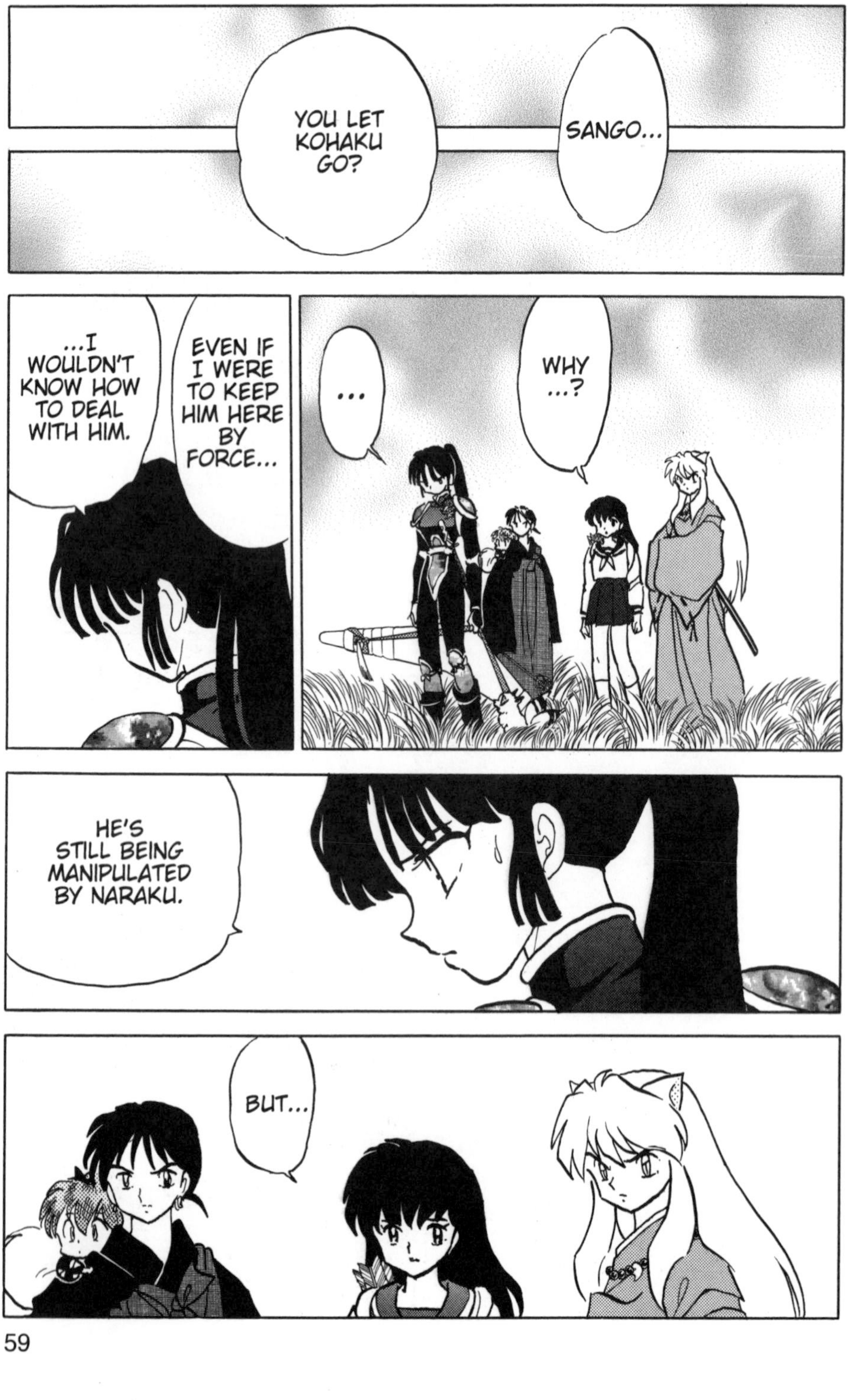
SANGO...
YOU LET KOHAKU GO?
WHY ...?
...
EVEN IF I WERE TO KEEP HIM HERE BY FORCE...
...I WOULDN'T KNOW HOW TO DEAL WITH HIM.
HE'S STILL BEING MANIPULATED BY NARAKU.
BUT...

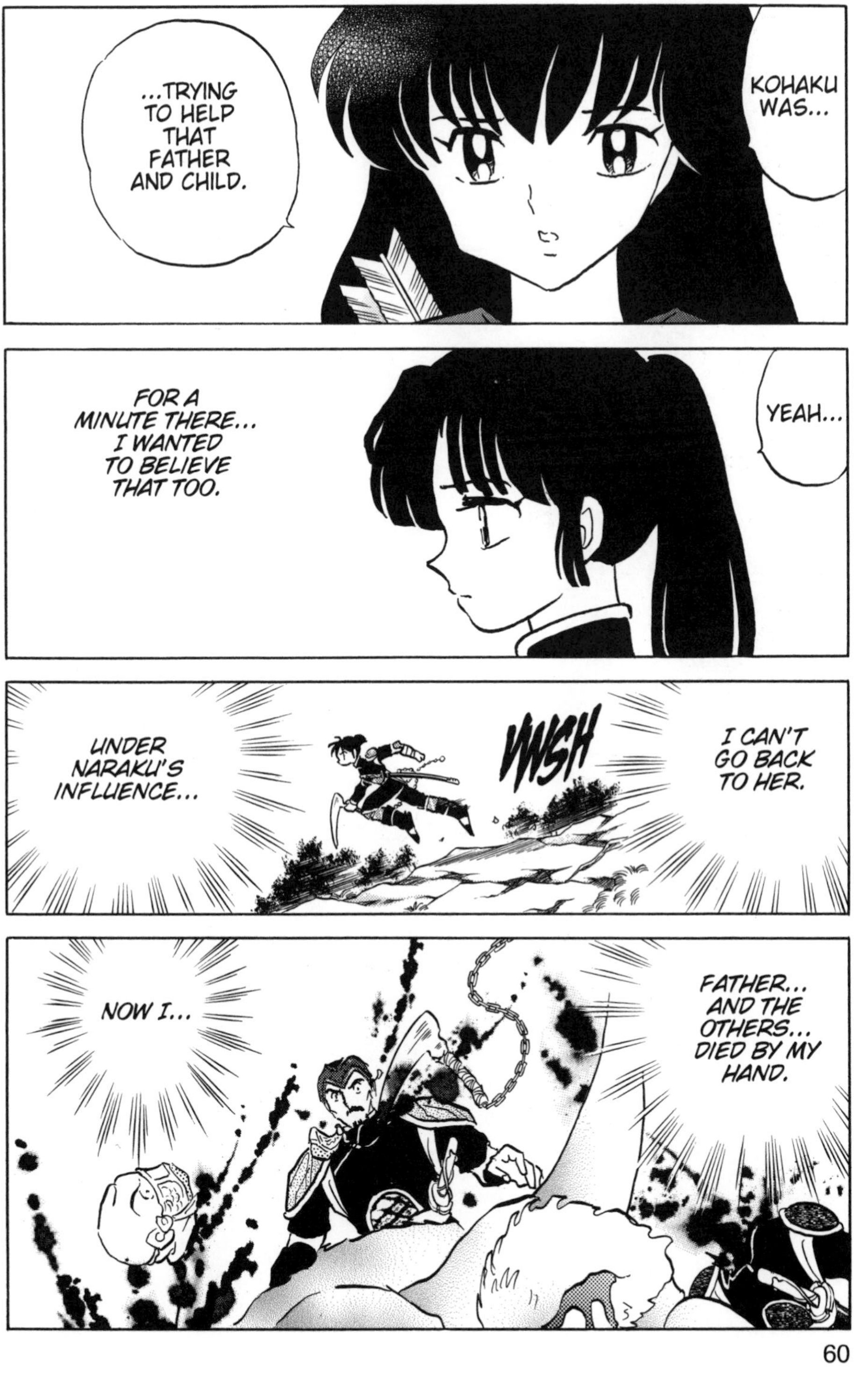
KOHAKU WAS...
...TRYING TO HELP THAT FATHER AND CHILD.
YEAH...
FOR A MINUTE THERE... I WANTED TO BELIEVE THAT TOO.
I CAN'T GO BACK TO HER.
VWSH
UNDER NARAKU'S INFLUENCE...
FATHER... AND THE OTHERS... DIED BY MY HAND.
NOW I...

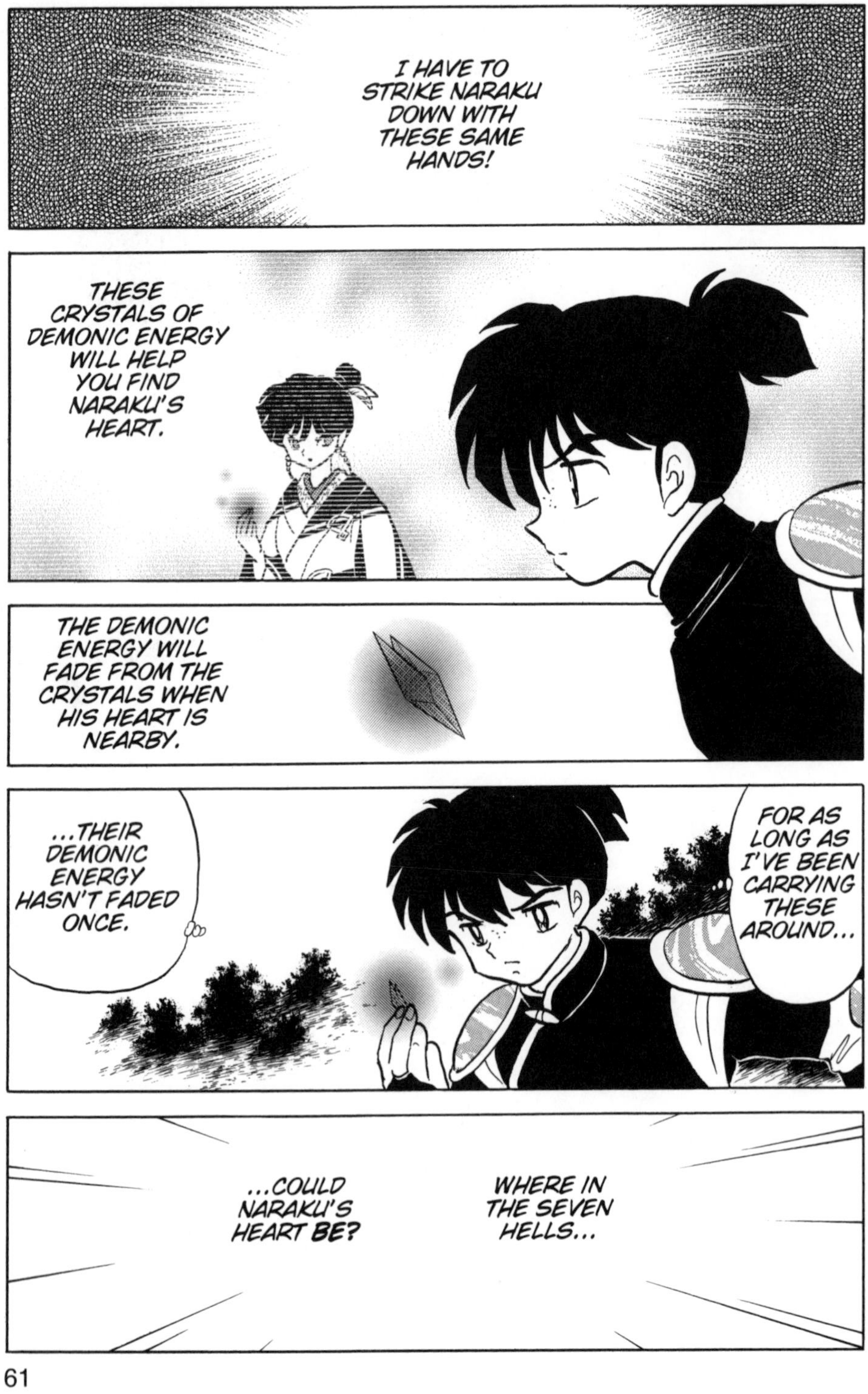
I HAVE TO STRIKE NARAKU DOWN WITH THESE SAME HANDS!
THESE CRYSTALS OF DEMONIC ENERGY WILL HELP YOU FIND NARAKU'S HEART.
THE DEMONIC ENERGY WILL FADE FROM THE CRYSTALS WHEN HIS HEART IS NEARBY.
FOR AS LONG AS I'VE BEEN CARRYING THESE AROUND...
...THEIR DEMONIC ENERGY HASN'T FADED ONCE.
WHERE IN THE SEVEN HELLS...
...COULD NARAKU'S HEART BE?

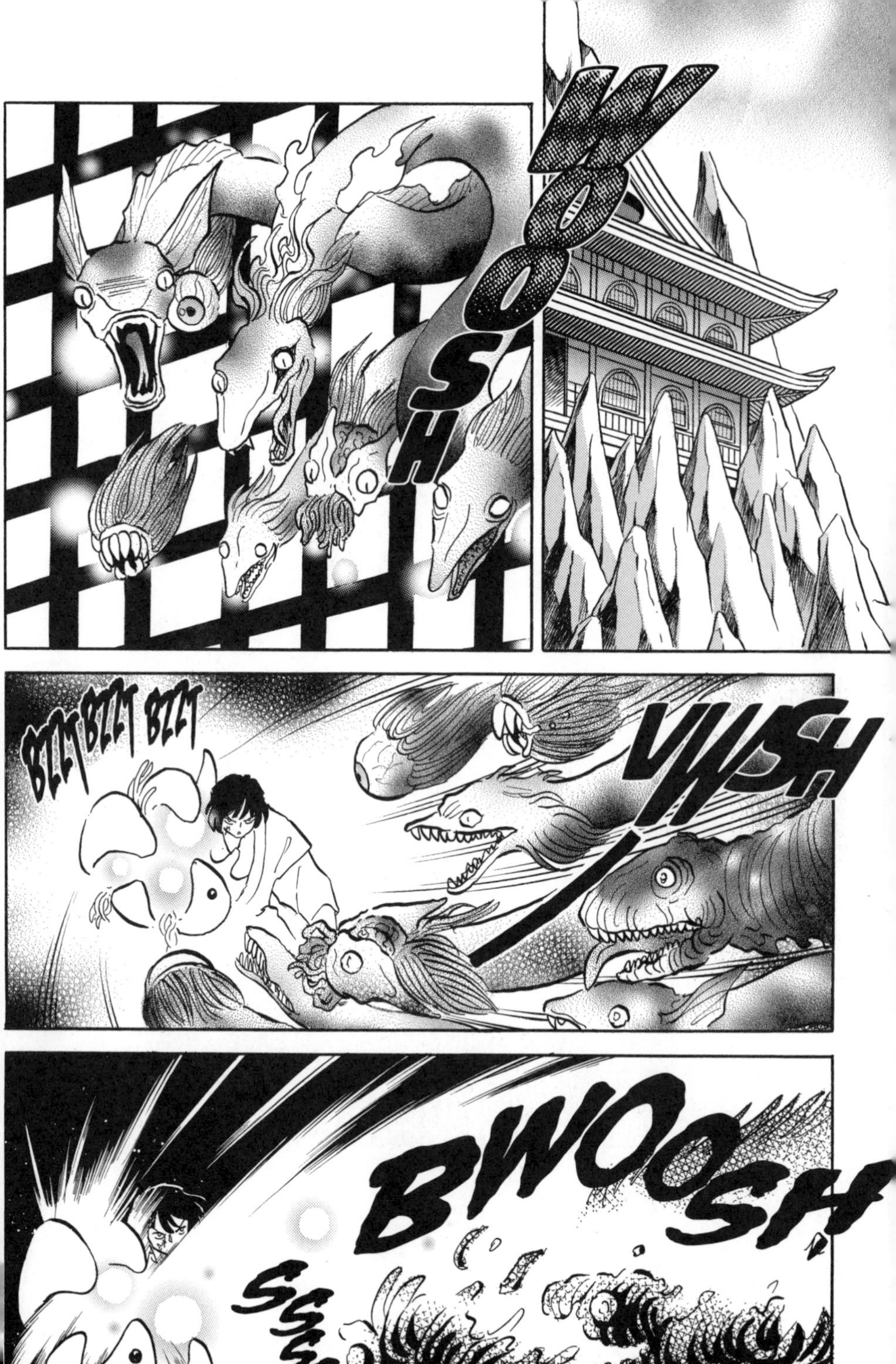
WHOOSH
VWSH
BZZT BZZT BZZT
BWOOSH
SSSSS

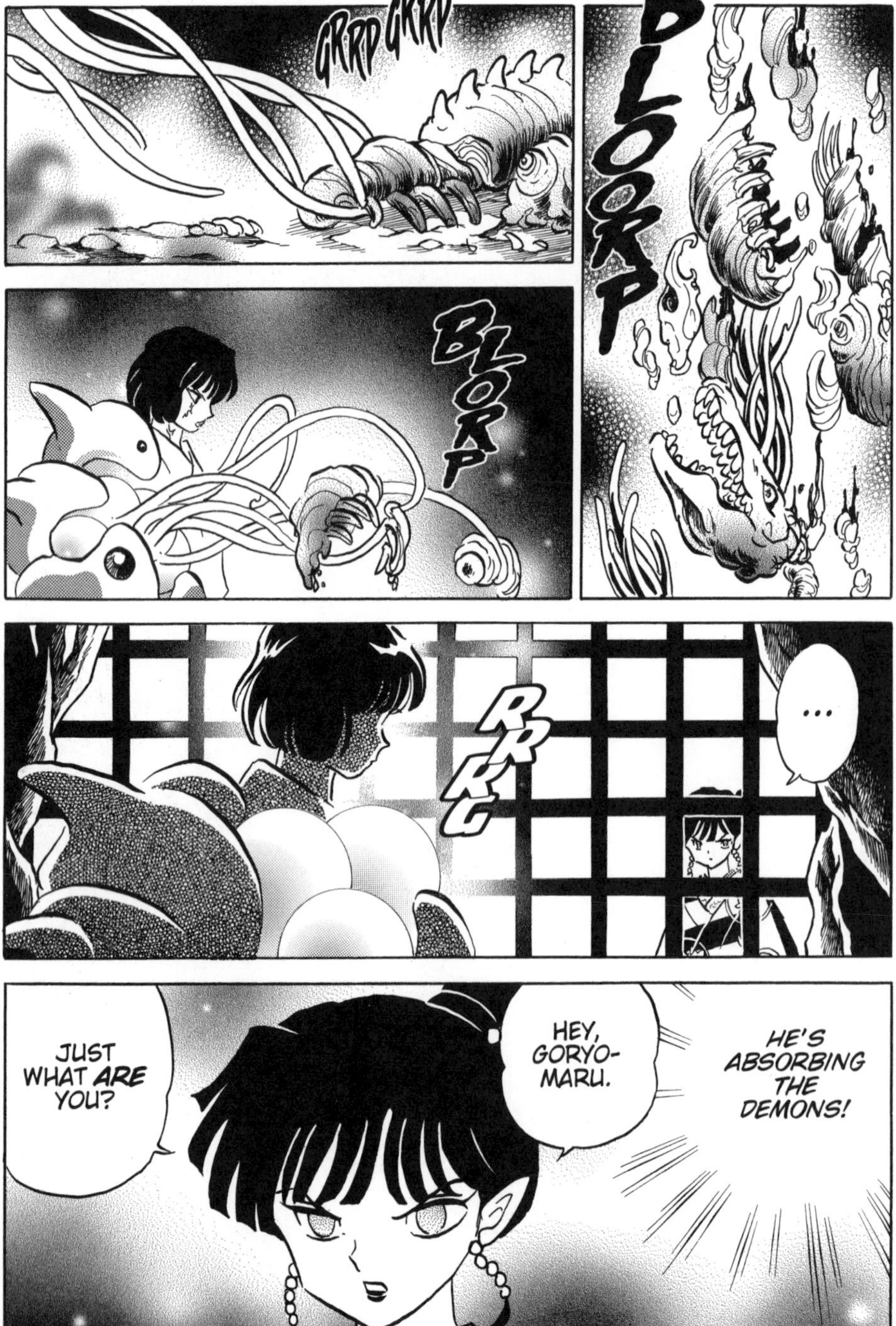
BLOORP
GRRP GRRP
BLORP
...
RRRG
HE'S ABSORBING THE DEMONS!
HEY, GORYO-MARU.
JUST WHAT ARE YOU?

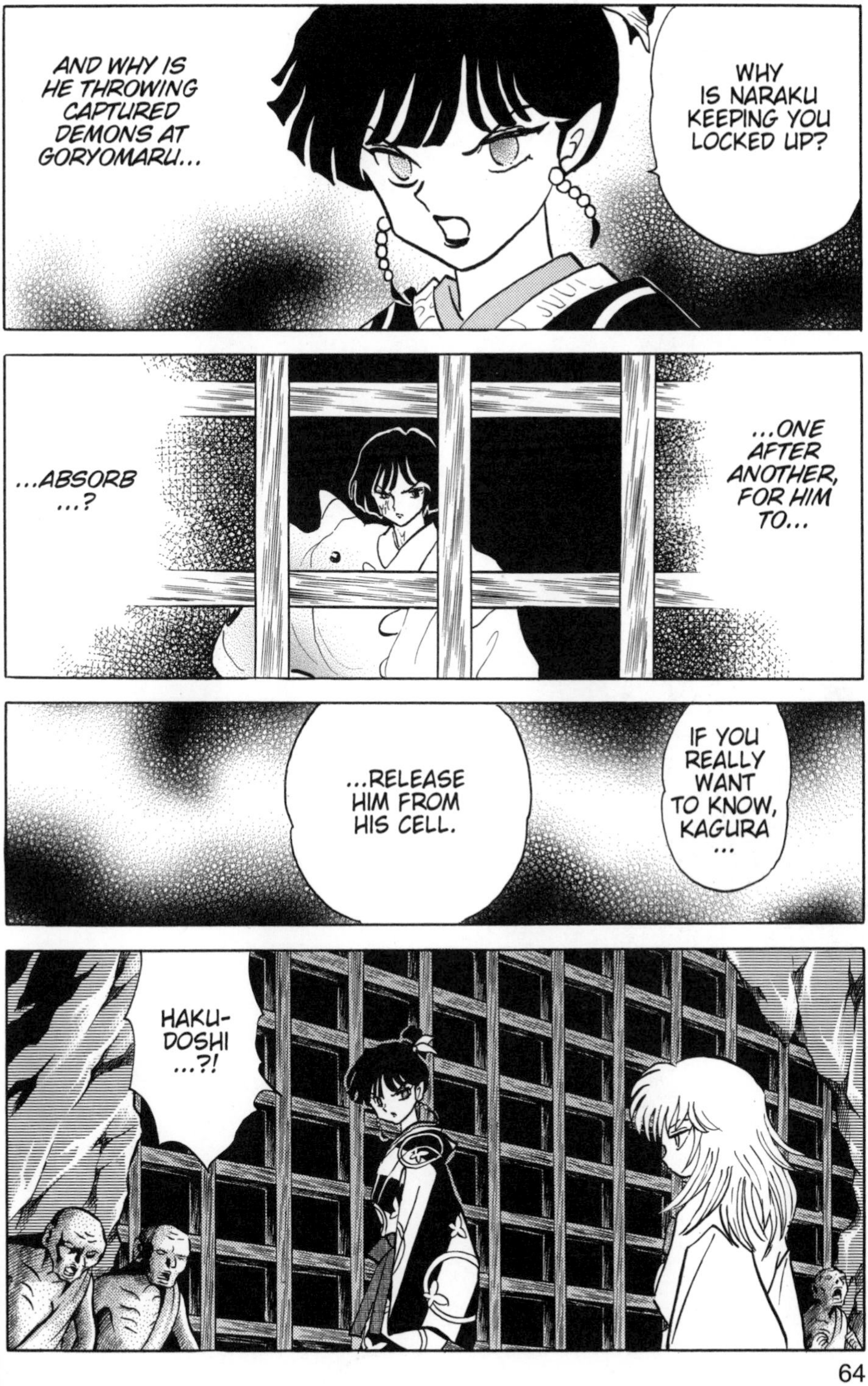
WHY IS NARAKU KEEPING YOU LOCKED UP?
AND WHY IS HE THROWING CAPTURED DEMONS AT GORYOMARU...
...ONE AFTER ANOTHER, FOR HIM TO...
...ABSORB ...?
IF YOU REALLY WANT TO KNOW, KAGURA ...
...RELEASE HIM FROM HIS CELL.
HAKU-DOSHI ...?!

SCROLL FOUR
ESCAPE

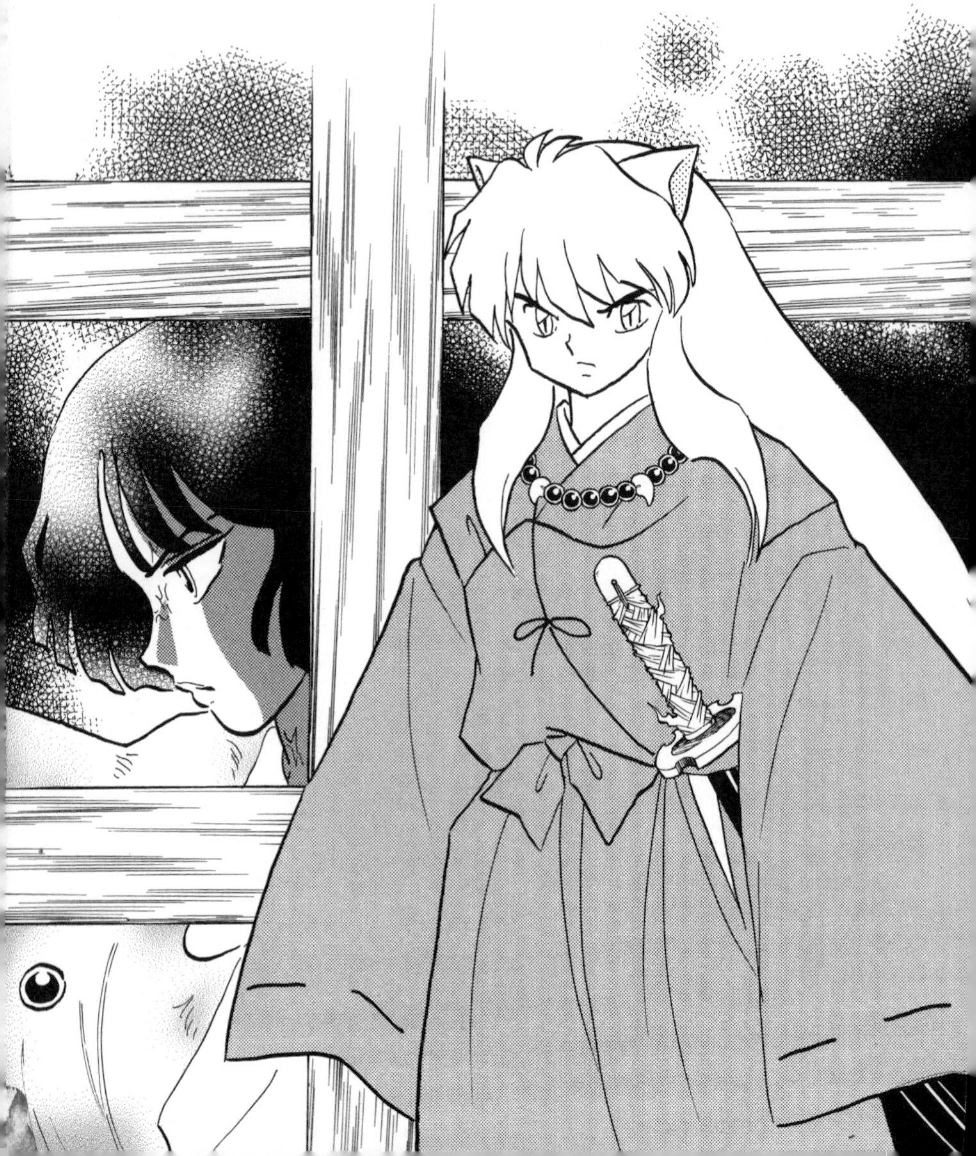

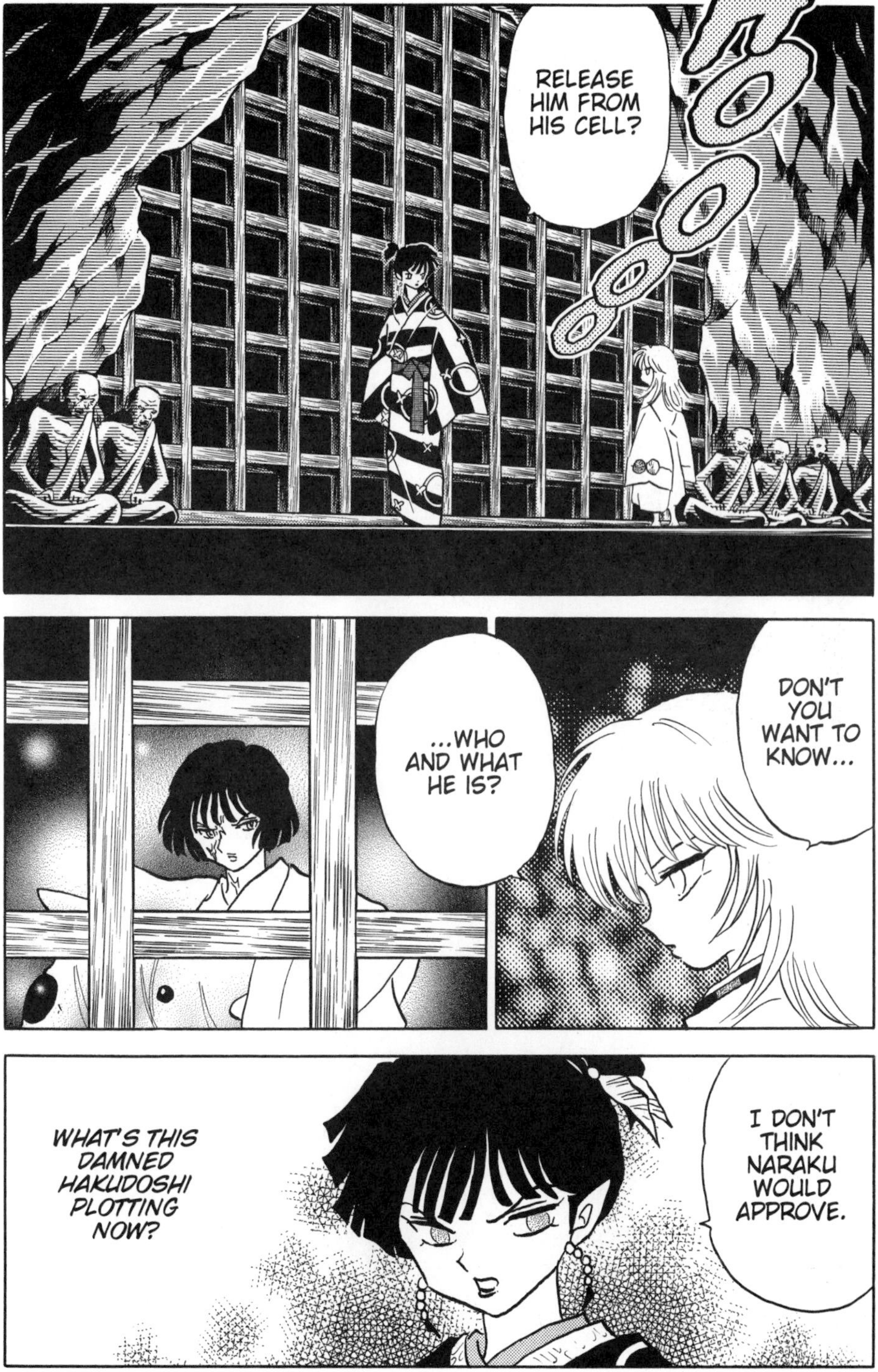

RELEASE HIM FROM HIS CELL?
DON'T YOU WANT TO KNOW...
...WHO AND WHAT HE IS?
I DON'T THINK NARAKU WOULD APPROVE.
WHAT'S THIS DAMNED HAKUDOSHI PLOTTING NOW?

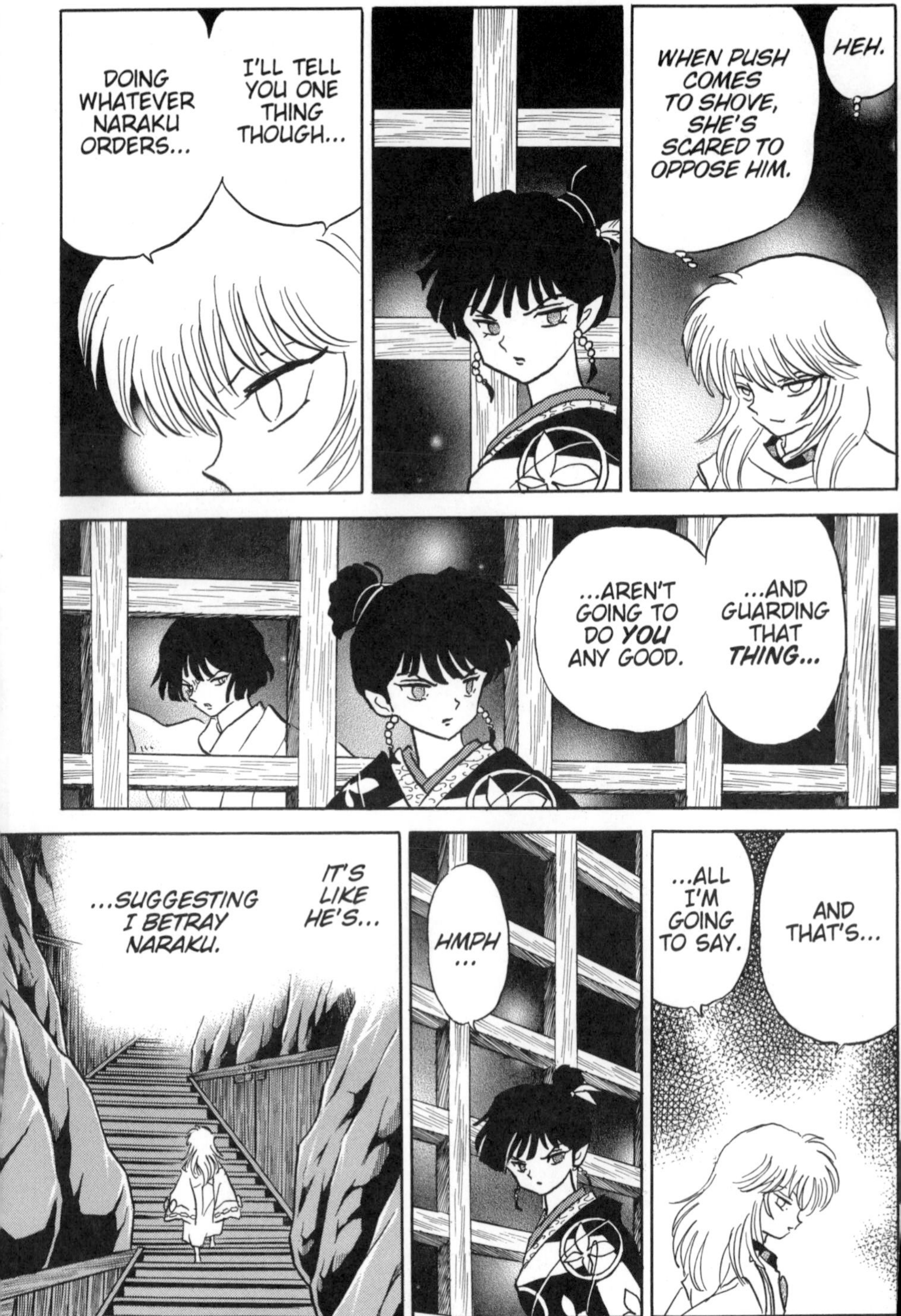
HEH.
WHEN PUSH COMES TO SHOVE, SHE'S SCARED TO OPPOSE HIM.
I'LL TELL YOU ONE THING THOUGH...
DOING WHATEVER NARAKU ORDERS...
...AND GUARDING THAT *THING*...
...AREN'T GOING TO DO *YOU* ANY GOOD.
AND THAT'S...
...ALL I'M GOING TO SAY.
HMPH...
IT'S LIKE HE'S...
...SUGGESTING I BETRAY NARAKU.

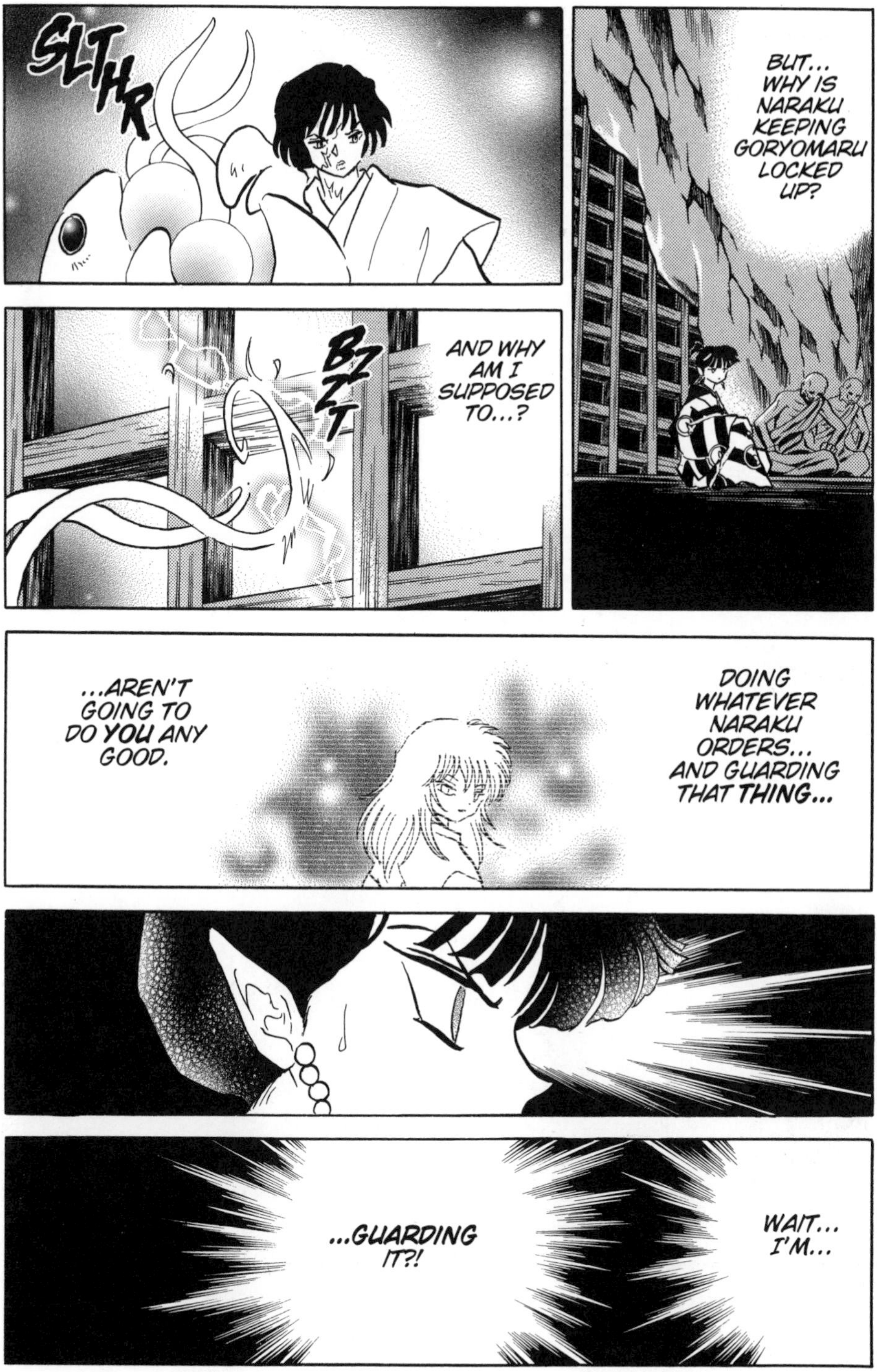
BUT... WHY IS NARAKU KEEPING GORYOMARU LOCKED UP?
SLTHR
BZZT
AND WHY AM I SUPPOSED TO...?
DOING WHATEVER NARAKU ORDERS... AND GUARDING THAT THING...
...AREN'T GOING TO DO YOU ANY GOOD.
WAIT... I'M...
...GUARDING IT?!

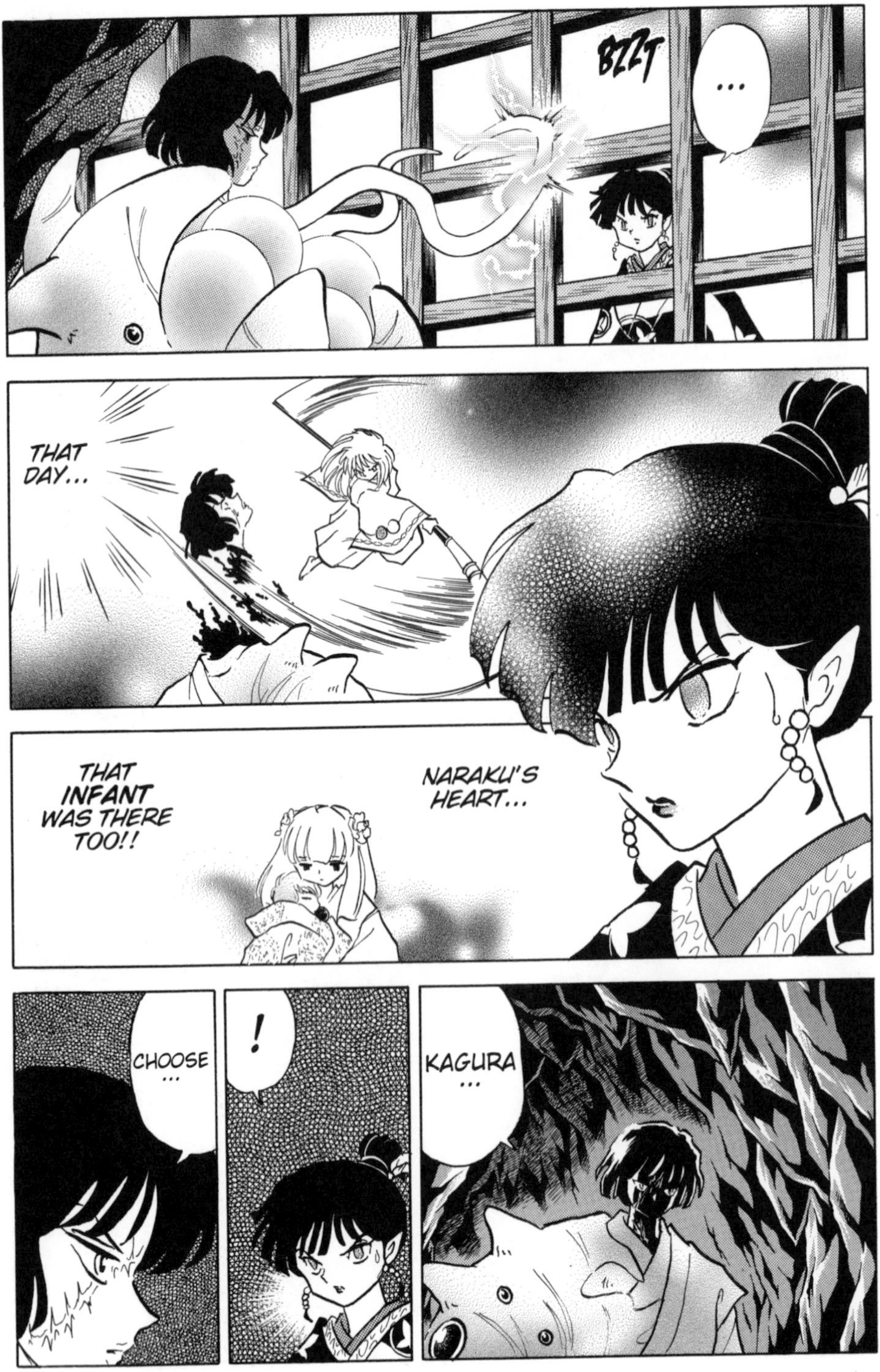
...
BZZT
THAT DAY...
NARAKU'S HEART...
THAT INFANT WAS THERE TOO!!
KAGURA ...
!
CHOOSE ...

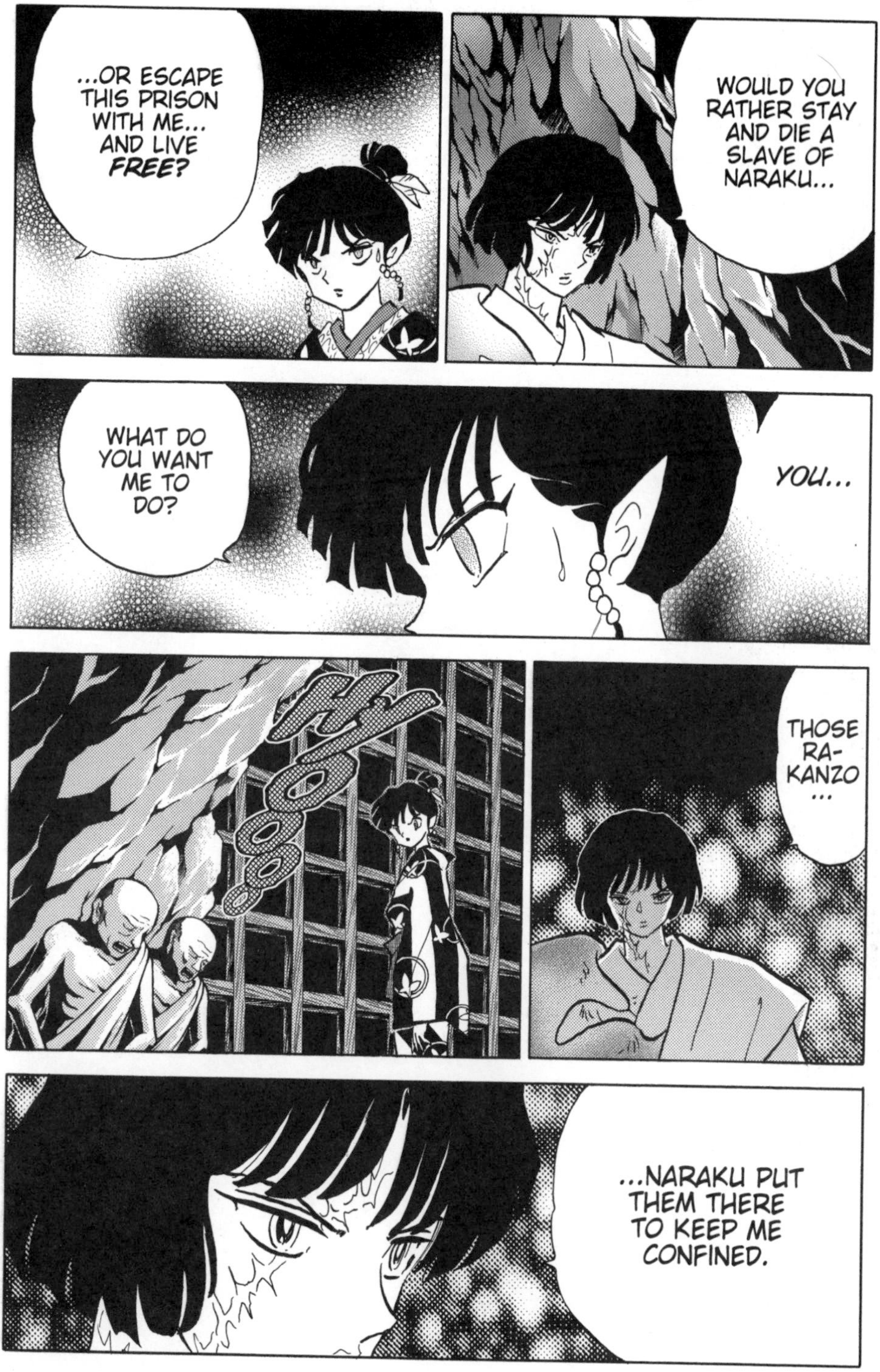
WOULD YOU RATHER STAY AND DIE A SLAVE OF NARAKU...
...OR ESCAPE THIS PRISON WITH ME... AND LIVE *FREE?*
YOU...
WHAT DO YOU WANT ME TO DO?
THOSE RA-KANZO ...
...NARAKU PUT THEM THERE TO KEEP ME CONFINED.

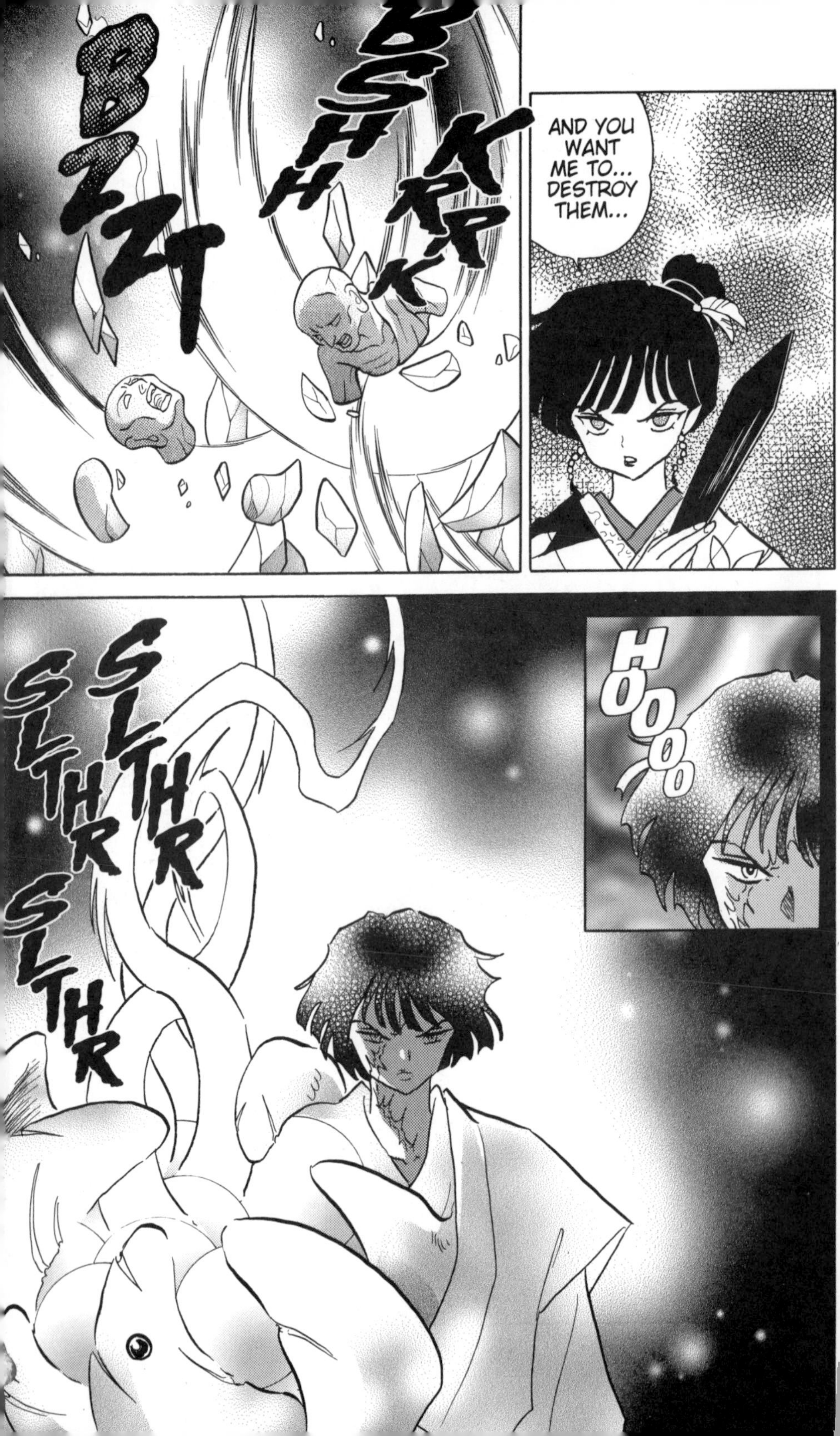
AND YOU WANT ME TO... DESTROY THEM...
BSHH
KRRK
BZZT
HOOOO
SLTHR
SLTHR

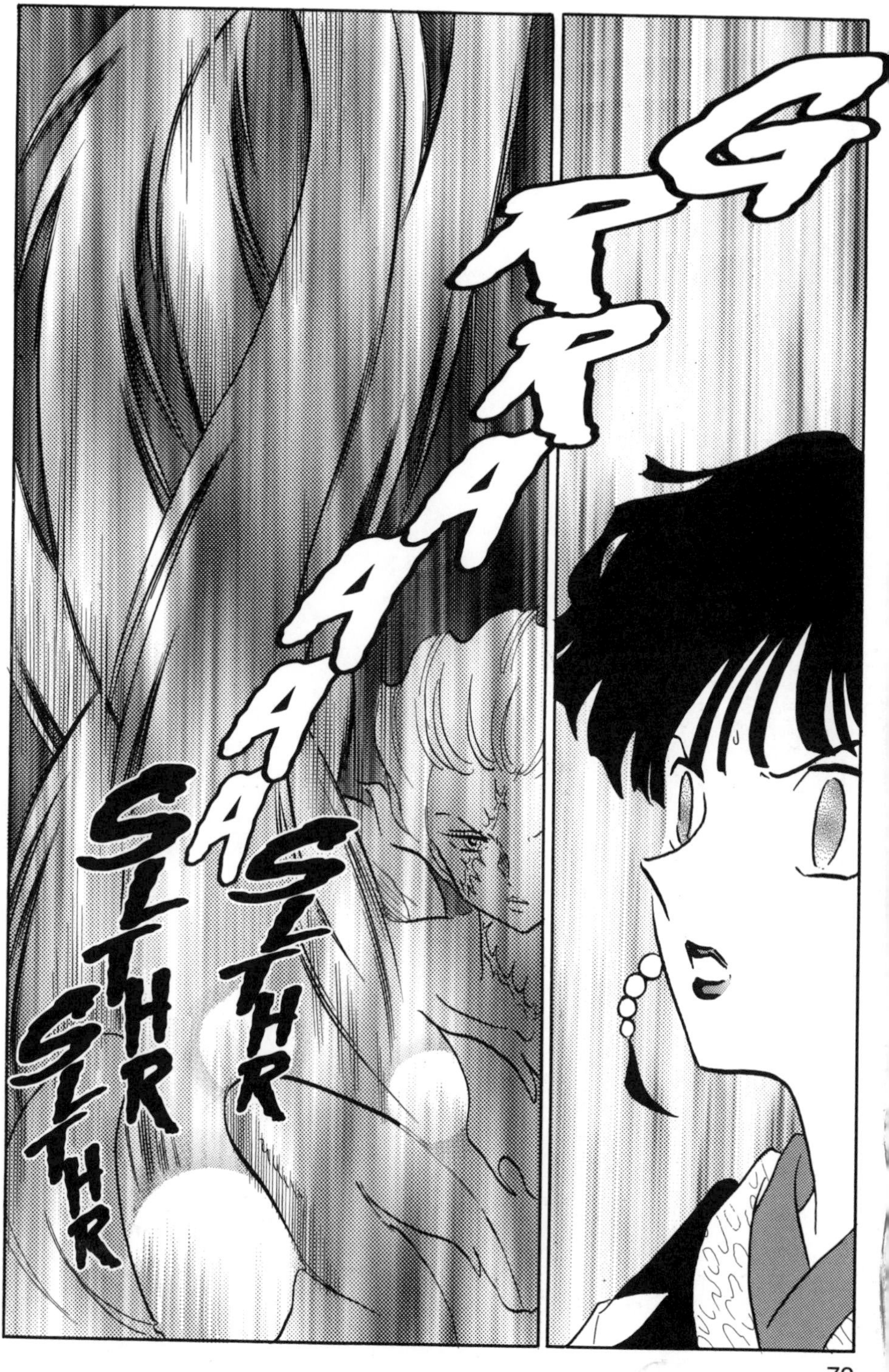
GRRAAAA
SA
SLTHR
SLTHR SLTHR

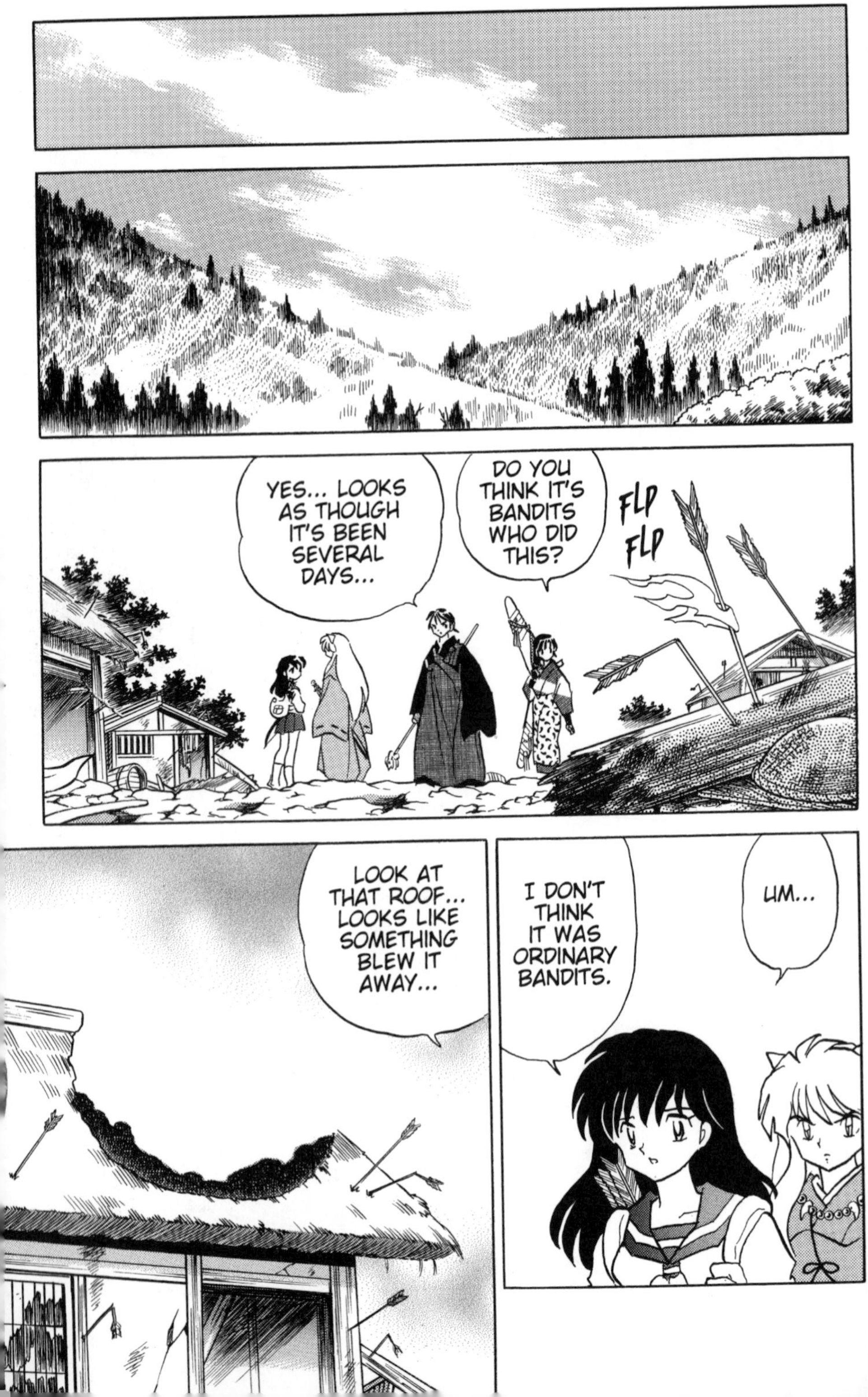
FLP FLP
DO YOU THINK IT'S BANDITS WHO DID THIS?
YES... LOOKS AS THOUGH IT'S BEEN SEVERAL DAYS...
UM...
I DON'T THINK IT WAS ORDINARY BANDITS.
LOOK AT THAT ROOF... LOOKS LIKE SOMETHING BLEW IT AWAY...

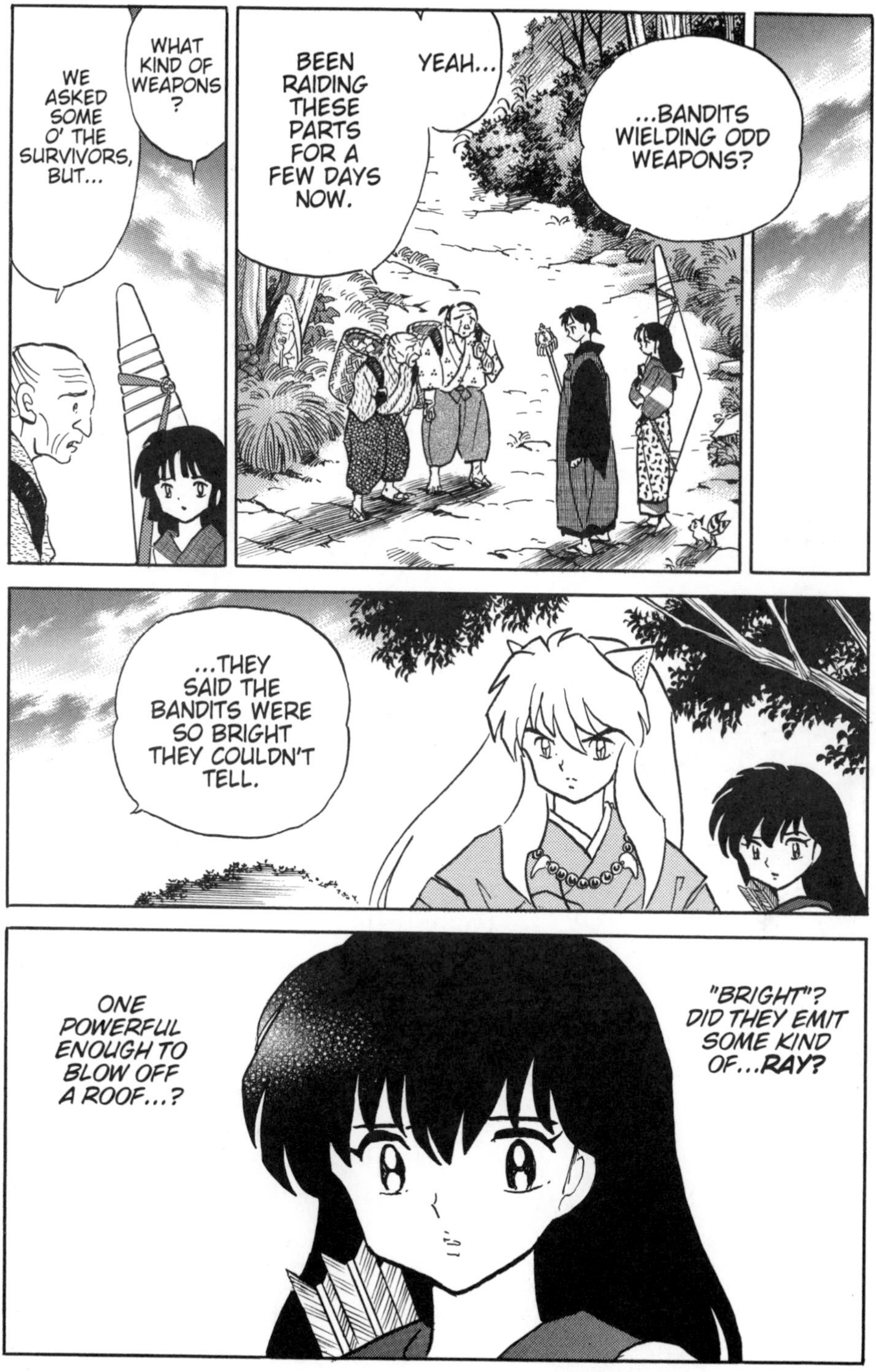
...BANDITS WIELDING ODD WEAPONS?
YEAH...
BEEN RAIDING THESE PARTS FOR A FEW DAYS NOW.
WHAT KIND OF WEAPONS?
WE ASKED SOME O' THE SURVIVORS, BUT...
...THEY SAID THE BANDITS WERE SO BRIGHT THEY COULDN'T TELL.
"BRIGHT"? DID THEY EMIT SOME KIND OF...*RAY?*
ONE POWERFUL ENOUGH TO BLOW OFF A ROOF...?

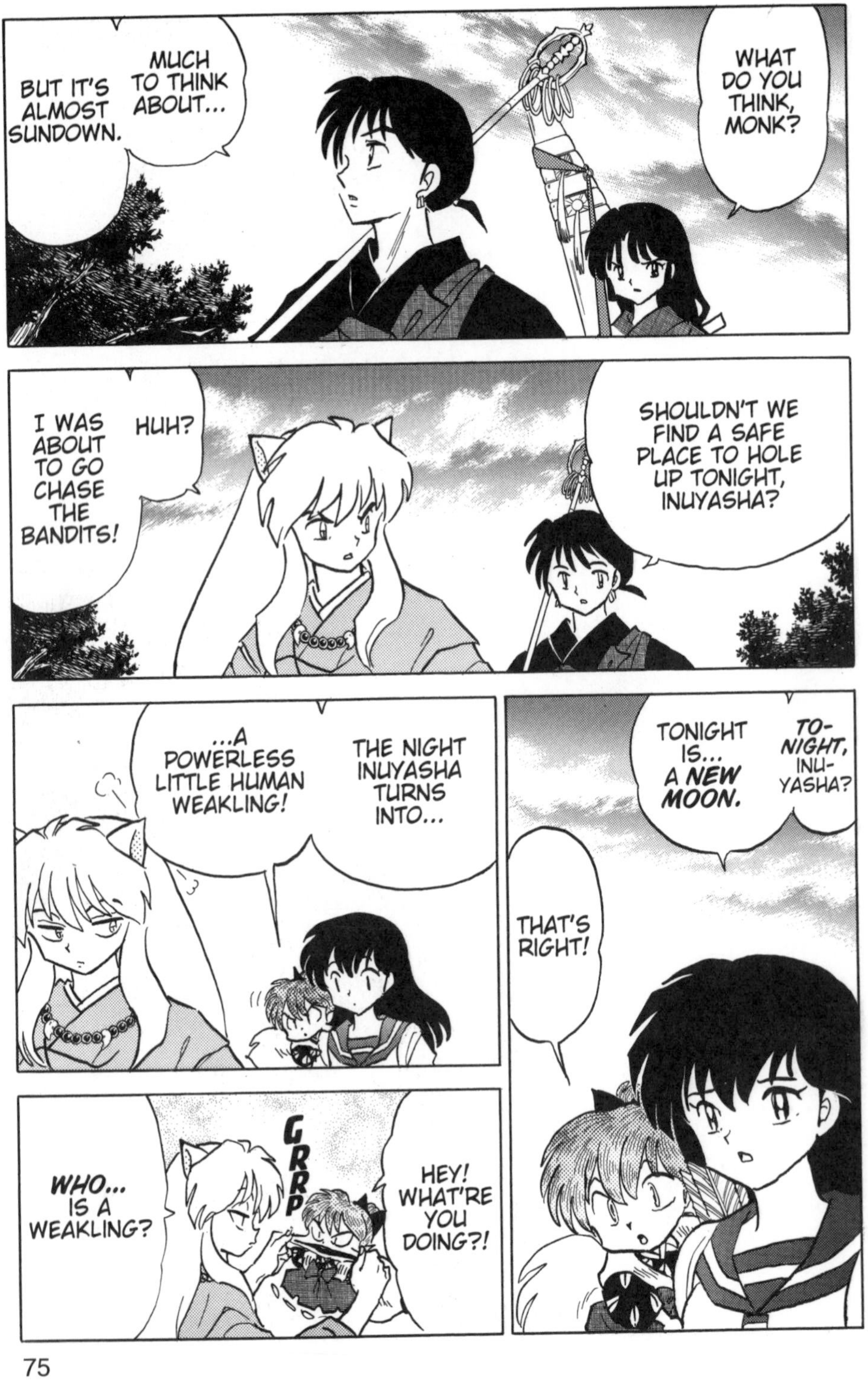
WHAT DO YOU THINK, MONK?
MUCH TO THINK ABOUT...
BUT IT'S ALMOST SUNDOWN.
SHOULDN'T WE FIND A SAFE PLACE TO HOLE UP TONIGHT, INUYASHA?
HUH?
I WAS ABOUT TO GO CHASE THE BANDITS!
TO-NIGHT, INU-YASHA?
TONIGHT IS... A *NEW MOON.*
THAT'S RIGHT!
THE NIGHT INUYASHA TURNS INTO...
...A POWERLESS LITTLE HUMAN WEAKLING!
HEY! WHAT'RE YOU DOING?!
GRRP
WHO... IS A WEAKLING?

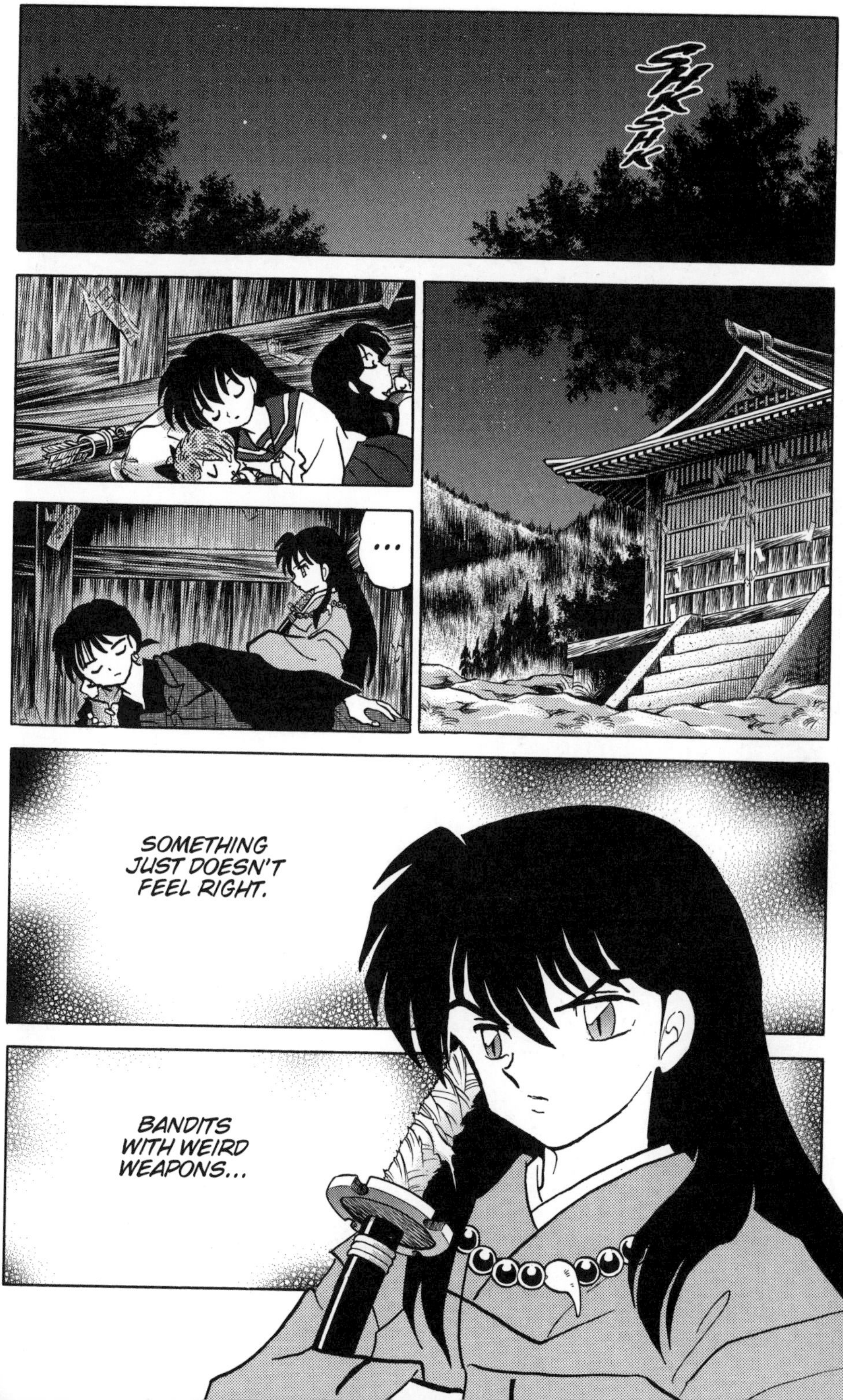
SHK SHK
...
SOMETHING JUST DOESN'T FEEL RIGHT.
BANDITS WITH WEIRD WEAPONS...

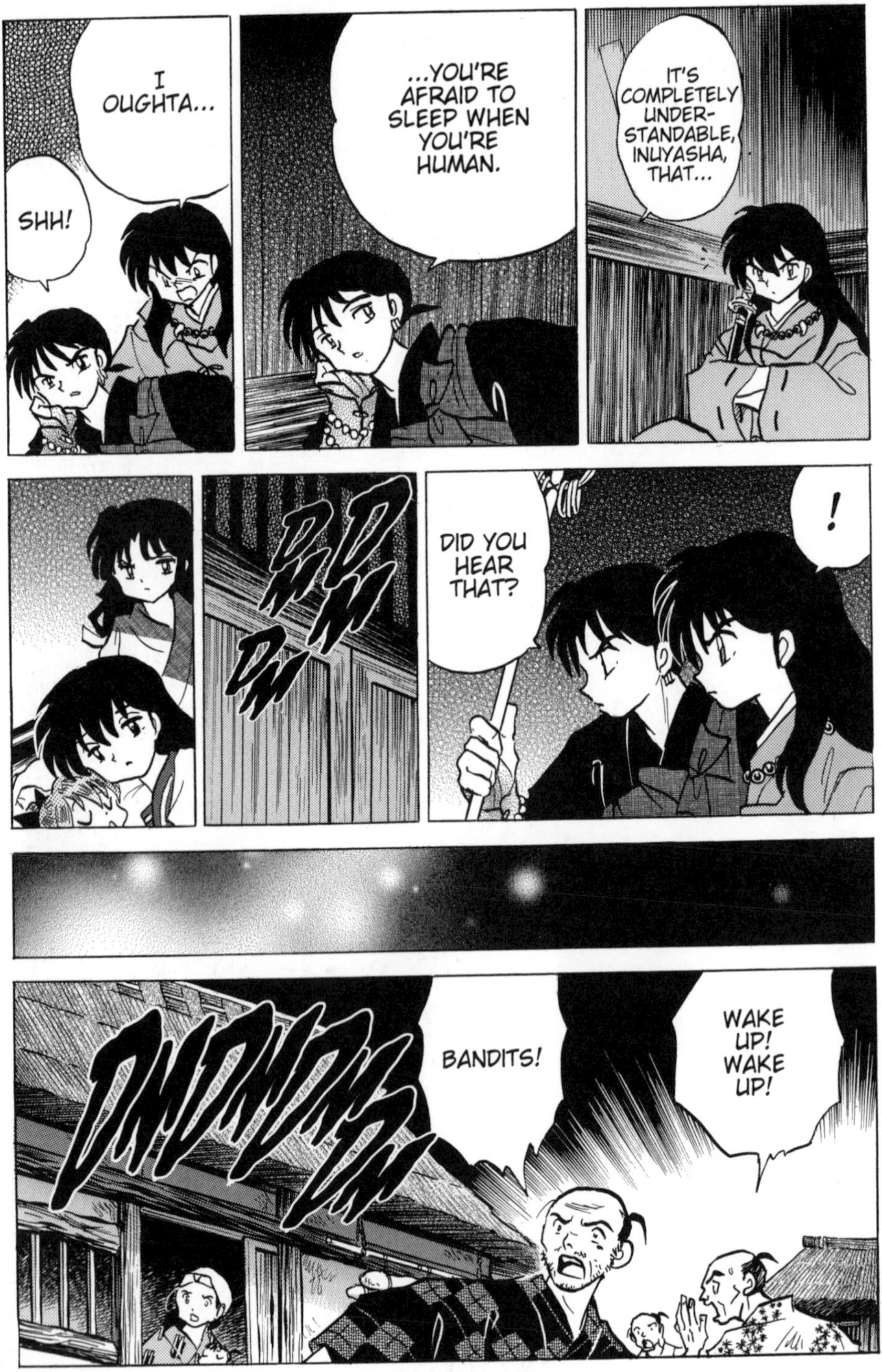
IT'S COMPLETELY UNDER-STANDABLE, INUYASHA, THAT...
...YOU'RE AFRAID TO SLEEP WHEN YOU'RE HUMAN.
I OUGHTA...
SHH!
!
DID YOU HEAR THAT?
WAKE UP! WAKE UP!
BANDITS!

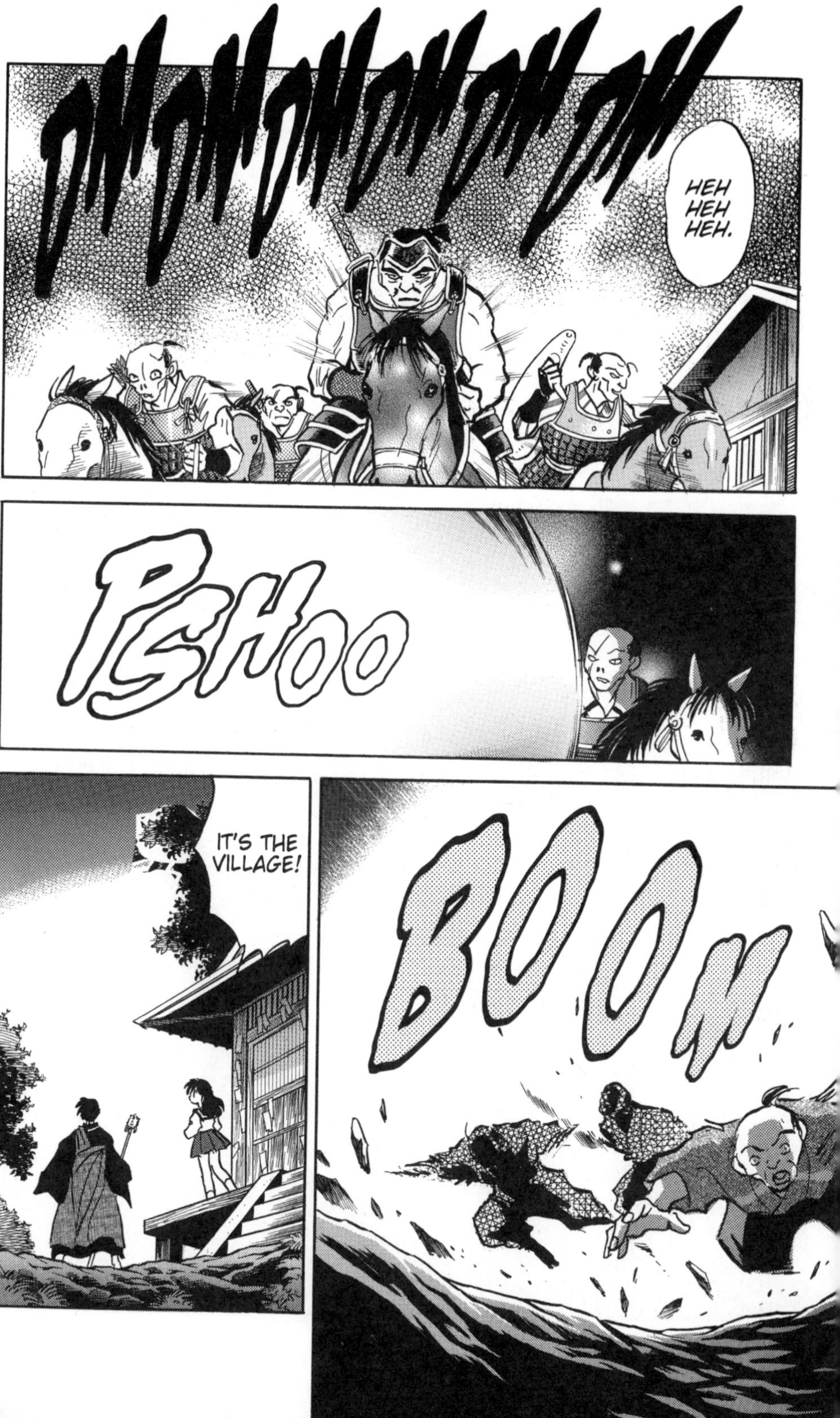
DN DN DN DN DN DN
HEH HEH HEH.
PSHOO
BOOM
IT'S THE VILLAGE!

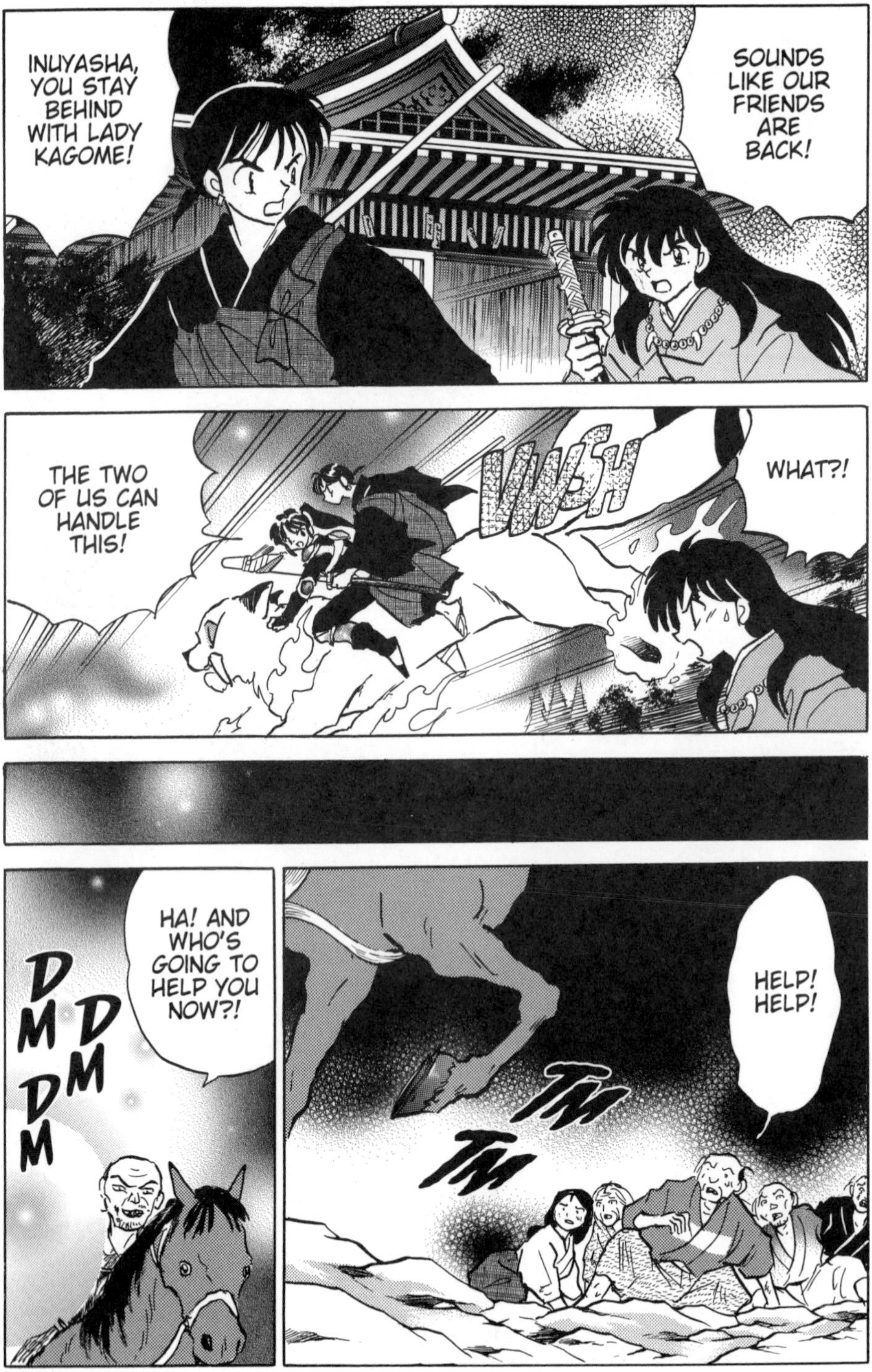
SOUNDS LIKE OUR FRIENDS ARE BACK!
INUYASHA, YOU STAY BEHIND WITH LADY KAGOME!
WHAT?!
VWSH
THE TWO OF US CAN HANDLE THIS!
HELP! HELP!
TM
TM
HA! AND WHO'S GOING TO HELP YOU NOW?!
DM DM DM DM

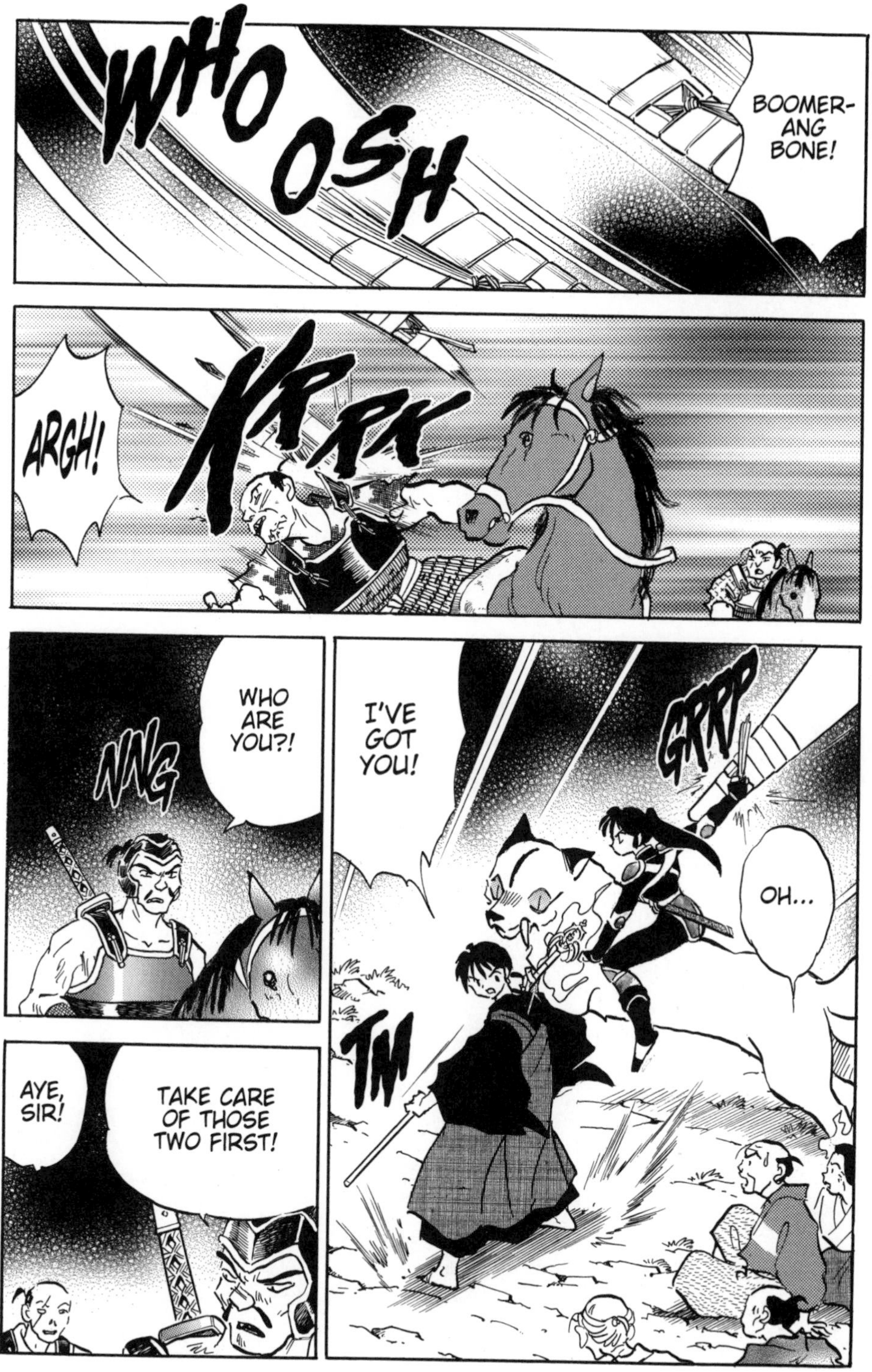
BOOMER-ANG BONE!
WHOOSH
KRRK
ARGH!
GRRP
I'VE GOT YOU!
OH...
TM
WHO ARE YOU?!
NNG
TAKE CARE OF THOSE TWO FIRST!
AYE, SIR!

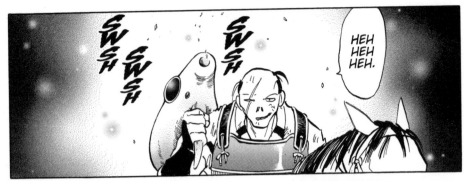

HEH HEH HEH.
SWSH
SWSH
SWSH
!
MONK! LOOK...!
GORYOMARU'S GORYO URNS!
SHK SHK
WHAT'S TAKING THEM SO LONG?
THEY JUST LEFT!

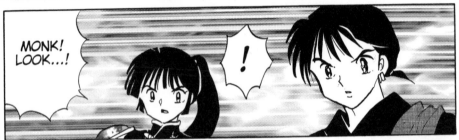

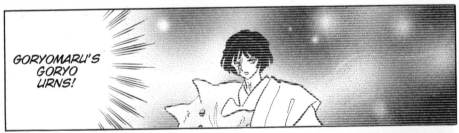

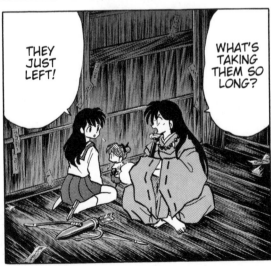

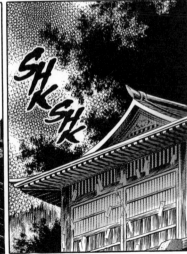

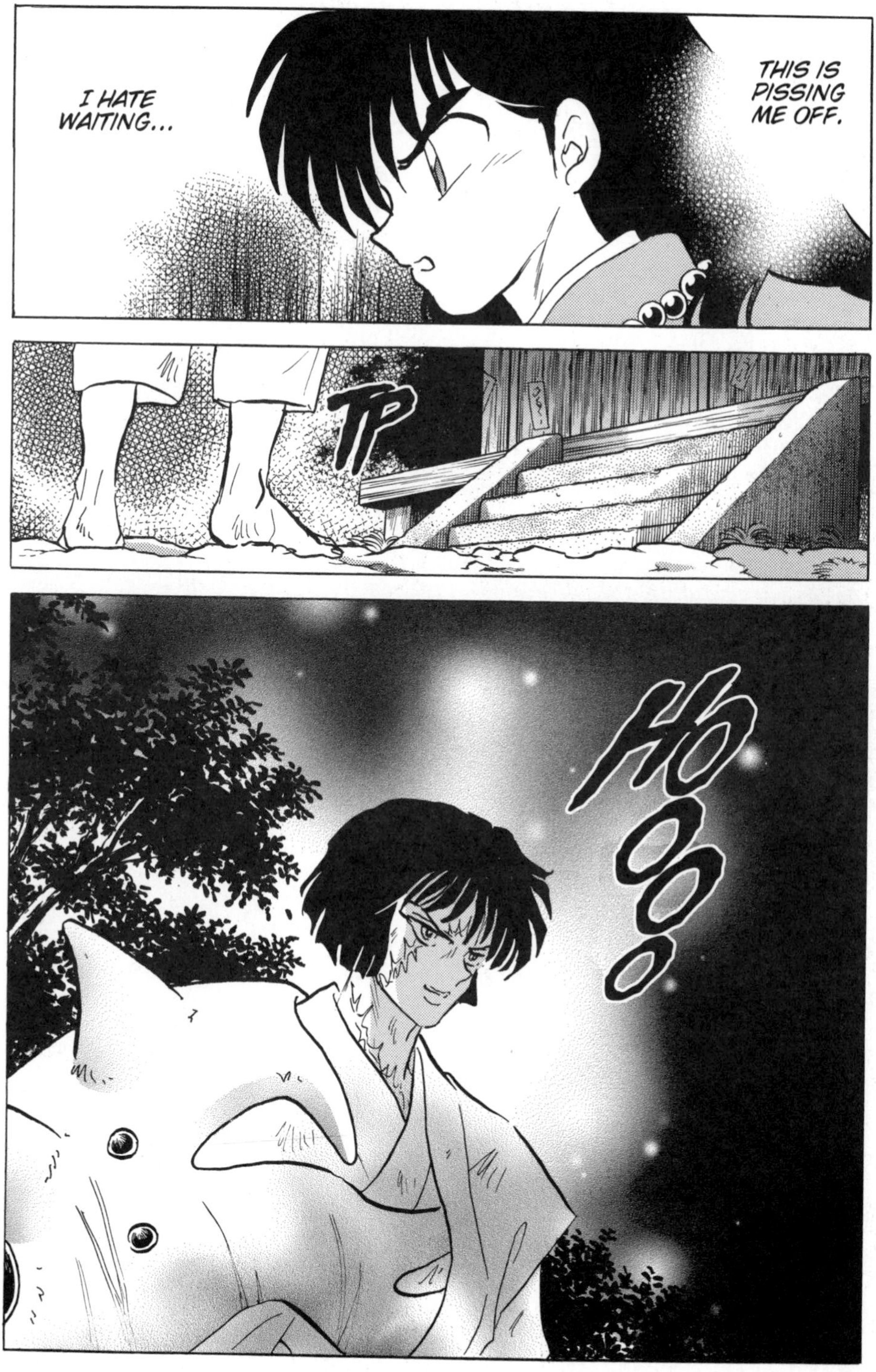
THIS IS PISSING ME OFF.
I HATE WAITING...
TP
HOOOO

SCROLL FIVE
GORYOMARU'S IDENTITY

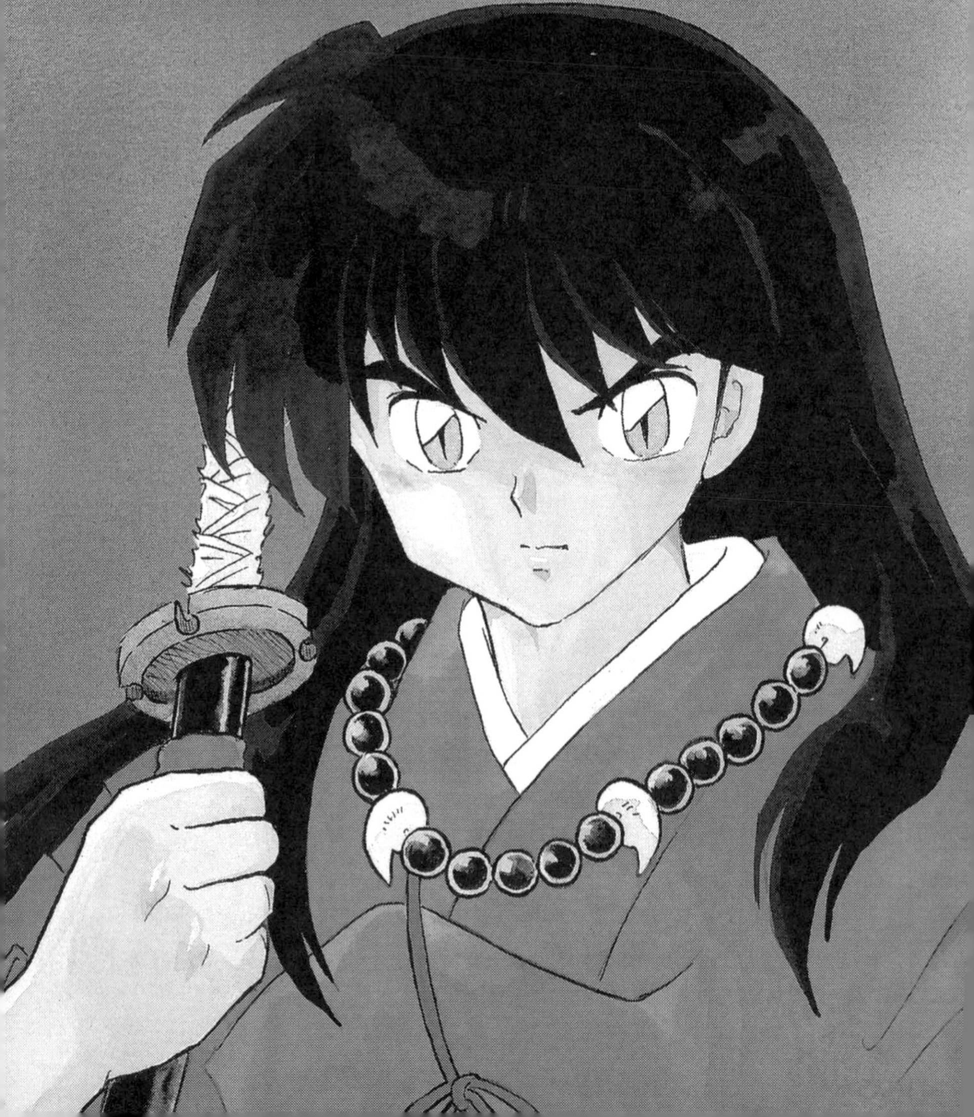

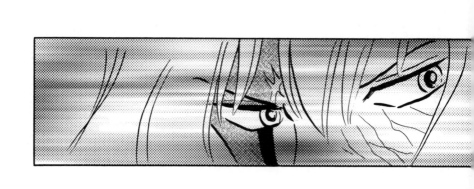

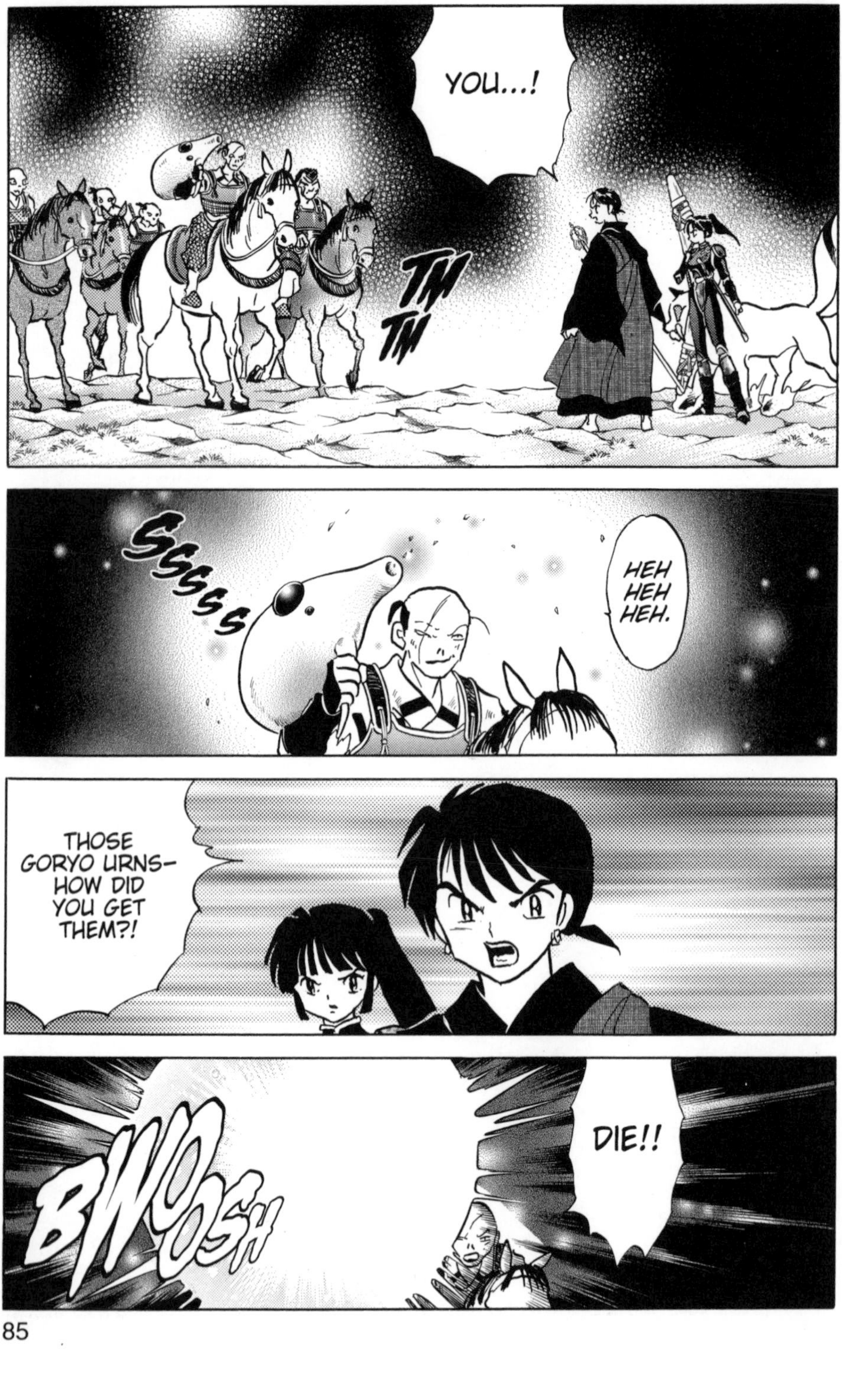
YOU...!
TM TM
HEH HEH HEH.
SSSSSS
THOSE GORYO URNS-HOW DID YOU GET THEM?!
DIE!!
BWOOSH

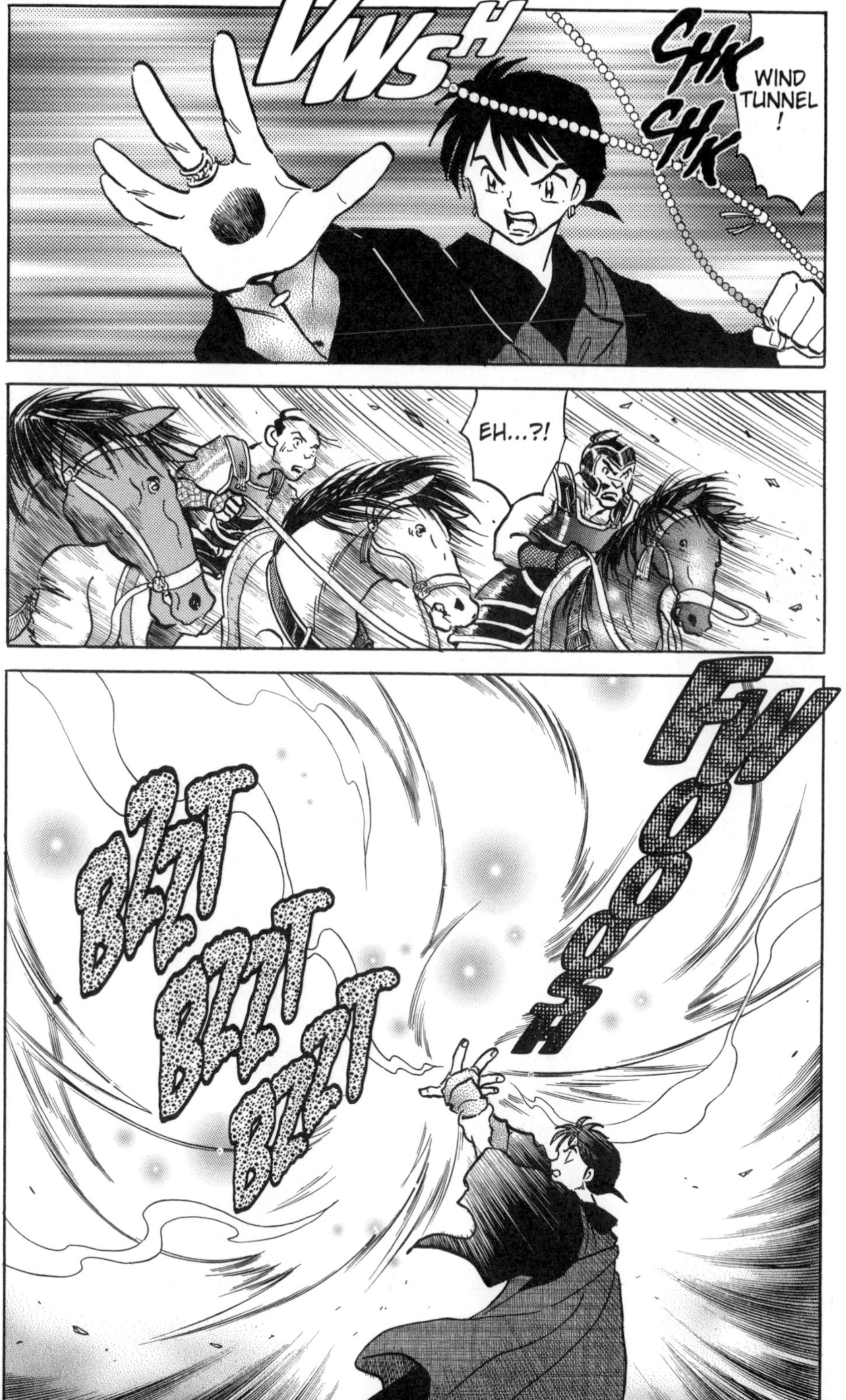
WIND TUNNEL !
CHK CHK
VWSH
EH...?!
FWOOOOSH
BZZT BZZT BZZT

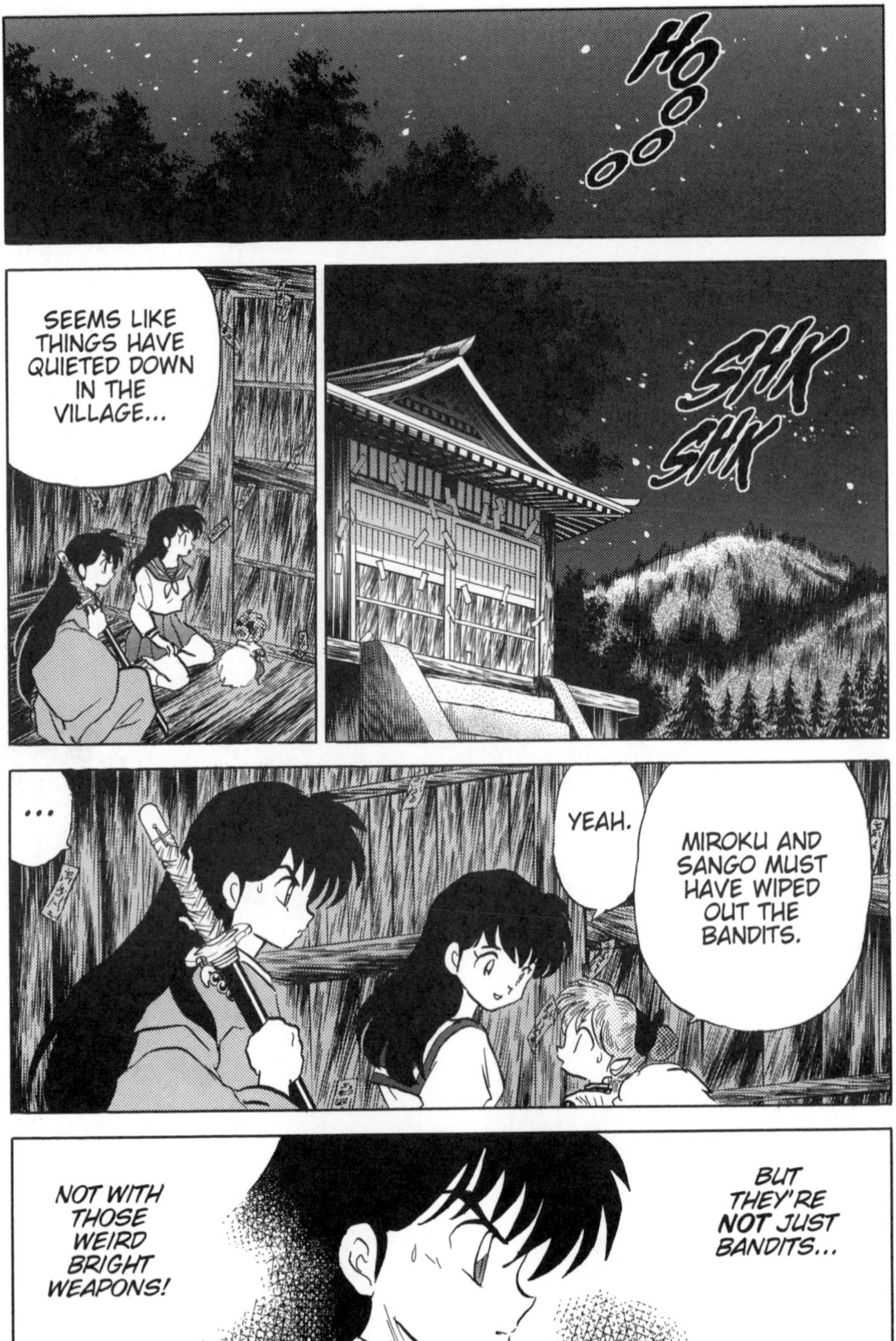
HOOOOO
SHK SHK
SEEMS LIKE THINGS HAVE QUIETED DOWN IN THE VILLAGE...
MIROKU AND SANGO MUST HAVE WIPED OUT THE BANDITS.
YEAH.
...
BUT THEY'RE **NOT** JUST BANDITS...
NOT WITH THOSE WEIRD BRIGHT WEAPONS!

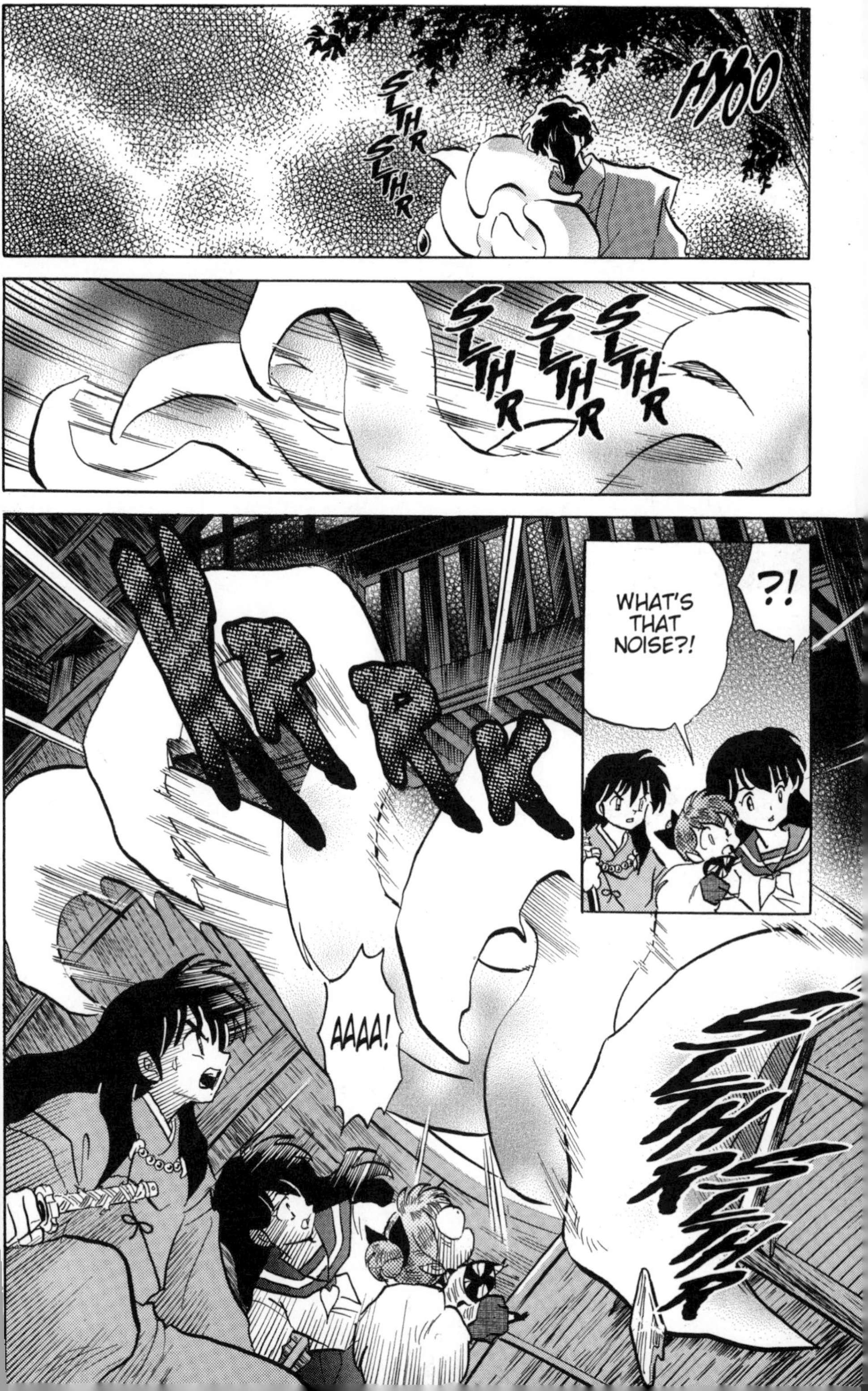
HYOO
SLTHR SLTHR
SLTHR SLTHR SLTHR
?!
WHAT'S THAT NOISE?!
VRRK
SLTHR SLTHR
AAAA!

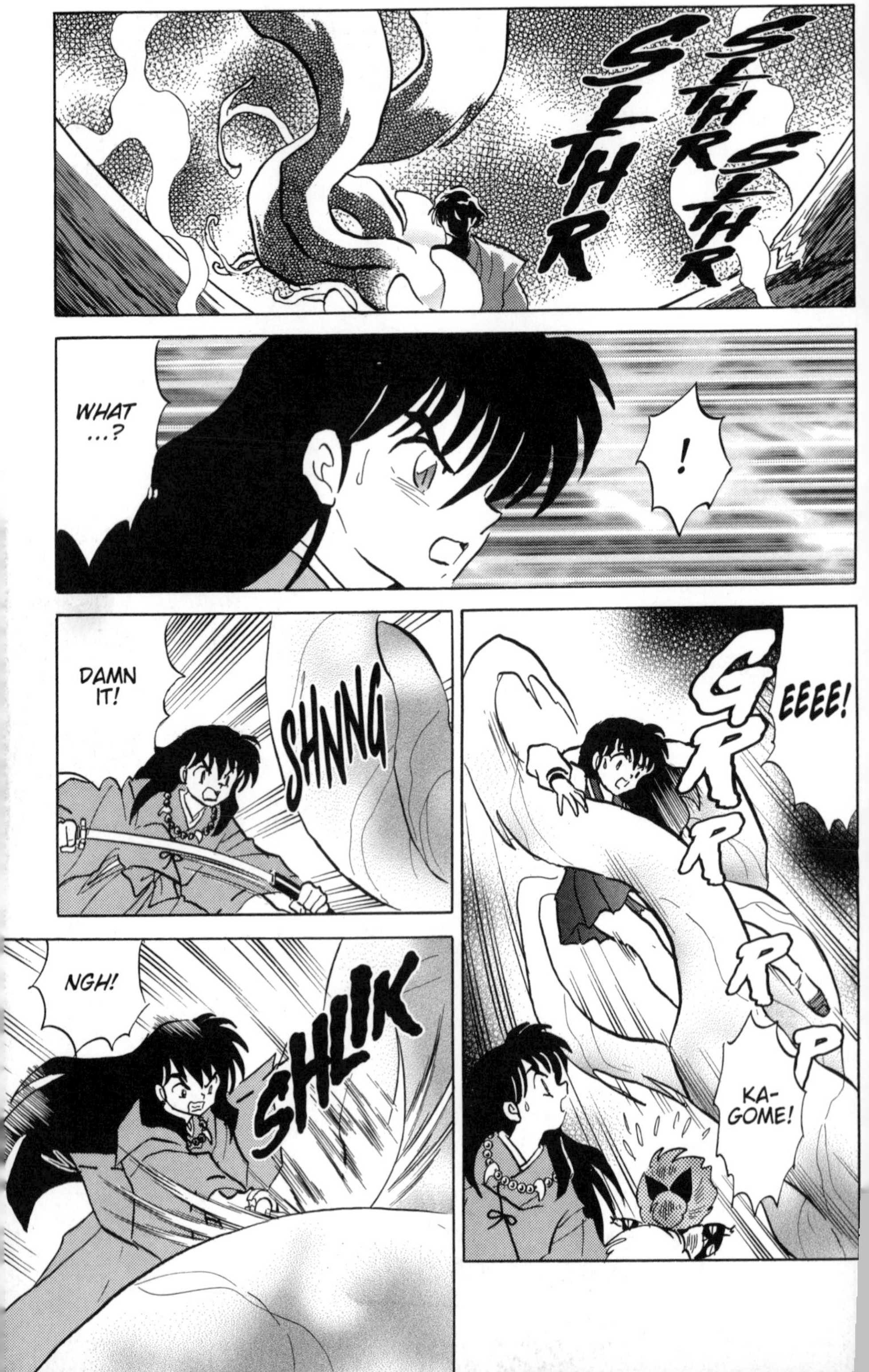
SLHR SLHR
SLHR
!
WHAT ...?
EEEE!
GRRRP
KA-GOME!
DAMN IT!
SHNNG
NGH!
SHLIK

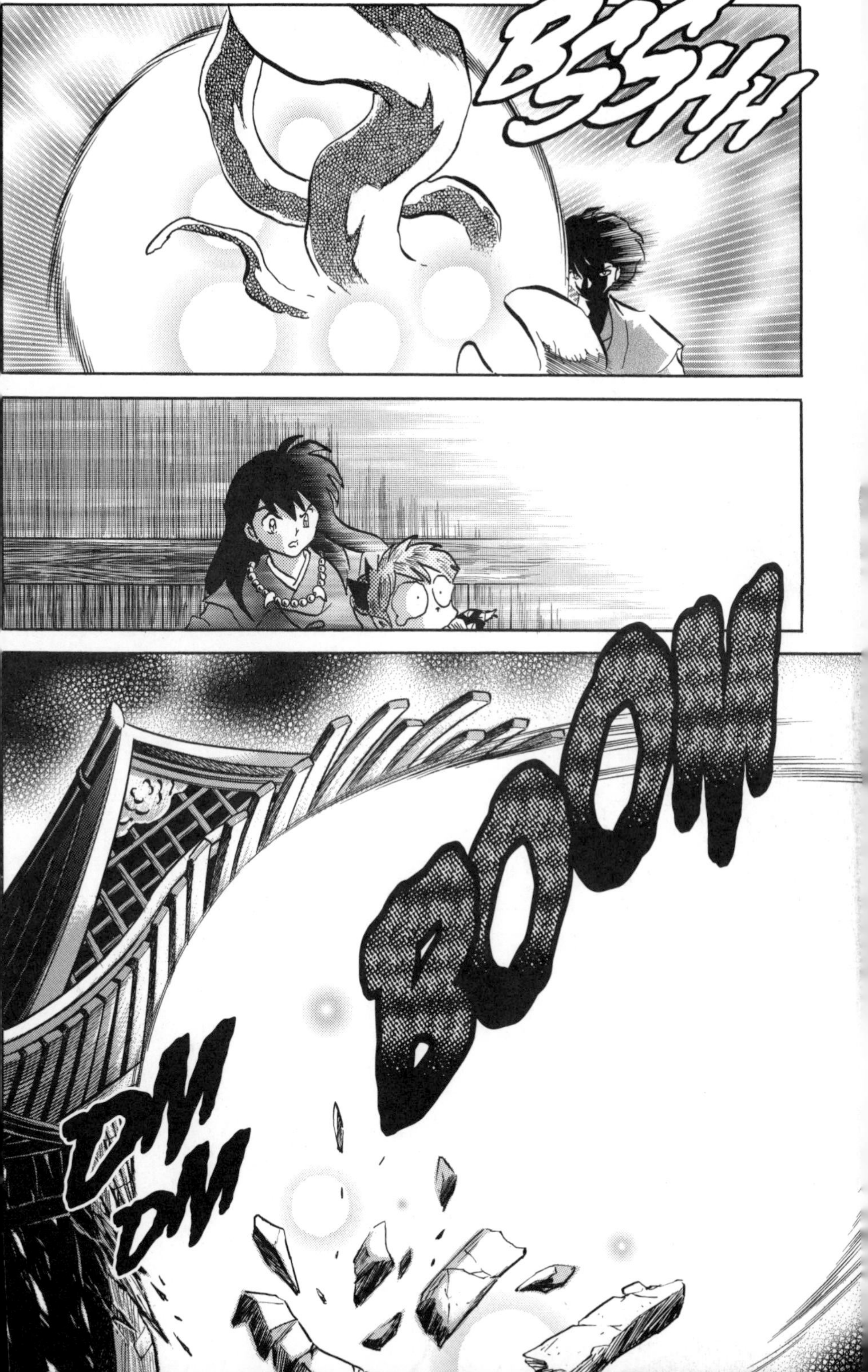
BSSHH
BOOOM
DM DM

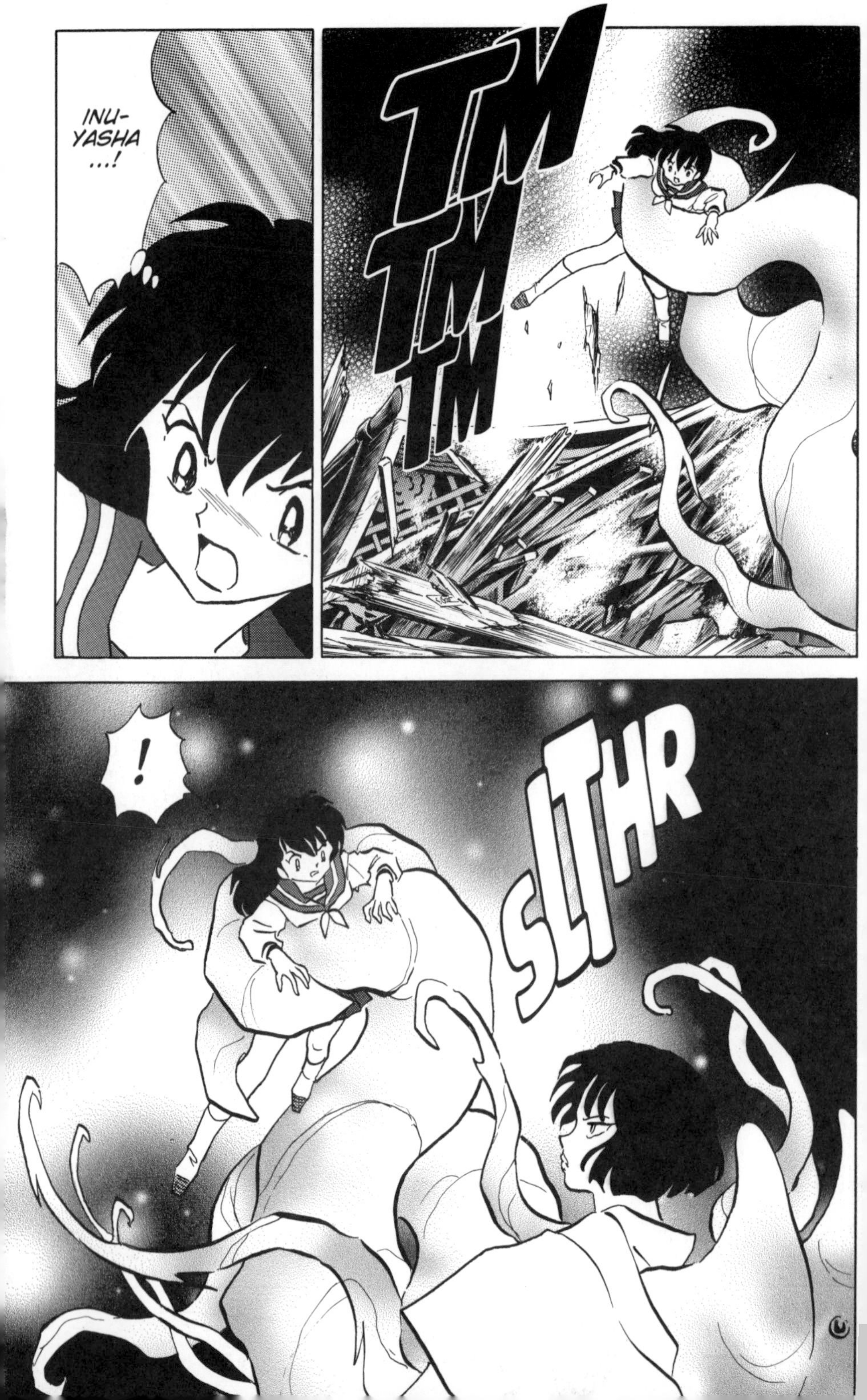
TM
TM
TM
INU-YASHA ...!
!
SLITHR

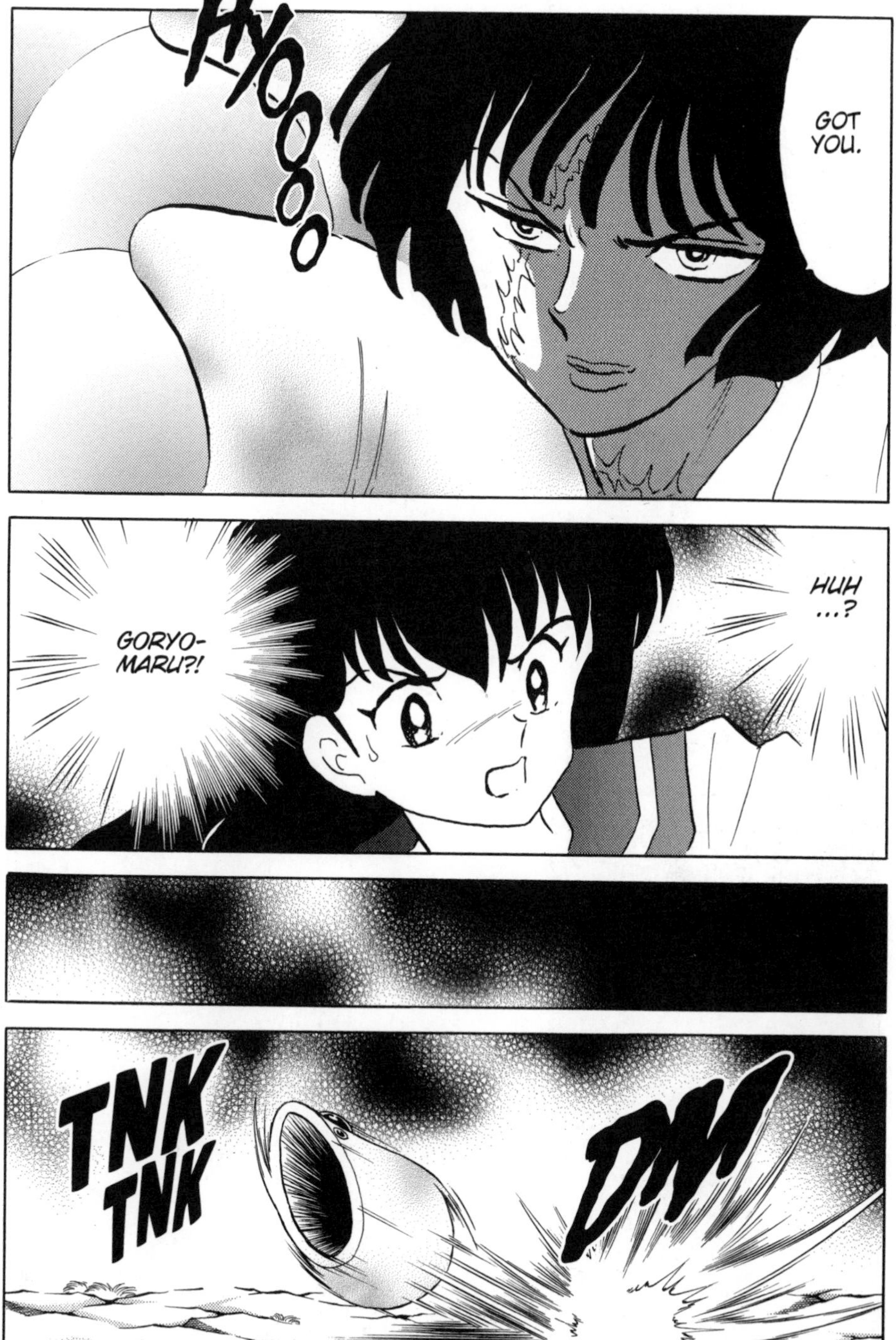
GOT YOU.
HYOOOO
HUH ...?
GORYO-MARU?!
DM
TNK TNK

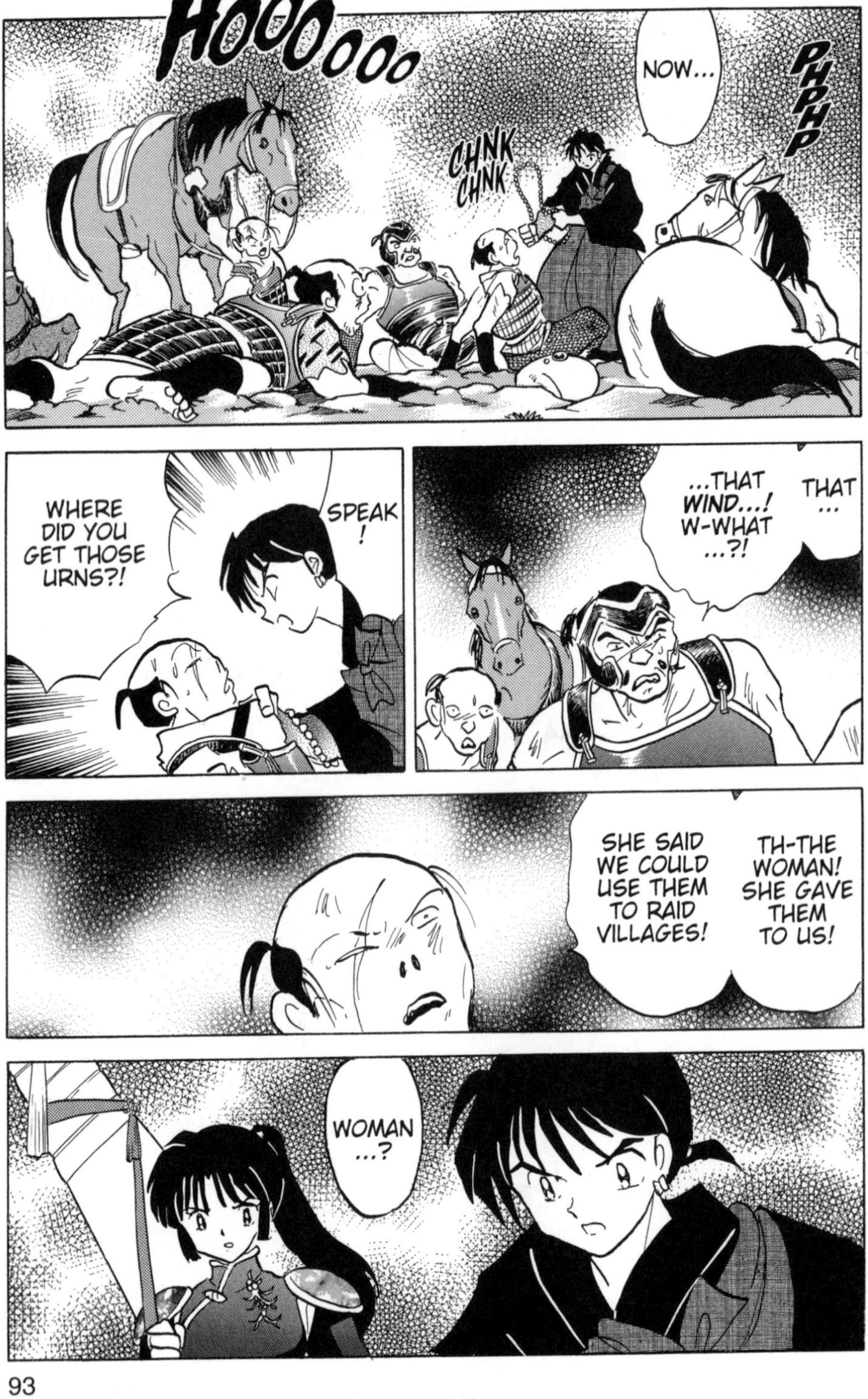
PHPHP
NOW...
CHNK CHNK
HOOOooo
THAT ...
...THAT WIND...! W-WHAT ...?!
SPEAK!
WHERE DID YOU GET THOSE URNS?!
TH-THE WOMAN! SHE GAVE THEM TO US!
SHE SAID WE COULD USE THEM TO RAID VILLAGES!
WOMAN ...?

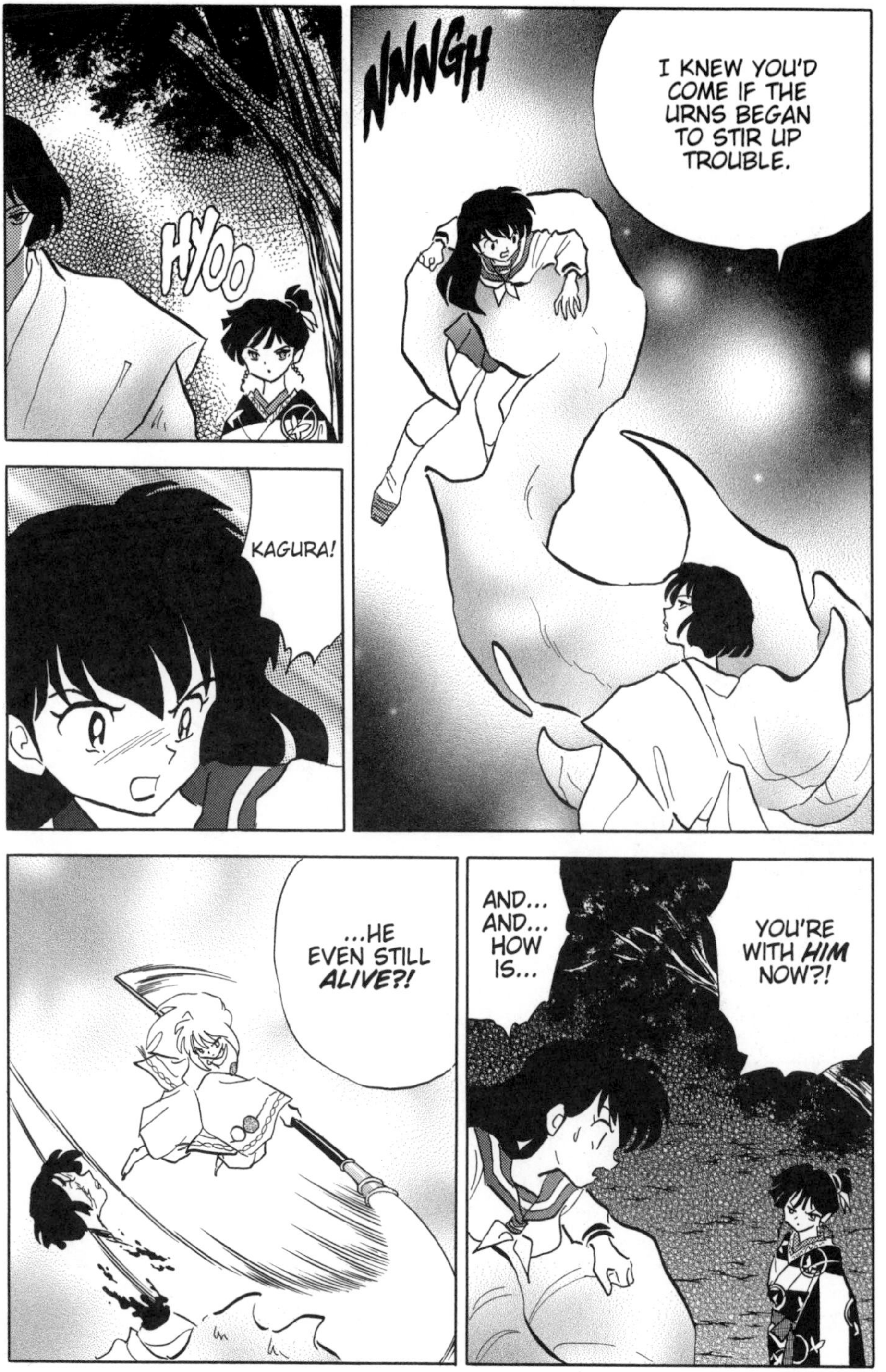
I KNEW YOU'D COME IF THE URNS BEGAN TO STIR UP TROUBLE.
NNNGH
HYOO
KAGURA!
YOU'RE WITH *HIM* NOW?!
AND... AND... HOW IS...
...HE EVEN STILL *ALIVE?!*

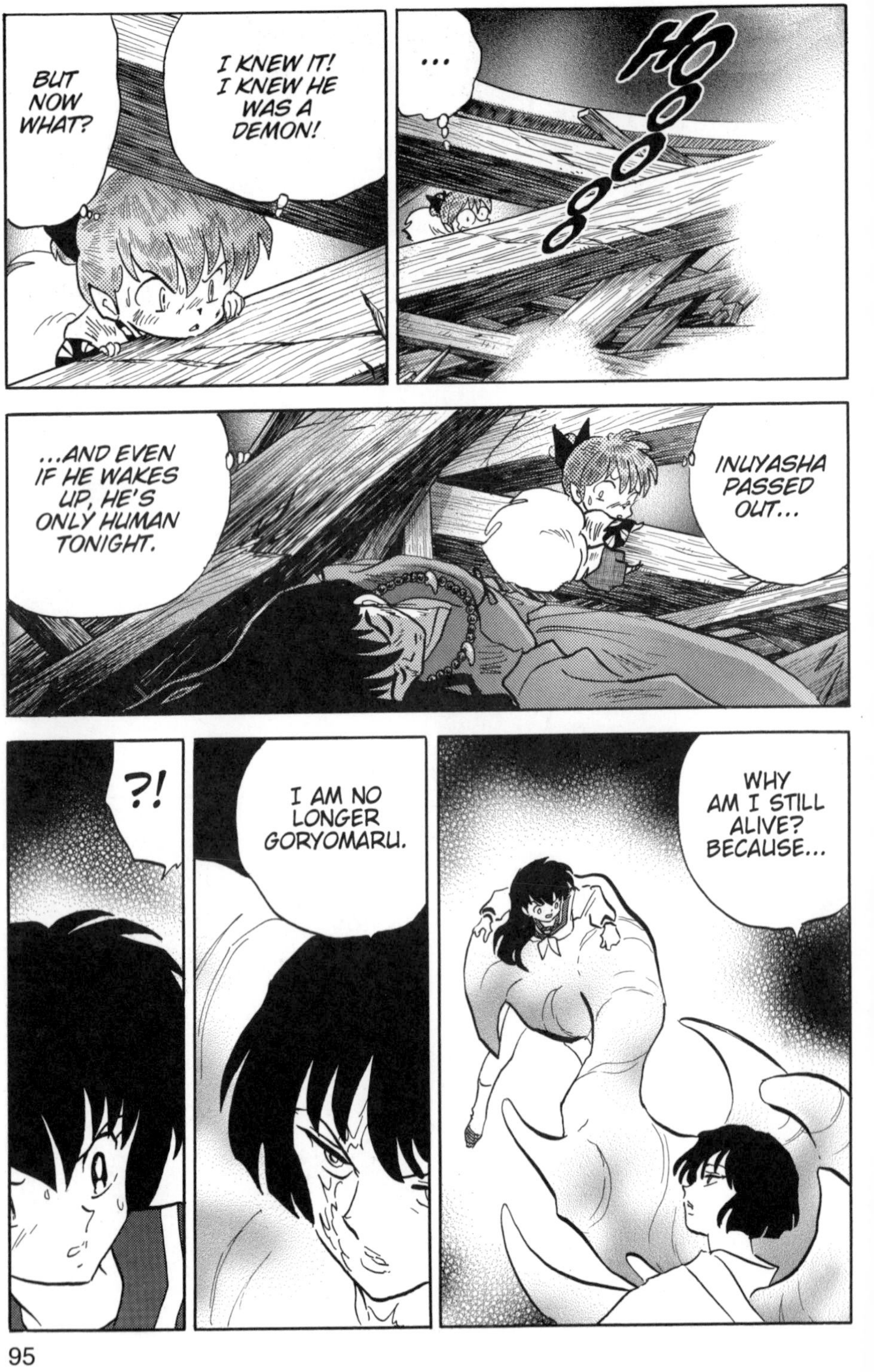
HOOOOO
...
I KNEW IT! I KNEW HE WAS A DEMON!
BUT NOW WHAT?
INUYASHA PASSED OUT...
...AND EVEN IF HE WAKES UP, HE'S ONLY HUMAN TONIGHT.
WHY AM I STILL ALIVE? BECAUSE...
I AM NO LONGER GORYOMARU.
?!

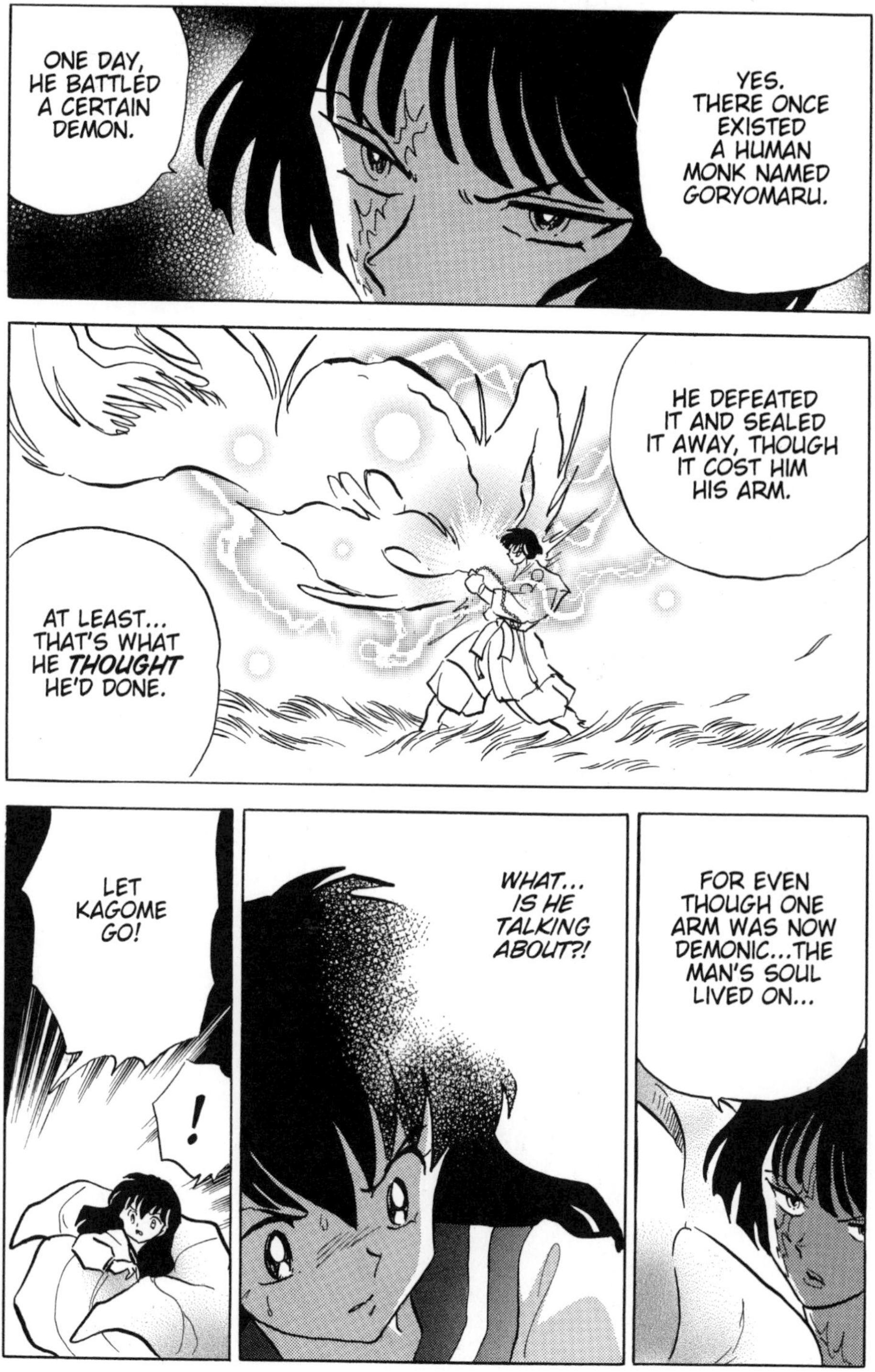
YES. THERE ONCE EXISTED A HUMAN MONK NAMED GORYOMARU.
ONE DAY, HE BATTLED A CERTAIN DEMON.
HE DEFEATED IT AND SEALED IT AWAY, THOUGH IT COST HIM HIS ARM.
AT LEAST... THAT'S WHAT HE *THOUGHT* HE'D DONE.
FOR EVEN THOUGH ONE ARM WAS NOW DEMONIC...THE MAN'S SOUL LIVED ON...
WHAT... IS HE TALKING ABOUT?!
LET KAGOME GO!
!

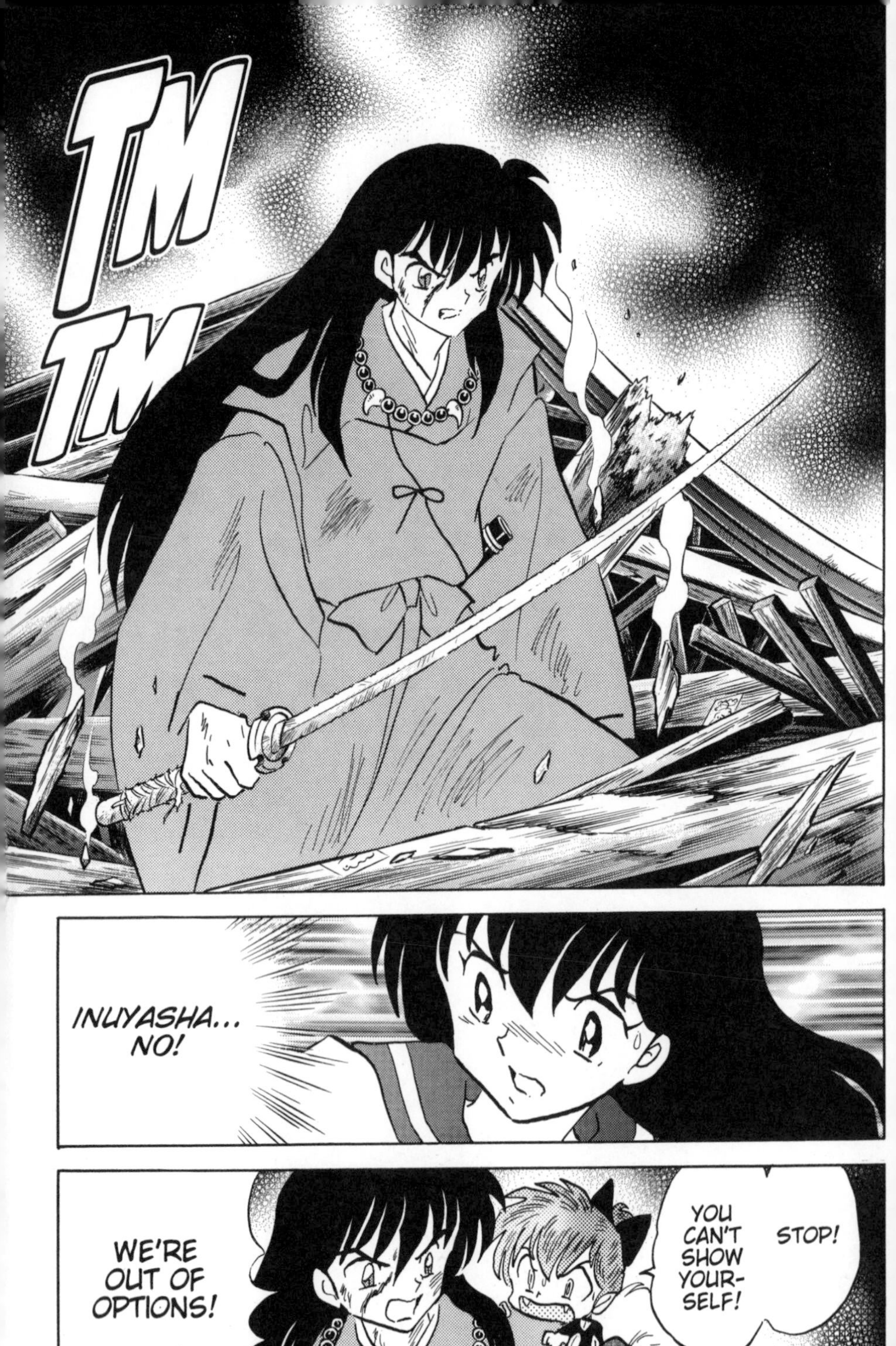
TM TM
INUYASHA... NO!
STOP!
YOU CAN'T SHOW YOUR-SELF!
WE'RE OUT OF OPTIONS!

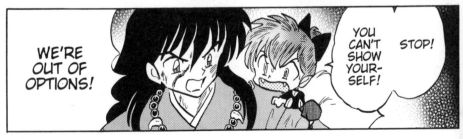

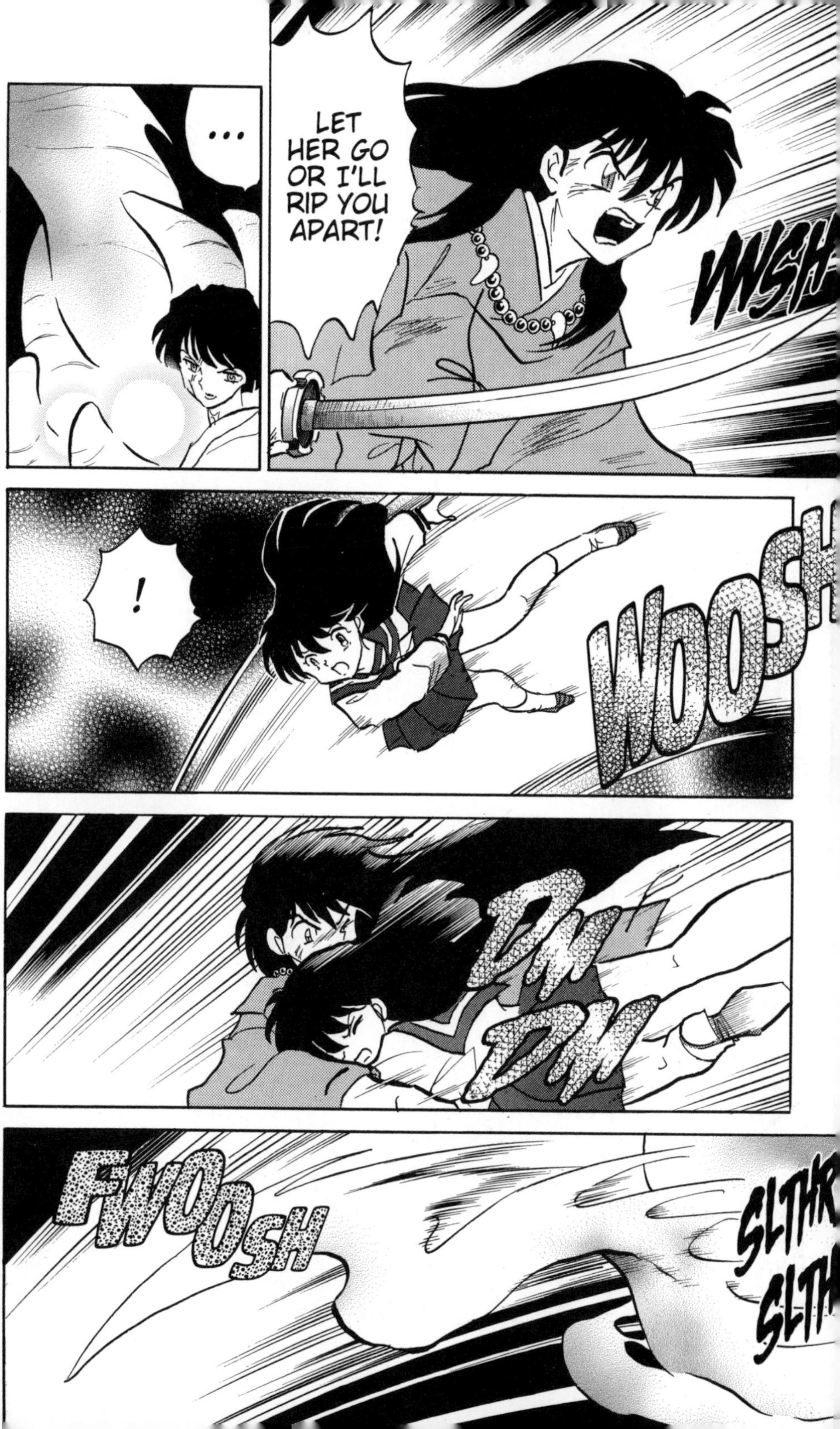
LET HER GO OR I'LL RIP YOU APART!
VWSH
...
!
WOOSH
DM
DM
FWOOSH
SLTHR
SLTH

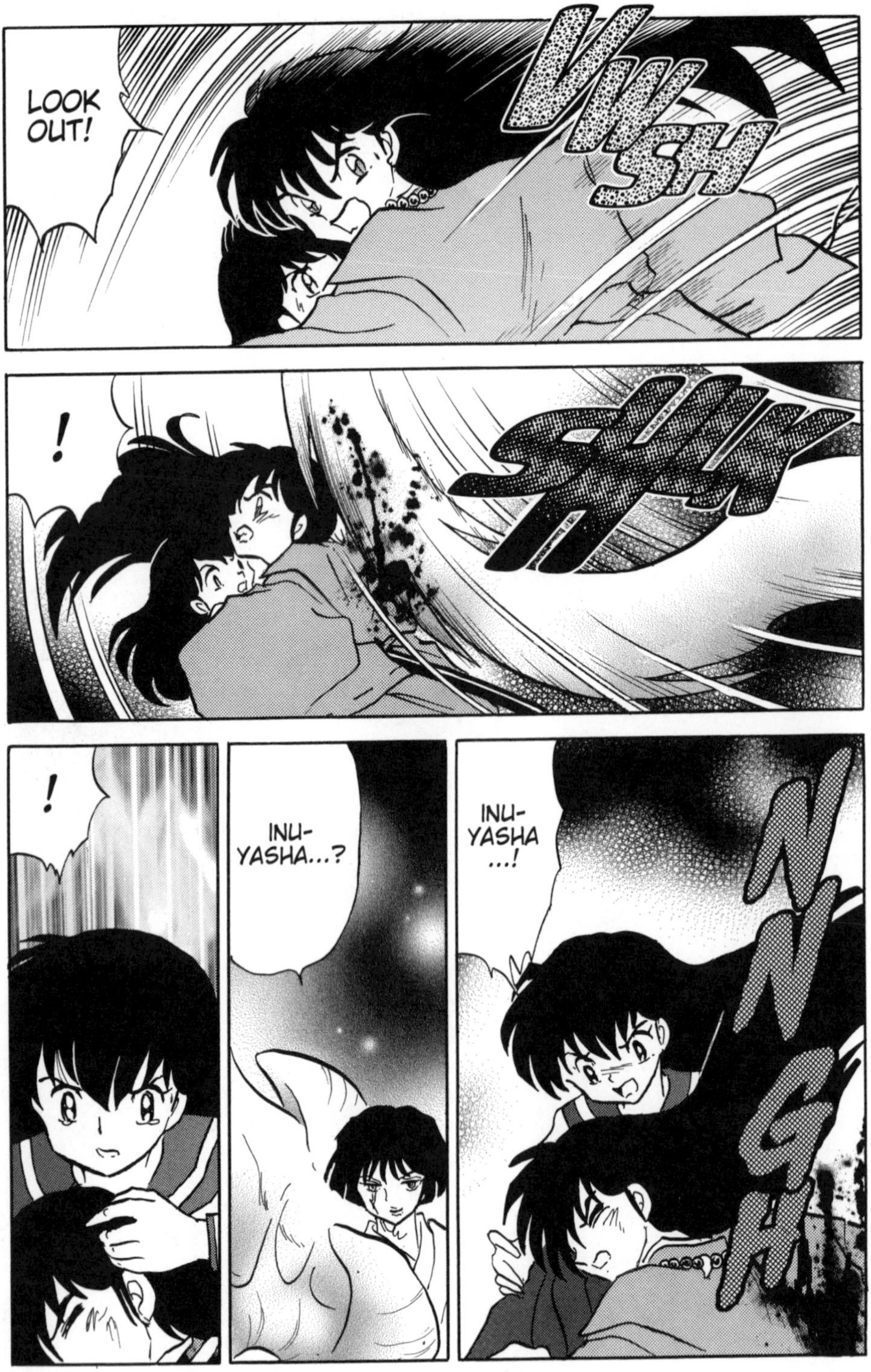
LOOK OUT!
VWSH
!
SHUK
INU-YASHA...!
NNGH
INU-YASHA...?
!

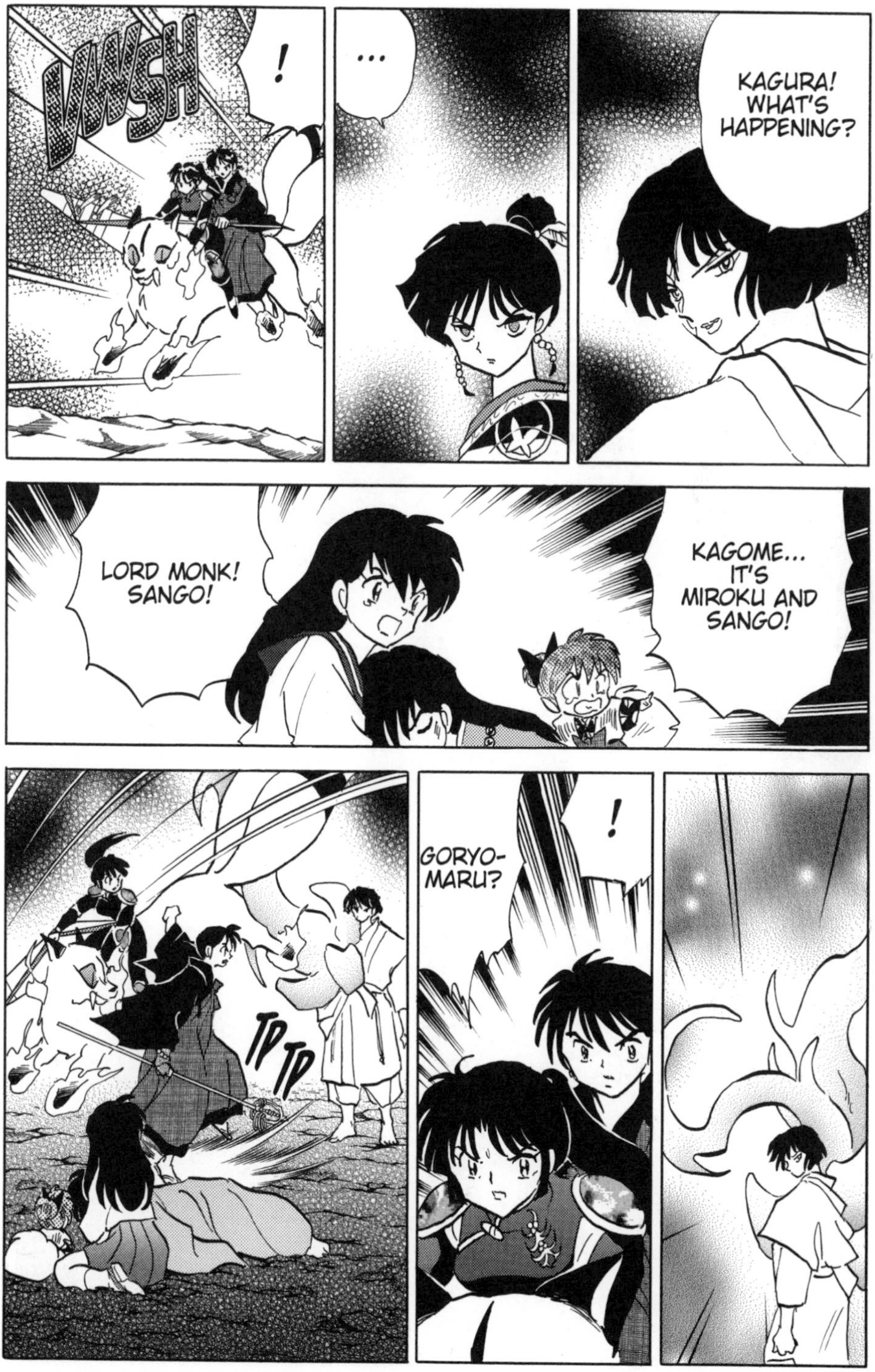
KAGURA! WHAT'S HAPPENING?
...
!
VWSH
KAGOME... IT'S MIROKU AND SANGO!
LORD MONK! SANGO!
!
GORYO-MARU?
TP TP

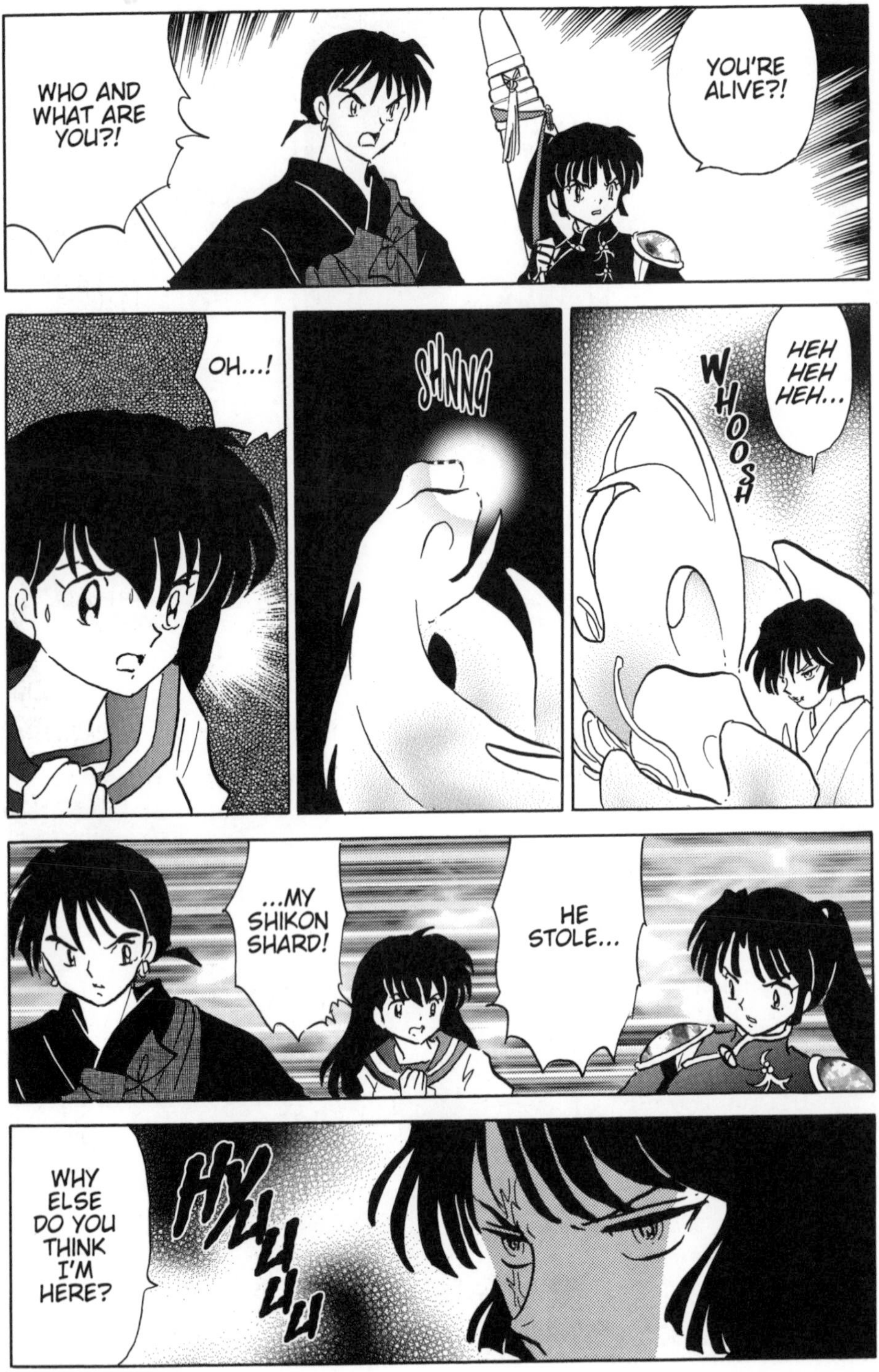
YOU'RE ALIVE?!
WHO AND WHAT ARE YOU?!
HEH HEH HEH...
WHOOSH
SHNNG
OH...!
HE STOLE...
...MY SHIKON SHARD!
HYUUUU
WHY ELSE DO YOU THINK I'M HERE?

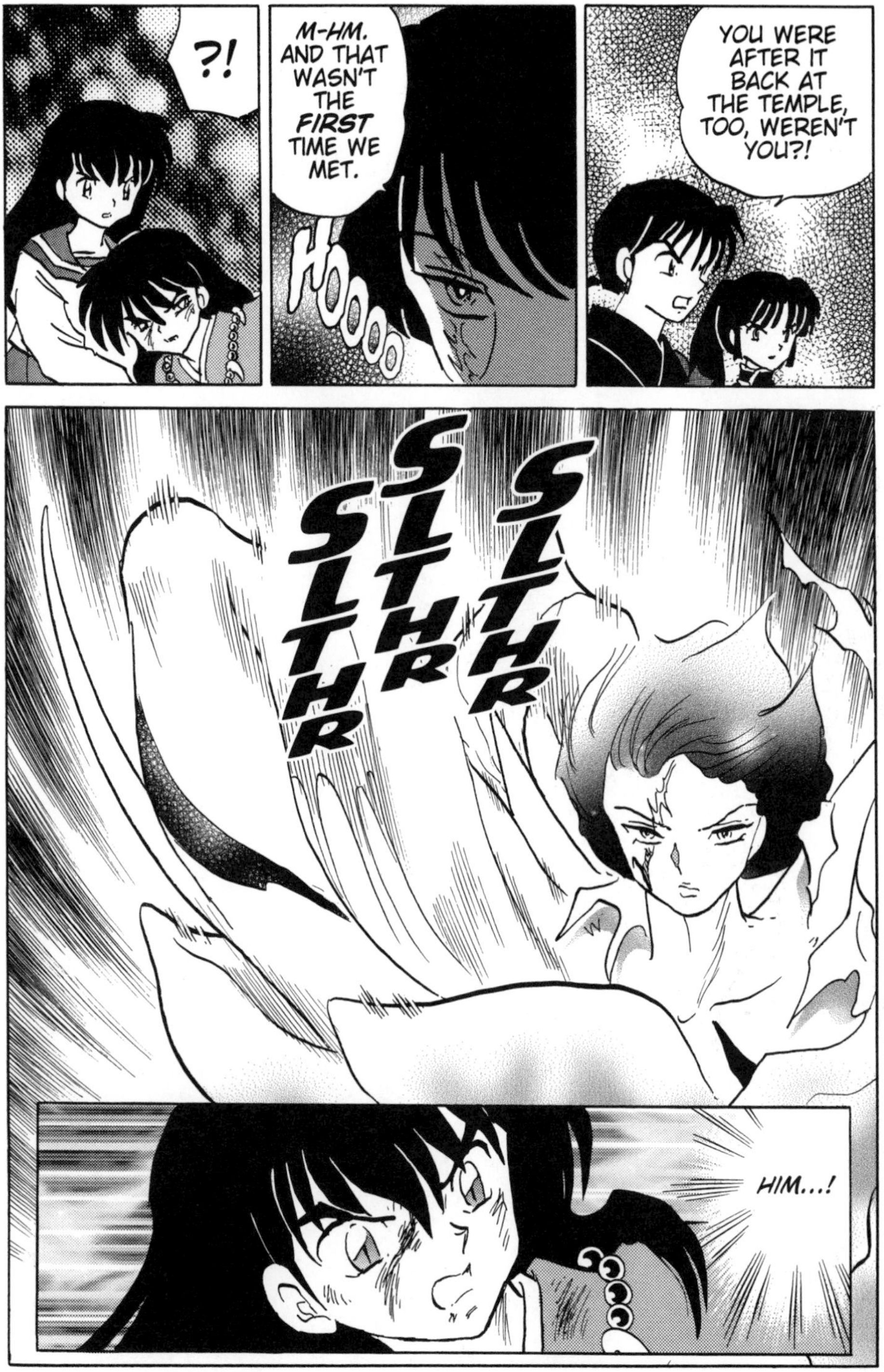
YOU WERE AFTER IT BACK AT THE TEMPLE, TOO, WEREN'T YOU?!
M-HM. AND THAT WASN'T THE *FIRST* TIME WE MET.
HOOOOO
?!
SLITHR
SLITHR
SLITHR
HIM...!

SCROLL SIX
METAMORPHOSIS

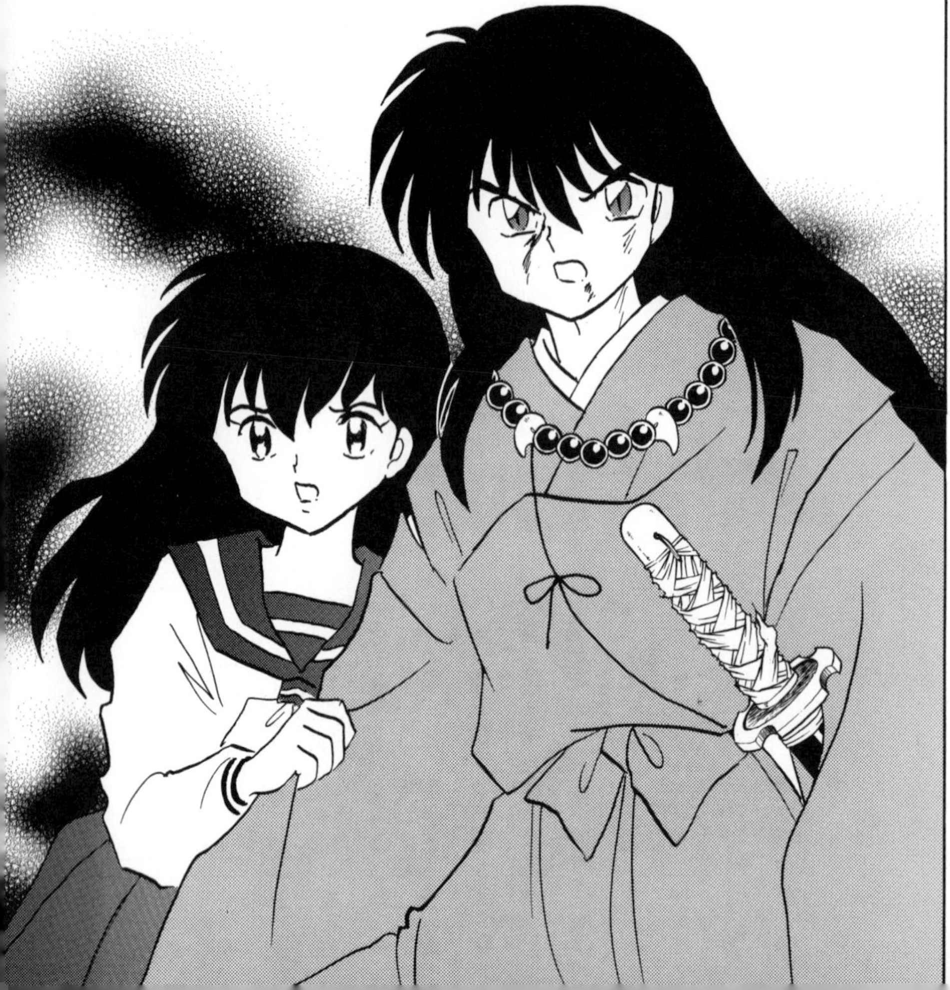

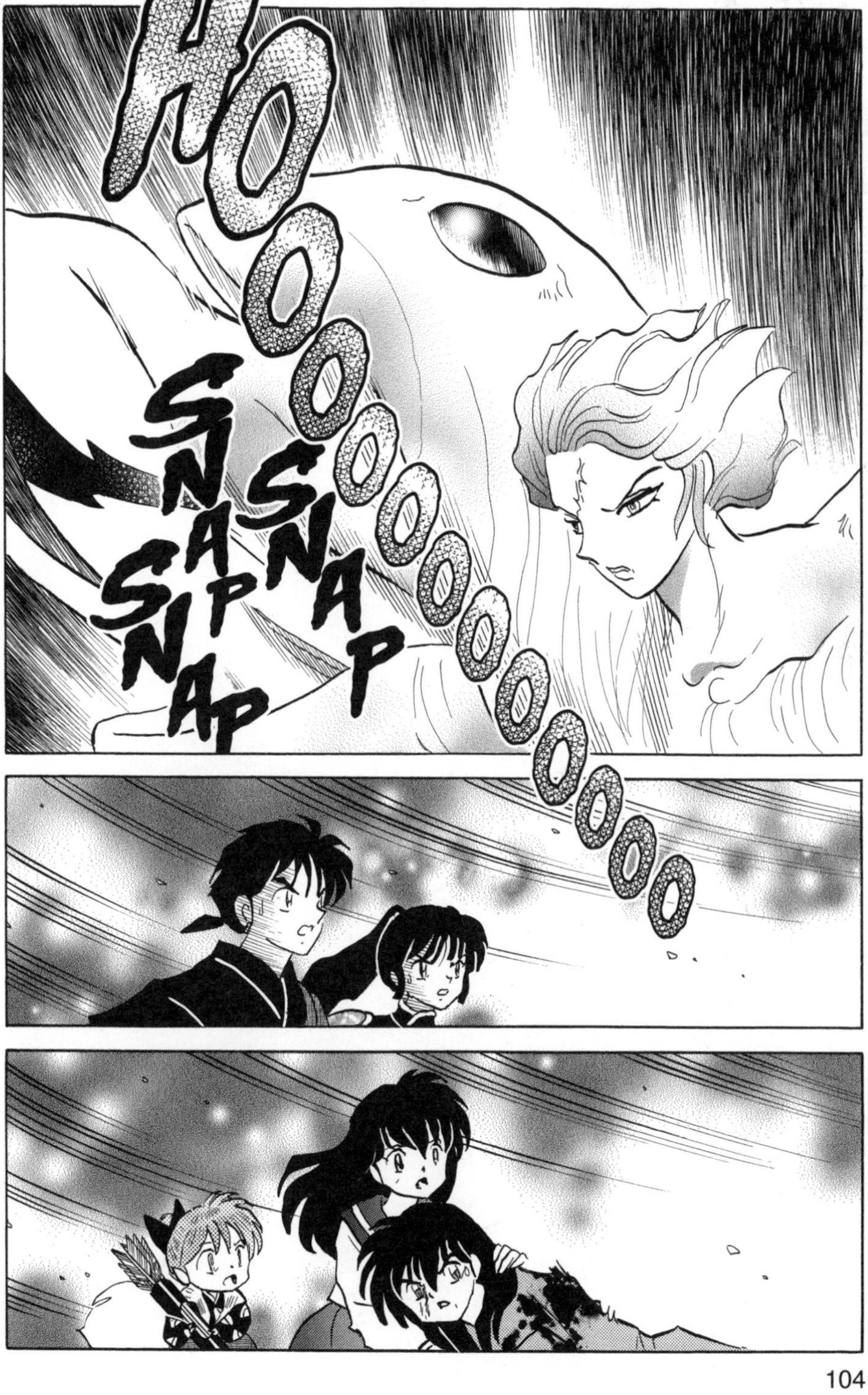
HOOOOOOOOOOOOOOOO
SNAP
SNAP
SNAP

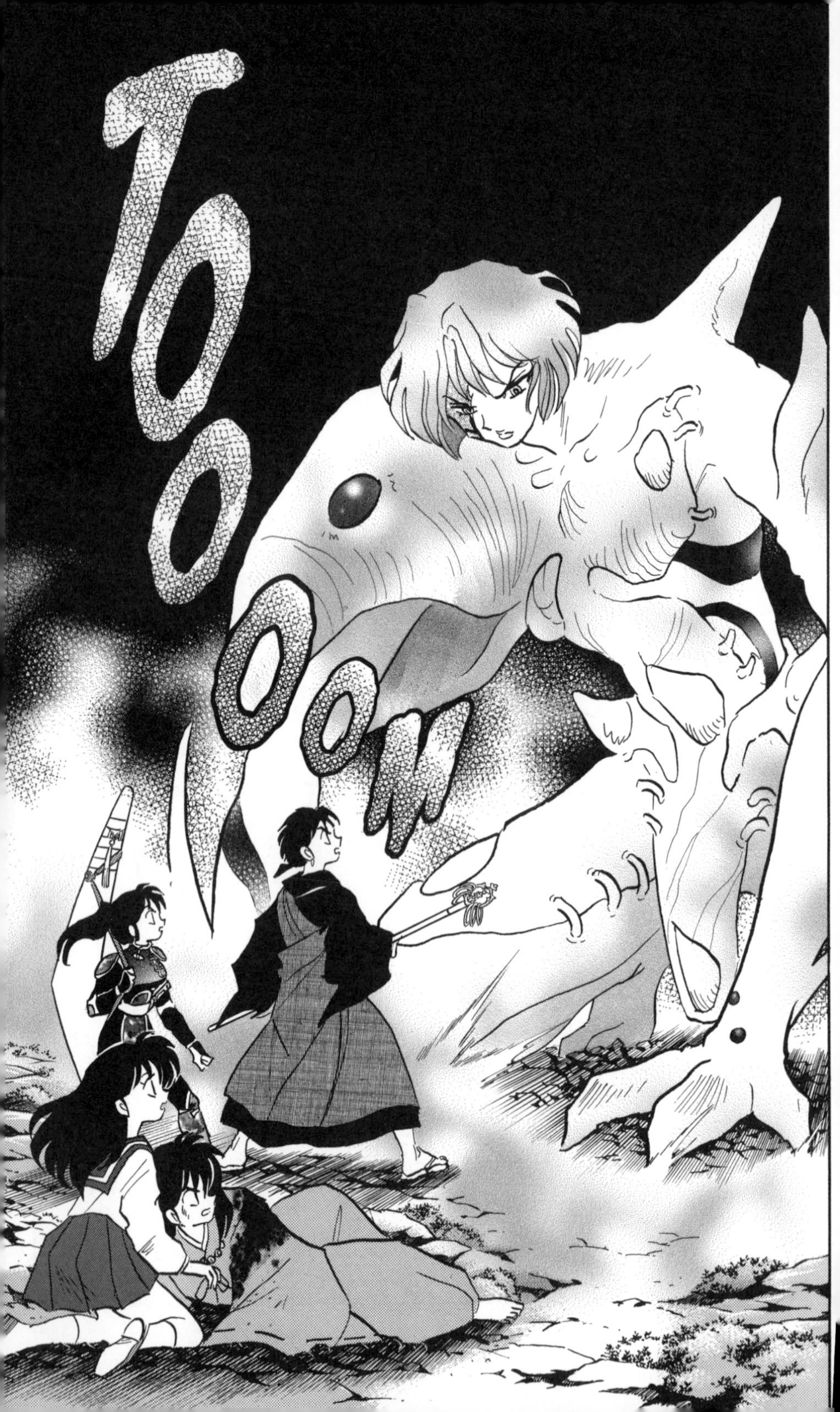
TOOOOOM

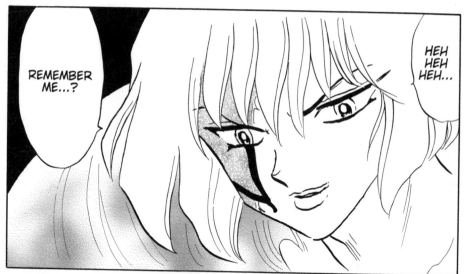

REMEMBER ME...?

HEH HEH HEH...

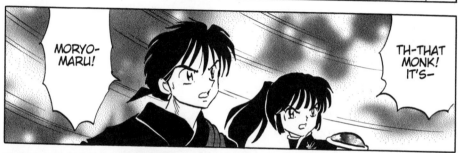

MORYO-MARU!

TH-THAT MONK! IT'S—

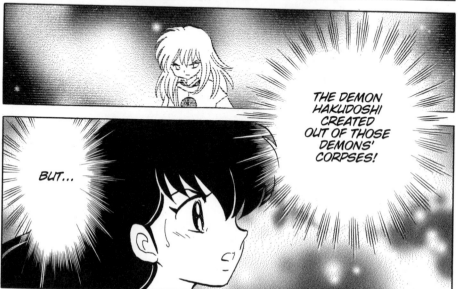

THE DEMON HAKUDOSHI CREATED OUT OF THOSE DEMONS' CORPSES!

BUT...

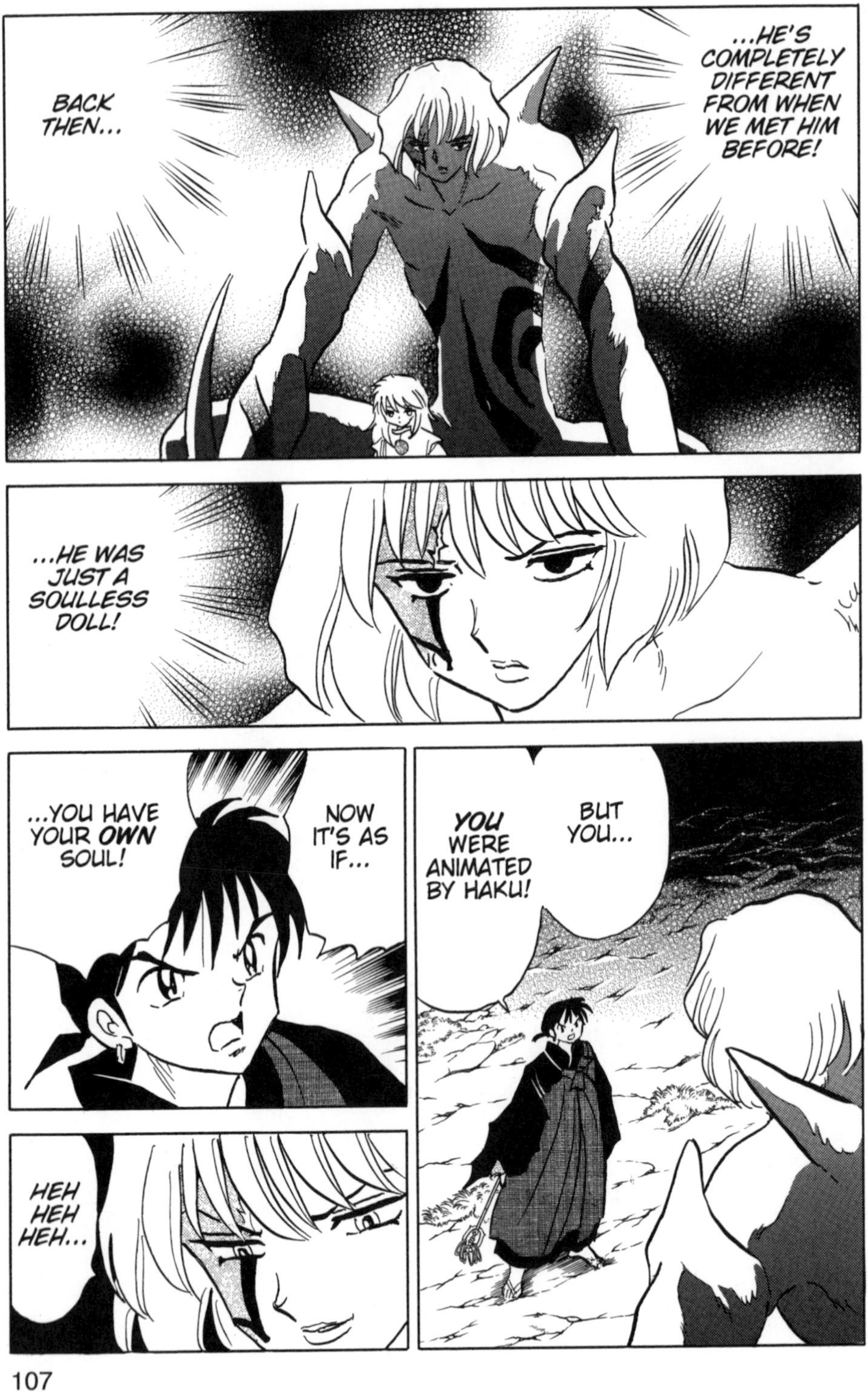
...HE'S COMPLETELY DIFFERENT FROM WHEN WE MET HIM BEFORE!
BACK THEN...
...HE WAS JUST A SOULLESS DOLL!
BUT YOU...
YOU WERE ANIMATED BY HAKU!
NOW IT'S AS IF...
...YOU HAVE YOUR *OWN* SOUL!
HEH HEH HEH...

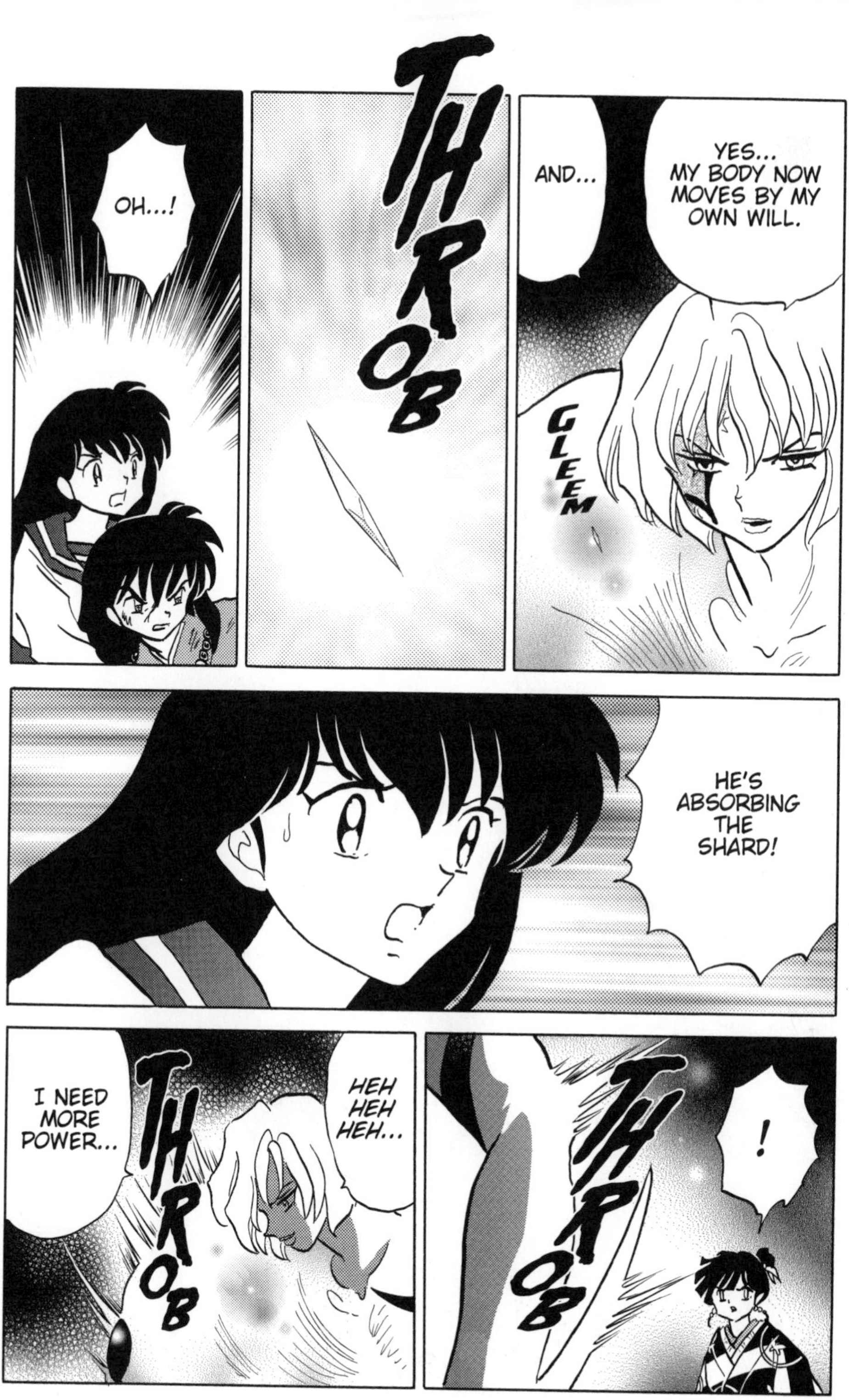
YES... MY BODY NOW MOVES BY MY OWN WILL.
AND...
GLEEM
THROB
OH...!
HE'S ABSORBING THE SHARD!
!
THROB
HEH HEH HEH...
I NEED MORE POWER...
THROB

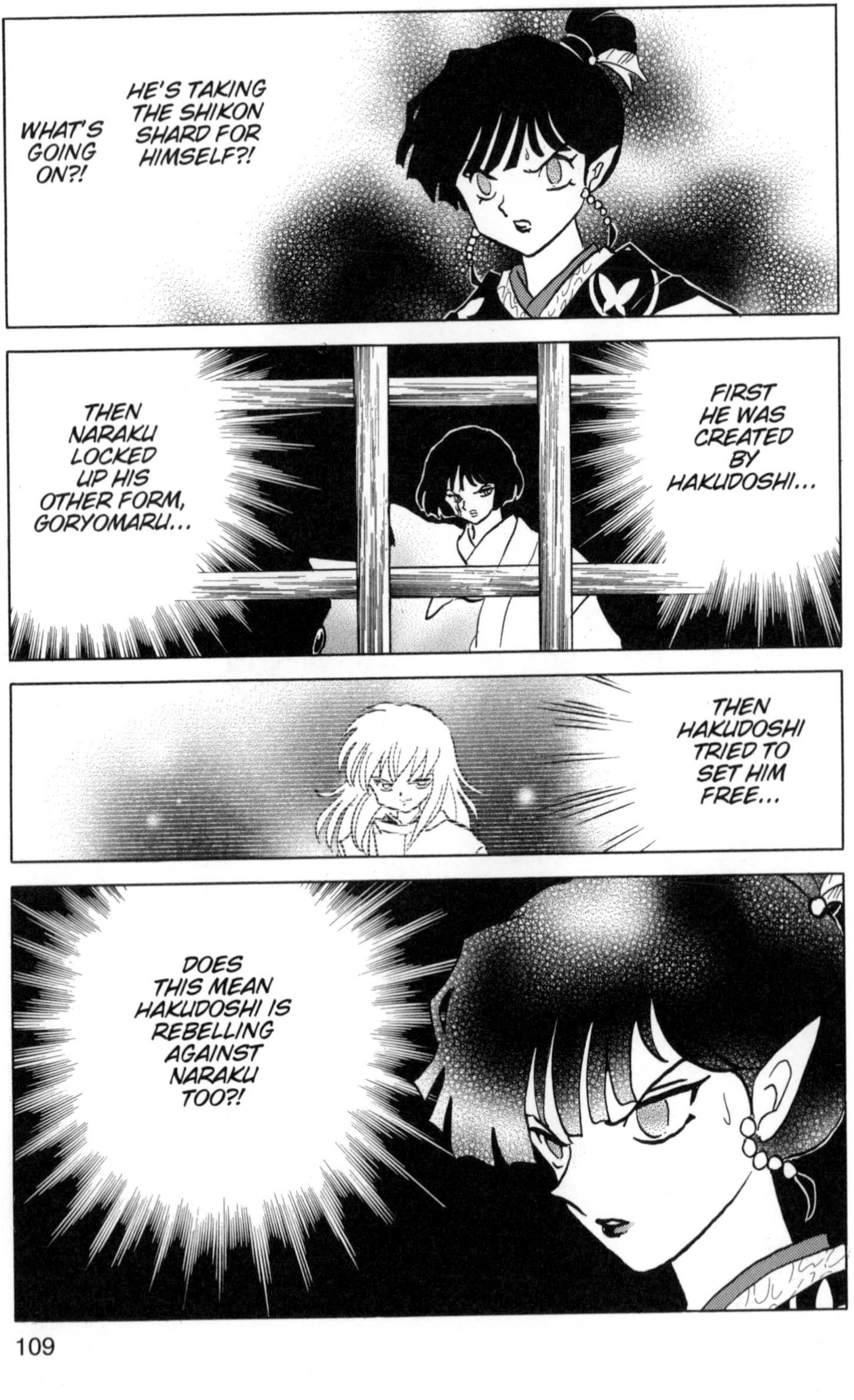
HE'S TAKING THE SHIKON SHARD FOR HIMSELF?!
WHAT'S GOING ON?!
FIRST HE WAS CREATED BY HAKUDOSHI...
THEN NARAKU LOCKED UP HIS OTHER FORM, GORYOMARU...
THEN HAKUDOSHI TRIED TO SET HIM FREE...
DOES THIS MEAN HAKUDOSHI IS REBELLING AGAINST NARAKU TOO?!

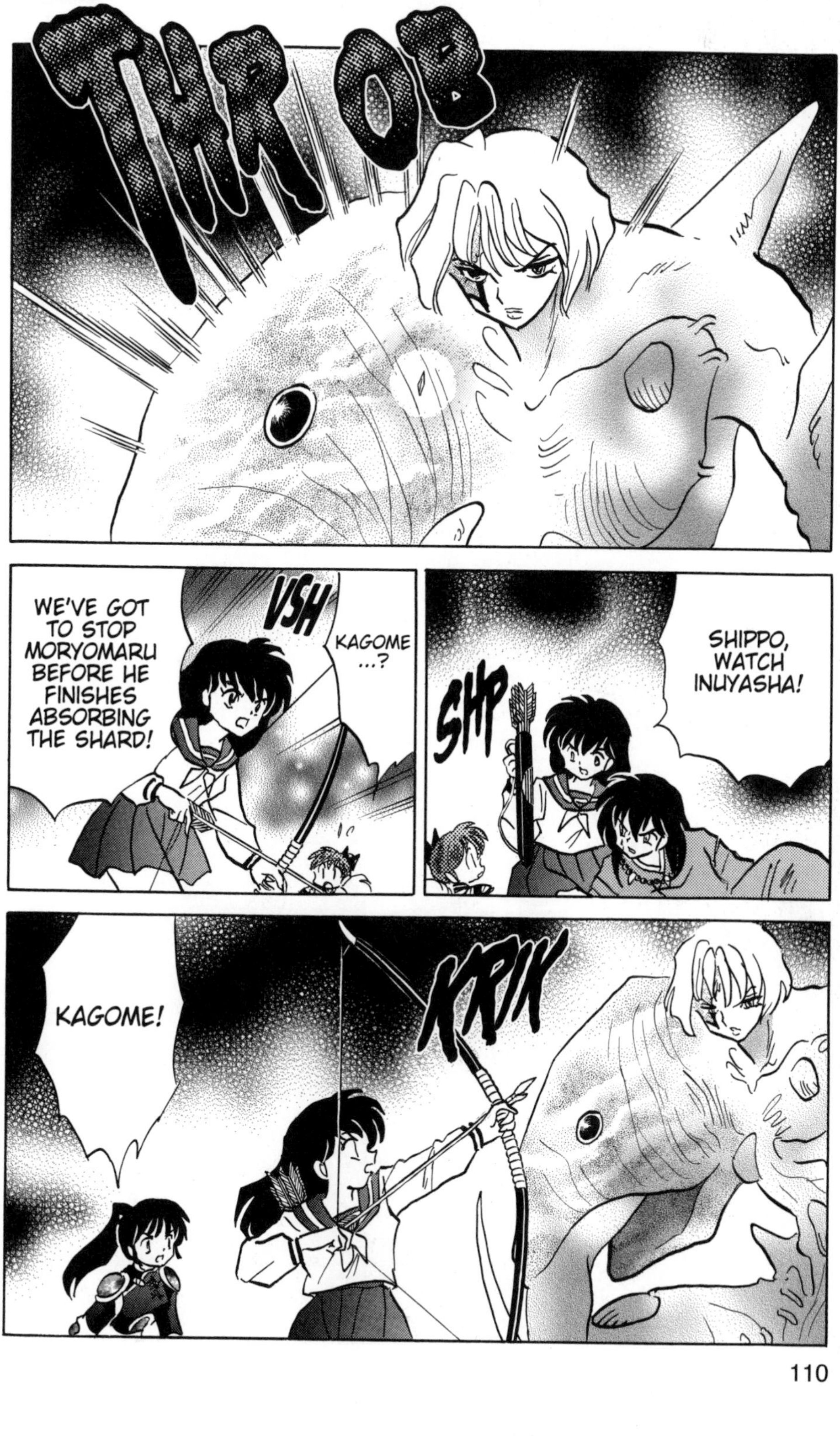
THROB
SHIPPO, WATCH INUYASHA!
SHP
VSH
KAGOME ...?
WE'VE GOT TO STOP MORYOMARU BEFORE HE FINISHES ABSORBING THE SHARD!
KRIK
KAGOME!

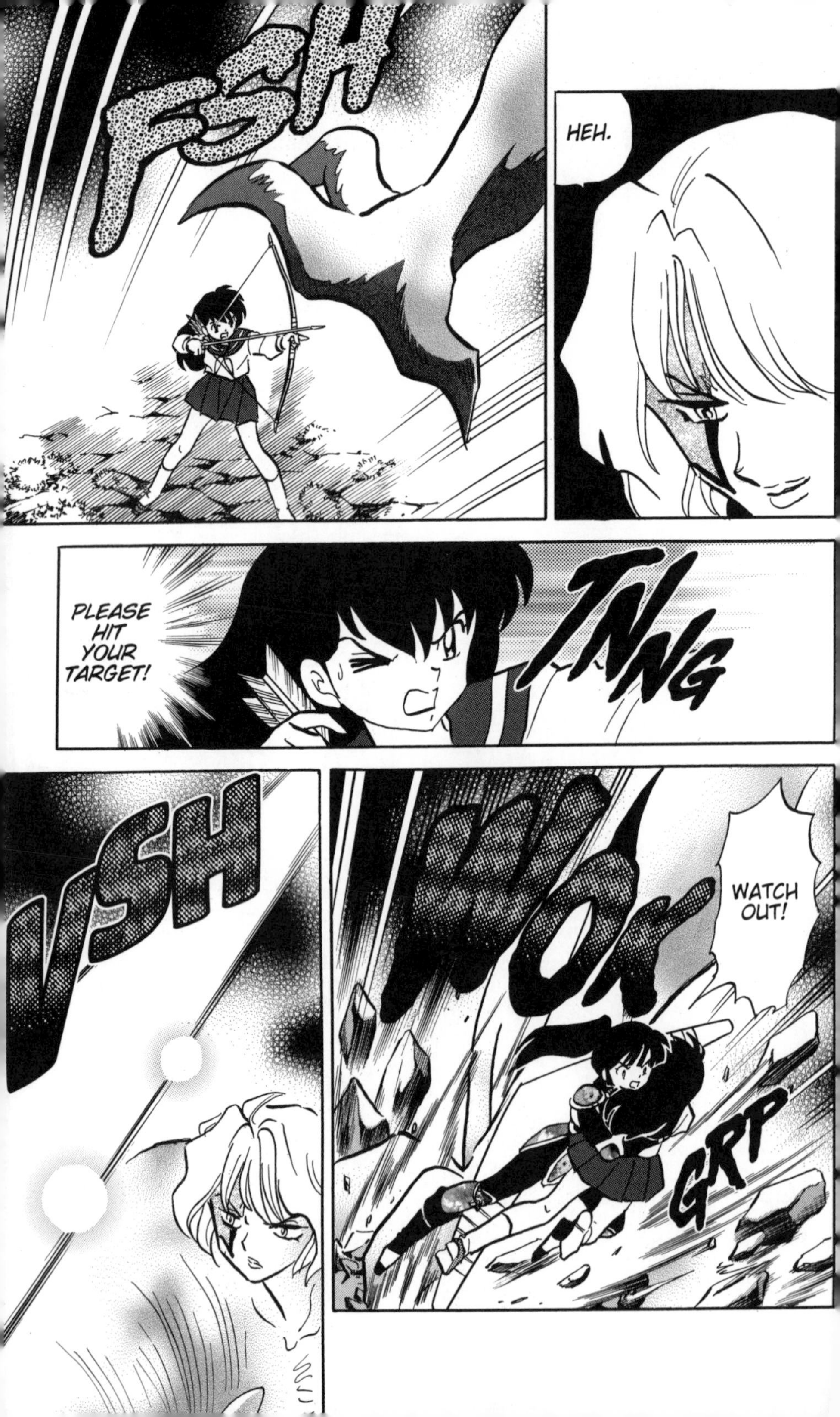
HEH.
FSH
TNNG
PLEASE HIT YOUR TARGET!
WATCH OUT!
GRP
VSH

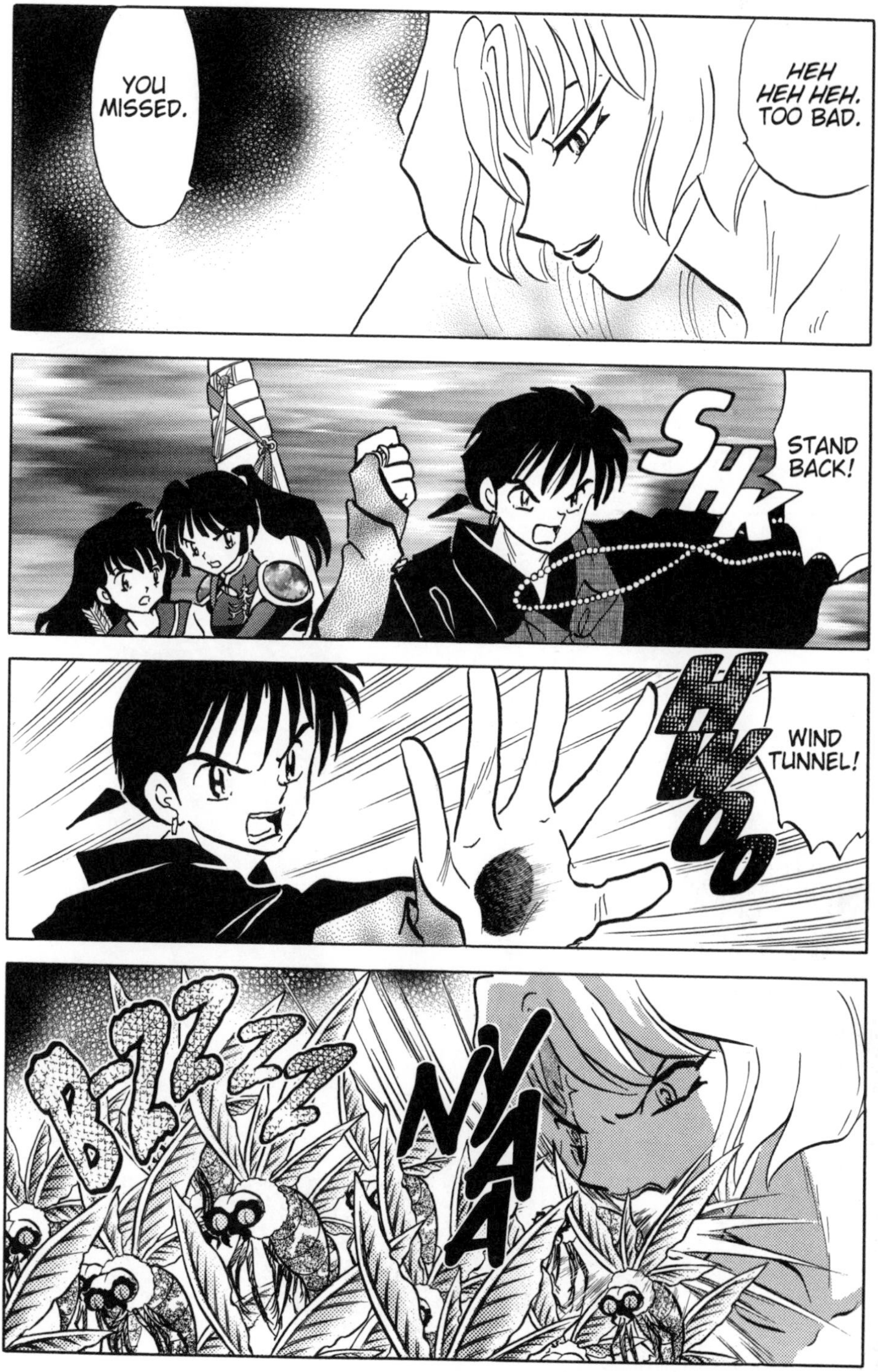

HEH HEH HEH. TOO BAD.
YOU MISSED.
STAND BACK!
SHK
WIND TUNNEL!
HWOO
NYAA
BZZZZ

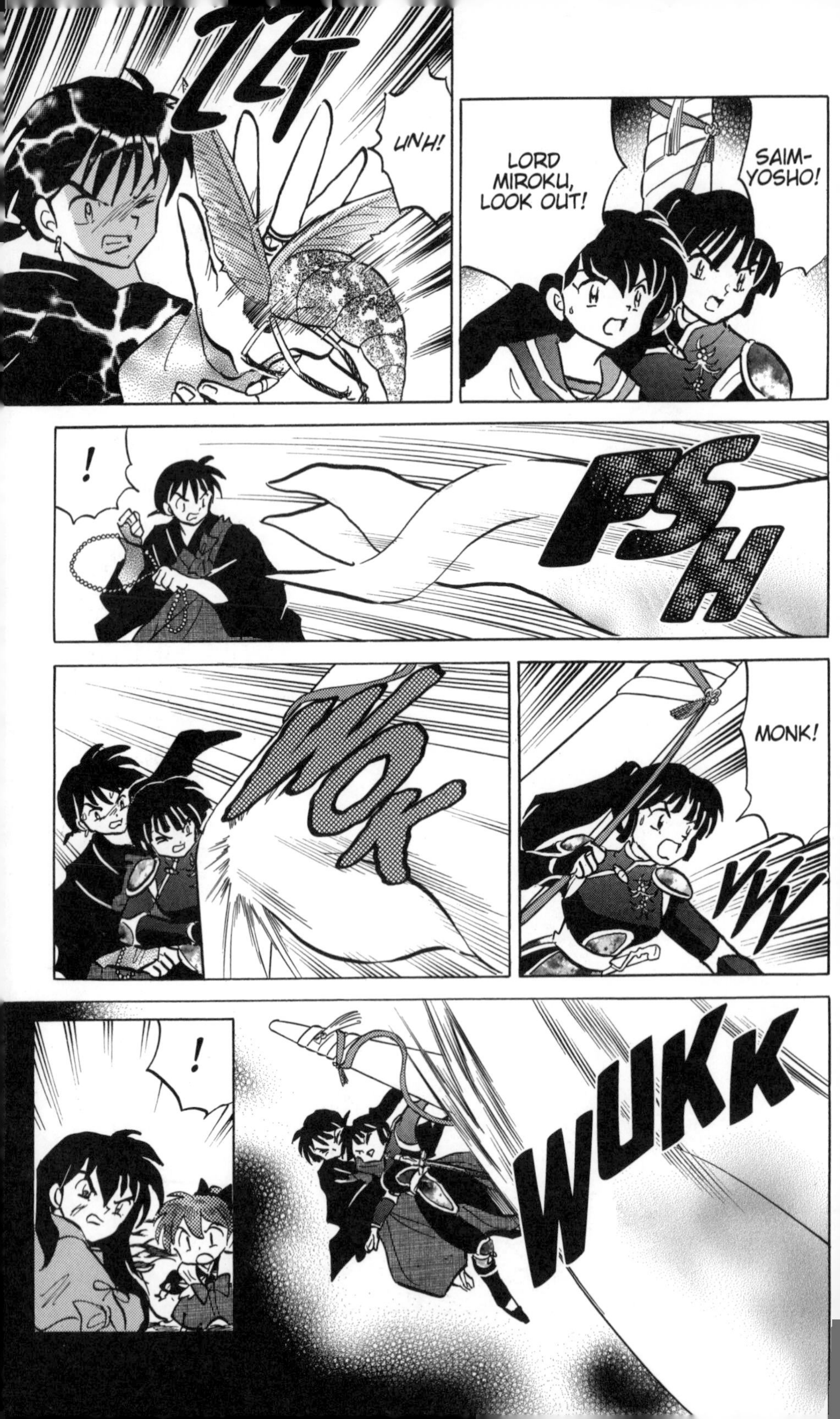
SAIM-YOSHO!
LORD MIROKU, LOOK OUT!
ZZT
UNH!
FSSH
!
MONK!
VVV
WHOK
WUKK
!

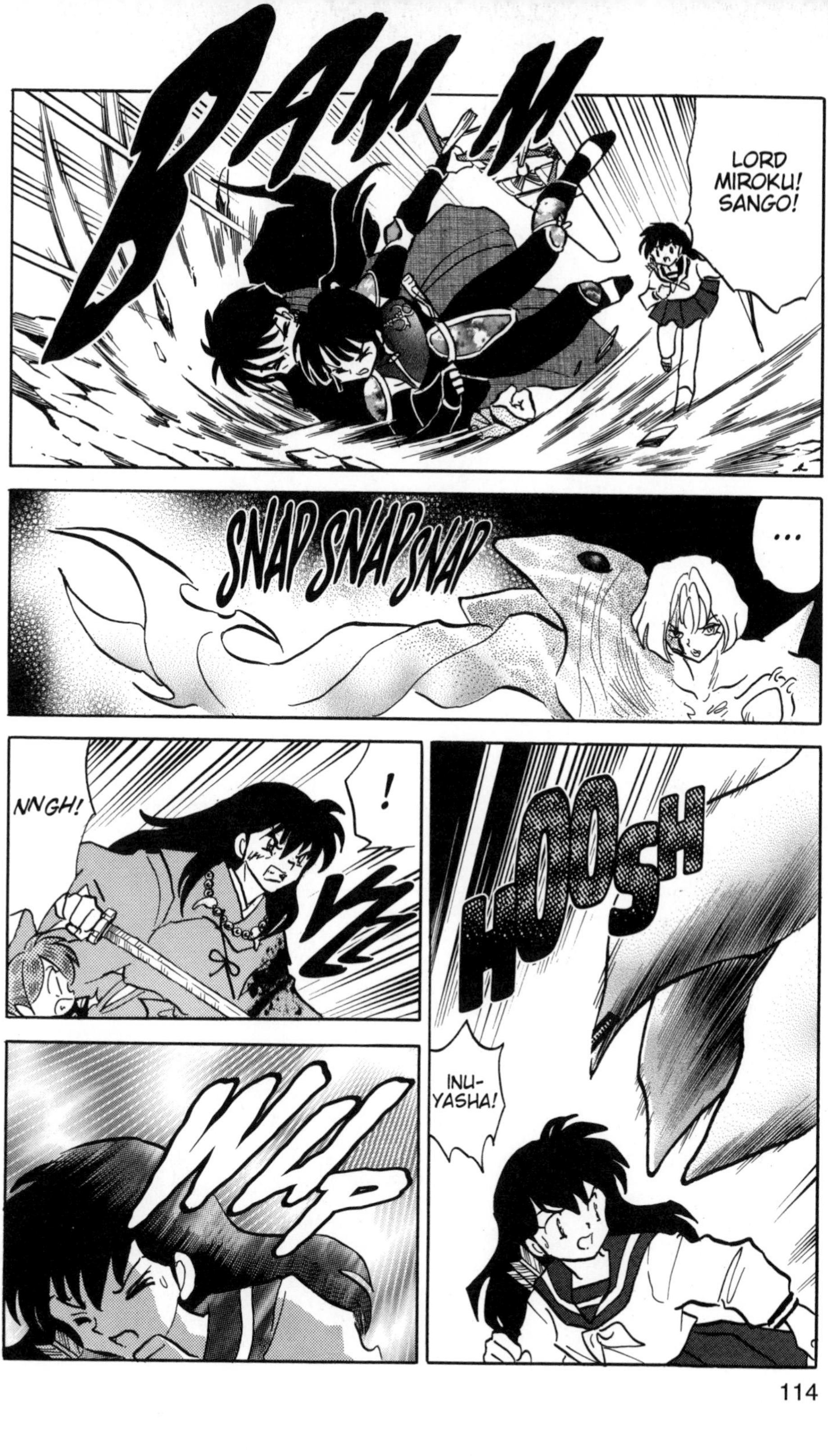

BAMM
LORD MIROKU! SANGO!
...
SNAP SNAP SNAP
WHOOSH
INU-YASHA!
!
NNGH!
WHIP

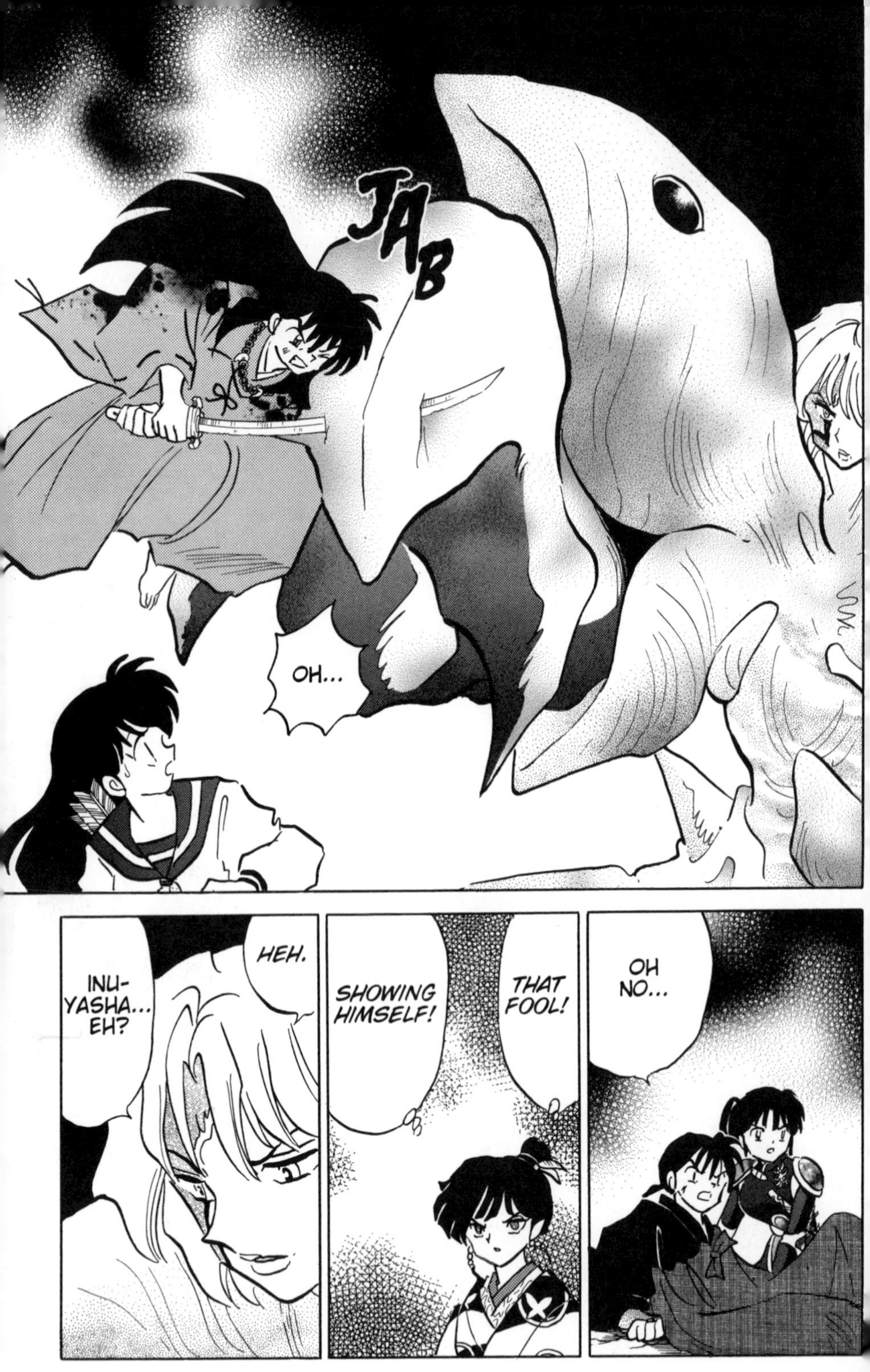
JAB
OH...
OH NO...
THAT FOOL!
SHOWING HIMSELF!
HEH.
INU-YASHA... EH?

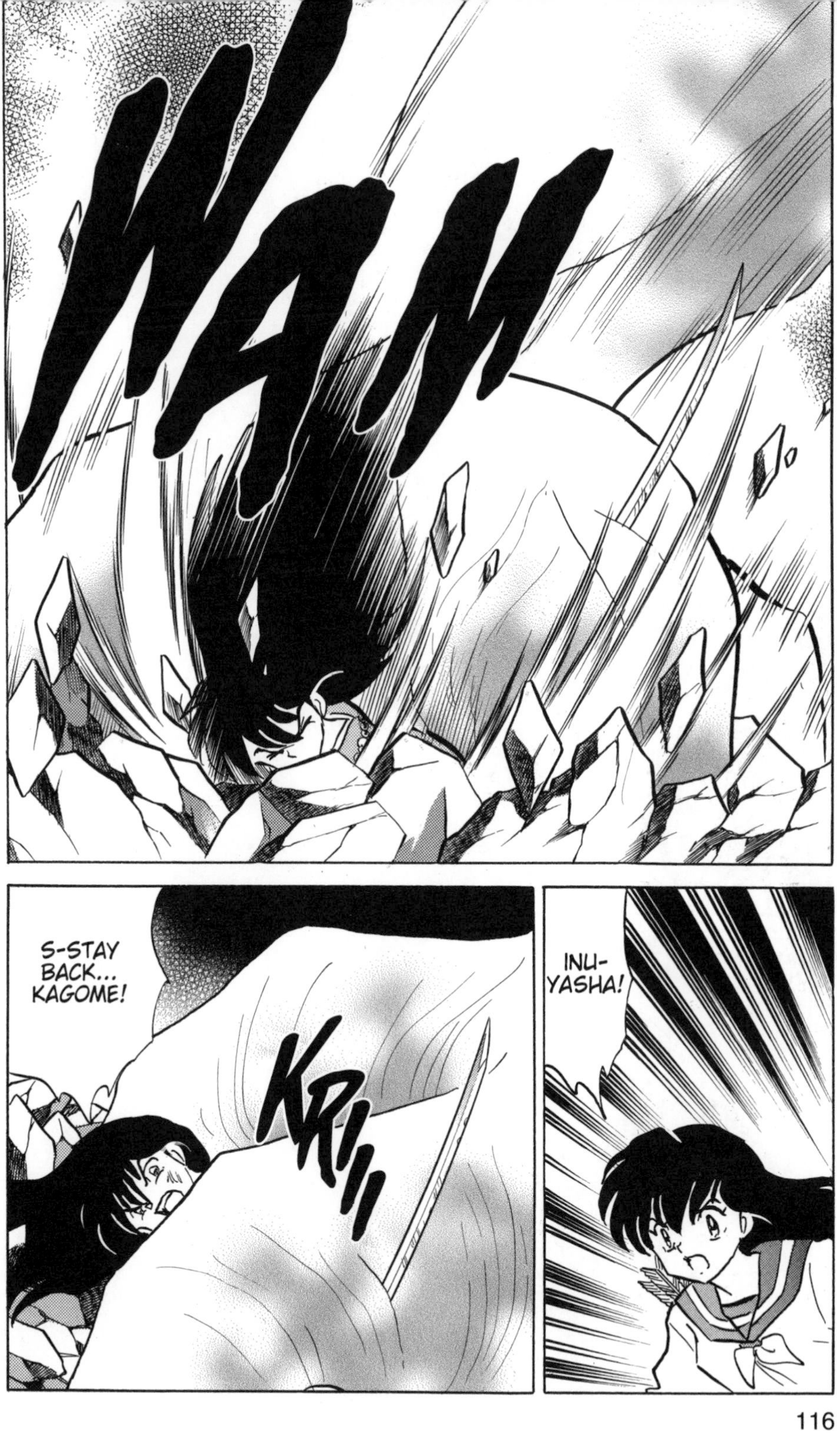
WHAM
INU-
YASHA!
S-STAY
BACK...
KAGOME!
KRIII

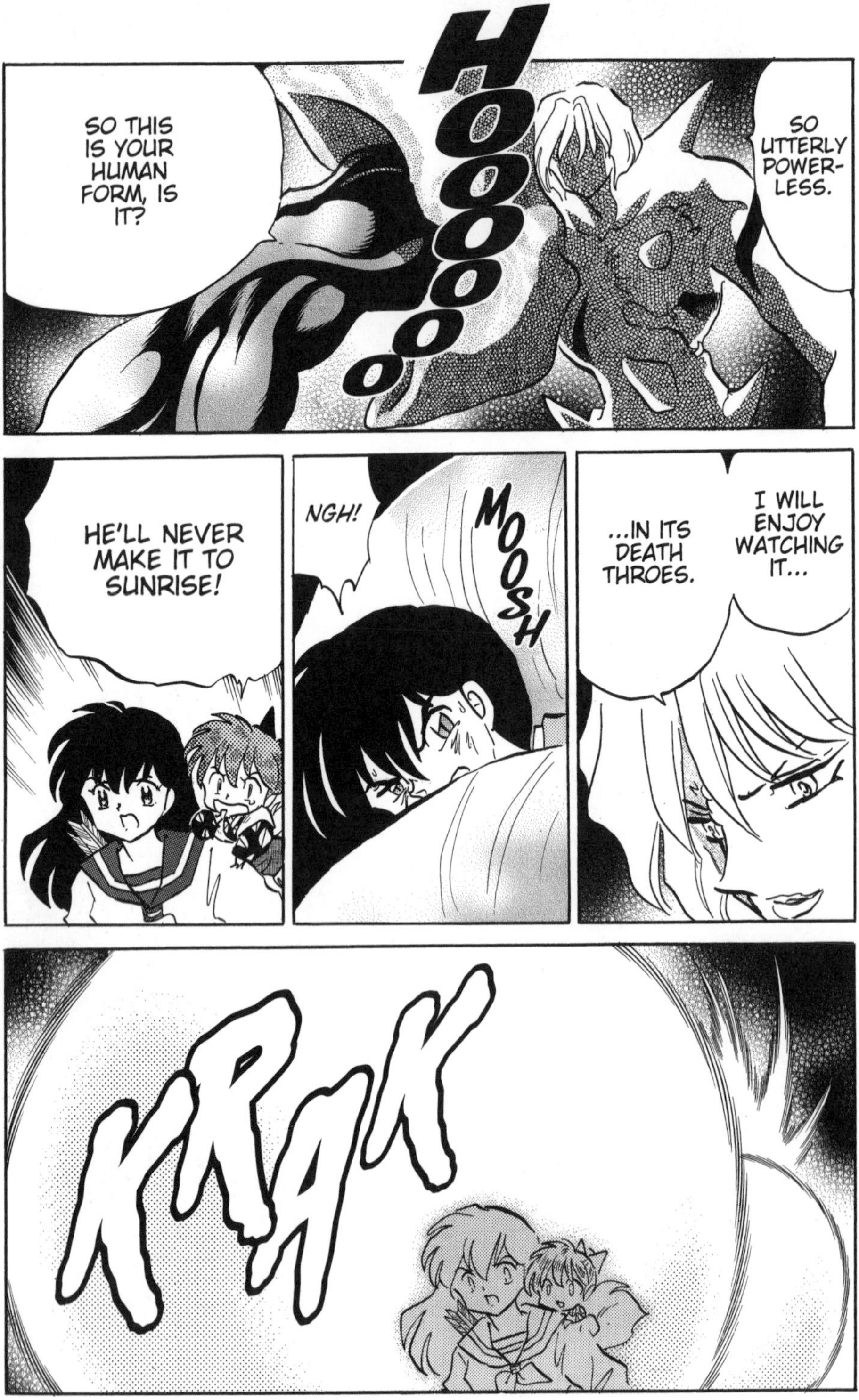

HOOOOOOO
SO UTTERLY POWER-LESS.
SO THIS IS YOUR HUMAN FORM, IS IT?
I WILL ENJOY WATCHING IT...
...IN ITS DEATH THROES.
MOOSH
NGH!
HE'LL NEVER MAKE IT TO SUNRISE!
KRAK

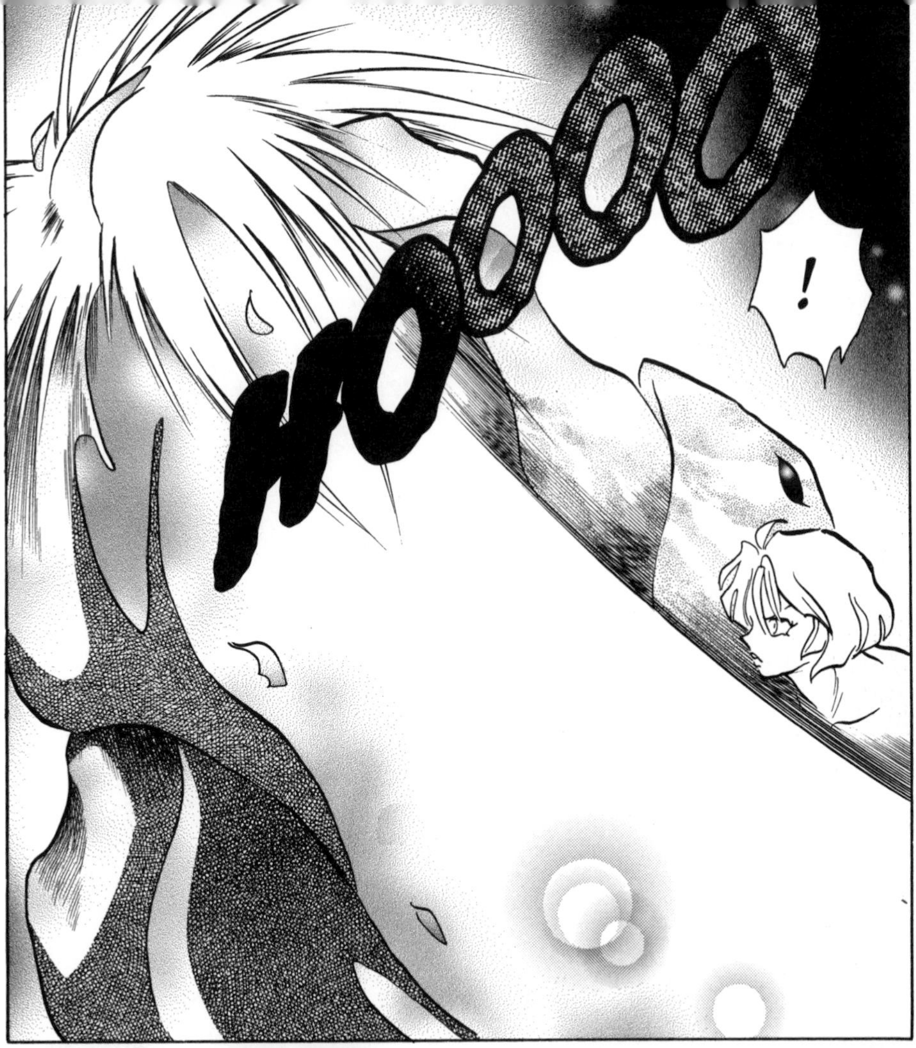
HOOOOOO
!

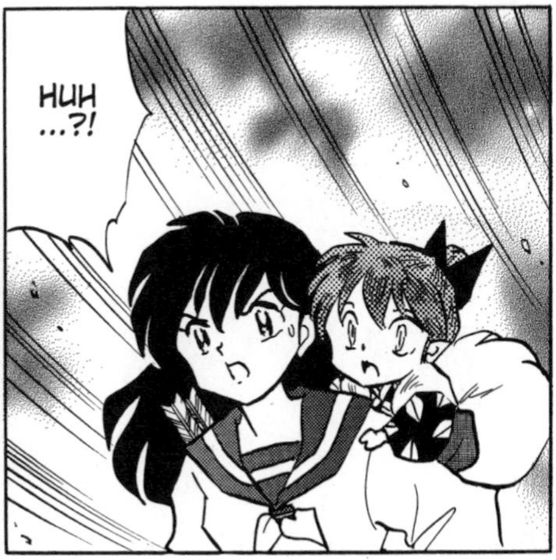
HUH ...?!

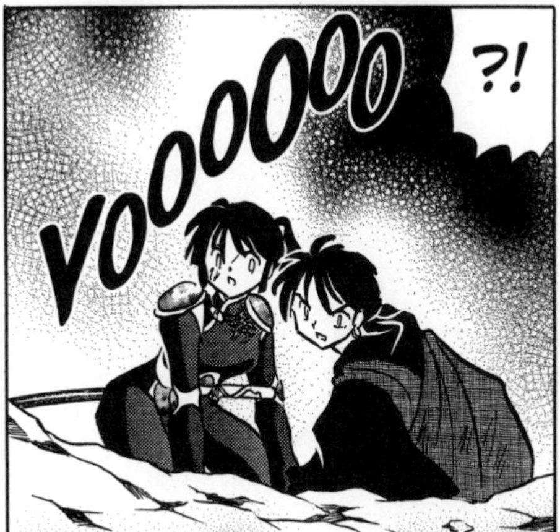
VOOOOOO
?!

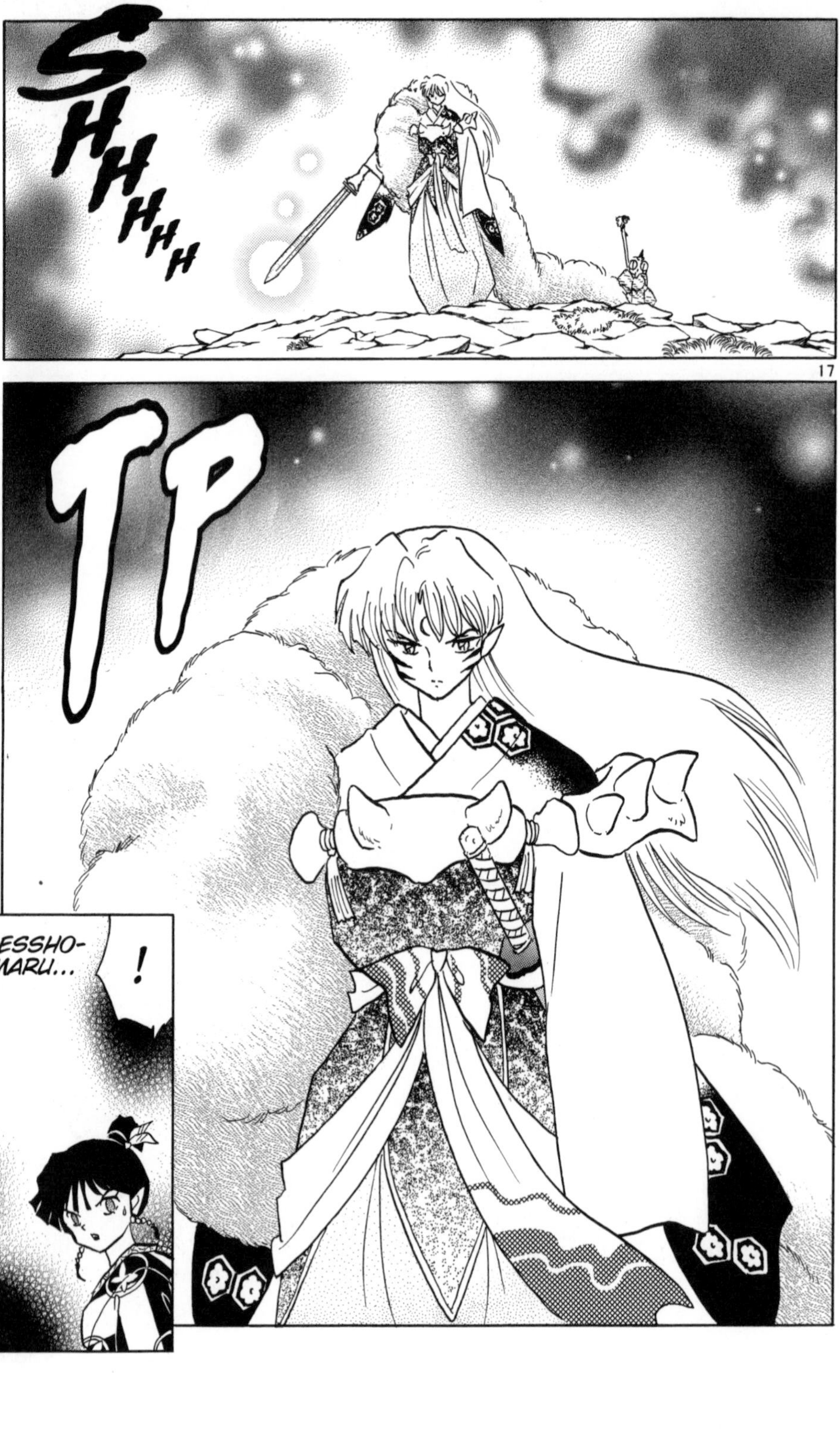
SHHHHH
TP
!
SESSHO-MARU...

17

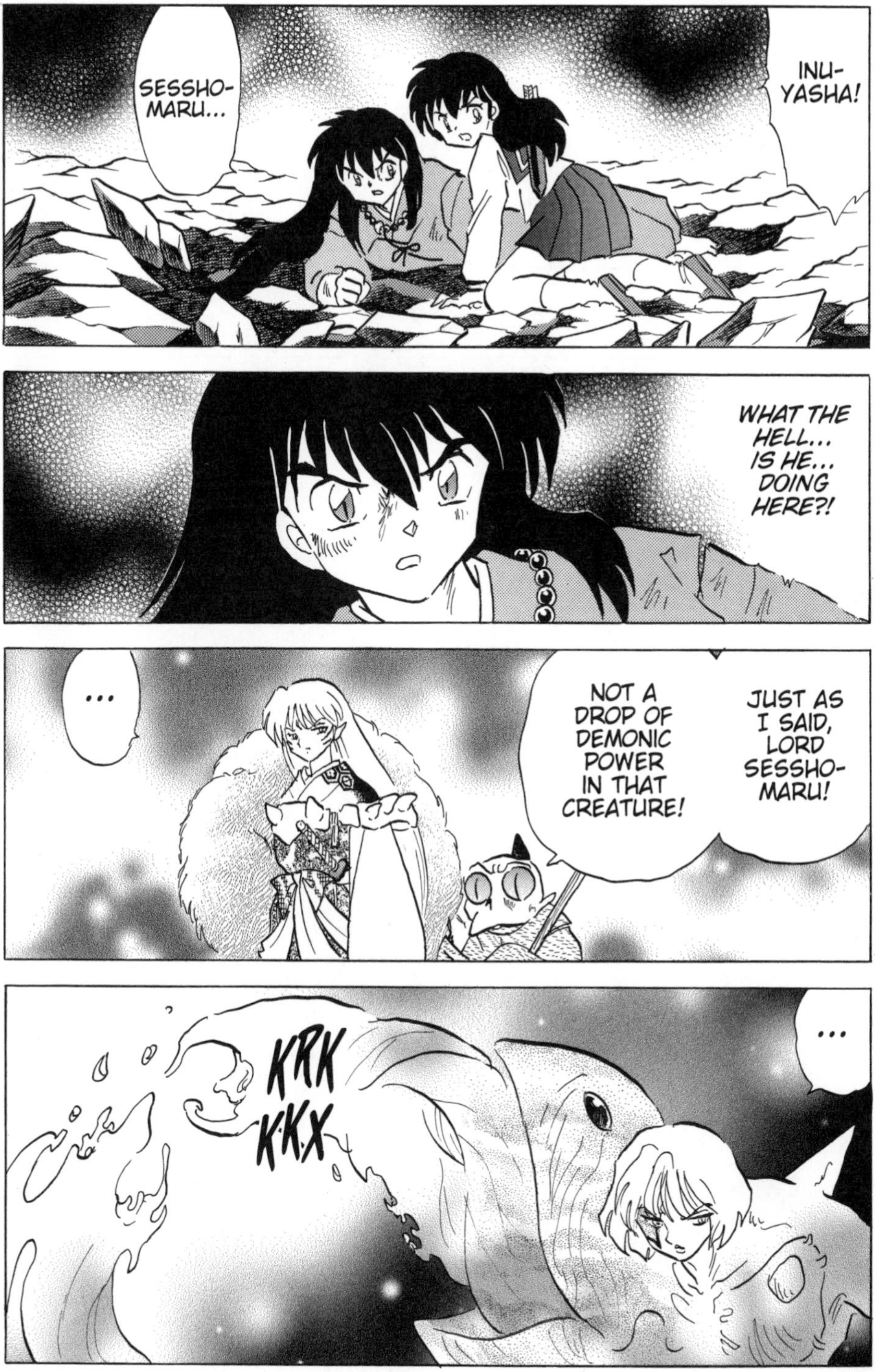
INU-YASHA!
SESSHO-MARU...
WHAT THE HELL... IS HE... DOING HERE?!
JUST AS I SAID, LORD SESSHO-MARU!
NOT A DROP OF DEMONIC POWER IN THAT CREATURE!
...
...
KRK K·K·X

SCROLL SEVEN
THE VANISHED DEMONIC ENERGY

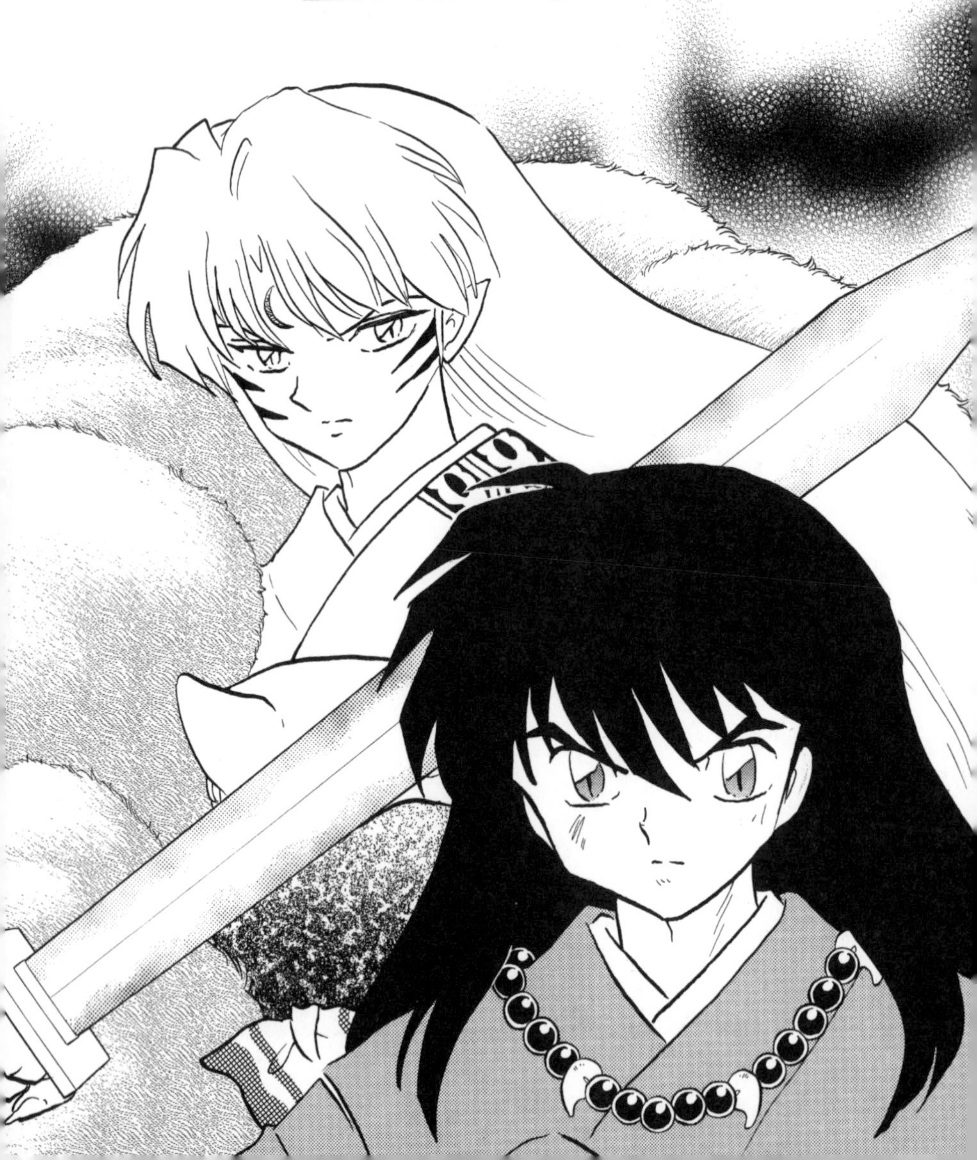

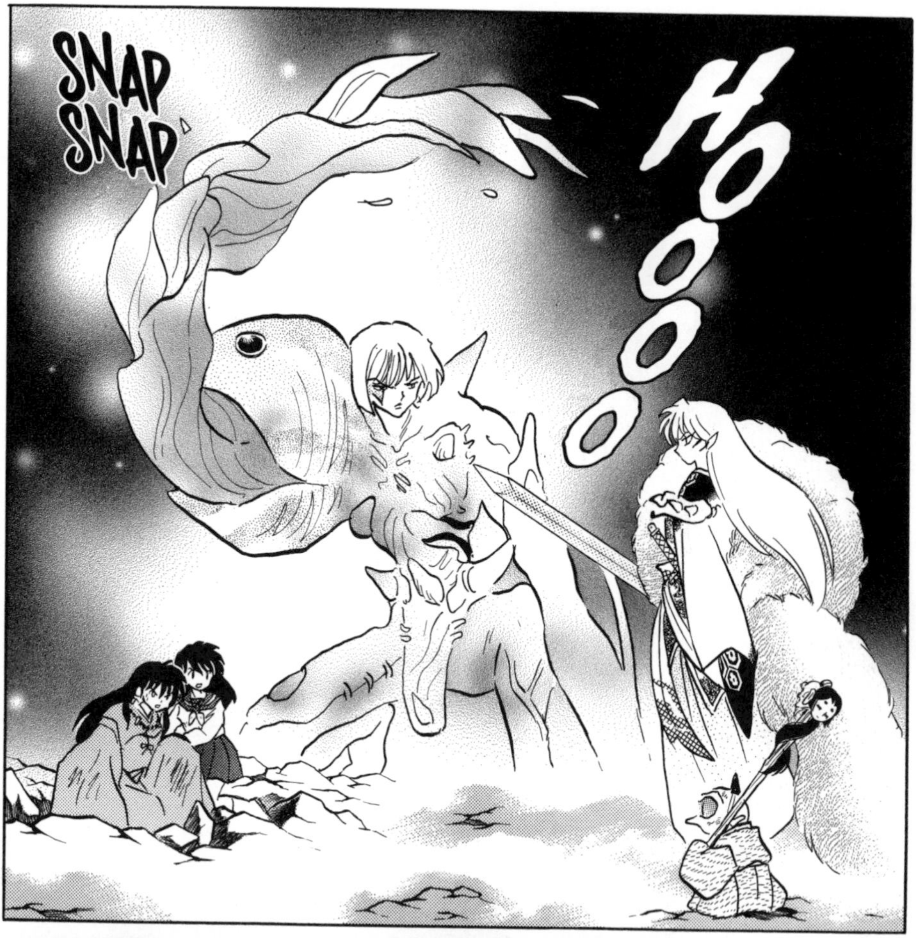
HOOOOO
SNAP SNAP

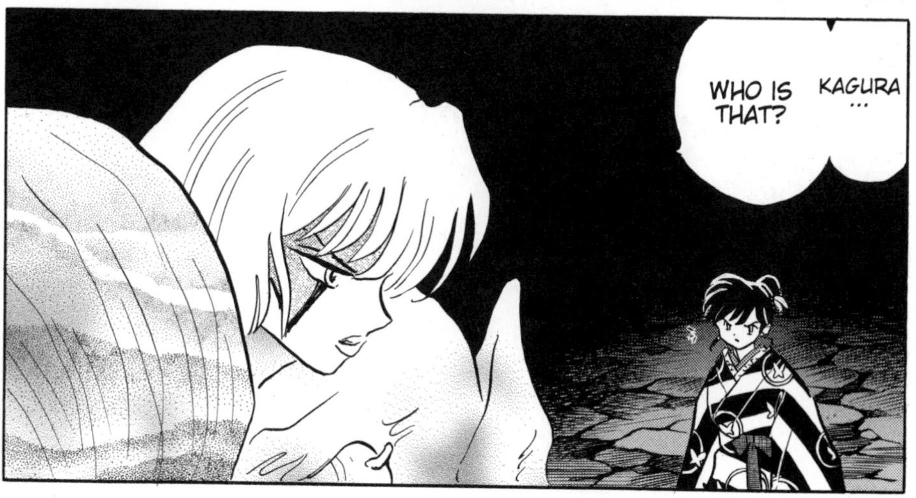
KAGURA ...
WHO IS THAT?

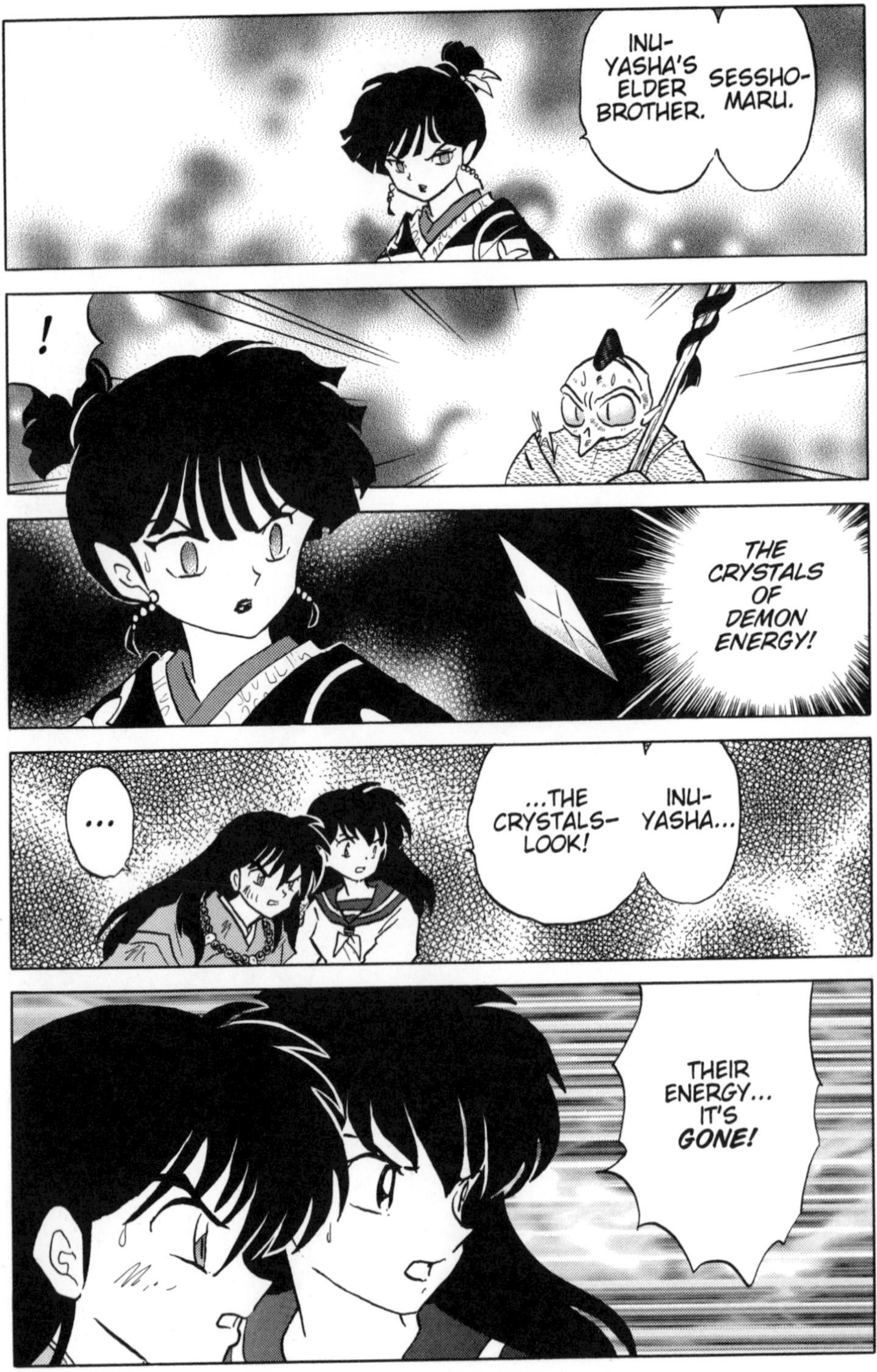
SESSHO-MARU.
INU-YASHA'S ELDER BROTHER.
!
THE CRYSTALS OF DEMON ENERGY!
INU-YASHA...
...THE CRYSTALS- LOOK!
...
THEIR ENERGY... IT'S *GONE!*

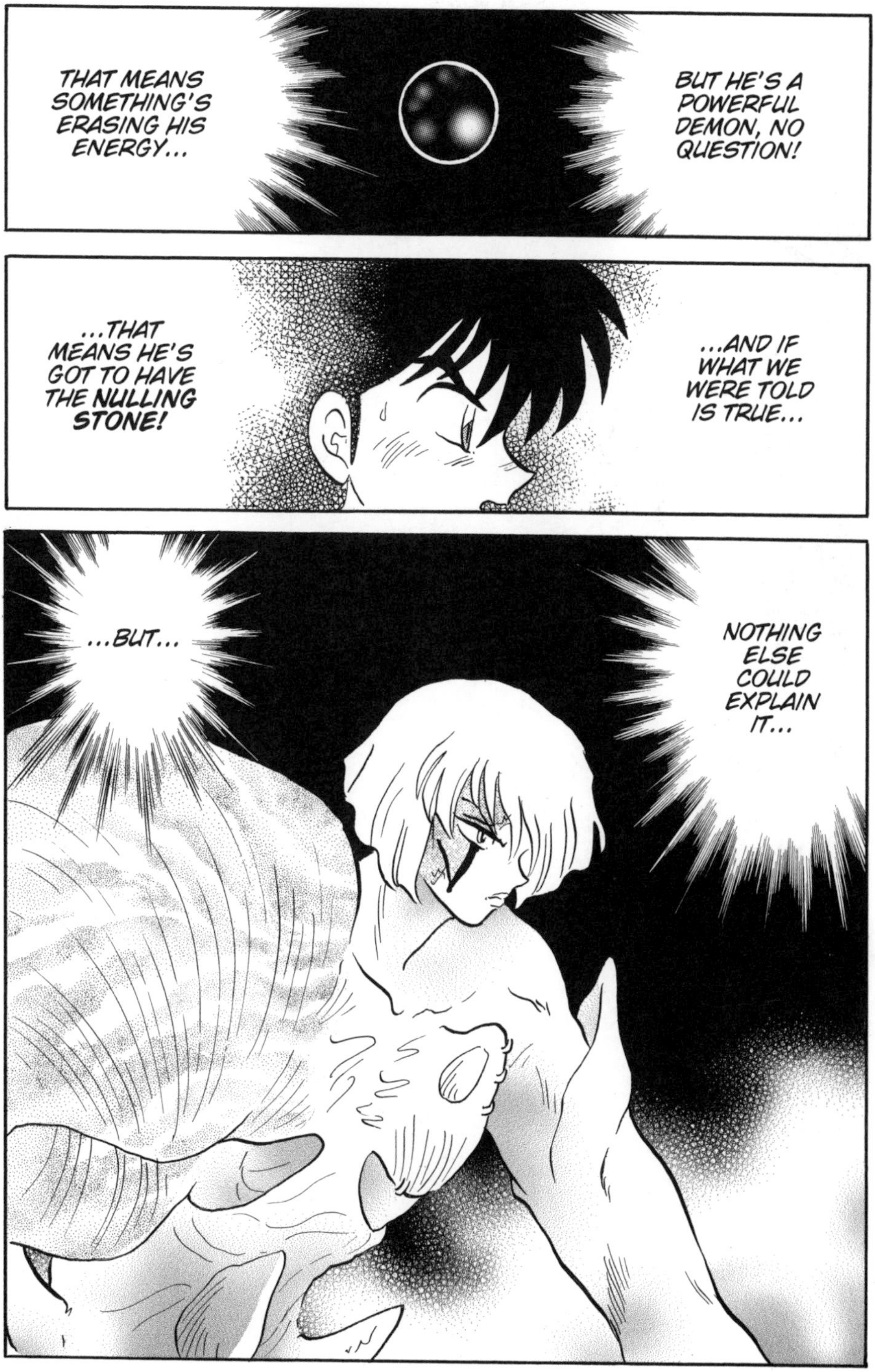
BUT HE'S A POWERFUL DEMON, NO QUESTION!
THAT MEANS SOMETHING'S ERASING HIS ENERGY...
...AND IF WHAT WE WERE TOLD IS TRUE...
...THAT MEANS HE'S GOT TO HAVE THE NULLING STONE!
NOTHING ELSE COULD EXPLAIN IT...
...BUT...

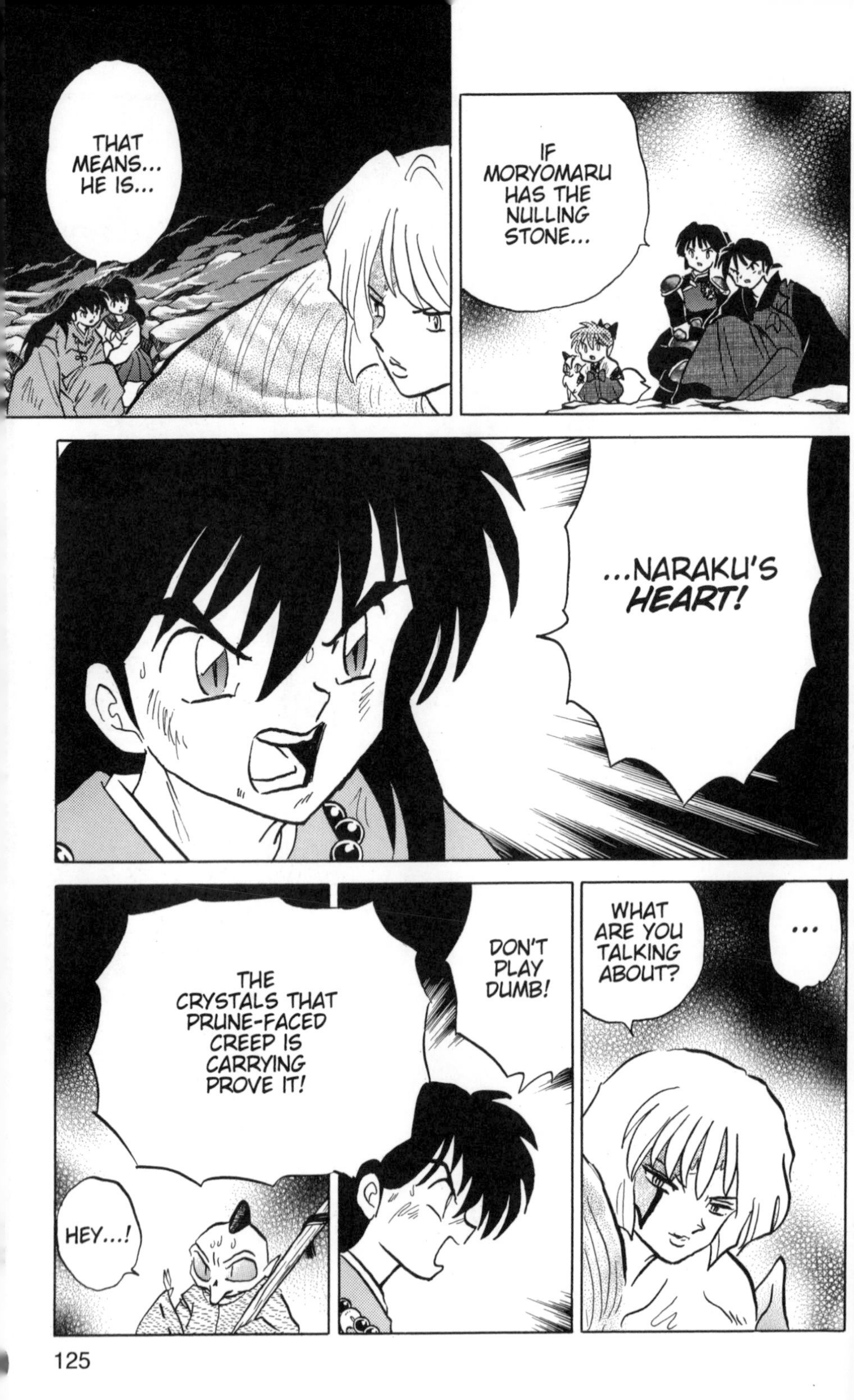
IF MORYOMARU HAS THE NULLING STONE...
THAT MEANS... HE IS...
...NARAKU'S *HEART!*
...
WHAT ARE YOU TALKING ABOUT?
DON'T PLAY DUMB!
THE CRYSTALS THAT PRUNE-FACED CREEP IS CARRYING PROVE IT!
HEY...!

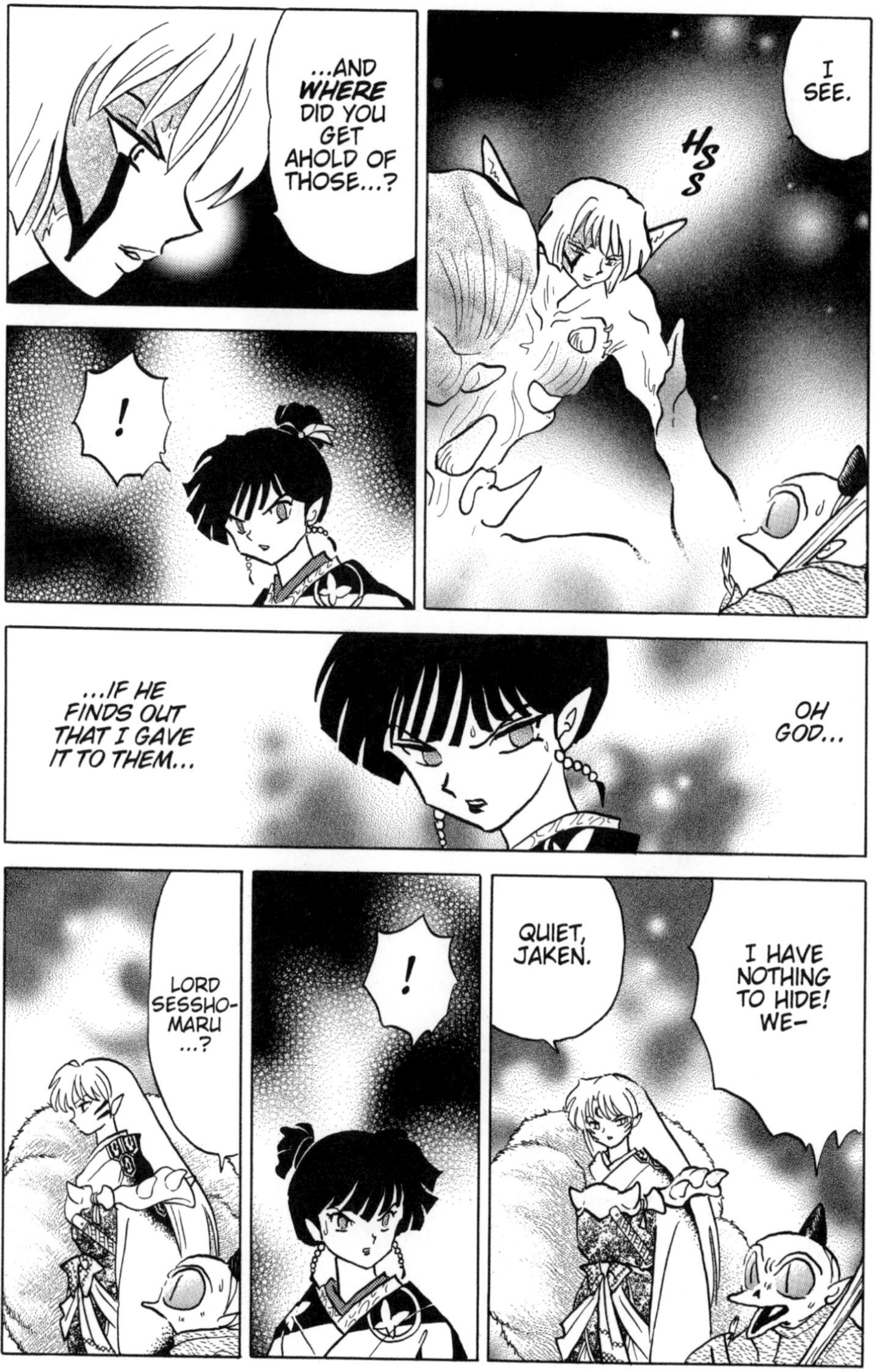
I SEE.
HSS
...AND **WHERE** DID YOU GET AHOLD OF THOSE...?
!
OH GOD...
...IF HE FINDS OUT THAT I GAVE IT TO THEM...
I HAVE NOTHING TO HIDE! WE–
QUIET, JAKEN.
!
LORD SESSHO-MARU ...?

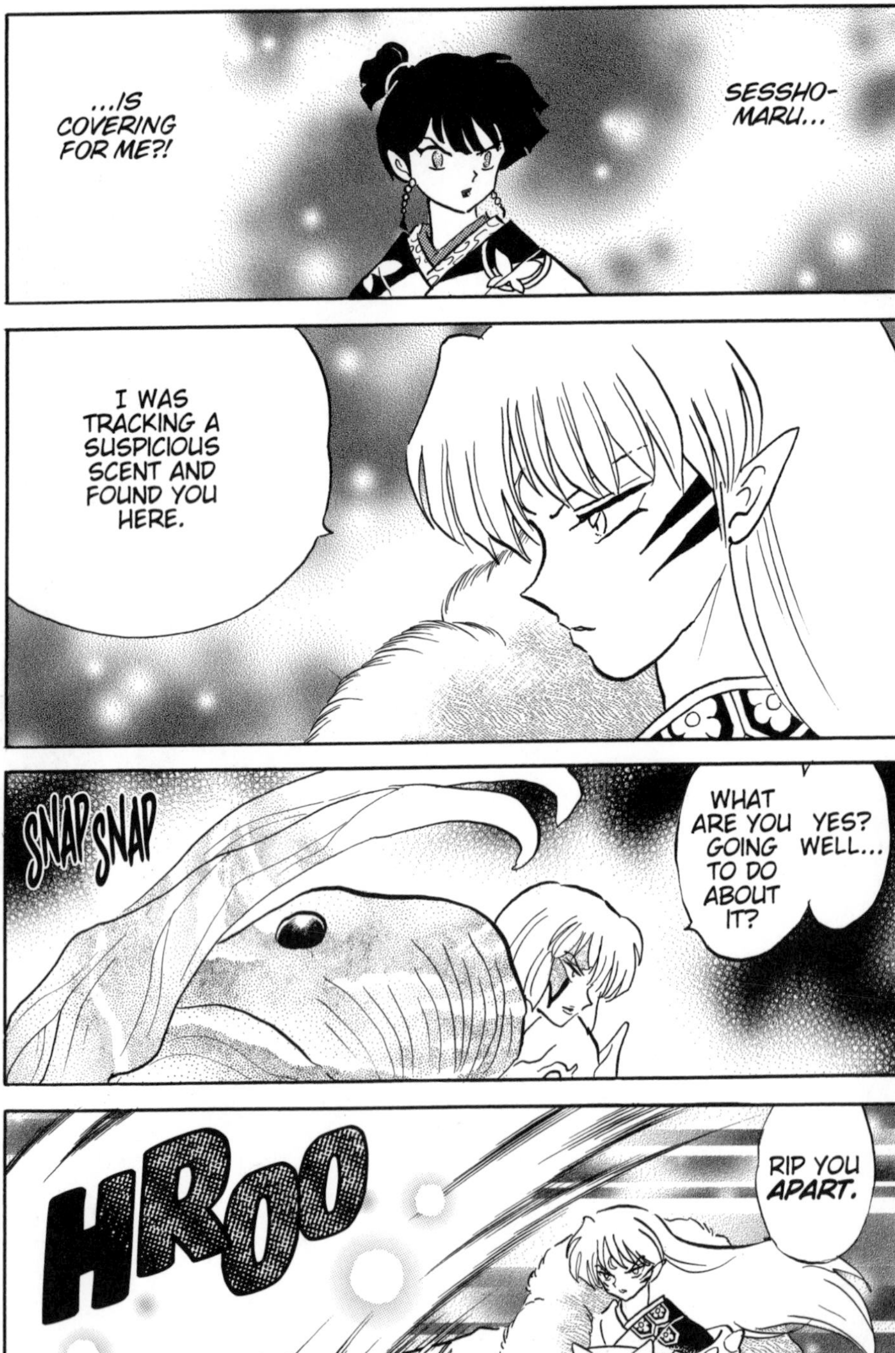
SESSHO-MARU...
...IS COVERING FOR ME?!
I WAS TRACKING A SUSPICIOUS SCENT AND FOUND YOU HERE.
YES? WELL...
WHAT ARE YOU GOING TO DO ABOUT IT?
SNAP SNAP
RIP YOU APART.
HROO

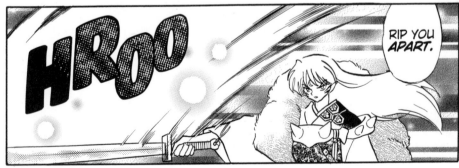

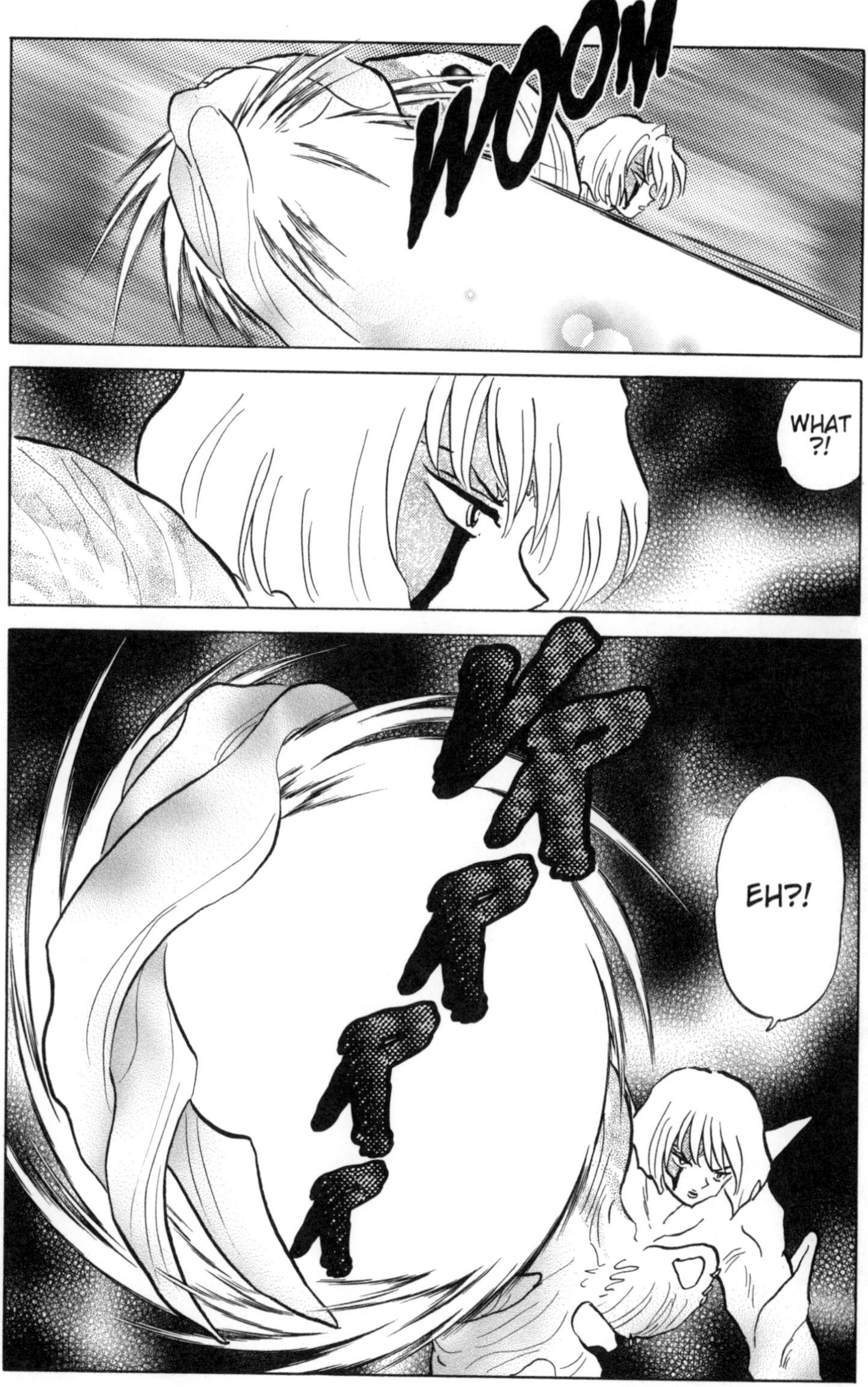
WOOM
WHAT ?!
EH?!

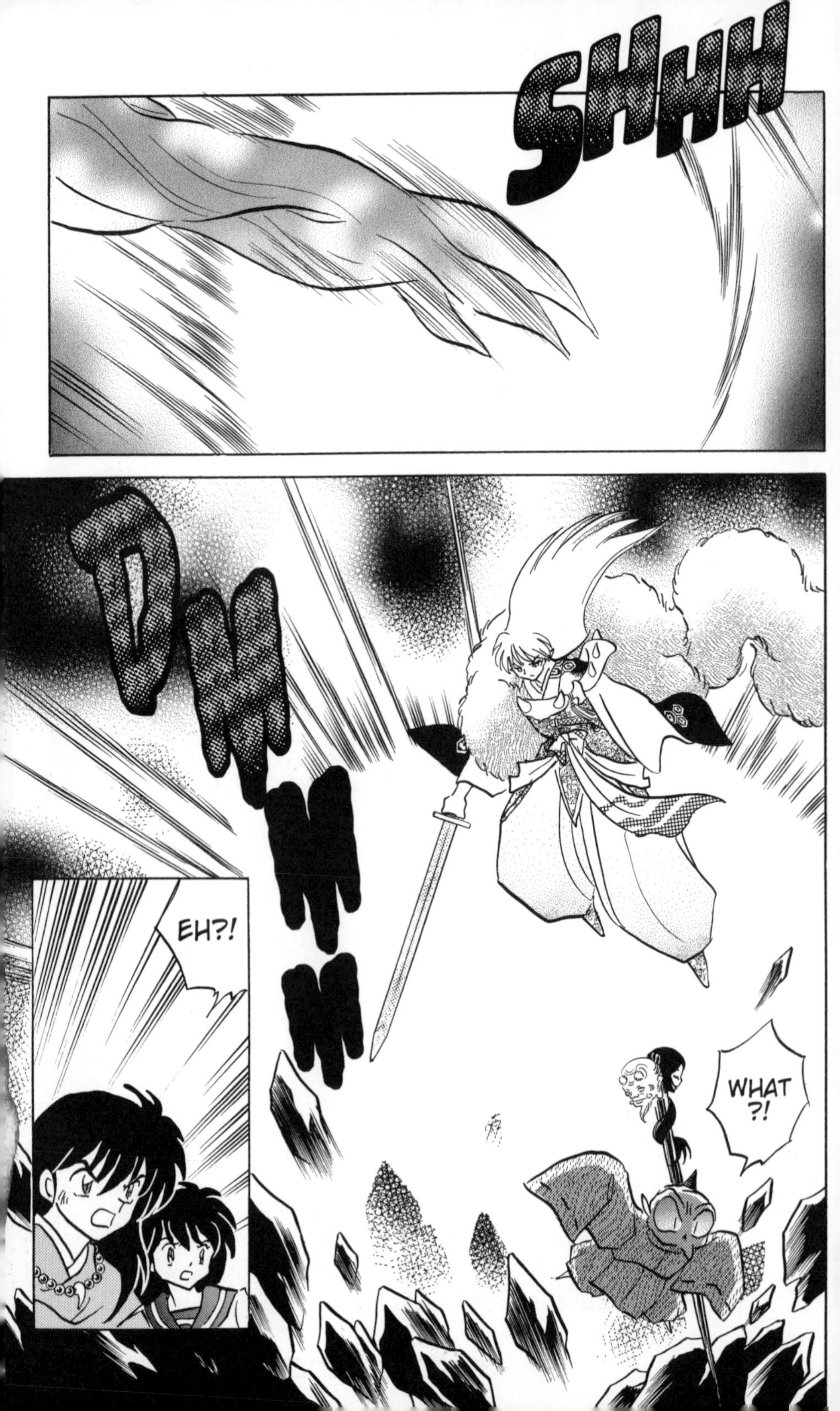
SHHH
DMMMM
WHAT?!
EH?!

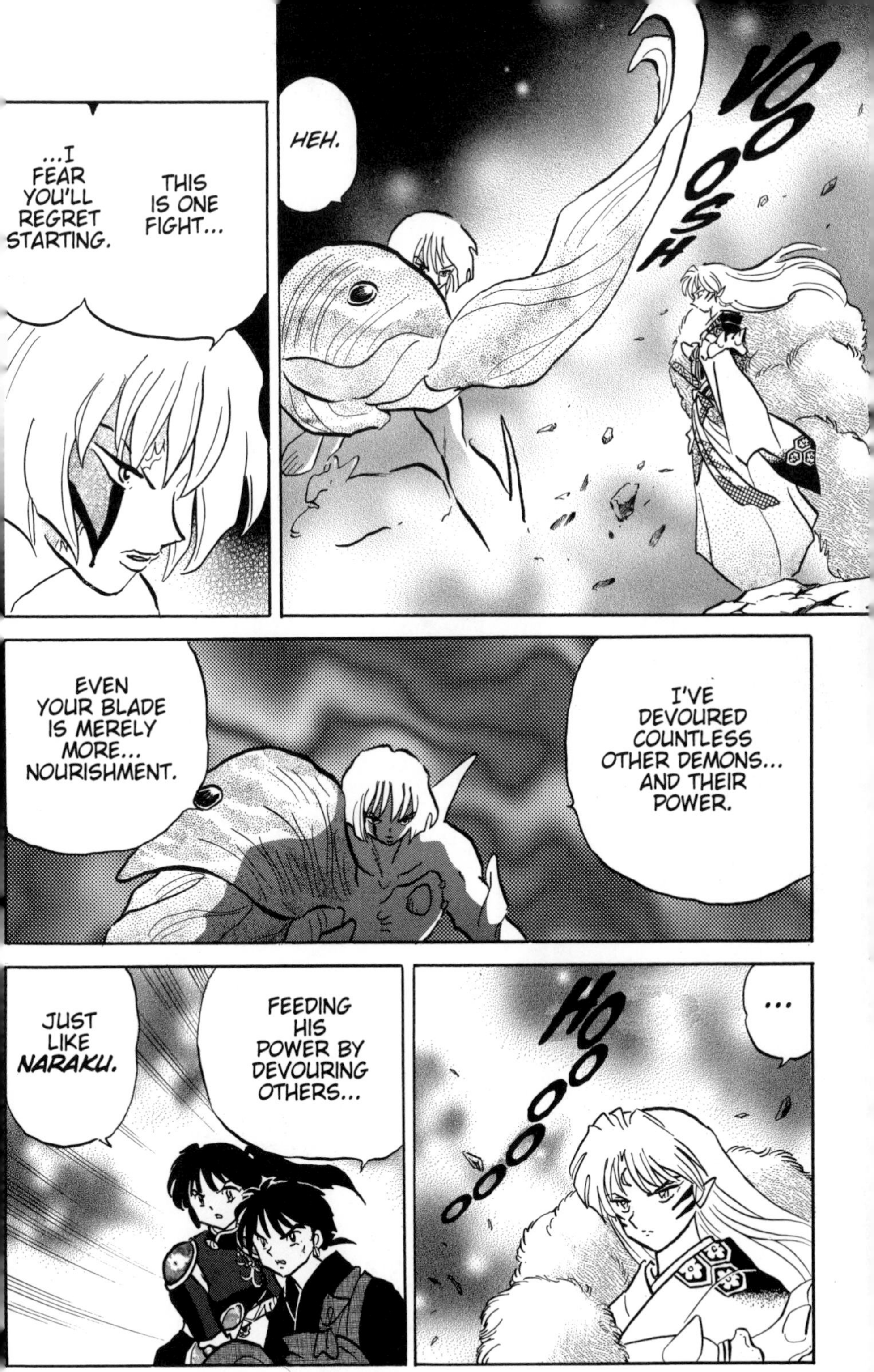
HEH.
VOOOSH
THIS IS ONE FIGHT...
...I FEAR YOU'LL REGRET STARTING.
I'VE DEVOURED COUNTLESS OTHER DEMONS... AND THEIR POWER.
EVEN YOUR BLADE IS MERELY MORE... NOURISHMENT.
...
HOOOOOOOO
FEEDING HIS POWER BY DEVOURING OTHERS...
JUST LIKE NARAKU.

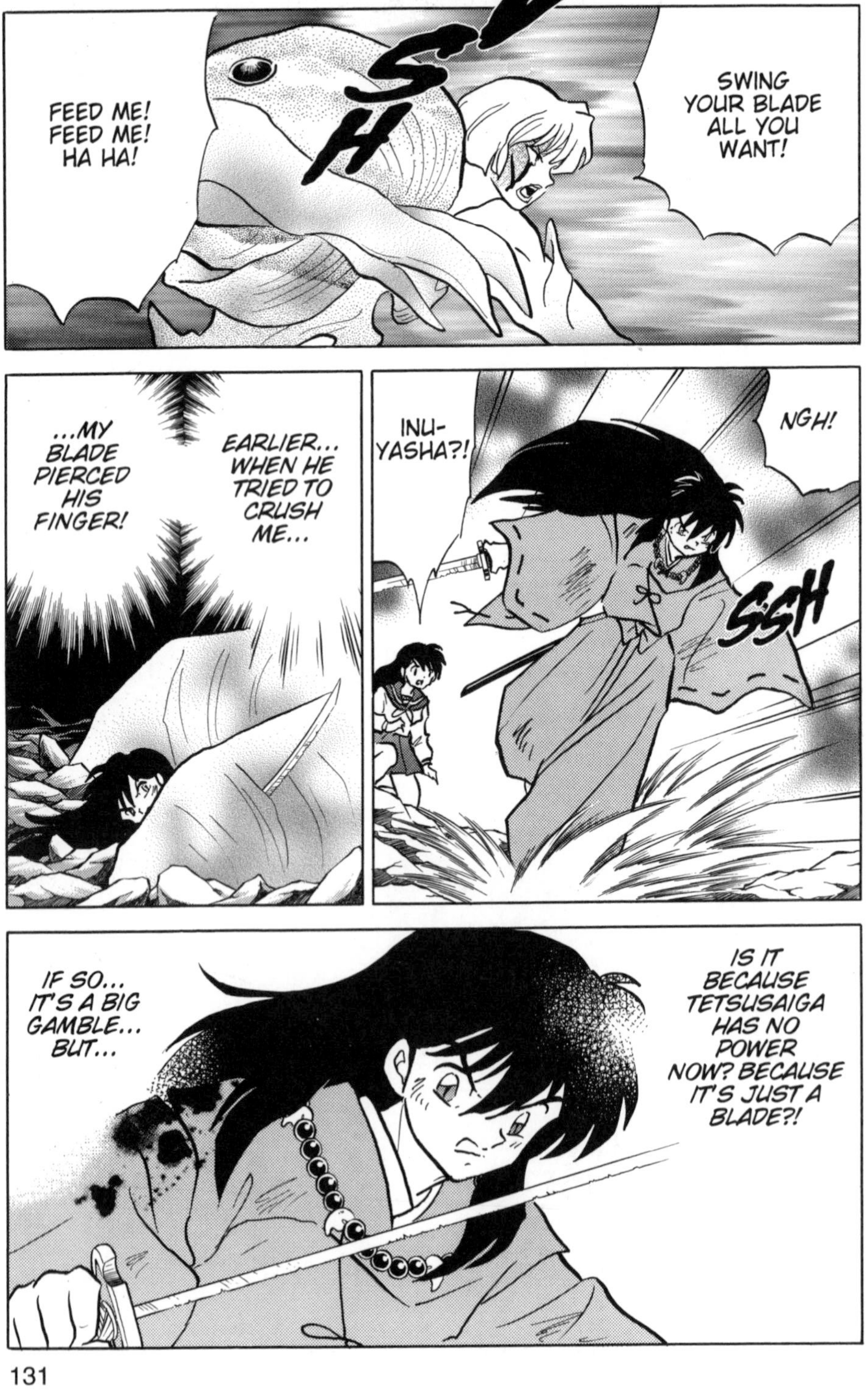
SWING YOUR BLADE ALL YOU WANT!
FEED ME! FEED ME! HA HA!
NGH!
SSH
INU-YASHA?!
EARLIER... WHEN HE TRIED TO CRUSH ME...
...MY BLADE PIERCED HIS FINGER!
IS IT BECAUSE TETSUSAIGA HAS NO POWER NOW? BECAUSE IT'S JUST A BLADE?!
IF SO... IT'S A BIG GAMBLE... BUT...

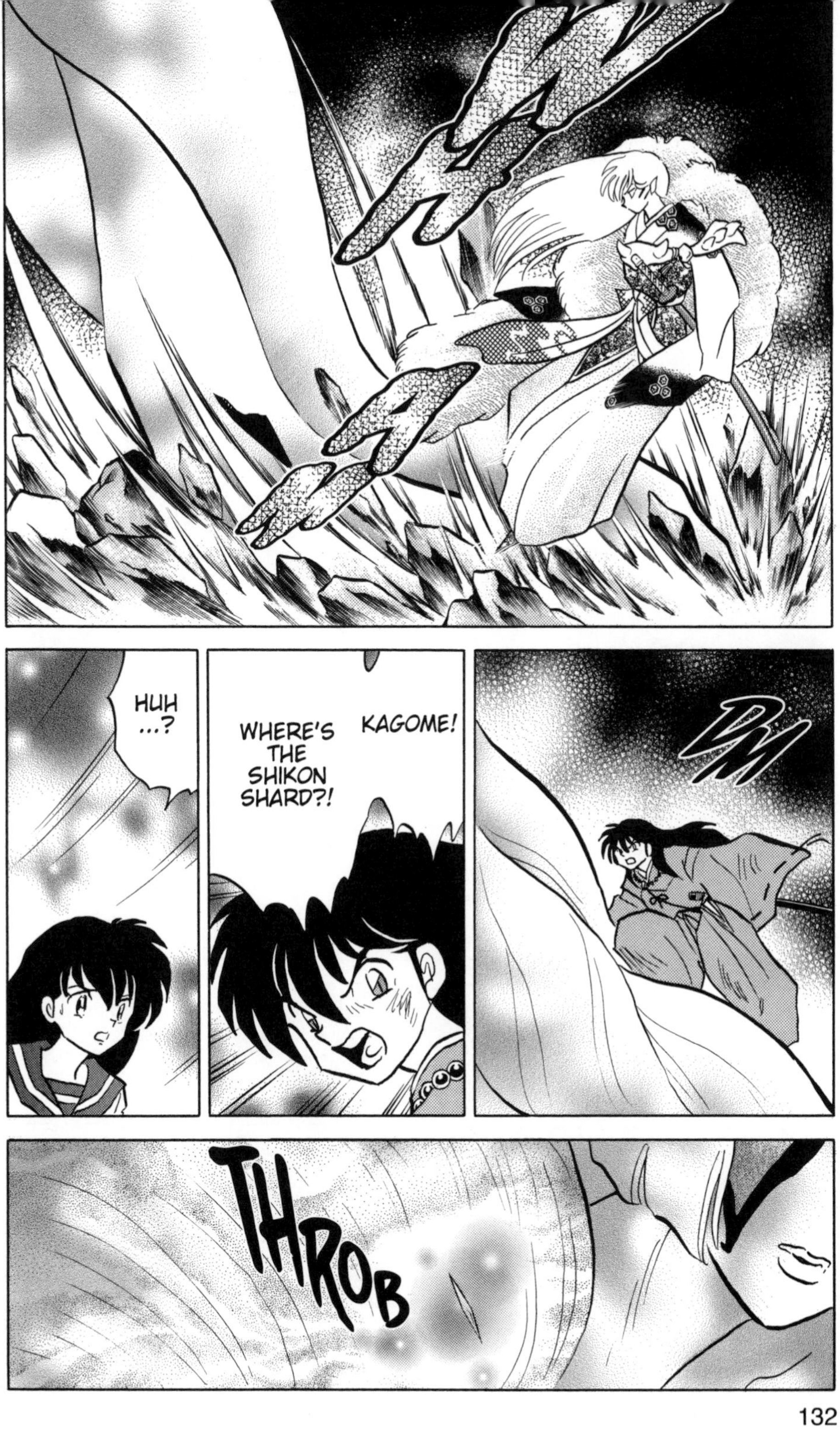
DM
KAGOME!
WHERE'S THE SHIKON SHARD?!
HUH ...?
THROB

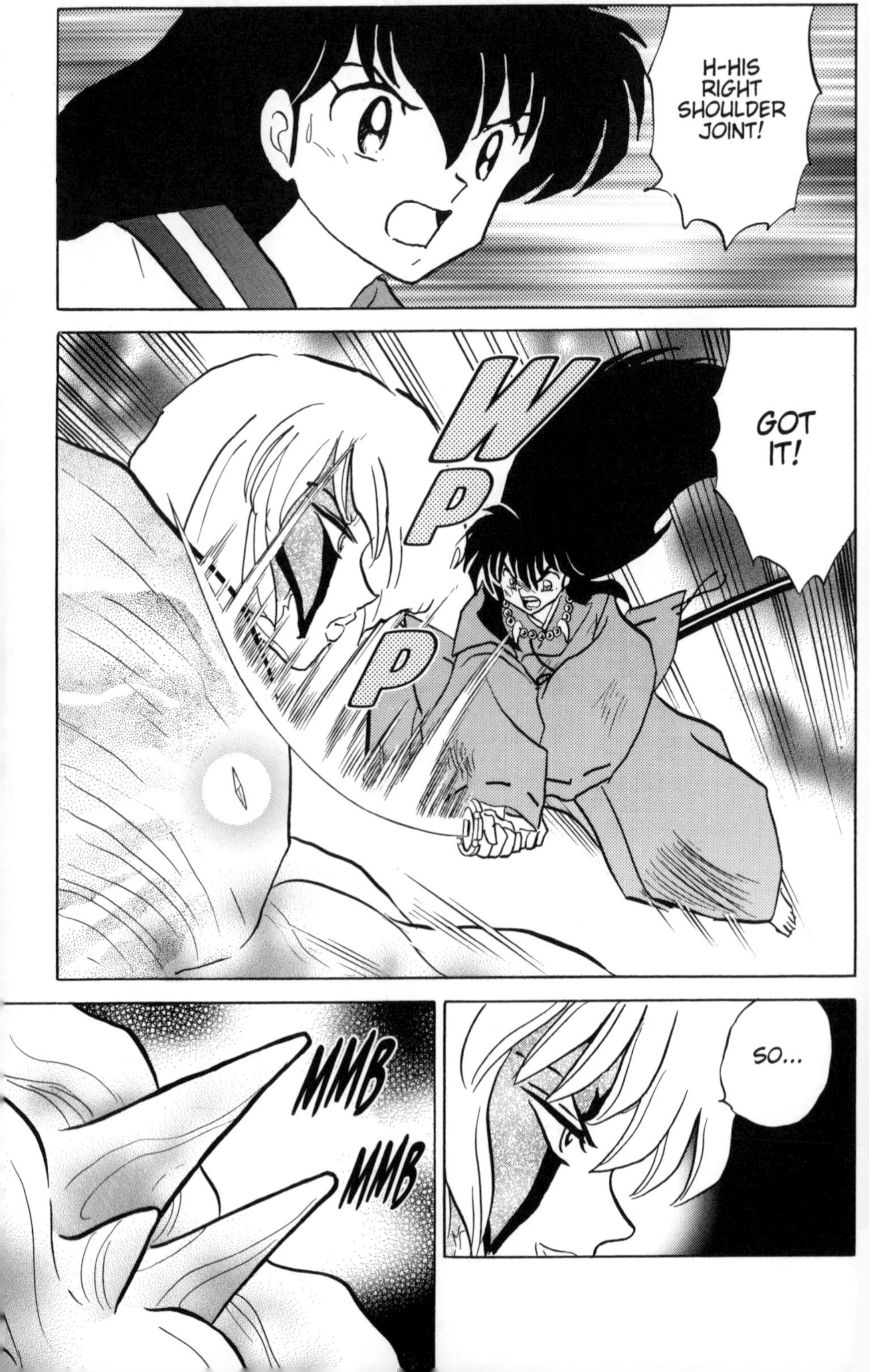
H-HIS RIGHT SHOULDER JOINT!
WPP
GOT IT!
SO...
MMB MMB

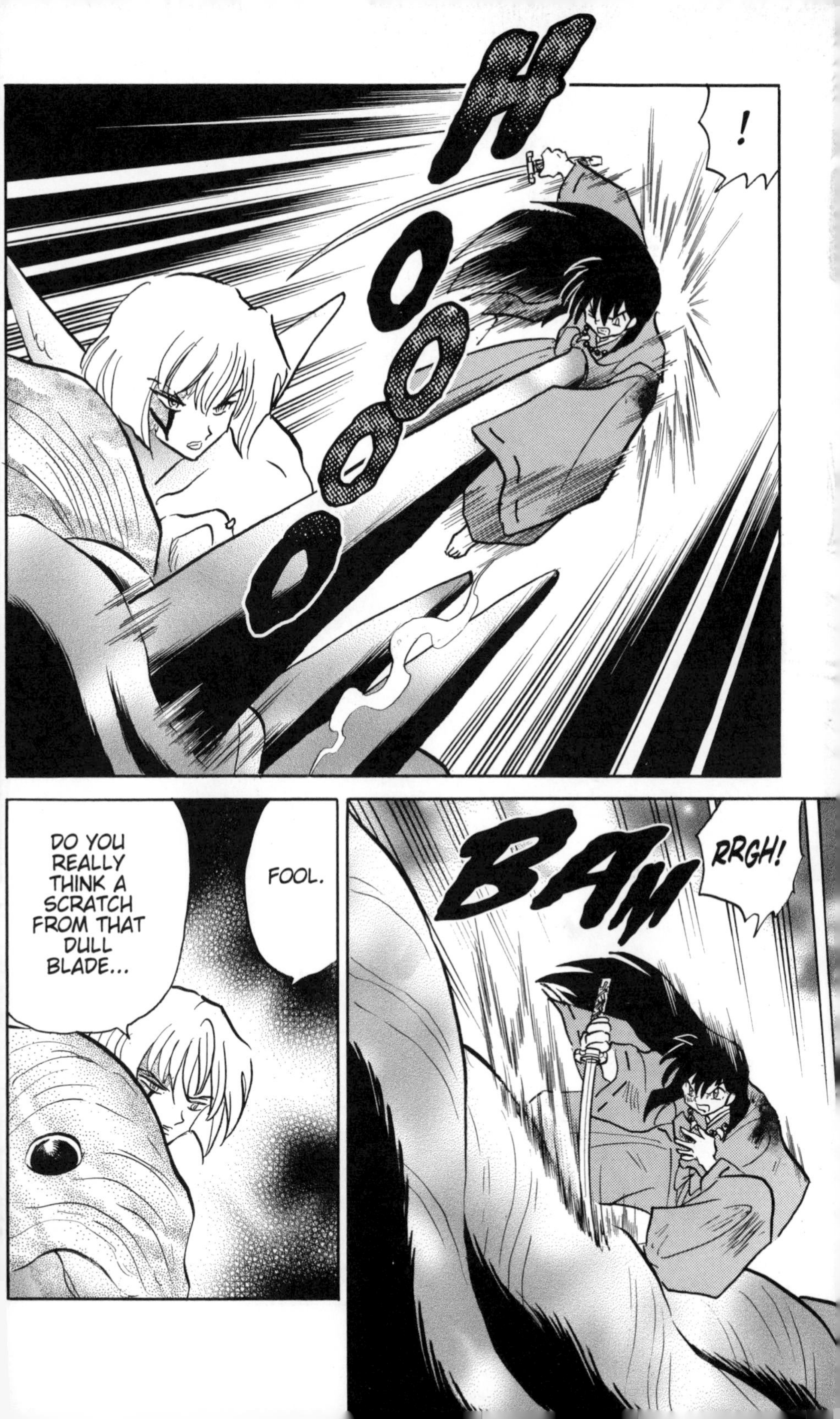

HOOOOO
!
BAM
RRGH!
FOOL.
DO YOU REALLY THINK A SCRATCH FROM THAT DULL BLADE...

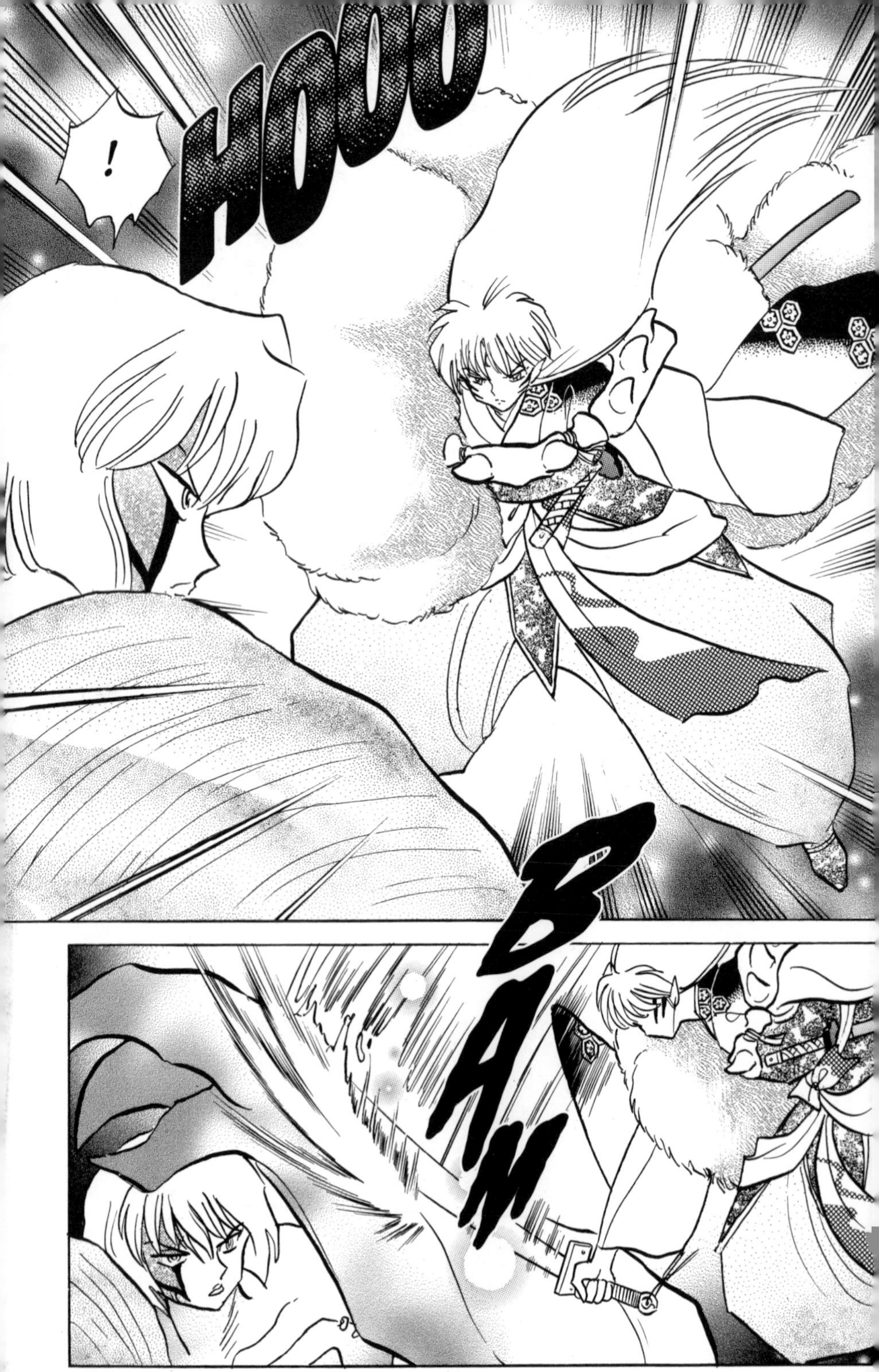
!
HOOO
BAM

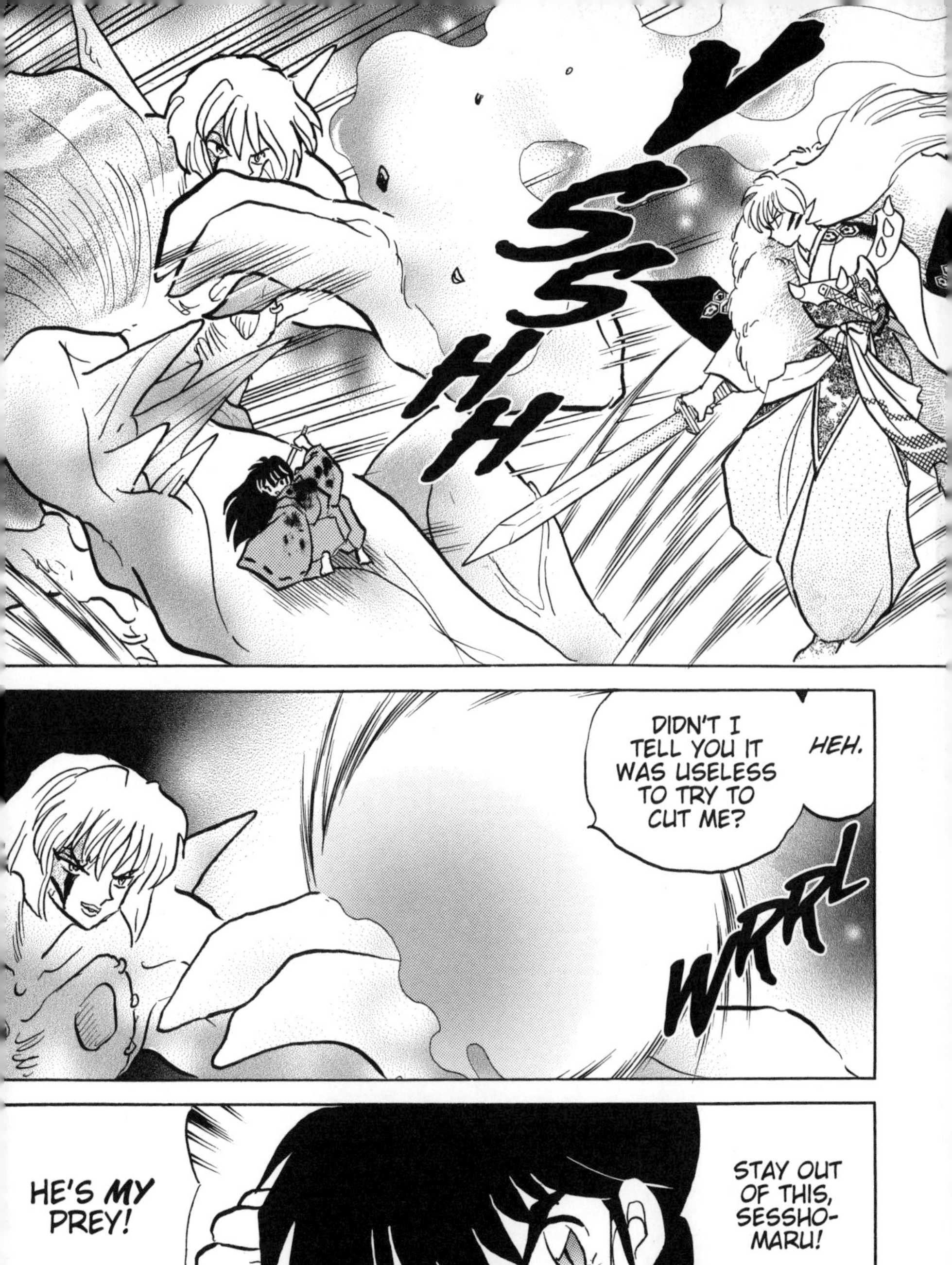
VSSHH
HEH.
DIDN'T I TELL YOU IT WAS USELESS TO TRY TO CUT ME?
WRRL
STAY OUT OF THIS, SESSHO-MARU!
HE'S *MY* PREY!

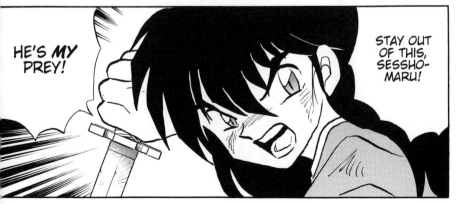

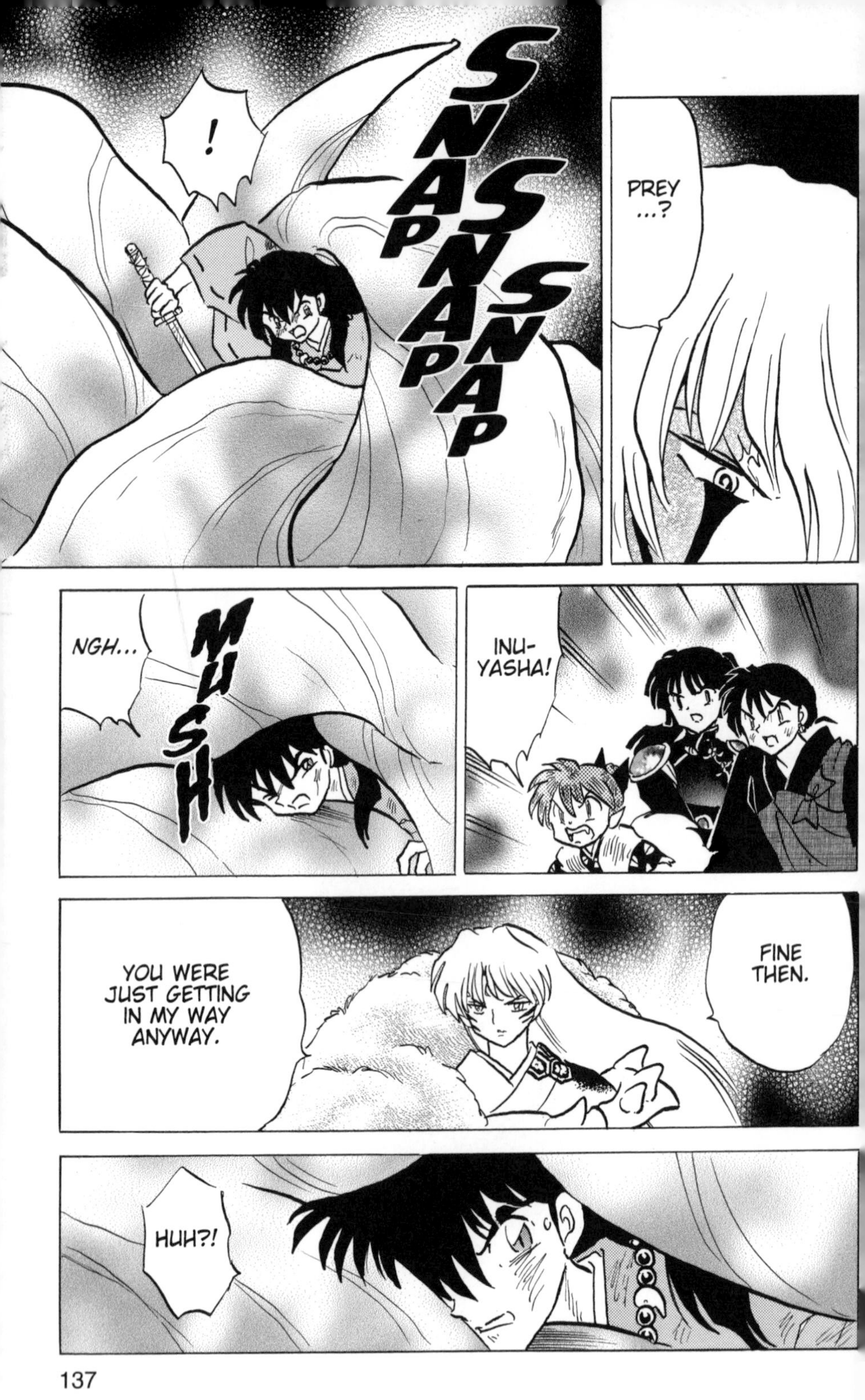

PREY ...?
!
SNAP
SNAP
SNAP
INU-YASHA!
NGH...
MUSH
FINE THEN.
YOU WERE JUST GETTING IN MY WAY ANYWAY.
HUH?!

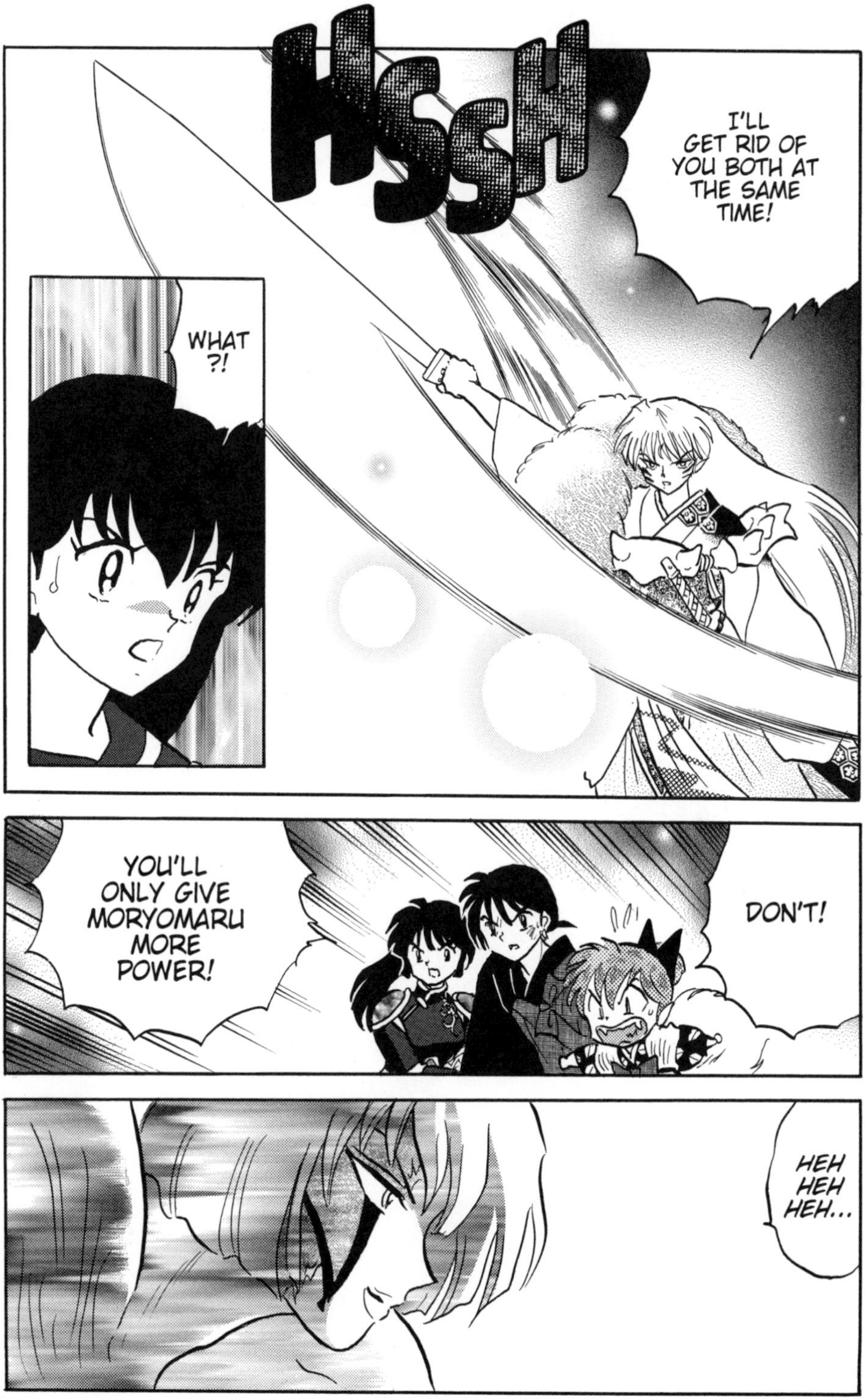
HSSH
I'LL GET RID OF YOU BOTH AT THE SAME TIME!
WHAT?!
DON'T!
YOU'LL ONLY GIVE MORYOMARU MORE POWER!
HEH HEH HEH...

SCROLL EIGHT
THE VESSEL

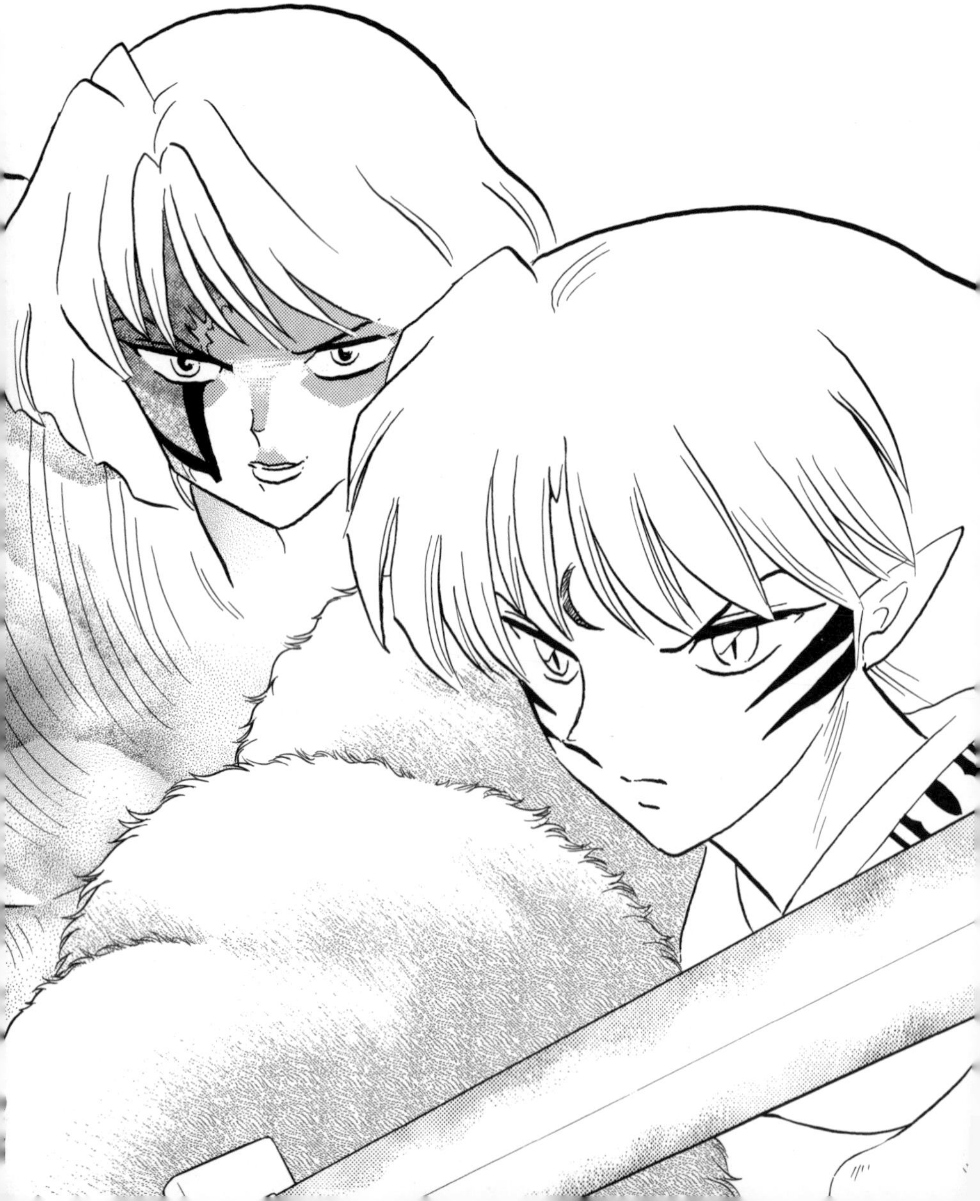

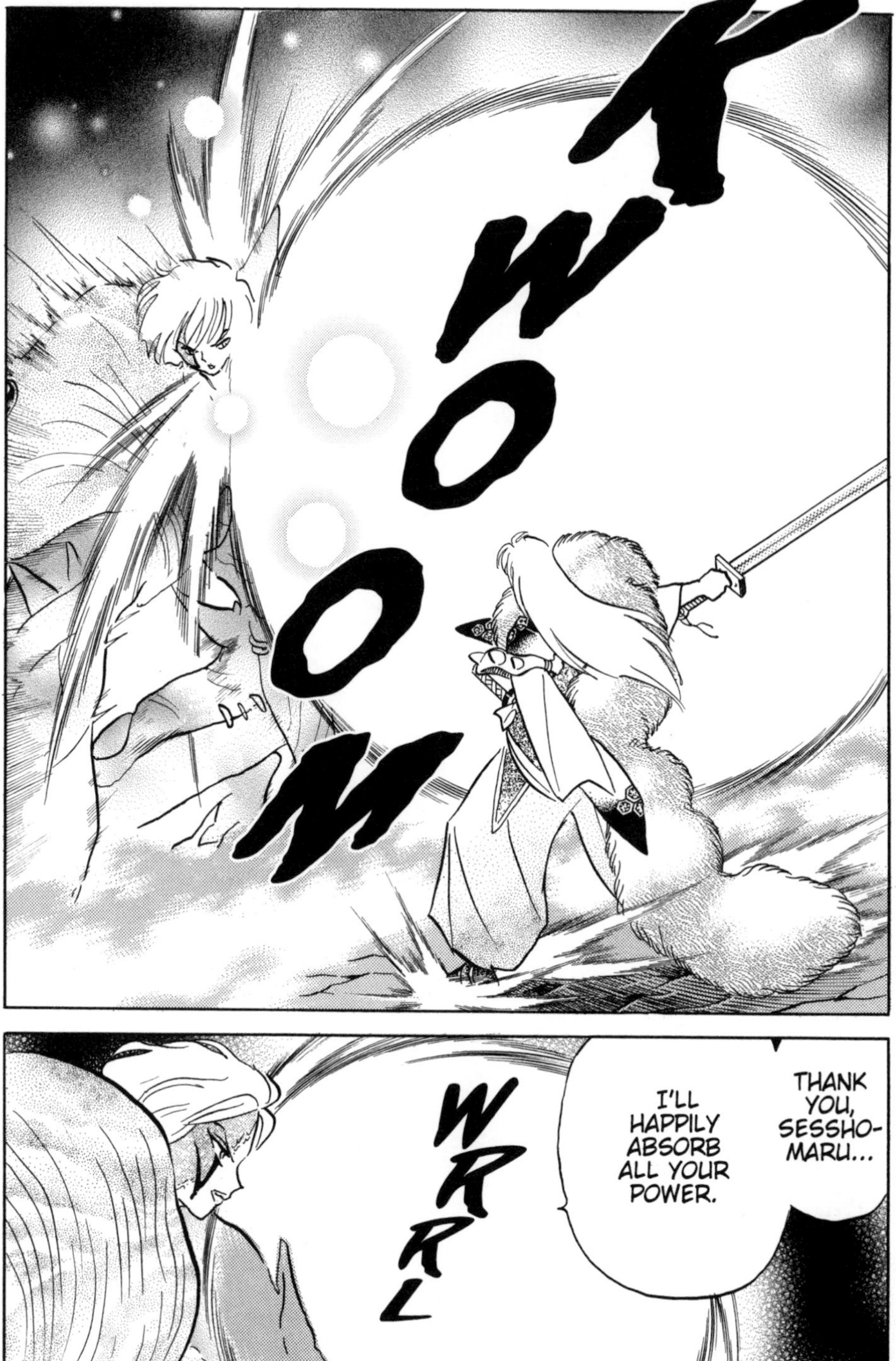
KWOOM
THANK YOU, SESSHO-MARU...
I'LL HAPPILY ABSORB ALL YOUR POWER.
WRRL

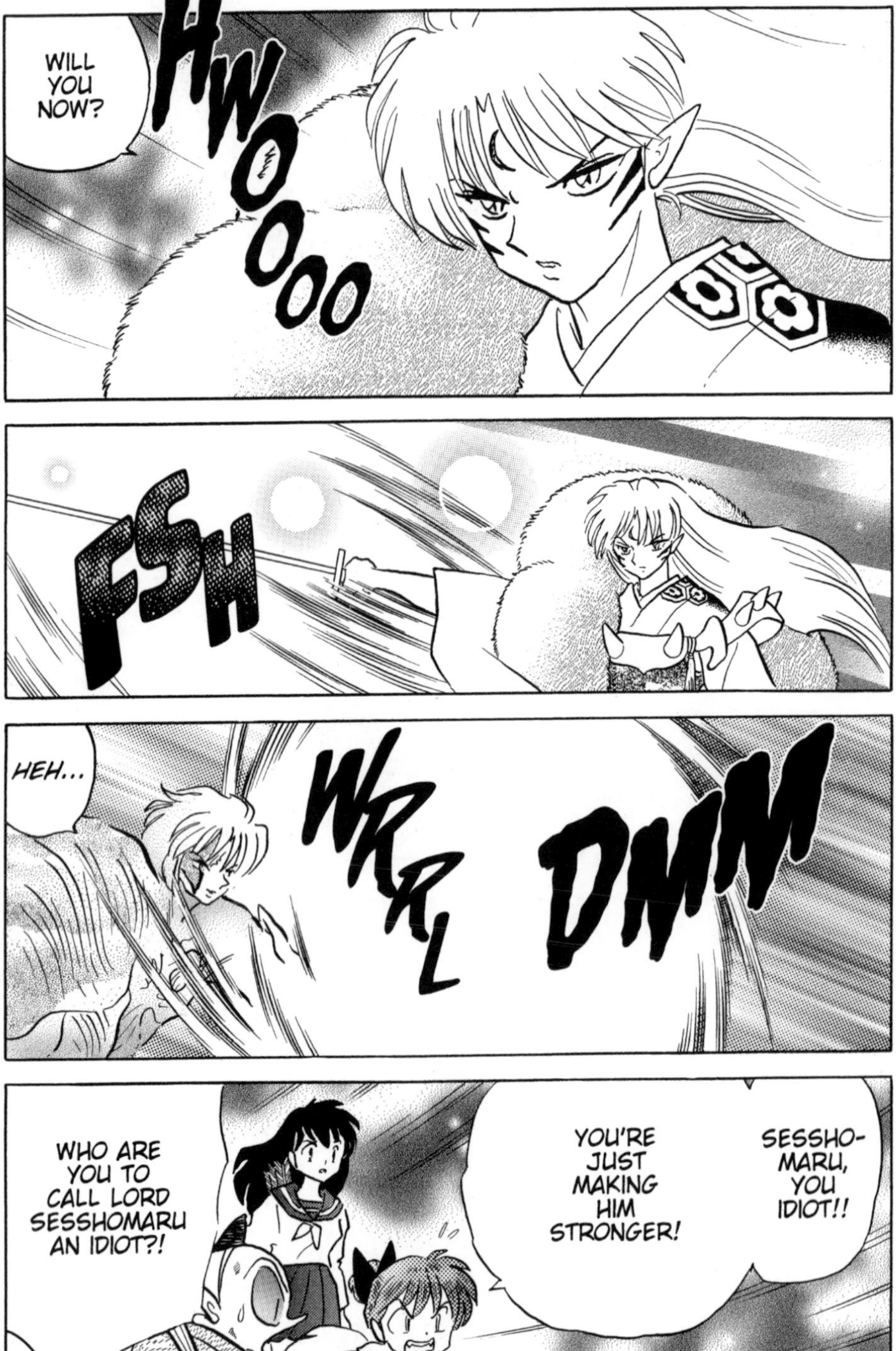
HWOOOO
WILL YOU NOW?
FSH
DMM
WRRL
HEH...
SESSHOMARU, YOU IDIOT!!
YOU'RE JUST MAKING HIM STRONGER!
WHO ARE YOU TO CALL LORD SESSHOMARU AN IDIOT?!

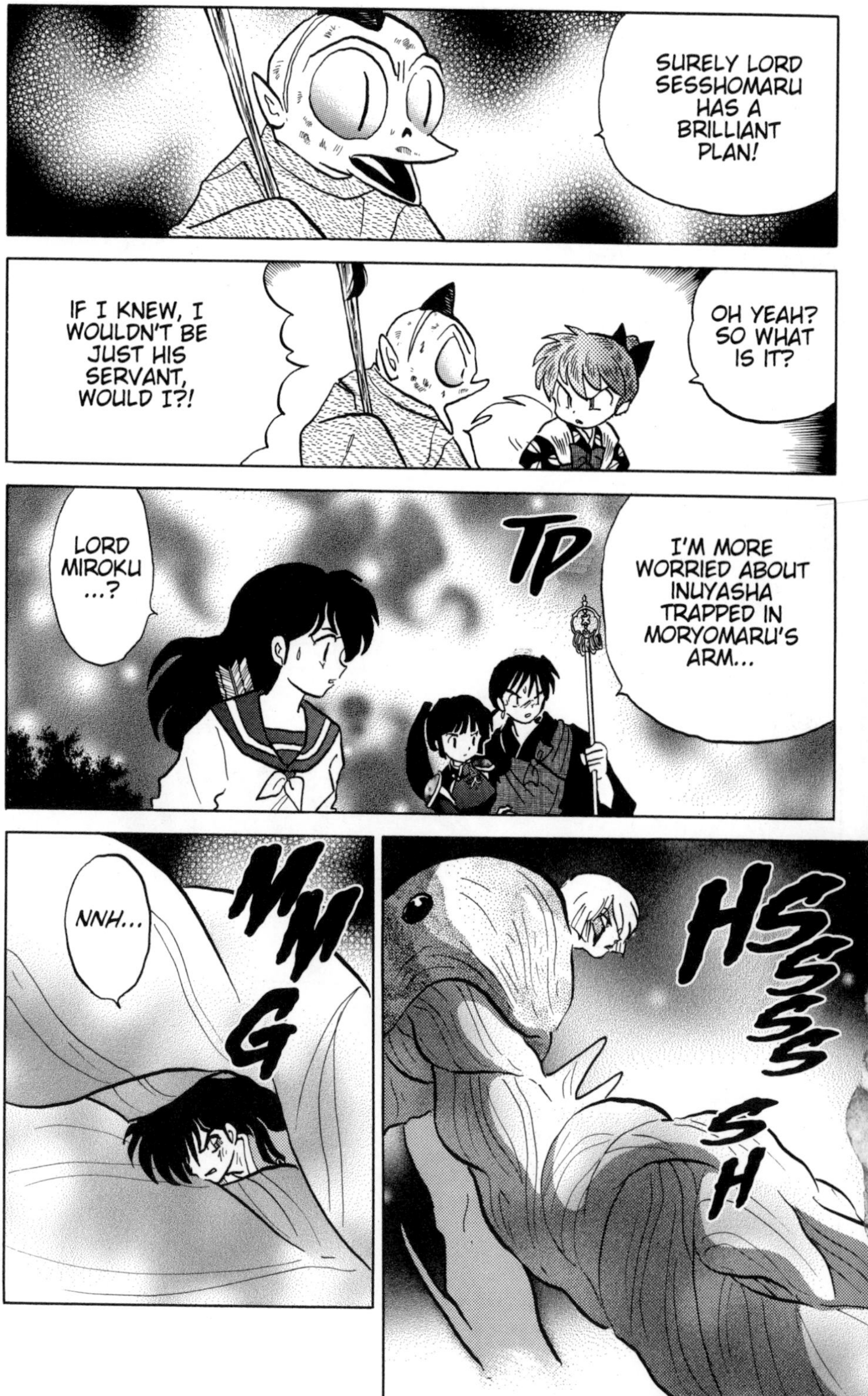
SURELY LORD SESSHOMARU HAS A BRILLIANT PLAN!
OH YEAH? SO WHAT IS IT?
IF I KNEW, I WOULDN'T BE JUST HIS SERVANT, WOULD I?!
I'M MORE WORRIED ABOUT INUYASHA TRAPPED IN MORYOMARU'S ARM...
TP
LORD MIROKU ...?
HSSSSSH
MMG
NNH...

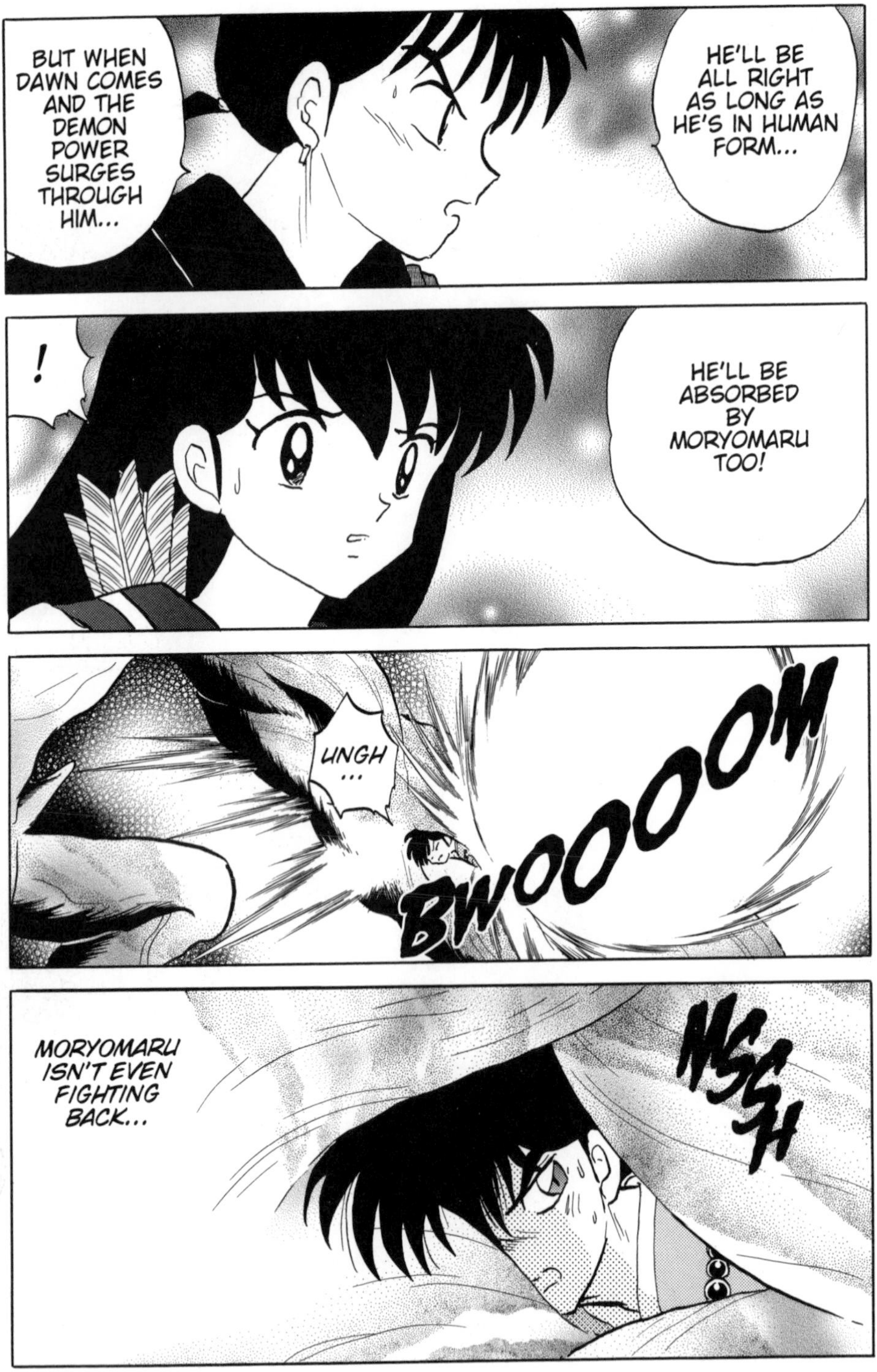
HE'LL BE ALL RIGHT AS LONG AS HE'S IN HUMAN FORM...
BUT WHEN DAWN COMES AND THE DEMON POWER SURGES THROUGH HIM...
HE'LL BE ABSORBED BY MORYOMARU TOO!
!
BWOOOOOOM
UNGH...
NSSH
MORYOMARU ISN'T EVEN FIGHTING BACK...

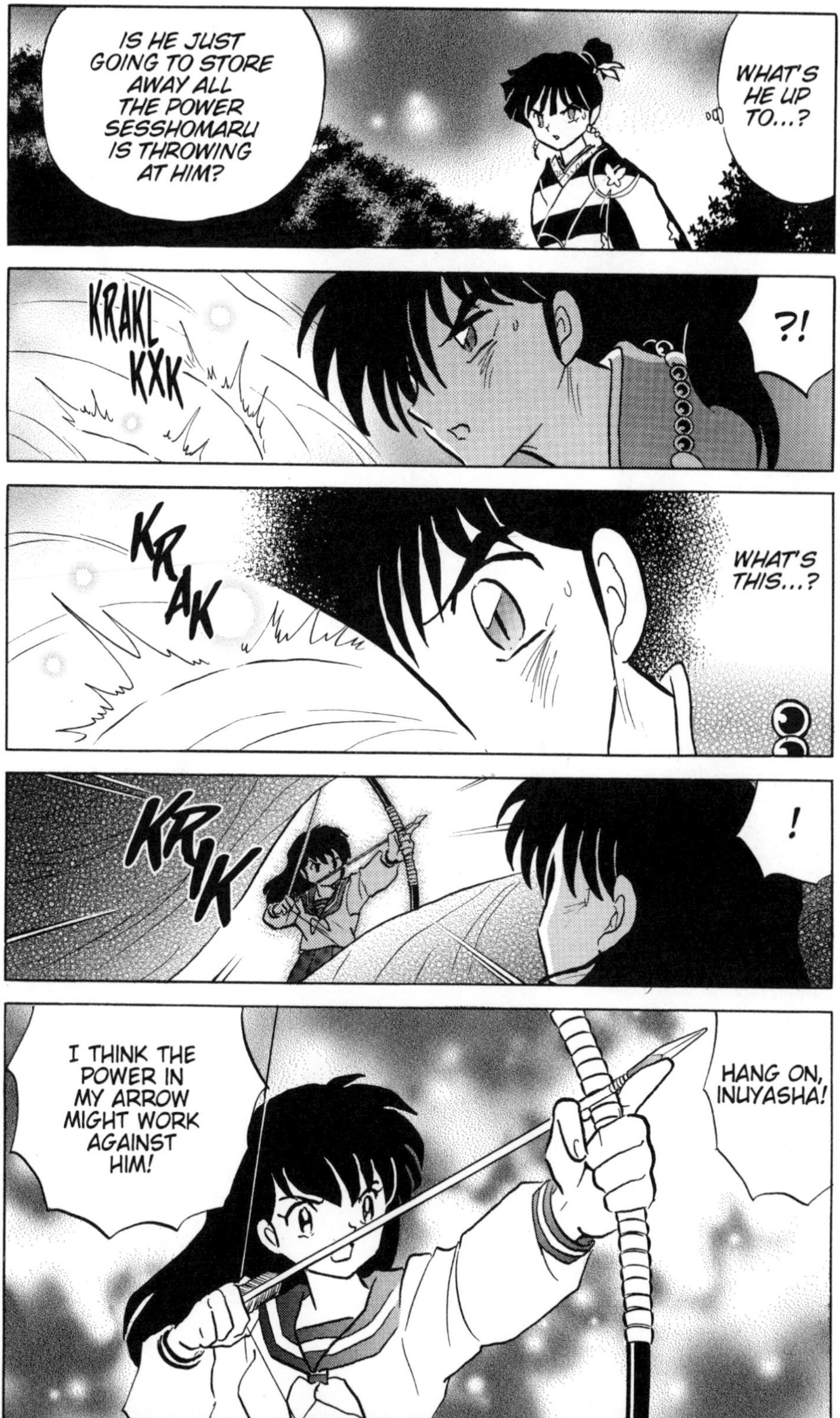
WHAT'S HE UP TO...?
IS HE JUST GOING TO STORE AWAY ALL THE POWER SESSHOMARU IS THROWING AT HIM?
?!
KRAKL KXK
WHAT'S THIS...?
KRAK
!
KRYK
HANG ON, INUYASHA!
I THINK THE POWER IN MY ARROW MIGHT WORK AGAINST HIM!

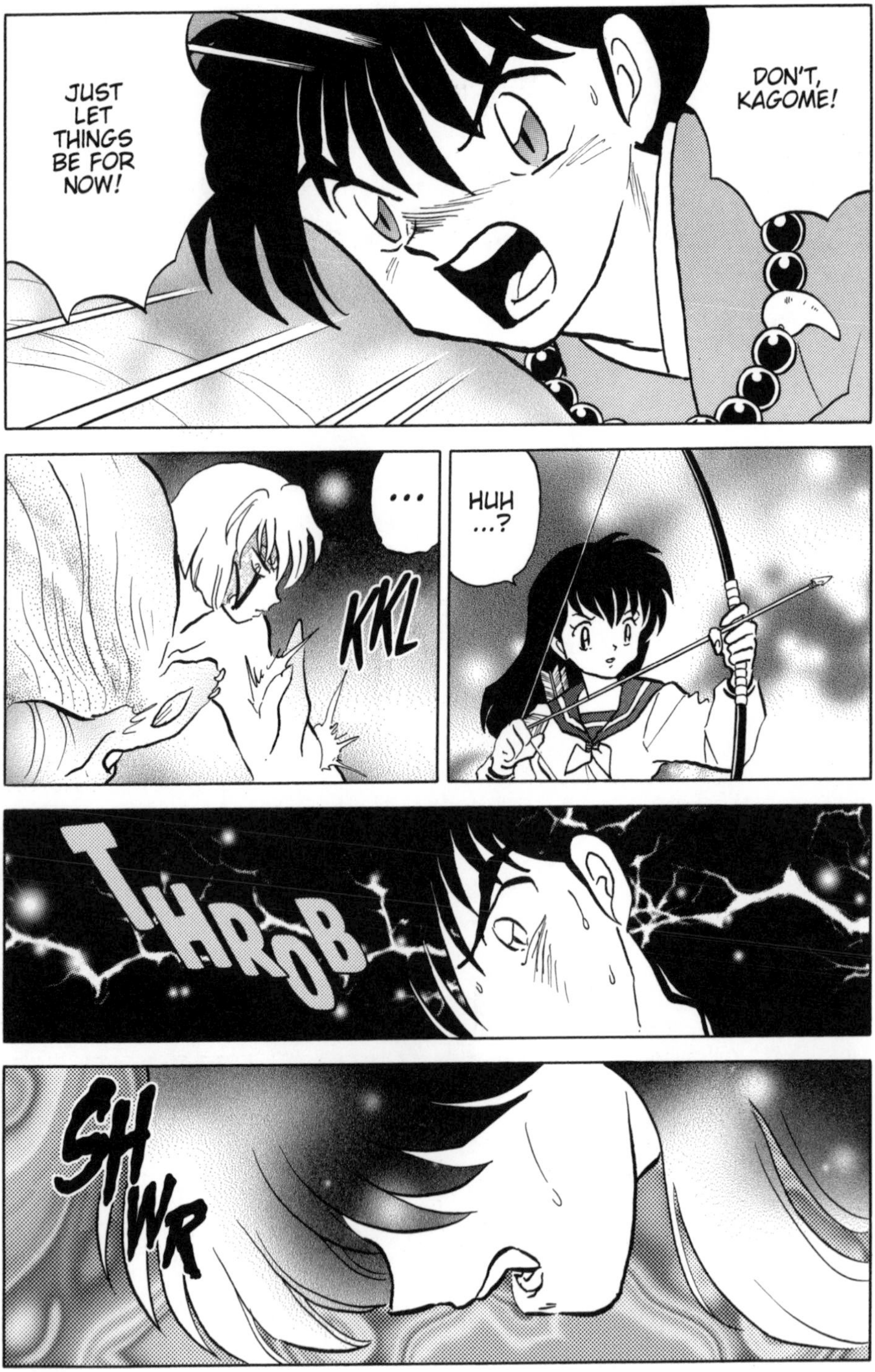
DON'T, KAGOME!
JUST LET THINGS BE FOR NOW!
HUH ...?
...
KKL
THROB
SHWR

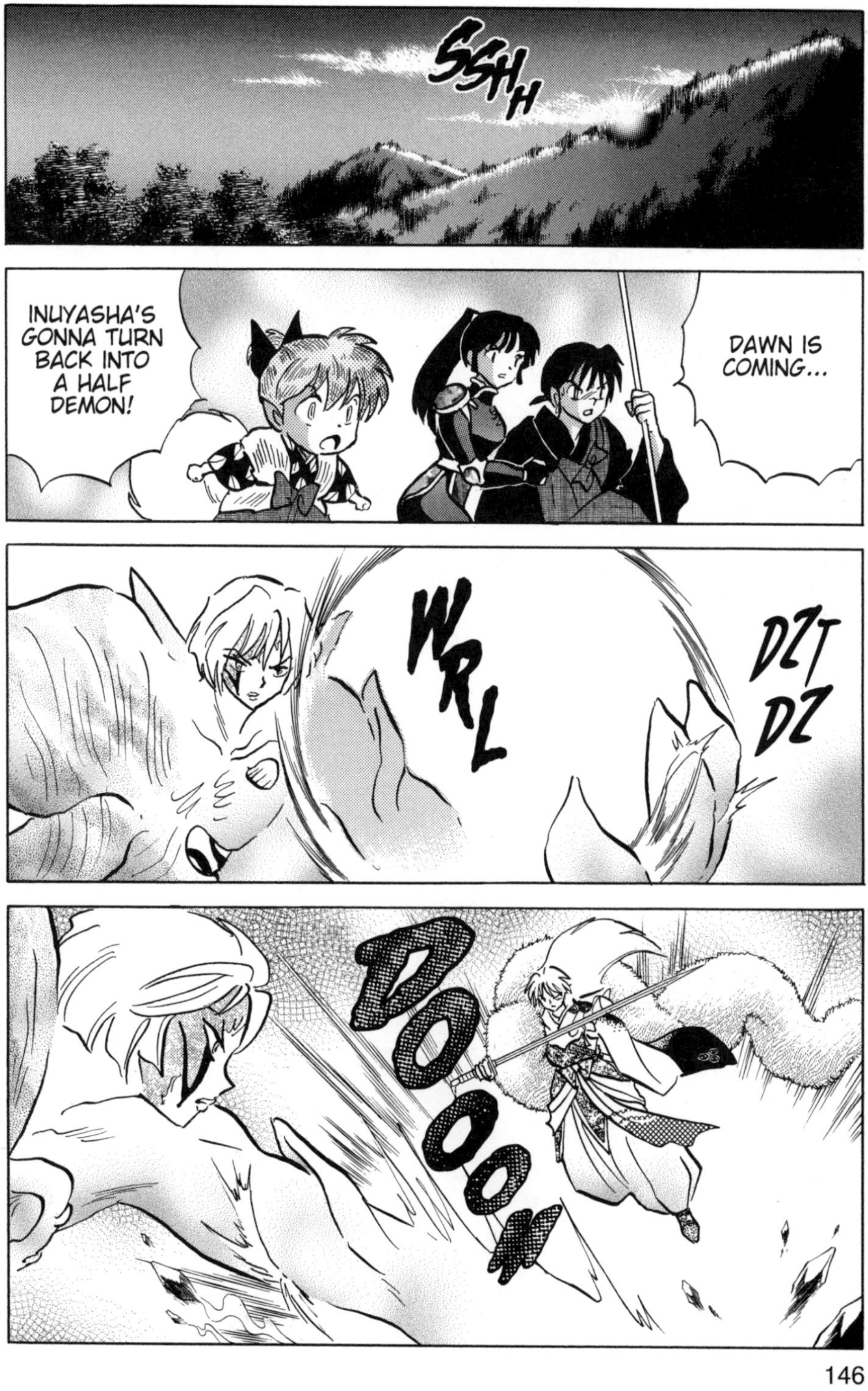
SSHH
DAWN IS COMING...
INUYASHA'S GONNA TURN BACK INTO A HALF DEMON!
DZT DZ
WRL
DOOOM

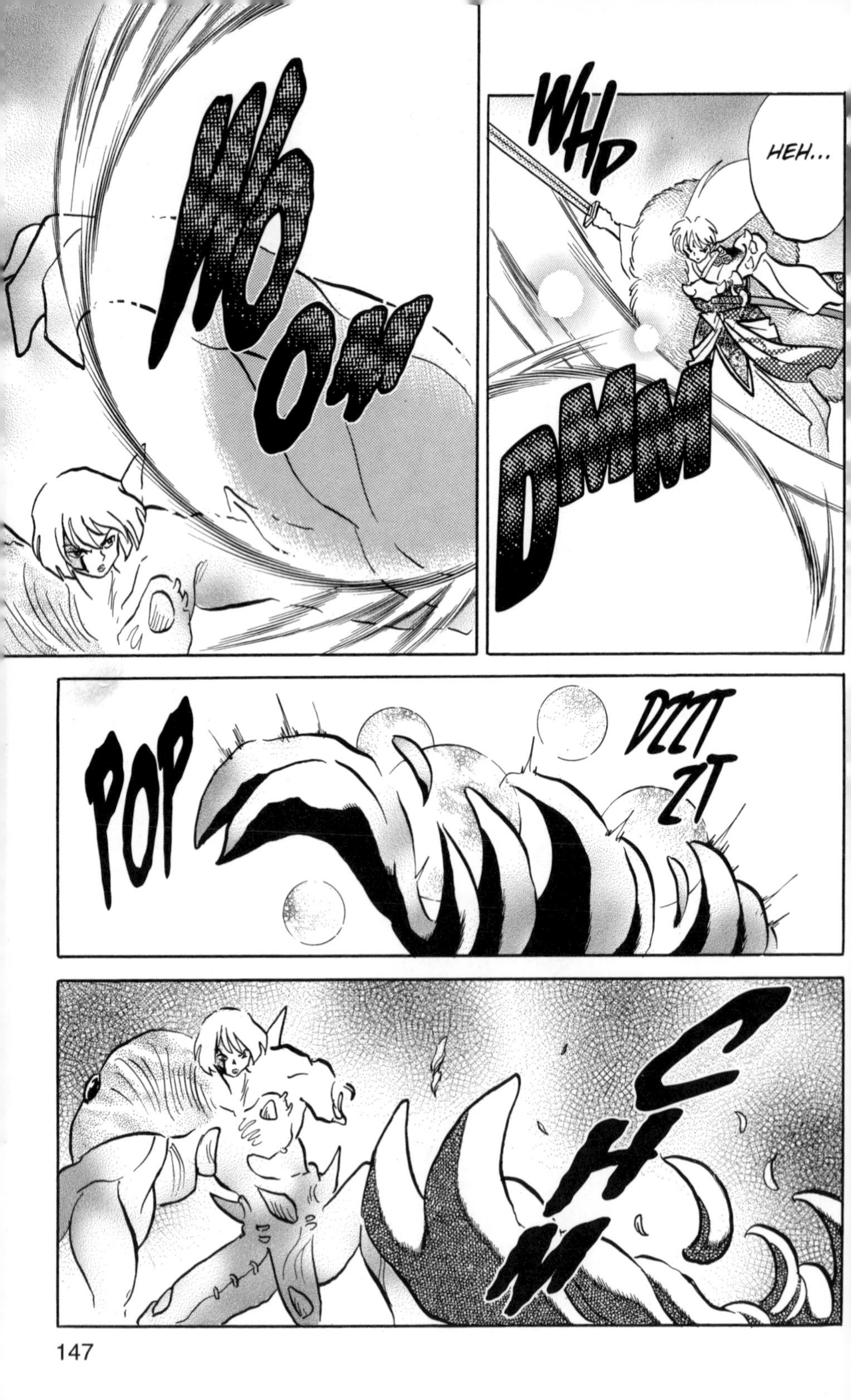
WHP
HEH...
DMM
WHOOM
DZZT
ZT
POP
CHM

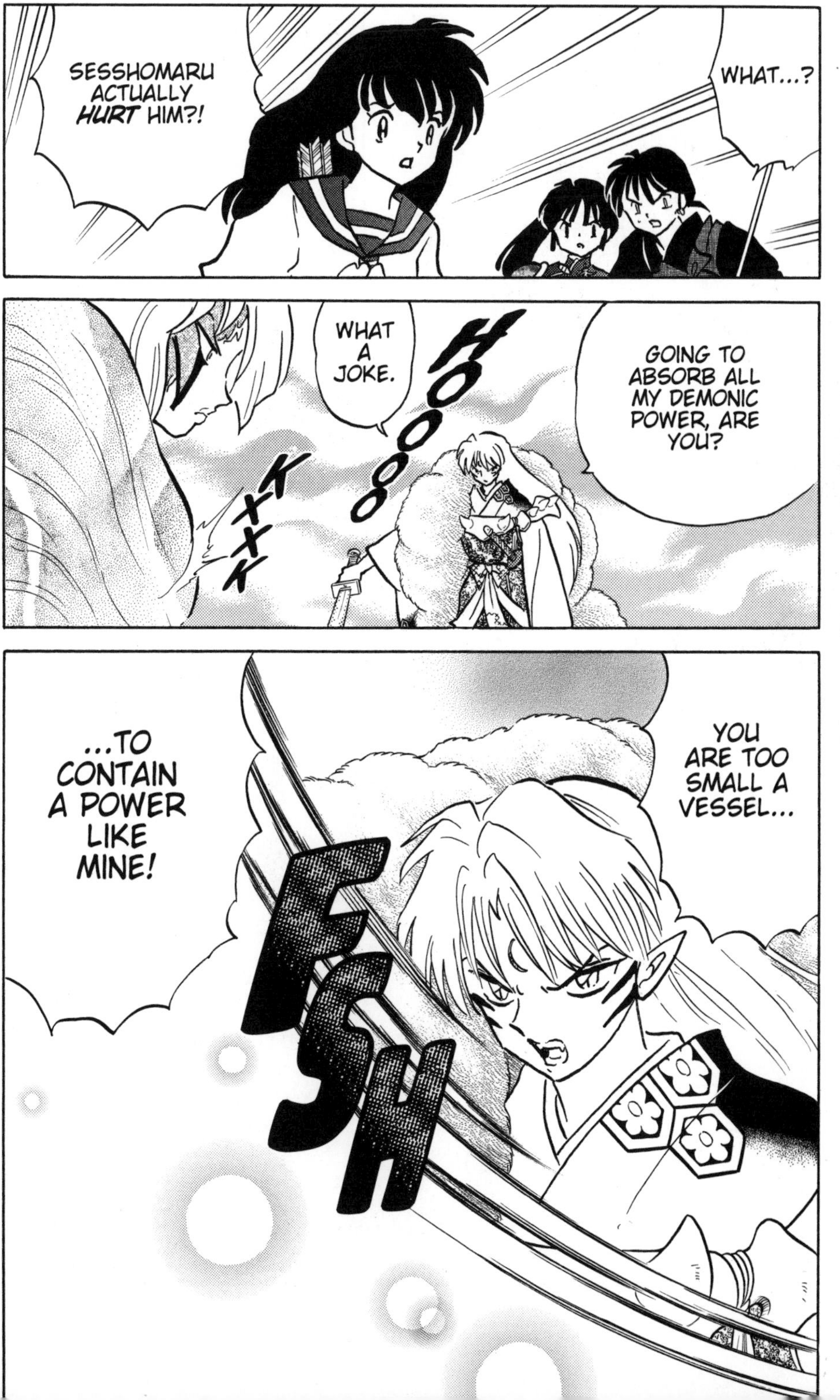
WHAT...?
SESSHOMARU ACTUALLY *HURT* HIM?!
GOING TO ABSORB ALL MY DEMONIC POWER, ARE YOU?
HOOOOO
WHAT A JOKE.
YOU ARE TOO SMALL A VESSEL...
...TO CONTAIN A POWER LIKE MINE!
FSSH

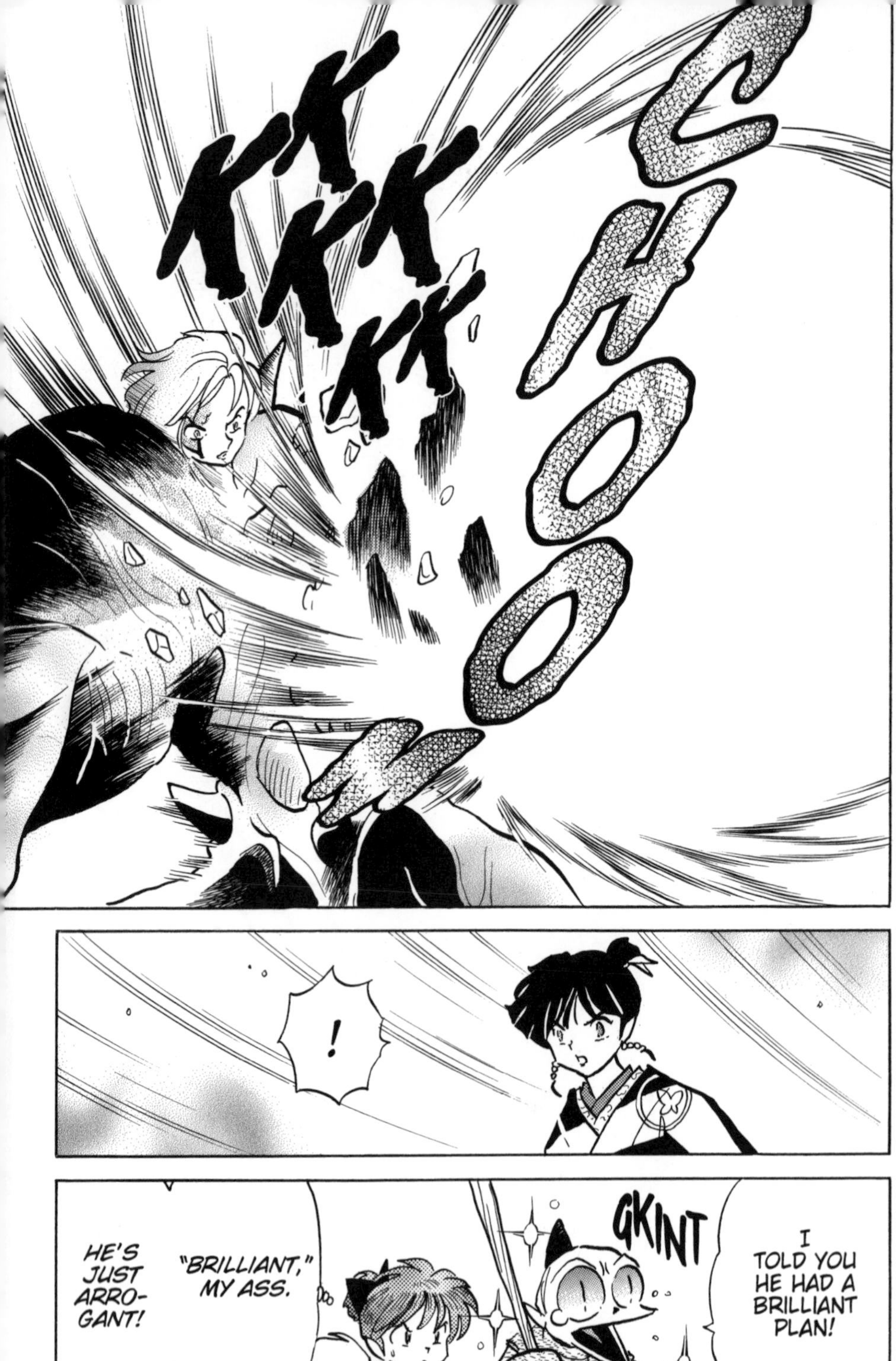
!
I TOLD YOU HE HAD A BRILLIANT PLAN!
GKINT
"BRILLIANT," MY ASS.
HE'S JUST ARRO-GANT!

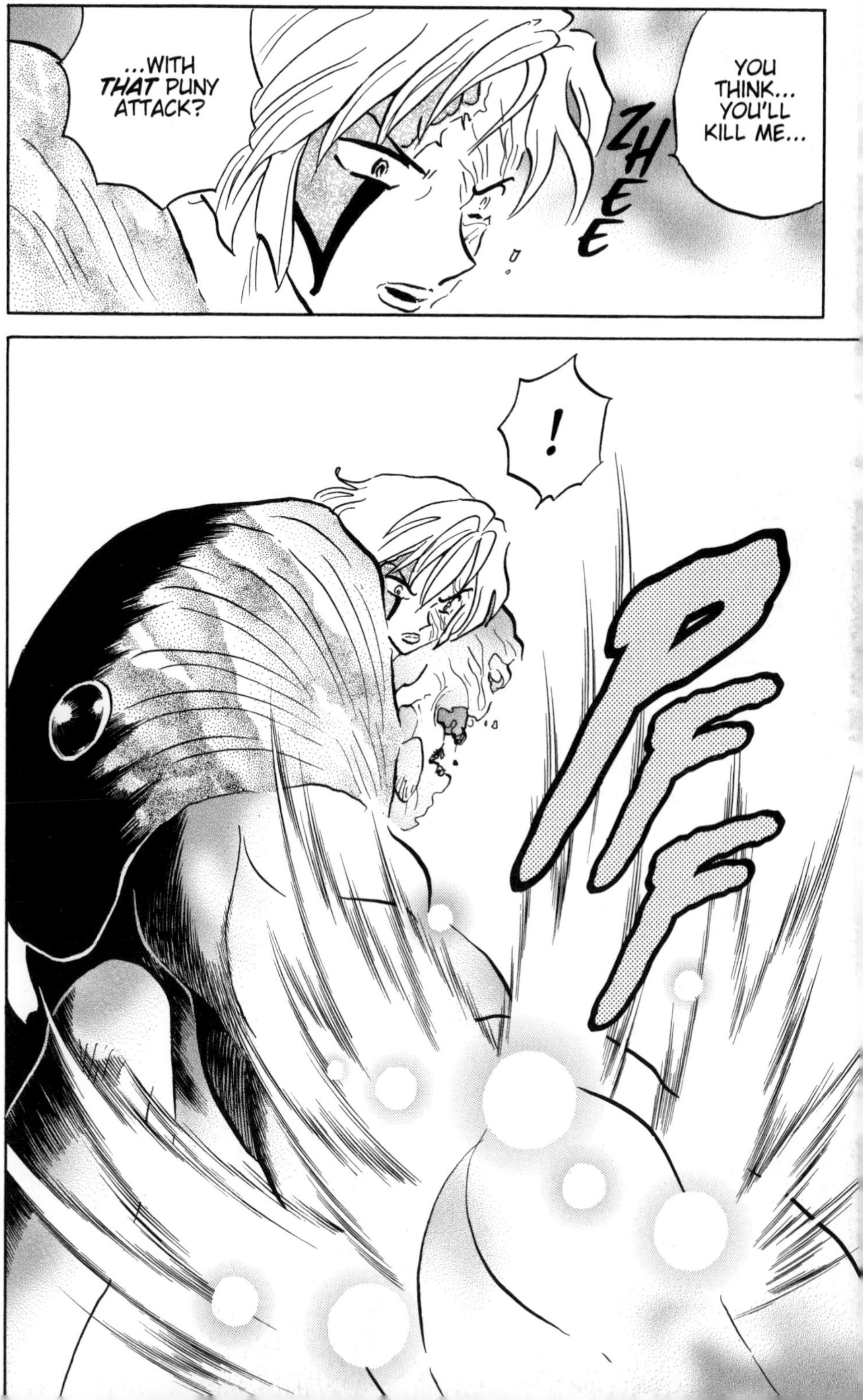
YOU THINK... YOU'LL KILL ME...
ZHEE
...WITH *THAT* PUNY ATTACK?
!
PFF

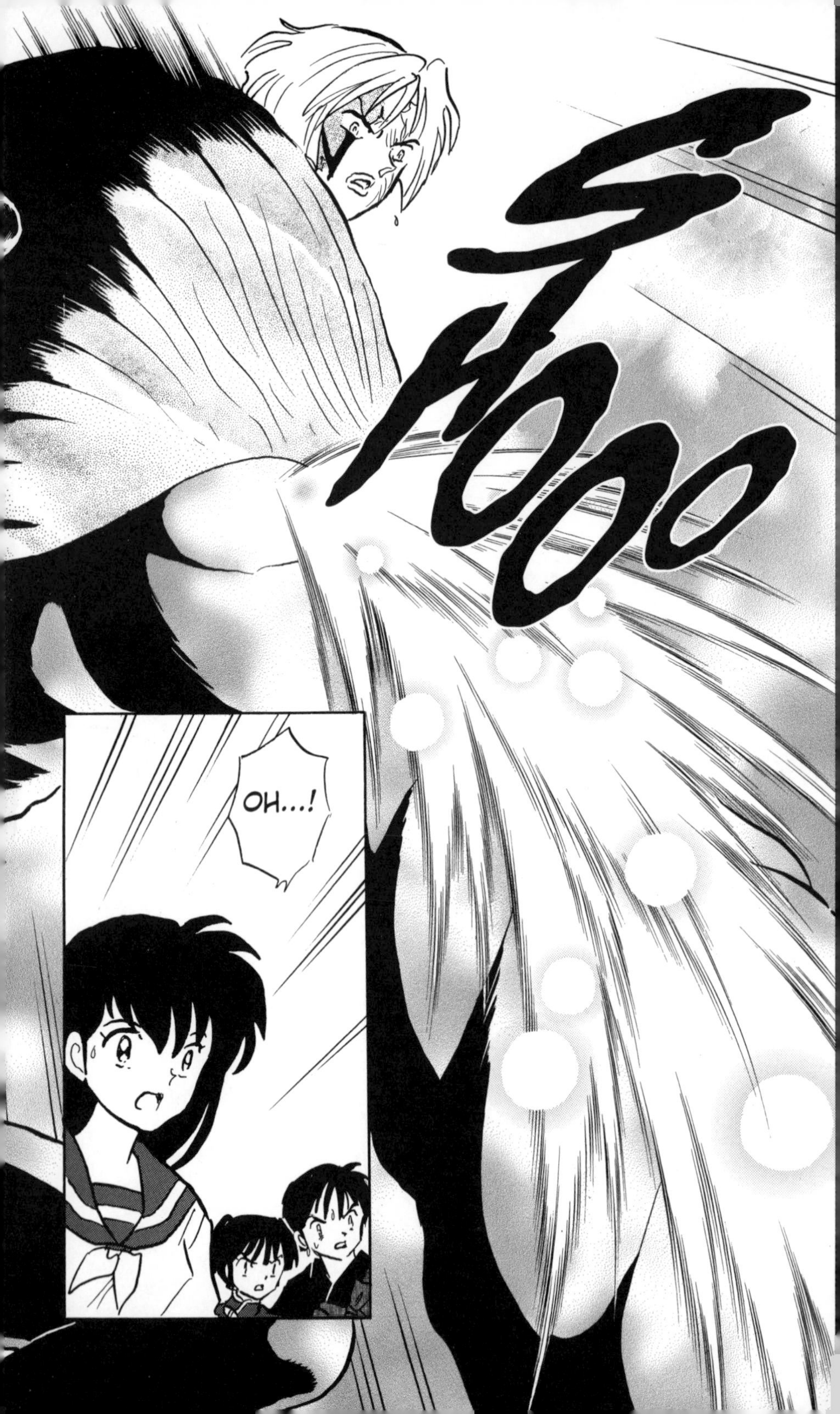
SHOOO
OH...!

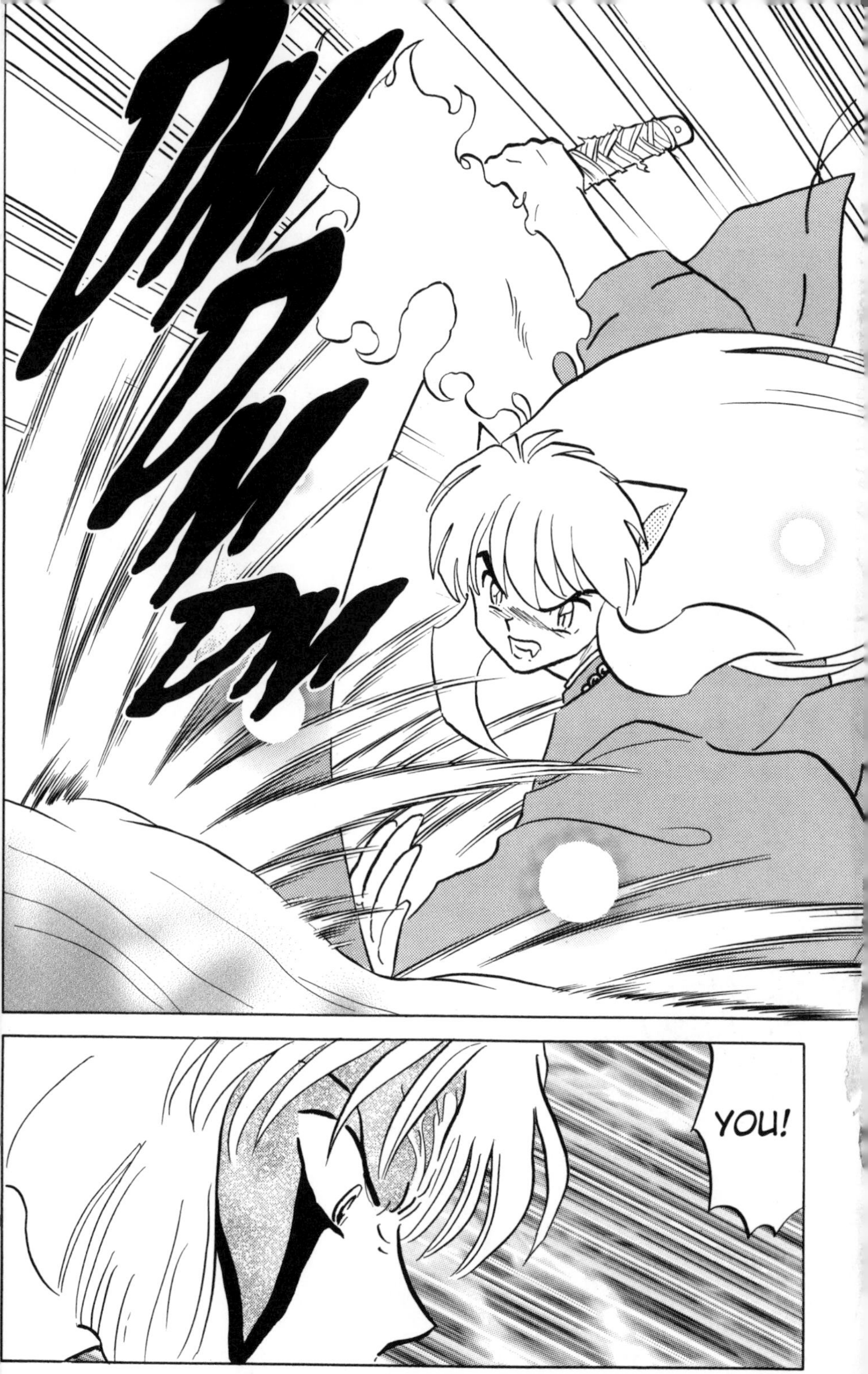
YOU!

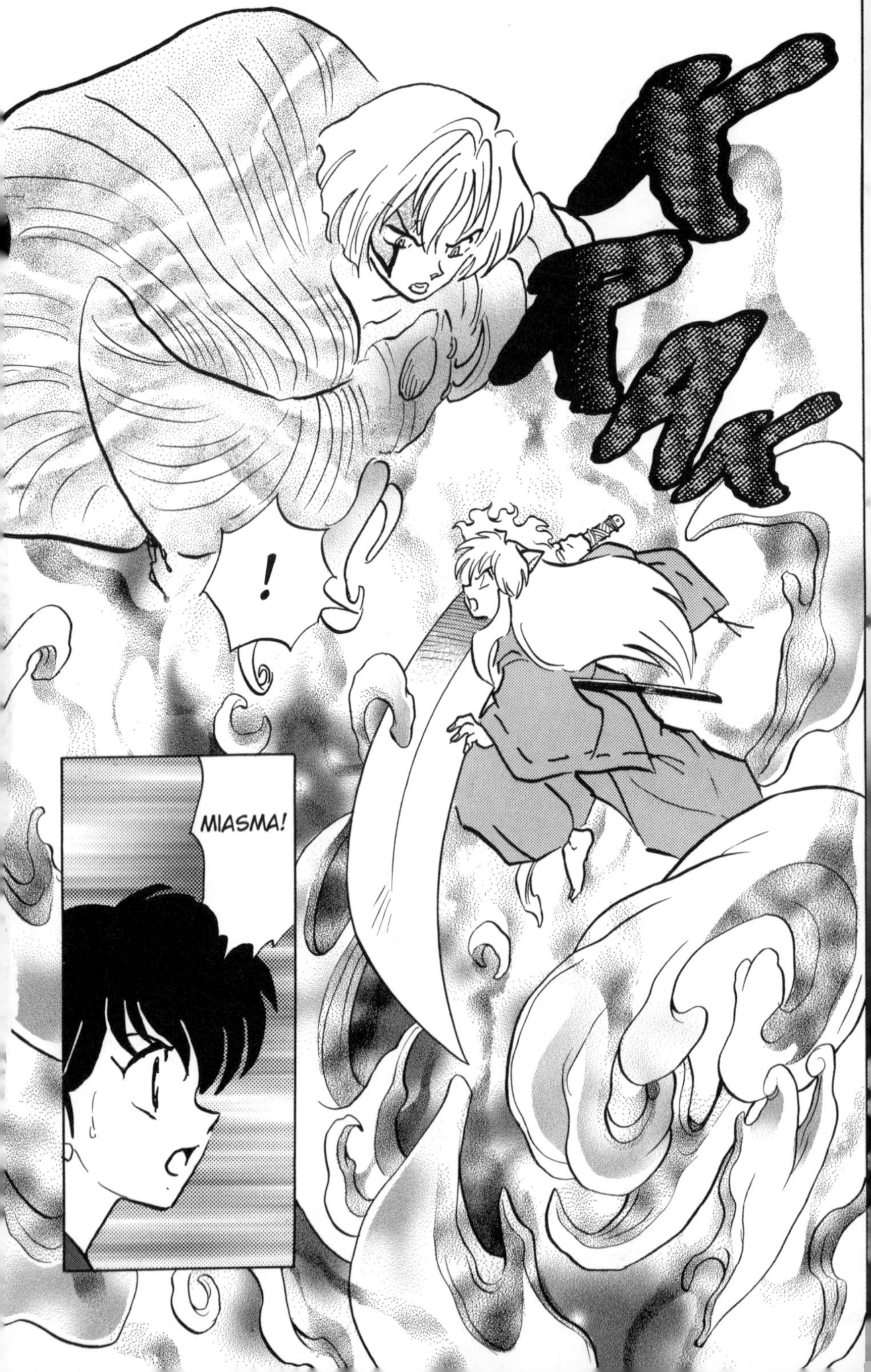
!
MIASMA!

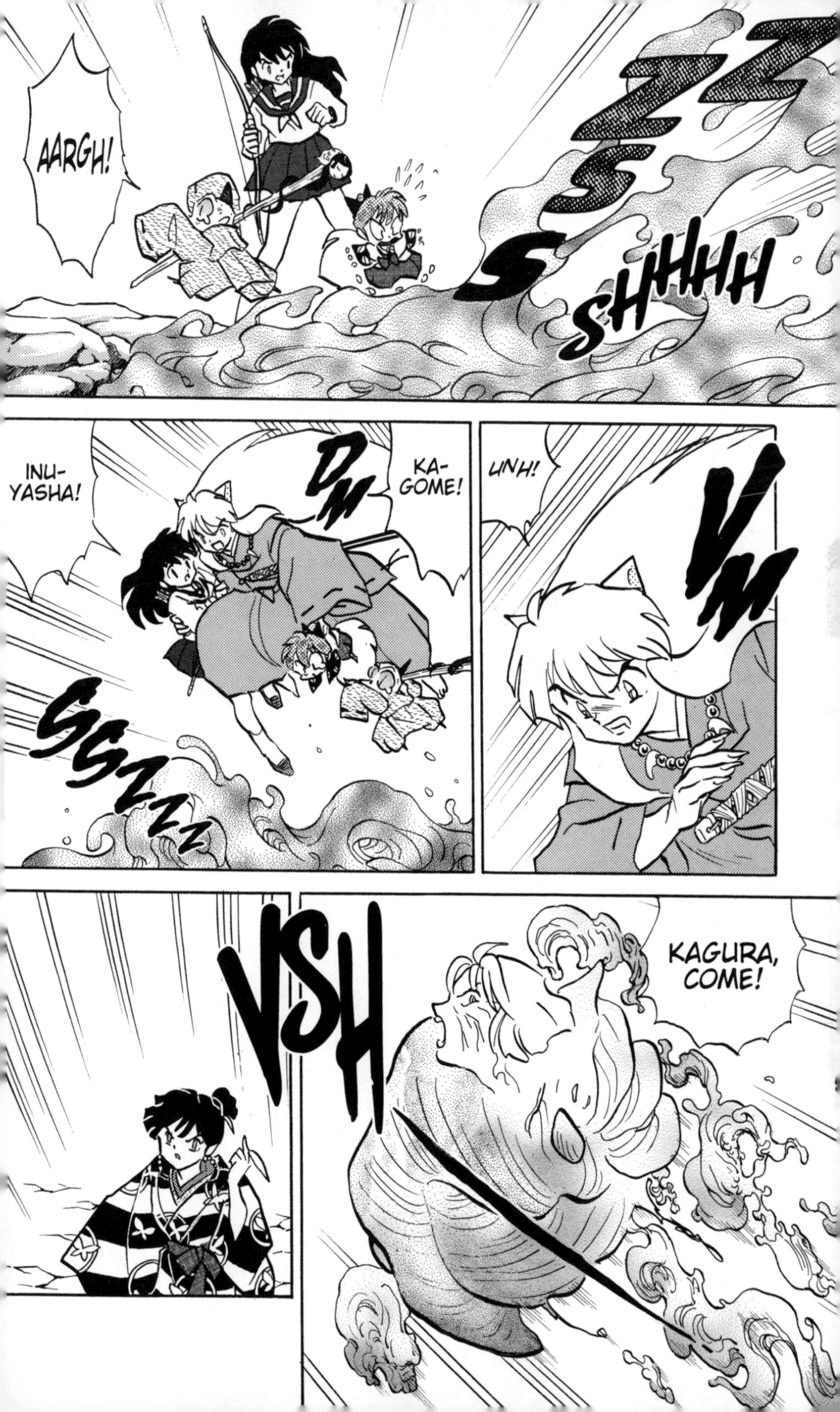
AARGH!
ZZZSS
SHHHHH
UNH!
VM
KA-GOME!
DM
INU-YASHA!
SSZZZZ
KAGURA, COME!
VSH

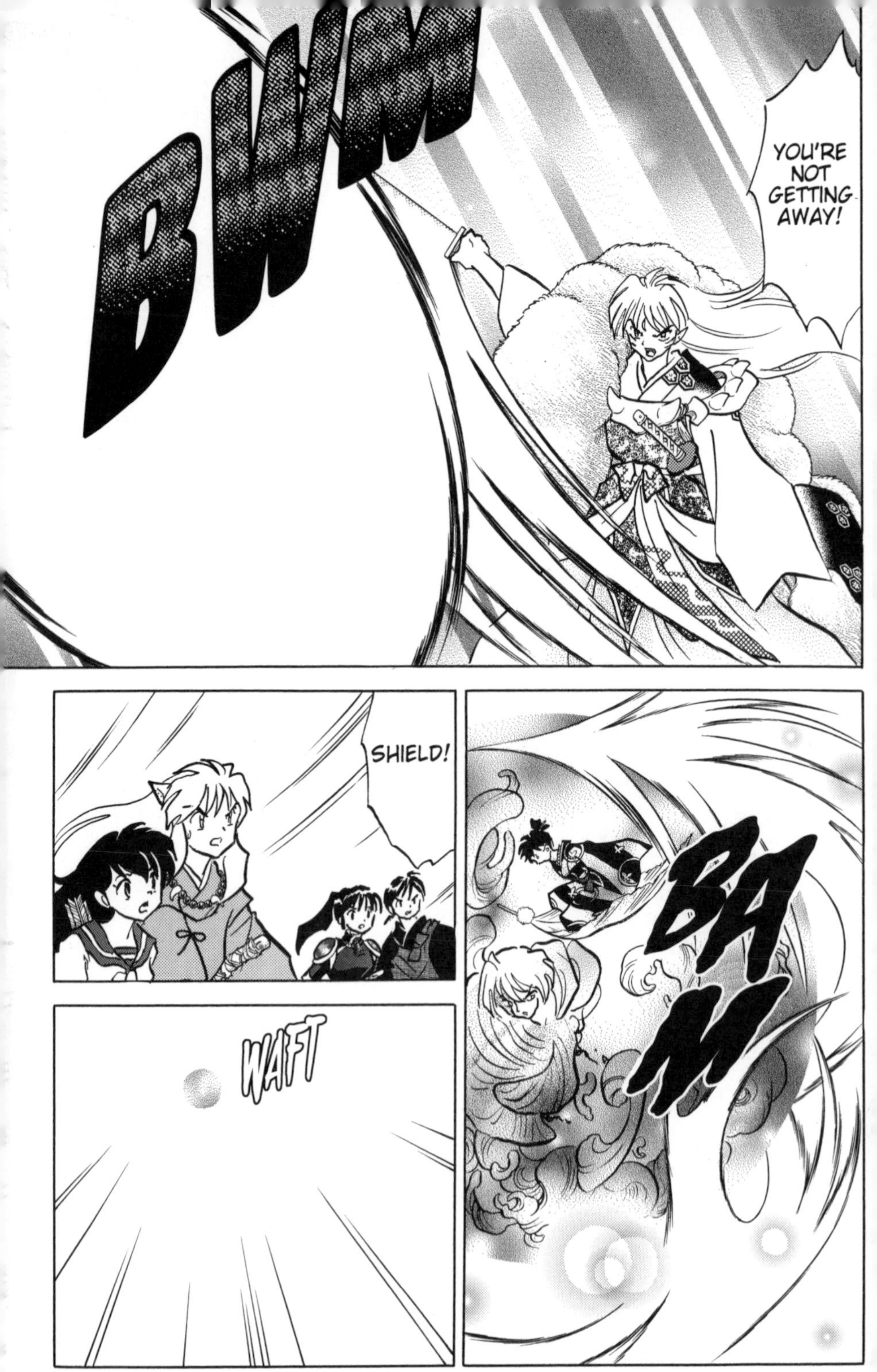
YOU'RE NOT GETTING AWAY!
BWM
BAM!
SHIELD!
WAFT

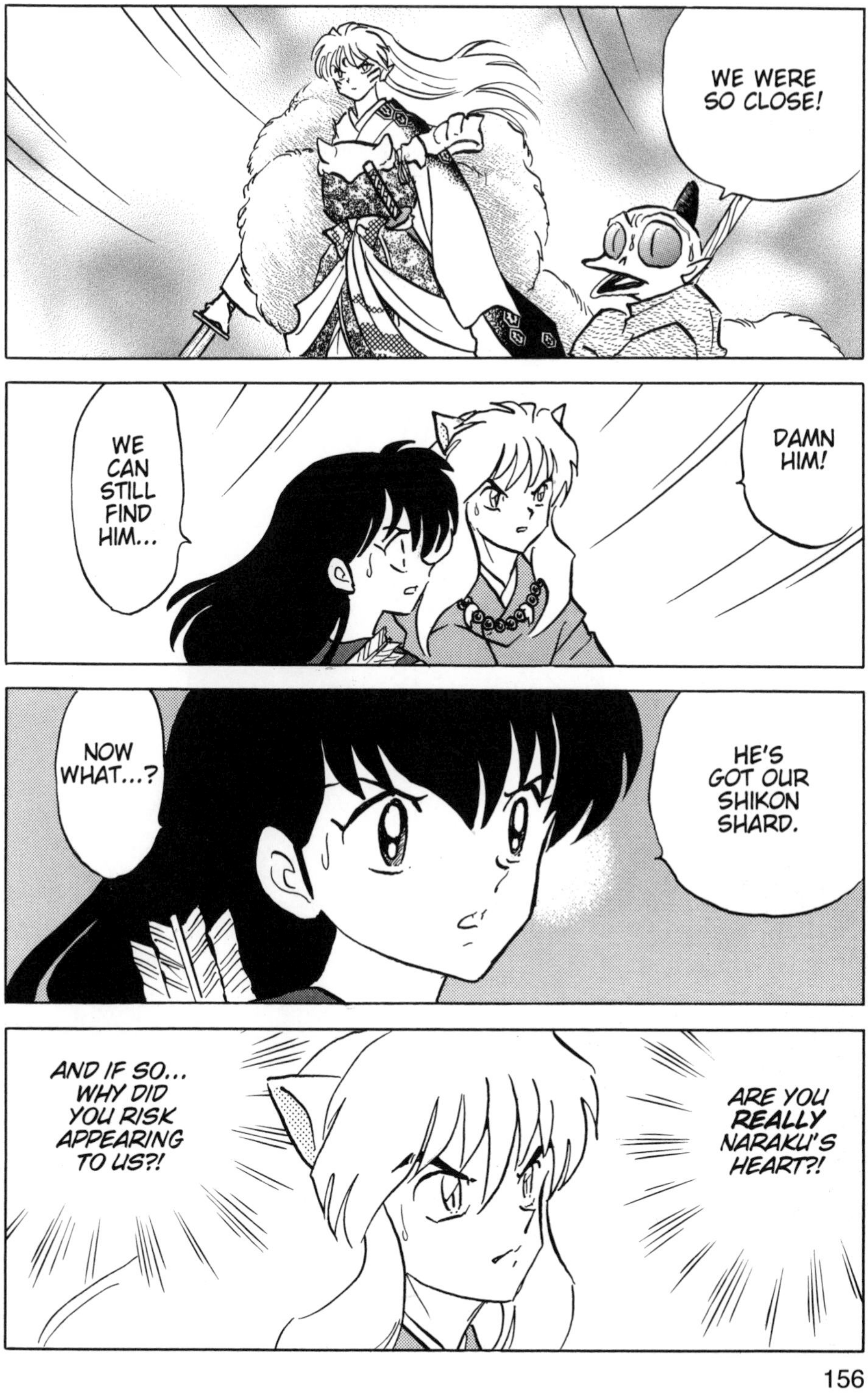
WE WERE SO CLOSE!
DAMN HIM!
WE CAN STILL FIND HIM...
HE'S GOT OUR SHIKON SHARD.
NOW WHAT...?
ARE YOU **REALLY** NARAKU'S HEART?!
AND IF SO... WHY DID YOU RISK APPEARING TO US?!

SCROLL NINE
THE LOCATION OF THE INFANT

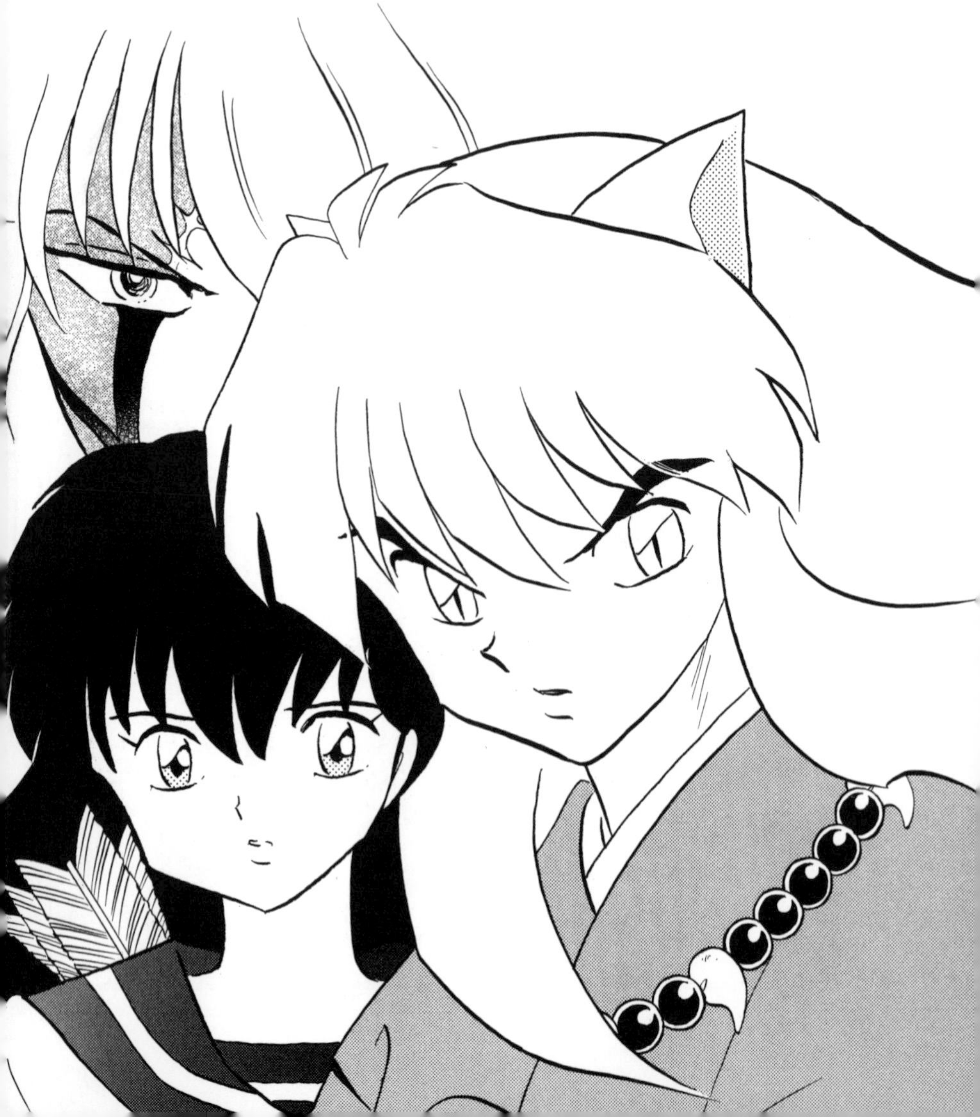

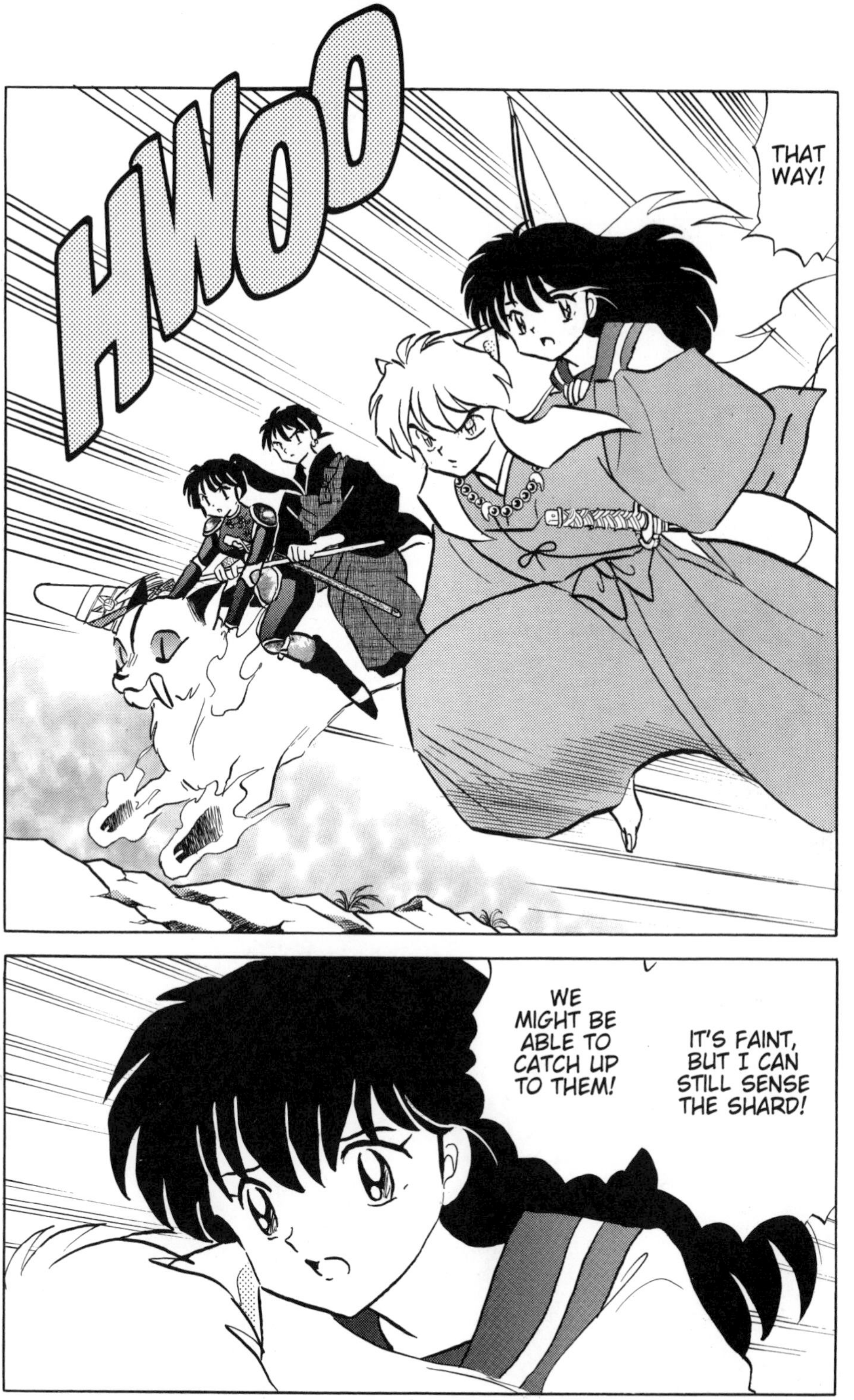
HWOO
THAT WAY!
IT'S FAINT, BUT I CAN STILL SENSE THE SHARD!
WE MIGHT BE ABLE TO CATCH UP TO THEM!

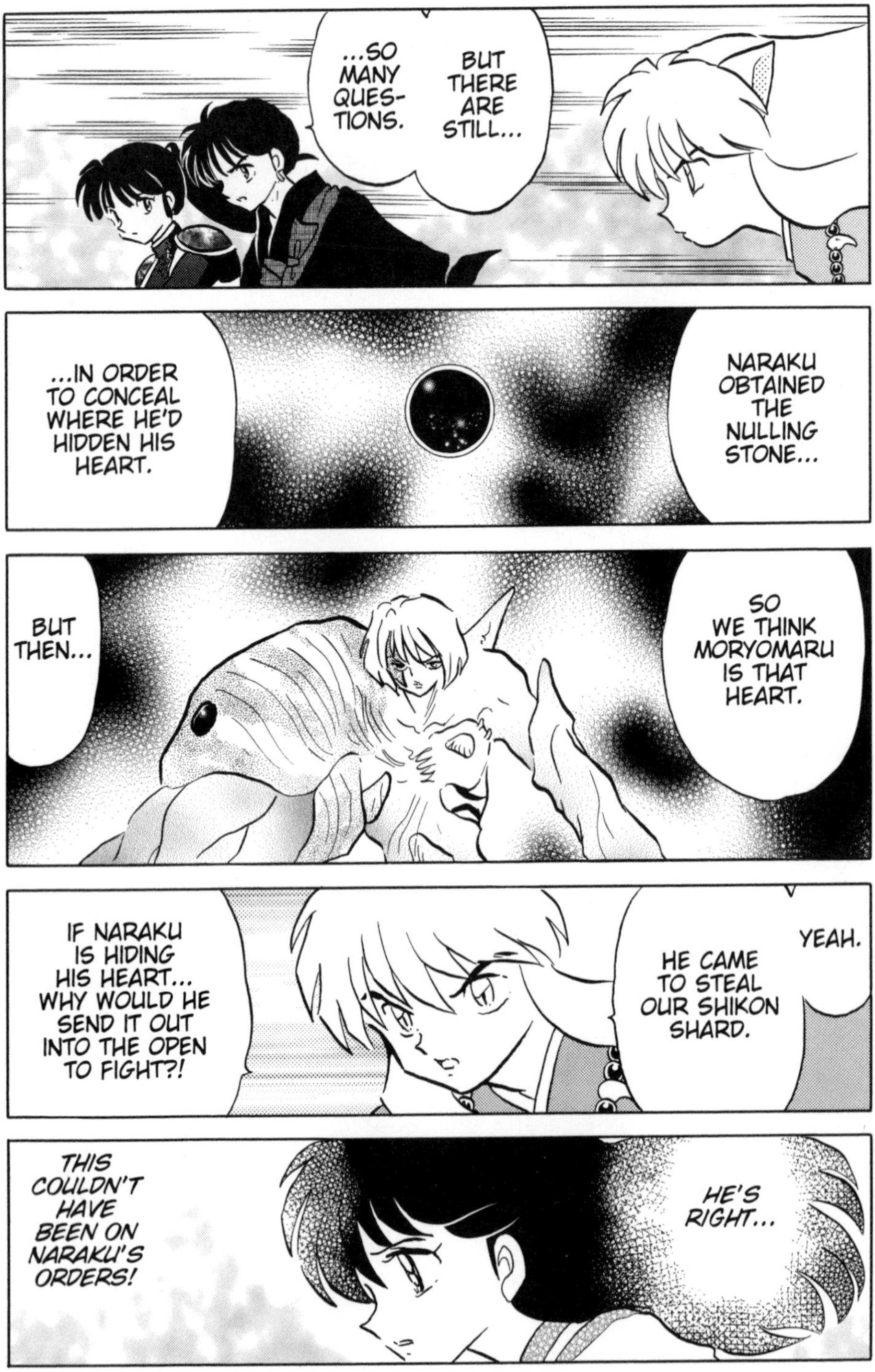
BUT THERE ARE STILL...
...SO MANY QUES-TIONS.
NARAKU OBTAINED THE NULLING STONE...
...IN ORDER TO CONCEAL WHERE HE'D HIDDEN HIS HEART.
SO WE THINK MORYOMARU IS THAT HEART.
BUT THEN...
YEAH.
HE CAME TO STEAL OUR SHIKON SHARD.
IF NARAKU IS HIDING HIS HEART... WHY WOULD HE SEND IT OUT INTO THE OPEN TO FIGHT?!
HE'S RIGHT...
THIS COULDN'T HAVE BEEN ON NARAKU'S ORDERS!

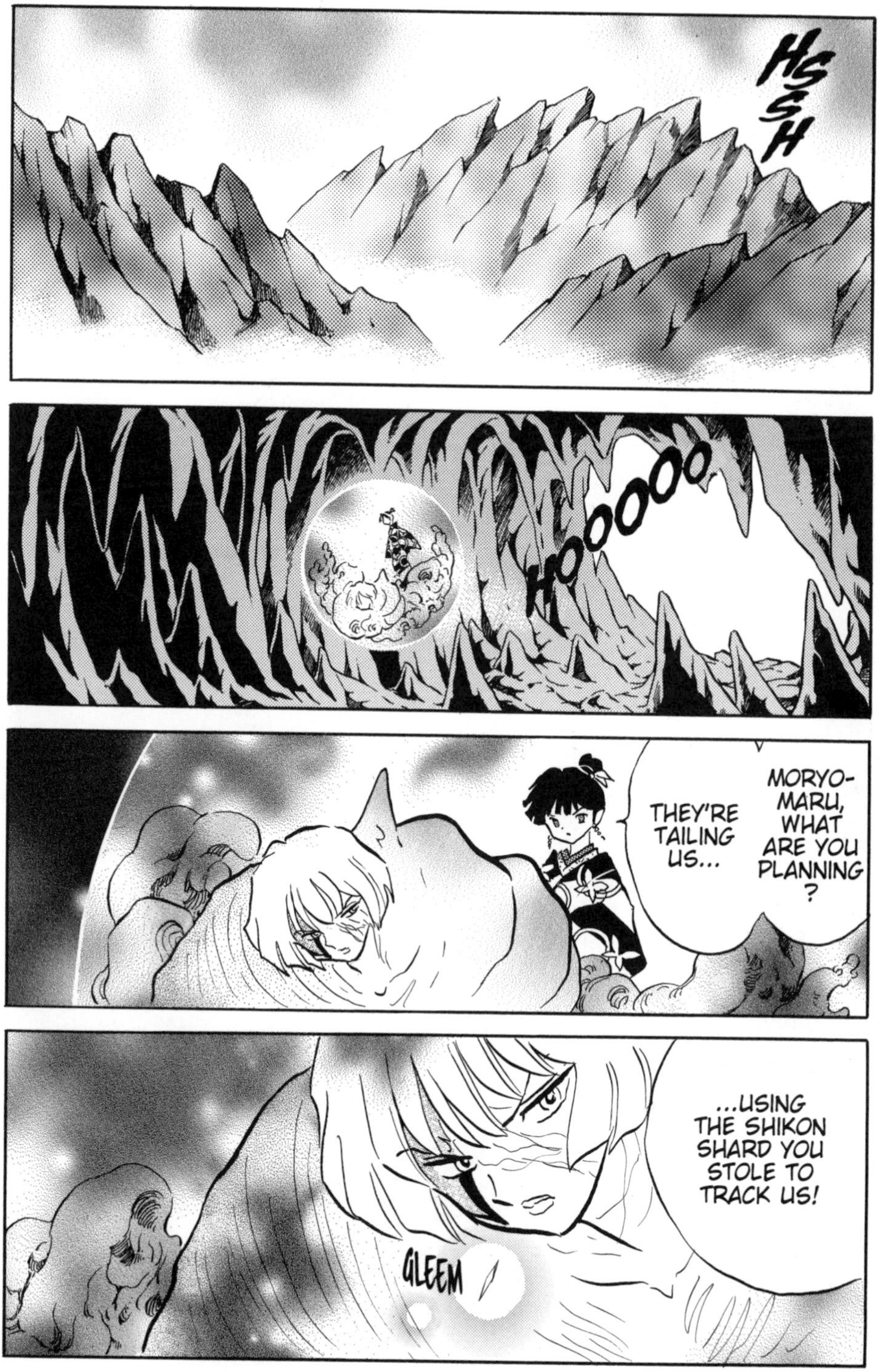

HSSH
HOOOOO
MORYO-MARU, WHAT ARE YOU PLANNING?
THEY'RE TAILING US...
...USING THE SHIKON SHARD YOU STOLE TO TRACK US!
GLEEM

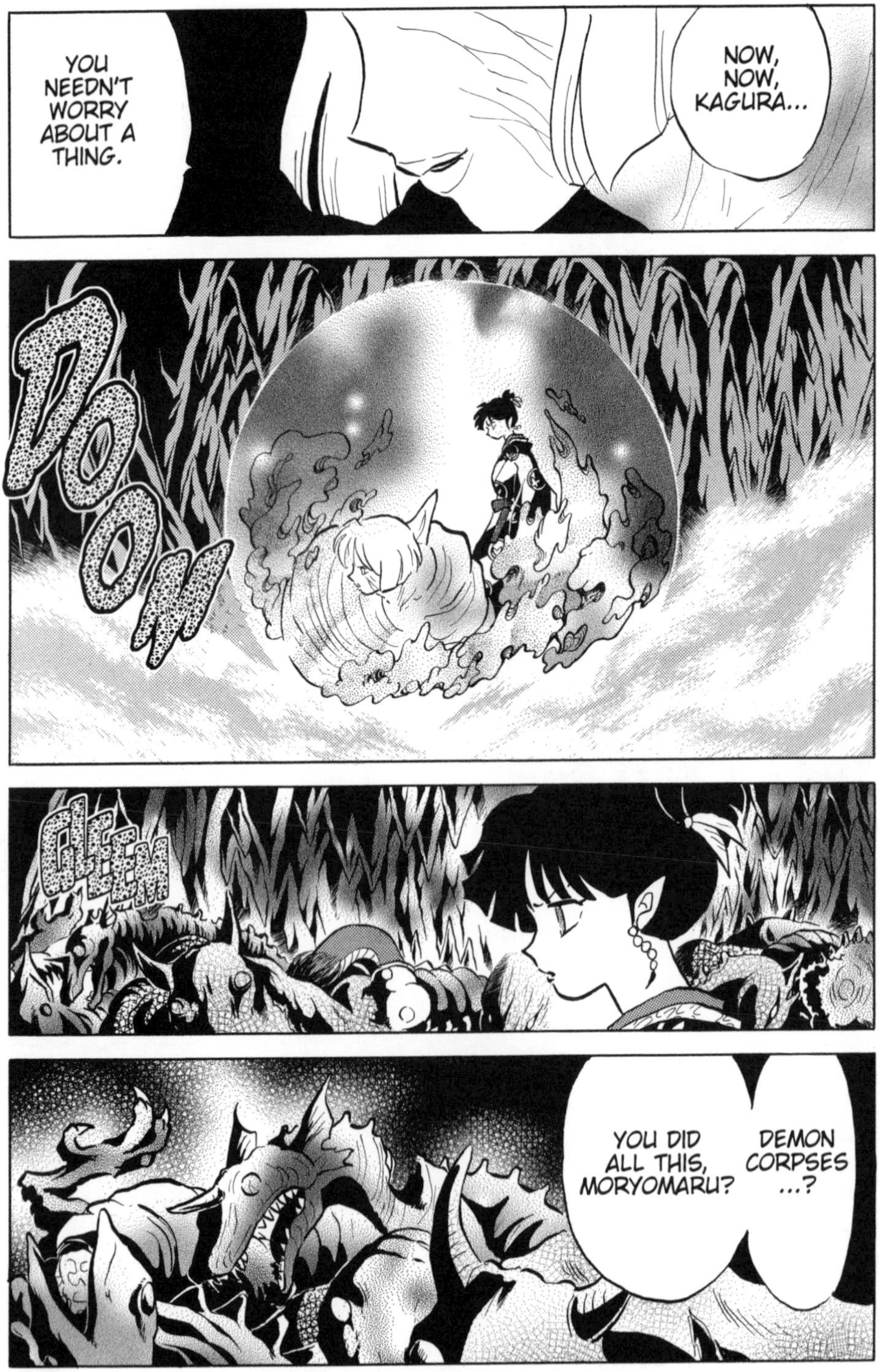
NOW, NOW, KAGURA...
YOU NEEDN'T WORRY ABOUT A THING.
DOOOM
GLEEM
DEMON CORPSES ...?
YOU DID ALL THIS, MORYOMARU?

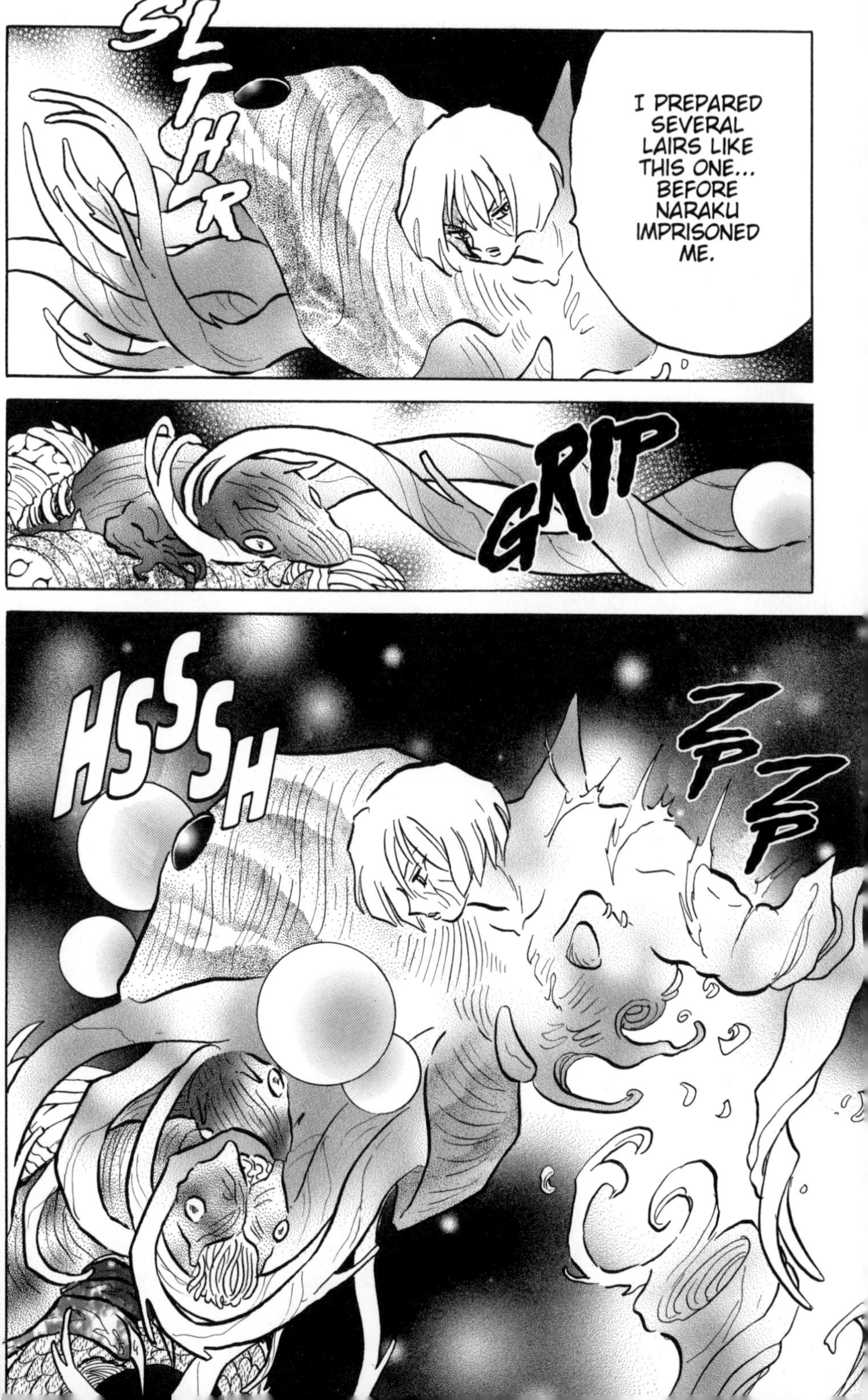
I PREPARED SEVERAL LAIRS LIKE THIS ONE... BEFORE NARAKU IMPRISONED ME.
SLTHR
GRIP
ZPZP
HSSSH

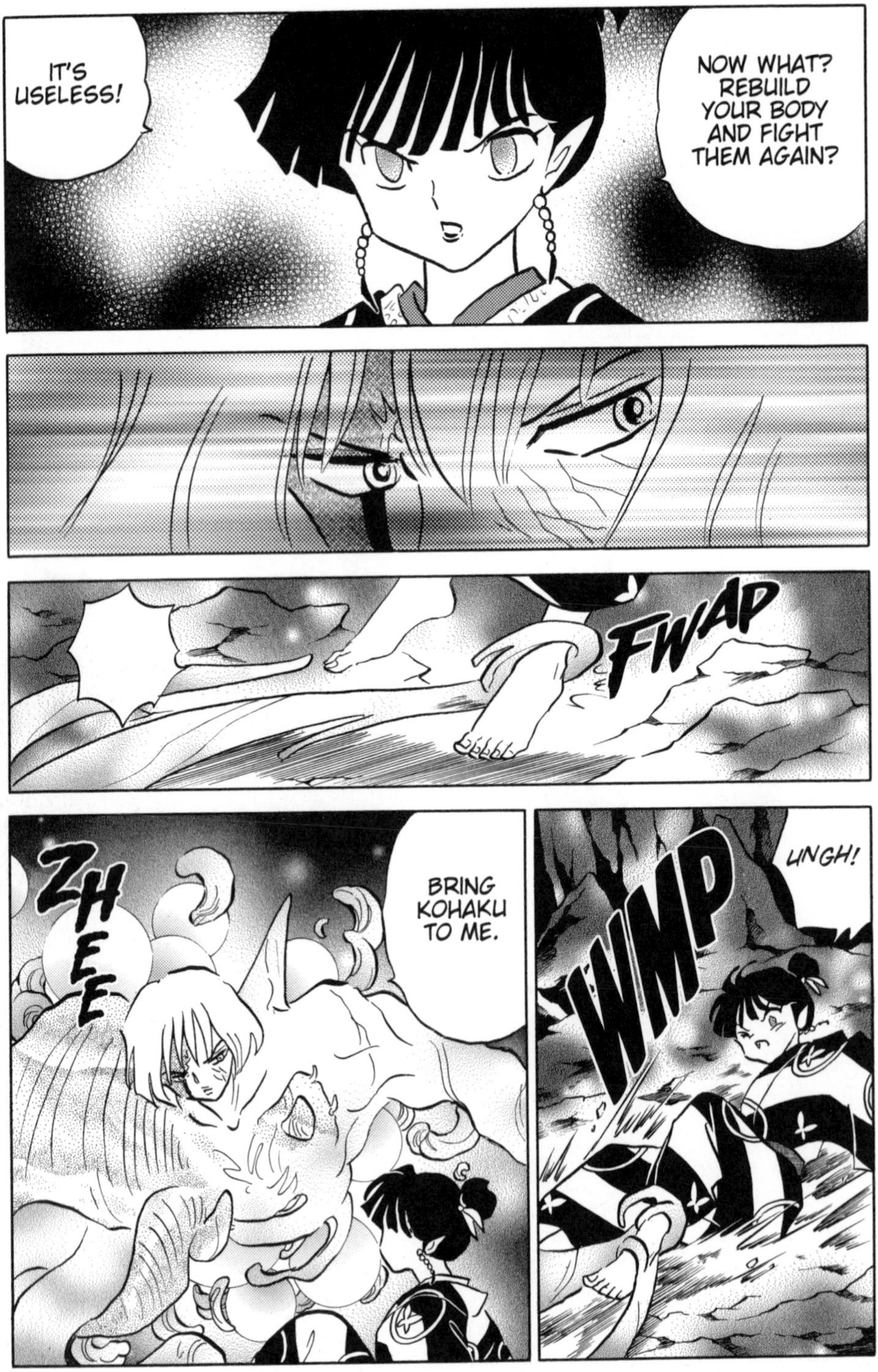
NOW WHAT? REBUILD YOUR BODY AND FIGHT THEM AGAIN?
IT'S USELESS!
FWAP
UNGH!
WMP
BRING KOHAKU TO ME.
ZHEE

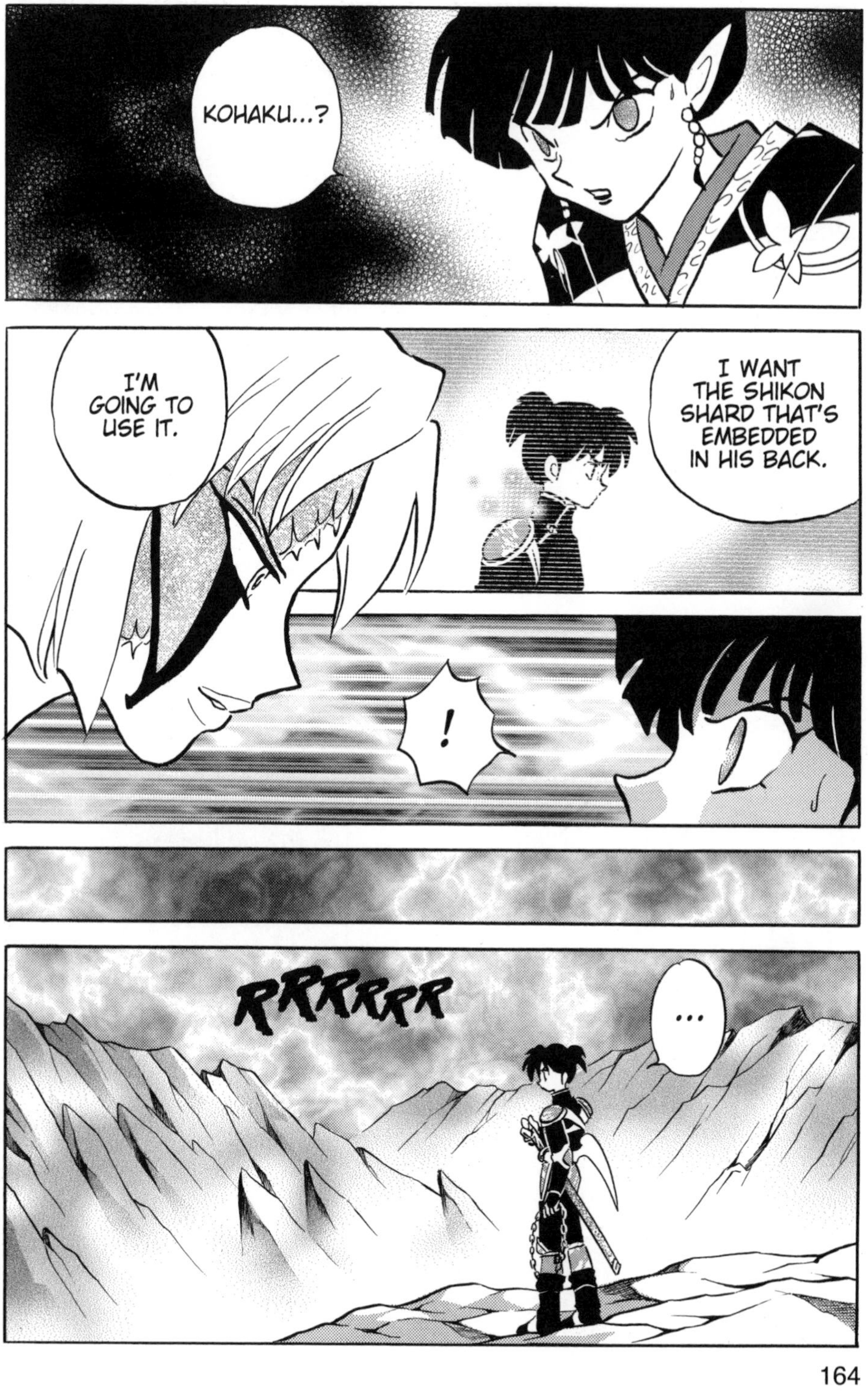
KOHAKU...?
I WANT THE SHIKON SHARD THAT'S EMBEDDED IN HIS BACK.
I'M GOING TO USE IT.
!
...
RRRRRR

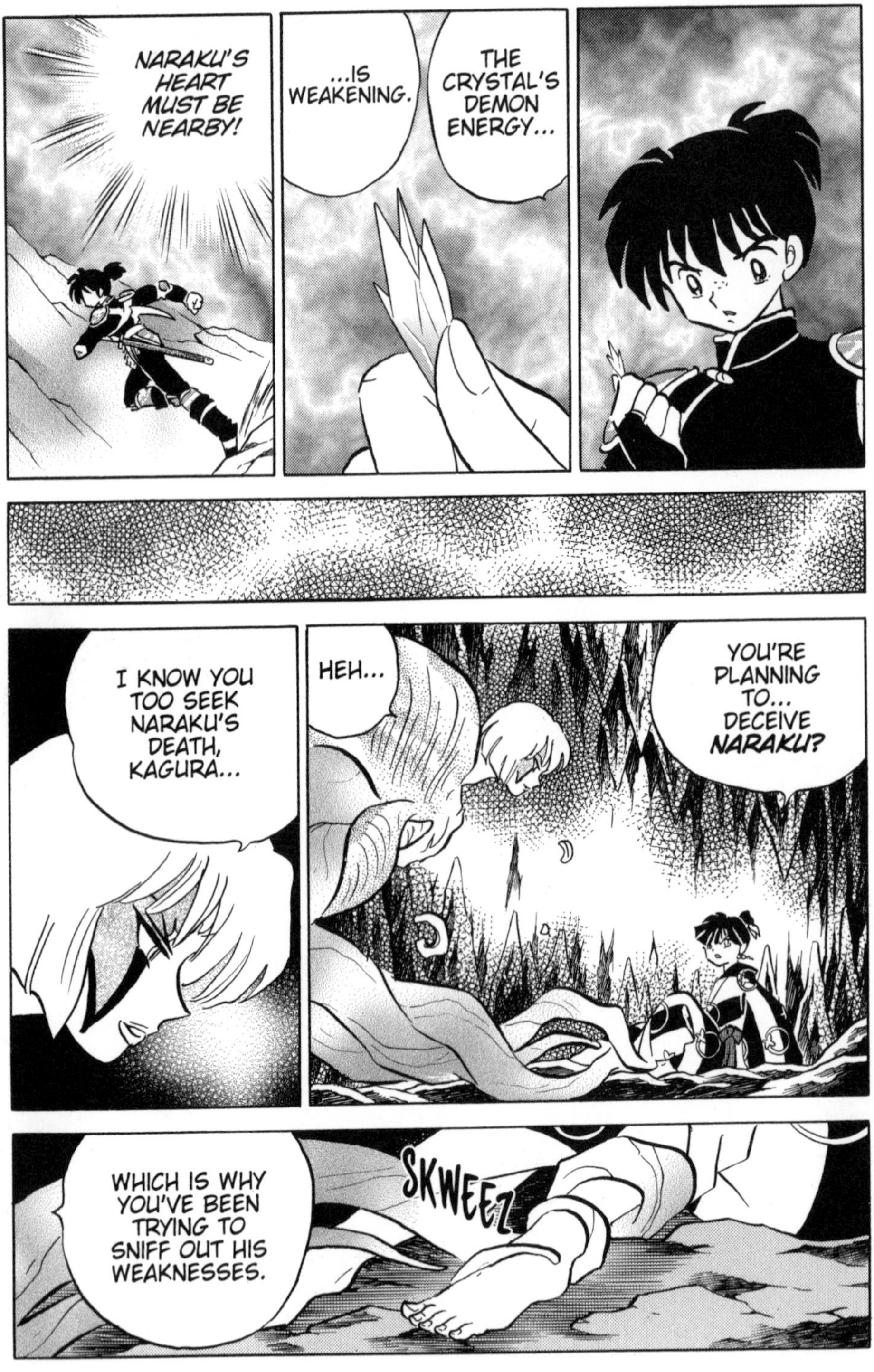
THE CRYSTAL'S DEMON ENERGY...
...IS WEAKENING.
NARAKU'S HEART MUST BE NEARBY!
YOU'RE PLANNING TO... DECEIVE NARAKU?
HEH...
I KNOW YOU TOO SEEK NARAKU'S DEATH, KAGURA...
SKWEEZ
WHICH IS WHY YOU'VE BEEN TRYING TO SNIFF OUT HIS WEAKNESSES.

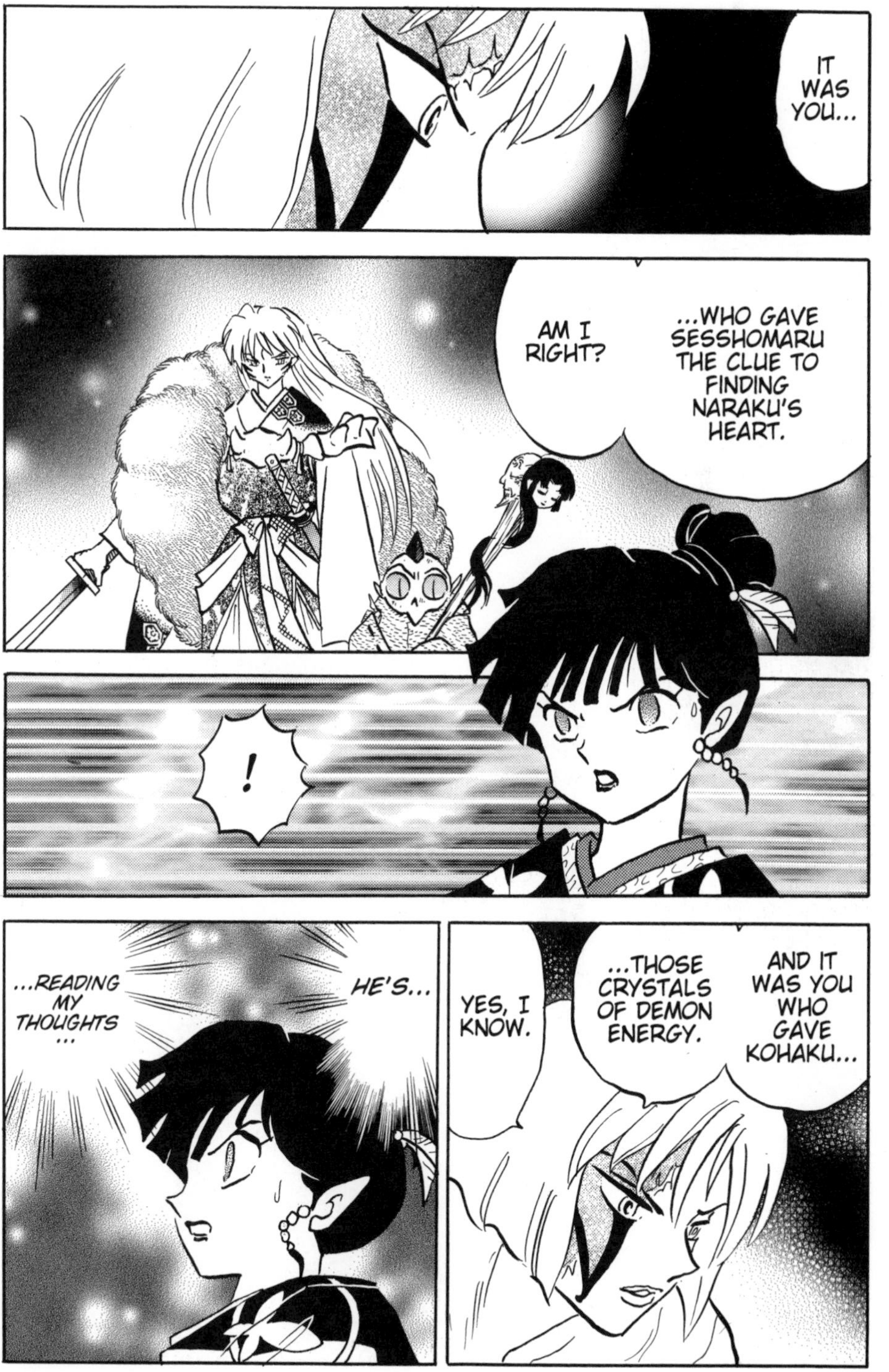
IT WAS YOU...
...WHO GAVE SESSHOMARU THE CLUE TO FINDING NARAKU'S HEART.
AM I RIGHT?
!
AND IT WAS YOU WHO GAVE KOHAKU...
...THOSE CRYSTALS OF DEMON ENERGY.
YES, I KNOW.
HE'S...
...READING MY THOUGHTS...

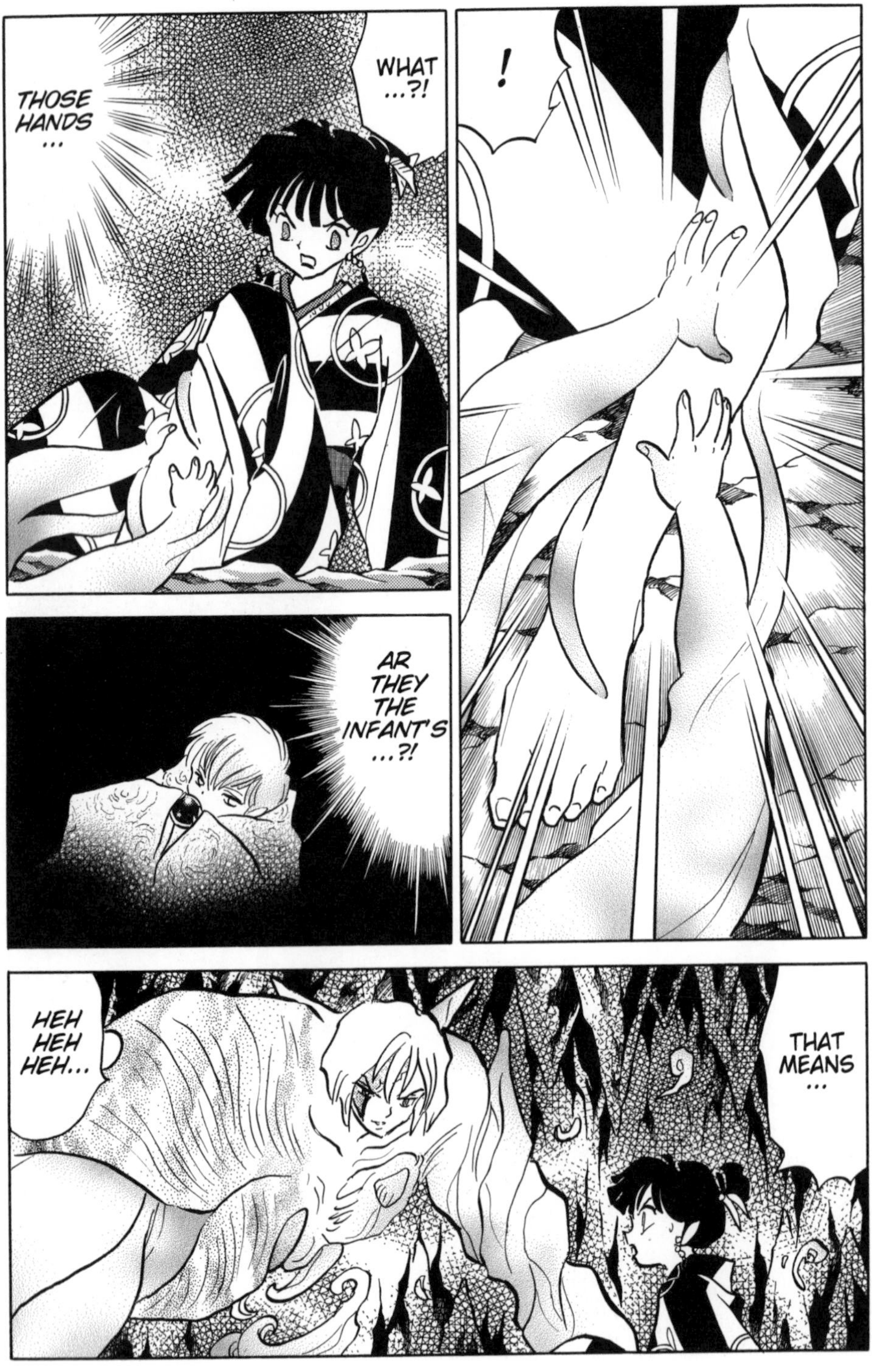
!
WHAT ...?!
THOSE HANDS ...
AR THEY THE INFANT'S ...?!
THAT MEANS ...
HEH HEH HEH...

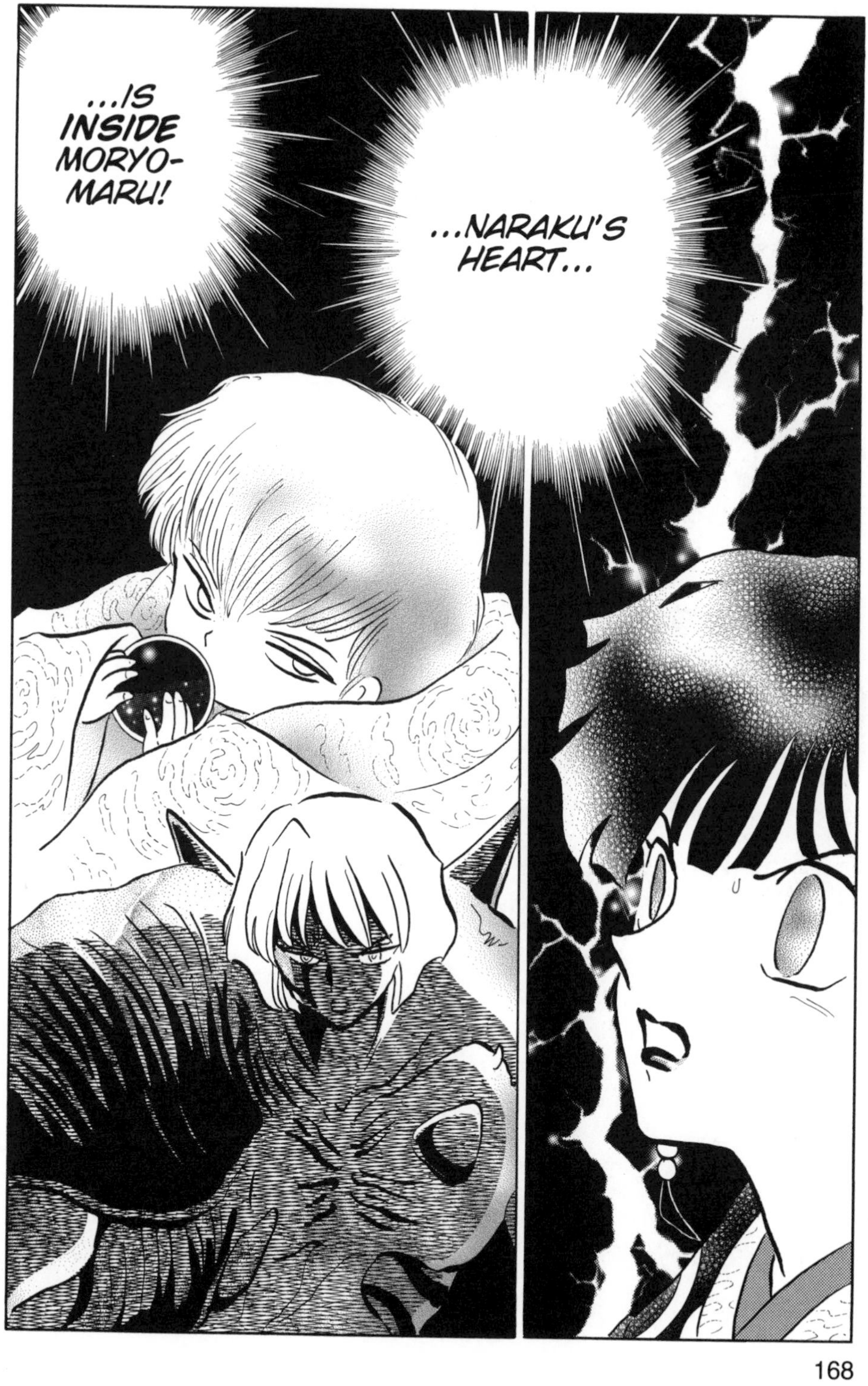
...NARAKU'S HEART...
...IS INSIDE MORYO-MARU!

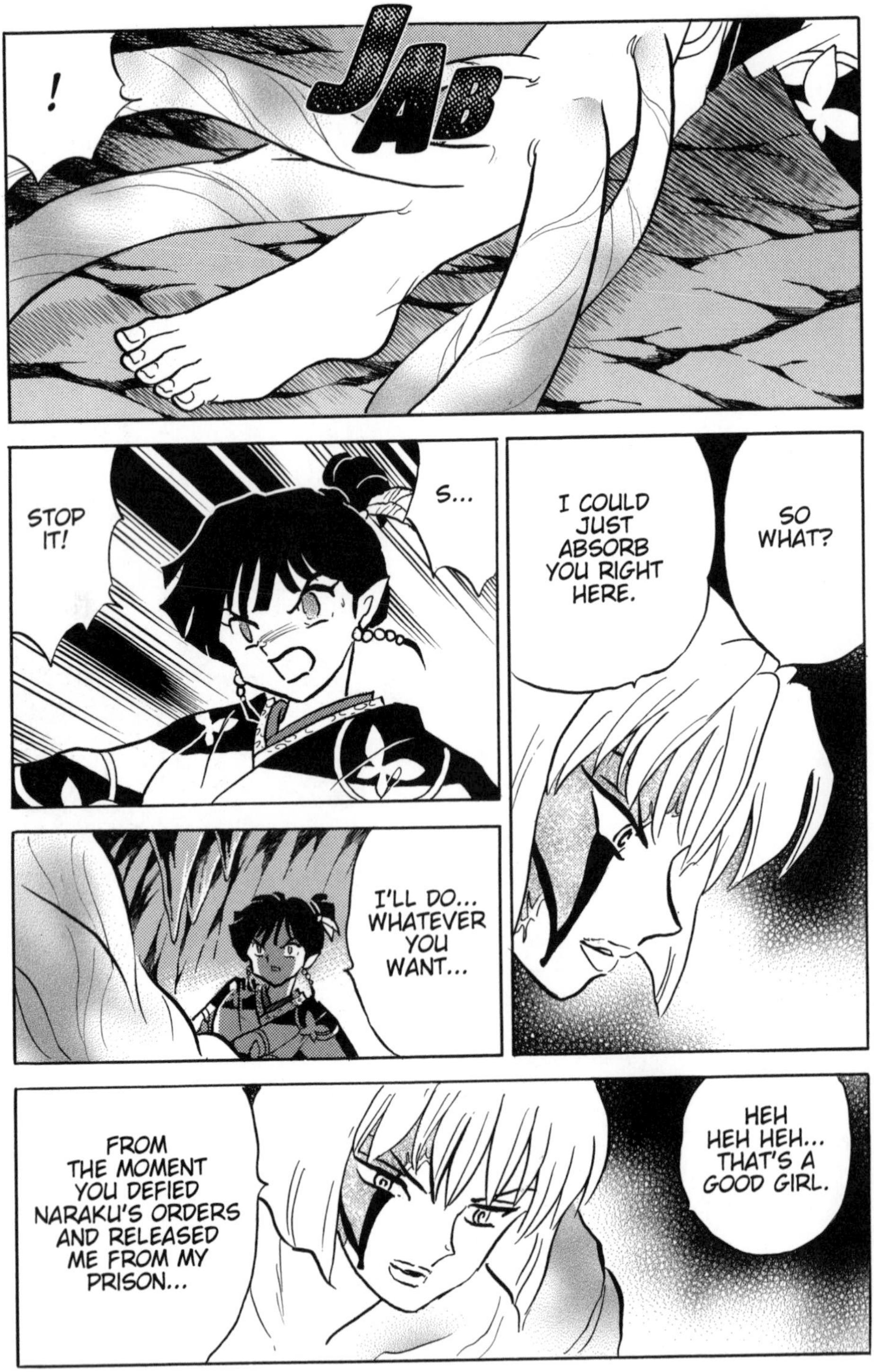
JAB
!
SO WHAT?
I COULD JUST ABSORB YOU RIGHT HERE.
S...
STOP IT!
I'LL DO... WHATEVER YOU WANT...
HEH HEH HEH... THAT'S A GOOD GIRL.
FROM THE MOMENT YOU DEFIED NARAKU'S ORDERS AND RELEASED ME FROM MY PRISON...

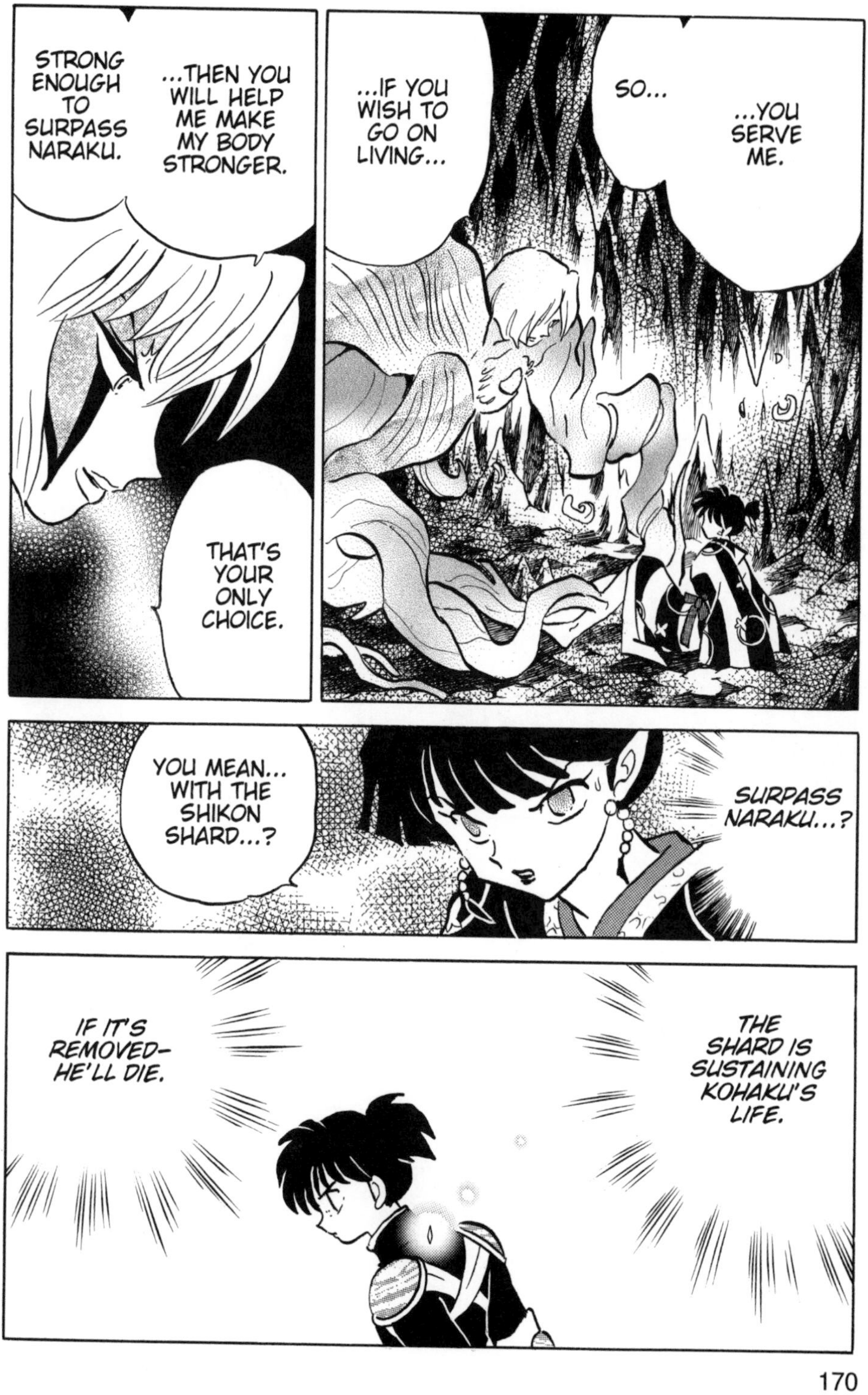
SO...
...YOU SERVE ME.
...IF YOU WISH TO GO ON LIVING...
...THEN YOU WILL HELP ME MAKE MY BODY STRONGER.
STRONG ENOUGH TO SURPASS NARAKU.
THAT'S YOUR ONLY CHOICE.
SURPASS NARAKU...?
YOU MEAN... WITH THE SHIKON SHARD...?
THE SHARD IS SUSTAINING KOHAKU'S LIFE.
IF IT'S REMOVED— HE'LL DIE.

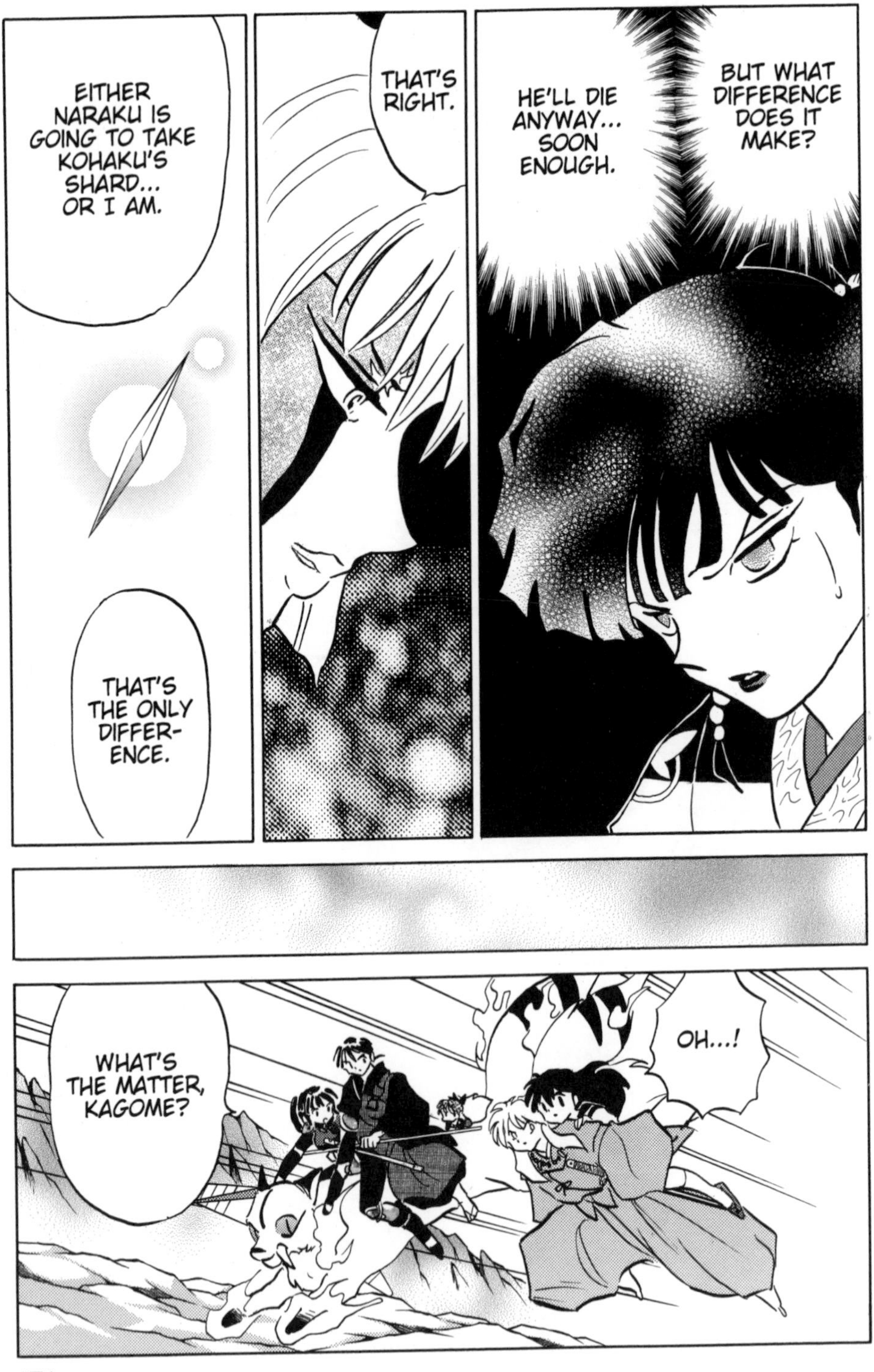
BUT WHAT DIFFERENCE DOES IT MAKE?
HE'LL DIE ANYWAY... SOON ENOUGH.
THAT'S RIGHT.
EITHER NARAKU IS GOING TO TAKE KOHAKU'S SHARD... OR I AM.
THAT'S THE ONLY DIFFER-ENCE.
OH...!
WHAT'S THE MATTER, KAGOME?

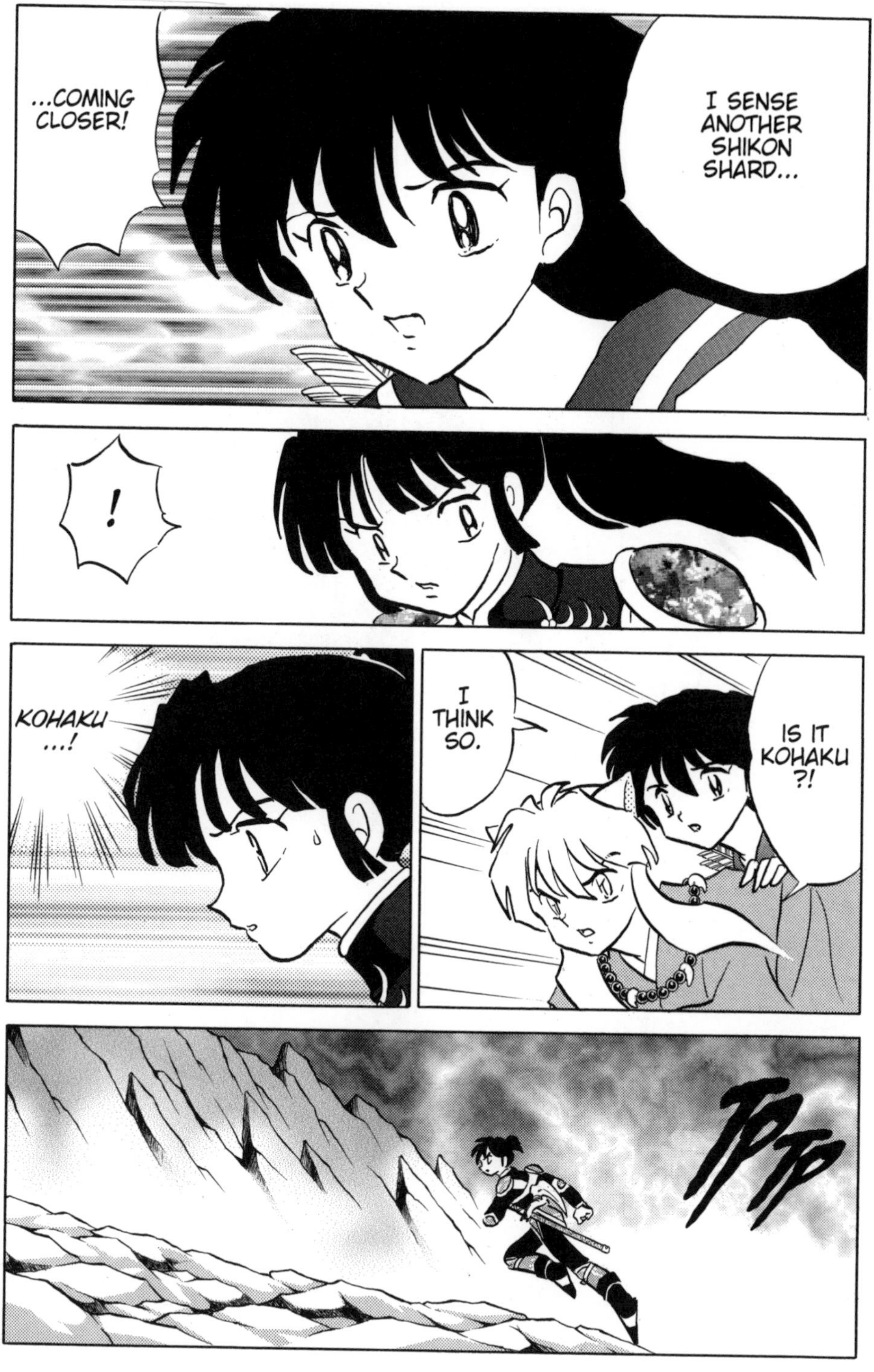
I SENSE ANOTHER SHIKON SHARD...
...COMING CLOSER!
!
IS IT KOHAKU ?!
I THINK SO.
KOHAKU ...!

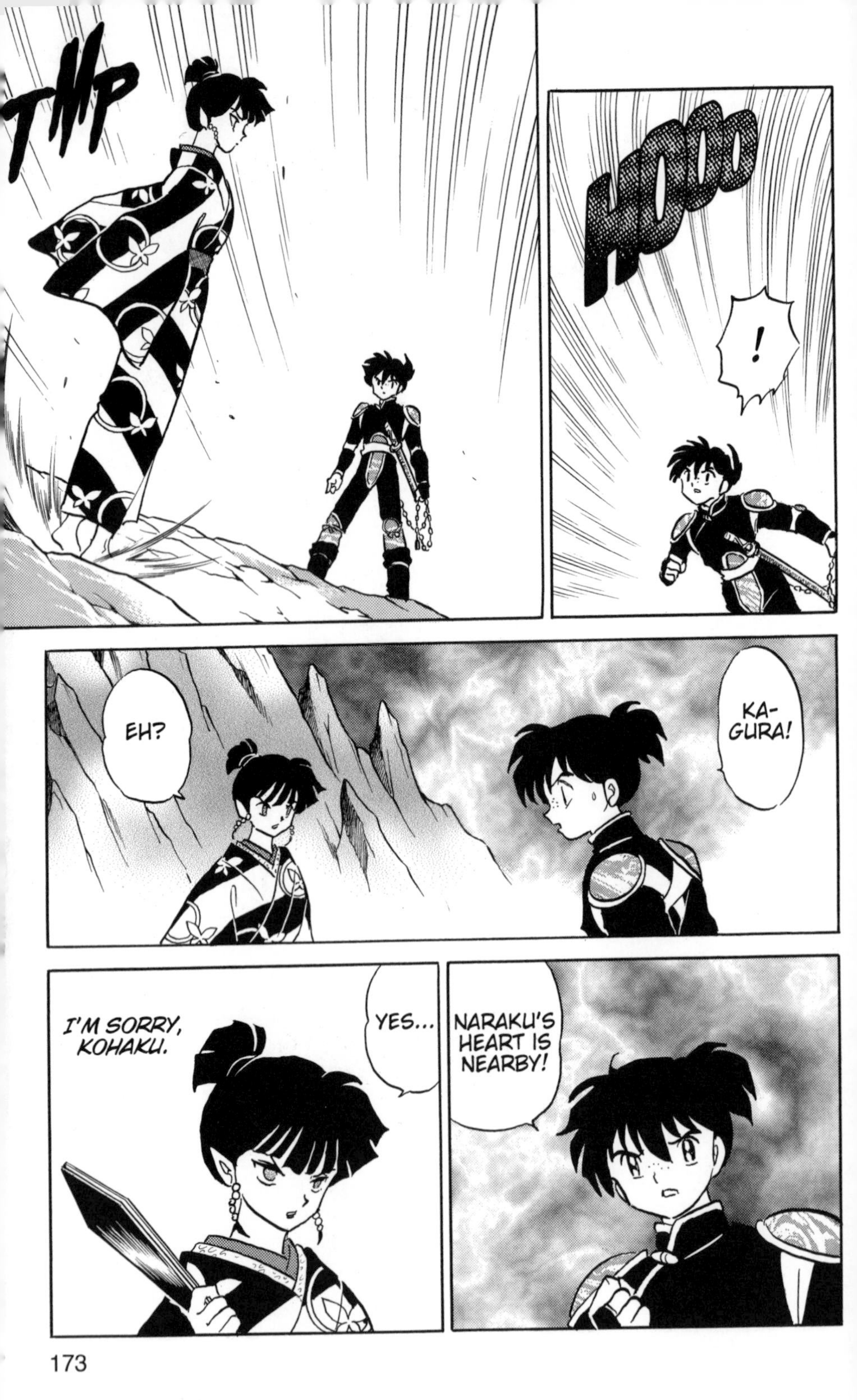
HOOO
!
THP
KA-GURA!
EH?
NARAKU'S HEART IS NEARBY!
YES...
I'M SORRY, KOHAKU.

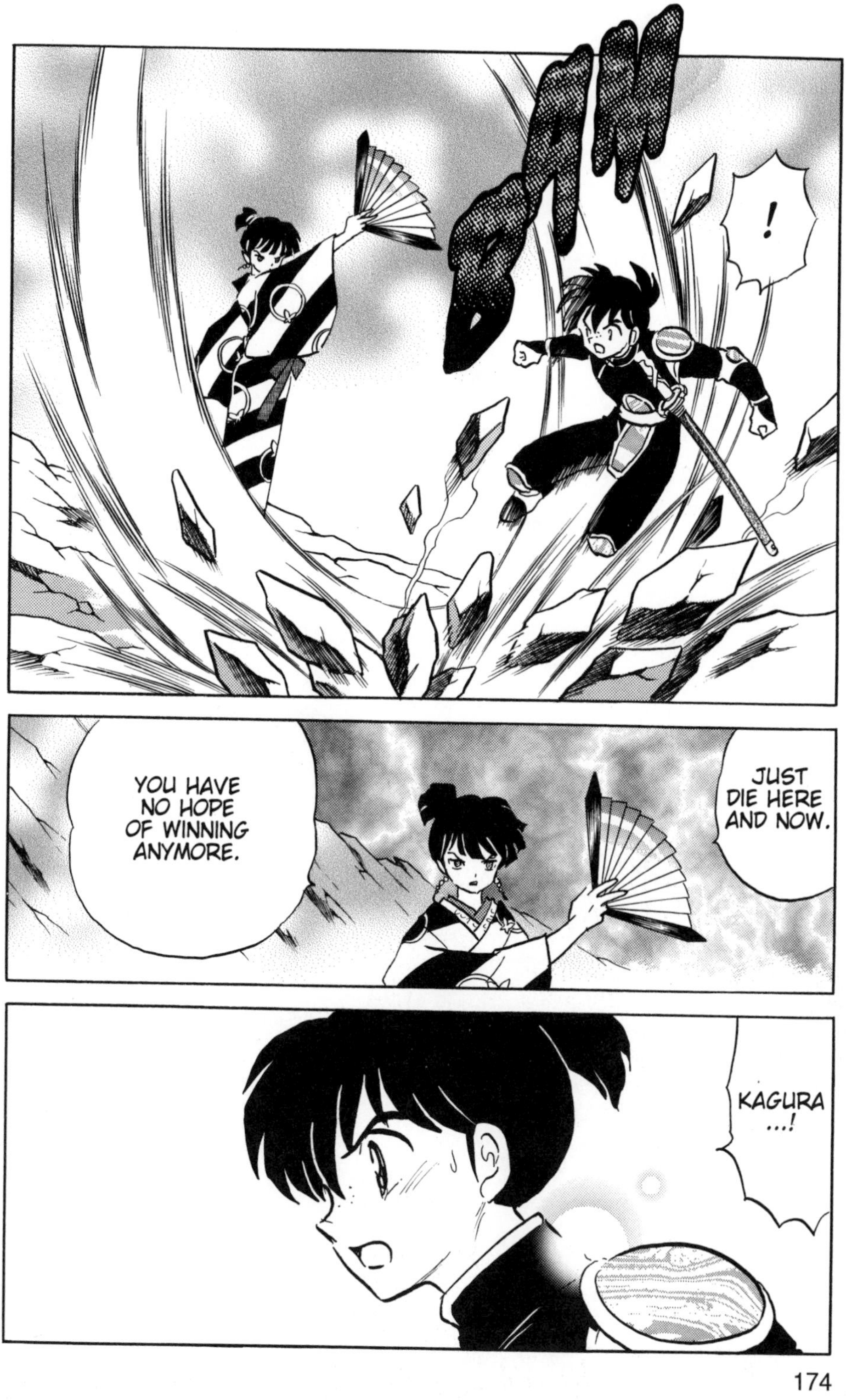
BAM
!
JUST DIE HERE AND NOW.
YOU HAVE NO HOPE OF WINNING ANYMORE.
KAGURA ...!

SCROLL TEN
KAGURA'S DECISION

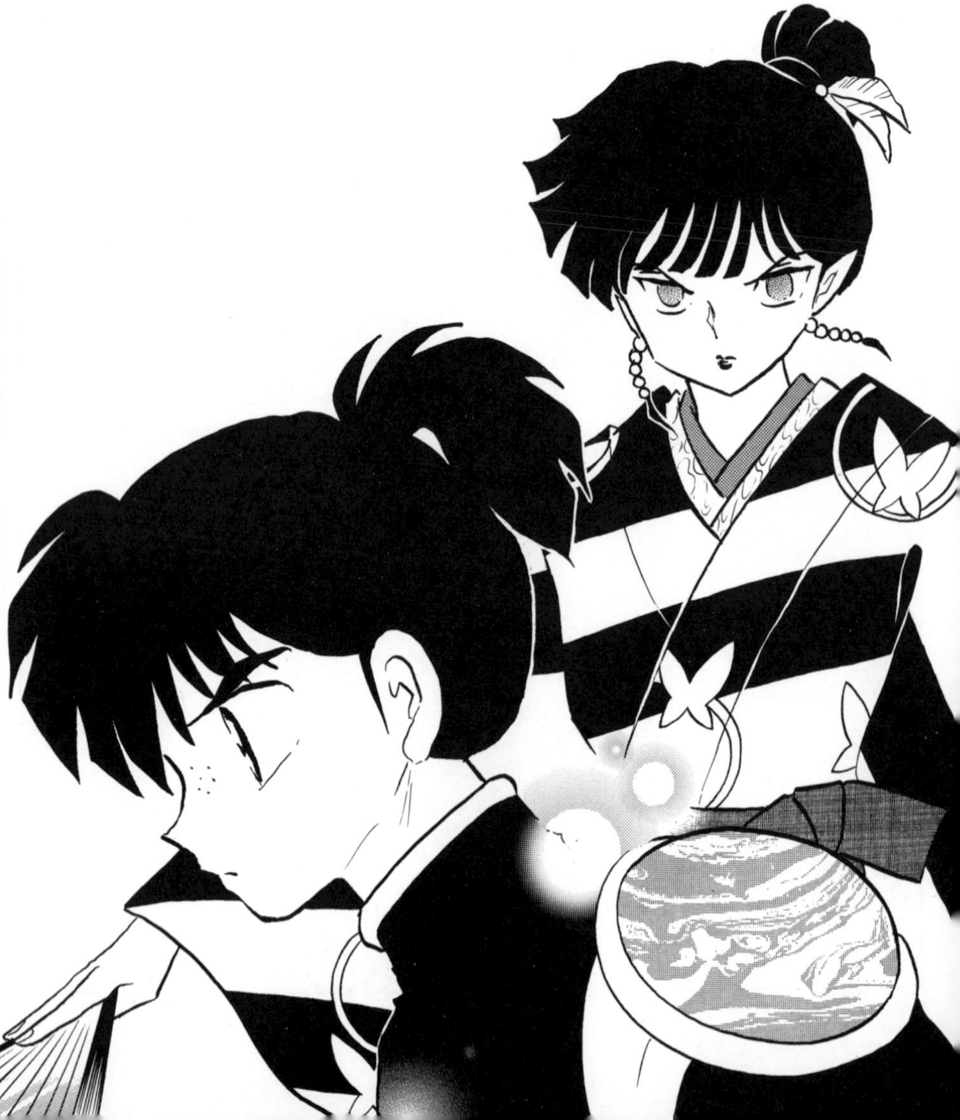

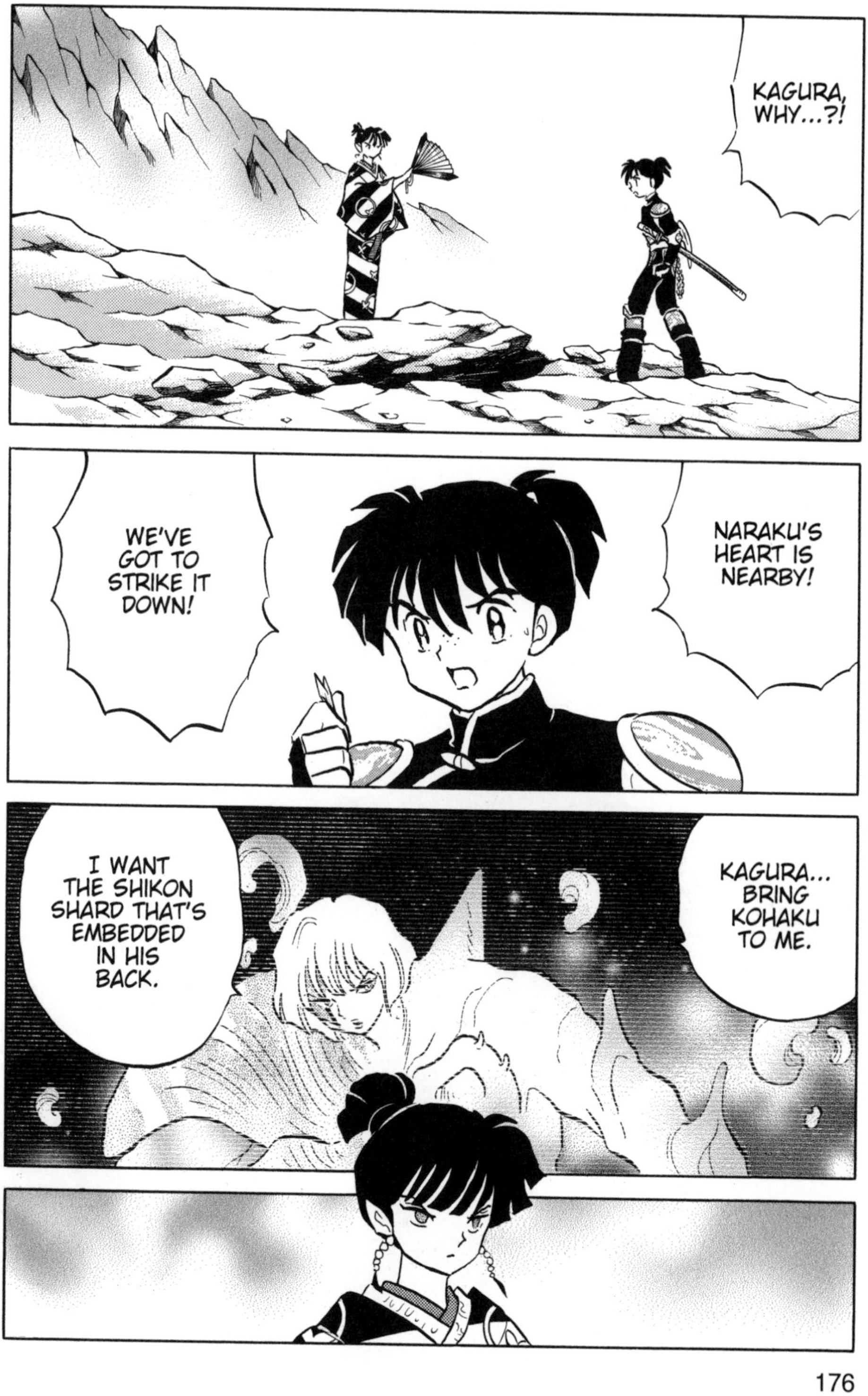
KAGURA, WHY...?!
NARAKU'S HEART IS NEARBY!
WE'VE GOT TO STRIKE IT DOWN!
KAGURA... BRING KOHAKU TO ME.
I WANT THE SHIKON SHARD THAT'S EMBEDDED IN HIS BACK.

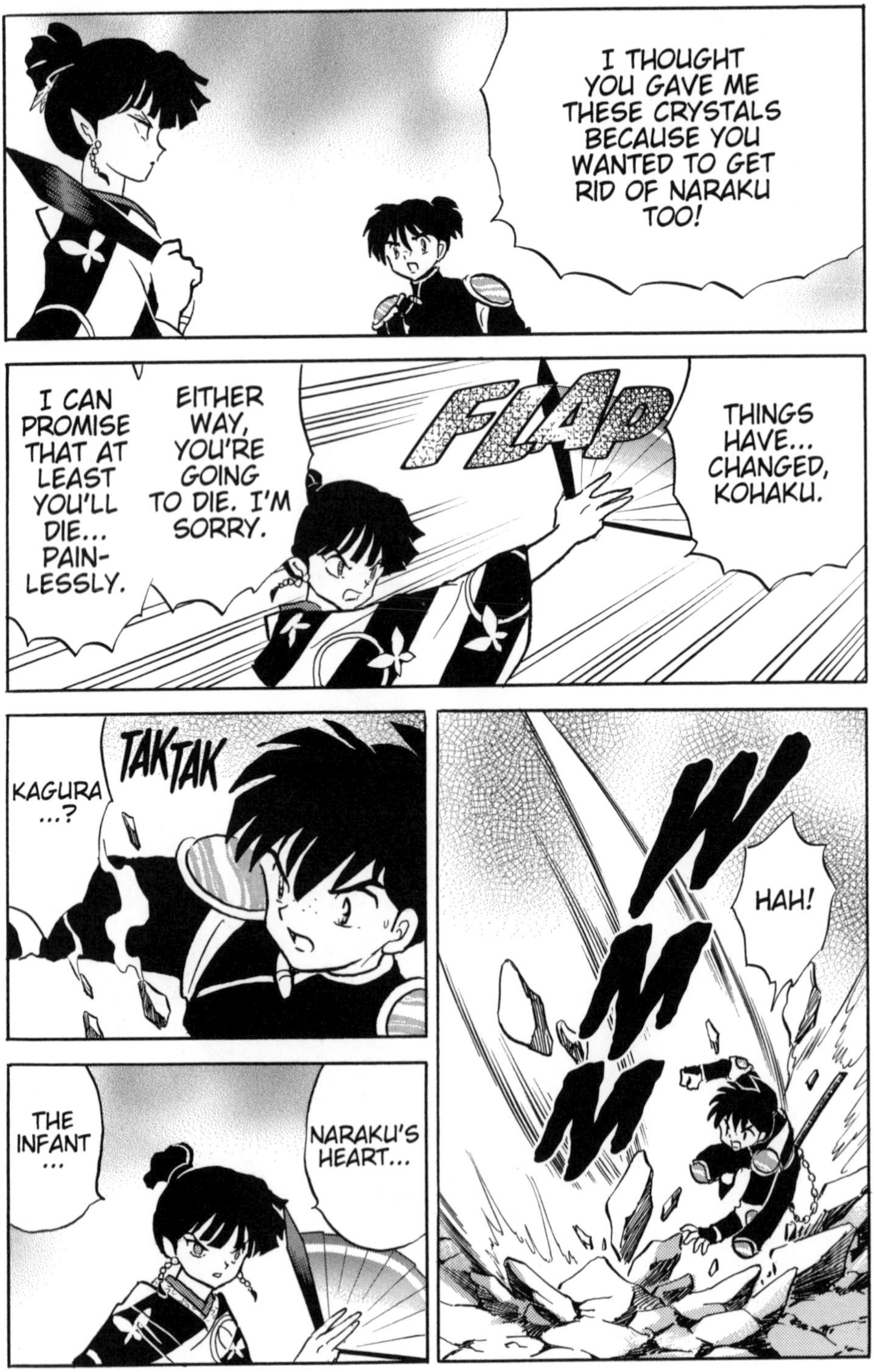

I THOUGHT YOU GAVE ME THESE CRYSTALS BECAUSE YOU WANTED TO GET RID OF NARAKU TOO!
THINGS HAVE... CHANGED, KOHAKU.
FLAP
EITHER WAY, YOU'RE GOING TO DIE. I'M SORRY.
I CAN PROMISE THAT AT LEAST YOU'LL DIE... PAIN-LESSLY.
HAH!
WMM
TAKTAK
KAGURA ...?
NARAKU'S HEART...
THE INFANT ...

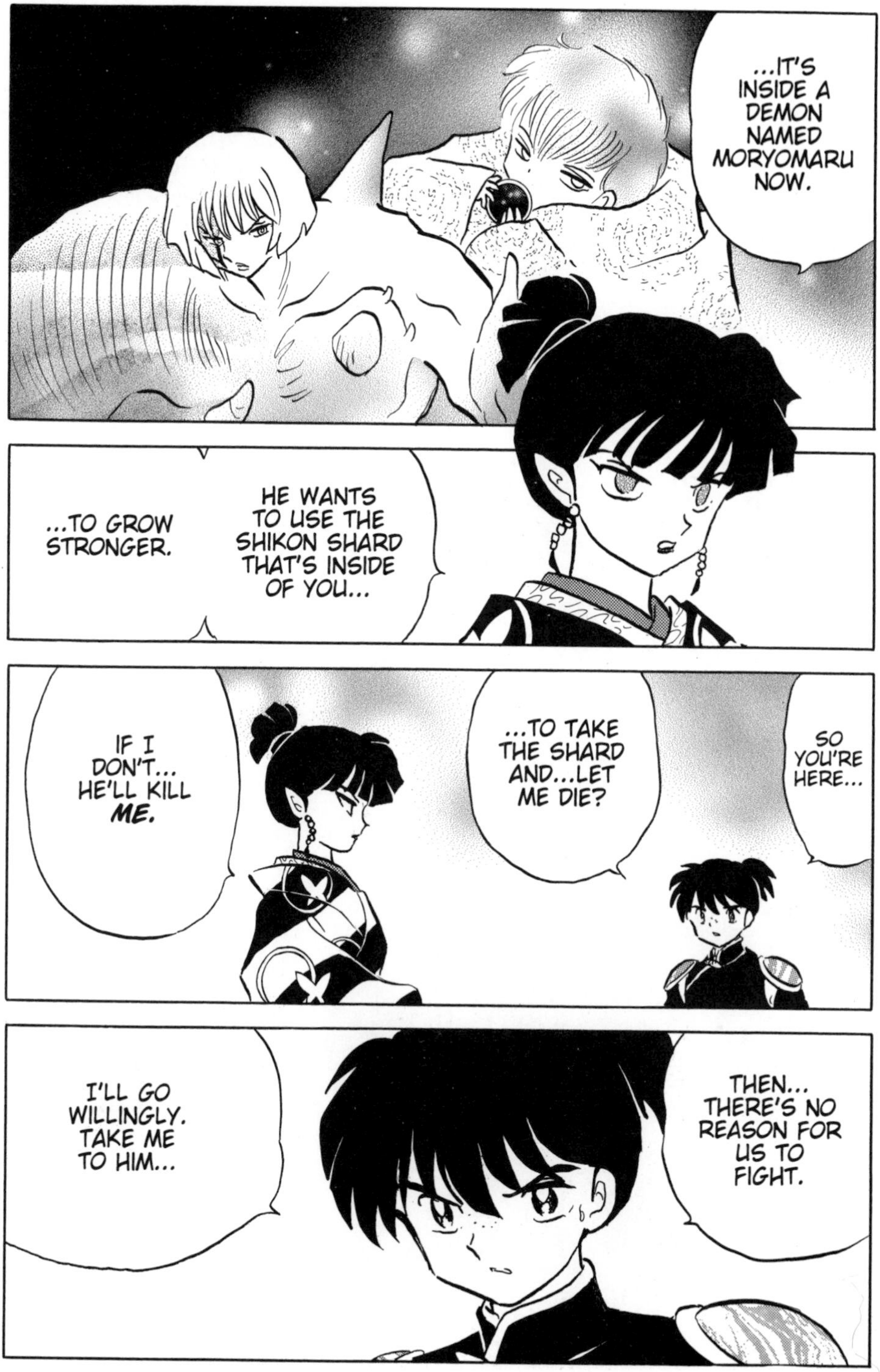
...IT'S INSIDE A DEMON NAMED MORYOMARU NOW.
HE WANTS TO USE THE SHIKON SHARD THAT'S INSIDE OF YOU...
...TO GROW STRONGER.
SO YOU'RE HERE...
...TO TAKE THE SHARD AND...LET ME DIE?
IF I DON'T... HE'LL KILL *ME.*
THEN... THERE'S NO REASON FOR US TO FIGHT.
I'LL GO WILLINGLY. TAKE ME TO HIM...

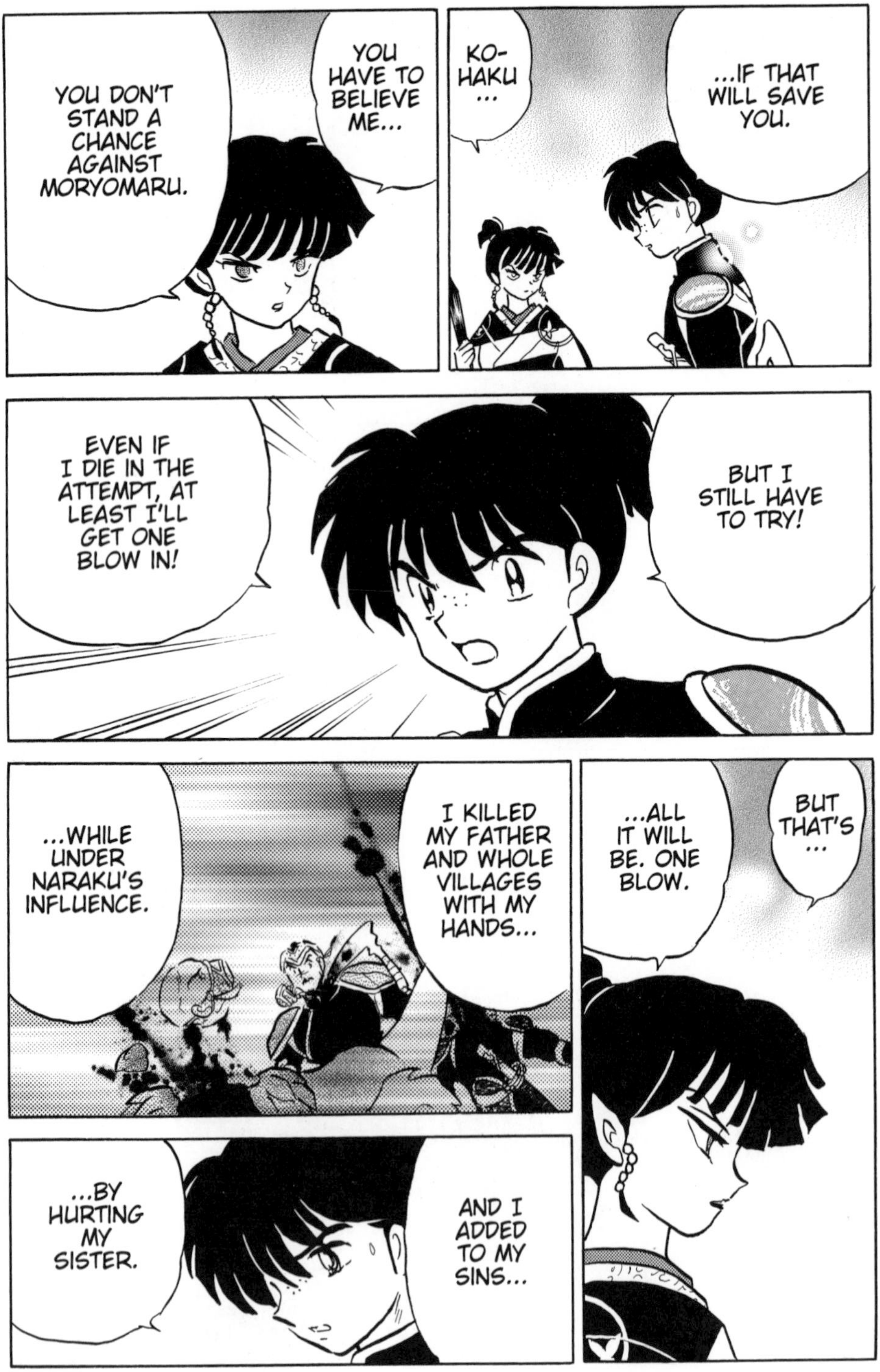
...IF THAT WILL SAVE YOU.
KO-HAKU ...
YOU HAVE TO BELIEVE ME...
YOU DON'T STAND A CHANCE AGAINST MORYOMARU.
BUT I STILL HAVE TO TRY!
EVEN IF I DIE IN THE ATTEMPT, AT LEAST I'LL GET ONE BLOW IN!
BUT THAT'S ...
...ALL IT WILL BE. ONE BLOW.
I KILLED MY FATHER AND WHOLE VILLAGES WITH MY HANDS...
...WHILE UNDER NARAKU'S INFLUENCE.
AND I ADDED TO MY SINS...
...BY HURTING MY SISTER.

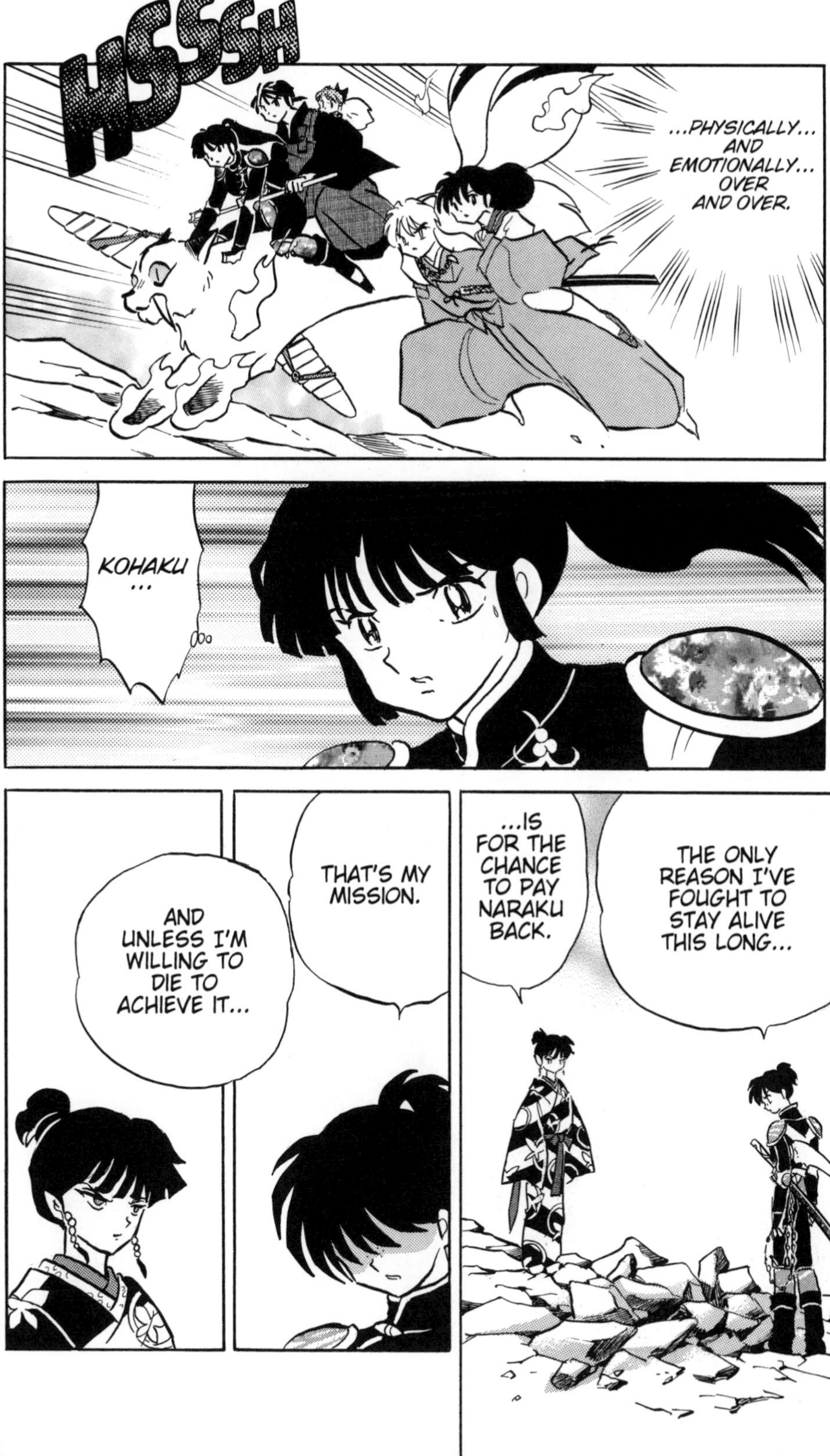
...PHYSICALLY... AND EMOTIONALLY... OVER AND OVER.
HSSSH
KOHAKU ...
THE ONLY REASON I'VE FOUGHT TO STAY ALIVE THIS LONG...
...IS FOR THE CHANCE TO PAY NARAKU BACK.
THAT'S MY MISSION.
AND UNLESS I'M WILLING TO DIE TO ACHIEVE IT...

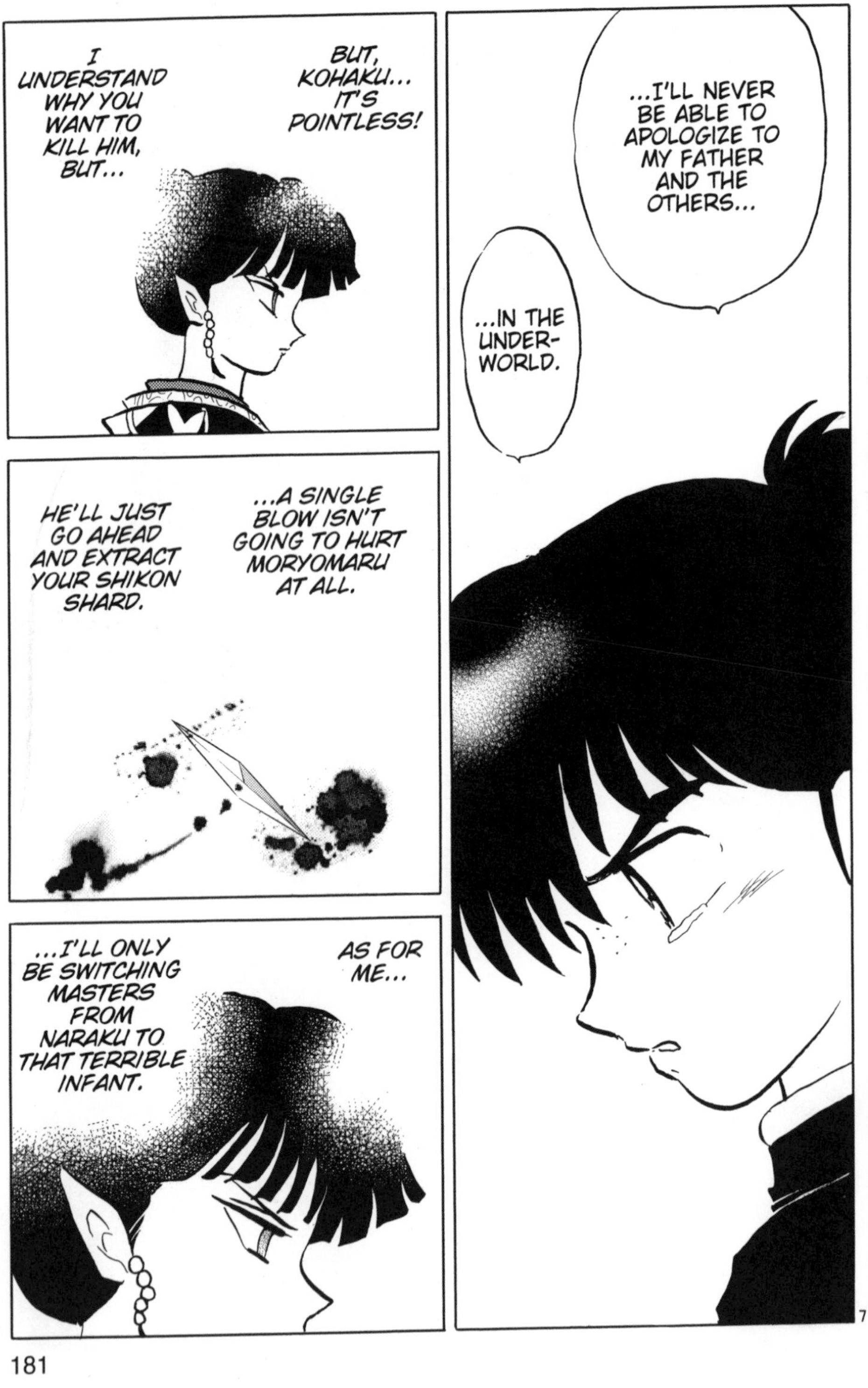
BUT, KOHAKU... IT'S POINTLESS!
I UNDERSTAND WHY YOU WANT TO KILL HIM, BUT...
...A SINGLE BLOW ISN'T GOING TO HURT MORYOMARU AT ALL.
HE'LL JUST GO AHEAD AND EXTRACT YOUR SHIKON SHARD.
AS FOR ME...
...I'LL ONLY BE SWITCHING MASTERS FROM NARAKU TO THAT TERRIBLE INFANT.
...I'LL NEVER BE ABLE TO APOLOGIZE TO MY FATHER AND THE OTHERS...
...IN THE UNDER-WORLD.

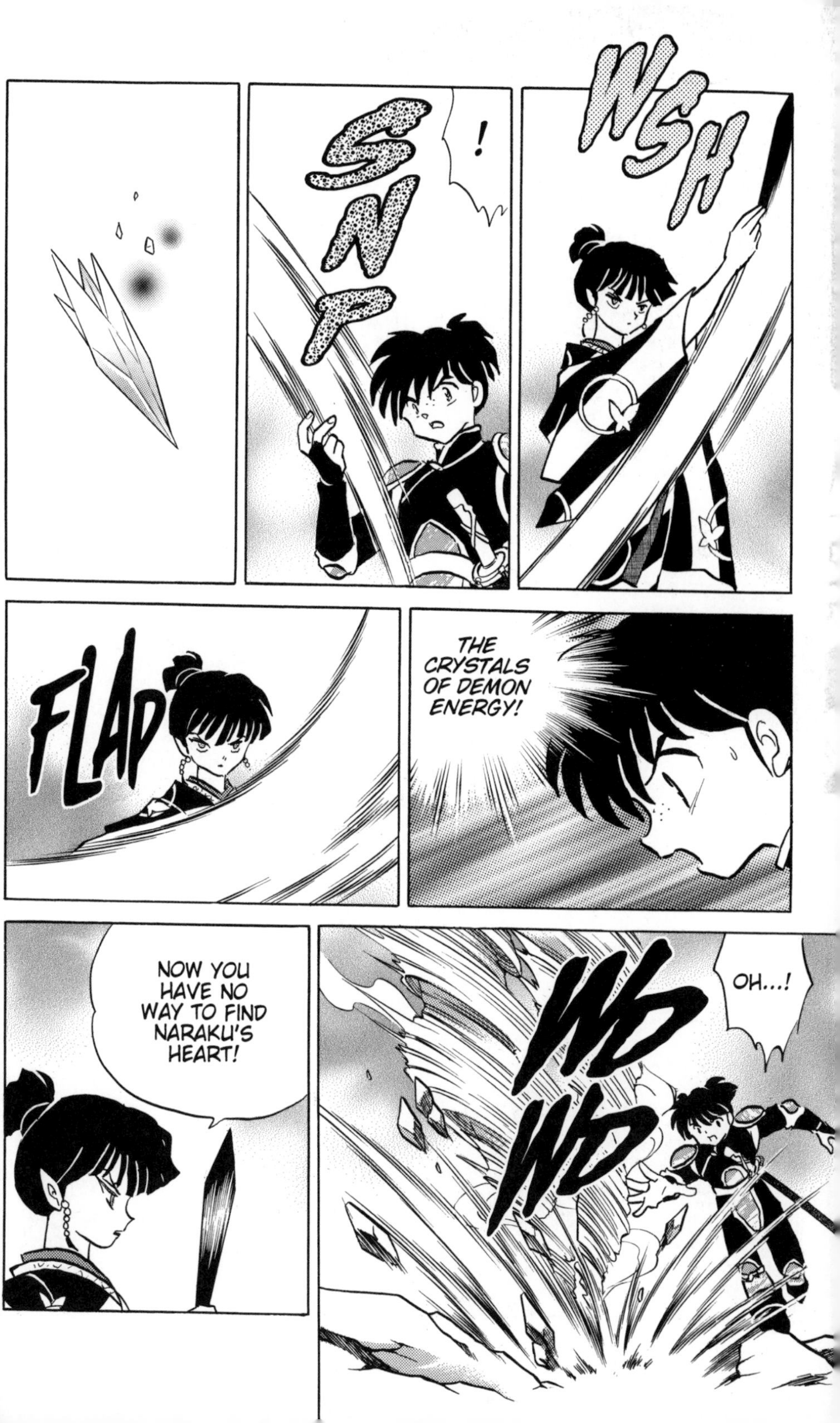
WSH
SNP
!
THE CRYSTALS OF DEMON ENERGY!
FLAP
OH...!
WO WO
NOW YOU HAVE NO WAY TO FIND NARAKU'S HEART!

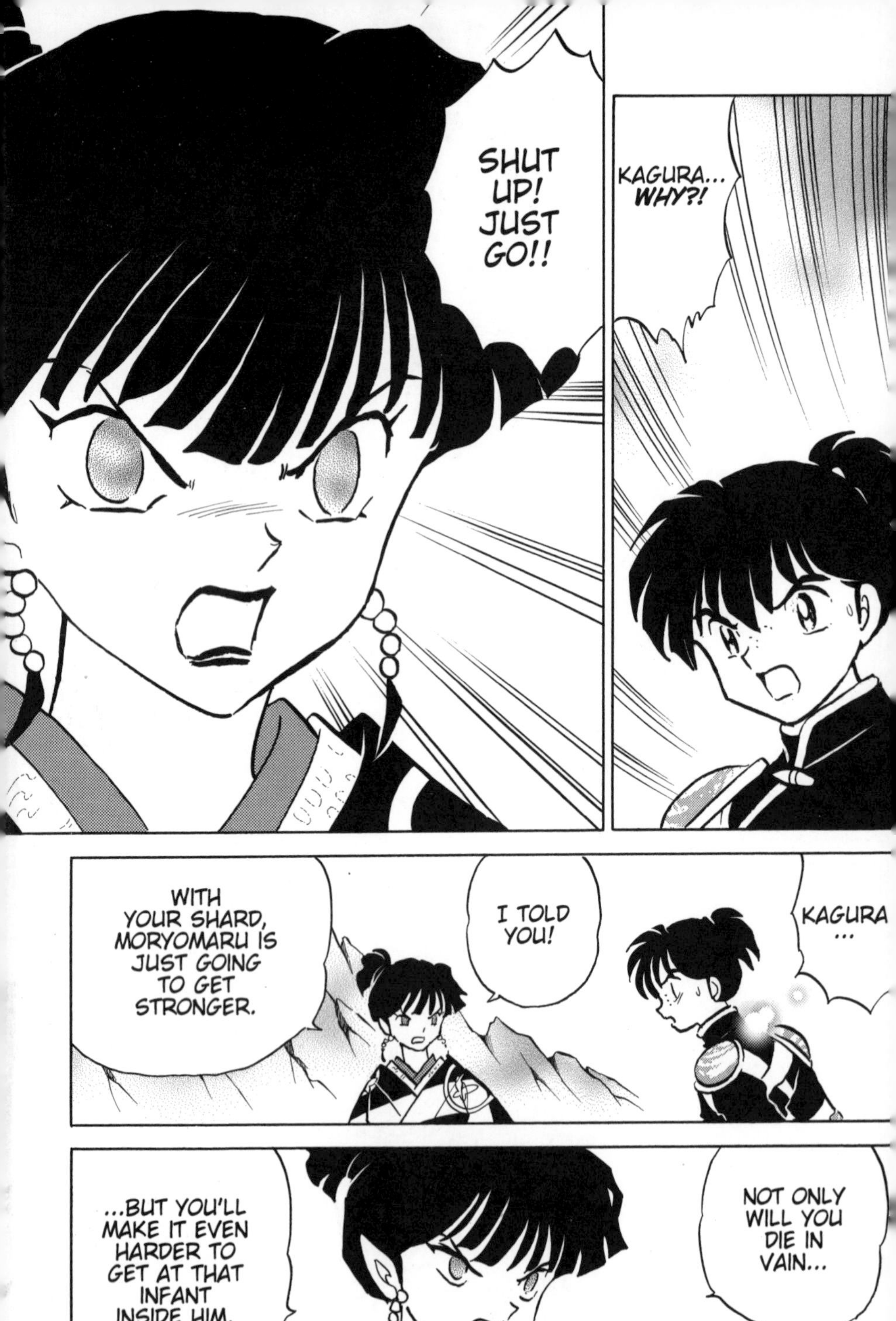
KAGURA... WHY?!
SHUT UP! JUST GO!!
KAGURA ...
I TOLD YOU!
WITH YOUR SHARD, MORYOMARU IS JUST GOING TO GET STRONGER.
NOT ONLY WILL YOU DIE IN VAIN...
...BUT YOU'LL MAKE IT EVEN HARDER TO GET AT THAT INFANT INSIDE HIM.

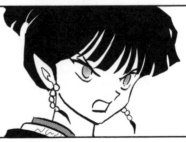

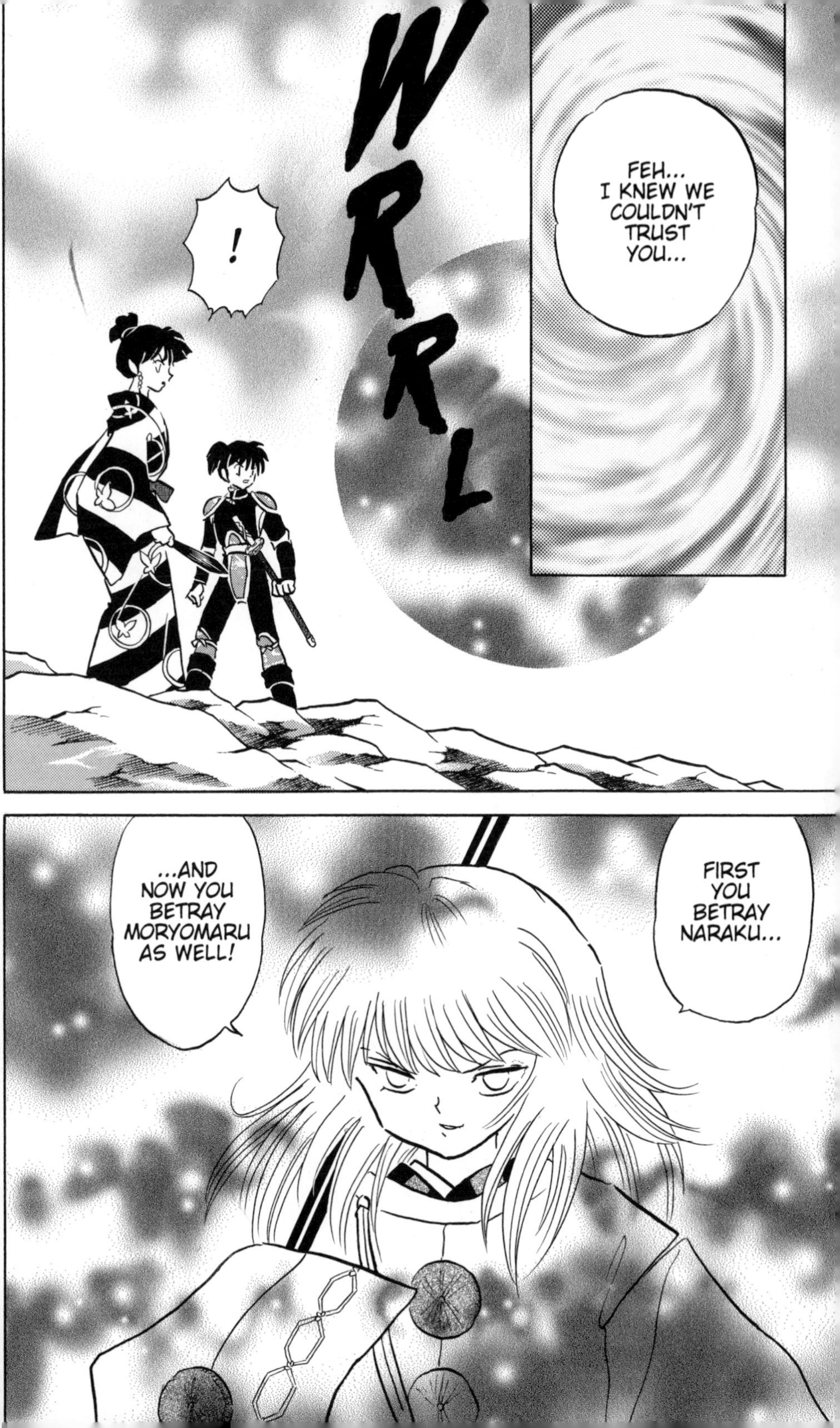
FEH... I KNEW WE COULDN'T TRUST YOU...
WRRL
!
FIRST YOU BETRAY NARAKU...
...AND NOW YOU BETRAY MORYOMARU AS WELL!

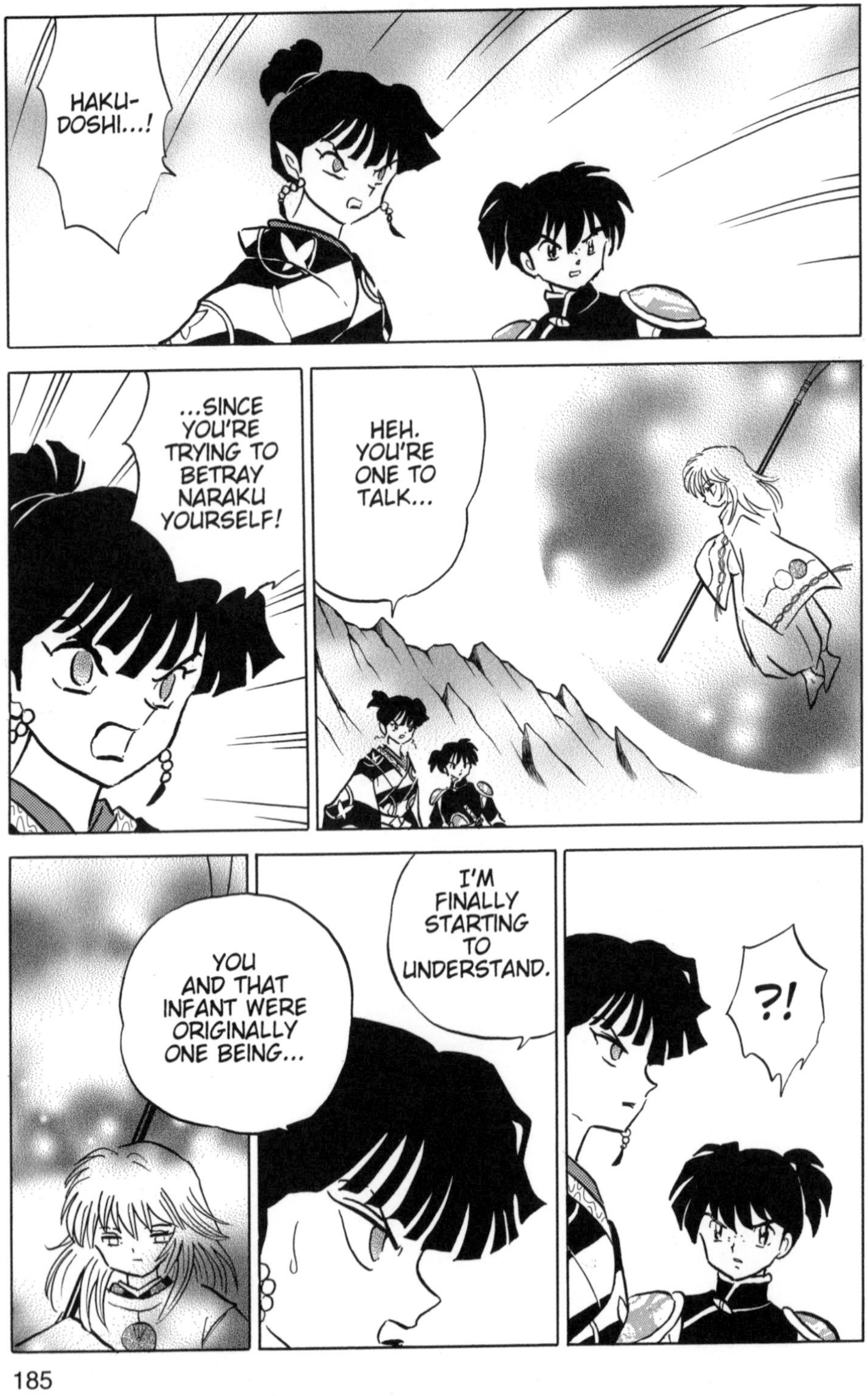
HAKU-DOSHI...!
HEH. YOU'RE ONE TO TALK...
...SINCE YOU'RE TRYING TO BETRAY NARAKU YOURSELF!
?!
I'M FINALLY STARTING TO UNDERSTAND.
YOU AND THAT INFANT WERE ORIGINALLY ONE BEING...

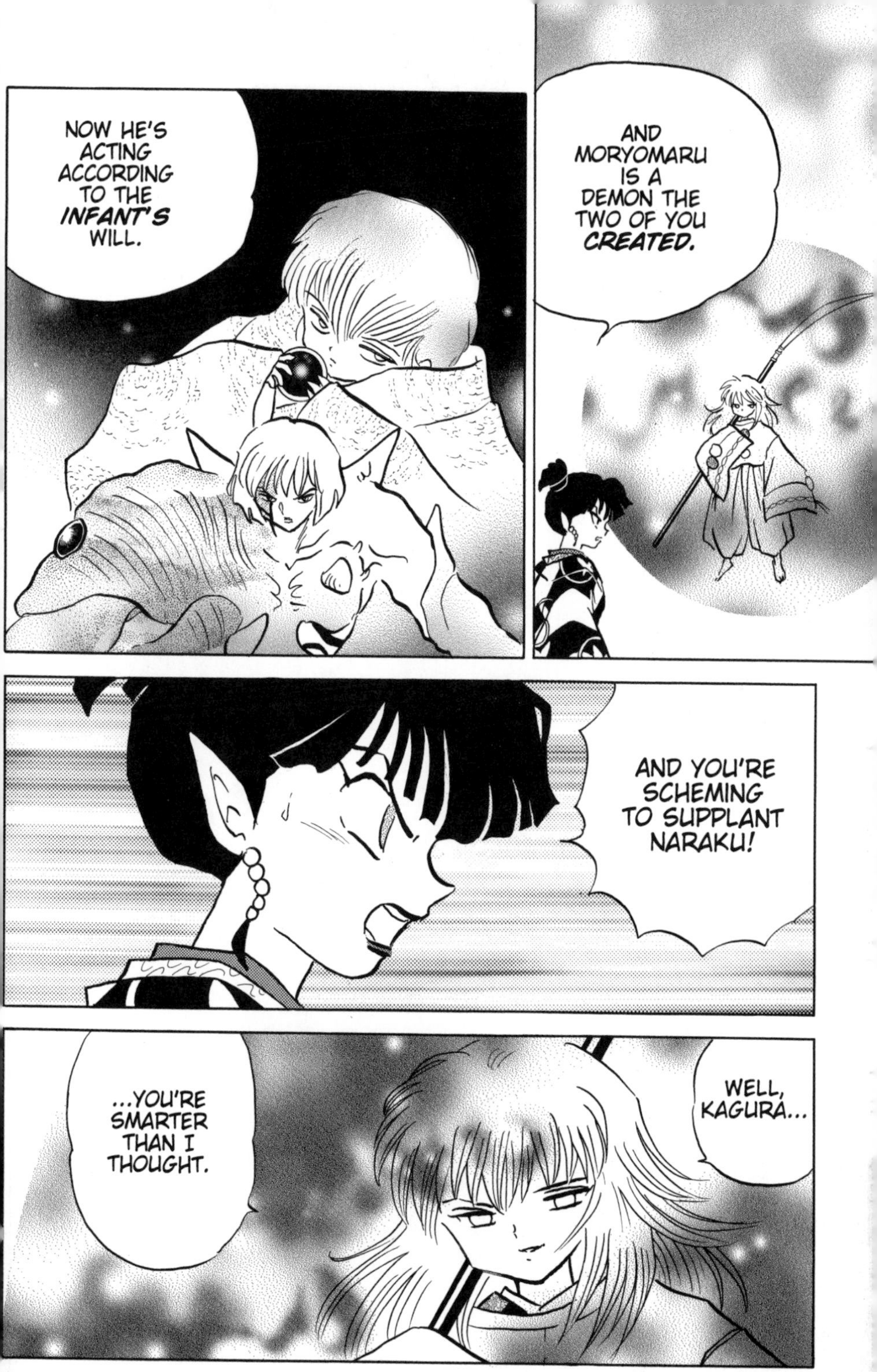
AND MORYOMARU IS A DEMON THE TWO OF YOU *CREATED.*
NOW HE'S ACTING ACCORDING TO THE *INFANT'S* WILL.
AND YOU'RE SCHEMING TO SUPPLANT NARAKU!
WELL, KAGURA...
...YOU'RE SMARTER THAN I THOUGHT.

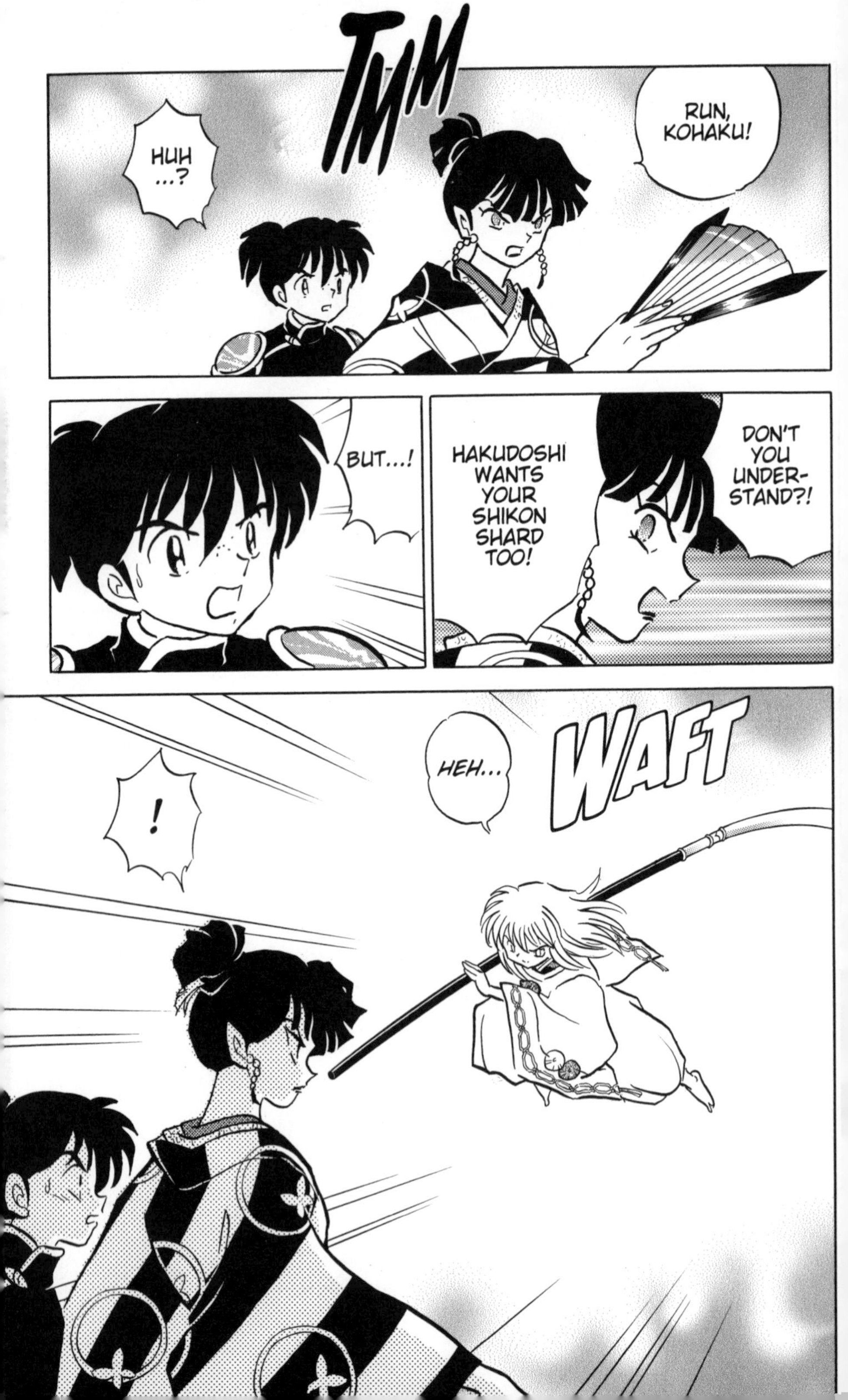
RUN, KOHAKU!
TMM
HUH...?
DON'T YOU UNDERSTAND?!
HAKUDOSHI WANTS YOUR SHIKON SHARD TOO!
BUT...!
WAFT
HEH...
!

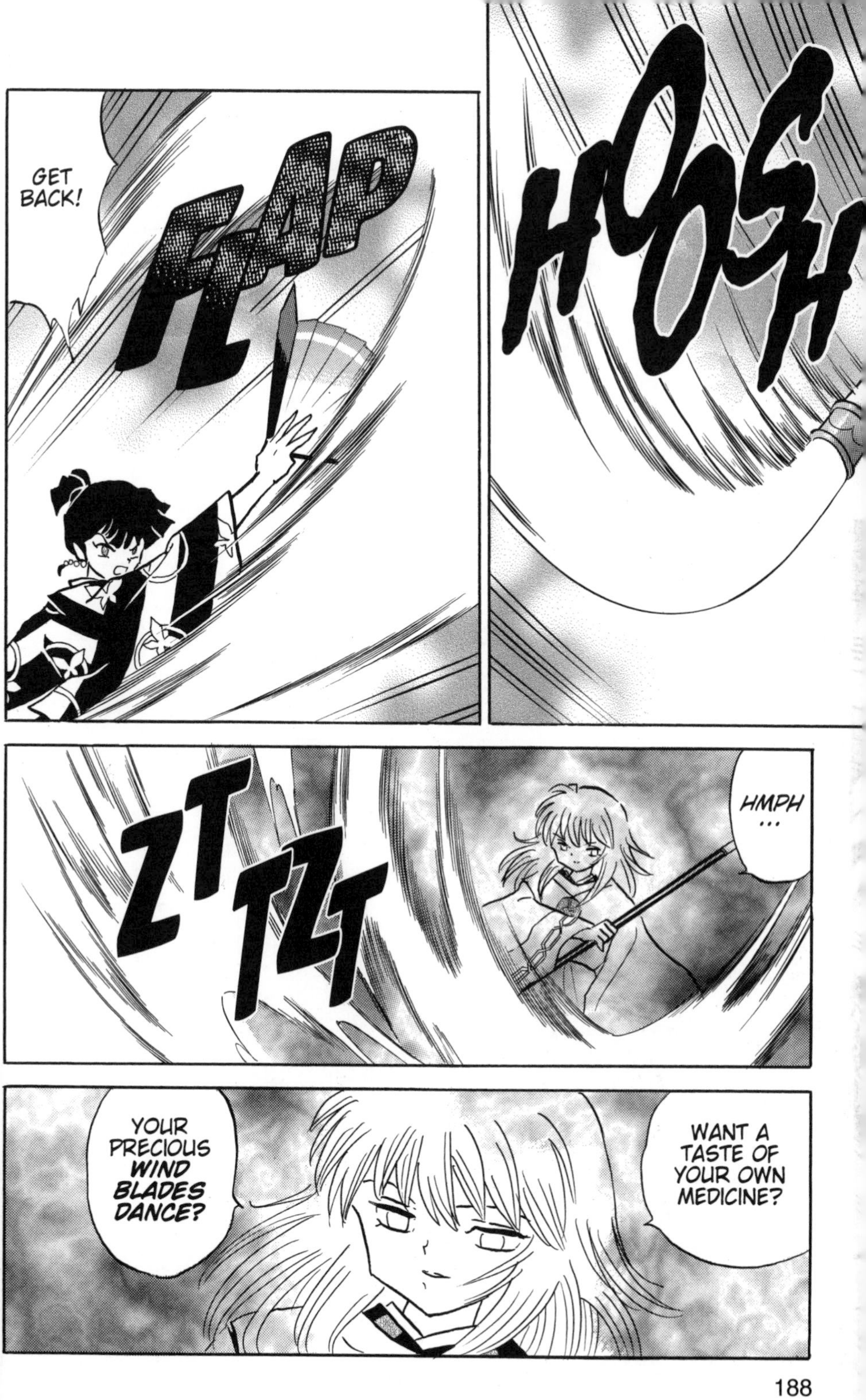
HOOSH
FLAP
GET BACK!
HMPH ...
ZT TZT
WANT A TASTE OF YOUR OWN MEDICINE?
YOUR PRECIOUS *WIND BLADES DANCE?*

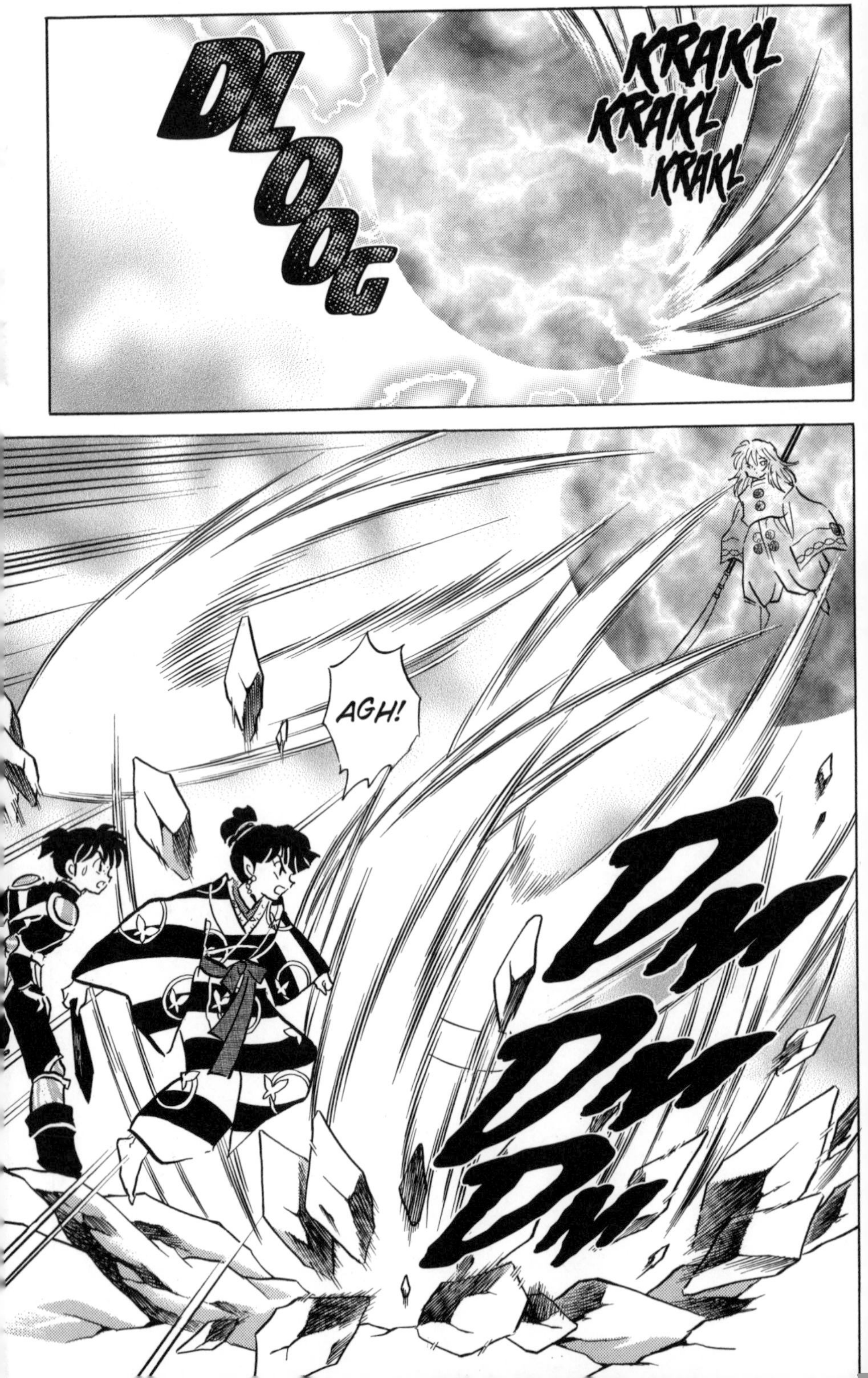
KRAKL
KRAKL
KRAKL
DLOOG
AGH!
DM
DM
DM

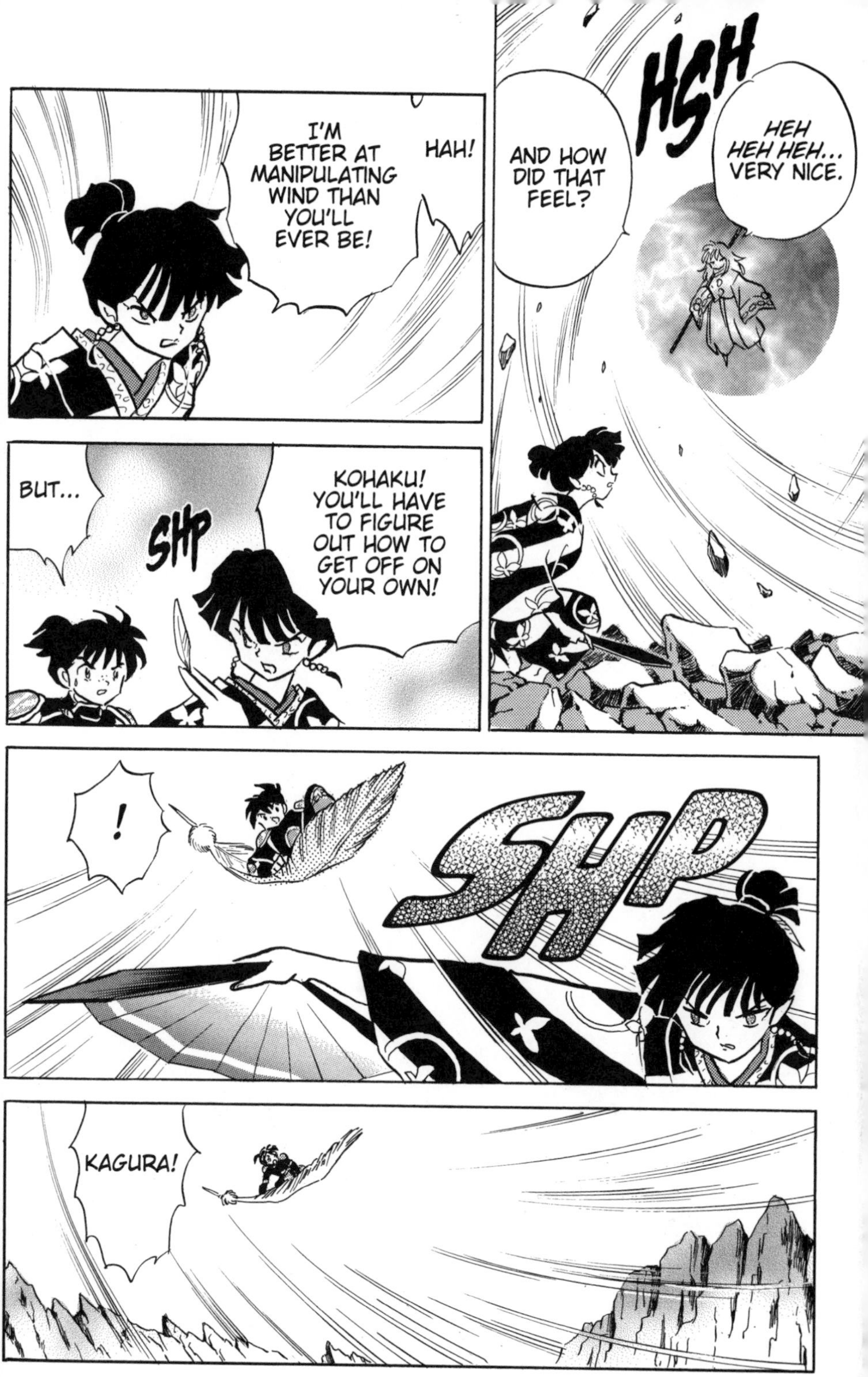
HSH
HEH HEH HEH... VERY NICE.
AND HOW DID THAT FEEL?
HAH!
I'M BETTER AT MANIPULATING WIND THAN YOU'LL EVER BE!
KOHAKU! YOU'LL HAVE TO FIGURE OUT HOW TO GET OFF ON YOUR OWN!
SHP
BUT...
SHP
!
KAGURA!

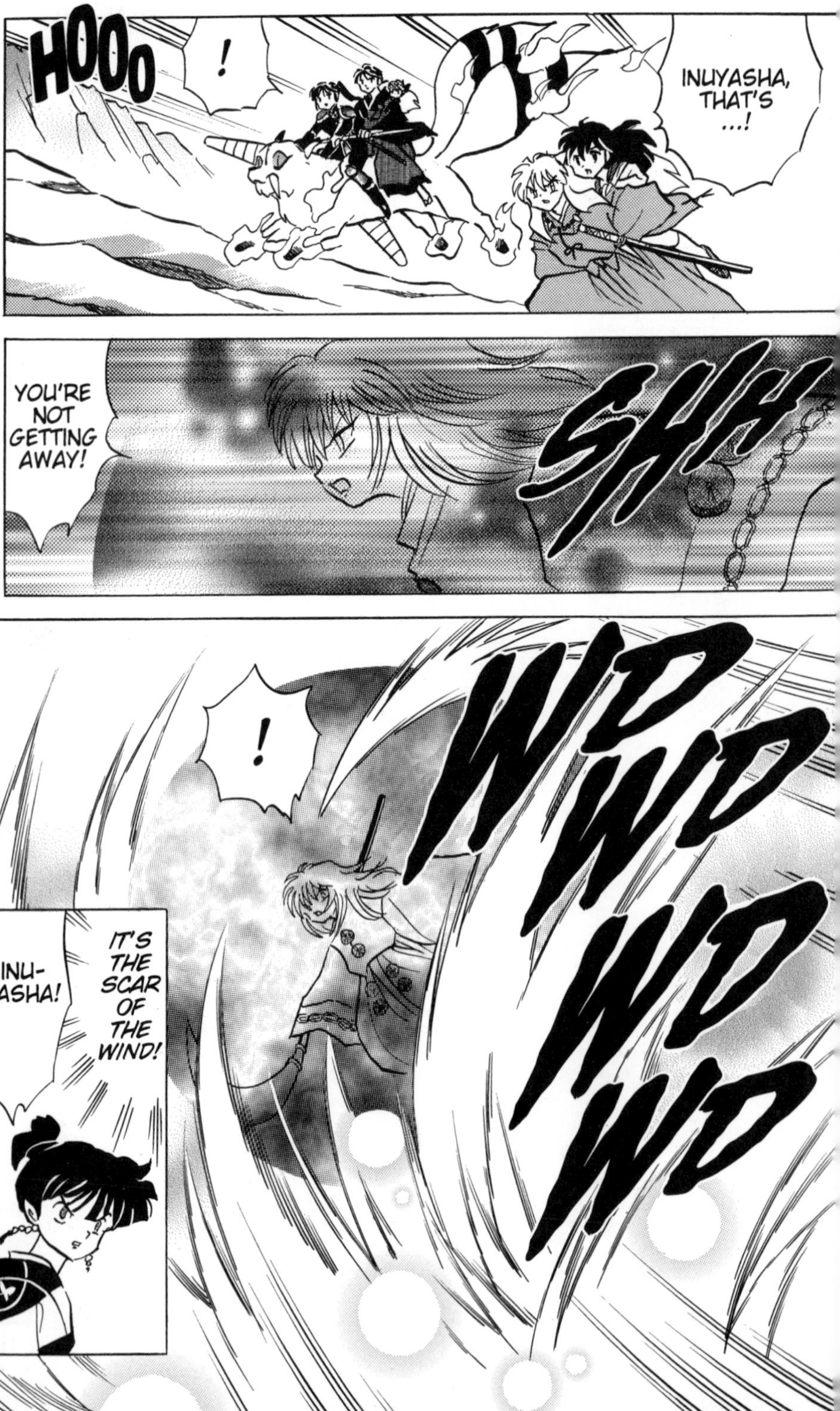
INUYASHA, THAT'S ...!
!
HOOO
SHH
YOU'RE NOT GETTING AWAY!
WID WID WID WID WID
!
IT'S THE SCAR OF THE WIND!
INU-YASHA!

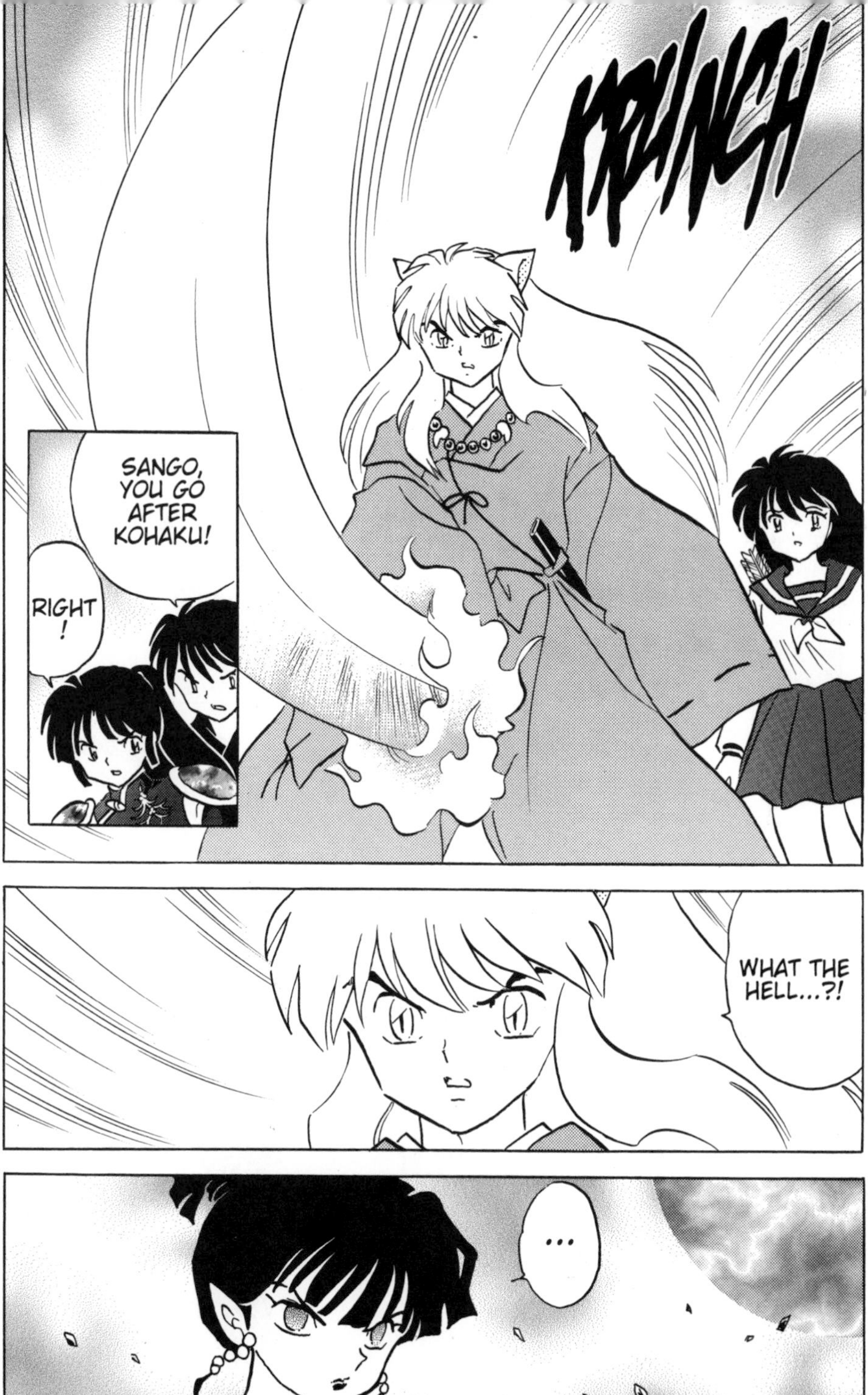
KRUNCH
SANGO, YOU GO AFTER KOHAKU!
RIGHT!
WHAT THE HELL...?!
...

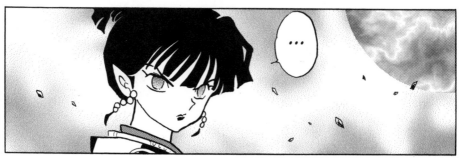

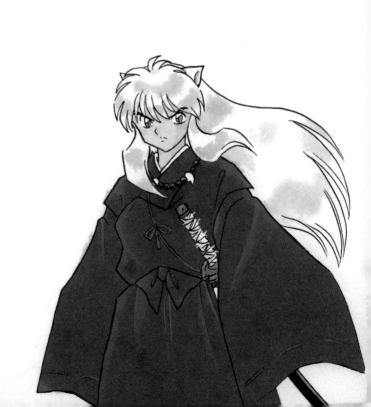

InuYasha

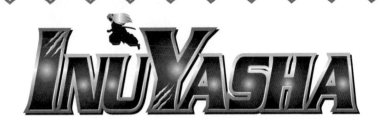

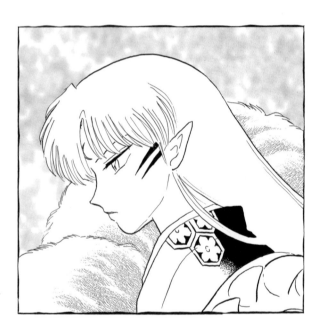

Volume 38

The Wind

SCROLL ONE
HAKUDOSHI'S SCHEME

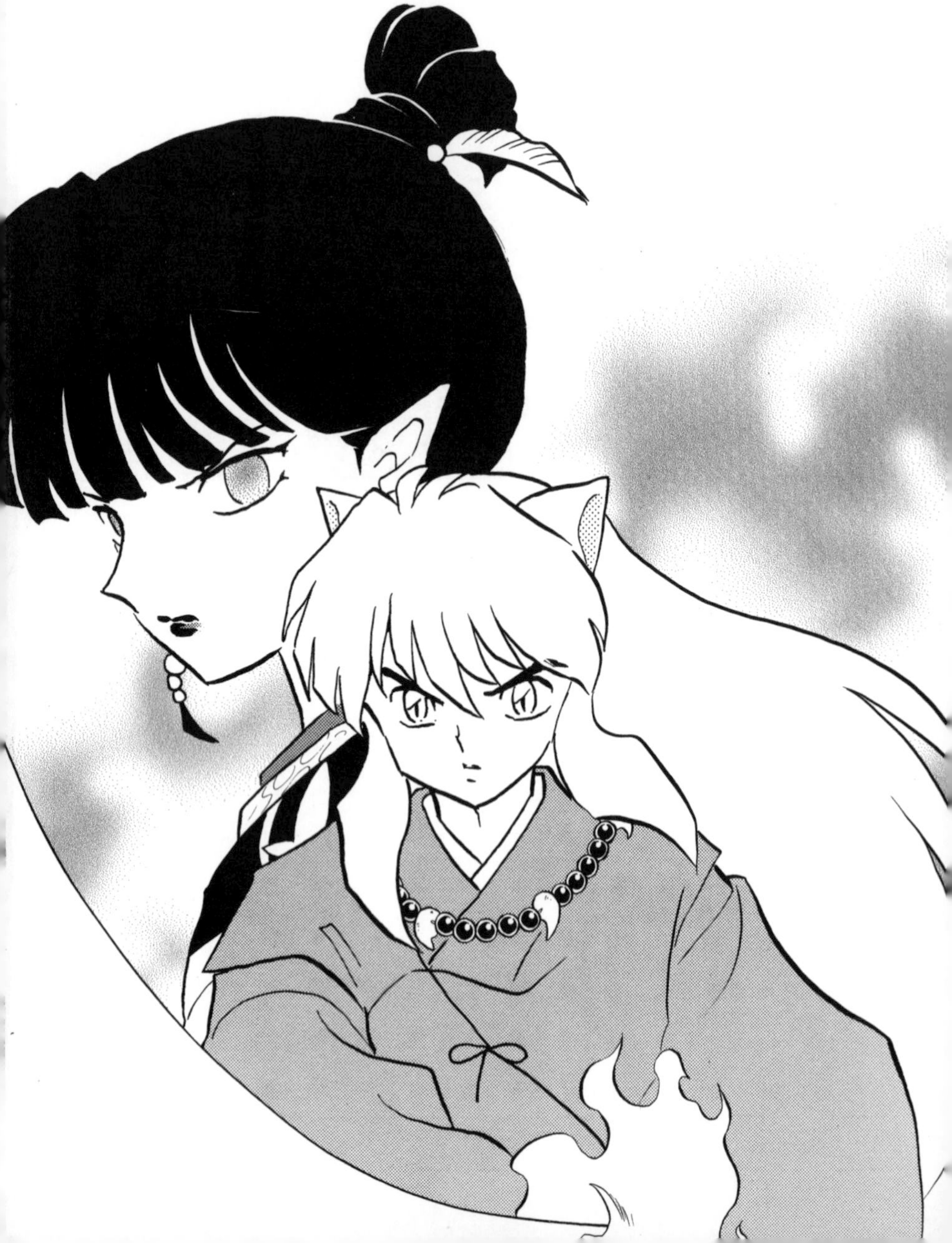

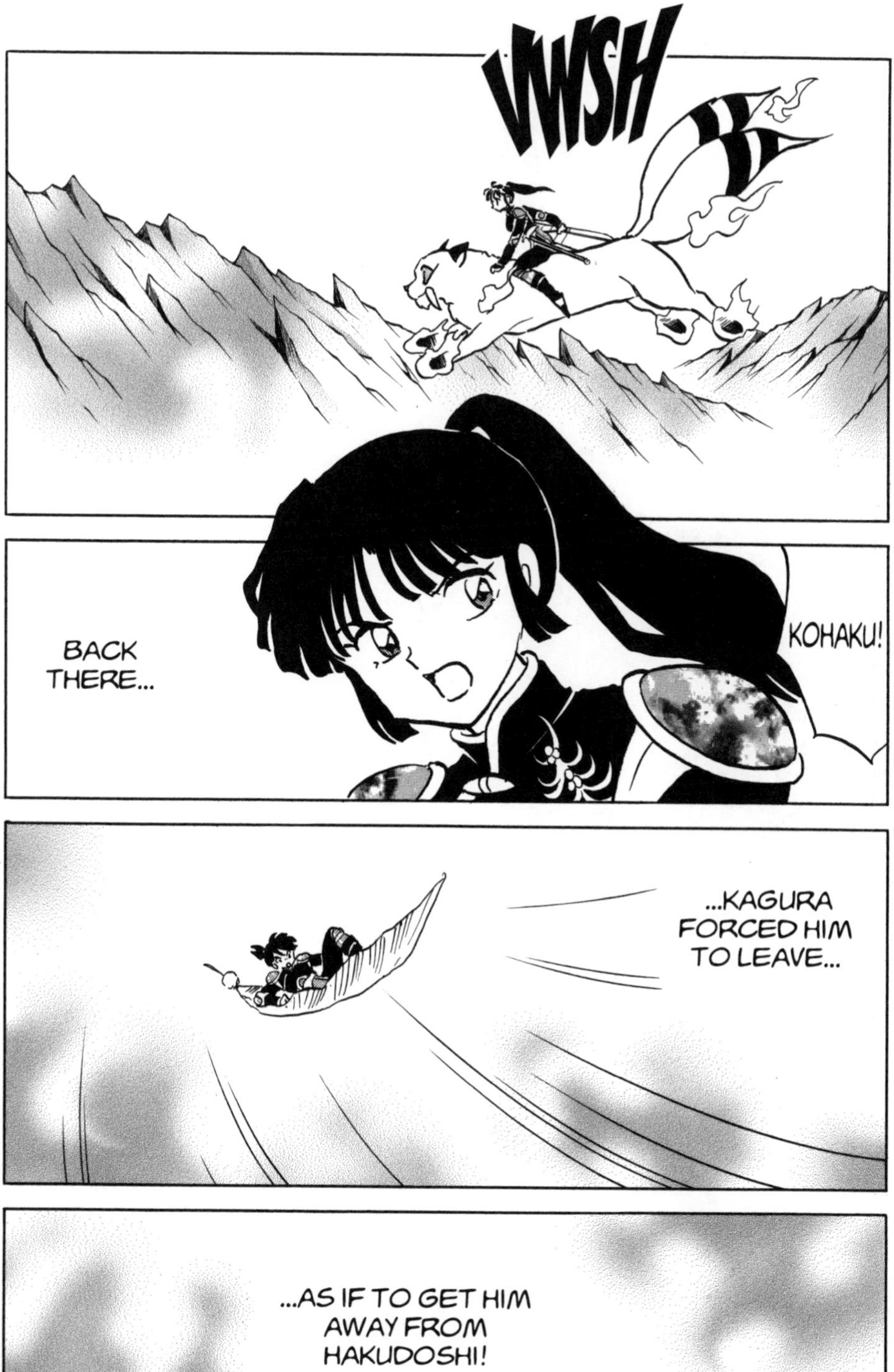
VWSH
KOHAKU!
BACK THERE...
...KAGURA FORCED HIM TO LEAVE...
...AS IF TO GET HIM AWAY FROM HAKUDOSHI!

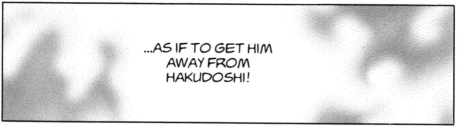

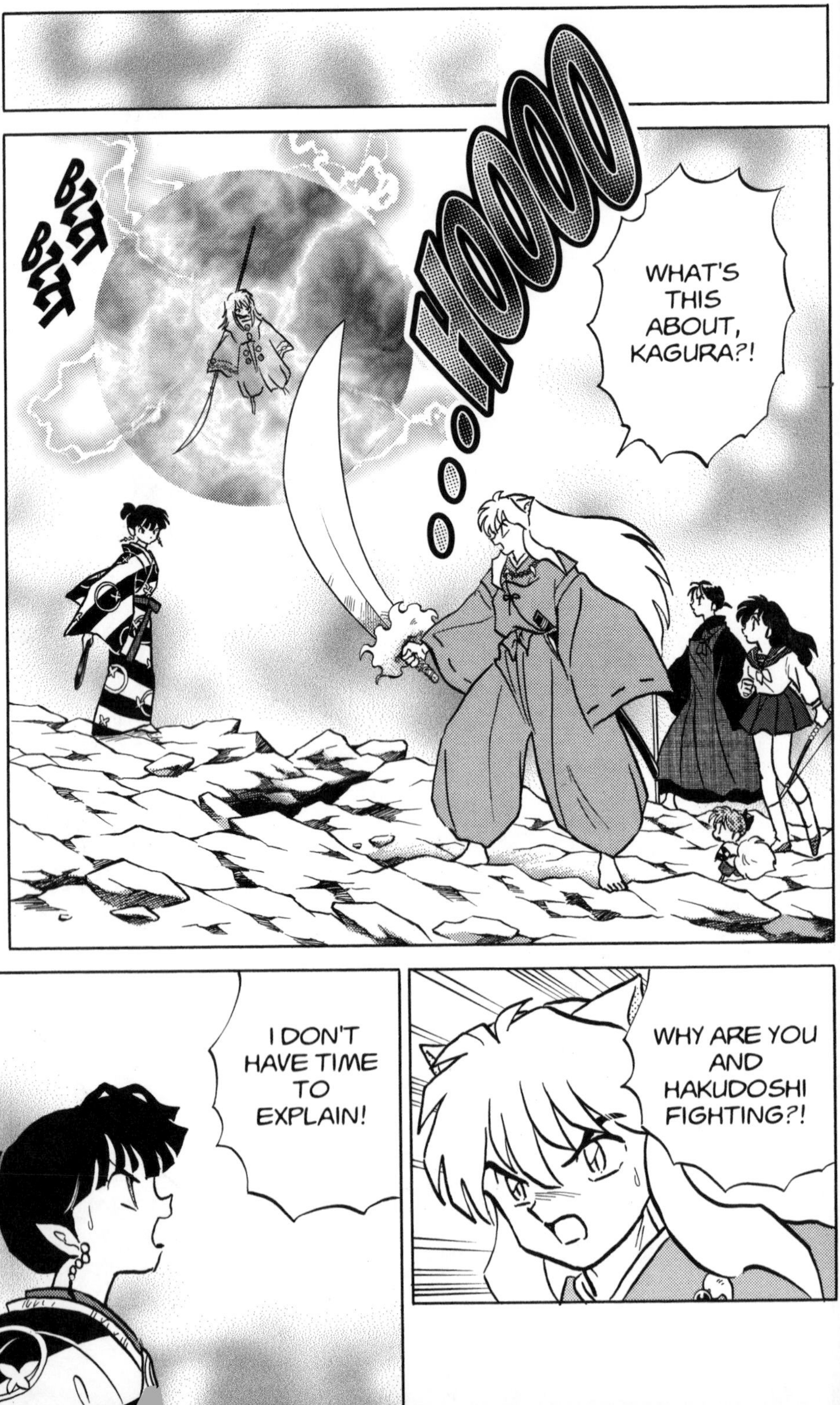
WHAT'S THIS ABOUT, KAGURA?!
...HOOOO
BZZT BZZT
WHY ARE YOU AND HAKUDOSHI FIGHTING?!
I DON'T HAVE TIME TO EXPLAIN!

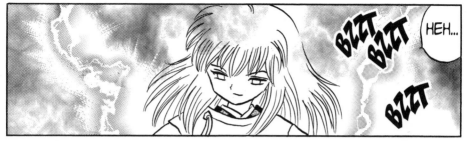

HEH...

BZZT BZZT

BZZT

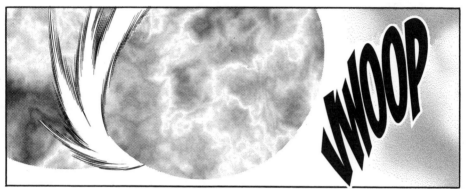

VWOOP

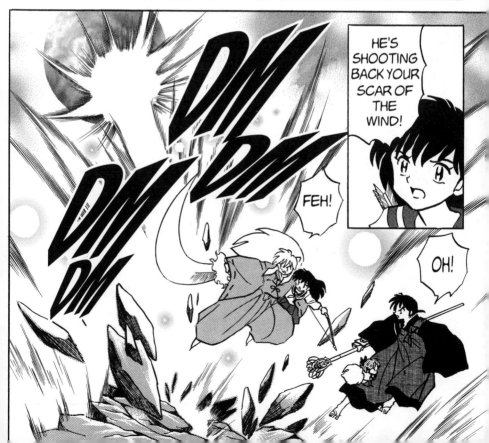

HE'S SHOOTING BACK YOUR SCAR OF THE WIND!

FEH!

OH!

DM DM DM DM

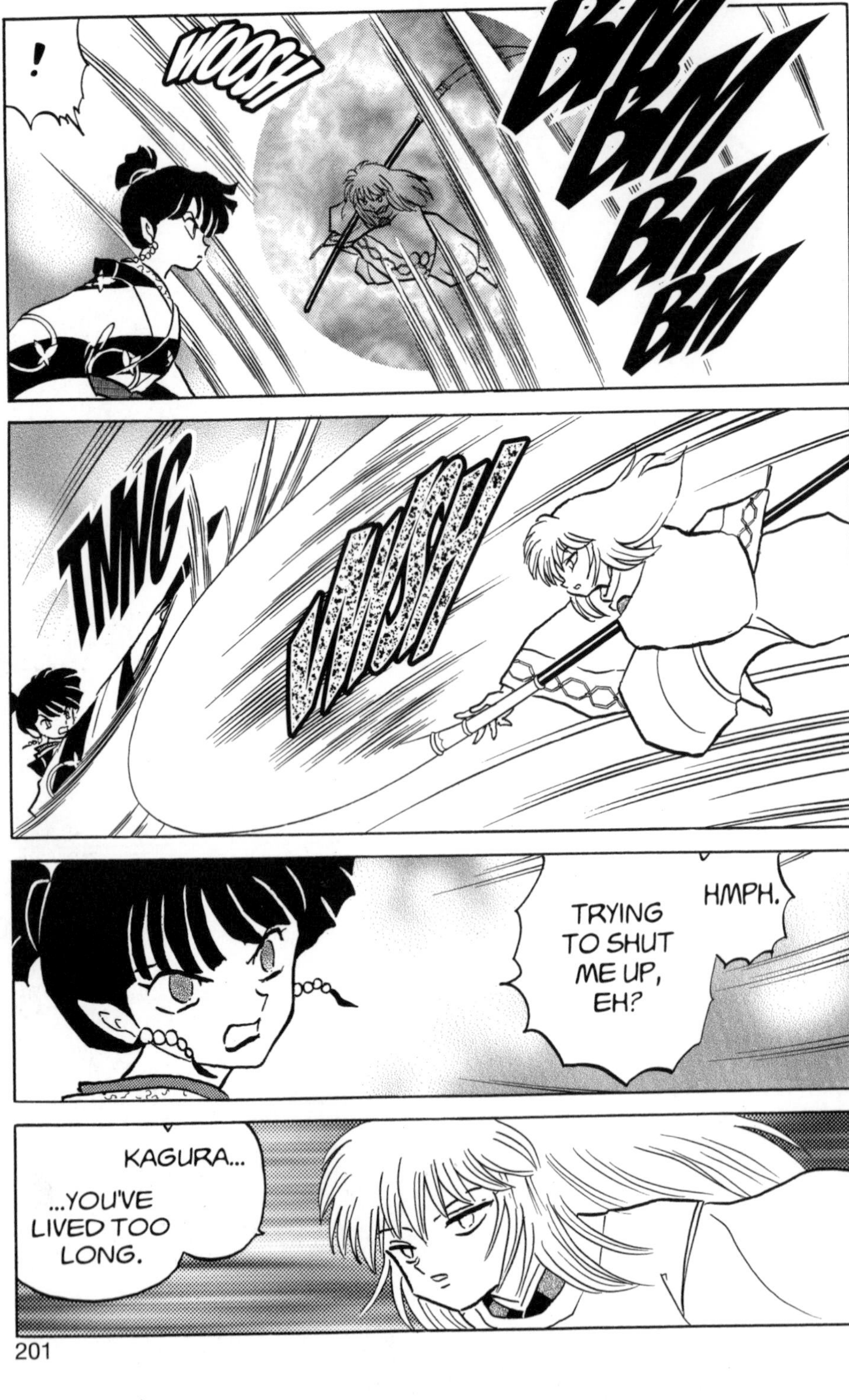
BAM BAM BAM BAM
WOOSH
!
TWNG...
HMPH.
TRYING TO SHUT ME UP, EH?
KAGURA...
...YOU'VE LIVED TOO LONG.

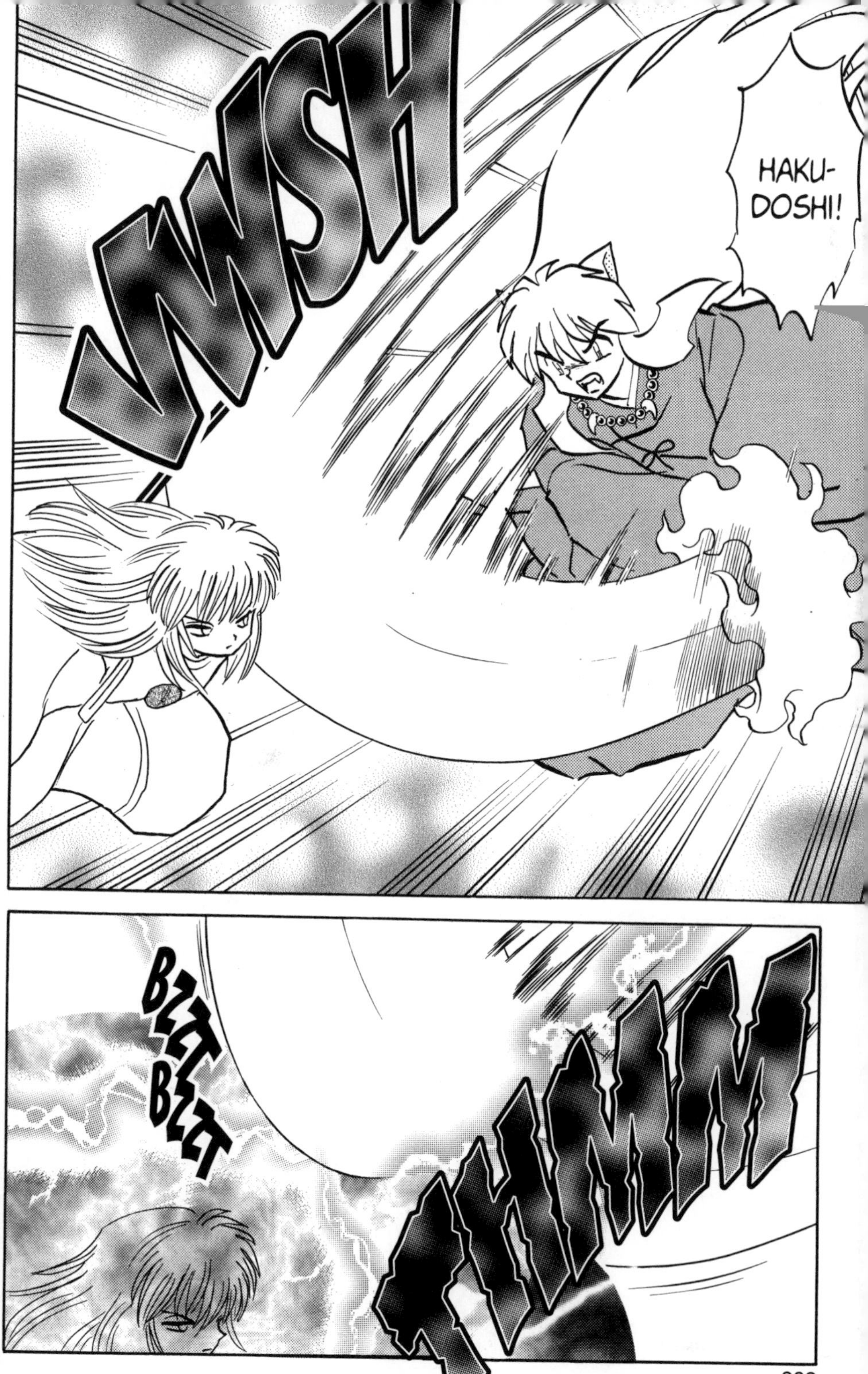
HAKU-
DOSHI!
VWSH
BZZT BZZT
THMM

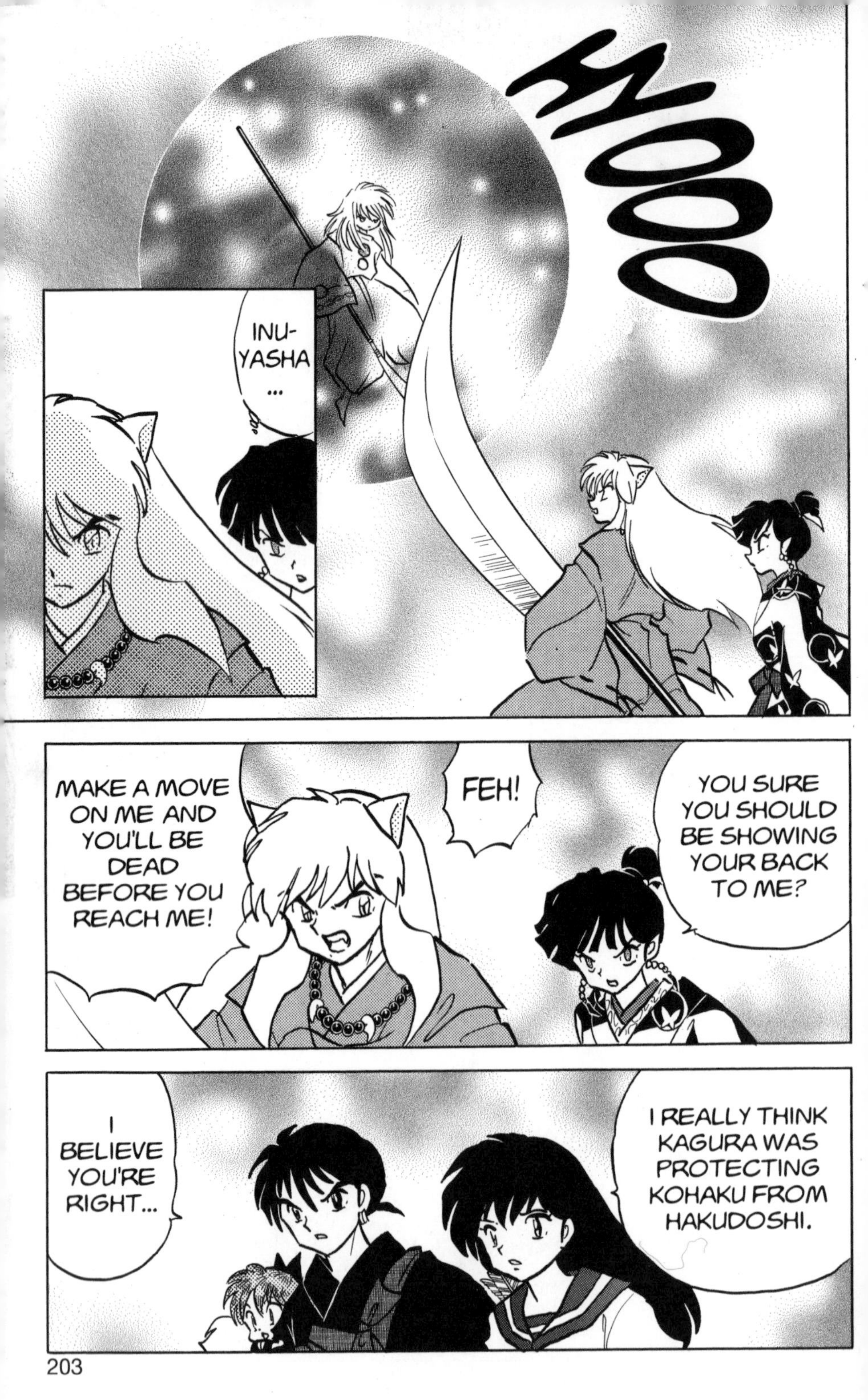
HYOOO
INU-YASHA ...
YOU SURE YOU SHOULD BE SHOWING YOUR BACK TO ME?
FEH!
MAKE A MOVE ON ME AND YOU'LL BE DEAD BEFORE YOU REACH ME!
I REALLY THINK KAGURA WAS PROTECTING KOHAKU FROM HAKUDOSHI.
I BELIEVE YOU'RE RIGHT...

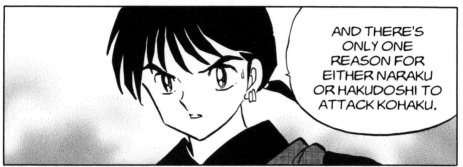

AND THERE'S ONLY ONE REASON FOR EITHER NARAKU OR HAKUDOSHI TO ATTACK KOHAKU.
TO GET THE SHIKON SHARD EMBEDDED IN HIM!
KAGURA! JUST SPIT OUT EVERYTHING YOU KNOW!
UNLESS YOU THINK YOU CAN TRUST HAKUDOSHI MORE.
I MEAN, MAYBE HE'S HANGING AROUND TO MAKE SURE YOU'RE OKAY...

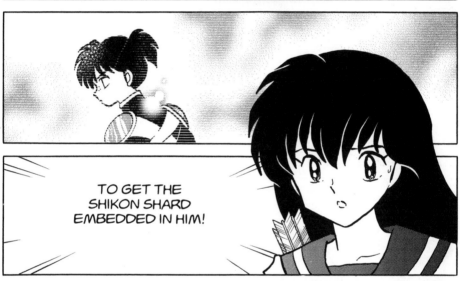

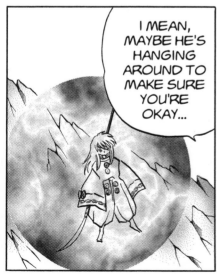

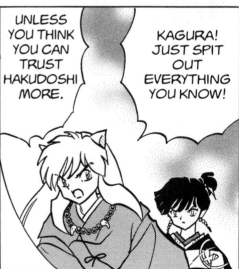

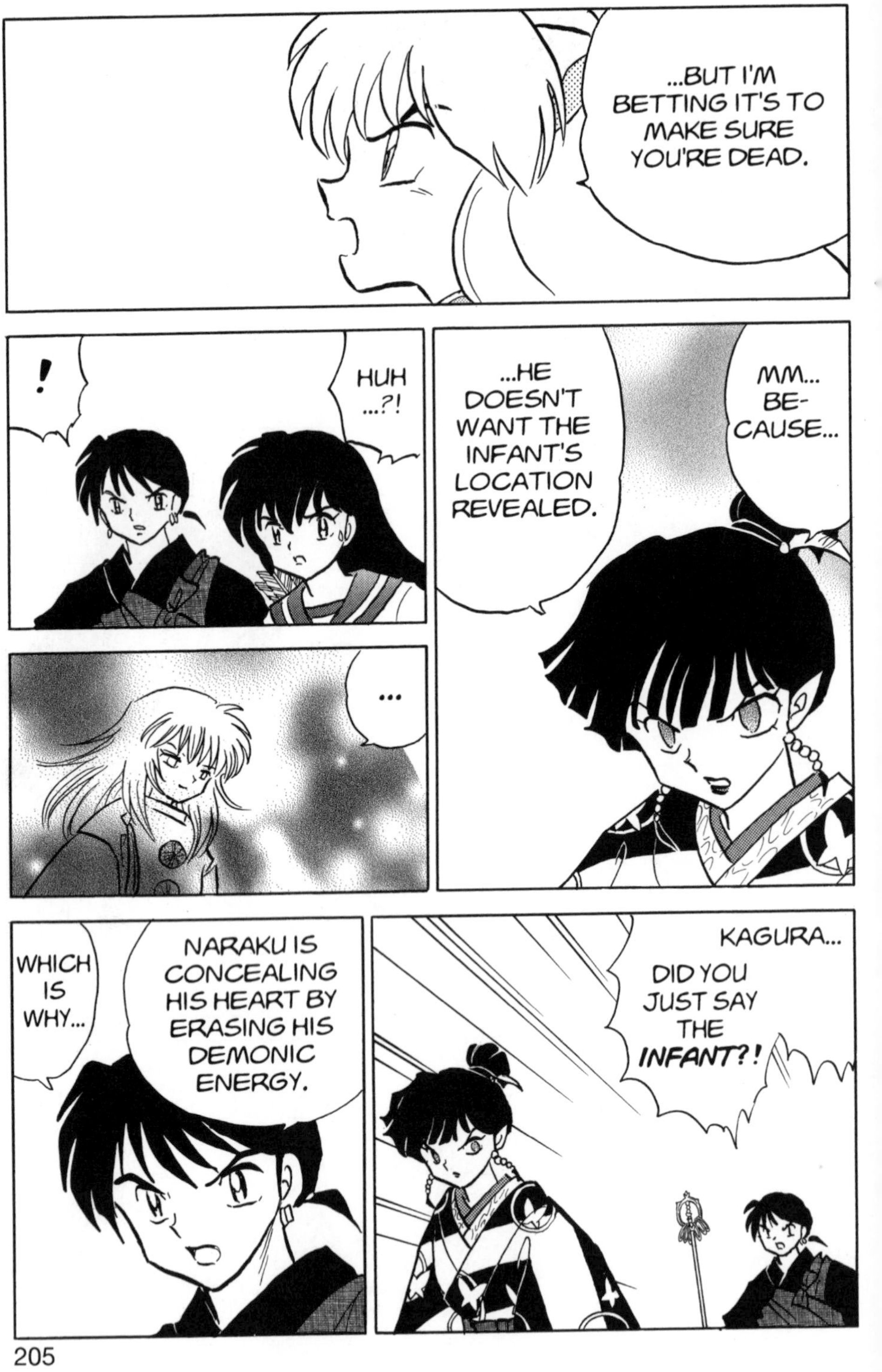
...BUT I'M BETTING IT'S TO MAKE SURE YOU'RE DEAD.
MM... BE-CAUSE...
...HE DOESN'T WANT THE INFANT'S LOCATION REVEALED.
HUH ...?!
!
...
KAGURA...
DID YOU JUST SAY THE *INFANT?!*
NARAKU IS CONCEALING HIS HEART BY ERASING HIS DEMONIC ENERGY.
WHICH IS WHY...

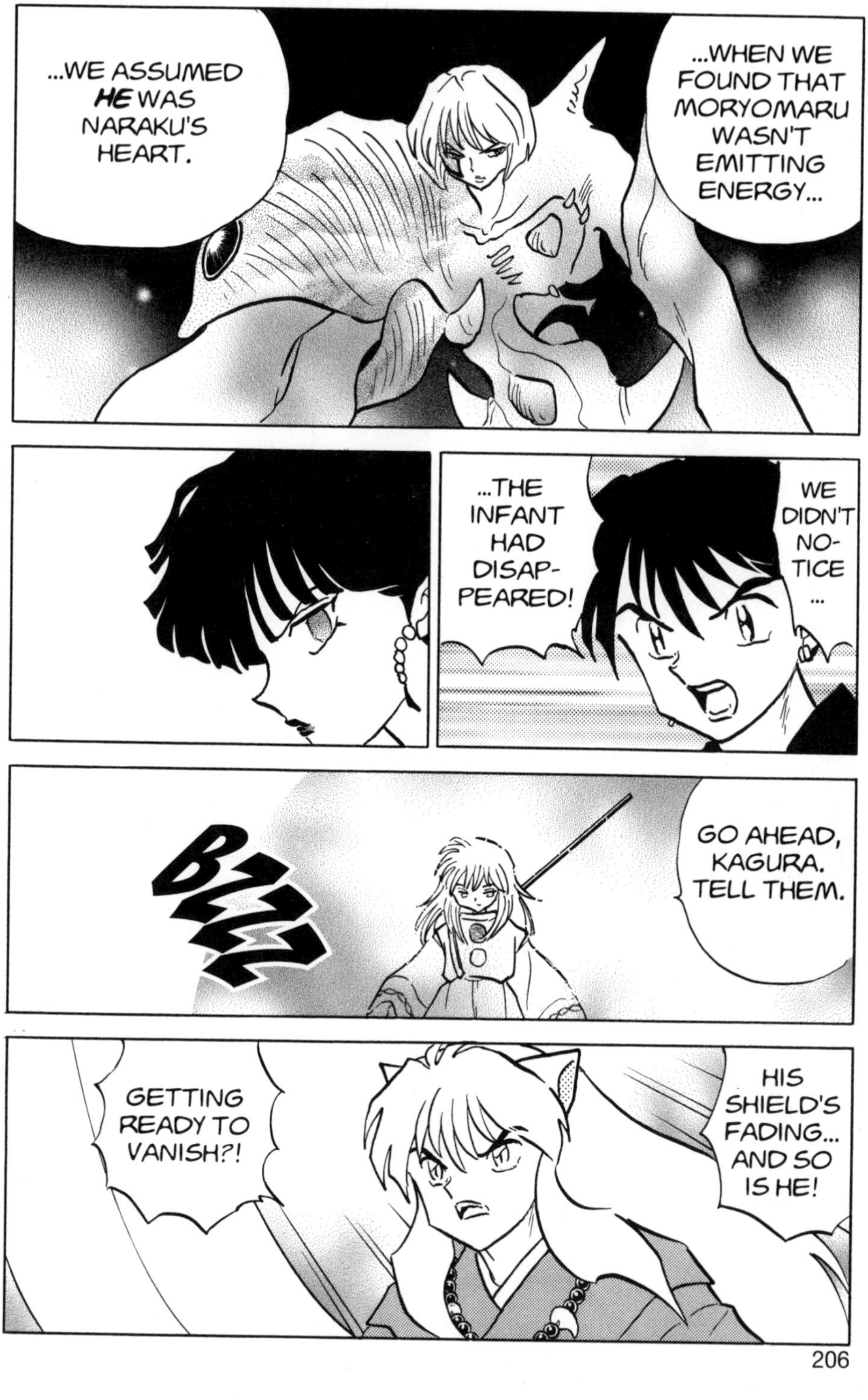
...WHEN WE FOUND THAT MORYOMARU WASN'T EMITTING ENERGY...
...WE ASSUMED HE WAS NARAKU'S HEART.
WE DIDN'T NO-TICE...
...THE INFANT HAD DISAP-PEARED!
GO AHEAD, KAGURA. TELL THEM.
BZZZ
HIS SHIELD'S FADING... AND SO IS HE!
GETTING READY TO VANISH?!

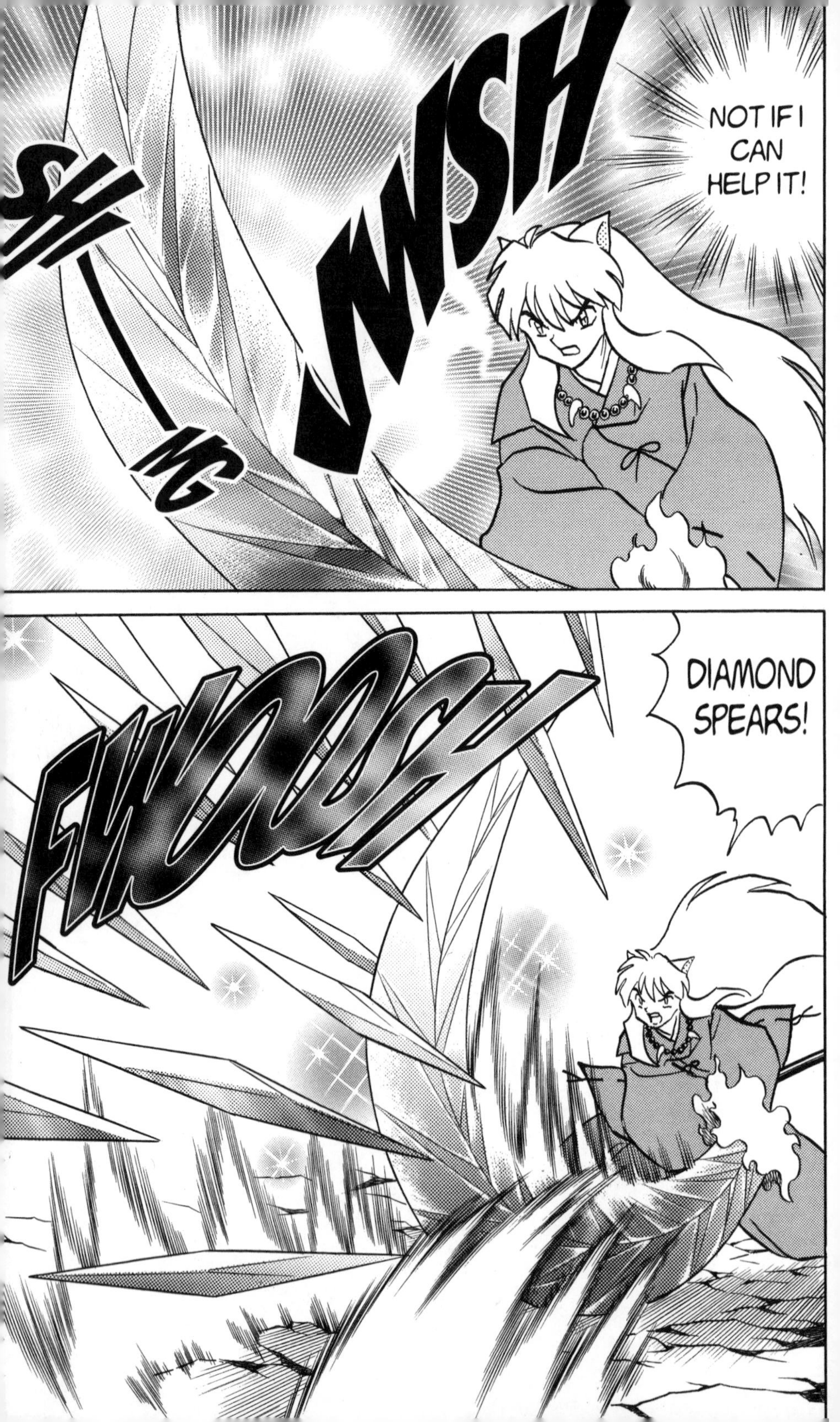
NOT IF I CAN HELP IT!
SWISH
SHI—NG
DIAMOND SPEARS!
FWOOSH

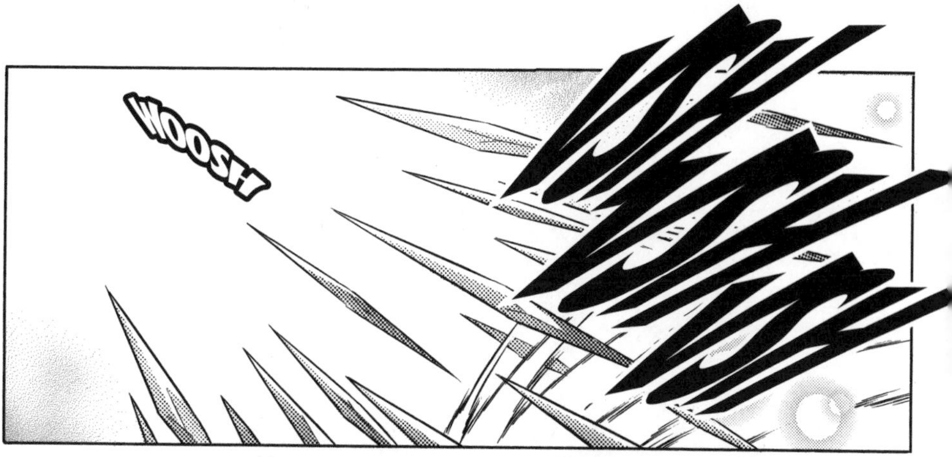
WOOSH
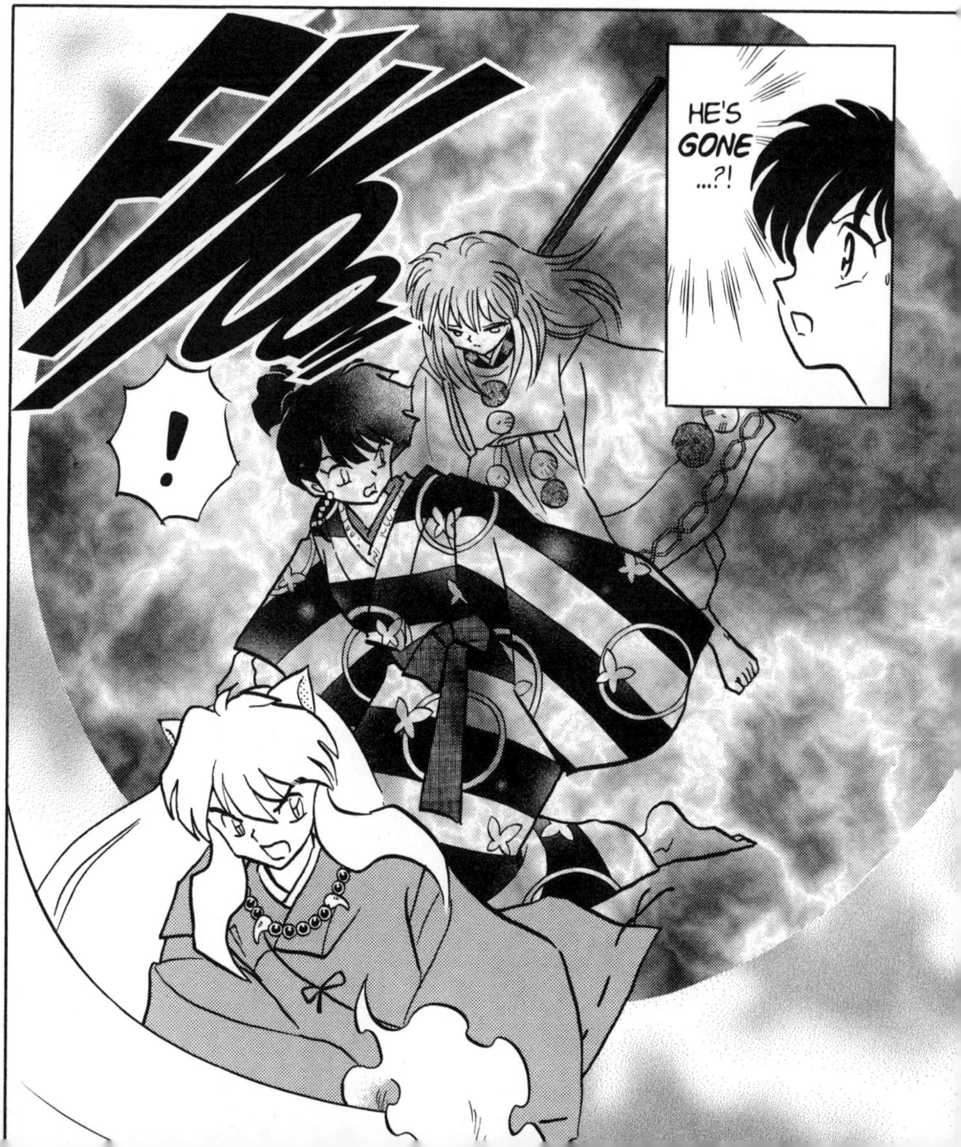
HE'S GONE ...?!
!

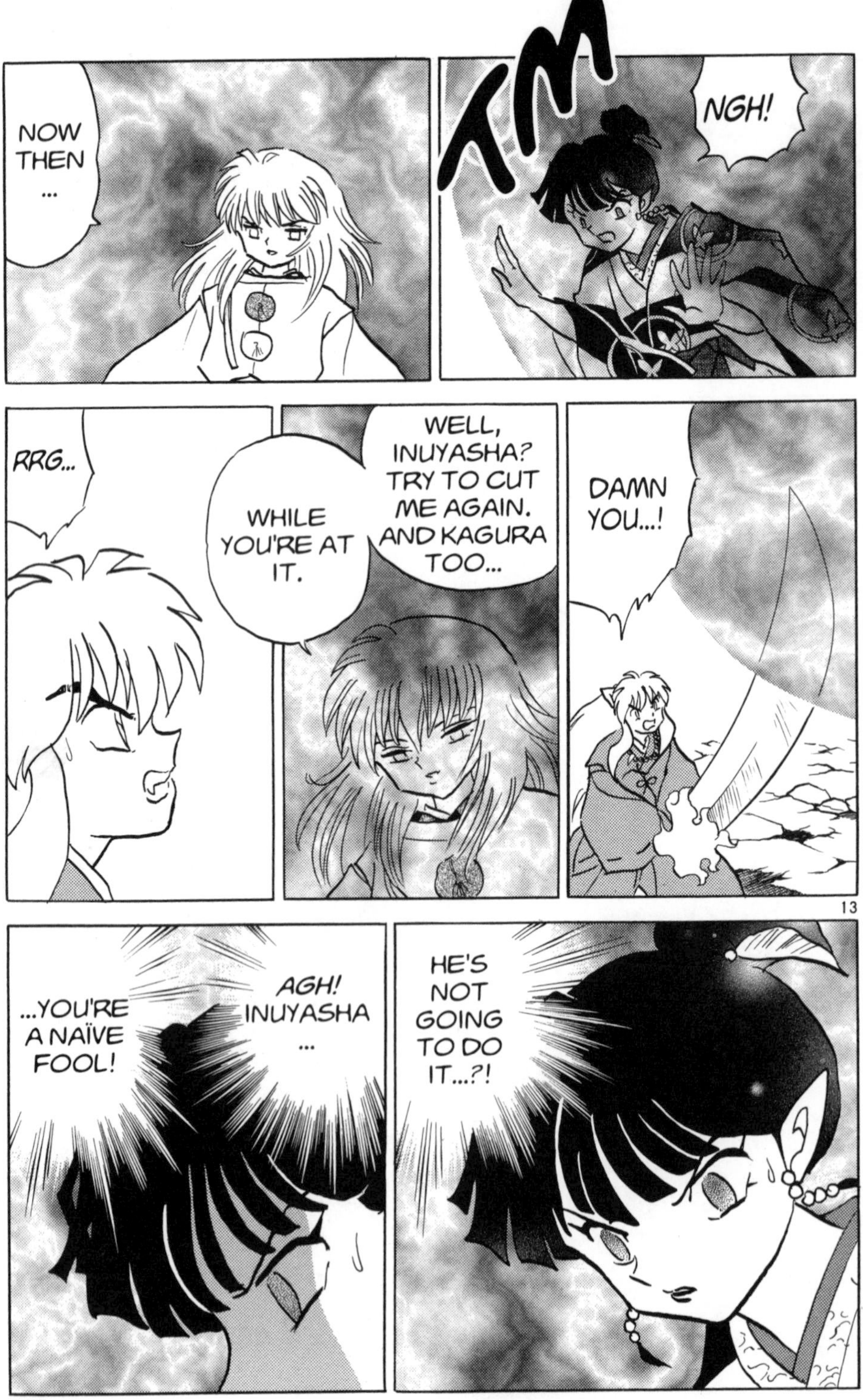
TM
NGH!
NOW THEN ...
DAMN YOU...!
WELL, INUYASHA? TRY TO CUT ME AGAIN. AND KAGURA TOO...
WHILE YOU'RE AT IT.
RRG...
HE'S NOT GOING TO DO IT...?!
AGH! INUYASHA ...
...YOU'RE A NAÏVE FOOL!

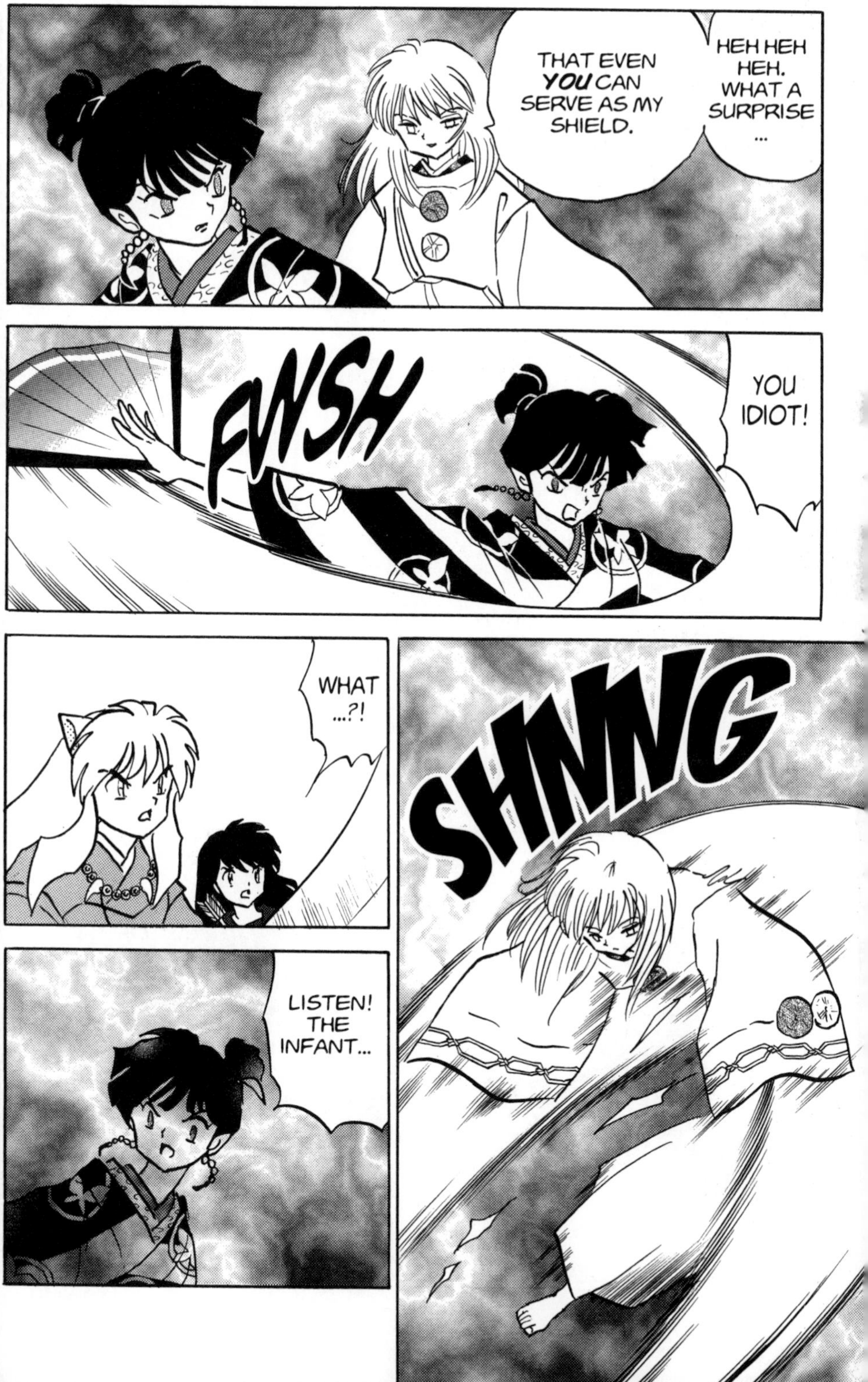
HEH HEH HEH. WHAT A SURPRISE ...
THAT EVEN YOU CAN SERVE AS MY SHIELD.
YOU IDIOT!
FWSH
SHNNG
WHAT ...?!
LISTEN! THE INFANT...

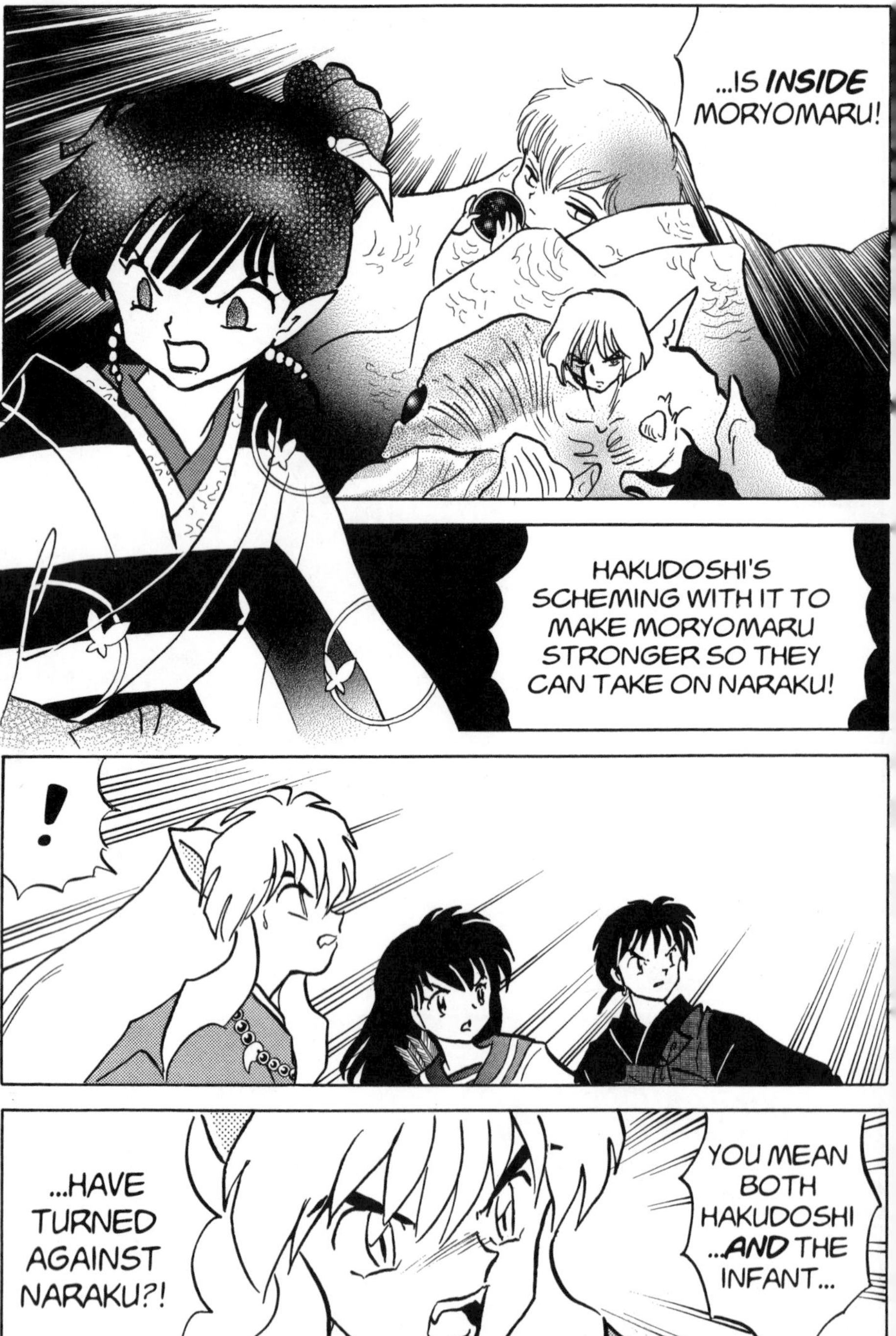

...IS **INSIDE** MORYOMARU!
HAKUDOSHI'S SCHEMING WITH IT TO MAKE MORYOMARU STRONGER SO THEY CAN TAKE ON NARAKU!
!
YOU MEAN BOTH HAKUDOSHI ...**AND** THE INFANT...
...HAVE TURNED AGAINST NARAKU?!

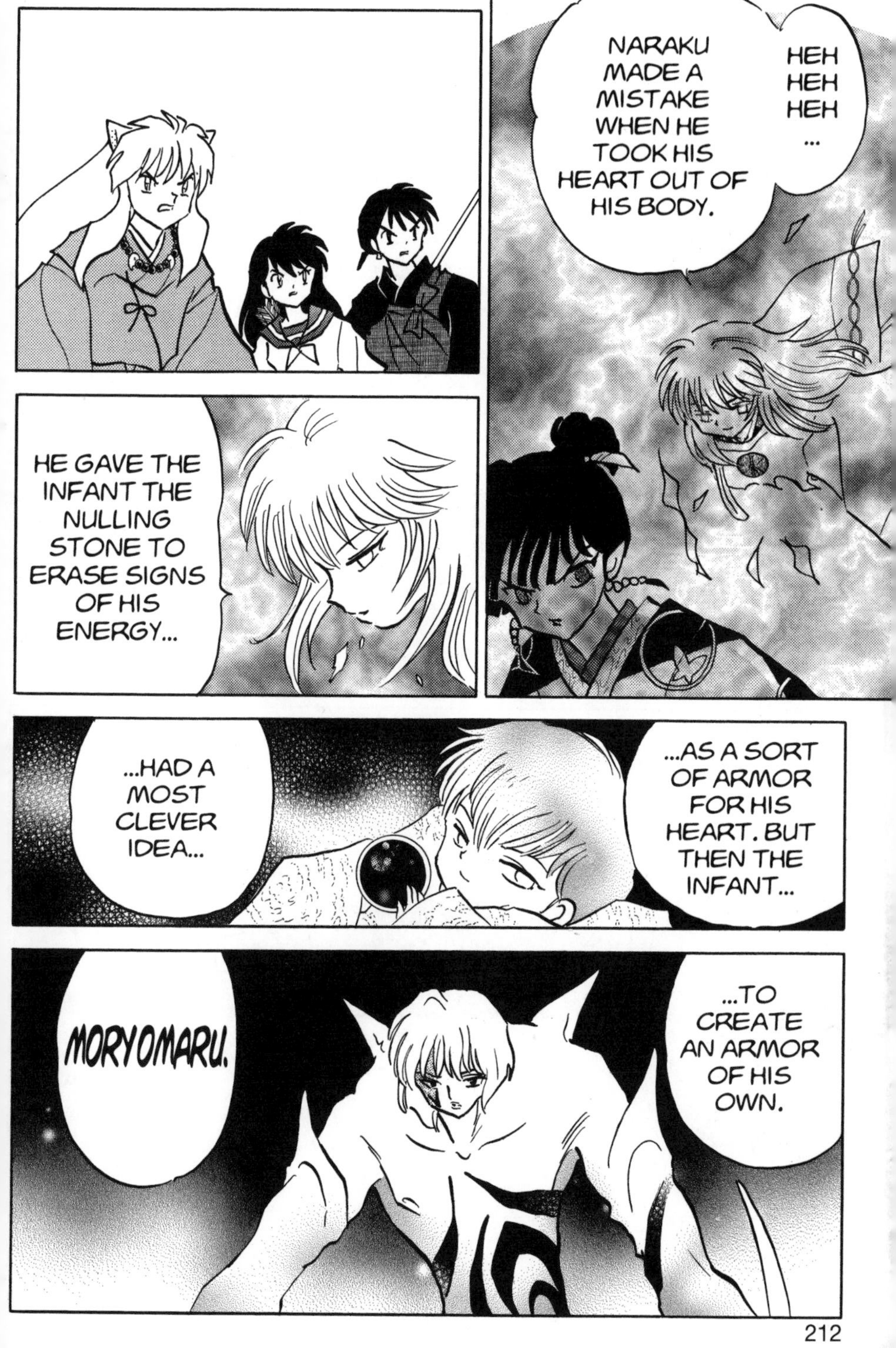
HEH HEH HEH...
NARAKU MADE A MISTAKE WHEN HE TOOK HIS HEART OUT OF HIS BODY.
HE GAVE THE INFANT THE NULLING STONE TO ERASE SIGNS OF HIS ENERGY...
...AS A SORT OF ARMOR FOR HIS HEART. BUT THEN THE INFANT...
...HAD A MOST CLEVER IDEA...
...TO CREATE AN ARMOR OF HIS OWN.
MORYOMARU.

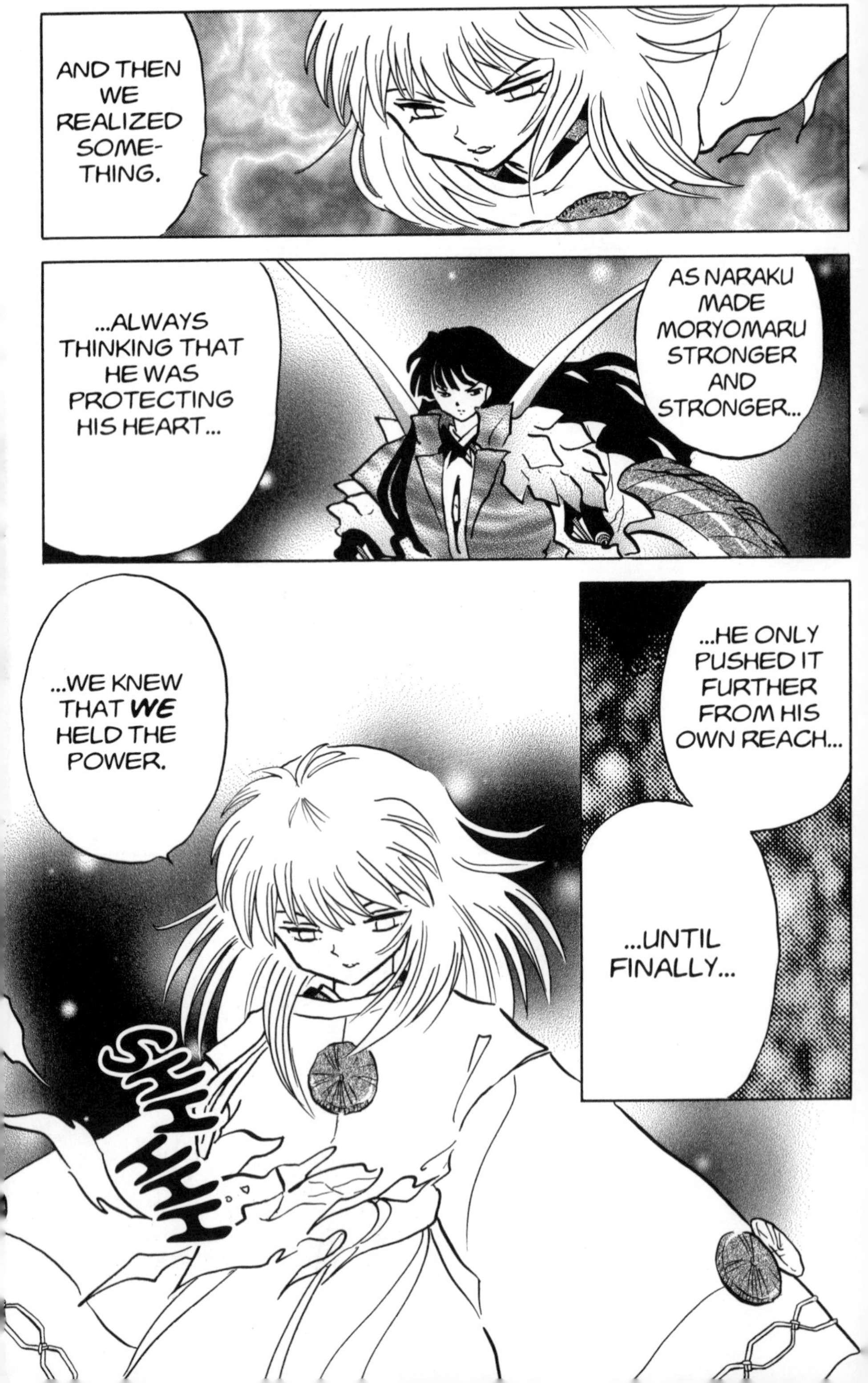
AND THEN WE REALIZED SOME-THING.
AS NARAKU MADE MORYOMARU STRONGER AND STRONGER...
...ALWAYS THINKING THAT HE WAS PROTECTING HIS HEART...
...HE ONLY PUSHED IT FURTHER FROM HIS OWN REACH...
...UNTIL FINALLY...
...WE KNEW THAT **WE** HELD THE POWER.
SHHHHHH

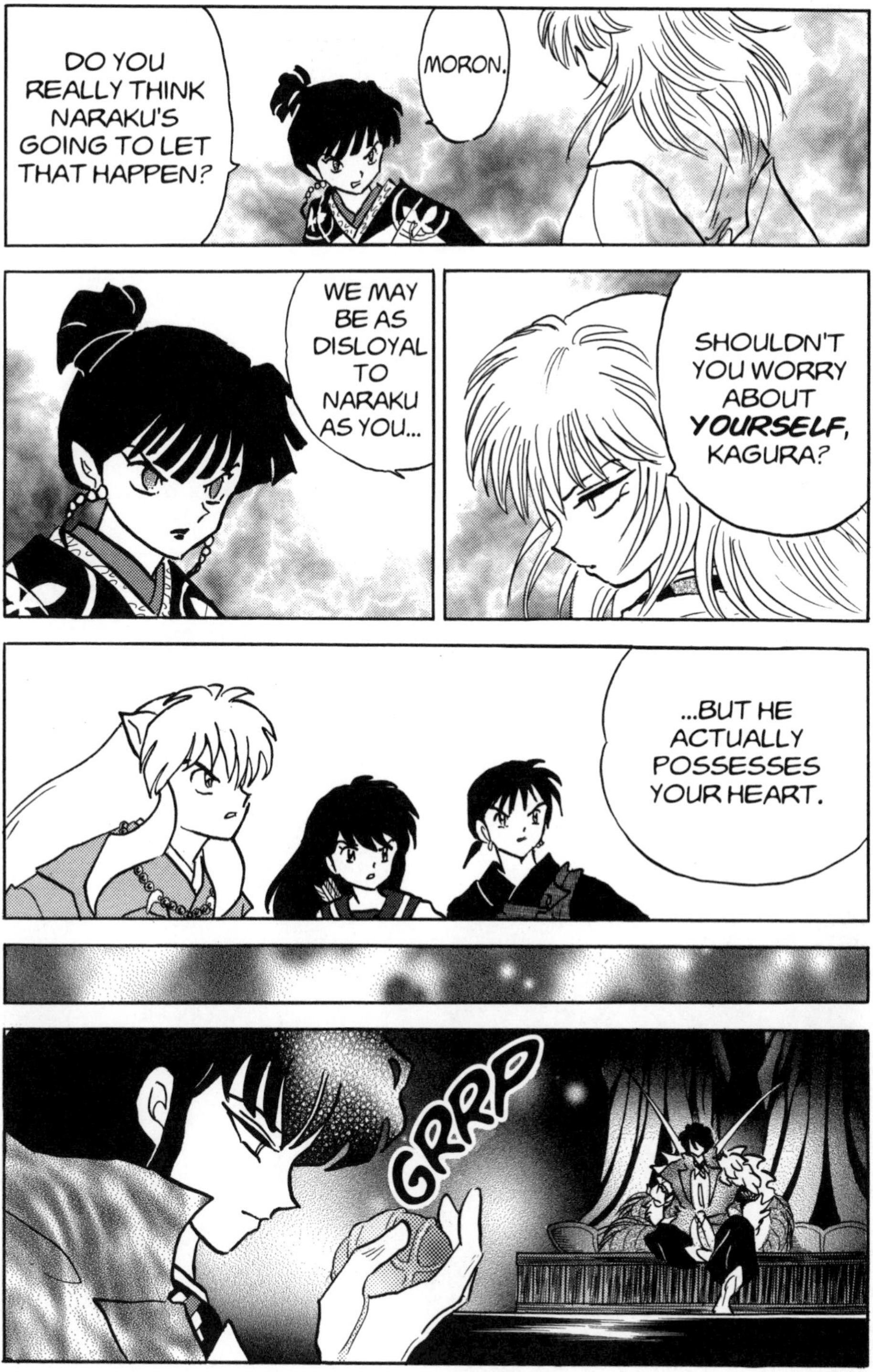
MORON.
DO YOU REALLY THINK NARAKU'S GOING TO LET THAT HAPPEN?
SHOULDN'T YOU WORRY ABOUT **YOURSELF**, KAGURA?
WE MAY BE AS DISLOYAL TO NARAKU AS YOU...
...BUT HE ACTUALLY POSSESSES YOUR HEART.
GRRP

SCROLL TWO
HAKUDOSHI'S END

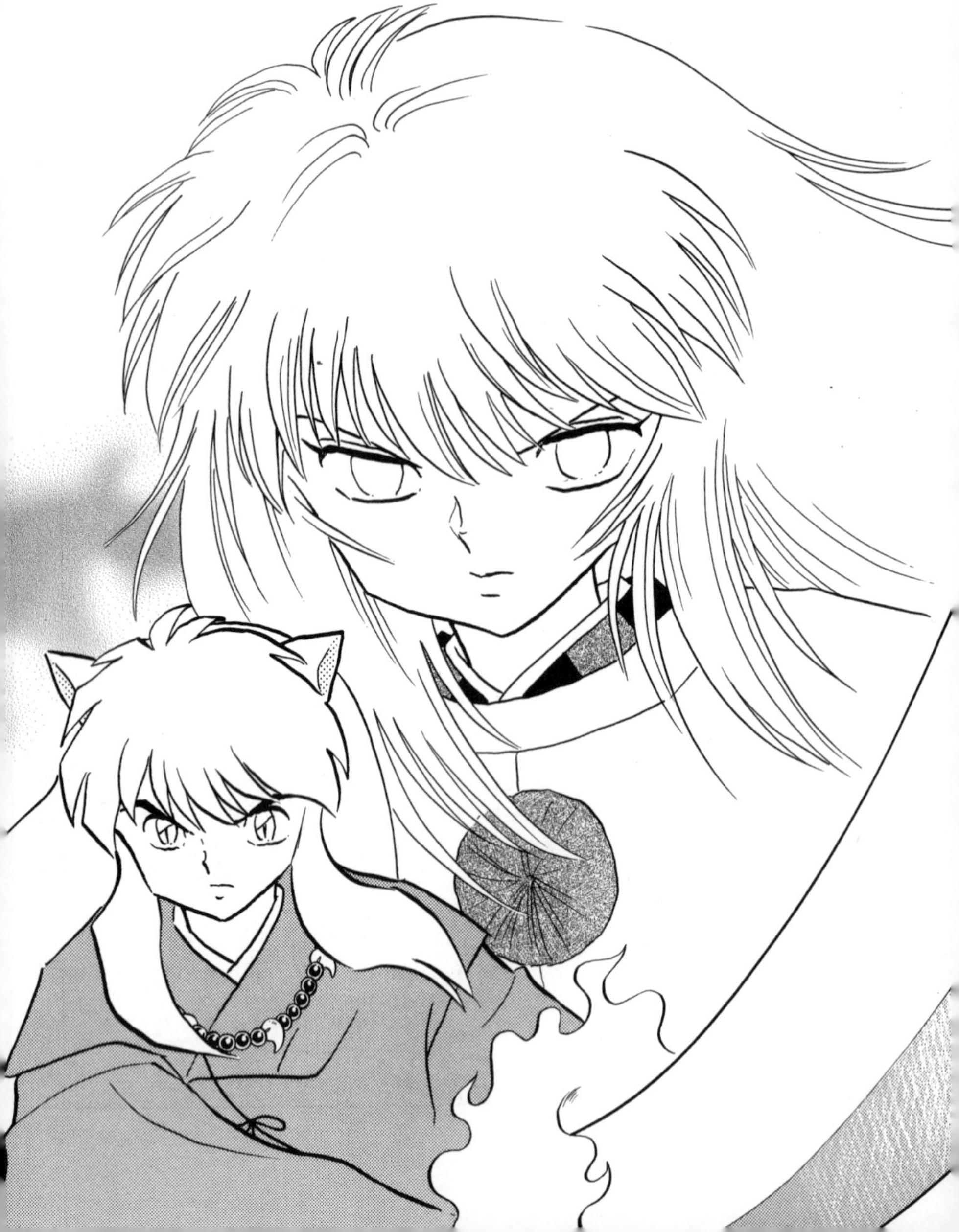

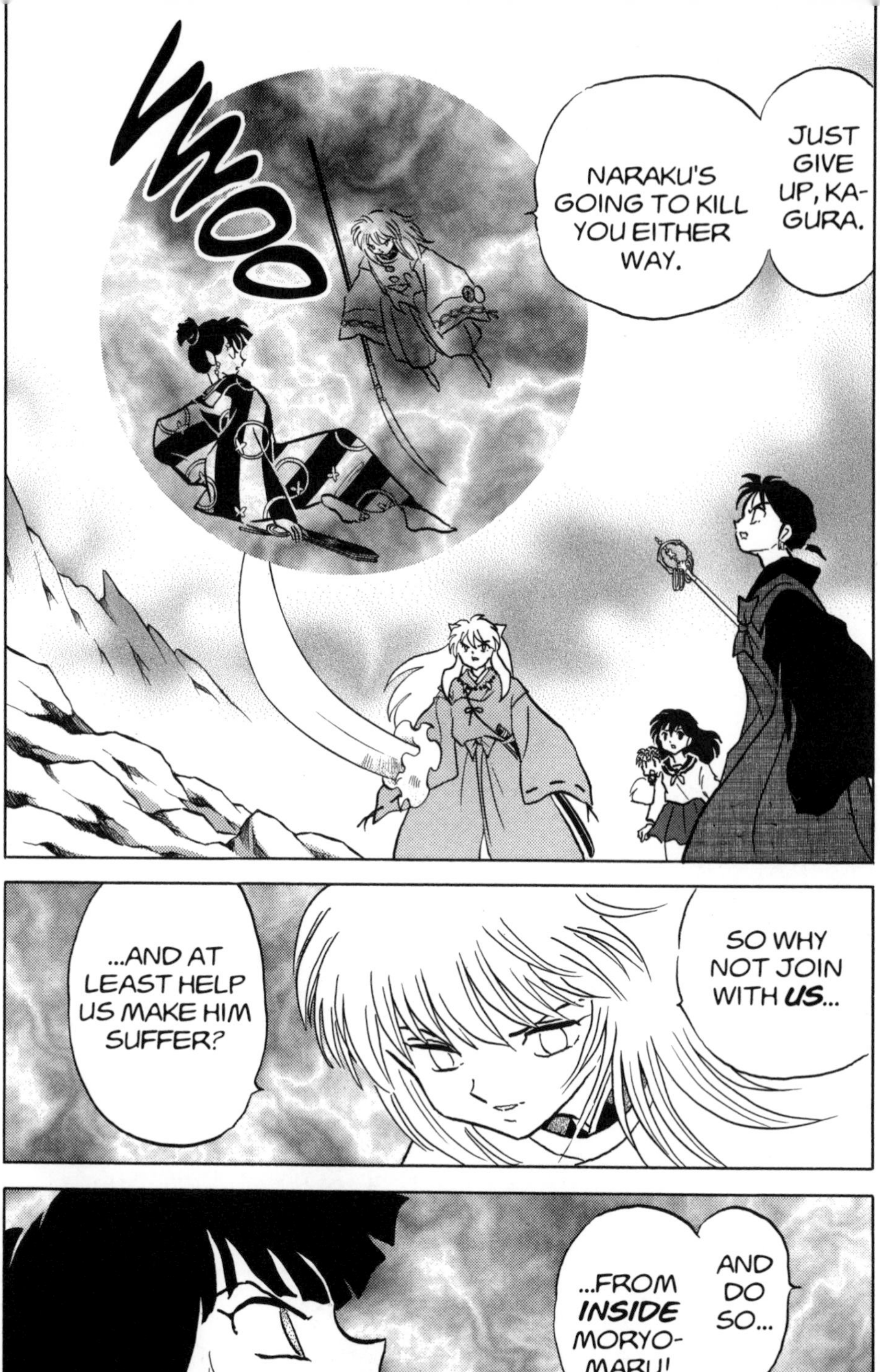
JUST GIVE UP, KA-GURA.
NARAKU'S GOING TO KILL YOU EITHER WAY.
VWOO
SO WHY NOT JOIN WITH ***US***...
...AND AT LEAST HELP US MAKE HIM SUFFER?
AND DO SO...
...FROM ***INSIDE*** MORYO-MARU!

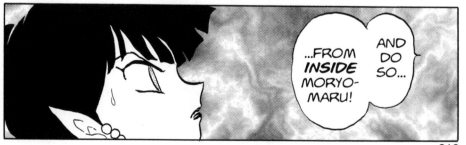

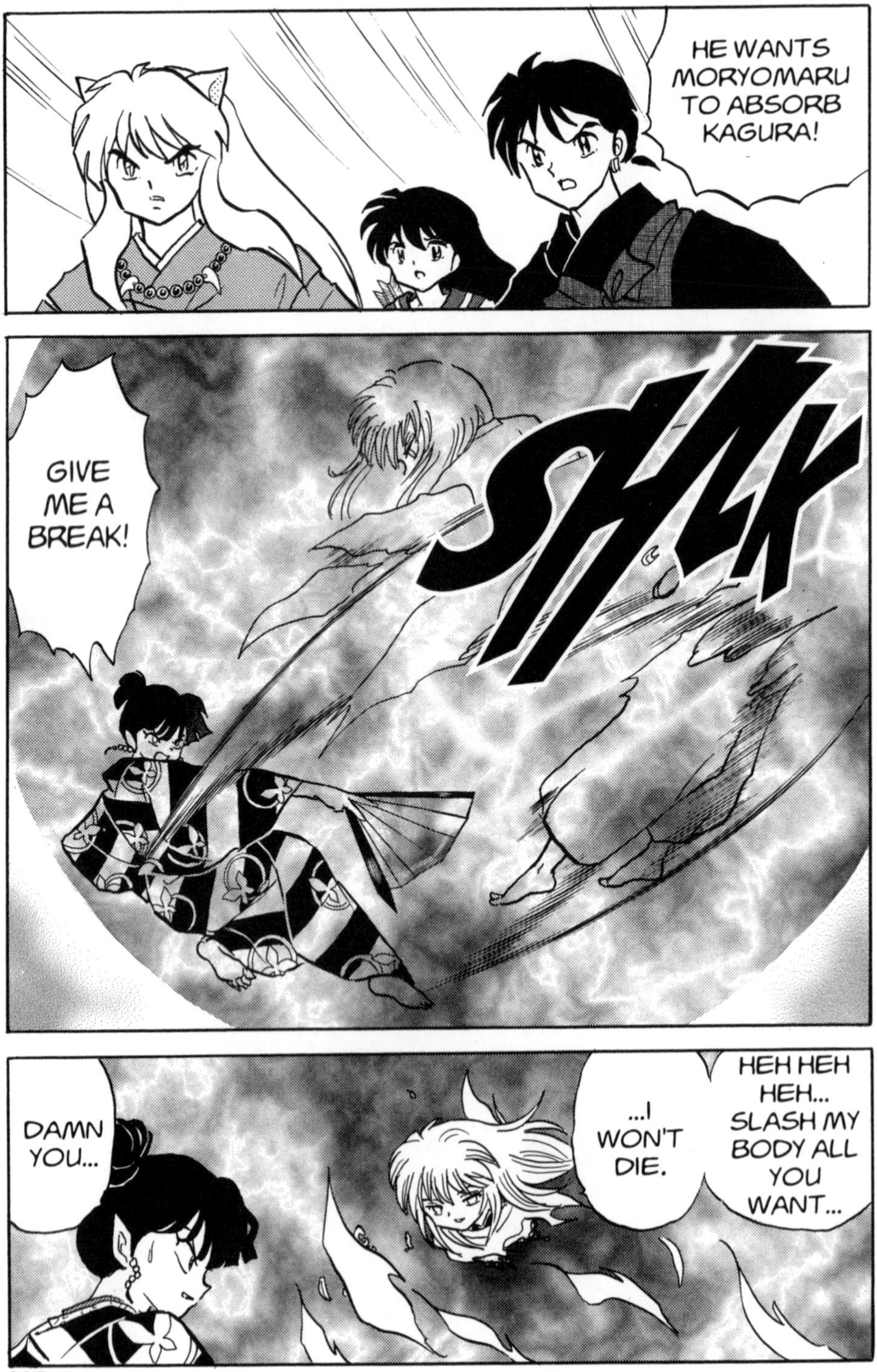
HE WANTS MORYOMARU TO ABSORB KAGURA!
SHAK
GIVE ME A BREAK!
HEH HEH HEH... SLASH MY BODY ALL YOU WANT...
...I WON'T DIE.
DAMN YOU...

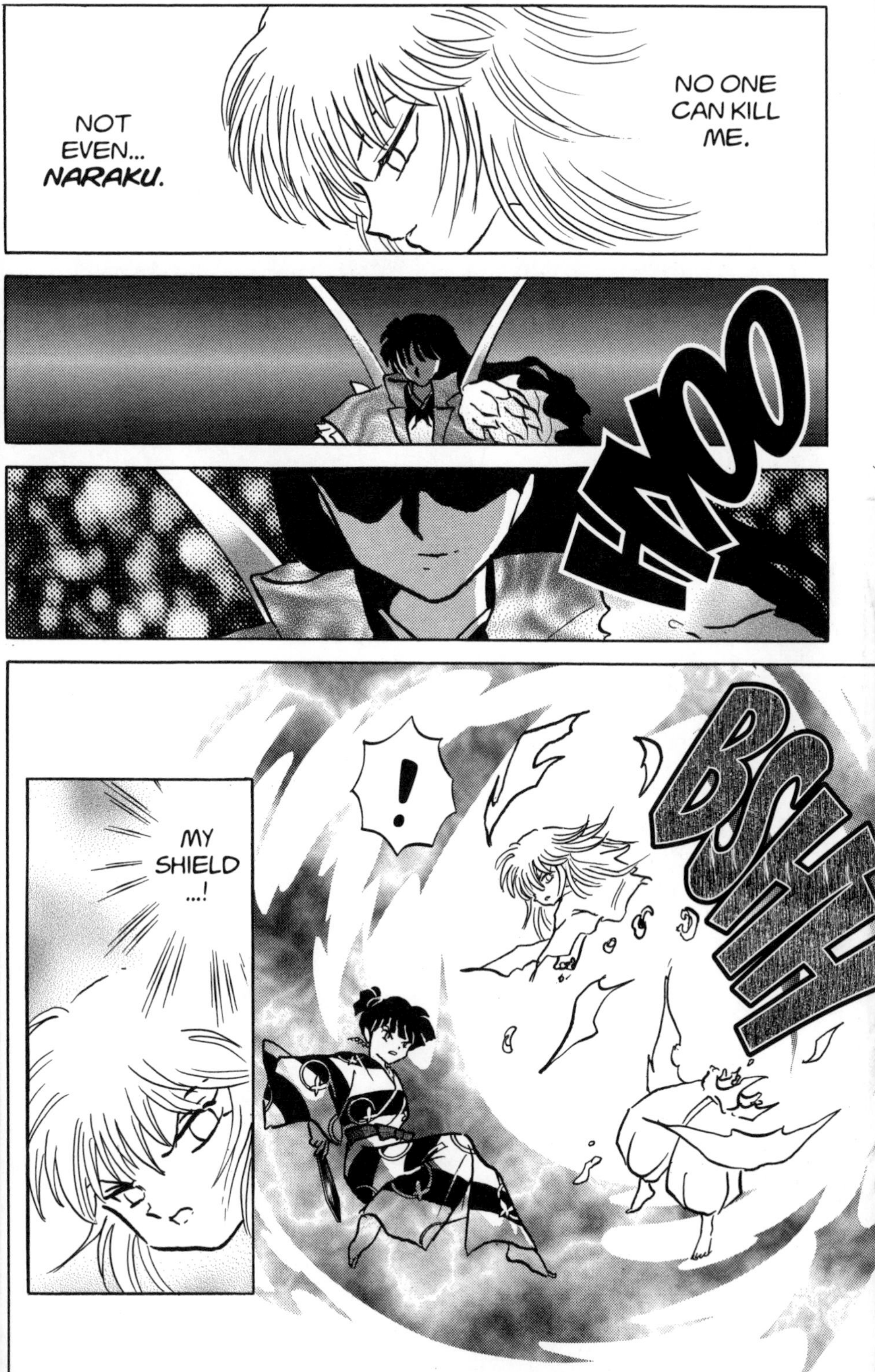
NO ONE CAN KILL ME.
NOT EVEN... ***NARAKU.***
WHOO
BSHH!
!
MY SHIELD ...!

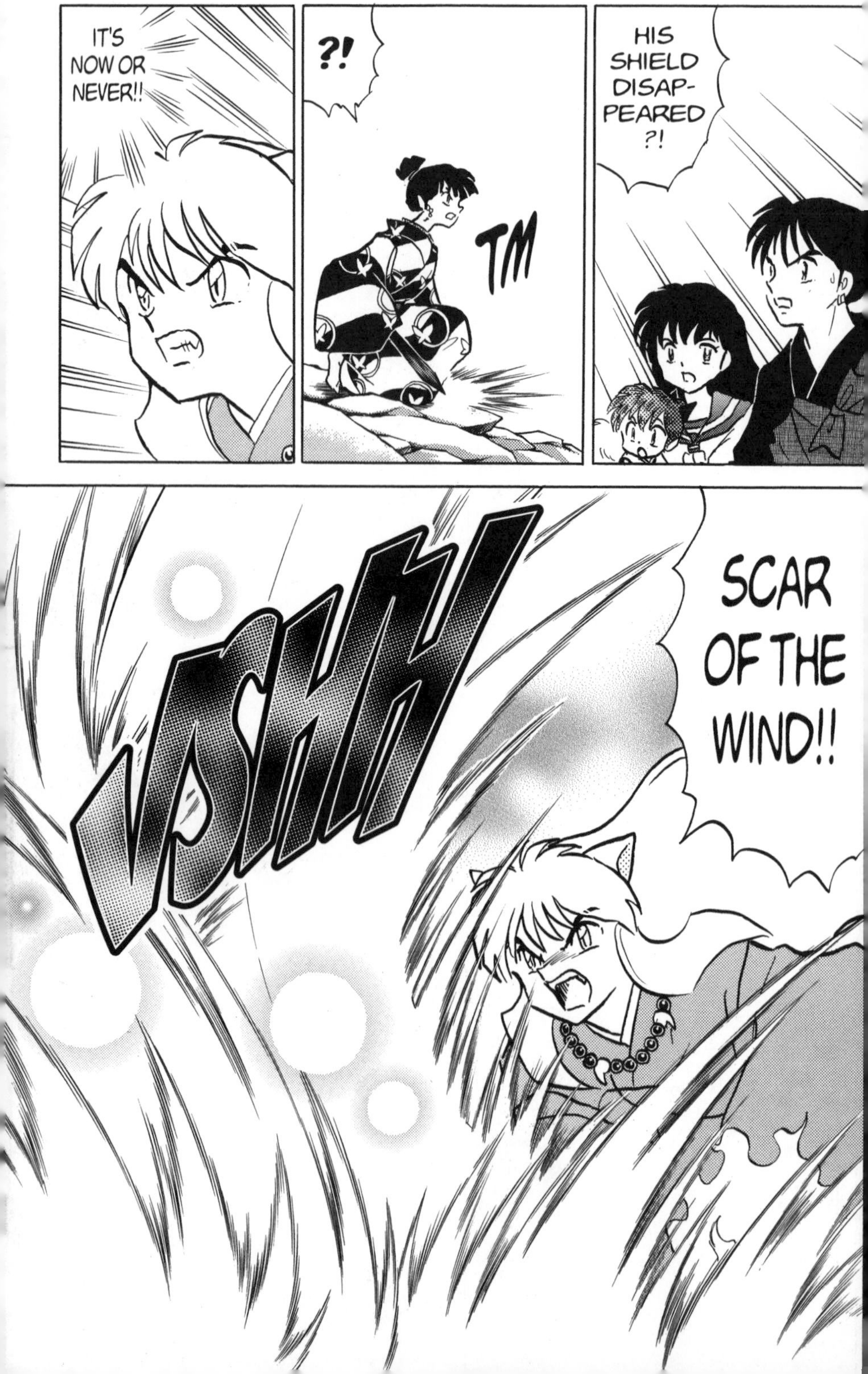
HIS SHIELD DISAP-PEARED ?!
?!
TM
IT'S NOW OR NEVER!!
SCAR OF THE WIND!!
VSHH

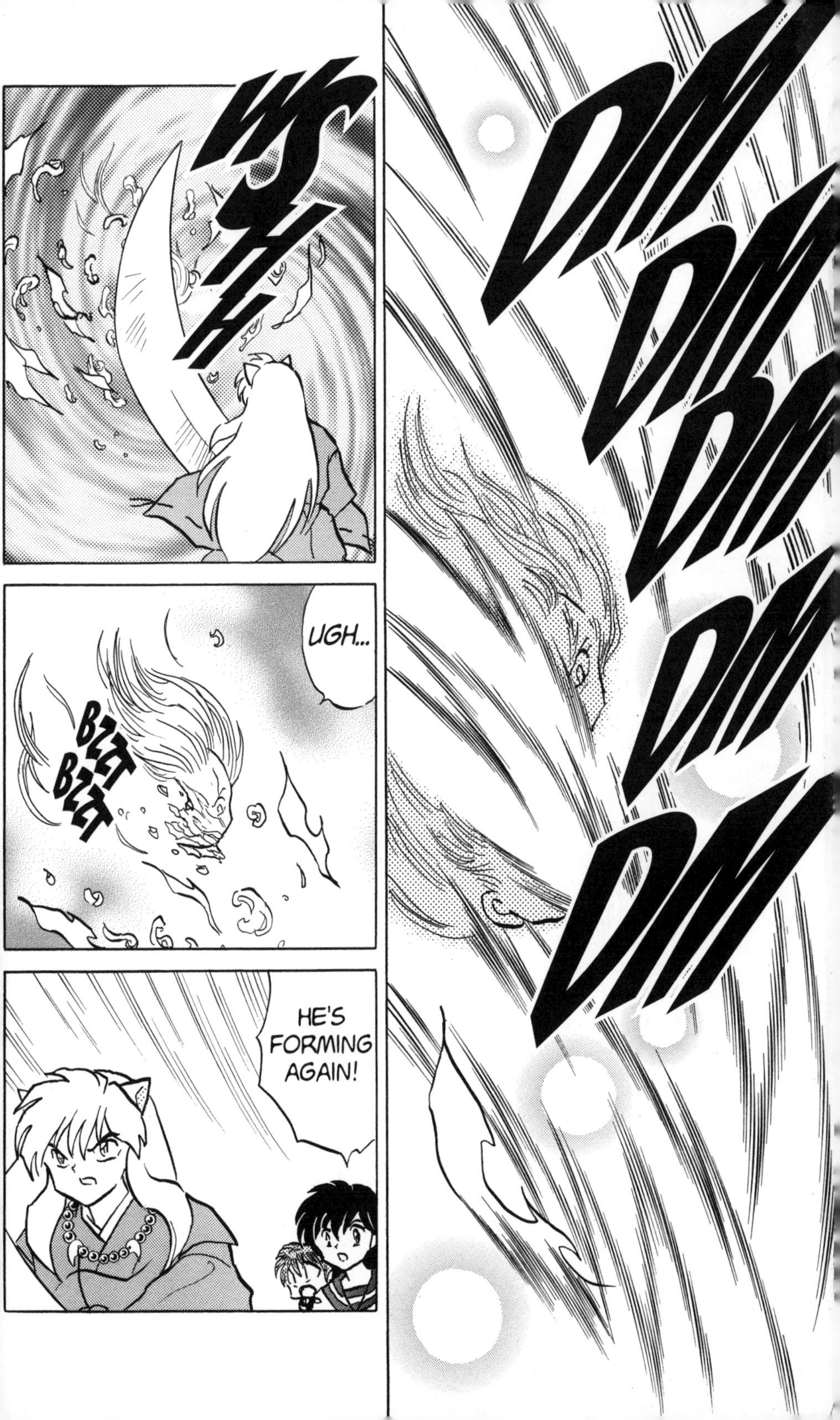
UGH...
BZZT
BZZT
HE'S FORMING AGAIN!

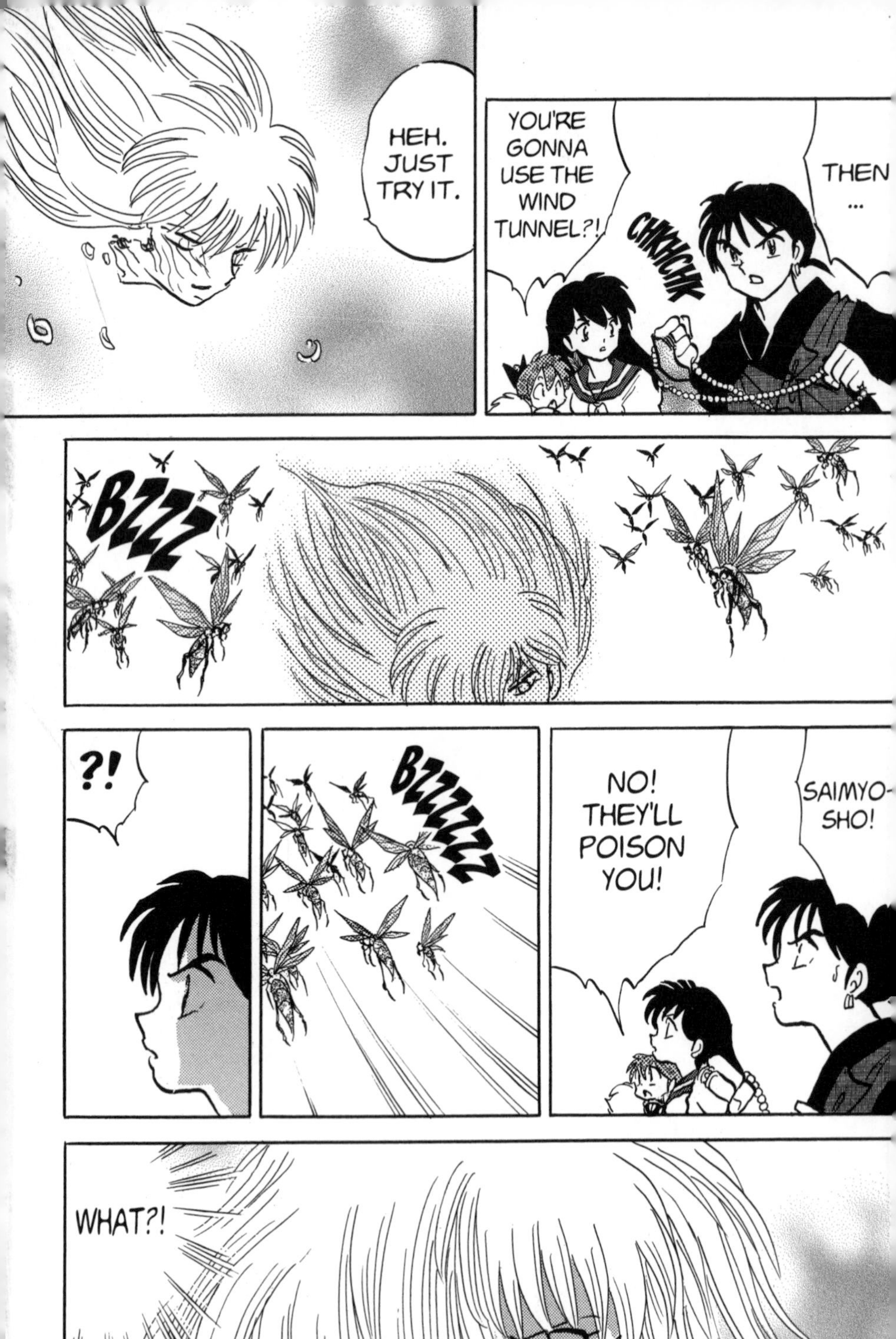
THEN ...
YOU'RE GONNA USE THE WIND TUNNEL?!
CHKHCHK
HEH. JUST TRY IT.
BZZZ
SAIMYO-SHO!
NO! THEY'LL POISON YOU!
BZZZZZZZ
?!
WHAT?!

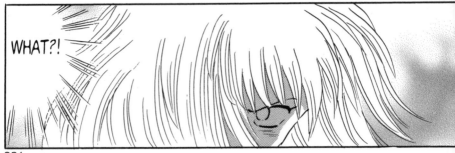

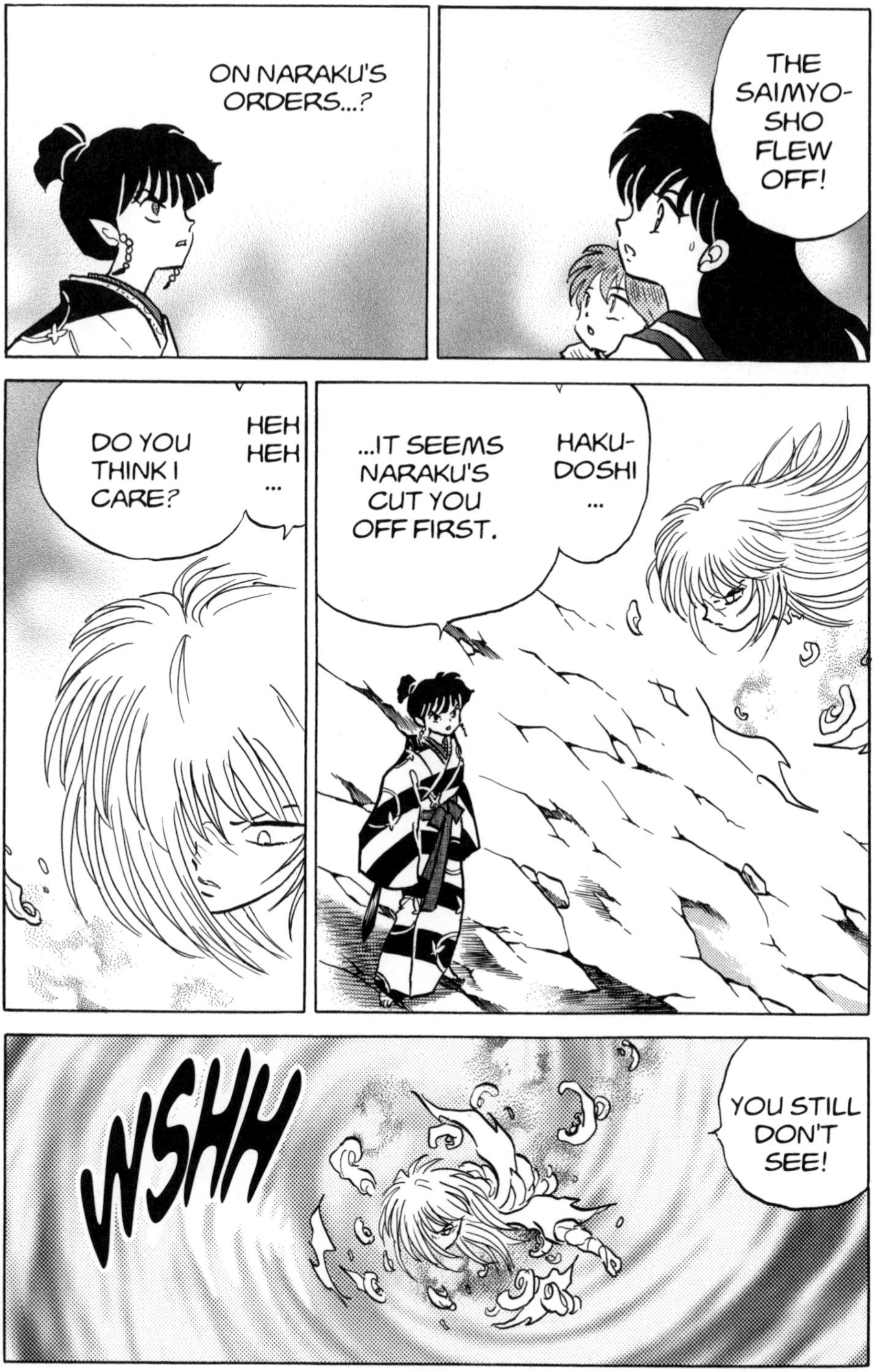
THE SAIMYO-SHO FLEW OFF!
ON NARAKU'S ORDERS...?
HAKU-DOSHI ...
...IT SEEMS NARAKU'S CUT YOU OFF FIRST.
HEH HEH ...
DO YOU THINK I CARE?
YOU STILL DON'T SEE!
WSHH

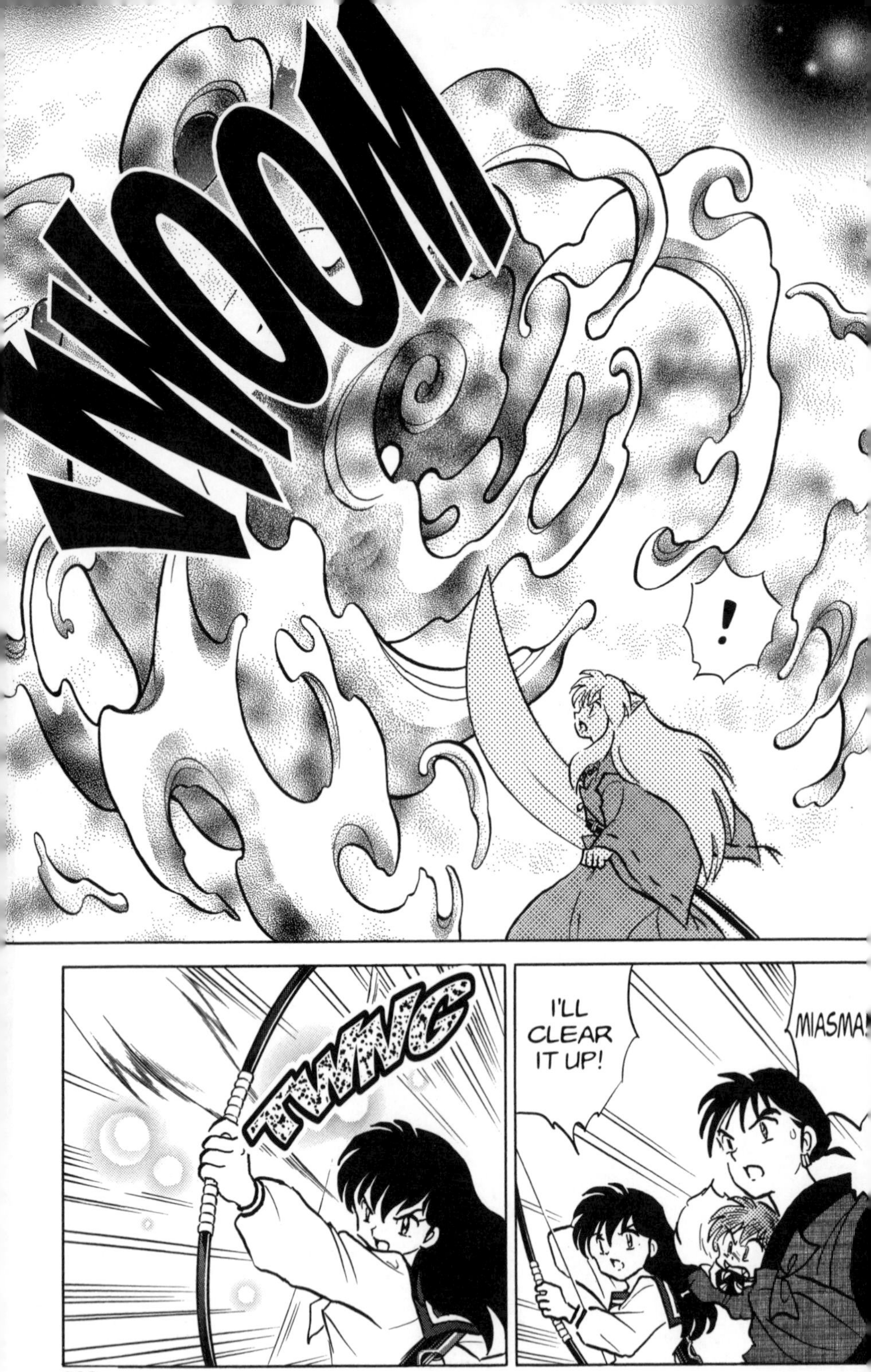
VWOOM
!
MIASMA!
I'LL CLEAR IT UP!
TWING

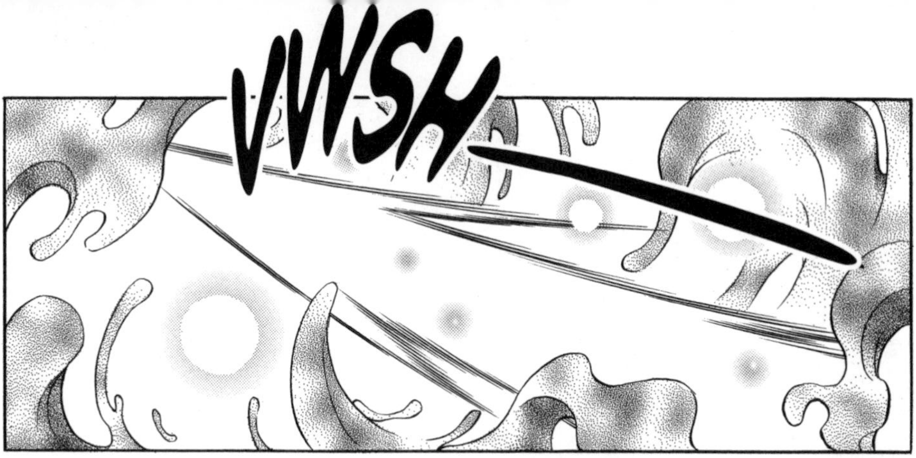
VWSH

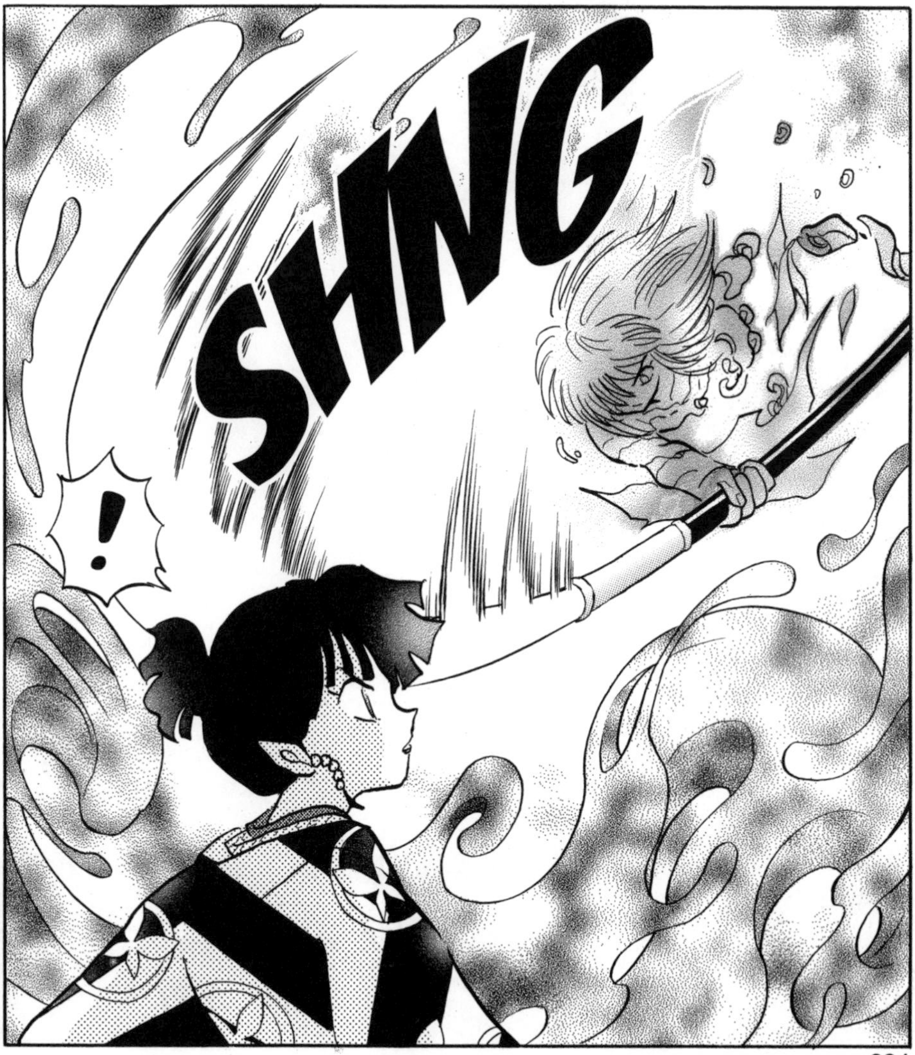
SHING
!

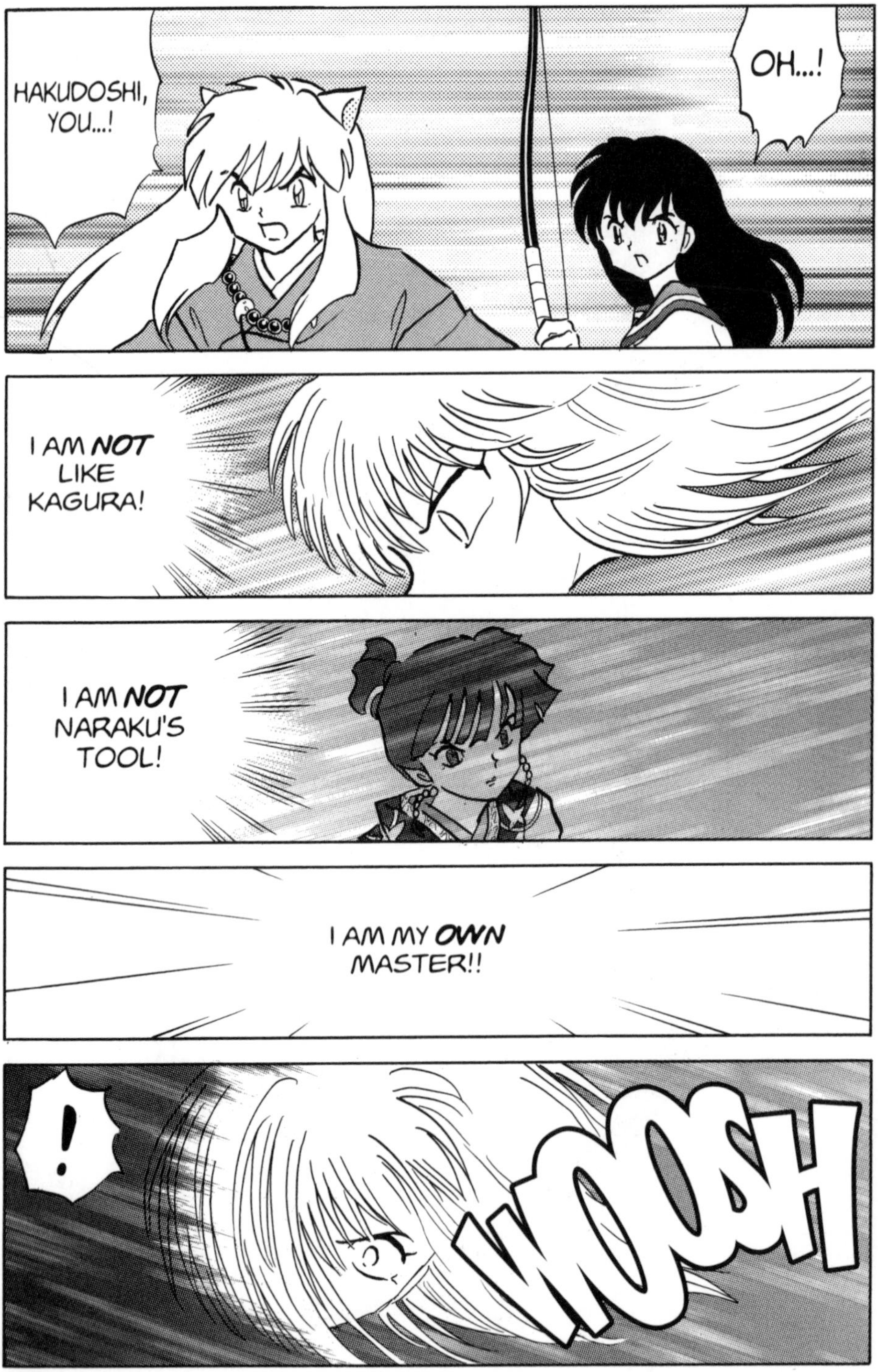

OH...!
HAKUDOSHI, YOU...!
I AM **NOT** LIKE KAGURA!
I AM **NOT** NARAKU'S TOOL!
I AM MY **OWN** MASTER!!
WOOSH
!

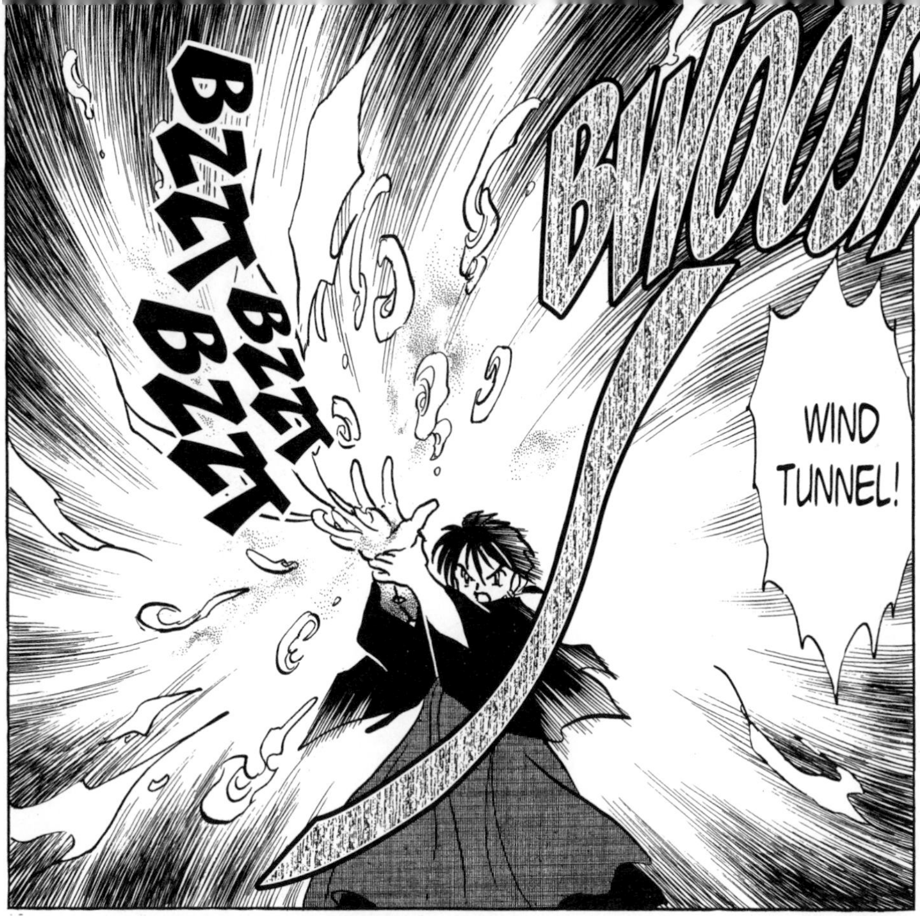
WIND TUNNEL!
BZZT BZZT BZZT

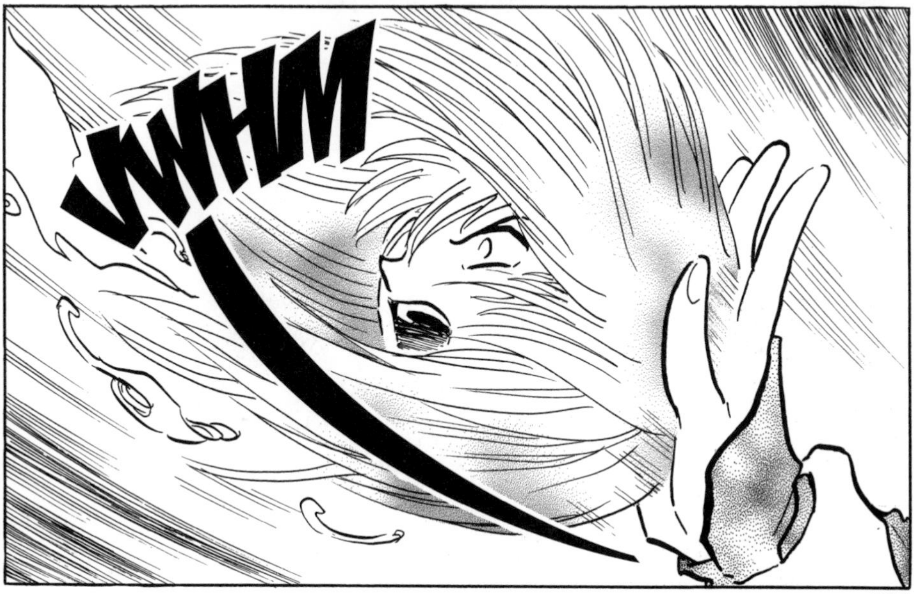
WHUM

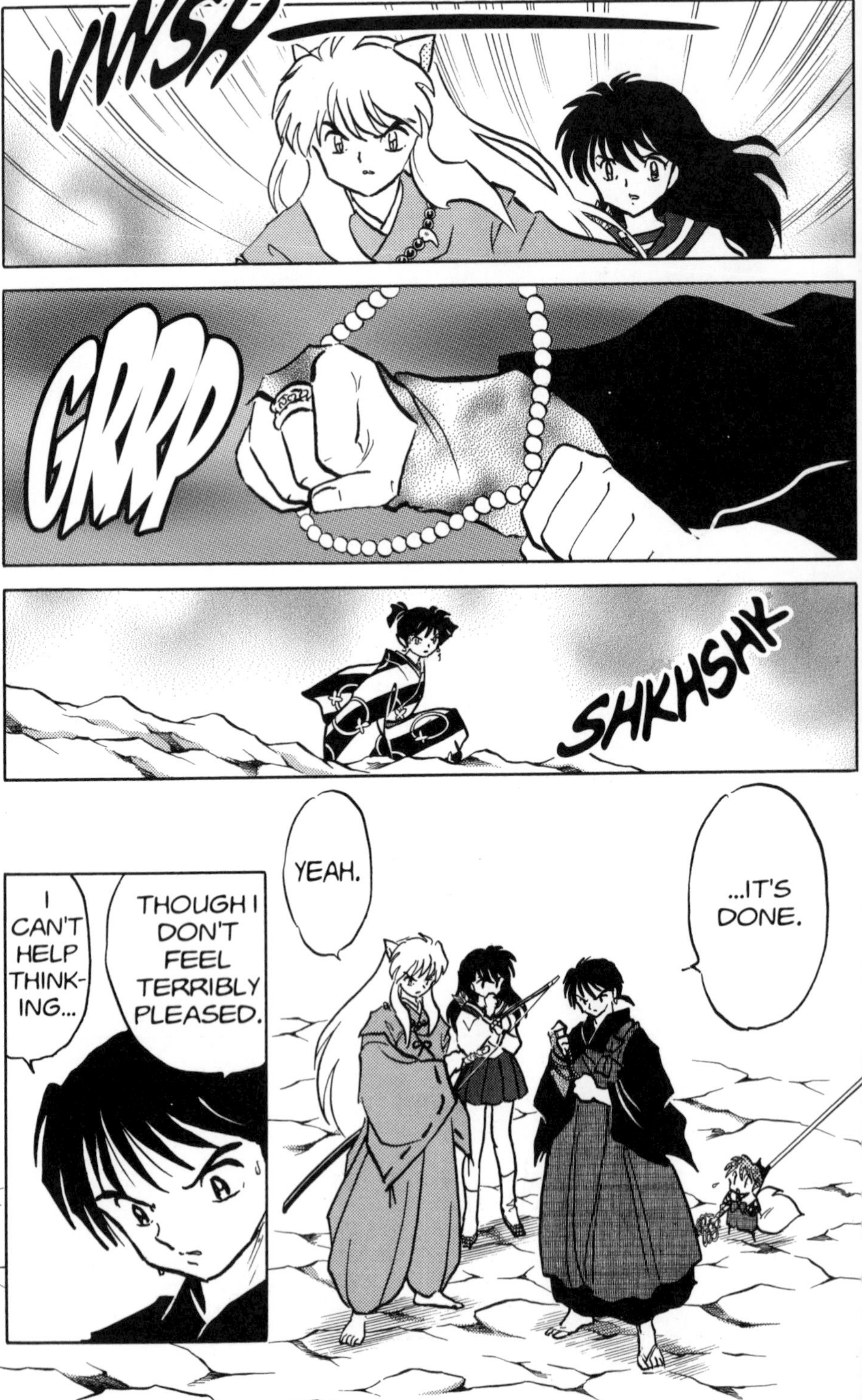
VVVSH
GRRP
SHKSHK
...IT'S DONE.
YEAH.
THOUGH I DON'T FEEL TERRIBLY PLEASED.
I CAN'T HELP THINKING...

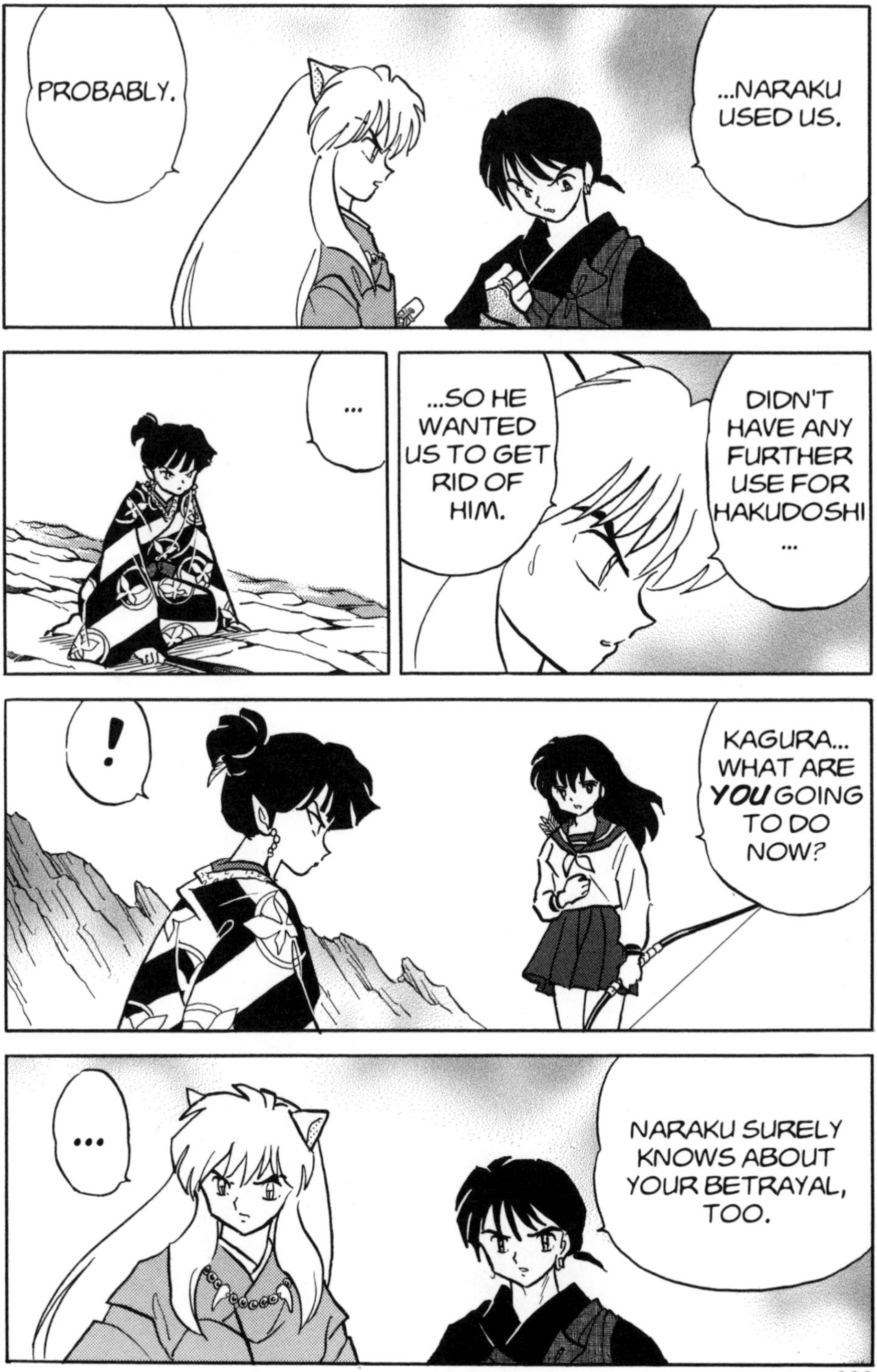
...NARAKU USED US.
PROBABLY.
DIDN'T HAVE ANY FURTHER USE FOR HAKUDOSHI ...
...SO HE WANTED US TO GET RID OF HIM.
...
KAGURA... WHAT ARE *YOU* GOING TO DO NOW?
!
NARAKU SURELY KNOWS ABOUT YOUR BETRAYAL, TOO.
...

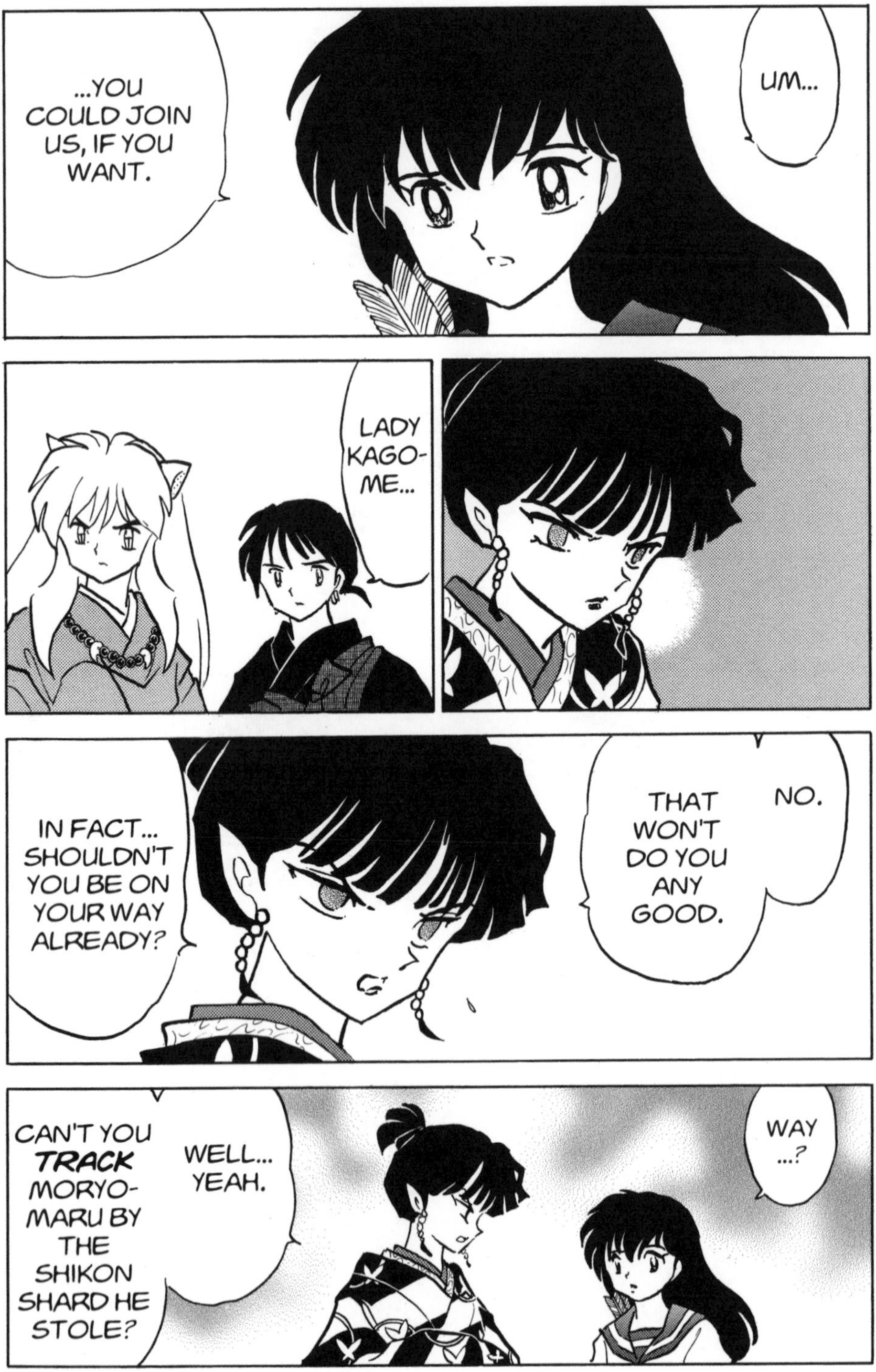
UM...
...YOU COULD JOIN US, IF YOU WANT.
LADY KAGOME...
NO.
THAT WON'T DO YOU ANY GOOD.
IN FACT... SHOULDN'T YOU BE ON YOUR WAY ALREADY?
WAY ...?
WELL... YEAH.
CAN'T YOU **TRACK** MORYOMARU BY THE SHIKON SHARD HE STOLE?

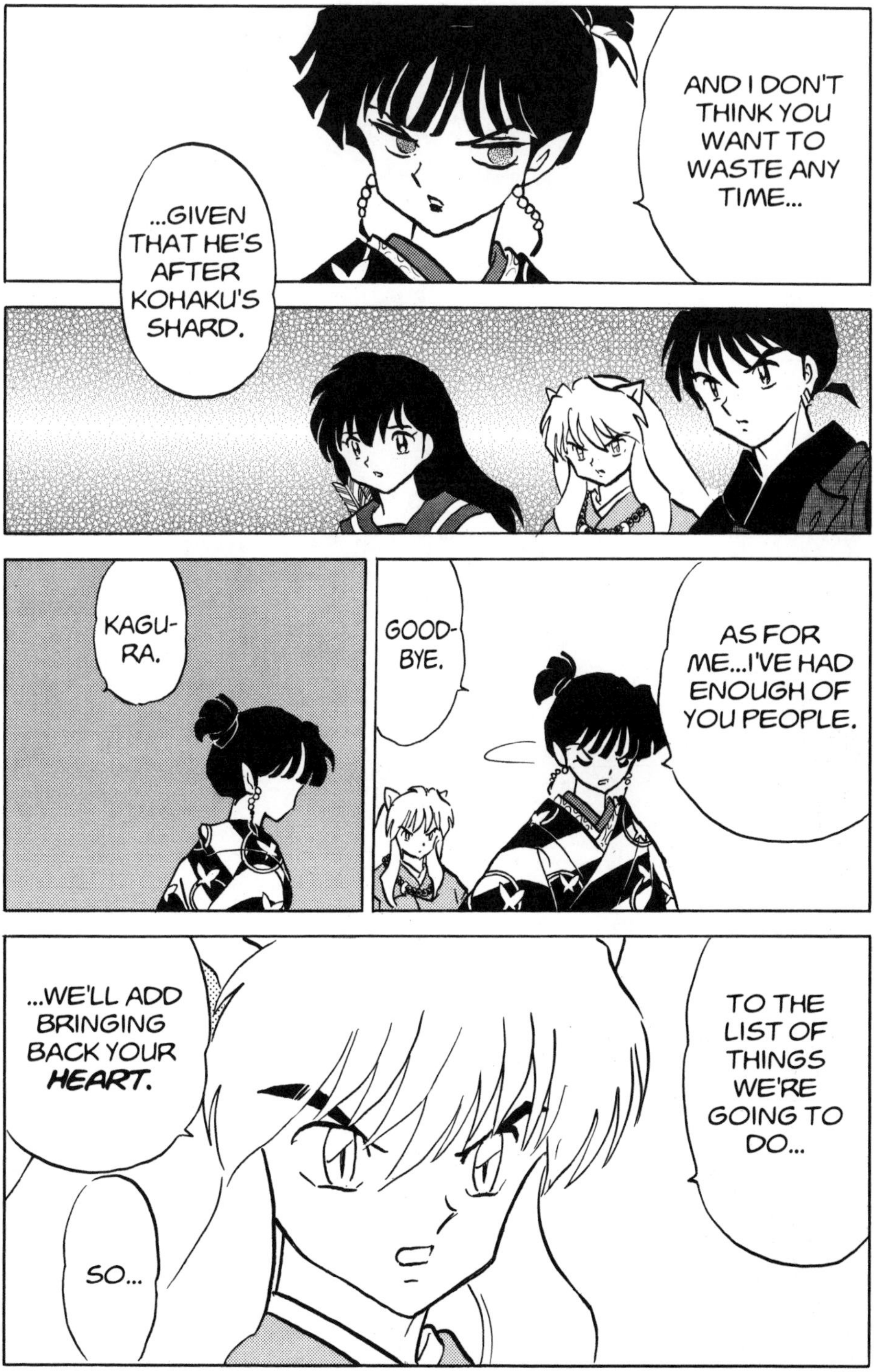
AND I DON'T THINK YOU WANT TO WASTE ANY TIME...
...GIVEN THAT HE'S AFTER KOHAKU'S SHARD.
AS FOR ME...I'VE HAD ENOUGH OF YOU PEOPLE.
GOOD-BYE.
KAGU-RA.
SO...
TO THE LIST OF THINGS WE'RE GOING TO DO...
...WE'LL ADD BRINGING BACK YOUR ***HEART***.

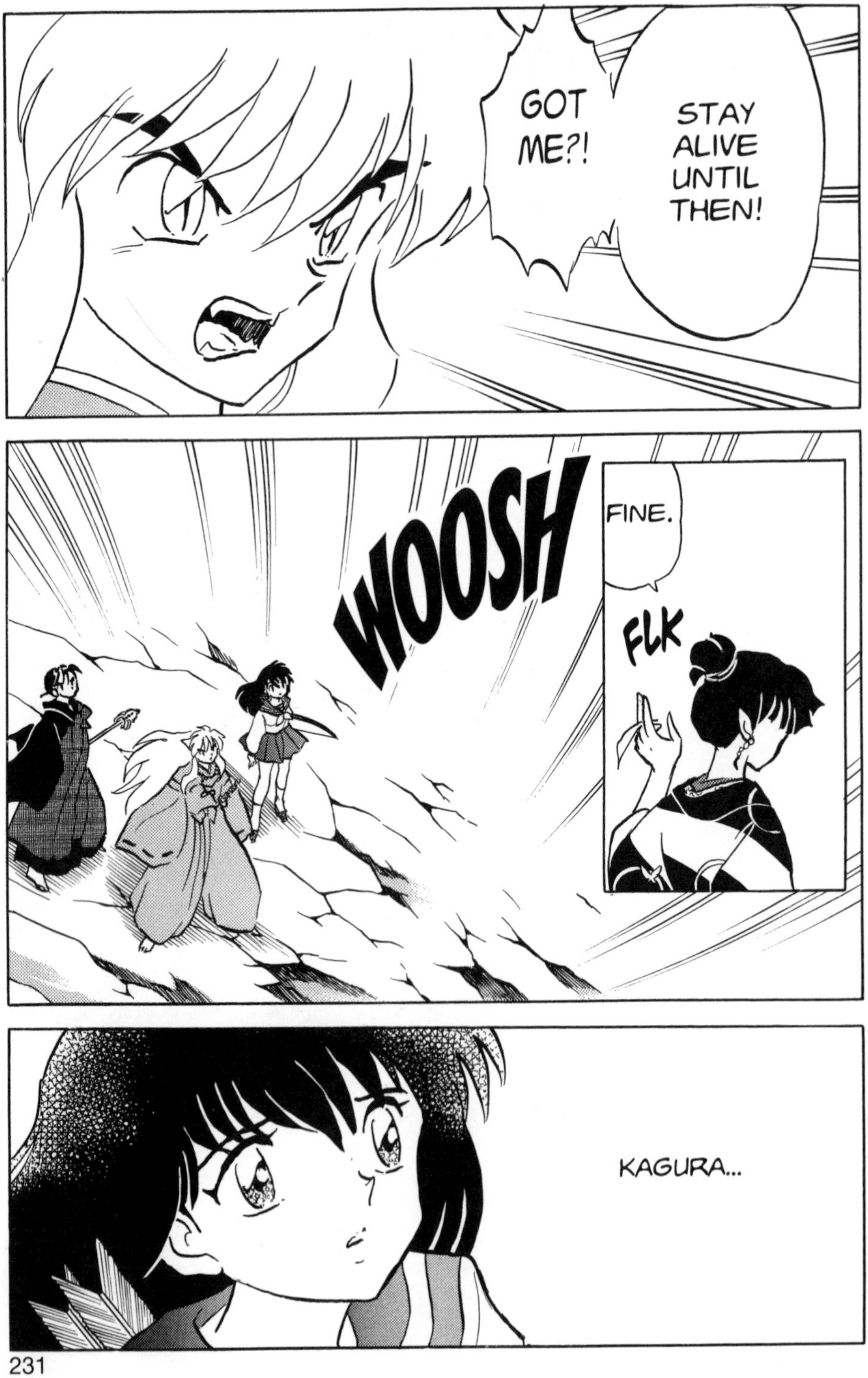
STAY ALIVE UNTIL THEN!
GOT ME?!
FINE.
FLK
WOOSH
KAGURA...

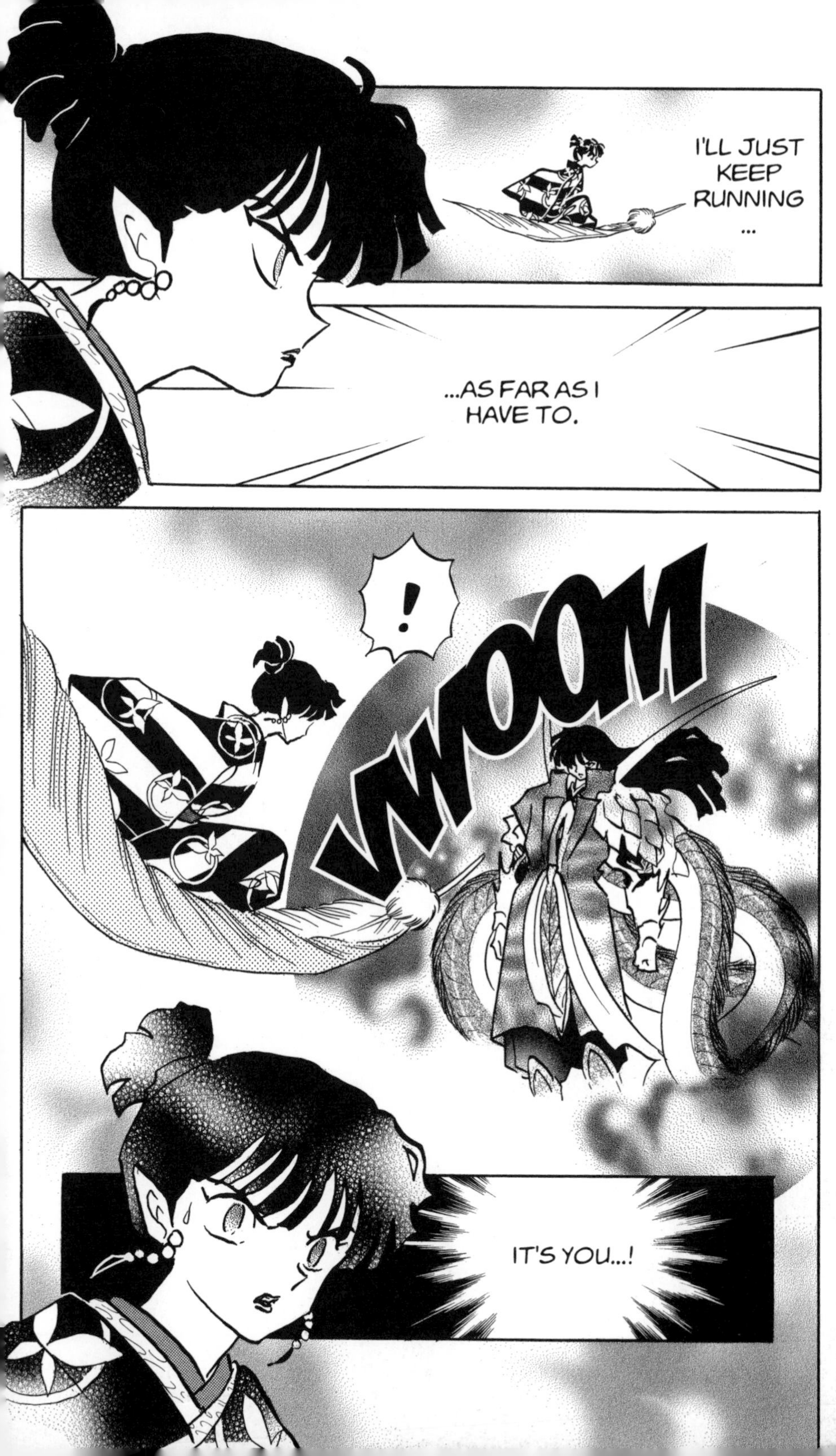
I'LL JUST KEEP RUNNING ...
...AS FAR AS I HAVE TO.
!
VWOOM
IT'S YOU...!

SCROLL THREE
KAGURA'S HEART

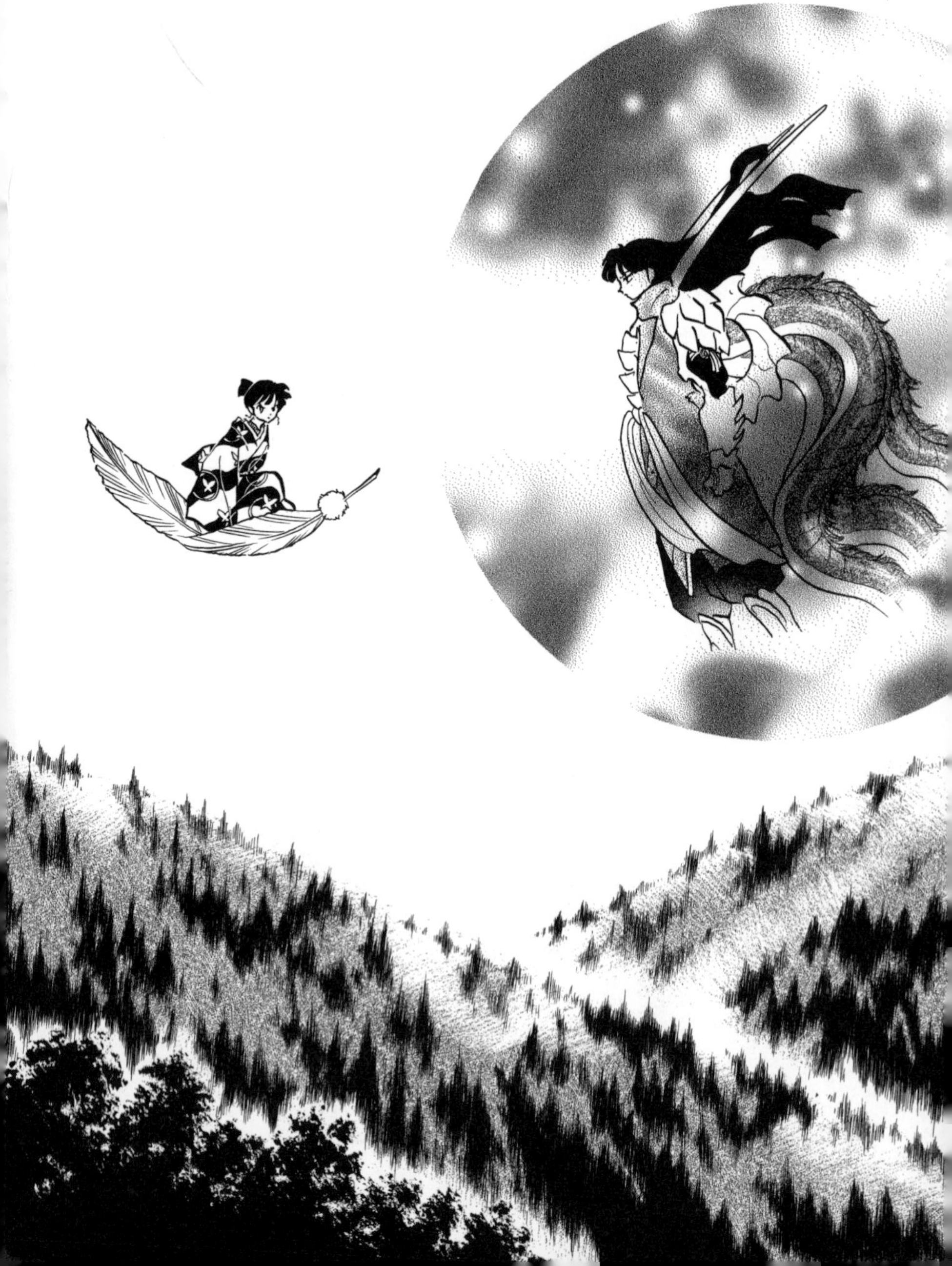

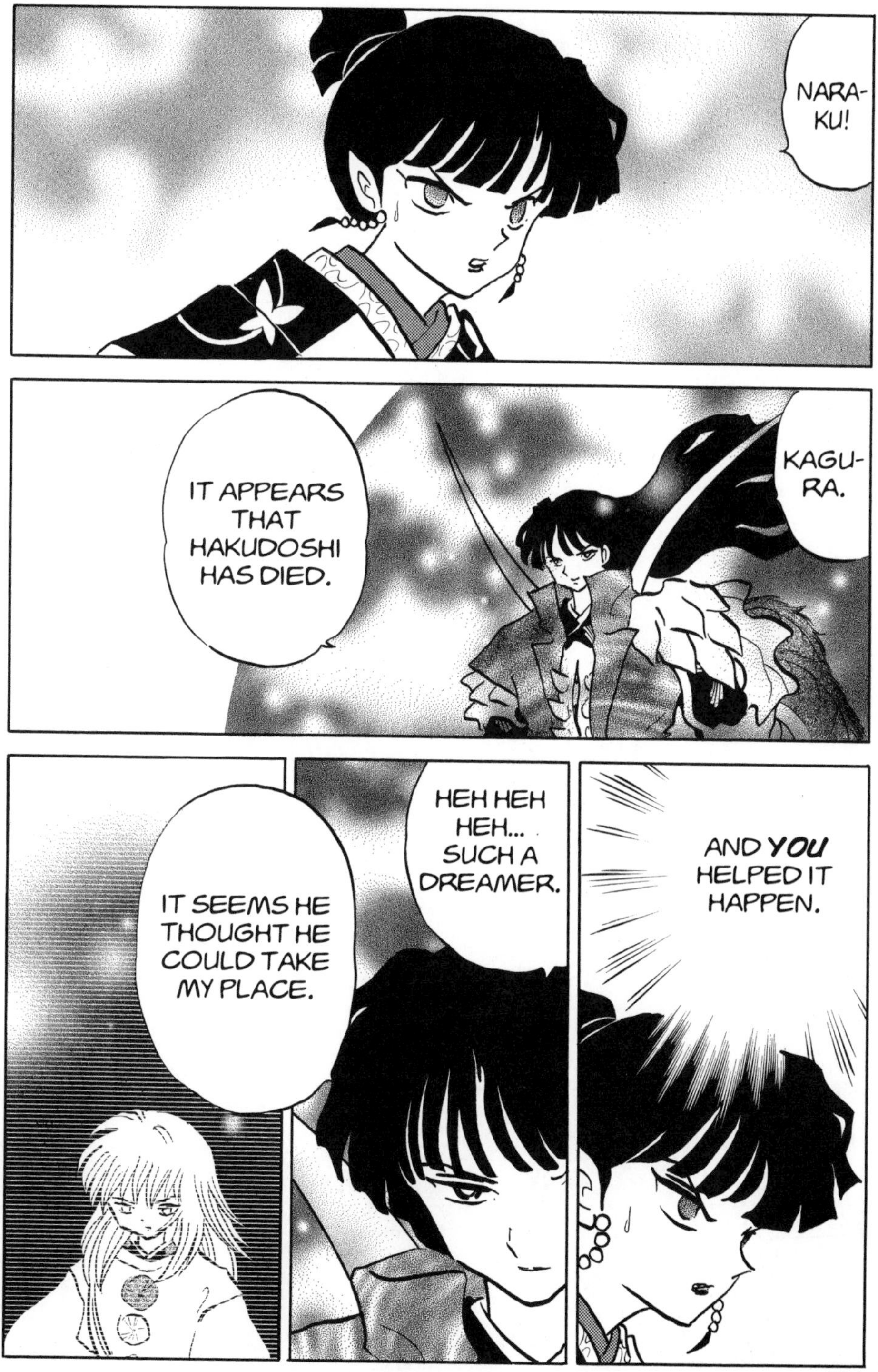
NARA-KU!
KAGU-RA.
IT APPEARS THAT HAKUDOSHI HAS DIED.
AND **YOU** HELPED IT HAPPEN.
HEH HEH HEH... SUCH A DREAMER.
IT SEEMS HE THOUGHT HE COULD TAKE MY PLACE.

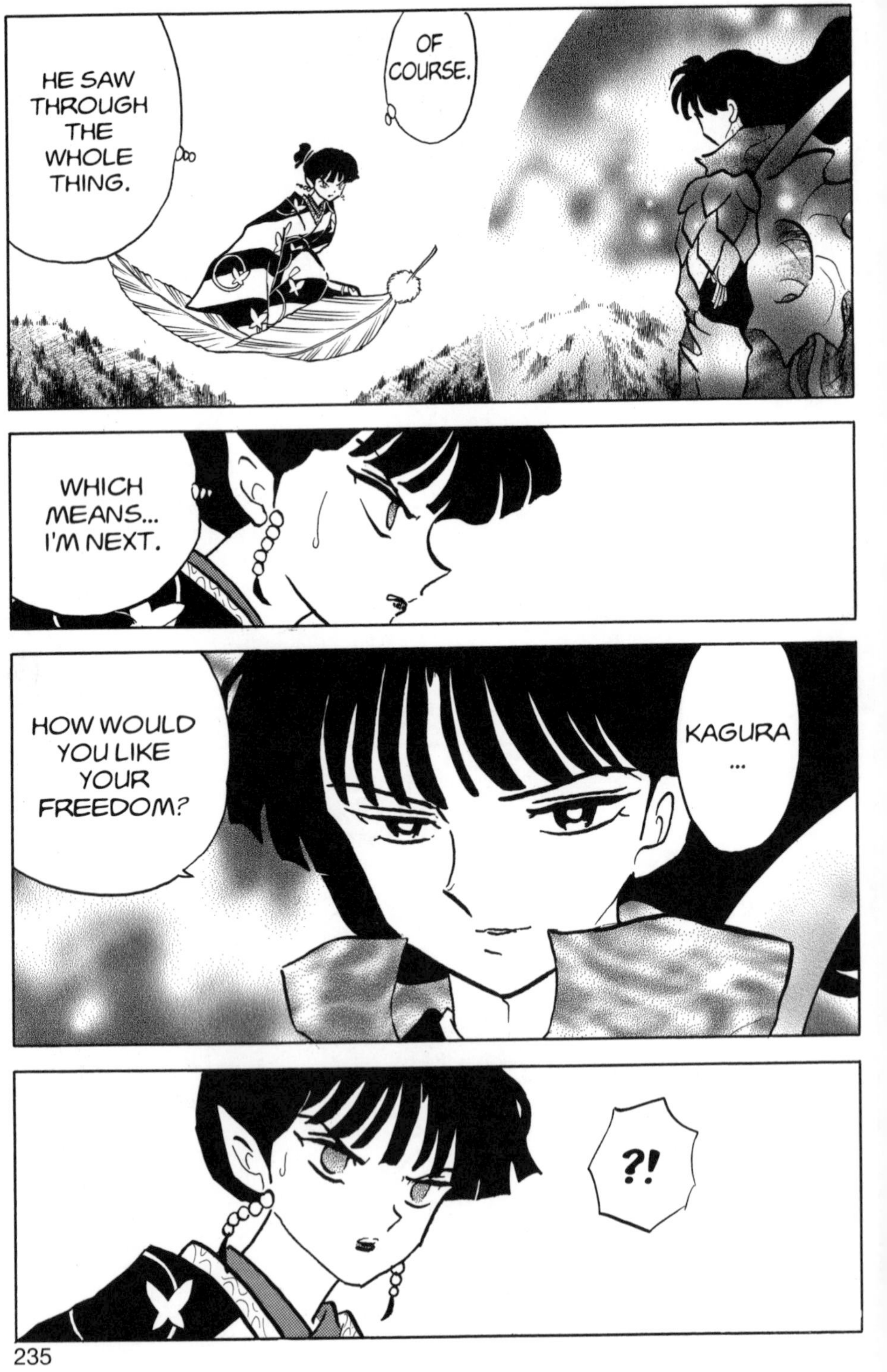
OF COURSE.
HE SAW THROUGH THE WHOLE THING.
WHICH MEANS... I'M NEXT.
KAGURA ...
HOW WOULD YOU LIKE YOUR FREEDOM?
?!

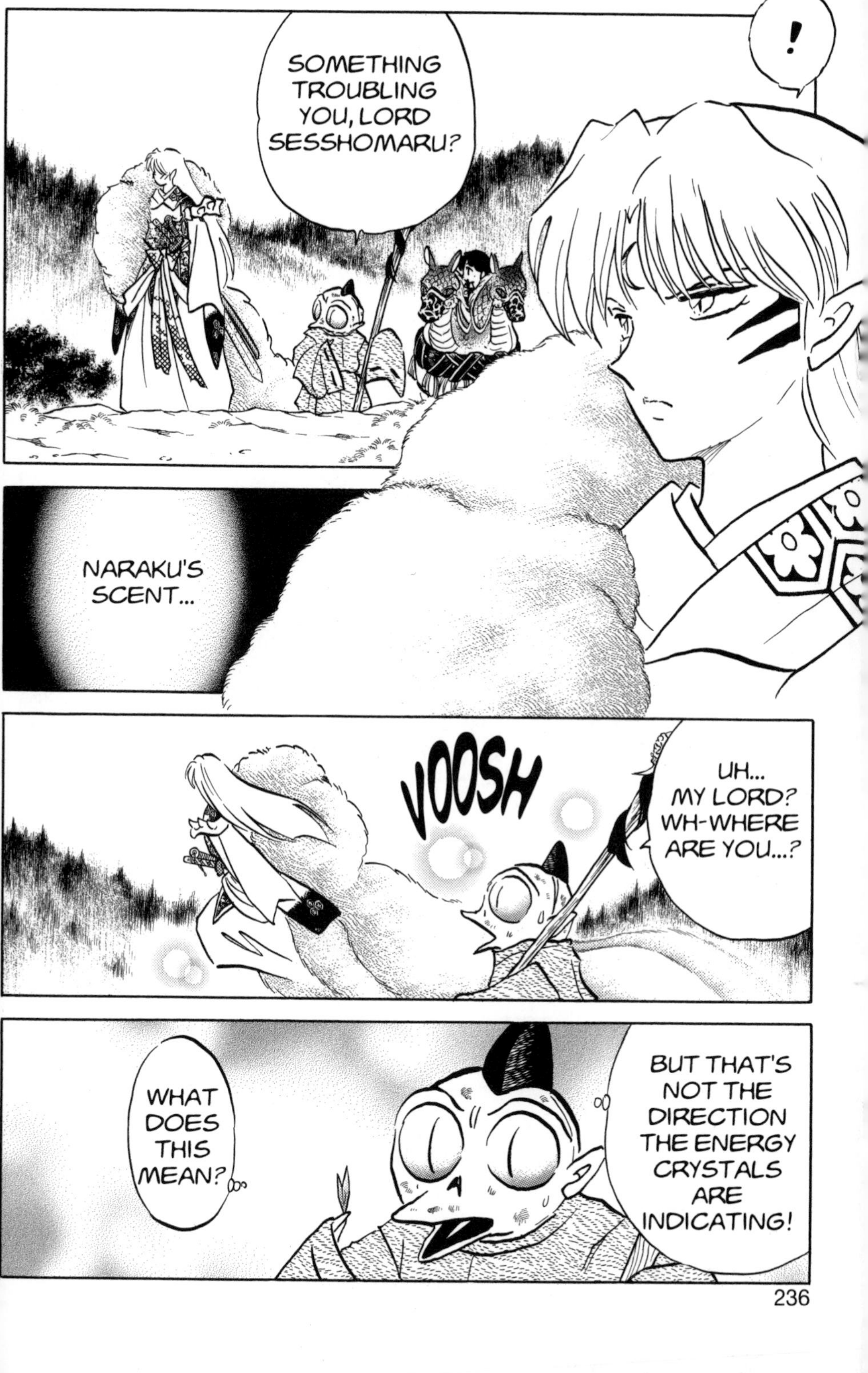
!
SOMETHING TROUBLING YOU, LORD SESSHOMARU?
NARAKU'S SCENT...
UH... MY LORD? WH-WHERE ARE YOU...?
VOOSH
BUT THAT'S NOT THE DIRECTION THE ENERGY CRYSTALS ARE INDICATING!
WHAT DOES THIS MEAN?

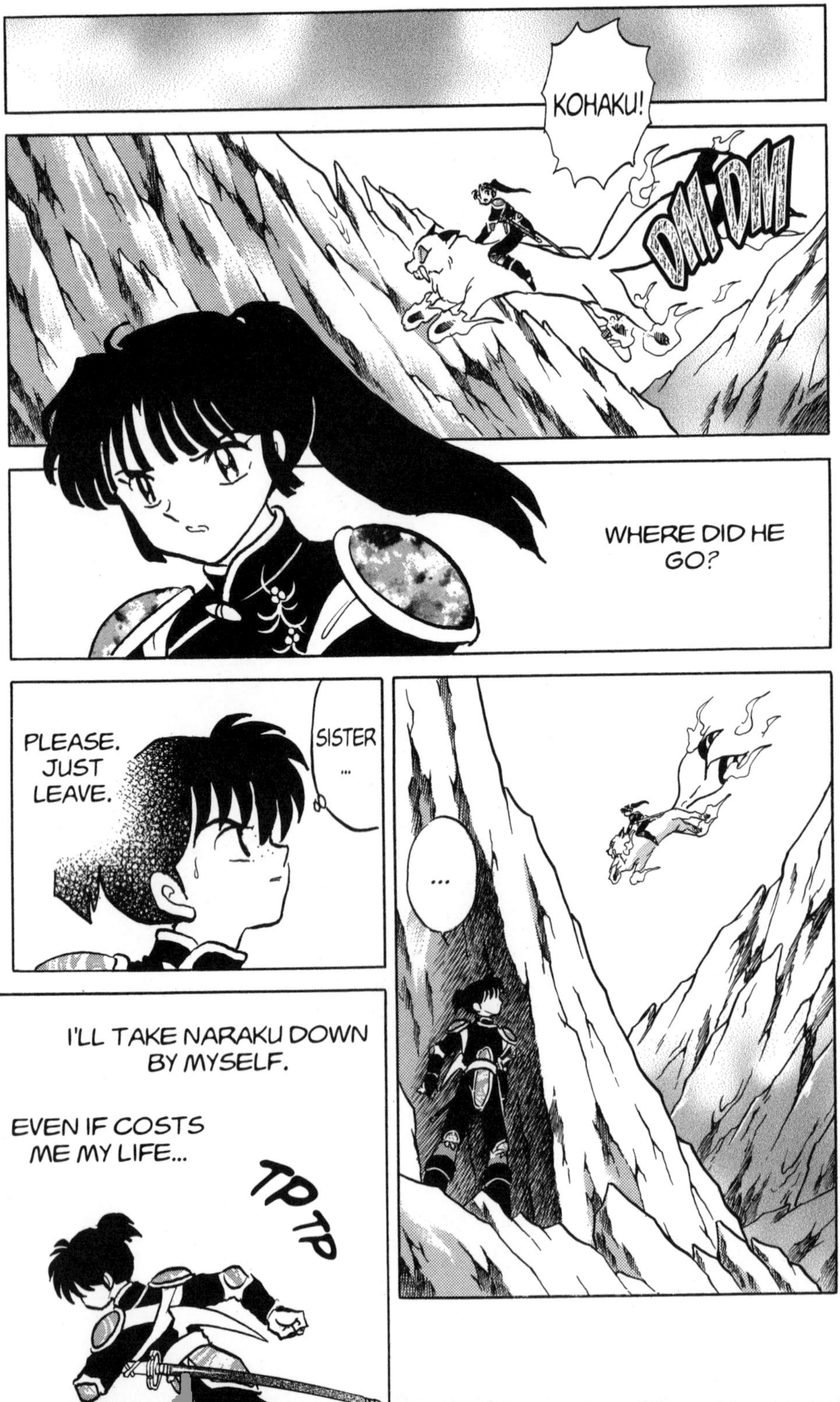

KOHAKU!
DM DM
WHERE DID HE GO?
...
SISTER ...
PLEASE. JUST LEAVE.
I'LL TAKE NARAKU DOWN BY MYSELF.
EVEN IF COSTS ME MY LIFE...
TP TP

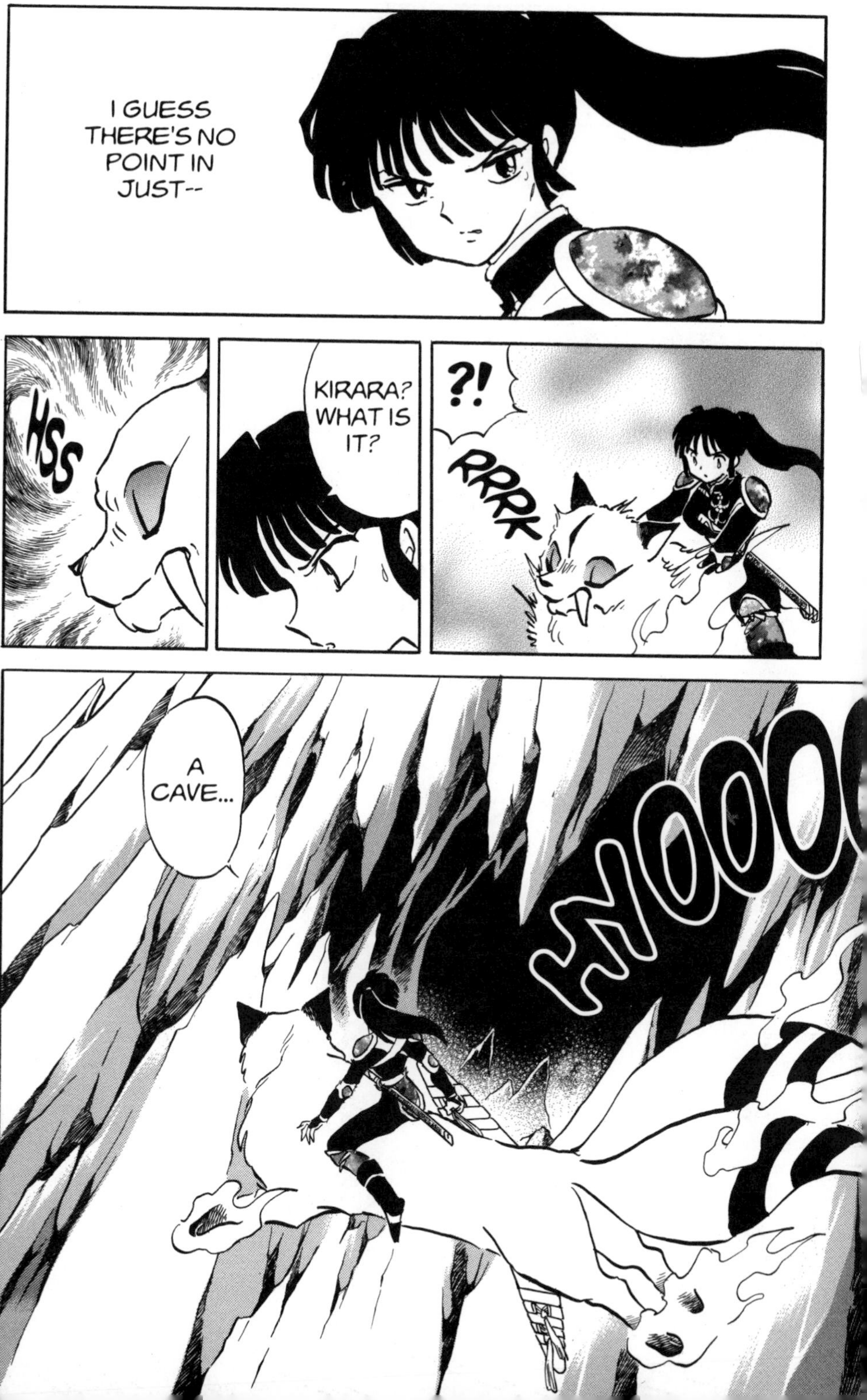
I GUESS THERE'S NO POINT IN JUST--
?!
RRRK
KIRARA? WHAT IS IT?
HSS
A CAVE...
HYOOO

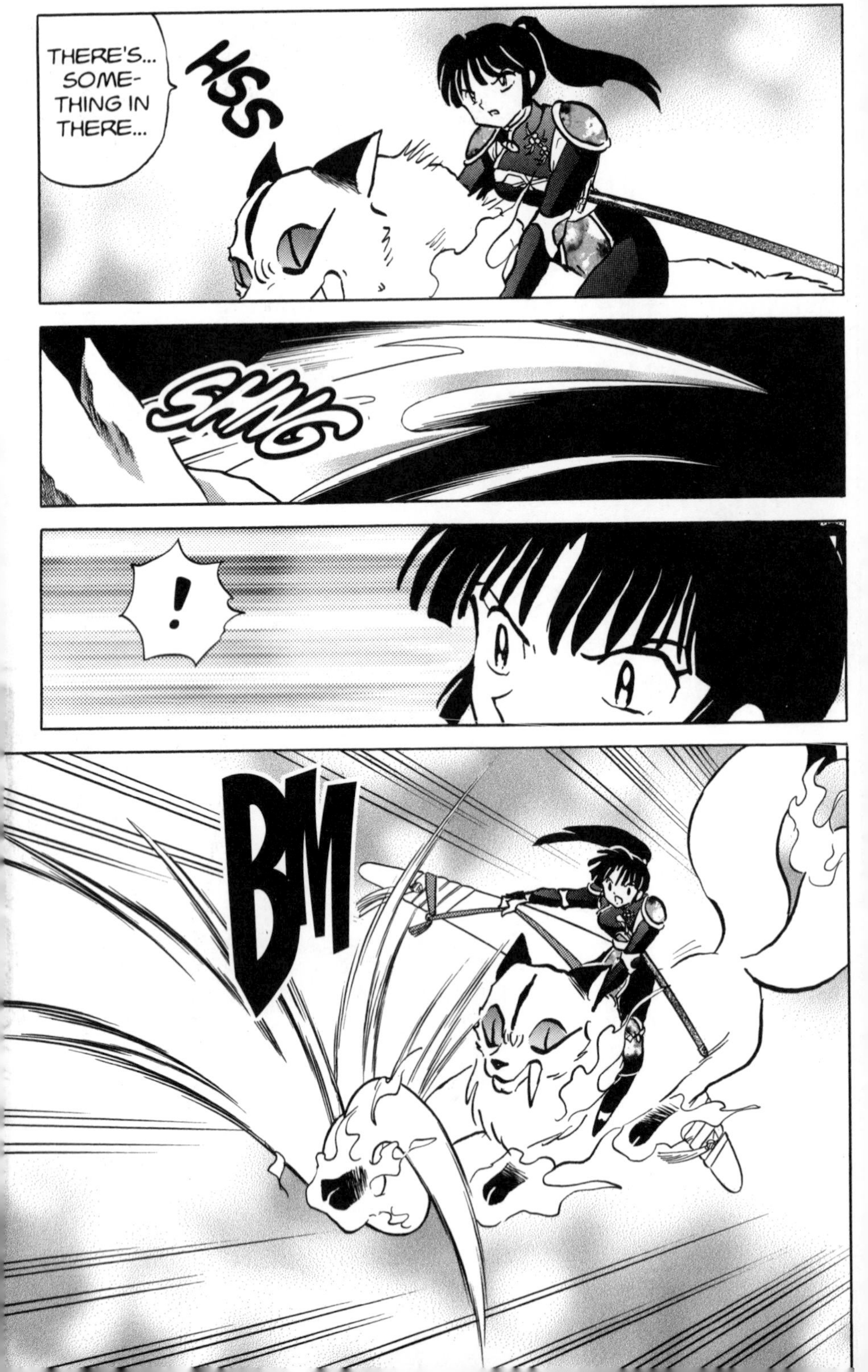
HSS
THERE'S... SOME-THING IN THERE...
SHING
!
BM

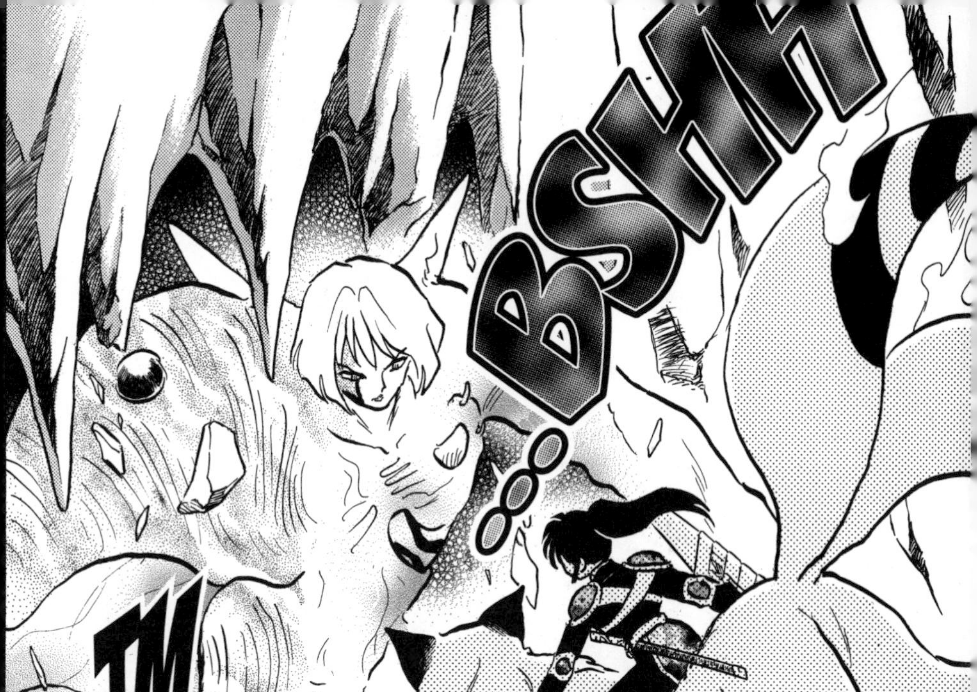
BSHH
TM TM TM
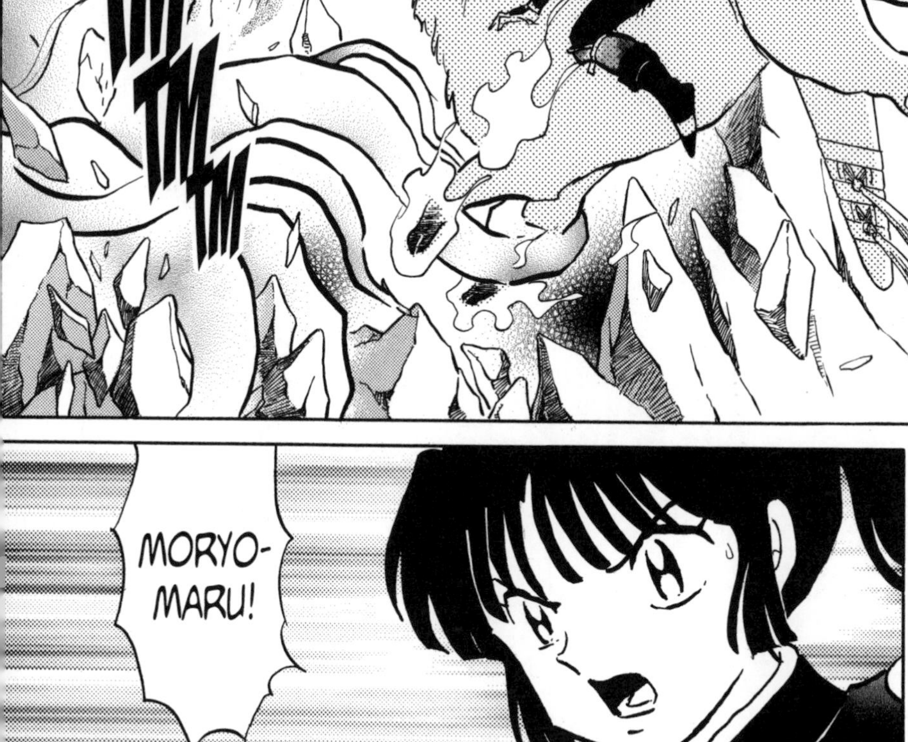
MORYO-
MARU!

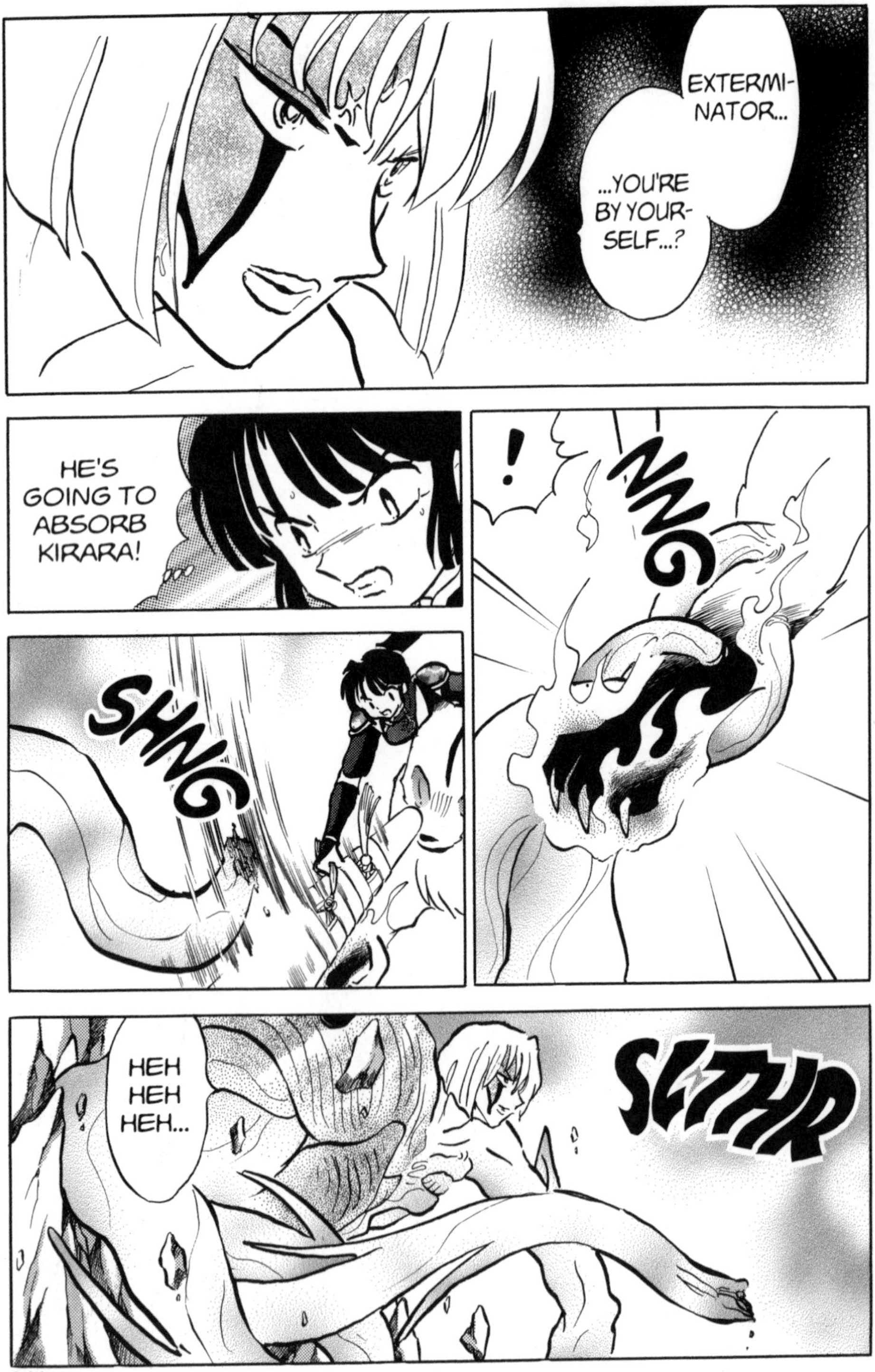
EXTERMINATOR...
...YOU'RE BY YOURSELF...?
!
HE'S GOING TO ABSORB KIRARA!
SHNG
SLTHR
HEH HEH HEH...

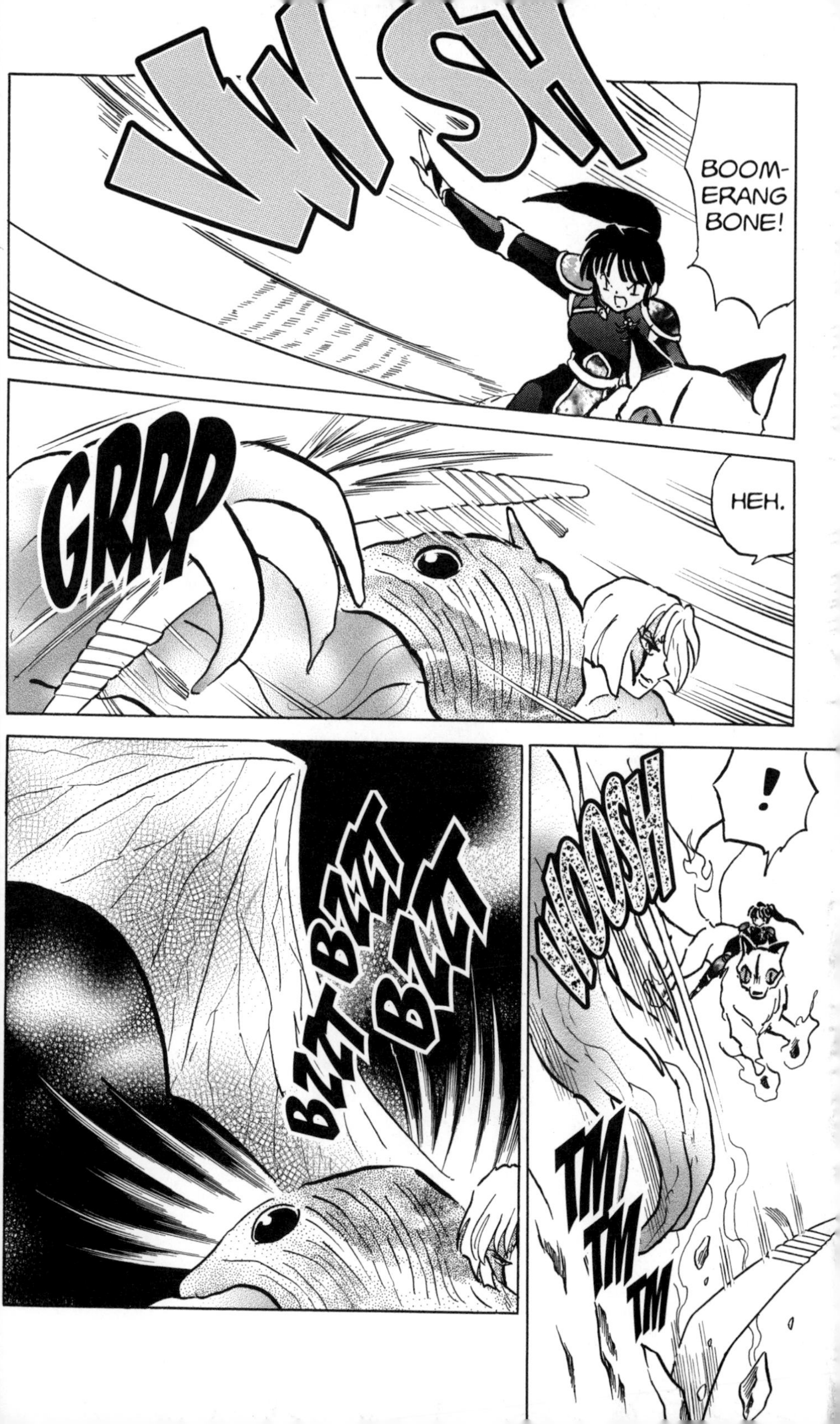
VWSH
BOOM-
ERANG
BONE!
GRRP
HEH.
!
WOOSH
TM
TM
TM
BZZT
BZZT
BZZT

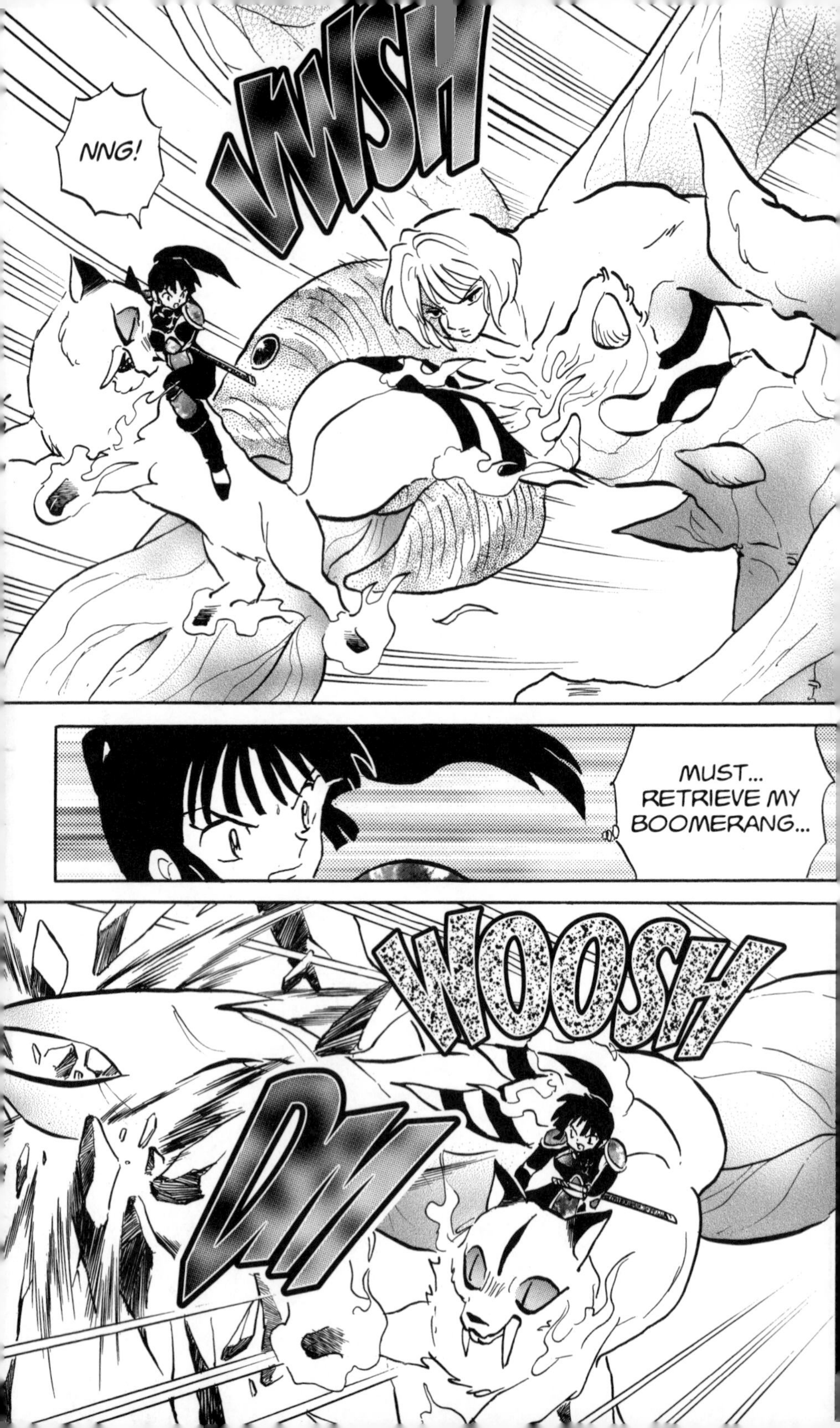
VWSH
NNG!
MUST... RETRIEVE MY BOOMERANG...
WOOSH
ZM

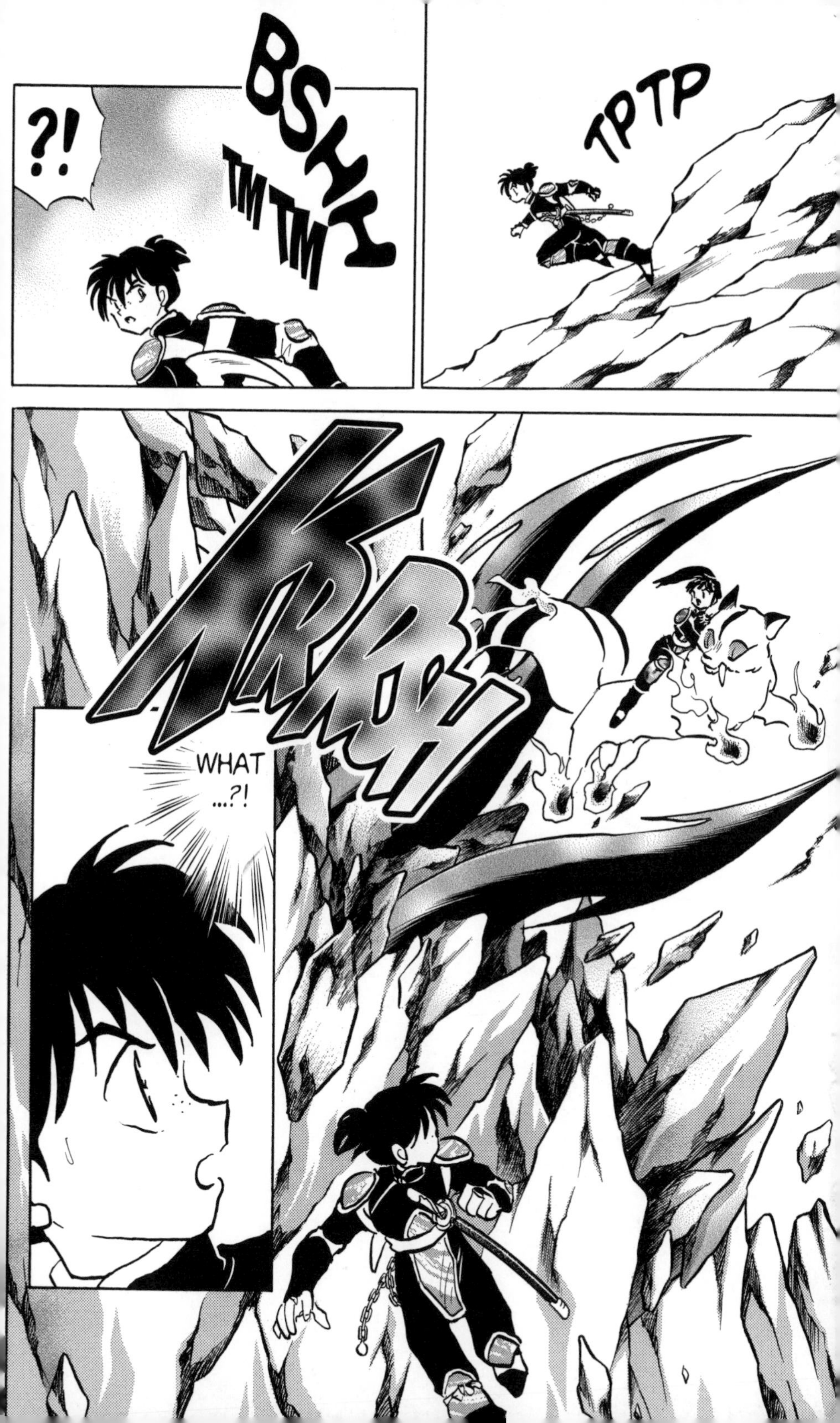
TPTP
?!
BSHH
TM TM
KRASH
WHAT ...?!

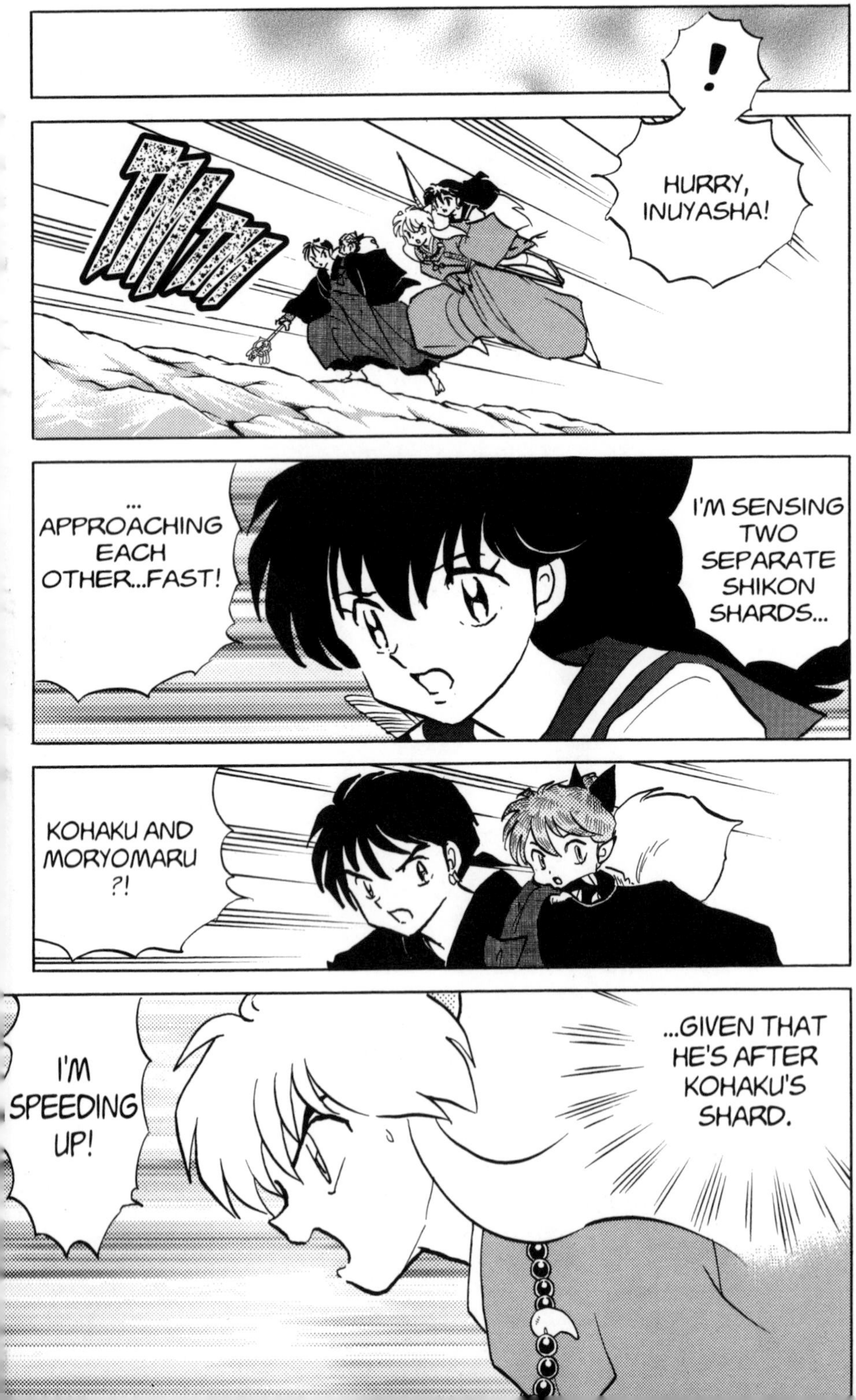
!
HURRY, INUYASHA!
I'M SENSING TWO SEPARATE SHIKON SHARDS...
...APPROACHING EACH OTHER...FAST!
KOHAKU AND MORYOMARU ?!
...GIVEN THAT HE'S AFTER KOHAKU'S SHARD.
I'M SPEEDING UP!

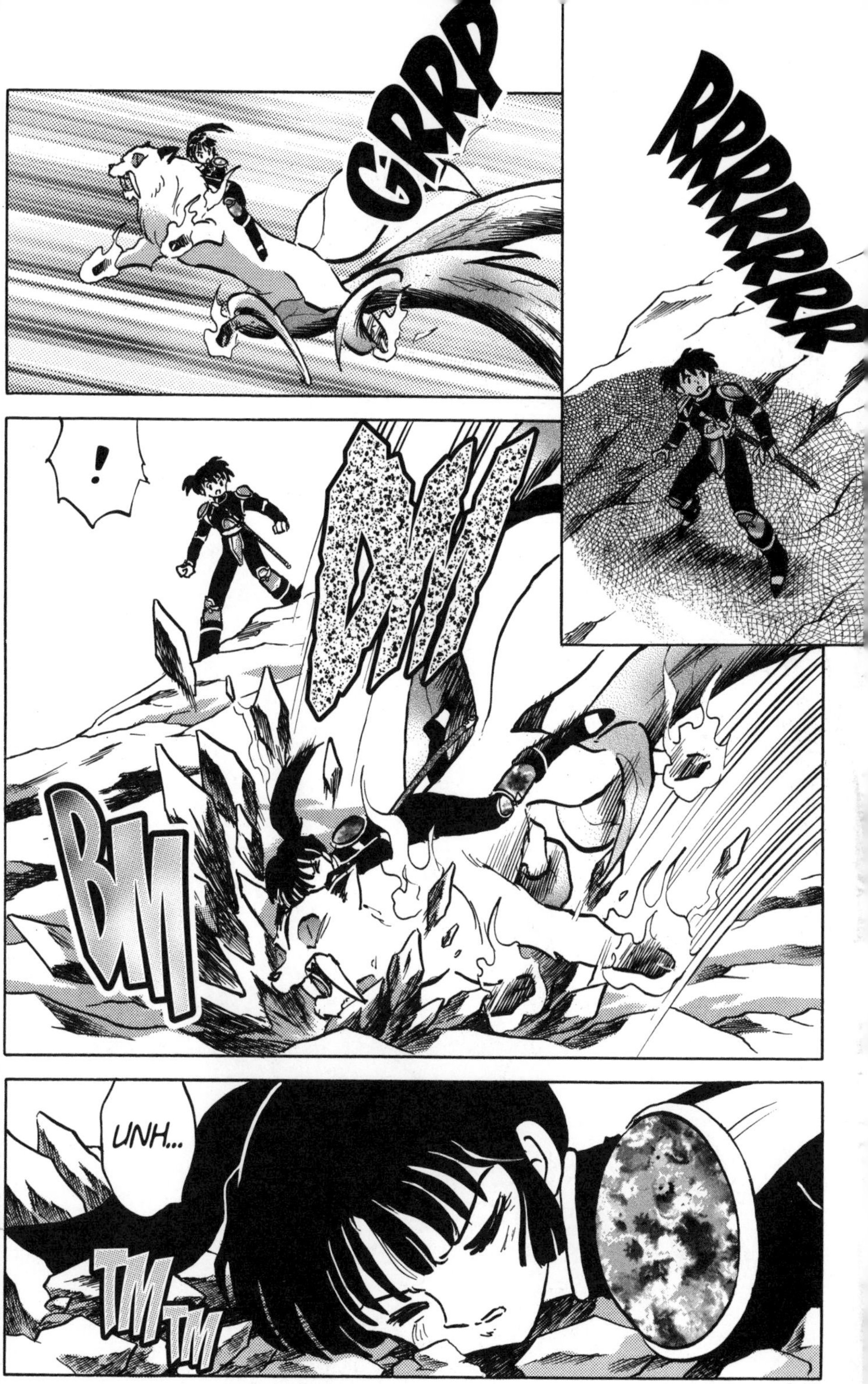
GRRP
RRRRRRRR
!
DM
BM
UNH...
TM TM

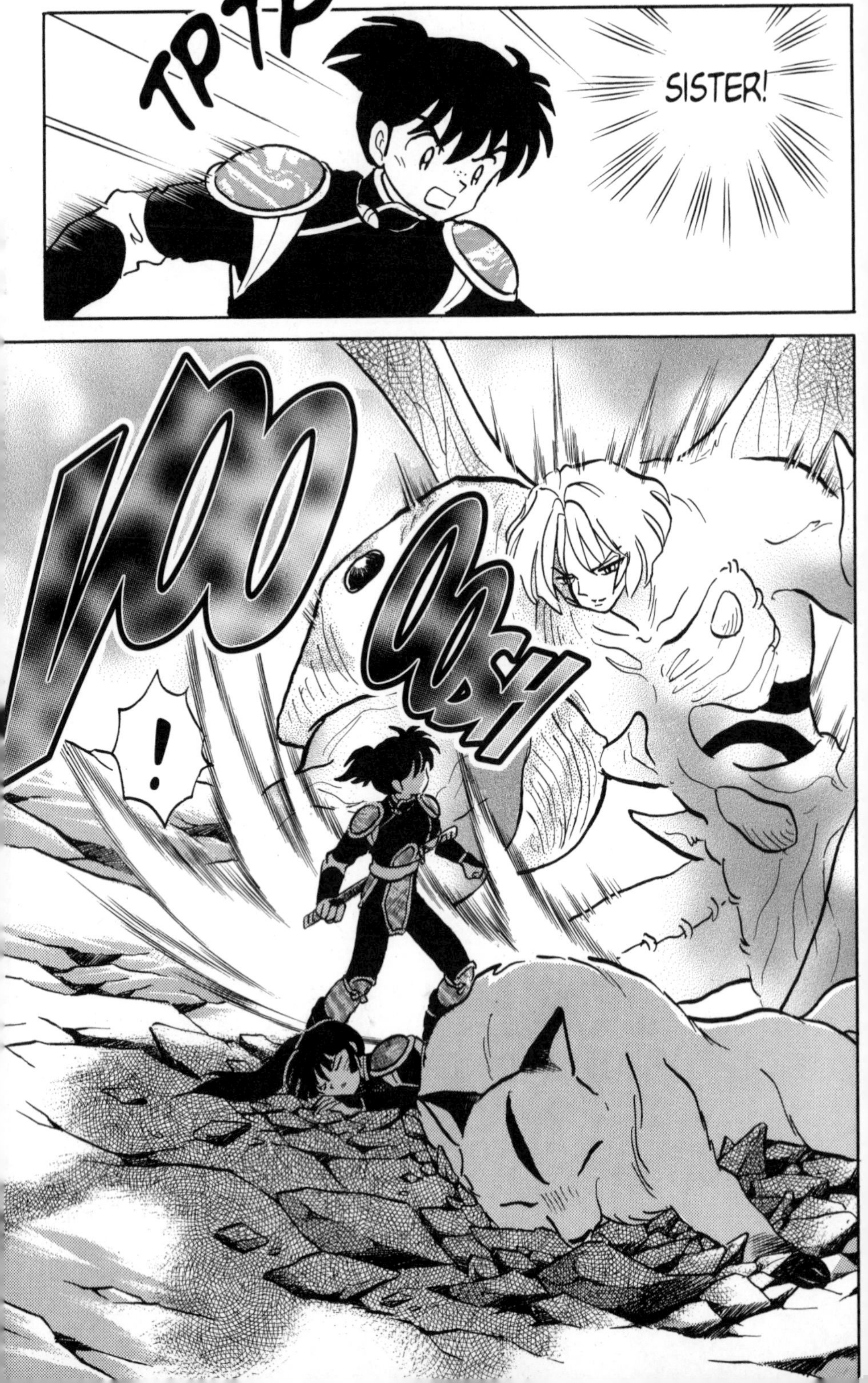
SISTER!
TPTP
!

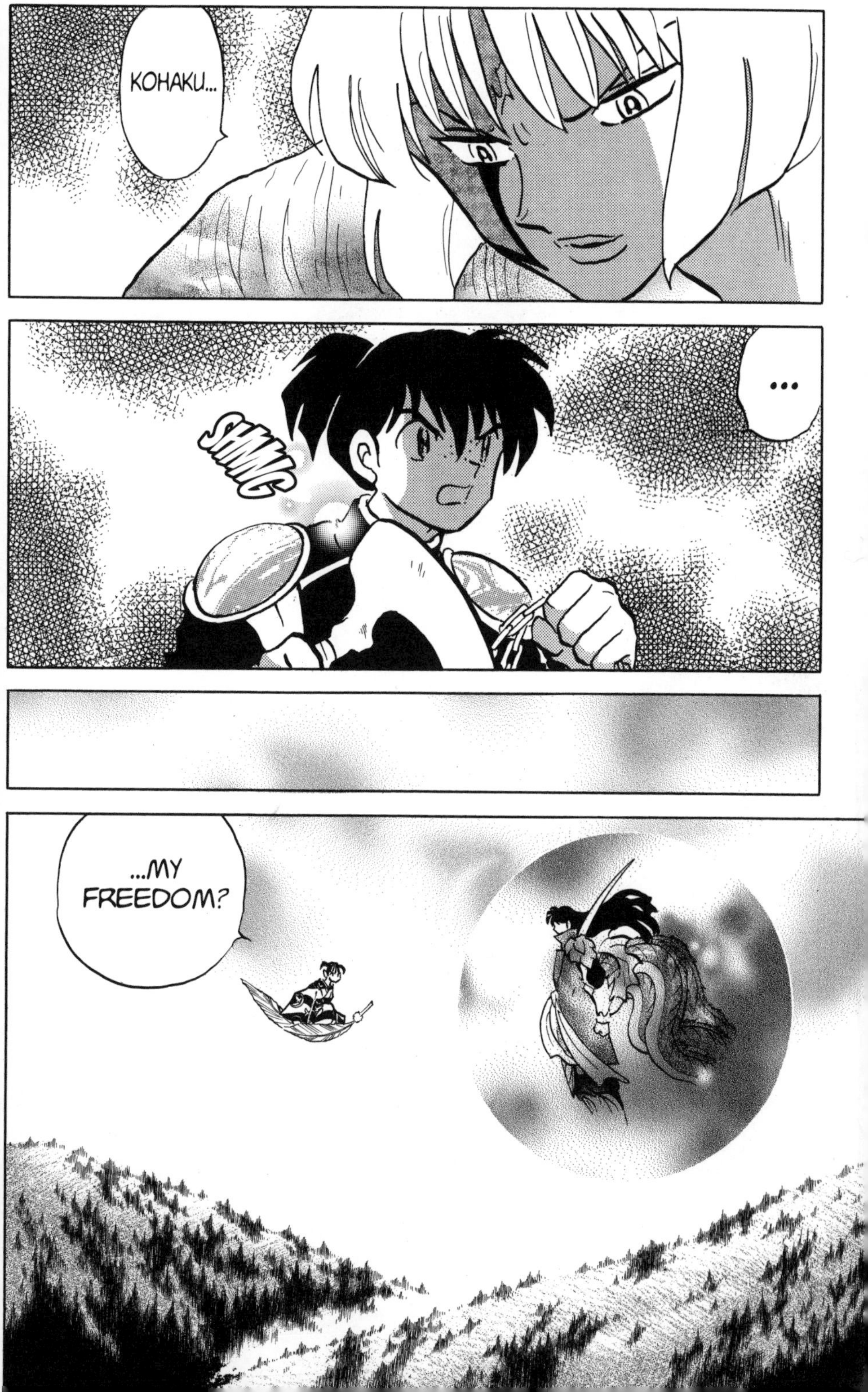
KOHAKU...
...
SHING
...MY FREEDOM?

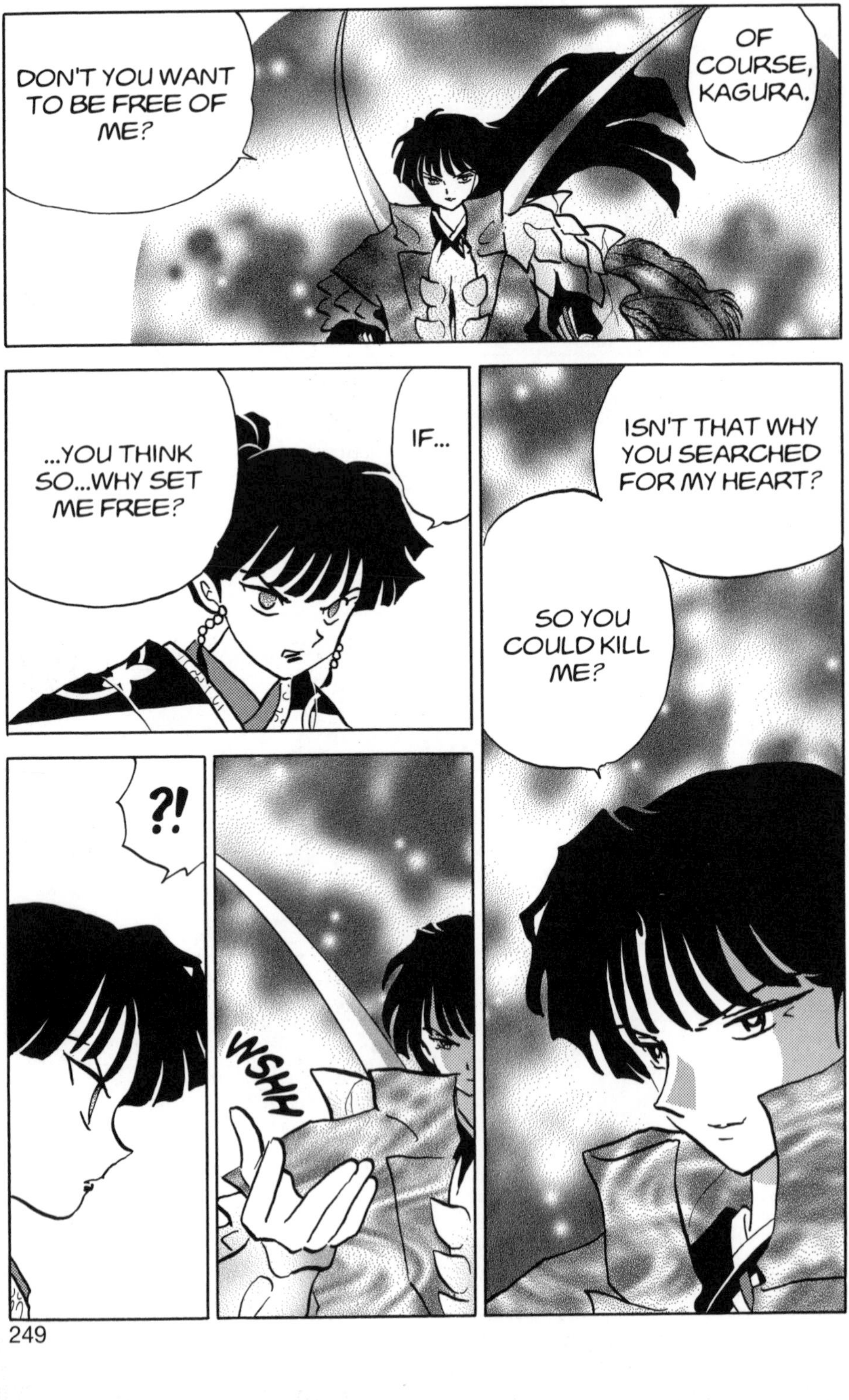
OF COURSE, KAGURA.
DON'T YOU WANT TO BE FREE OF ME?
ISN'T THAT WHY YOU SEARCHED FOR MY HEART?
SO YOU COULD KILL ME?
IF...
...YOU THINK SO...WHY SET ME FREE?
WSHH
?!

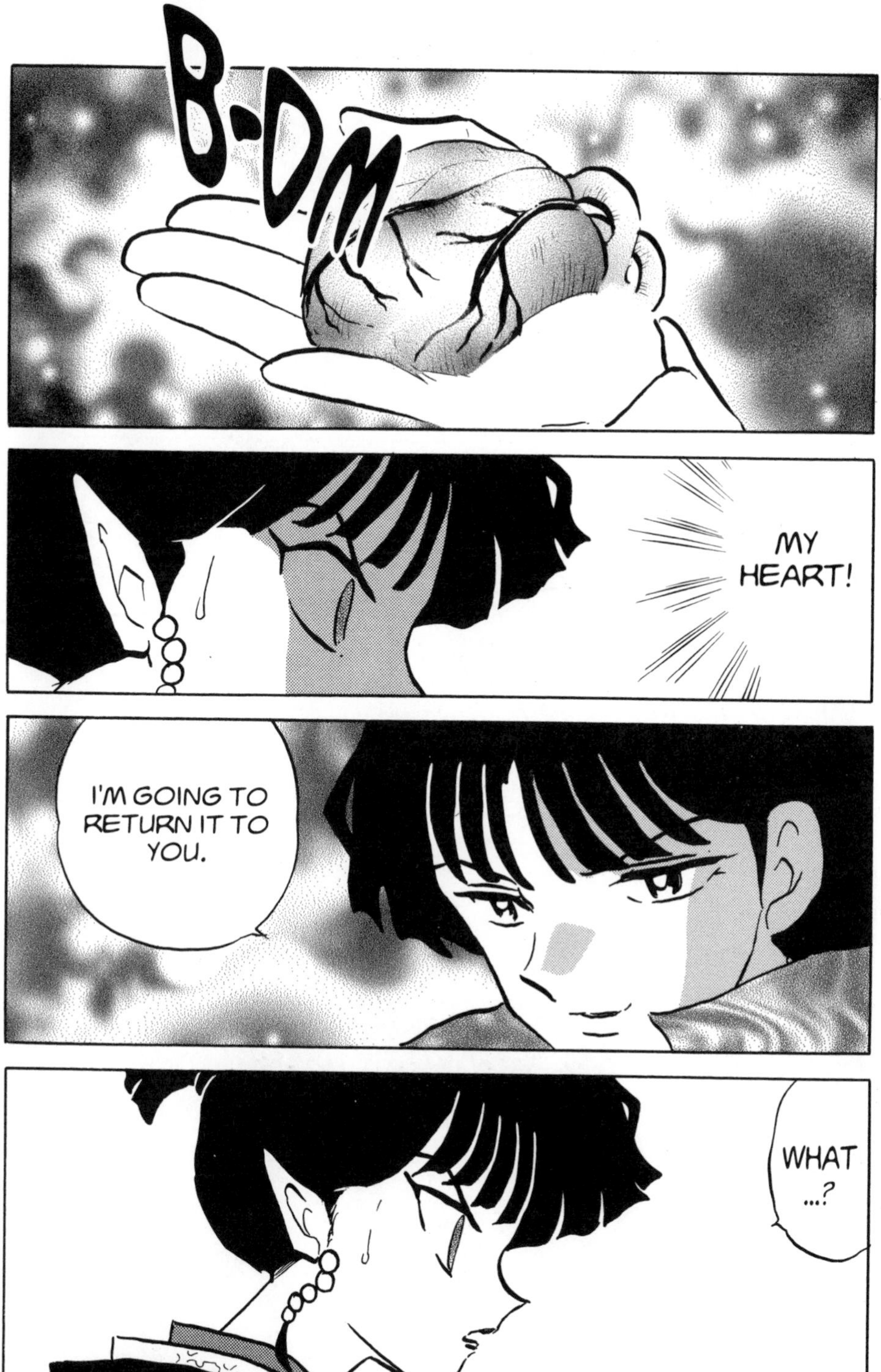
B-DM
MY HEART!
I'M GOING TO RETURN IT TO YOU.
WHAT ...?

SCROLL FOUR
PAIN WITHOUT END

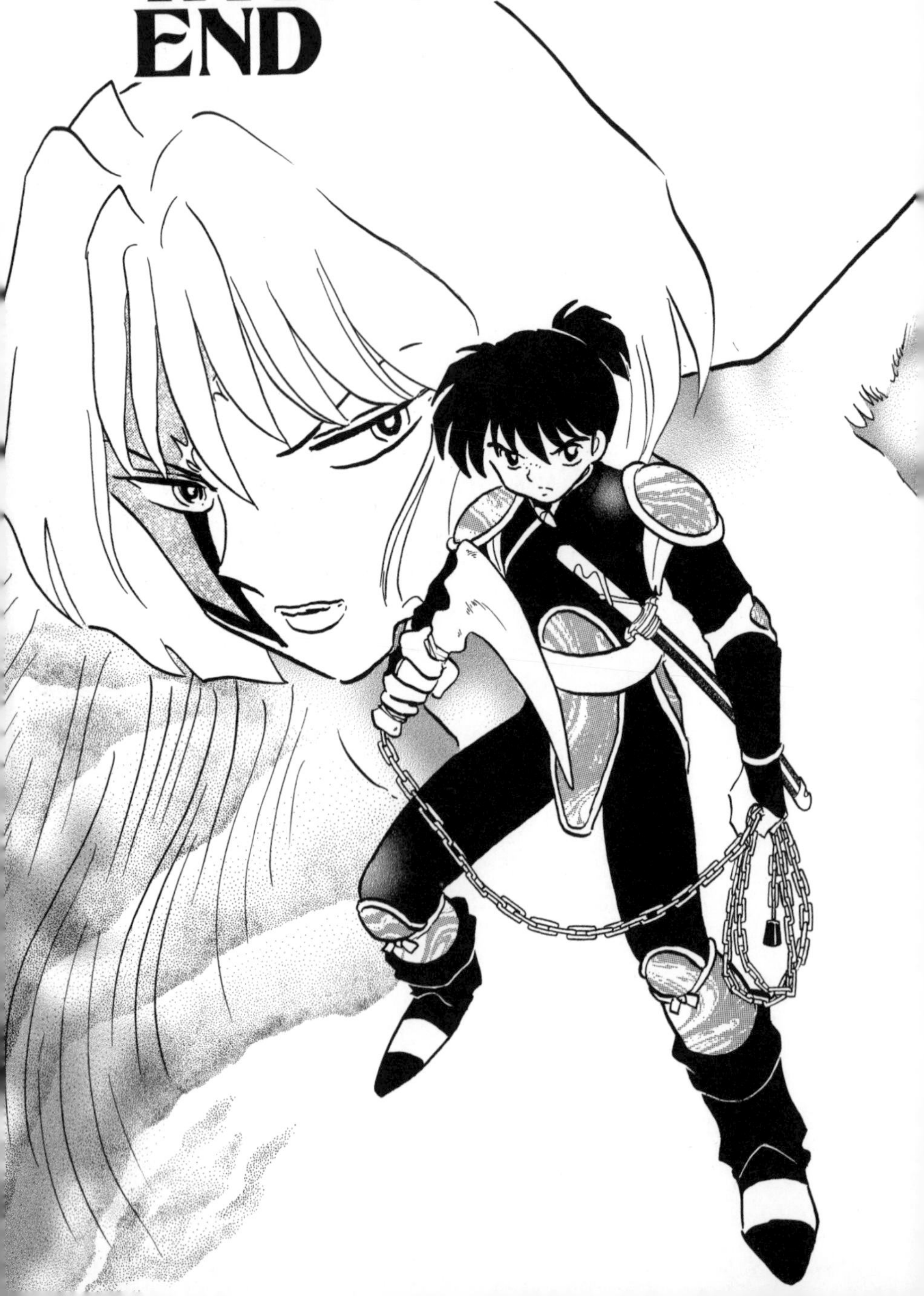

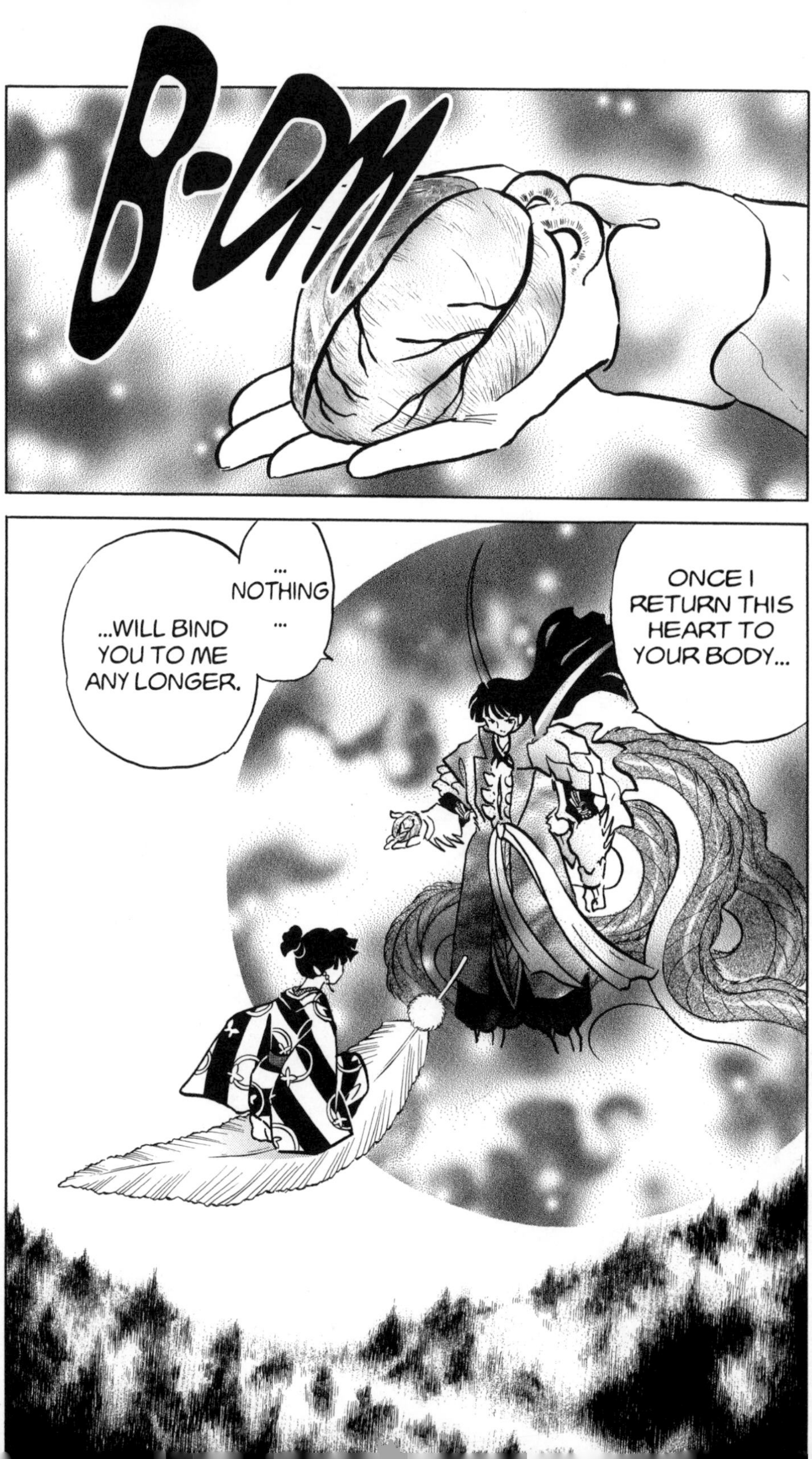
B-DM
ONCE I RETURN THIS HEART TO YOUR BODY...
... NOTHING ...
...WILL BIND YOU TO ME ANY LONGER.

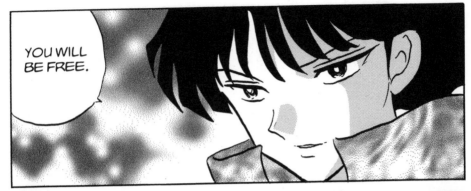

YOU WILL BE FREE.

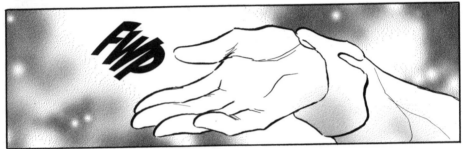

FWP

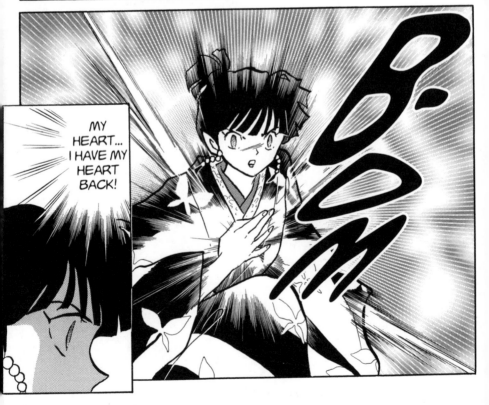

MY HEART... I HAVE MY HEART BACK!

BOOM

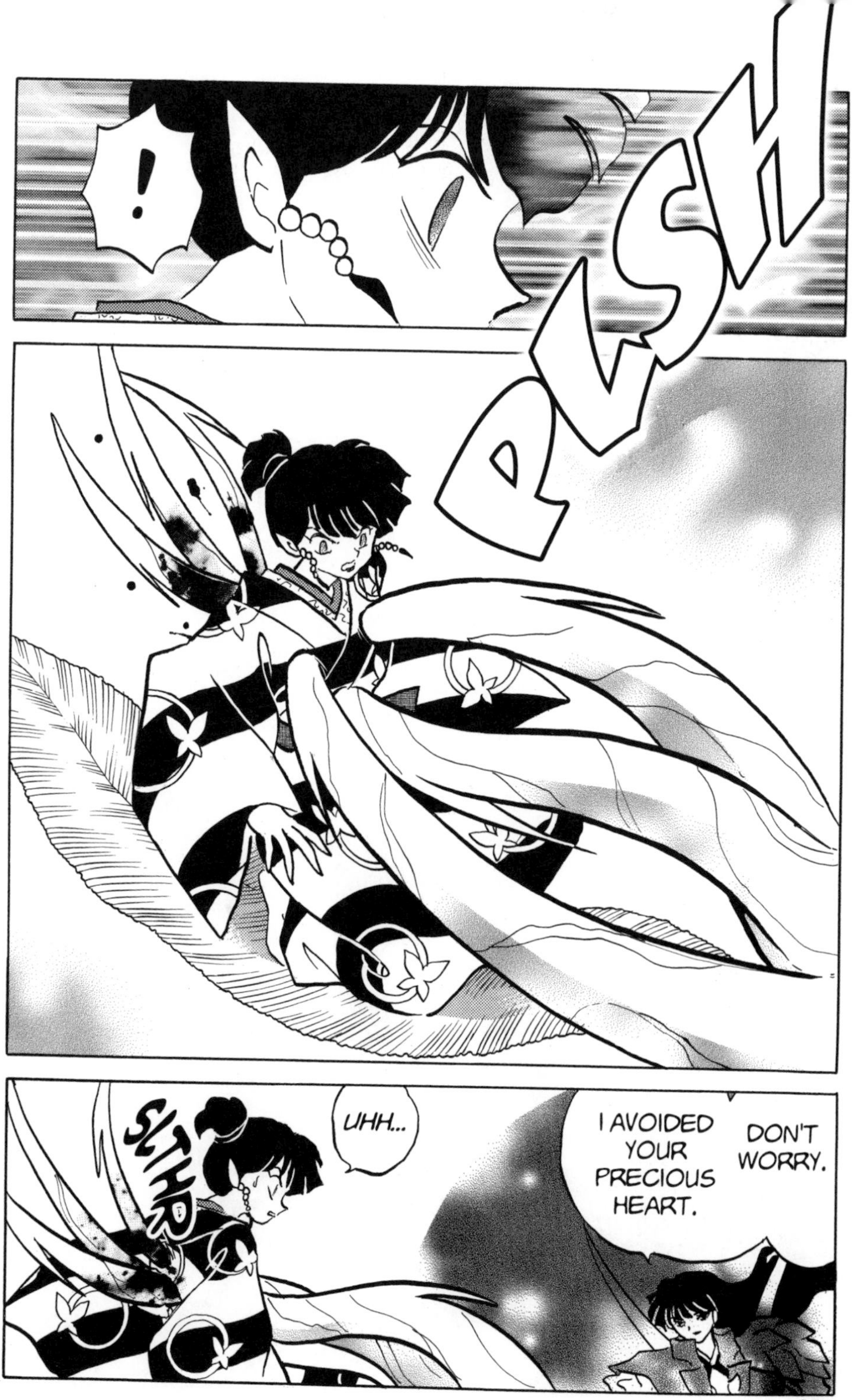
!
PESH
DON'T WORRY.
I AVOIDED YOUR PRECIOUS HEART.
UHH...
SLTHR

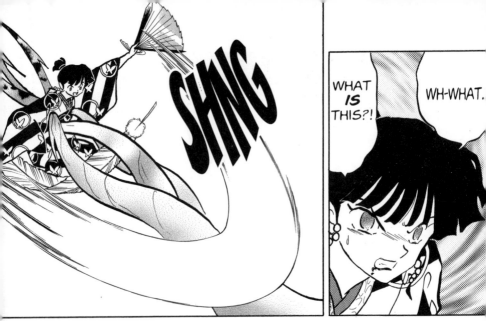

SHNG

WHAT **IS** THIS?!

WH-WHAT.

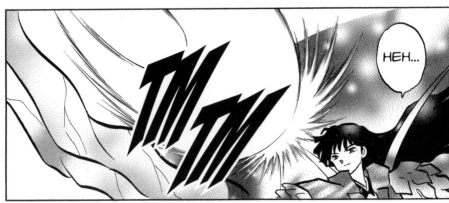

TM TM

HEH...

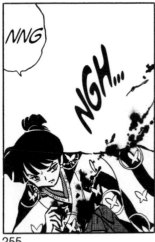

NNG

NGH....

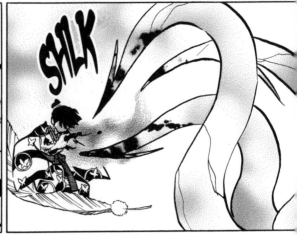

SHLK

255

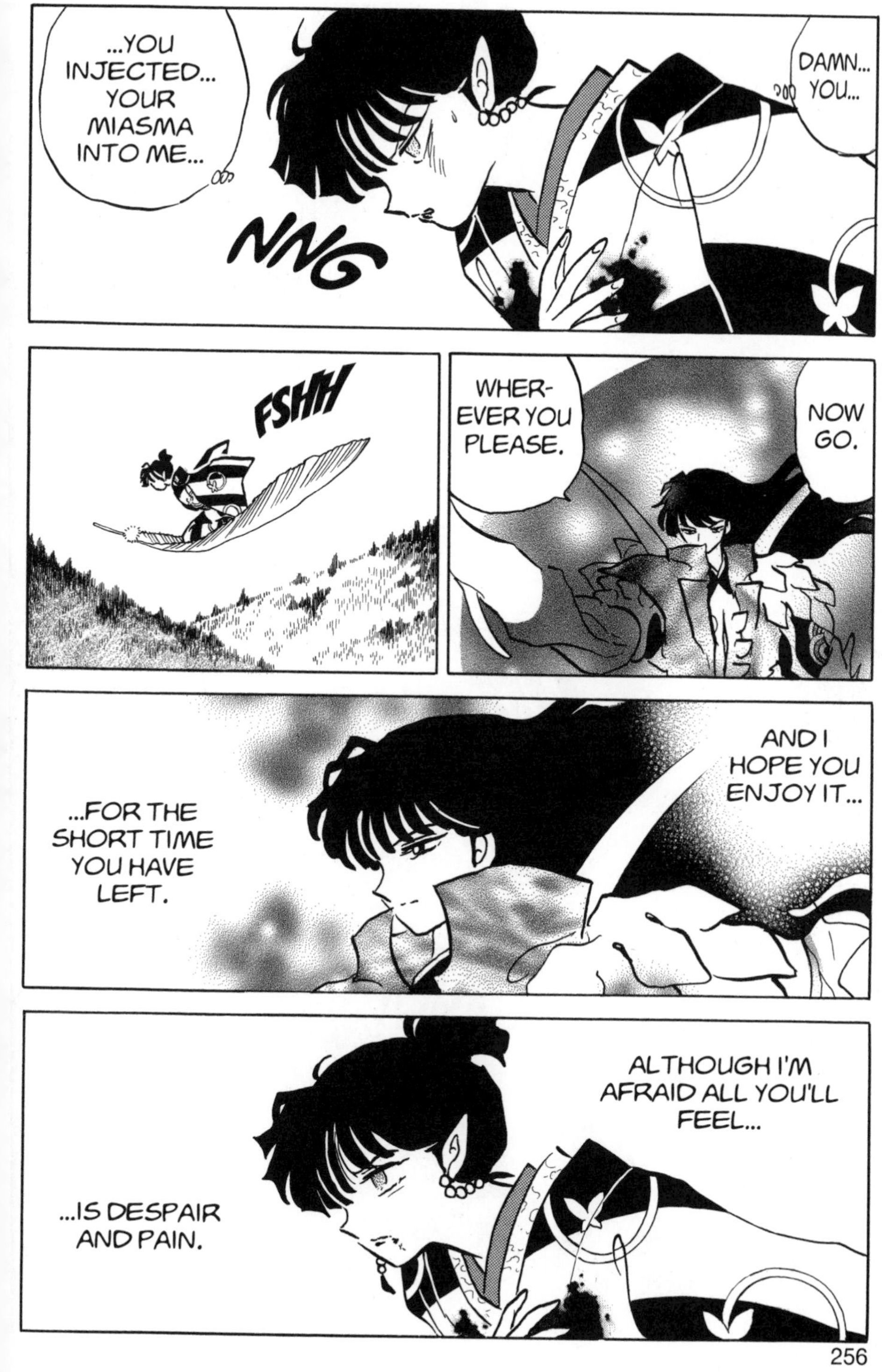
DAMN... YOU...
...YOU INJECTED... YOUR MIASMA INTO ME...
NNG
NOW GO.
WHER-EVER YOU PLEASE.
FSHH
AND I HOPE YOU ENJOY IT...
...FOR THE SHORT TIME YOU HAVE LEFT.
ALTHOUGH I'M AFRAID ALL YOU'LL FEEL...
...IS DESPAIR AND PAIN.

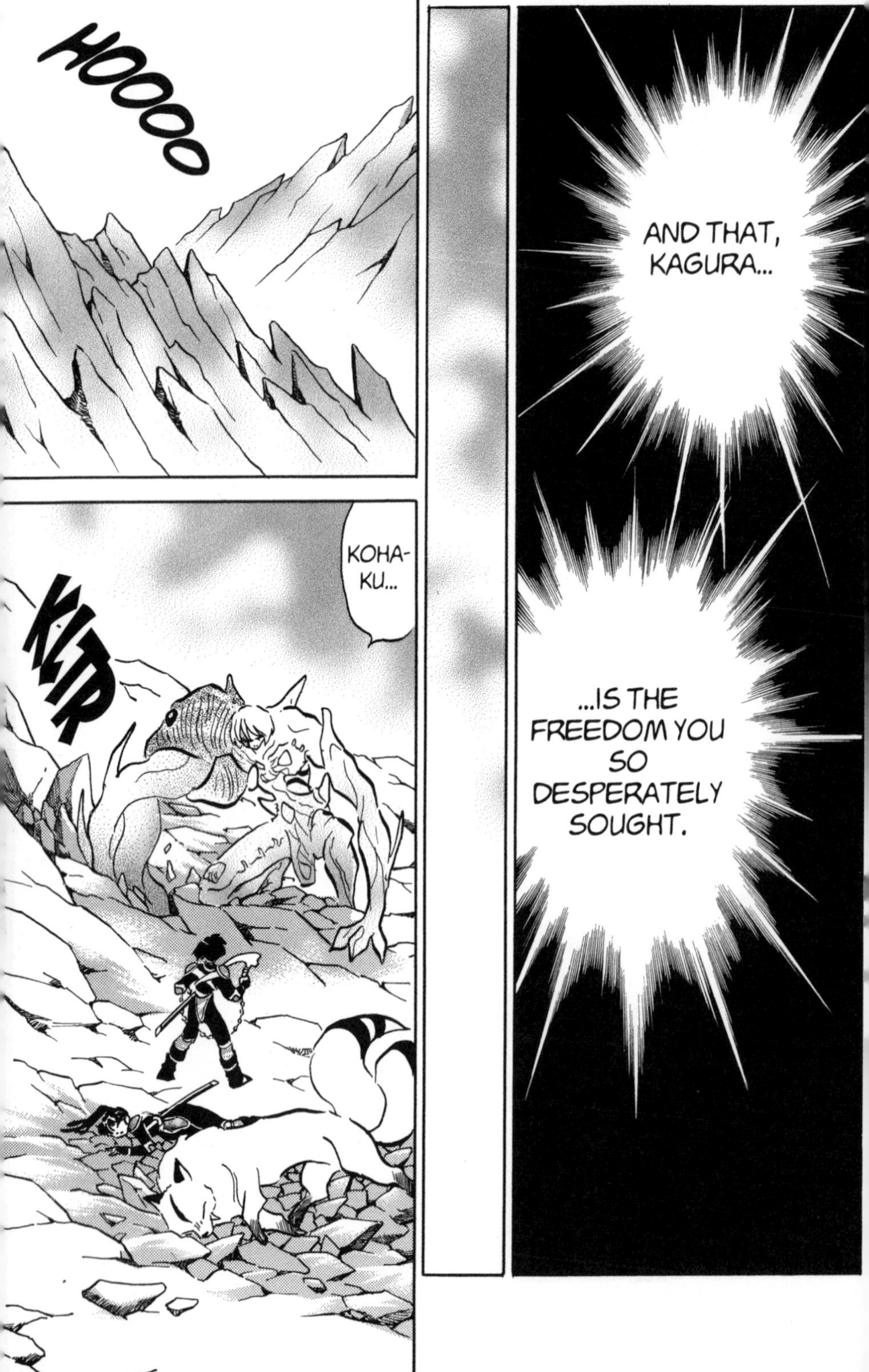
AND THAT, KAGURA...
...IS THE FREEDOM YOU SO DESPERATELY SOUGHT.
HOOOO
KOHA-KU...
KLTR

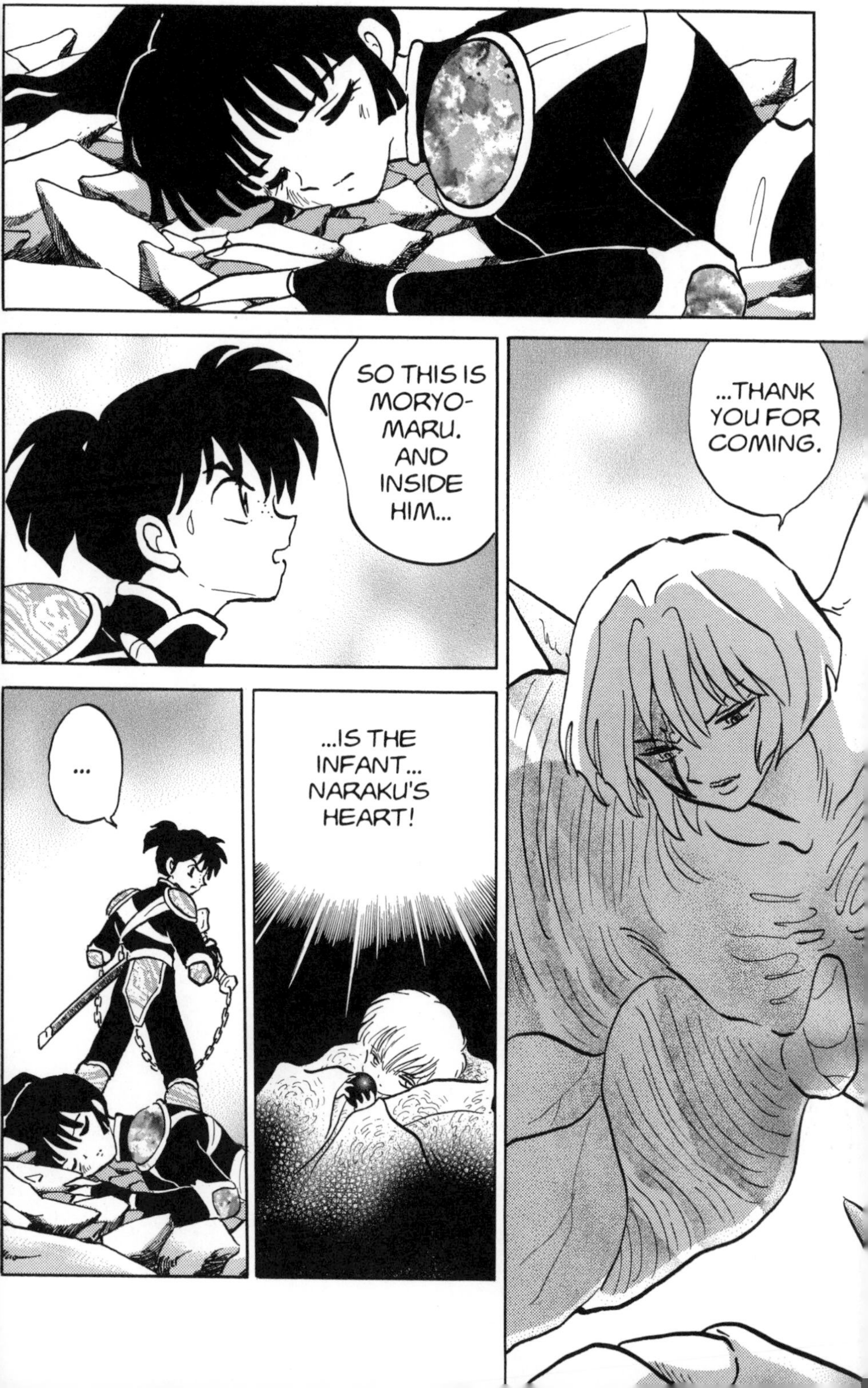
...THANK YOU FOR COMING.
SO THIS IS MORYO-MARU. AND INSIDE HIM...
...IS THE INFANT... NARAKU'S HEART!
...

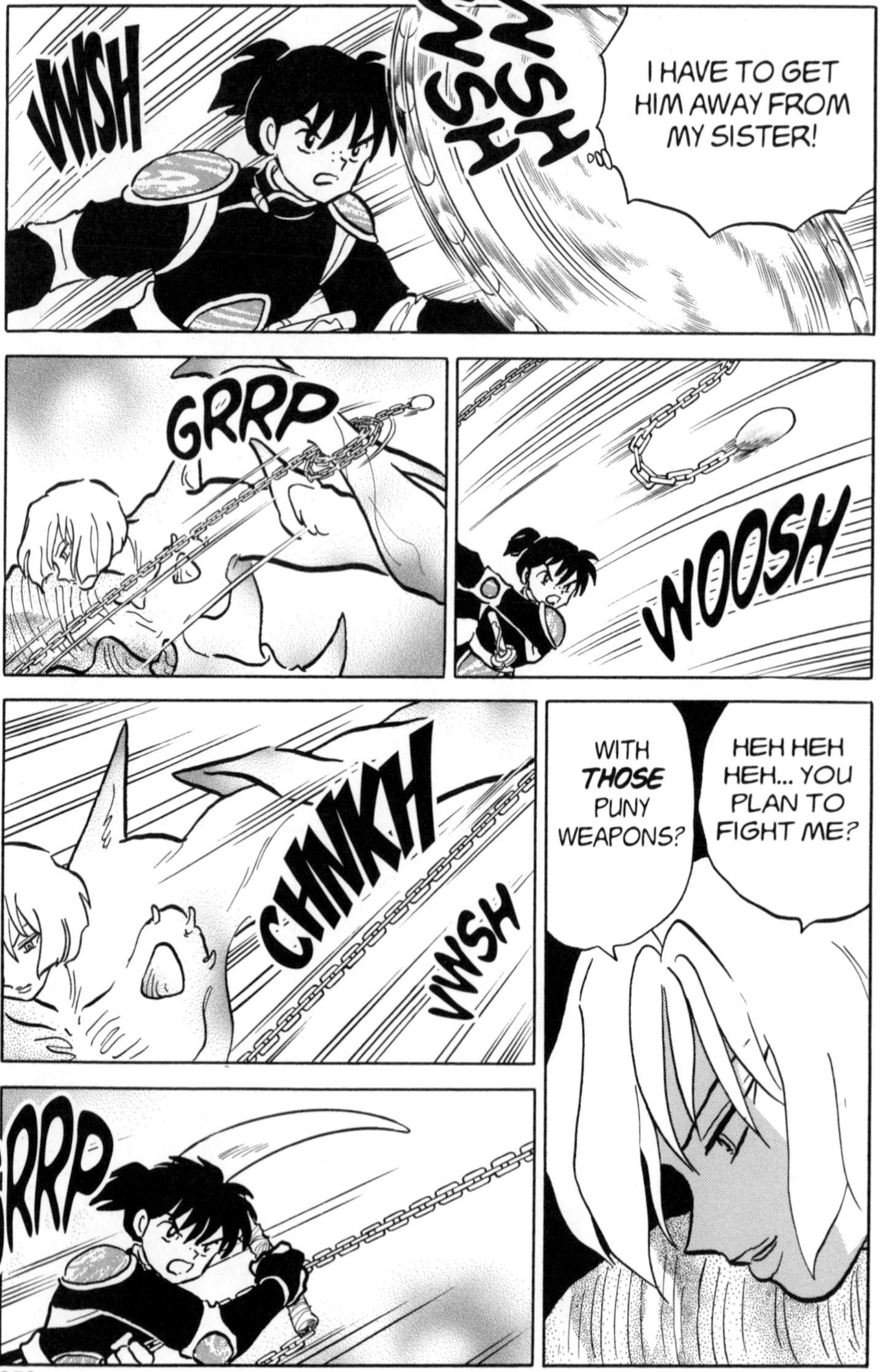
I HAVE TO GET HIM AWAY FROM MY SISTER!
WSH WSH
VWSH
WOOSH
GRRP
HEH HEH HEH... YOU PLAN TO FIGHT ME?
WITH ***THOSE*** PUNY WEAPONS?
VWSH
CHNKH
GRRP

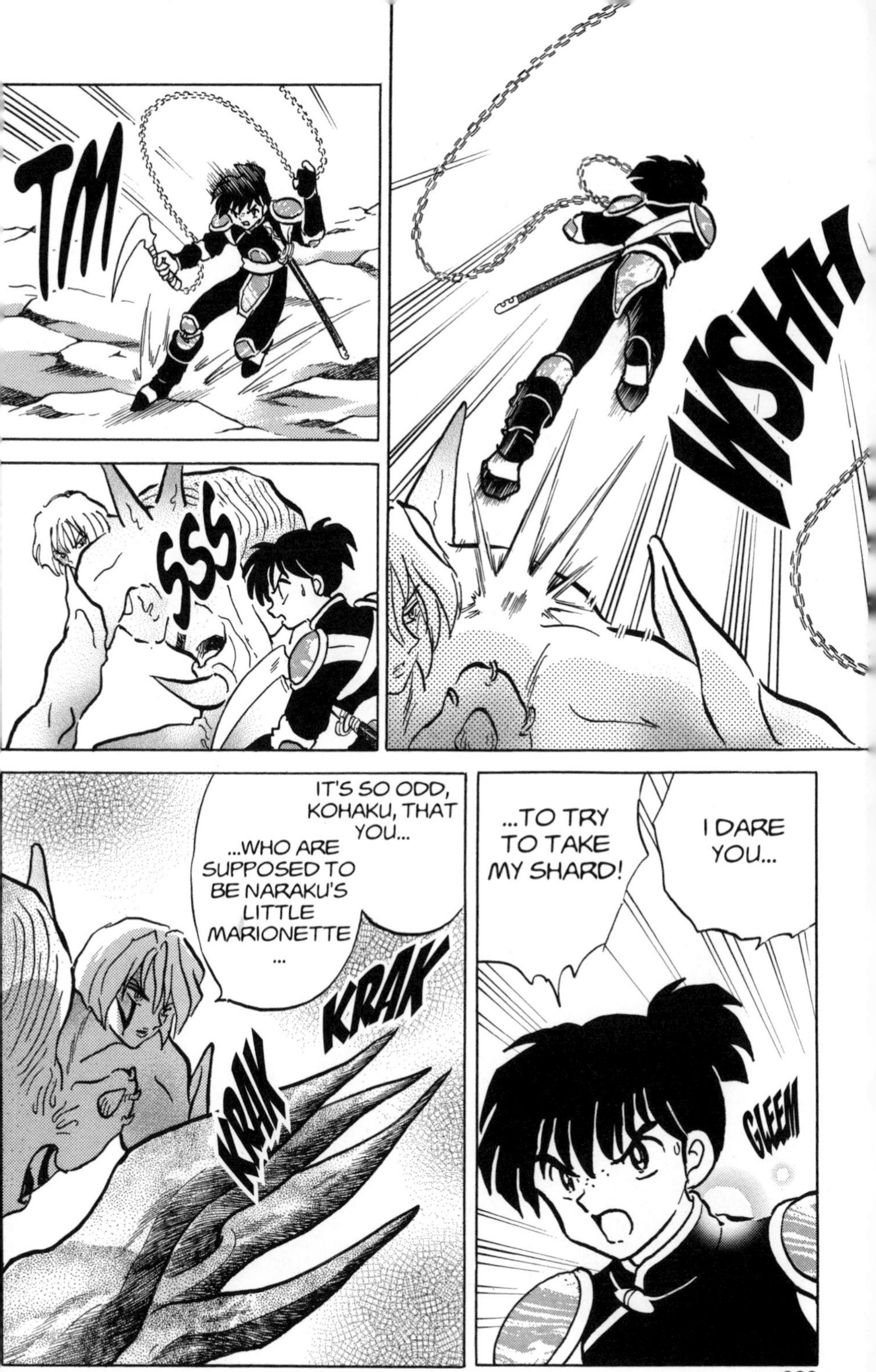
WSHH
TM
SSS
I DARE YOU...
...TO TRY TO TAKE MY SHARD!
GLEEM
IT'S SO ODD, KOHAKU, THAT YOU...
...WHO ARE SUPPOSED TO BE NARAKU'S LITTLE MARIONETTE ...
KRAK
KRAK

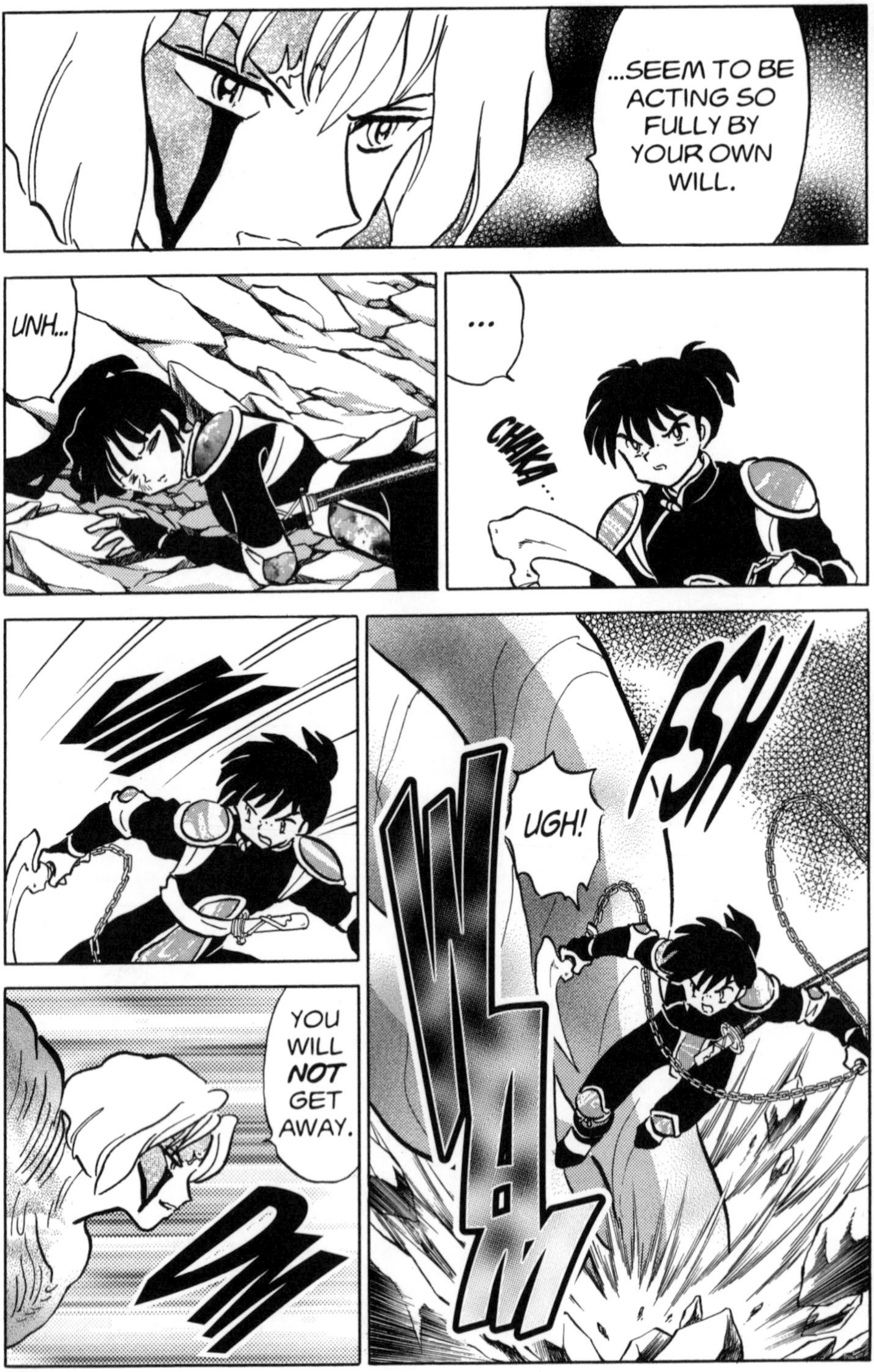
...SEEM TO BE ACTING SO FULLY BY YOUR OWN WILL.
...
CHAKA...
UNH...
FSH
UGH!
WHAM
YOU WILL **NOT** GET AWAY.

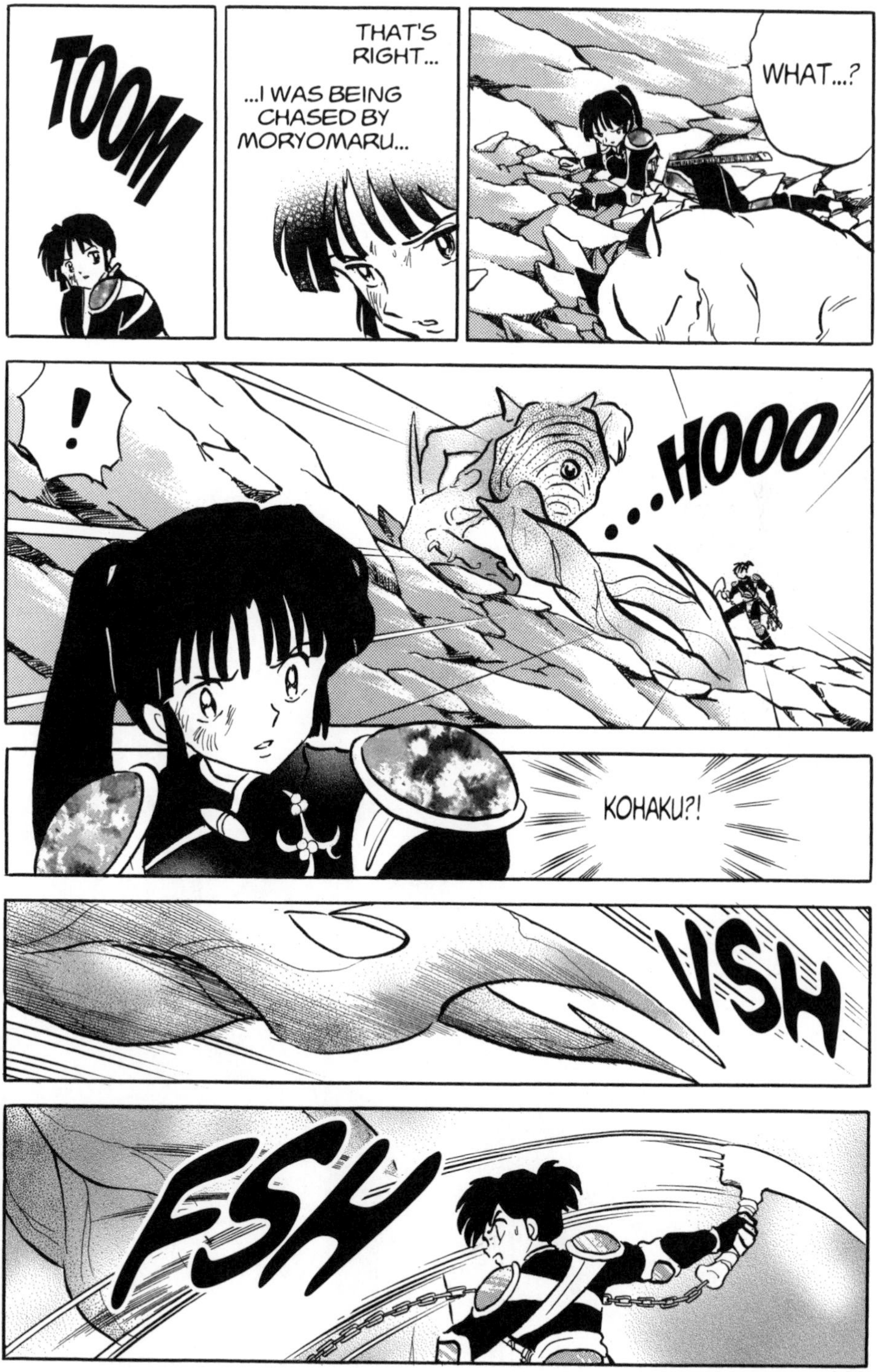
WHAT...?
THAT'S RIGHT...
...I WAS BEING CHASED BY MORYOMARU...
TOOM
...HOOO
!
KOHAKU?!
VSH
FSH

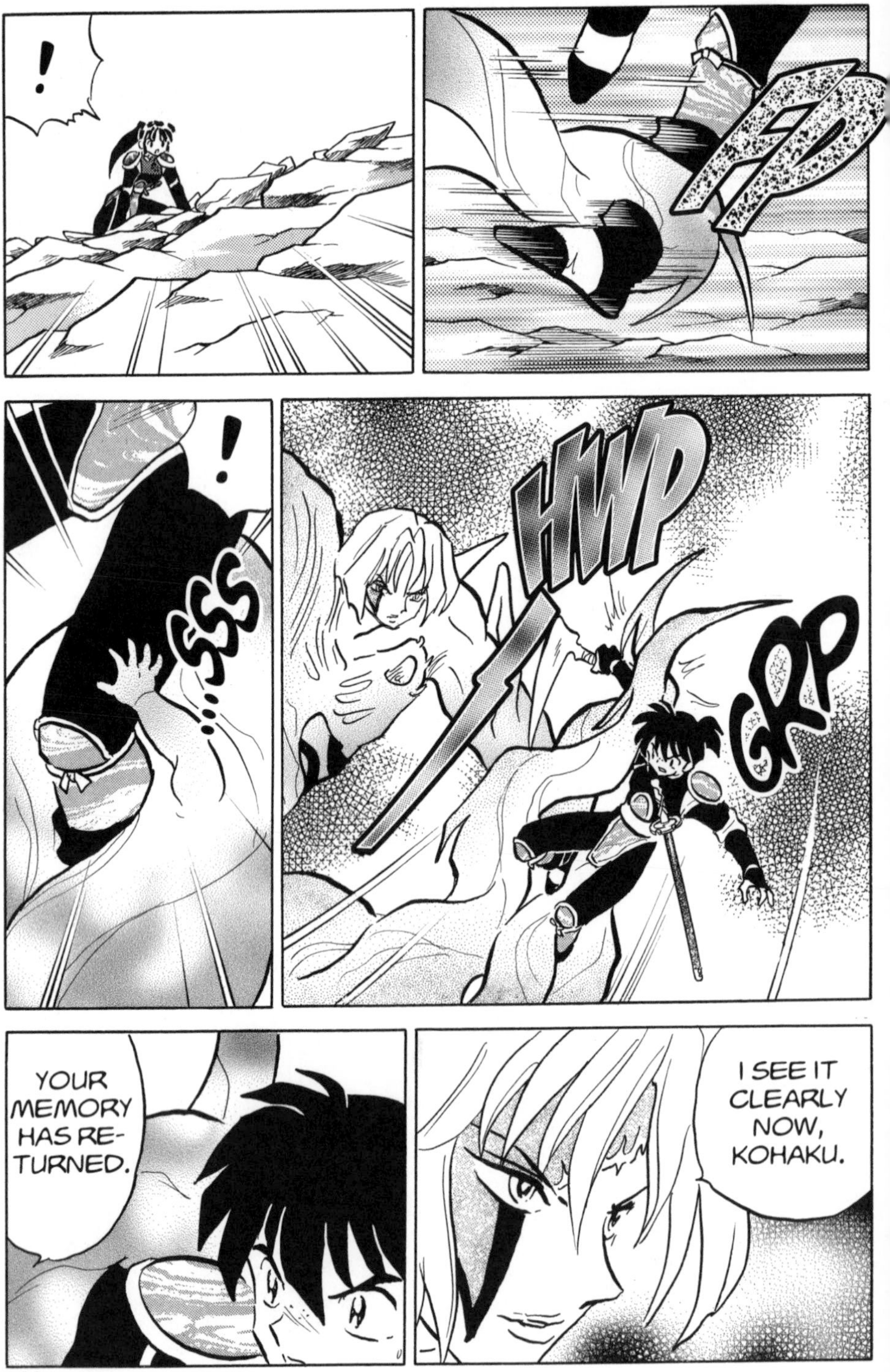
FP
!
HWP
GRP
!
SSS...
I SEE IT CLEARLY NOW, KOHAKU.
YOUR MEMORY HAS RE-TURNED.

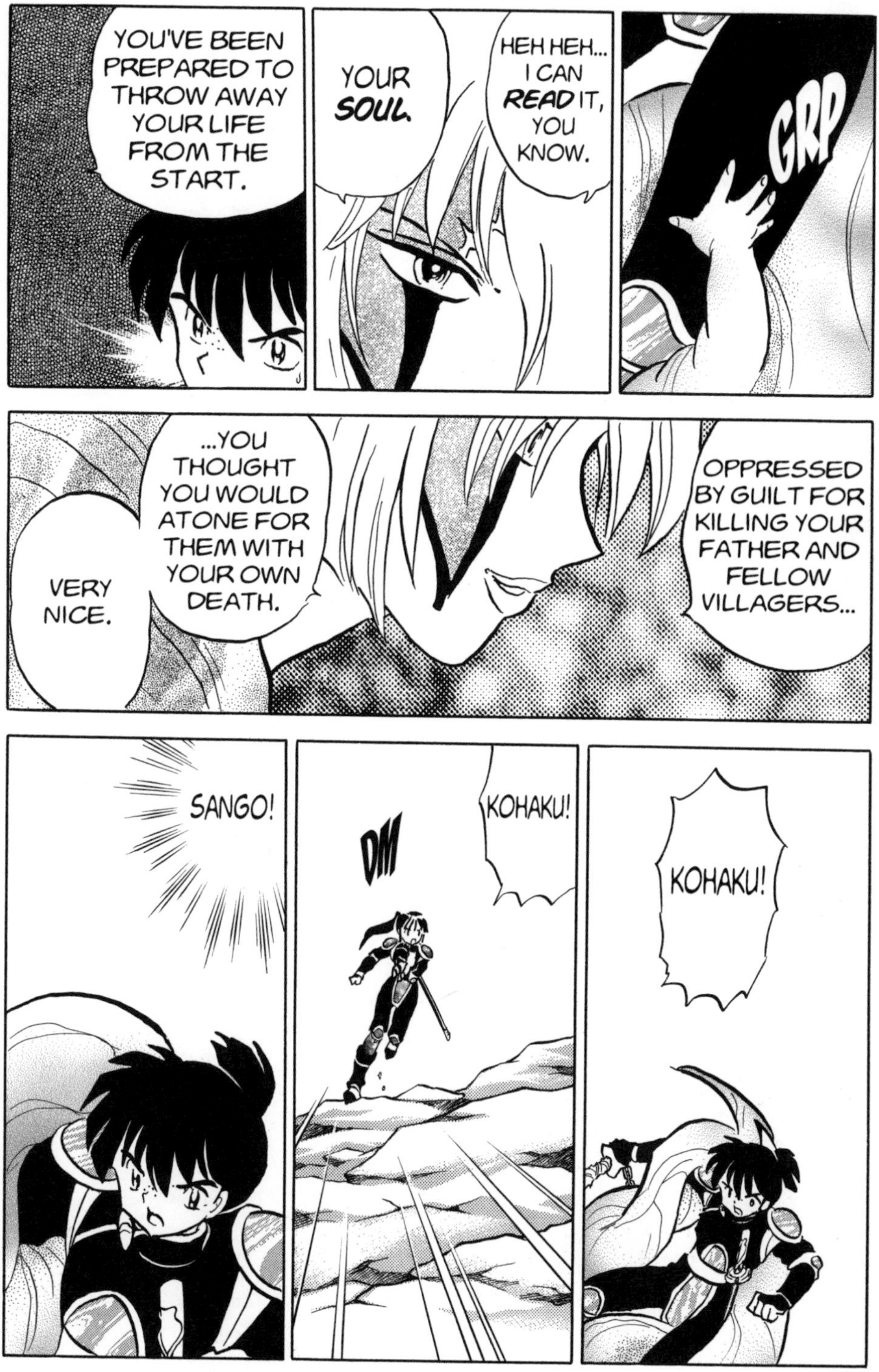
GRP
HEH HEH... I CAN READ IT, YOU KNOW.
YOUR SOUL.
YOU'VE BEEN PREPARED TO THROW AWAY YOUR LIFE FROM THE START.
OPPRESSED BY GUILT FOR KILLING YOUR FATHER AND FELLOW VILLAGERS...
...YOU THOUGHT YOU WOULD ATONE FOR THEM WITH YOUR OWN DEATH.
VERY NICE.
KOHAKU!
KOHAKU!
DM
SANGO!

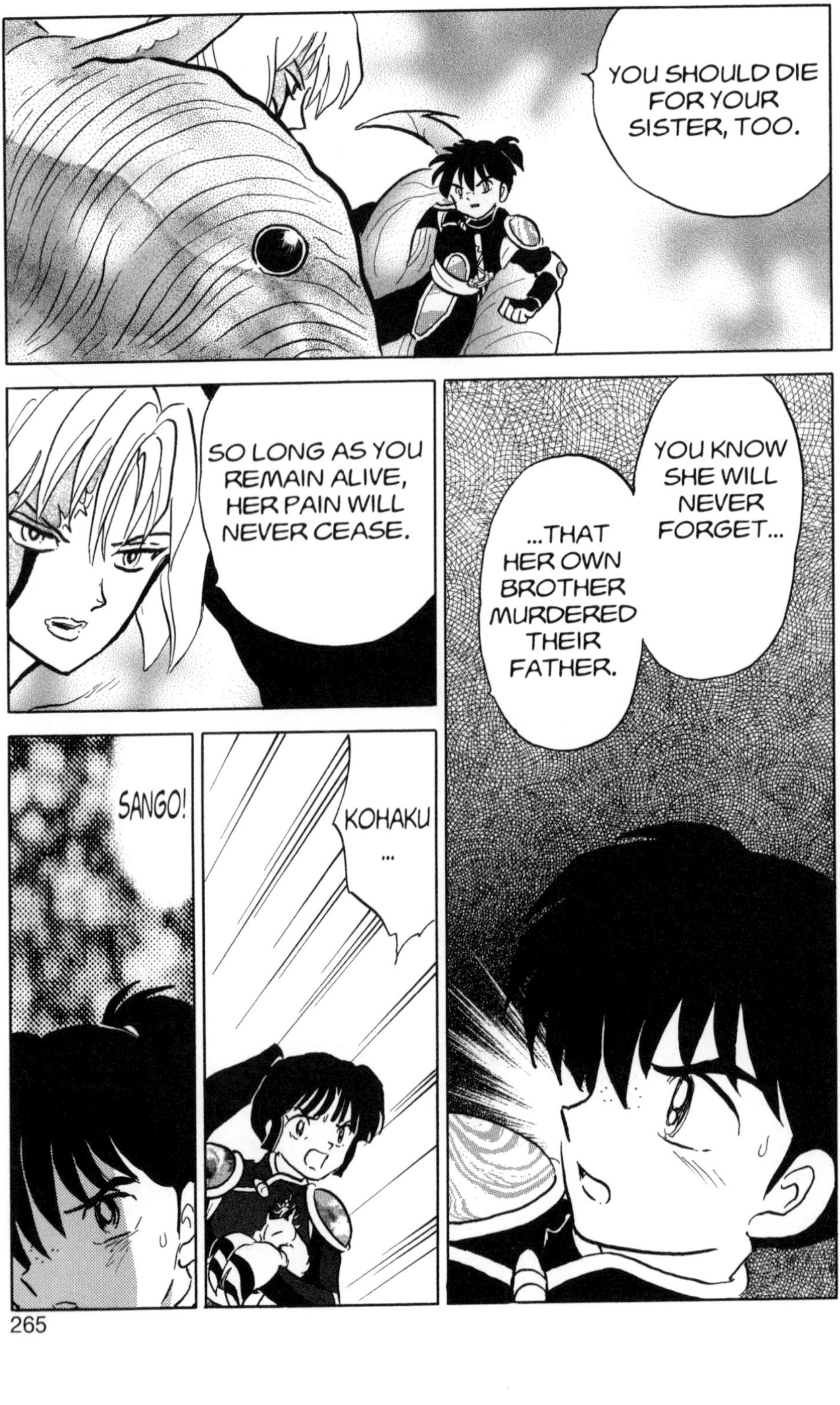
YOU SHOULD DIE FOR YOUR SISTER, TOO.
YOU KNOW SHE WILL NEVER FORGET...
...THAT HER OWN BROTHER MURDERED THEIR FATHER.
SO LONG AS YOU REMAIN ALIVE, HER PAIN WILL NEVER CEASE.
KOHAKU ...
SANGO!

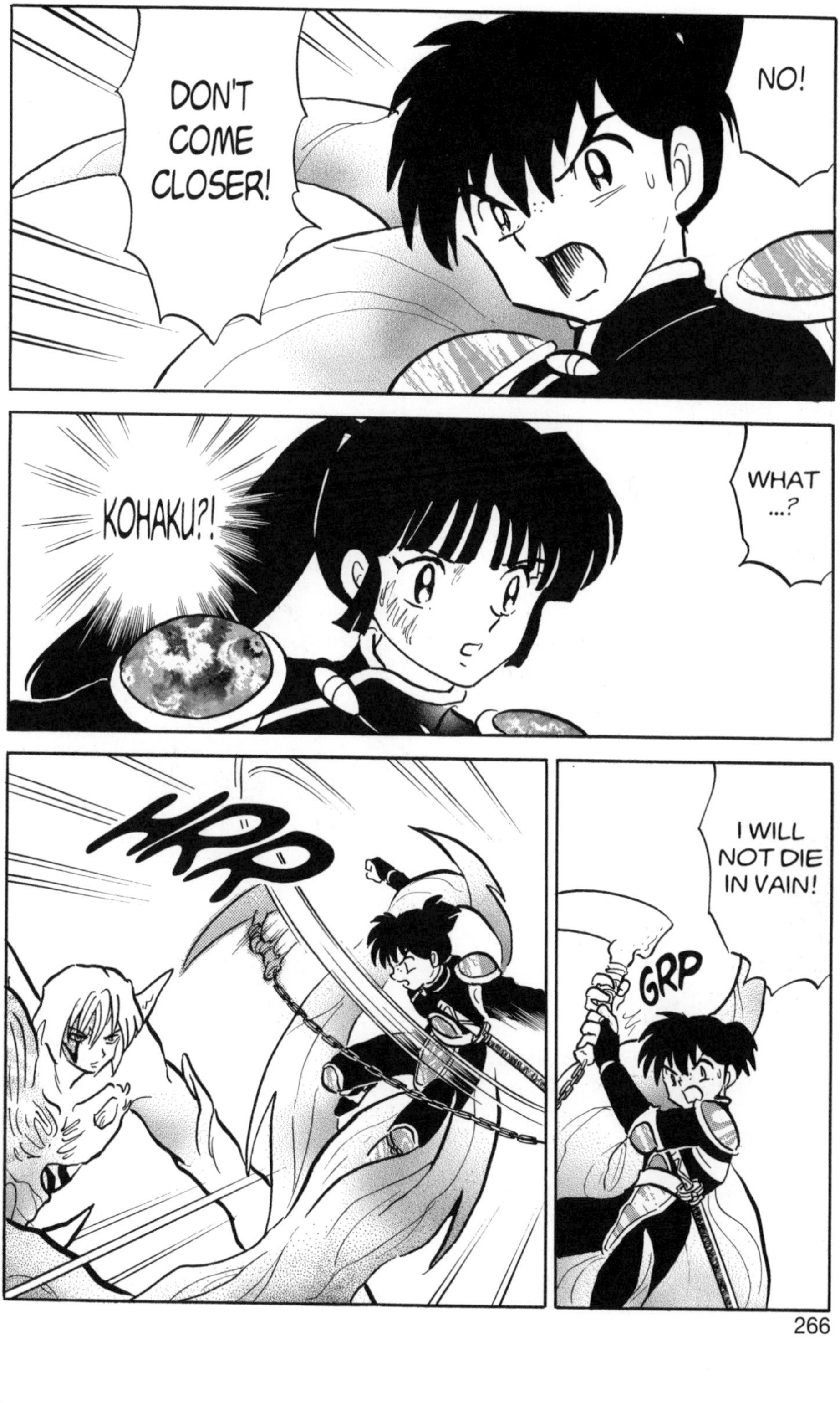
NO!
DON'T COME CLOSER!
WHAT ...?
KOHAKU?!
I WILL NOT DIE IN VAIN!
GRP
HRR

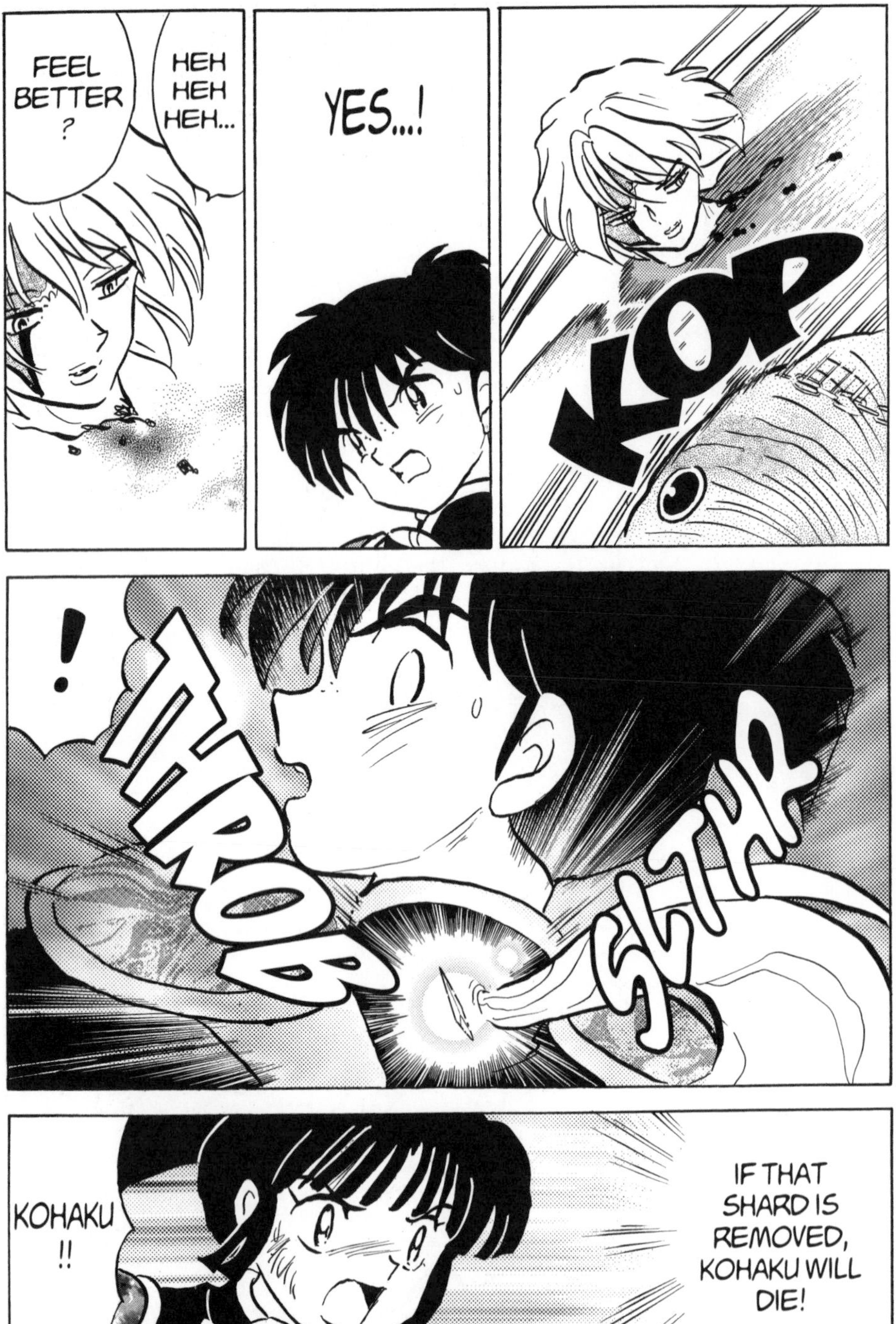
KOP
YES...!
HEH HEH HEH...
FEEL BETTER ?
SLTHR
!
THROB
IF THAT SHARD IS REMOVED, KOHAKU WILL DIE!
KOHAKU !!

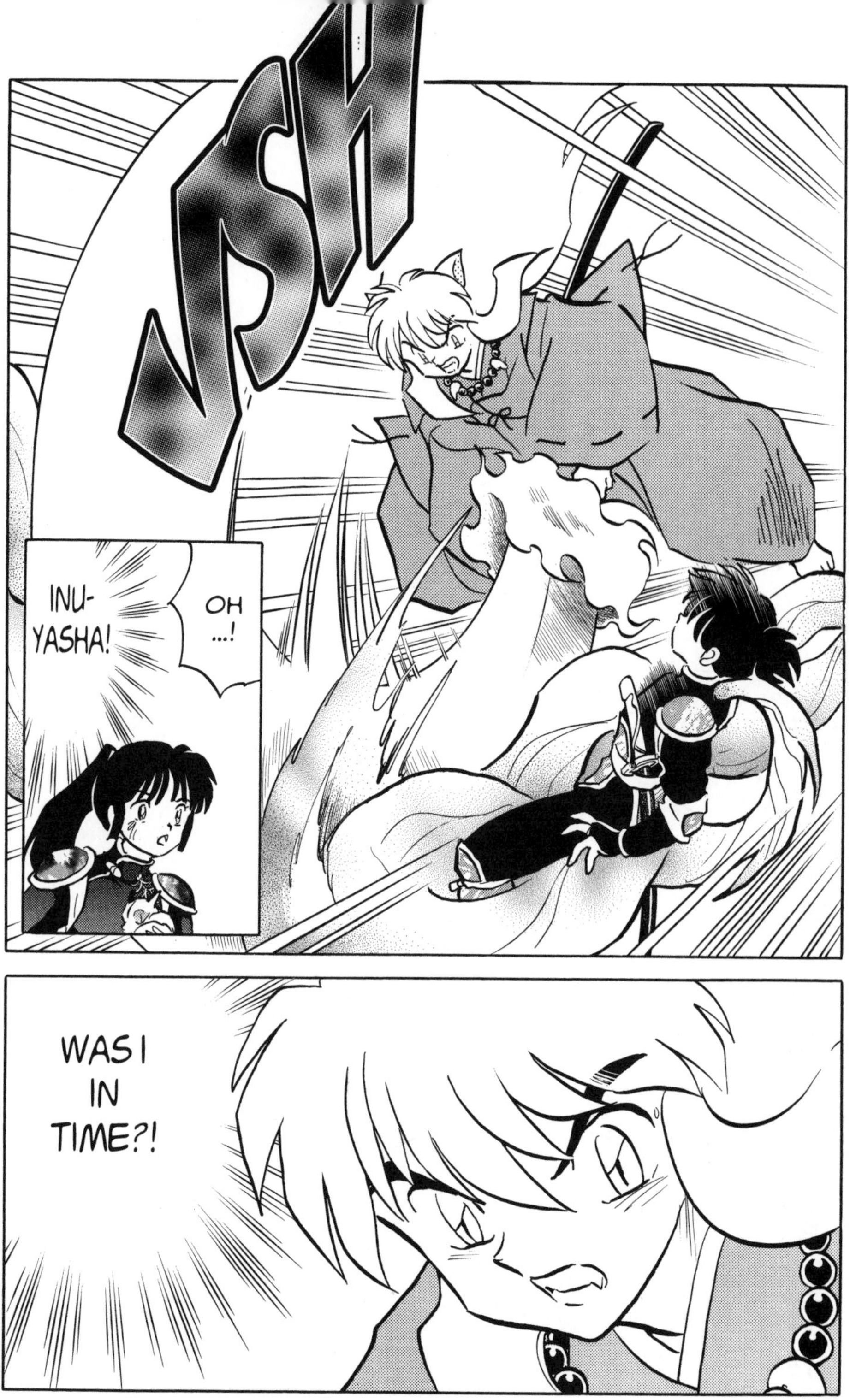
VSH
OH ...!
INU-YASHA!
WAS I IN TIME?!

SCROLL FIVE
SIBLINGS

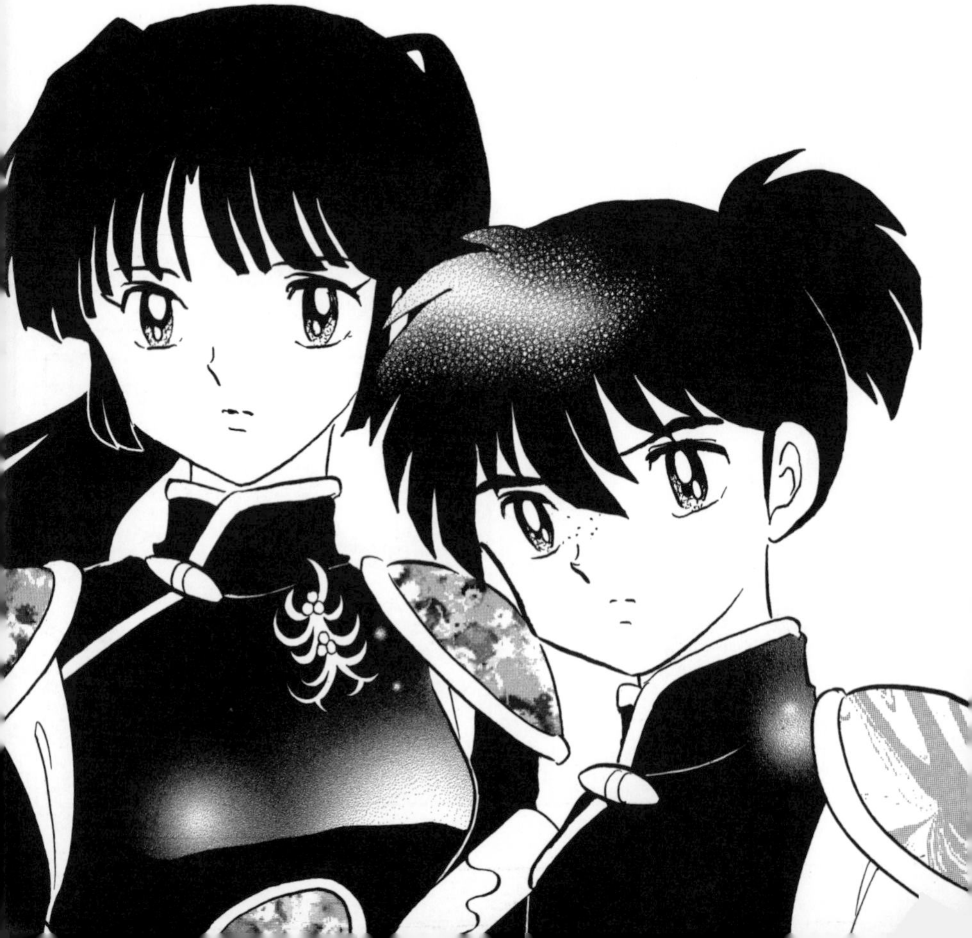

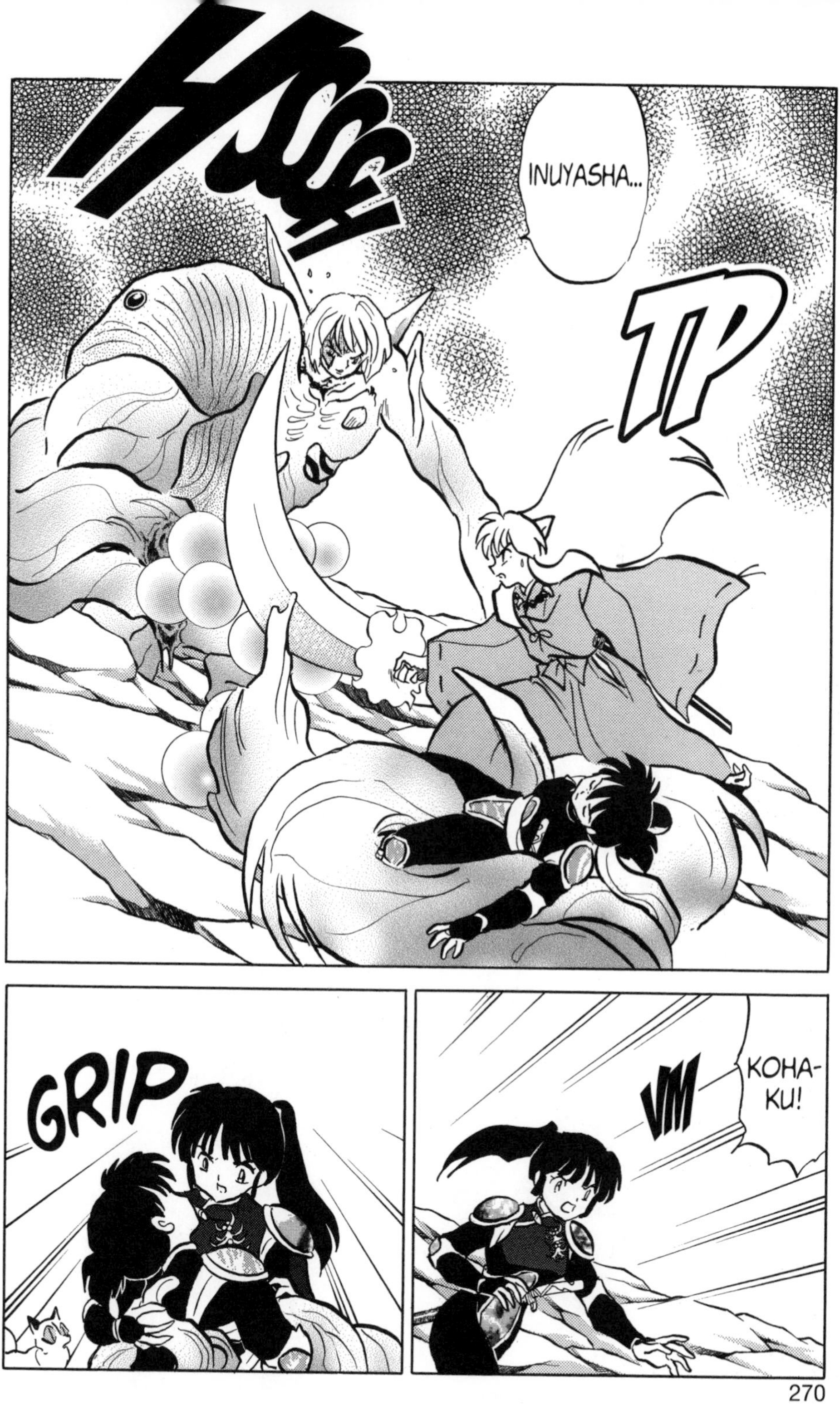
INUYASHA...
TP
KOHA-
KU!
VM
GRIP

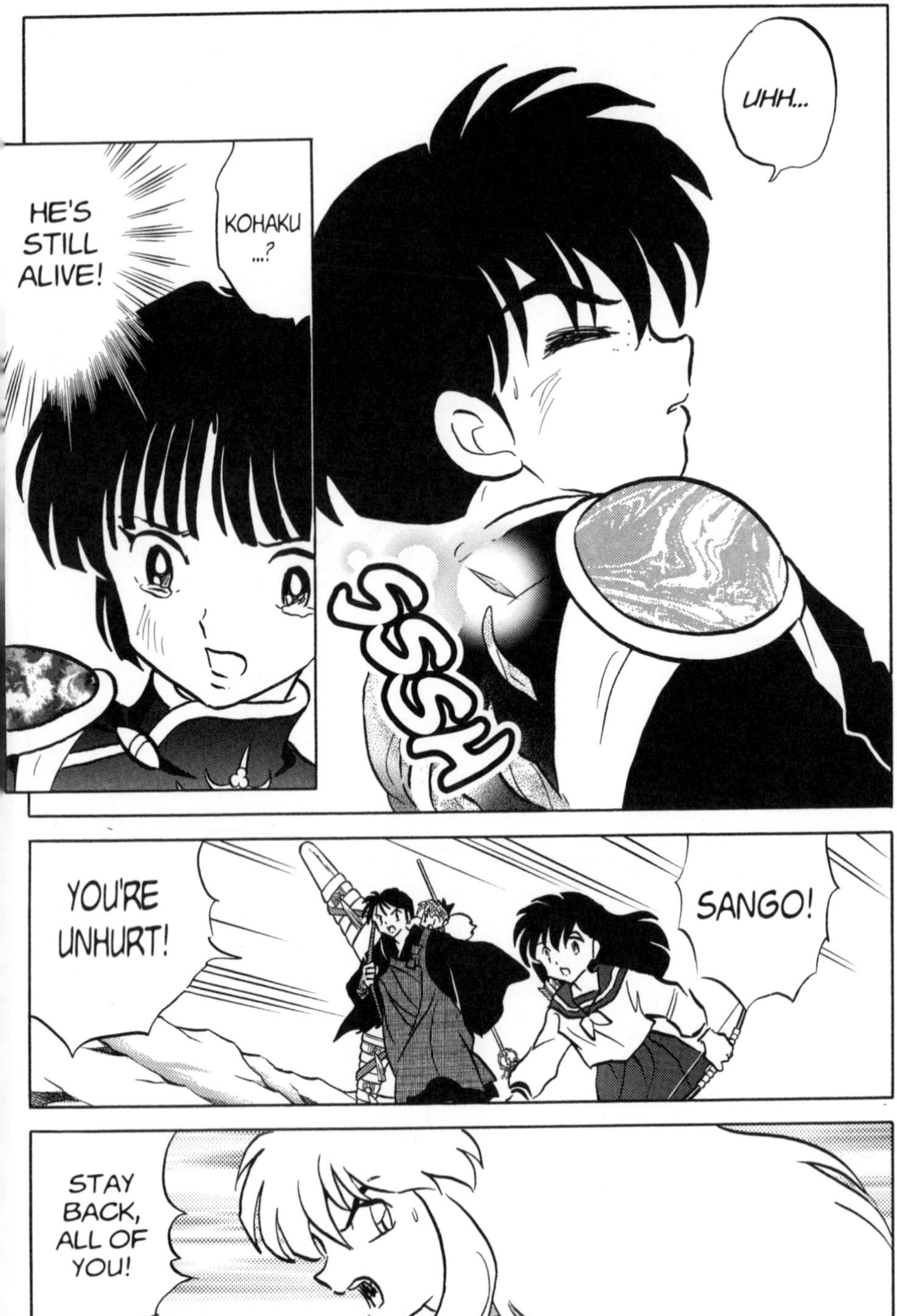
UHH...
SSSH
KOHAKU ...?
HE'S STILL ALIVE!
SANGO!
YOU'RE UNHURT!
STAY BACK, ALL OF YOU!

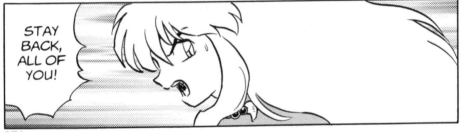

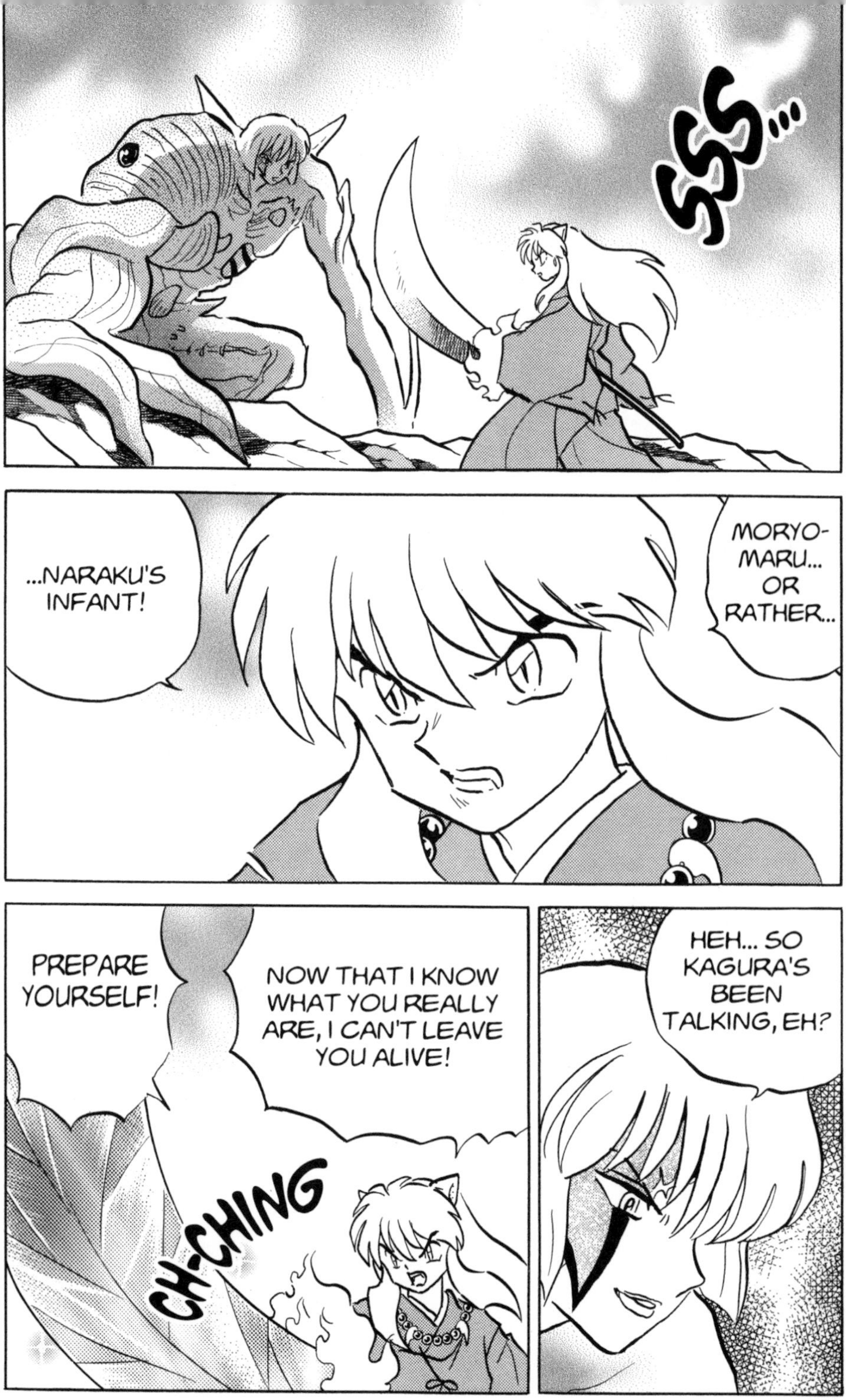
SSS...
MORYO-MARU... OR RATHER...
...NARAKU'S INFANT!
HEH... SO KAGURA'S BEEN TALKING, EH?
NOW THAT I KNOW WHAT YOU REALLY ARE, I CAN'T LEAVE YOU ALIVE!
PREPARE YOURSELF!
CH-CHING

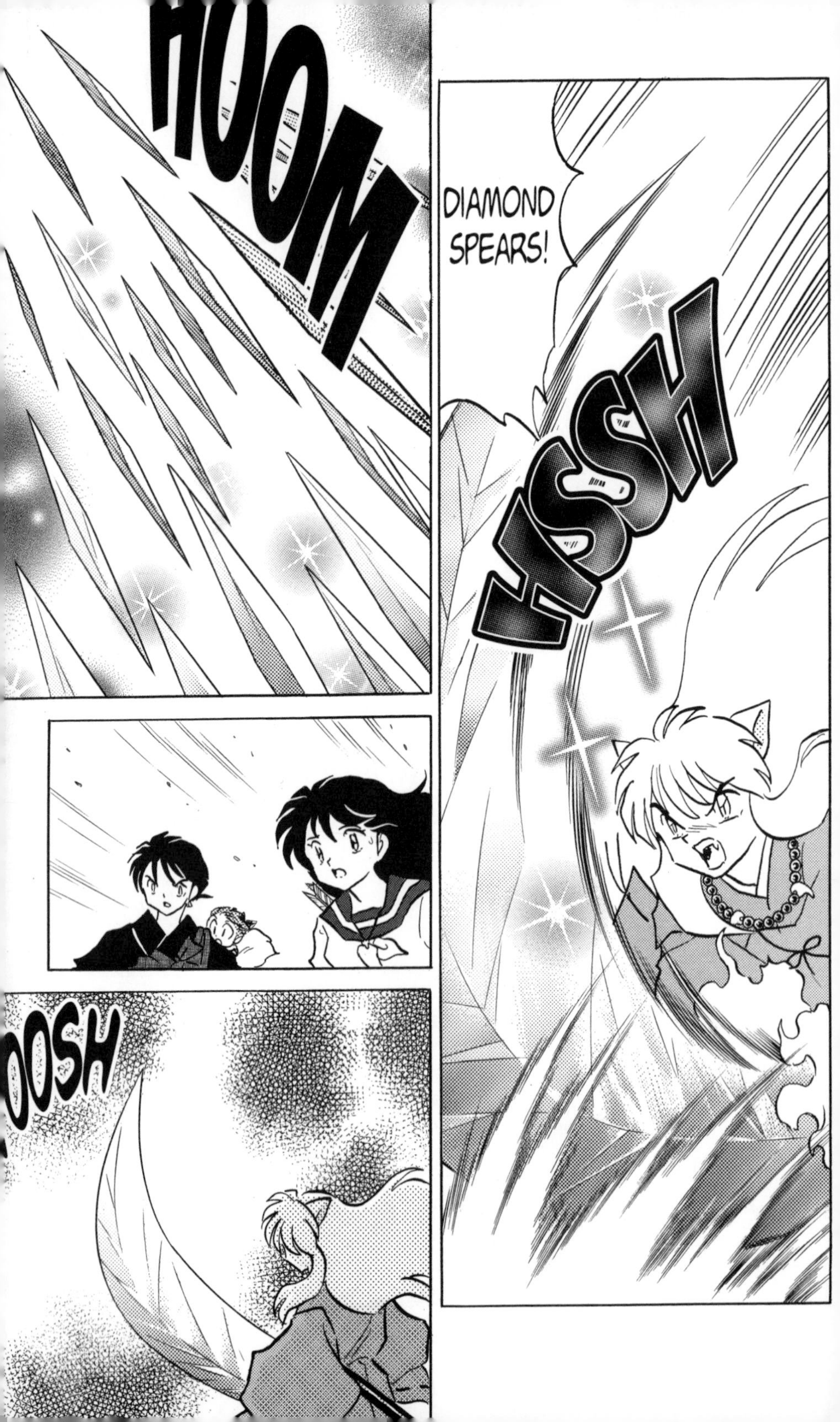
DIAMOND SPEARS!
HISSH
HOOM
OOSH

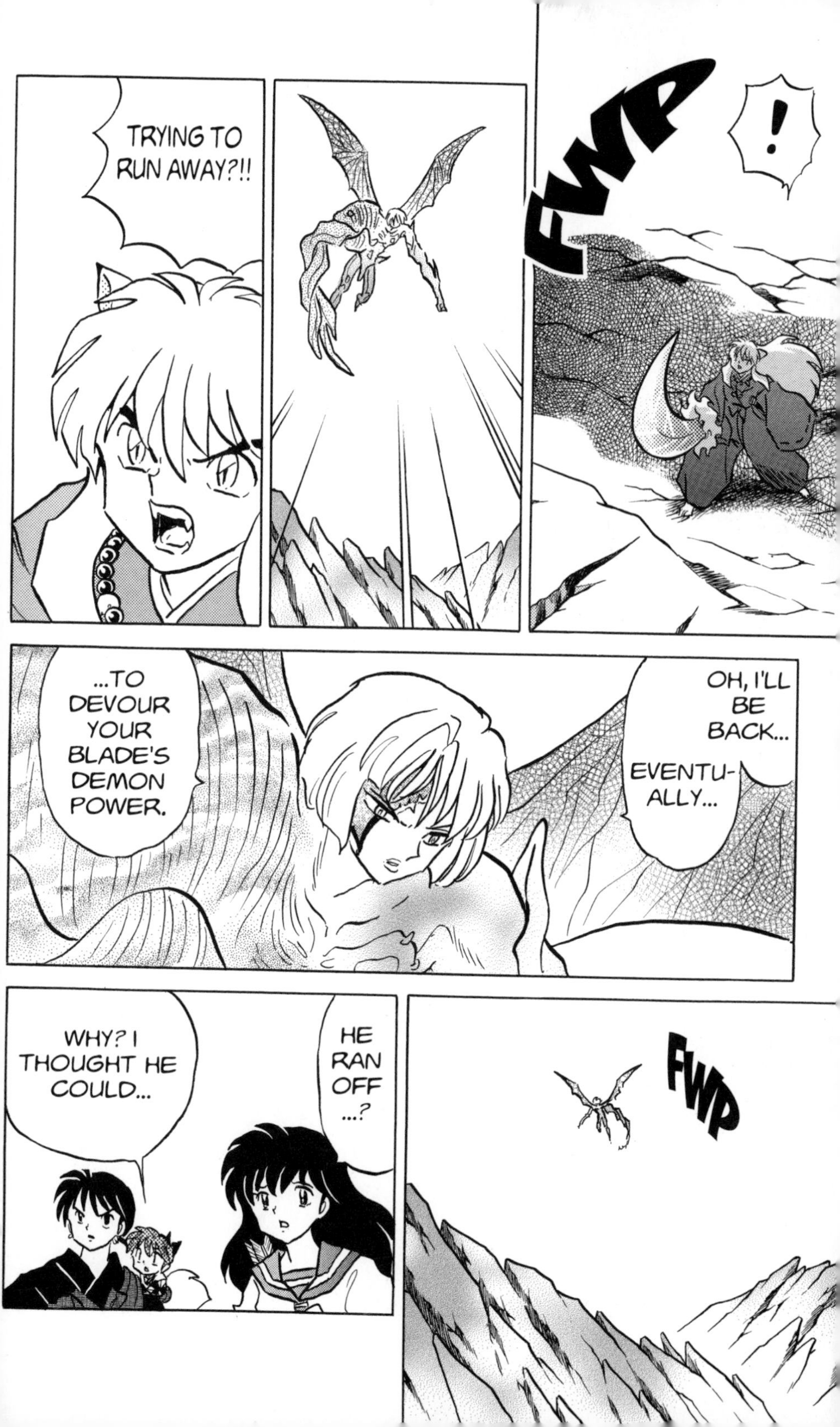
FWP
!
TRYING TO RUN AWAY?!!
OH, I'LL BE BACK...
EVENTU-ALLY...
...TO DEVOUR YOUR BLADE'S DEMON POWER.
FWP
HE RAN OFF ...?
WHY? I THOUGHT HE COULD...

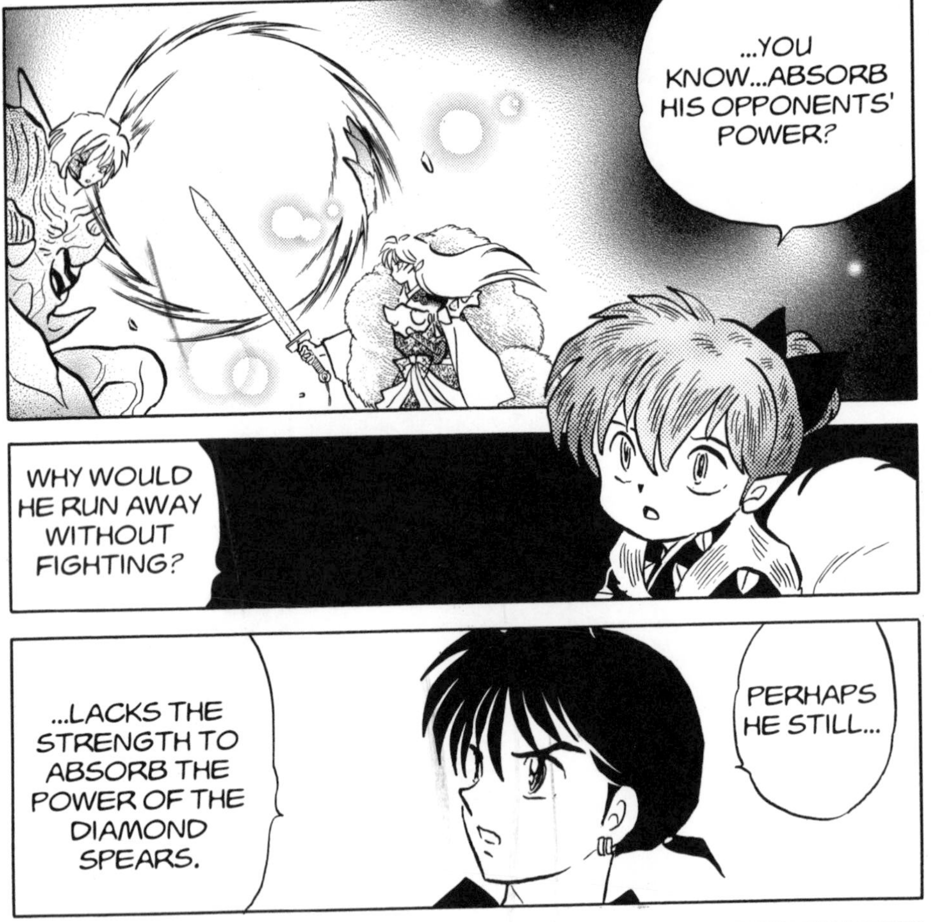
...YOU KNOW...ABSORB HIS OPPONENTS' POWER?
WHY WOULD HE RUN AWAY WITHOUT FIGHTING?
PERHAPS HE STILL...
...LACKS THE STRENGTH TO ABSORB THE POWER OF THE DIAMOND SPEARS.
YOU'RE PRO-BABLY RIGHT.
WHICH IS WHY HE WAS TRYING TO TAKE KOHAKU'S SHIKON SHARD...TO INCREASE HIS STRENGTH.
NNH...

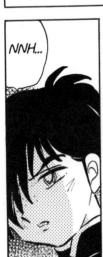

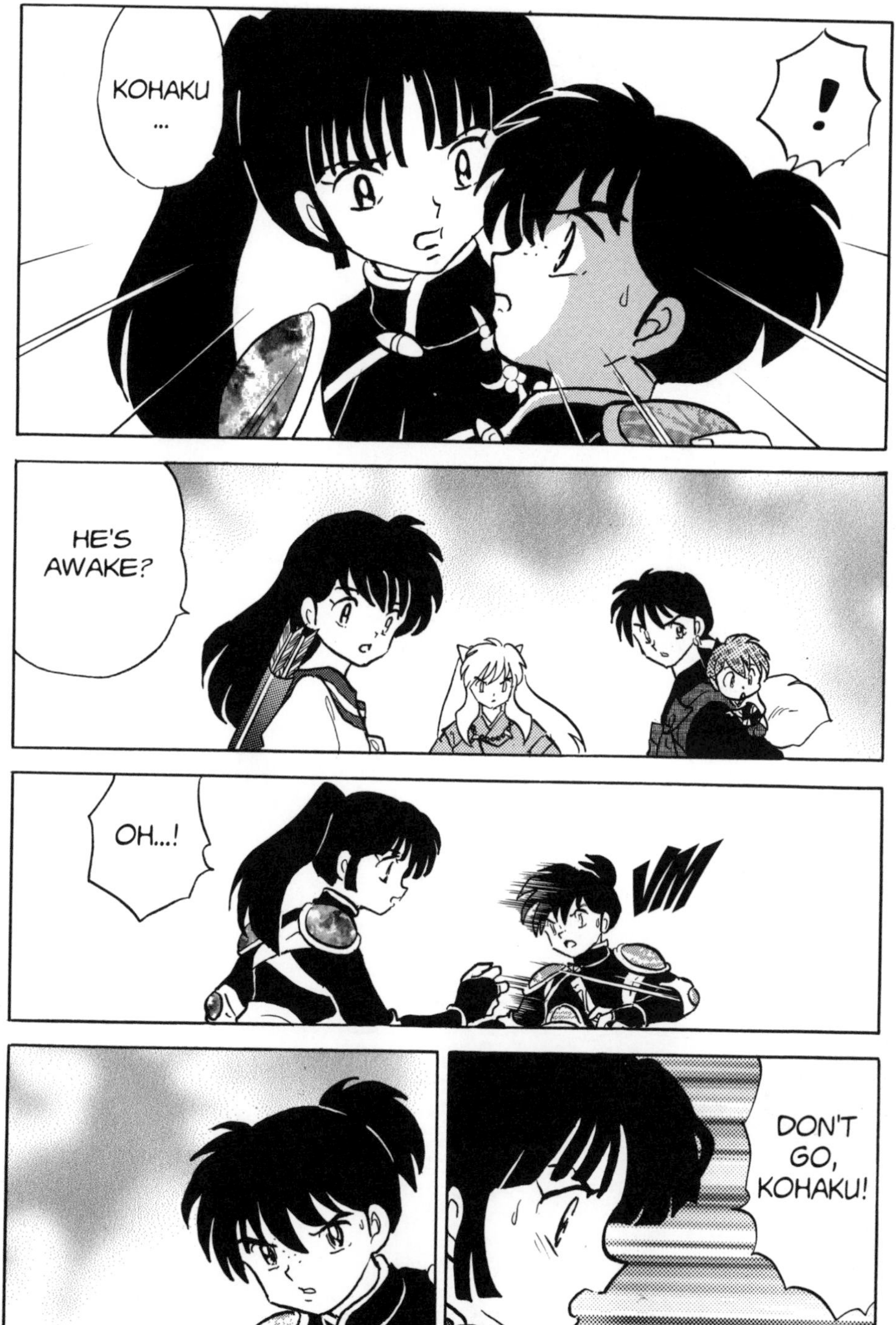
!
KOHAKU ...
HE'S AWAKE?
VM
OH...!
DON'T GO, KOHAKU!

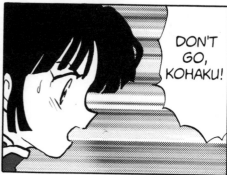

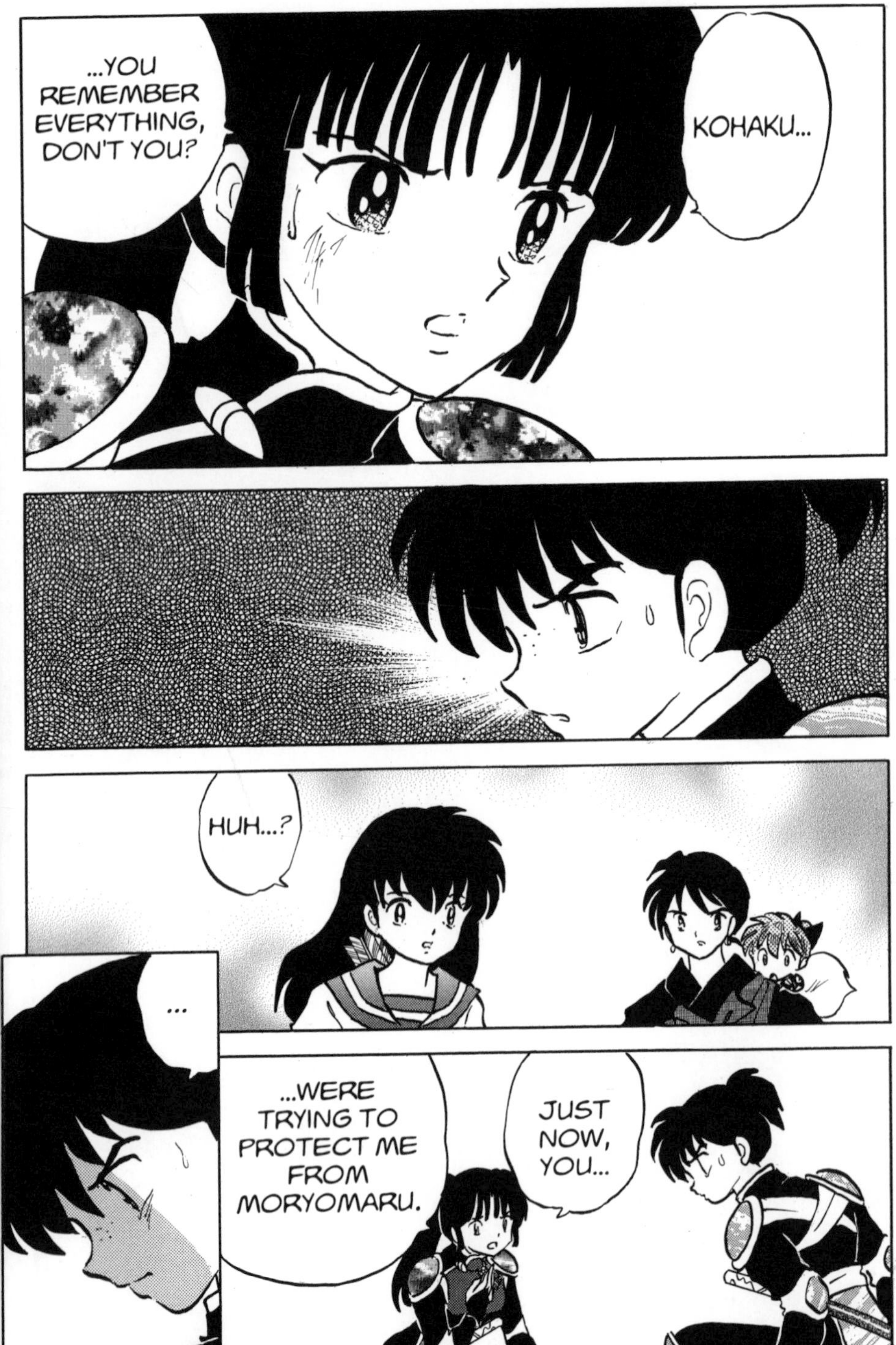
KOHAKU...
...YOU REMEMBER EVERYTHING, DON'T YOU?
HUH...?
JUST NOW, YOU...
...WERE TRYING TO PROTECT ME FROM MORYOMARU.
...

SANGO... SISTER...
KOHAKU!

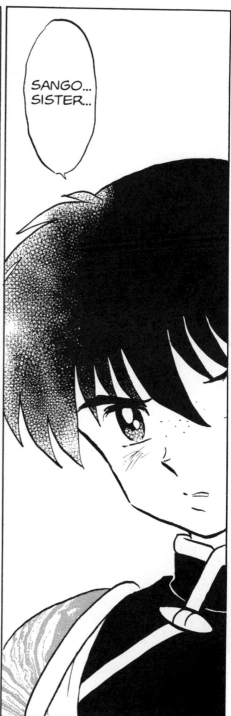

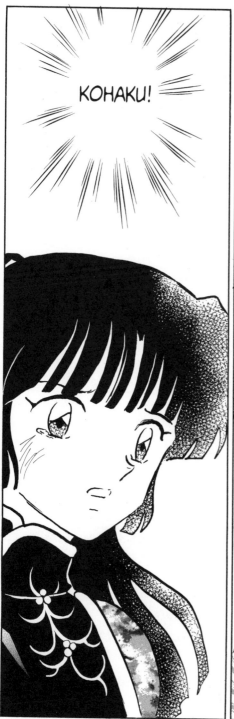

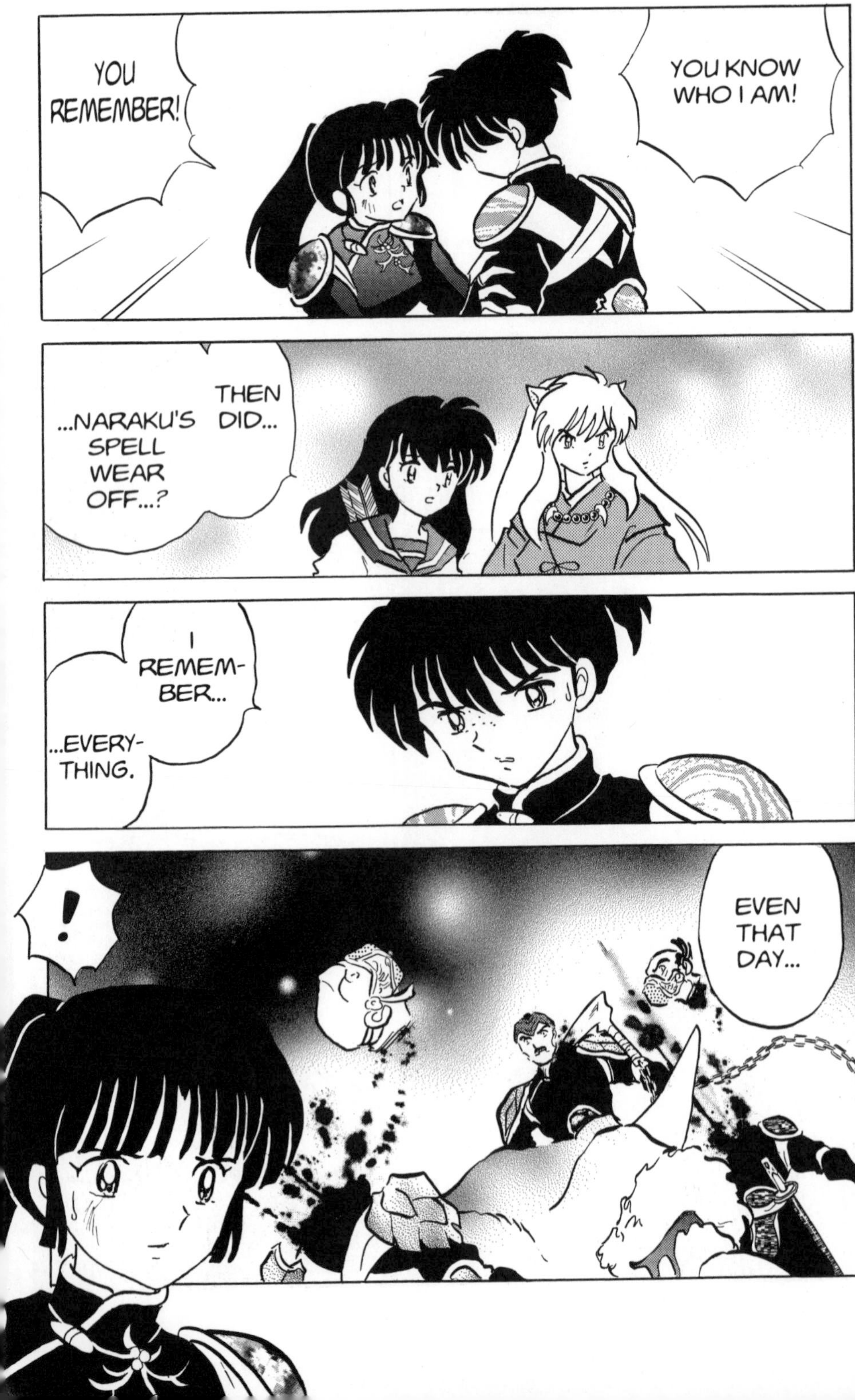
YOU KNOW WHO I AM!
YOU REMEMBER!
THEN DID... ...NARAKU'S SPELL WEAR OFF...?
I REMEMBER...
...EVERYTHING.
EVEN THAT DAY...
!

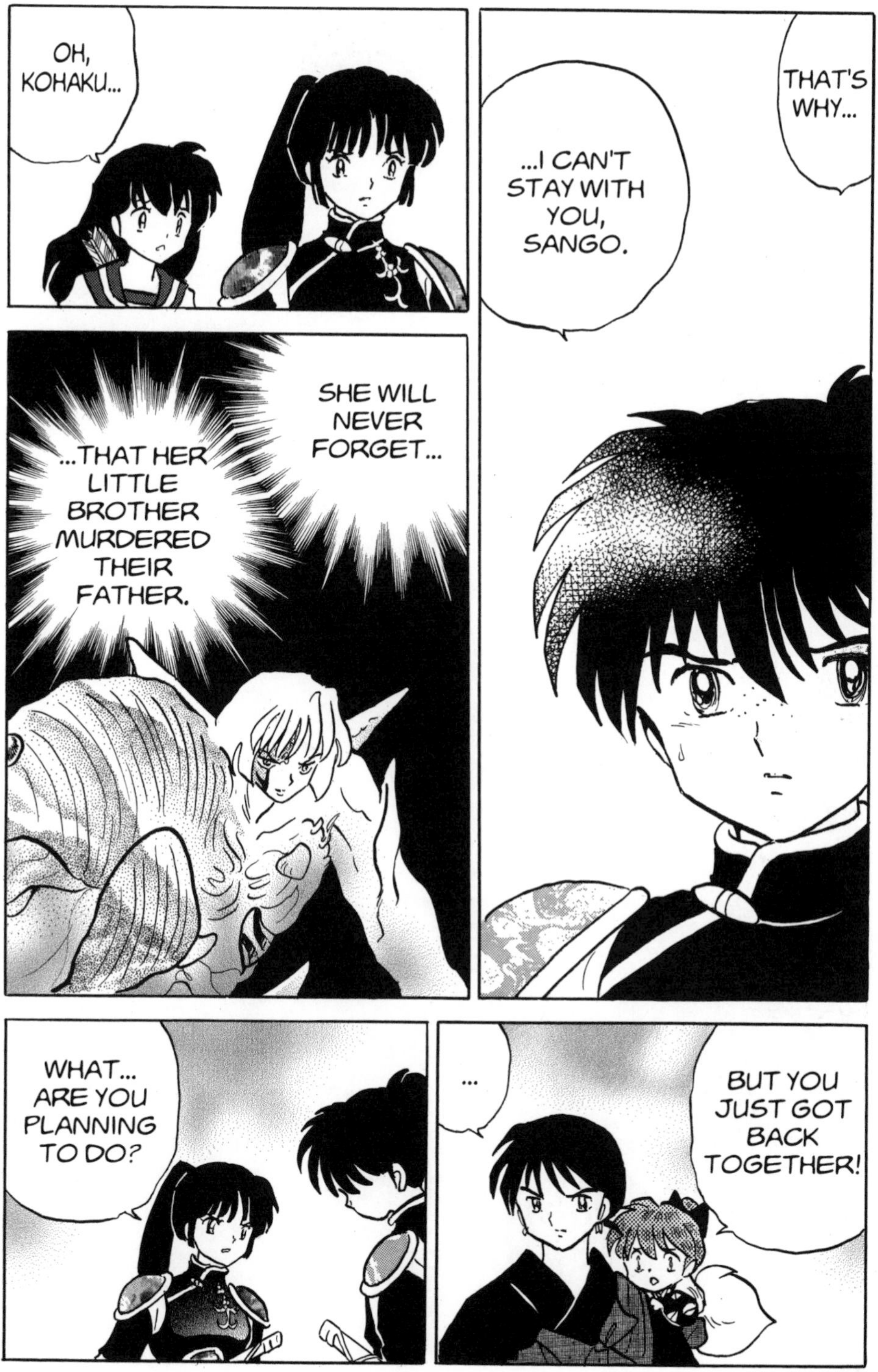
THAT'S WHY...
...I CAN'T STAY WITH YOU, SANGO.
OH, KOHAKU...
SHE WILL NEVER FORGET...
...THAT HER LITTLE BROTHER MURDERED THEIR FATHER.
BUT YOU JUST GOT BACK TOGETHER!
...
WHAT... ARE YOU PLANNING TO DO?

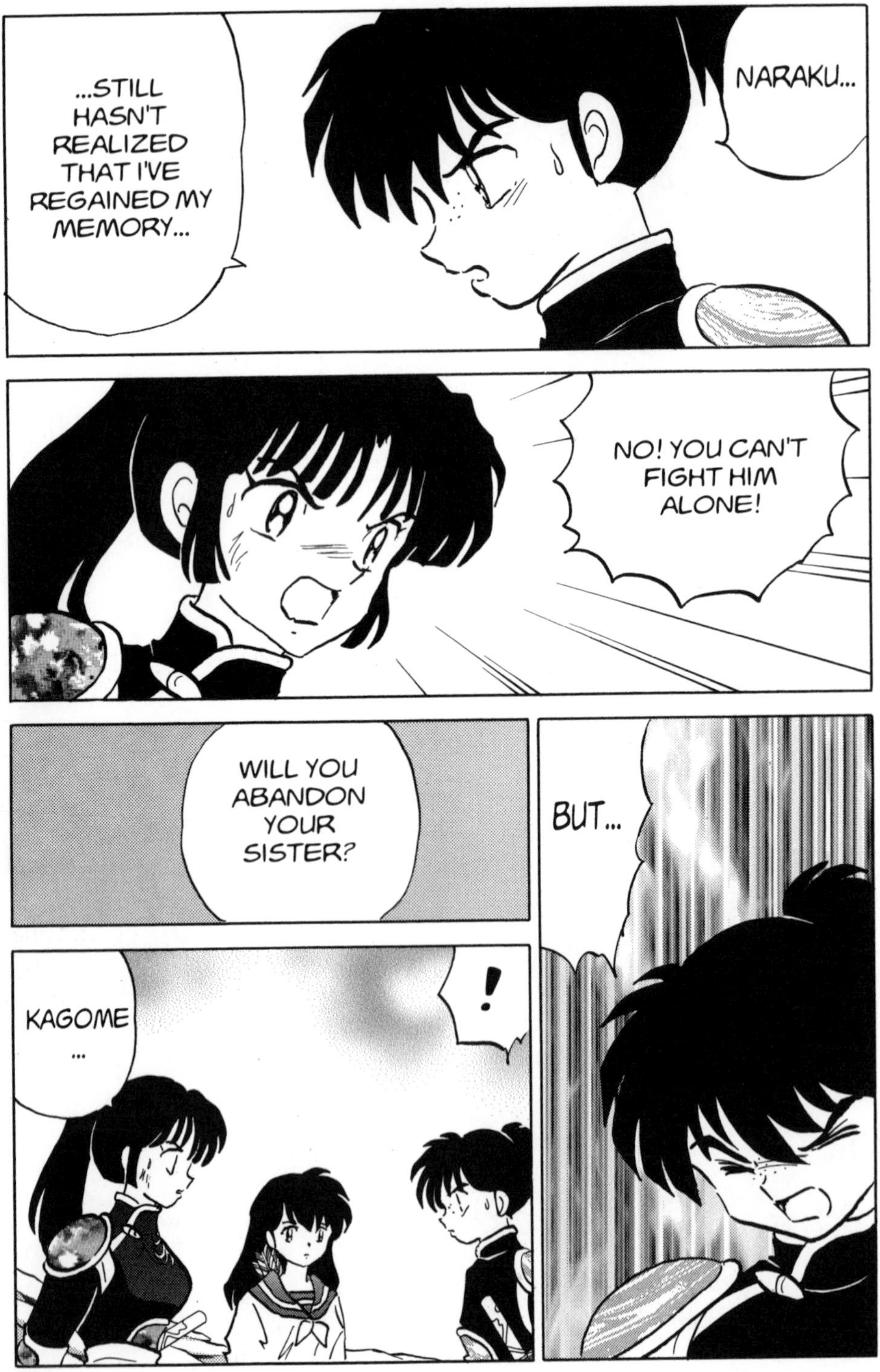
NARAKU...
...STILL HASN'T REALIZED THAT I'VE REGAINED MY MEMORY...
NO! YOU CAN'T FIGHT HIM ALONE!
BUT...
WILL YOU ABANDON YOUR SISTER?
!
KAGOME ...

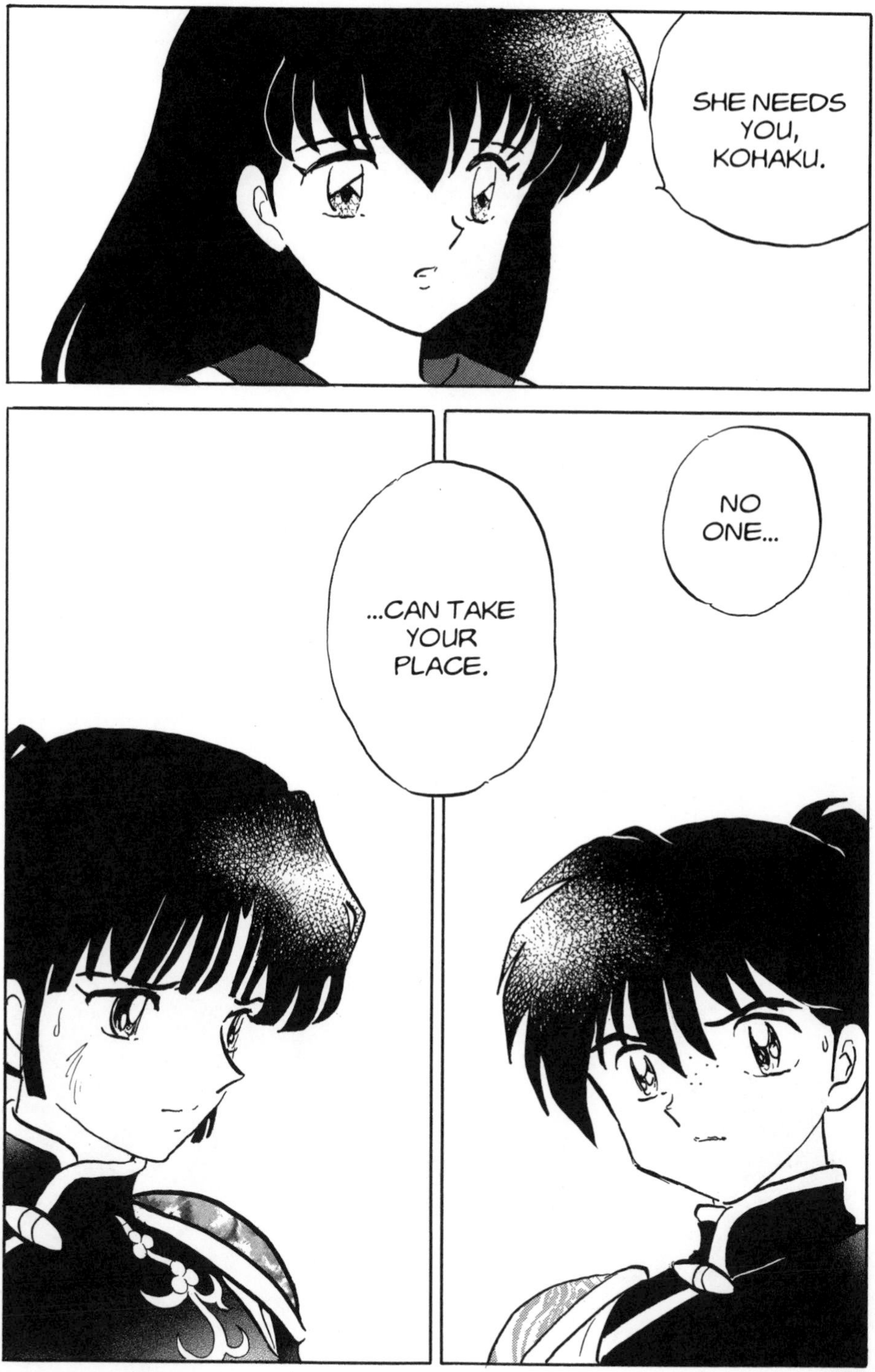
SHE NEEDS YOU, KOHAKU.
NO ONE...
...CAN TAKE YOUR PLACE.

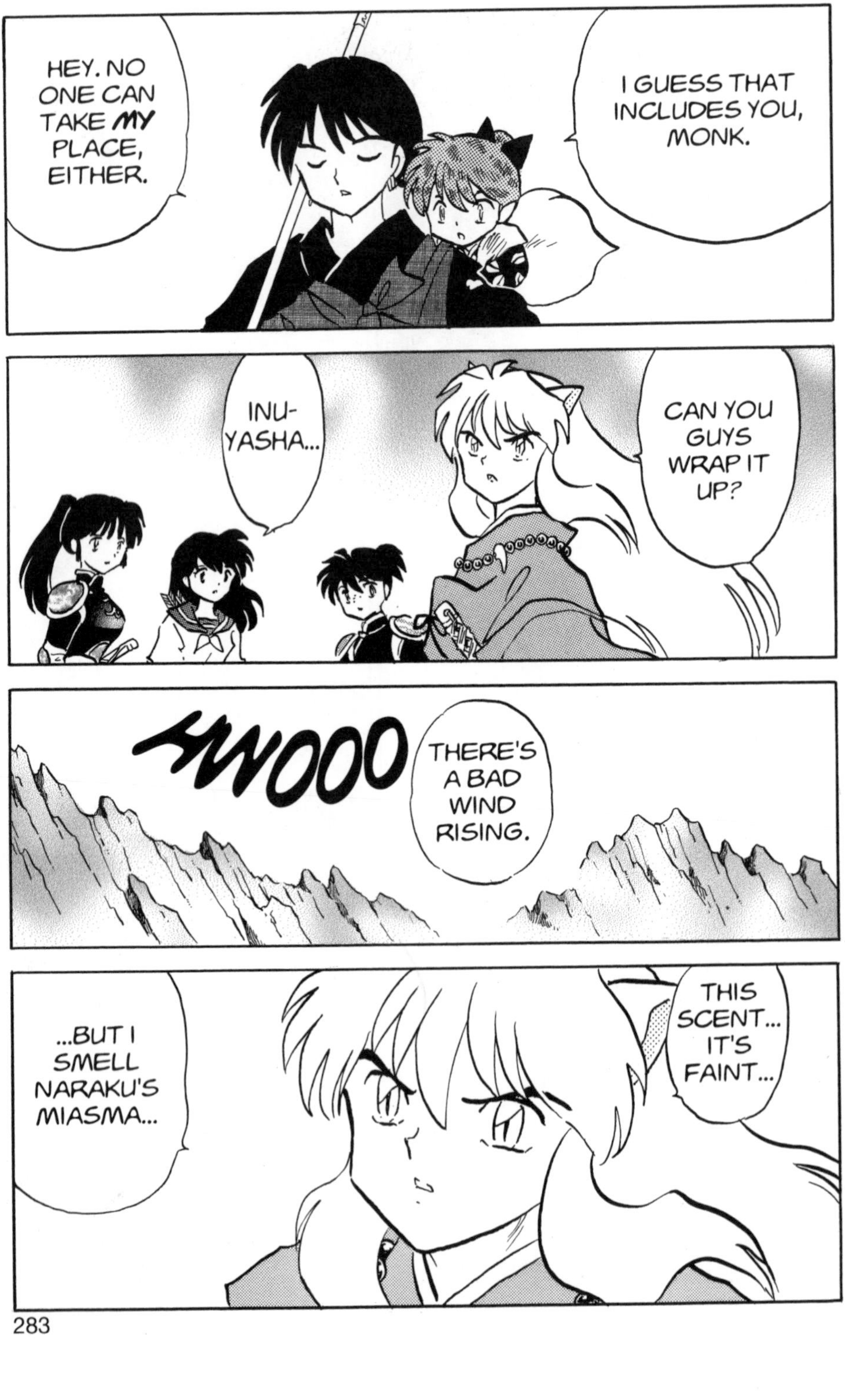
I GUESS THAT INCLUDES YOU, MONK.
HEY. NO ONE CAN TAKE *MY* PLACE, EITHER.
CAN YOU GUYS WRAP IT UP?
INU-YASHA...
THERE'S A BAD WIND RISING.
HWOOO
THIS SCENT... IT'S FAINT...
...BUT I SMELL NARAKU'S MIASMA...

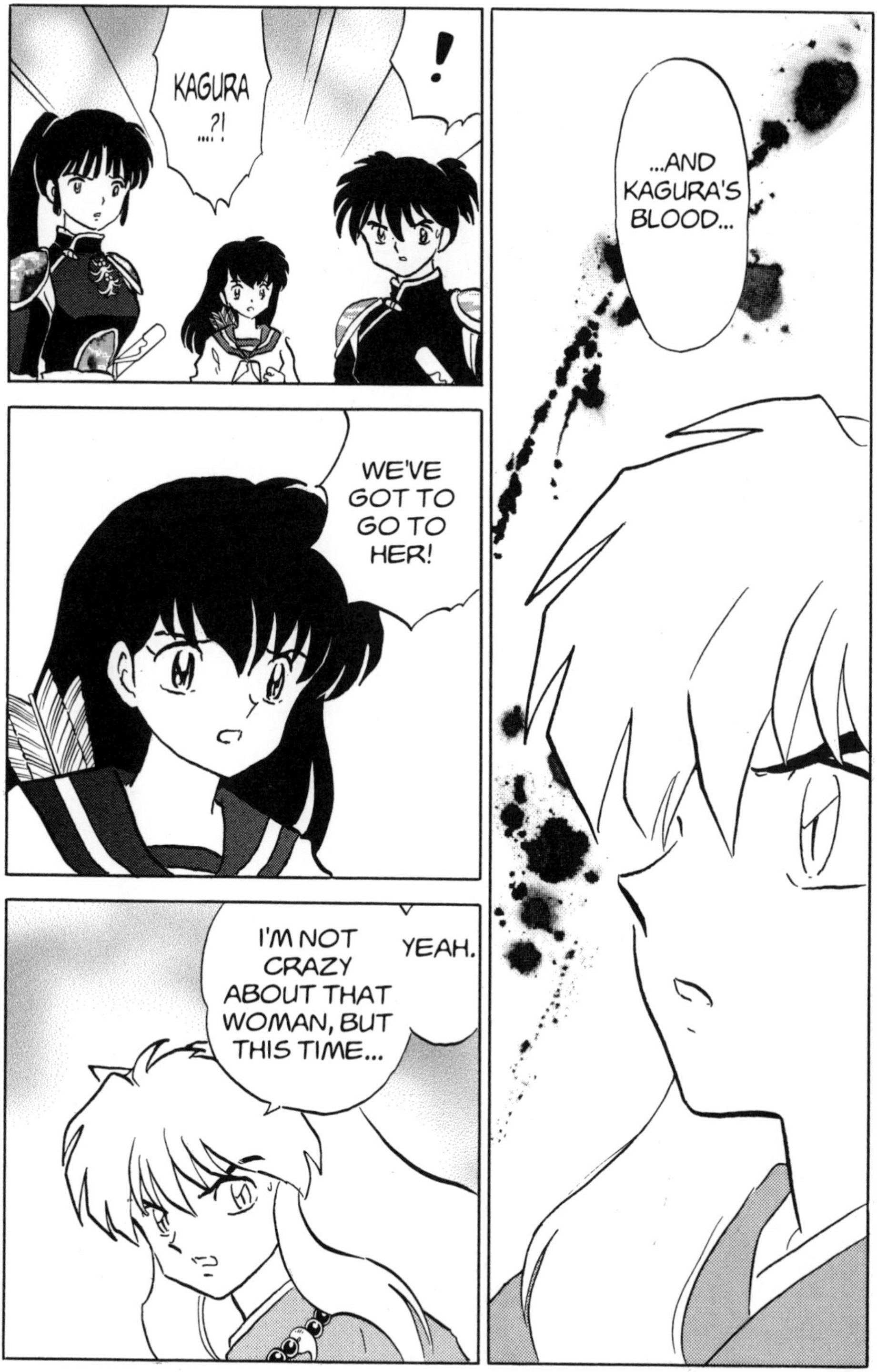
...AND KAGURA'S BLOOD...
!
KAGURA ..?!
....?!
WE'VE GOT TO GO TO HER!
YEAH.
I'M NOT CRAZY ABOUT THAT WOMAN, BUT THIS TIME...

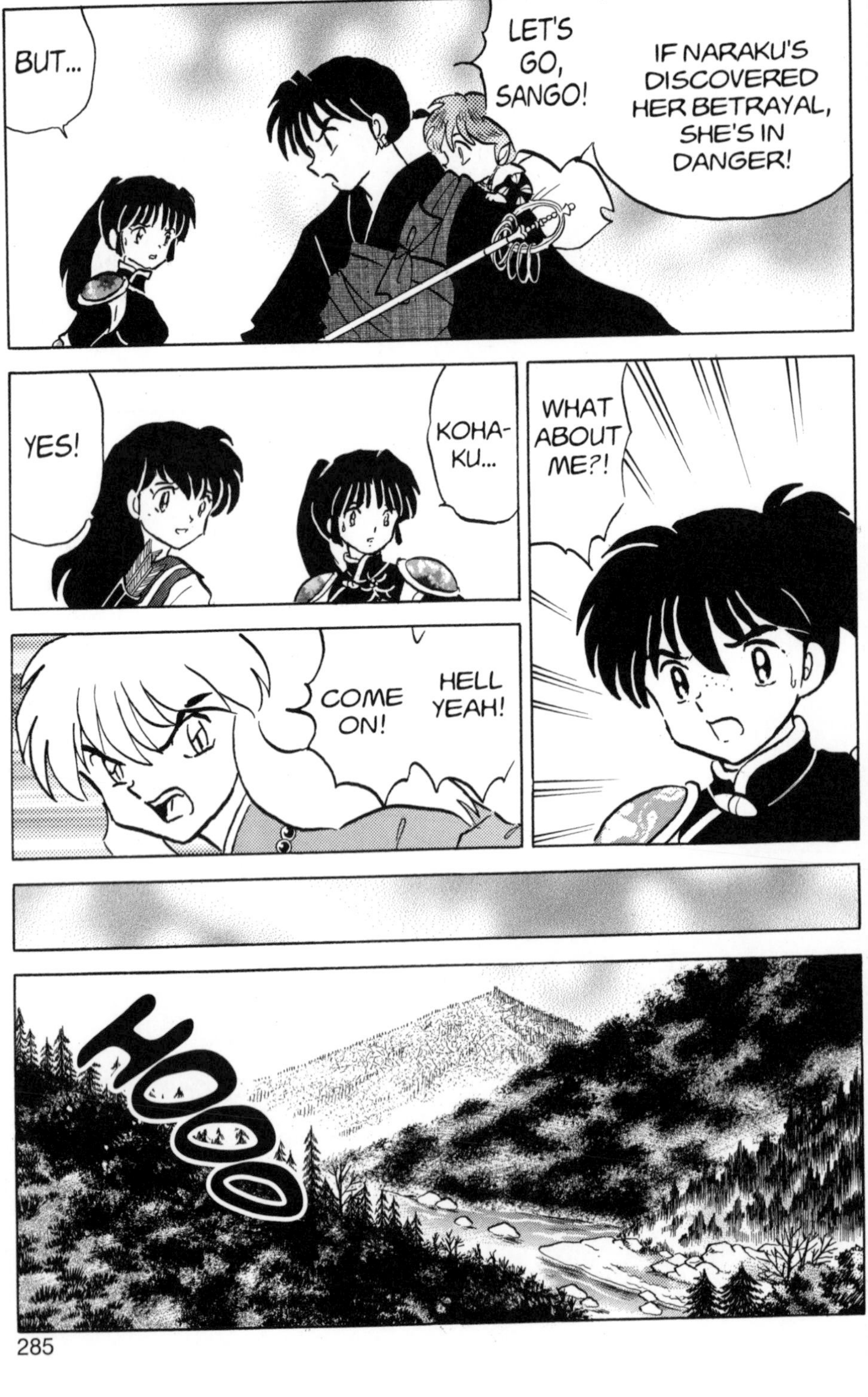
IF NARAKU'S DISCOVERED HER BETRAYAL, SHE'S IN DANGER!
LET'S GO, SANGO!
BUT...
WHAT ABOUT ME?!
KOHAKU...
YES!
HELL YEAH!
COME ON!
HOOO

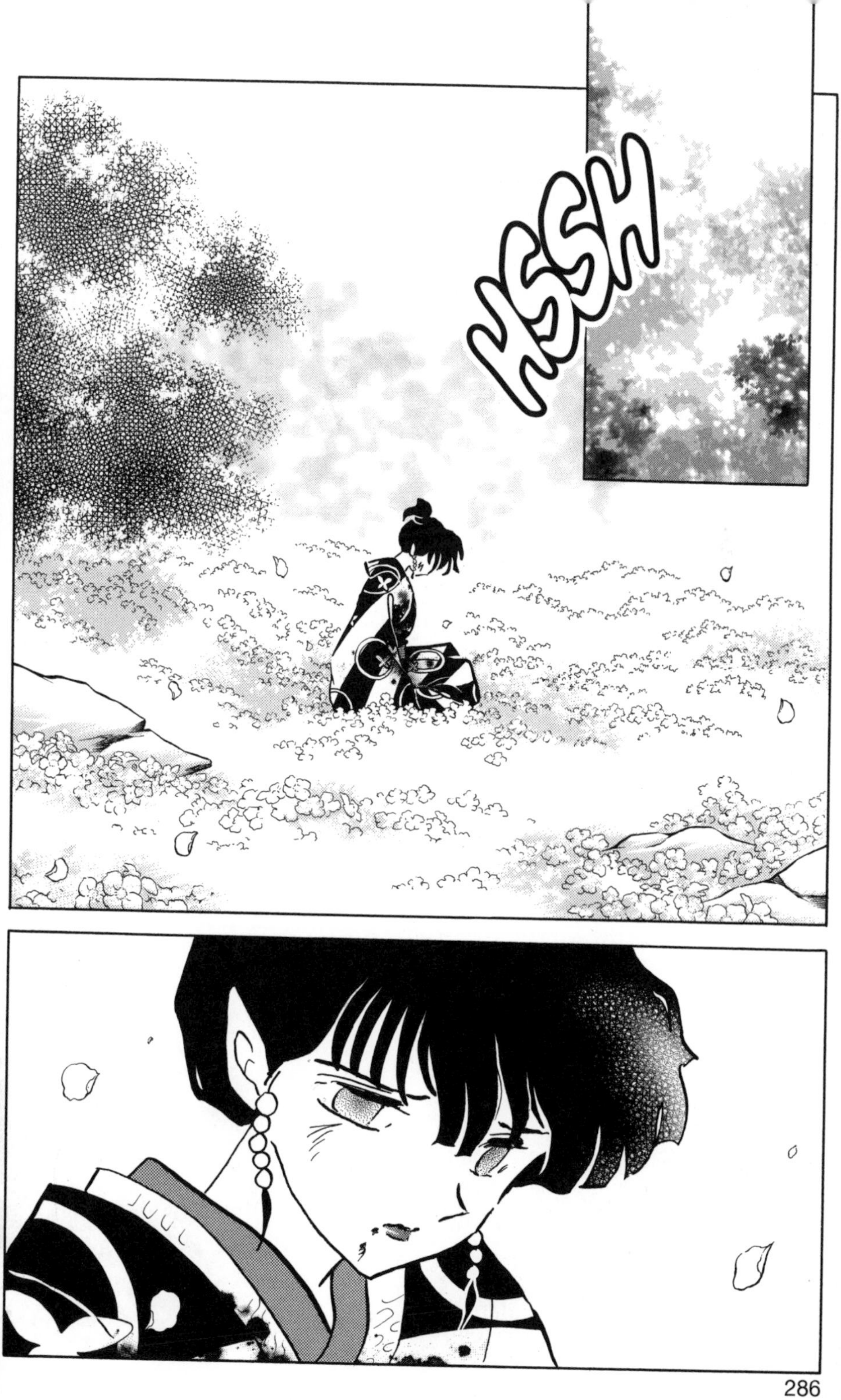
HSSH

SCROLL SIX
THE WIND

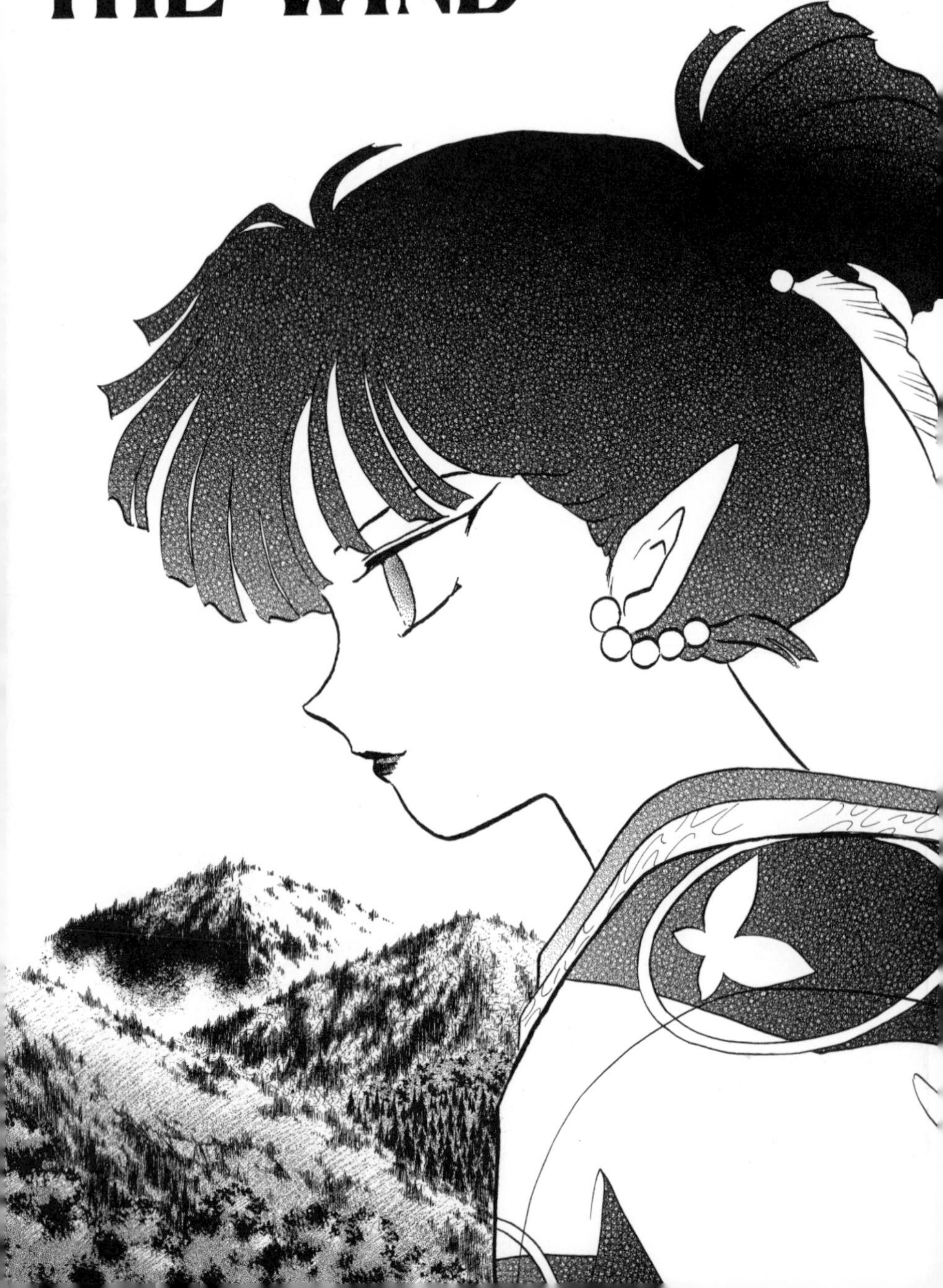

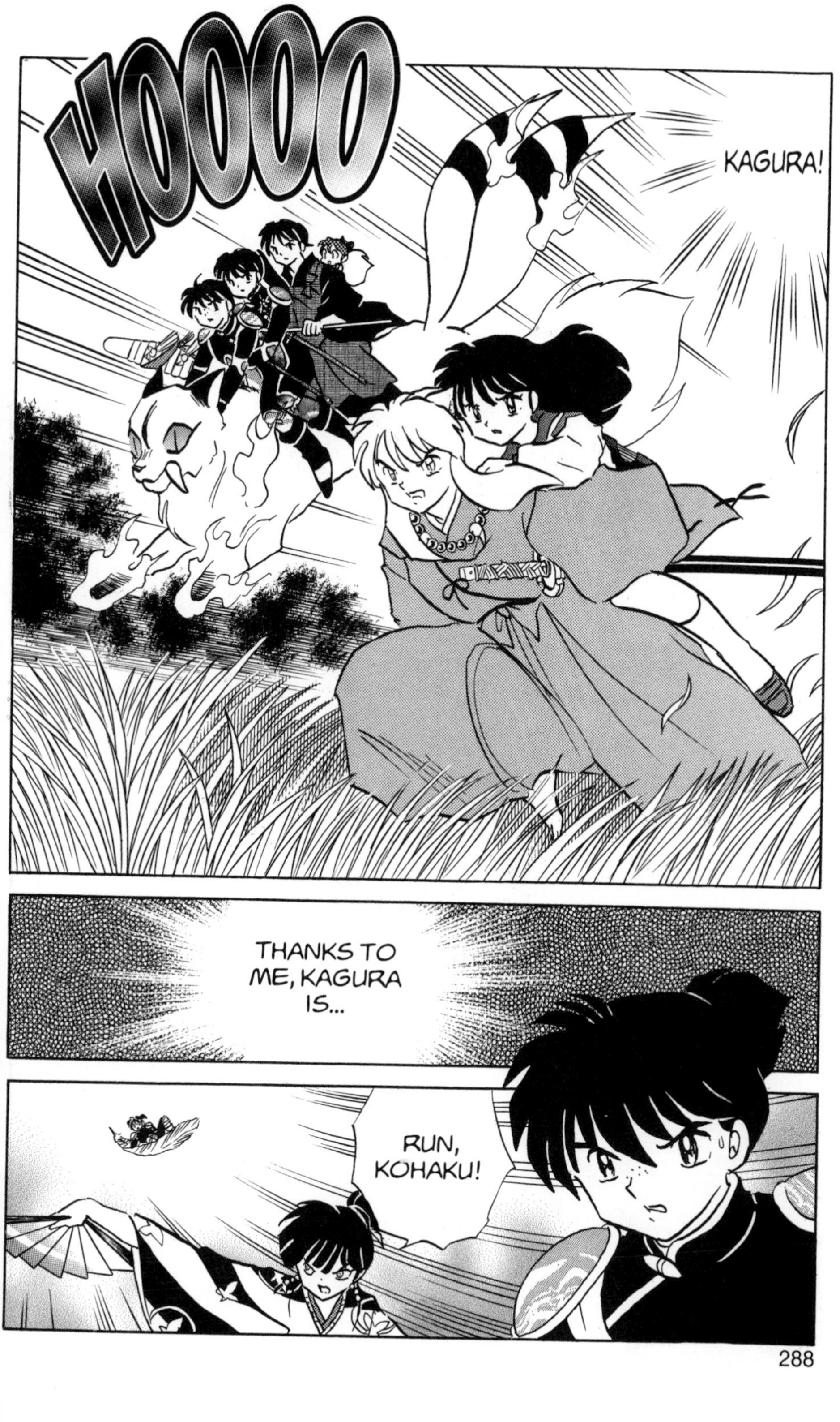
HOOOO
KAGURA!
THANKS TO ME, KAGURA IS...
RUN, KOHAKU!

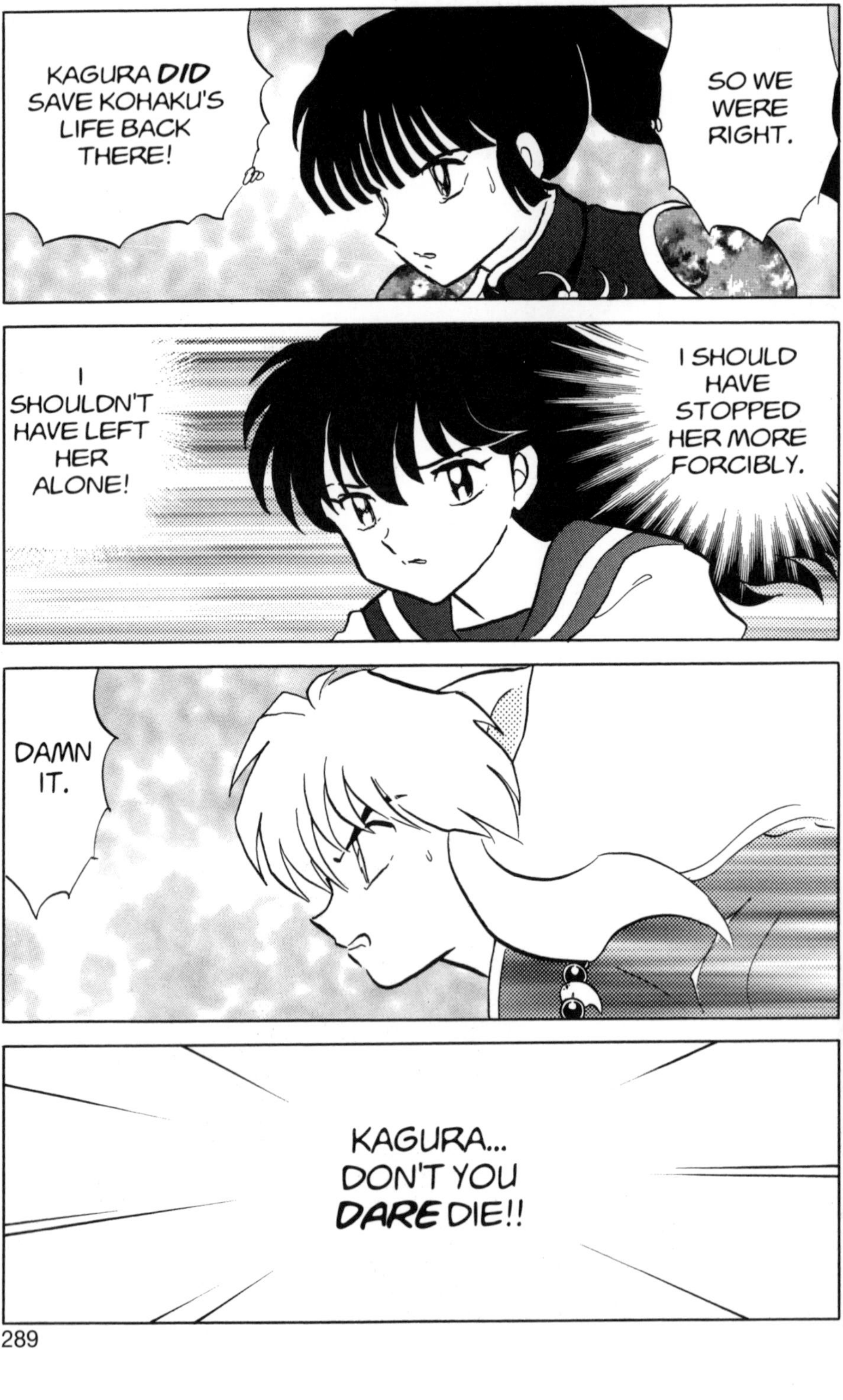
SO WE WERE RIGHT.
KAGURA DID SAVE KOHAKU'S LIFE BACK THERE!
I SHOULD HAVE STOPPED HER MORE FORCIBLY.
I SHOULDN'T HAVE LEFT HER ALONE!
DAMN IT.
KAGURA... DON'T YOU DARE DIE!!

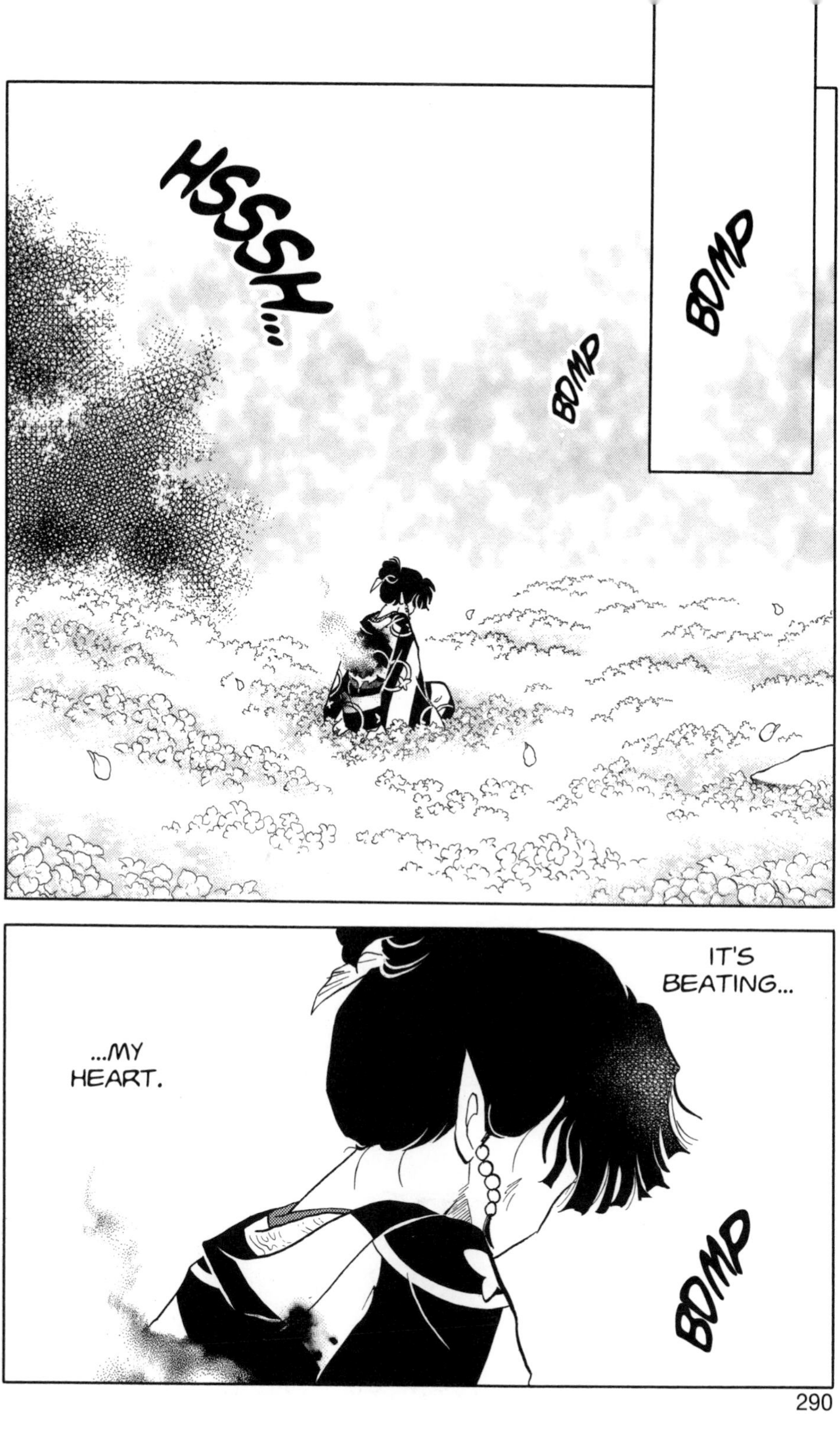
BOMP
BOMP
HSSSH...
IT'S BEATING...
...MY HEART.
BOMP

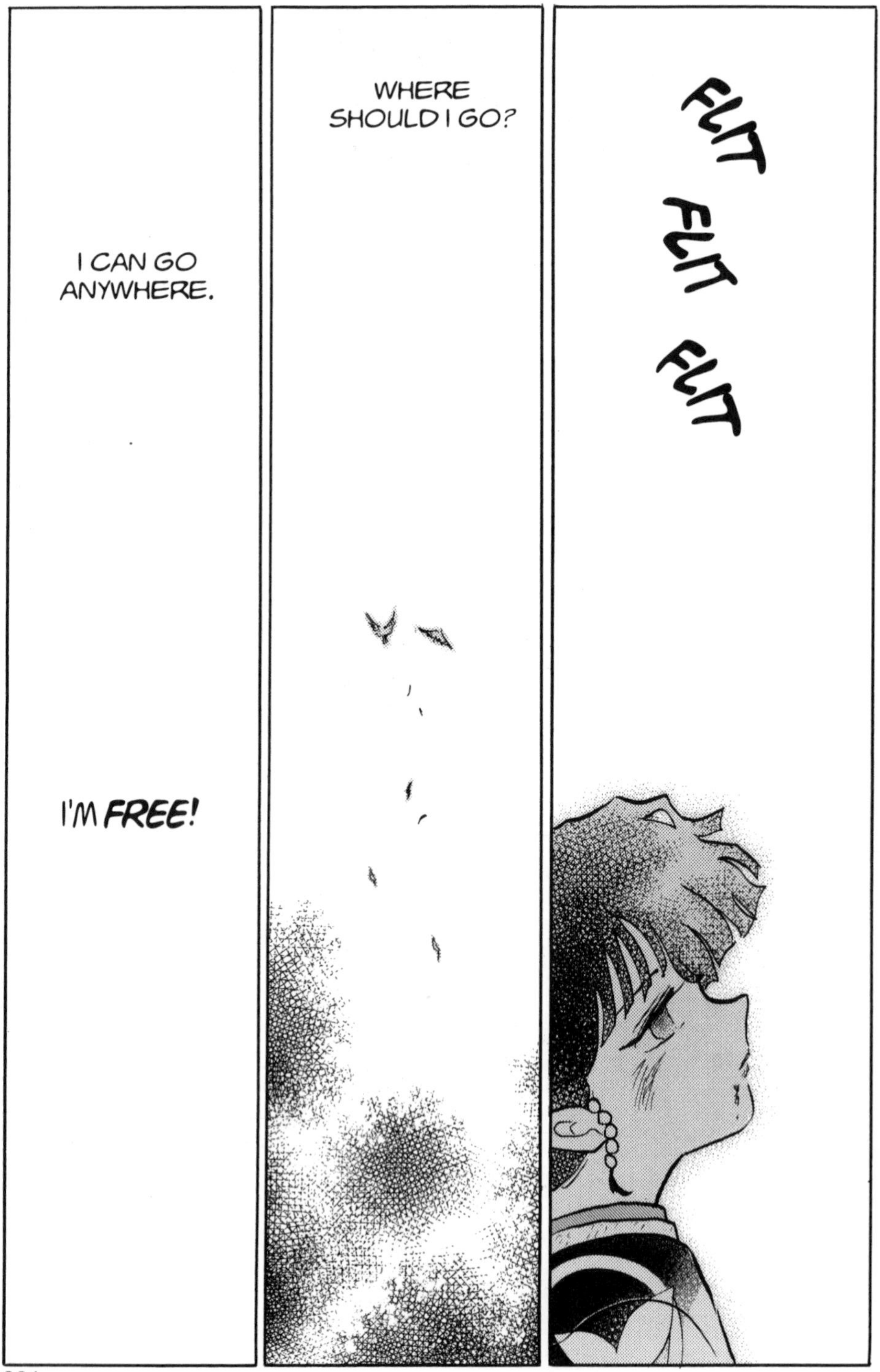
FLIT FLIT FLIT
WHERE SHOULD I GO?
I CAN GO ANYWHERE.
I'M **FREE!**

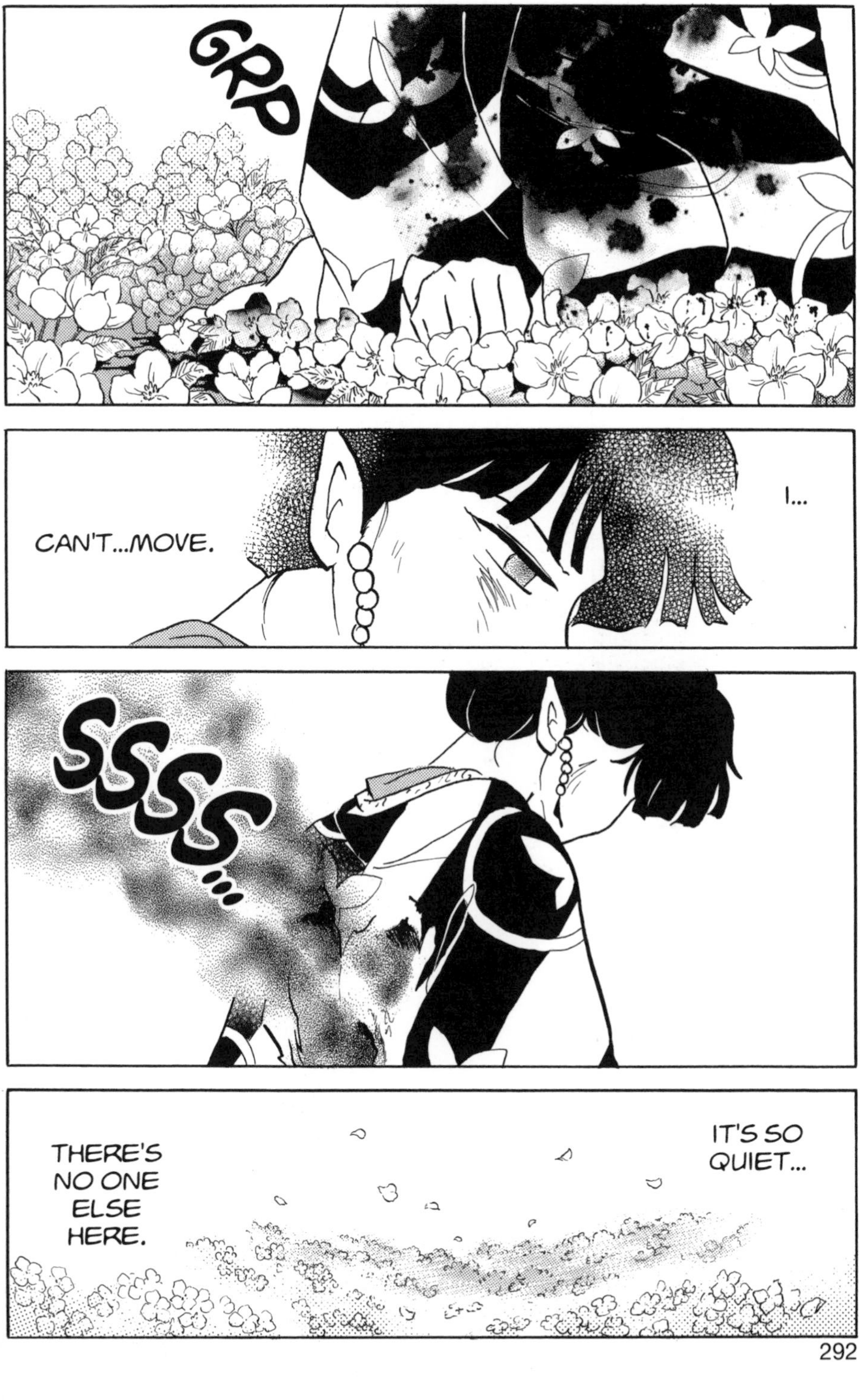
GRP
I...
CAN'T...MOVE.
SSSS...
IT'S SO QUIET...
THERE'S NO ONE ELSE HERE.

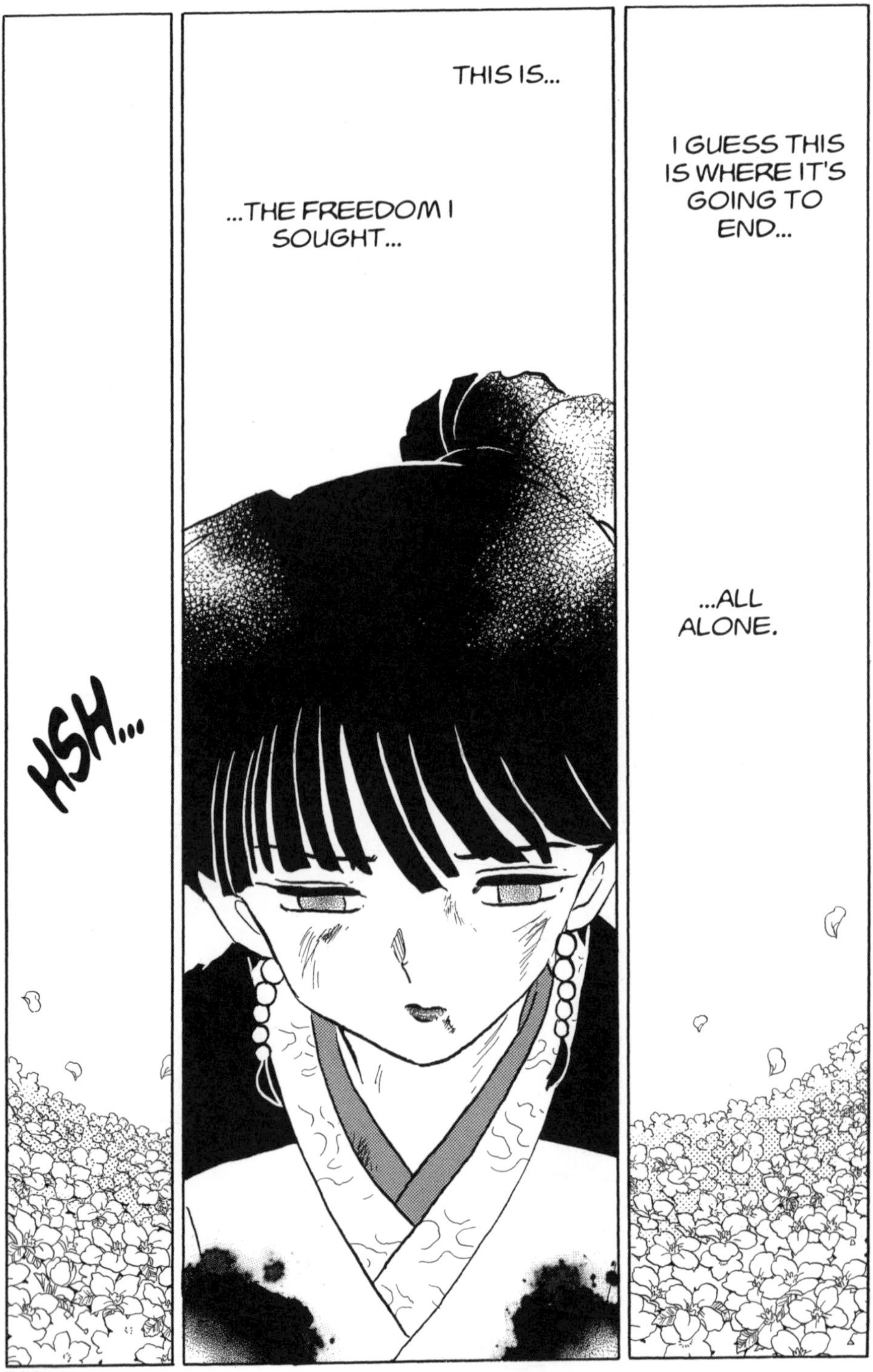
I GUESS THIS IS WHERE IT'S GOING TO END...
...ALL ALONE.
THIS IS...
...THE FREEDOM I SOUGHT...
HSH...

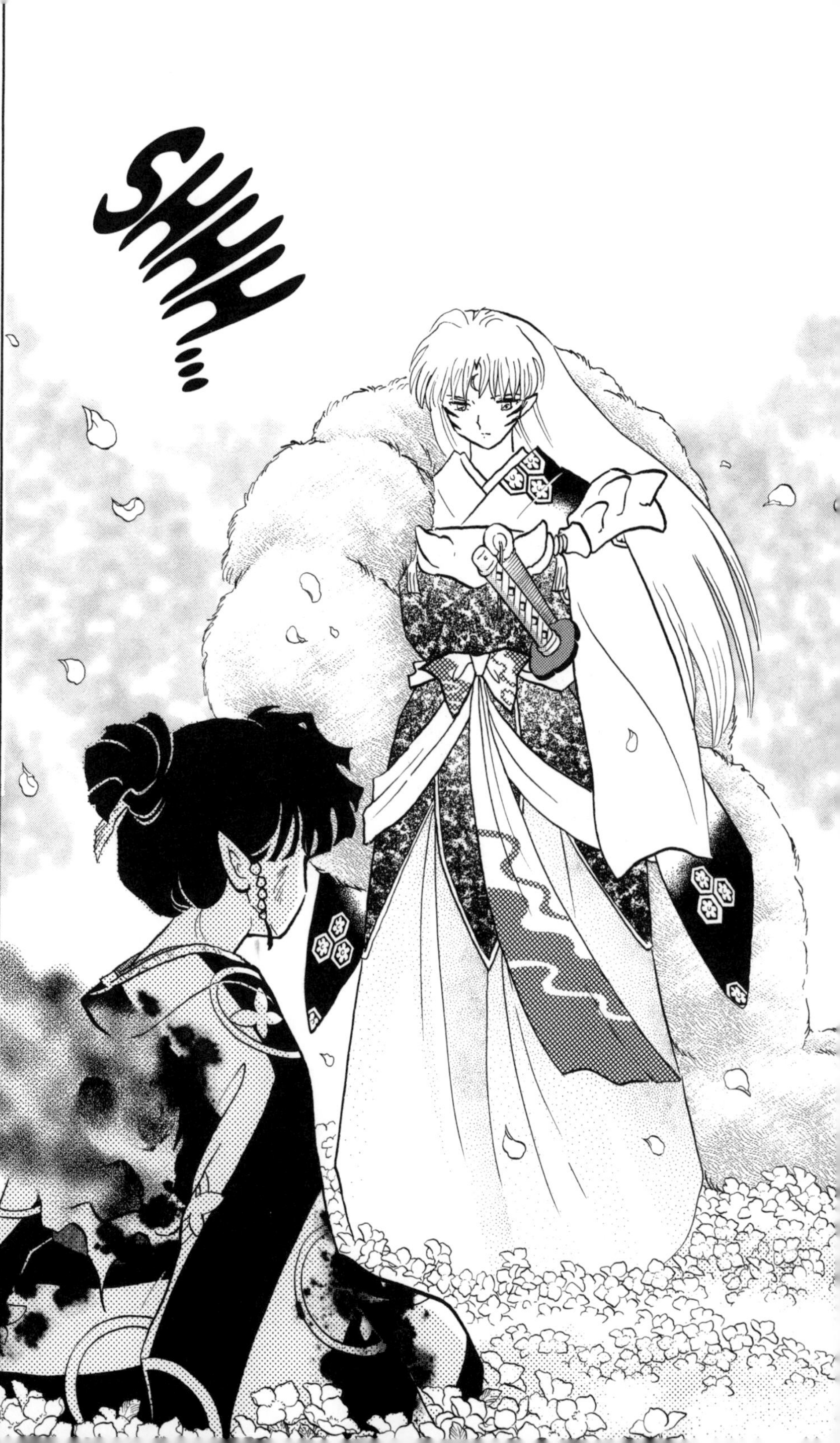
SHHH...

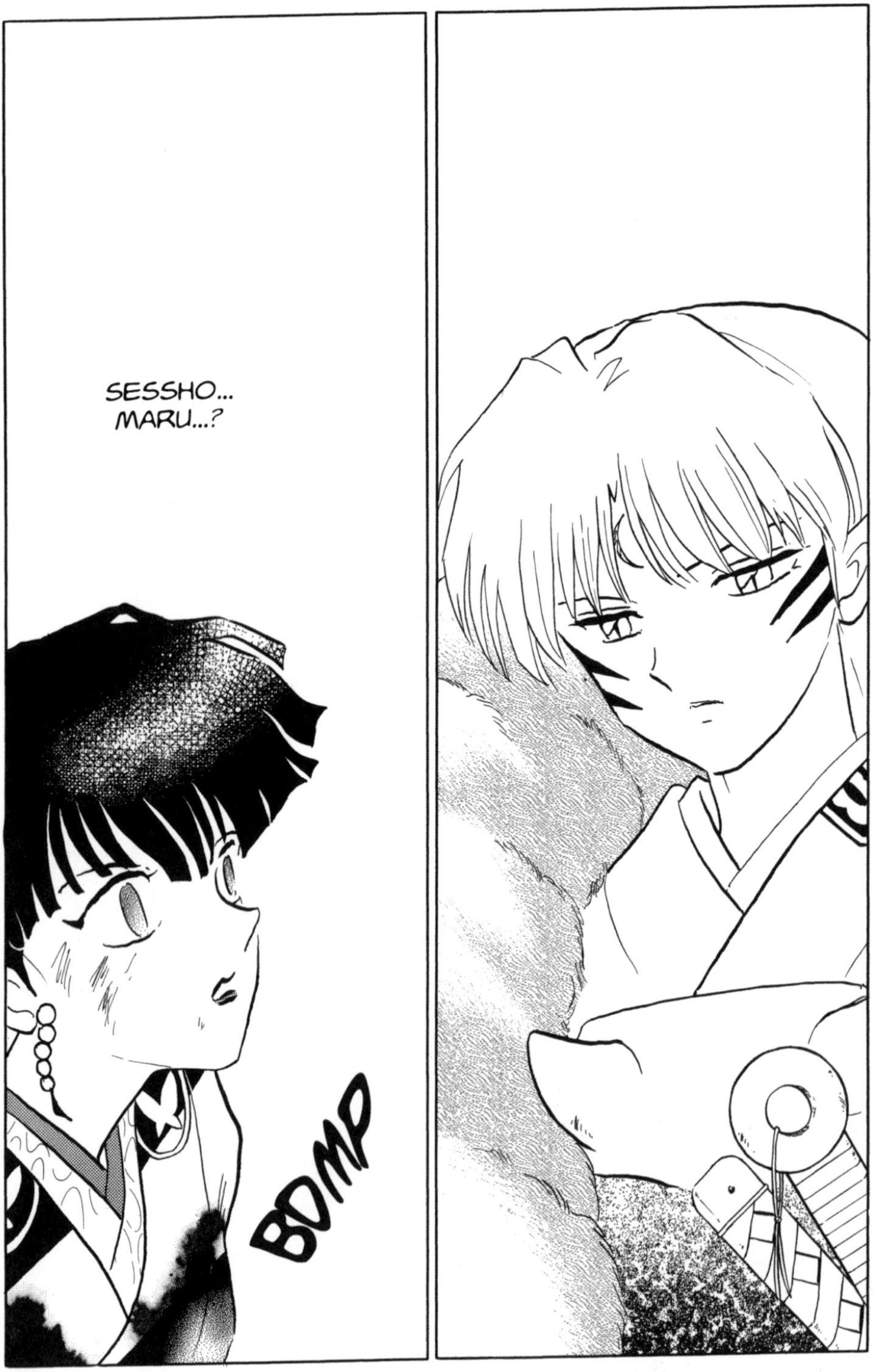
SESSHO...
MARU...?
BDMP

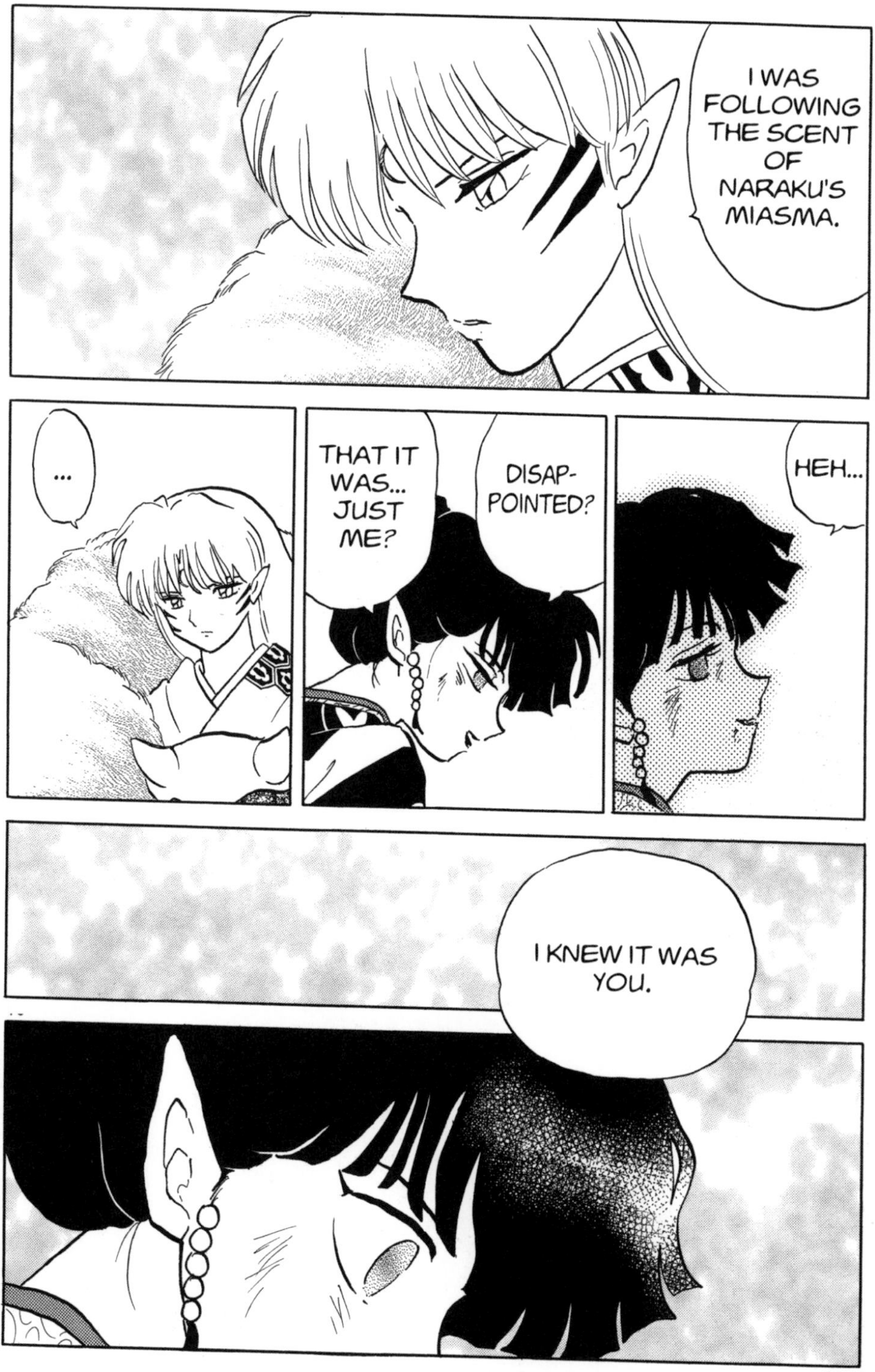
I WAS FOLLOWING THE SCENT OF NARAKU'S MIASMA.
HEH...
DISAP-POINTED?
THAT IT WAS... JUST ME?
...
I KNEW IT WAS YOU.

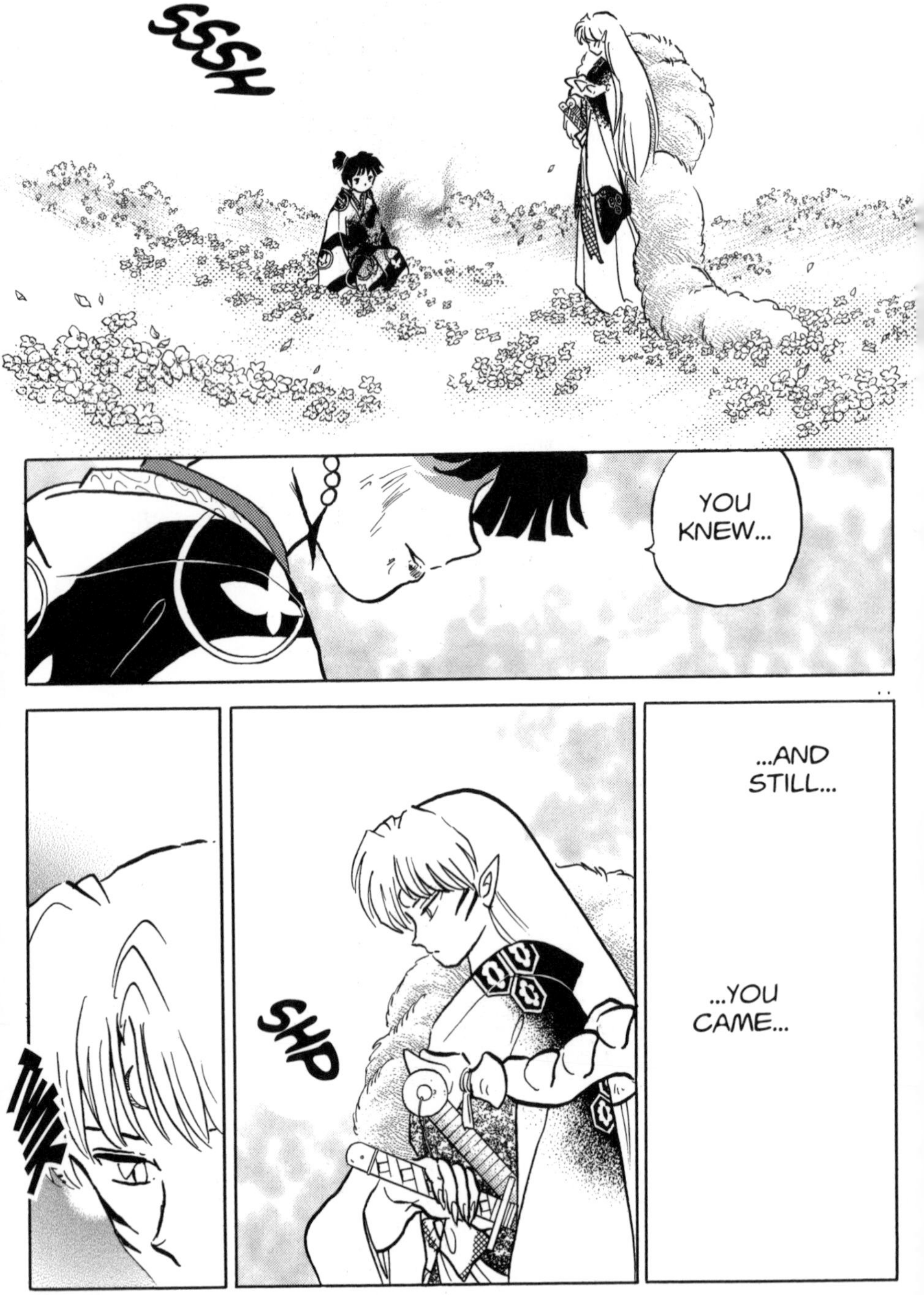
SSSH
YOU KNEW...
...AND STILL...
...YOU CAME...
SHP
TWIK

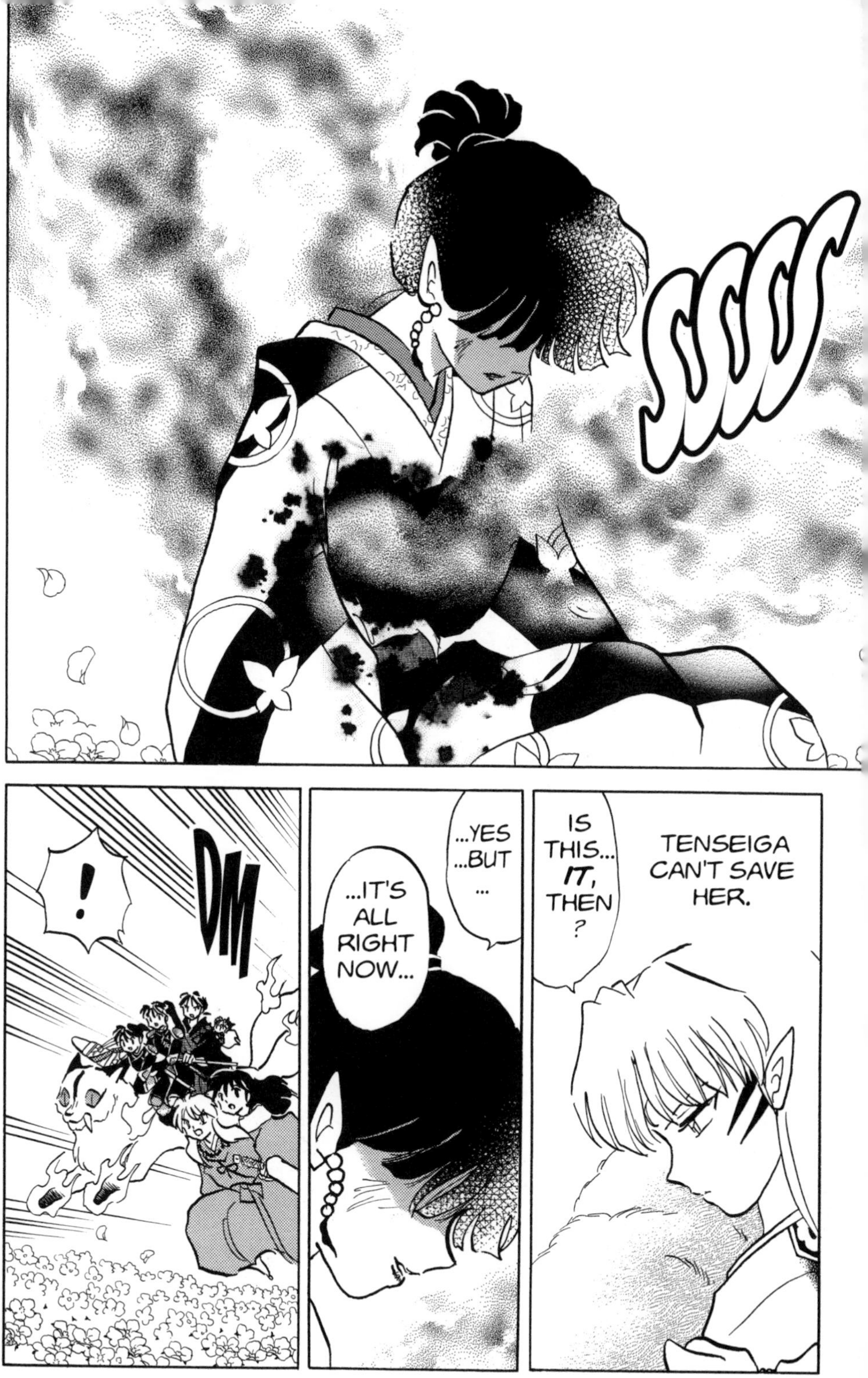
SSSS
TENSEIGA CAN'T SAVE HER.
IS THIS... *IT*, THEN?
...YES ...BUT ...
...IT'S ALL RIGHT NOW...
DM
!

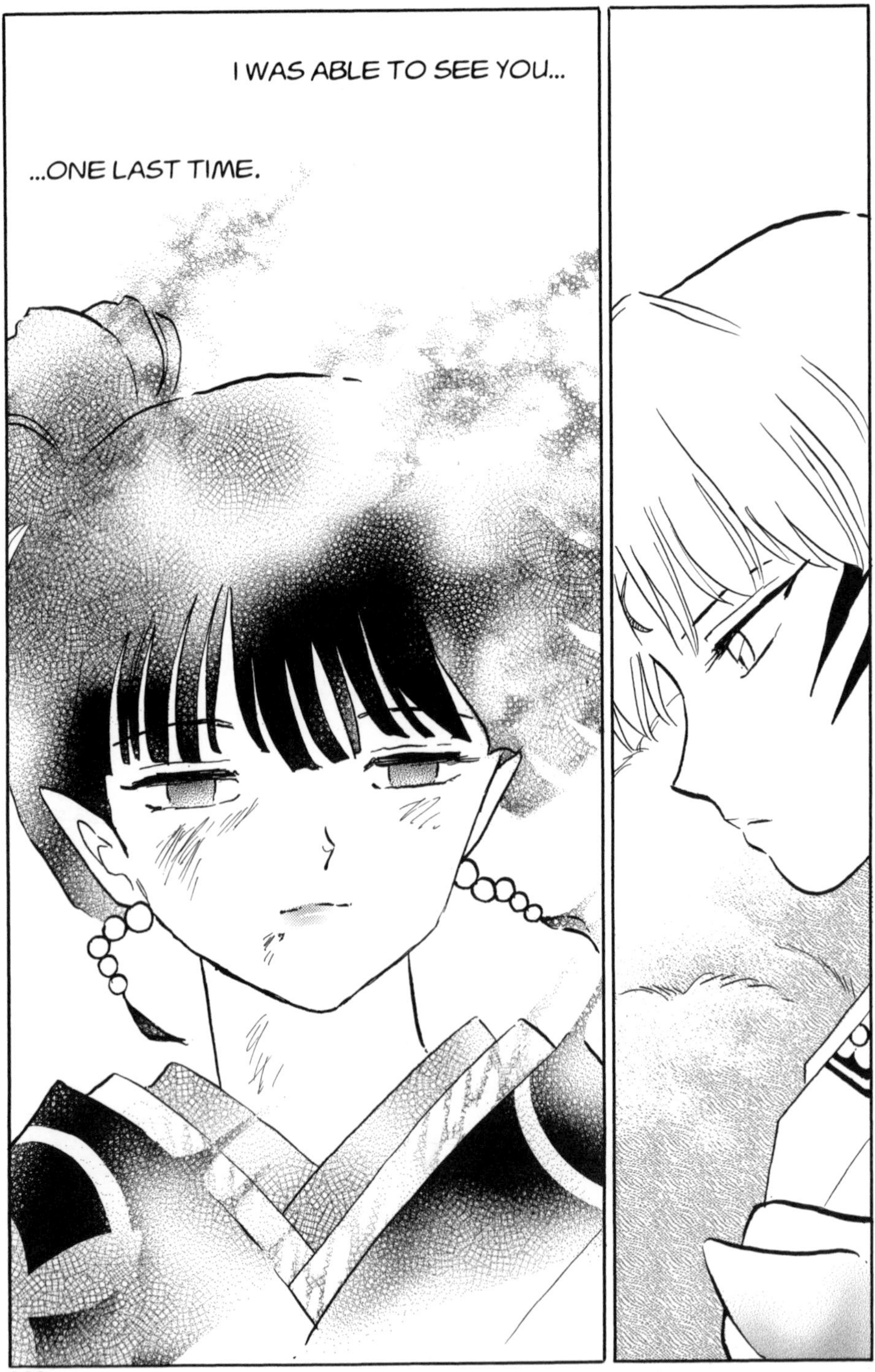
I WAS ABLE TO SEE YOU...
...ONE LAST TIME.

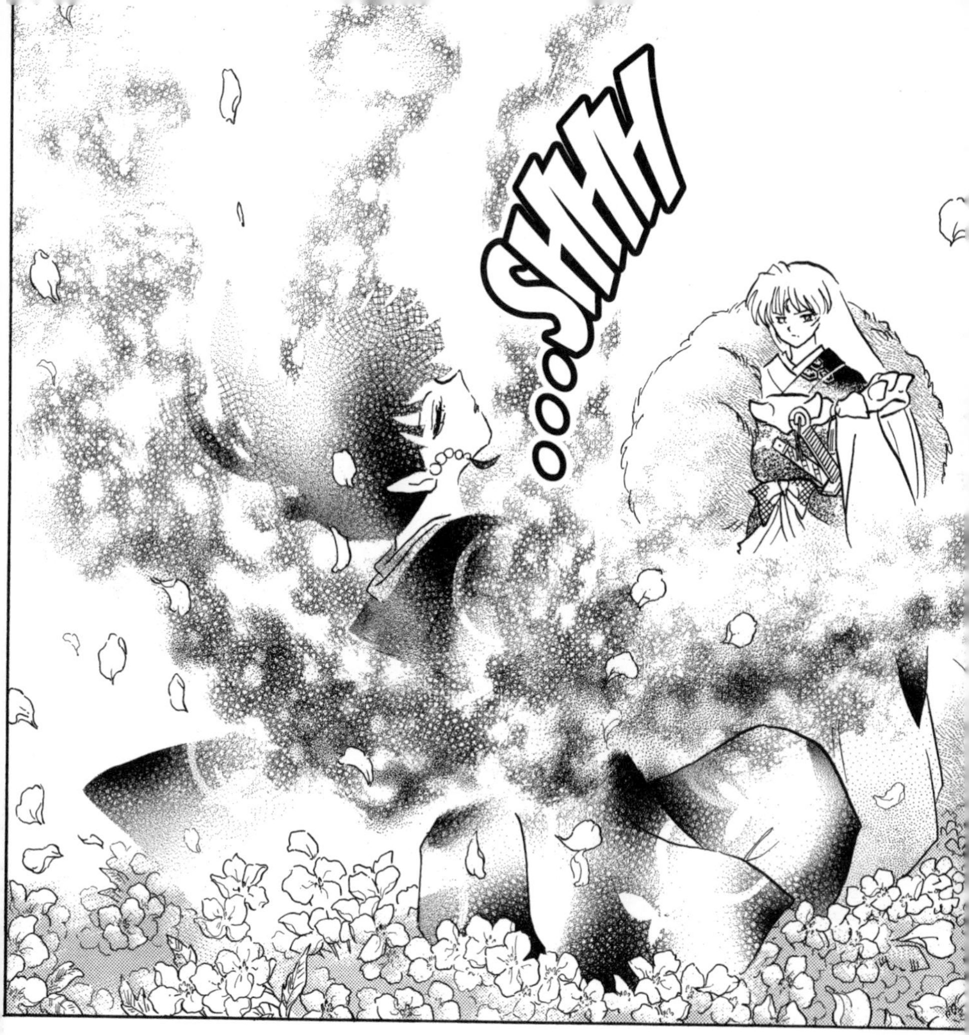
OOOSHHH
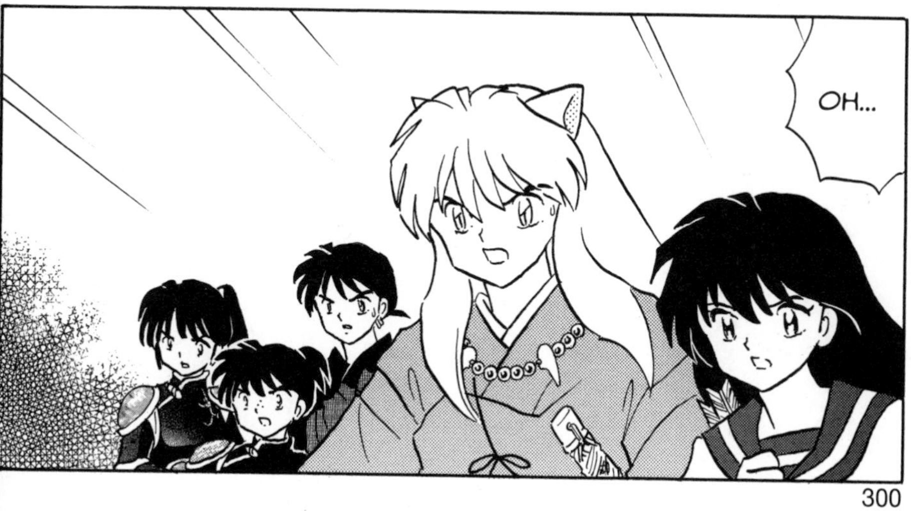
OH...

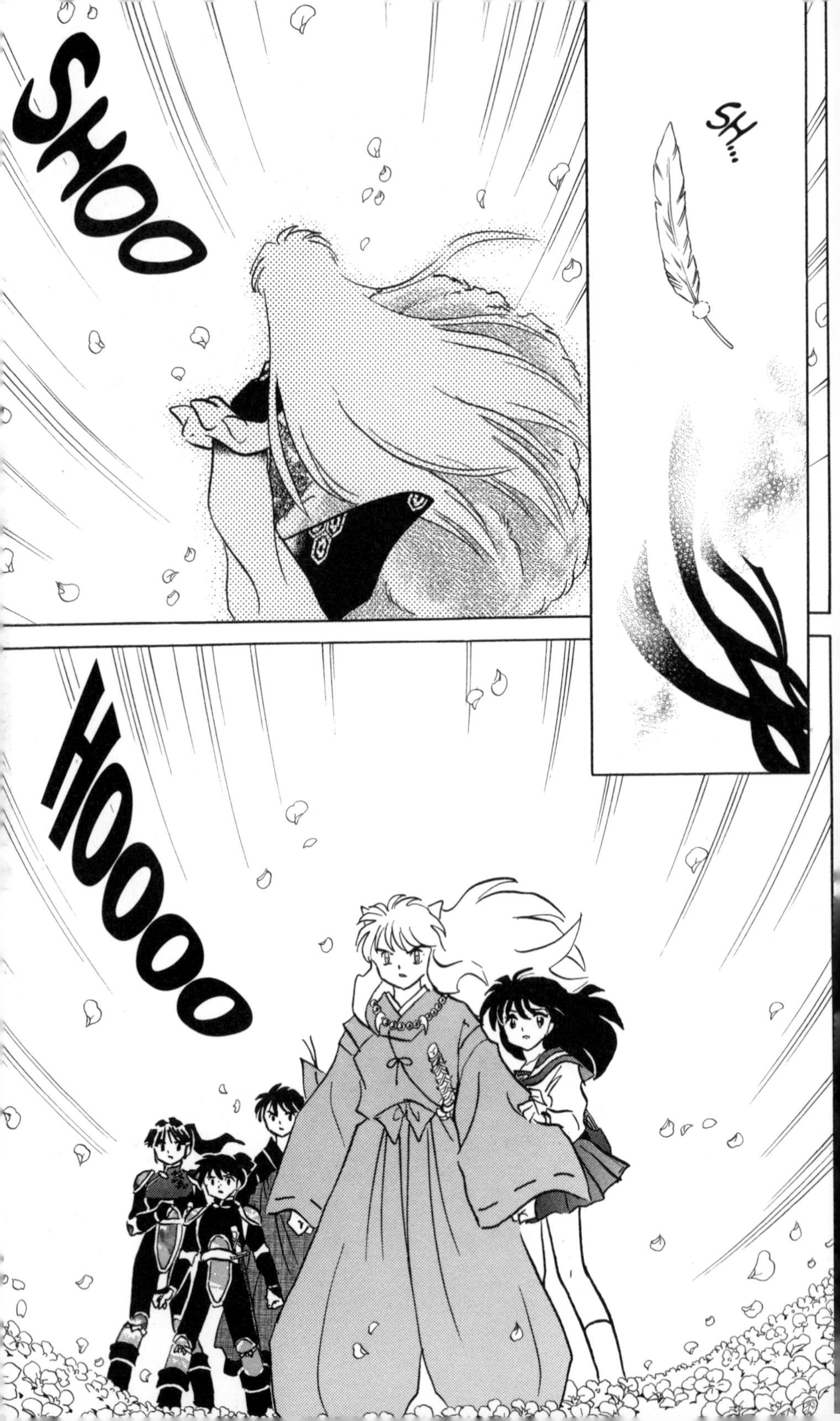
SH...
SHOO
HOOOOO

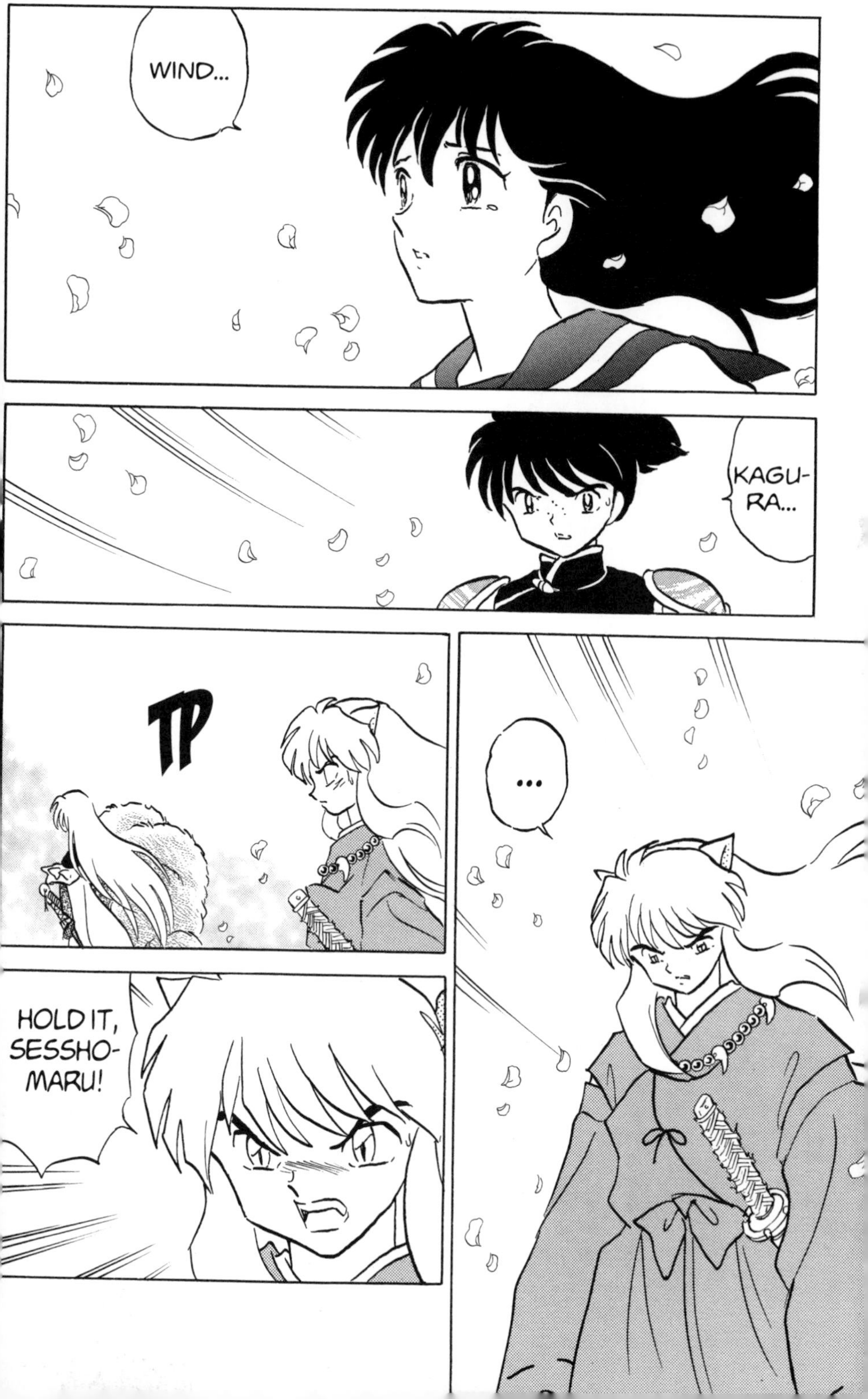
WIND...
KAGU-RA...
...
TP
HOLD IT, SESSHO-MARU!

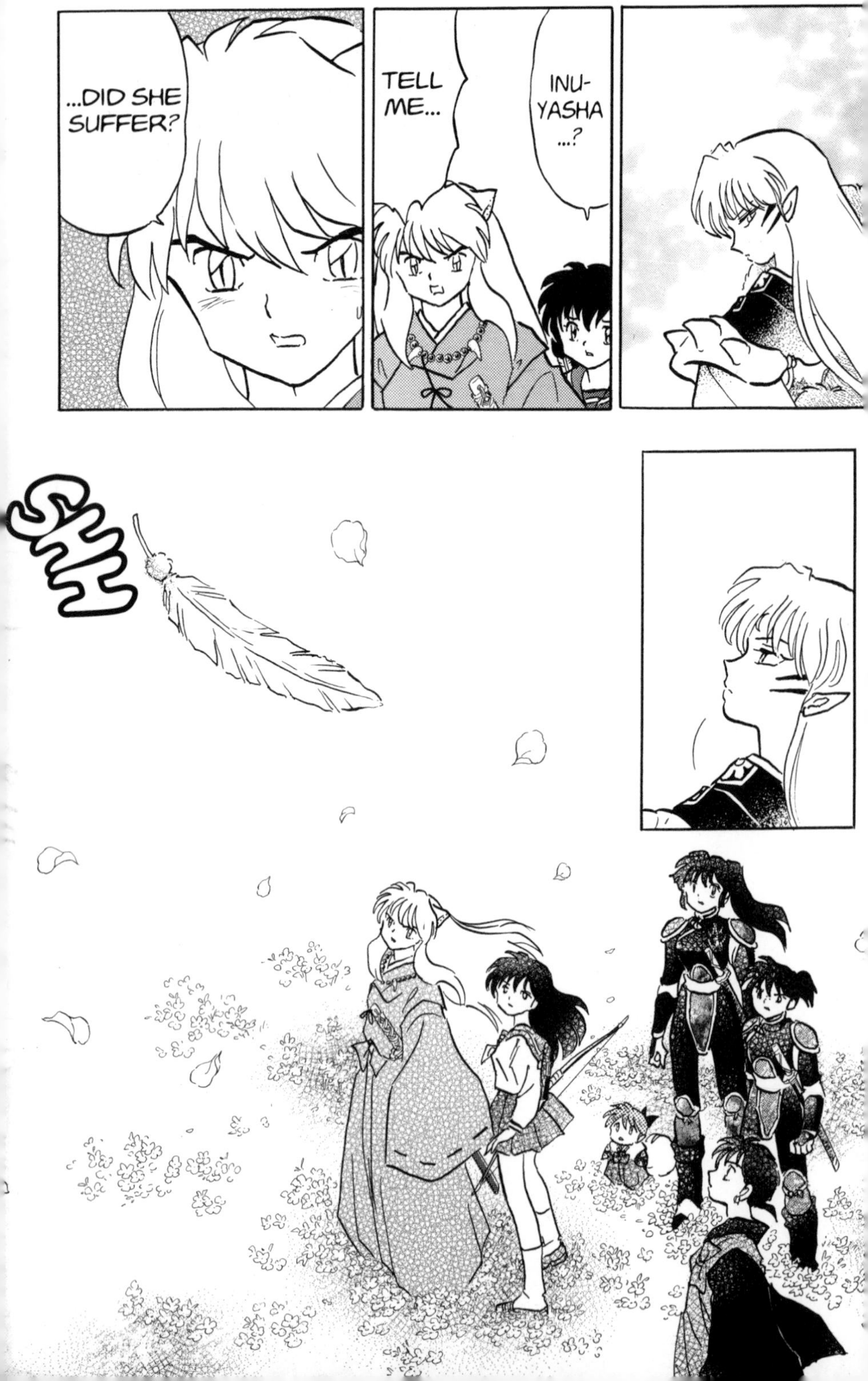
INU-YASHA ...?
TELL ME...
...DID SHE SUFFER?
SHH

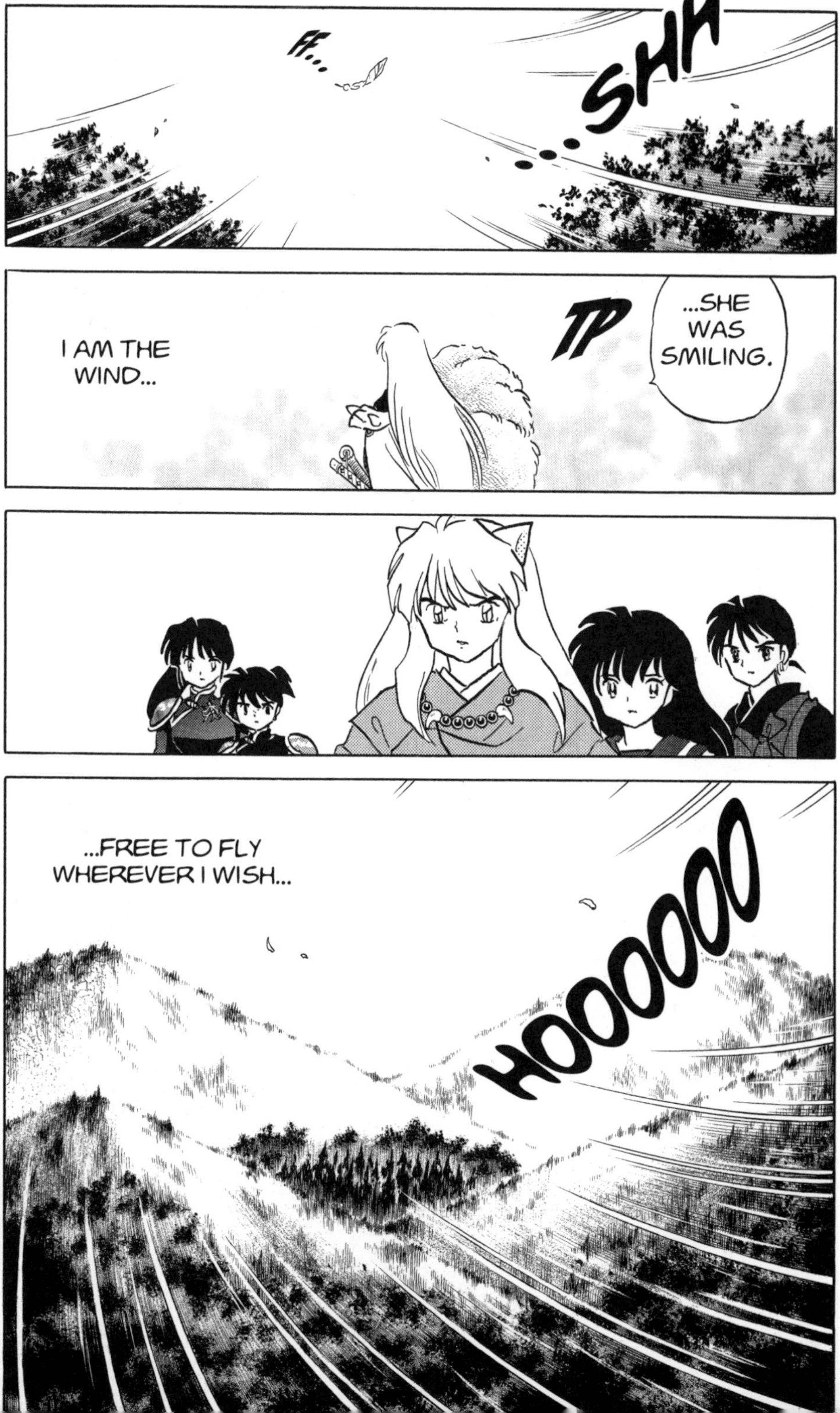
FF... ...SHH
...SHE WAS SMILING.
TP
I AM THE WIND...
HOOOOOO
...FREE TO FLY WHEREVER I WISH...

SCROLL SEVEN
THE HOLE IN HER CHEST

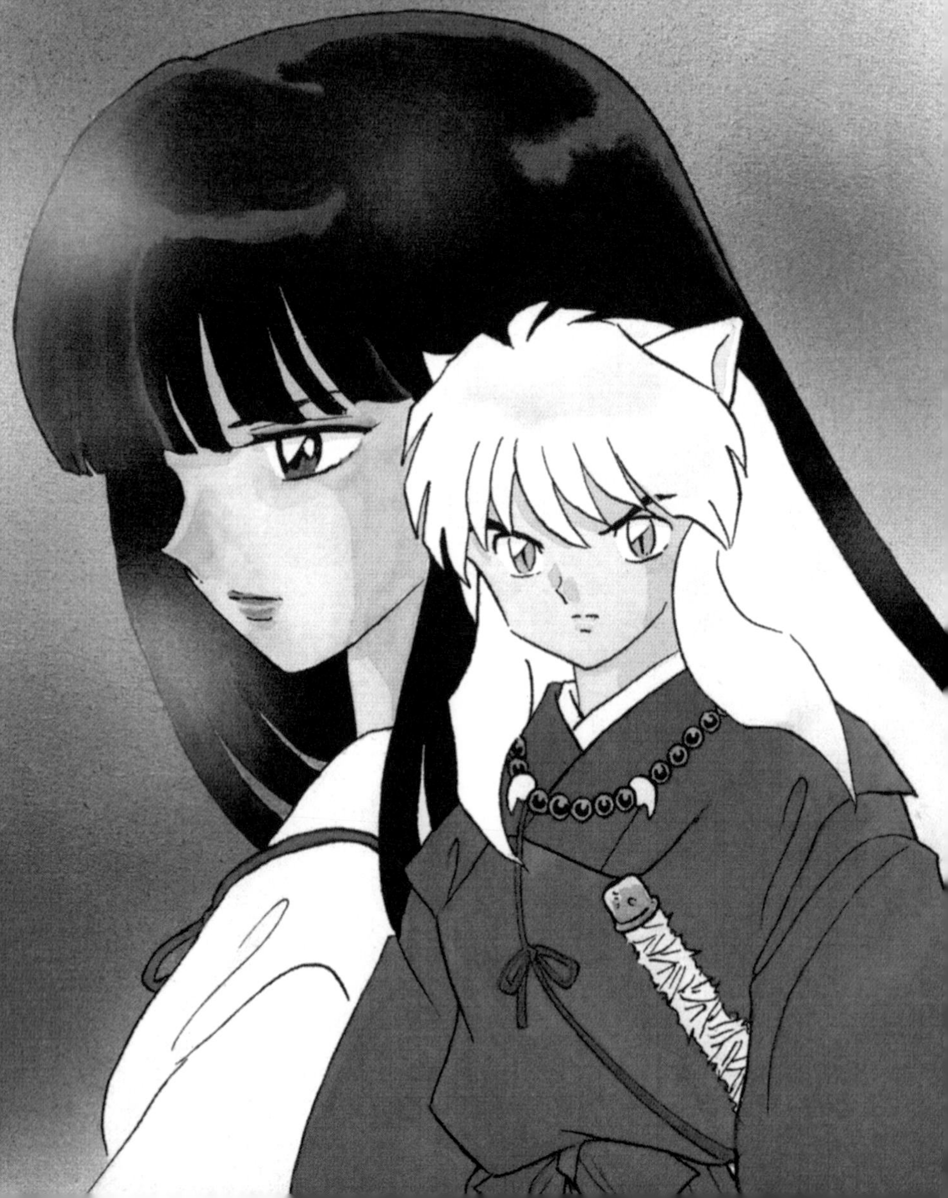

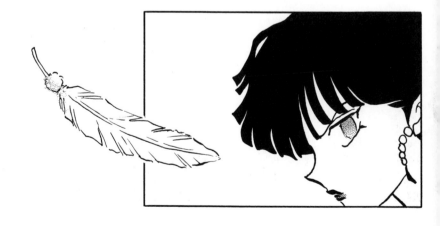

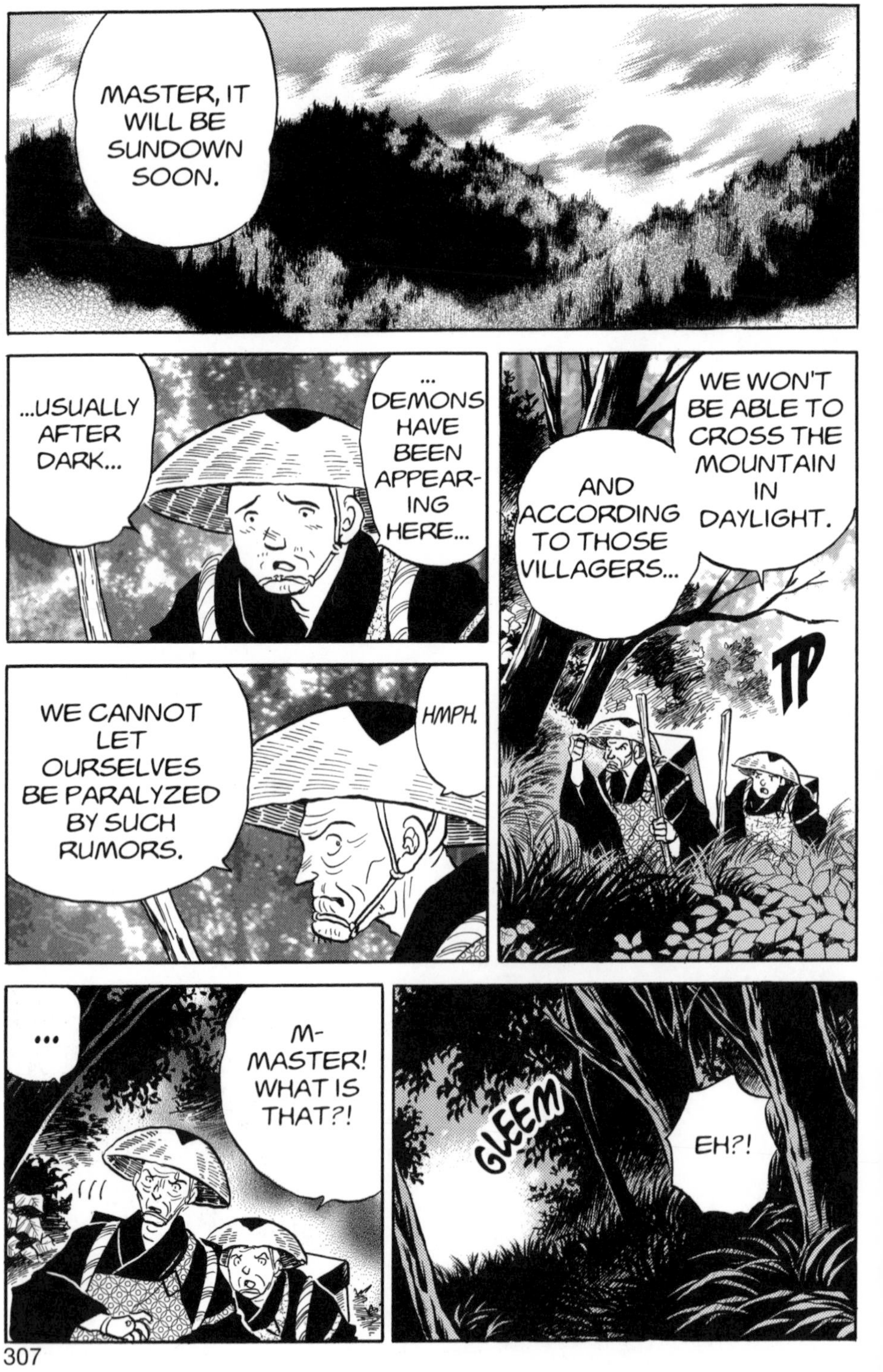
MASTER, IT WILL BE SUNDOWN SOON.
WE WON'T BE ABLE TO CROSS THE MOUNTAIN IN DAYLIGHT.
AND ACCORDING TO THOSE VILLAGERS...
TP
... DEMONS HAVE BEEN APPEAR-ING HERE...
...USUALLY AFTER DARK...
HMPH.
WE CANNOT LET OURSELVES BE PARALYZED BY SUCH RUMORS.
EH?!
GLEEM
M-MASTER! WHAT IS THAT?!
...

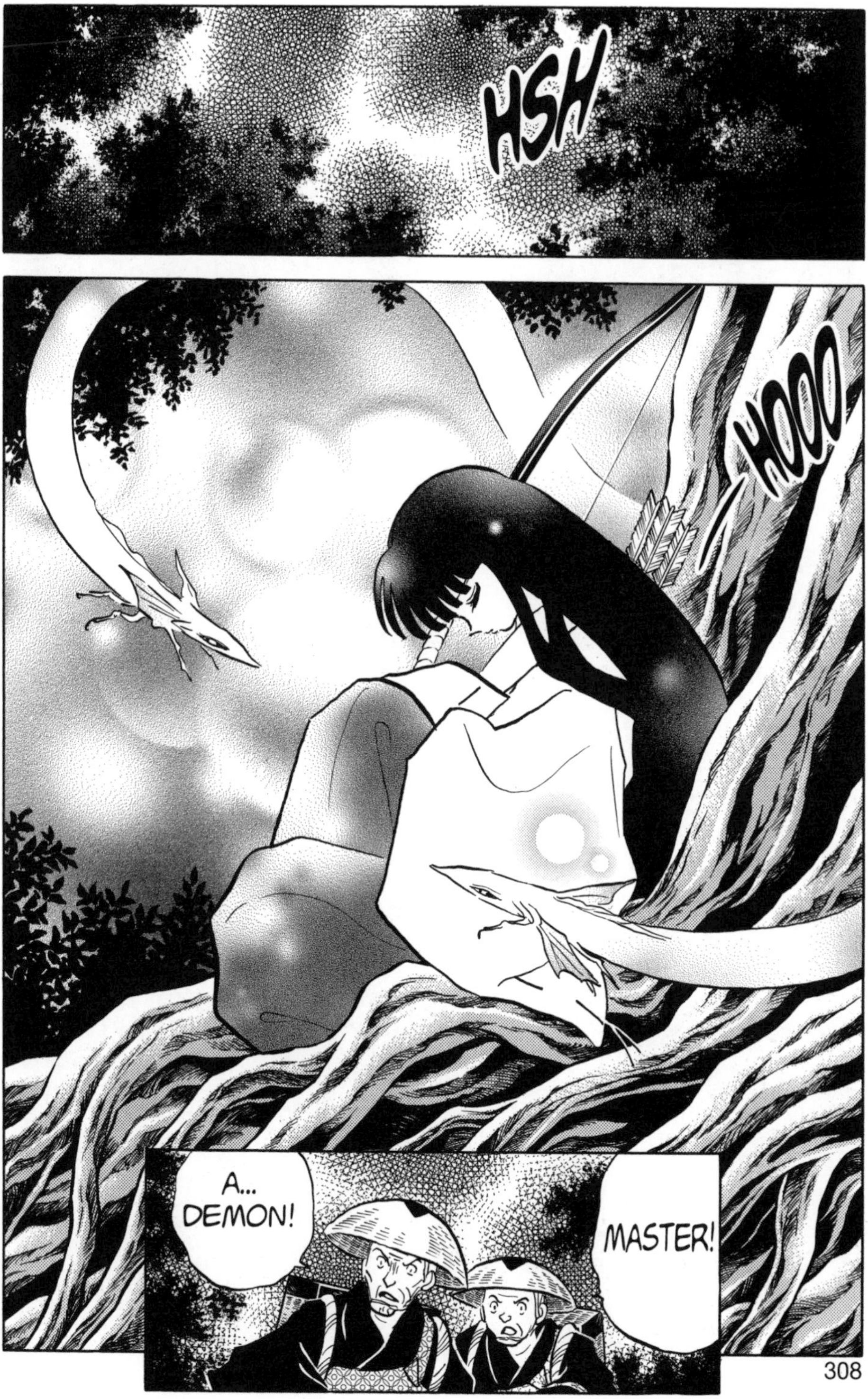
HSH
HOOO
MASTER!
A... DEMON!

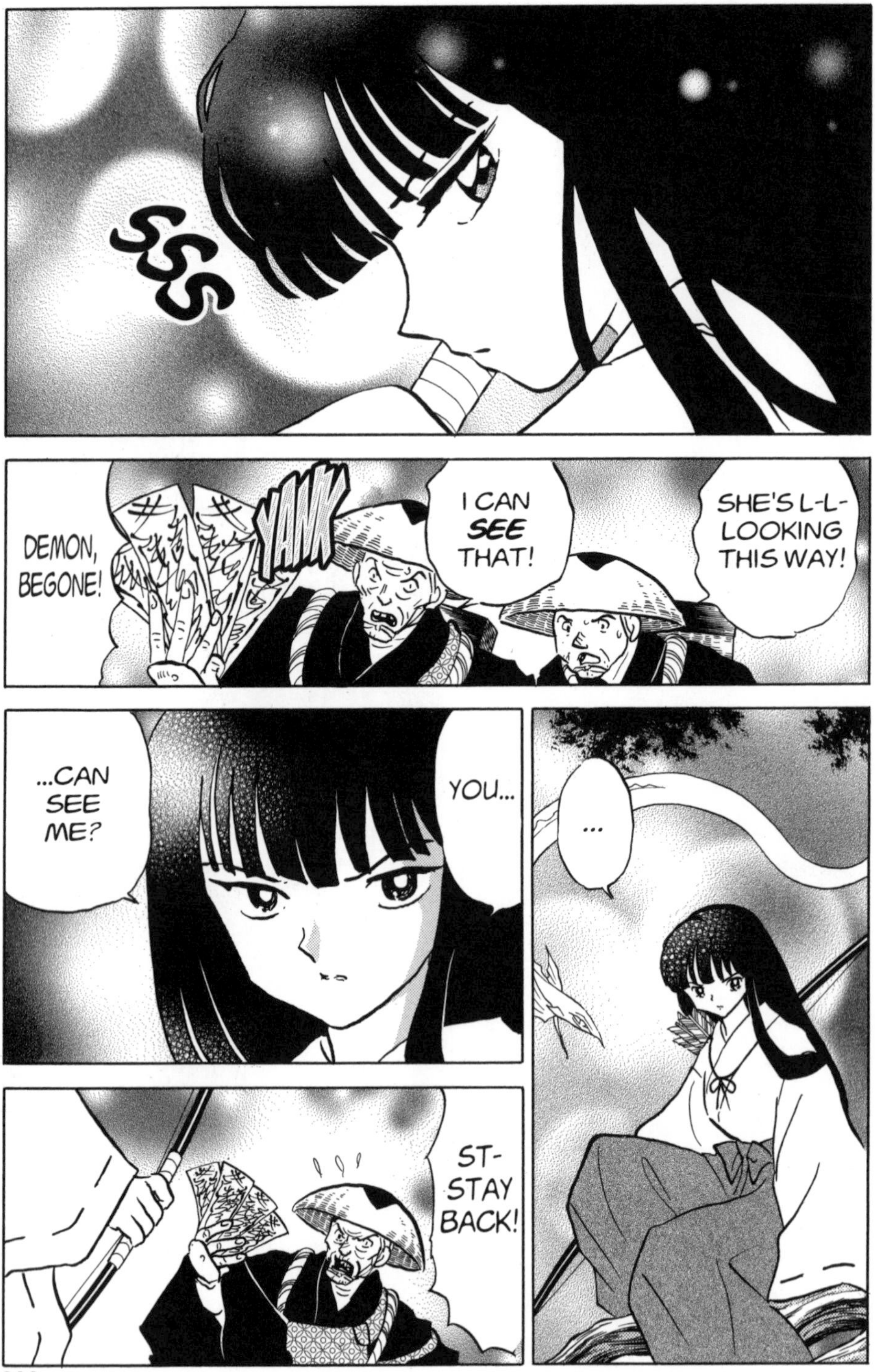
SSS
SHE'S L-L-LOOKING THIS WAY!
I CAN SEE THAT!
YANK
DEMON, BEGONE!
...
YOU...
...CAN SEE ME?
ST-STAY BACK!

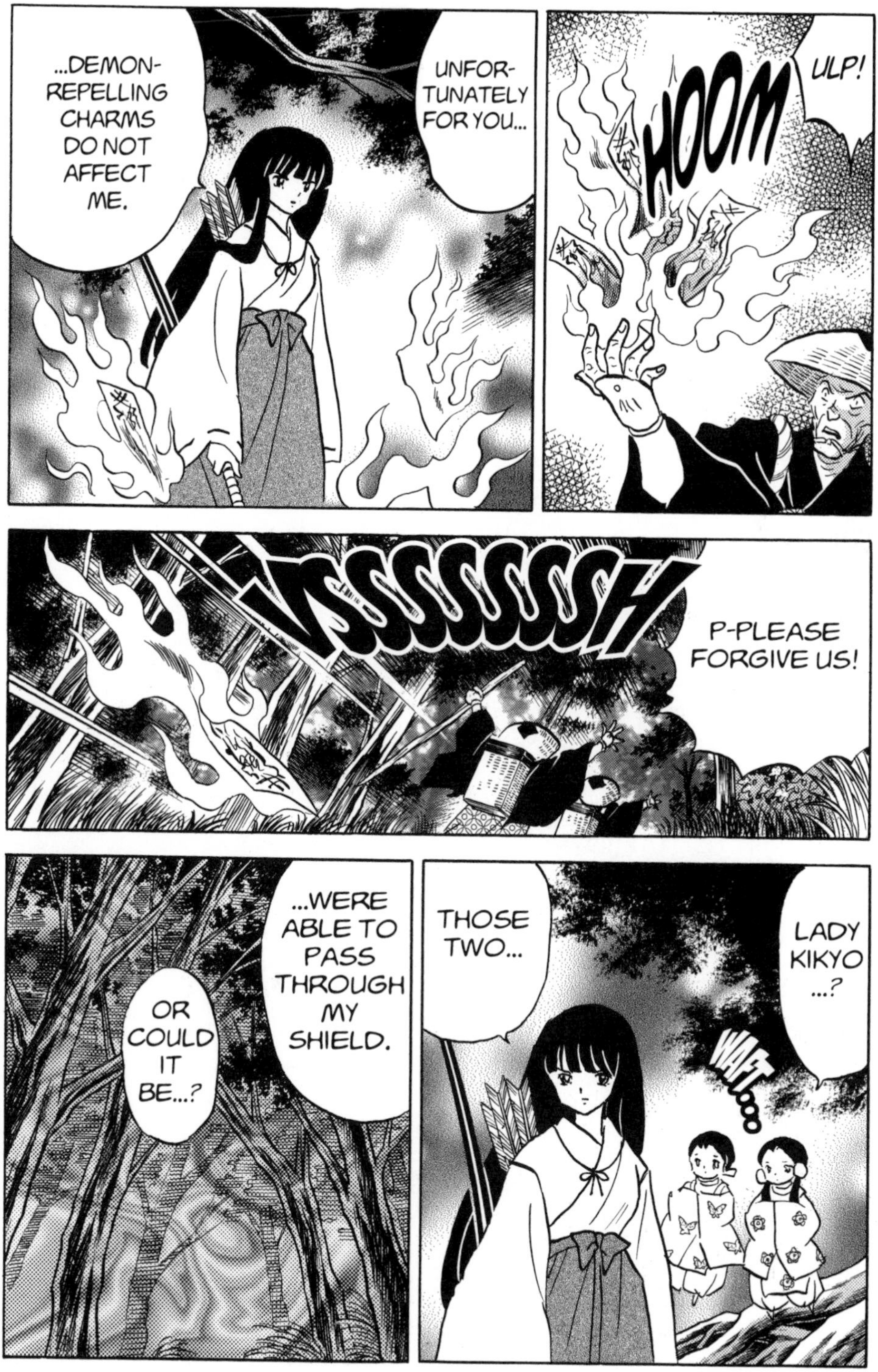
ULP!
HOOM
UNFORTUNATELY FOR YOU...
...DEMON-REPELLING CHARMS DO NOT AFFECT ME.
P-PLEASE FORGIVE US!
VSSSSSSSH
LADY KIKYO...?
WAFT...
THOSE TWO...
...WERE ABLE TO PASS THROUGH MY SHIELD.
OR COULD IT BE...?

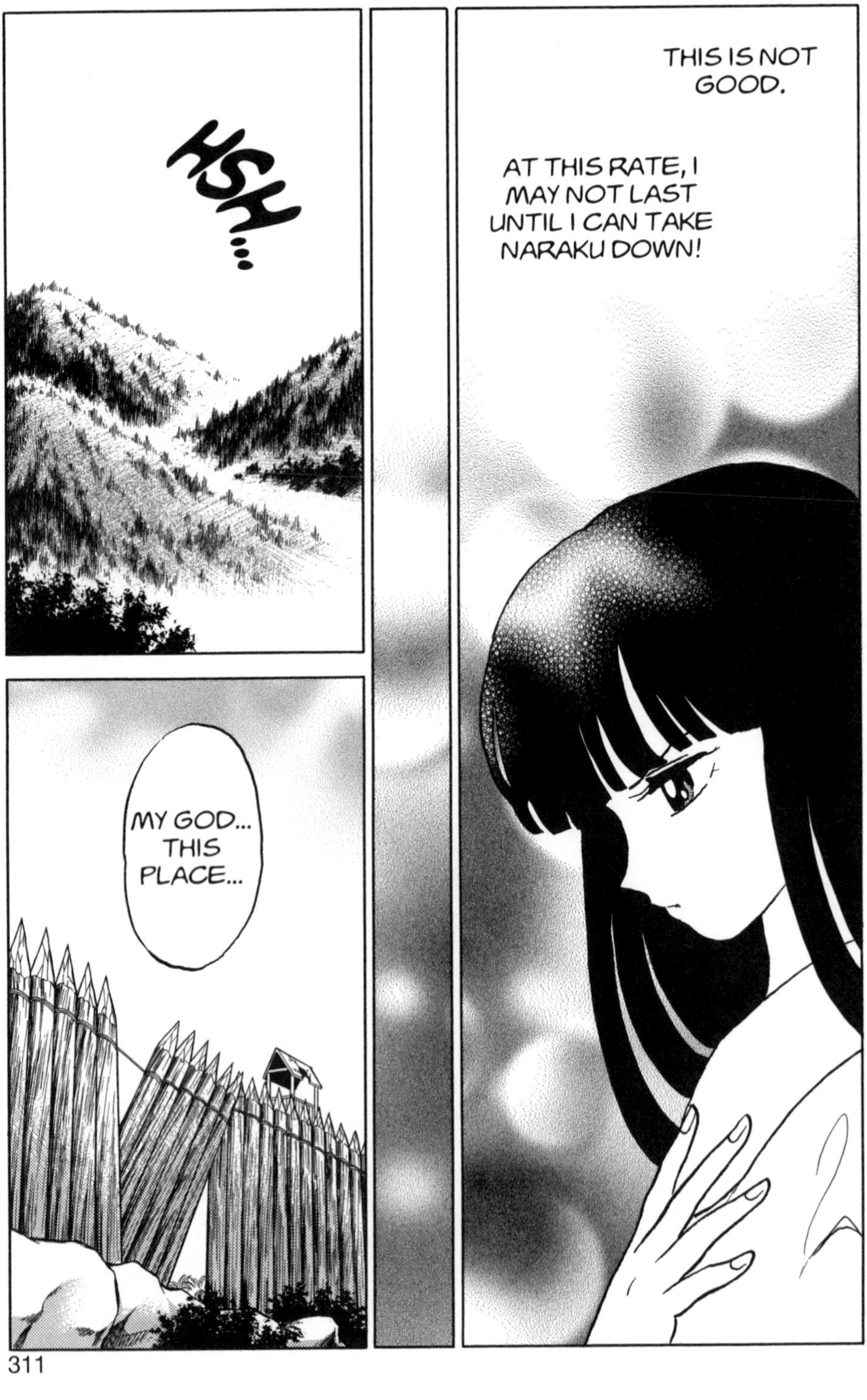
THIS IS NOT GOOD.
AT THIS RATE, I MAY NOT LAST UNTIL I CAN TAKE NARAKU DOWN!
HSH...
MY GOD... THIS PLACE...

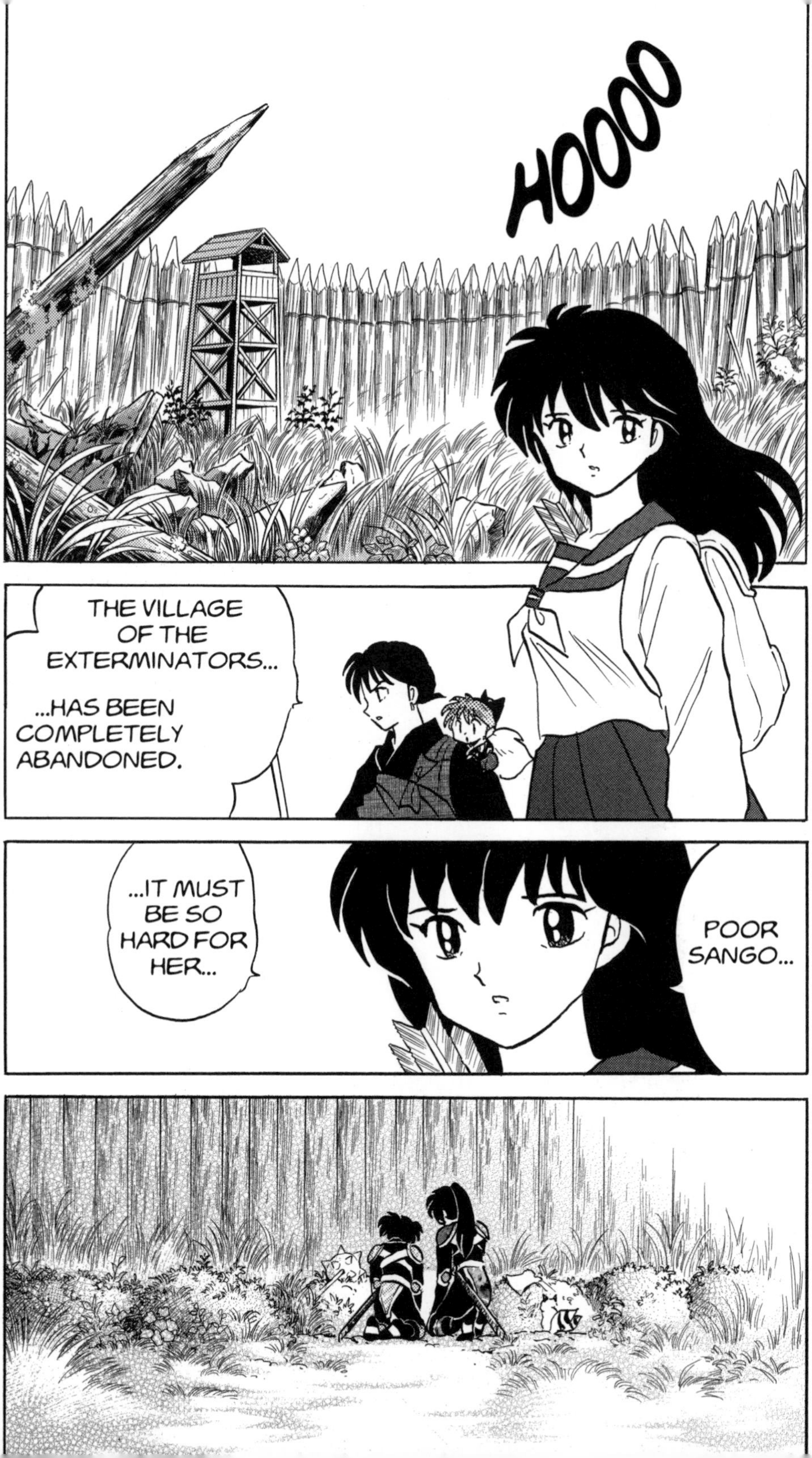
HOOOO
THE VILLAGE OF THE EXTERMINATORS...
...HAS BEEN COMPLETELY ABANDONED.
POOR SANGO...
...IT MUST BE SO HARD FOR HER...

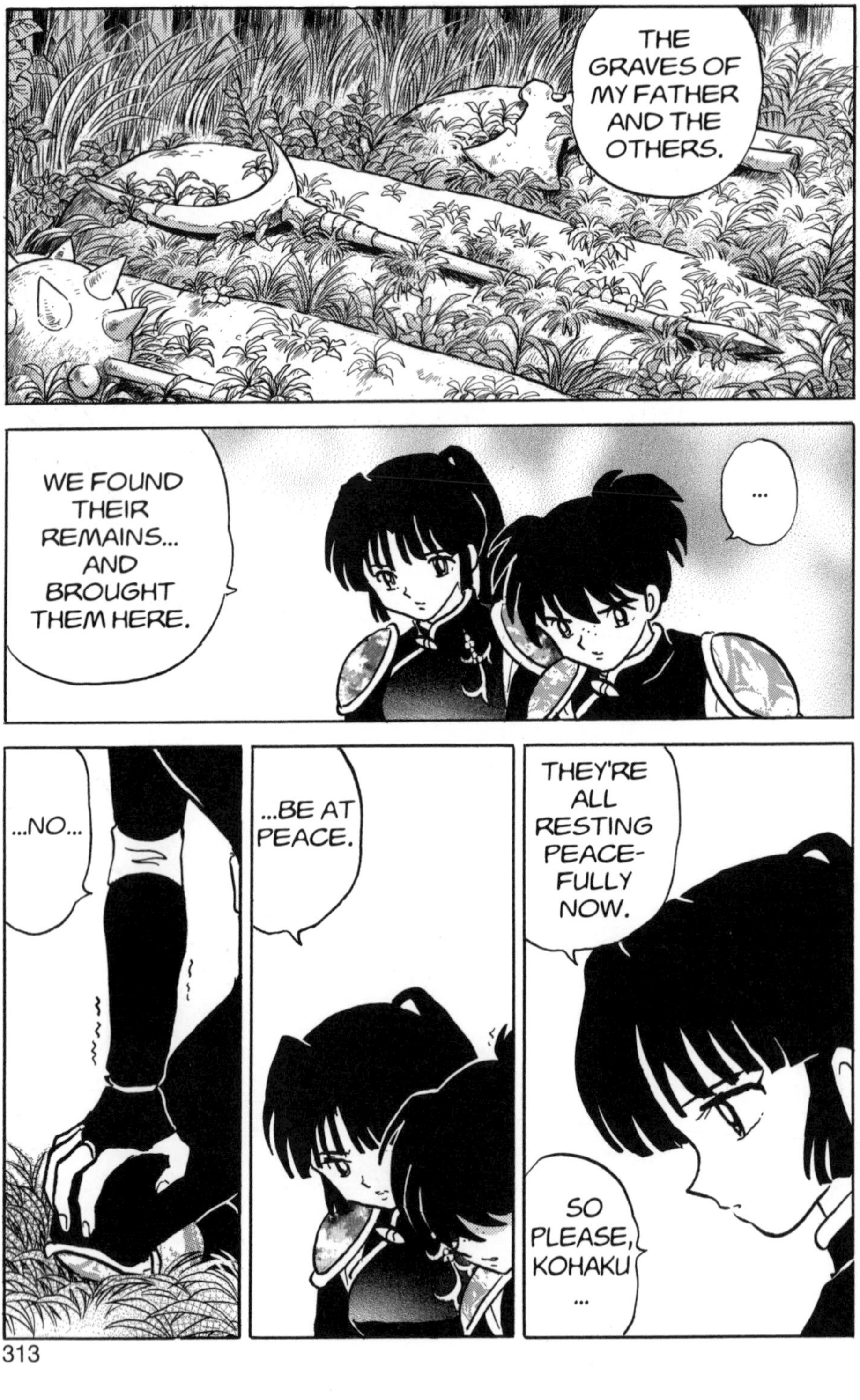
THE GRAVES OF MY FATHER AND THE OTHERS.
...
WE FOUND THEIR REMAINS... AND BROUGHT THEM HERE.
THEY'RE ALL RESTING PEACE-FULLY NOW.
SO PLEASE, KOHAKU ...
...BE AT PEACE.
...NO...

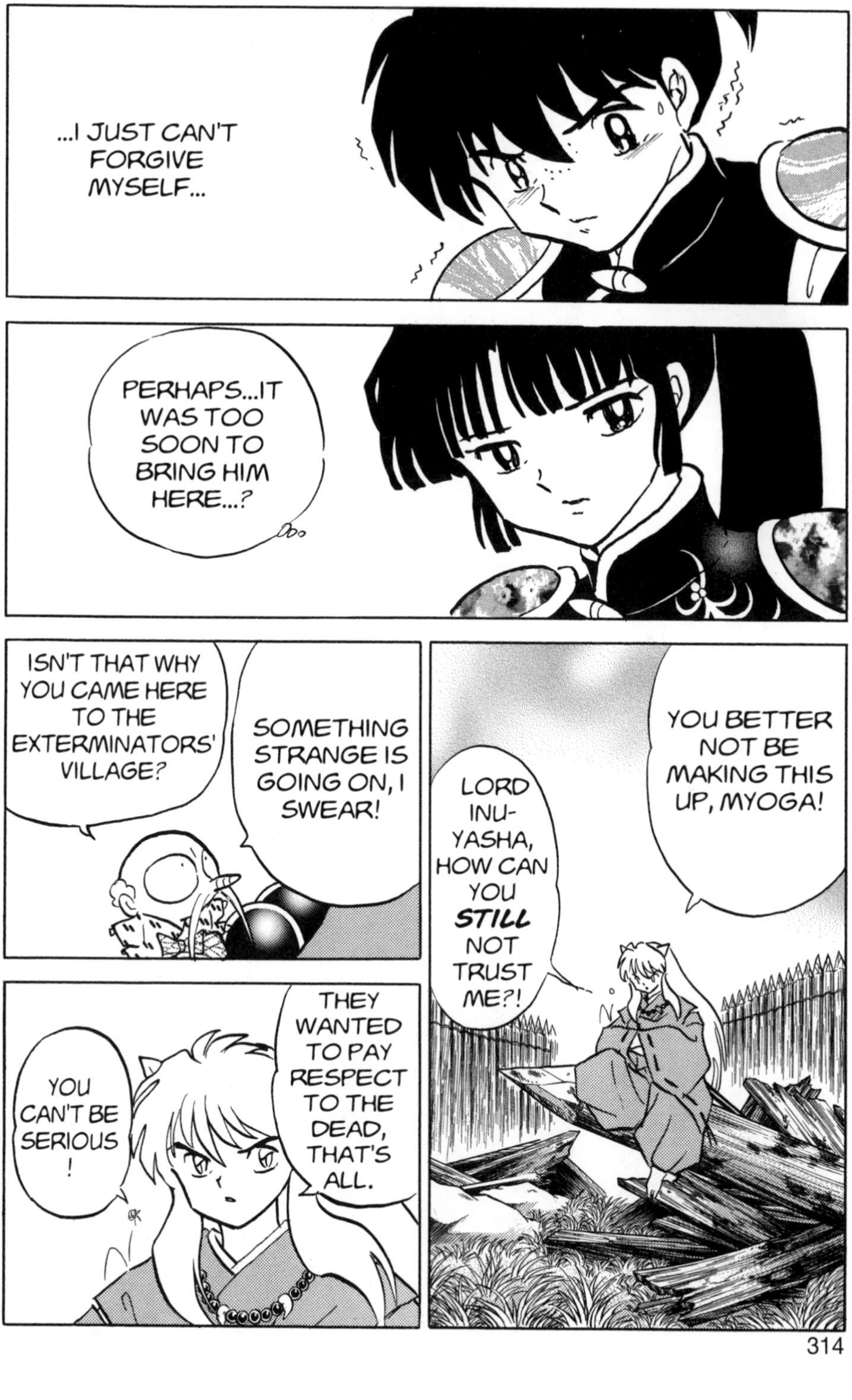
...I JUST CAN'T FORGIVE MYSELF...
PERHAPS...IT WAS TOO SOON TO BRING HIM HERE...?
YOU BETTER NOT BE MAKING THIS UP, MYOGA!
LORD INU-YASHA, HOW CAN YOU **STILL** NOT TRUST ME?!
SOMETHING STRANGE IS GOING ON, I SWEAR!
ISN'T THAT WHY YOU CAME HERE TO THE EXTERMINATORS' VILLAGE?
THEY WANTED TO PAY RESPECT TO THE DEAD, THAT'S ALL.
YOU CAN'T BE SERIOUS!

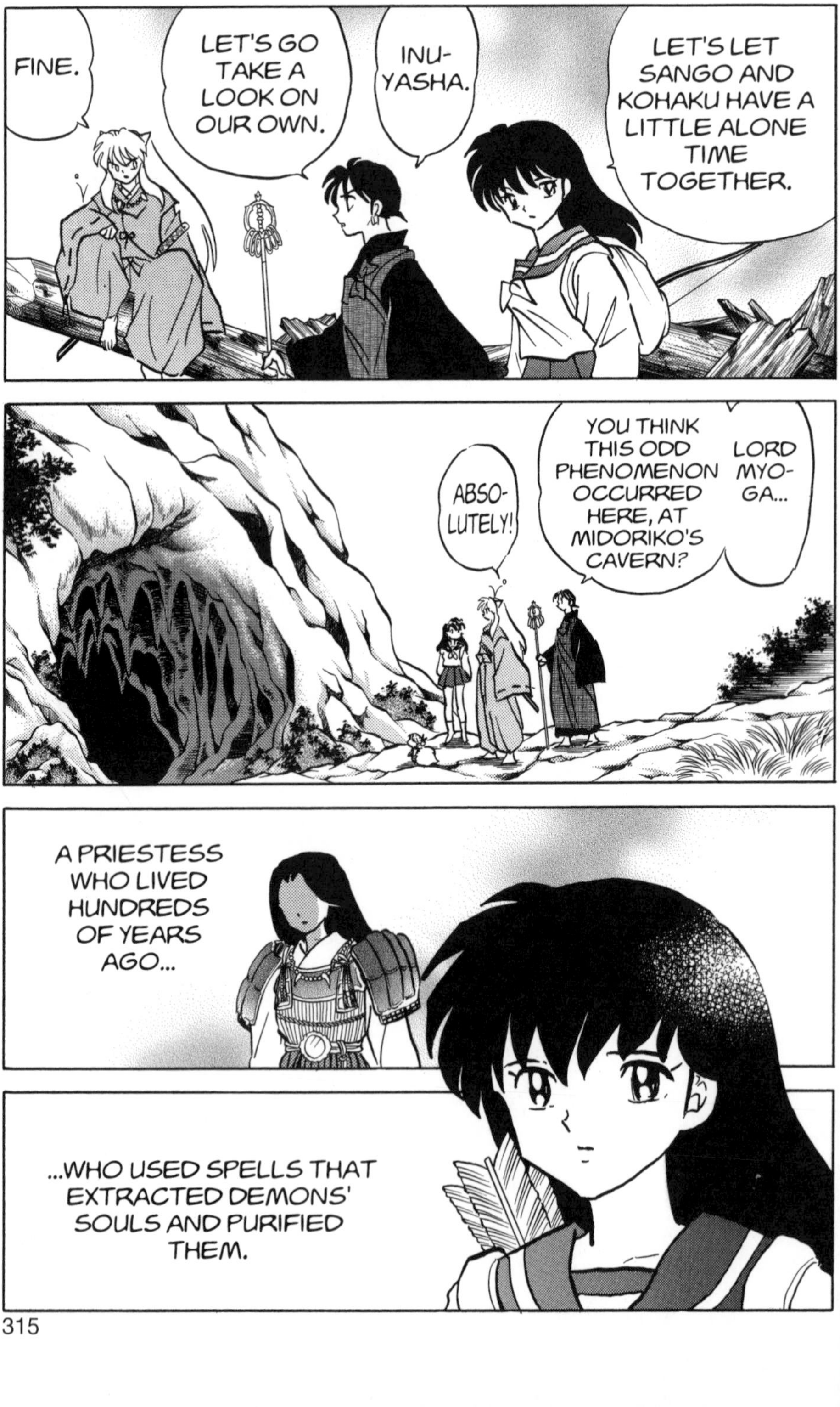
LET'S LET SANGO AND KOHAKU HAVE A LITTLE ALONE TIME TOGETHER.
INU-YASHA.
LET'S GO TAKE A LOOK ON OUR OWN.
FINE.
LORD MYO-GA...
YOU THINK THIS ODD PHENOMENON OCCURRED HERE, AT MIDORIKO'S CAVERN?
ABSO-LUTELY!
A PRIESTESS WHO LIVED HUNDREDS OF YEARS AGO...
...WHO USED SPELLS THAT EXTRACTED DEMONS' SOULS AND PURIFIED THEM.

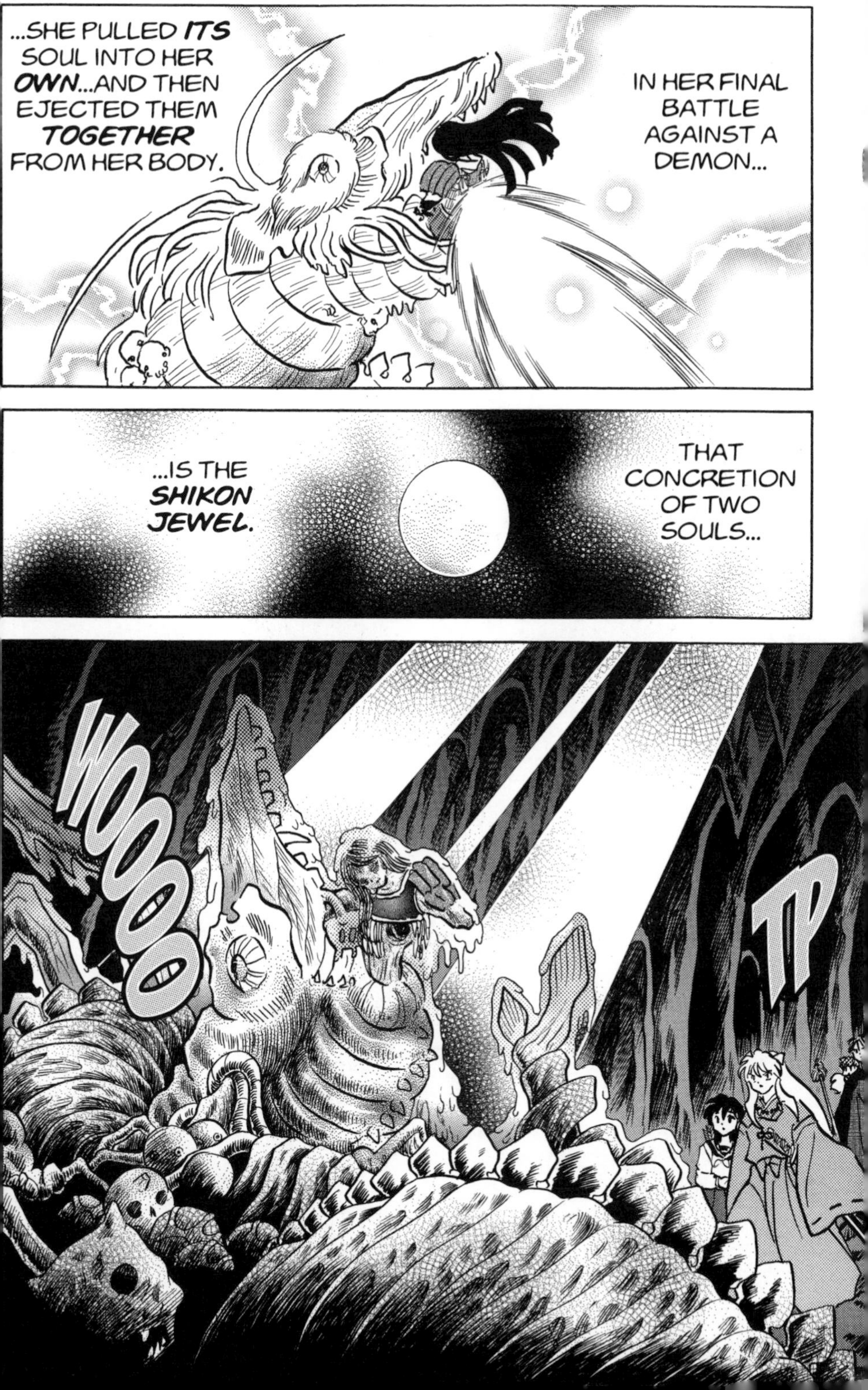
IN HER FINAL BATTLE AGAINST A DEMON...
...SHE PULLED ITS SOUL INTO HER OWN...AND THEN EJECTED THEM TOGETHER FROM HER BODY.
THAT CONCRETION OF TWO SOULS...
...IS THE SHIKON JEWEL.
TP
WOOOOO

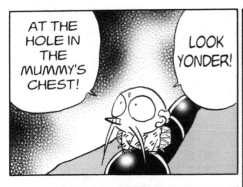

LOOK YONDER!

AT THE HOLE IN THE MUMMY'S CHEST!

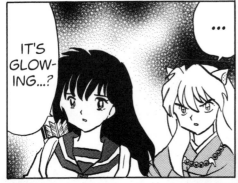

IT'S GLOW- ING....?

...

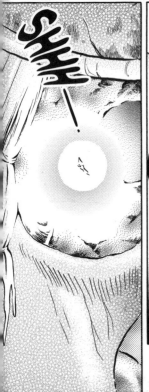

SHHH

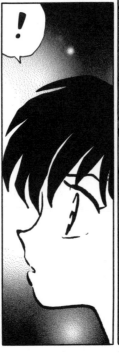

!

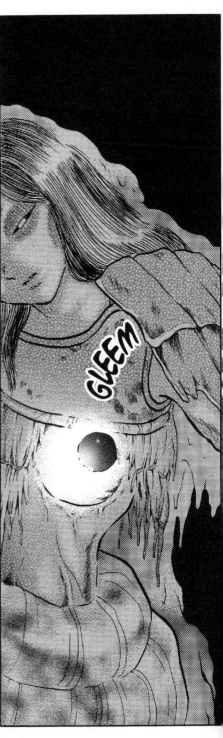

GUEEM

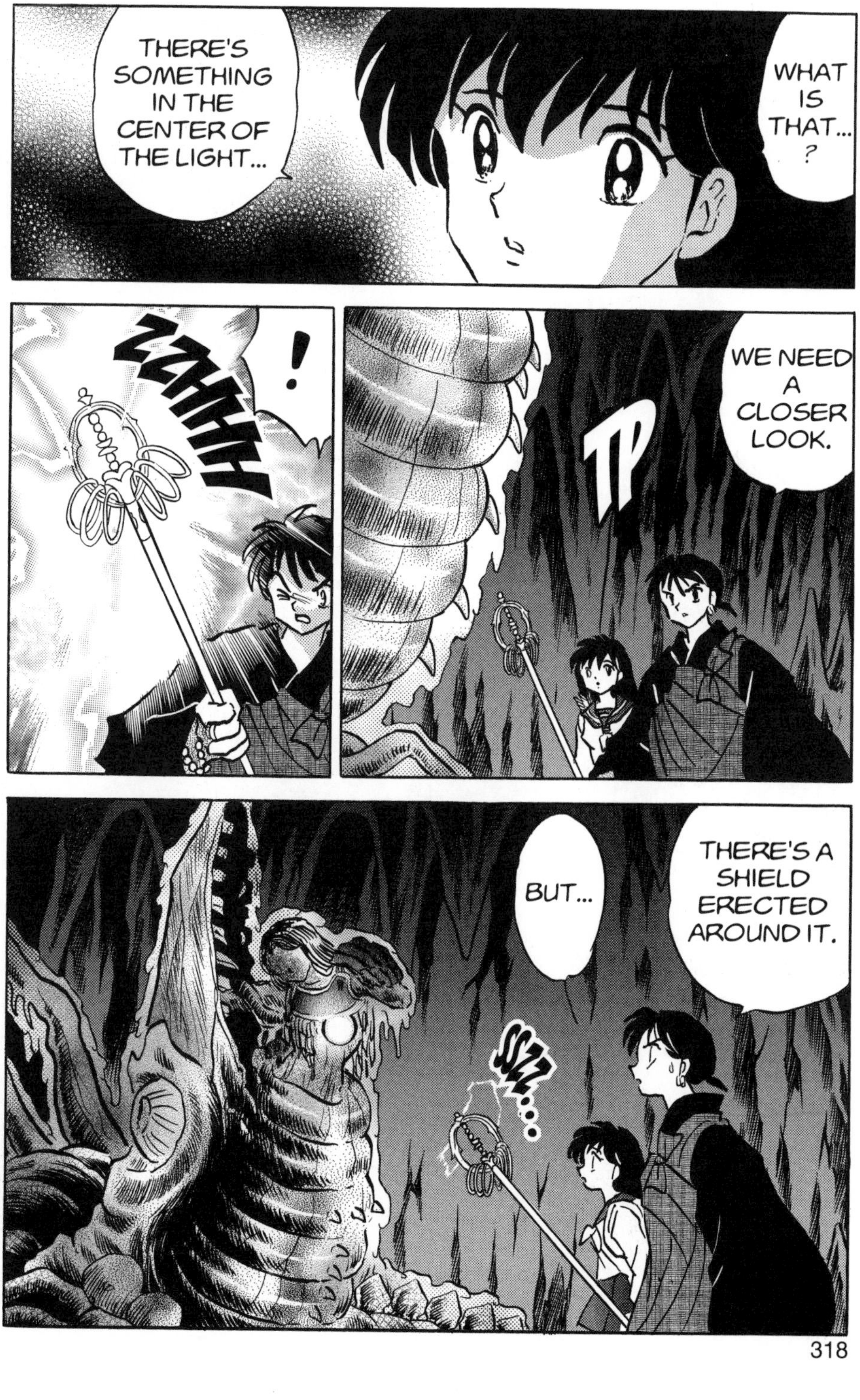

WHAT IS THAT...?
THERE'S SOMETHING IN THE CENTER OF THE LIGHT...
WE NEED A CLOSER LOOK.
TP
!
ZZHHHH
THERE'S A SHIELD ERECTED AROUND IT.
BUT...
SSZZ...

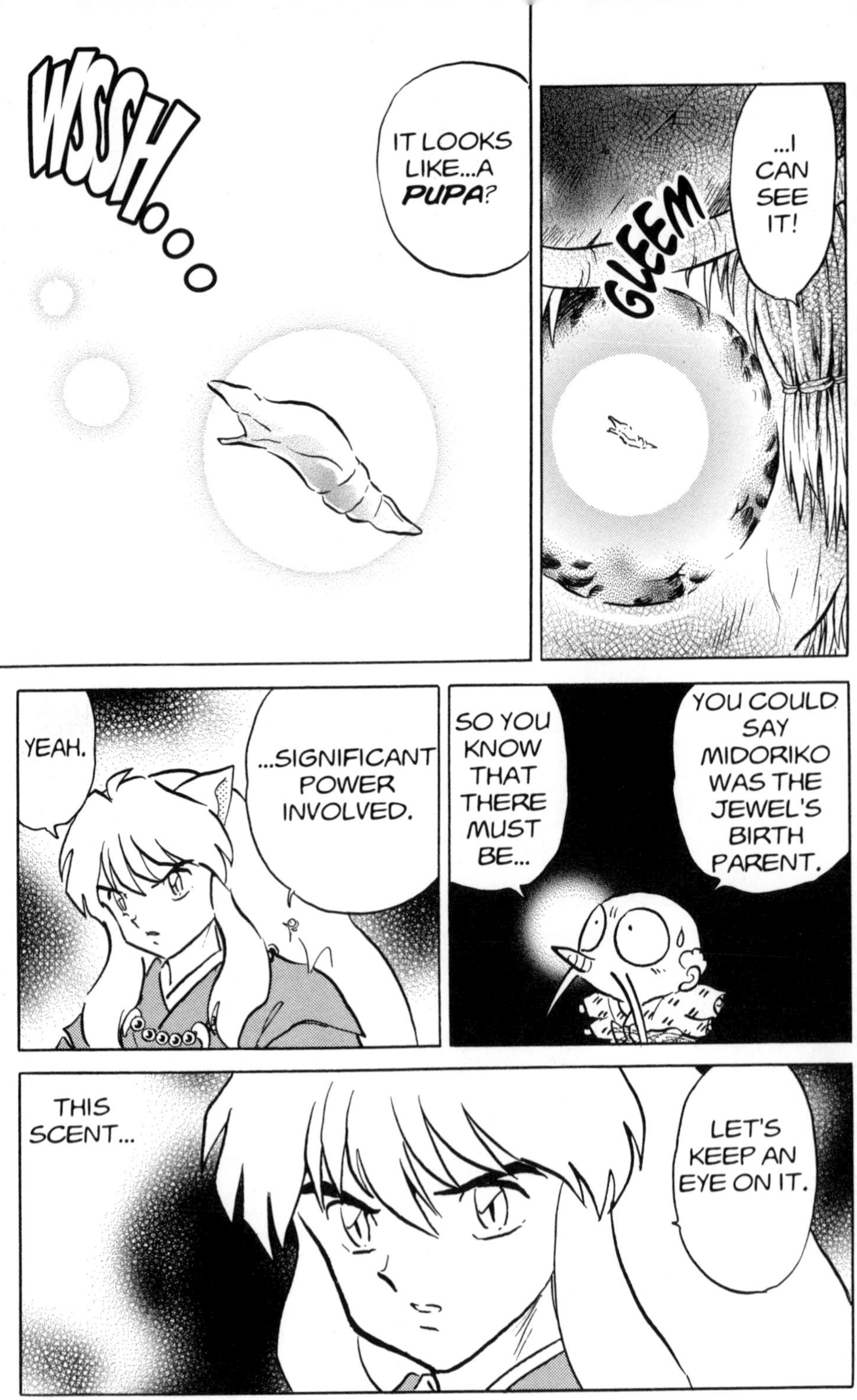
...I CAN SEE IT!
GLEEM
IT LOOKS LIKE...A *PUPA*?
WSSH
YOU COULD SAY MIDORIKO WAS THE JEWEL'S BIRTH PARENT.
SO YOU KNOW THAT THERE MUST BE...
...SIGNIFICANT POWER INVOLVED.
YEAH.
LET'S KEEP AN EYE ON IT.
THIS SCENT...

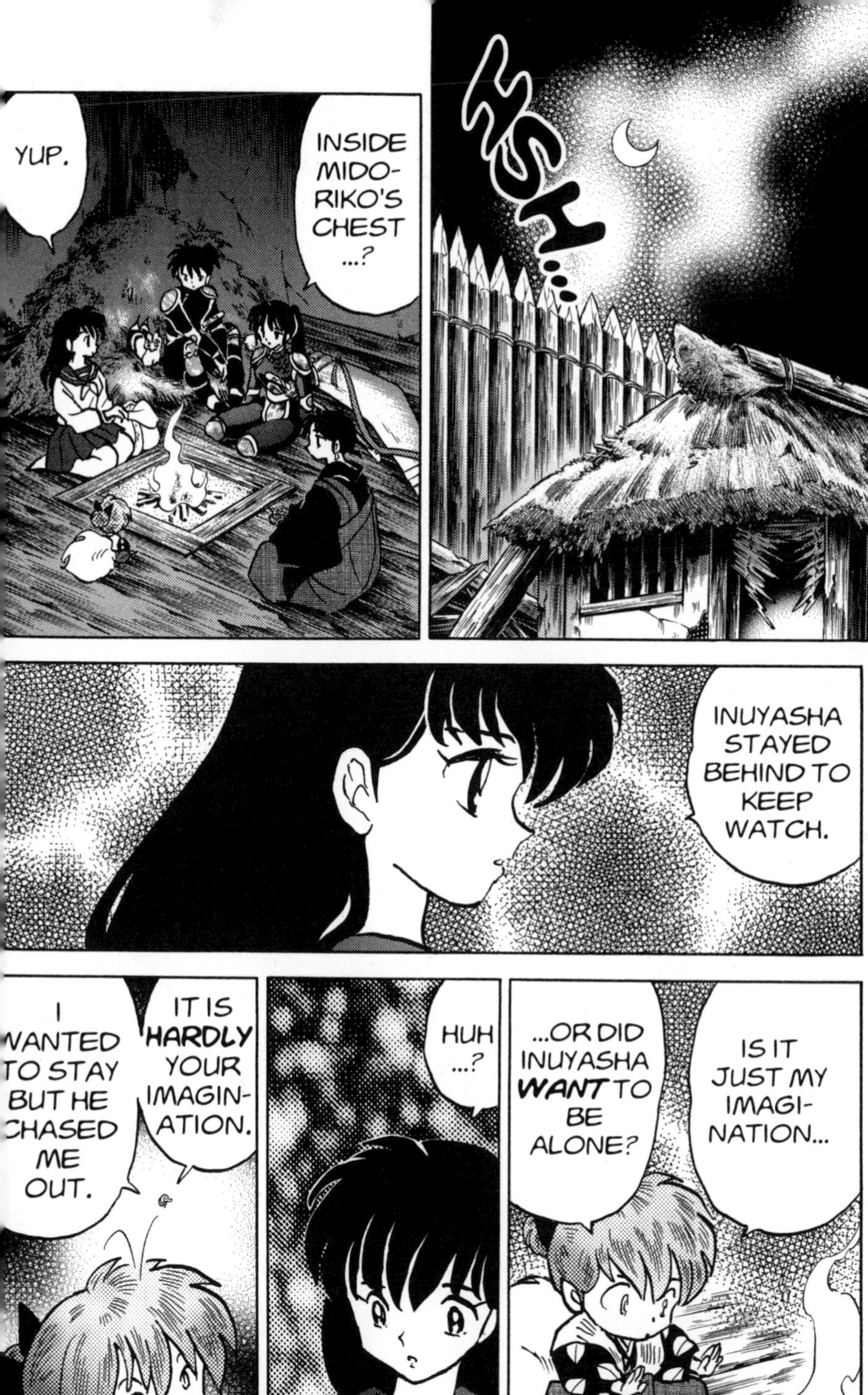
HSH...
INSIDE MIDO-RIKO'S CHEST ...?
YUP.
INUYASHA STAYED BEHIND TO KEEP WATCH.
IS IT JUST MY IMAGI-NATION...
...OR DID INUYASHA WANT TO BE ALONE?
HUH ...?
IT IS HARDLY YOUR IMAGIN-ATION.
I WANTED TO STAY BUT HE CHASED ME OUT.

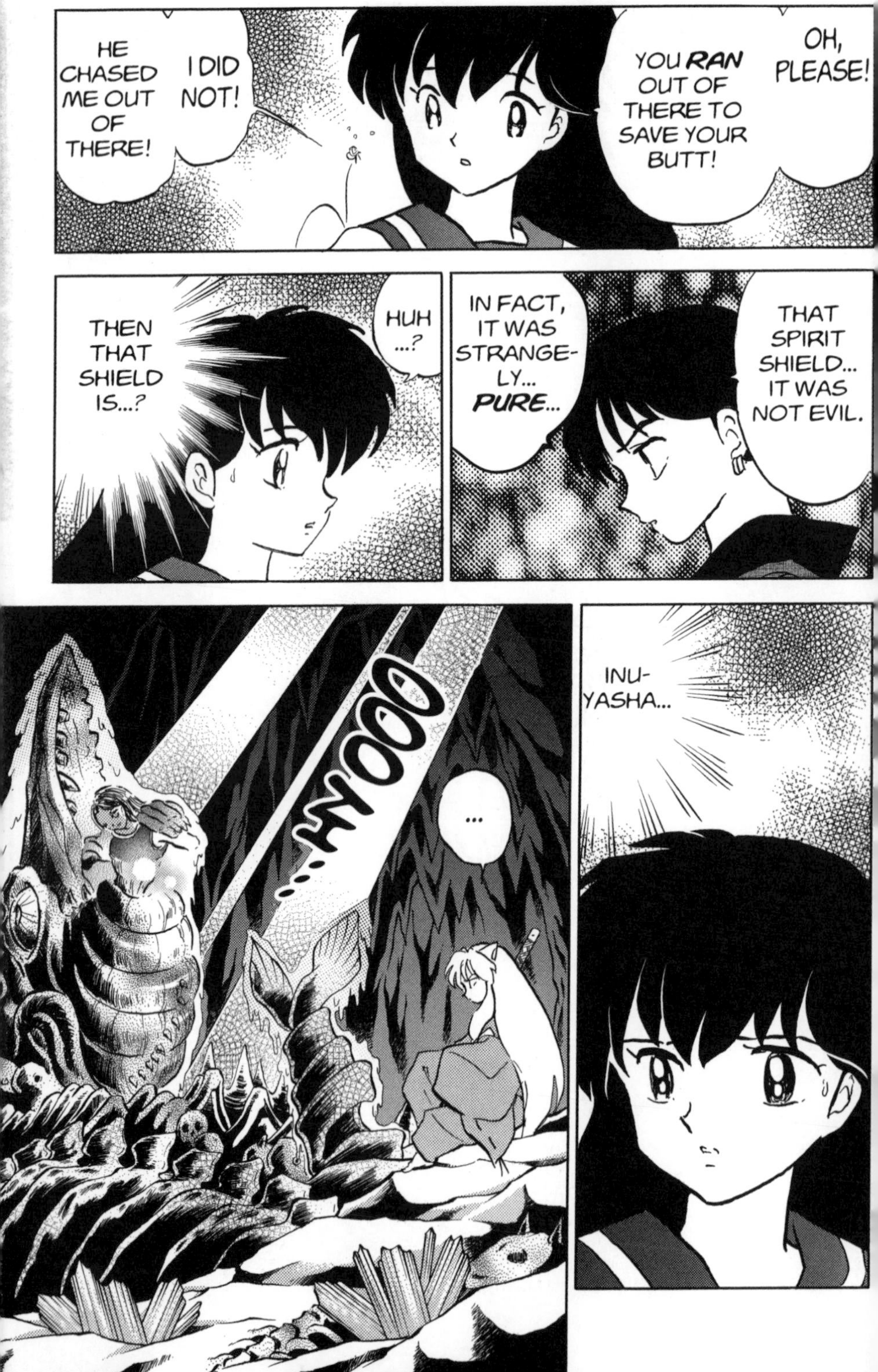
OH, PLEASE!
YOU **RAN** OUT OF THERE TO SAVE YOUR BUTT!
I DID NOT!
HE CHASED ME OUT OF THERE!
THAT SPIRIT SHIELD... IT WAS NOT EVIL.
IN FACT, IT WAS STRANGE-LY... **PURE**...
HUH ...?
THEN THAT SHIELD IS...?
INU-YASHA...
OOOOH...
...

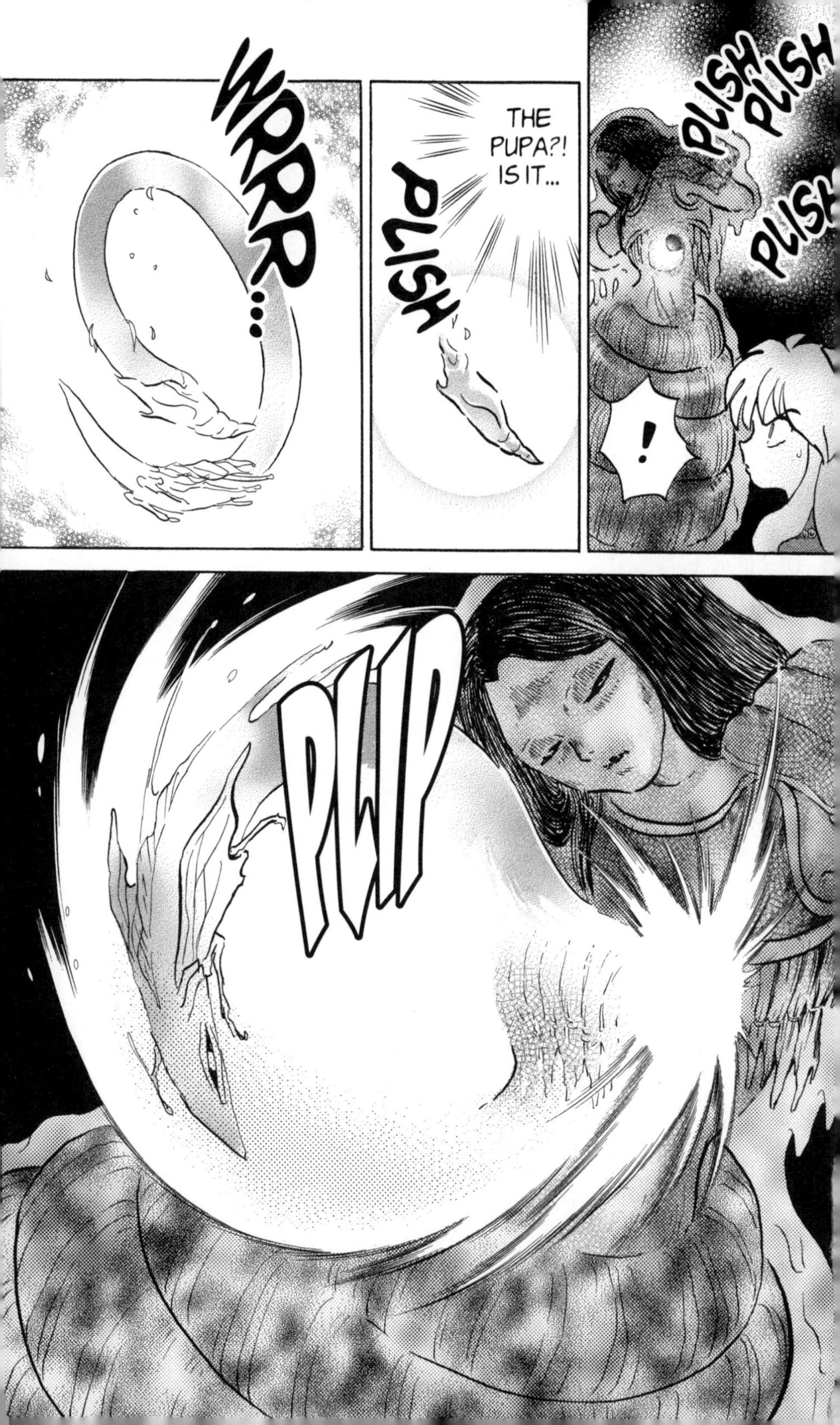
PLISH PLISH
PLISH
!
THE PUPA?! IS IT...
PLISH
WRRR...
PLIP

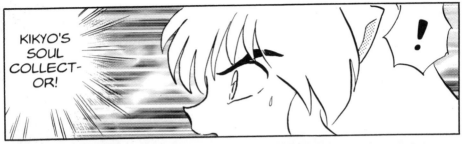

KIKYO'S SOUL COLLECTOR!

!

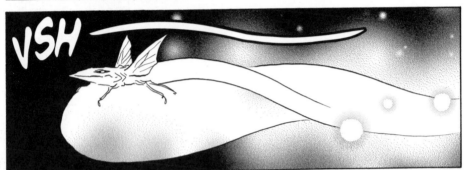

VSH

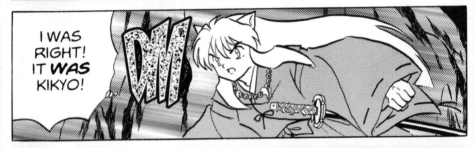

I WAS RIGHT! IT **WAS** KIKYO!

DM

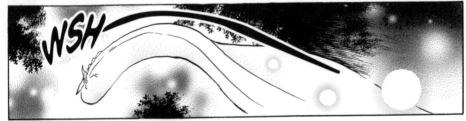

WSH

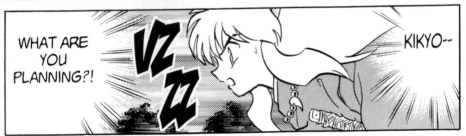

WHAT ARE YOU PLANNING?!

VZ ZZ

KIKYO--

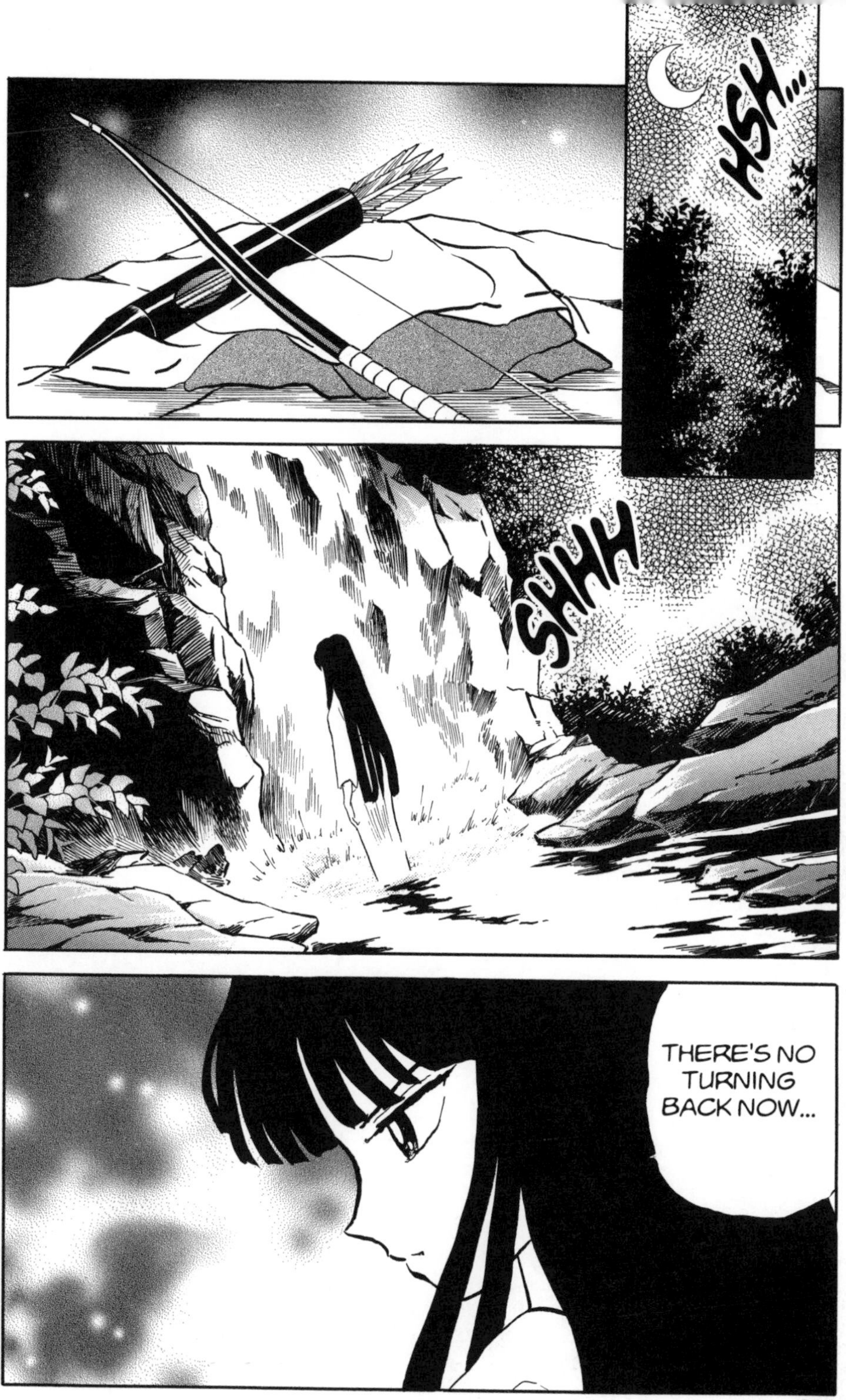
HSH...
SHHH
THERE'S NO TURNING BACK NOW...

SCROLL EIGHT
THE SAME SOUL

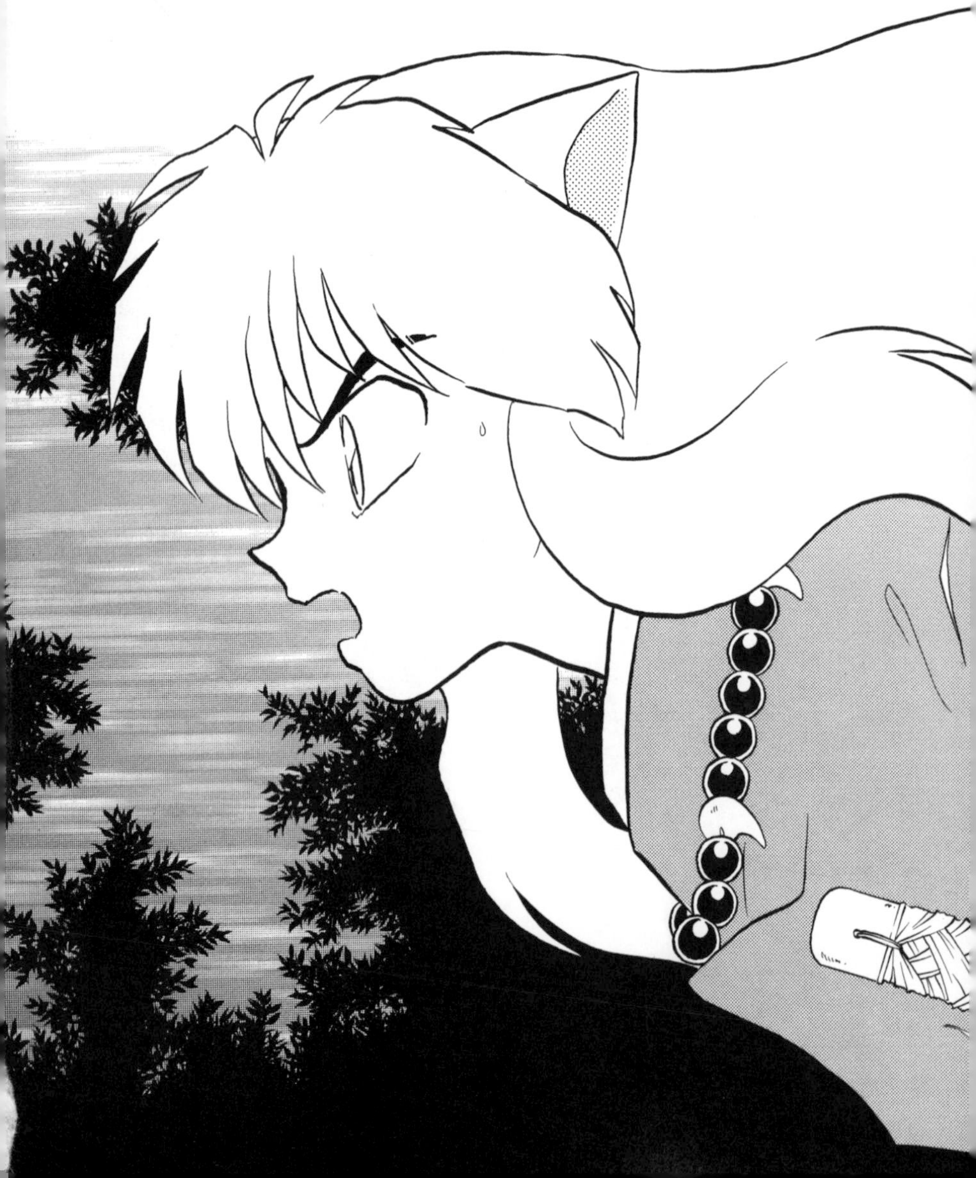

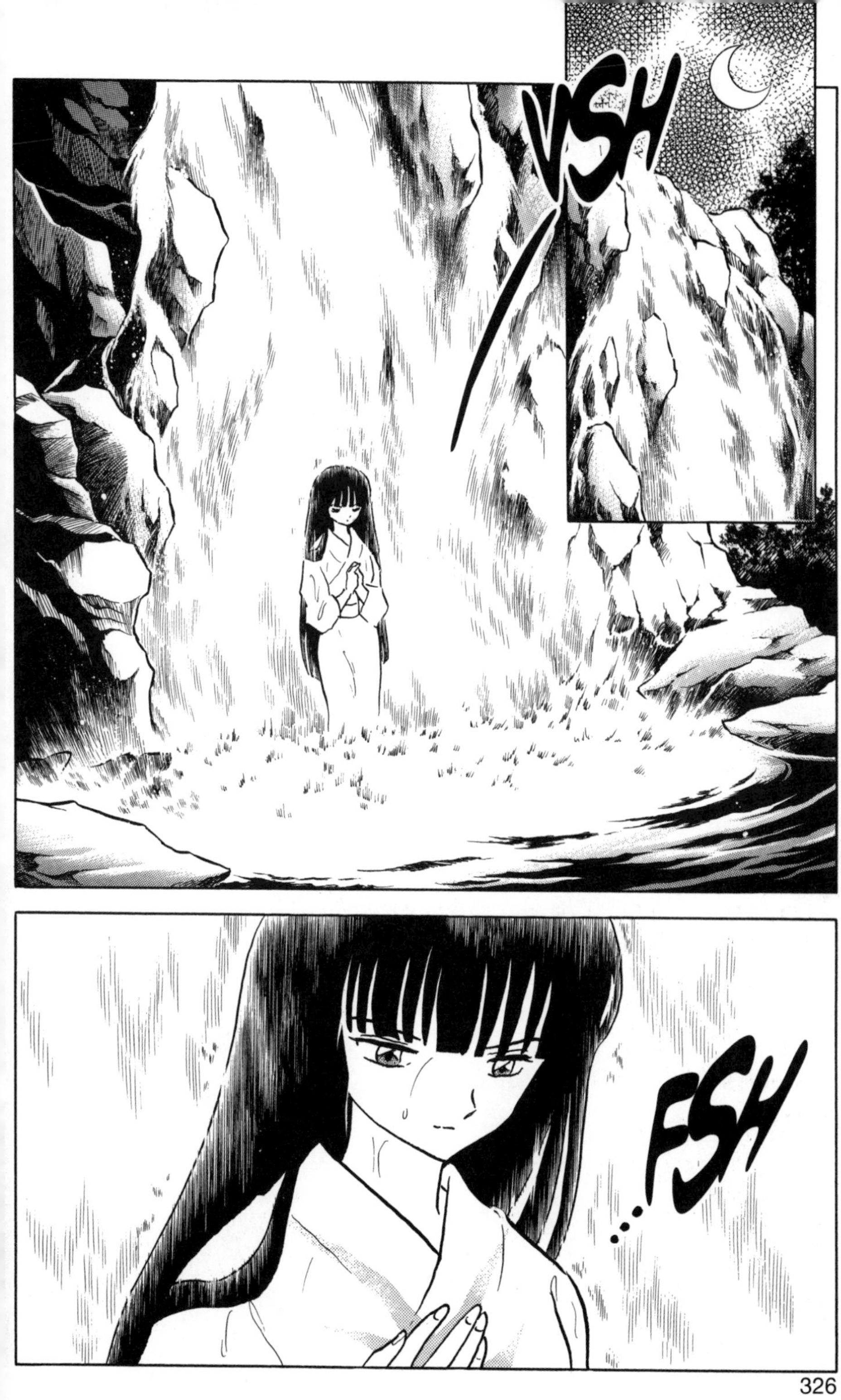
VSH
...FSH

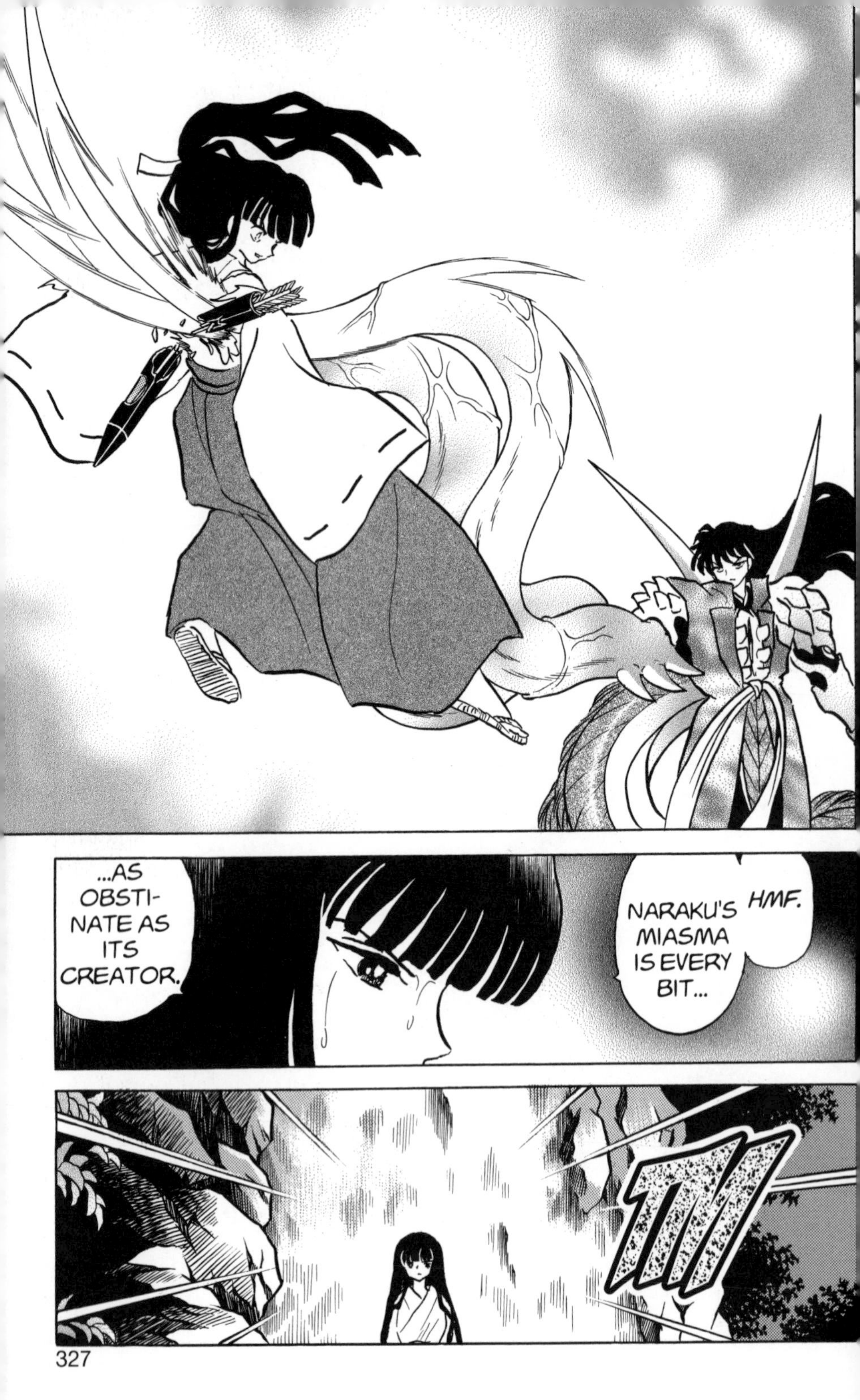
HMF.
NARAKU'S MIASMA IS EVERY BIT...
...AS OBSTINATE AS ITS CREATOR.

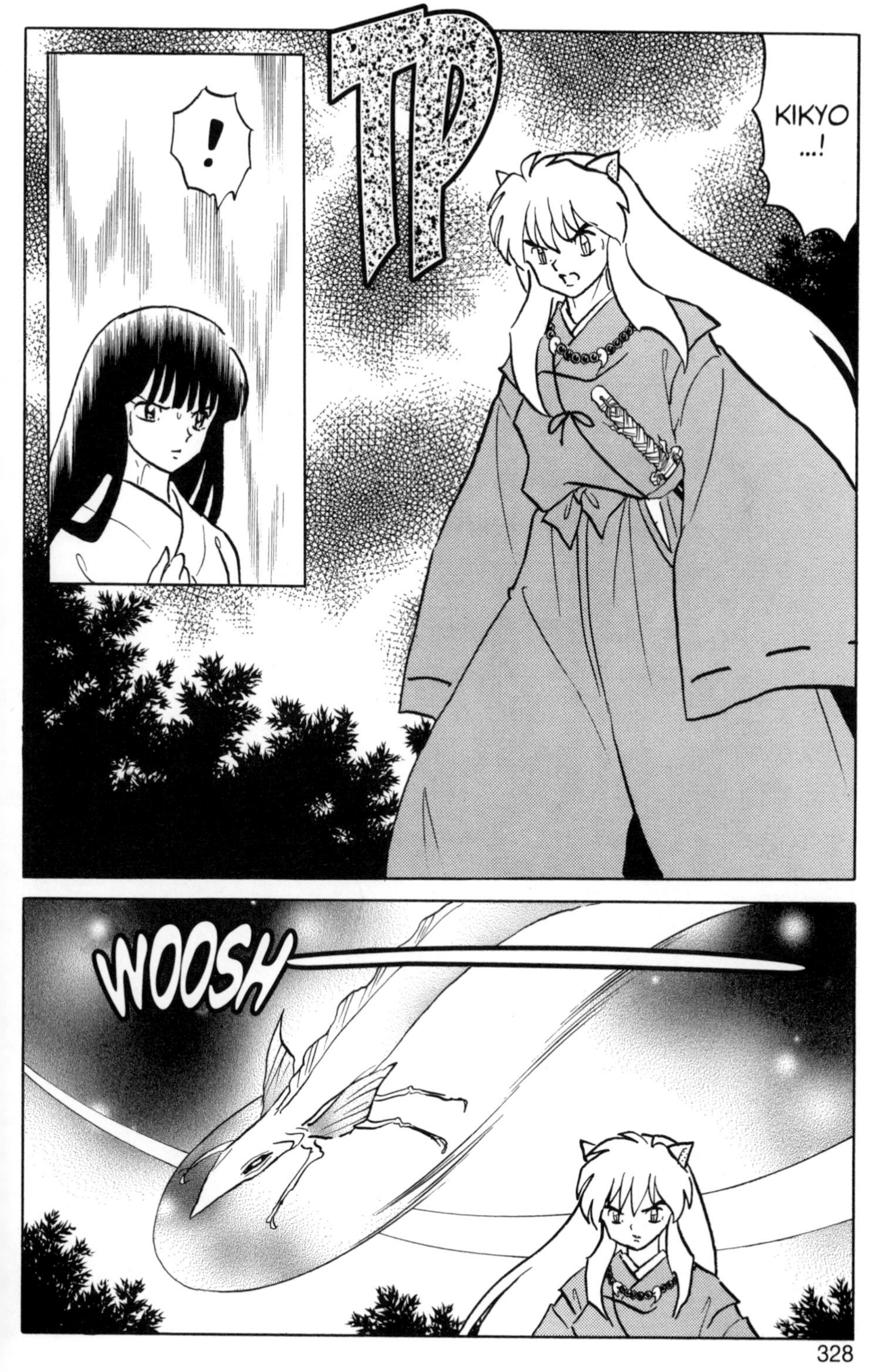
KIKYO ...!
TP
!
WOOSH

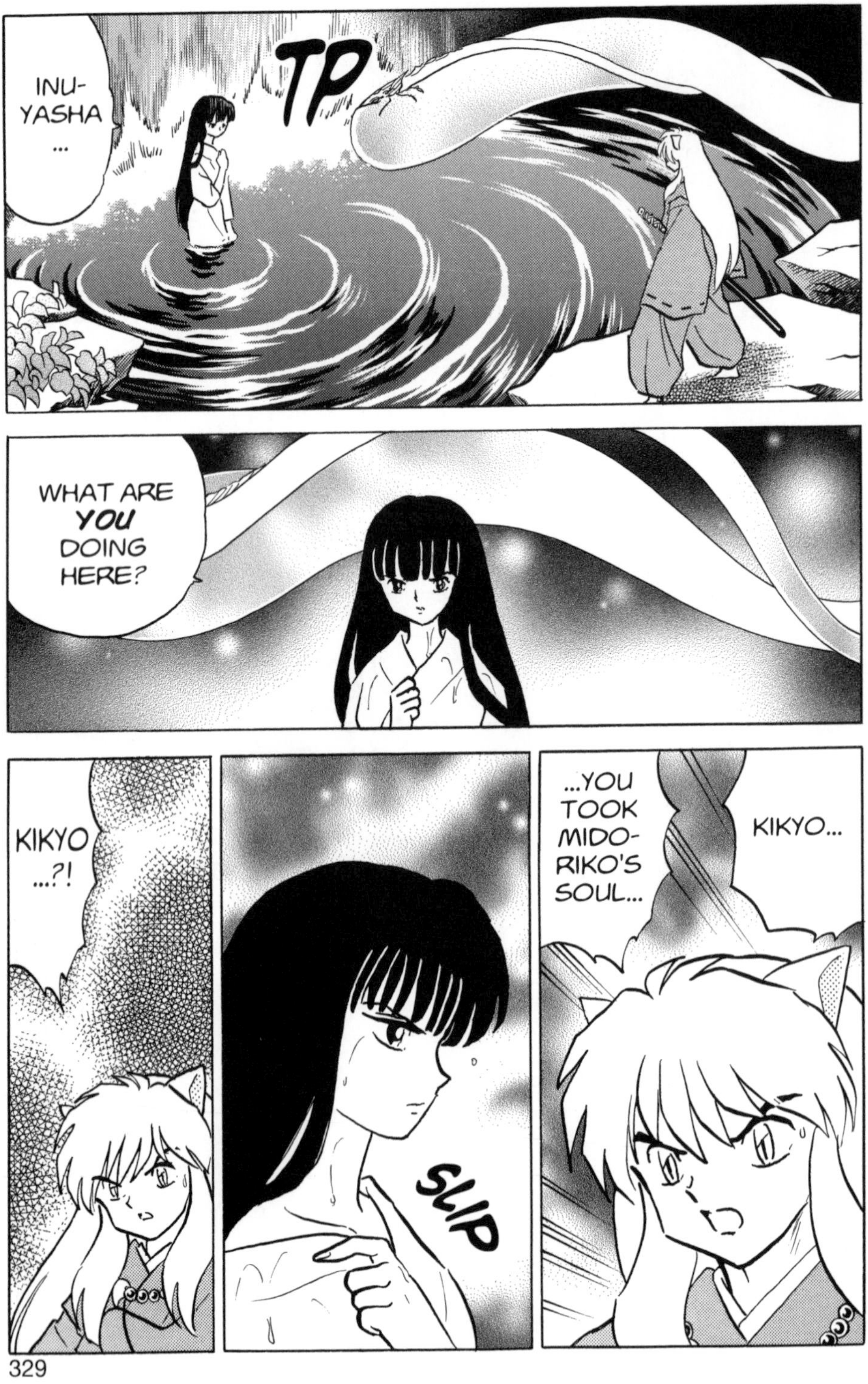

INU-YASHA...
TP
WHAT ARE YOU DOING HERE?
KIKYO...
...YOU TOOK MIDO-RIKO'S SOUL...
SLIP
KIKYO...?!

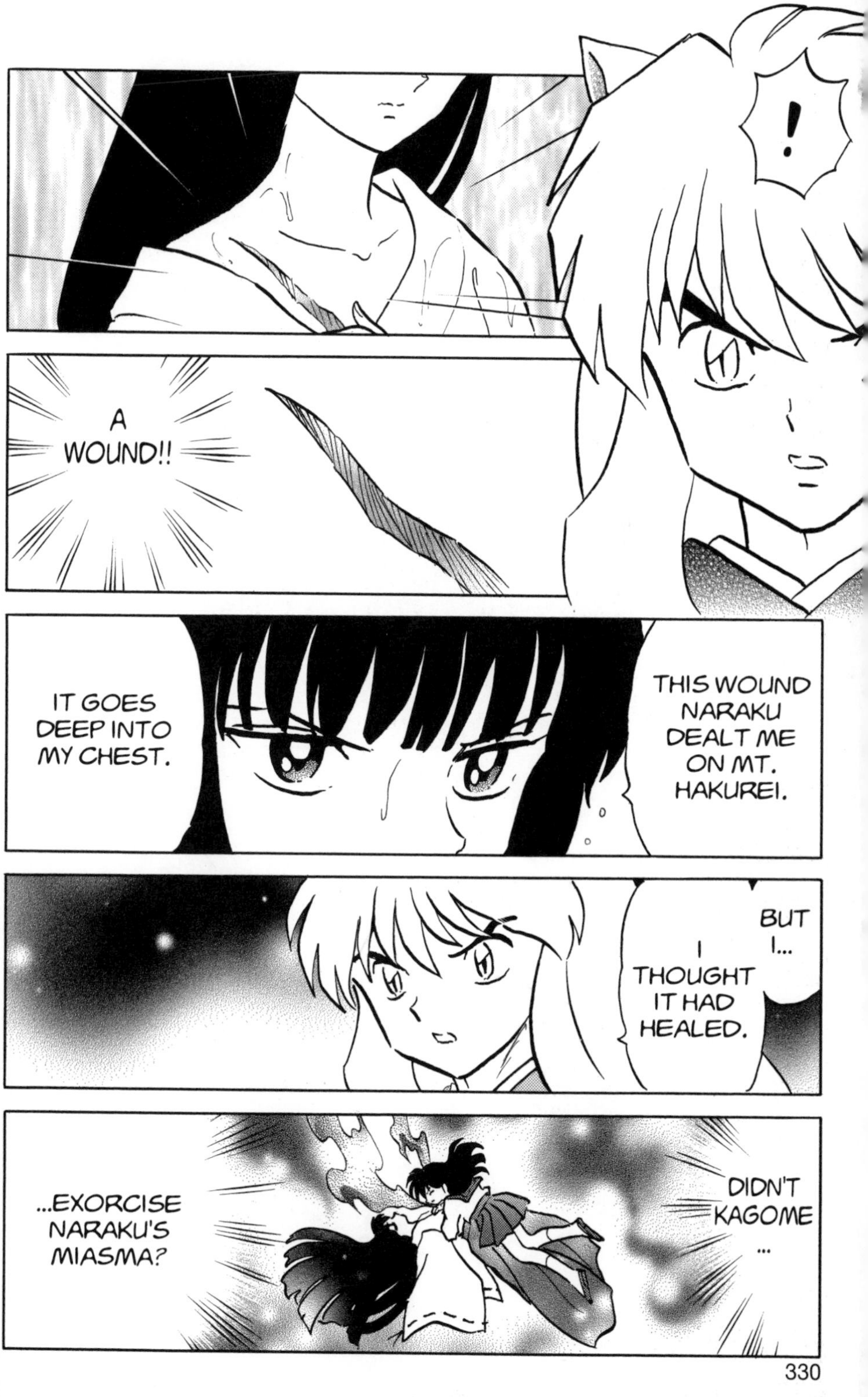
!
A WOUND!!
THIS WOUND NARAKU DEALT ME ON MT. HAKUREI.
IT GOES DEEP INTO MY CHEST.
BUT I...
I THOUGHT IT HAD HEALED.
DIDN'T KAGOME ...
...EXORCISE NARAKU'S MIASMA?

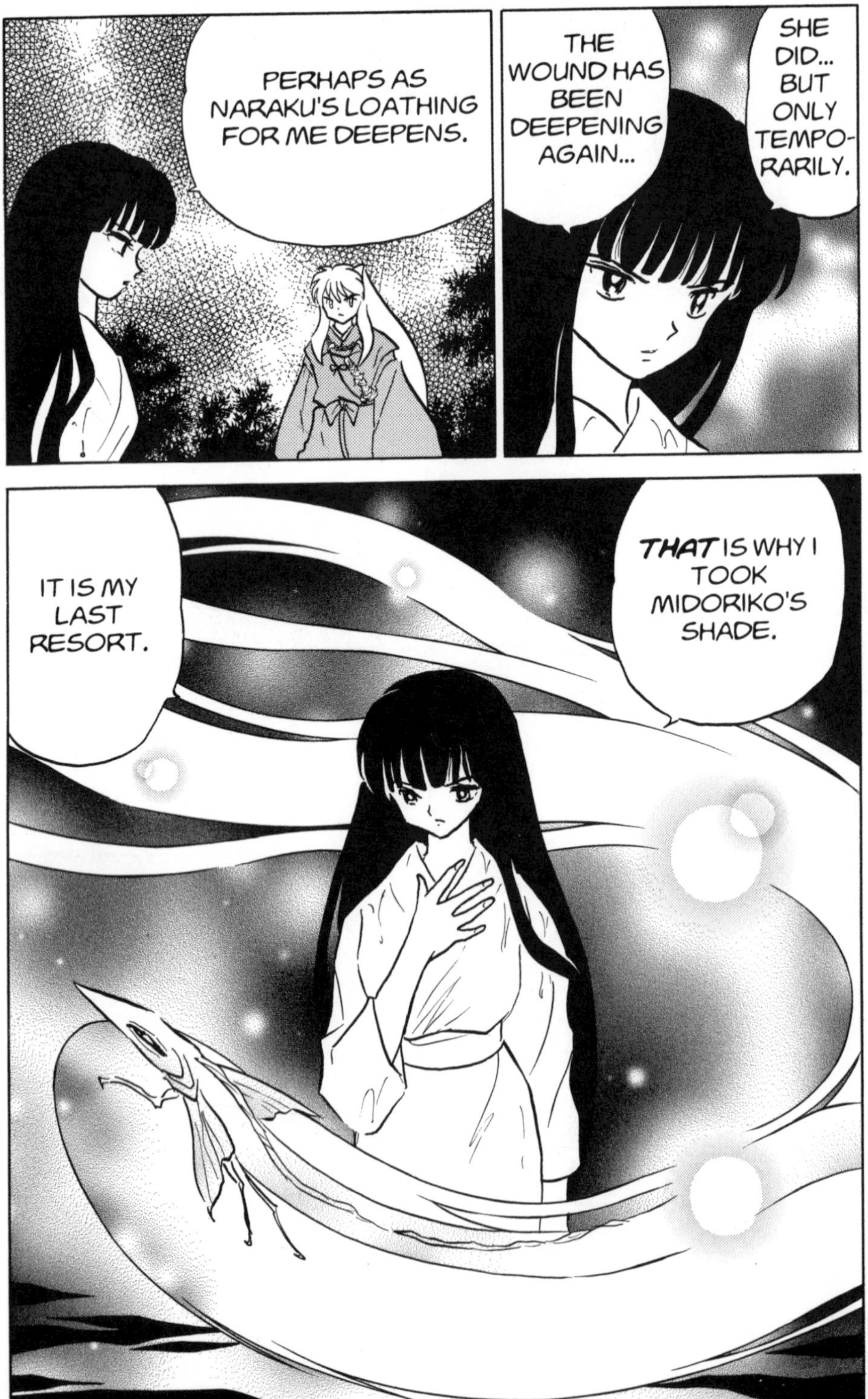
SHE DID... BUT ONLY TEMPORARILY.
THE WOUND HAS BEEN DEEPENING AGAIN...
PERHAPS AS NARAKU'S LOATHING FOR ME DEEPENS.
THAT IS WHY I TOOK MIDORIKO'S SHADE.
IT IS MY LAST RESORT.

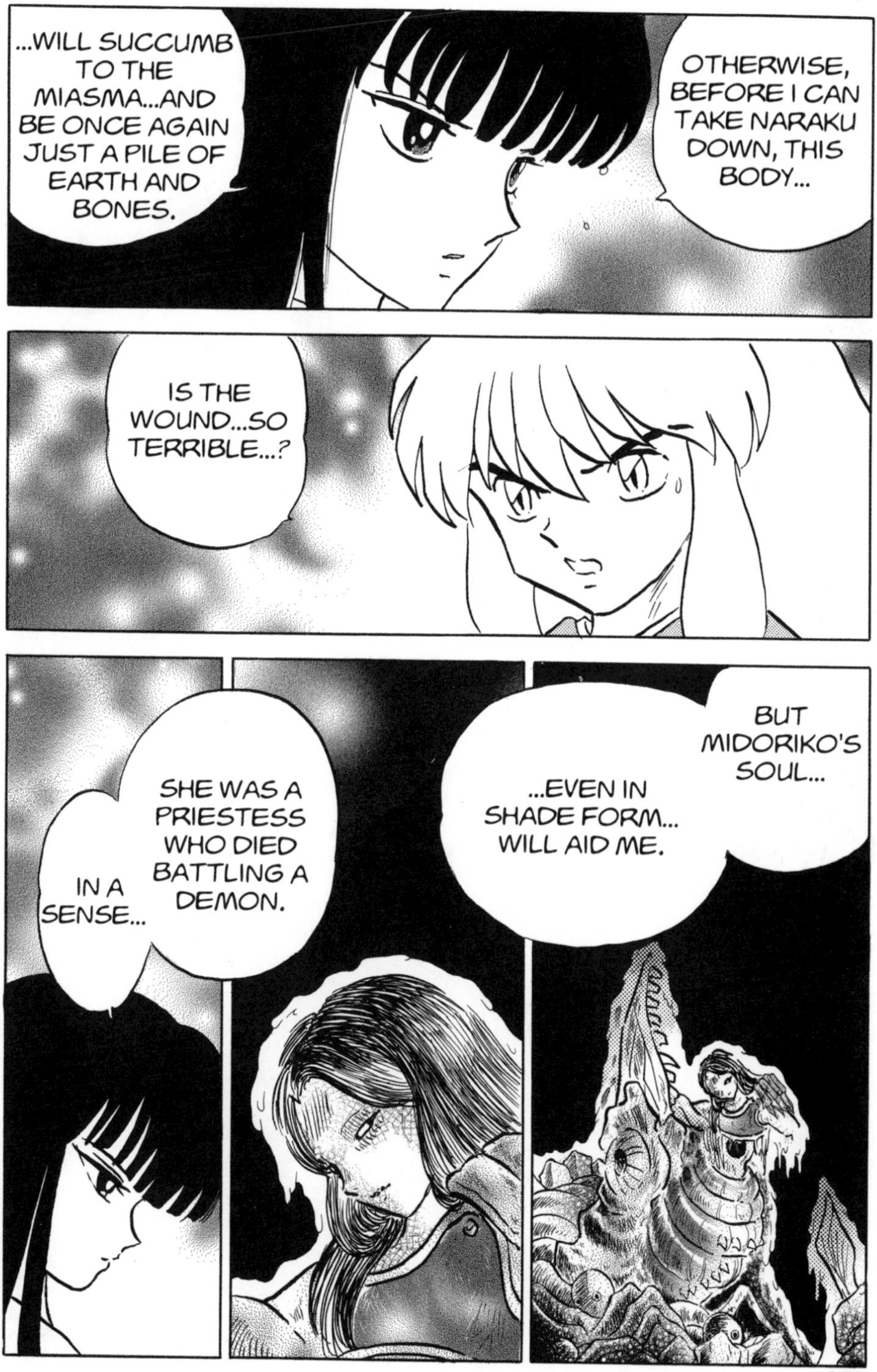
OTHERWISE, BEFORE I CAN TAKE NARAKU DOWN, THIS BODY...
...WILL SUCCUMB TO THE MIASMA...AND BE ONCE AGAIN JUST A PILE OF EARTH AND BONES.
IS THE WOUND...SO TERRIBLE...?
BUT MIDORIKO'S SOUL...
...EVEN IN SHADE FORM... WILL AID ME.
IN A SENSE... SHE WAS A PRIESTESS WHO DIED BATTLING A DEMON.

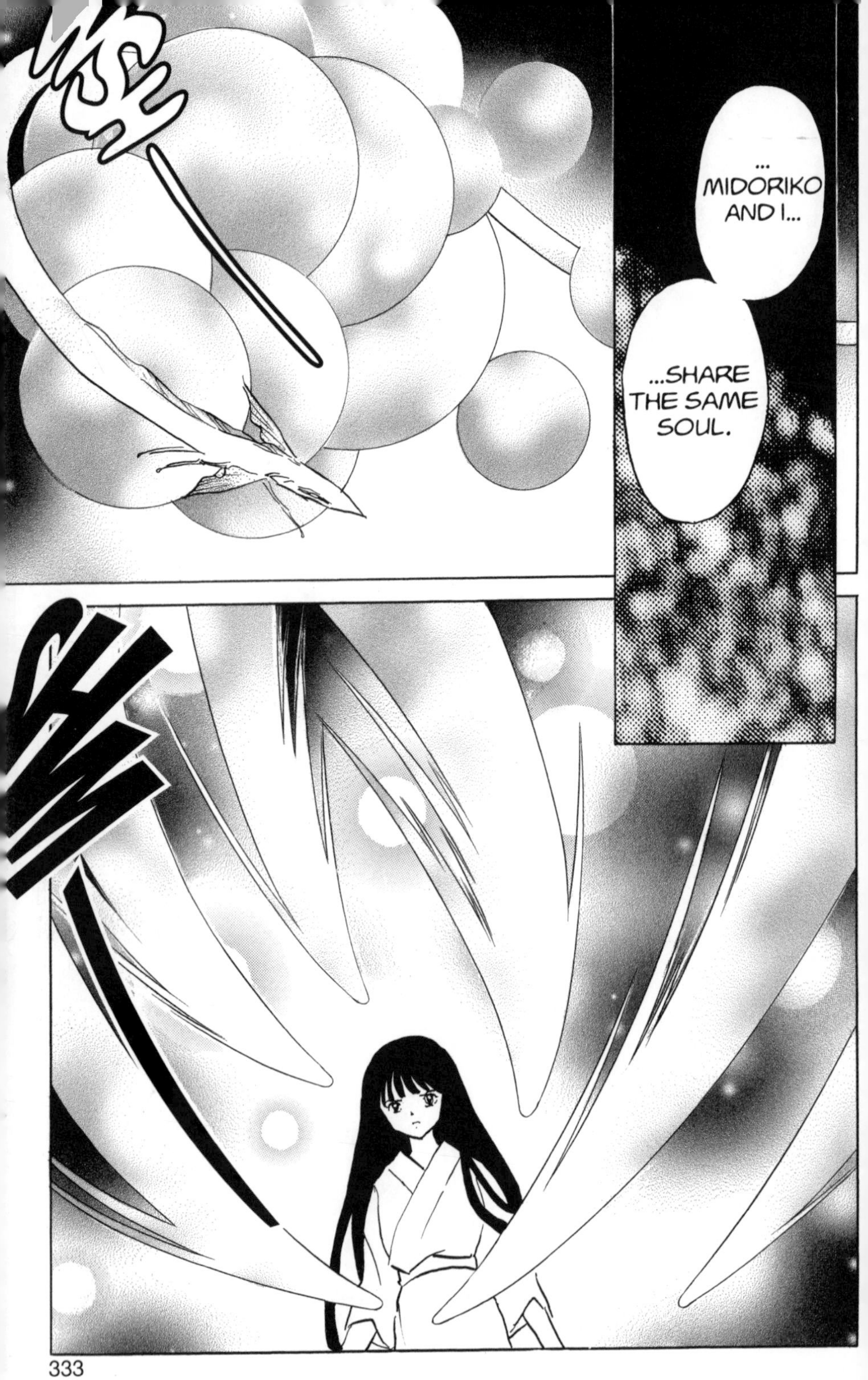
...MIDORIKO AND I...
...SHARE THE SAME SOUL.

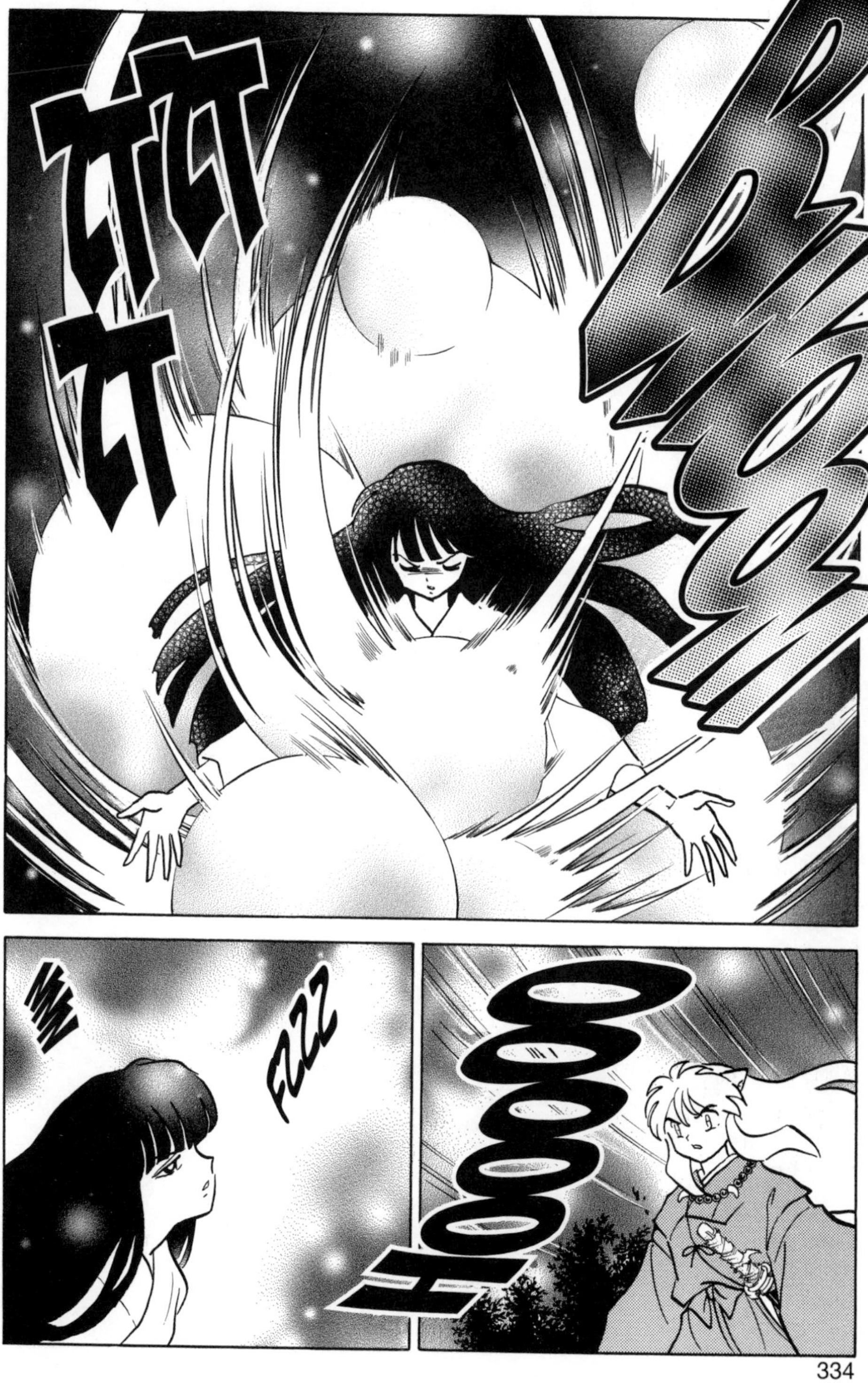
HOOOOOO
FZZZ

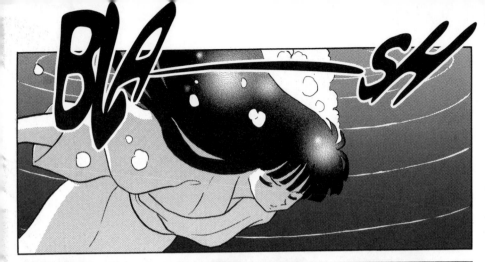

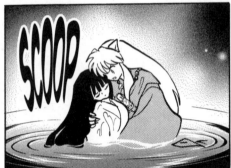

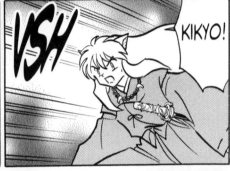

KIKYO!

...IT'S CLOSING UP...!

THE WOUND...

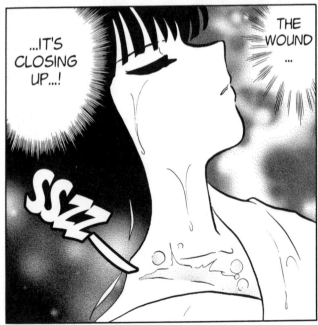

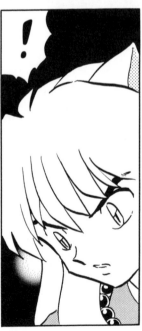

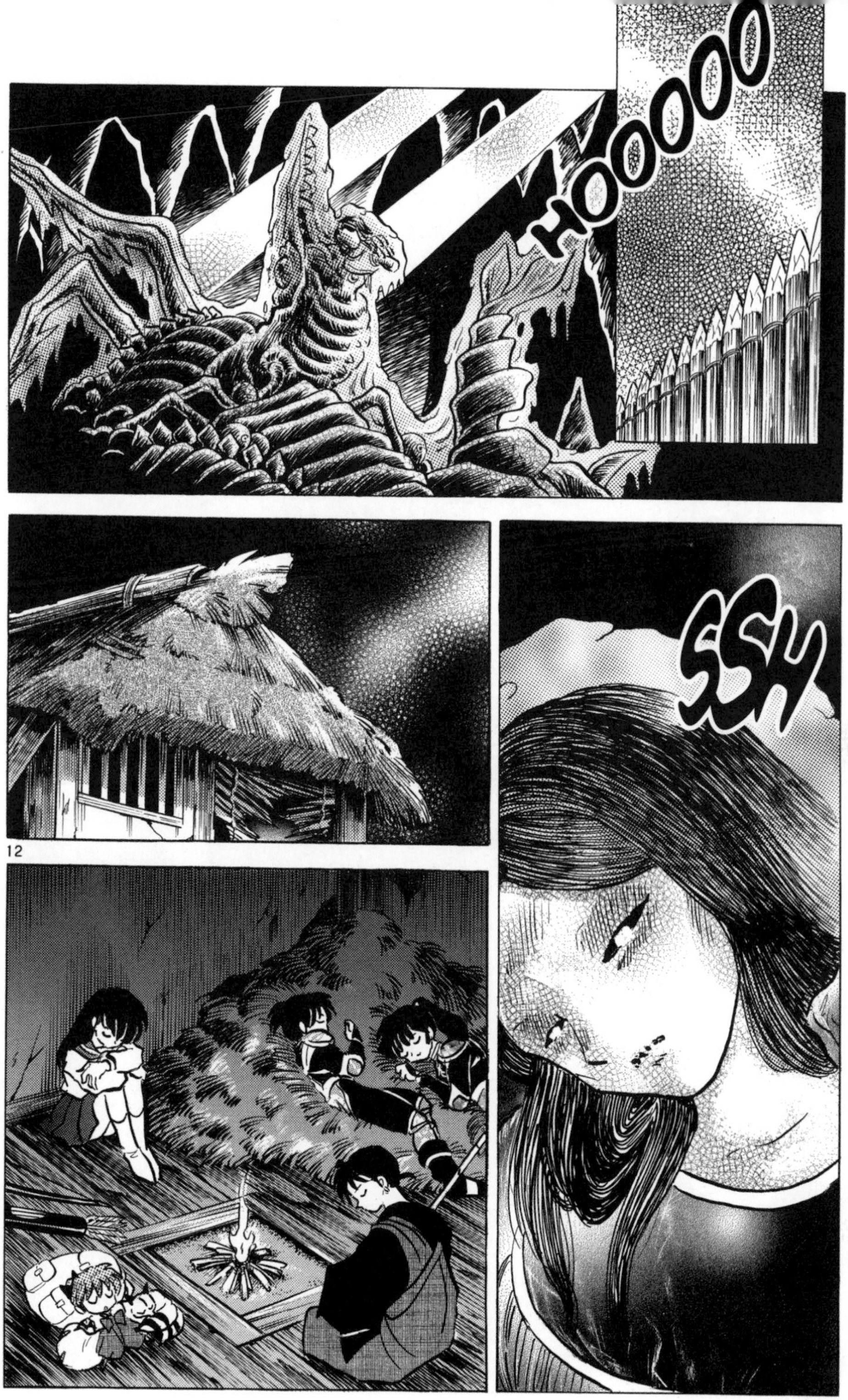
HOOOOOO
SSH

12

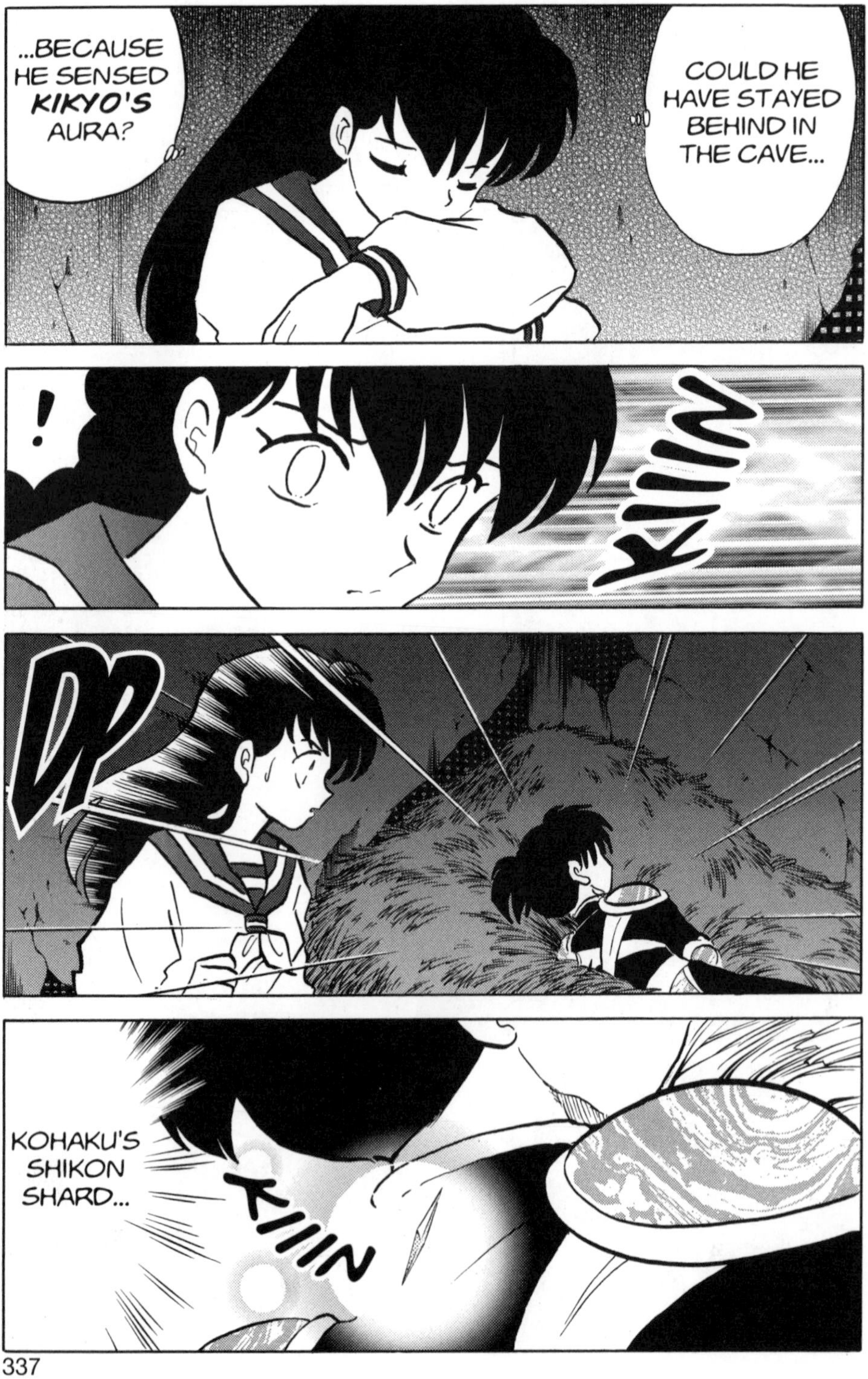
COULD HE HAVE STAYED BEHIND IN THE CAVE...
...BECAUSE HE SENSED **KIKYO'S** AURA?
KIIIN
!
DP
KOHAKU'S SHIKON SHARD...
KIIIN

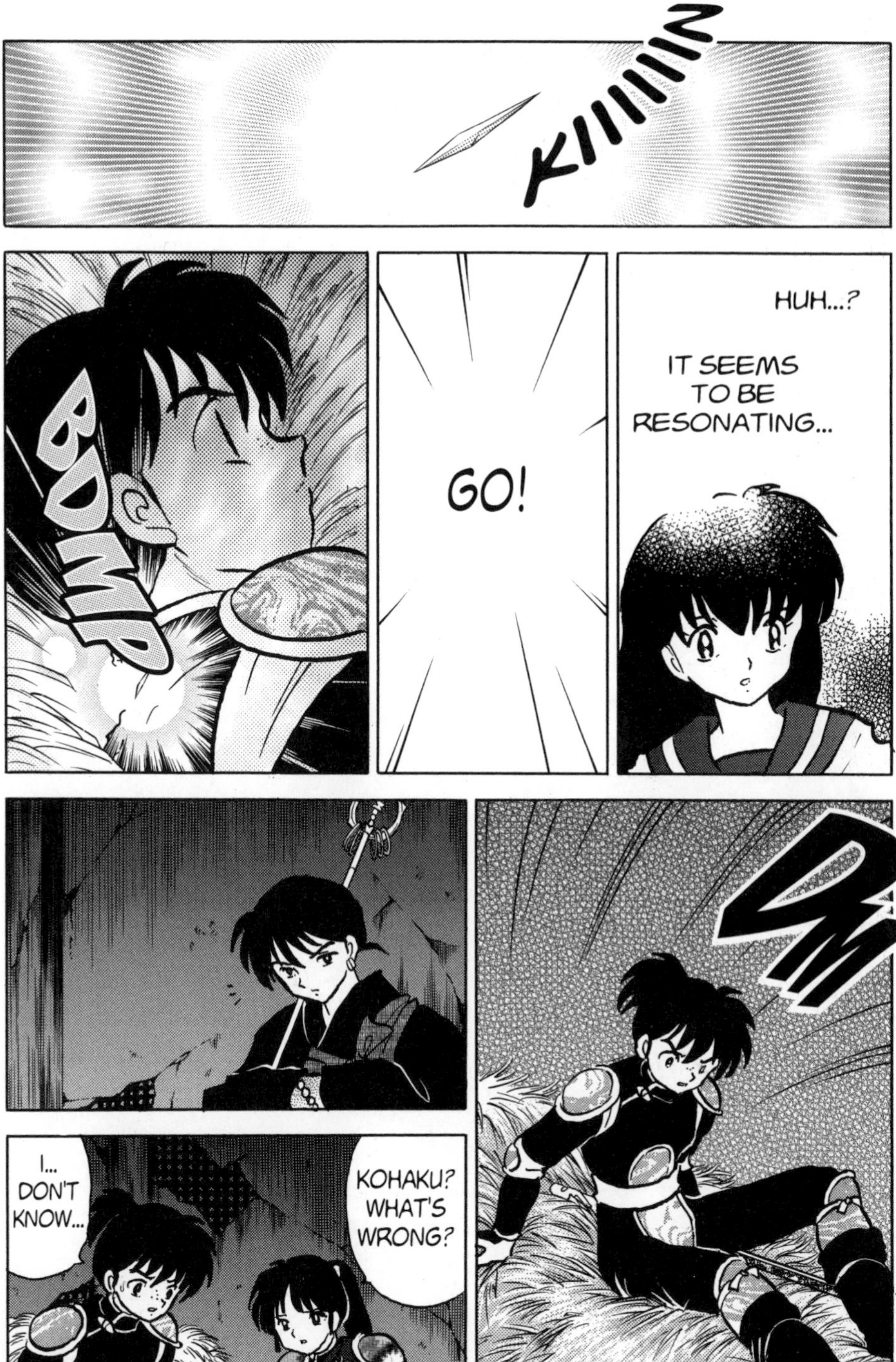
KIIIIIN
HUH...?
IT SEEMS TO BE RESONATING...
GO!
BDMP
DM
KOHAKU? WHAT'S WRONG?
I... DON'T KNOW...

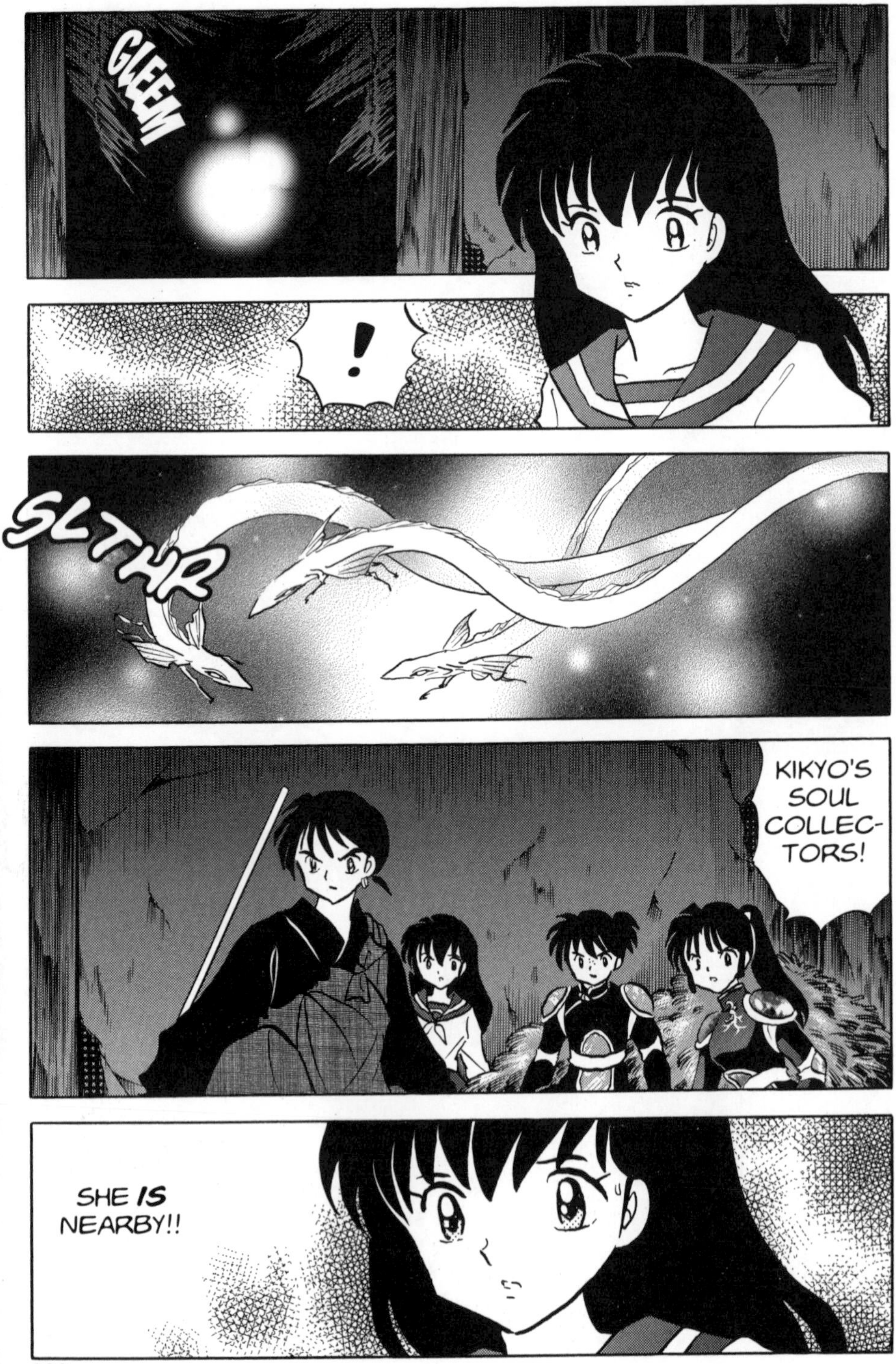
GLEEM
!
SLTHR
KIKYO'S SOUL COLLECTORS!
SHE IS NEARBY!!

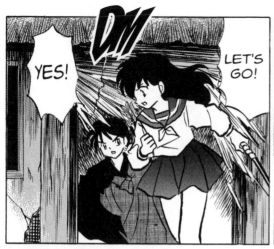

YES!

LET'S GO!

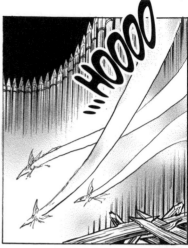

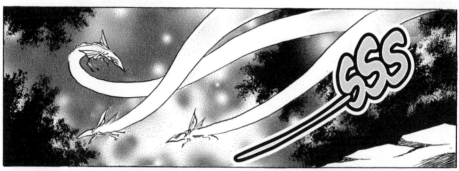

BUT...

I THINK THEY'RE LEADING US!

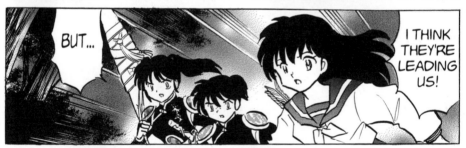

OH!

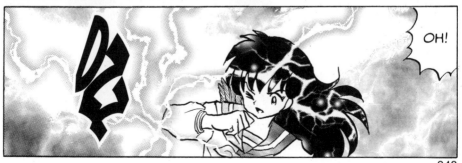

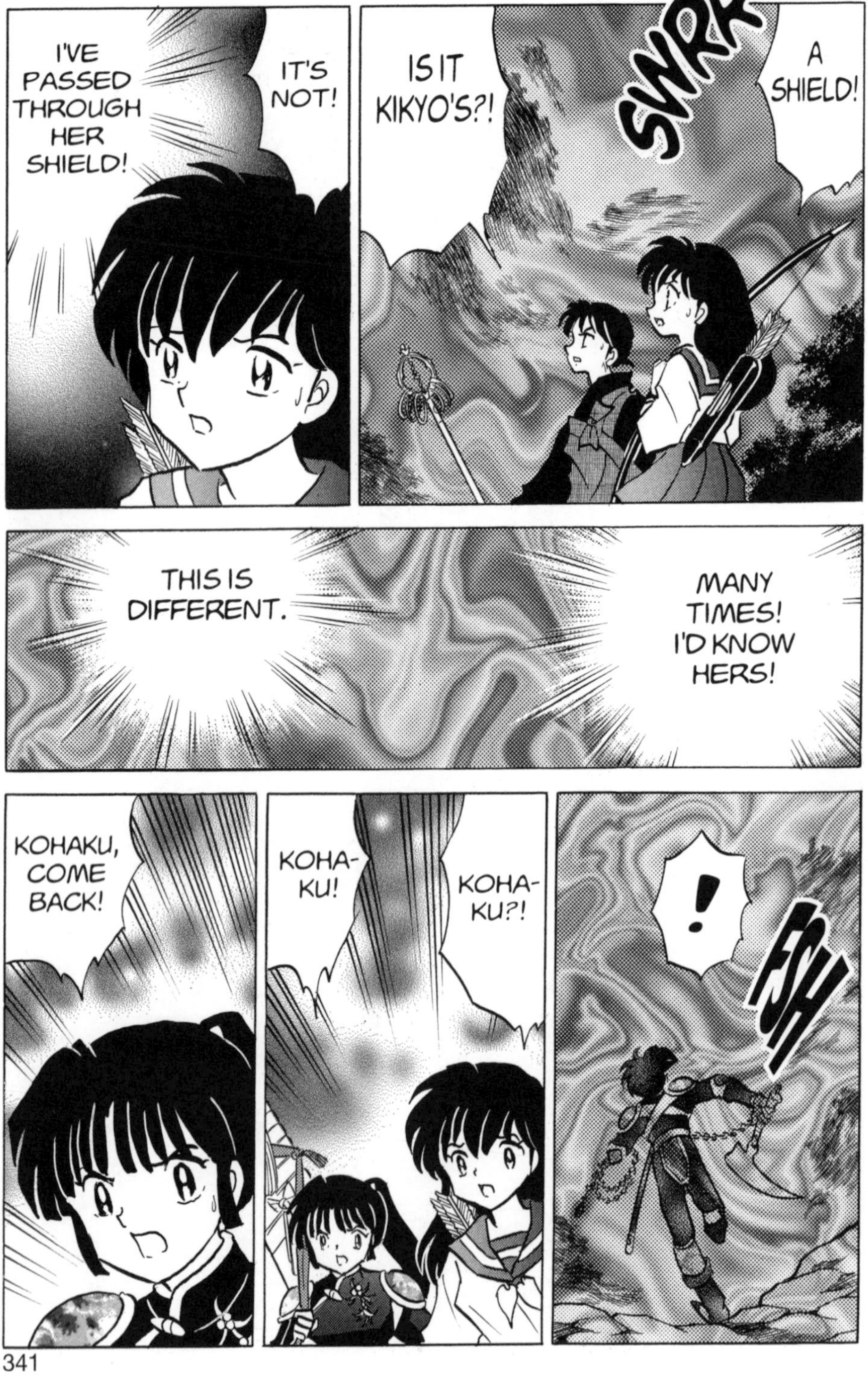
A SHIELD!
SWRR
IS IT KIKYO'S?!
IT'S NOT!
I'VE PASSED THROUGH HER SHIELD!
MANY TIMES! I'D KNOW HERS!
THIS IS DIFFERENT.
!
FSH
KOHA-KU?!
KOHA-KU!
KOHAKU, COME BACK!

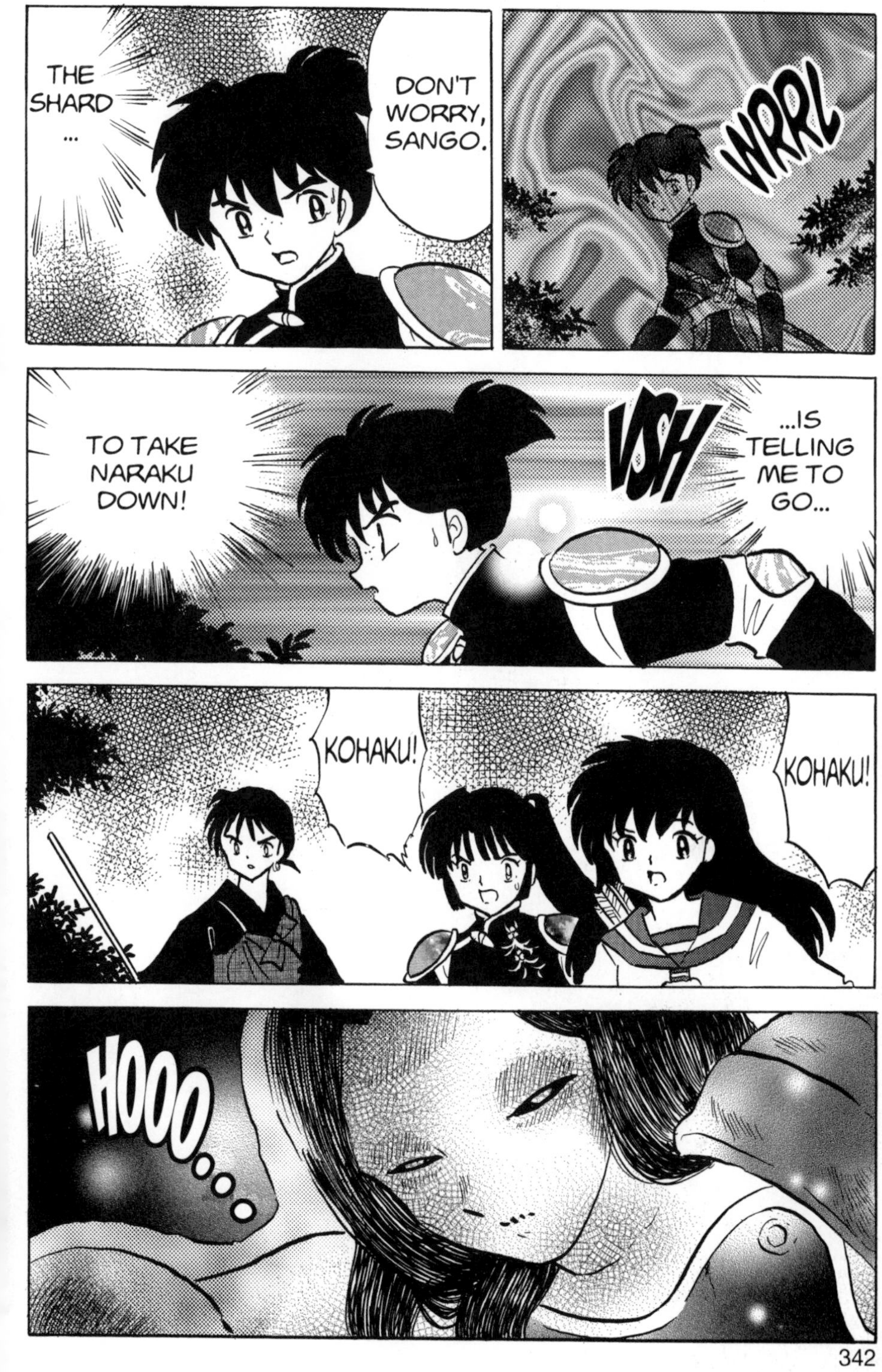
WRRL
DON'T WORRY, SANGO.
THE SHARD ...
...IS TELLING ME TO GO...
VSH
TO TAKE NARAKU DOWN!
KOHAKU!
KOHAKU!
HOOO....

SCROLL NINE
MISSION

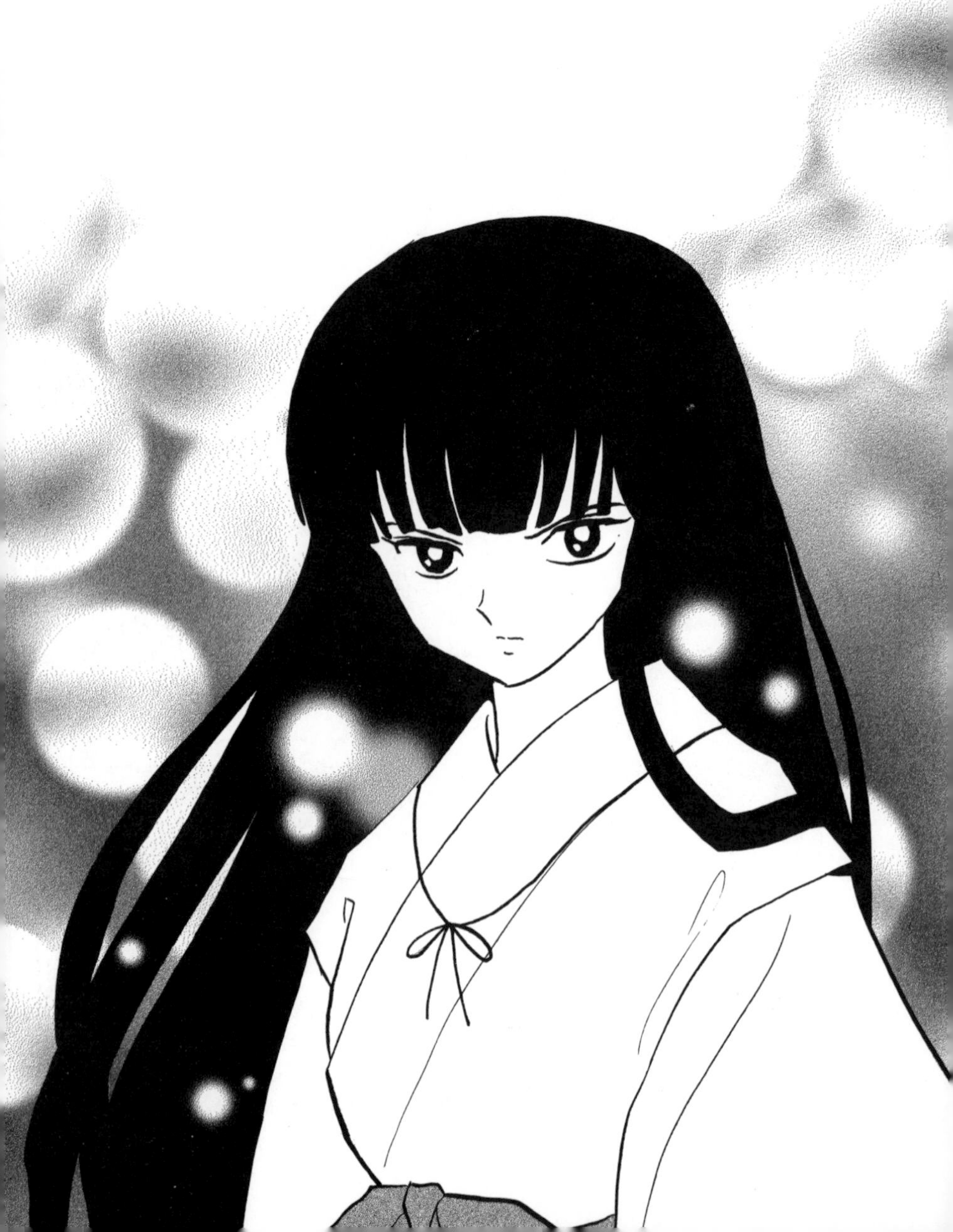

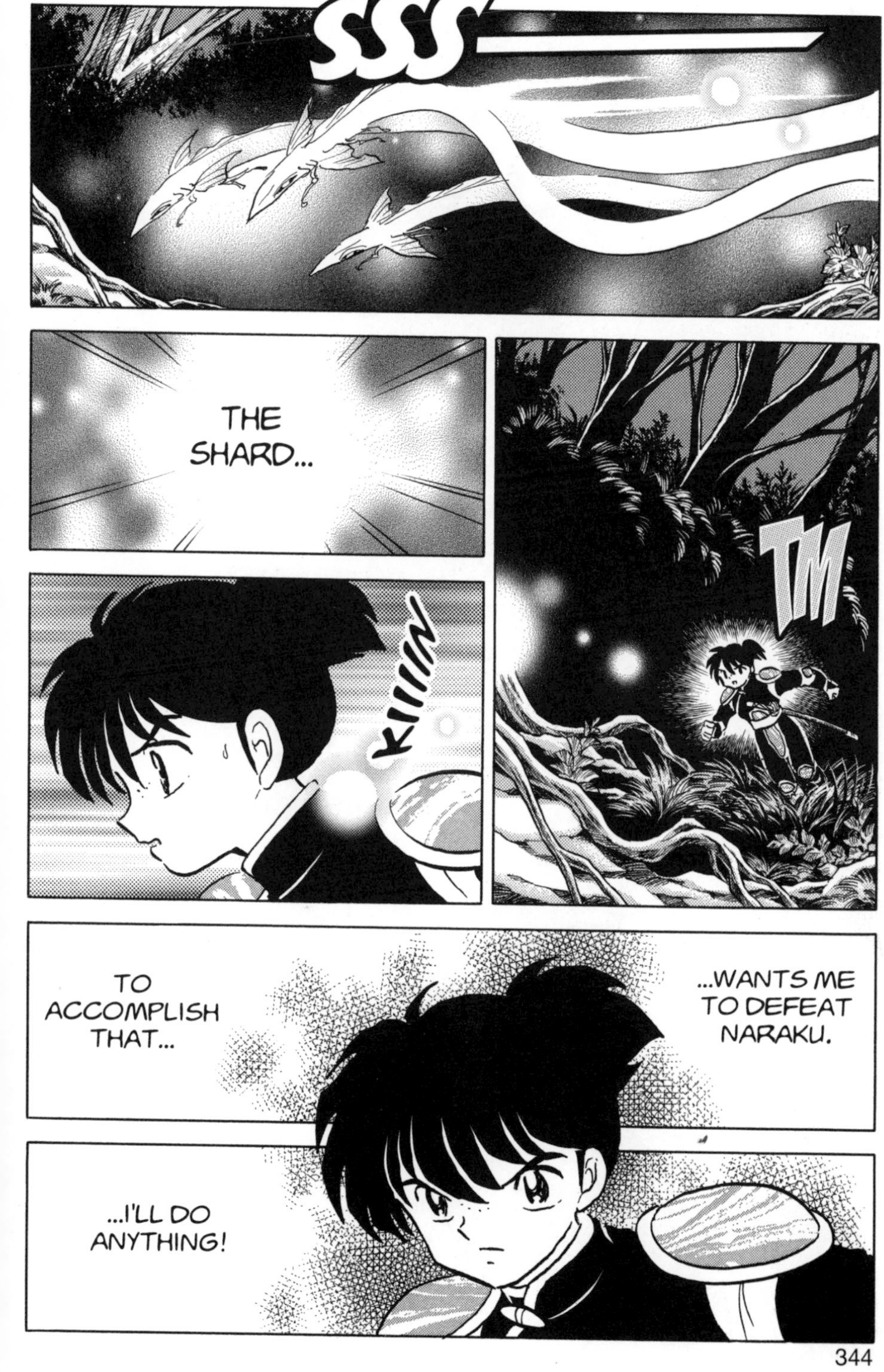
SSS
TM
THE SHARD...
KIIIIN
...WANTS ME TO DEFEAT NARAKU.
TO ACCOMPLISH THAT...
...I'LL DO ANYTHING!

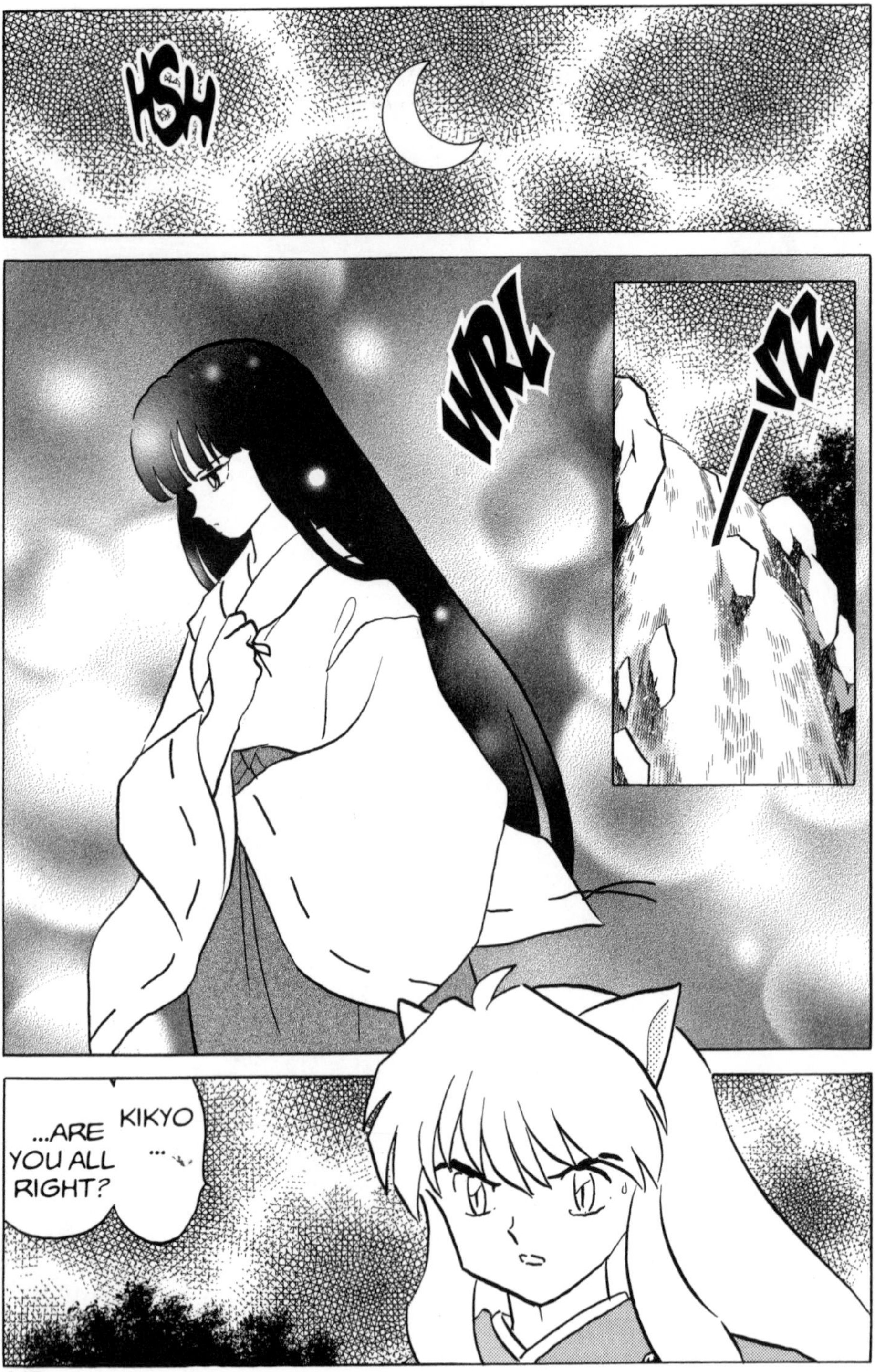
HSH
VZZ
WRL
KIKYO ...
...ARE YOU ALL RIGHT?

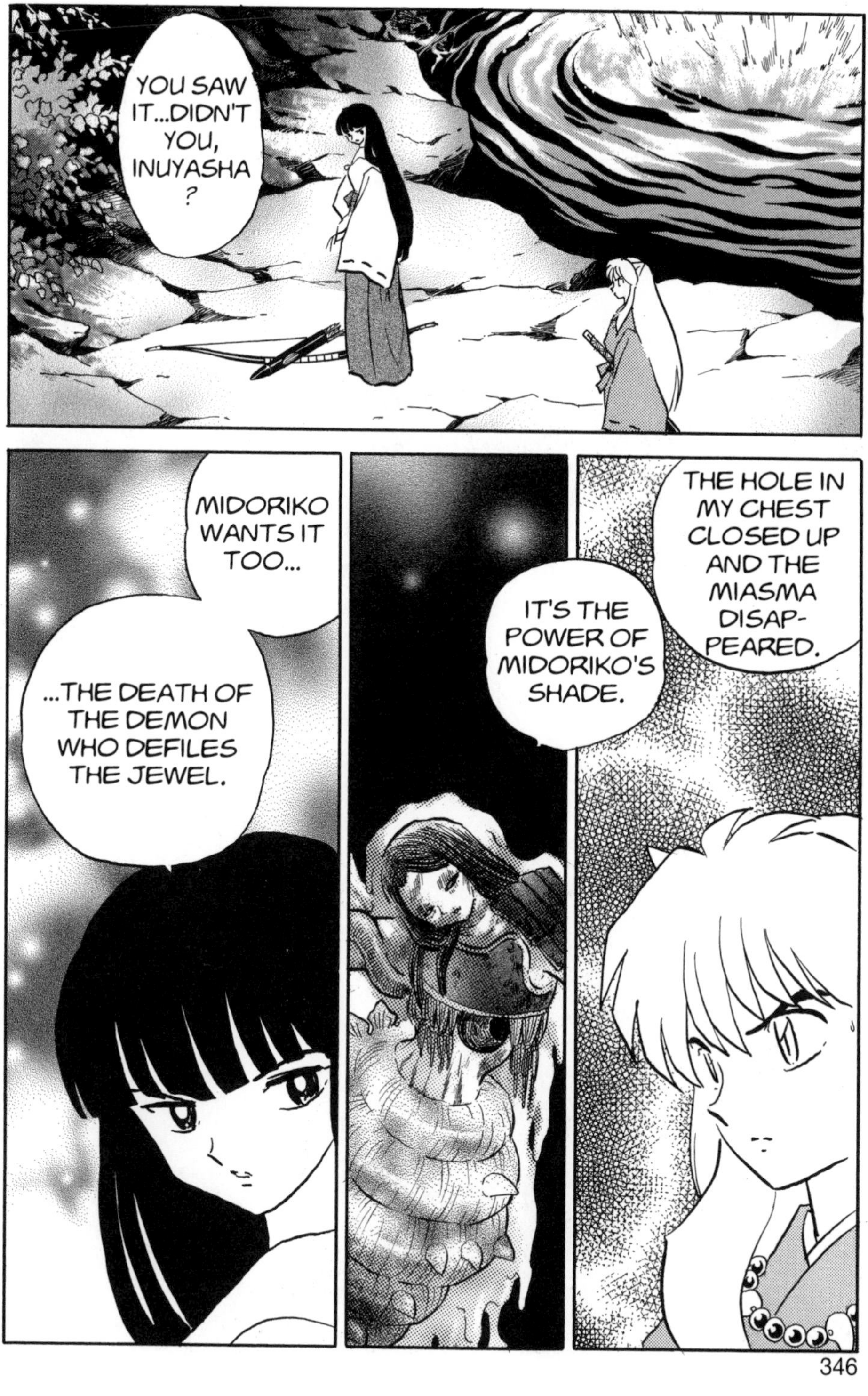
YOU SAW IT...DIDN'T YOU, INUYASHA?
THE HOLE IN MY CHEST CLOSED UP AND THE MIASMA DISAP-PEARED.
IT'S THE POWER OF MIDORIKO'S SHADE.
MIDORIKO WANTS IT TOO...
...THE DEATH OF THE DEMON WHO DEFILES THE JEWEL.

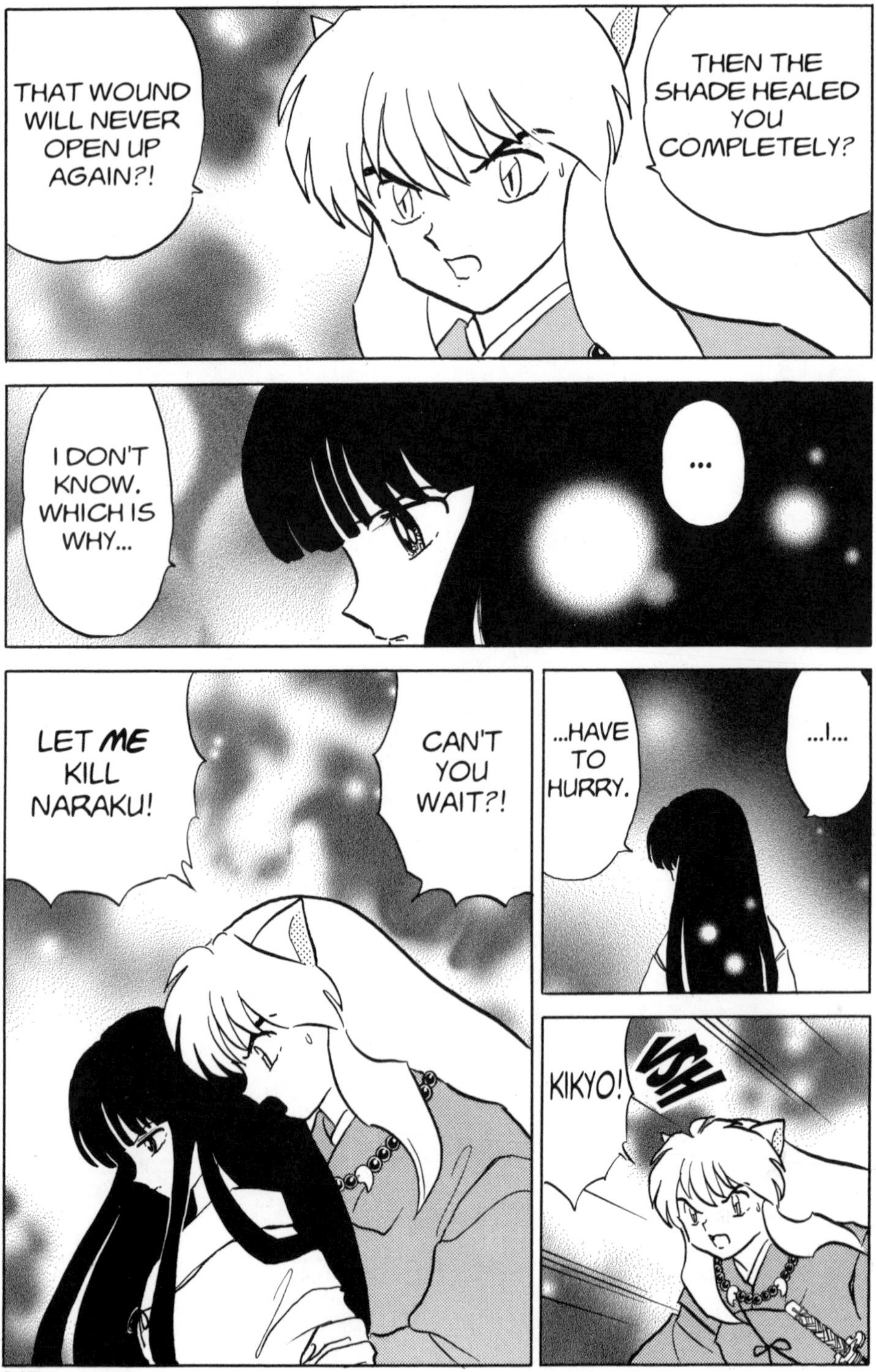
THEN THE SHADE HEALED YOU COMPLETELY?
THAT WOUND WILL NEVER OPEN UP AGAIN?!
...
I DON'T KNOW. WHICH IS WHY...
...I...
...HAVE TO HURRY.
VSH
KIKYO!
CAN'T YOU WAIT?!
LET *ME* KILL NARAKU!

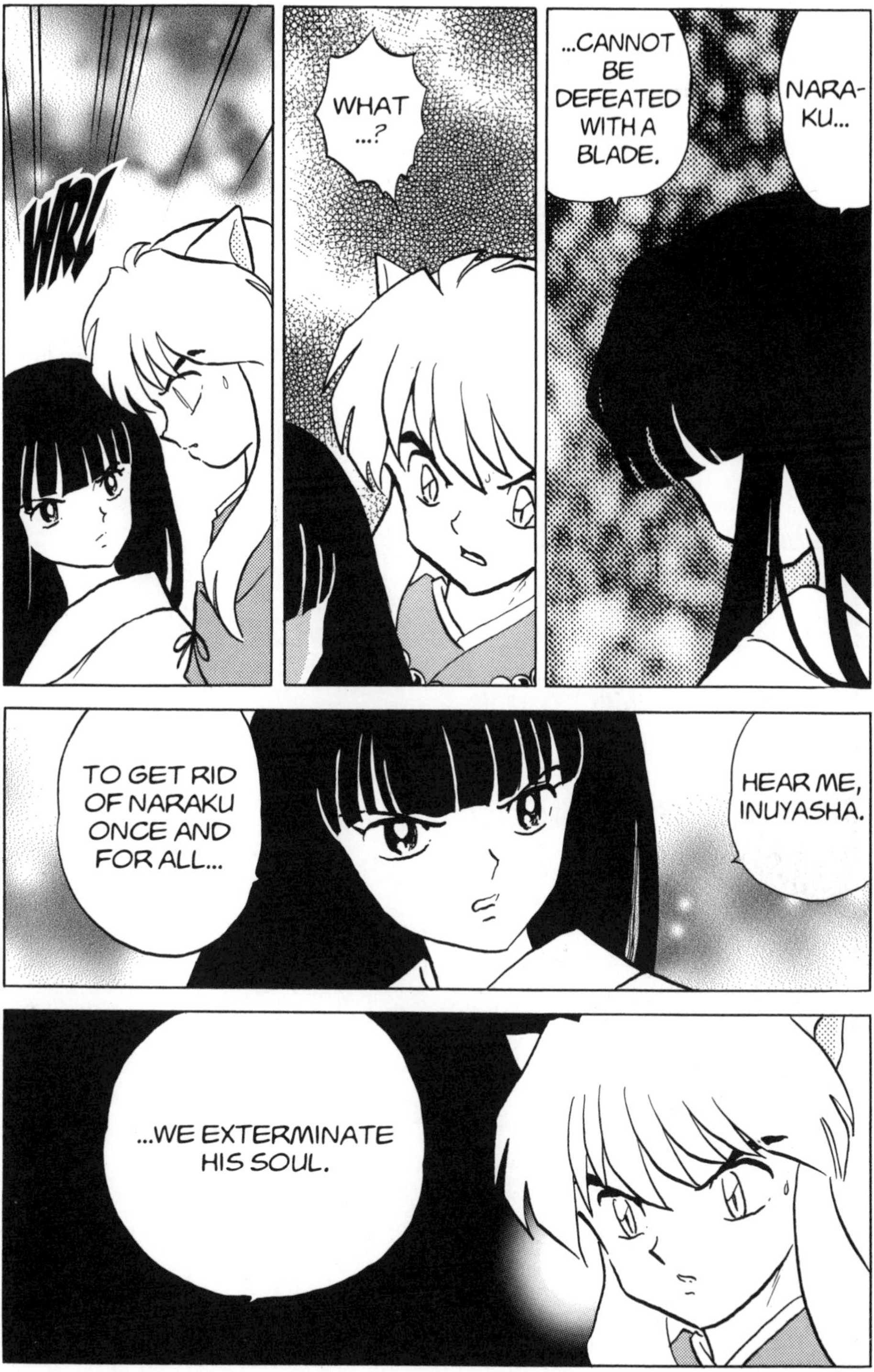
NARA-KU...
...CANNOT BE DEFEATED WITH A BLADE.
WHAT ...?
WRL
HEAR ME, INUYASHA.
TO GET RID OF NARAKU ONCE AND FOR ALL...
...WE EXTERMINATE HIS SOUL.

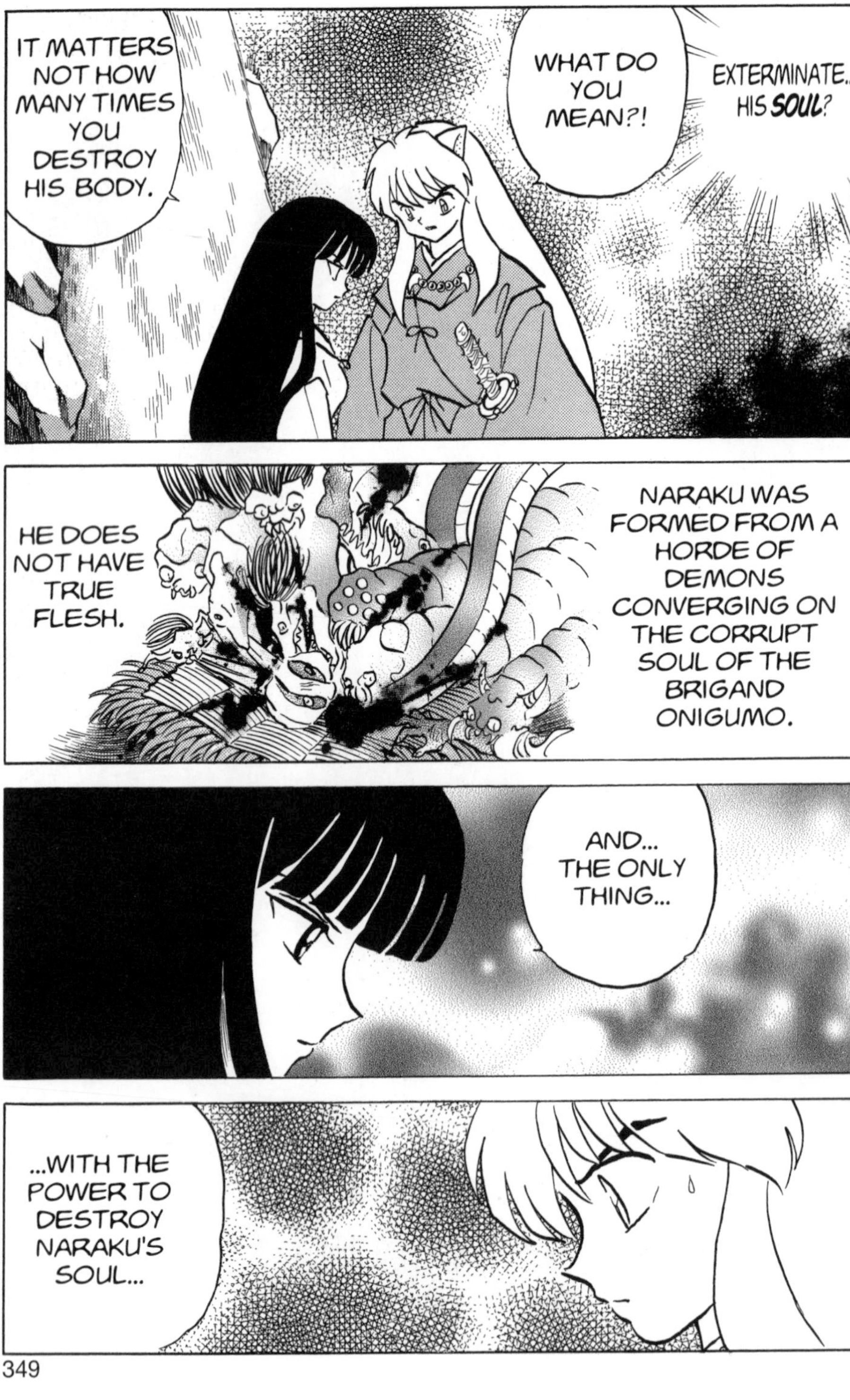
EXTERMINATE... HIS **SOUL**?
WHAT DO YOU MEAN?!
IT MATTERS NOT HOW MANY TIMES YOU DESTROY HIS BODY.
NARAKU WAS FORMED FROM A HORDE OF DEMONS CONVERGING ON THE CORRUPT SOUL OF THE BRIGAND ONIGUMO.
HE DOES NOT HAVE TRUE FLESH.
AND... THE ONLY THING...
...WITH THE POWER TO DESTROY NARAKU'S SOUL...

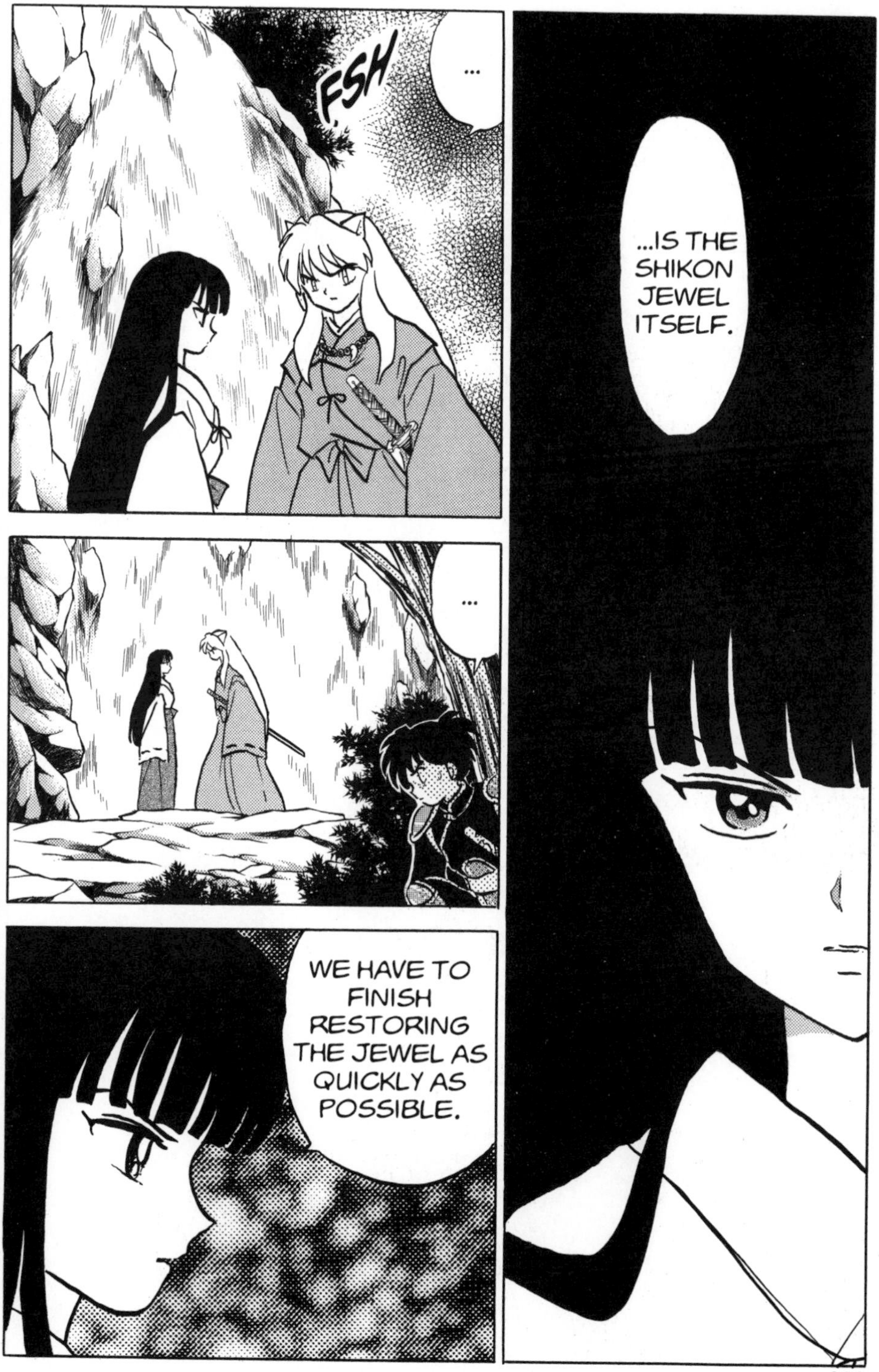
...IS THE SHIKON JEWEL ITSELF.
...
FSH
...
WE HAVE TO FINISH RESTORING THE JEWEL AS QUICKLY AS POSSIBLE.

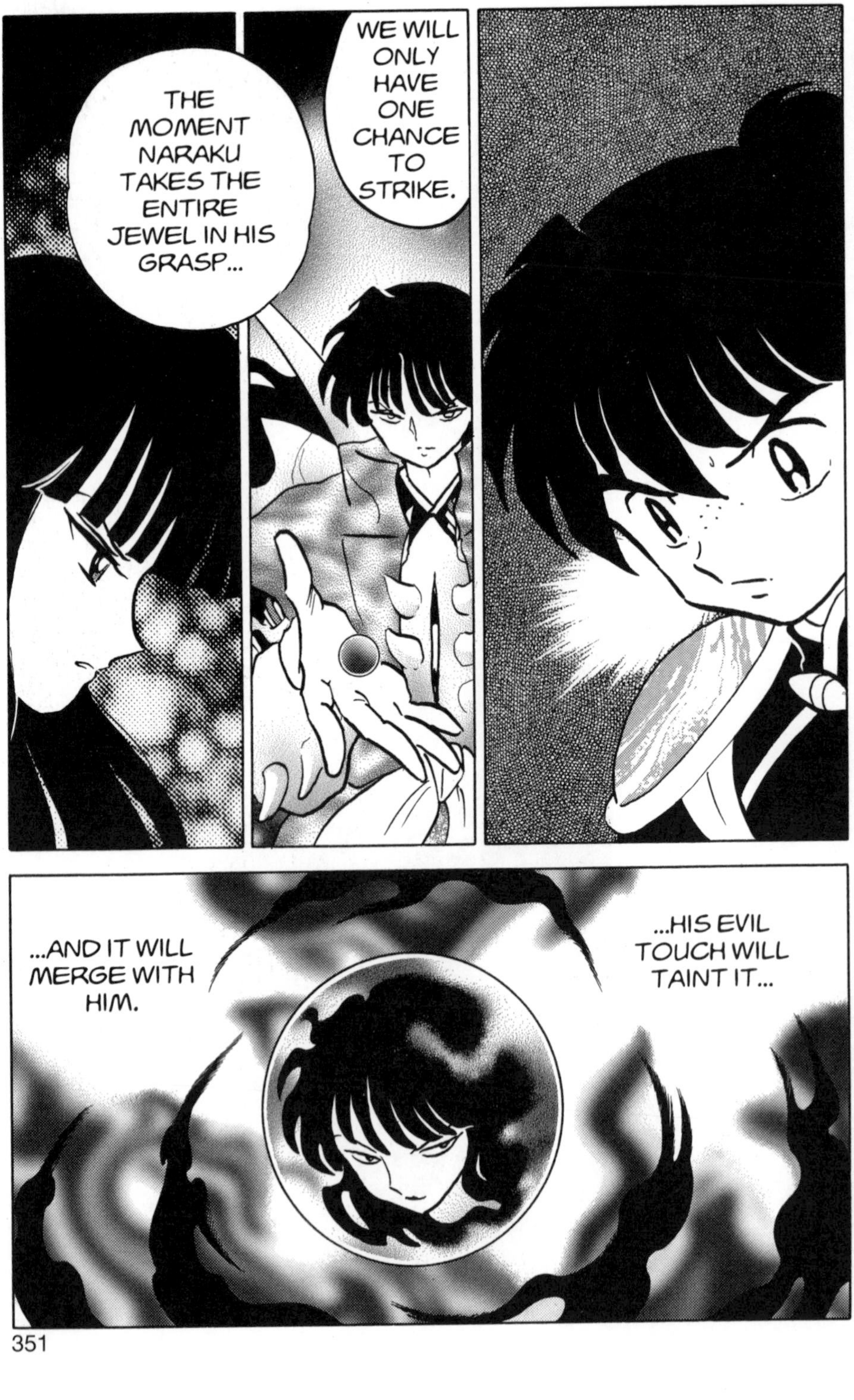
WE WILL ONLY HAVE ONE CHANCE TO STRIKE.
THE MOMENT NARAKU TAKES THE ENTIRE JEWEL IN HIS GRASP...
...HIS EVIL TOUCH WILL TAINT IT...
...AND IT WILL MERGE WITH HIM.

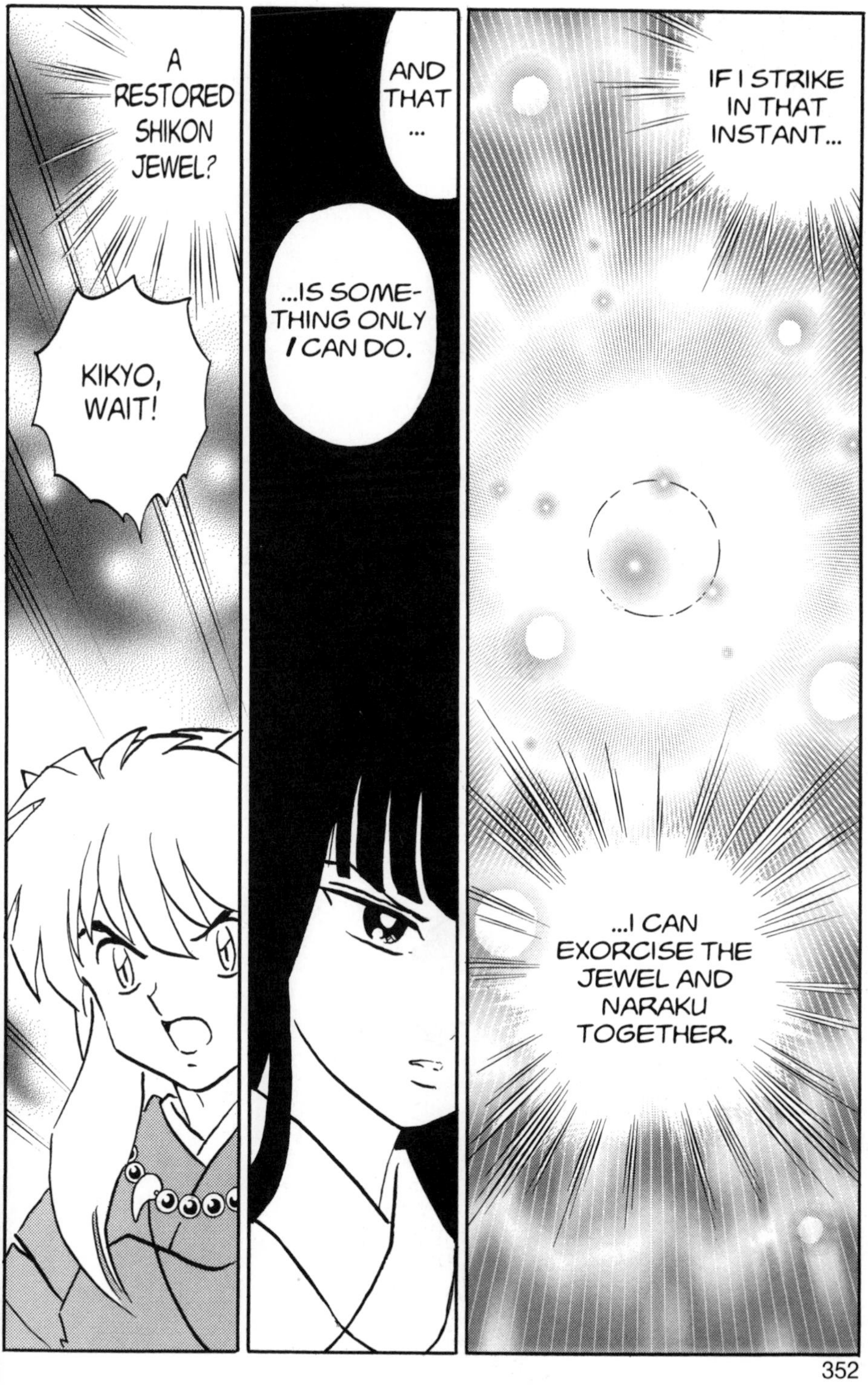
IF I STRIKE IN THAT INSTANT...
...I CAN EXORCISE THE JEWEL AND NARAKU TOGETHER.
AND THAT ...
...IS SOME-THING ONLY *I* CAN DO.
A RESTORED SHIKON JEWEL?
KIKYO, WAIT!

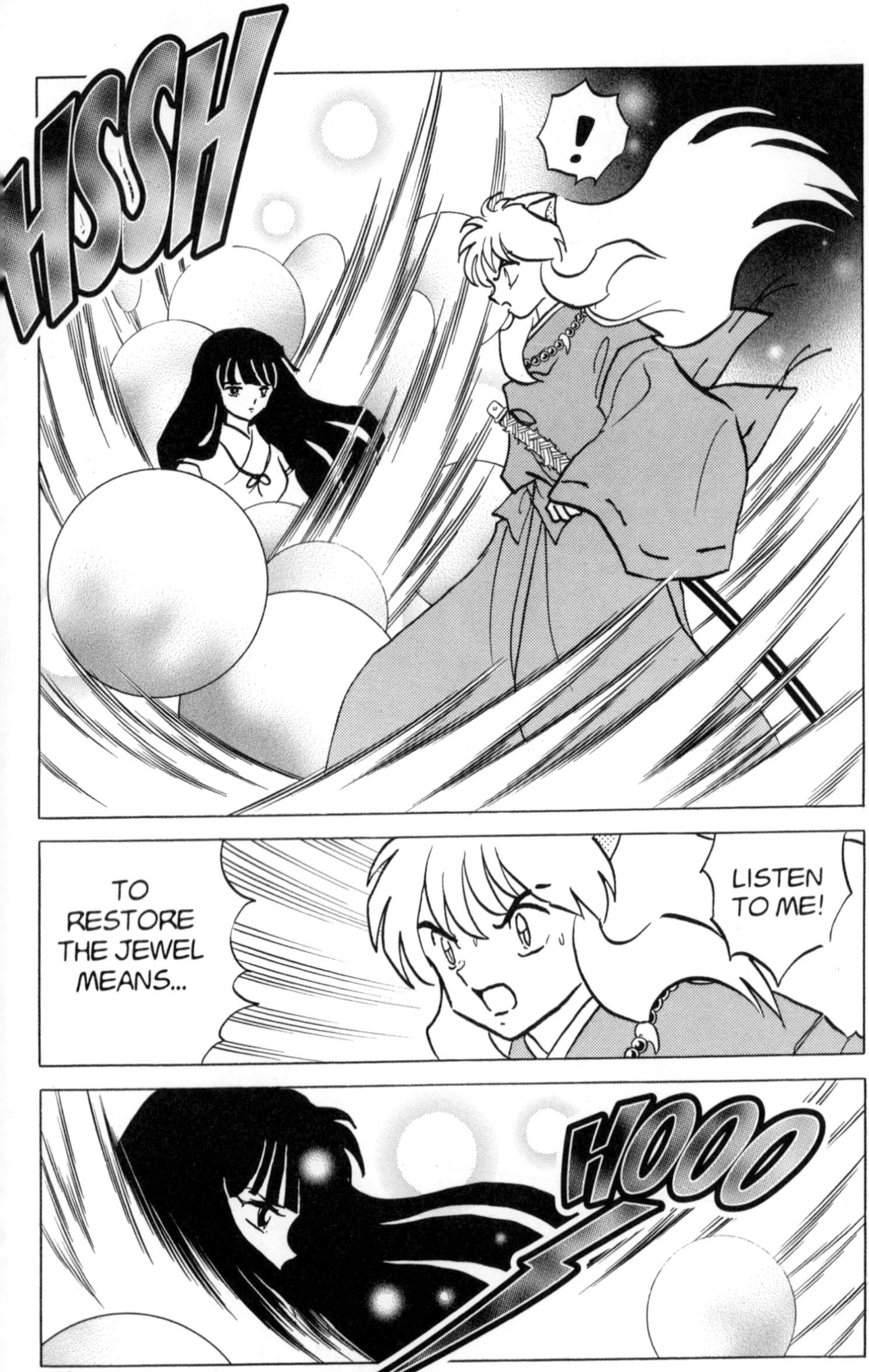
HSSH
!
LISTEN TO ME!
TO RESTORE THE JEWEL MEANS...
HOOO

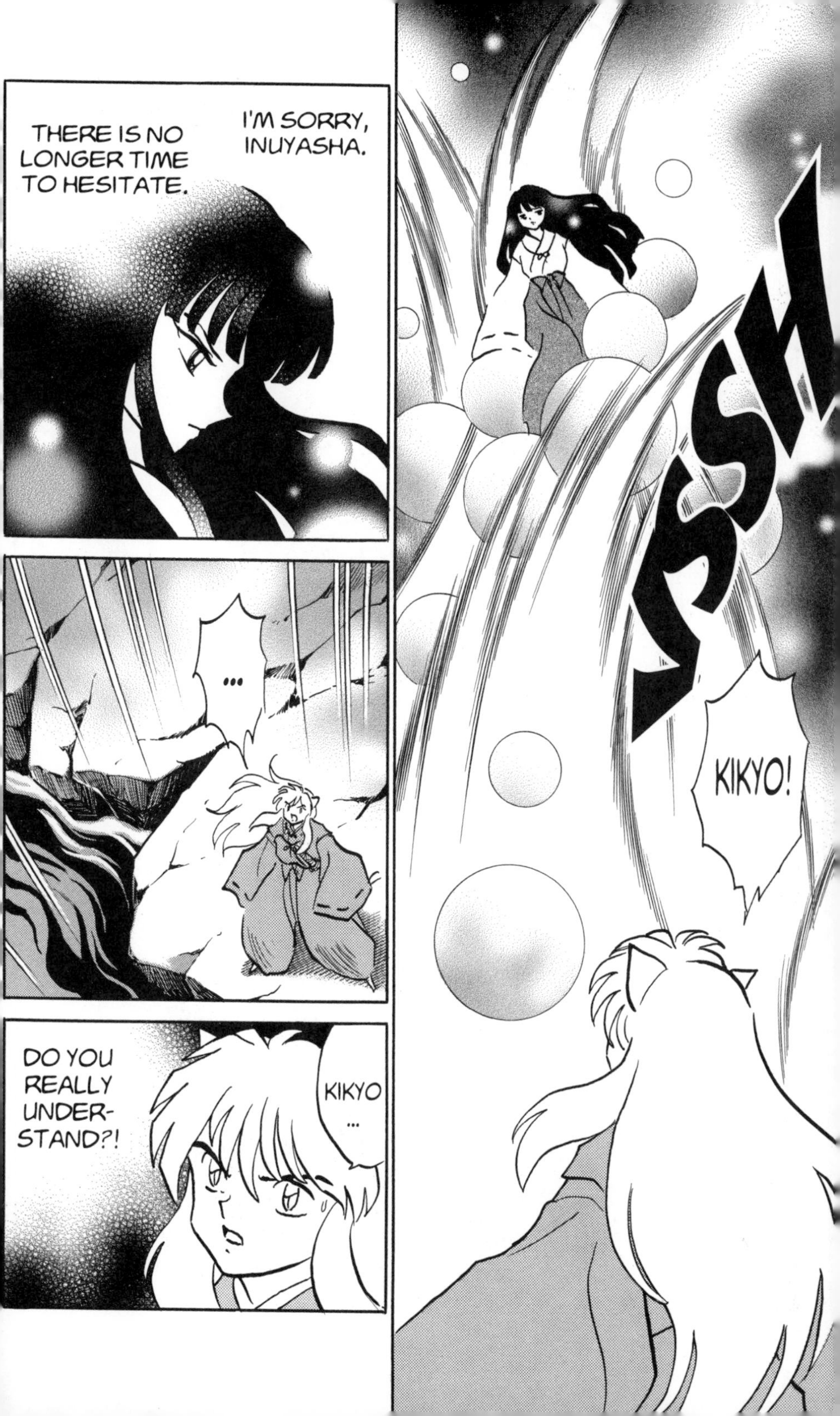
VSSH!
KIKYO!
I'M SORRY, INUYASHA.
THERE IS NO LONGER TIME TO HESITATE.
...
KIKYO ...
DO YOU REALLY UNDER-STAND?!

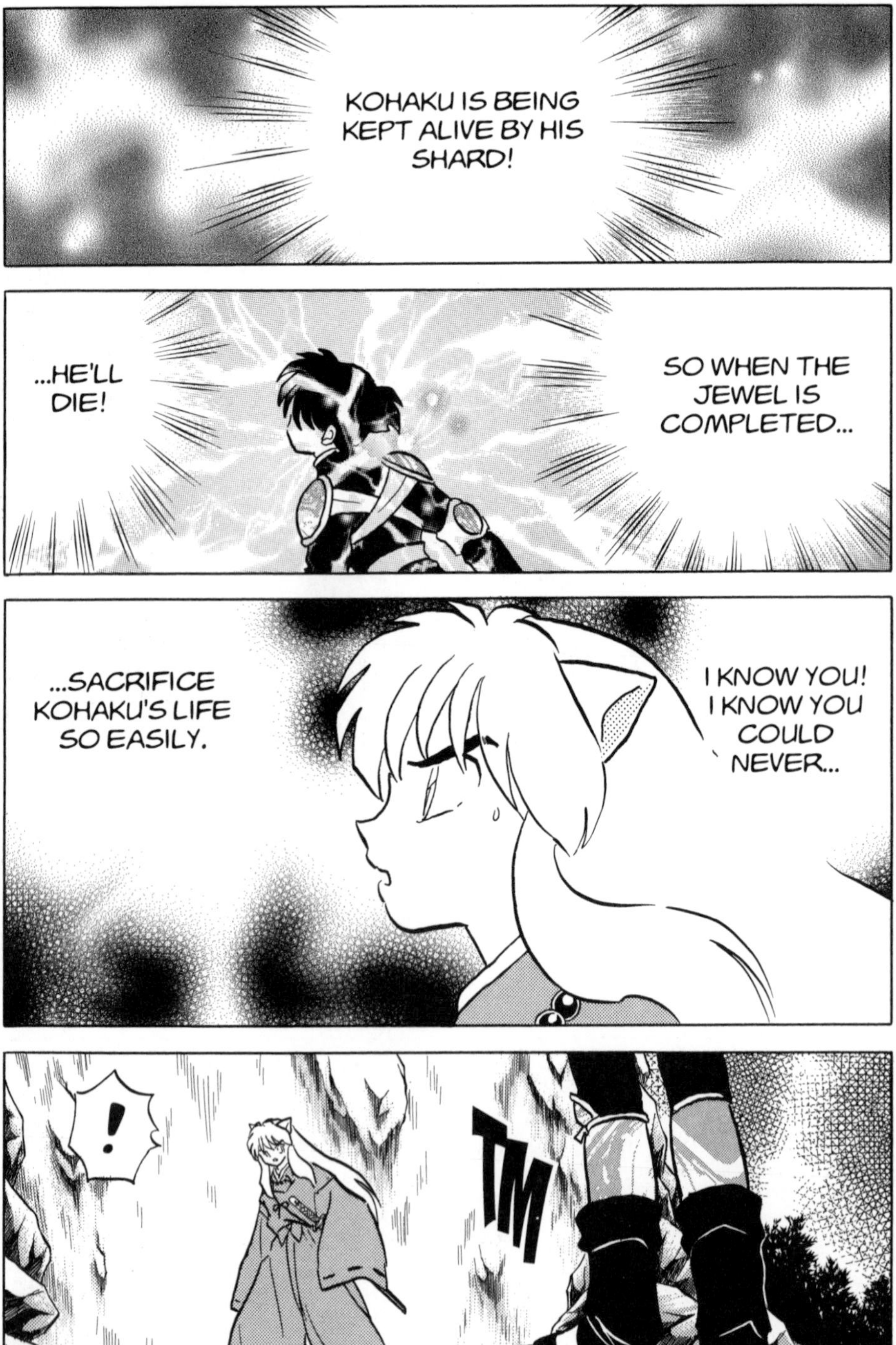
KOHAKU IS BEING KEPT ALIVE BY HIS SHARD!
SO WHEN THE JEWEL IS COMPLETED...
...HE'LL DIE!
I KNOW YOU! I KNOW YOU COULD NEVER...
...SACRIFICE KOHAKU'S LIFE SO EASILY.
TM
!

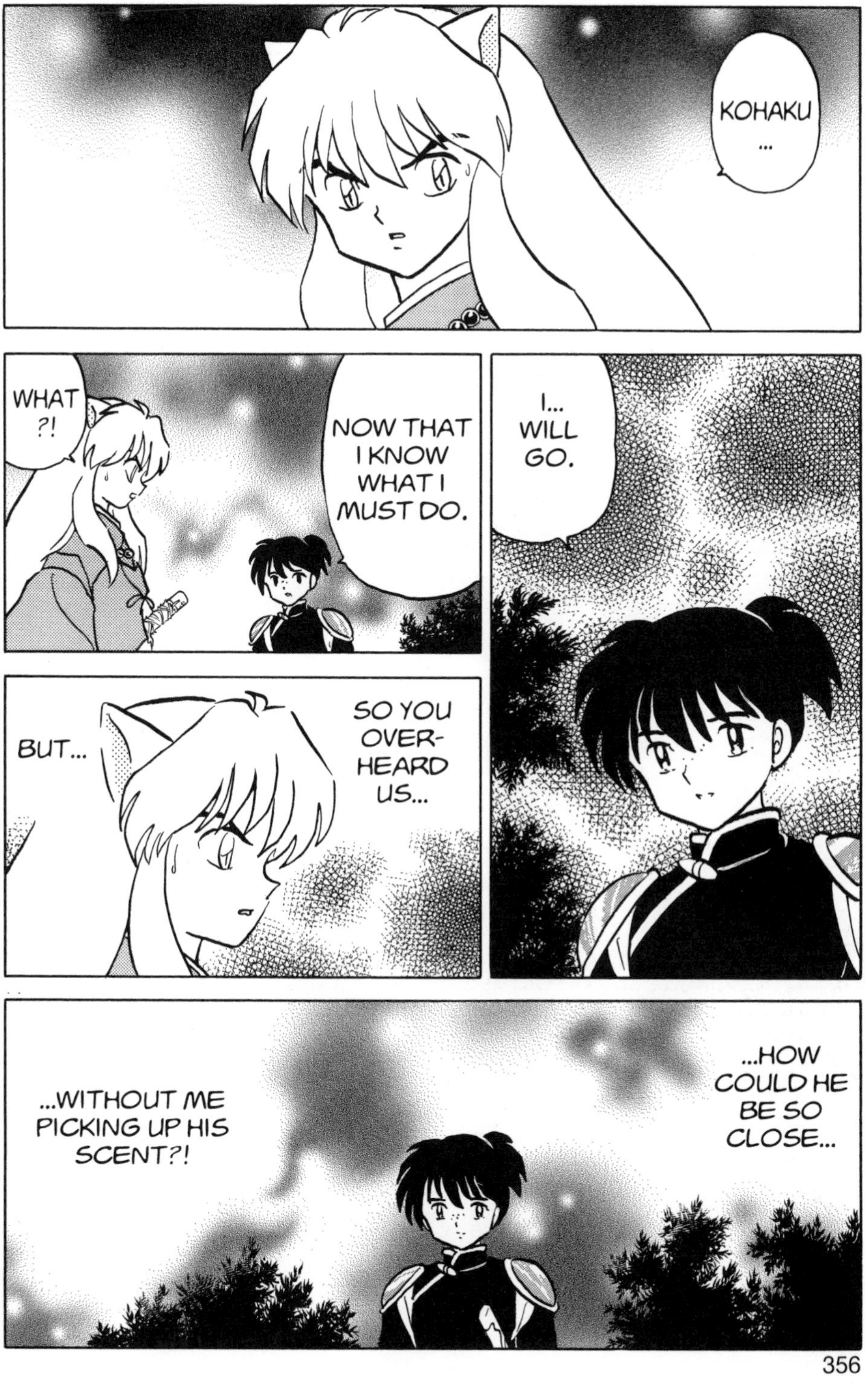
KOHAKU ...
I... WILL GO.
NOW THAT I KNOW WHAT I MUST DO.
WHAT ?!
SO YOU OVER-HEARD US...
BUT...
...HOW COULD HE BE SO CLOSE...
...WITHOUT ME PICKING UP HIS SCENT?!

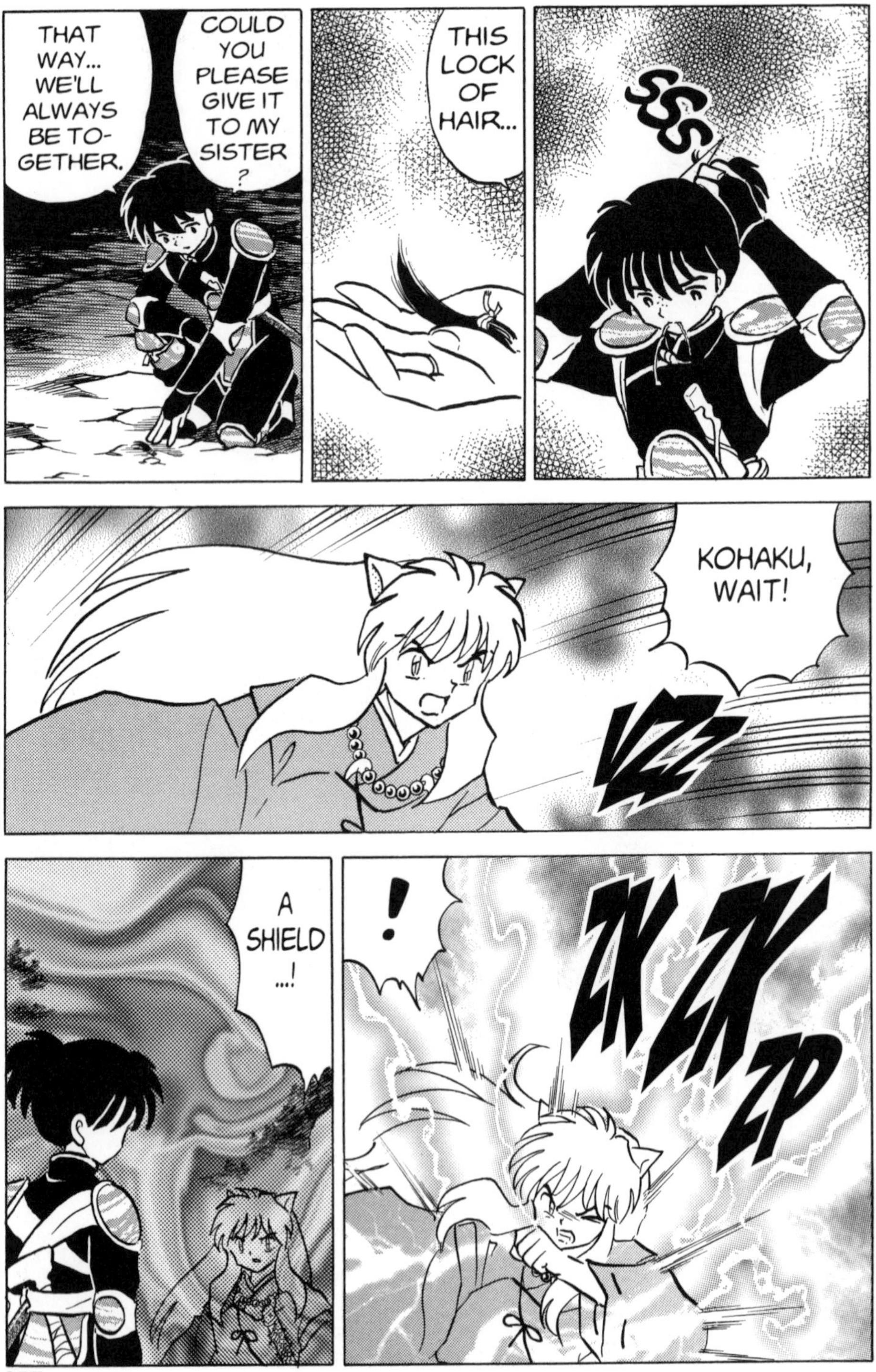
SSS
THIS LOCK OF HAIR...
COULD YOU PLEASE GIVE IT TO MY SISTER?
THAT WAY... WE'LL ALWAYS BE TOGETHER.
KOHAKU, WAIT!
!
ZK ZK ZP
A SHIELD ...!

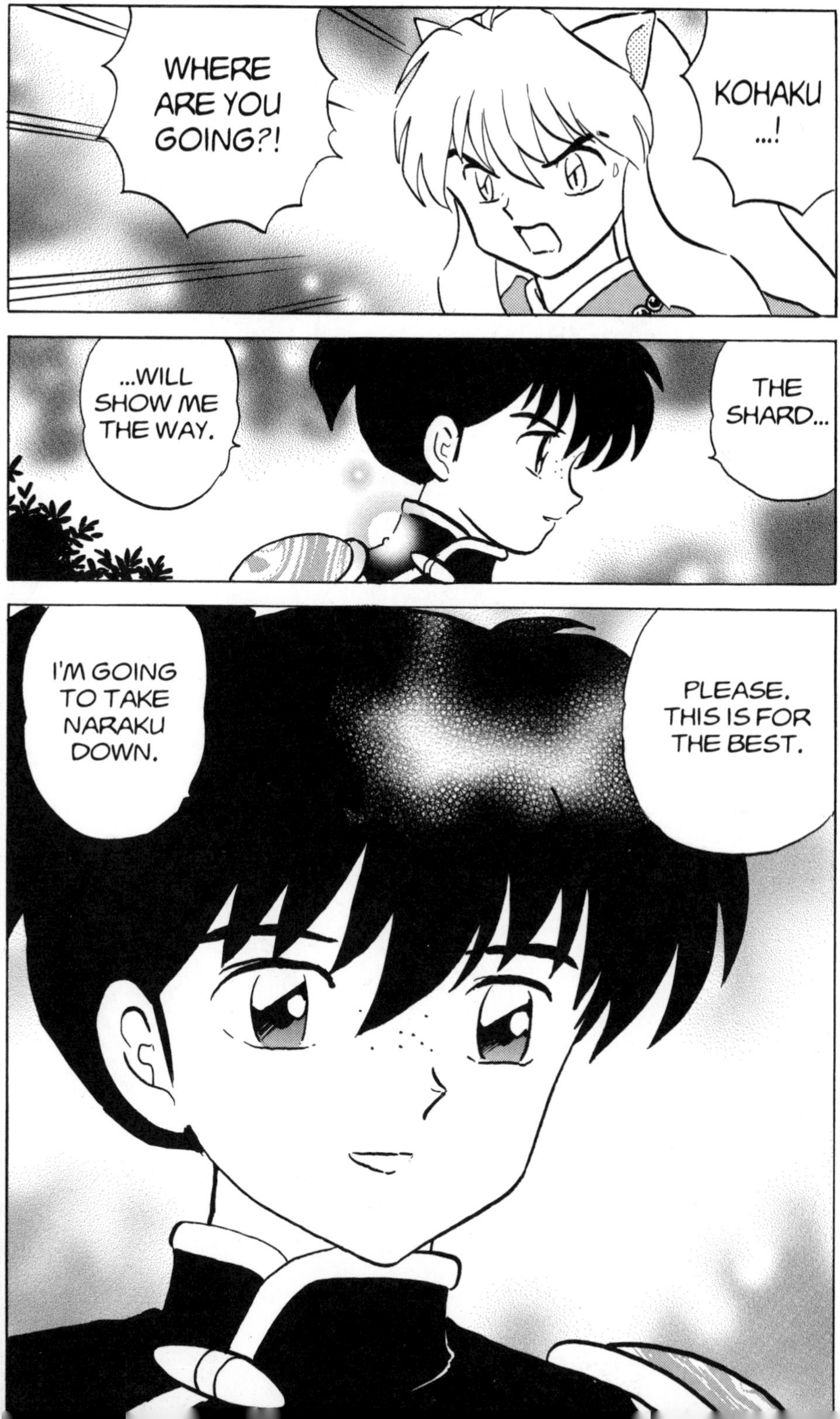
KOHAKU ...!
WHERE ARE YOU GOING?!
THE SHARD...
...WILL SHOW ME THE WAY.
PLEASE. THIS IS FOR THE BEST.
I'M GOING TO TAKE NARAKU DOWN.

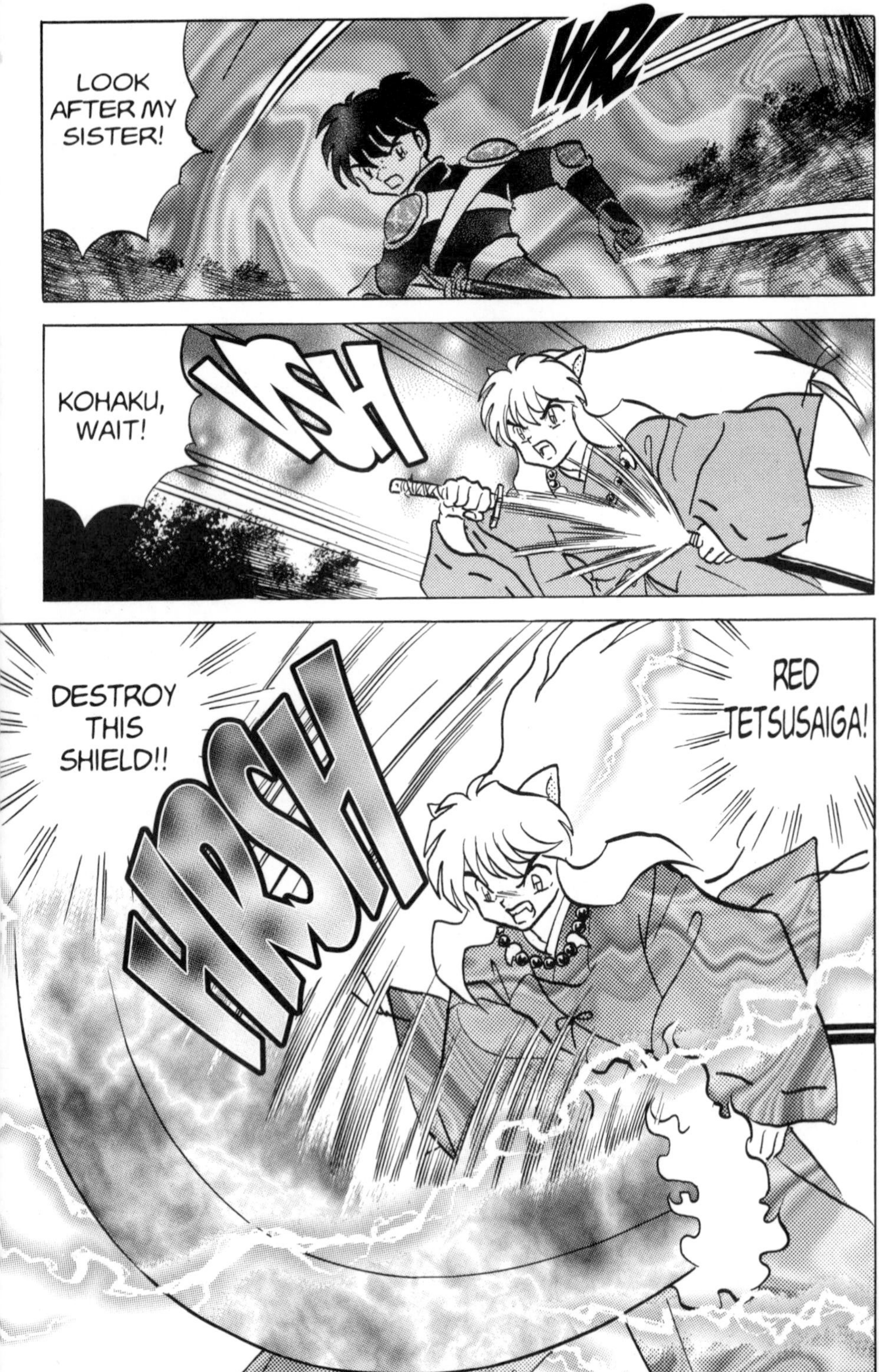
LOOK AFTER MY SISTER!
KOHAKU, WAIT!
RED TETSUSAIGA!
DESTROY THIS SHIELD!!

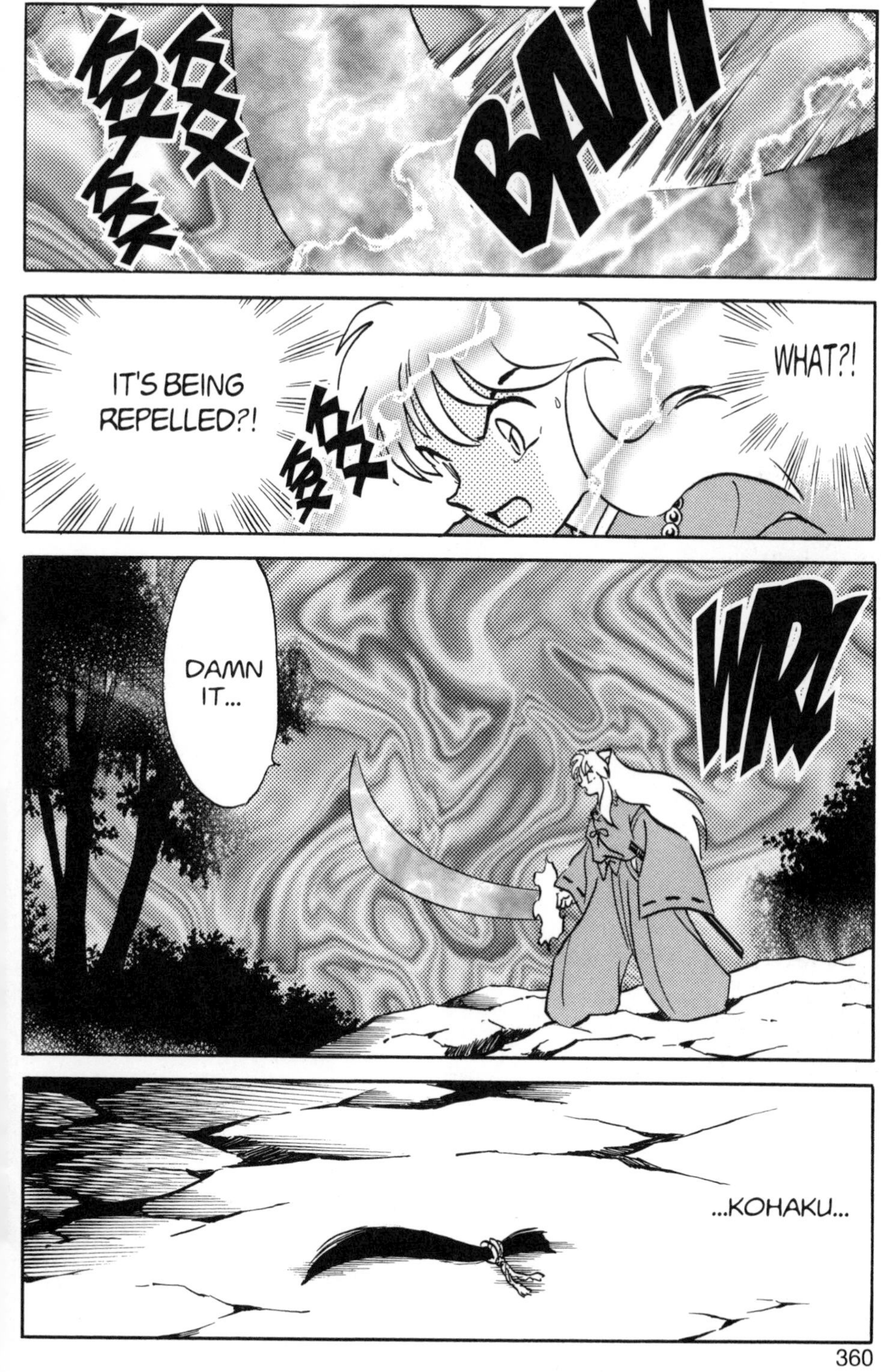
BAM
WHAT?!
IT'S BEING REPELLED?!
DAMN IT...
...KOHAKU...

SCROLL TEN
THE OROCHI'S LAIR

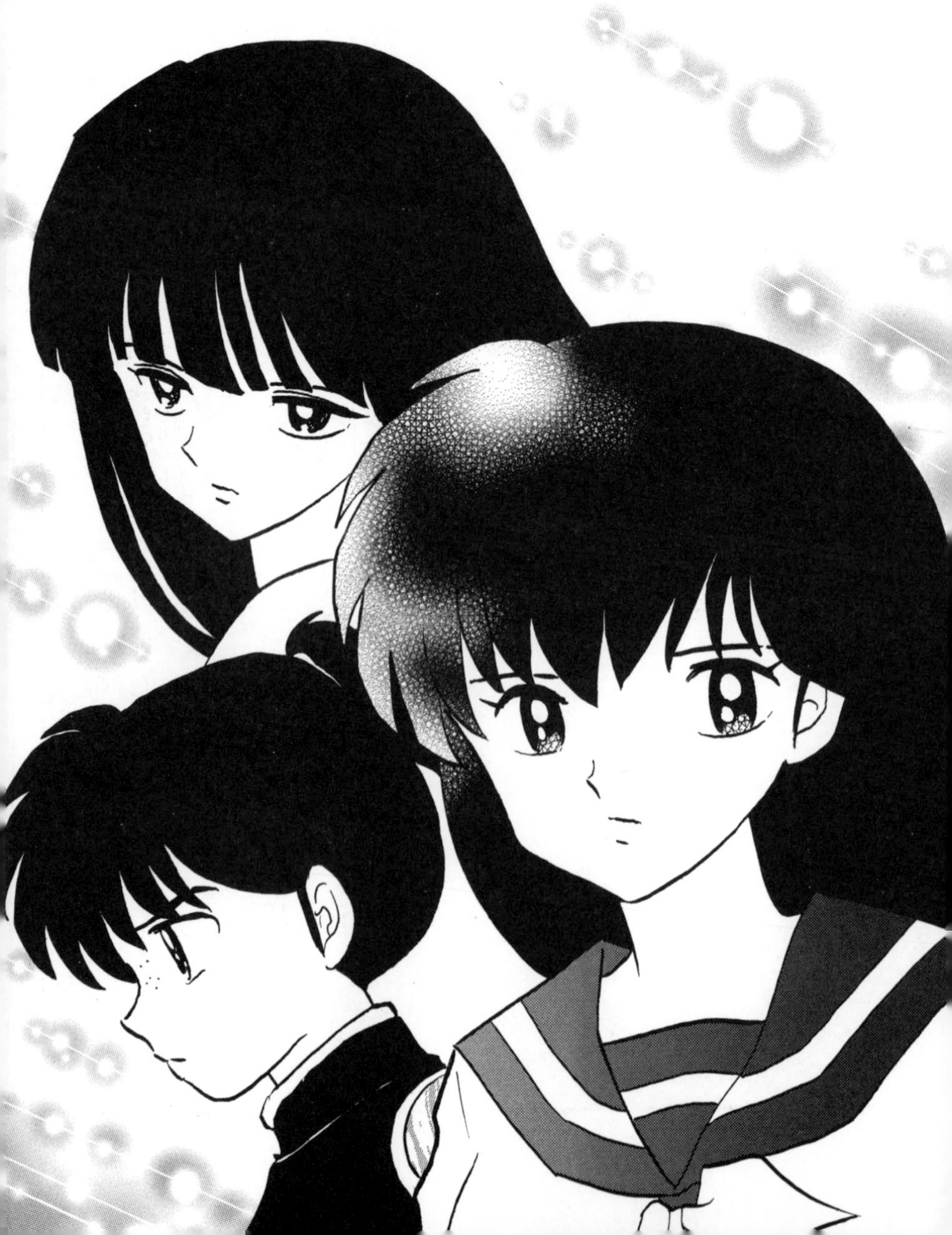

NOW THAT I KNOW WHAT I MUST DO...
I... WILL GO.
KOHA-KU...
...WHERE DID YOU GO, ALL BY YOUR-SELF...?
I'M SO SORRY, SANGO...
I COULDN'T STOP HIM.

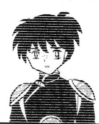

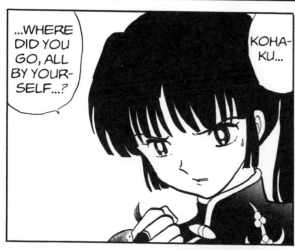

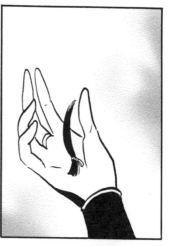

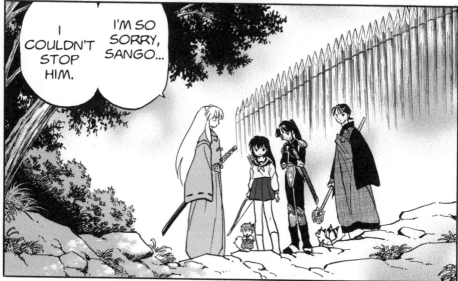

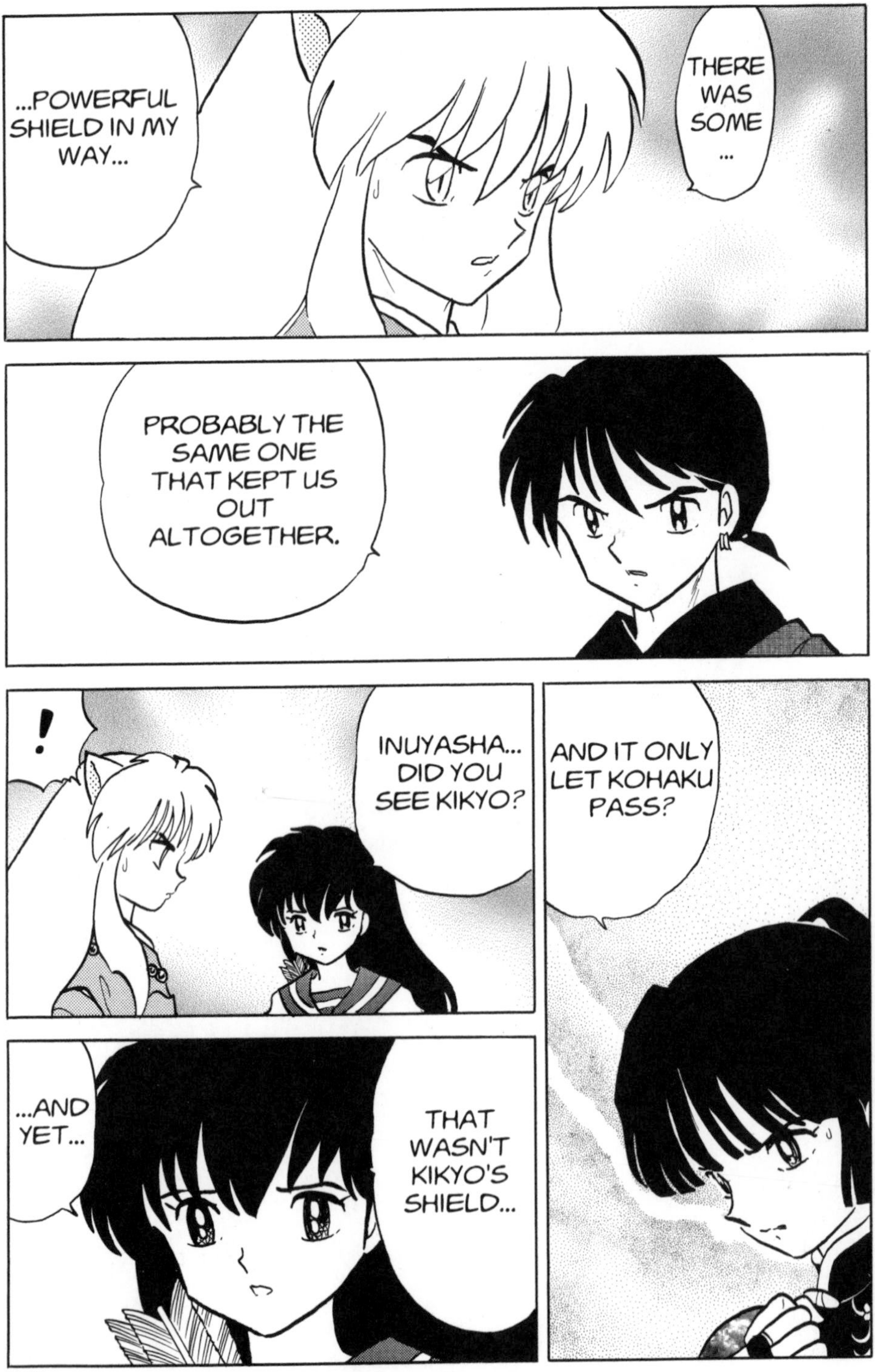
THERE WAS SOME ...
...POWERFUL SHIELD IN MY WAY...
PROBABLY THE SAME ONE THAT KEPT US OUT ALTOGETHER.
AND IT ONLY LET KOHAKU PASS?
INUYASHA... DID YOU SEE KIKYO?
!
THAT WASN'T KIKYO'S SHIELD...
...AND YET...

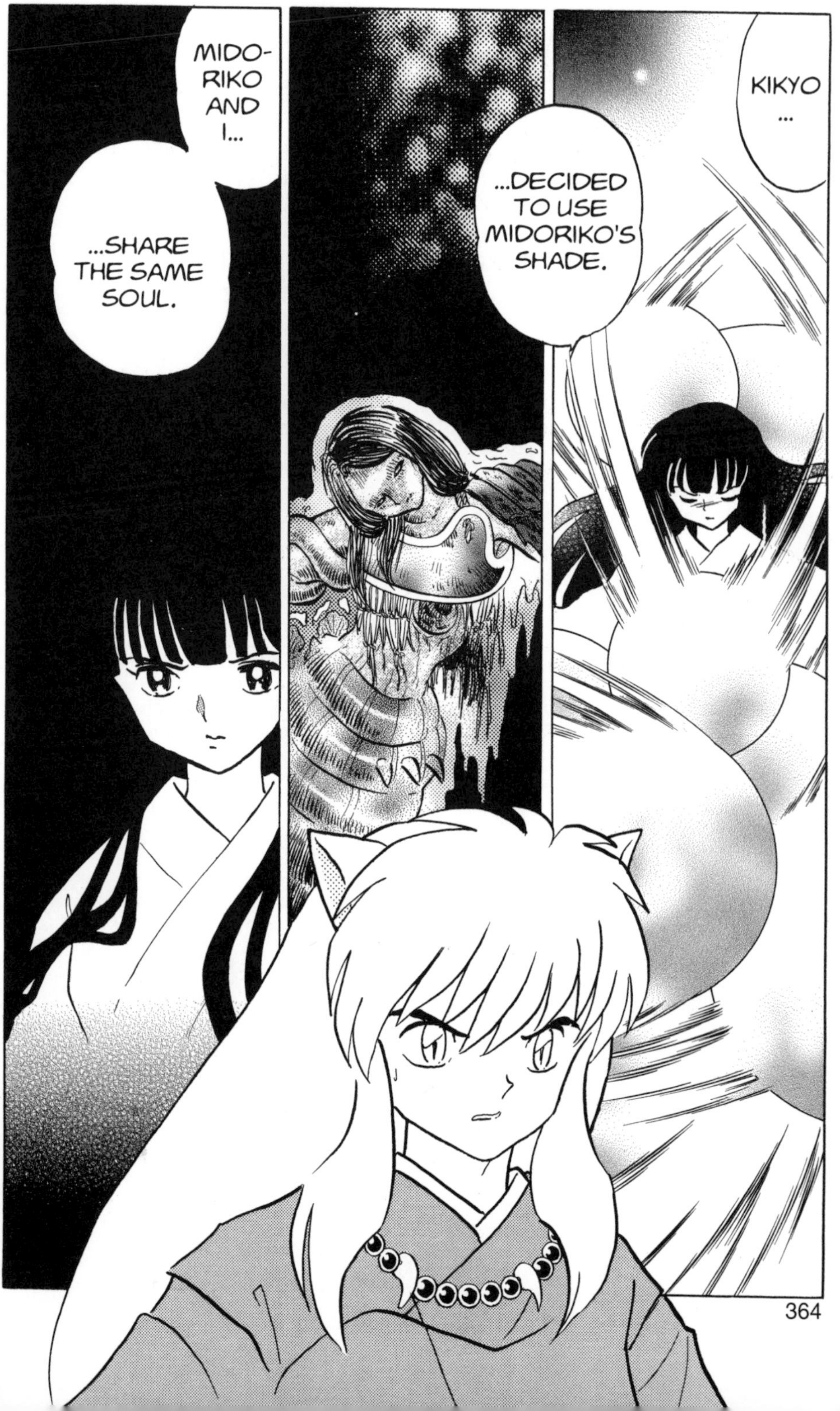
KIKYO ...
...DECIDED TO USE MIDORIKO'S SHADE.
MIDO-RIKO AND I...
...SHARE THE SAME SOUL.

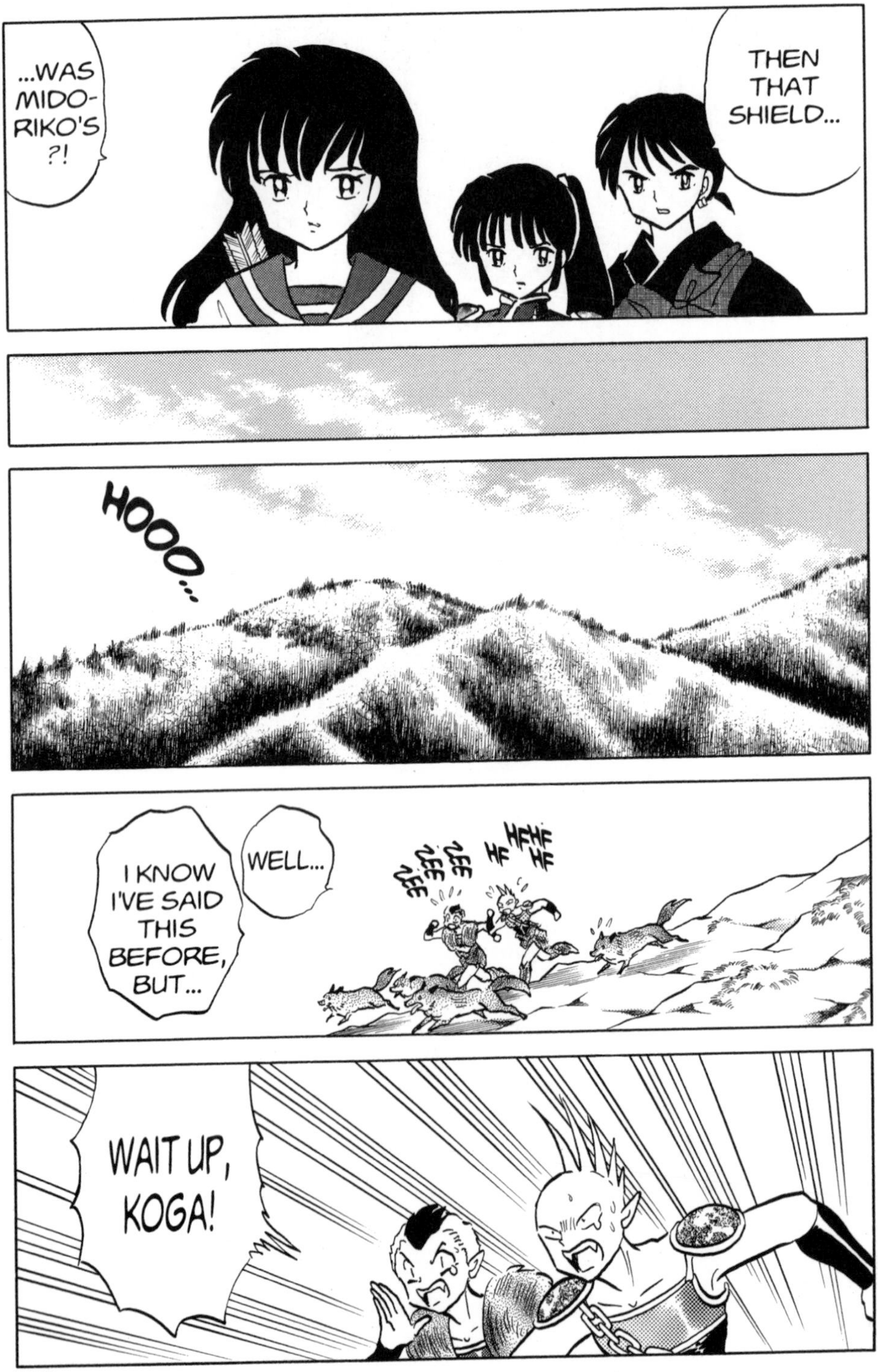
THEN THAT SHIELD...
...WAS MIDO-RIKO'S ?!
HOOOO...
HF HF HF HF
ZEE ZEE ZEE
WELL...
I KNOW I'VE SAID THIS BEFORE, BUT...
WAIT UP, KOGA!

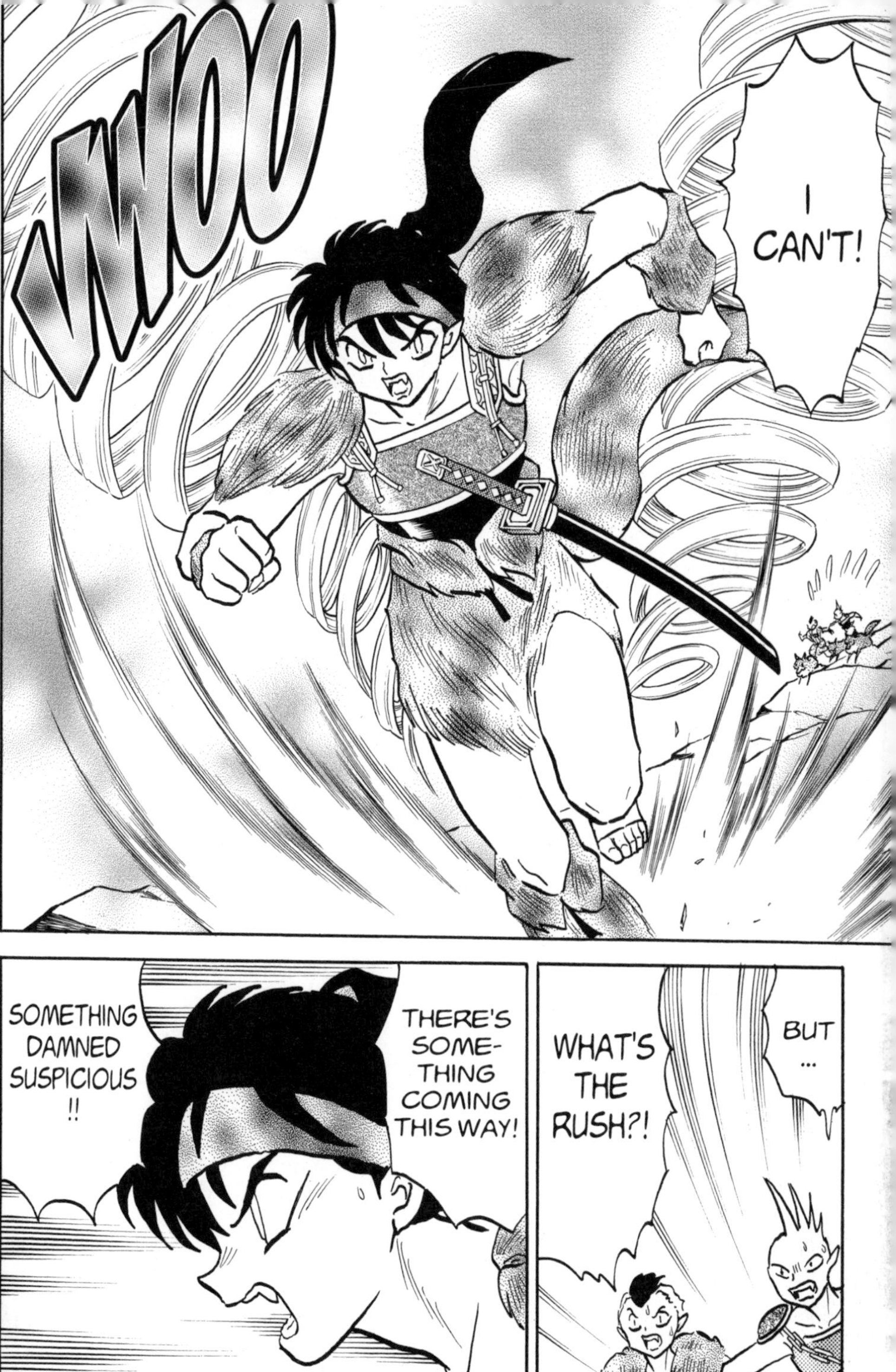
WHOO
I CAN'T!
BUT ...
WHAT'S THE RUSH?!
THERE'S SOMETHING COMING THIS WAY!
SOMETHING DAMNED SUSPICIOUS!!

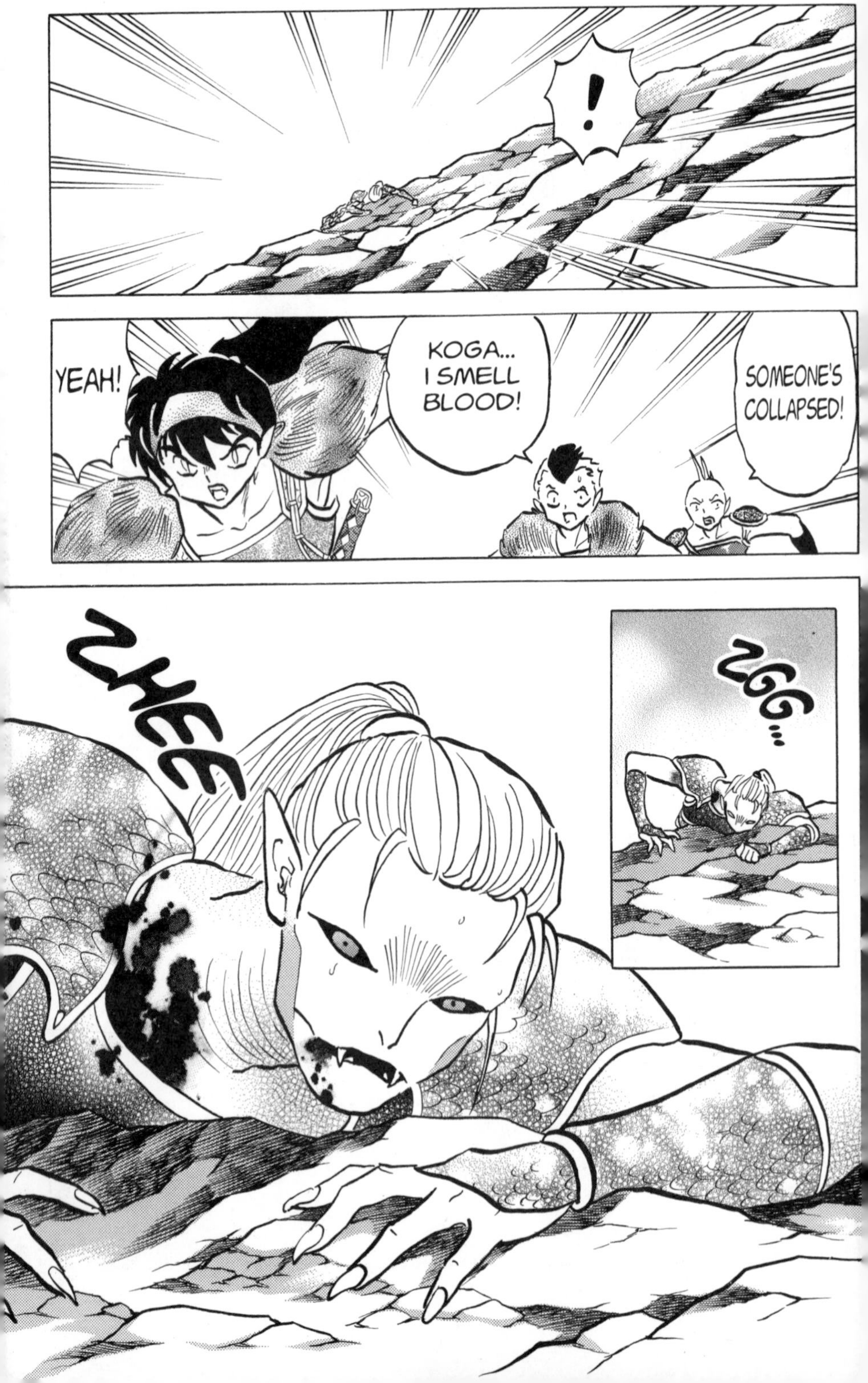
!
SOMEONE'S COLLAPSED!
KOGA... I SMELL BLOOD!
YEAH!
ZGG...
ZHEE

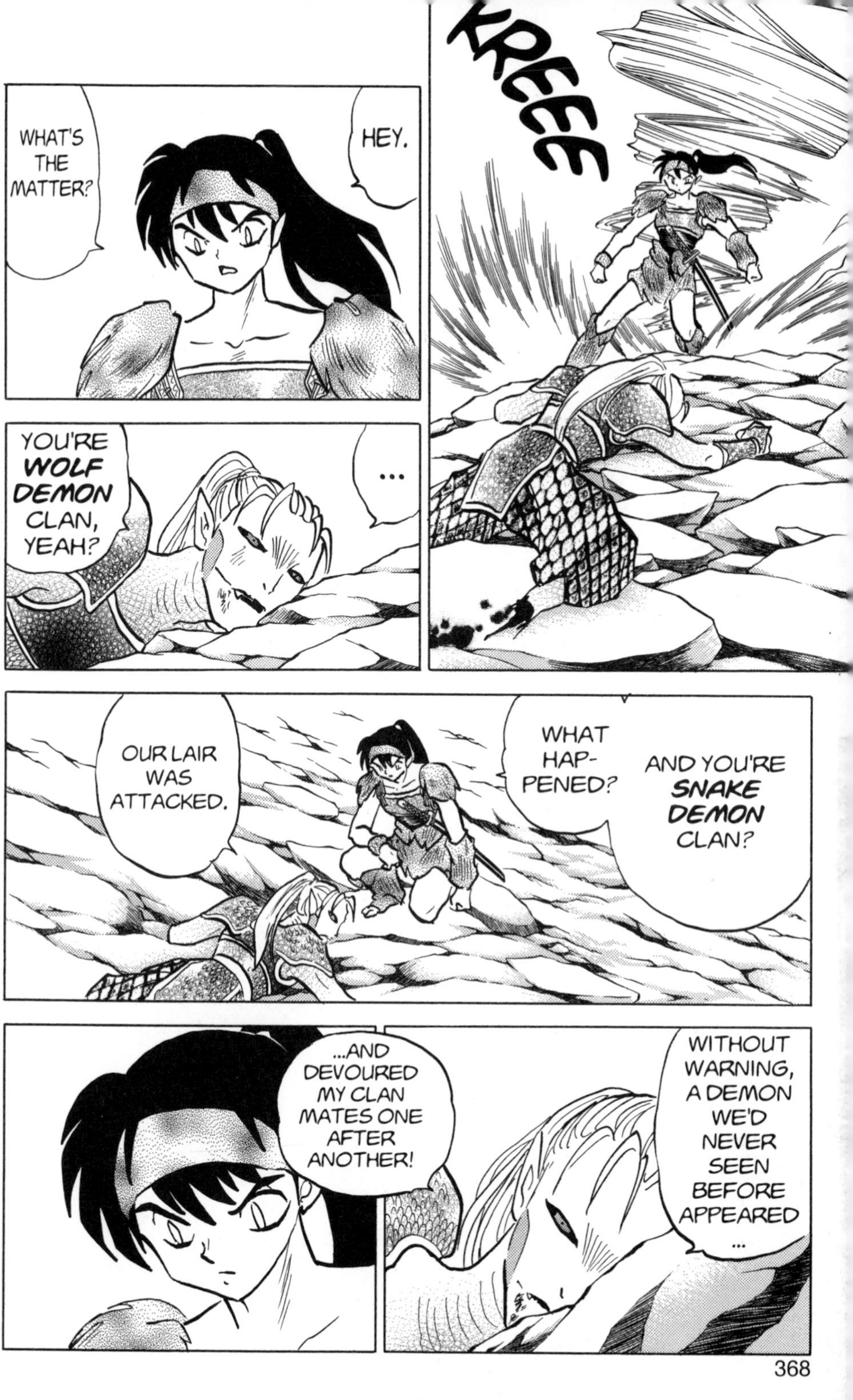
KREEE
HEY.
WHAT'S THE MATTER?
...
YOU'RE **WOLF DEMON** CLAN, YEAH?
AND YOU'RE **SNAKE DEMON** CLAN?
WHAT HAP-PENED?
OUR LAIR WAS ATTACKED.
WITHOUT WARNING, A DEMON WE'D NEVER SEEN BEFORE APPEARED ...
...AND DEVOURED MY CLAN MATES ONE AFTER ANOTHER!

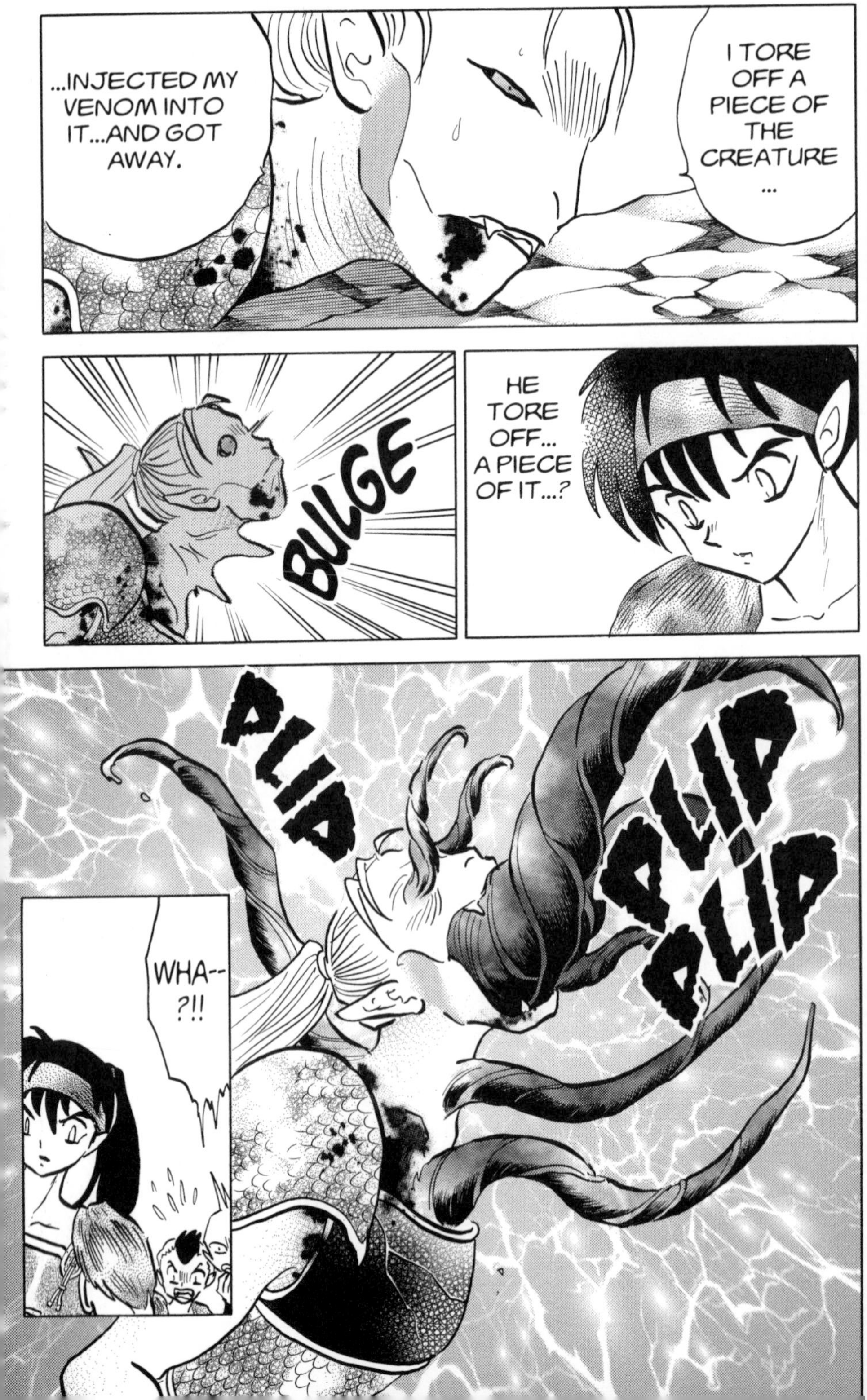
I TORE OFF A PIECE OF THE CREATURE ...
...INJECTED MY VENOM INTO IT...AND GOT AWAY.
HE TORE OFF... A PIECE OF IT...?
BULGE
PLIP
PLIP
PLIP
WHA-- ?!!

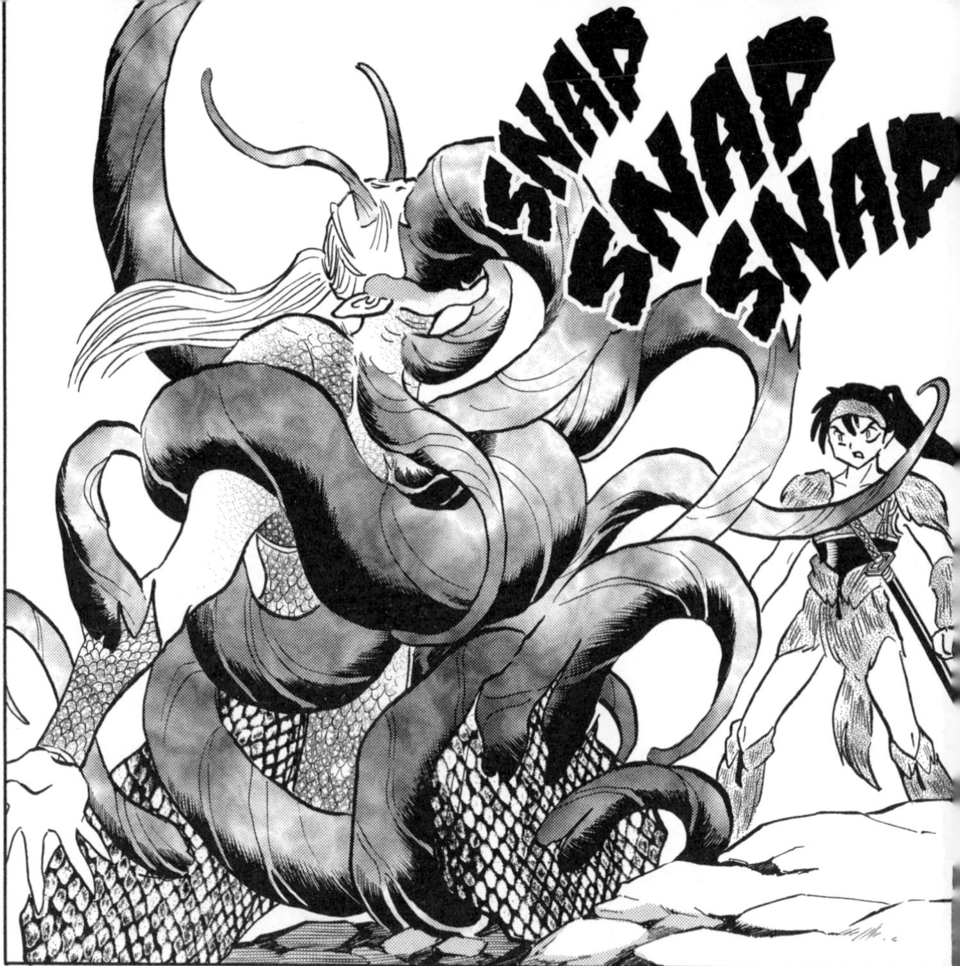
SNAP SNAP SNAP
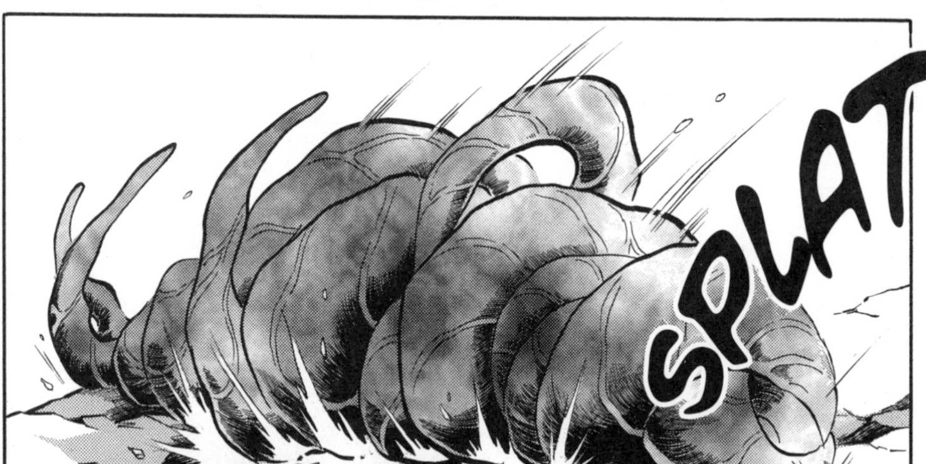
SPLAT

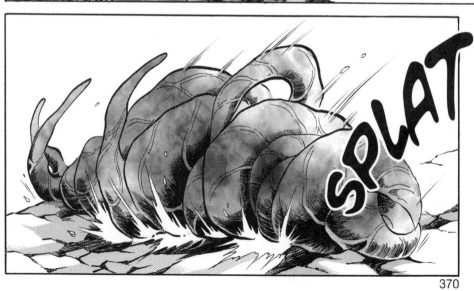

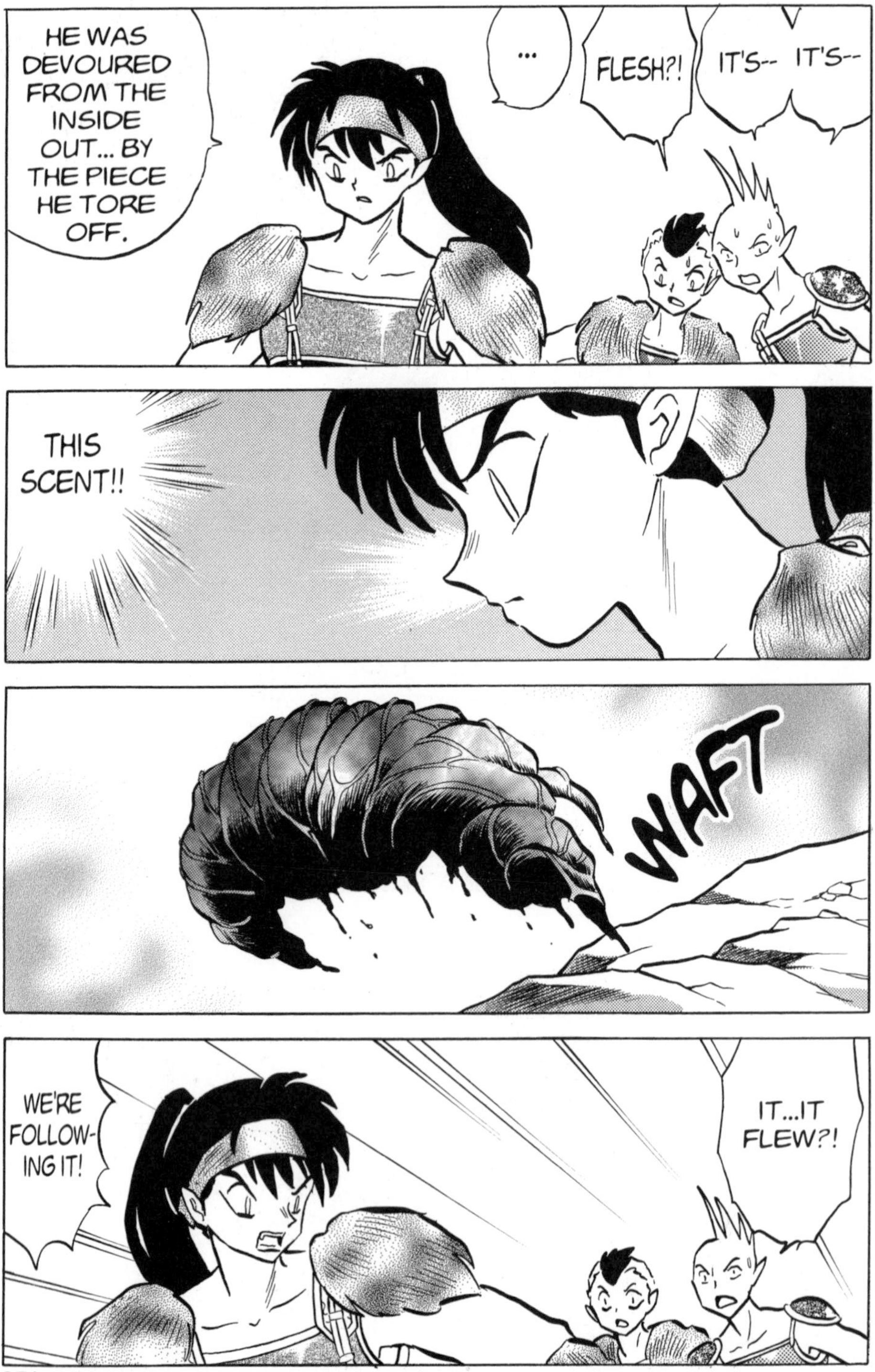
IT'S-- IT'S--
FLESH?!
...
HE WAS DEVOURED FROM THE INSIDE OUT... BY THE PIECE HE TORE OFF.
THIS SCENT!!
WAFT
IT...IT FLEW?!
WE'RE FOLLOW-ING IT!

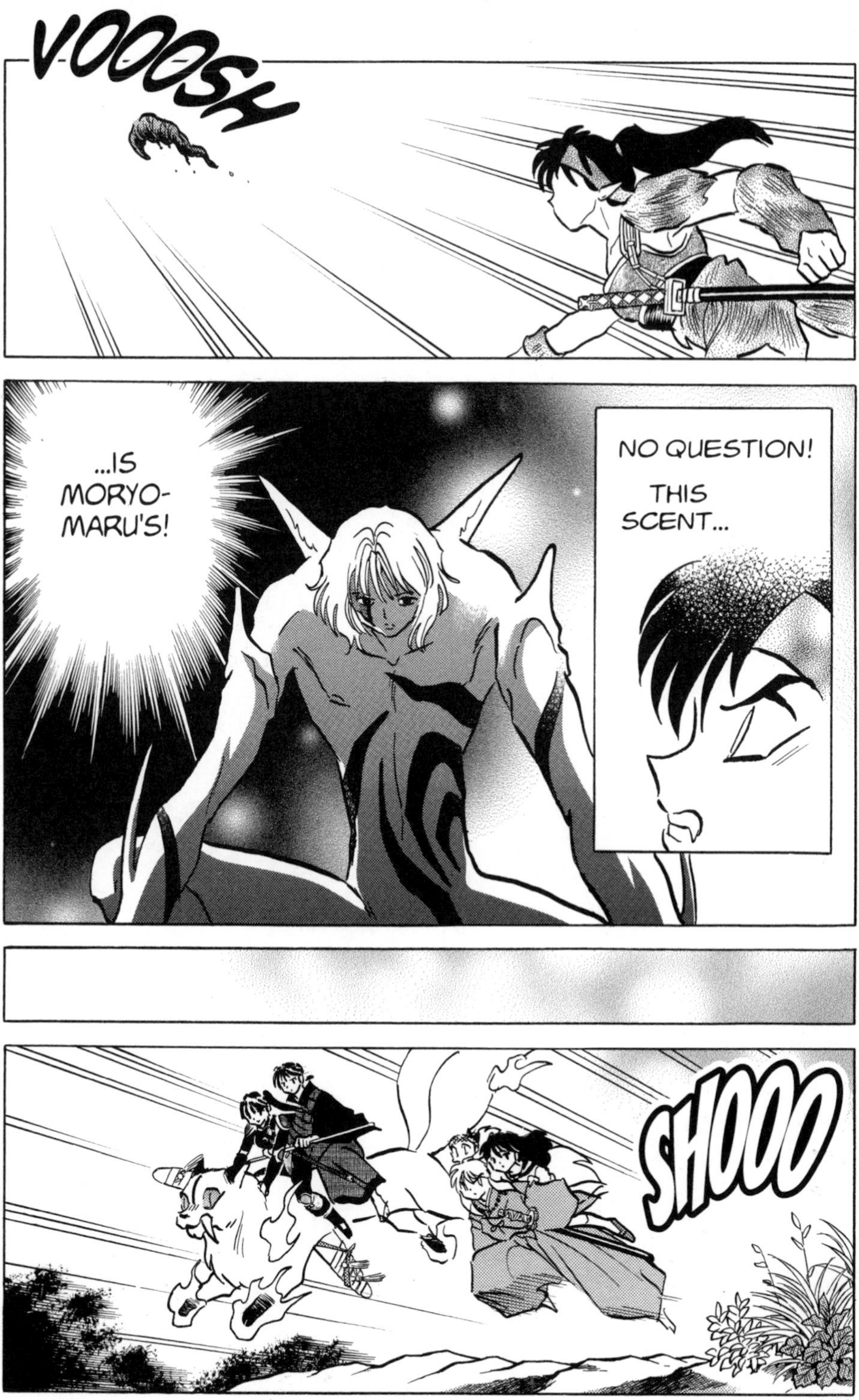
V-OOOSH
NO QUESTION!
THIS SCENT...
...IS MORYO-MARU'S!
SHOOO

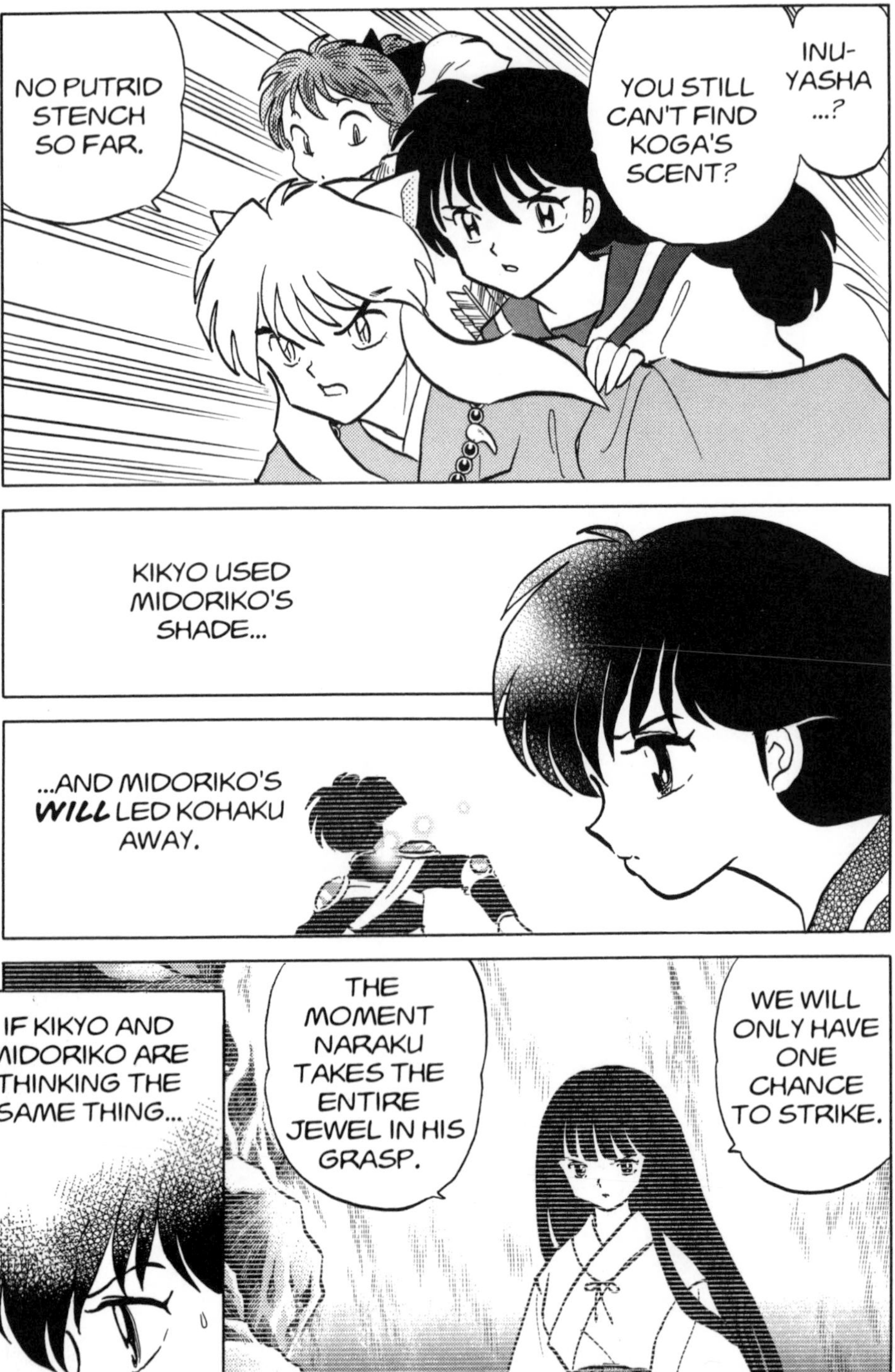
INU-YASHA ...?
YOU STILL CAN'T FIND KOGA'S SCENT?
NO PUTRID STENCH SO FAR.
KIKYO USED MIDORIKO'S SHADE...
...AND MIDORIKO'S WILL LED KOHAKU AWAY.
WE WILL ONLY HAVE ONE CHANCE TO STRIKE.
THE MOMENT NARAKU TAKES THE ENTIRE JEWEL IN HIS GRASP.
IF KIKYO AND MIDORIKO ARE THINKING THE SAME THING...

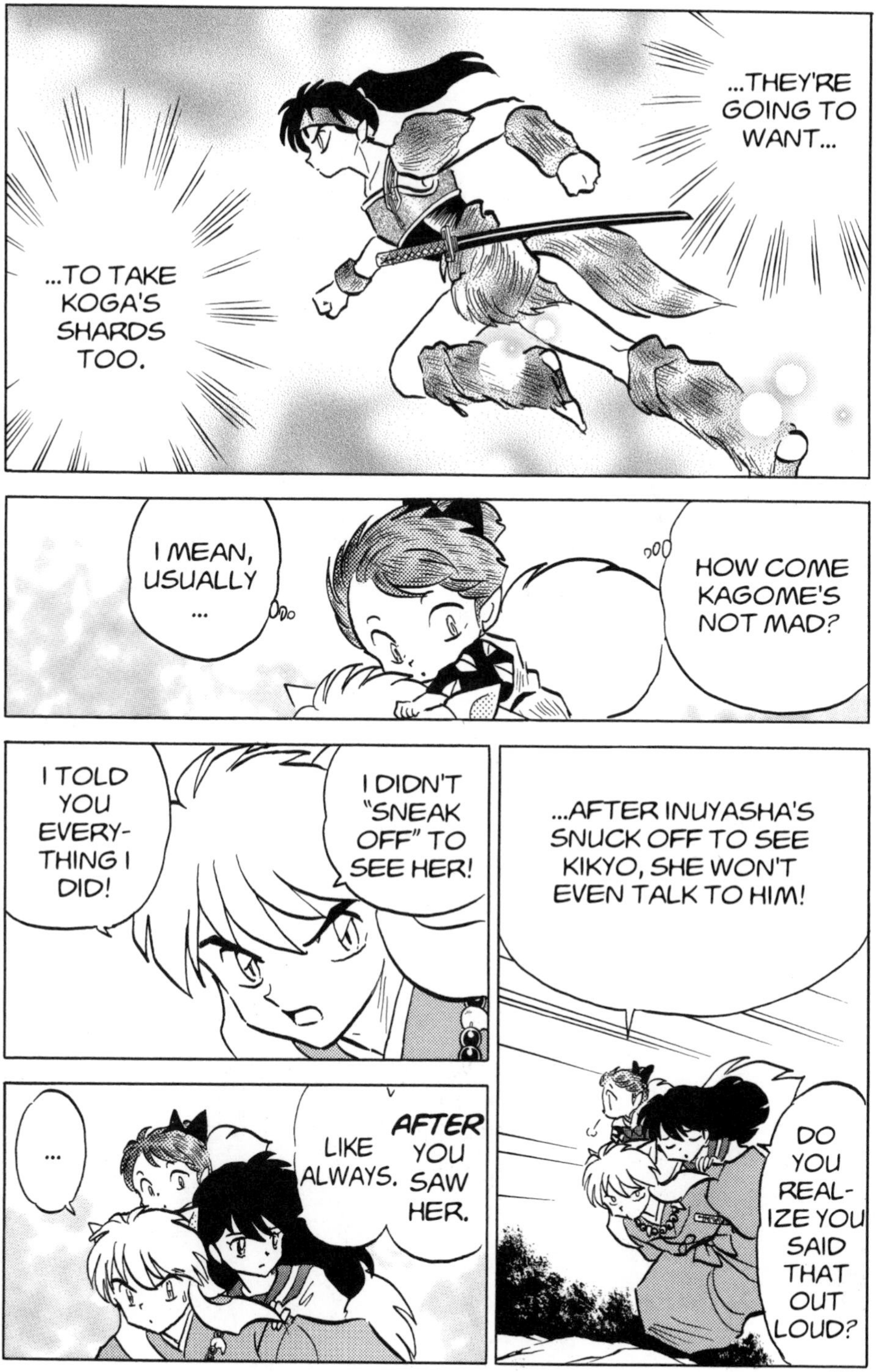
...THEY'RE GOING TO WANT...
...TO TAKE KOGA'S SHARDS TOO.
HOW COME KAGOME'S NOT MAD?
I MEAN, USUALLY ...
...AFTER INUYASHA'S SNUCK OFF TO SEE KIKYO, SHE WON'T EVEN TALK TO HIM!
DO YOU REALIZE YOU SAID THAT OUT LOUD?
I DIDN'T "SNEAK OFF" TO SEE HER!
I TOLD YOU EVERYTHING I DID!
AFTER YOU SAW HER.
LIKE ALWAYS.
...

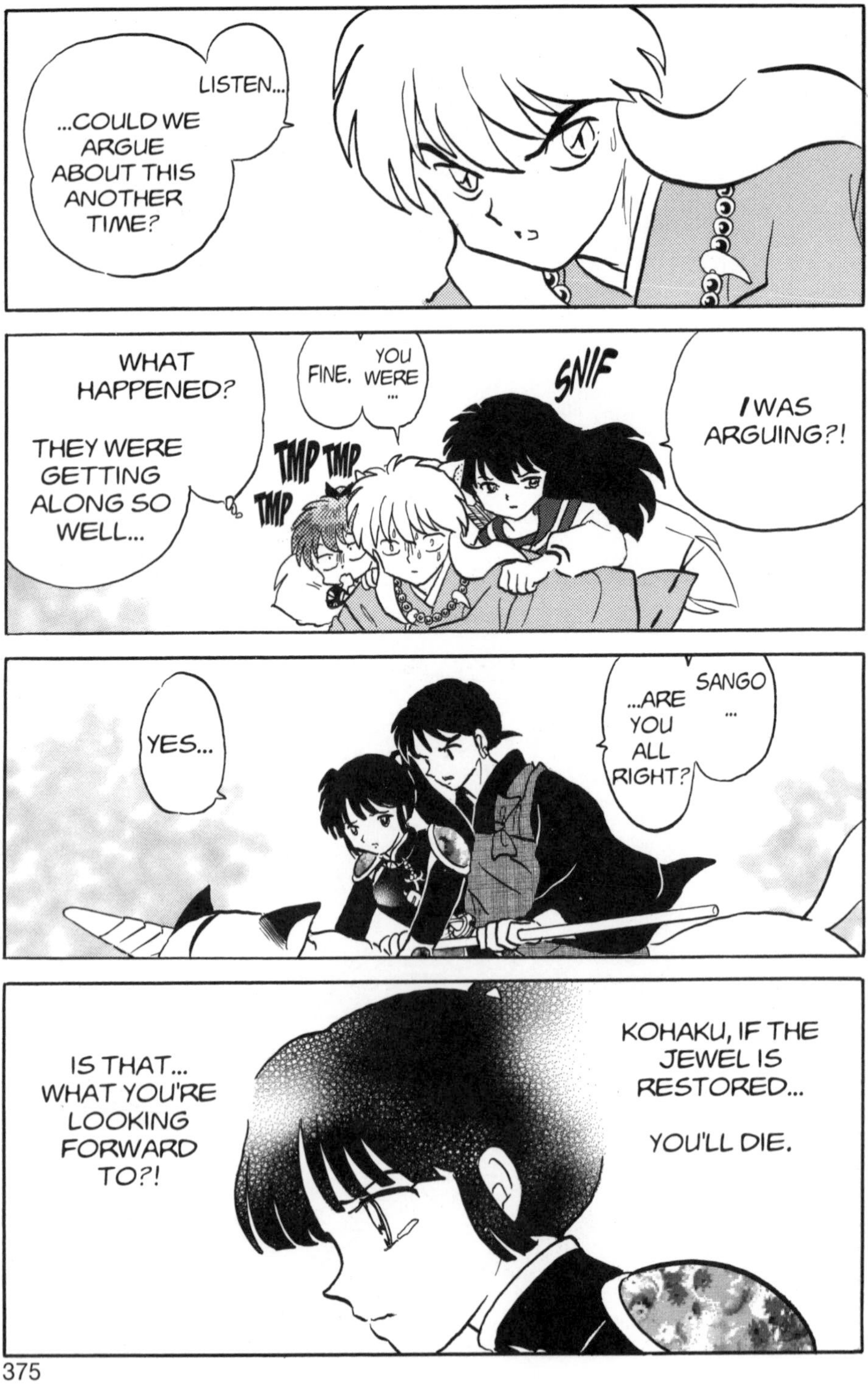
LISTEN... ...COULD WE ARGUE ABOUT THIS ANOTHER TIME?
I WAS ARGUING?!
SNIF
YOU WERE... FINE.
TMP TMP TMP
WHAT HAPPENED? THEY WERE GETTING ALONG SO WELL...
SANGO... ...ARE YOU ALL RIGHT?
YES...
KOHAKU, IF THE JEWEL IS RESTORED... YOU'LL DIE.
IS THAT... WHAT YOU'RE LOOKING FORWARD TO?!

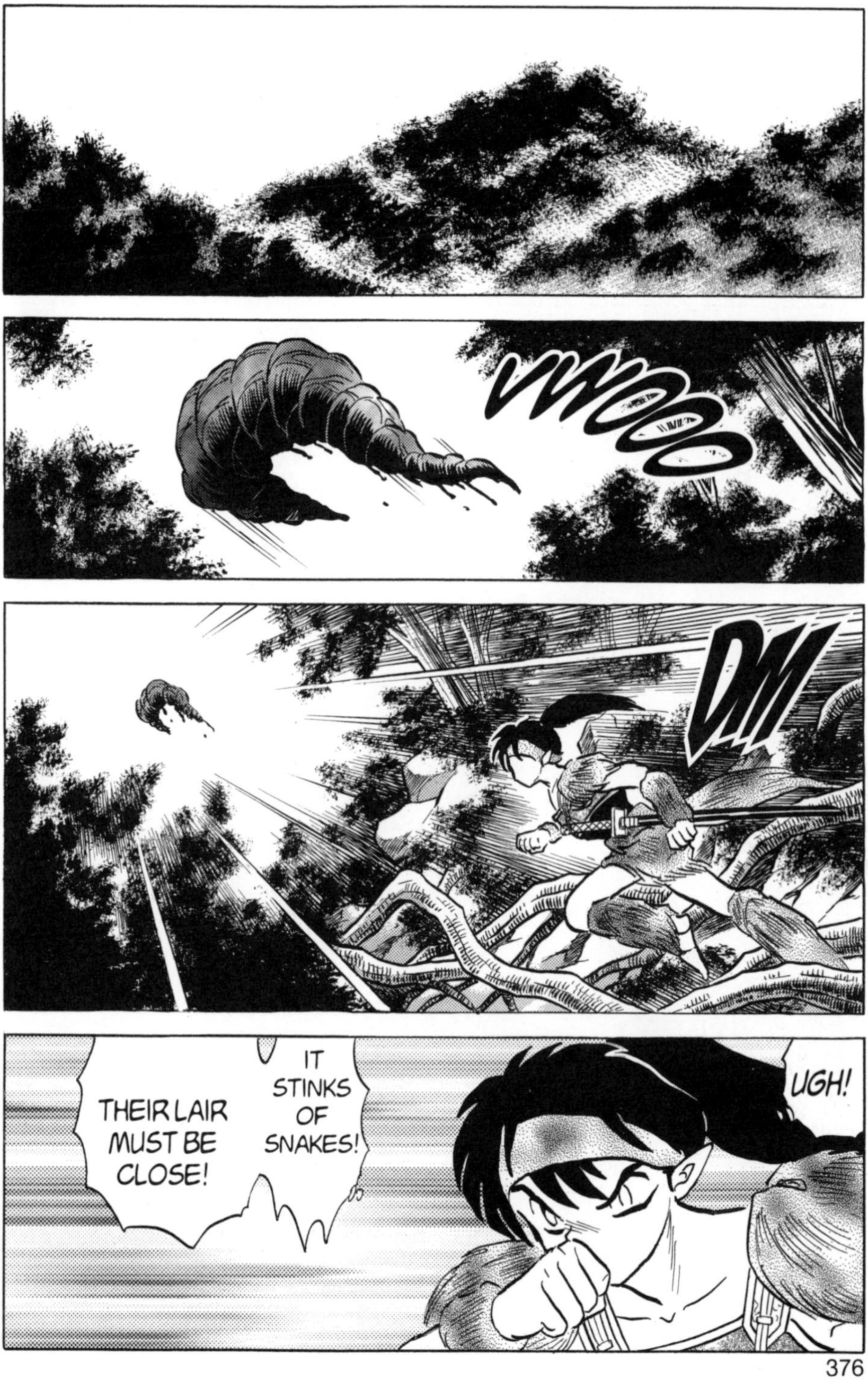
VWOOO
DM
UGH!
IT STINKS OF SNAKES!
THEIR LAIR MUST BE CLOSE!

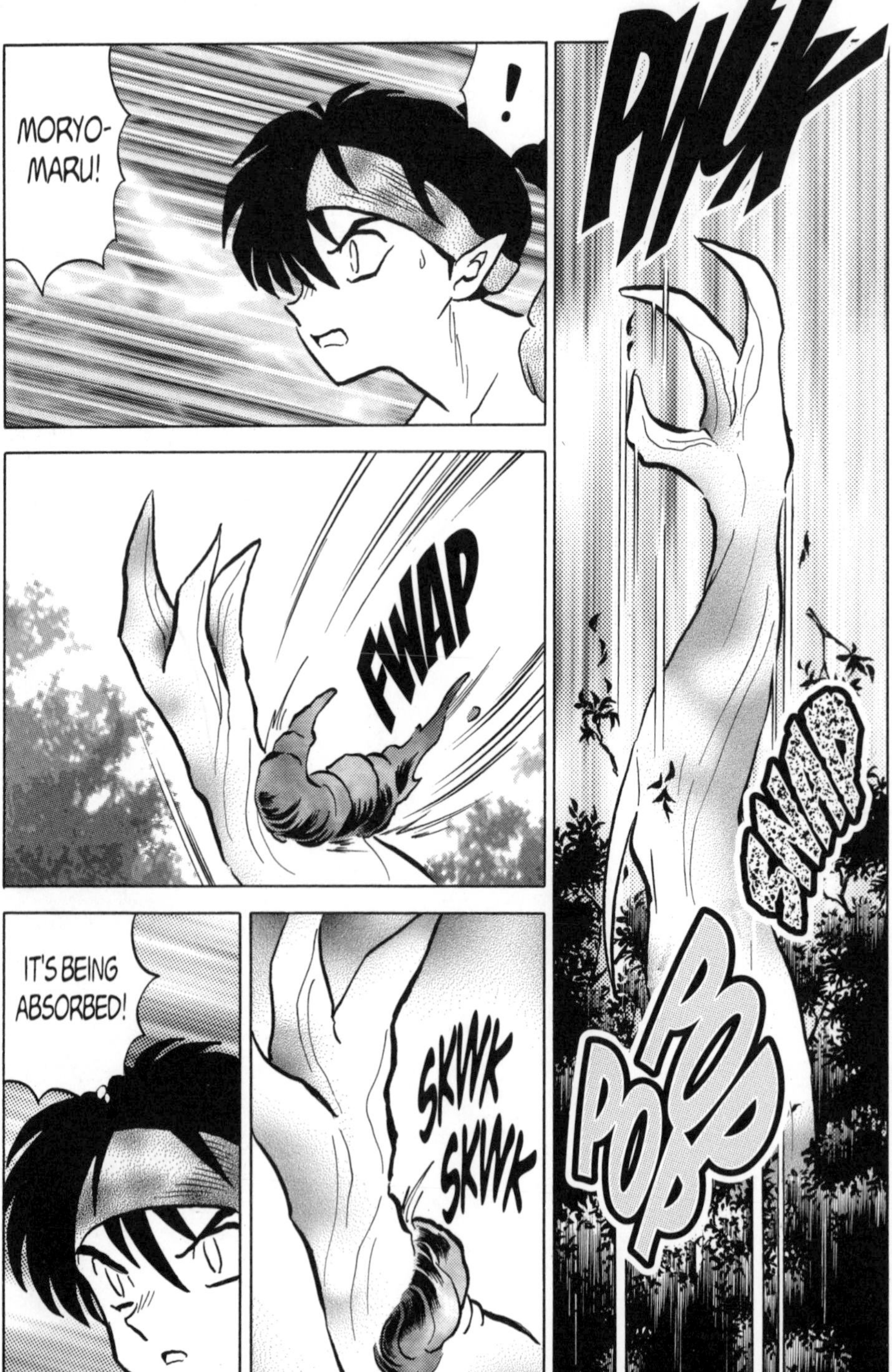
PIKK
SNAP
POP POP
!
MORYO-MARU!
FWAP
SKWK SKWK
IT'S BEING ABSORBED!

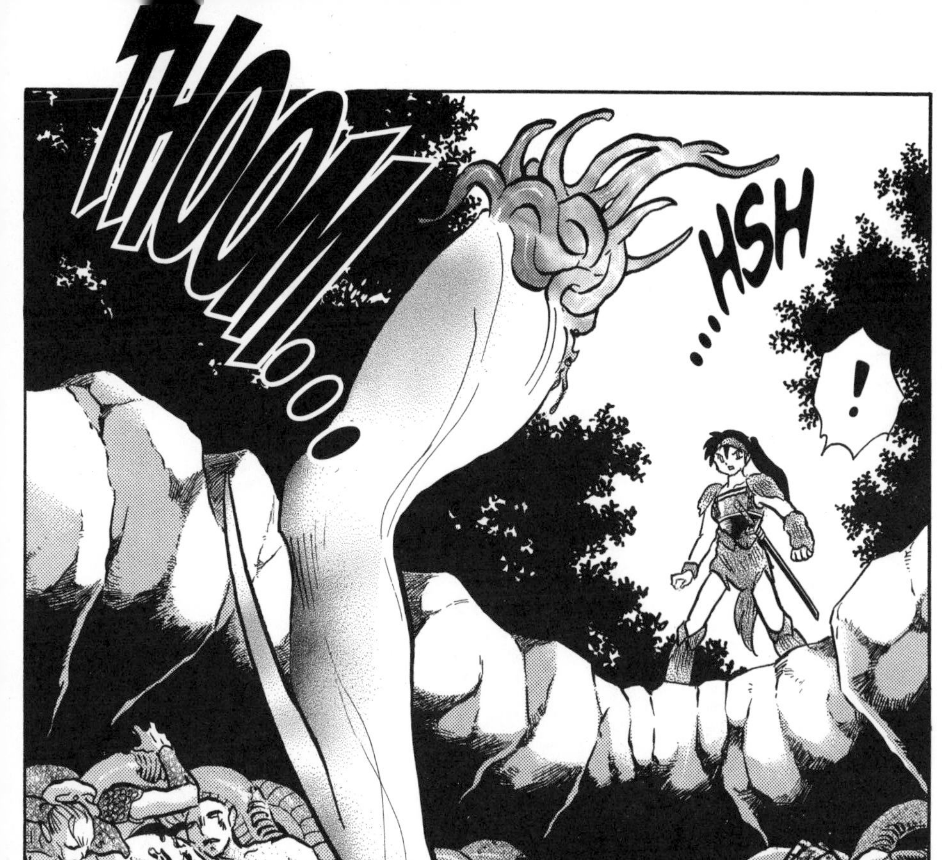
THOOM...
...HSH
!

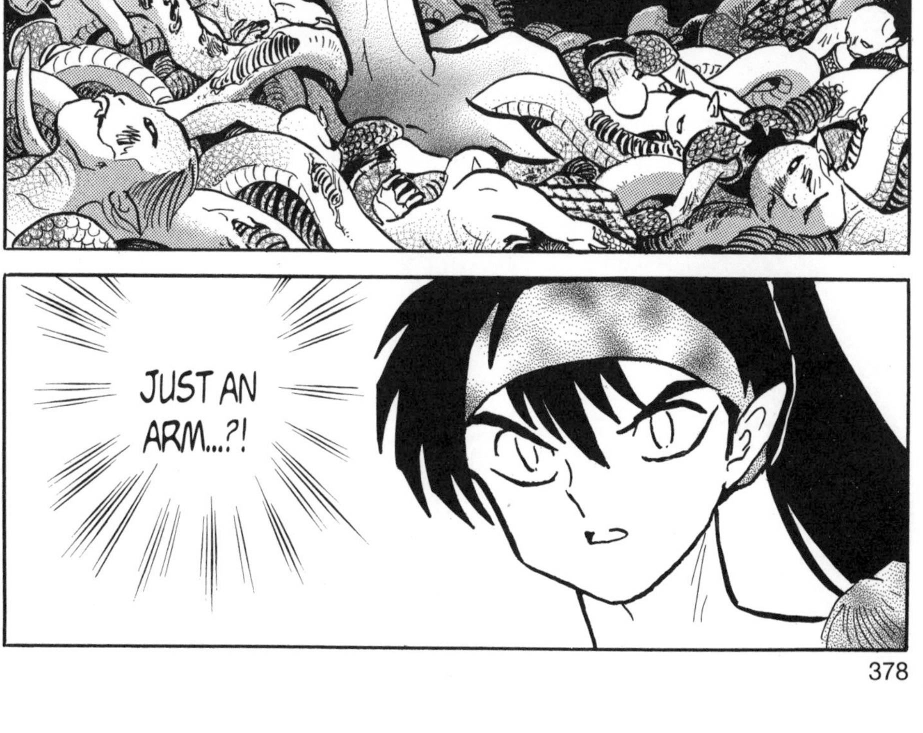
JUST AN ARM...?!

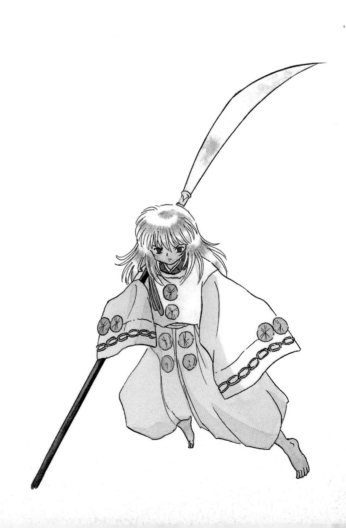

InuYasha

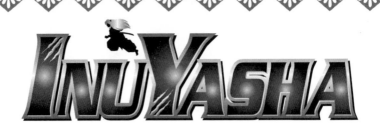

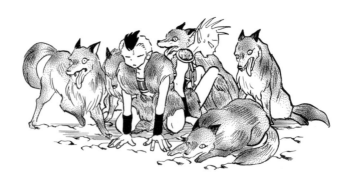

Volume 39

Changing Shard

SCROLL ONE
CHANGING SHARD

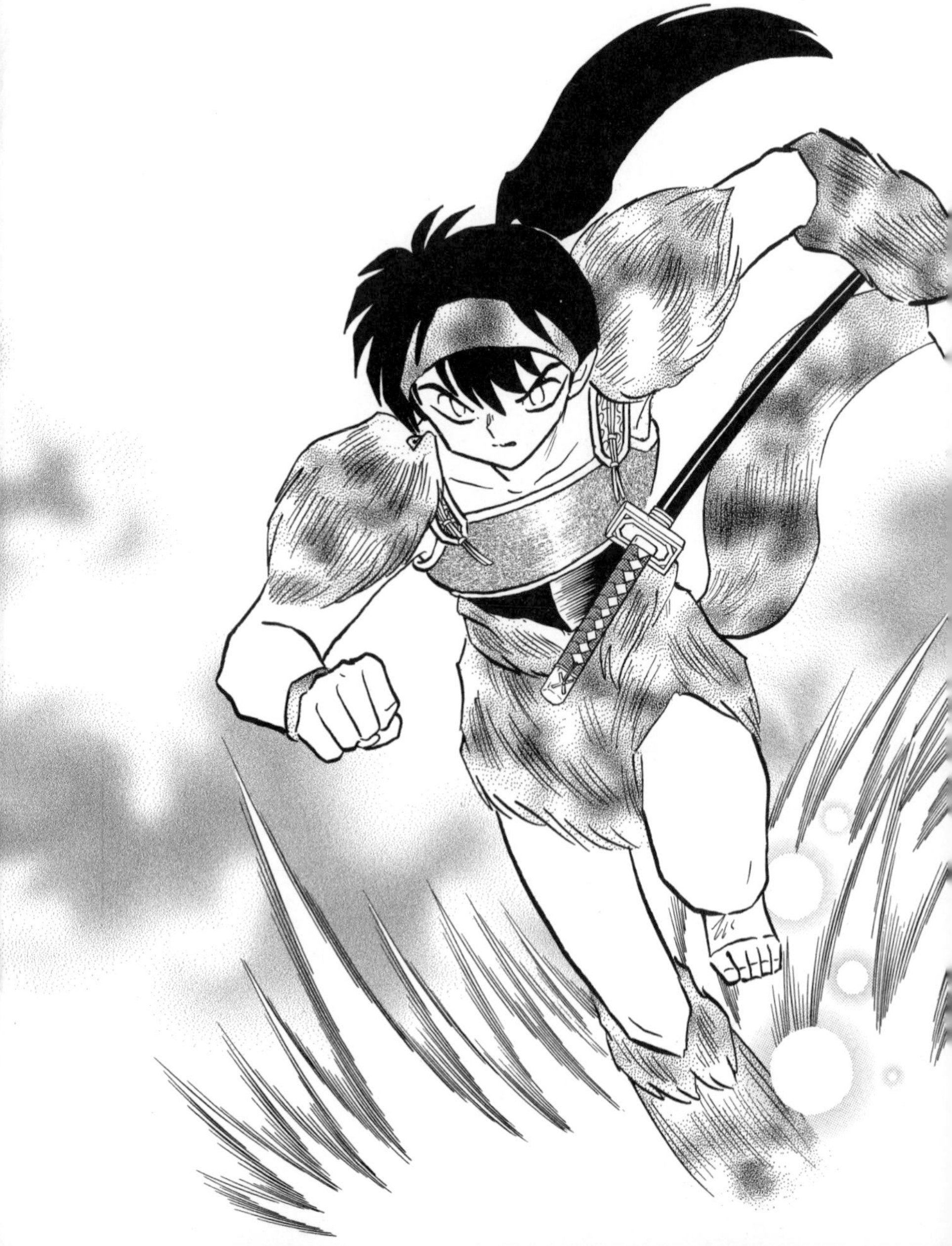

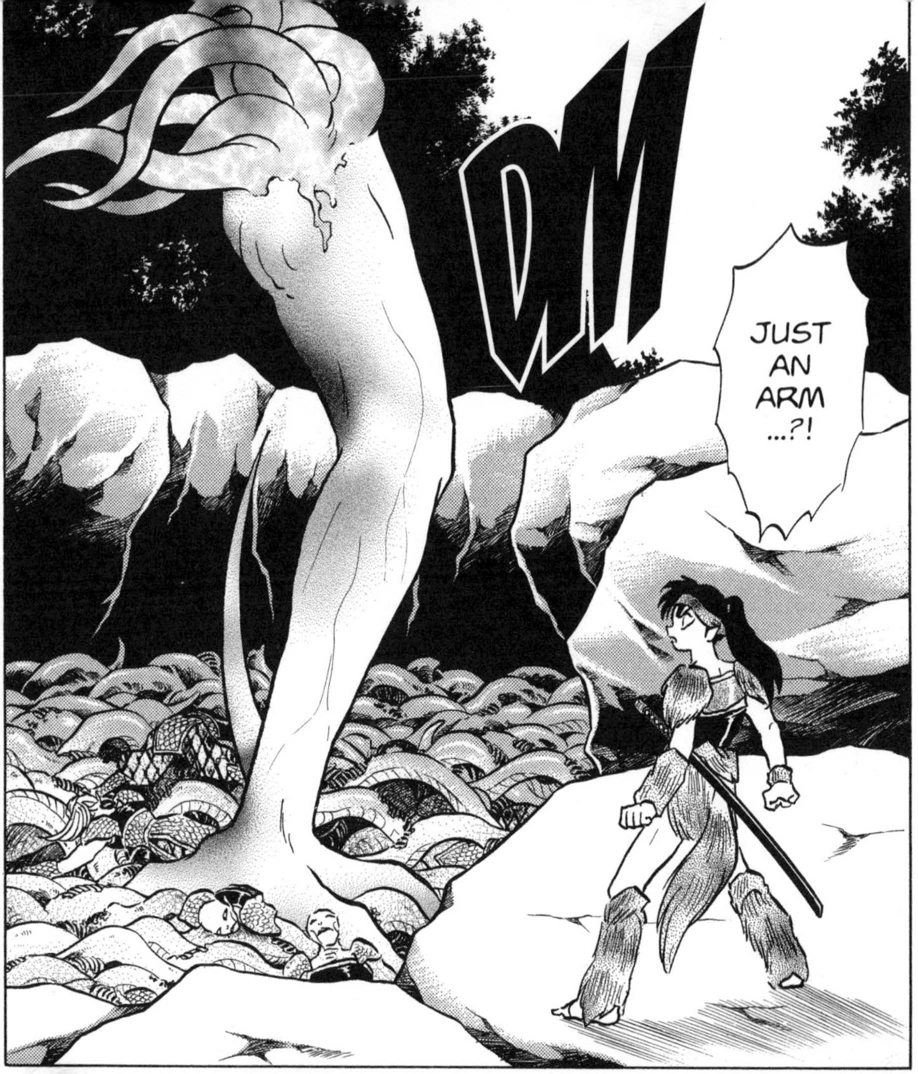
DM
JUST AN ARM ...?!

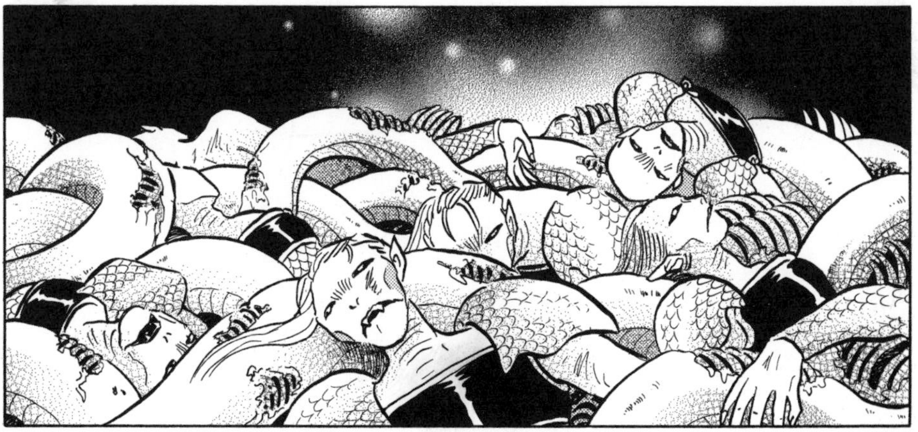

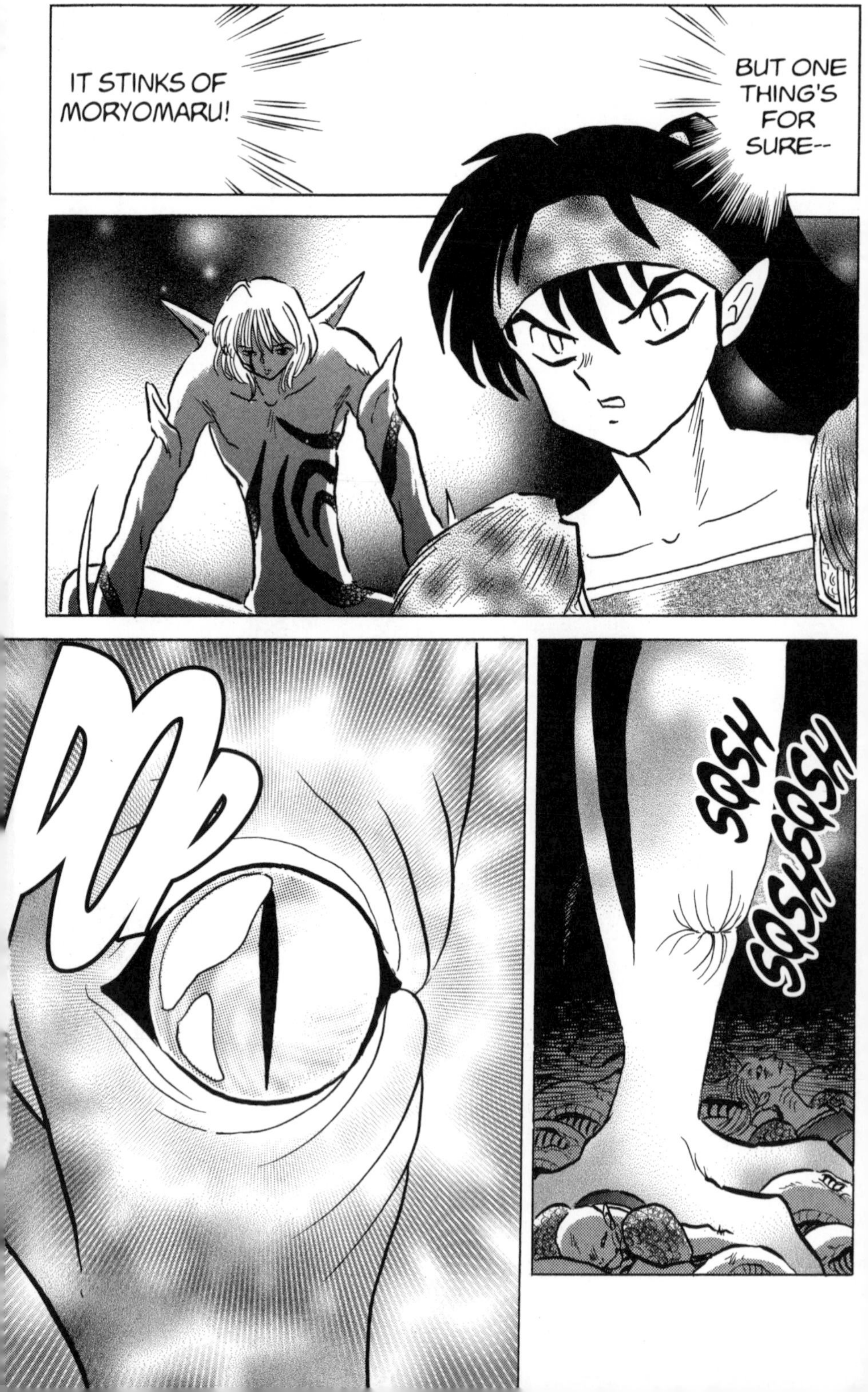
IT STINKS OF MORYOMARU!
BUT ONE THING'S FOR SURE--
SOSH
SOSHSOSH

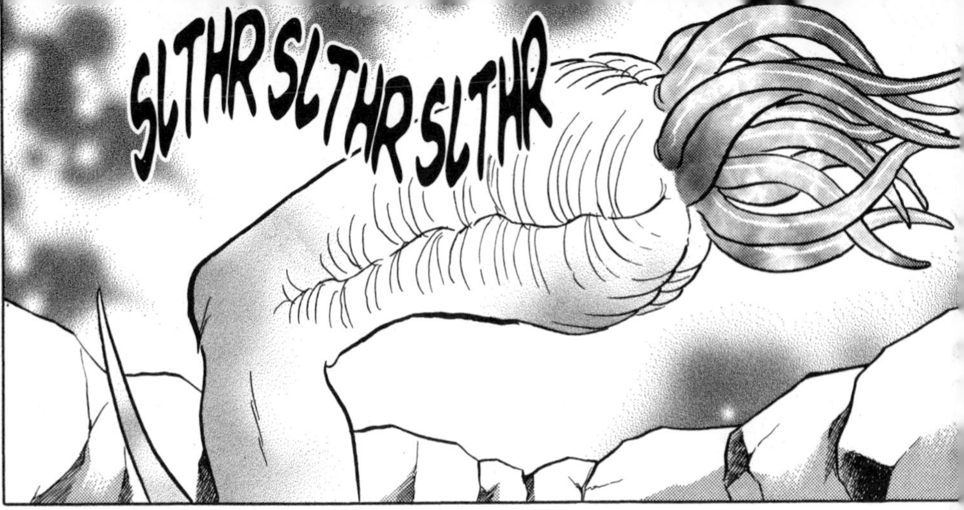
SLTHR SLTHR SLTHR
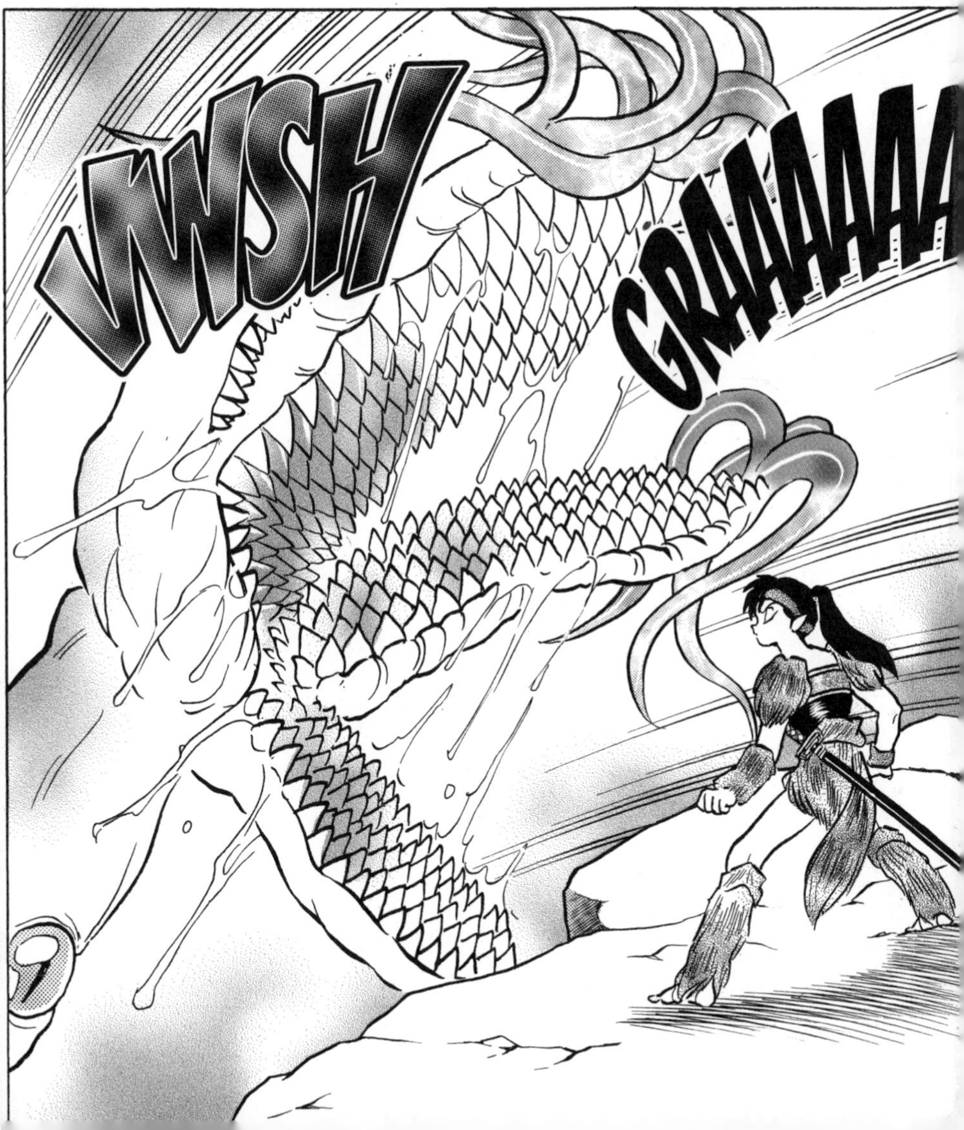
GRAAAAAA
VWISH

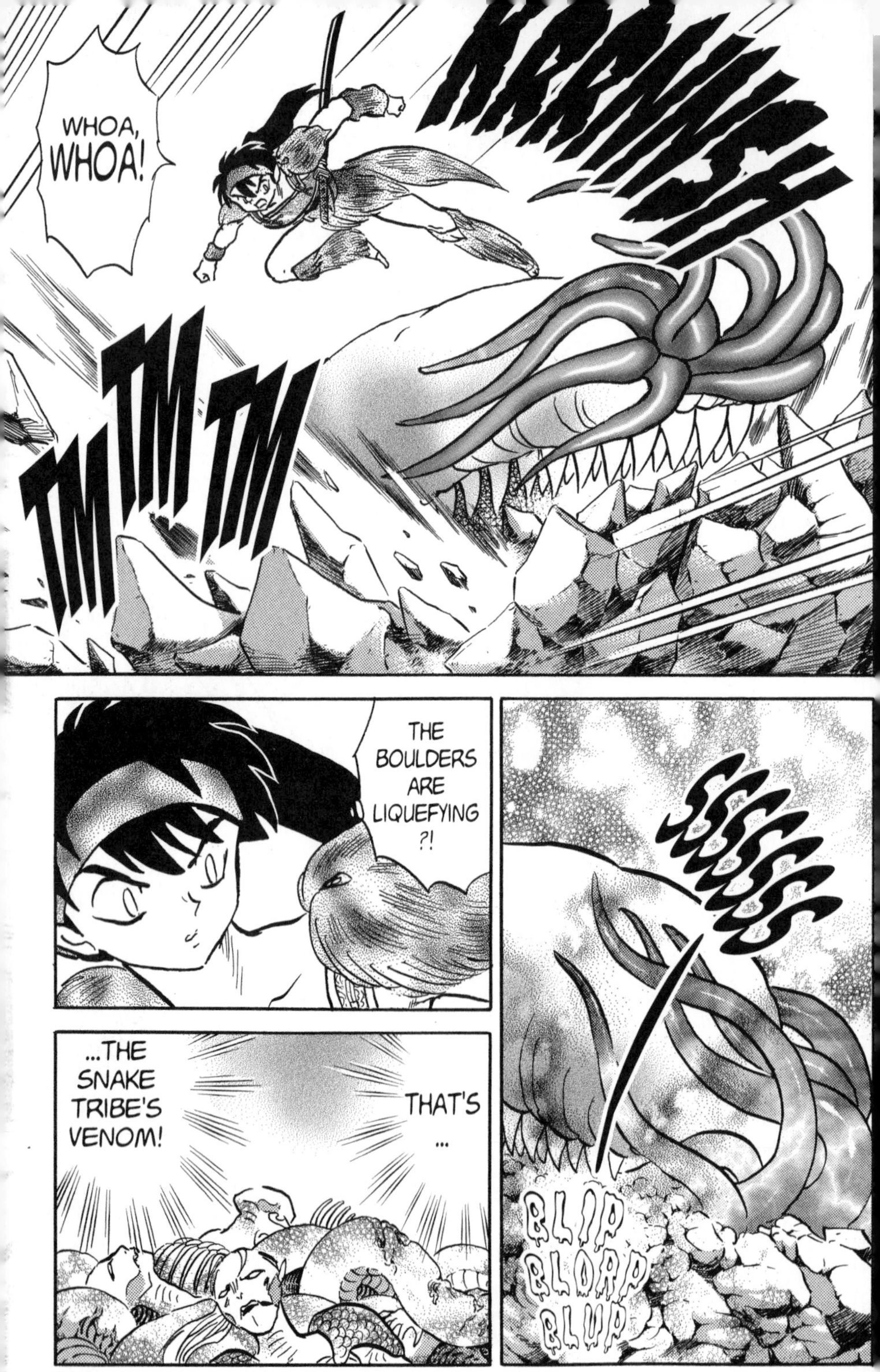
WHOA, WHOA!
TM TM TM
SSSSSS
BLIP BLORP BLUP
THE BOULDERS ARE LIQUEFYING ?!
THAT'S ...
...THE SNAKE TRIBE'S VENOM!

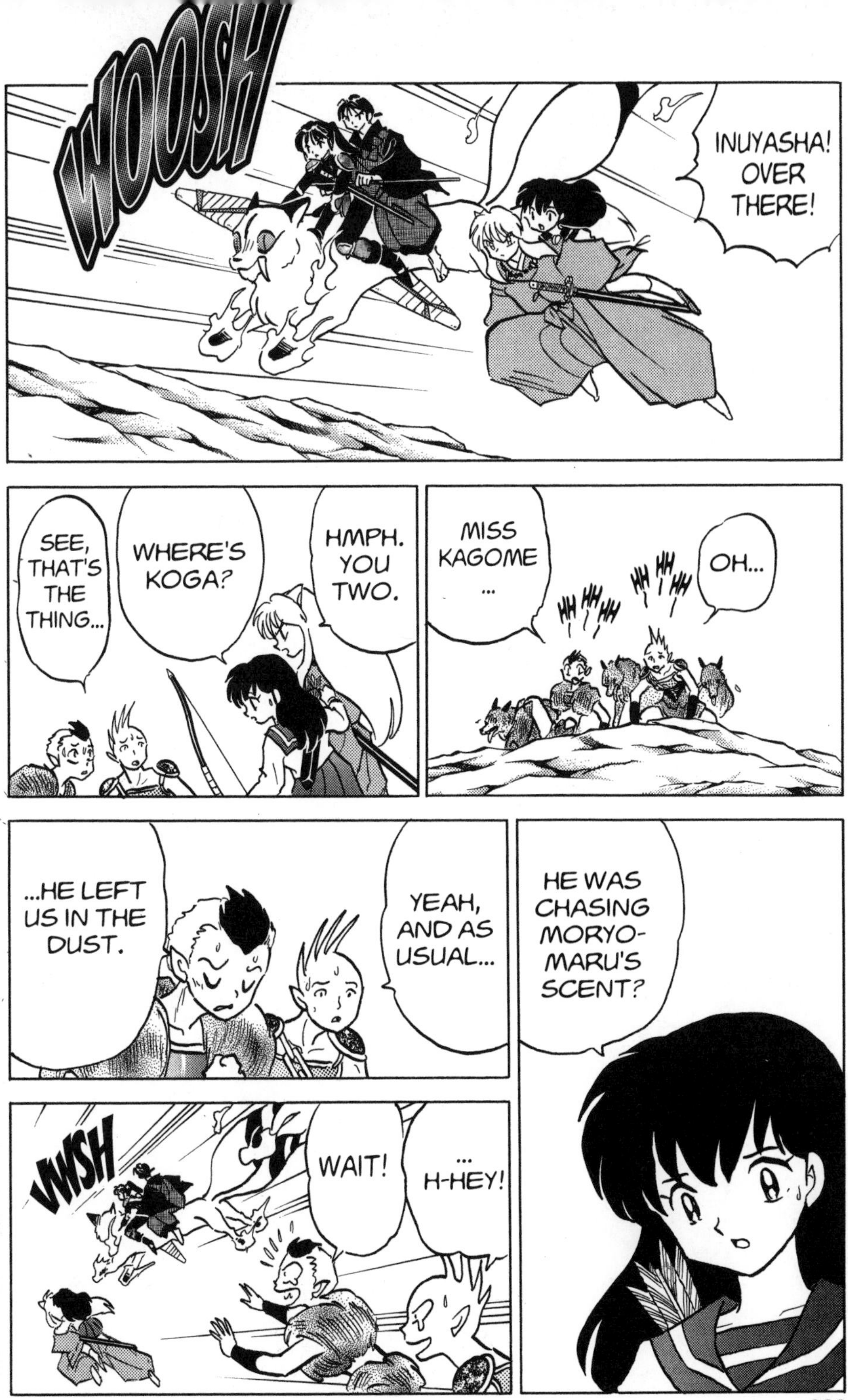
INUYASHA! OVER THERE!
WOOSH
OH...
MISS KAGOME ...
HH HH HH
HH HH HH
HMPH. YOU TWO.
WHERE'S KOGA?
SEE, THAT'S THE THING...
HE WAS CHASING MORYO-MARU'S SCENT?
YEAH, AND AS USUAL...
...HE LEFT US IN THE DUST.
... H-HEY!
WAIT!
VWSH

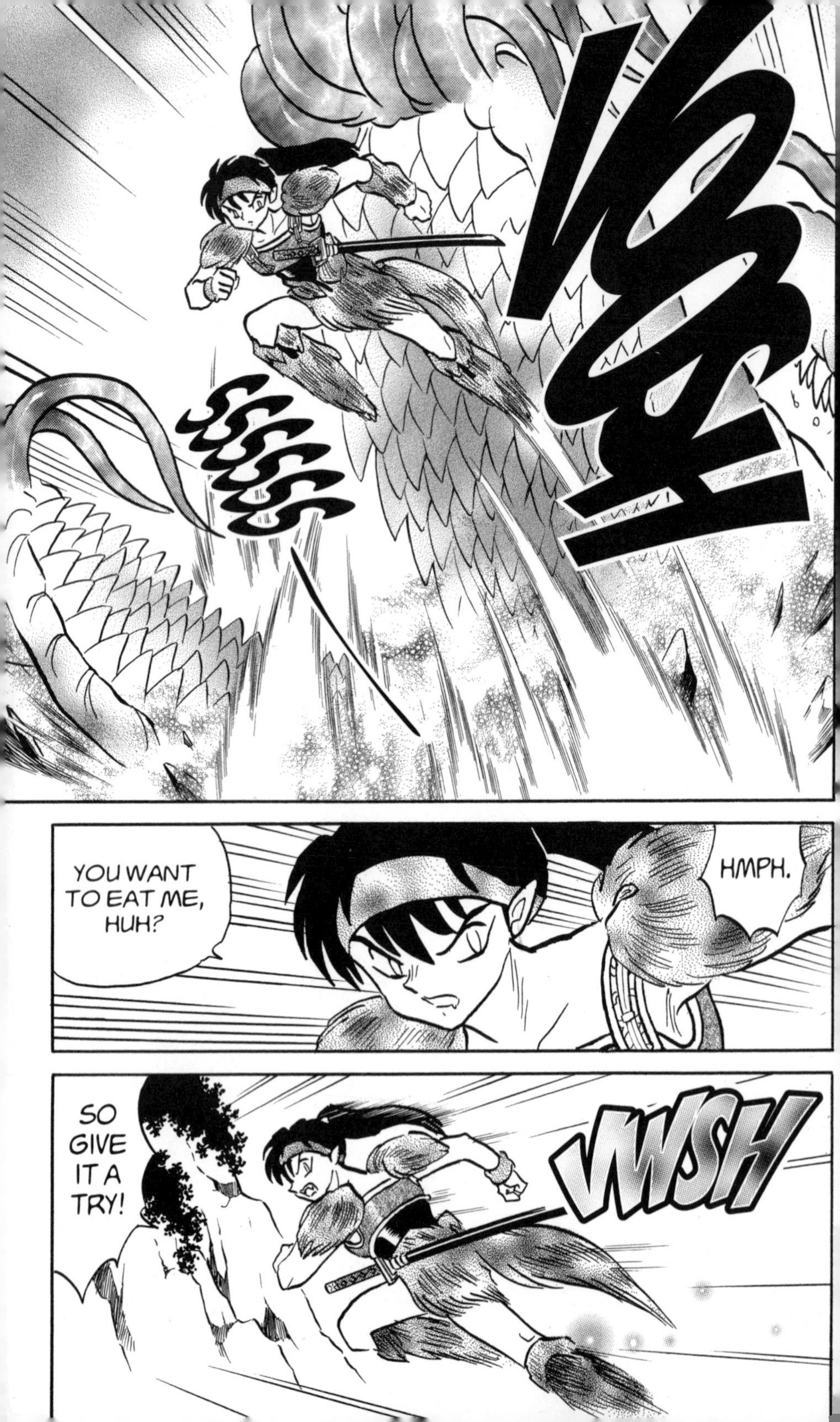
VOOSH!
SSSSSS
HMPH.
YOU WANT TO EAT ME, HUH?
SO GIVE IT A TRY!
VWSH

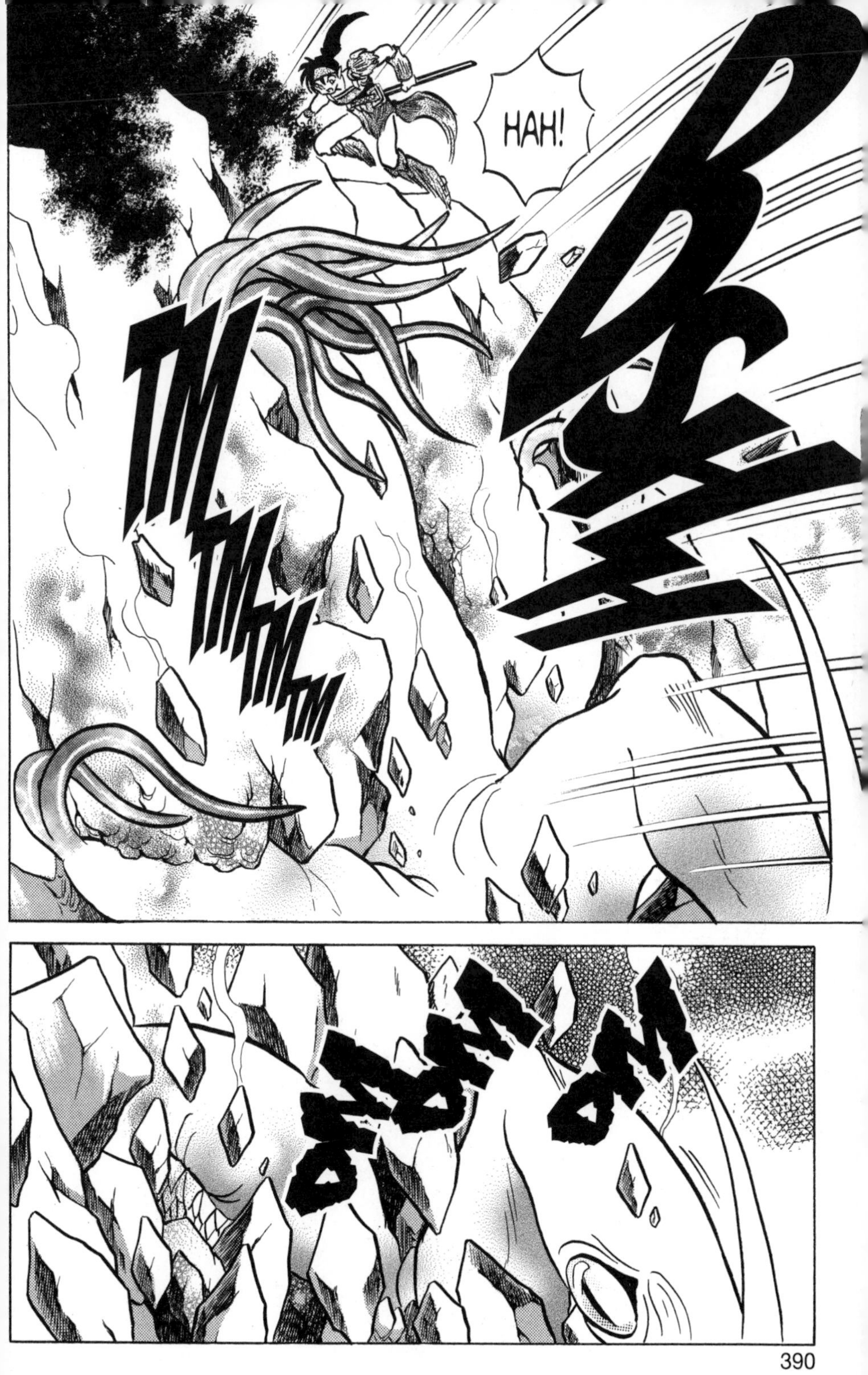
HAH!

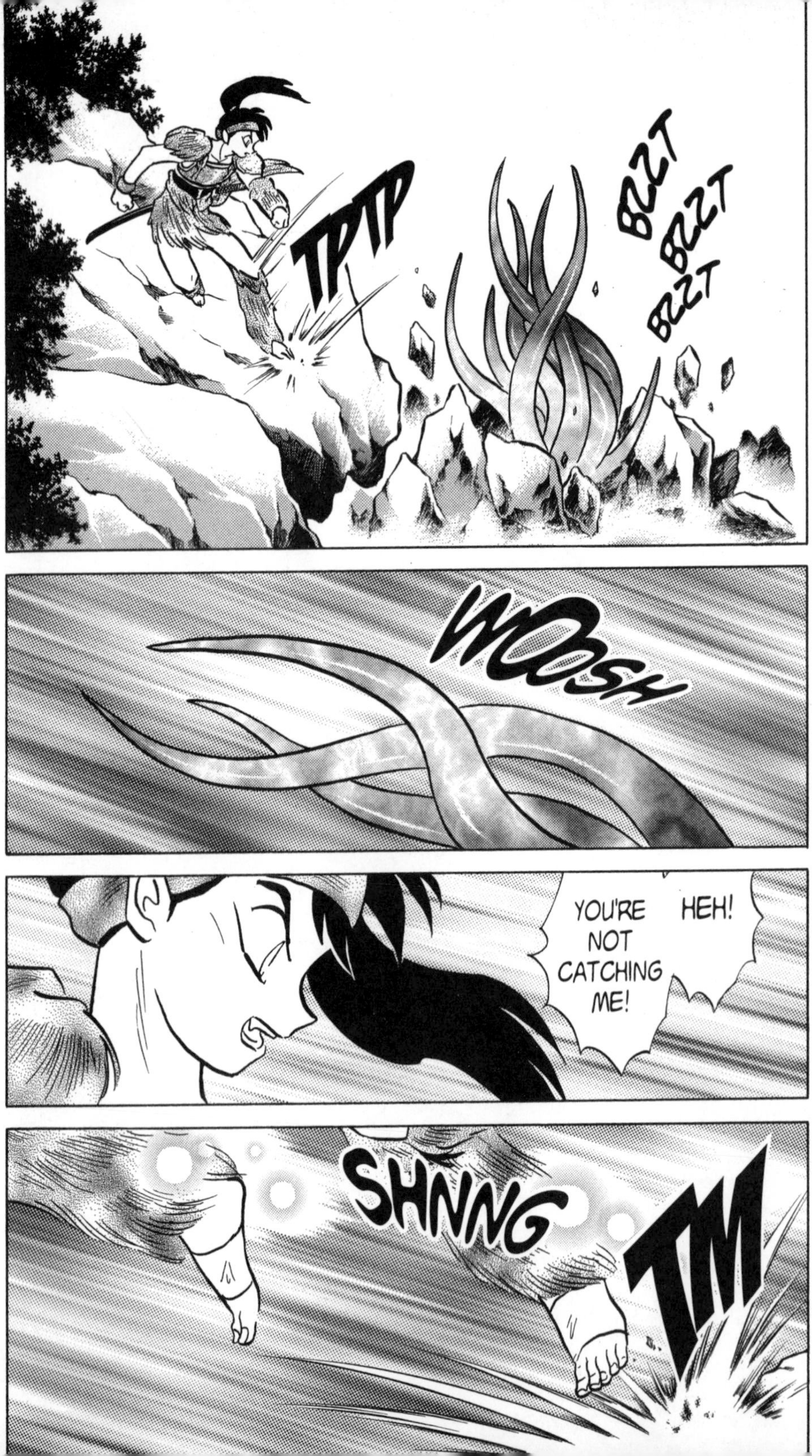
BZZT
BZZT
BZZT
TPTP
WOOSH
HEH!
YOU'RE NOT CATCHING ME!
TM
SHNNG

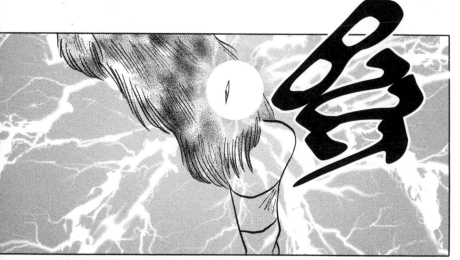

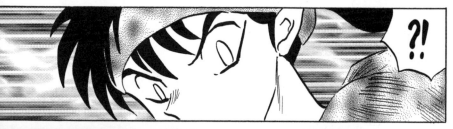

?!

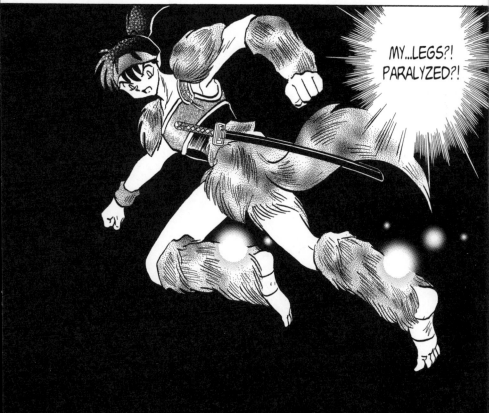

MY...LEGS?!
PARALYZED?!

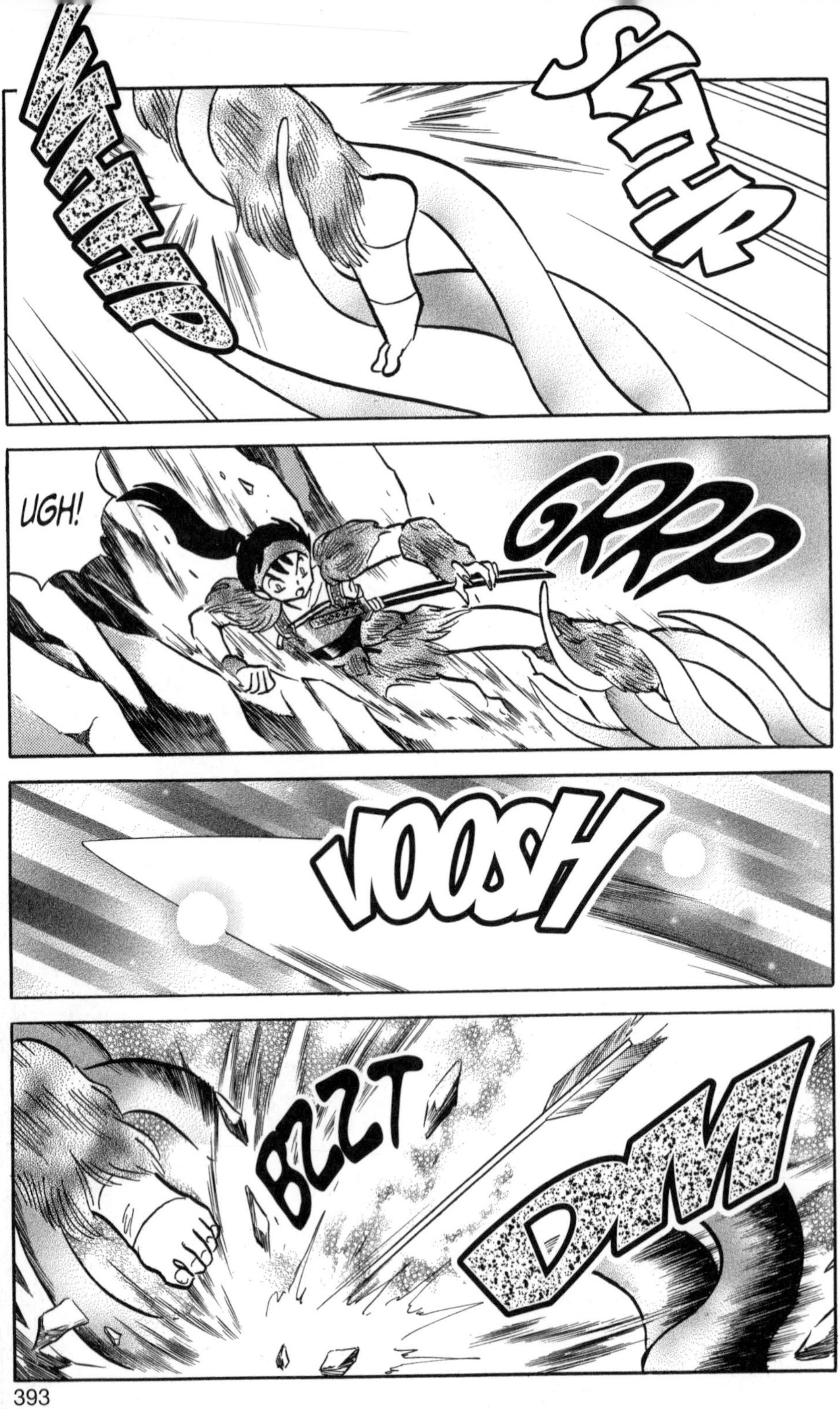
UGH!
GRPP
VOOSH
BZZT

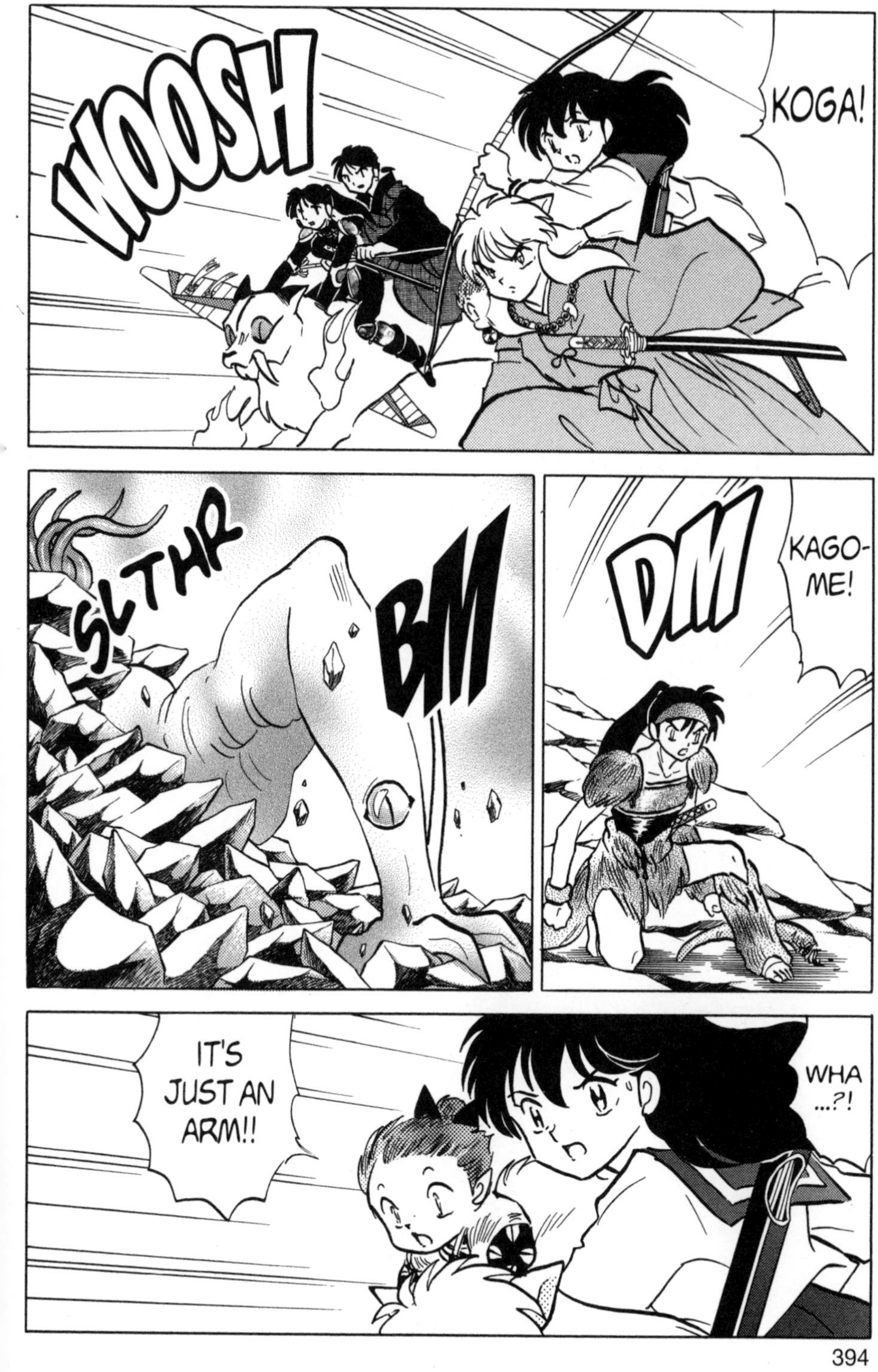
KOGA!
WOOSH
KAGO-ME!
DM
BM
SLTHR
WHA ...?!
IT'S JUST AN ARM!!

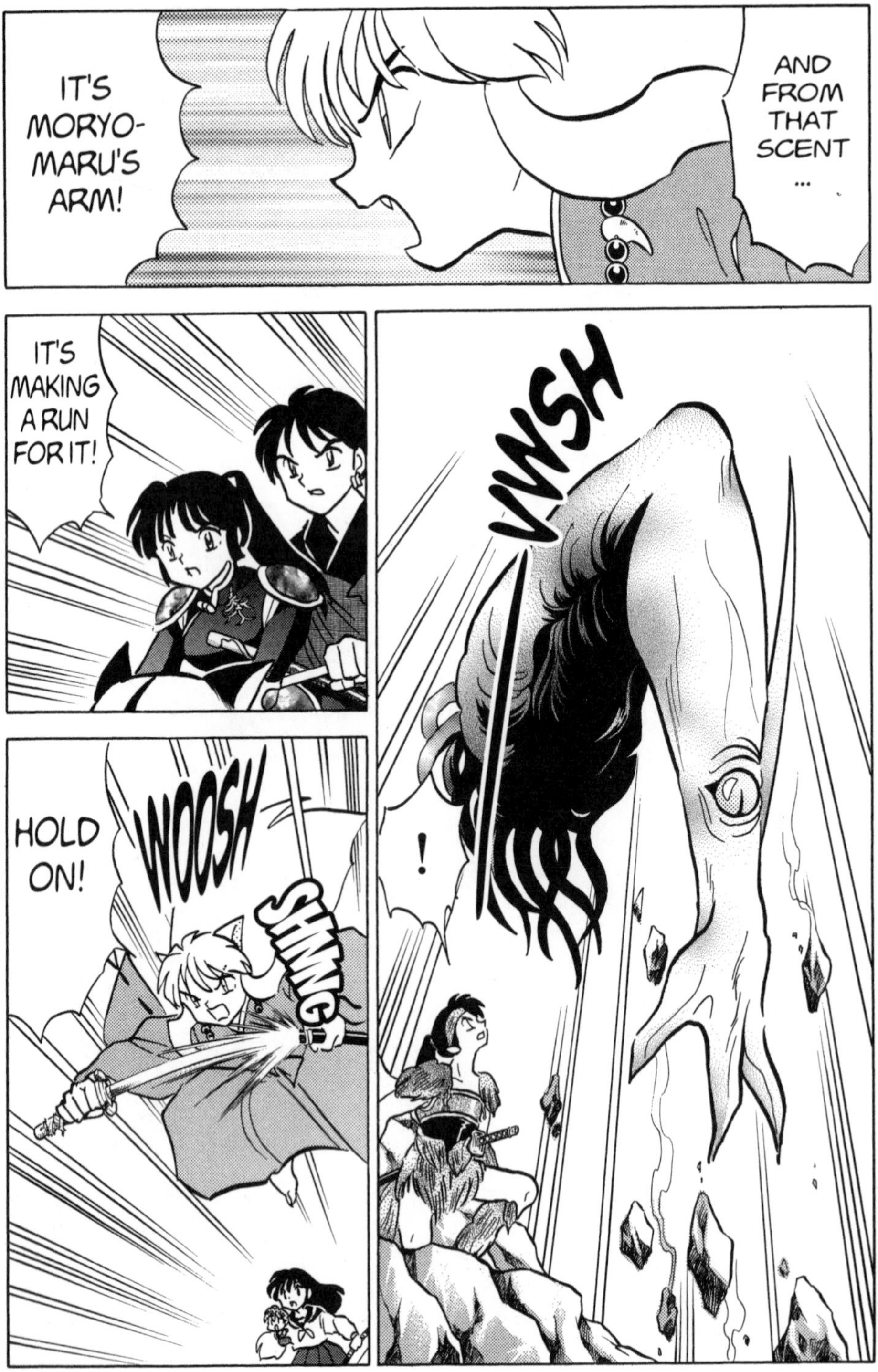
AND FROM THAT SCENT ...
IT'S MORYO-MARU'S ARM!
VWSH
!
IT'S MAKING A RUN FOR IT!
WOOSH
HOLD ON!
SHING

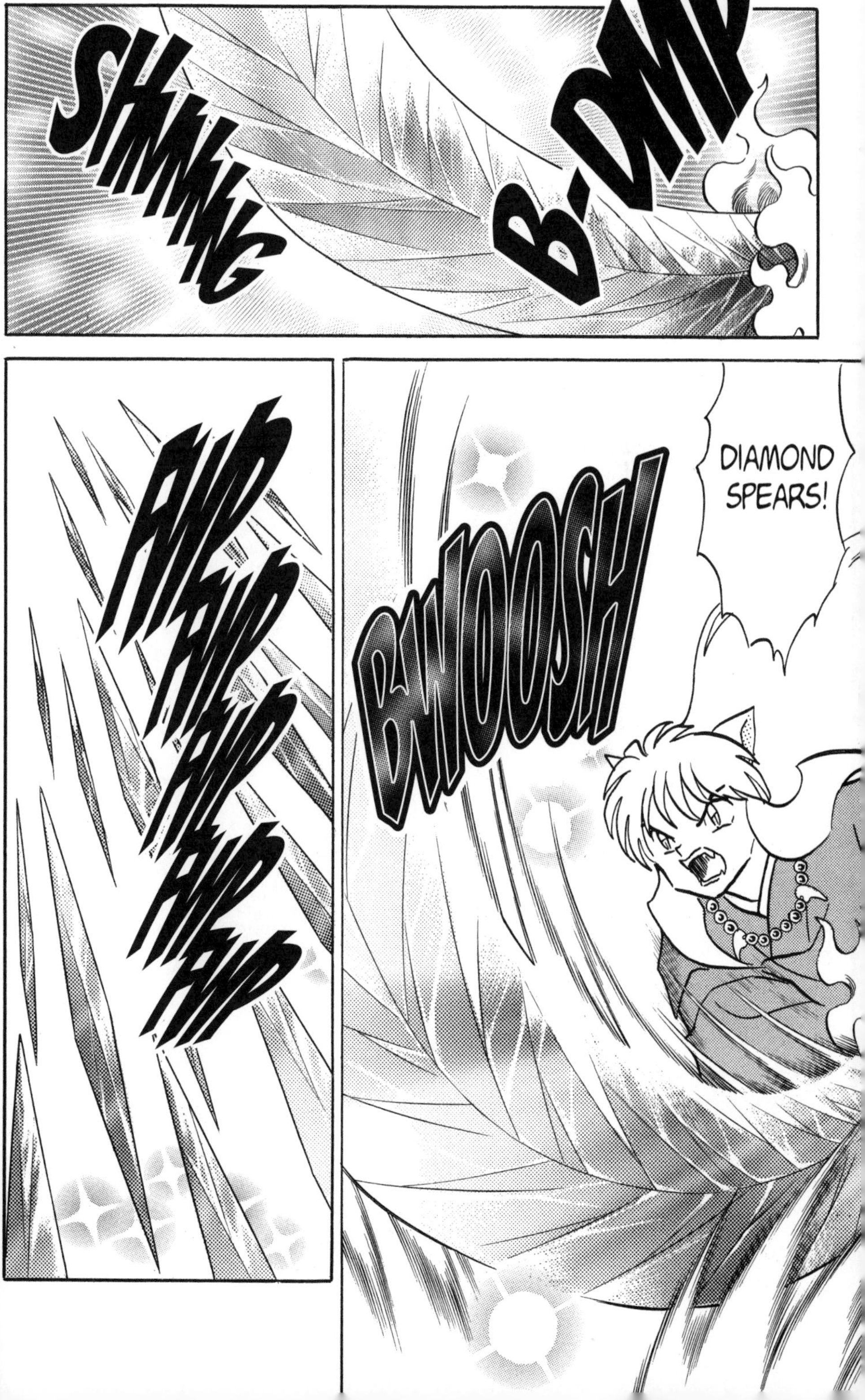
B-DMP
SHINNNG
DIAMOND SPEARS!
BWOOSH
PWD PWD PWD PWD

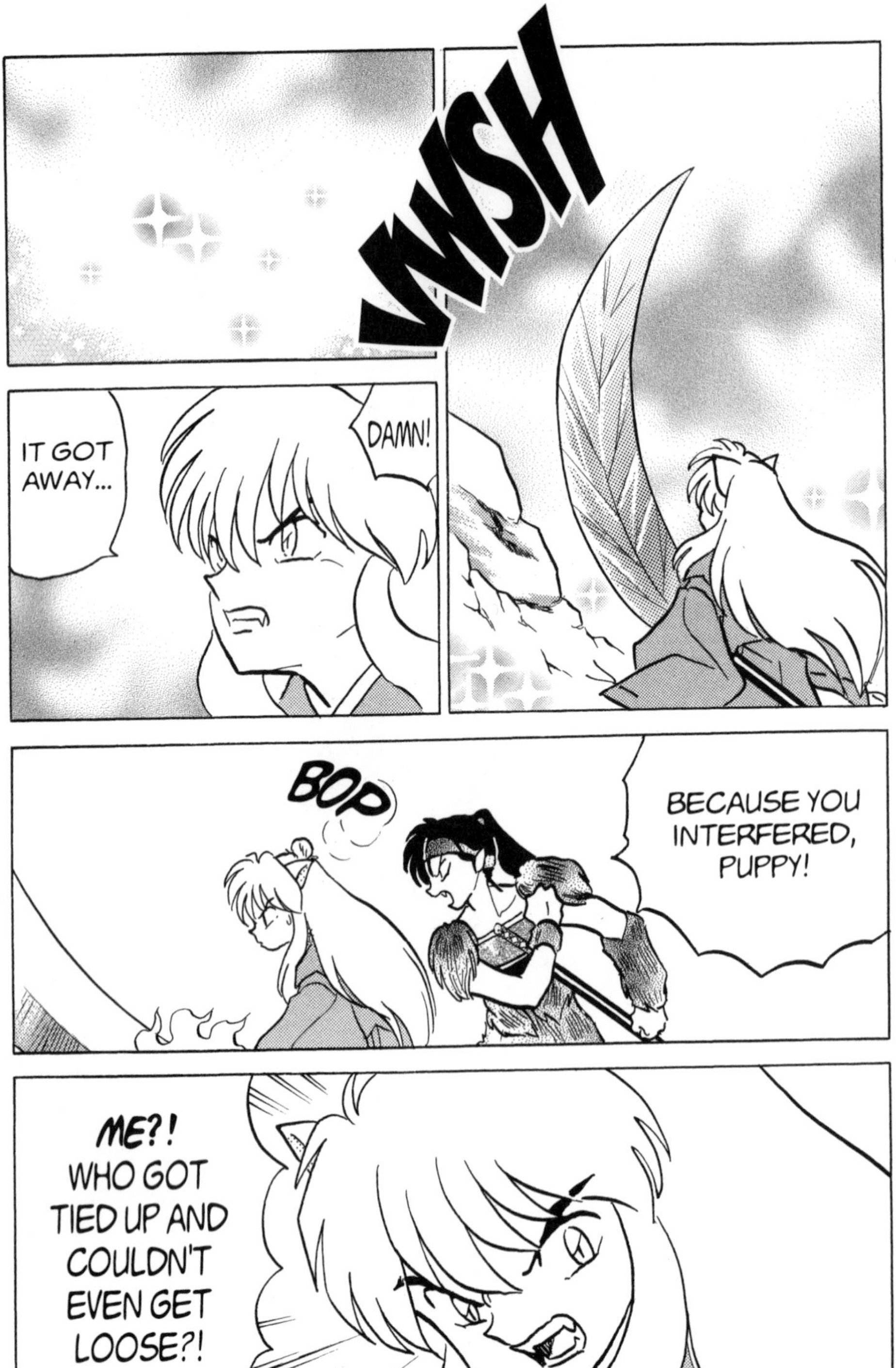
VWSH
DAMN!
IT GOT AWAY...
BECAUSE YOU INTERFERED, PUPPY!
BOP
ME?! WHO GOT TIED UP AND COULDN'T EVEN GET LOOSE?!

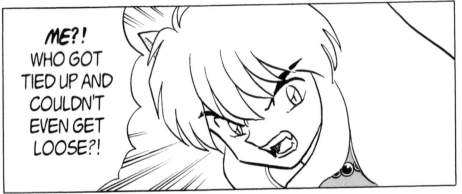

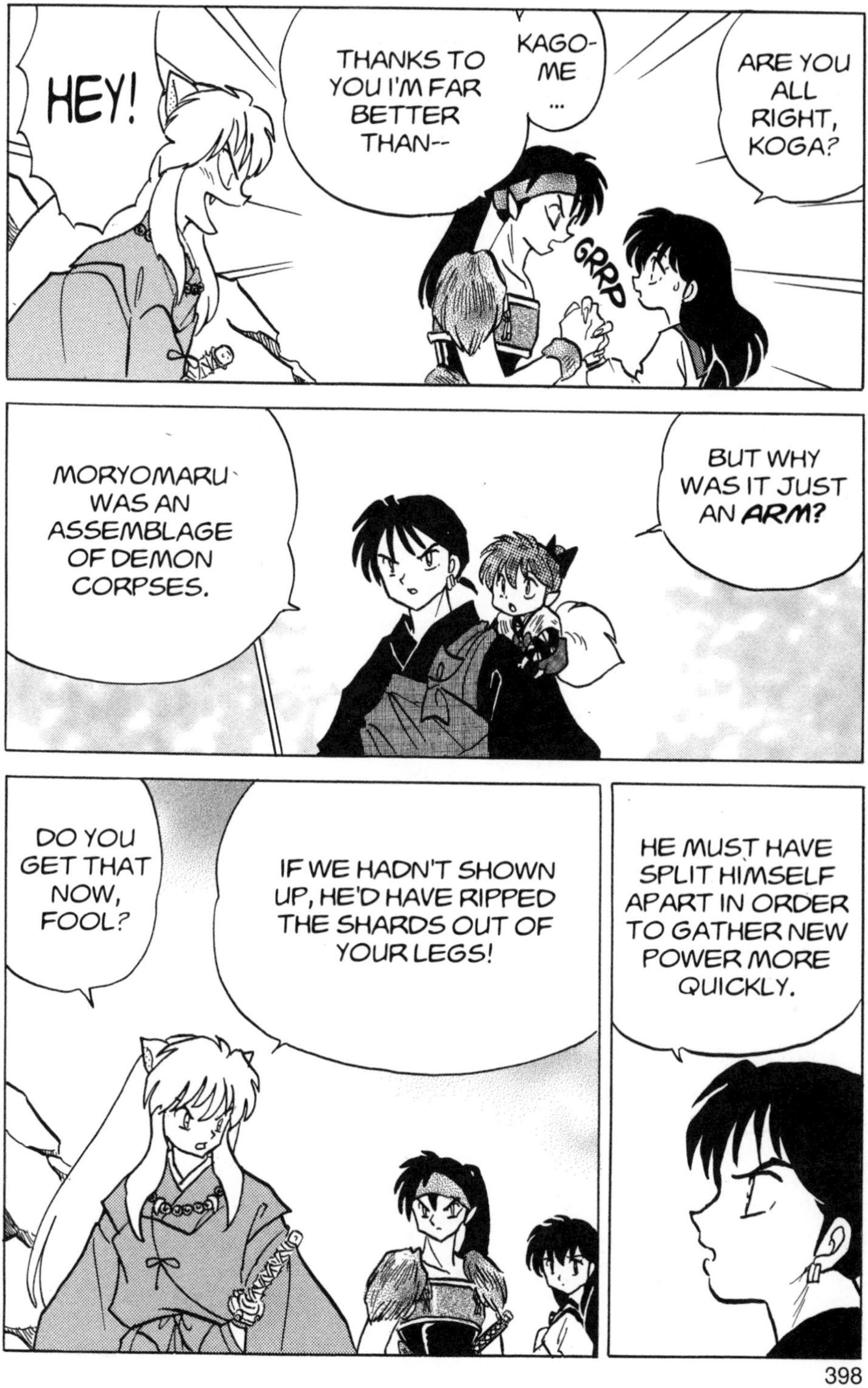
ARE YOU ALL RIGHT, KOGA?
KAGOME ...
THANKS TO YOU I'M FAR BETTER THAN--
GRRP
HEY!
BUT WHY WAS IT JUST AN ARM?
MORYOMARU WAS AN ASSEMBLAGE OF DEMON CORPSES.
HE MUST HAVE SPLIT HIMSELF APART IN ORDER TO GATHER NEW POWER MORE QUICKLY.
IF WE HADN'T SHOWN UP, HE'D HAVE RIPPED THE SHARDS OUT OF YOUR LEGS!
DO YOU GET THAT NOW, FOOL?

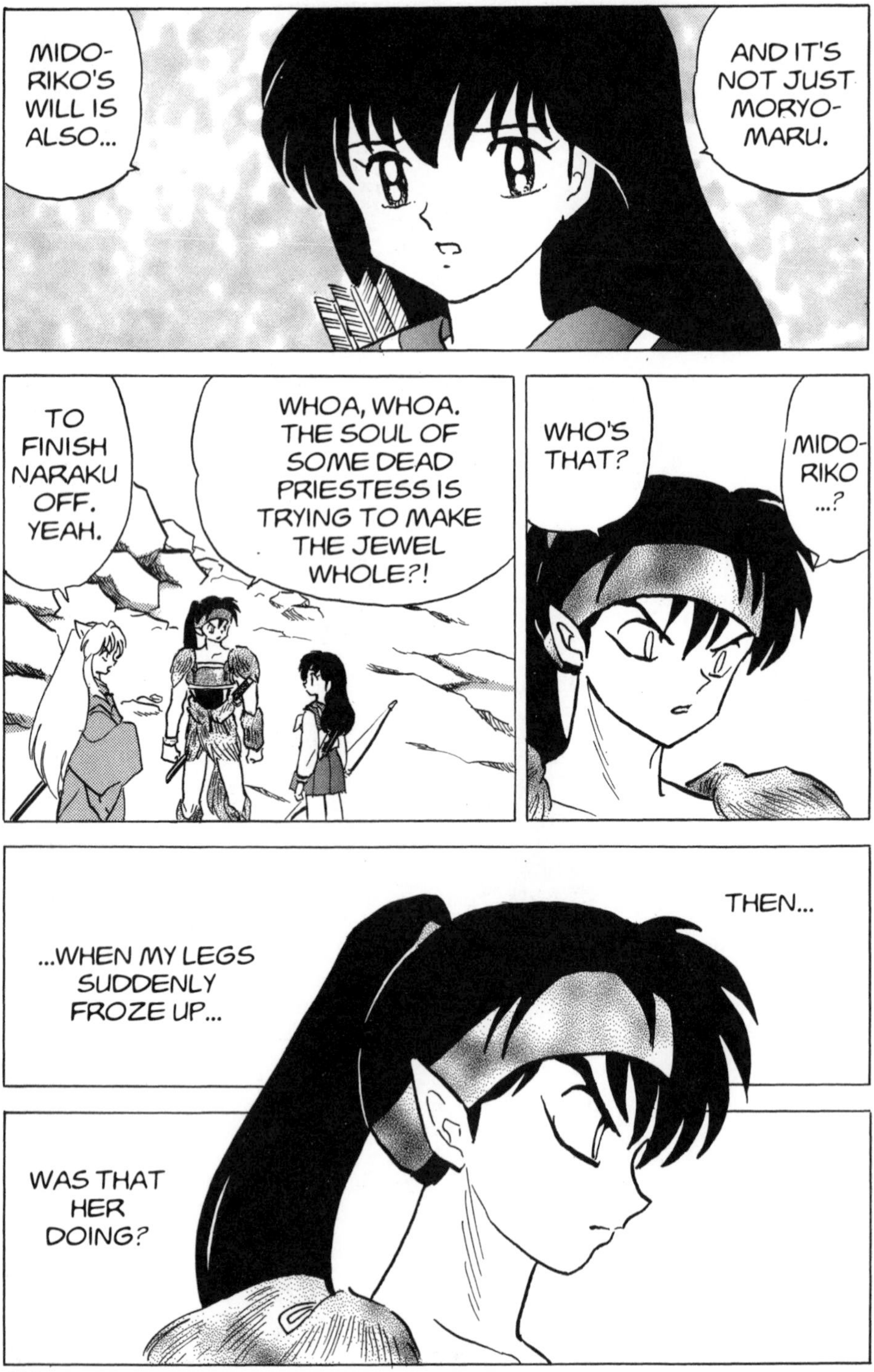
AND IT'S NOT JUST MORYO-MARU.
MIDO-RIKO'S WILL IS ALSO...
MIDO-RIKO ...?
WHO'S THAT?
WHOA, WHOA. THE SOUL OF SOME DEAD PRIESTESS IS TRYING TO MAKE THE JEWEL WHOLE?!
TO FINISH NARAKU OFF. YEAH.
THEN...
...WHEN MY LEGS SUDDENLY FROZE UP...
WAS THAT HER DOING?

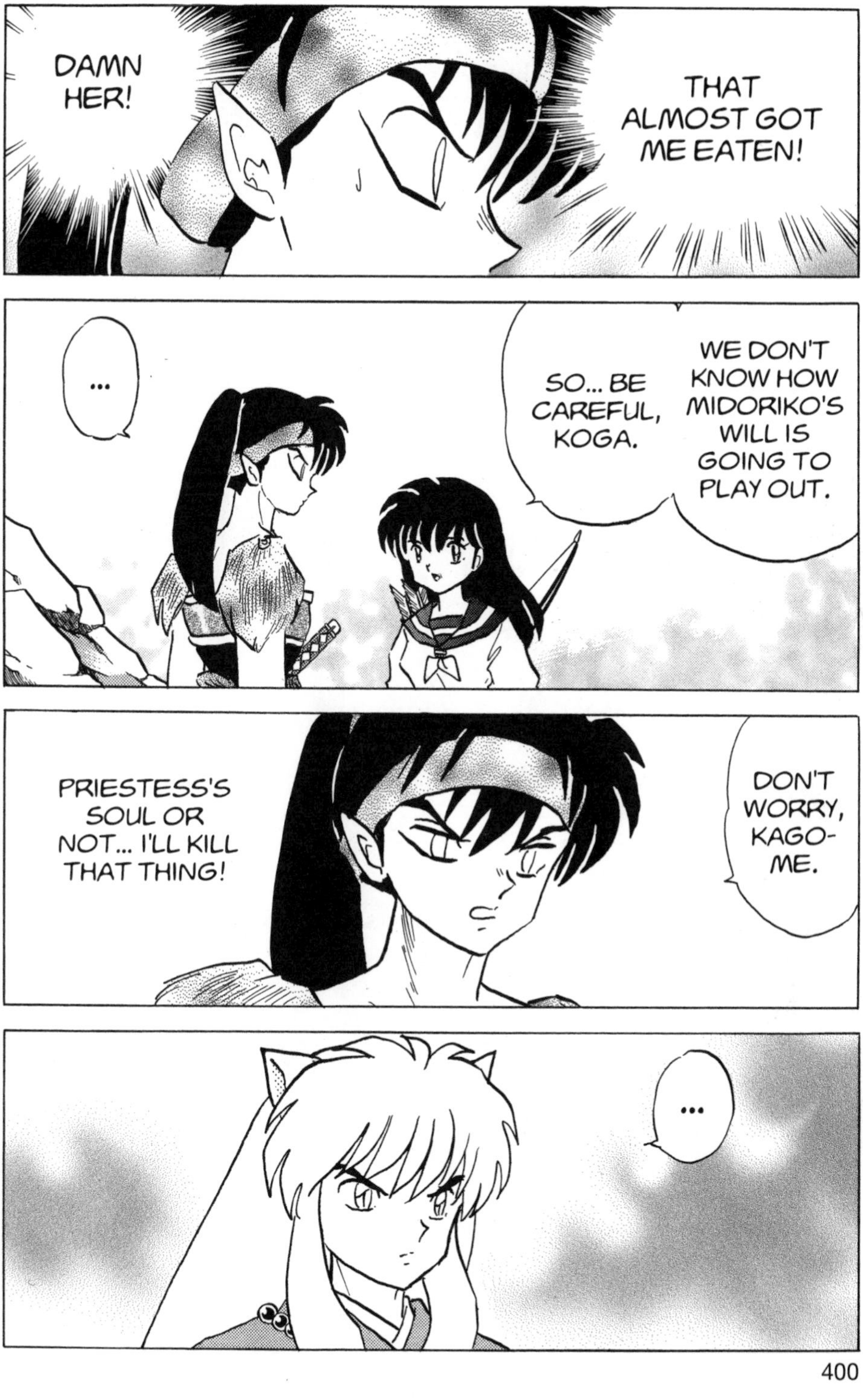
THAT ALMOST GOT ME EATEN!
DAMN HER!
WE DON'T KNOW HOW MIDORIKO'S WILL IS GOING TO PLAY OUT.
SO... BE CAREFUL, KOGA.
...
DON'T WORRY, KAGO-ME.
PRIESTESS'S SOUL OR NOT... I'LL KILL THAT THING!
...

SCROLL TWO
THE BURIAL GROUND OF THE WOLVES

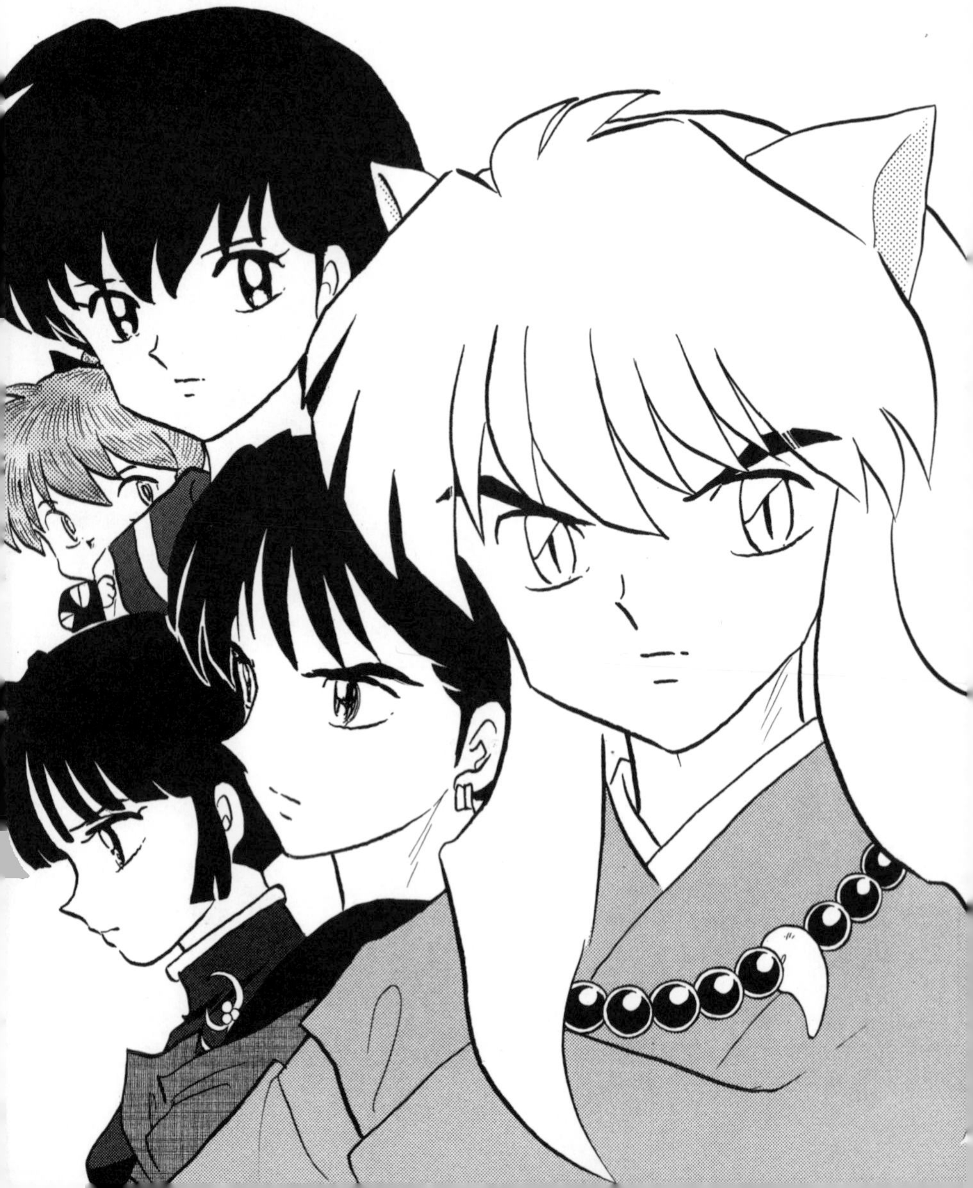

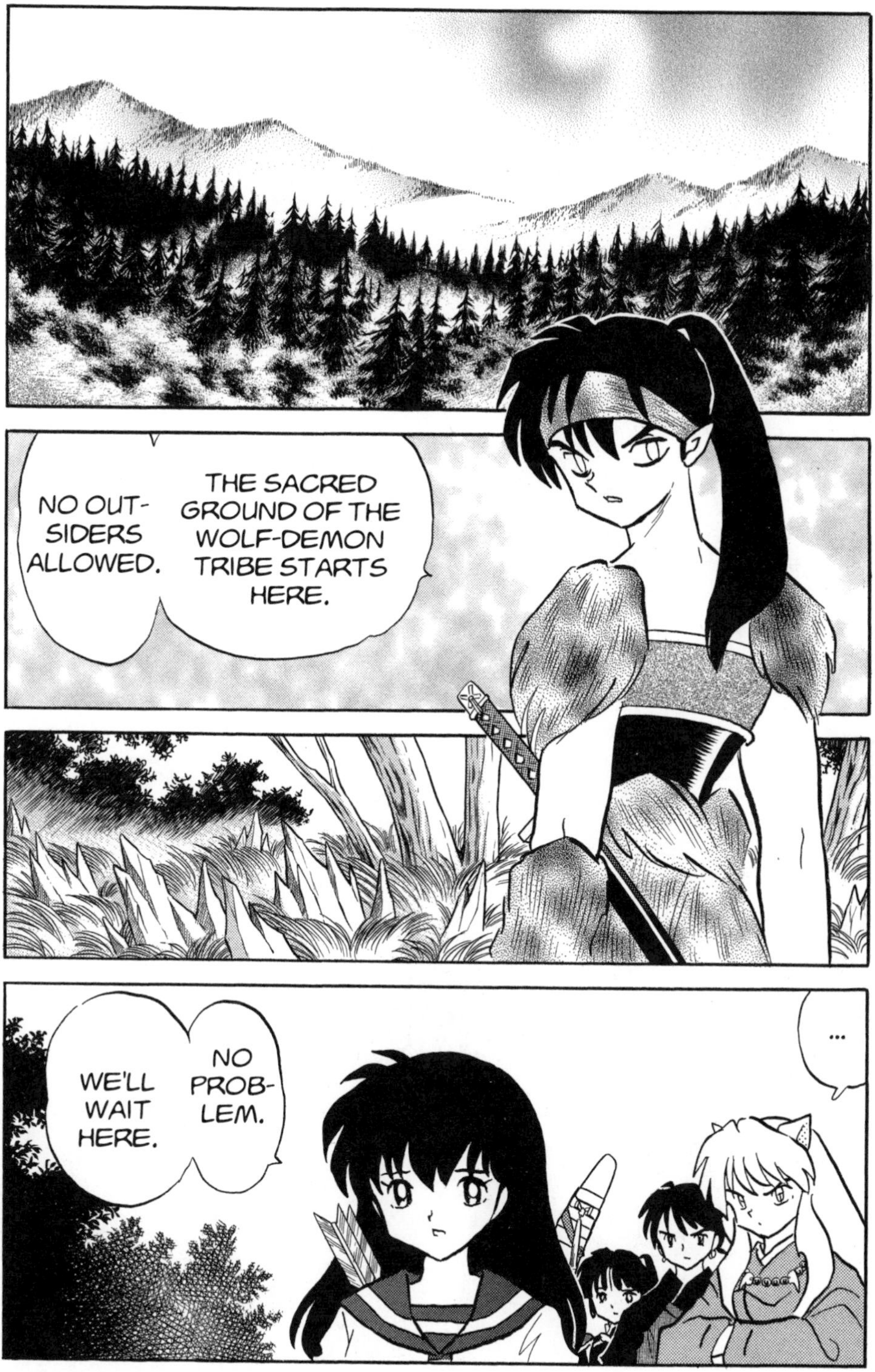
THE SACRED GROUND OF THE WOLF-DEMON TRIBE STARTS HERE.
NO OUT-SIDERS ALLOWED.
...
NO PROB-LEM.
WE'LL WAIT HERE.

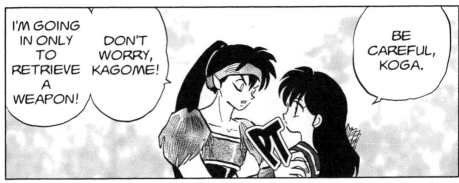

BE CAREFUL, KOGA.
DON'T WORRY, KAGOME!
I'M GOING IN ONLY TO RETRIEVE A WEAPON!
PT
WILL YOU JUST HURRY UP AND ***GO?!***
FWSH
K-KOGA...
YOU'RE GOING TO RETRIEVE A WEAPON? Y-YOU...
...D-DON'T MEAN THE ONE IN THE BURIAL GROUNDS ?!
BURIAL GROUNDS ...?
THE ANCESTRAL TOMBS.
THIS WEAPON'S EN-SHRINED THERE.
BUT WE NEED IT NOW.

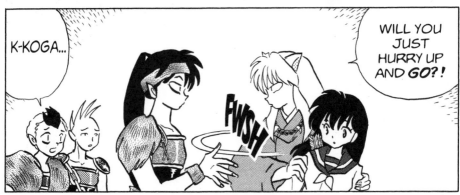

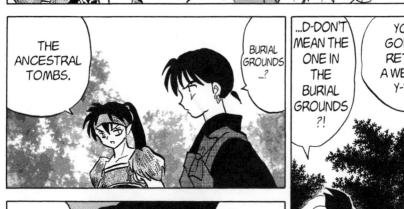

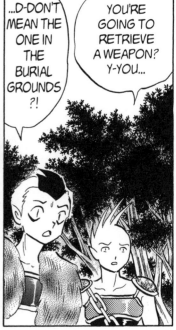

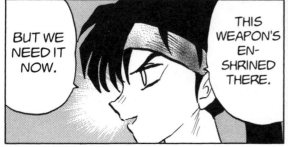

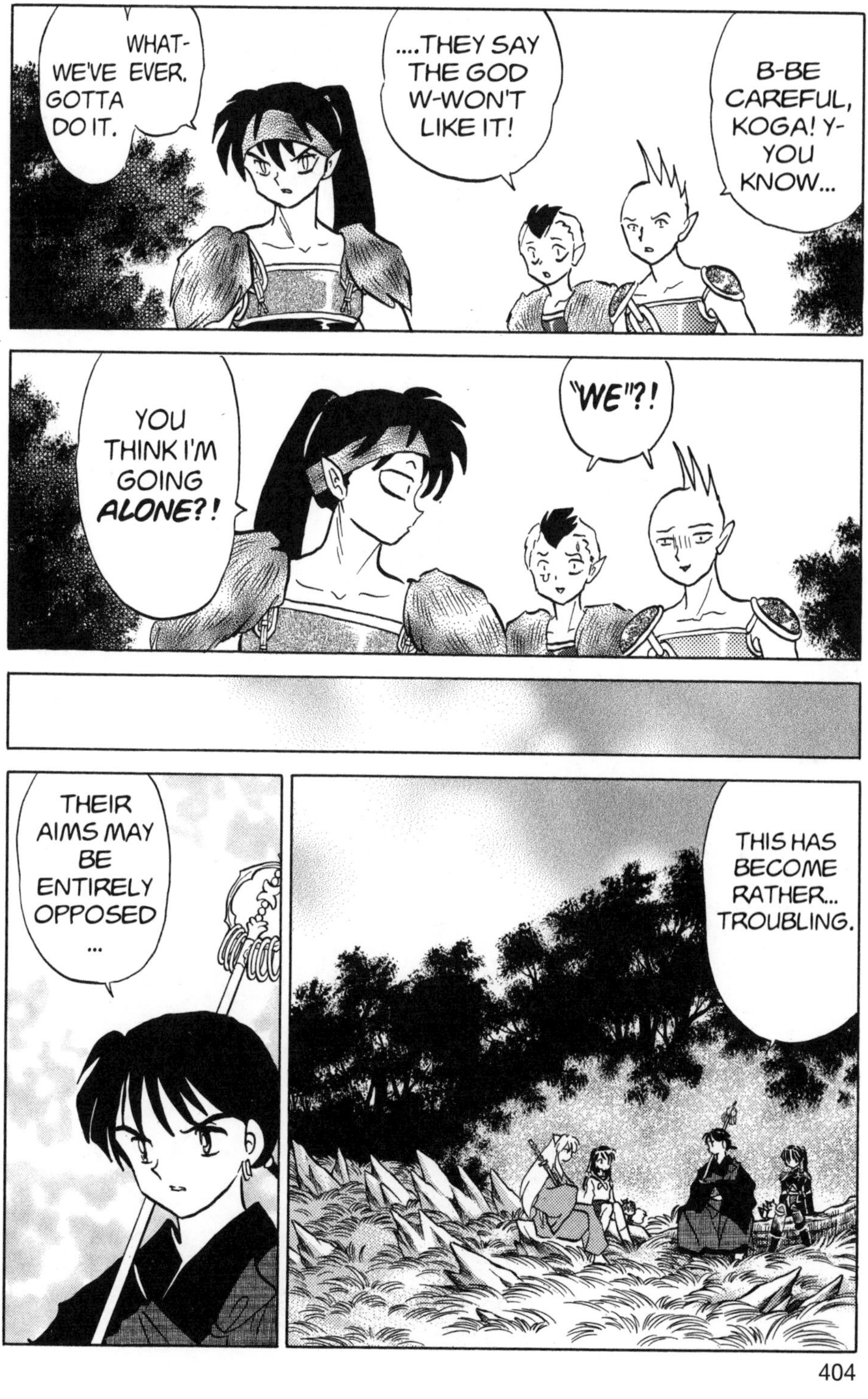
B-BE CAREFUL, KOGA! Y-YOU KNOW...
....THEY SAY THE GOD W-WON'T LIKE IT!
WHAT-EVER. WE'VE GOTTA DO IT.
"WE"?!
YOU THINK I'M GOING ALONE?!
THIS HAS BECOME RATHER... TROUBLING.
THEIR AIMS MAY BE ENTIRELY OPPOSED ...

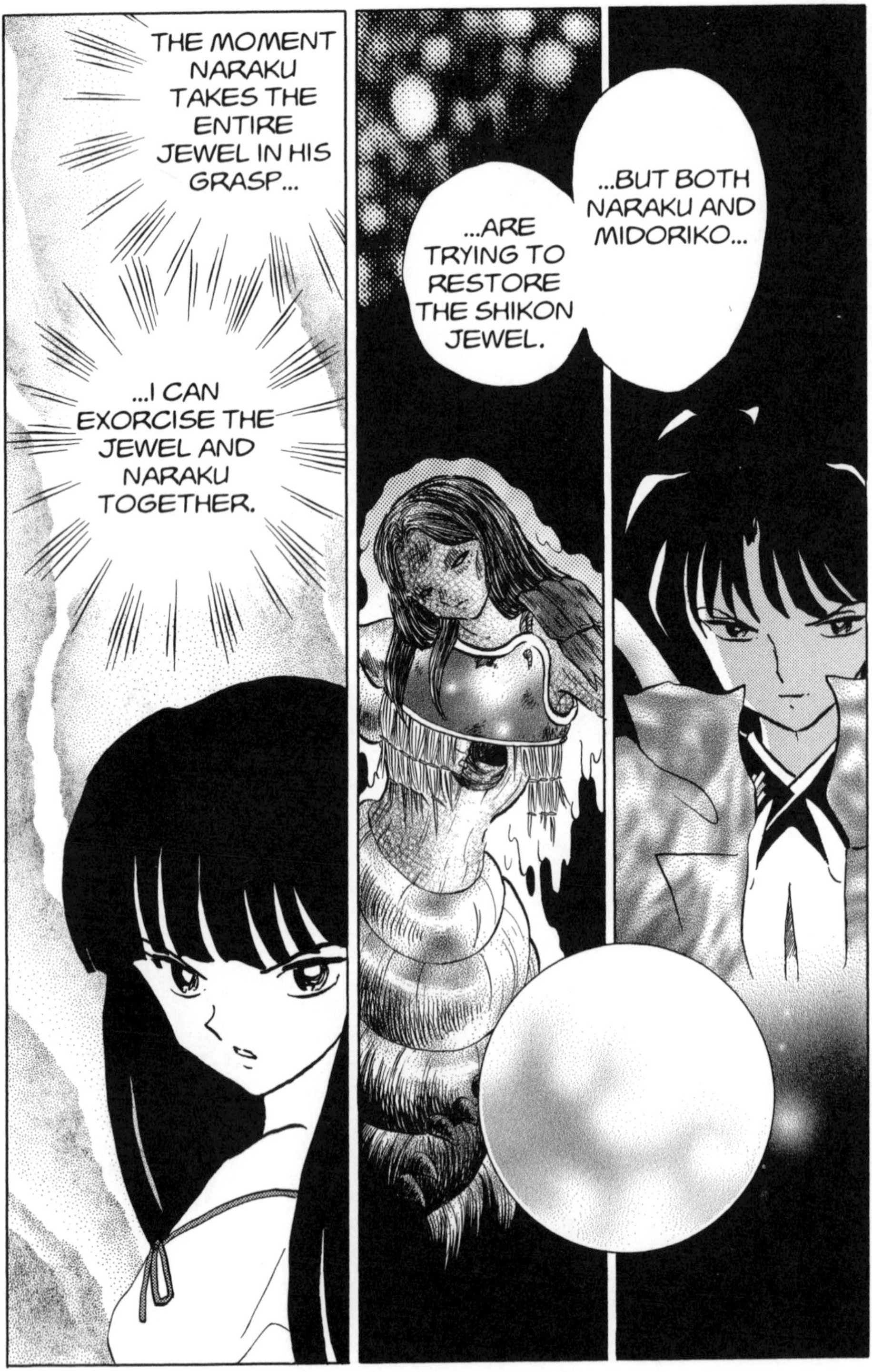
...BUT BOTH NARAKU AND MIDORIKO...
...ARE TRYING TO RESTORE THE SHIKON JEWEL.
THE MOMENT NARAKU TAKES THE ENTIRE JEWEL IN HIS GRASP...
...I CAN EXORCISE THE JEWEL AND NARAKU TOGETHER.

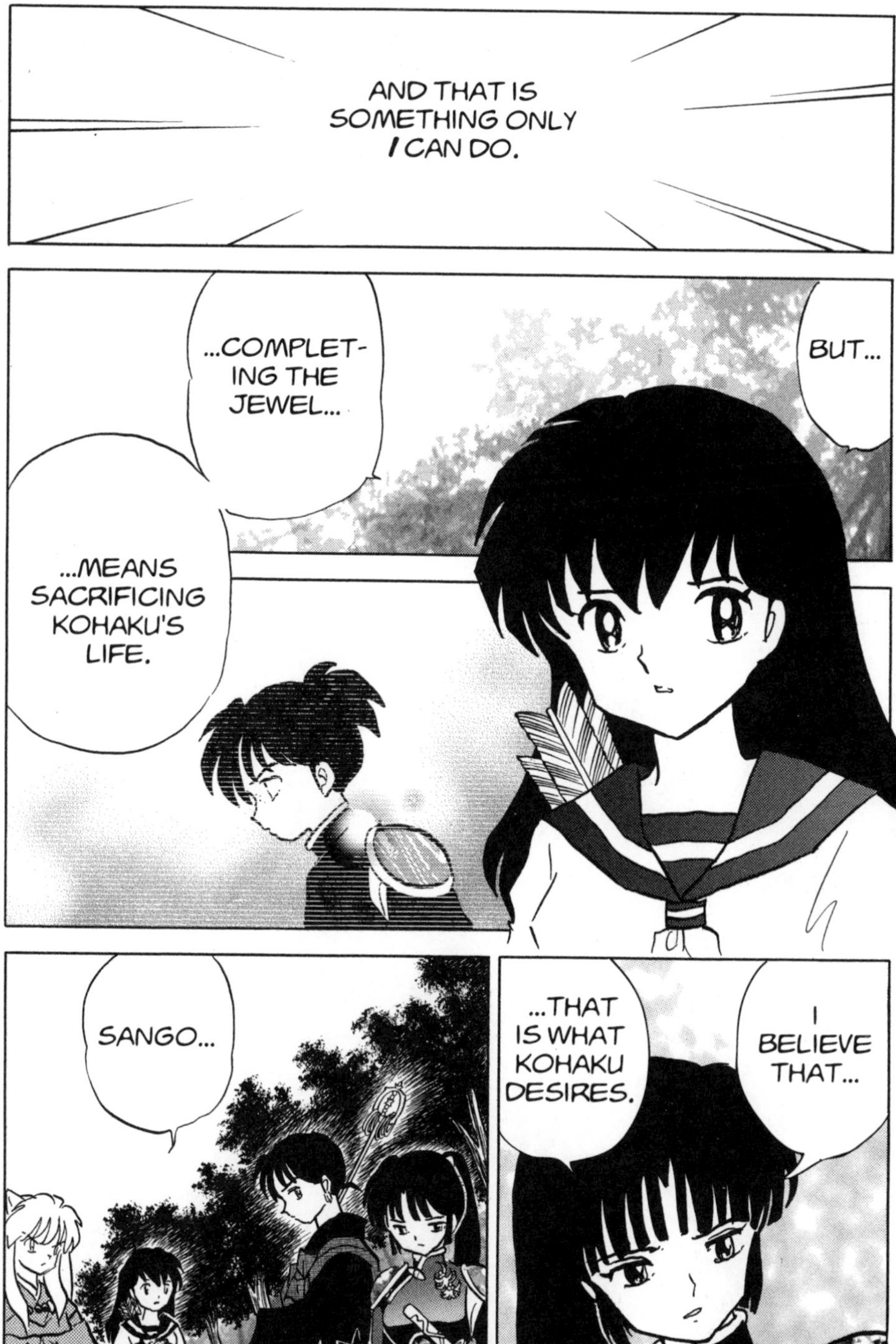
AND THAT IS SOMETHING ONLY *I* CAN DO.
BUT...
...COMPLETING THE JEWEL...
...MEANS SACRIFICING KOHAKU'S LIFE.
I BELIEVE THAT...
...THAT IS WHAT KOHAKU DESIRES.
SANGO...

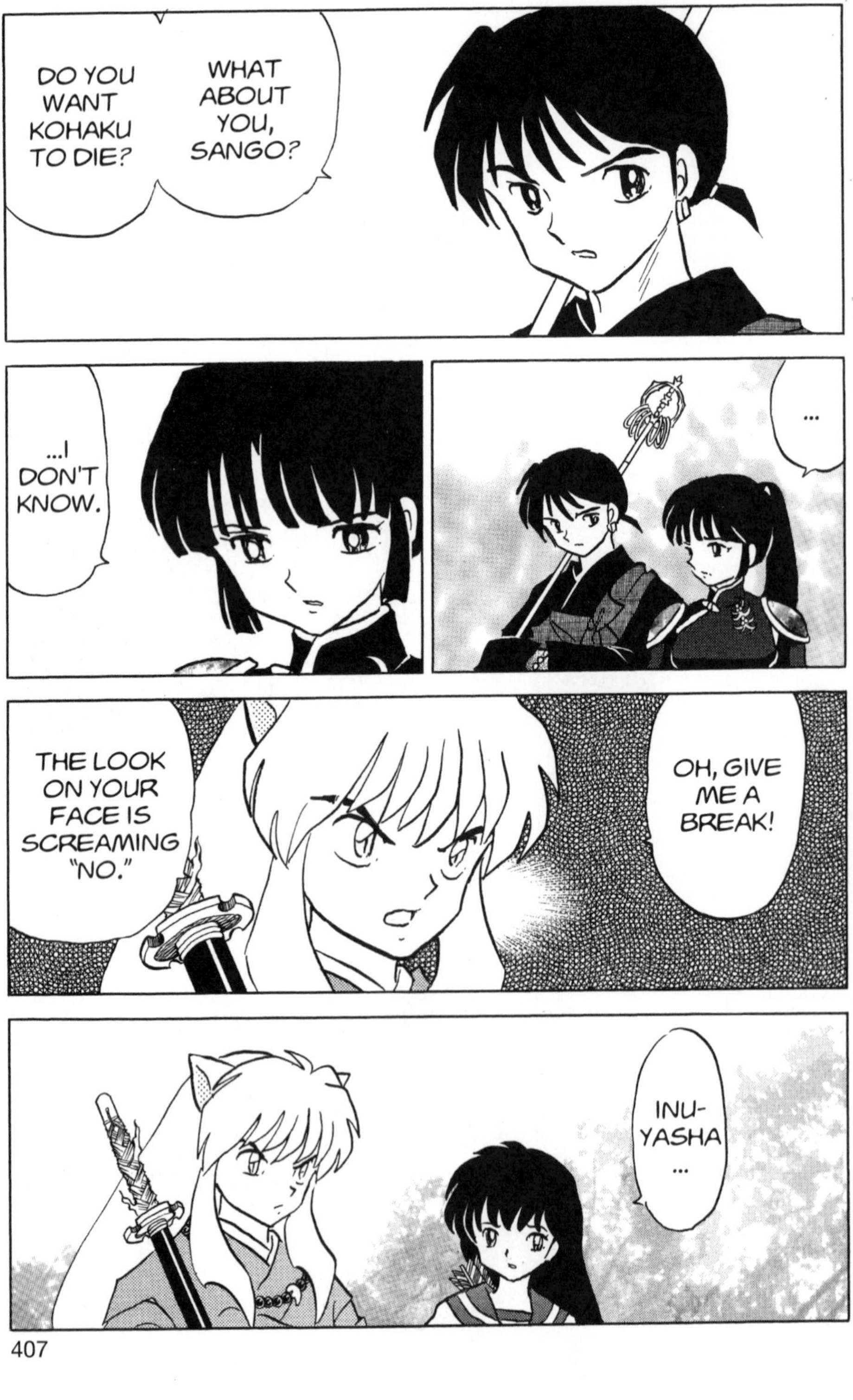
WHAT ABOUT YOU, SANGO?
DO YOU WANT KOHAKU TO DIE?
...
...I DON'T KNOW.
OH, GIVE ME A BREAK!
THE LOOK ON YOUR FACE IS SCREAMING "NO."
INU-YASHA ...

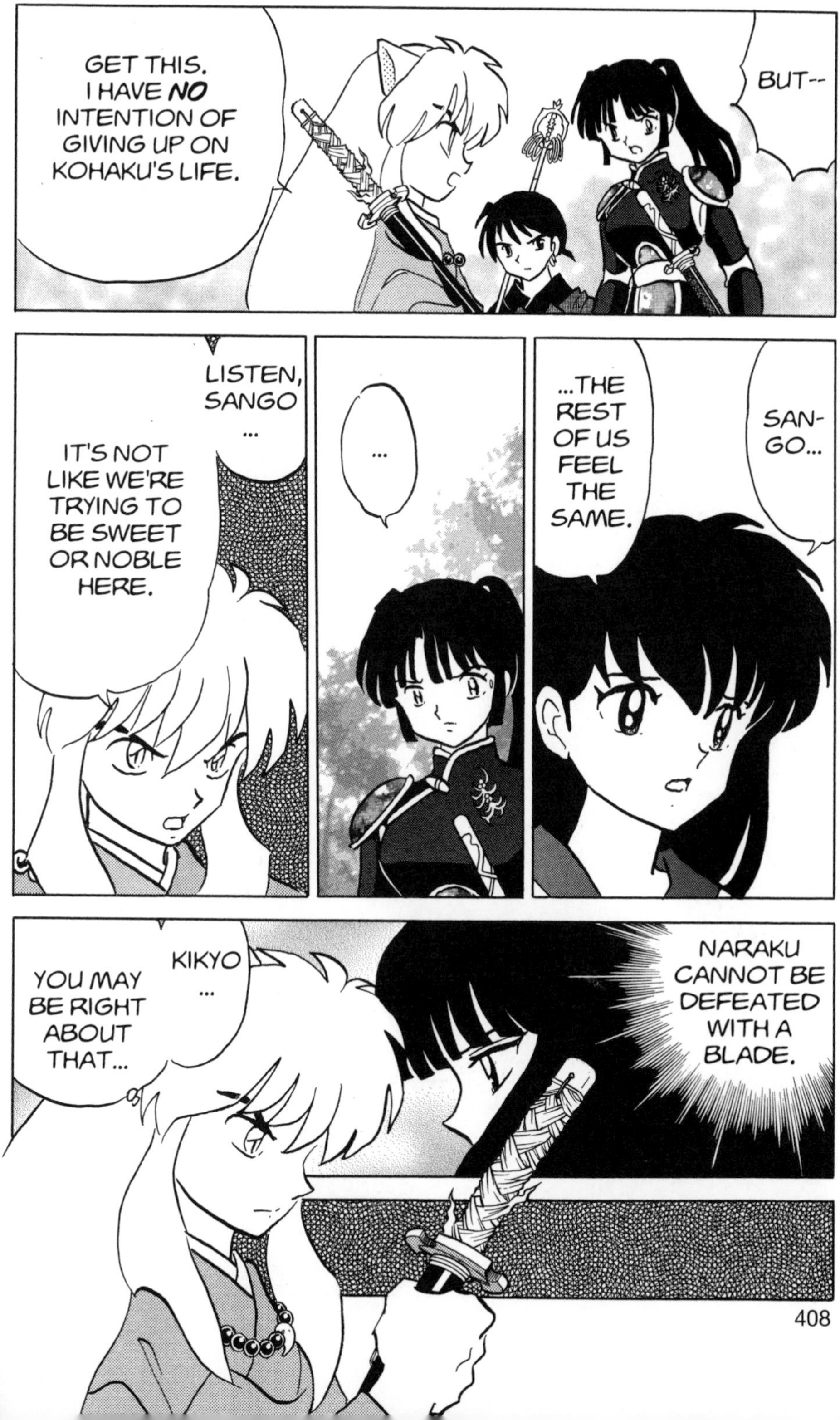
BUT--
GET THIS. I HAVE **NO** INTENTION OF GIVING UP ON KOHAKU'S LIFE.
SAN-GO...
...THE REST OF US FEEL THE SAME.
...
LISTEN, SANGO ...
IT'S NOT LIKE WE'RE TRYING TO BE SWEET OR NOBLE HERE.
NARAKU CANNOT BE DEFEATED WITH A BLADE.
KIKYO ...
YOU MAY BE RIGHT ABOUT THAT...

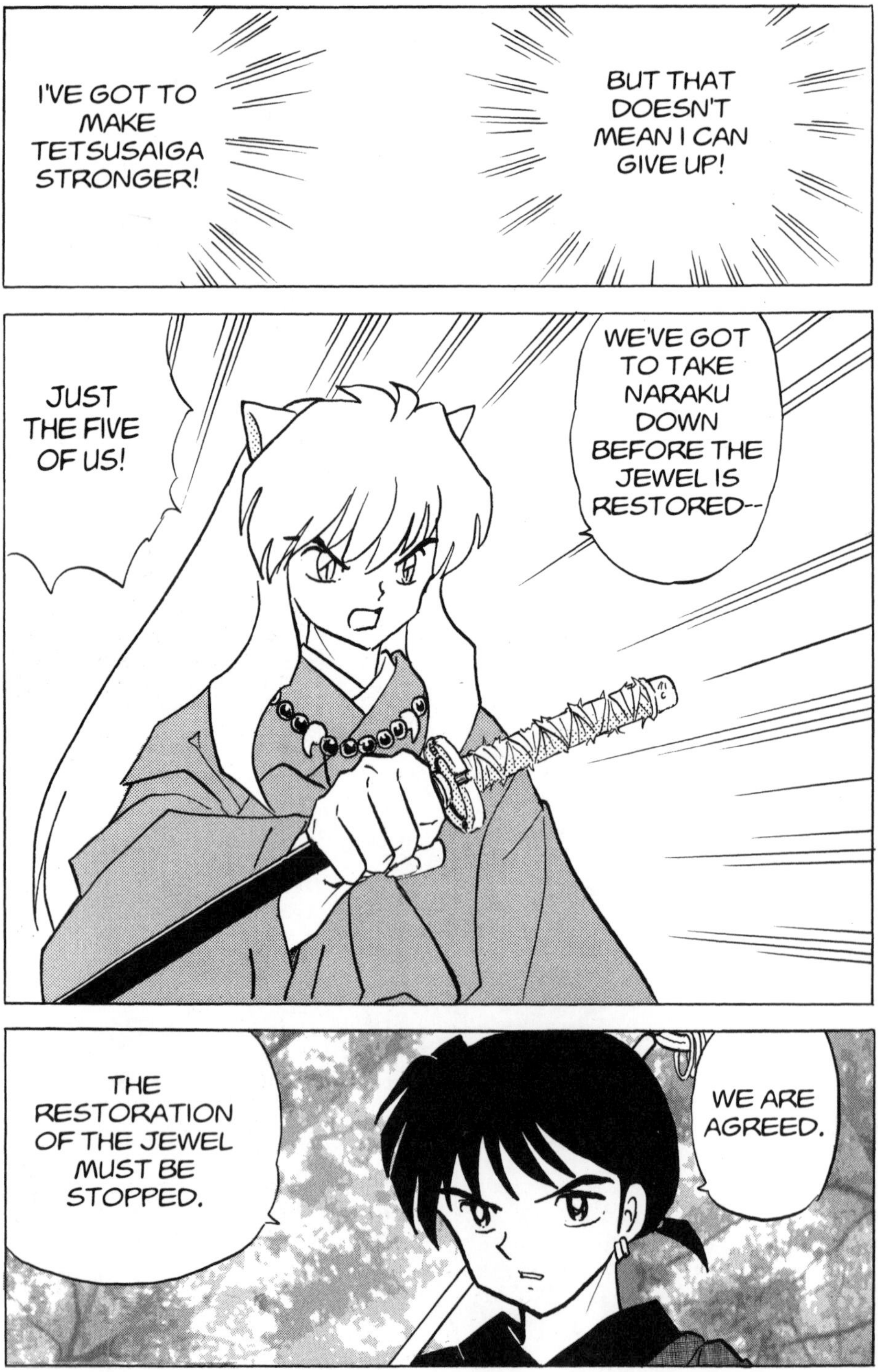
BUT THAT DOESN'T MEAN I CAN GIVE UP!
I'VE GOT TO MAKE TETSUSAIGA STRONGER!
WE'VE GOT TO TAKE NARAKU DOWN BEFORE THE JEWEL IS RESTORED--
JUST THE FIVE OF US!
WE ARE AGREED.
THE RESTORATION OF THE JEWEL MUST BE STOPPED.

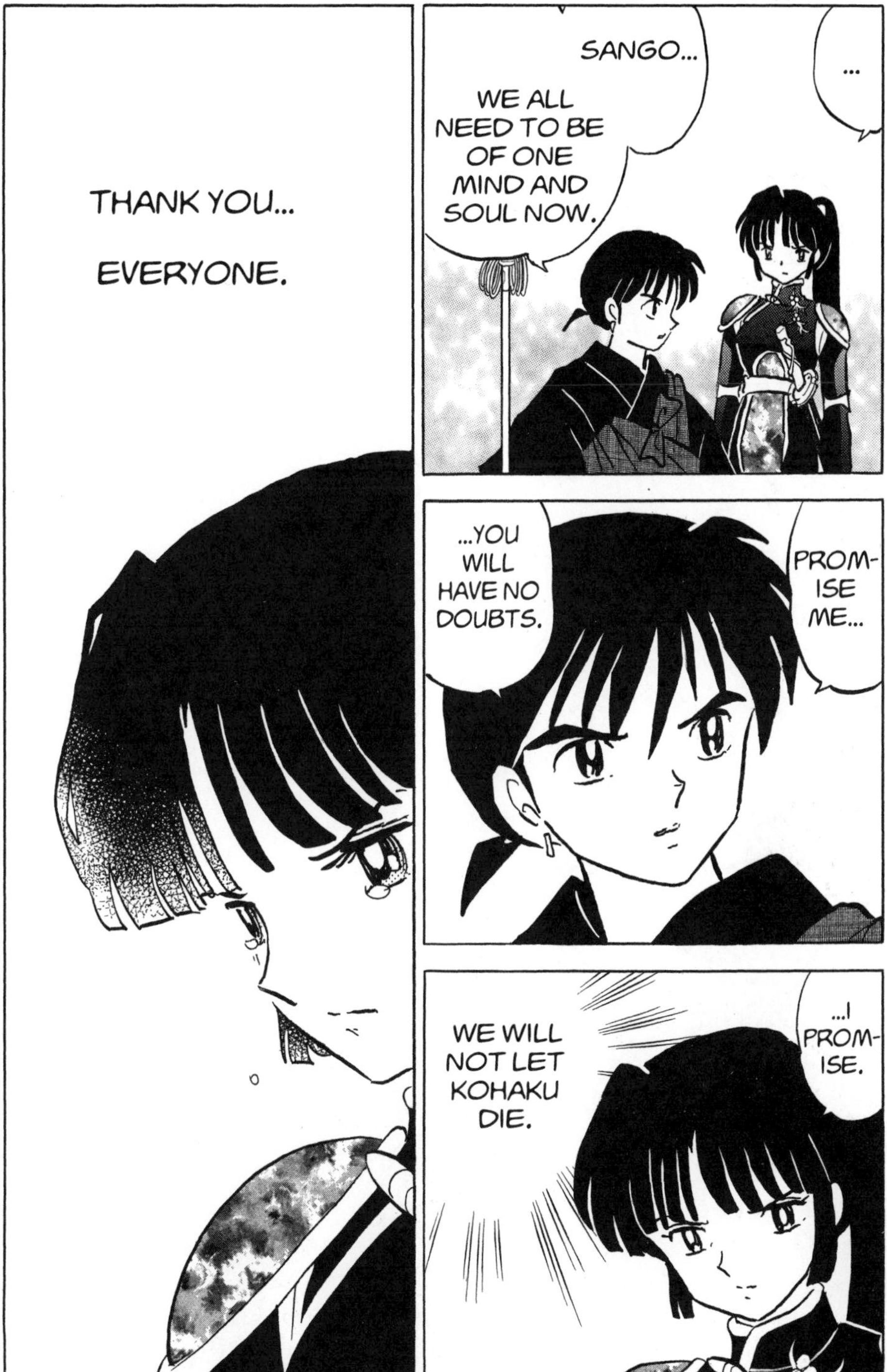
...
SANGO...
WE ALL NEED TO BE OF ONE MIND AND SOUL NOW.
PROMISE ME...
...YOU WILL HAVE NO DOUBTS.
...I PROMISE.
WE WILL NOT LET KOHAKU DIE.
THANK YOU...
EVERYONE.

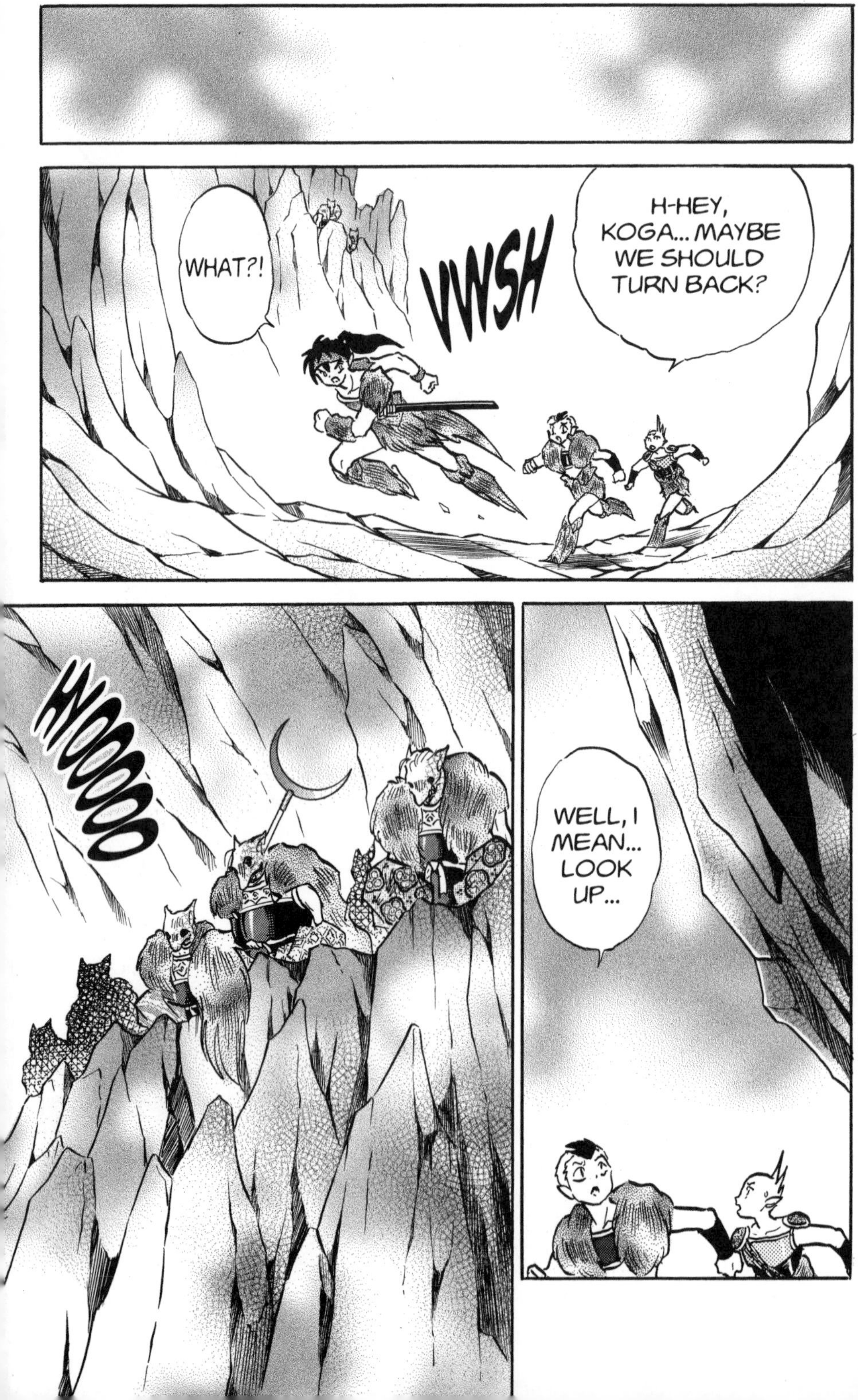
H-HEY, KOGA... MAYBE WE SHOULD TURN BACK?
VWSH
WHAT?!
WELL, I MEAN... LOOK UP...
HYOOOOO

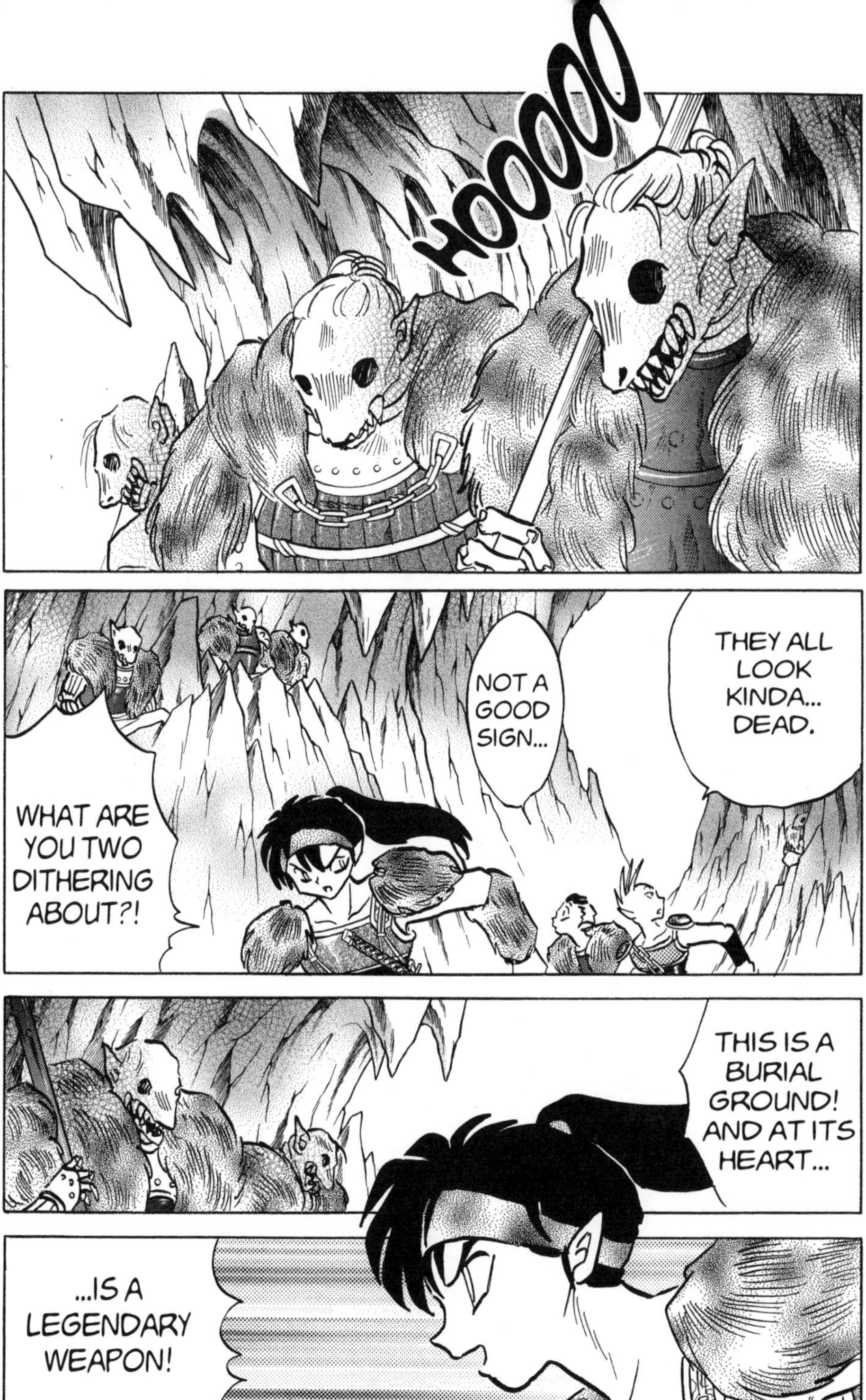
HOOOOO
THEY ALL LOOK KINDA... DEAD.
NOT A GOOD SIGN...
WHAT ARE YOU TWO DITHERING ABOUT?!
THIS IS A BURIAL GROUND! AND AT ITS HEART...
...IS A LEGENDARY WEAPON!

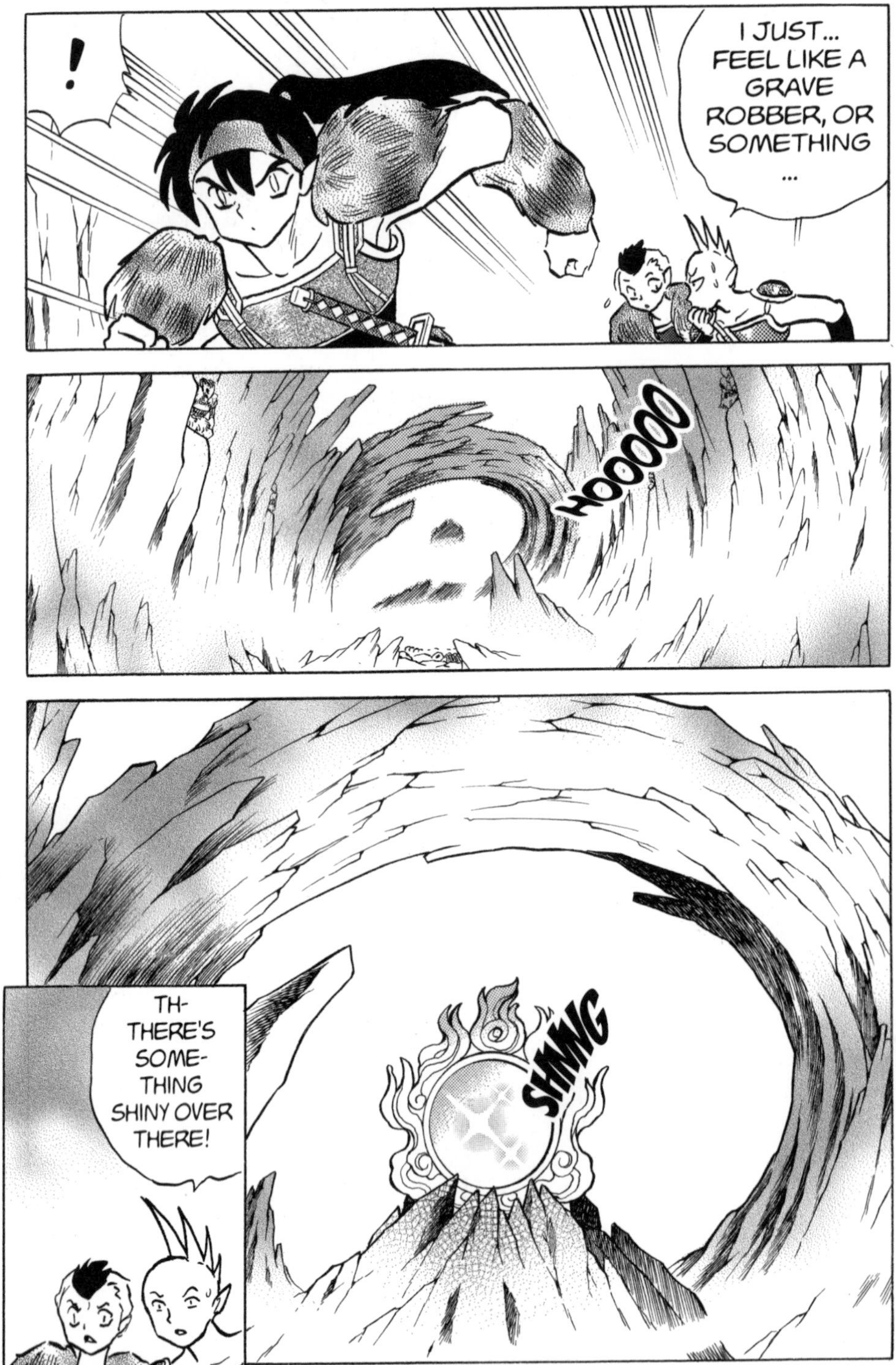
I JUST... FEEL LIKE A GRAVE ROBBER, OR SOMETHING ...
!
HOOOOO
SHING
TH- THERE'S SOME- THING SHINY OVER THERE!

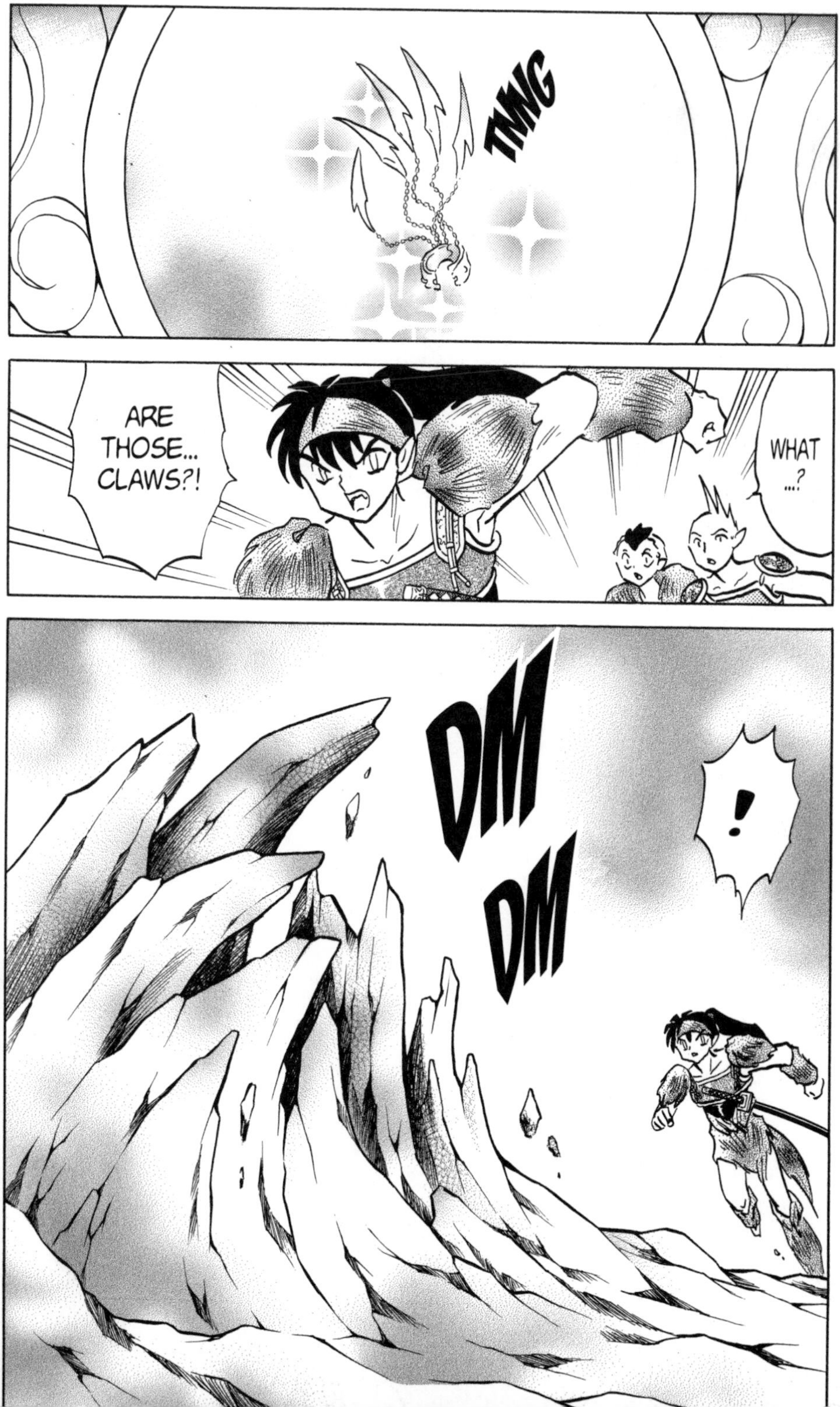
TWNG
WHAT ...?
ARE THOSE... CLAWS?!
!
DM DM

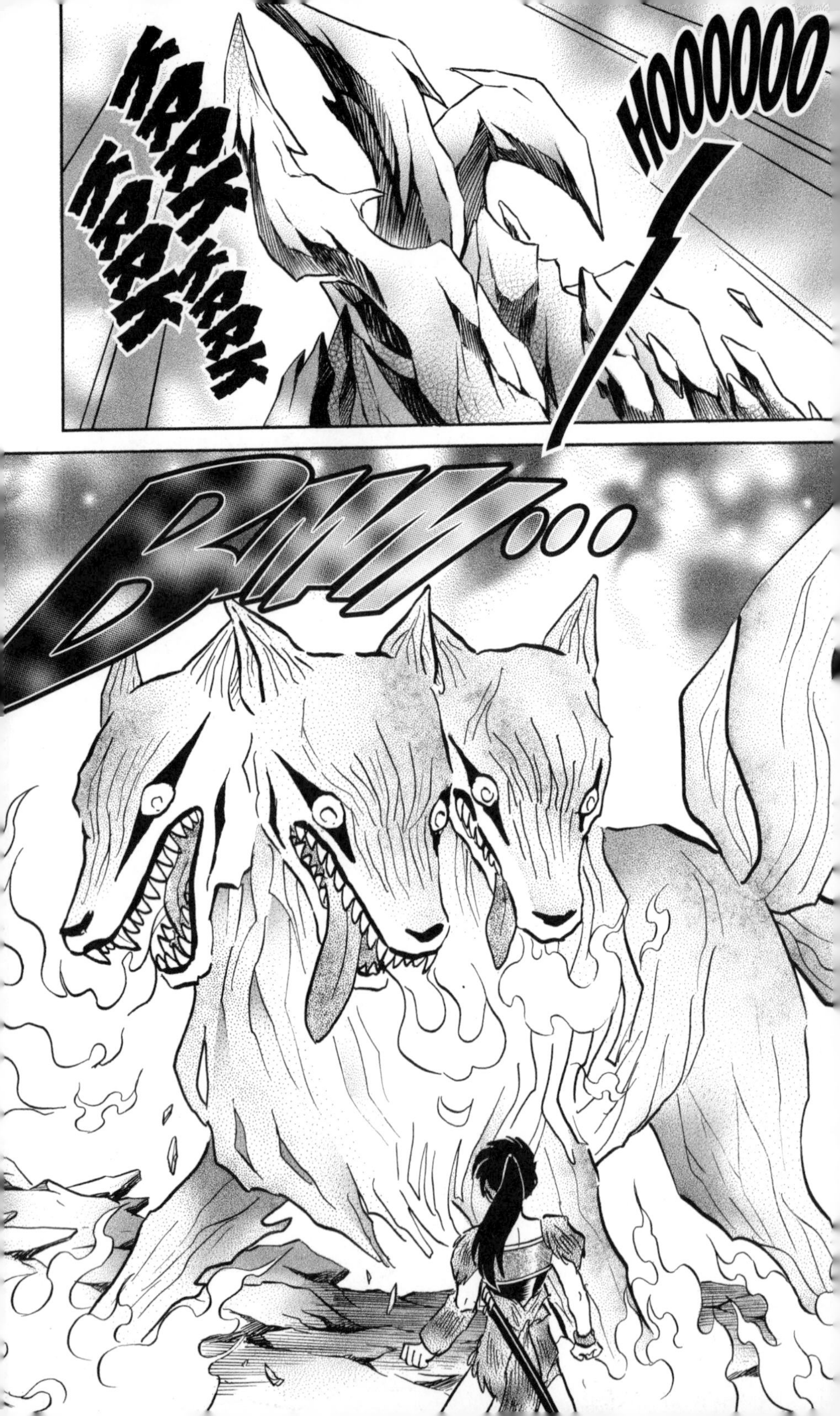
HOOOOOO
KRAK KRAK KRAK KRAK
BMM...

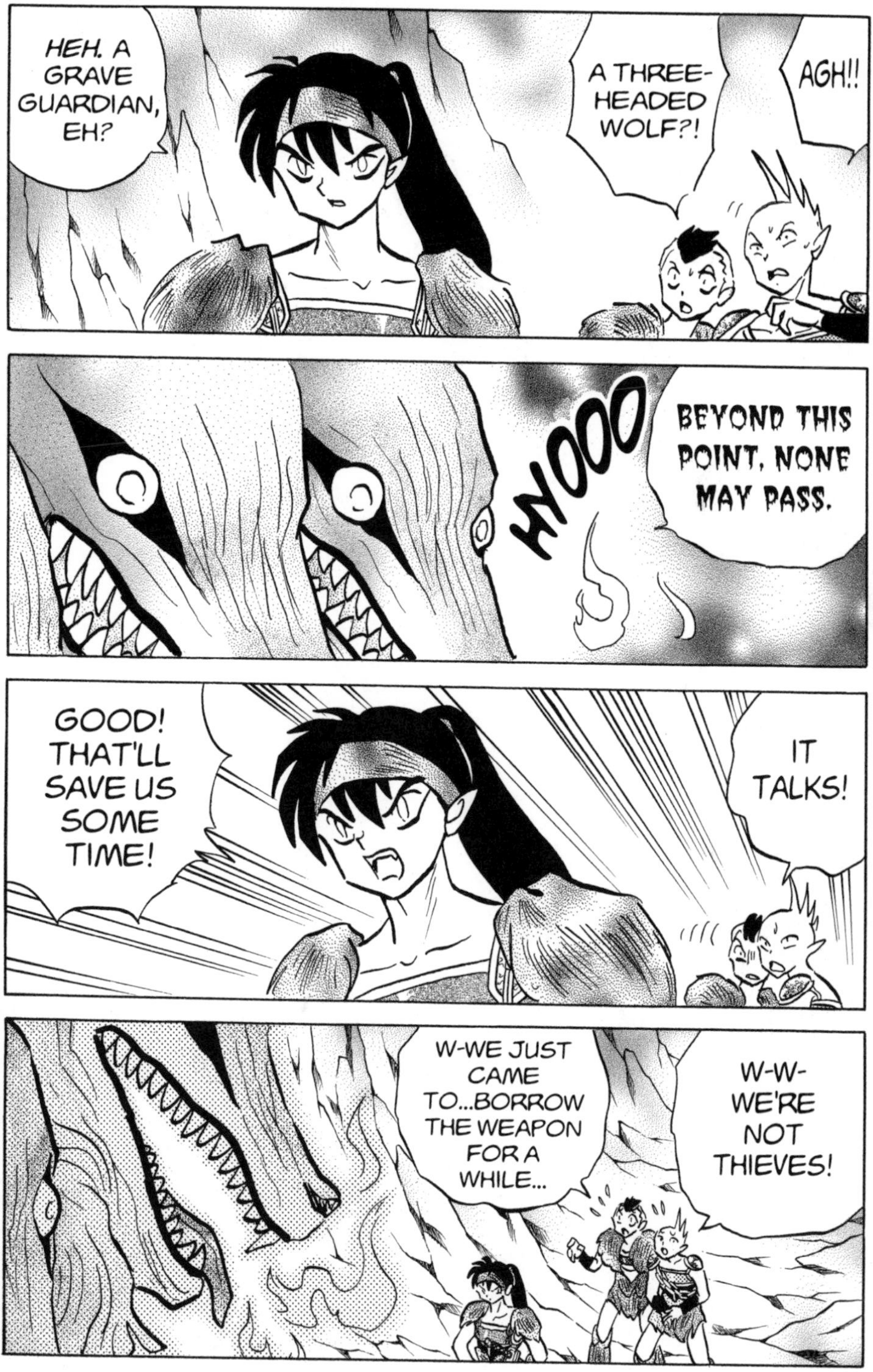
AGH!!
A THREE-HEADED WOLF?!
HEH. A GRAVE GUARDIAN, EH?
BEYOND THIS POINT, NONE MAY PASS.
HYOOO
IT TALKS!
GOOD! THAT'LL SAVE US SOME TIME!
W-W-WE'RE NOT THIEVES!
W-WE JUST CAME TO...BORROW THE WEAPON FOR A WHILE...

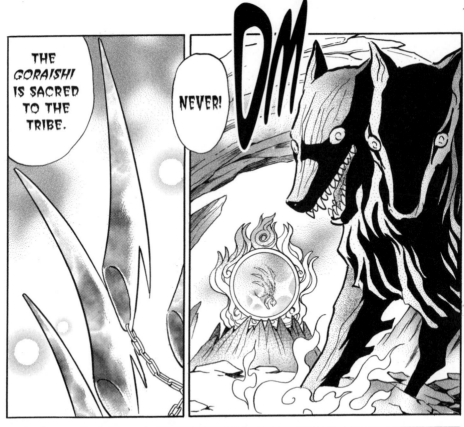

THE *GORAISHI* IS SACRED TO THE TRIBE.

NEVER!

OM

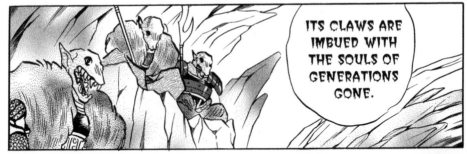

ITS CLAWS ARE IMBUED WITH THE SOULS OF GENERATIONS GONE.

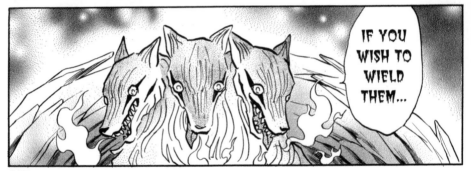

IF YOU WISH TO WIELD THEM...

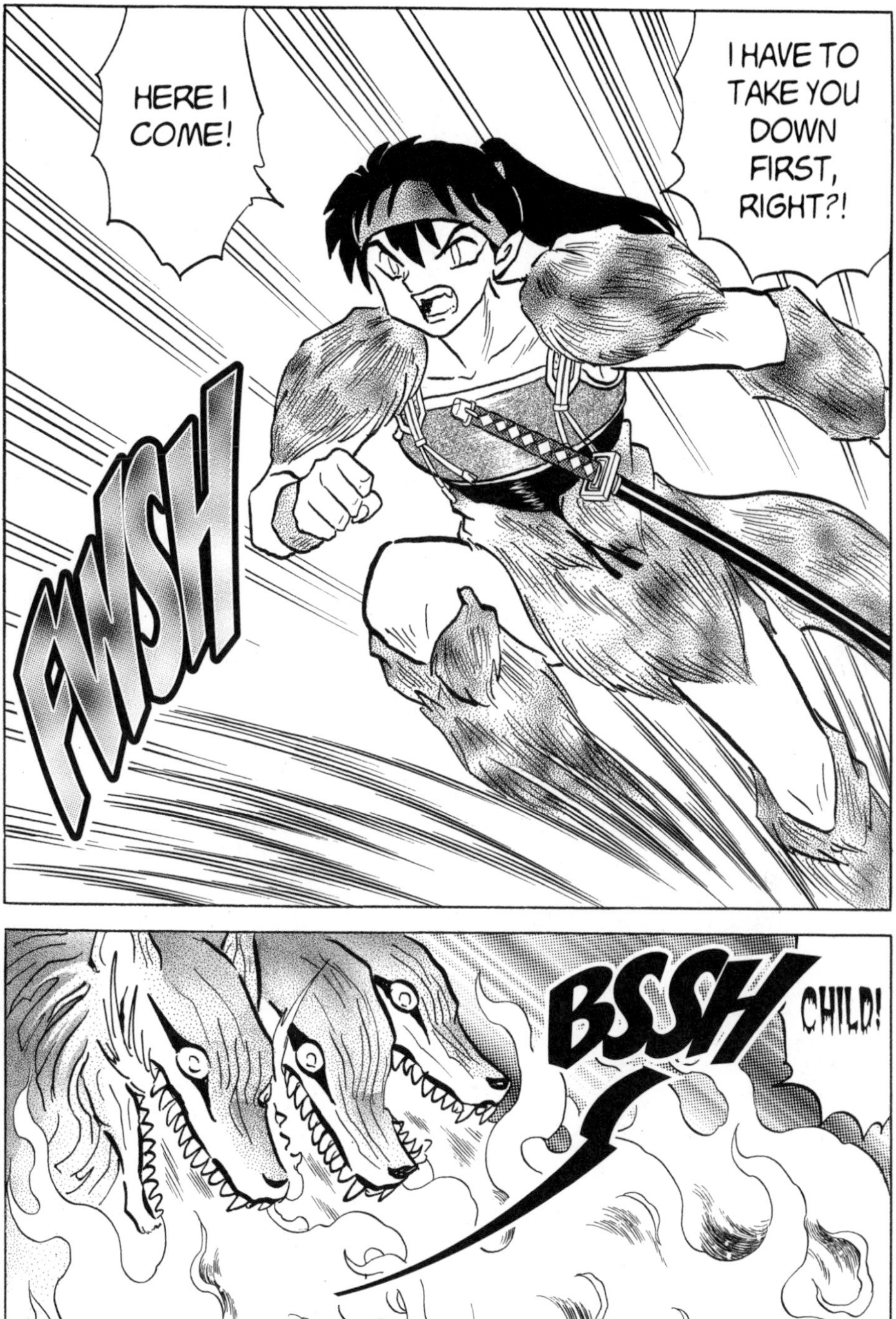
I HAVE TO TAKE YOU DOWN FIRST, RIGHT?!
HERE I COME!
FWSH
CHILD!
BSSH

SCROLL THREE
THE GUARDIAN OF THE TREASURE

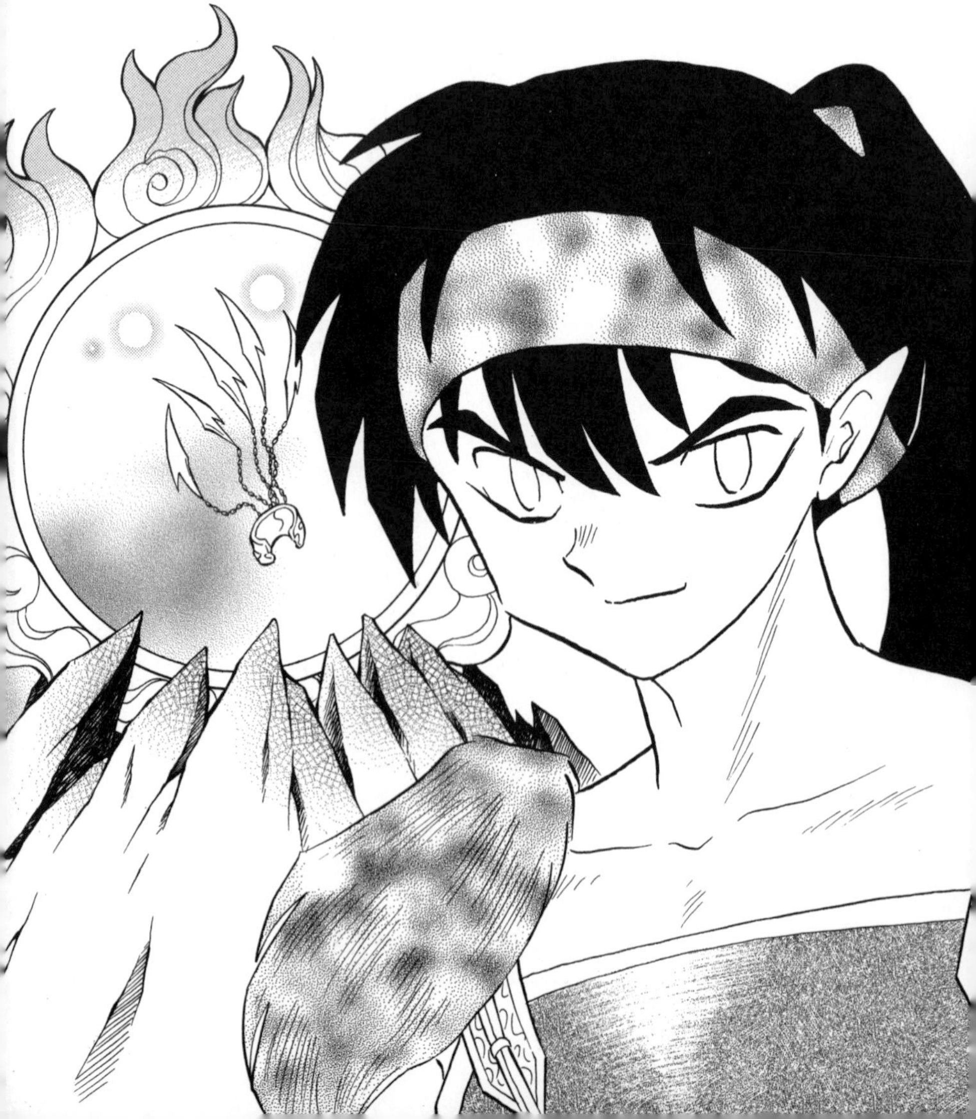

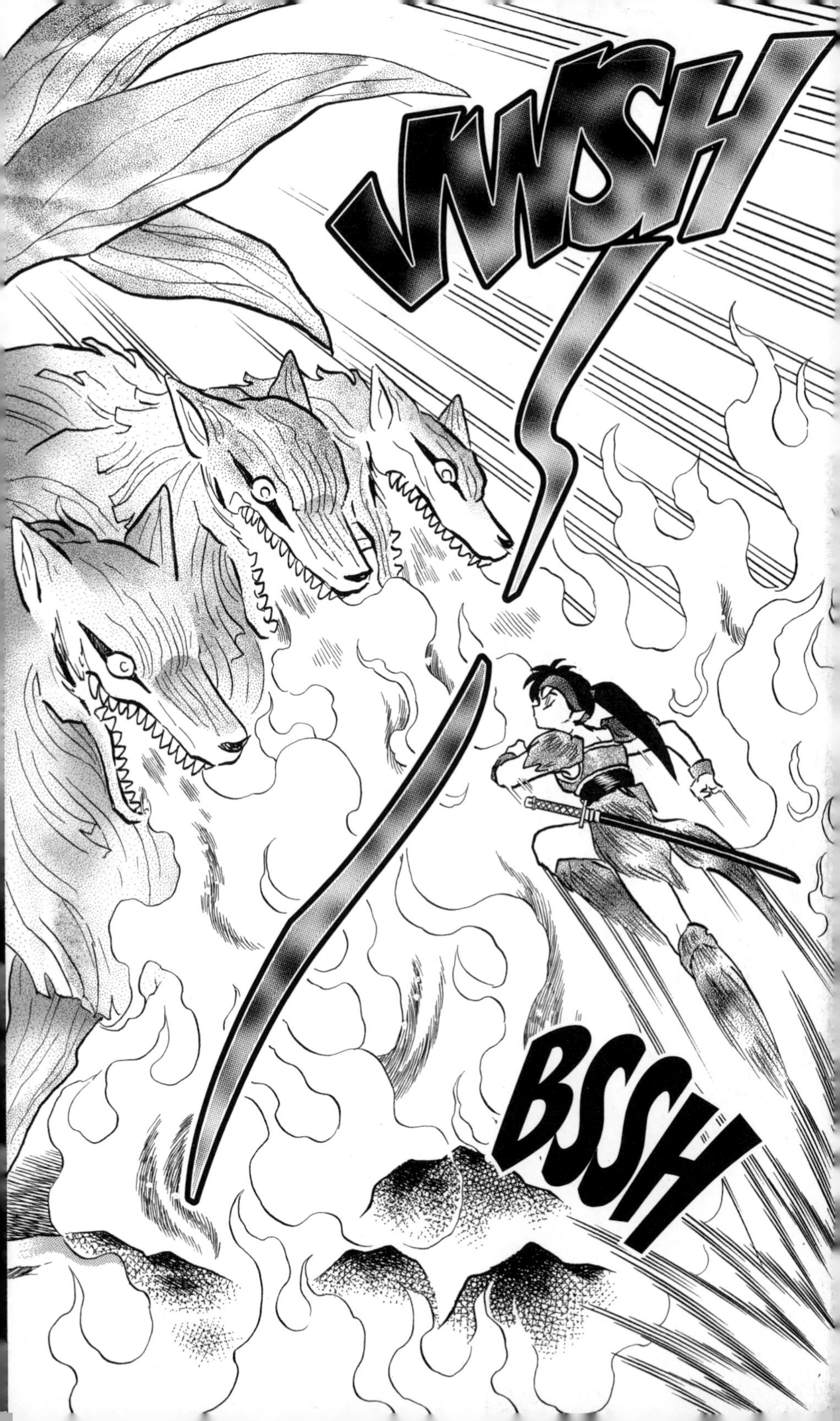
VWOSH
BSSH

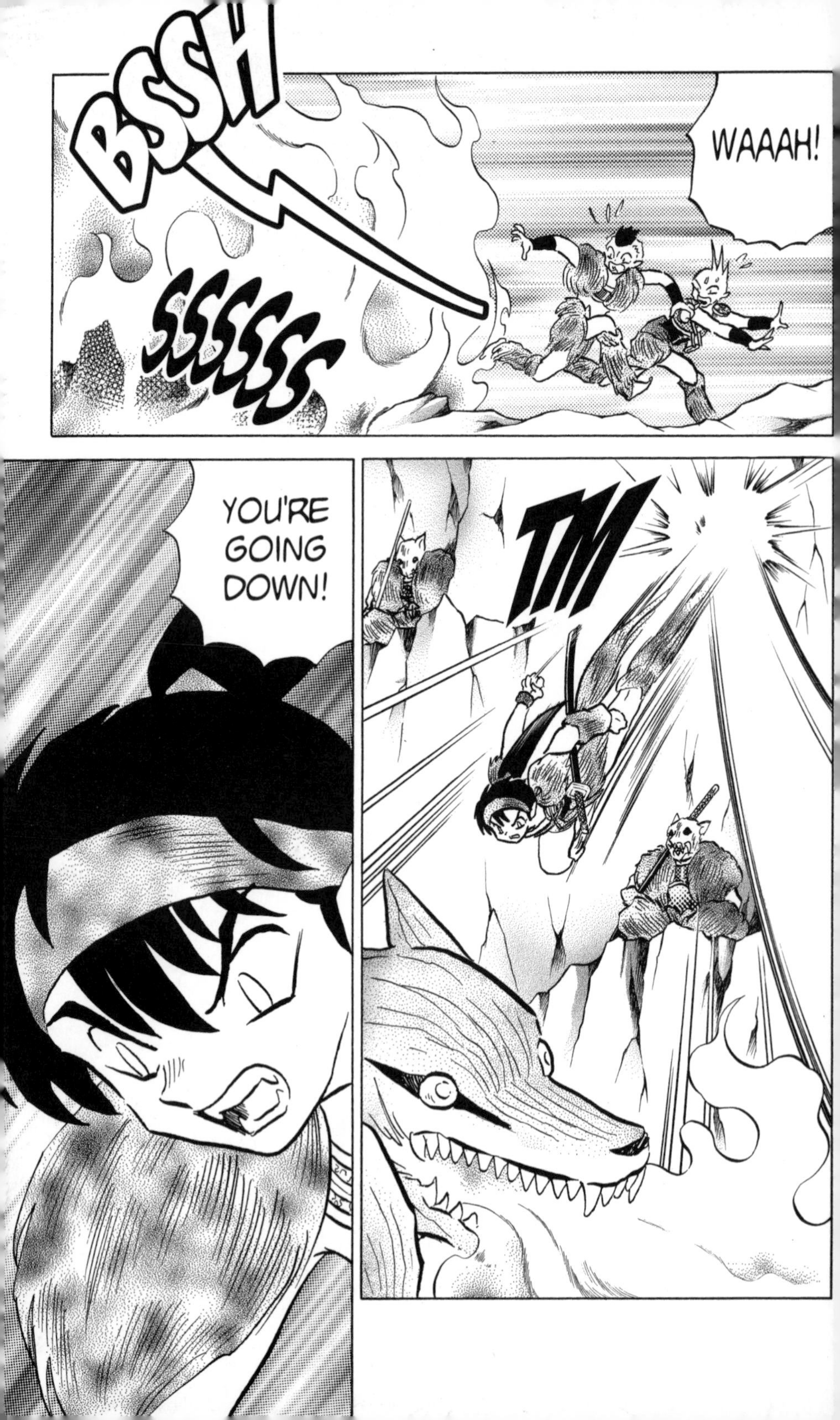
BSSH
SSSSSS
WAAAH!
TM
YOU'RE GOING DOWN!

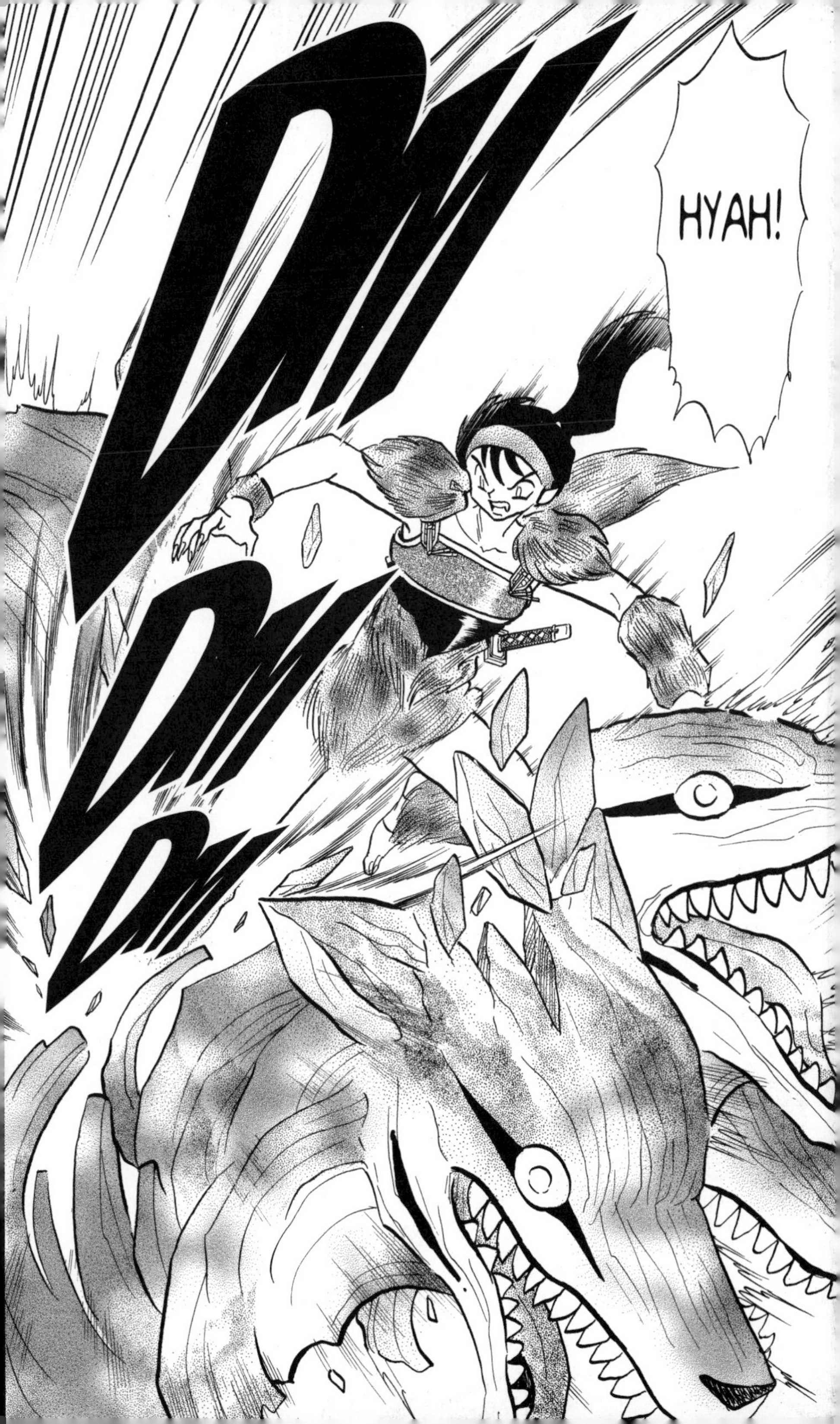
HYAH!

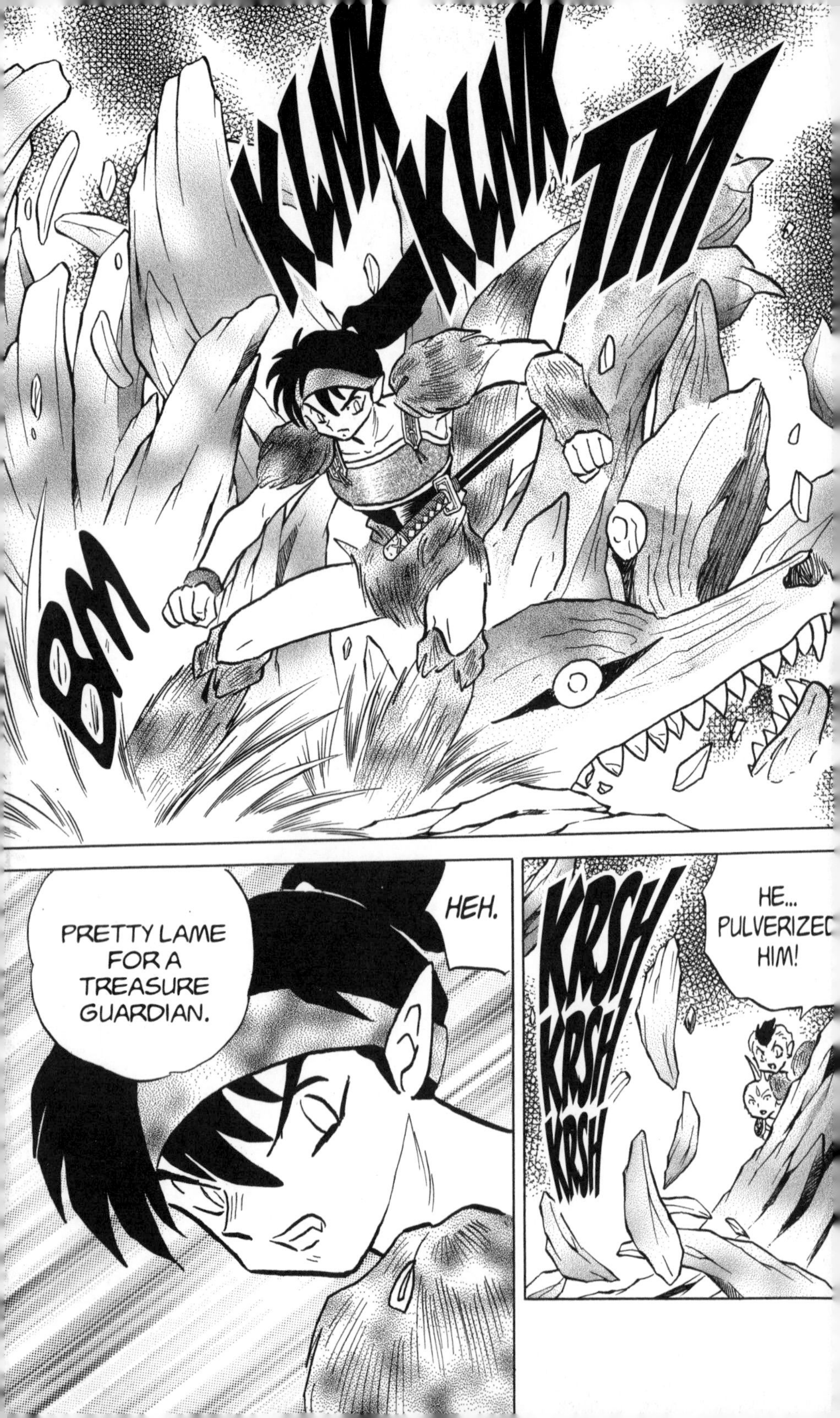
KRSH KRSH KRSH KRSH
HE... PULVERIZED HIM!
HEH.
PRETTY LAME FOR A TREASURE GUARDIAN.

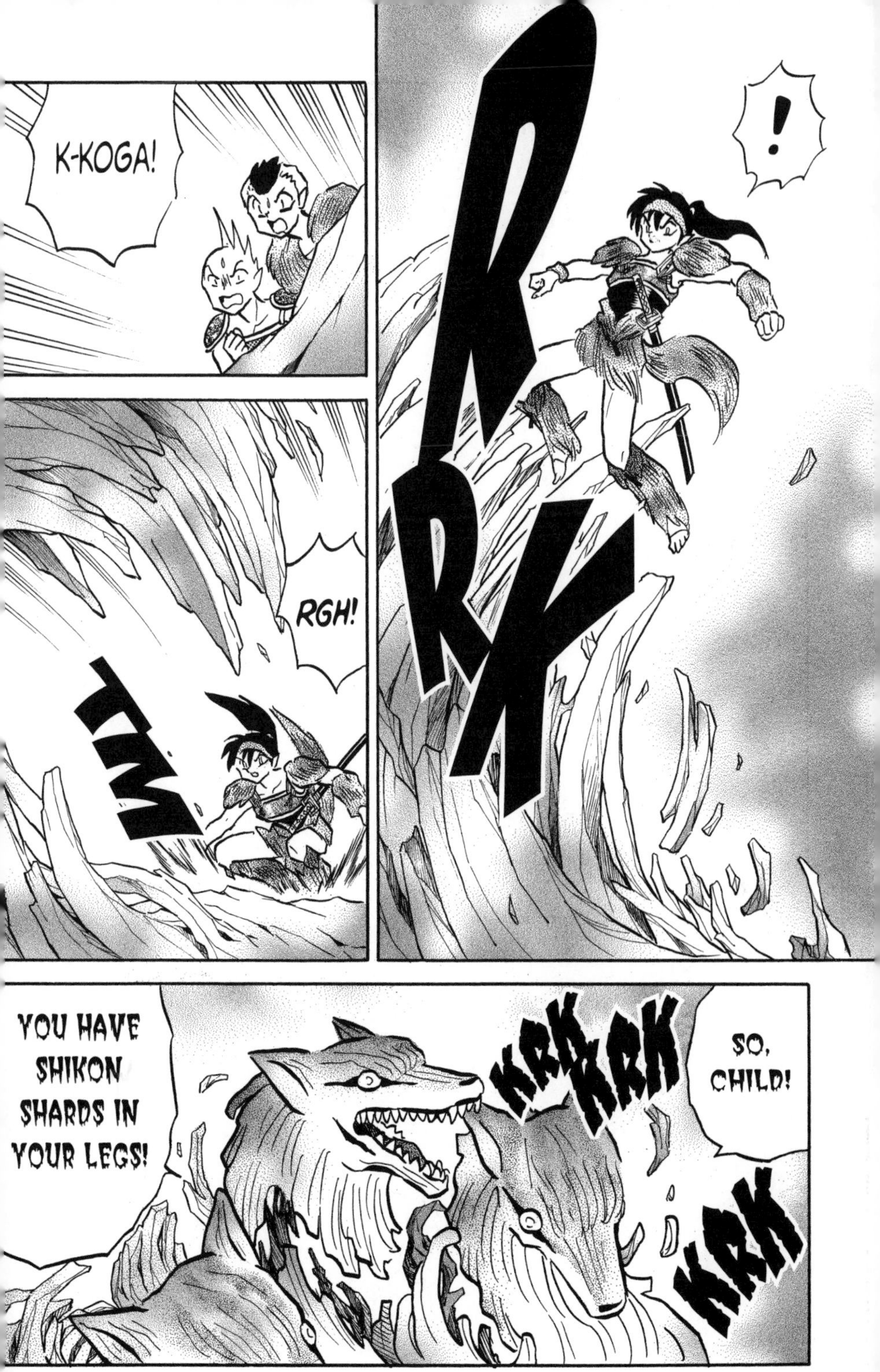
!
RRK
K-KOGA!
RGH!
TWM
SO, CHILD!
KRK KRK
KRK
YOU HAVE SHIKON SHARDS IN YOUR LEGS!

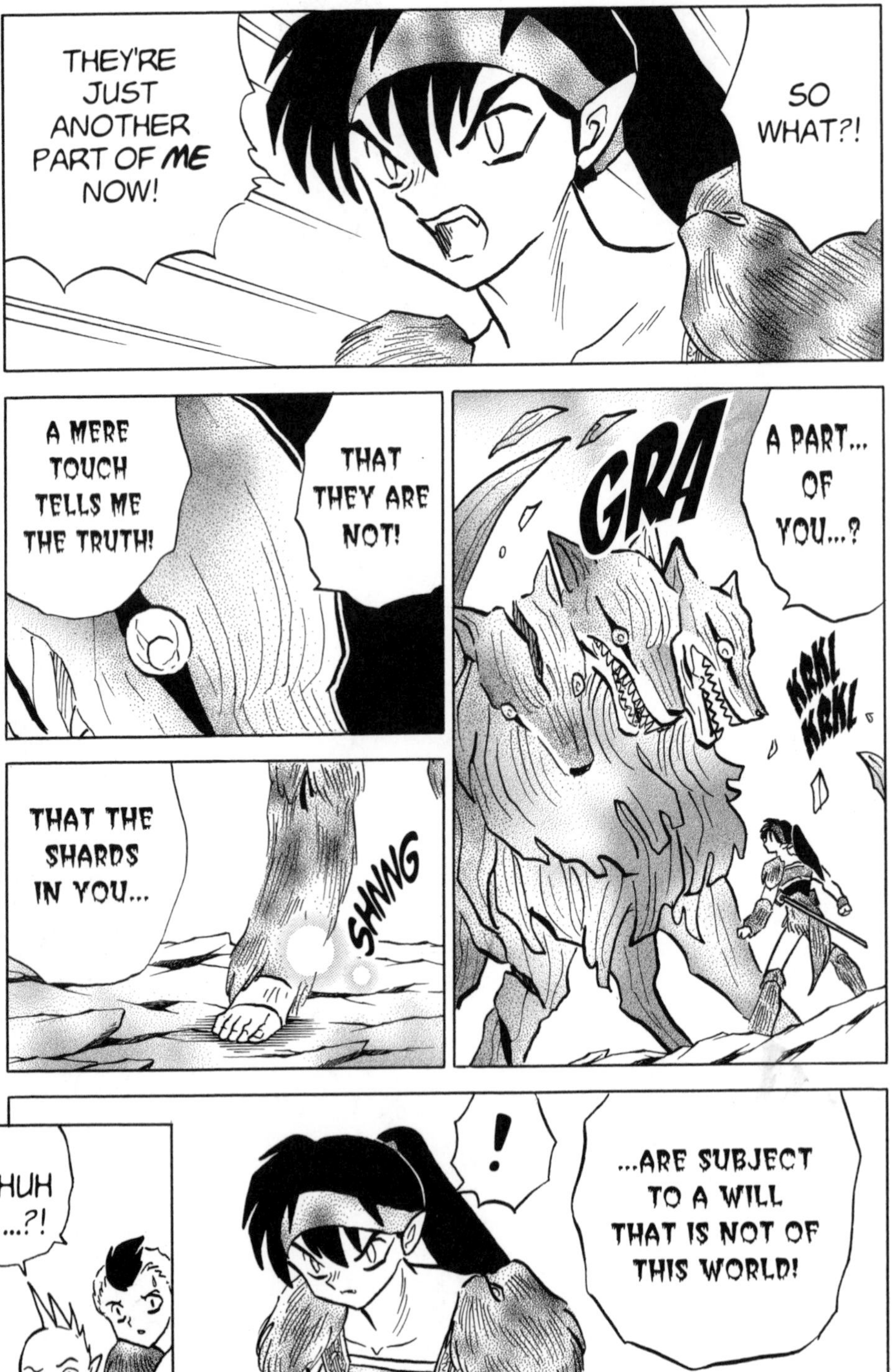
SO WHAT?!
THEY'RE JUST ANOTHER PART OF ME NOW!
A PART... OF YOU...?
GRA
KRKL KRKL
THAT THEY ARE NOT!
A MERE TOUCH TELLS ME THE TRUTH!
SHNNG
THAT THE SHARDS IN YOU...
...ARE SUBJECT TO A WILL THAT IS NOT OF THIS WORLD!
!
HUH ...?!

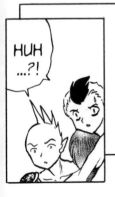

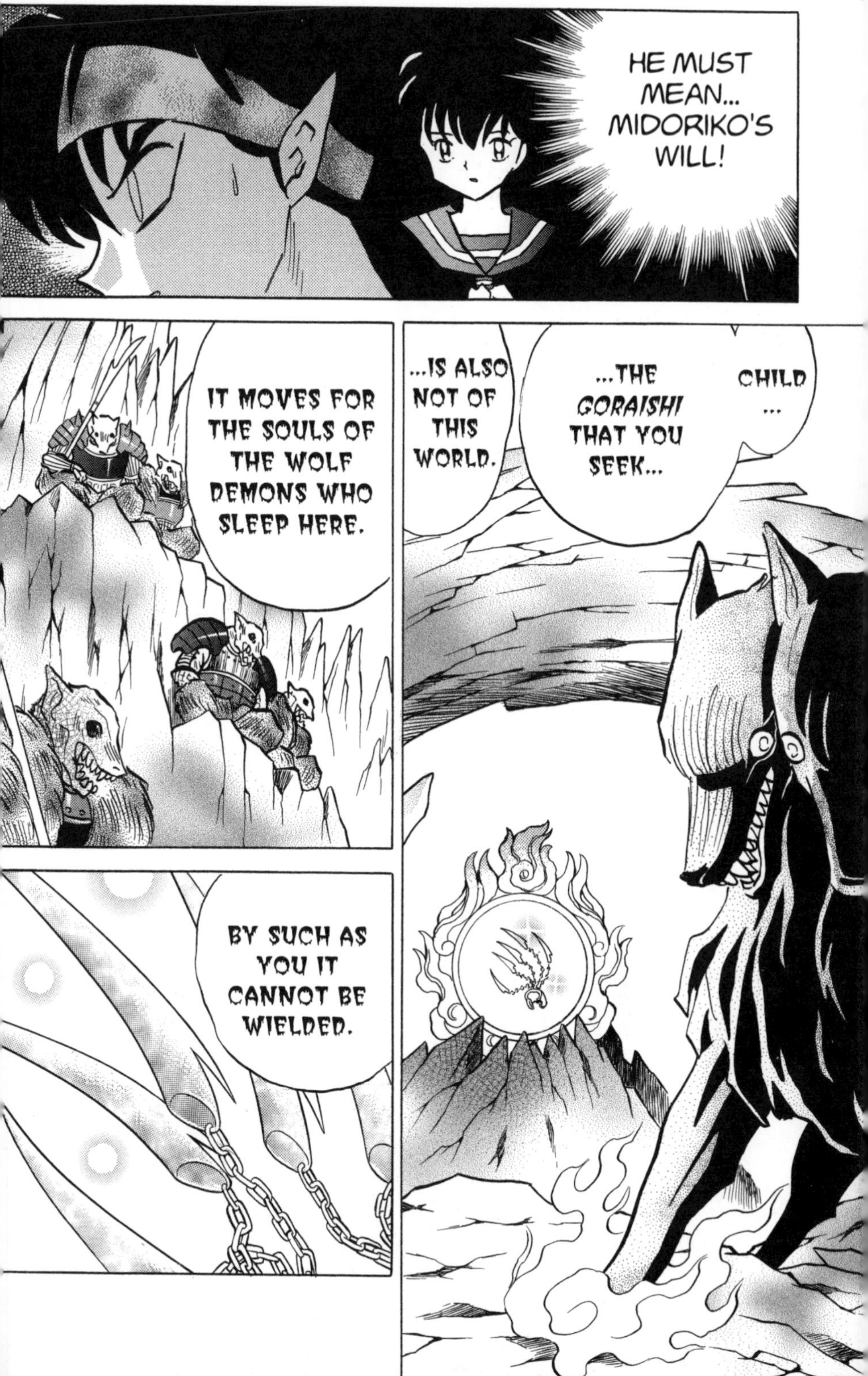
HE MUST MEAN... MIDORIKO'S WILL!
CHILD ...
...THE *GORAISHI* THAT YOU SEEK...
...IS ALSO NOT OF THIS WORLD.
IT MOVES FOR THE SOULS OF THE WOLF DEMONS WHO SLEEP HERE.
BY SUCH AS YOU IT CANNOT BE WIELDED.

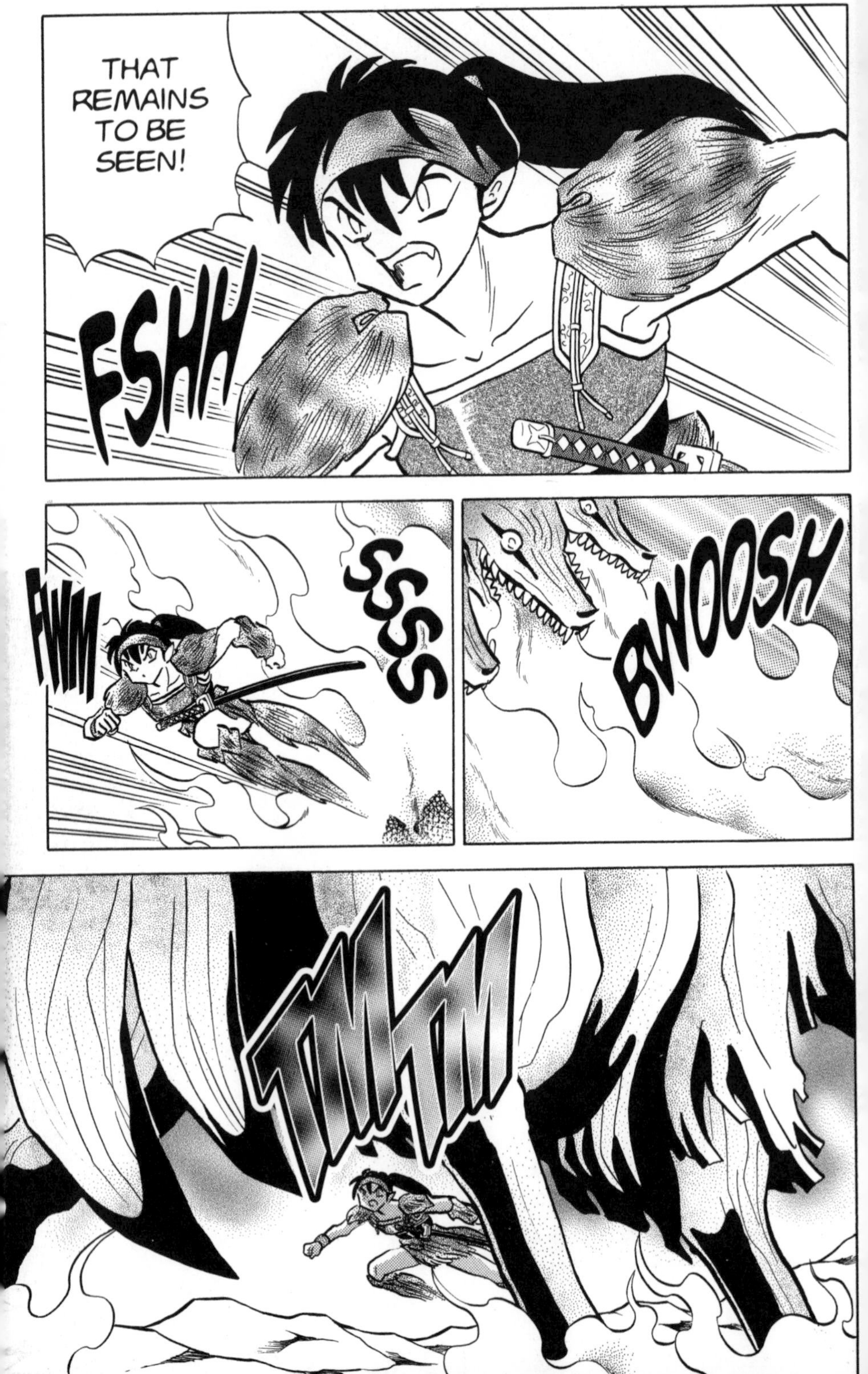
THAT REMAINS TO BE SEEN!
FSHH
BWOOSH
SSSS
FWM

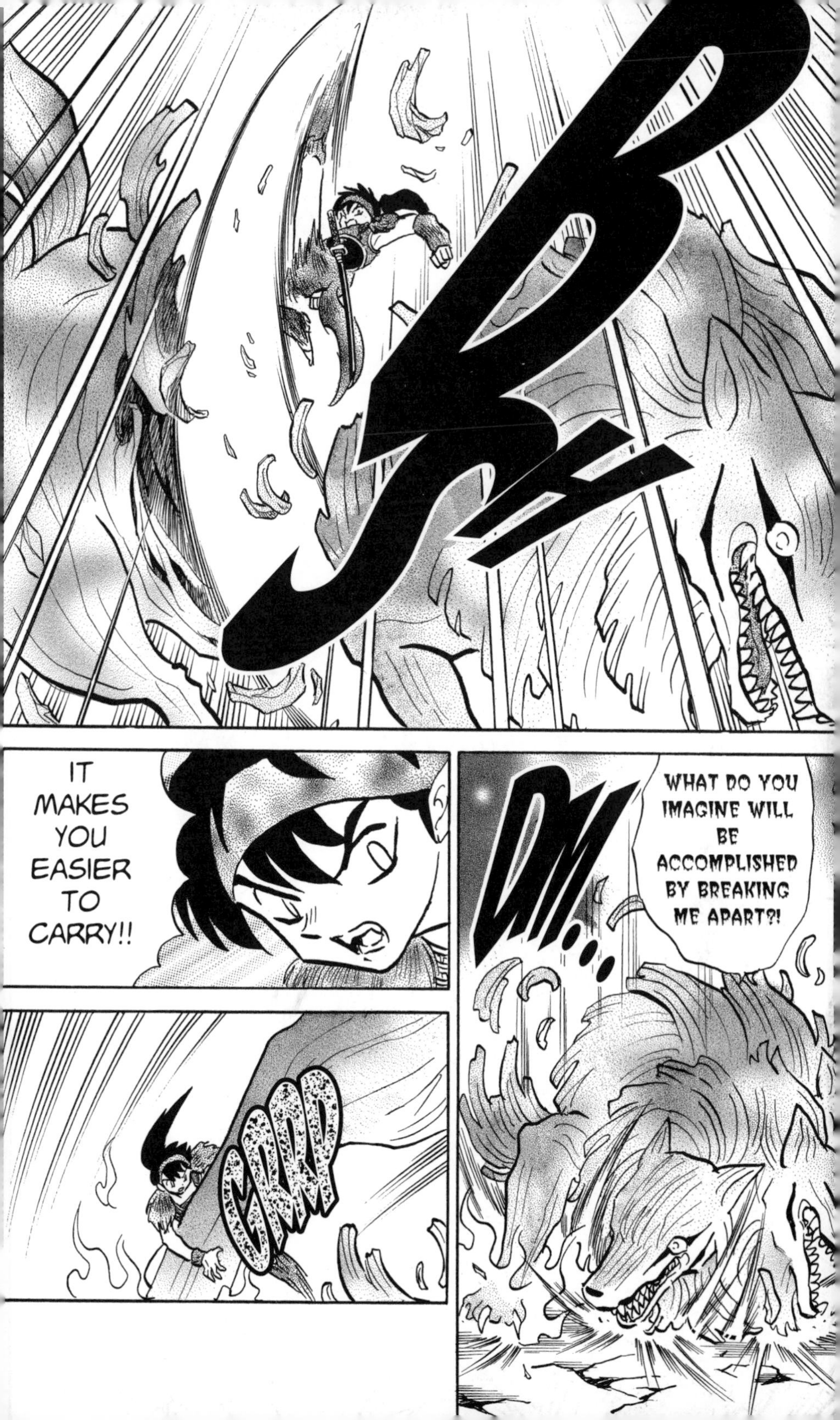
WHAT DO YOU IMAGINE WILL BE ACCOMPLISHED BY BREAKING ME APART?!
IT MAKES YOU EASIER TO CARRY!!

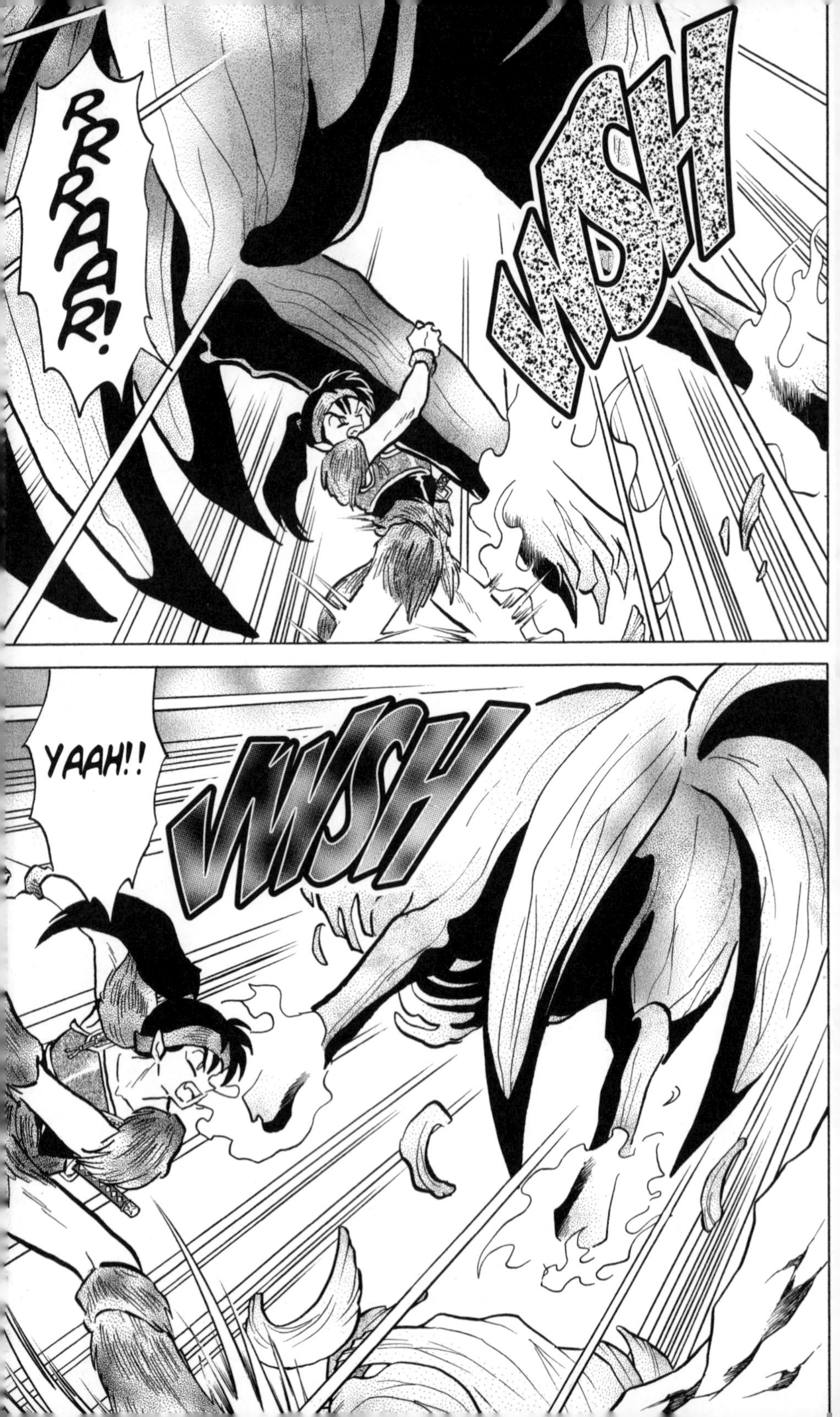
WOSH
RRRAAAR!
WHOSH
YAAH!!

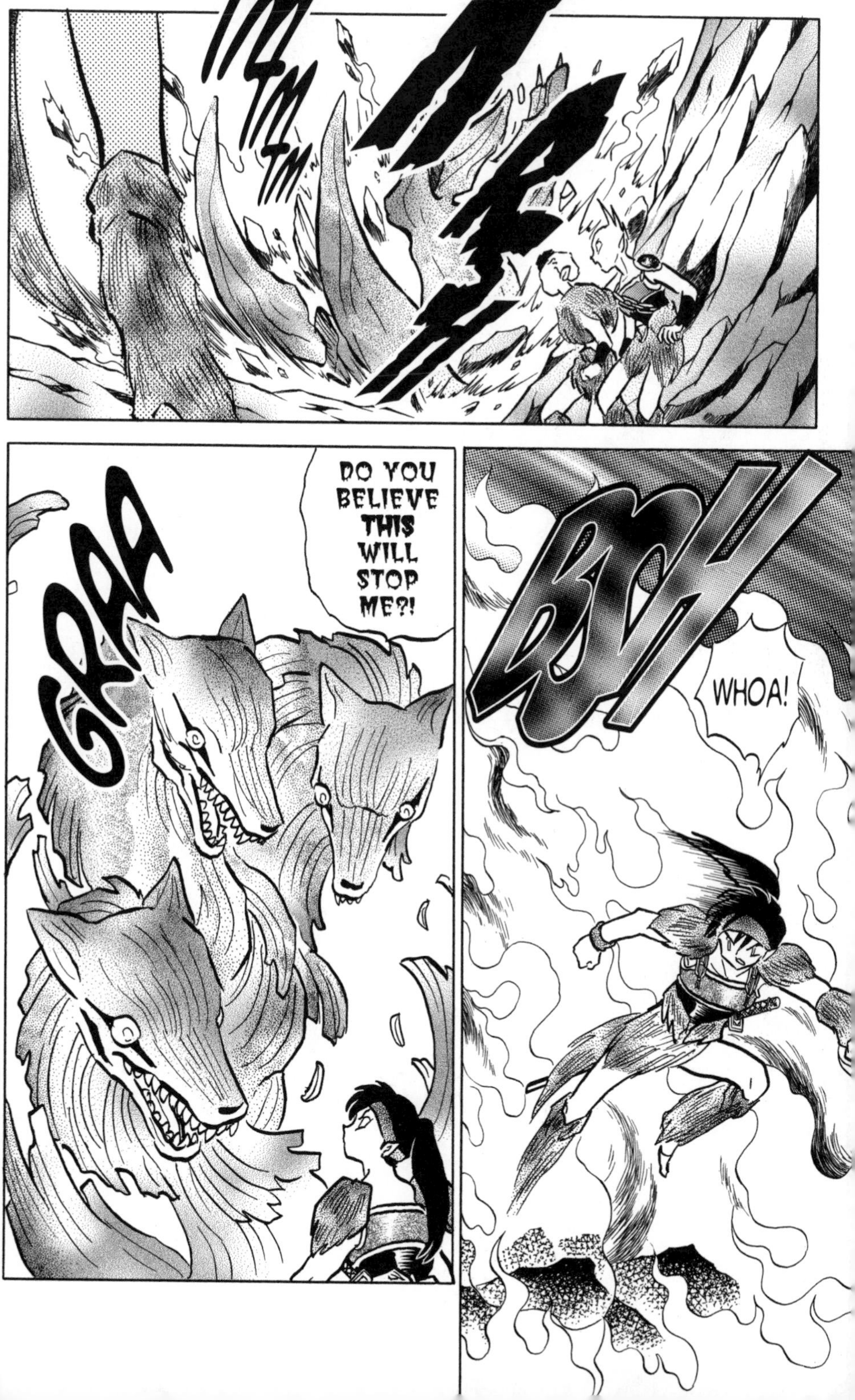
WHOA!
GRRA
DO YOU BELIEVE THIS WILL STOP ME?!

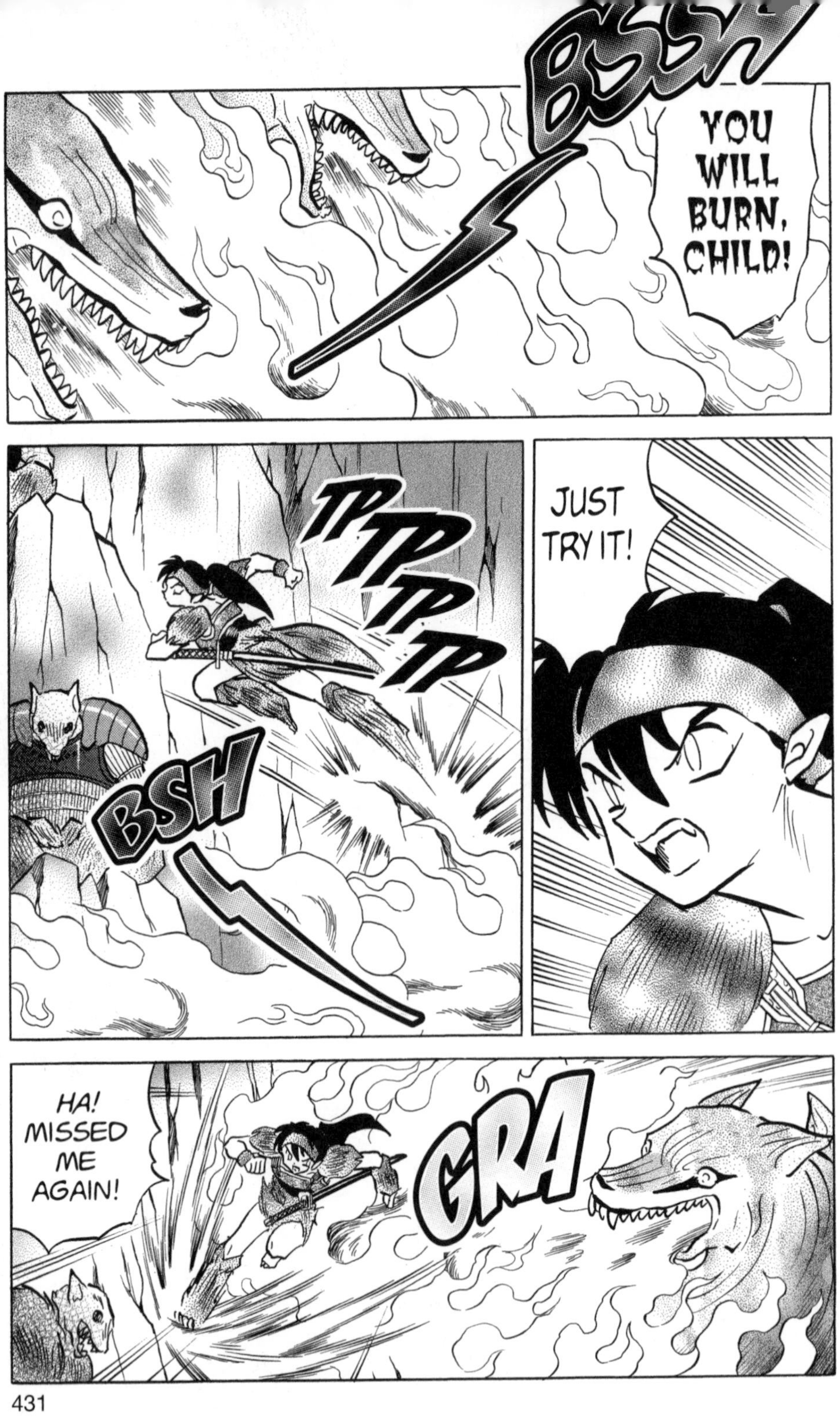
BSSH
YOU WILL BURN, CHILD!
JUST TRY IT!
TP TP TP TP TP
BSH
GRA
HA! MISSED ME AGAIN!

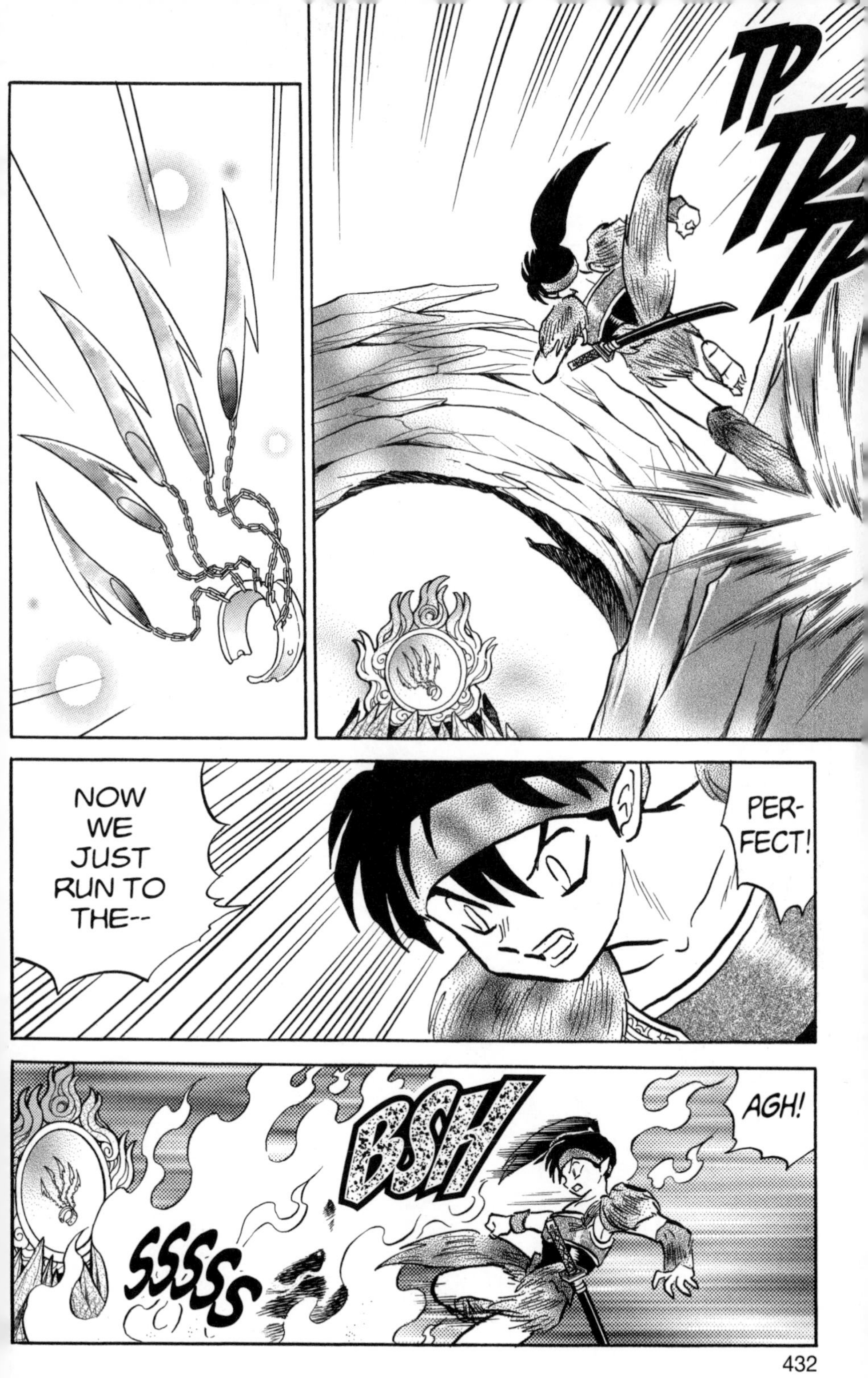
TP TP TP
PER-FECT!
NOW WE JUST RUN TO THE--
AGH!
BSH
SSSSS

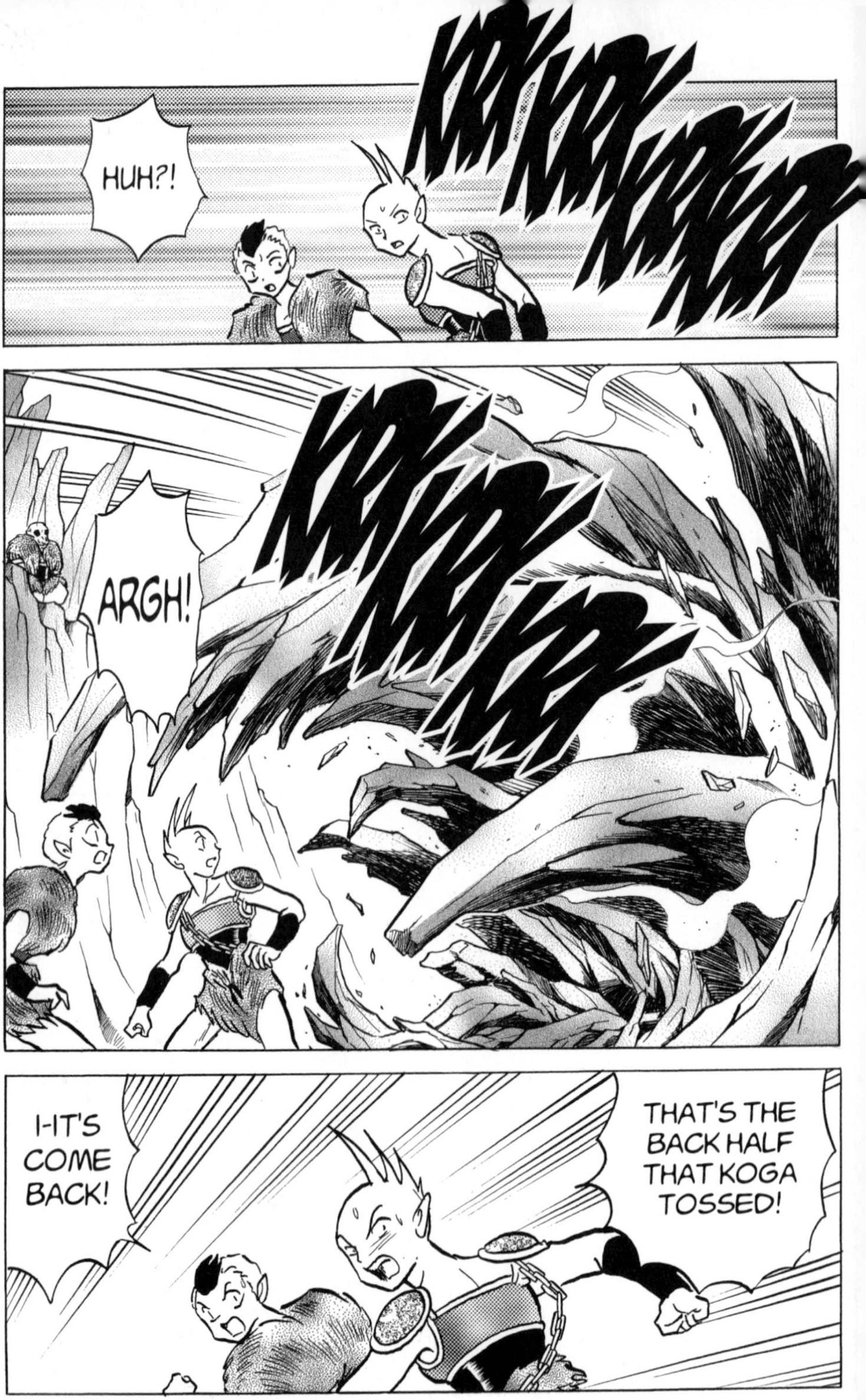
HUH?!
ARGH!
THAT'S THE BACK HALF THAT KOGA TOSSED!
I-IT'S COME BACK!

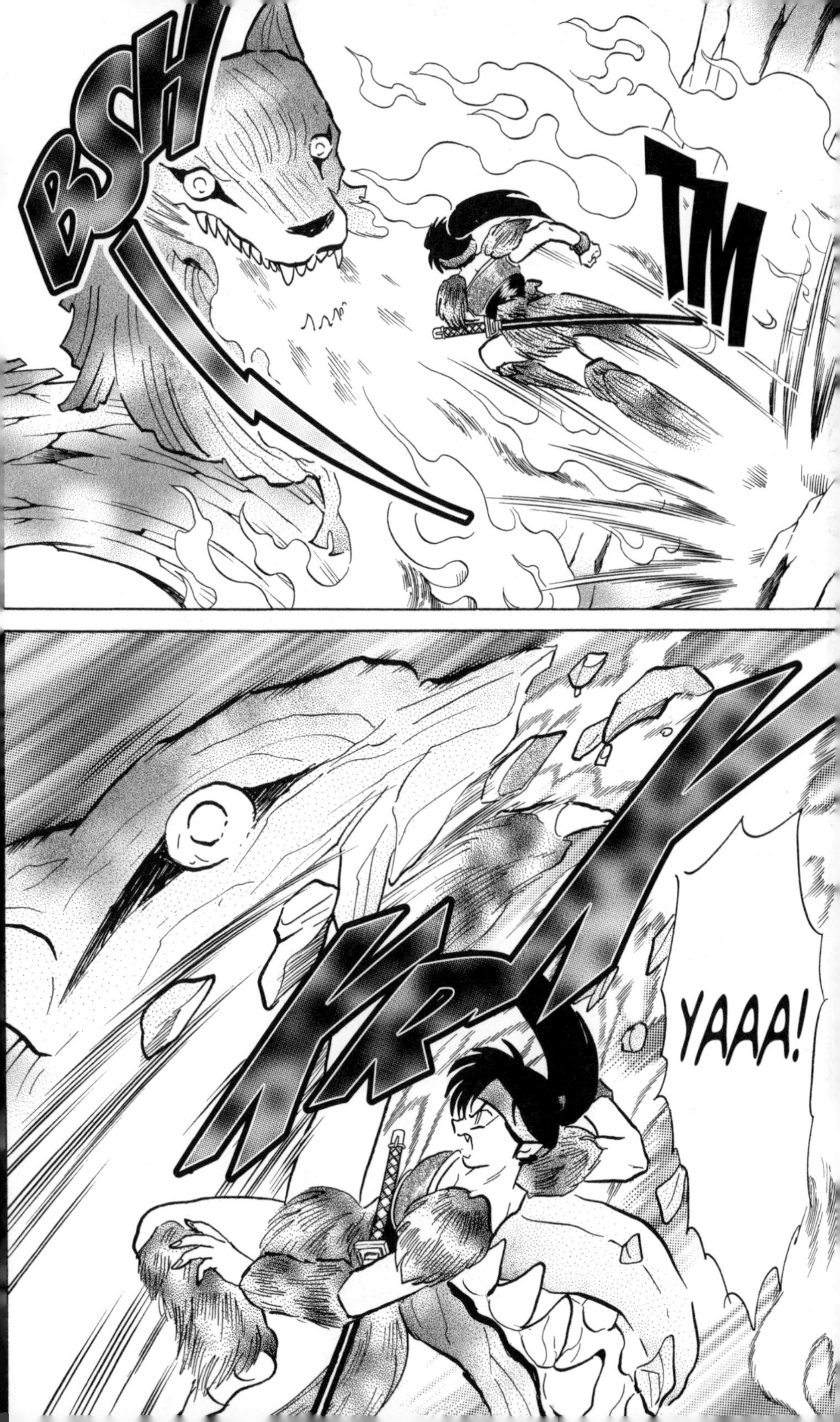
TM
BSCH
YAAA!

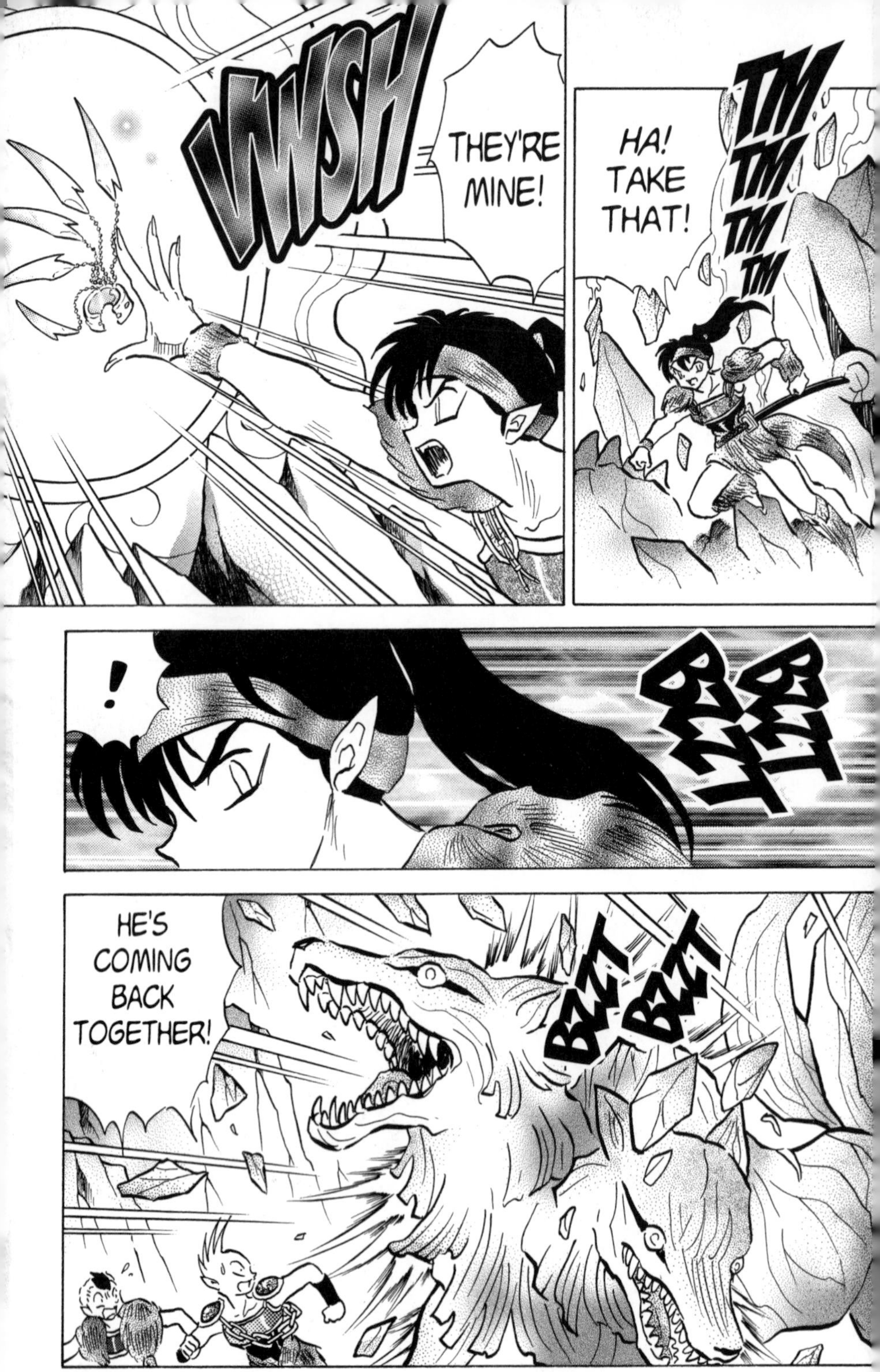
HA! TAKE THAT!
TM TM TM TM
VWSH
THEY'RE MINE!
BZZT BZZT
!
BZZT BZZT
HE'S COMING BACK TOGETHER!

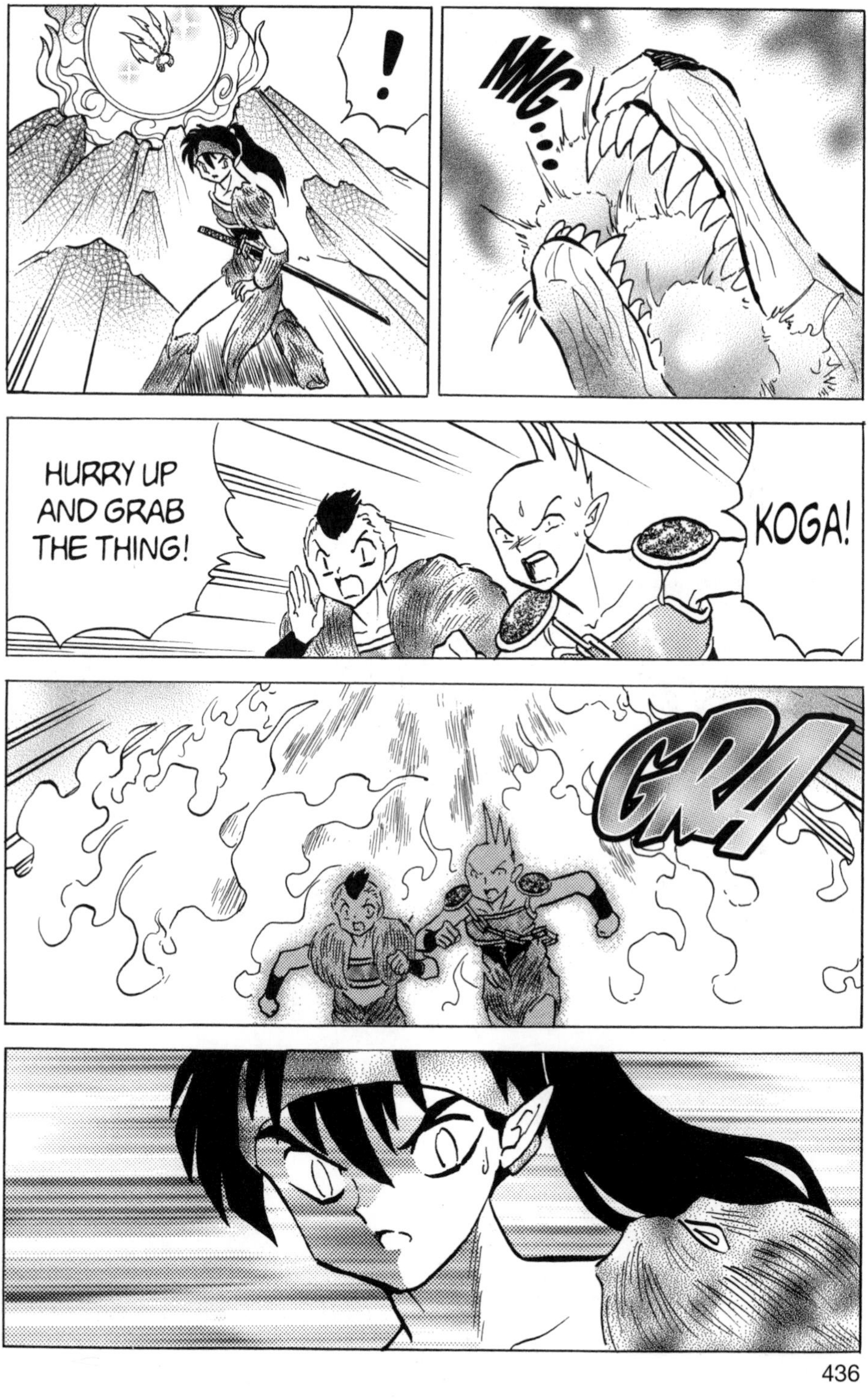
MNG...
!
KOGA!
HURRY UP AND GRAB THE THING!
GRA

SCROLL FOUR
GORAISHI

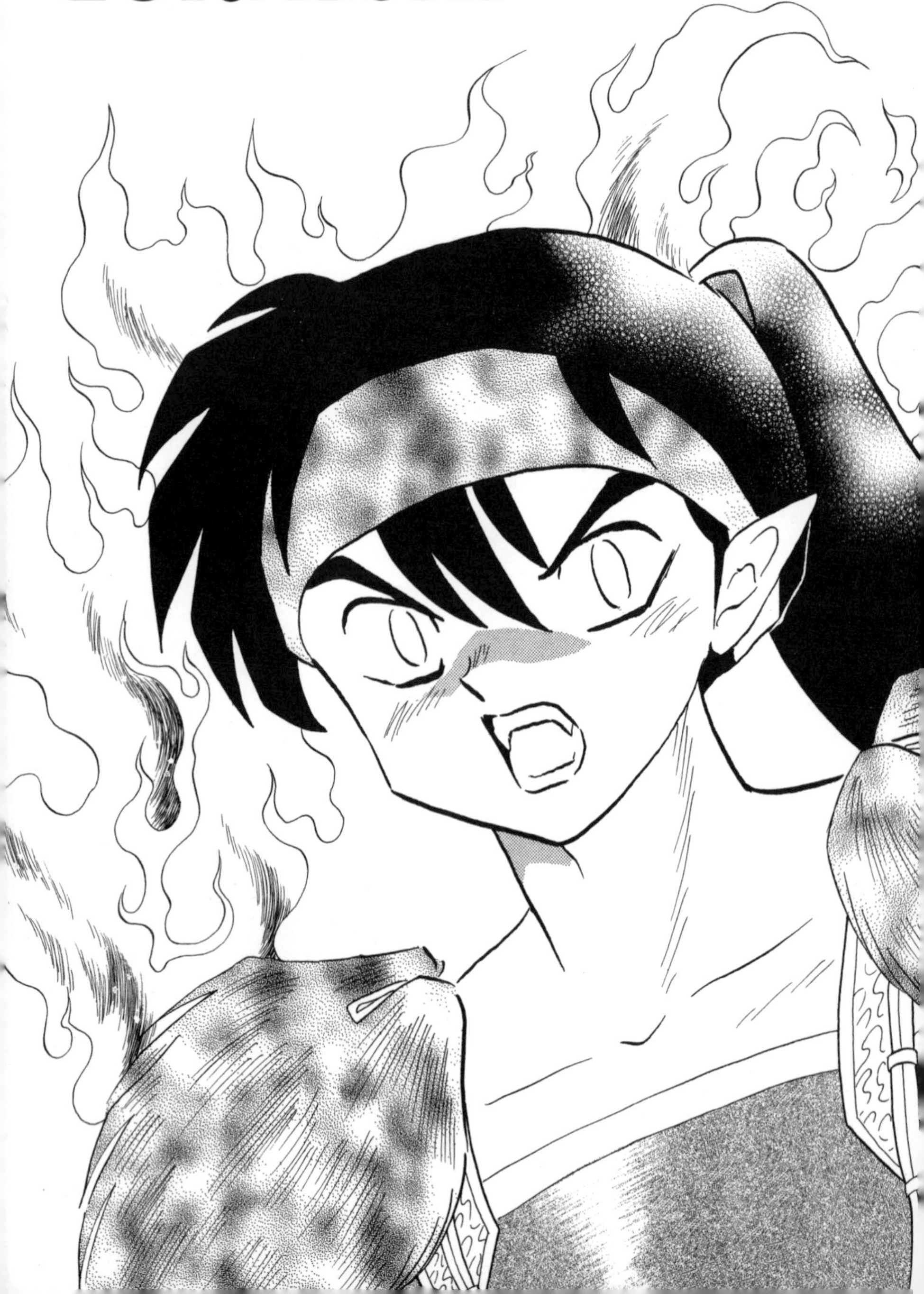

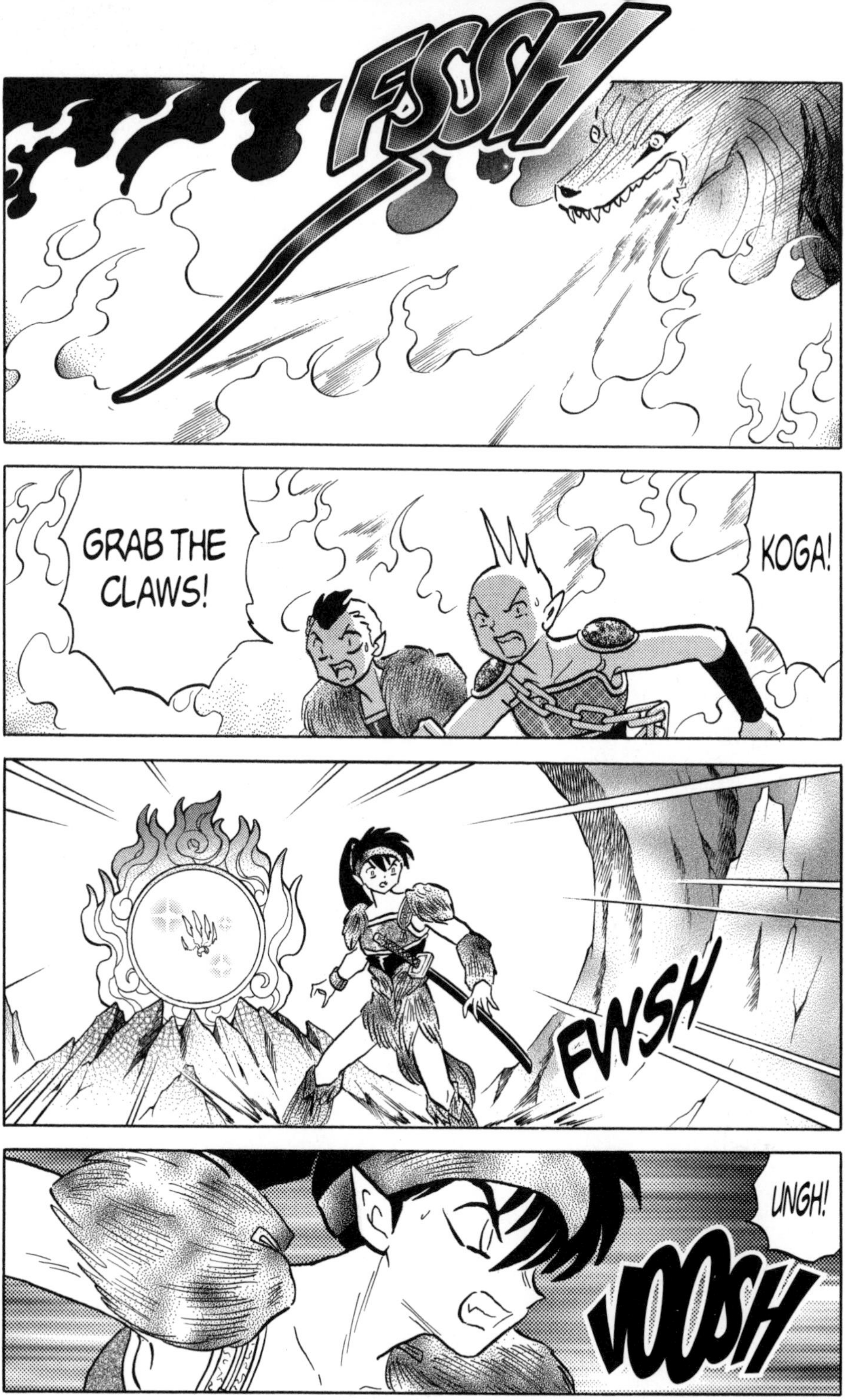
FSSH
KOGA!
GRAB THE CLAWS!
FWSH
UNGH!
VOOSH

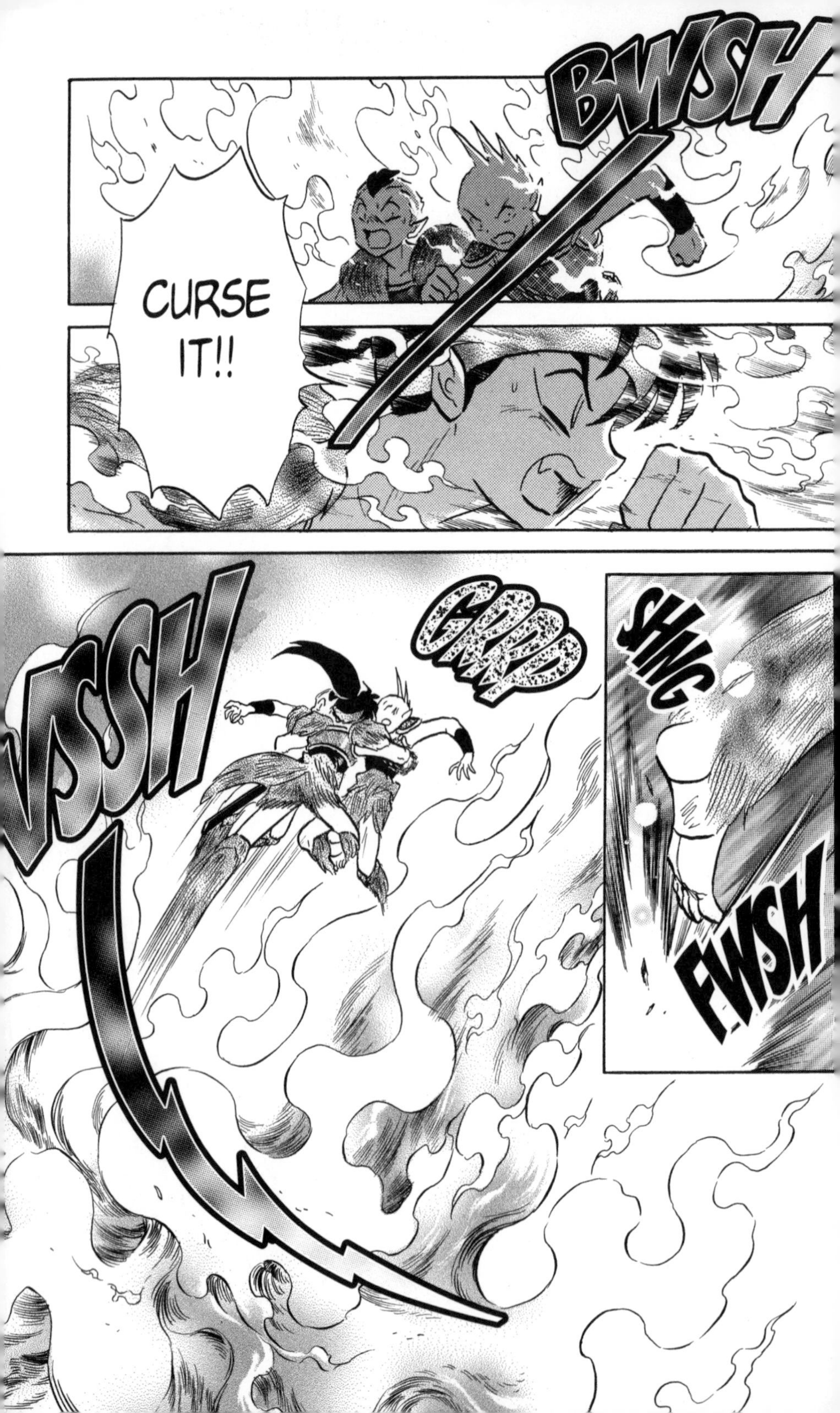
BWSH
CURSE IT!!
SHING
FWSH
GRRP
VSSH

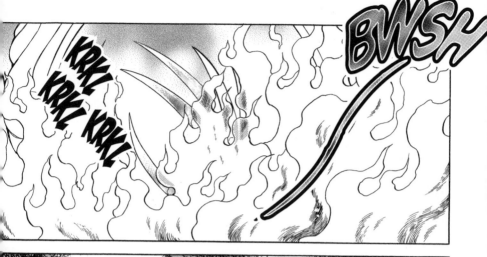

KRK! KRK! KRK!

BWSH

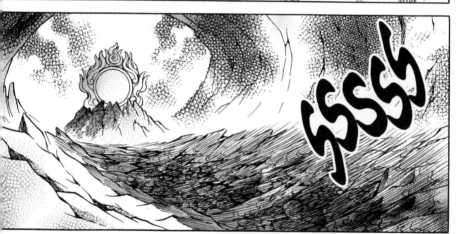

SSSS

THAT WAS TOO CLOSE...

S-SORRY, KOGA.

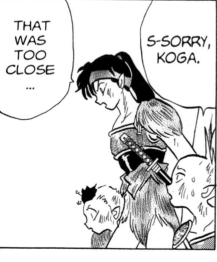

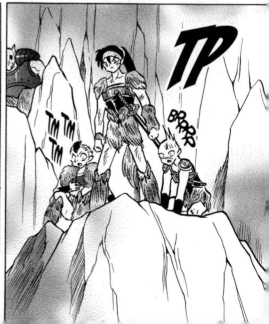

TP

TM TM TM

BRRRR

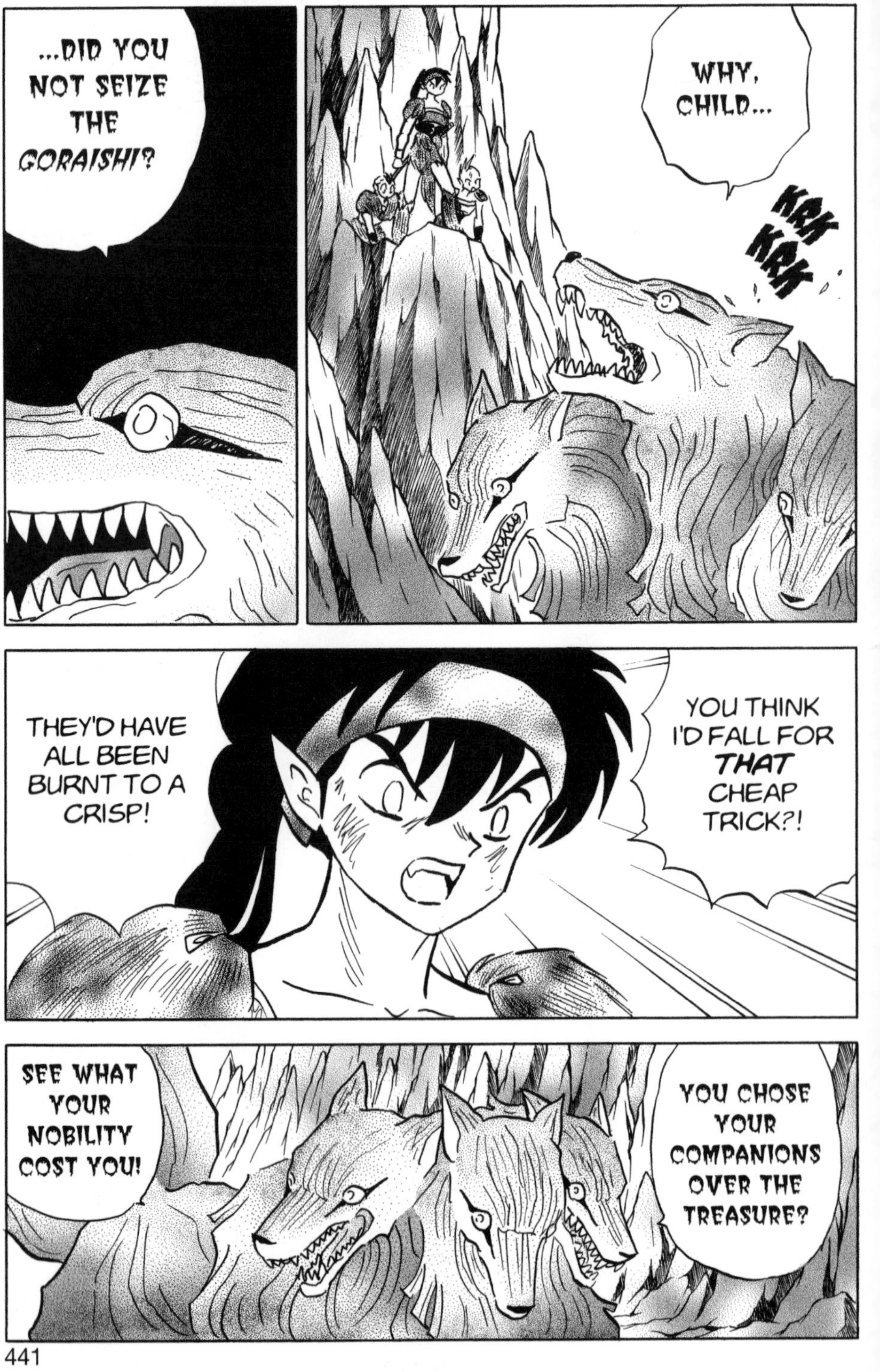
WHY, CHILD...
KRK KRK
...DID YOU NOT SEIZE THE *GORAISHI*?
YOU THINK I'D FALL FOR *THAT* CHEAP TRICK?!
THEY'D HAVE ALL BEEN BURNT TO A CRISP!
YOU CHOSE YOUR COMPANIONS OVER THE TREASURE?
SEE WHAT YOUR NOBILITY COST YOU!

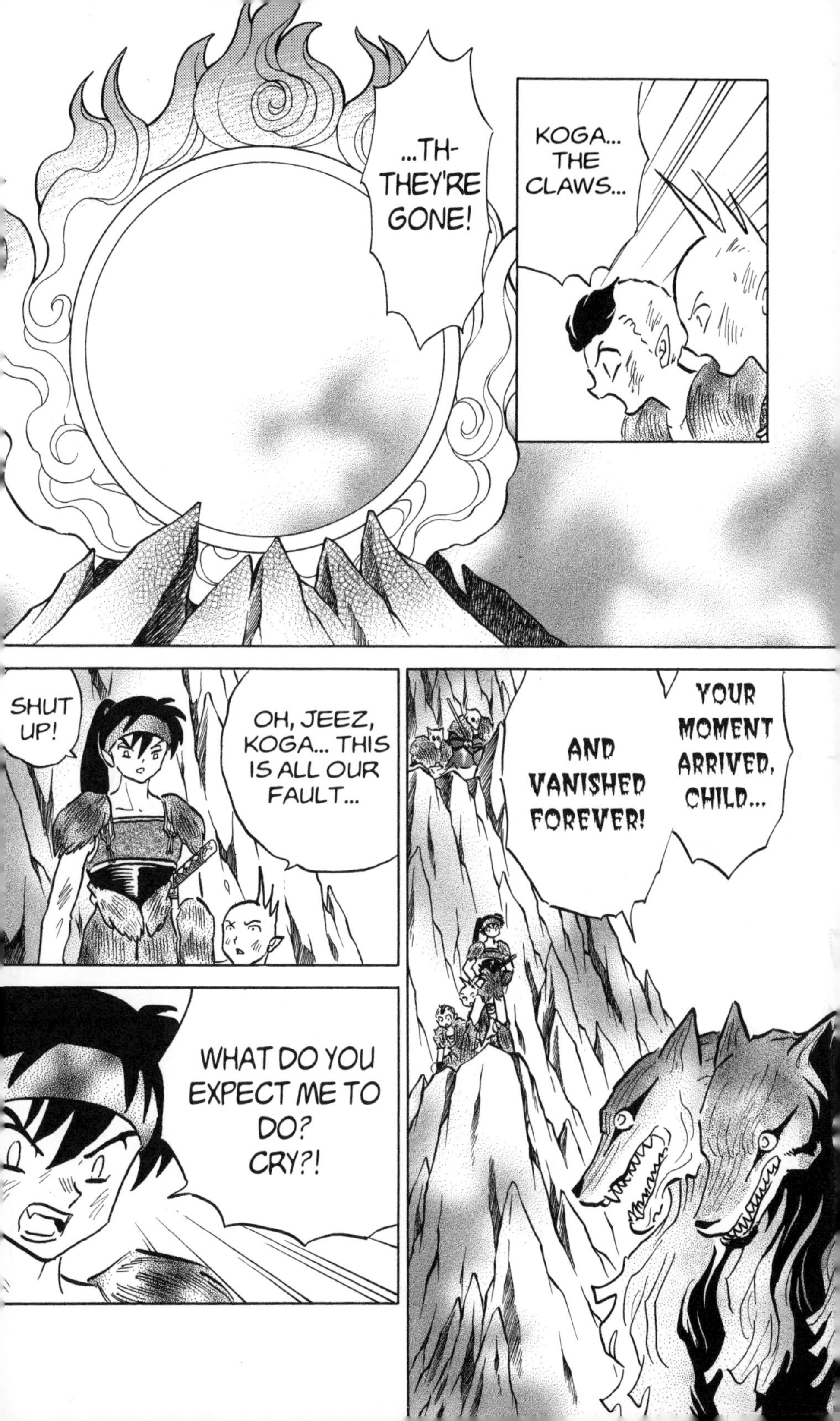
KOGA... THE CLAWS...
...TH- THEY'RE GONE!
YOUR MOMENT ARRIVED, CHILD...
AND VANISHED FOREVER!
OH, JEEZ, KOGA... THIS IS ALL OUR FAULT...
SHUT UP!
WHAT DO YOU EXPECT ME TO DO? CRY?!

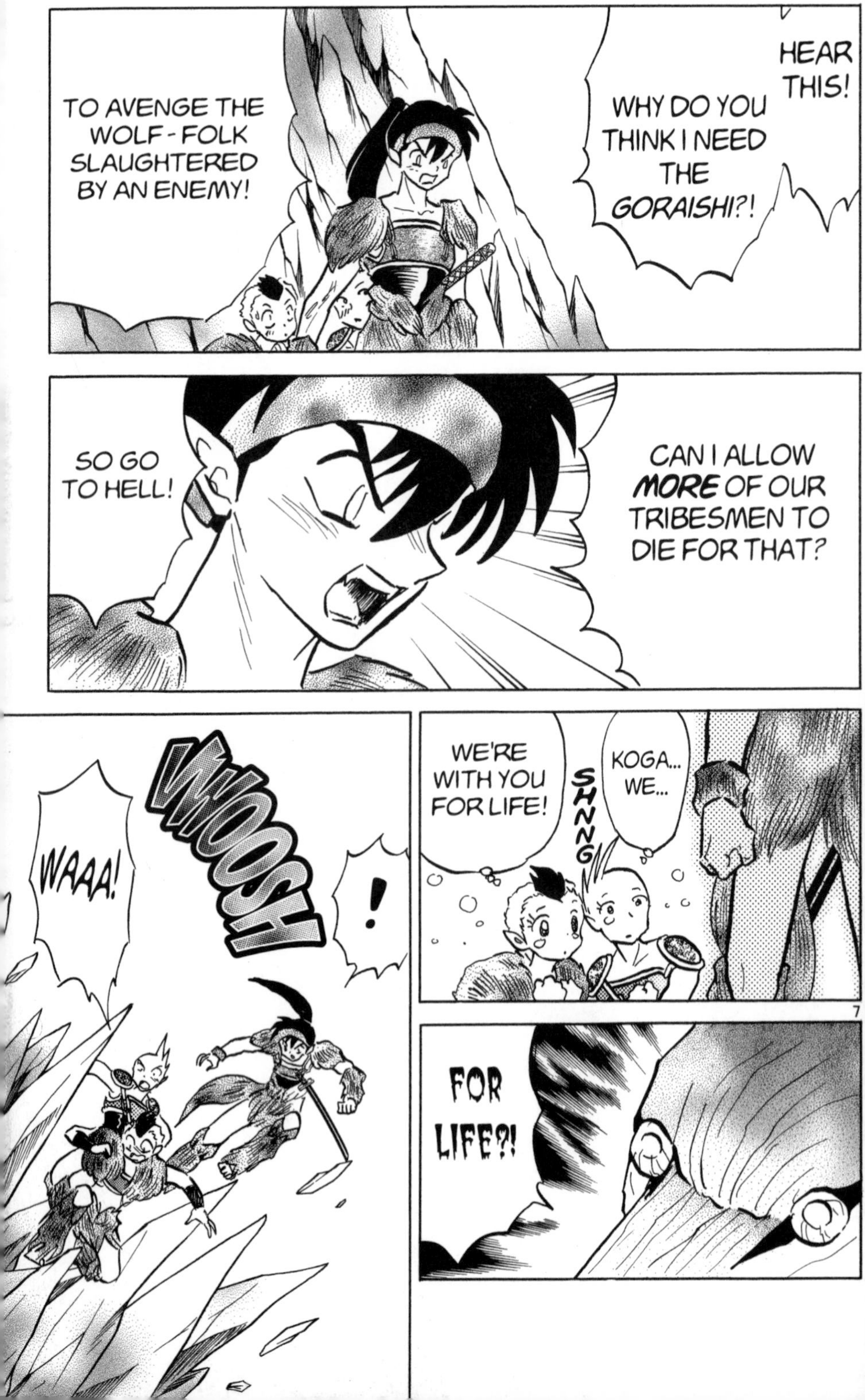
HEAR THIS!
WHY DO YOU THINK I NEED THE GORAISHI?!
TO AVENGE THE WOLF-FOLK SLAUGHTERED BY AN ENEMY!
CAN I ALLOW MORE OF OUR TRIBESMEN TO DIE FOR THAT?
SO GO TO HELL!
KOGA... WE...
SHNNG
WE'RE WITH YOU FOR LIFE!
FOR LIFE?!
!
WHOOSH!
WAAA!

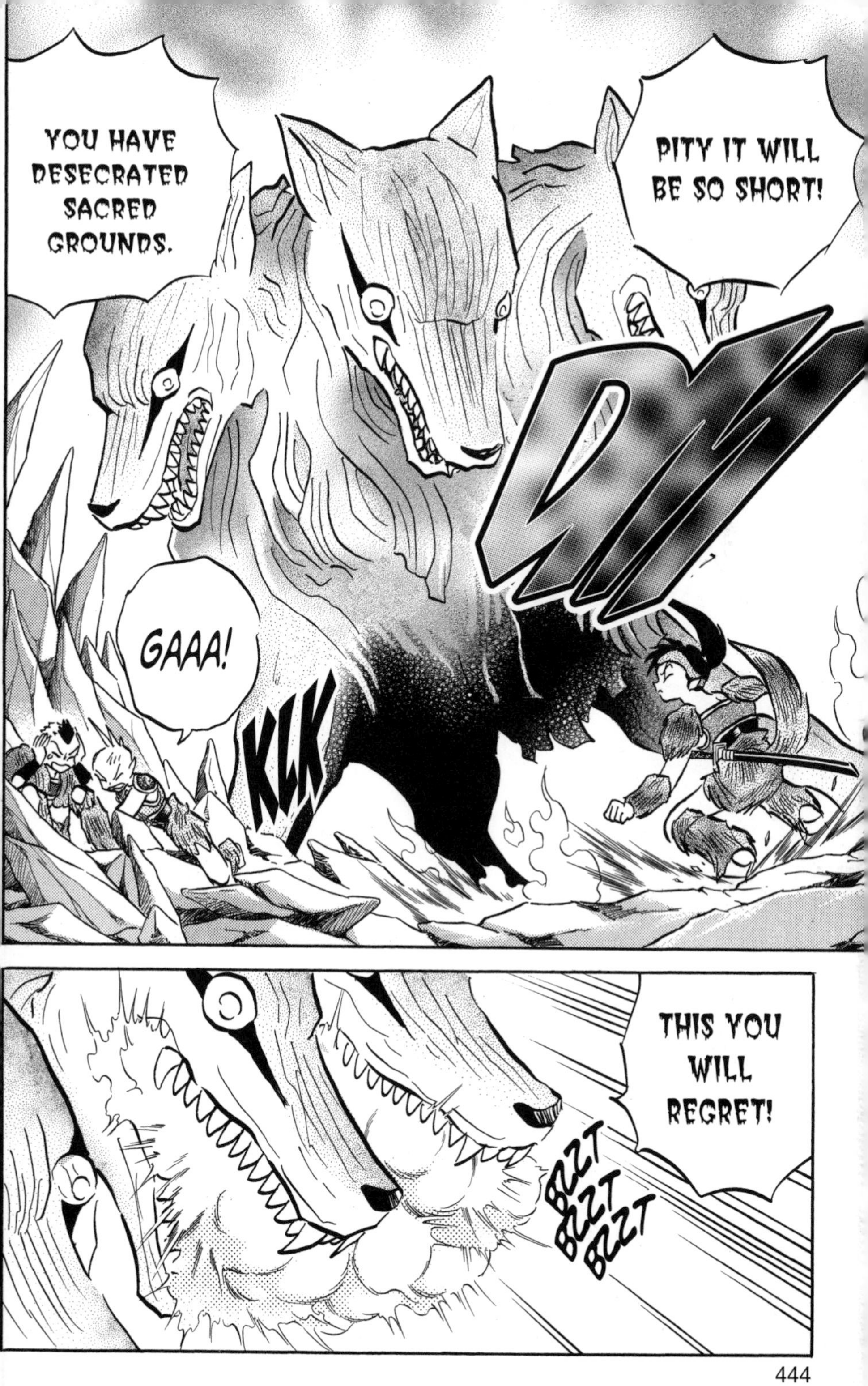
PITY IT WILL BE SO SHORT!
YOU HAVE DESECRATED SACRED GROUNDS.
GAAA!
KLK
THIS YOU WILL REGRET!
BZZT BZZT BZZT

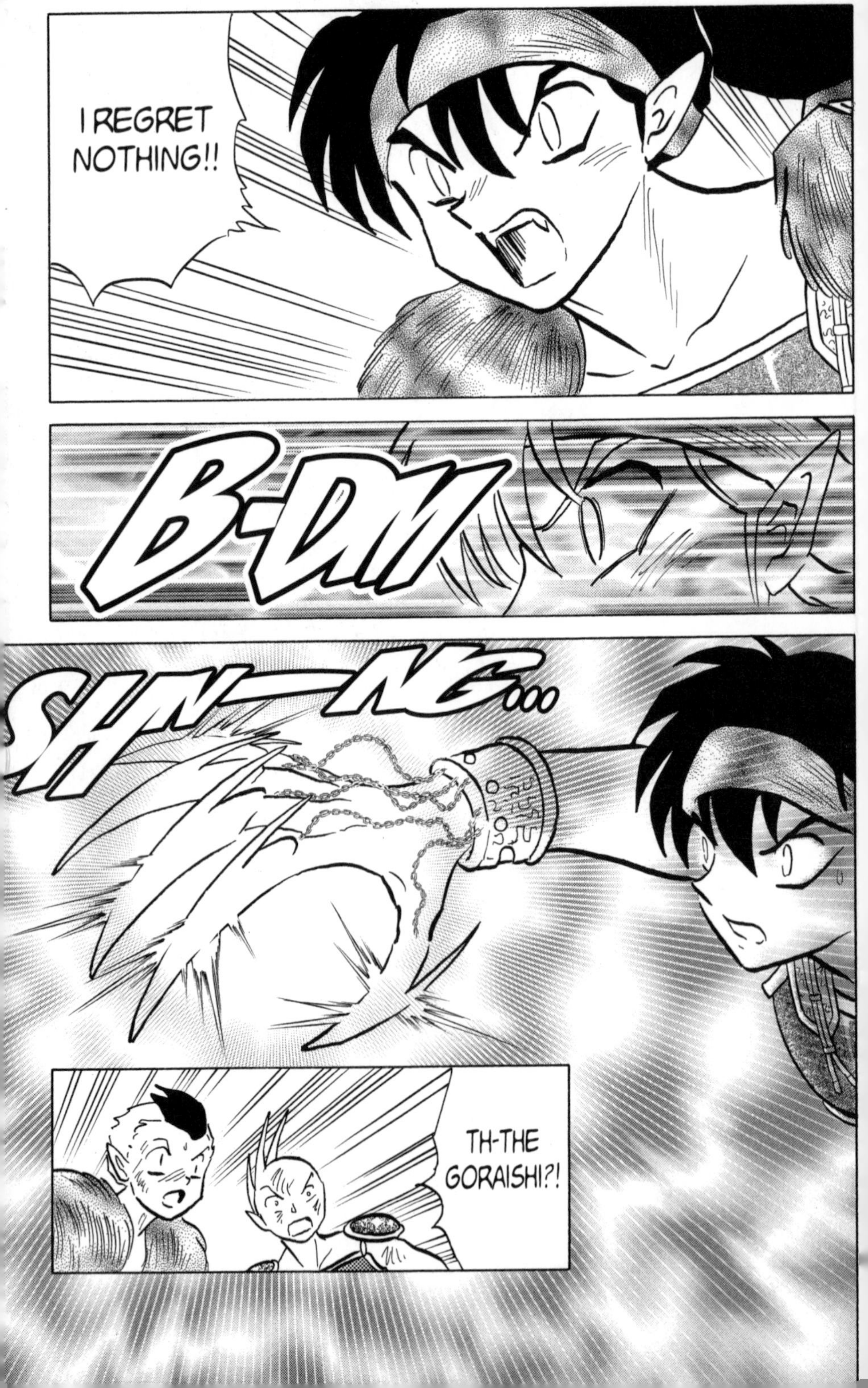
I REGRET NOTHING!!
B-DM
SHN—NG...
TH-THE GORAISHI?!

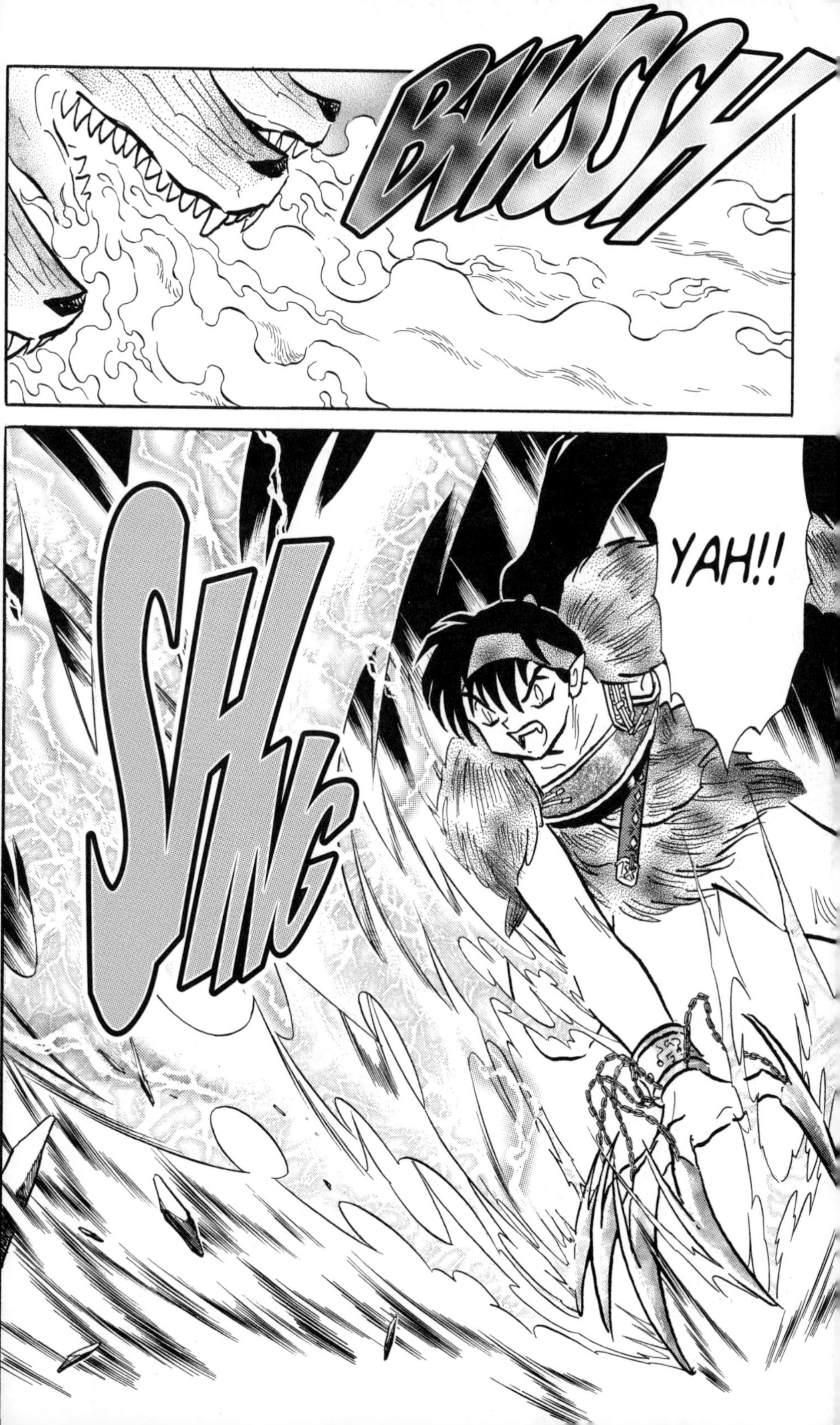
YAH!!

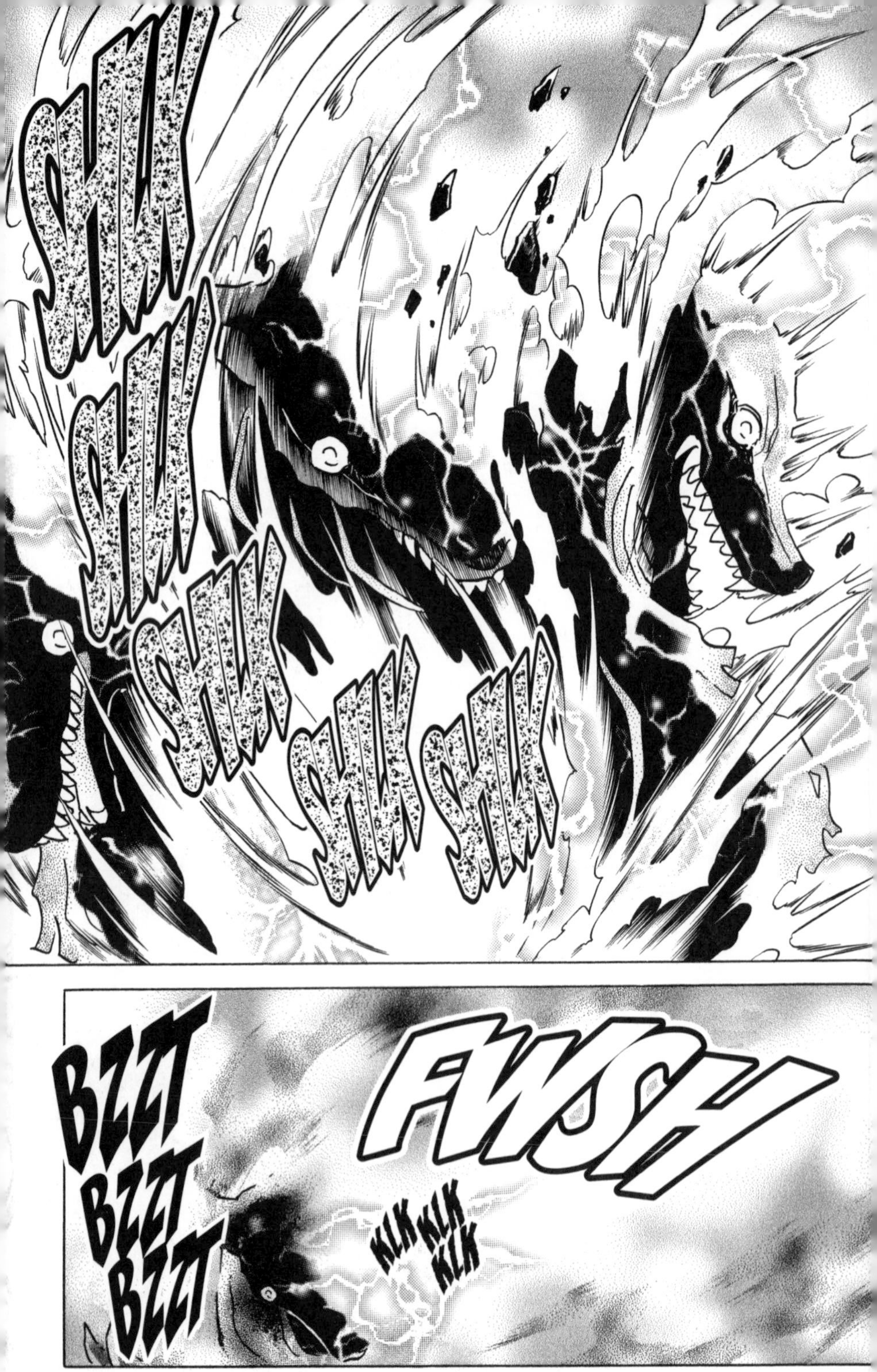
SHLK
SHLK
SHLK
SHLK
SHLK
FWSH
KLK KLK KLK
BZZT BZZT BZZT

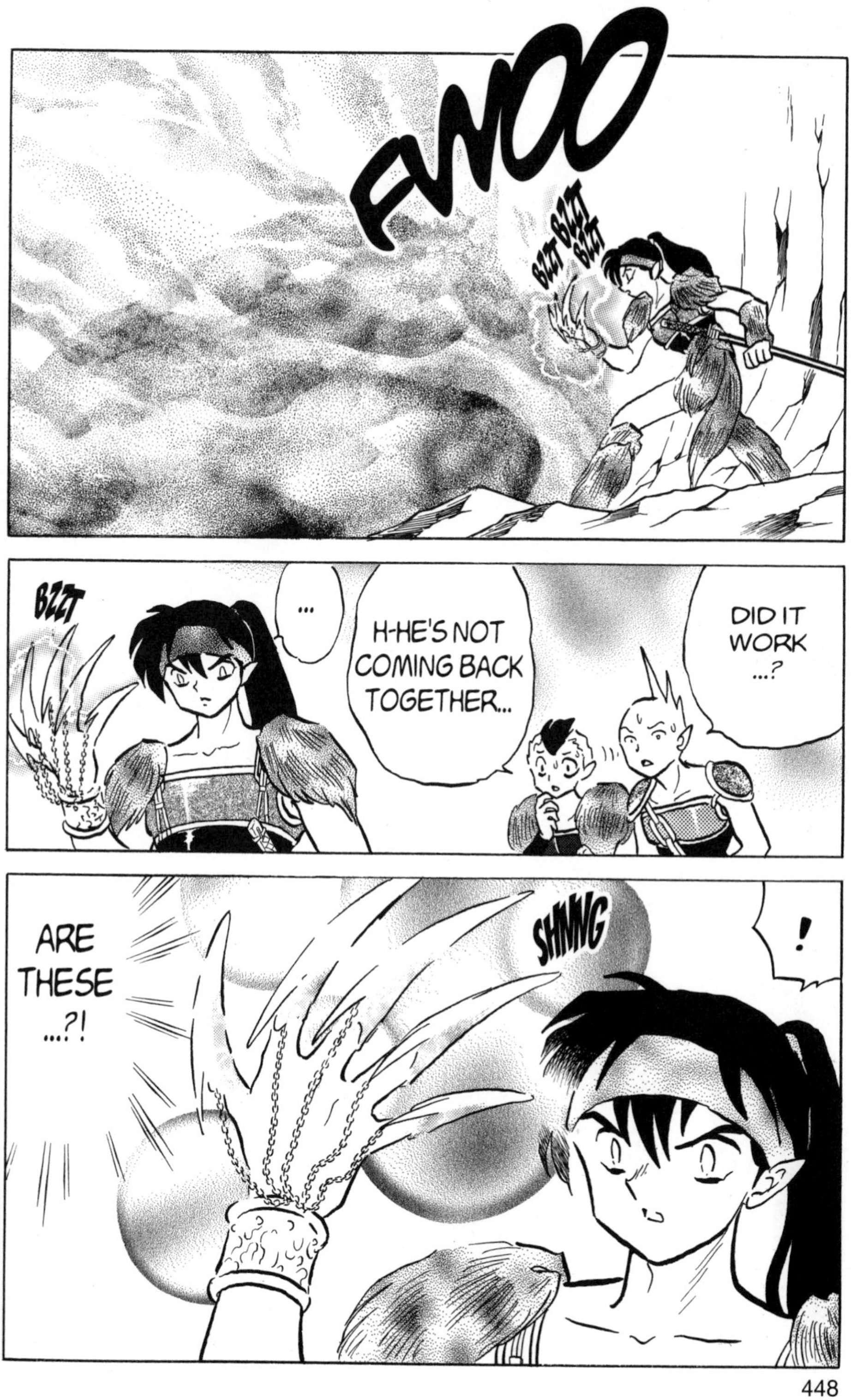
FWOO
BZZT BZZT BZZT
DID IT WORK ...?
H-HE'S NOT COMING BACK TOGETHER...
...
BZZT
!
SHNNG
ARE THESE ...?!

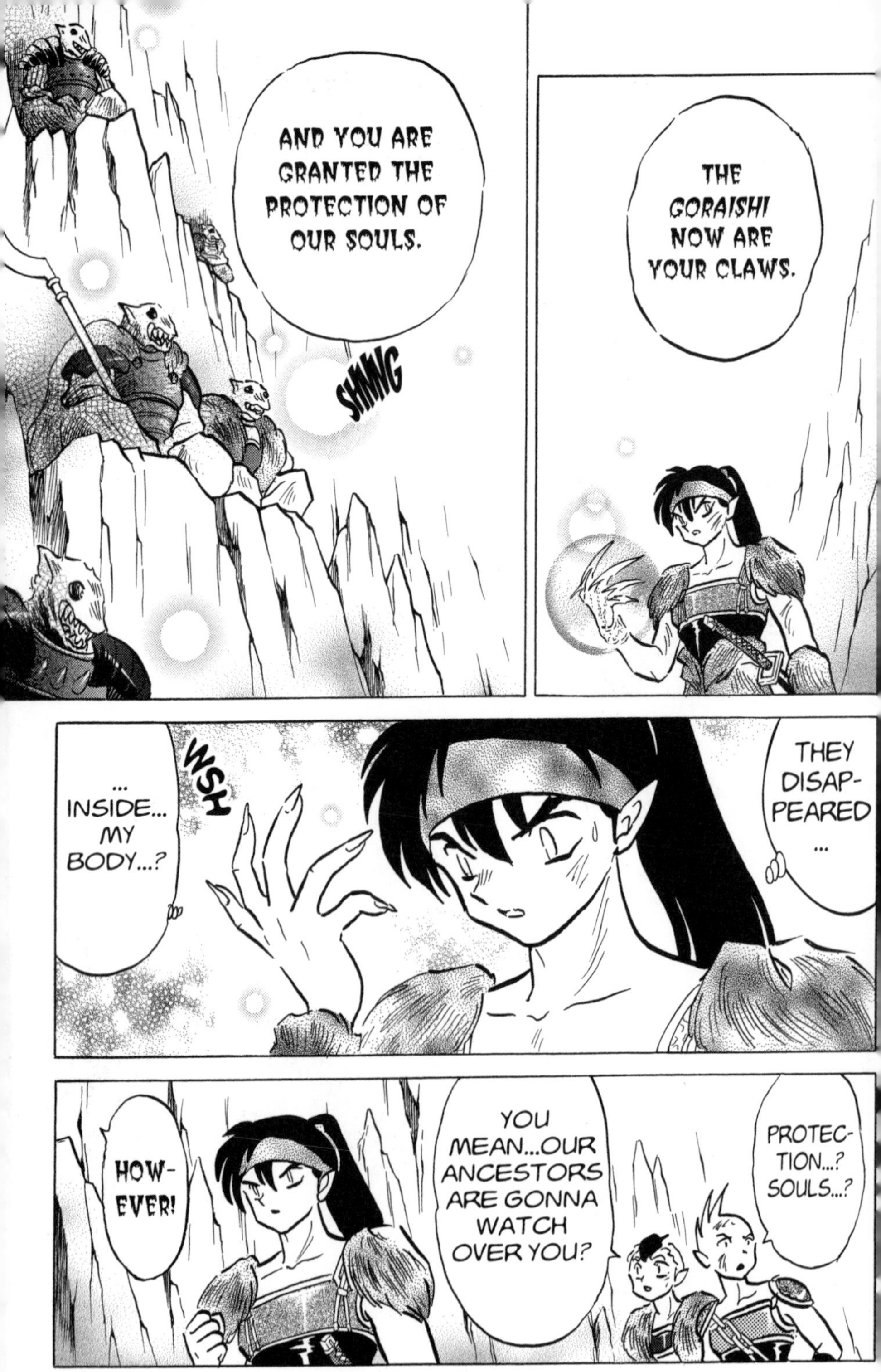
THE GORAISHI NOW ARE YOUR CLAWS.
AND YOU ARE GRANTED THE PROTECTION OF OUR SOULS.
SHNNG
THEY DISAP-PEARED ...
WSH
... INSIDE... MY BODY...?
PROTEC-TION...? SOULS...?
YOU MEAN...OUR ANCESTORS ARE GONNA WATCH OVER YOU?
HOW-EVER!

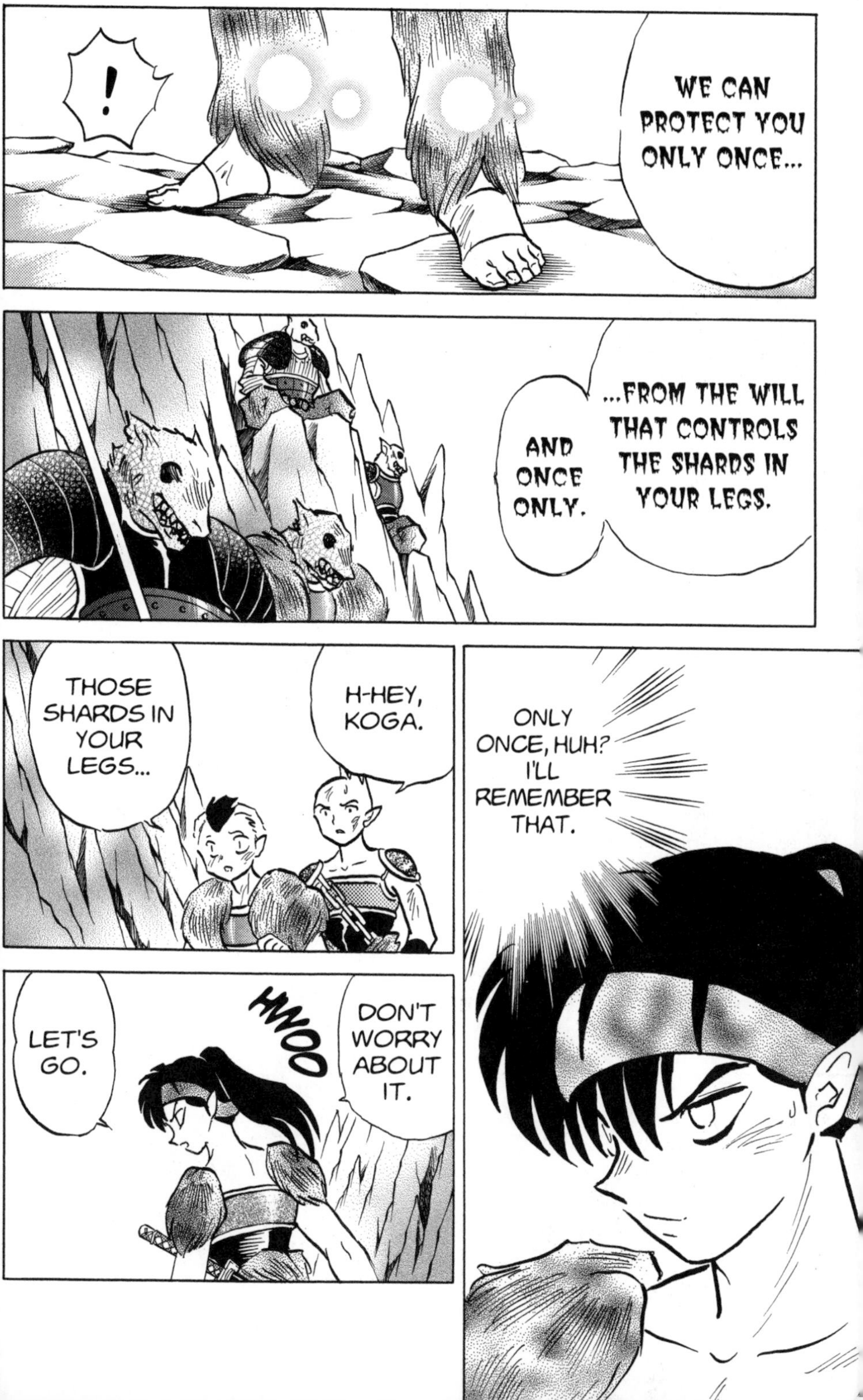

WE CAN PROTECT YOU ONLY ONCE...
!
...FROM THE WILL THAT CONTROLS THE SHARDS IN YOUR LEGS.
AND ONCE ONLY.
ONLY ONCE, HUH? I'LL REMEMBER THAT.
H-HEY, KOGA.
THOSE SHARDS IN YOUR LEGS...
DON'T WORRY ABOUT IT.
HWOO
LET'S GO.

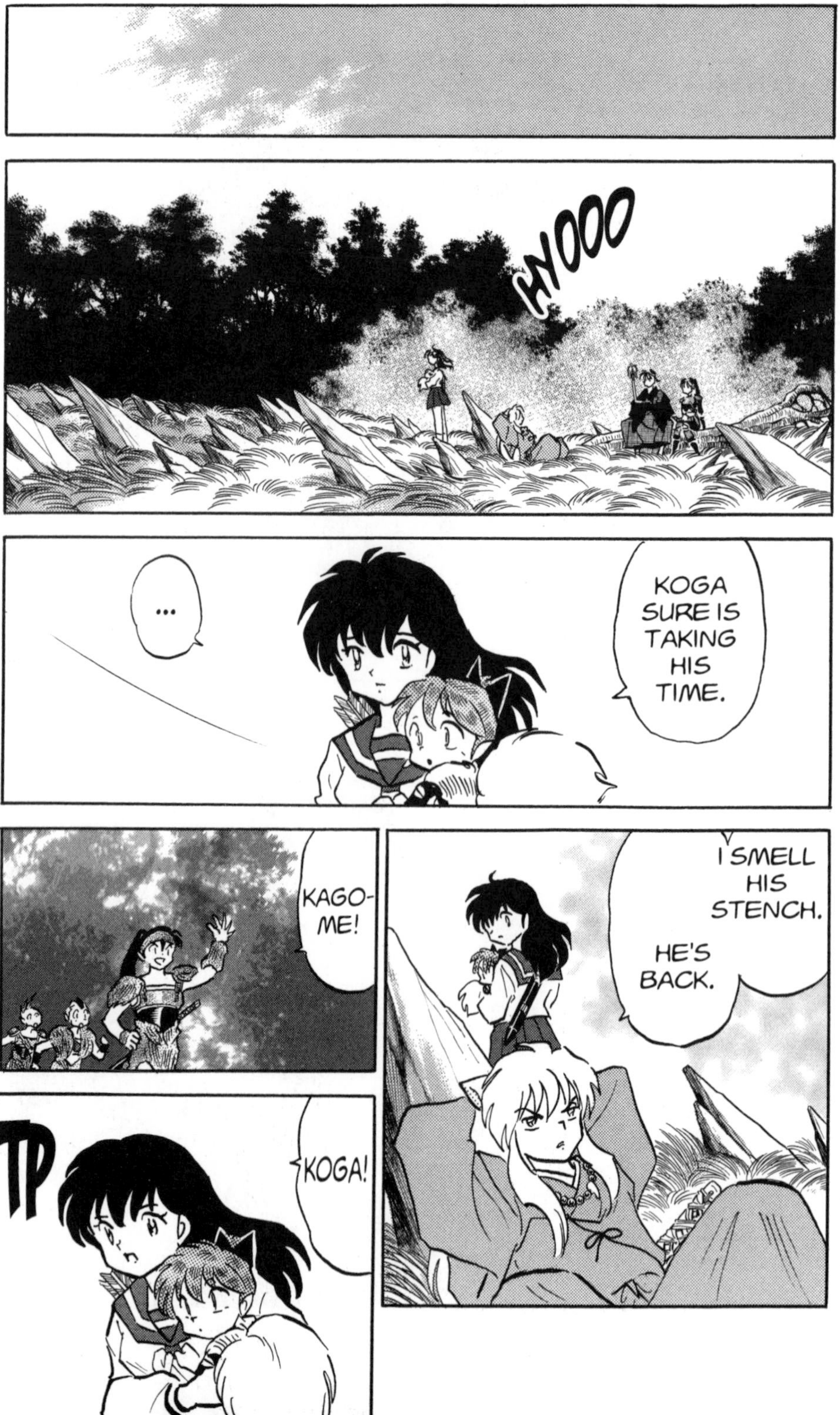
HYOOO
KOGA SURE IS TAKING HIS TIME.
...
I SMELL HIS STENCH.
HE'S BACK.
KAGO-ME!
KOGA!
TP

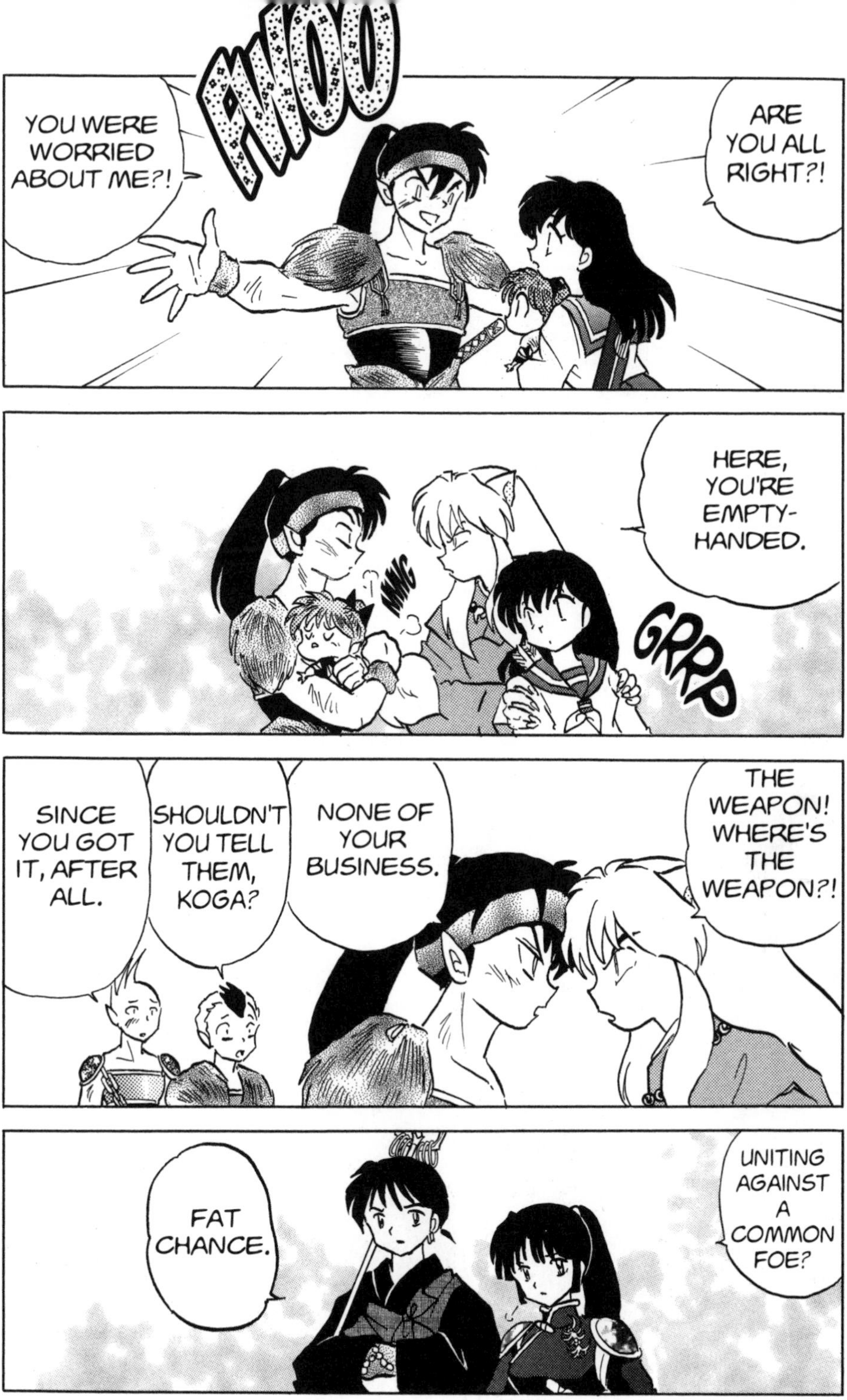
ARE YOU ALL RIGHT?!
AWOO
YOU WERE WORRIED ABOUT ME?!
HERE, YOU'RE EMPTY-HANDED.
GRRP
MNG
THE WEAPON! WHERE'S THE WEAPON?!
NONE OF YOUR BUSINESS.
SHOULDN'T YOU TELL THEM, KOGA?
SINCE YOU GOT IT, AFTER ALL.
UNITING AGAINST A COMMON FOE?
FAT CHANCE.

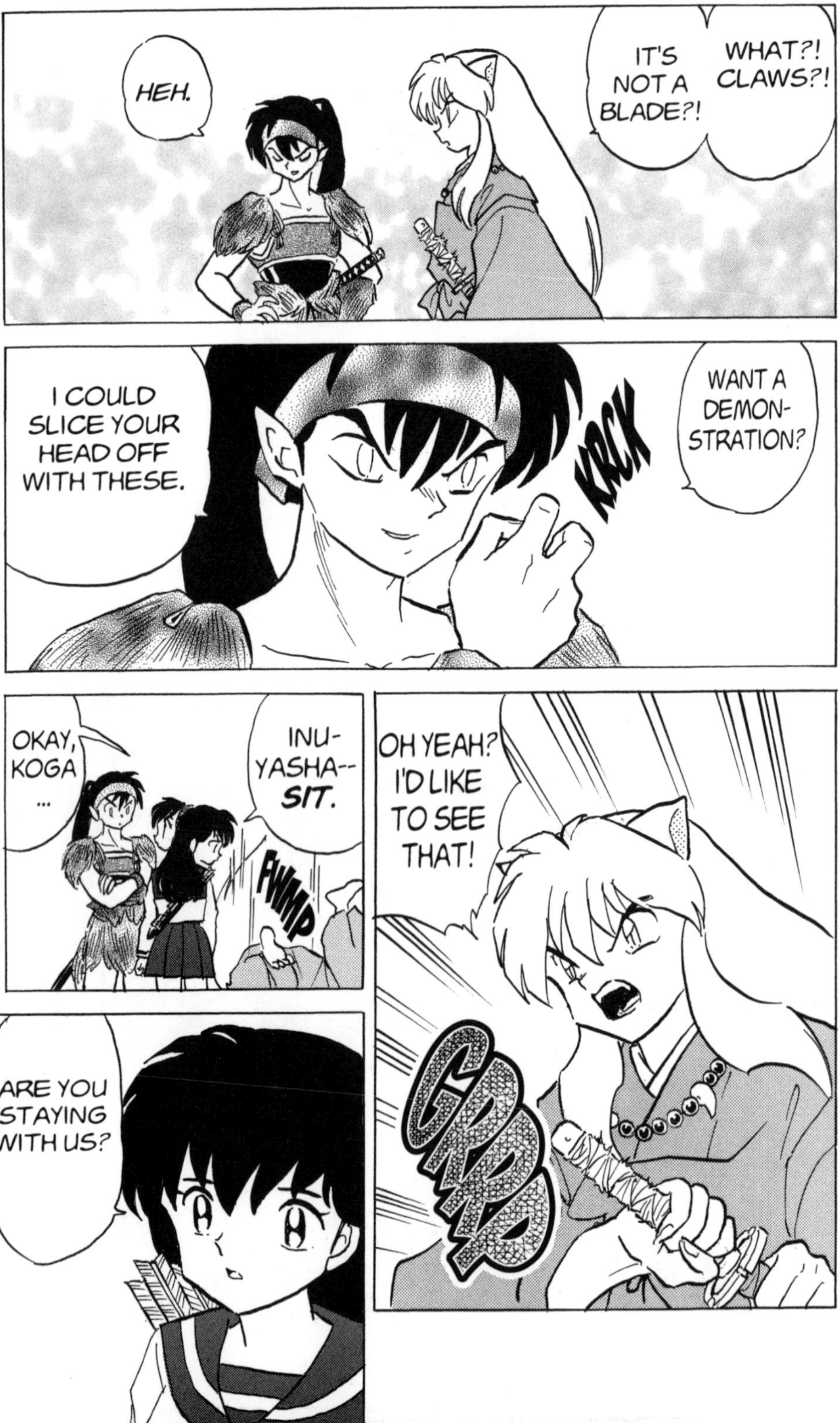
WHAT?! CLAWS?!
IT'S NOT A BLADE?!
HEH.
WANT A DEMON-STRATION?
KRCK
I COULD SLICE YOUR HEAD OFF WITH THESE.
OH YEAH? I'D LIKE TO SEE THAT!
GRRP
INU-YASHA-- **SIT**.
OKAY, KOGA ...
FWMP
ARE YOU STAYING WITH US?

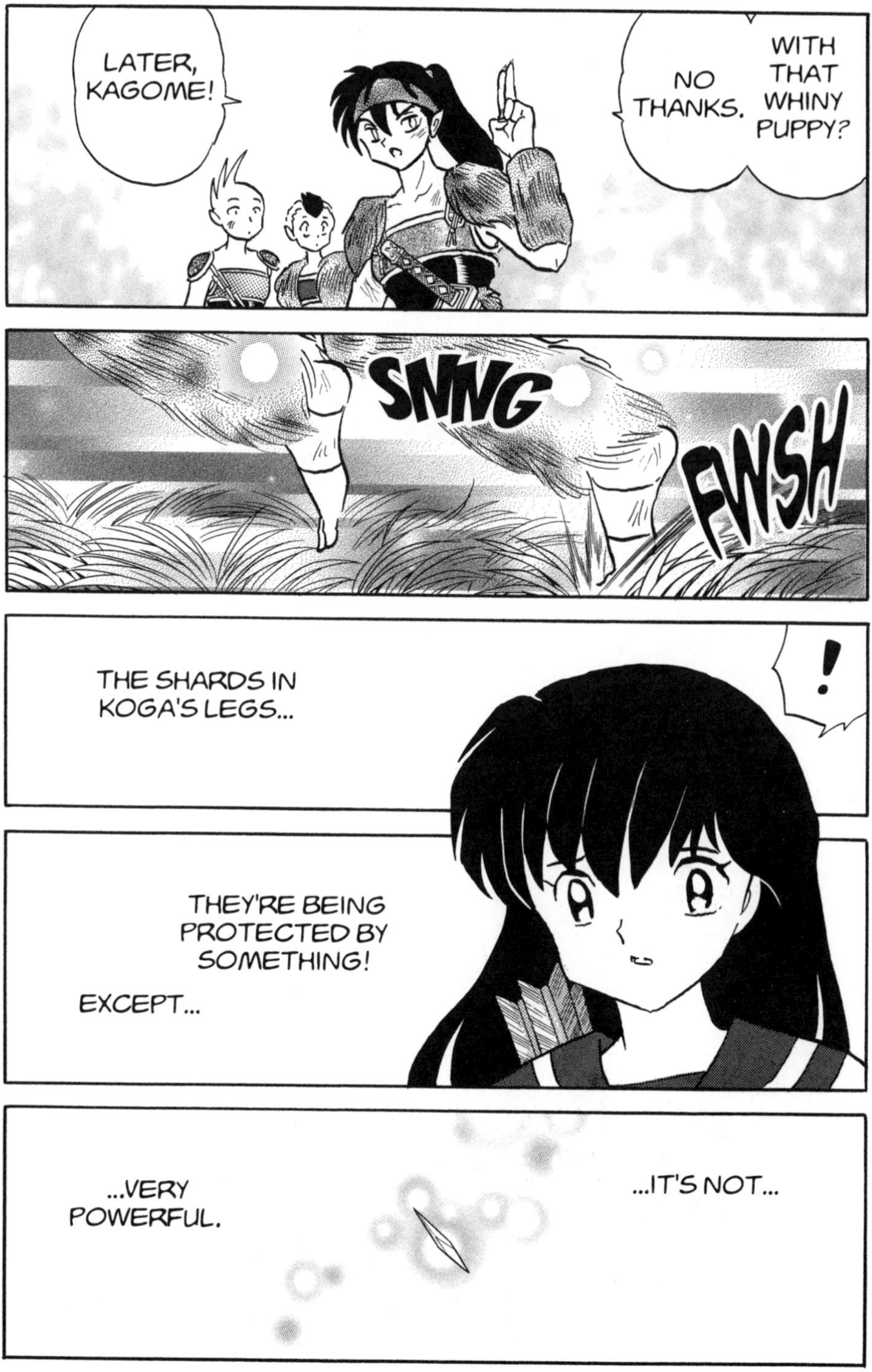
NO THANKS. WITH THAT WHINY PUPPY?
LATER, KAGOME!
FWSH
SNNG
!
THE SHARDS IN KOGA'S LEGS...
THEY'RE BEING PROTECTED BY SOMETHING!
EXCEPT...
...IT'S NOT...
...VERY POWERFUL.

SCROLL FIVE
MUJINA

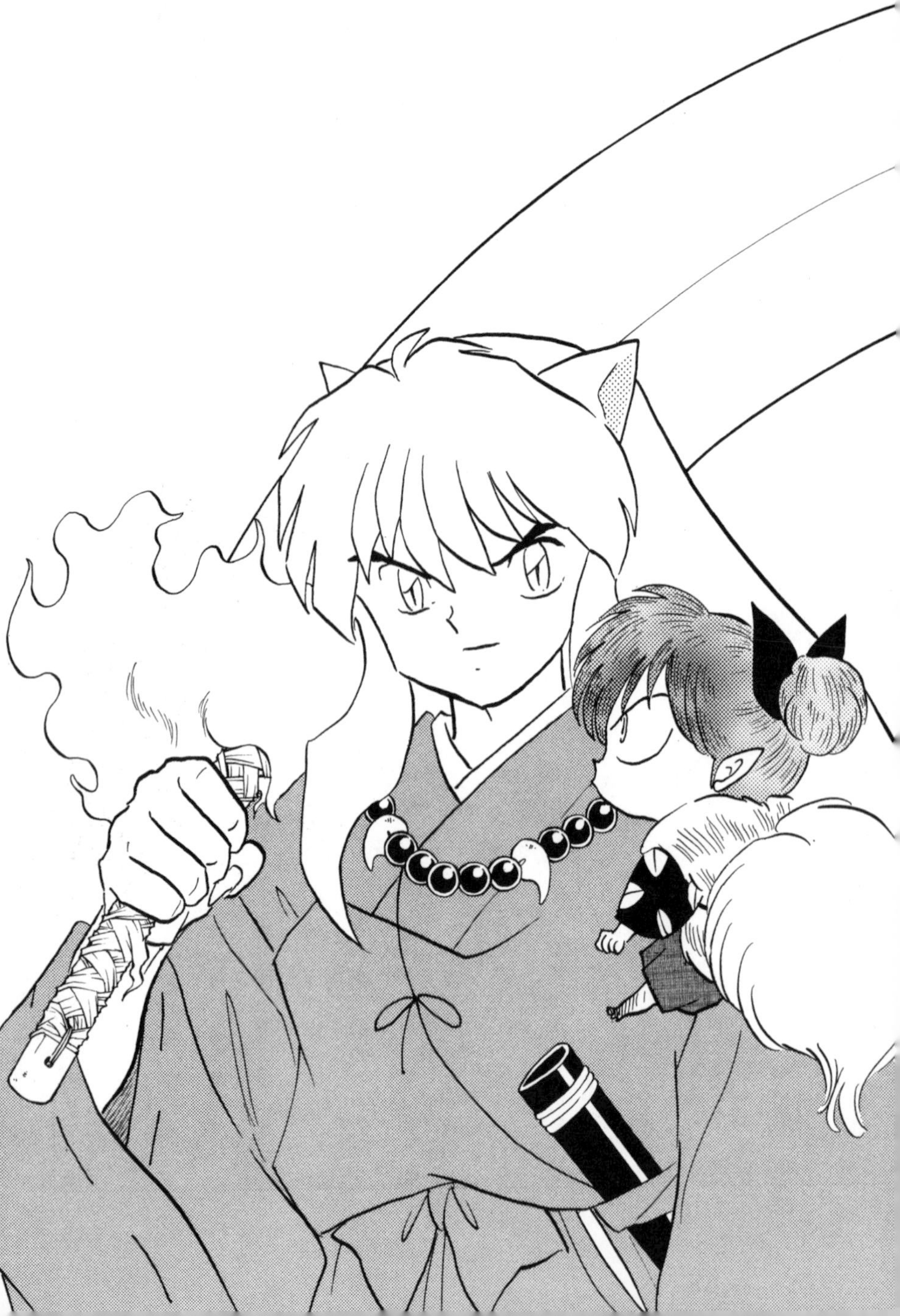

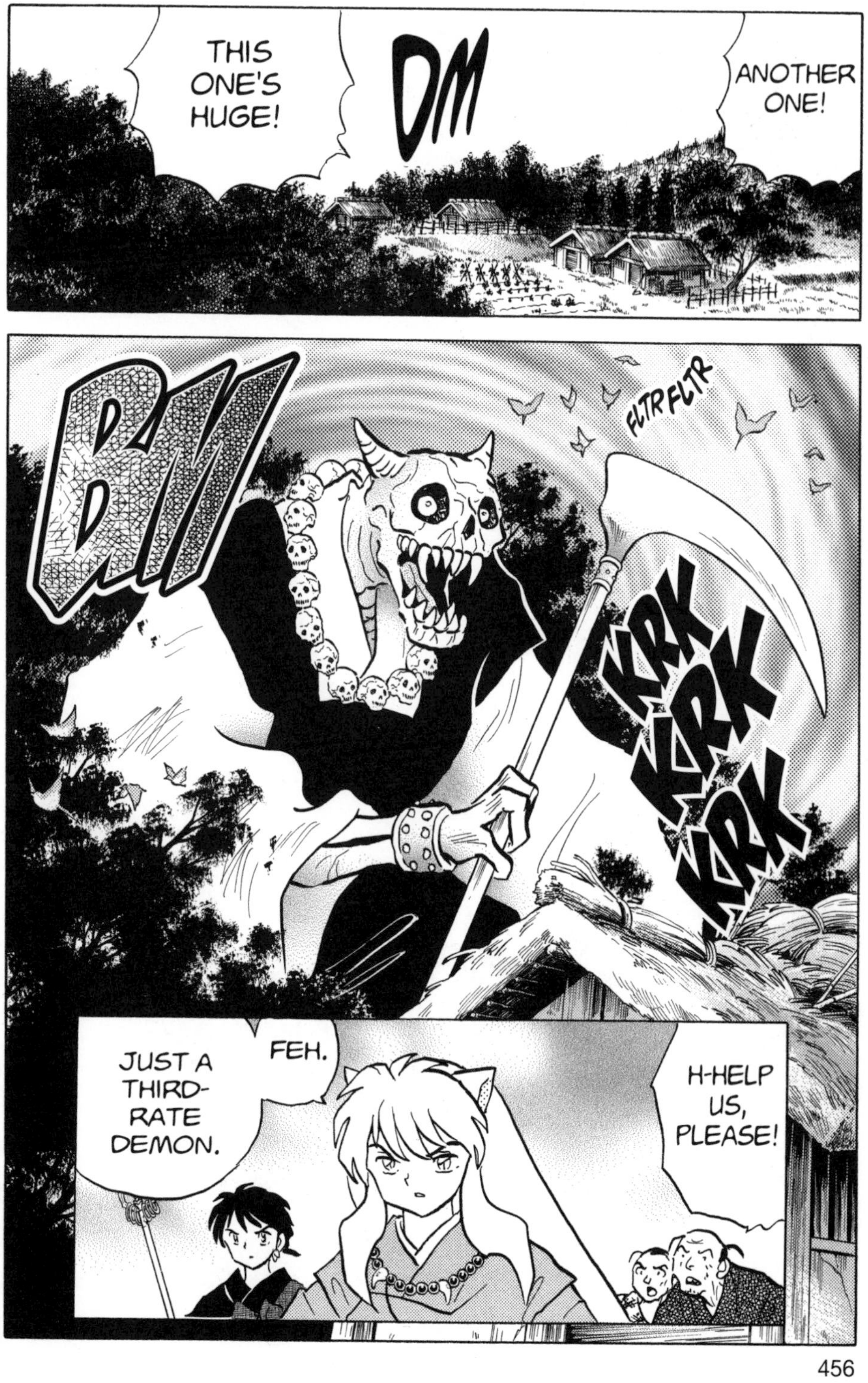
ANOTHER ONE!
DM
THIS ONE'S HUGE!
FLTR FLTR
KRK KRK KRK
BM
H-HELP US, PLEASE!
FEH.
JUST A THIRD-RATE DEMON.

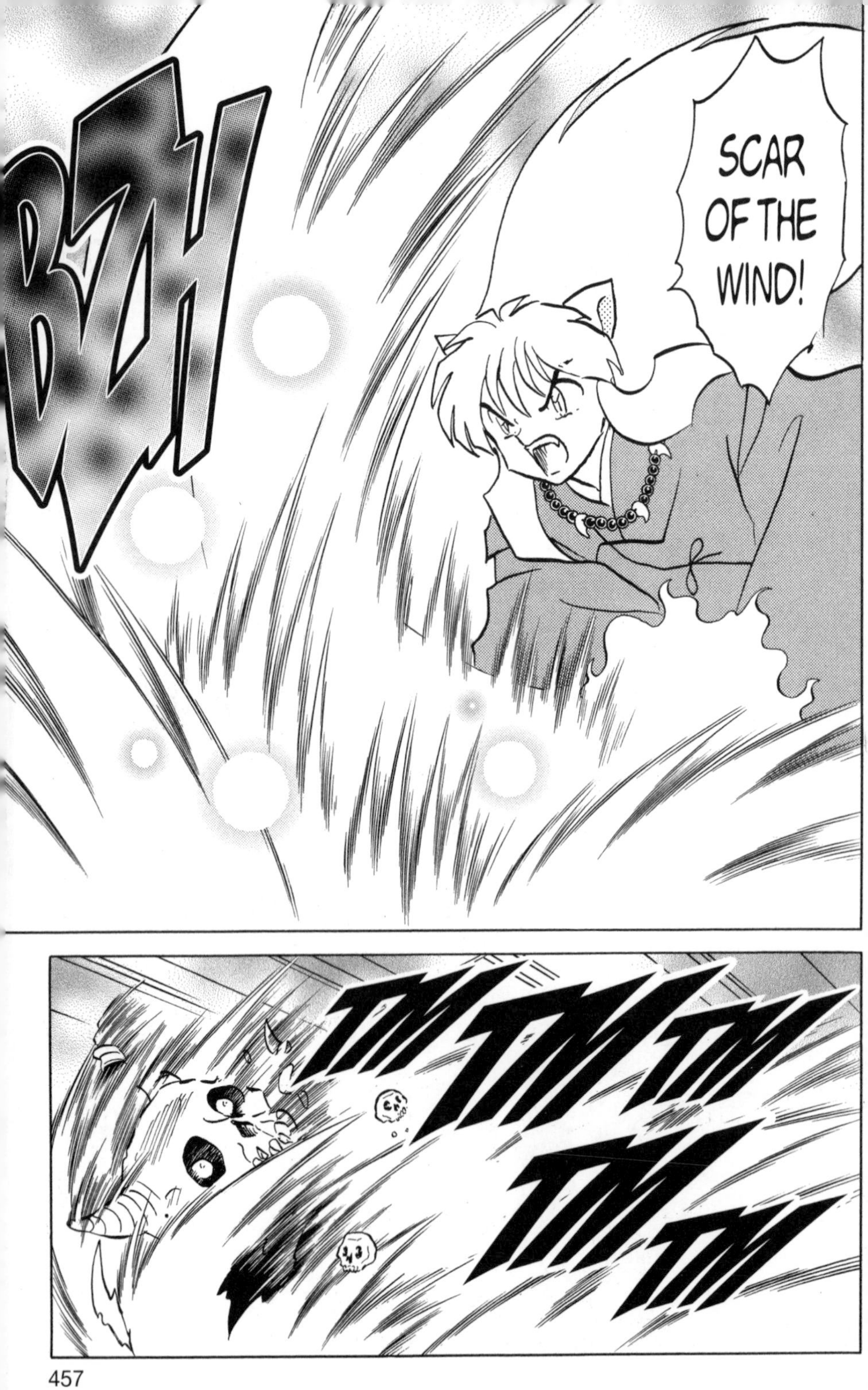
SCAR OF THE WIND!
BZH

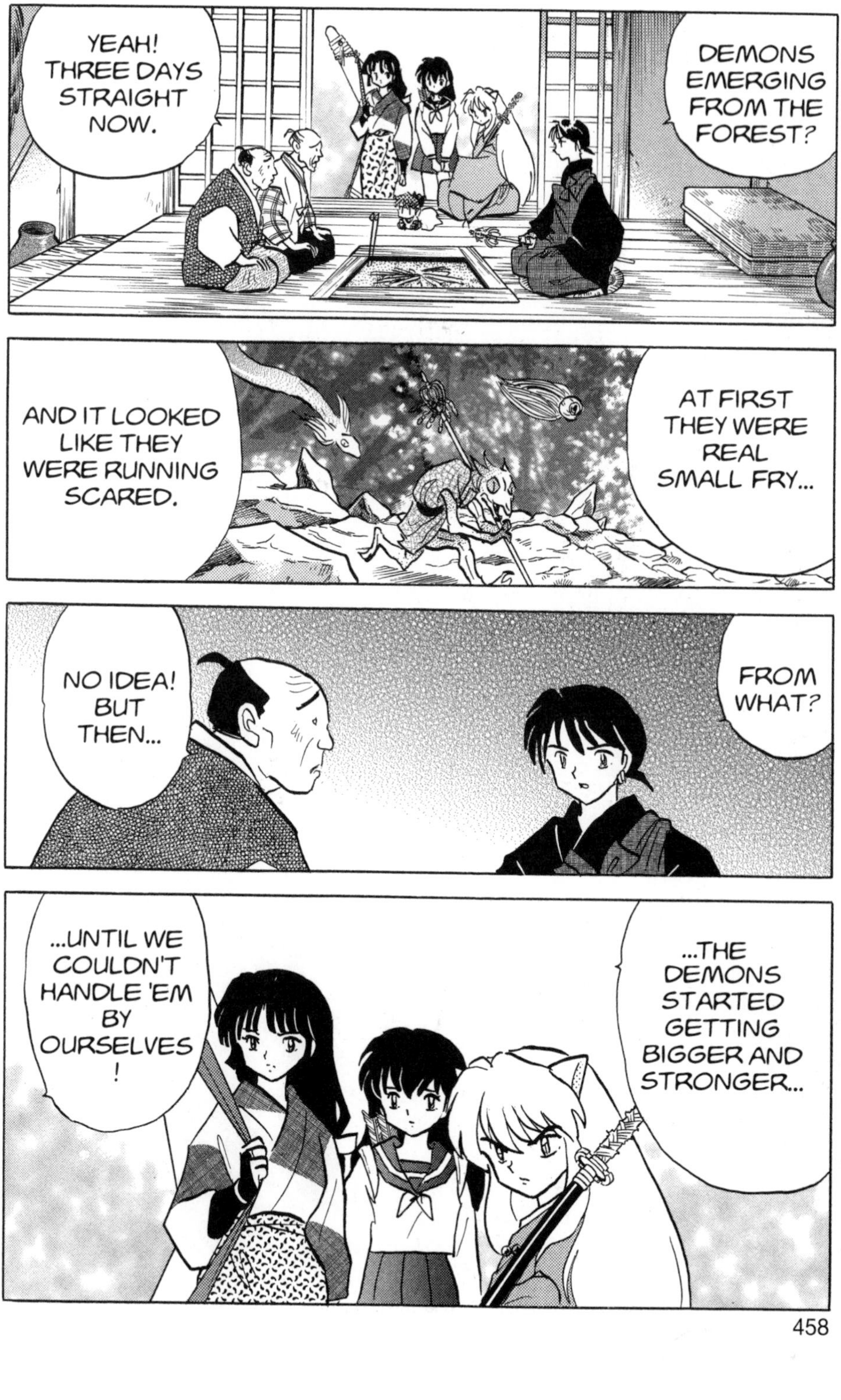
DEMONS EMERGING FROM THE FOREST?
YEAH! THREE DAYS STRAIGHT NOW.
AT FIRST THEY WERE REAL SMALL FRY...
AND IT LOOKED LIKE THEY WERE RUNNING SCARED.
FROM WHAT?
NO IDEA! BUT THEN...
...THE DEMONS STARTED GETTING BIGGER AND STRONGER...
...UNTIL WE COULDN'T HANDLE 'EM BY OURSELVES!

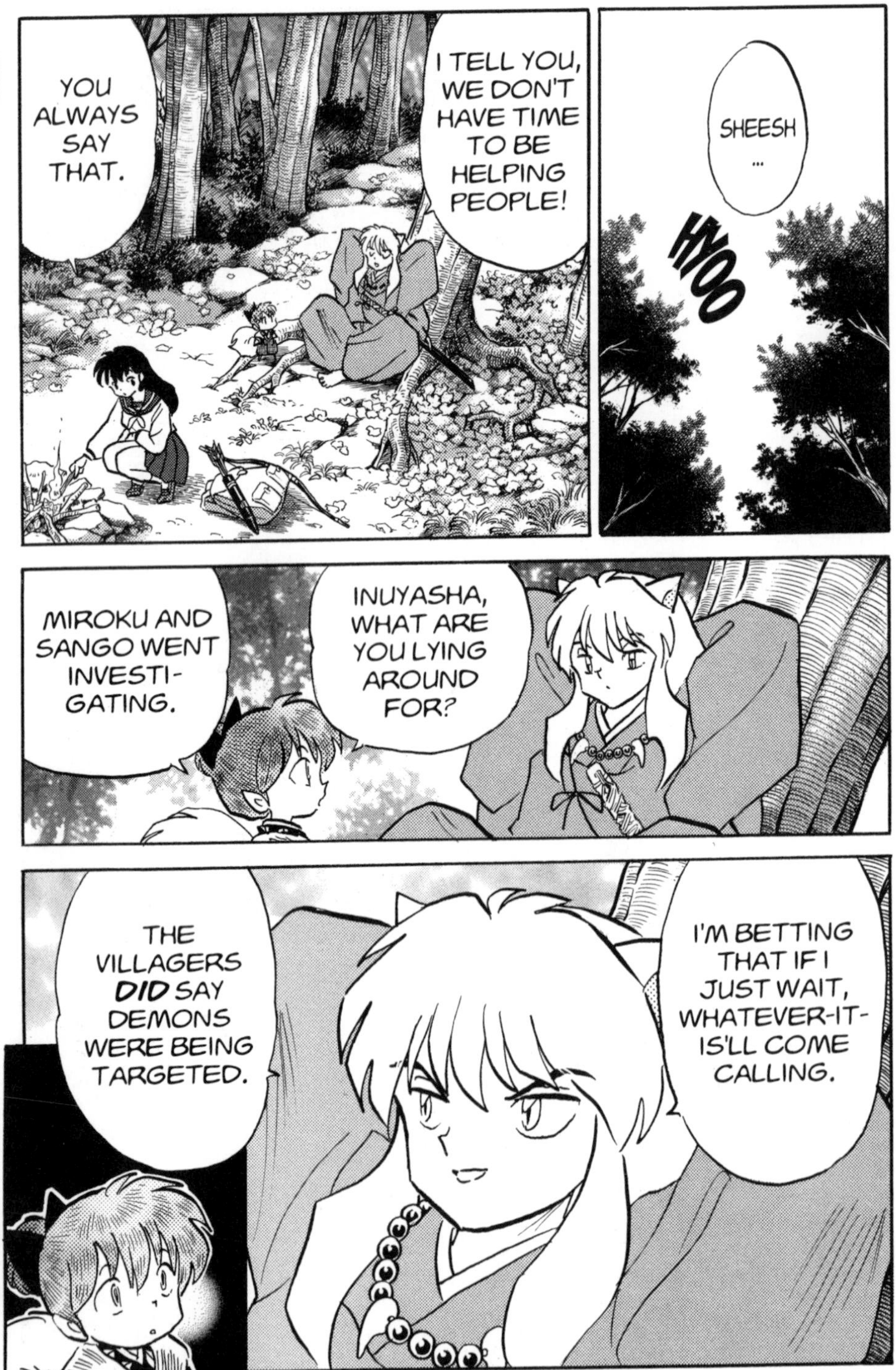
SHEESH ...
HYOO
I TELL YOU, WE DON'T HAVE TIME TO BE HELPING PEOPLE!
YOU ALWAYS SAY THAT.
INUYASHA, WHAT ARE YOU LYING AROUND FOR?
MIROKU AND SANGO WENT INVESTI-GATING.
I'M BETTING THAT IF I JUST WAIT, WHATEVER-IT-IS'LL COME CALLING.
THE VILLAGERS **DID** SAY DEMONS WERE BEING TARGETED.

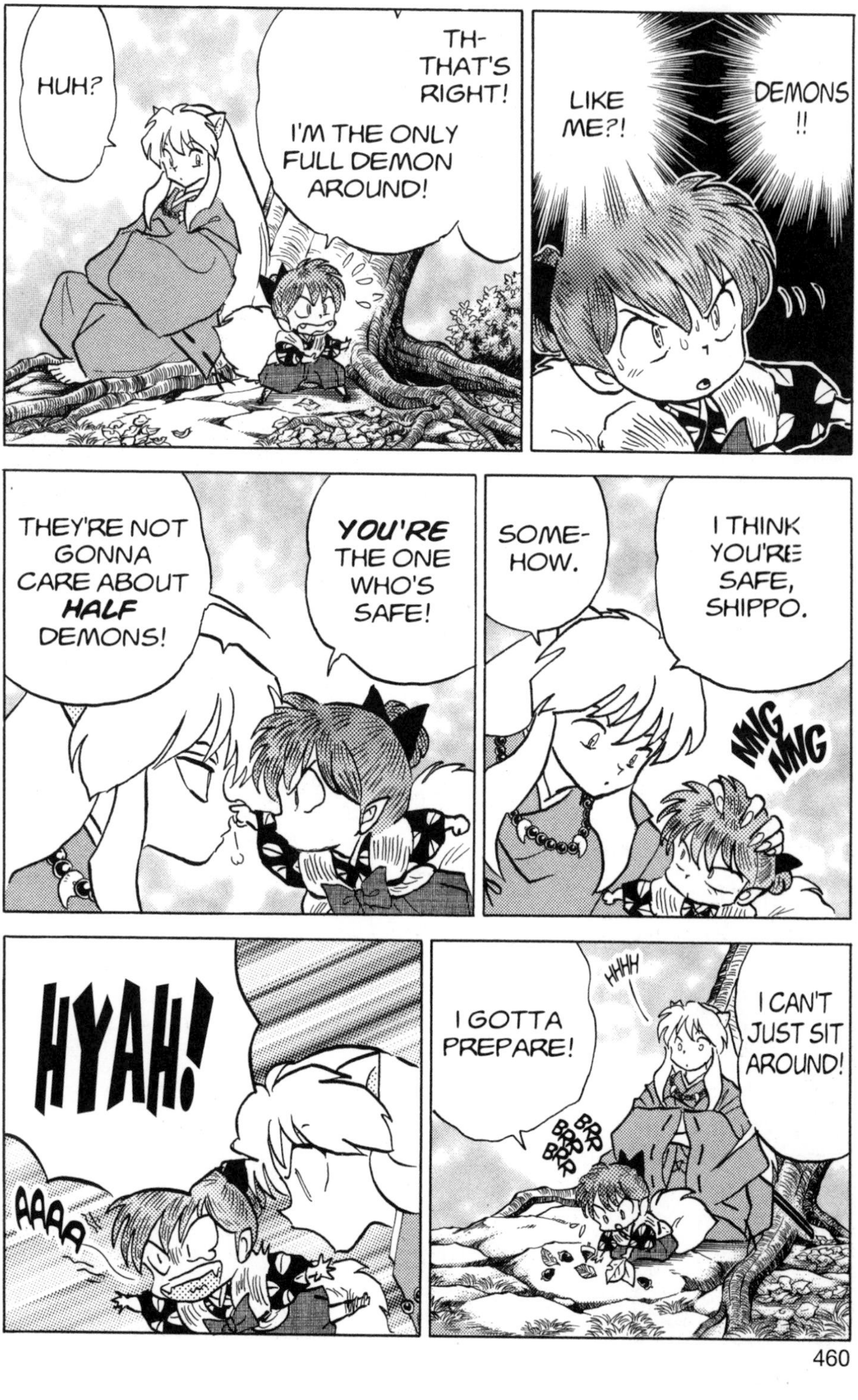
DEMONS !!
LIKE ME?!
TH- THAT'S RIGHT!
I'M THE ONLY FULL DEMON AROUND!
HUH?
I THINK YOU'RE SAFE, SHIPPO.
SOME-HOW.
MNG MNG
YOU'RE THE ONE WHO'S SAFE!
THEY'RE NOT GONNA CARE ABOUT HALF DEMONS!
I CAN'T JUST SIT AROUND!
HHHH
I GOTTA PREPARE!
BRR BRR BRR
HYAH!
AAAA

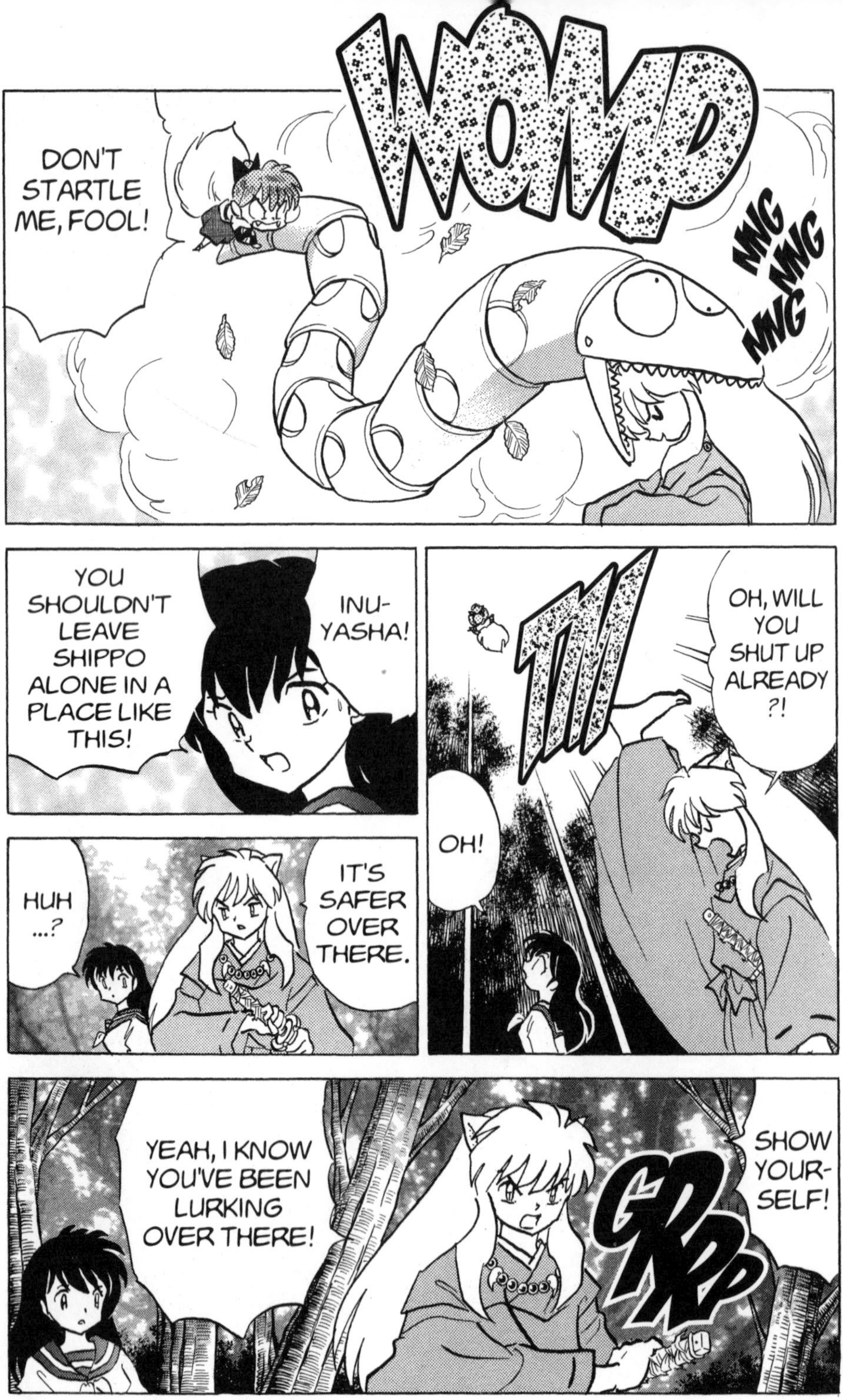
WOMP
MNG MNG MNG
DON'T STARTLE ME, FOOL!
OH, WILL YOU SHUT UP ALREADY?!
TM
OH!
INU-YASHA!
YOU SHOULDN'T LEAVE SHIPPO ALONE IN A PLACE LIKE THIS!
IT'S SAFER OVER THERE.
HUH...?
SHOW YOURSELF!
YEAH, I KNOW YOU'VE BEEN LURKING OVER THERE!

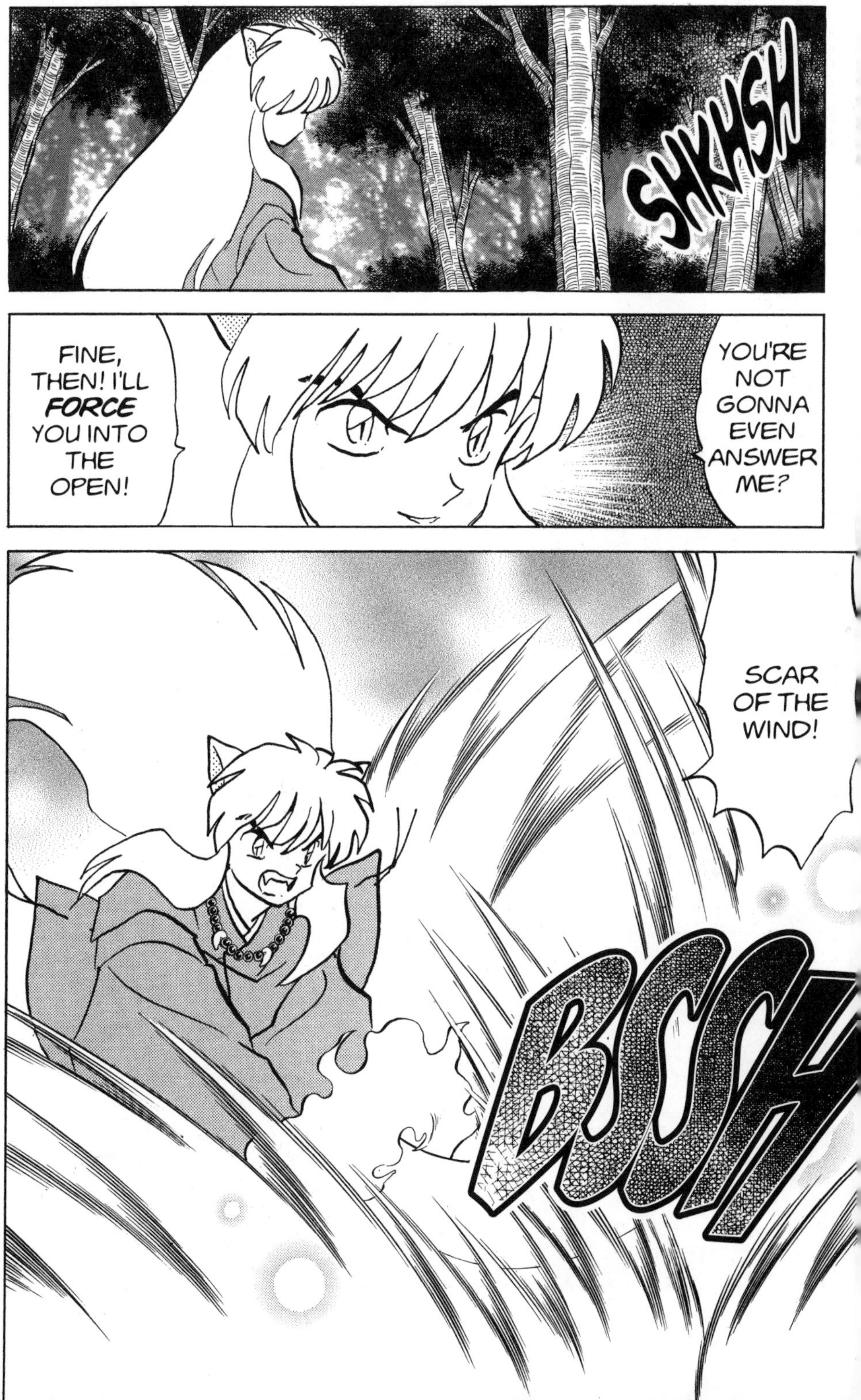
SHKSH
YOU'RE NOT GONNA EVEN ANSWER ME?
FINE, THEN! I'LL **FORCE** YOU INTO THE OPEN!
SCAR OF THE WIND!
BOO

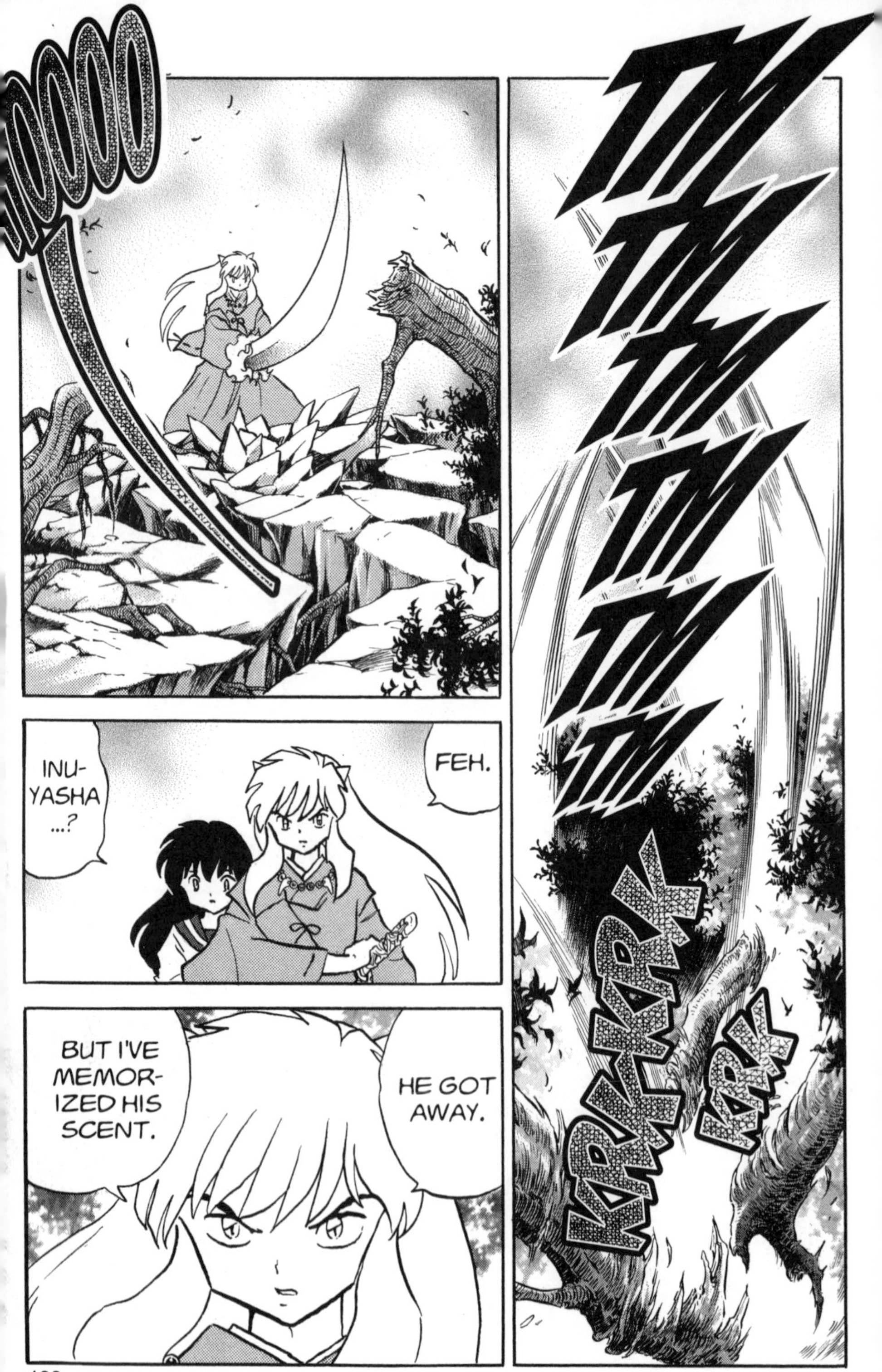
FEH.
INU-YASHA ...?
HE GOT AWAY.
BUT I'VE MEMORIZED HIS SCENT.

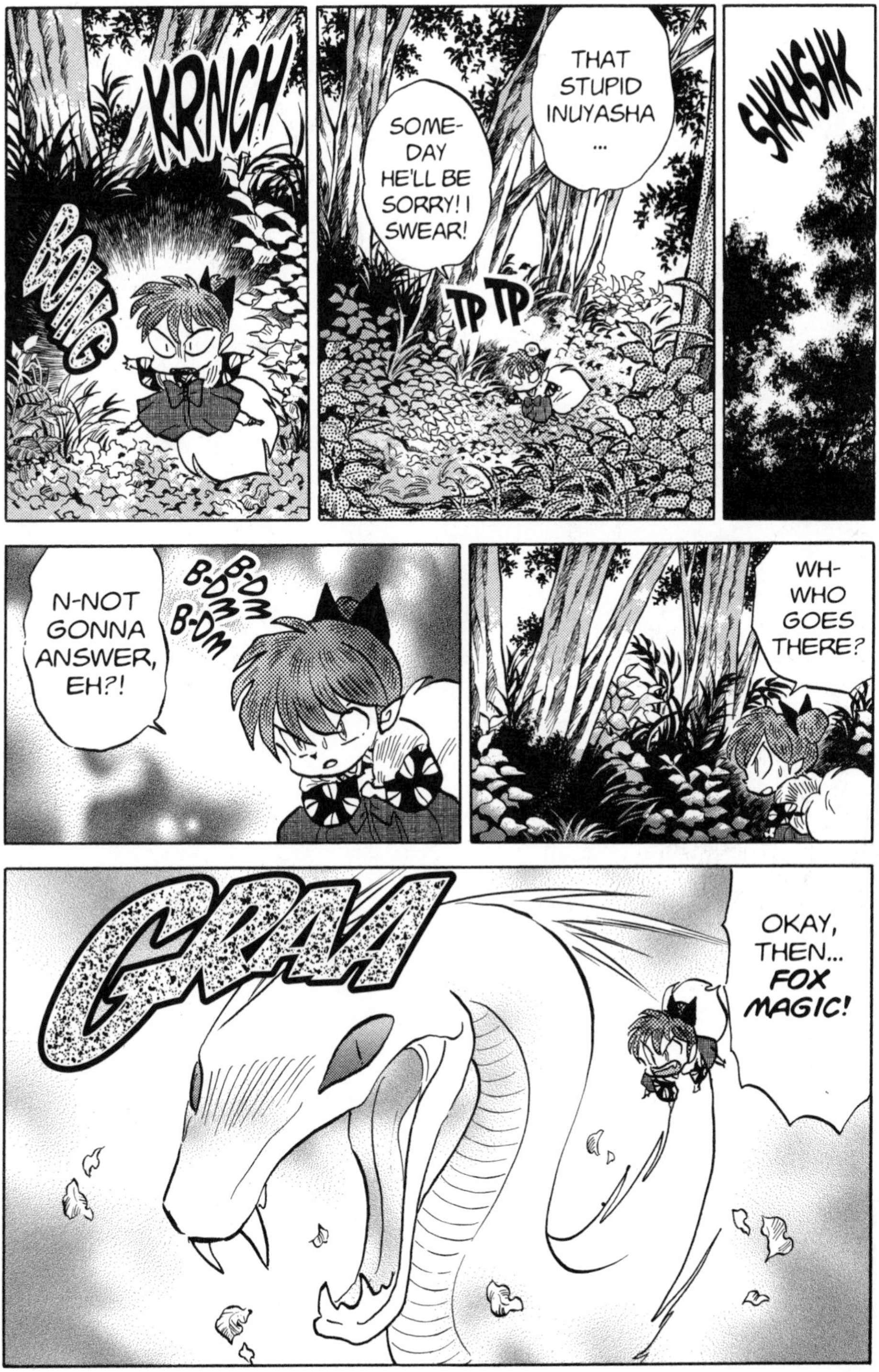
SHKSHK
THAT STUPID INUYASHA ...
SOME-DAY HE'LL BE SORRY!! I SWEAR!
TP TP
KRNCH
BOING
WH-WHO GOES THERE?
N-NOT GONNA ANSWER, EH?!
B-DM B-DM B-DM
OKAY, THEN... ***FOX MAGIC!***
GRAM

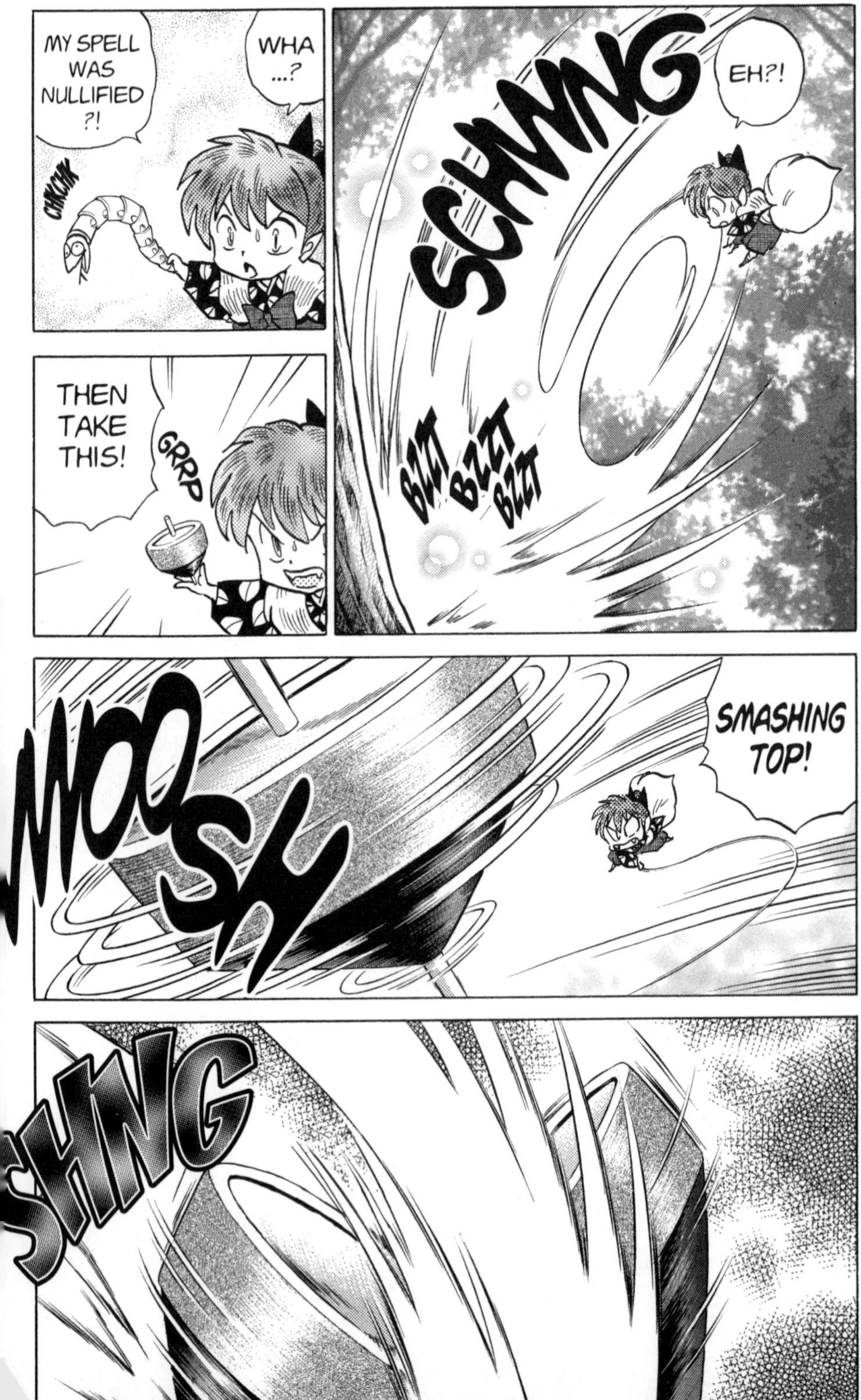
EH?!
SCHWNG
BZZT BZZT BZZT
WHA ...?
MY SPELL WAS NULLIFIED ?!
CHKCHK
THEN TAKE THIS!
GRRP
SMASHING TOP!
WHOOSH
SHING

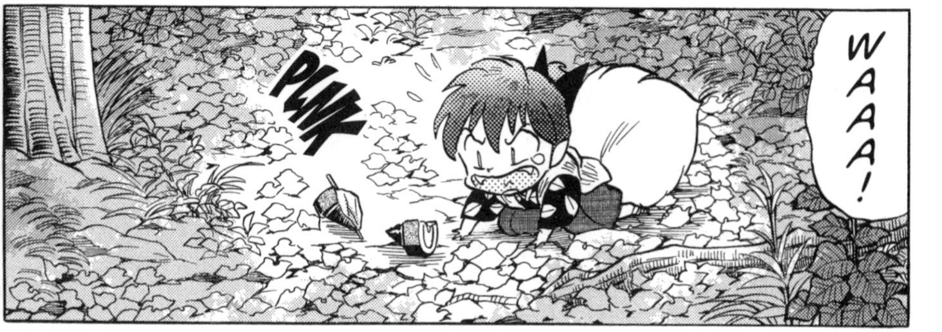
WAAAA!
PLINK
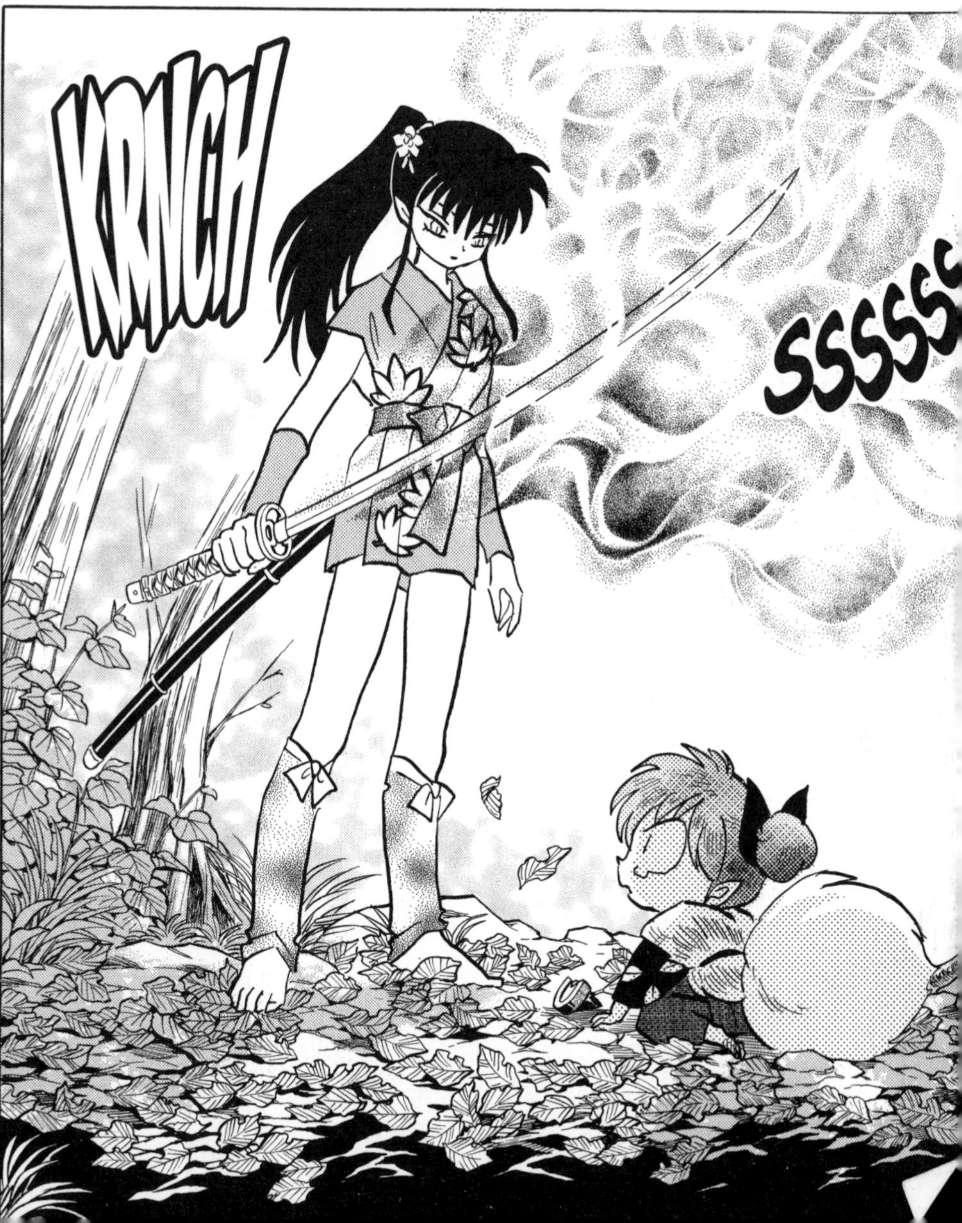
SSSSSS
KRNCH

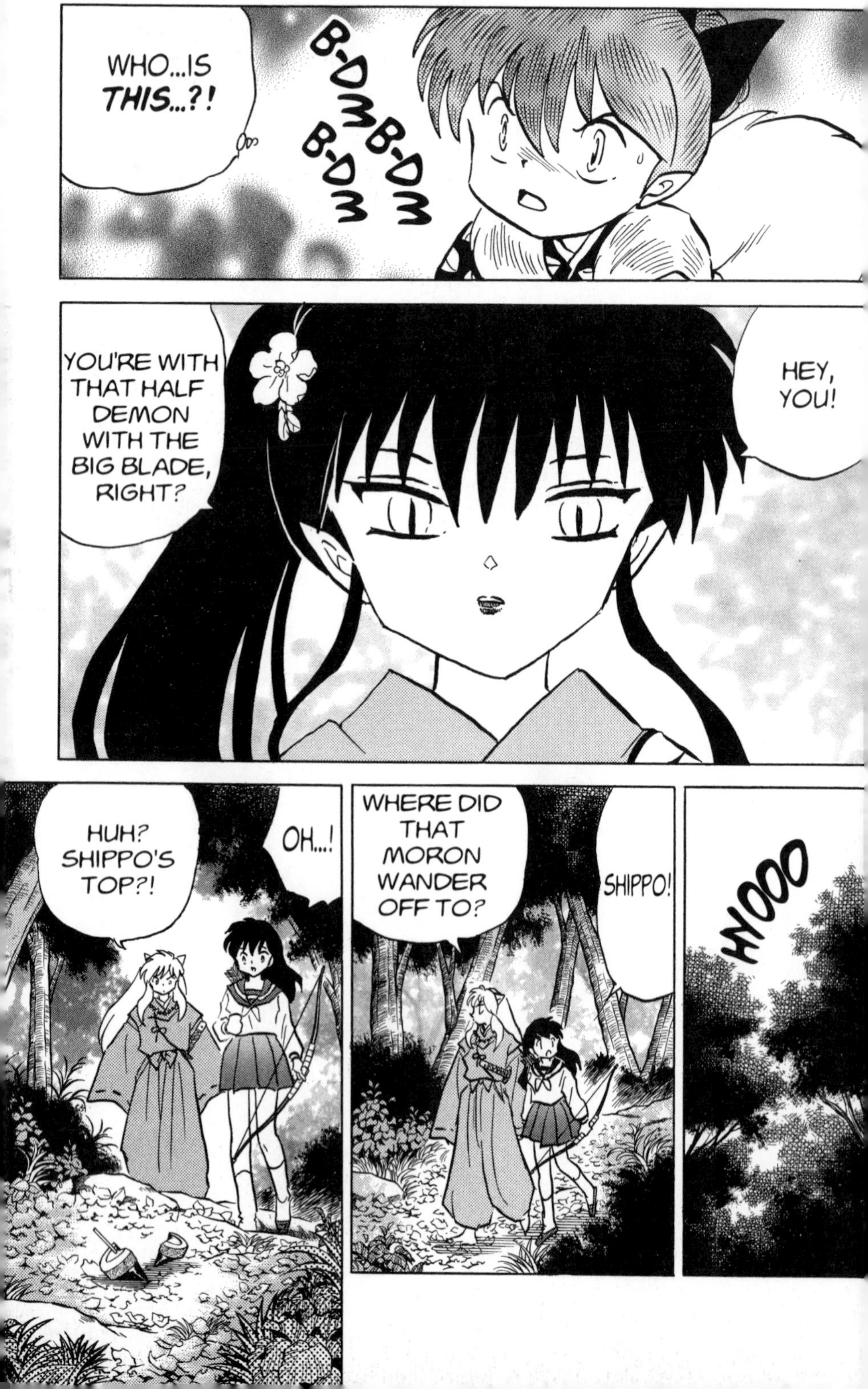
B-DMB-DM B-DM
WHO...IS THIS...?!
HEY, YOU!
YOU'RE WITH THAT HALF DEMON WITH THE BIG BLADE, RIGHT?
HYOOO
SHIPPO!
WHERE DID THAT MORON WANDER OFF TO?
OH...!
HUH? SHIPPO'S TOP?!

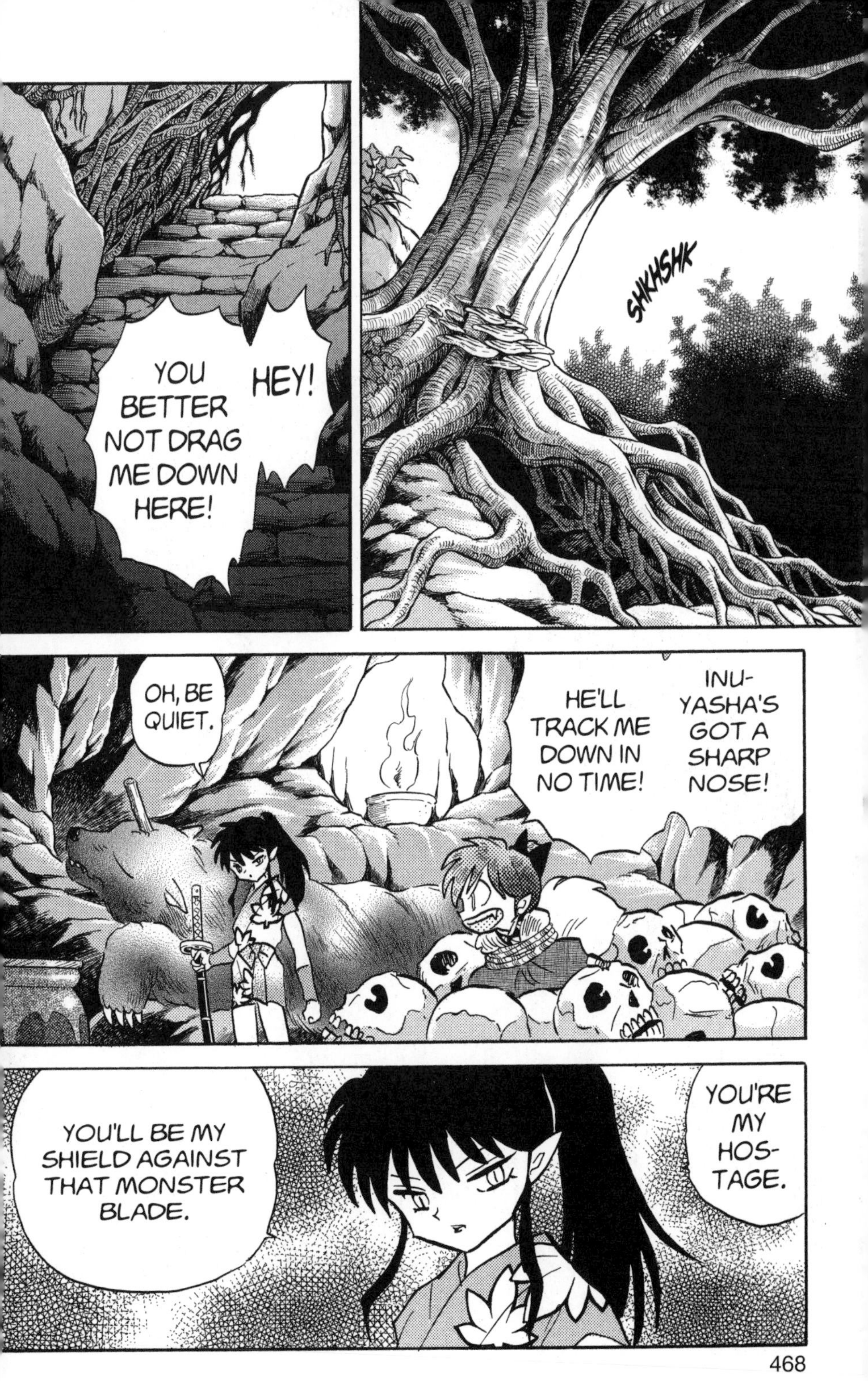
SHKHSHK
HEY!
YOU BETTER NOT DRAG ME DOWN HERE!
INU-YASHA'S GOT A SHARP NOSE!
HE'LL TRACK ME DOWN IN NO TIME!
OH, BE QUIET.
YOU'RE MY HOS-TAGE.
YOU'LL BE MY SHIELD AGAINST THAT MONSTER BLADE.

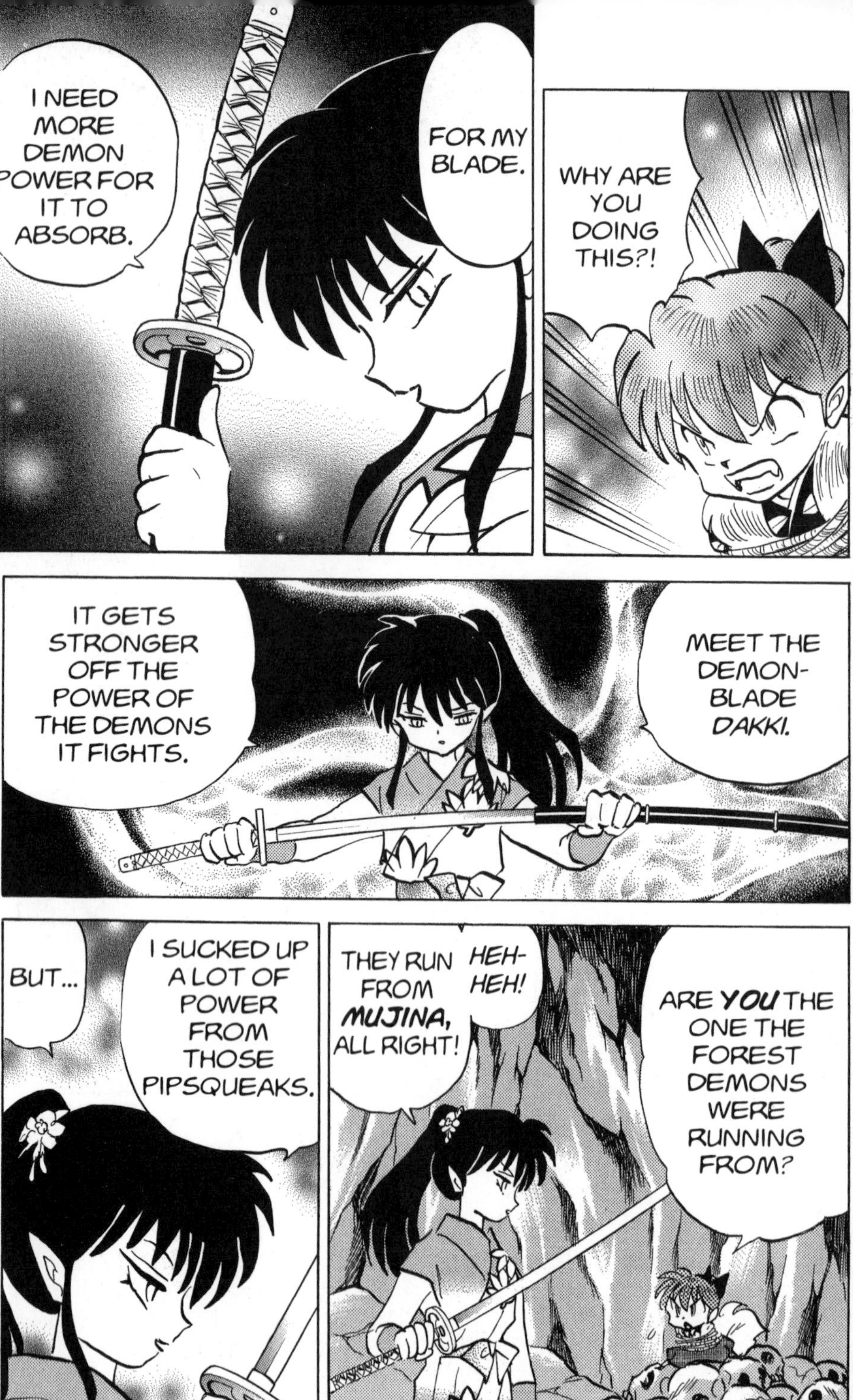
WHY ARE YOU DOING THIS?!
FOR MY BLADE.
I NEED MORE DEMON POWER FOR IT TO ABSORB.
MEET THE DEMON-BLADE *DAKKI*.
IT GETS STRONGER OFF THE POWER OF THE DEMONS IT FIGHTS.
ARE ***YOU*** THE ONE THE FOREST DEMONS WERE RUNNING FROM?
HEH-HEH!
THEY RUN FROM ***MUJINA***, ALL RIGHT!
I SUCKED UP A LOT OF POWER FROM THOSE PIPSQUEAKS.
BUT...

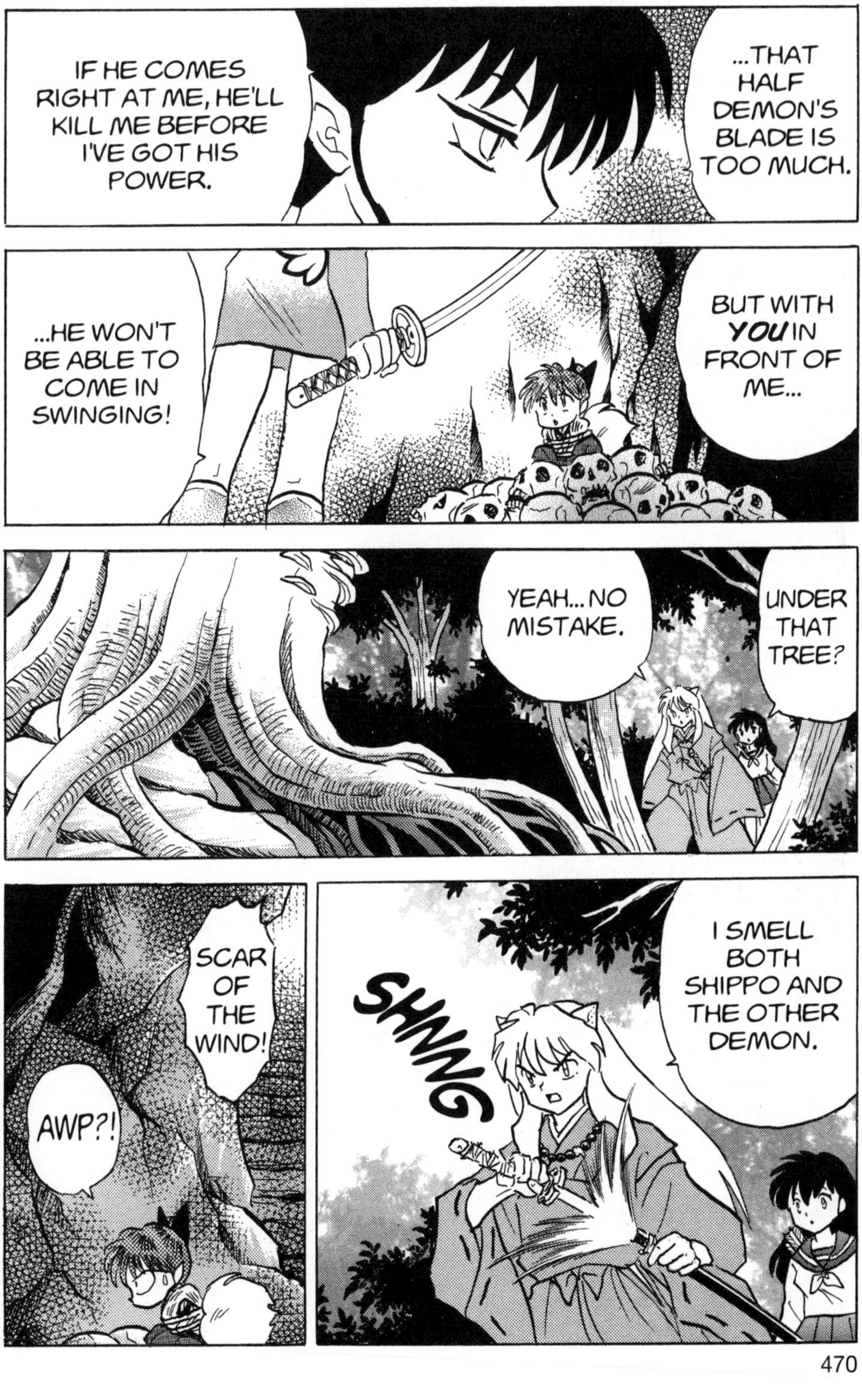
...THAT HALF DEMON'S BLADE IS TOO MUCH.
IF HE COMES RIGHT AT ME, HE'LL KILL ME BEFORE I'VE GOT HIS POWER.
BUT WITH *YOU* IN FRONT OF ME...
...HE WON'T BE ABLE TO COME IN SWINGING!
UNDER THAT TREE?
YEAH... NO MISTAKE.
I SMELL BOTH SHIPPO AND THE OTHER DEMON.
SHING
SCAR OF THE WIND!
AWP?!

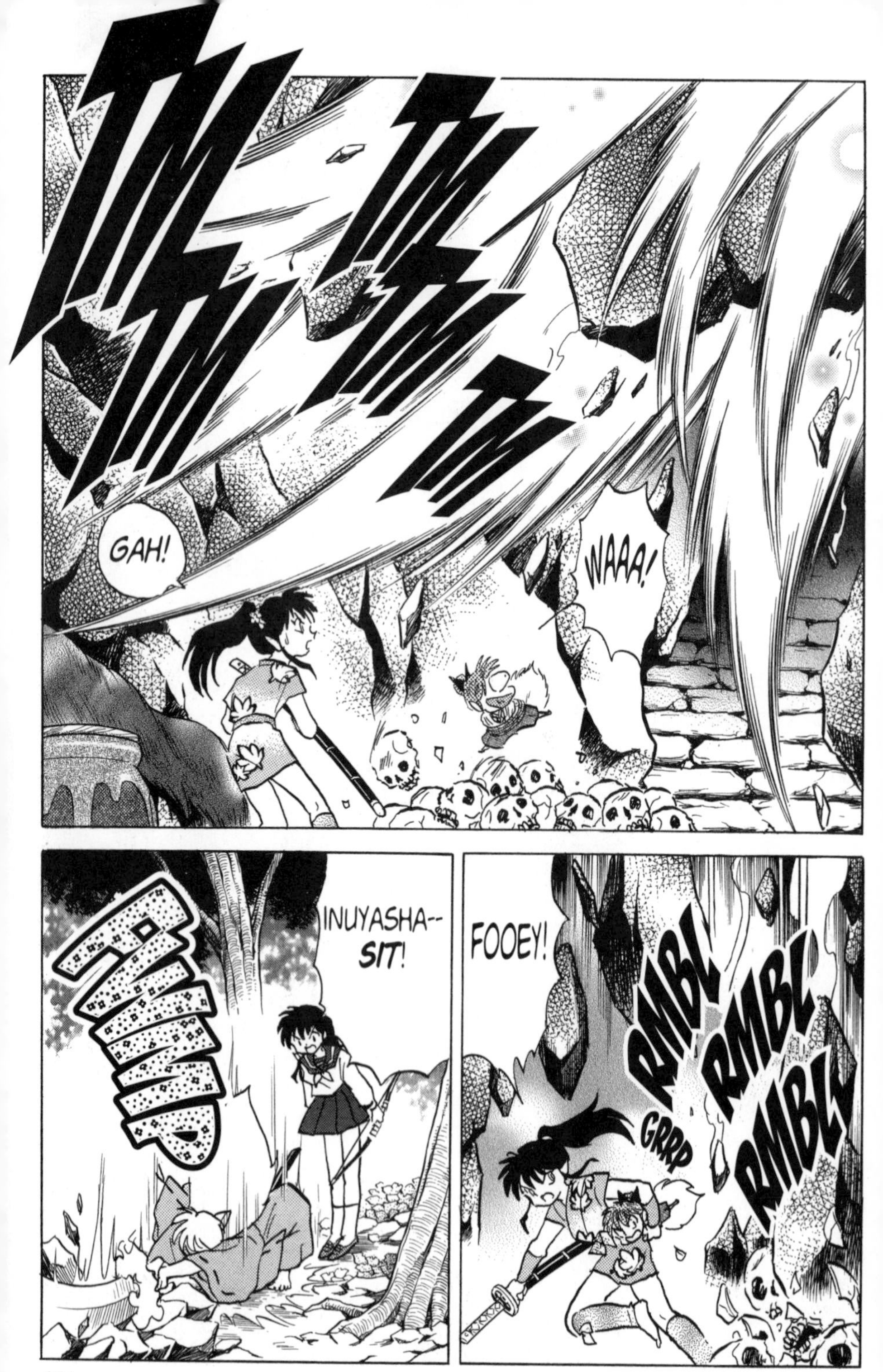
WAAA!
GAH!
FOOEY!
RMBL
RMBL
RMBL
GRRP
INUYASHA--
SIT!

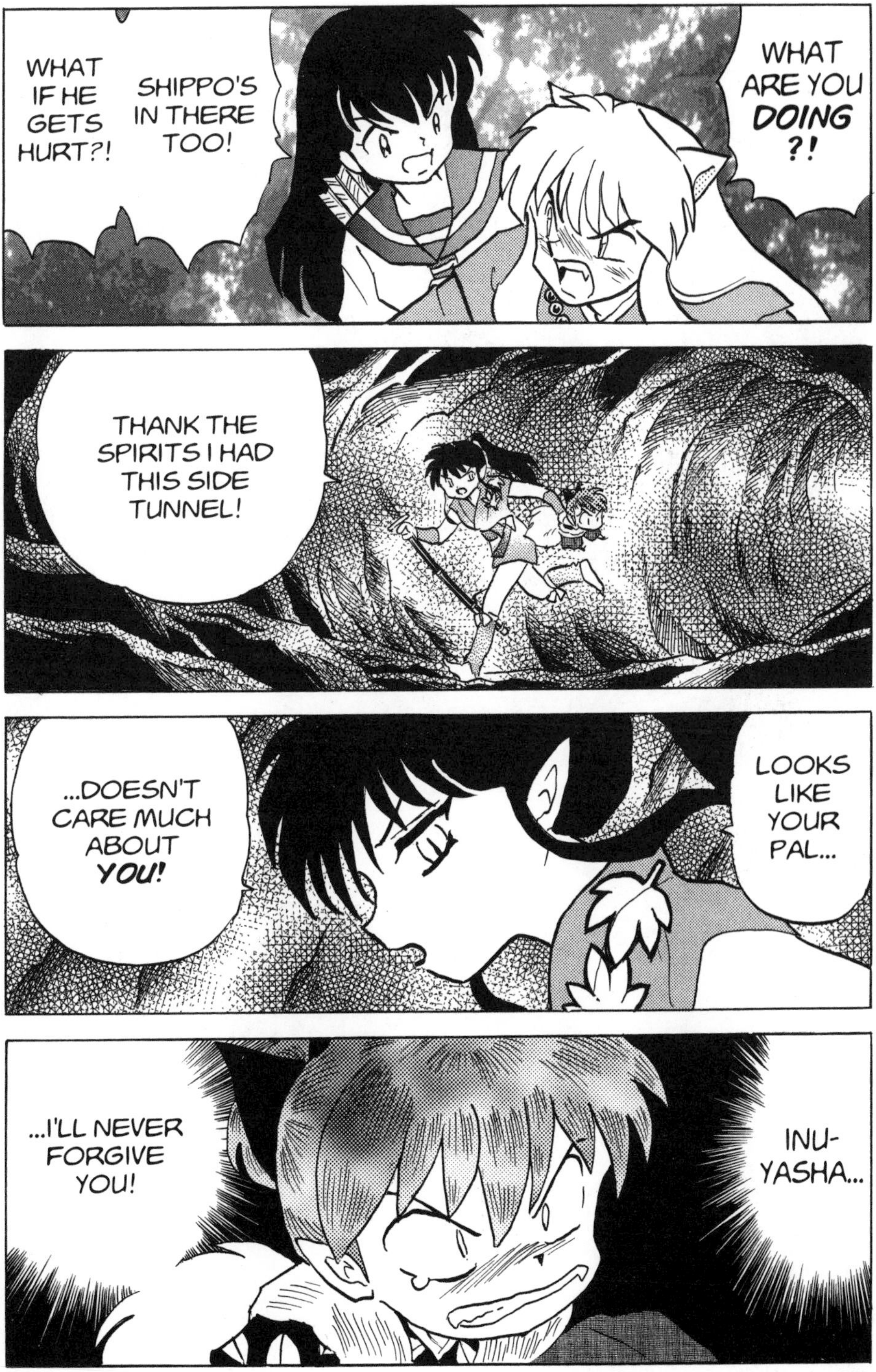
WHAT ARE YOU **DOING** ?!
SHIPPO'S IN THERE TOO!
WHAT IF HE GETS HURT?!
THANK THE SPIRITS I HAD THIS SIDE TUNNEL!
LOOKS LIKE YOUR PAL...
...DOESN'T CARE MUCH ABOUT **YOU!**
INU-YASHA...
...I'LL NEVER FORGIVE YOU!

SCROLL SIX
CAUSES

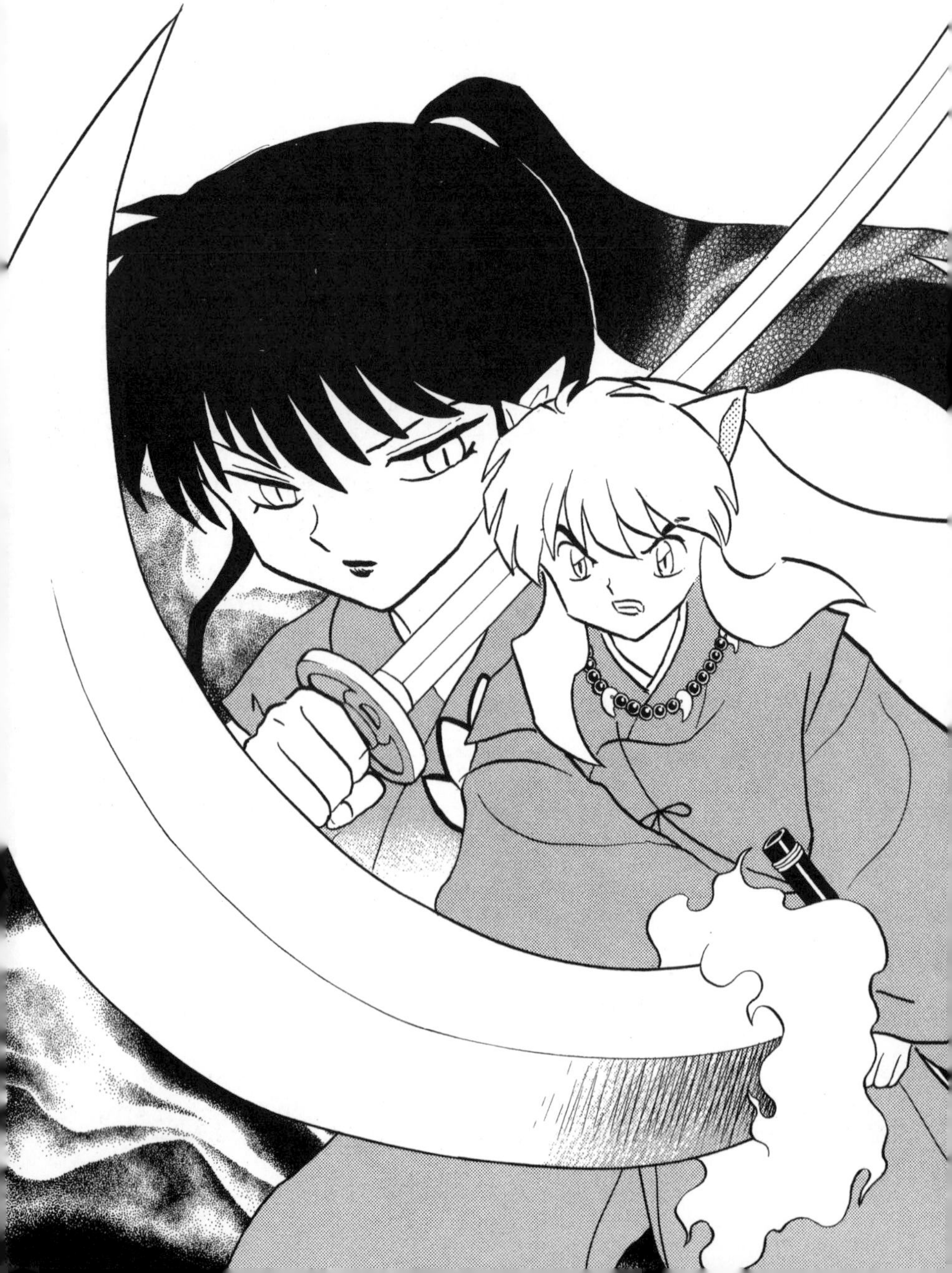

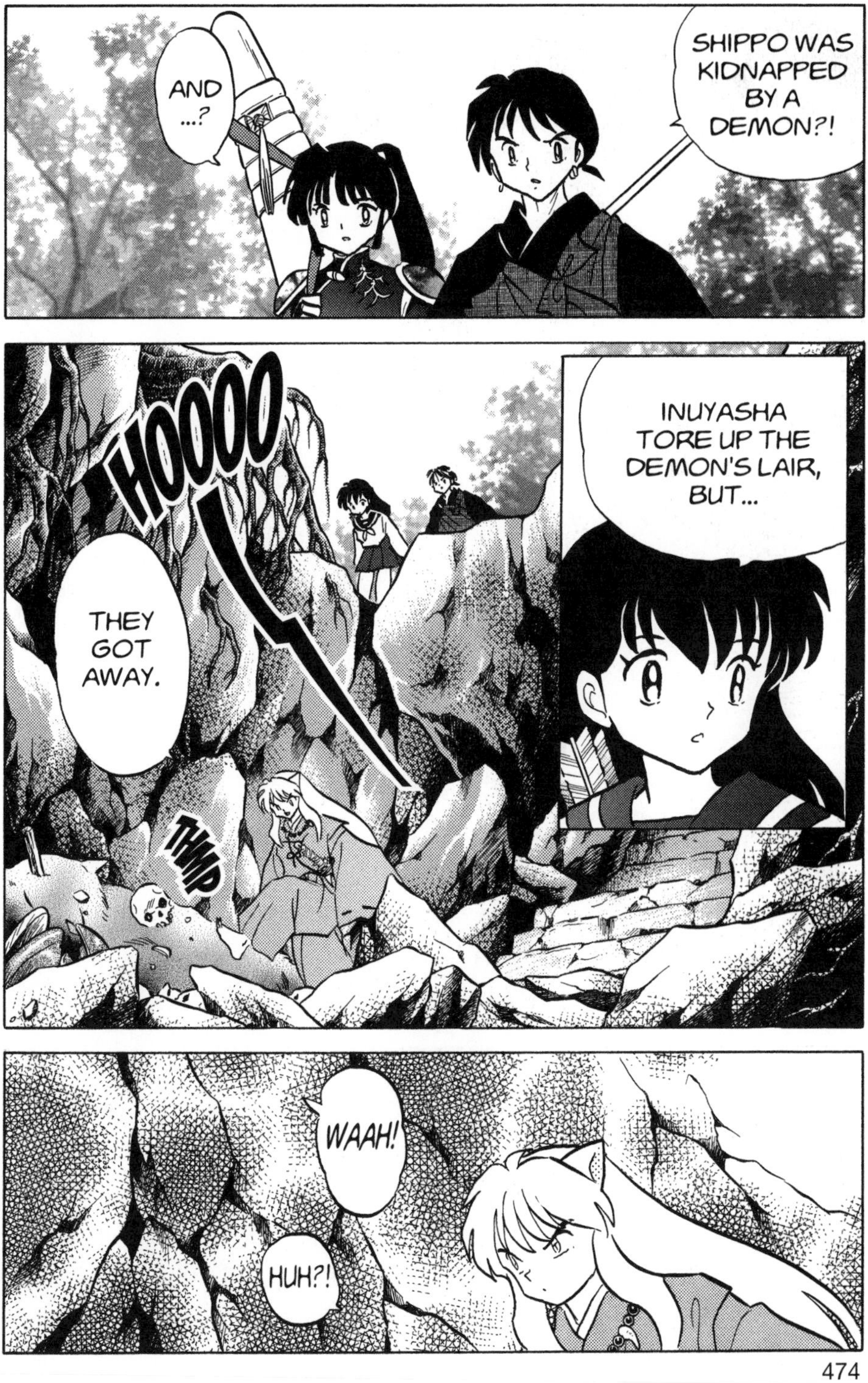
SHIPPO WAS KIDNAPPED BY A DEMON?!
AND ...?
INUYASHA TORE UP THE DEMON'S LAIR, BUT...
HOOOO
THEY GOT AWAY.
THMP
WAAH!
HUH?!

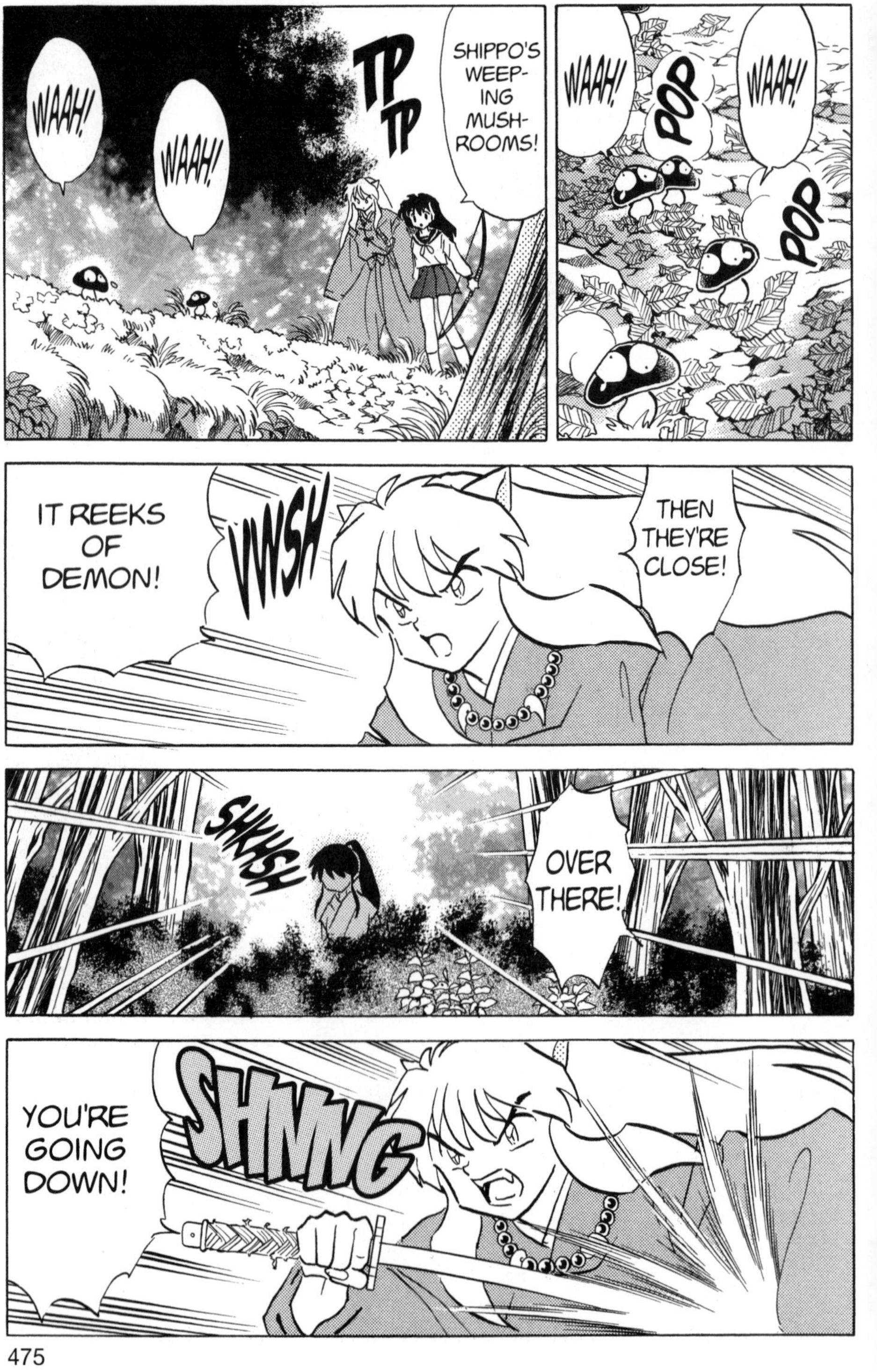
WAAH!
POP
WAAH!
POP
SHIPPO'S WEEP-ING MUSH-ROOMS!
TP TP
WAAH!
WAAH!
THEN THEY'RE CLOSE!
VWSH
IT REEKS OF DEMON!
OVER THERE!
SHKSH
SHING
YOU'RE GOING DOWN!

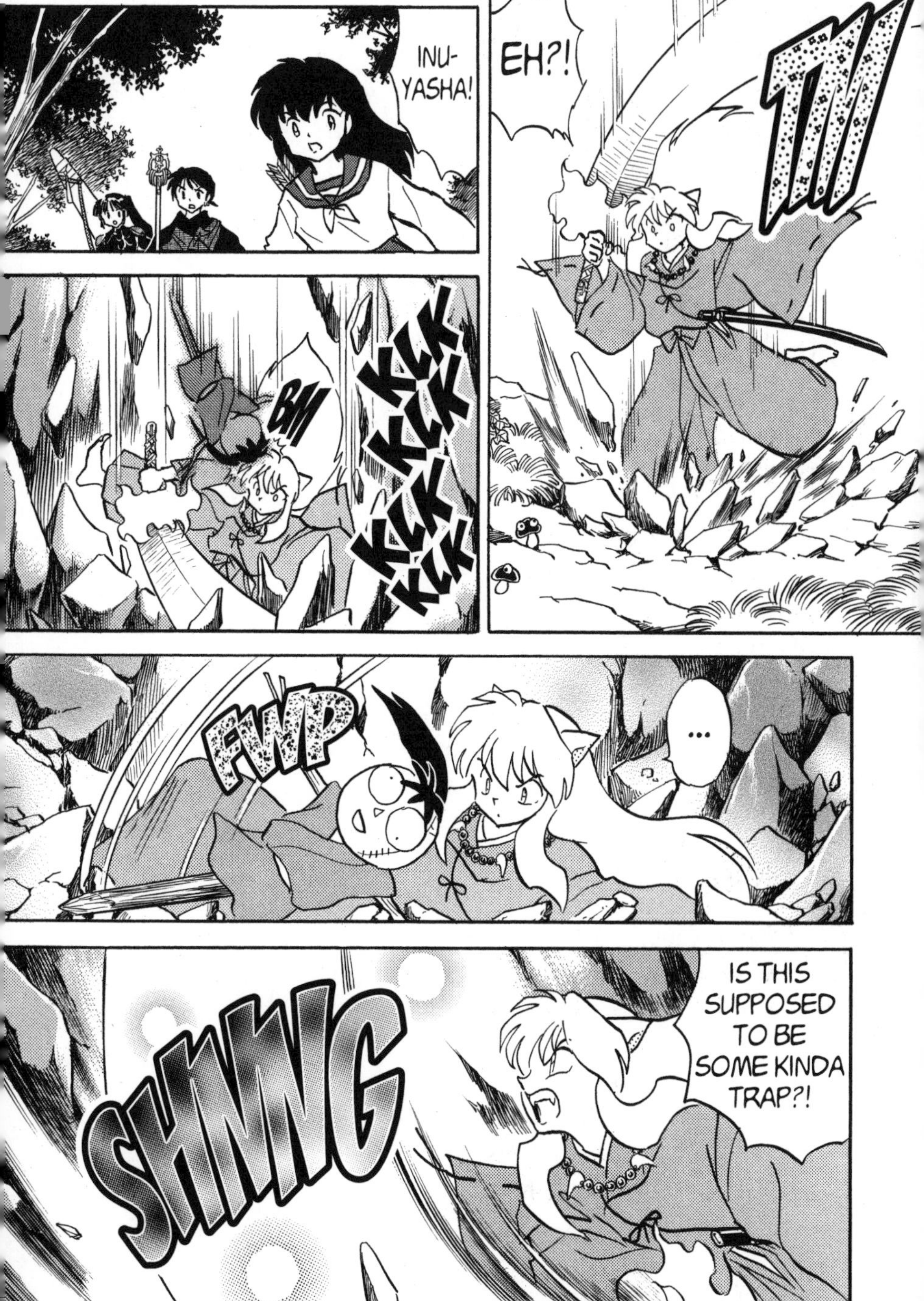
EH?!
INU-YASHA!
KLK KLK KLK KLK
BM
...
FWP
IS THIS SUPPOSED TO BE SOME KINDA TRAP?!
SHNNG

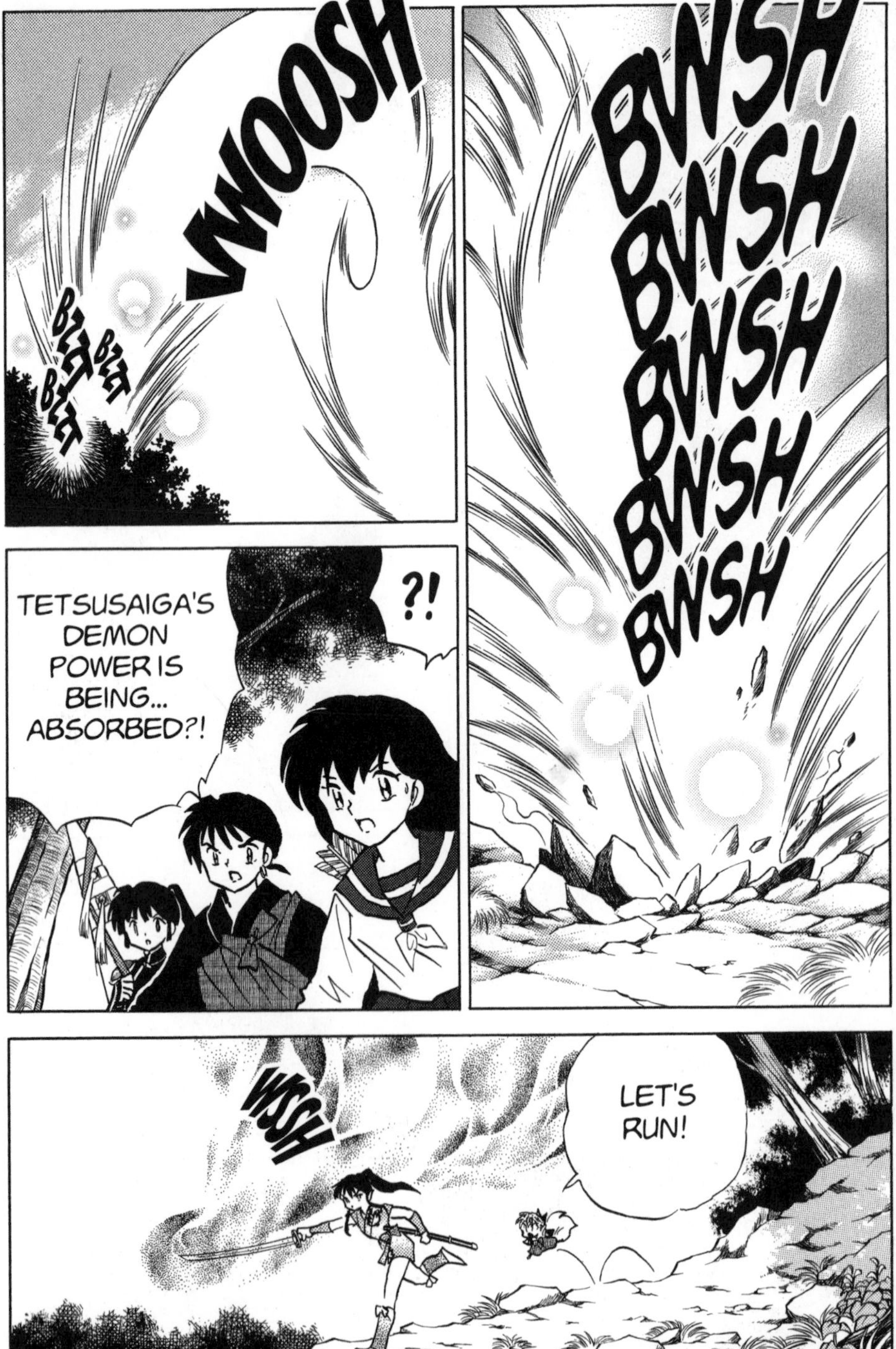
BWSH
BWSH
BWSH
BWSH
BWSH
BWSH
VWOOSH
BLZT BLZT BLZT
?!
TETSUSAIGA'S DEMON POWER IS BEING... ABSORBED?!
LET'S RUN!
WSSH

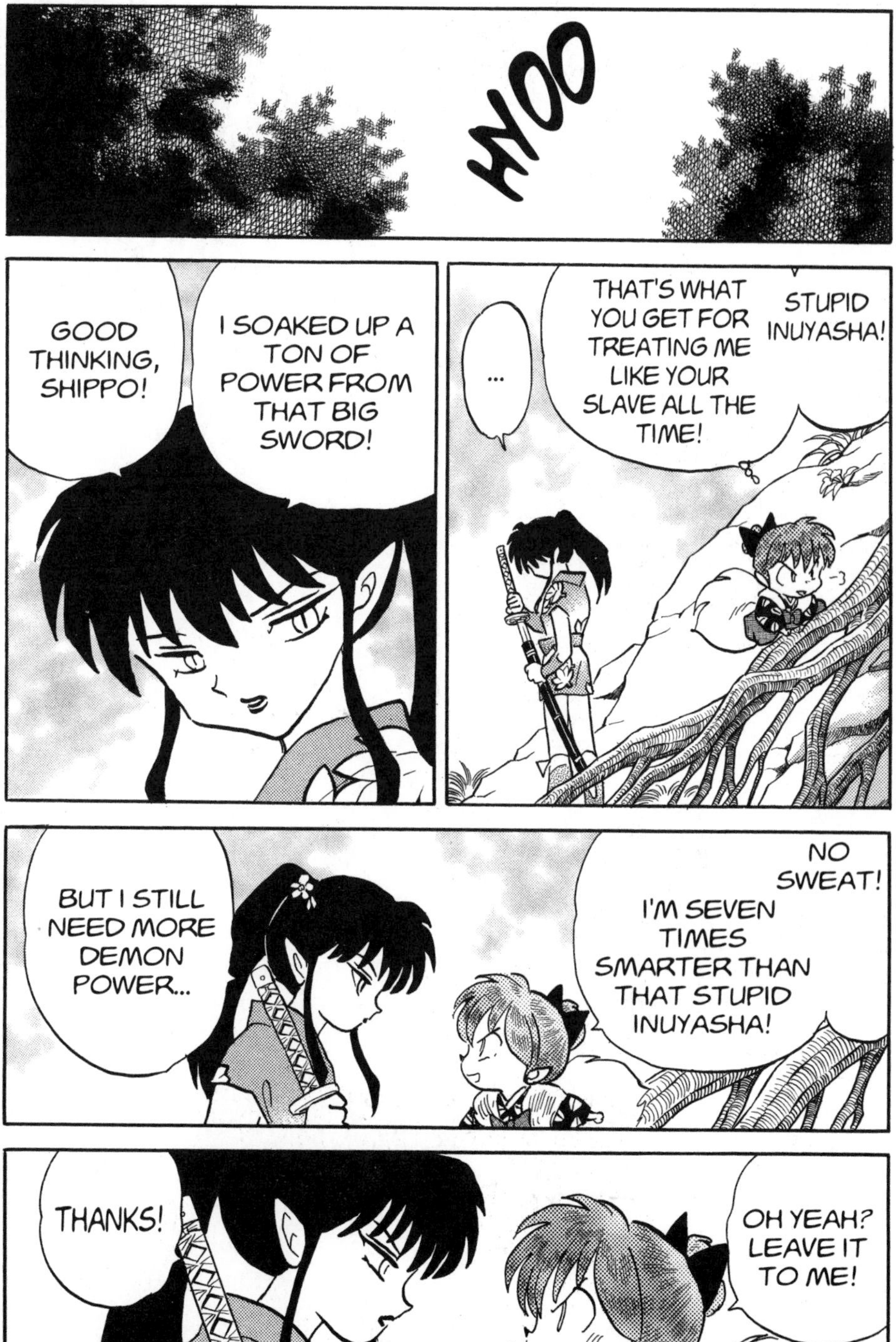
HYOO
STUPID INUYASHA!
THAT'S WHAT YOU GET FOR TREATING ME LIKE YOUR SLAVE ALL THE TIME!
...
I SOAKED UP A TON OF POWER FROM THAT BIG SWORD!
GOOD THINKING, SHIPPO!
NO SWEAT!
I'M SEVEN TIMES SMARTER THAN THAT STUPID INUYASHA!
BUT I STILL NEED MORE DEMON POWER...
OH YEAH? LEAVE IT TO ME!
THANKS!

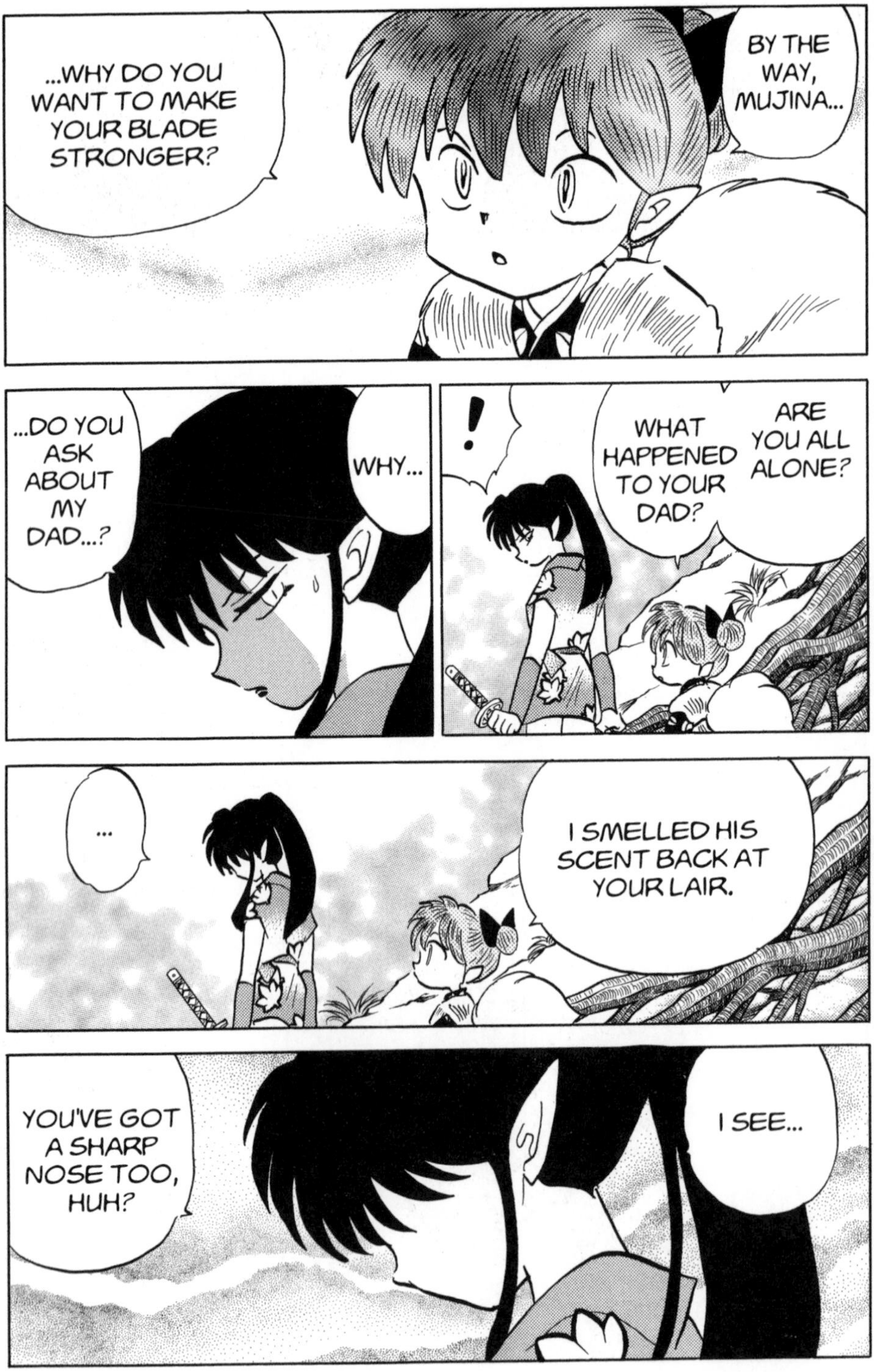
BY THE WAY, MUJINA...
...WHY DO YOU WANT TO MAKE YOUR BLADE STRONGER?
ARE YOU ALL ALONE?
WHAT HAPPENED TO YOUR DAD?
!
WHY...
...DO YOU ASK ABOUT MY DAD...?
I SMELLED HIS SCENT BACK AT YOUR LAIR.
...
I SEE...
YOU'VE GOT A SHARP NOSE TOO, HUH?

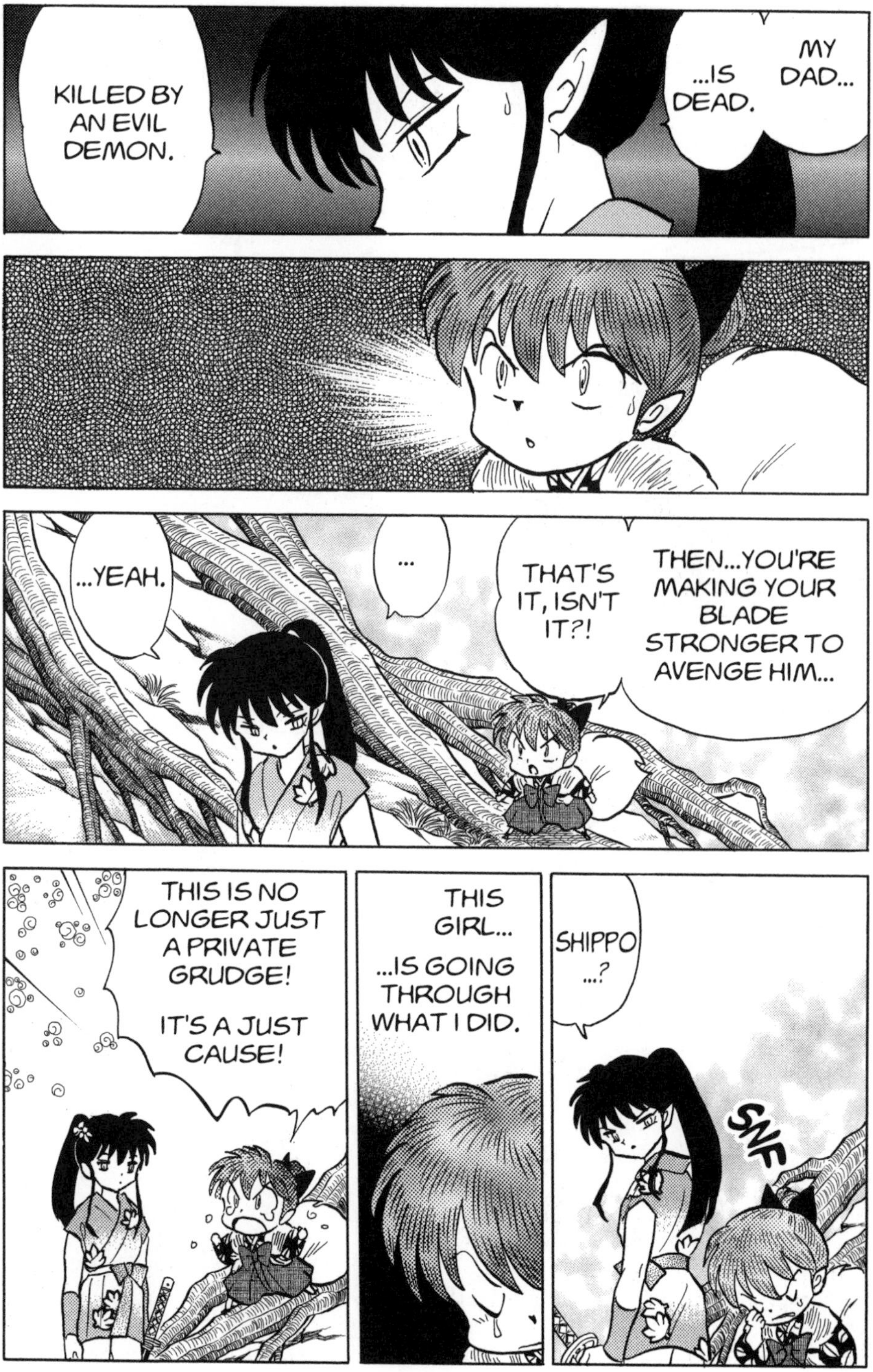
MY DAD...
...IS DEAD.
KILLED BY AN EVIL DEMON.
THEN...YOU'RE MAKING YOUR BLADE STRONGER TO AVENGE HIM...
THAT'S IT, ISN'T IT?!
...
...YEAH.
SHIPPO ...?
SNF
THIS GIRL...
...IS GOING THROUGH WHAT I DID.
THIS IS NO LONGER JUST A PRIVATE GRUDGE!
IT'S A JUST CAUSE!

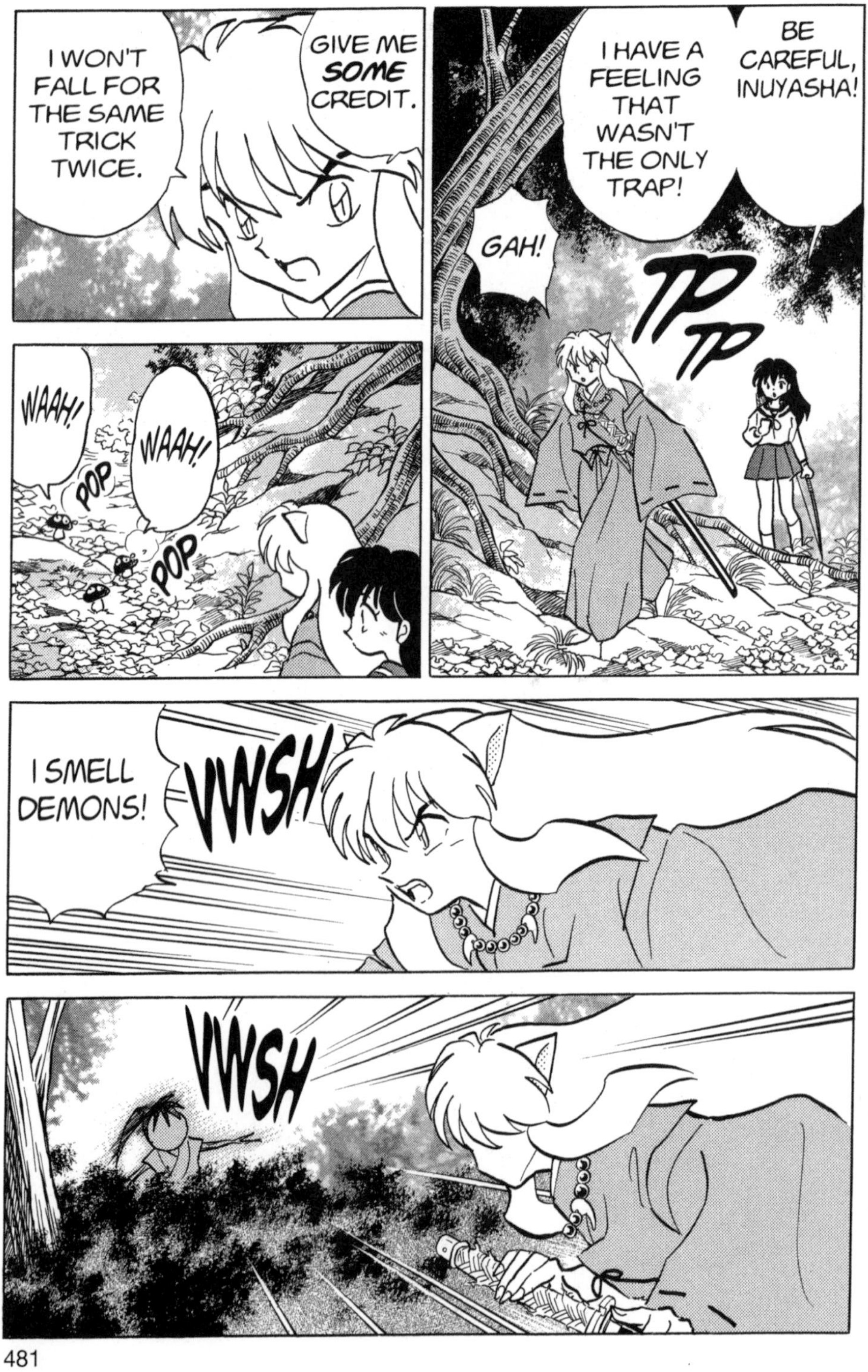
BE CAREFUL, INUYASHA!
I HAVE A FEELING THAT WASN'T THE ONLY TRAP!
GAH!
TP TP
GIVE ME *SOME* CREDIT.
I WON'T FALL FOR THE SAME TRICK TWICE.
WAAH!
WAAH!
POP
POP
VWSH
I SMELL DEMONS!
VWSH

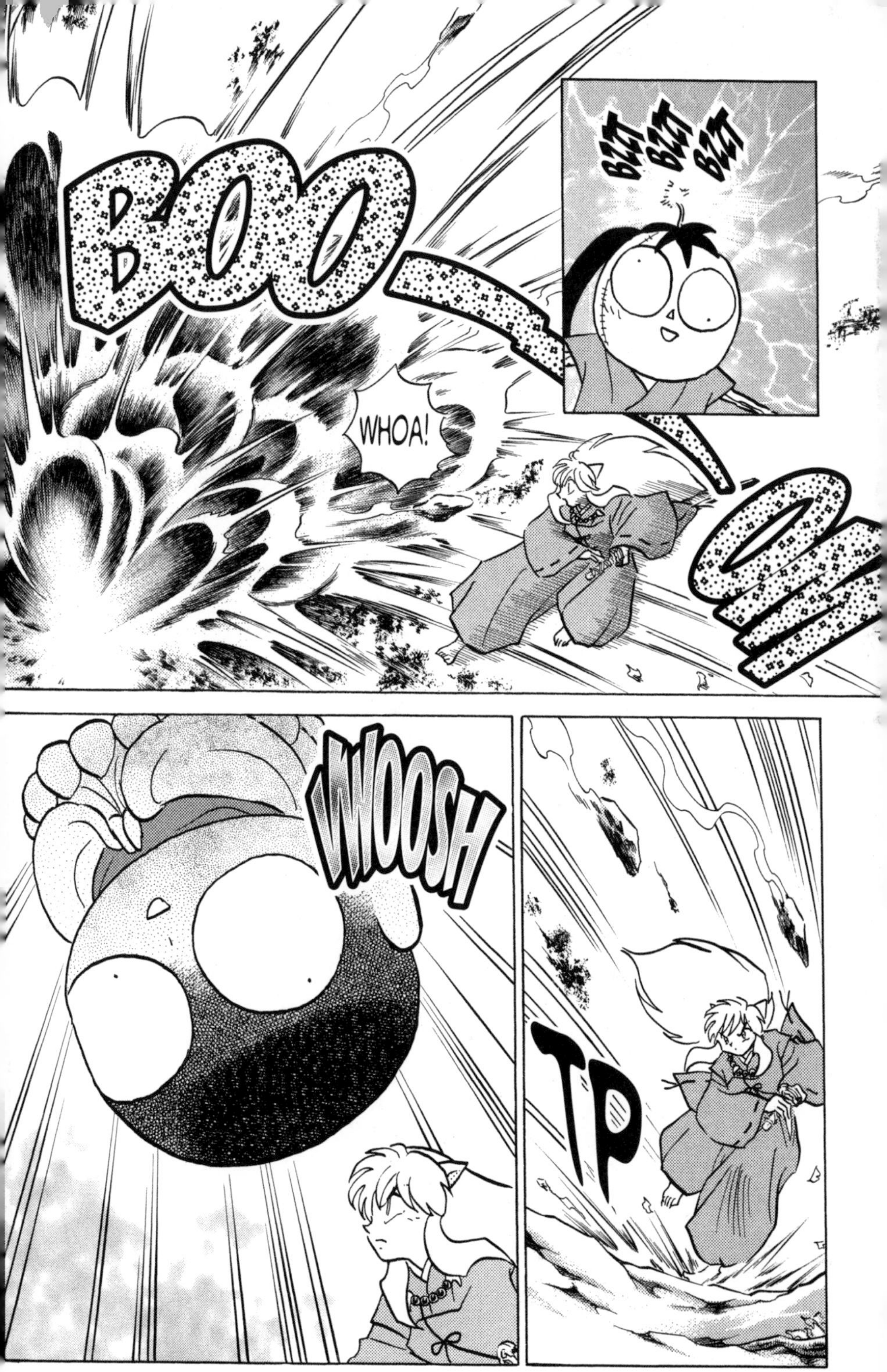
BZZT BZZT BZZT
BOO—OM
WHOA!
TP
WHOOSH

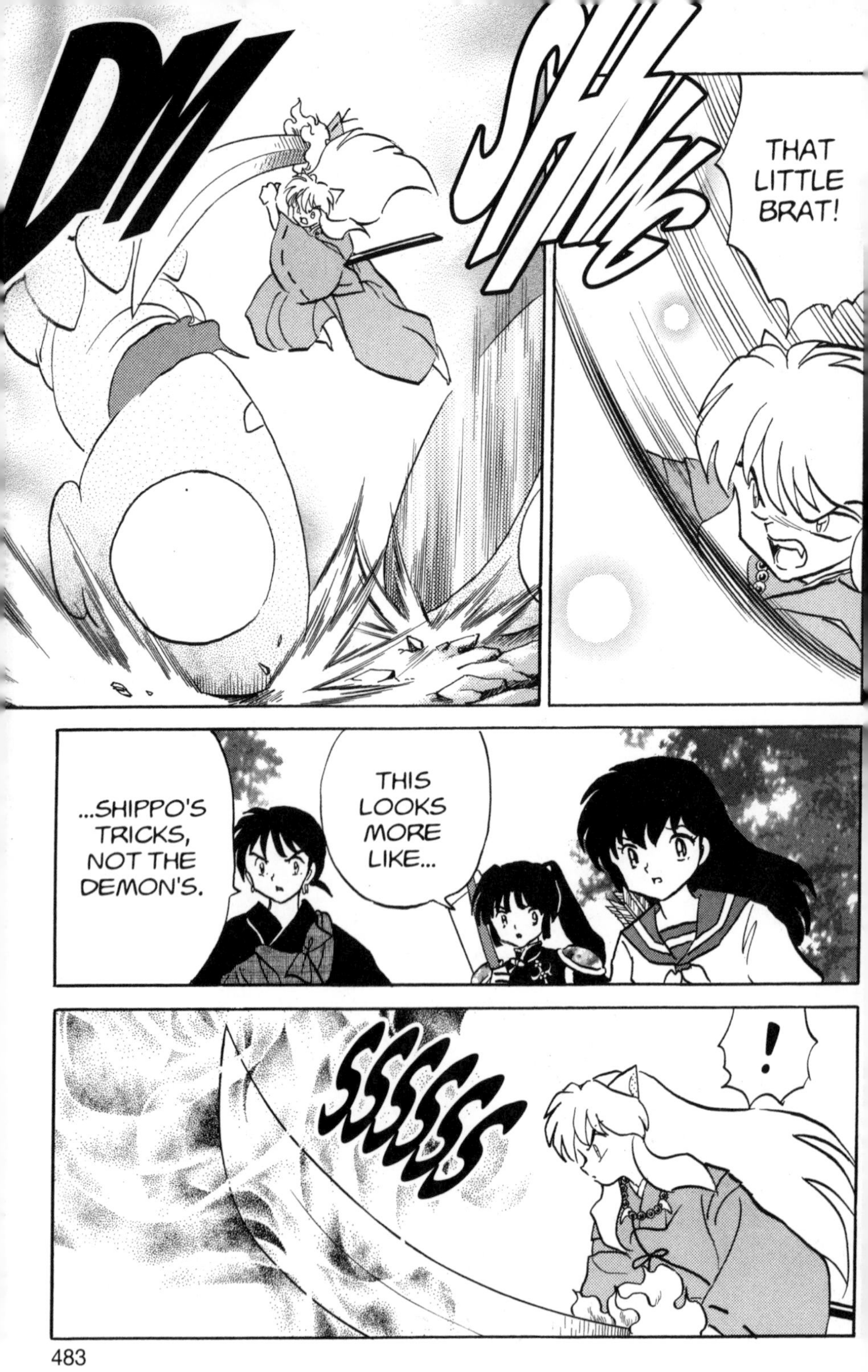
THAT LITTLE BRAT!
SHING
DM
THIS LOOKS MORE LIKE...
...SHIPPO'S TRICKS, NOT THE DEMON'S.
!
SSSSS

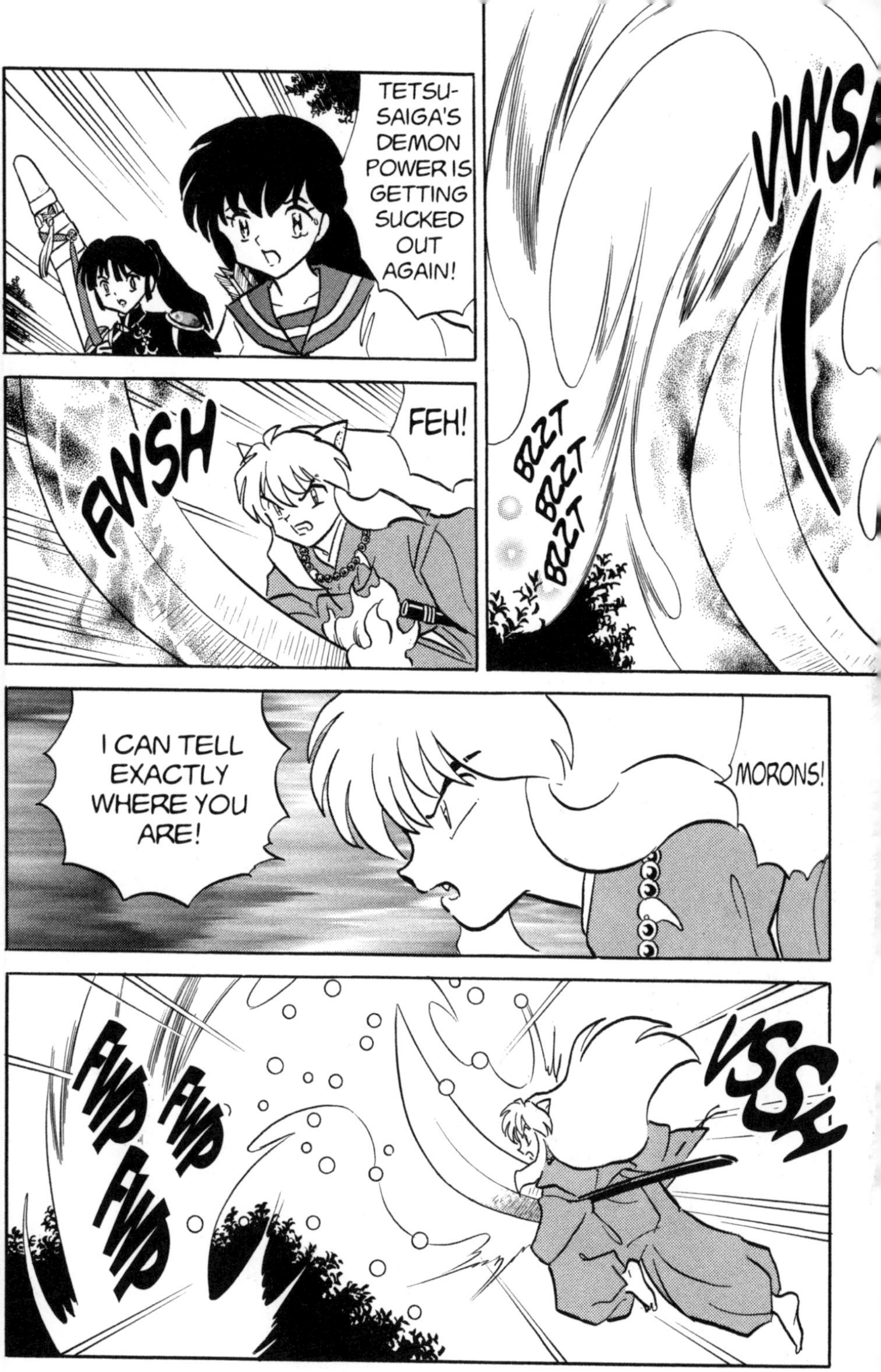
BZZT
BZZT
BZZT
TETSU-SAIGA'S DEMON POWER IS GETTING SUCKED OUT AGAIN!
FEH!
FWSH
MORONS!
I CAN TELL EXACTLY WHERE YOU ARE!
VSSH
FWP
FWP
FWP

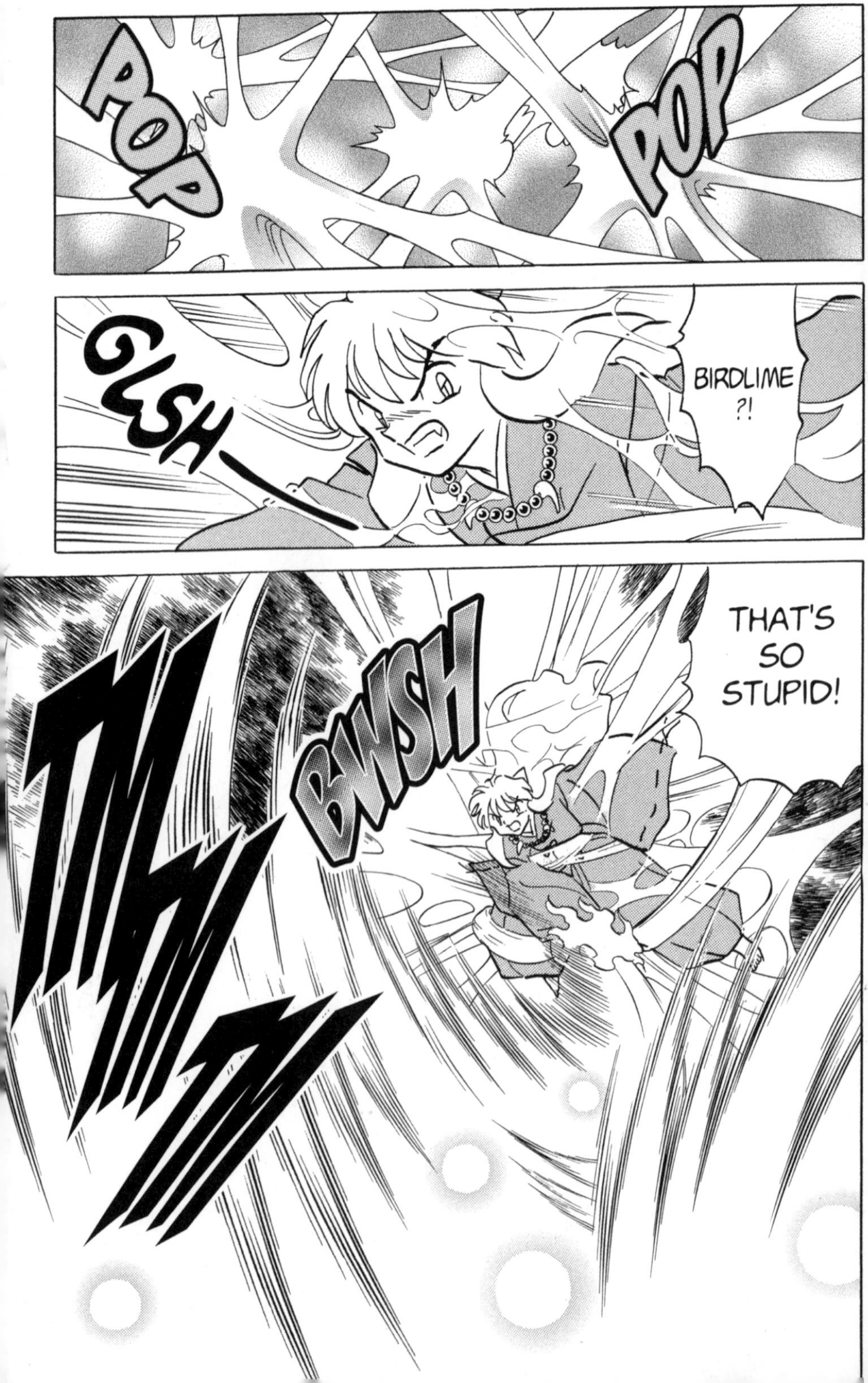
POP
POP
BIRDLIME ?!
GLSH
THAT'S SO STUPID!
BWSH
THWM

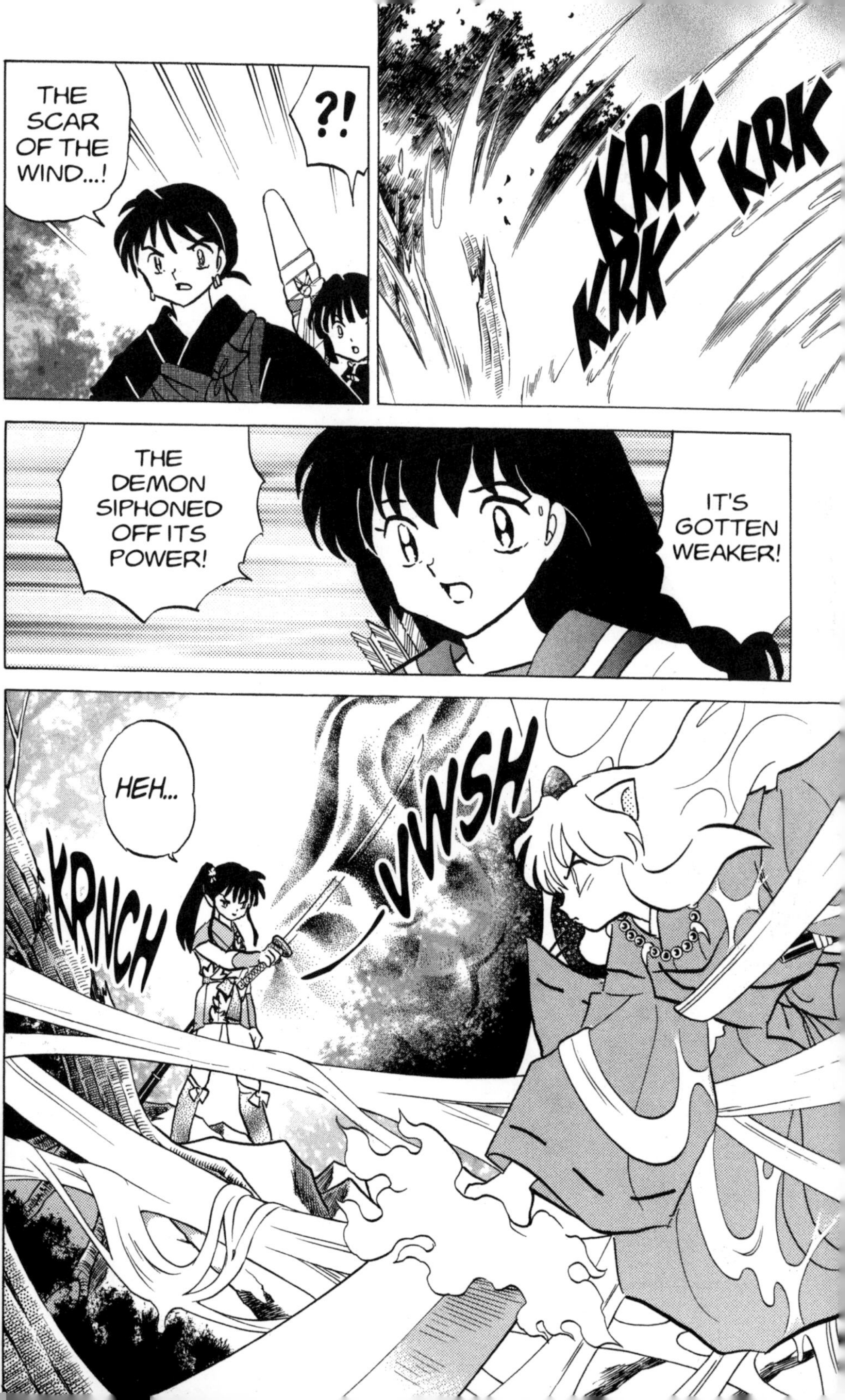
KRK KRK KRK KRK
?!
THE SCAR OF THE WIND...!
IT'S GOTTEN WEAKER!
THE DEMON SIPHONED OFF ITS POWER!
VVNSH
HEH...
KRNCH

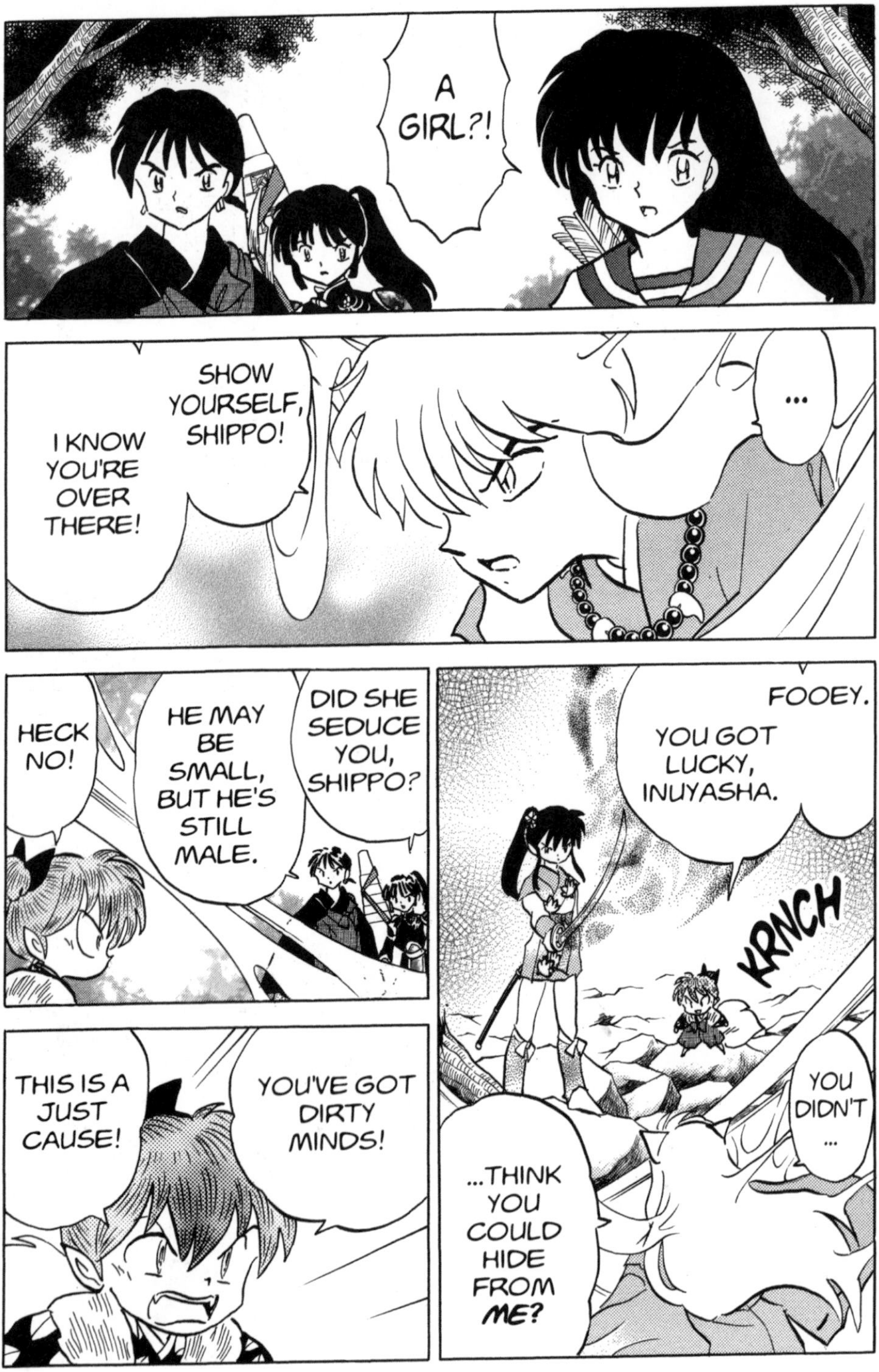
A GIRL?!
...
SHOW YOURSELF, SHIPPO!
I KNOW YOU'RE OVER THERE!
FOOEY.
YOU GOT LUCKY, INUYASHA.
KRNCH
YOU DIDN'T ...
...THINK YOU COULD HIDE FROM ME?
DID SHE SEDUCE YOU, SHIPPO?
HE MAY BE SMALL, BUT HE'S STILL MALE.
HECK NO!
YOU'VE GOT DIRTY MINDS!
THIS IS A JUST CAUSE!

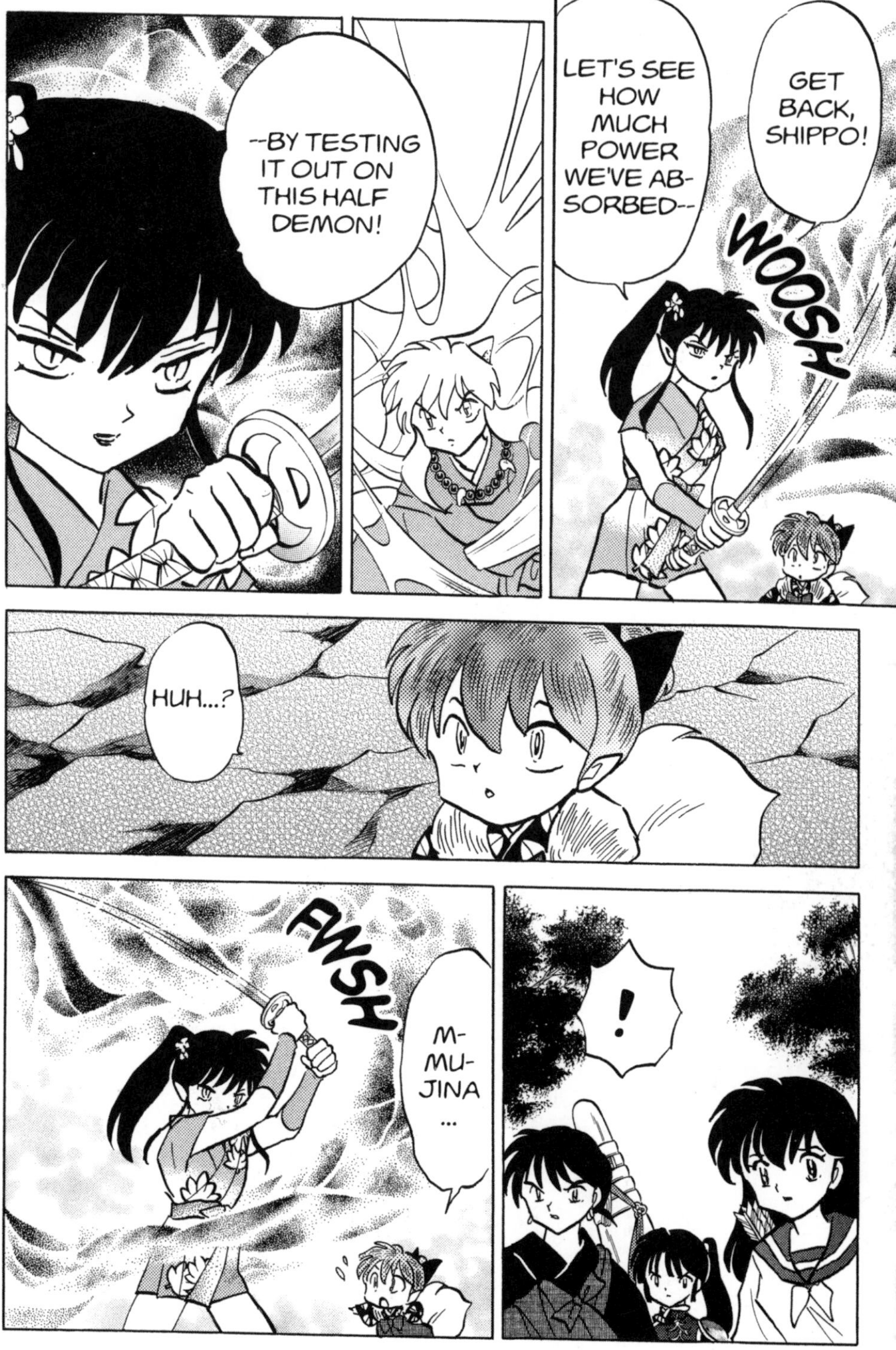
GET BACK, SHIPPO!
LET'S SEE HOW MUCH POWER WE'VE ABSORBED--
WOOSH
--BY TESTING IT OUT ON THIS HALF DEMON!
HUH...?
!
FWSH
M-MU-JINA...

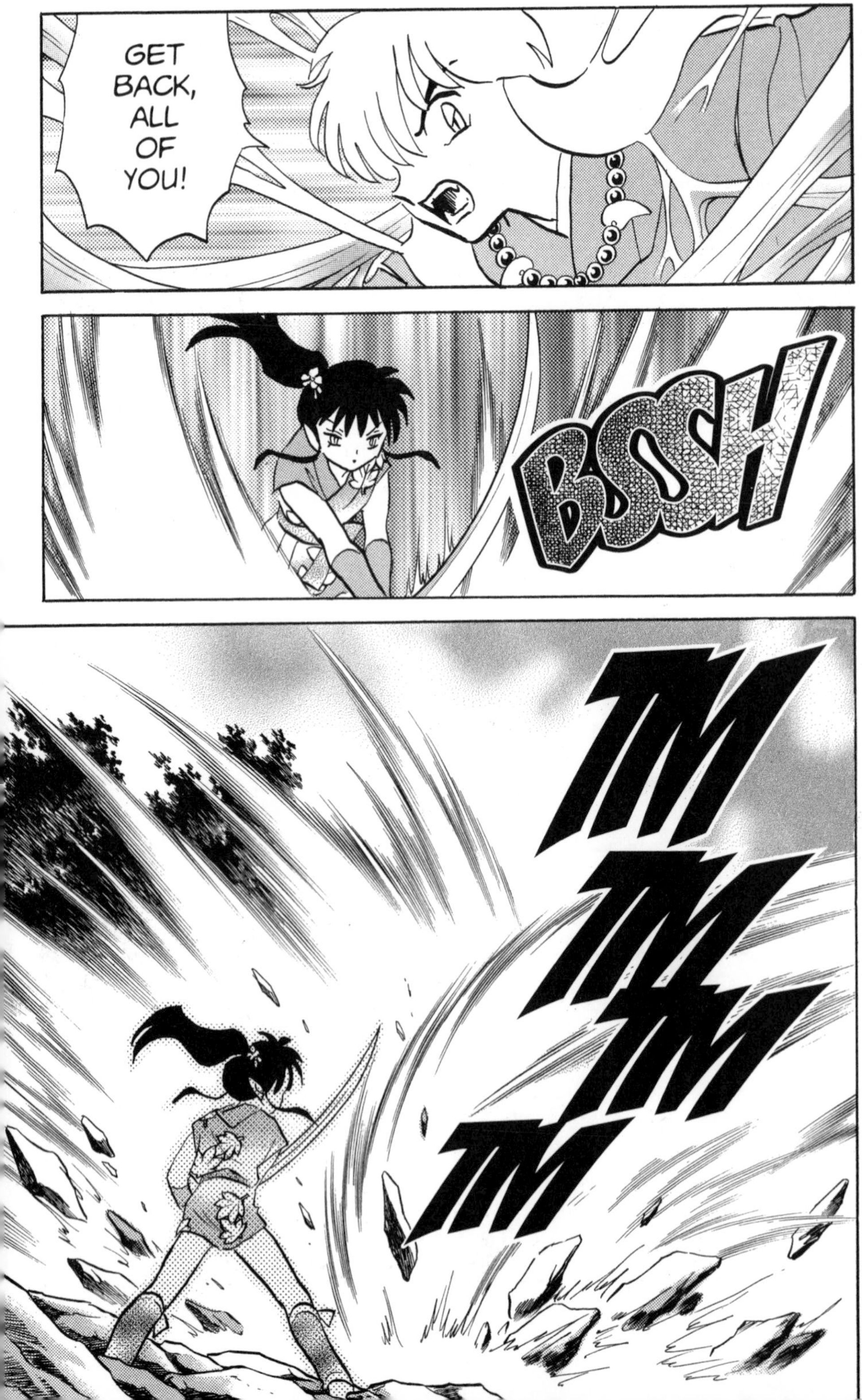
GET BACK, ALL OF YOU!
BOSH
TM TM TM TM

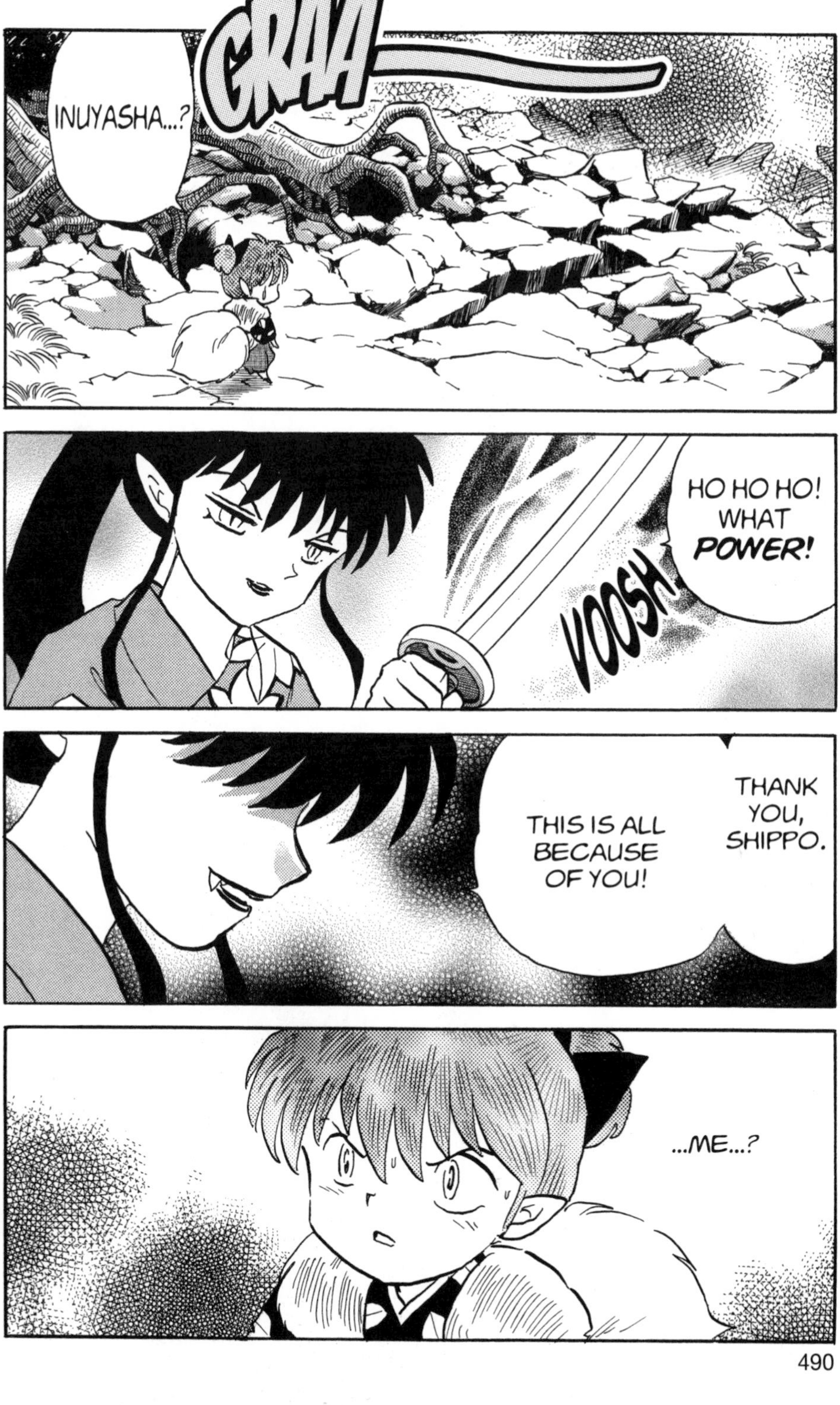

GRAA
INUYASHA...?
HO HO HO! WHAT POWER!
VOOSH
THANK YOU, SHIPPO.
THIS IS ALL BECAUSE OF YOU!
...ME...?

SCROLL SEVEN
DAKKI

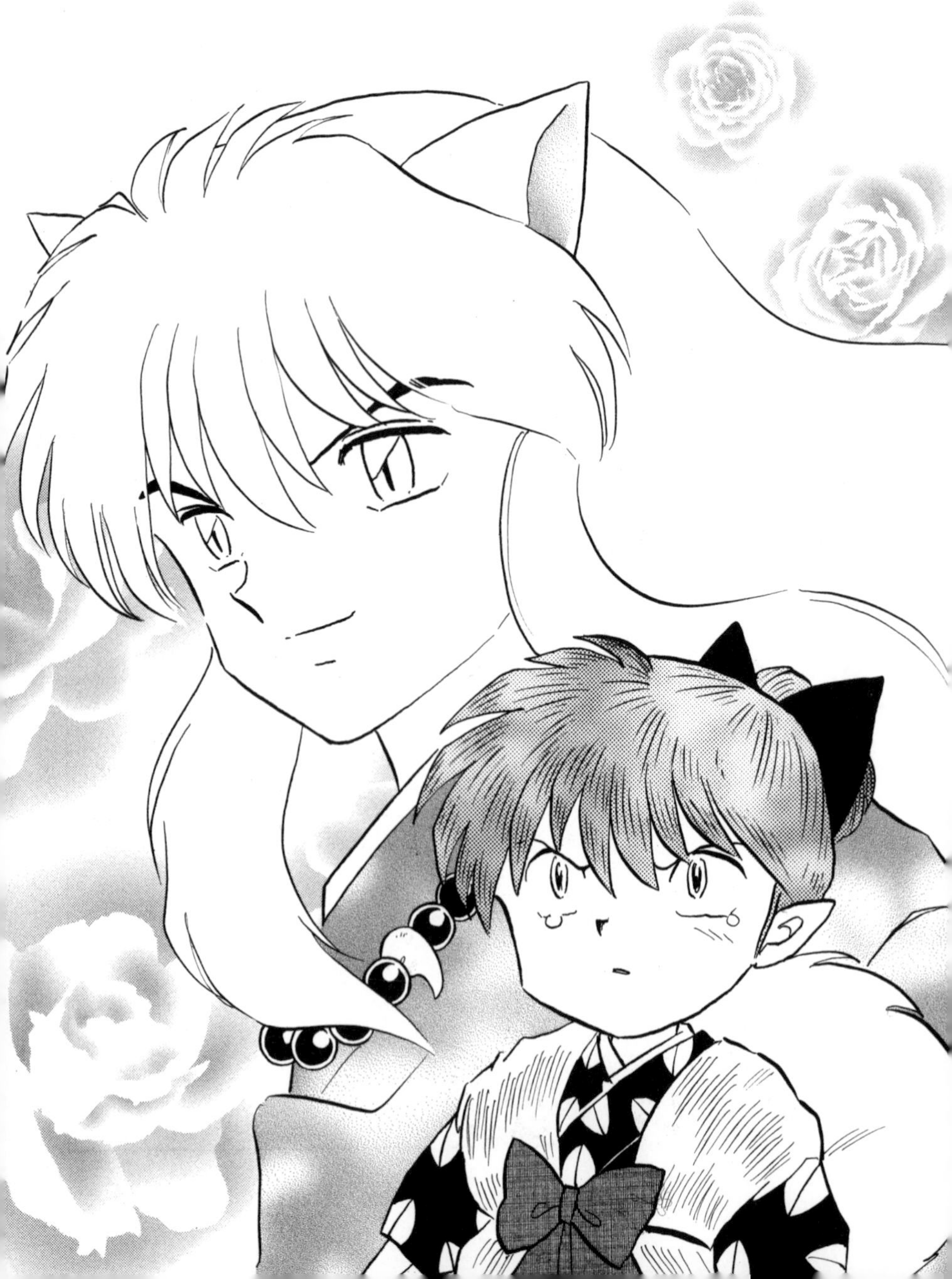

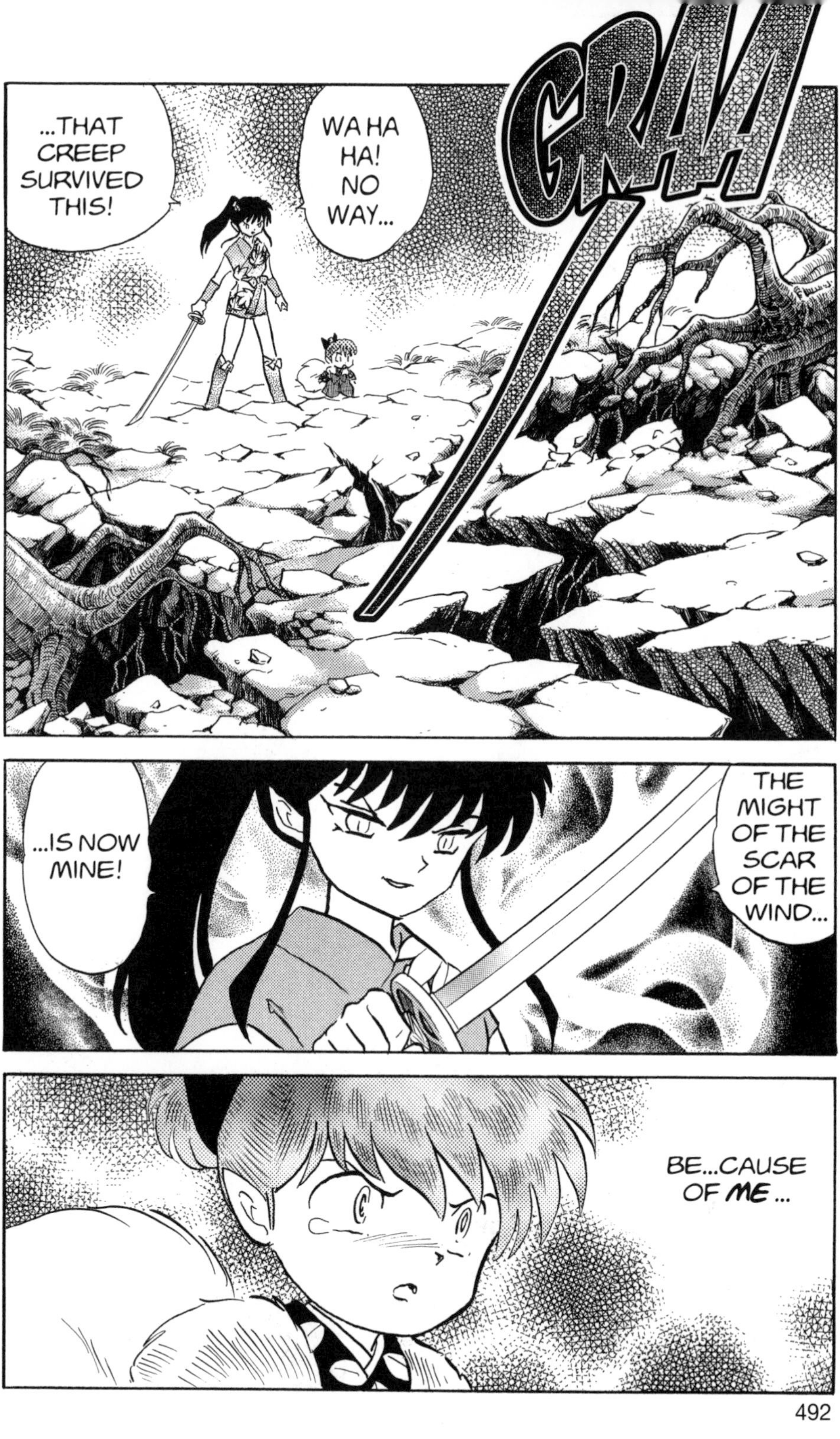
GRAM
WA HA HA! NO WAY...
...THAT CREEP SURVIVED THIS!
THE MIGHT OF THE SCAR OF THE WIND...
...IS NOW MINE!
BE...CAUSE OF *ME*...

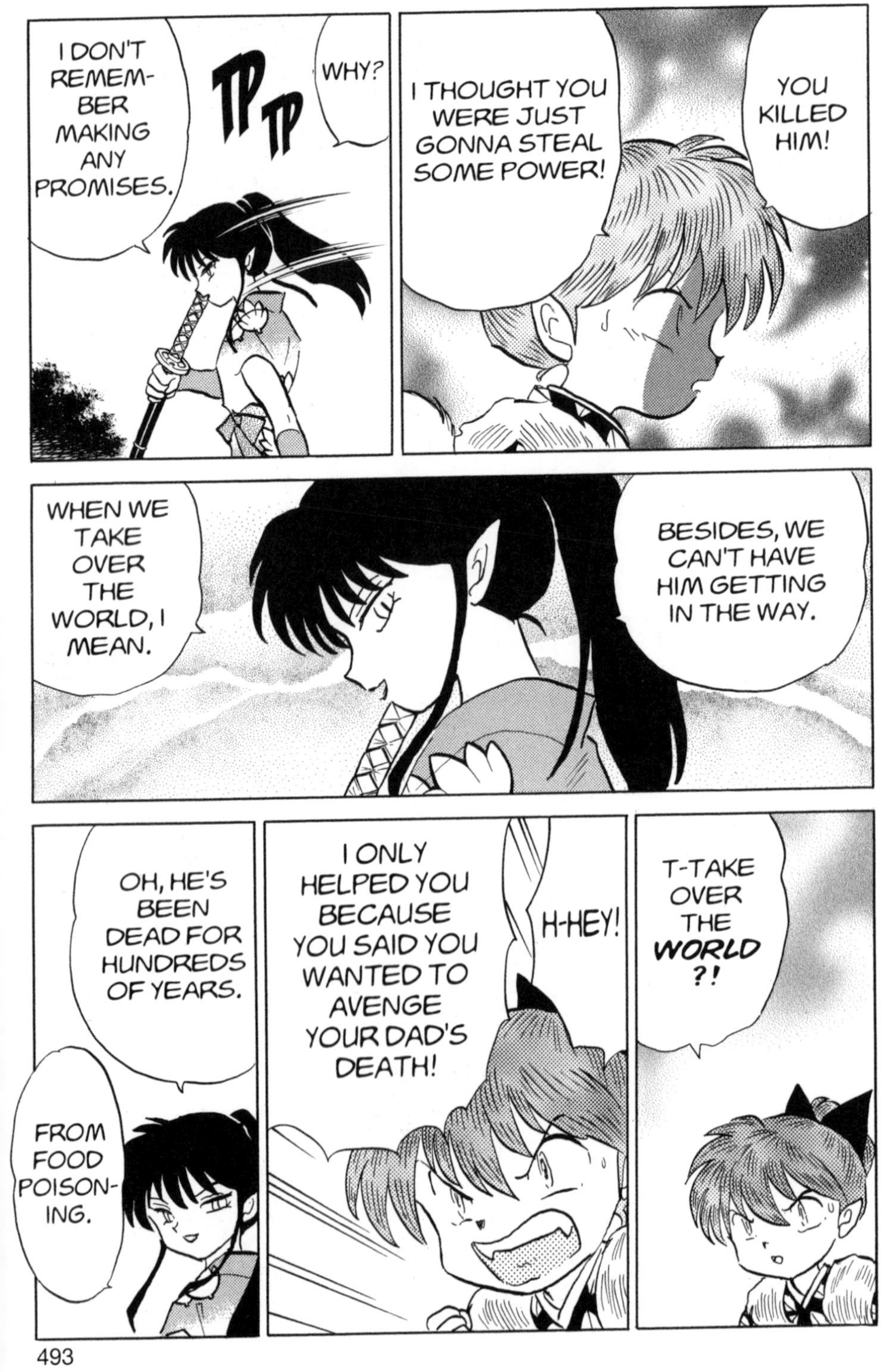
YOU KILLED HIM!
I THOUGHT YOU WERE JUST GONNA STEAL SOME POWER!
WHY?
TP TP
I DON'T REMEMBER MAKING ANY PROMISES.
BESIDES, WE CAN'T HAVE HIM GETTING IN THE WAY.
WHEN WE TAKE OVER THE WORLD, I MEAN.
T-TAKE OVER THE *WORLD* ?!
H-HEY!
I ONLY HELPED YOU BECAUSE YOU SAID YOU WANTED TO AVENGE YOUR DAD'S DEATH!
OH, HE'S BEEN DEAD FOR HUNDREDS OF YEARS.
FROM FOOD POISONING.

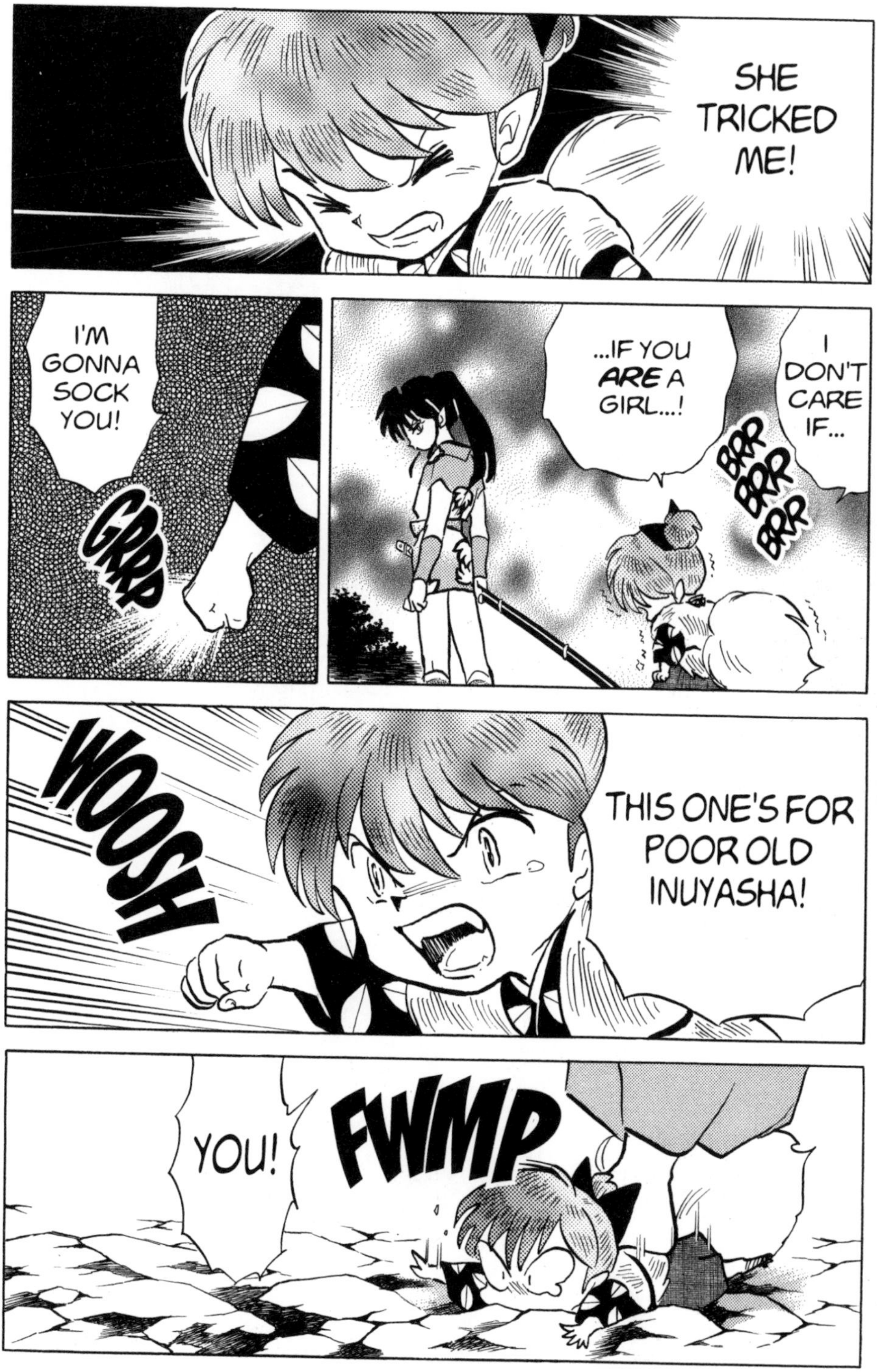
SHE TRICKED ME!
I DON'T CARE IF...
...IF YOU ARE A GIRL...!
BRR BRR BRR
I'M GONNA SOCK YOU!
GRRP
THIS ONE'S FOR POOR OLD INUYASHA!
WOOSH
FWMP
YOU!

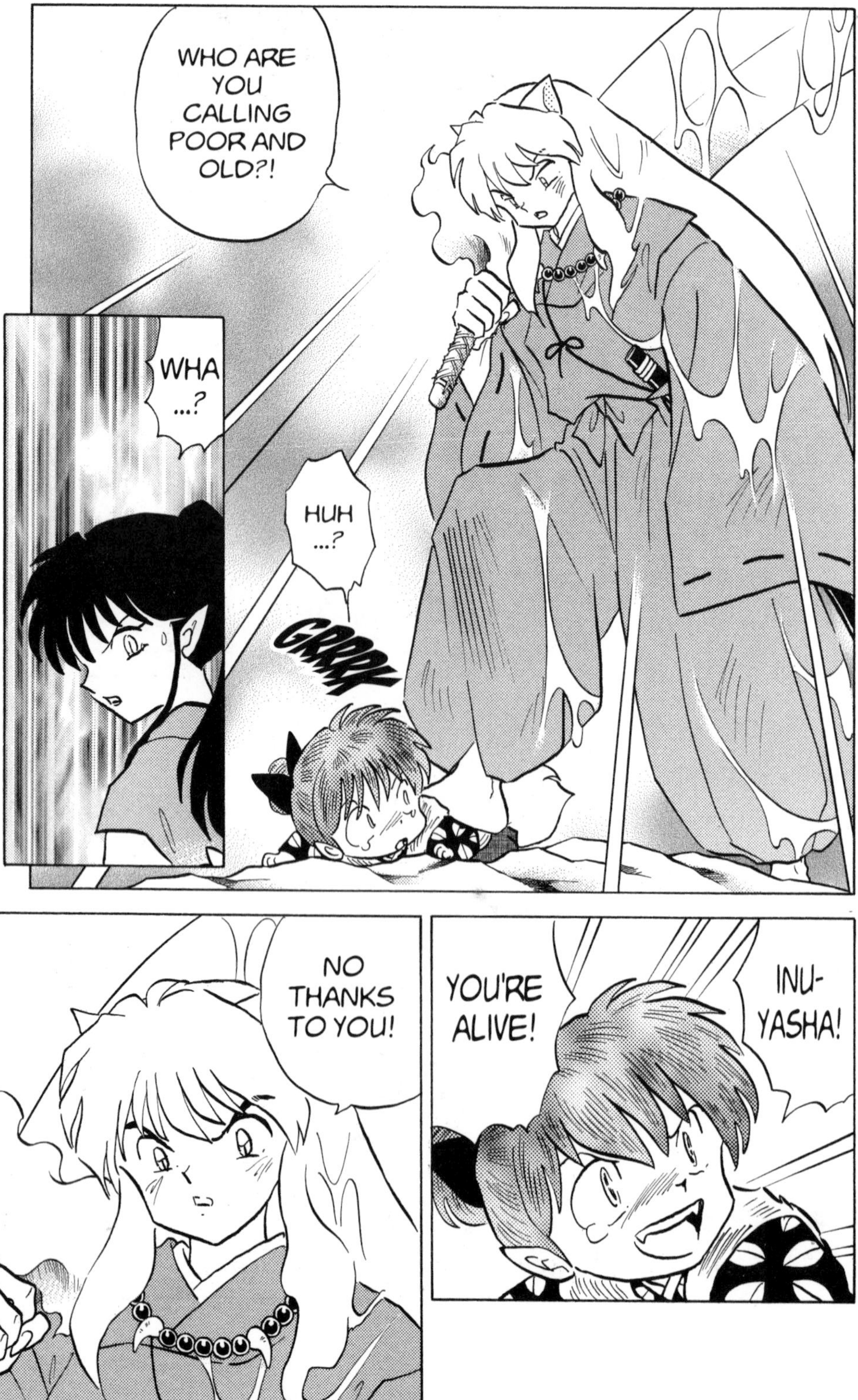
WHO ARE YOU CALLING POOR AND OLD?!
HUH ...?
GRRRK
WHA ...?
INU-YASHA!
YOU'RE ALIVE!
NO THANKS TO YOU!

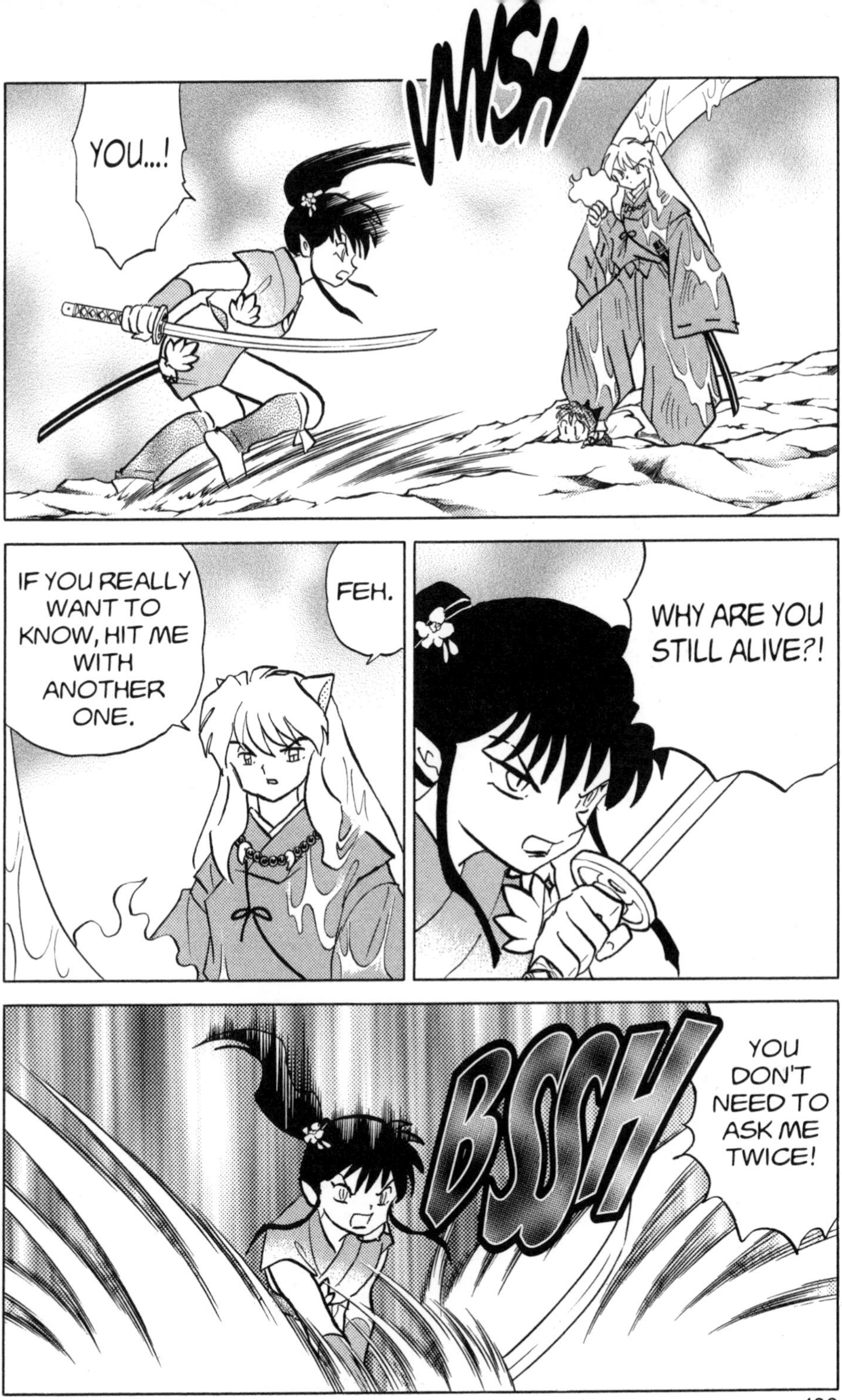
VWSH
YOU...!
WHY ARE YOU STILL ALIVE?!
FEH.
IF YOU REALLY WANT TO KNOW, HIT ME WITH ANOTHER ONE.
YOU DON'T NEED TO ASK ME TWICE!
BSCH

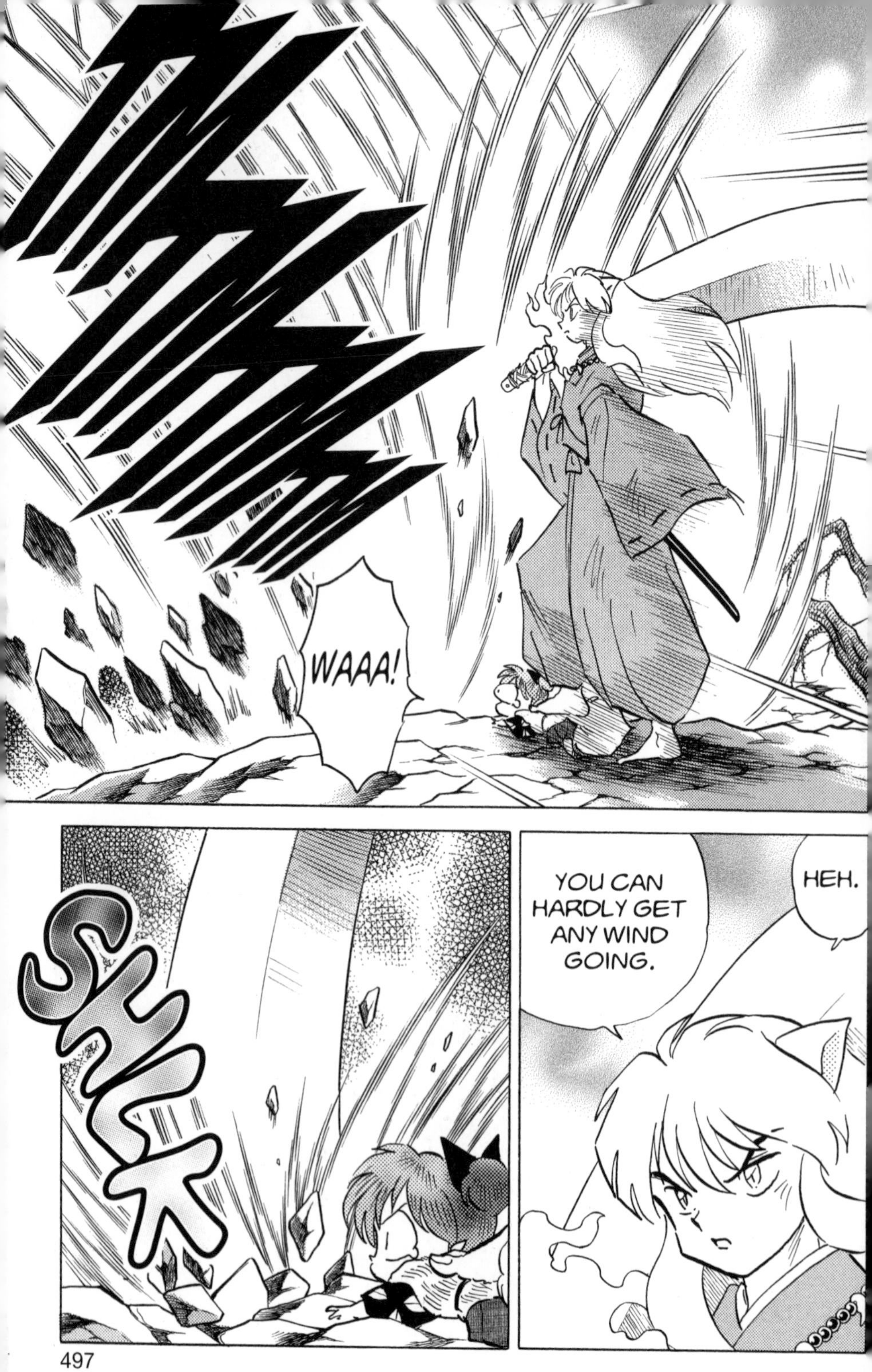
WAAA!
HEH.
YOU CAN HARDLY GET ANY WIND GOING.
SHUK

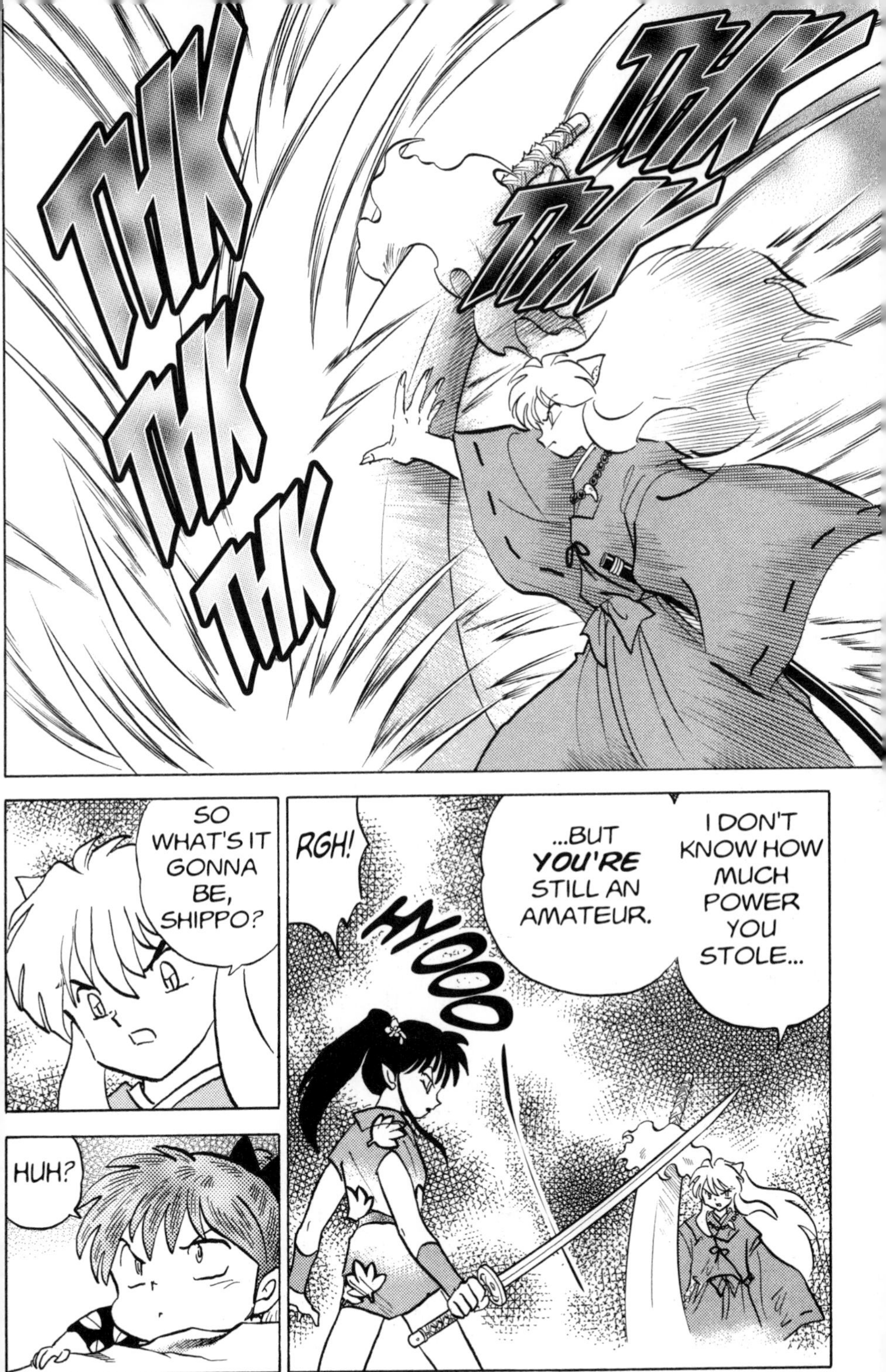
THK THK
THK THK THK
I DON'T KNOW HOW MUCH POWER YOU STOLE...
...BUT **YOU'RE** STILL AN AMATEUR.
RGH!
HYOOO
SO WHAT'S IT GONNA BE, SHIPPO?
HUH?

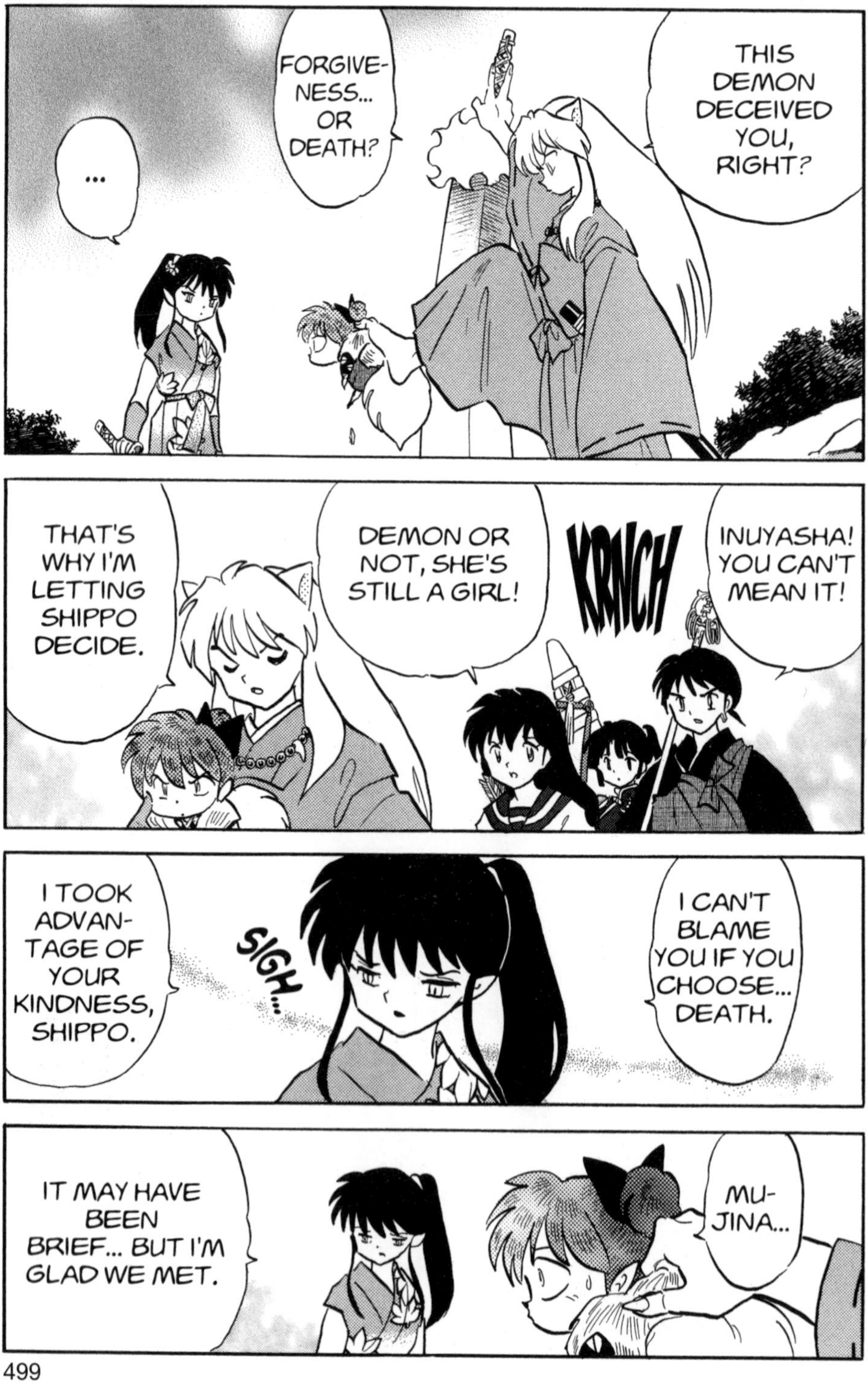
THIS DEMON DECEIVED YOU, RIGHT?
FORGIVENESS... OR DEATH?
...
INUYASHA! YOU CAN'T MEAN IT!
KRNCH
DEMON OR NOT, SHE'S STILL A GIRL!
THAT'S WHY I'M LETTING SHIPPO DECIDE.
I CAN'T BLAME YOU IF YOU CHOOSE... DEATH.
SIGH...
I TOOK ADVANTAGE OF YOUR KINDNESS, SHIPPO.
MUJINA...
IT MAY HAVE BEEN BRIEF... BUT I'M GLAD WE MET.

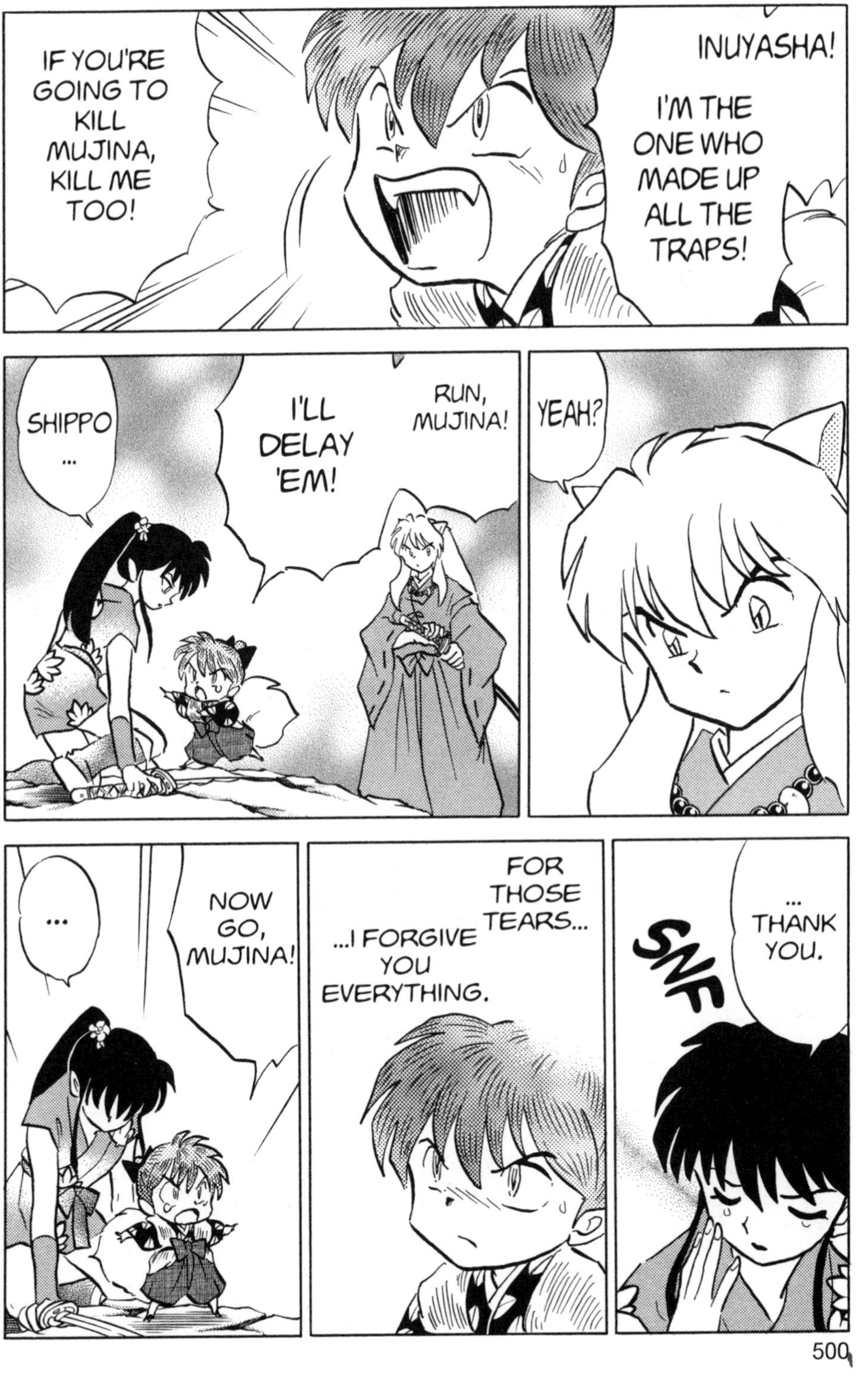
INUYASHA!
I'M THE ONE WHO MADE UP ALL THE TRAPS!
IF YOU'RE GOING TO KILL MUJINA, KILL ME TOO!
YEAH?
RUN, MUJINA!
I'LL DELAY 'EM!
SHIPPO ...
... THANK YOU.
SNF
FOR THOSE TEARS...
...I FORGIVE YOU EVERYTHING.
NOW GO, MUJINA!
...

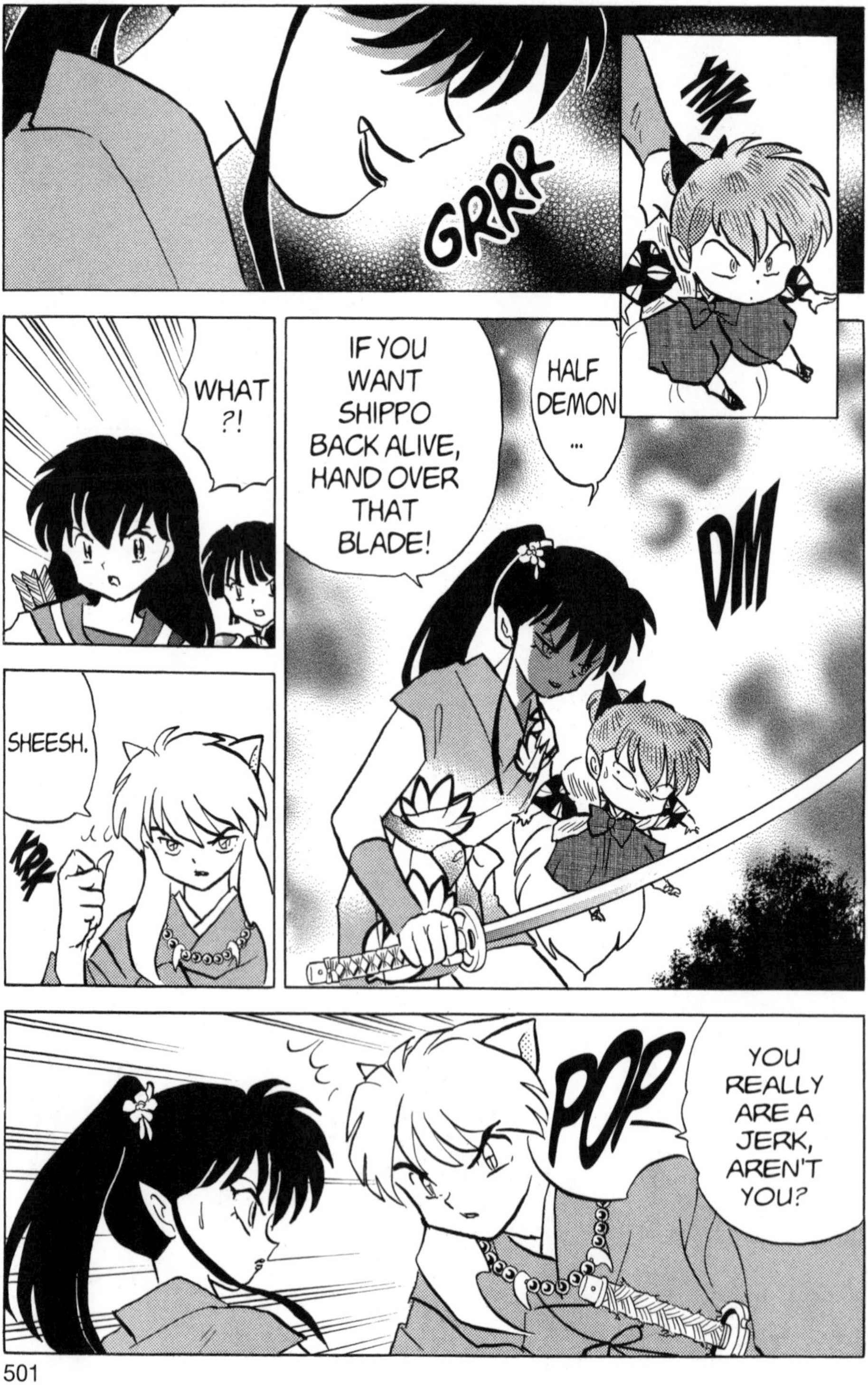
YNK
GRRR
HALF DEMON ...
IF YOU WANT SHIPPO BACK ALIVE, HAND OVER THAT BLADE!
DM
WHAT ?!
SHEESH.
KRK
POP
YOU REALLY ARE A JERK, AREN'T YOU?

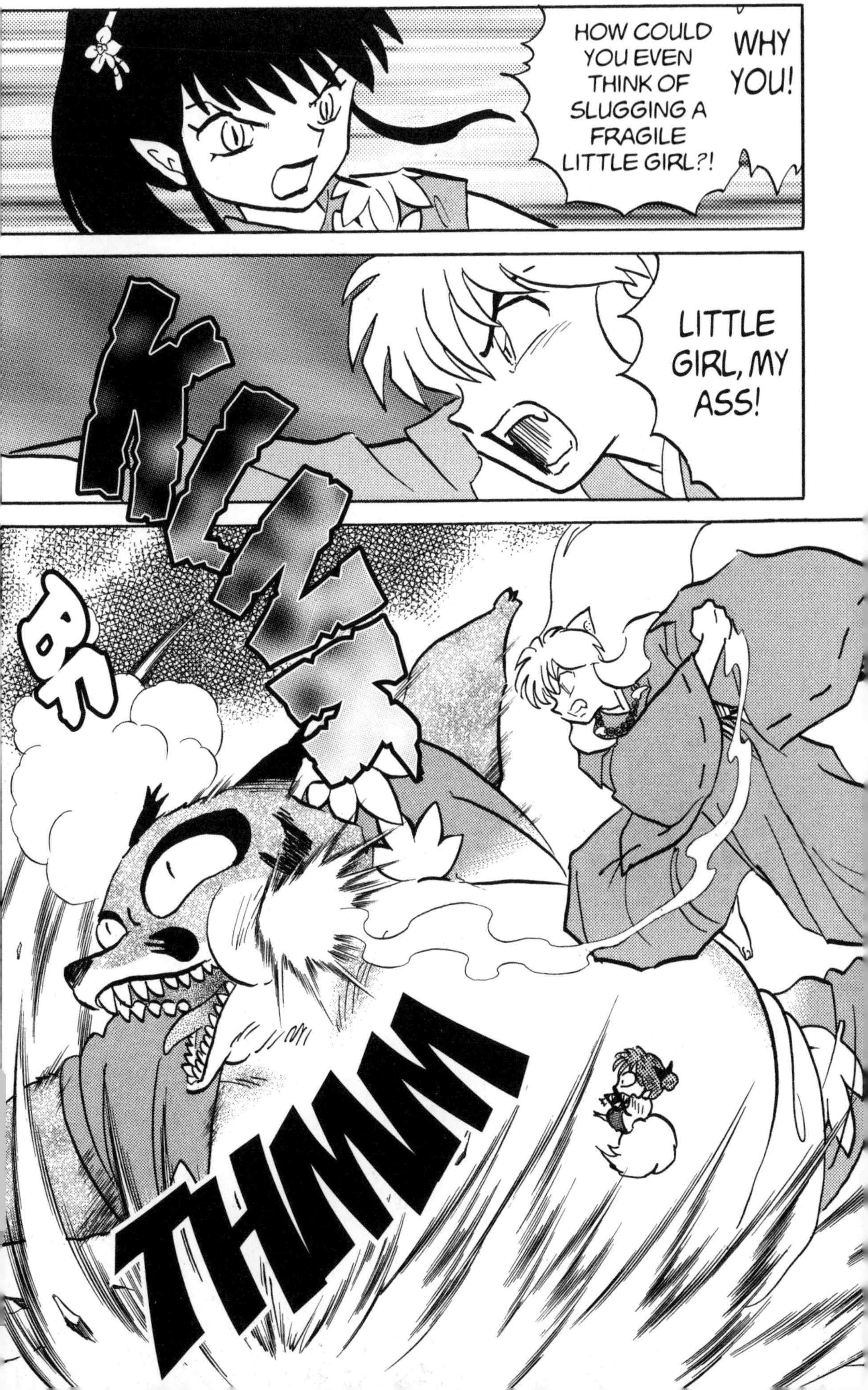
WHY YOU!
HOW COULD YOU EVEN THINK OF SLUGGING A FRAGILE LITTLE GIRL?!
LITTLE GIRL, MY ASS!
BF
THMM

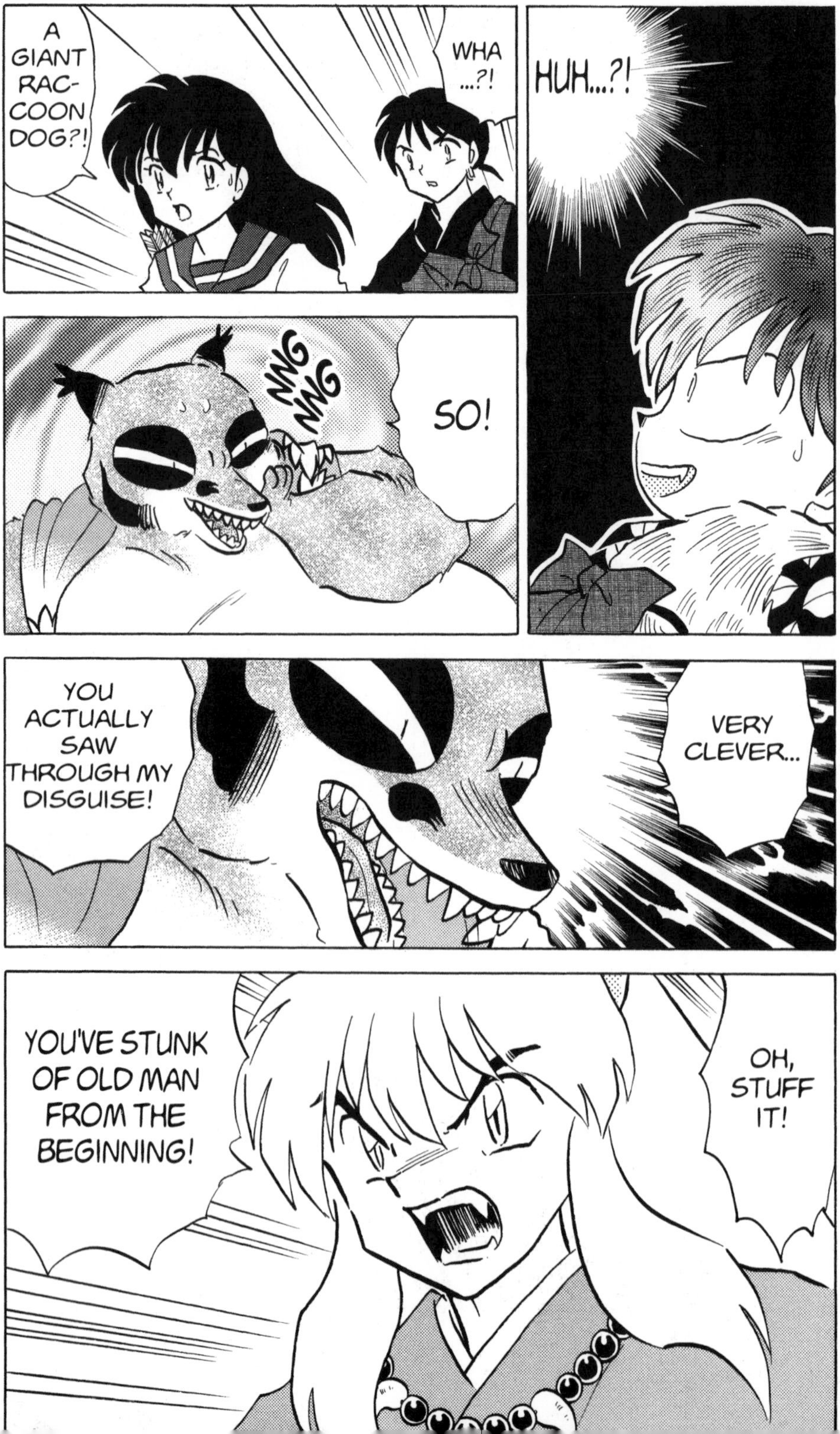
HUH...?!
WHA ...?!
A GIANT RAC-COON DOG?!
SO!
NNG NNG
VERY CLEVER...
YOU ACTUALLY SAW THROUGH MY DISGUISE!
OH, STUFF IT!
YOU'VE STUNK OF OLD MAN FROM THE BEGINNING!

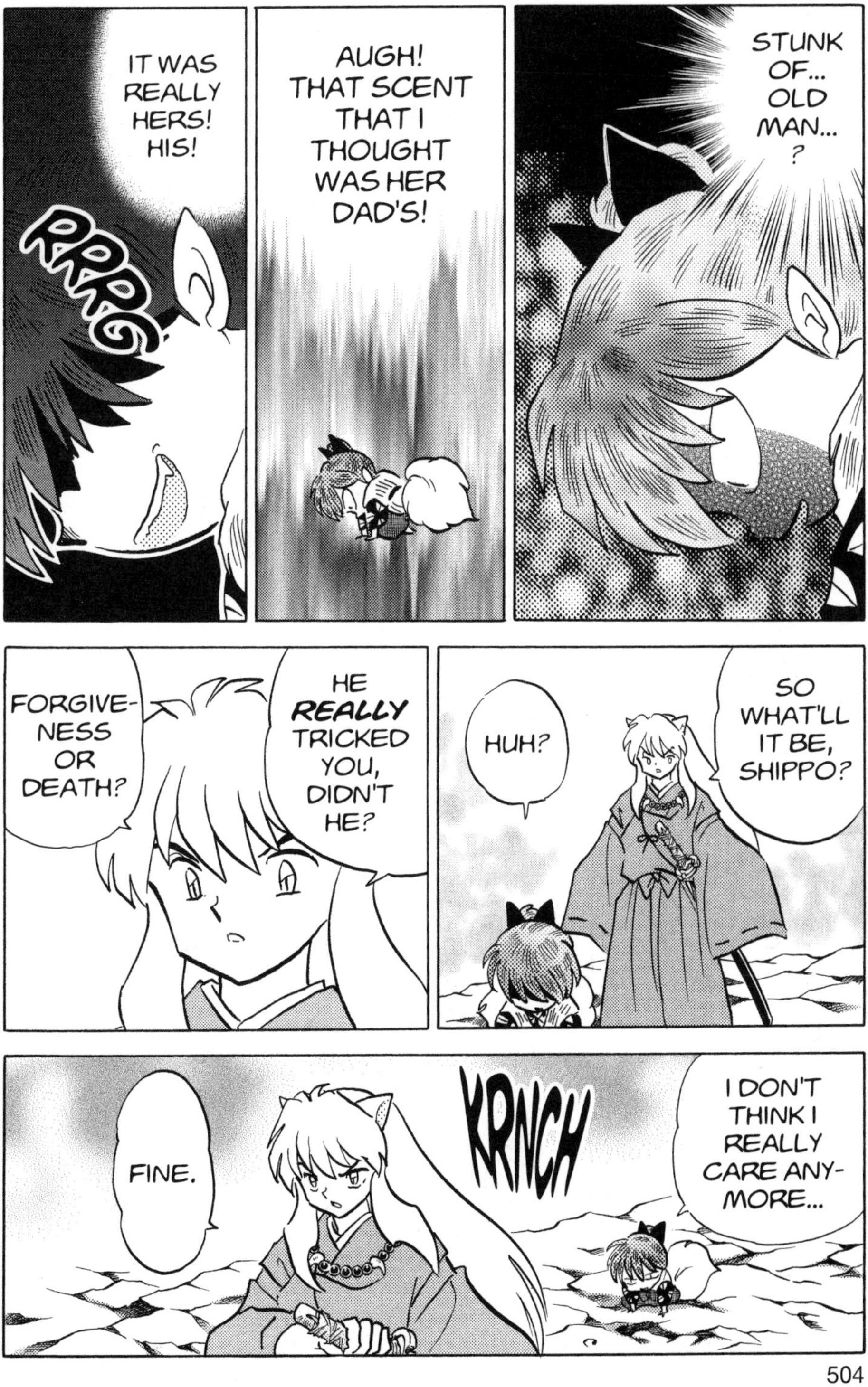
STUNK OF... OLD MAN... ?
AUGH! THAT SCENT THAT I THOUGHT WAS HER DAD'S!
IT WAS REALLY HERS! HIS!
RRRG
SO WHAT'LL IT BE, SHIPPO?
HUH?
HE **REALLY** TRICKED YOU, DIDN'T HE?
FORGIVE-NESS OR DEATH?
I DON'T THINK I REALLY CARE ANY-MORE...
KRNCH
FINE.

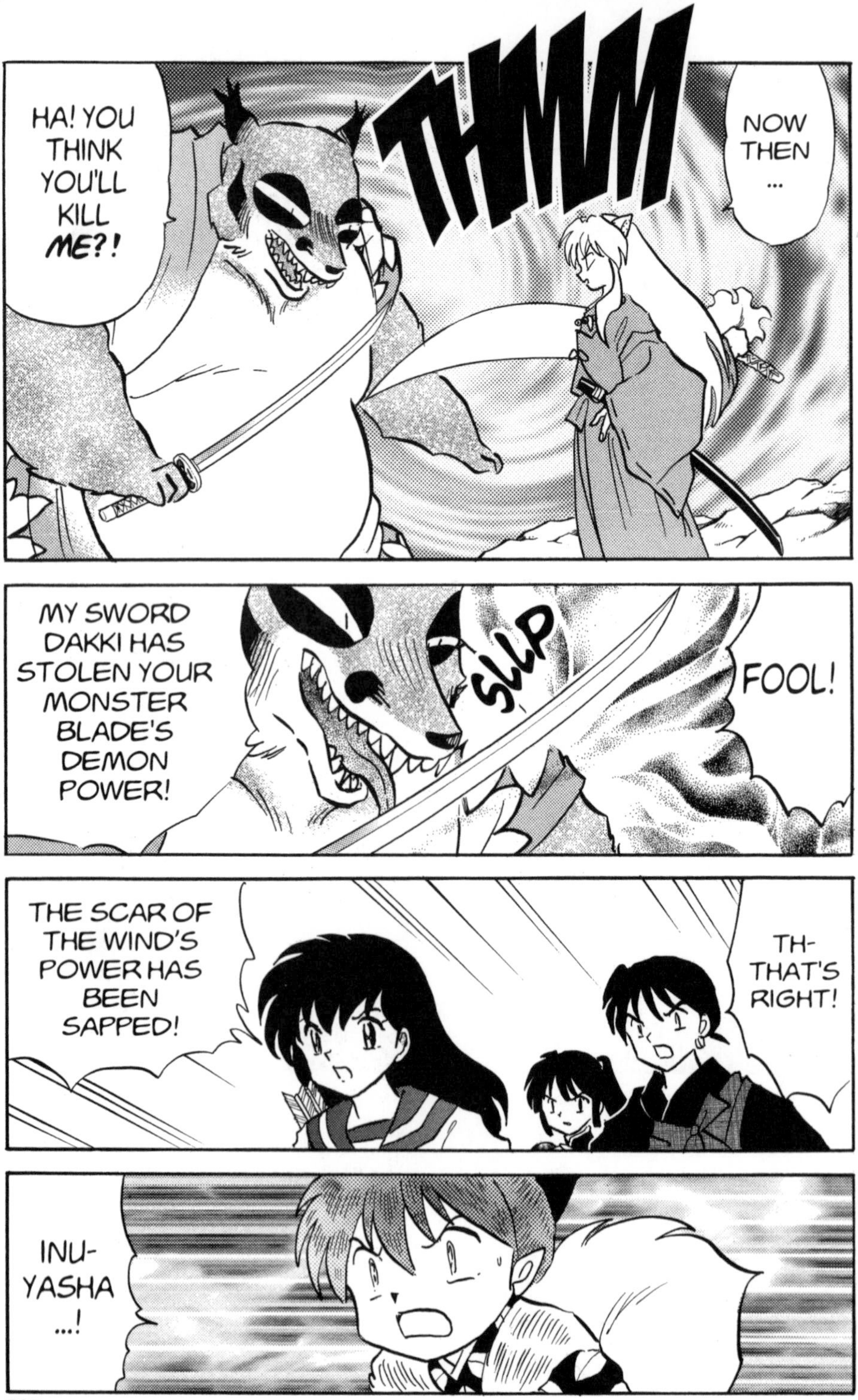
NOW THEN ...
THMM
HA! YOU THINK YOU'LL KILL ME?!
FOOL!
SLLP
MY SWORD DAKKI HAS STOLEN YOUR MONSTER BLADE'S DEMON POWER!
TH- THAT'S RIGHT!
THE SCAR OF THE WIND'S POWER HAS BEEN SAPPED!
INU- YASHA ...!

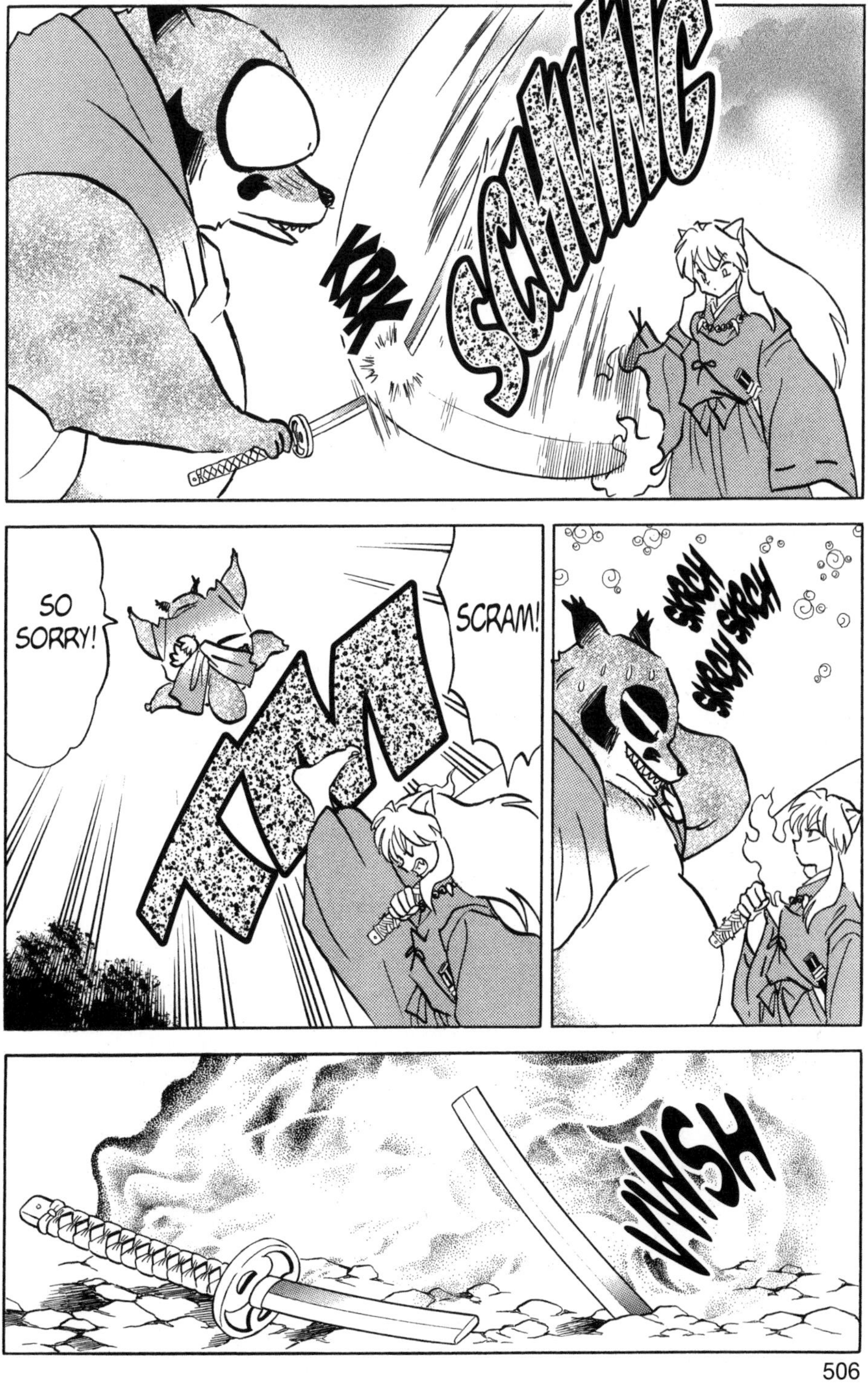
SCHWING
KRK
SKRCH SKRCH SKRCH SKRCH
SCRAM!
SO SORRY!
VWSH

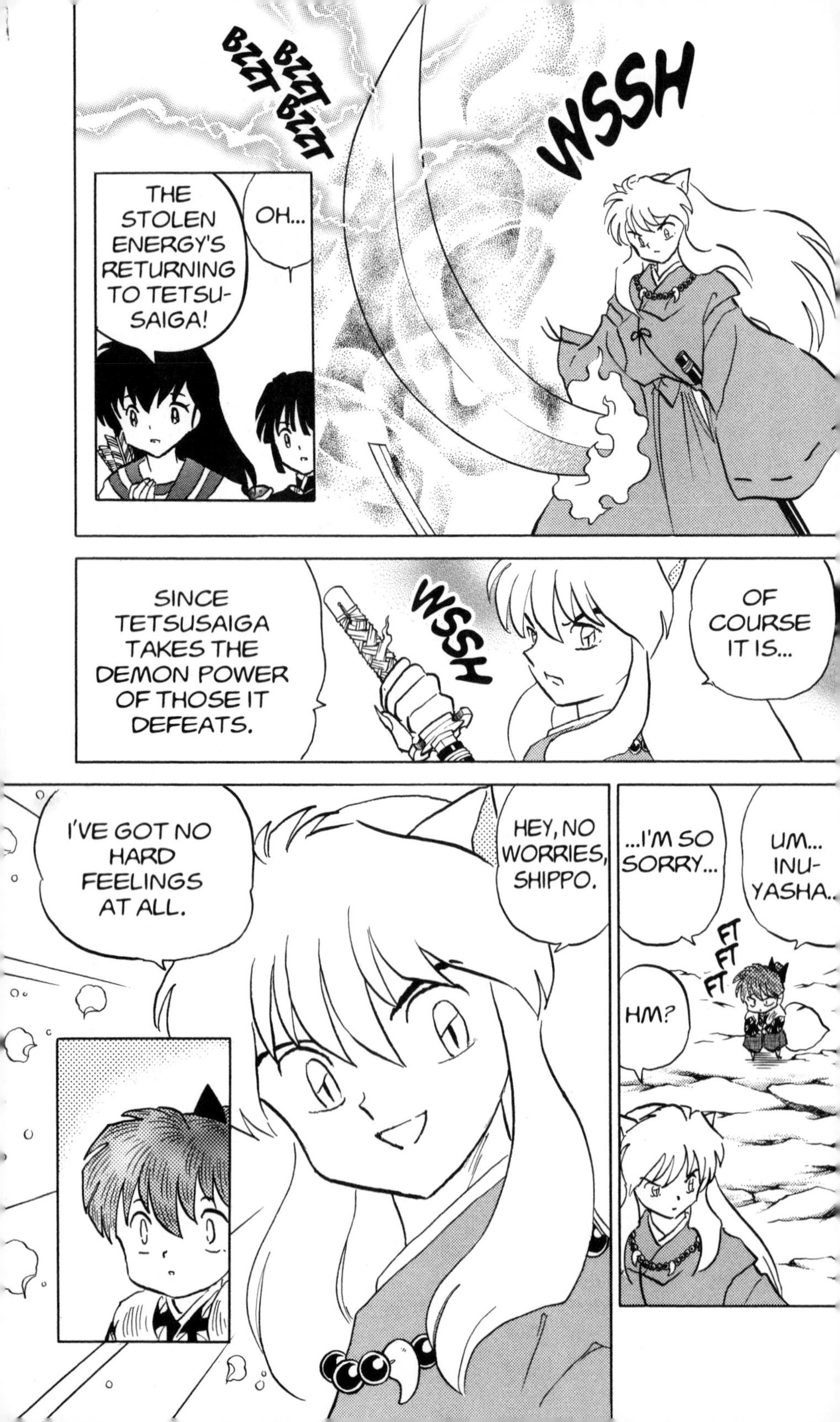
WSSH
BZZT BZZT
OH...
THE STOLEN ENERGY'S RETURNING TO TETSU-SAIGA!
OF COURSE IT IS...
WSSH
SINCE TETSUSAIGA TAKES THE DEMON POWER OF THOSE IT DEFEATS.
UM... INU-YASHA...
...I'M SO SORRY...
FT FT FT
HM?
HEY, NO WORRIES, SHIPPO.
I'VE GOT NO HARD FEELINGS AT ALL.

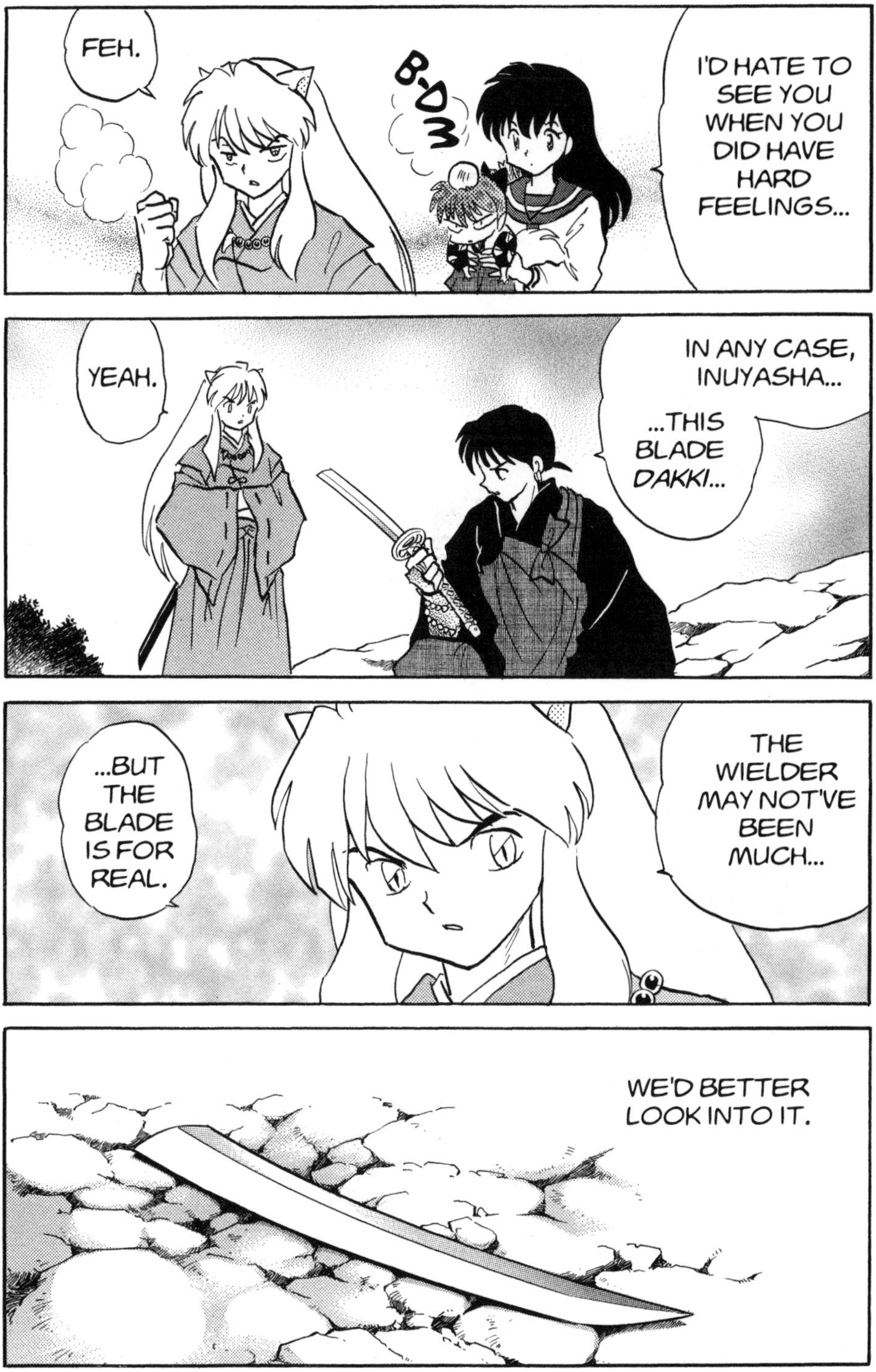
I'D HATE TO SEE YOU WHEN YOU DID HAVE HARD FEELINGS...
B-DM
FEH.
IN ANY CASE, INUYASHA...
...THIS BLADE DAKKI...
YEAH.
THE WIELDER MAY NOT'VE BEEN MUCH...
...BUT THE BLADE IS FOR REAL.
WE'D BETTER LOOK INTO IT.

SCROLL EIGHT
TOSHU

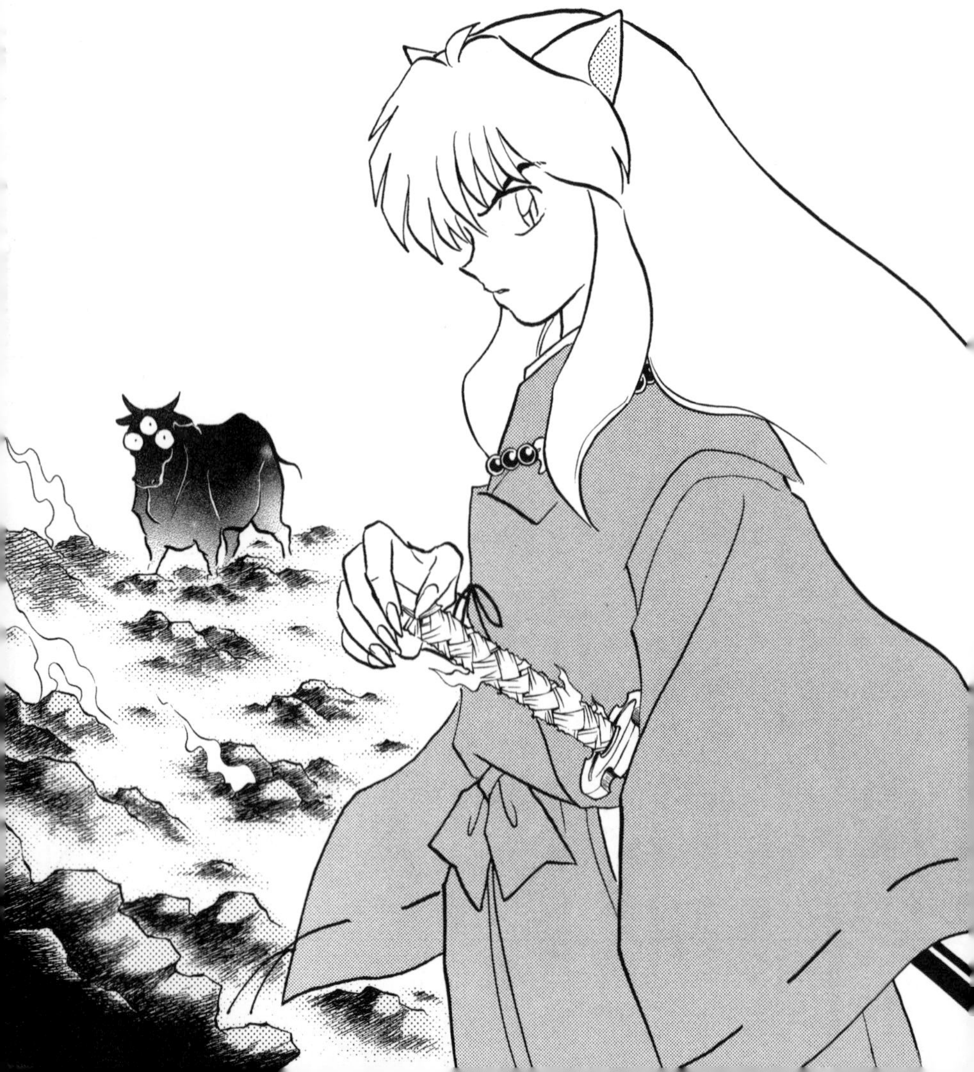

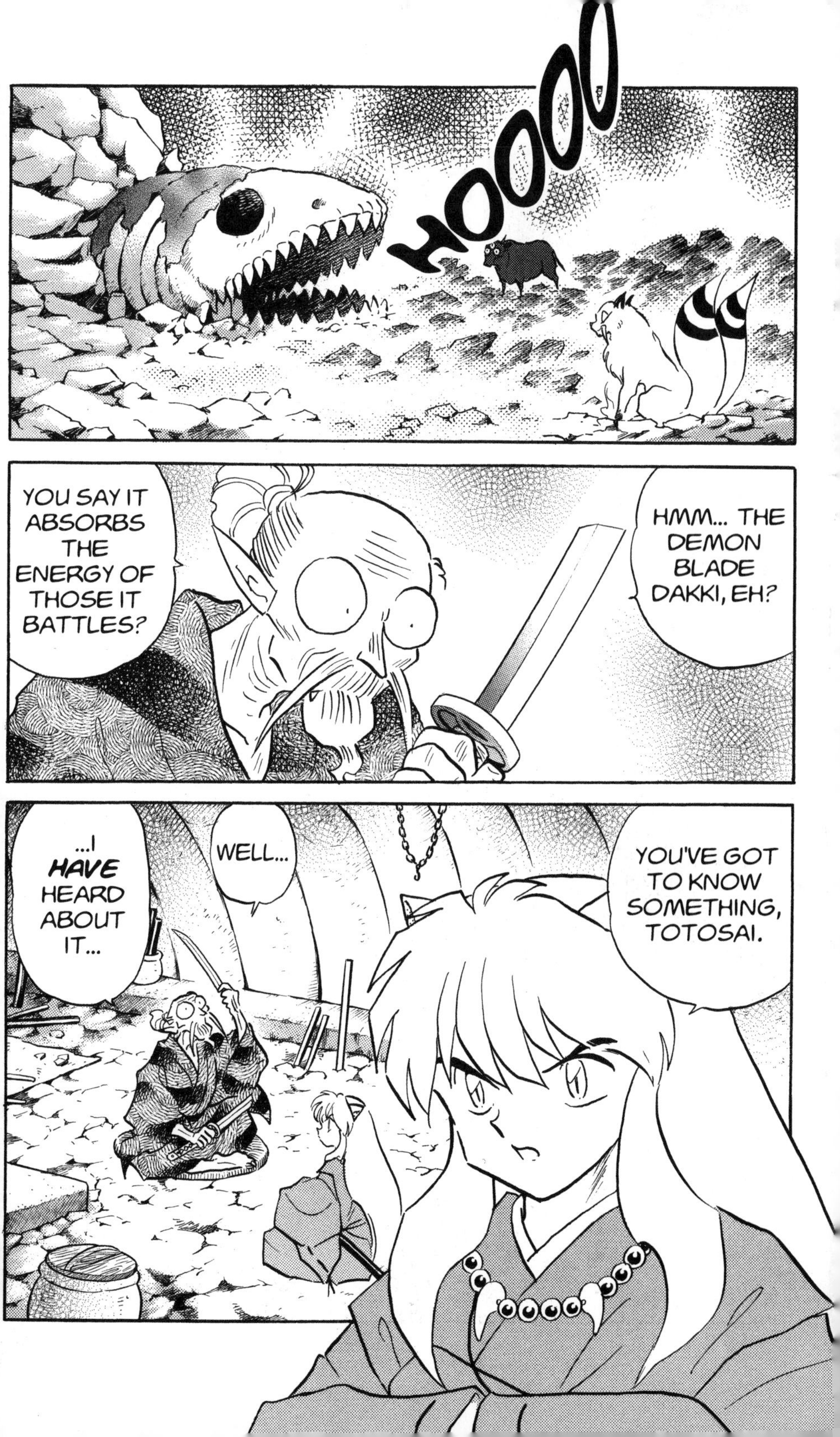
HOOOO
HMM... THE DEMON BLADE DAKKI, EH?
YOU SAY IT ABSORBS THE ENERGY OF THOSE IT BATTLES?
YOU'VE GOT TO KNOW SOMETHING, TOTOSAI.
WELL...
...I **HAVE** HEARD ABOUT IT...

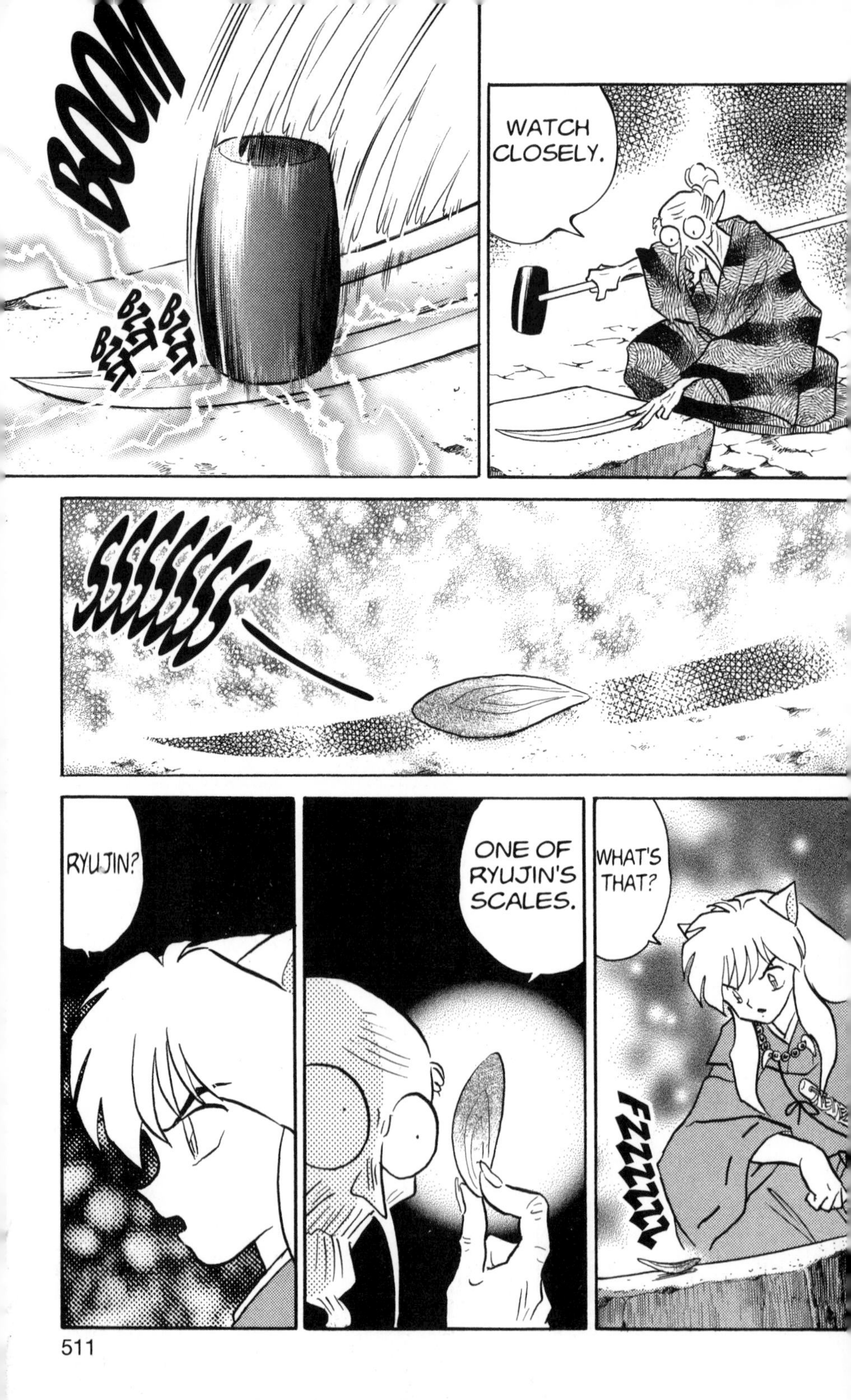
WATCH CLOSELY.
BOOM
BZZT BZZT BZZT
SSSSSSS
WHAT'S THAT?
FZZZZZ
ONE OF RYUJIN'S SCALES.
RYUJIN?

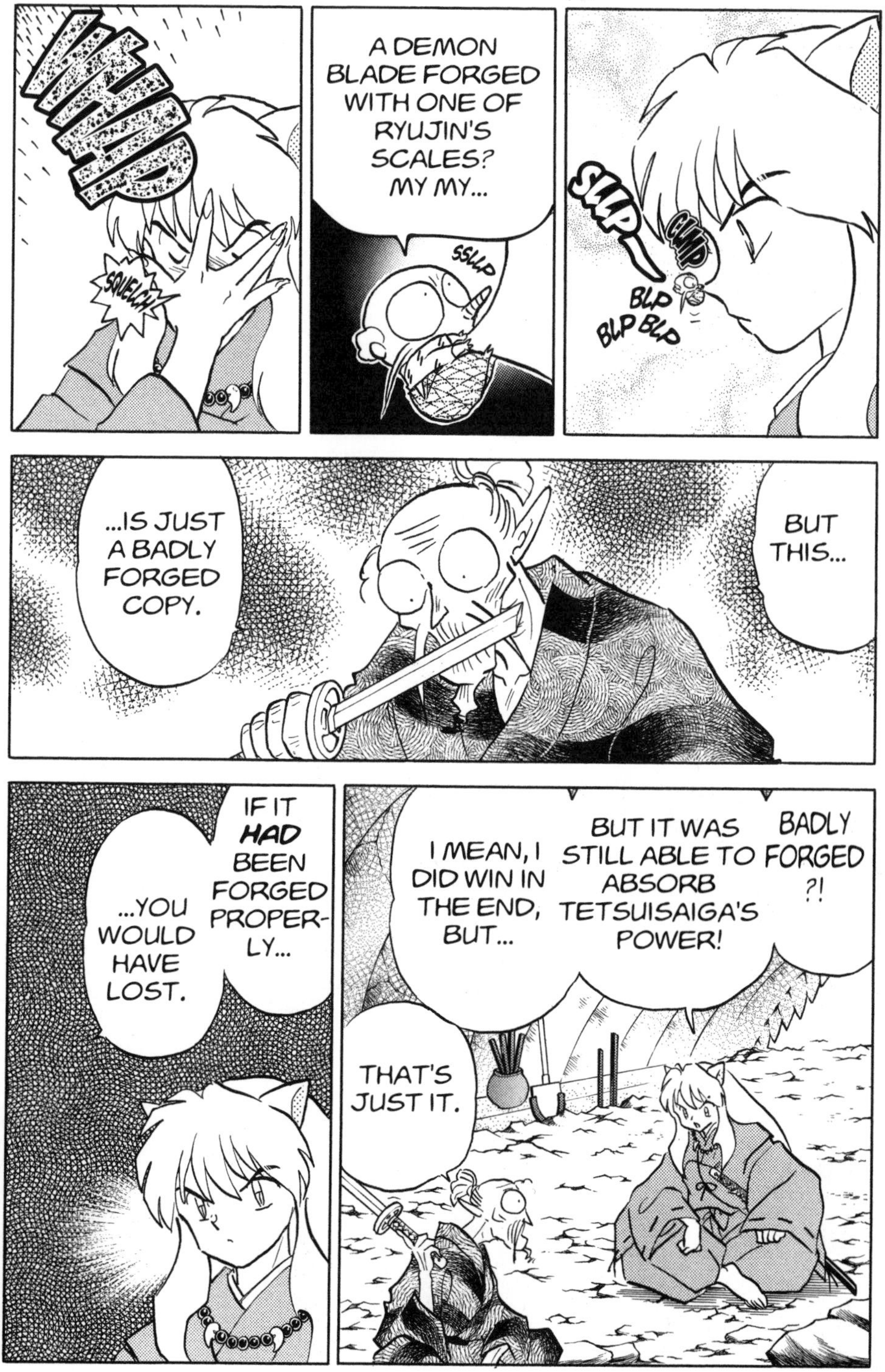
SLRP
GLMP
BLP
BLP BLP
A DEMON BLADE FORGED WITH ONE OF RYUJIN'S SCALES? MY MY...
SSLLP
WHAP
SQUELCH
BUT THIS...
...IS JUST A BADLY FORGED COPY.
BADLY FORGED ?!
BUT IT WAS STILL ABLE TO ABSORB TETSUISAIGA'S POWER!
I MEAN, I DID WIN IN THE END, BUT...
THAT'S JUST IT.
IF IT **HAD** BEEN FORGED PROPER-LY...
...YOU WOULD HAVE LOST.

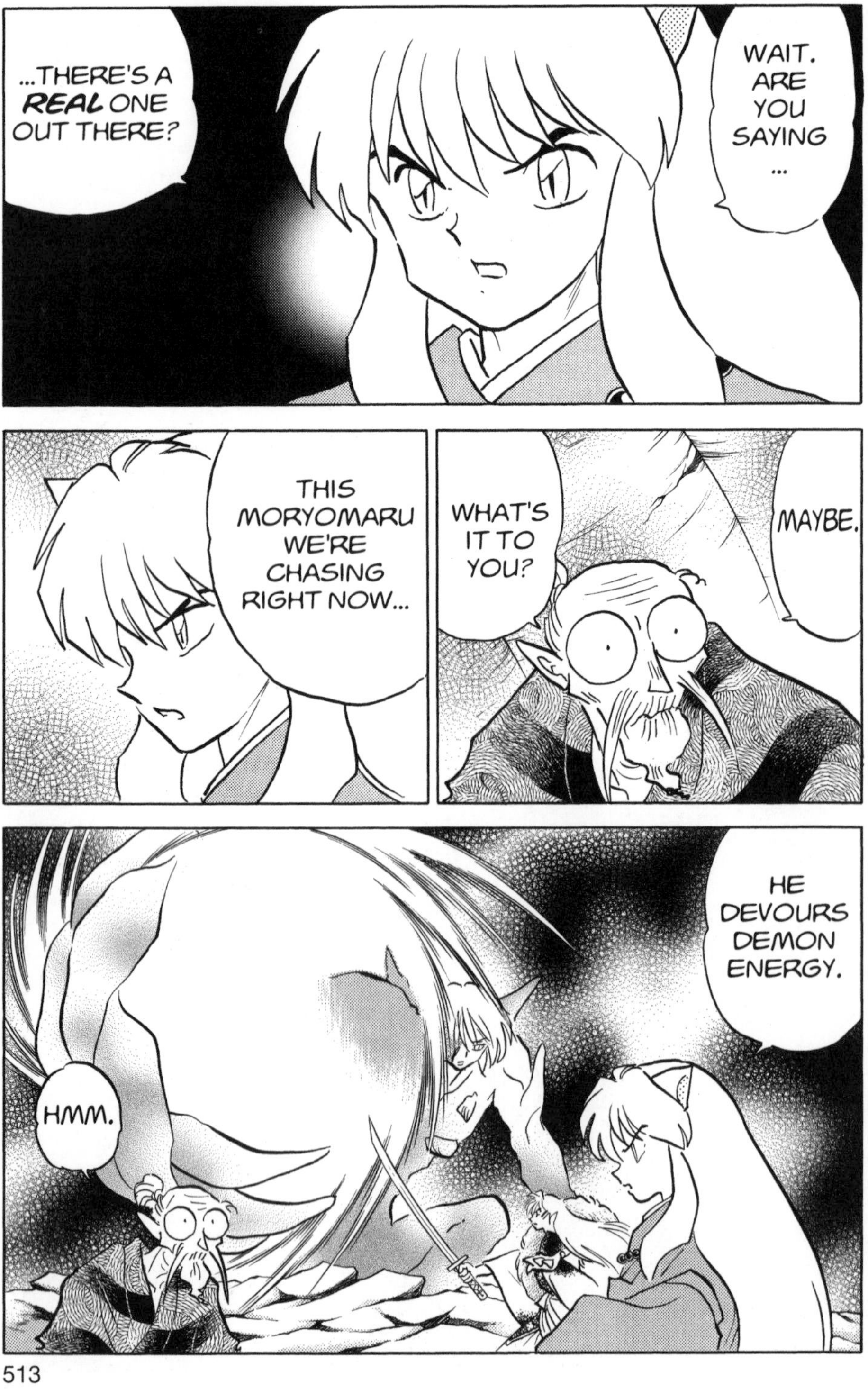
WAIT. ARE YOU SAYING ...
...THERE'S A **REAL** ONE OUT THERE?
MAYBE.
WHAT'S IT TO YOU?
THIS MORYOMARU WE'RE CHASING RIGHT NOW...
HE DEVOURS DEMON ENERGY.
HMM.

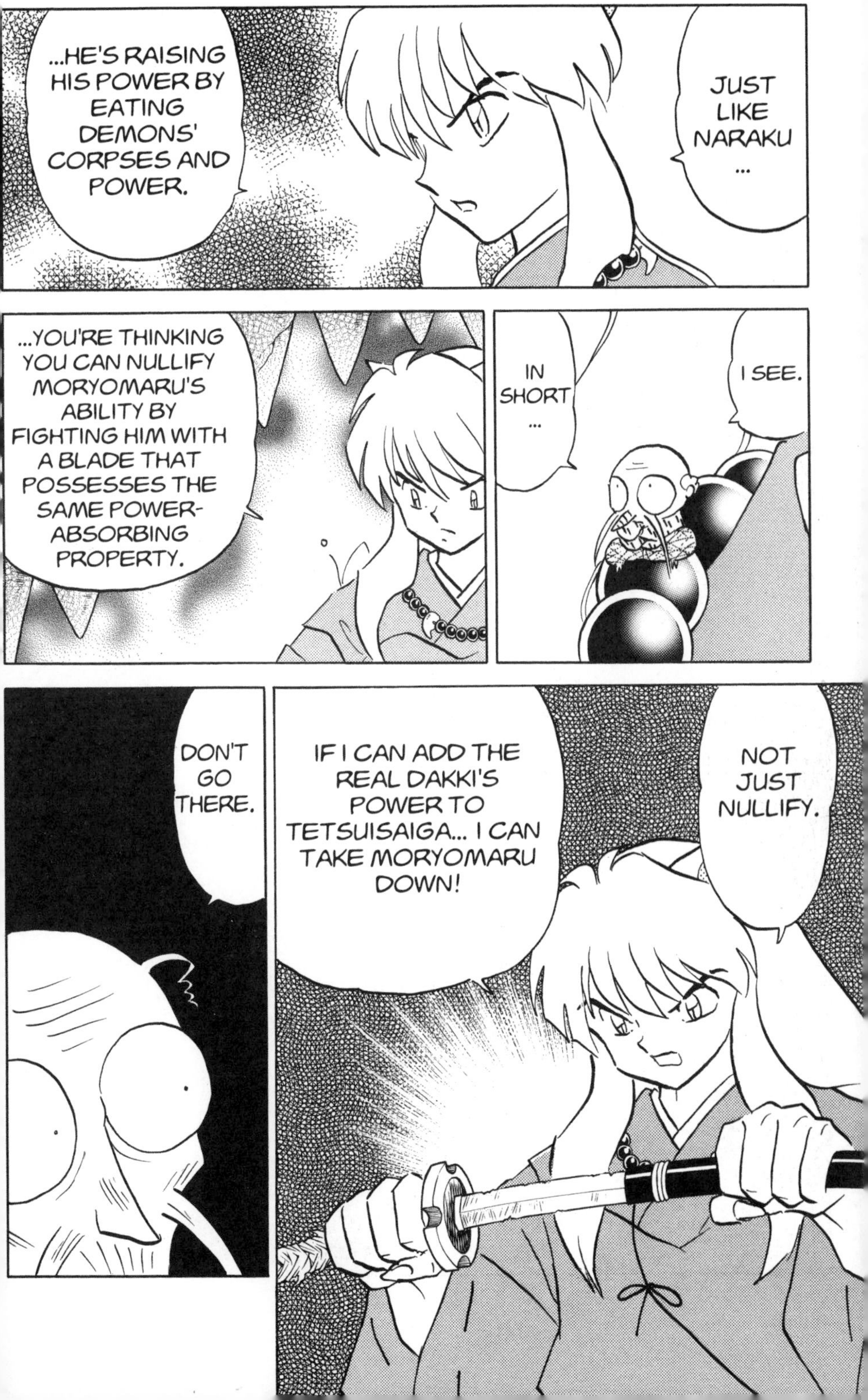
JUST LIKE NARAKU...
...HE'S RAISING HIS POWER BY EATING DEMONS' CORPSES AND POWER.
I SEE.
IN SHORT...
...YOU'RE THINKING YOU CAN NULLIFY MORYOMARU'S ABILITY BY FIGHTING HIM WITH A BLADE THAT POSSESSES THE SAME POWER-ABSORBING PROPERTY.
NOT JUST NULLIFY.
IF I CAN ADD THE REAL DAKKI'S POWER TO TETSUISAIGA... I CAN TAKE MORYOMARU DOWN!
DON'T GO THERE.

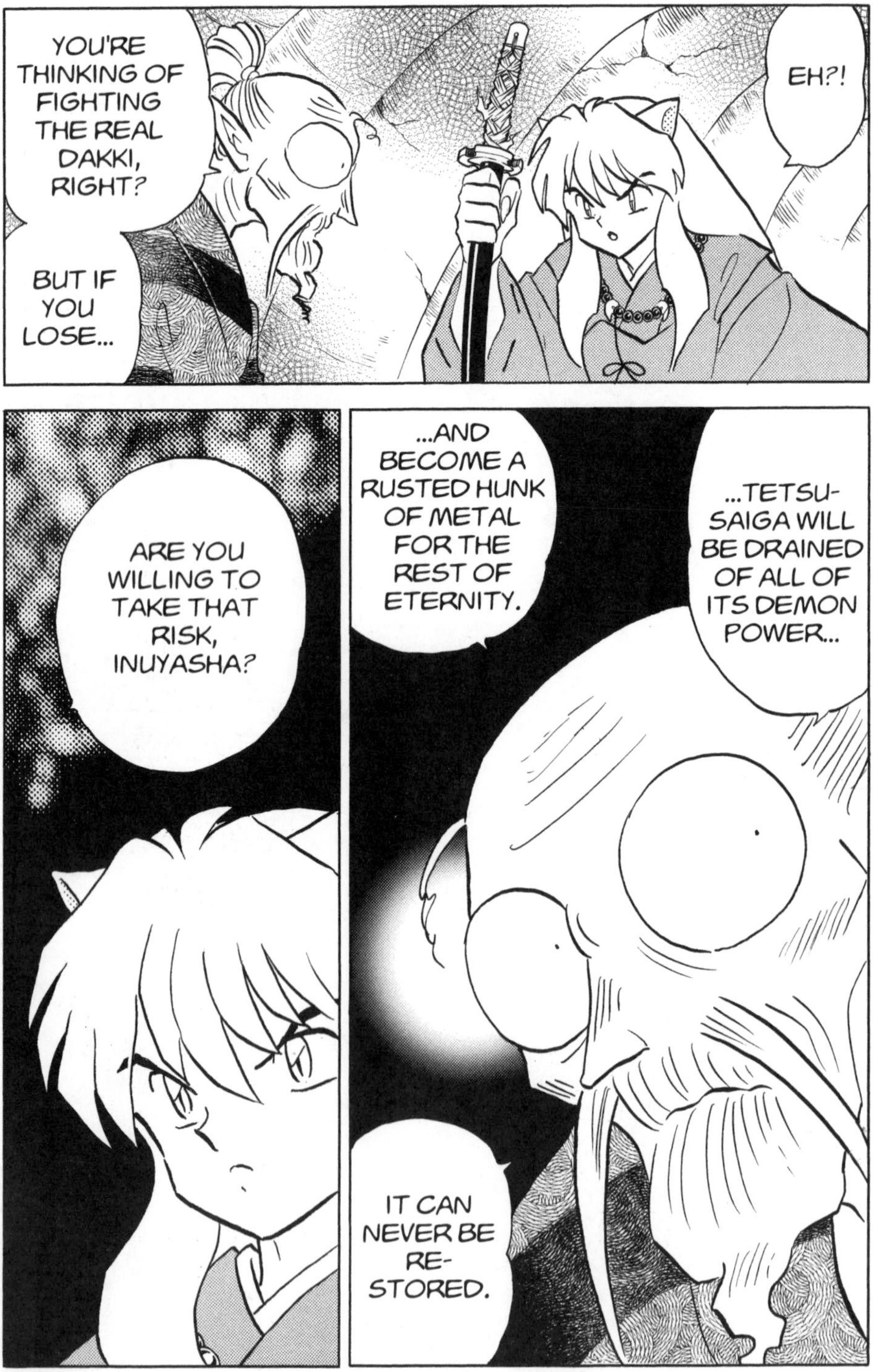
EH?!
YOU'RE THINKING OF FIGHTING THE REAL DAKKI, RIGHT?
BUT IF YOU LOSE...
...TETSU-SAIGA WILL BE DRAINED OF ALL OF ITS DEMON POWER...
...AND BECOME A RUSTED HUNK OF METAL FOR THE REST OF ETERNITY.
IT CAN NEVER BE RE-STORED.
ARE YOU WILLING TO TAKE THAT RISK, INUYASHA?

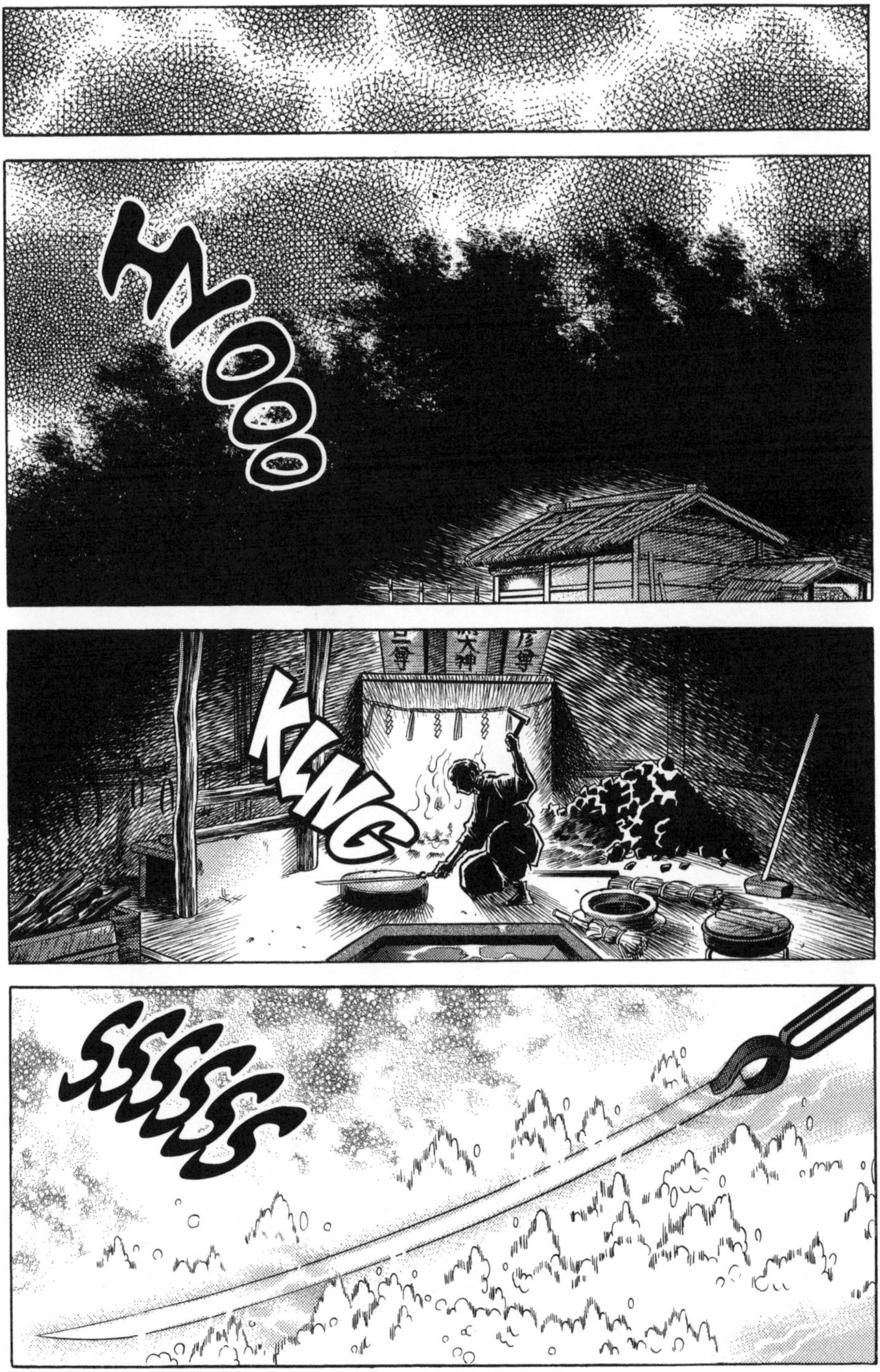
HYOOO
KLNG
SSSSS

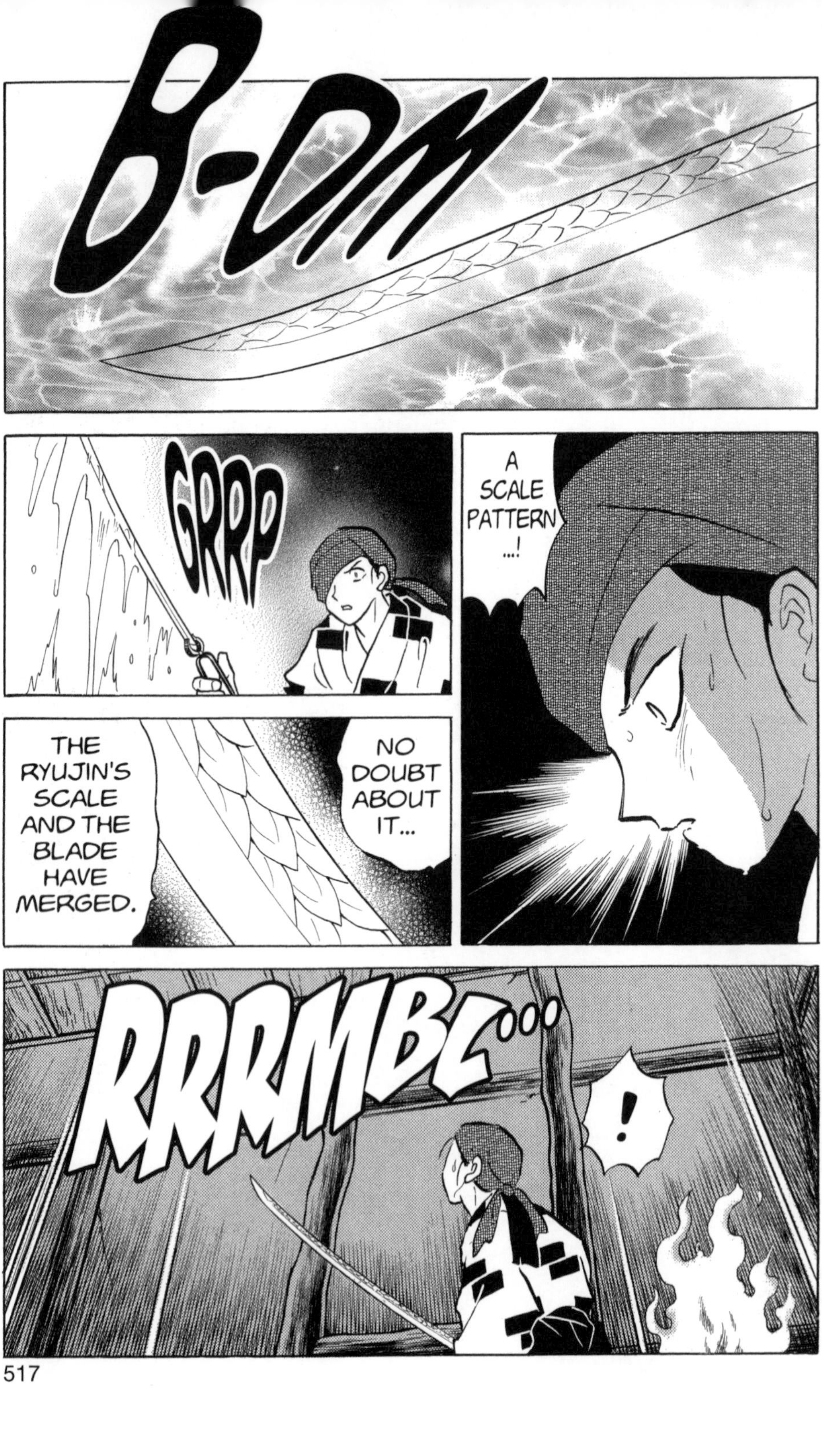
B-DM
A SCALE PATTERN ...!
GRRP
NO DOUBT ABOUT IT...
THE RYUJIN'S SCALE AND THE BLADE HAVE MERGED.
RRRMBL...
!

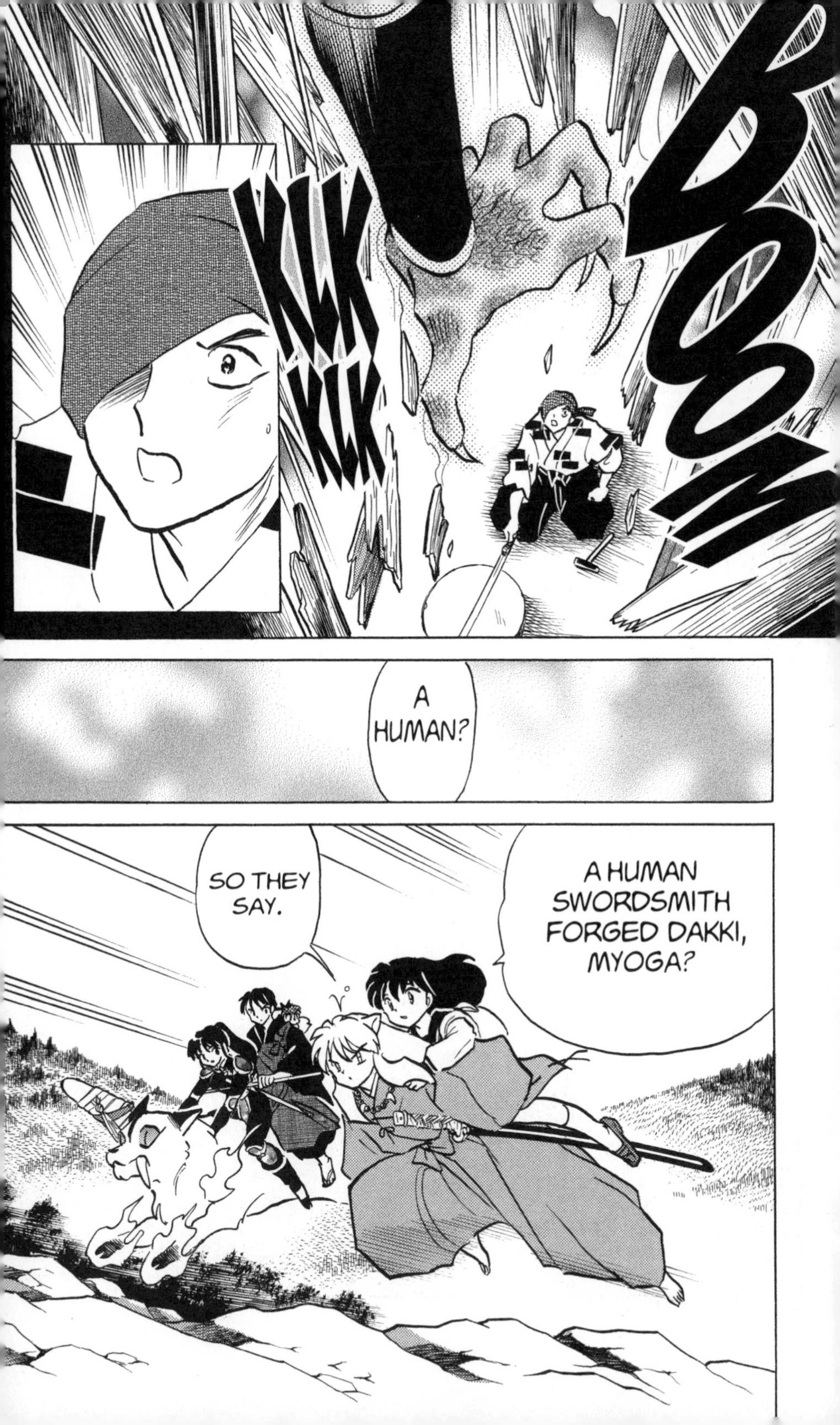
BOOM!!
KLK KLK
A HUMAN?
A HUMAN SWORDSMITH FORGED DAKKI, MYOGA?
SO THEY SAY.

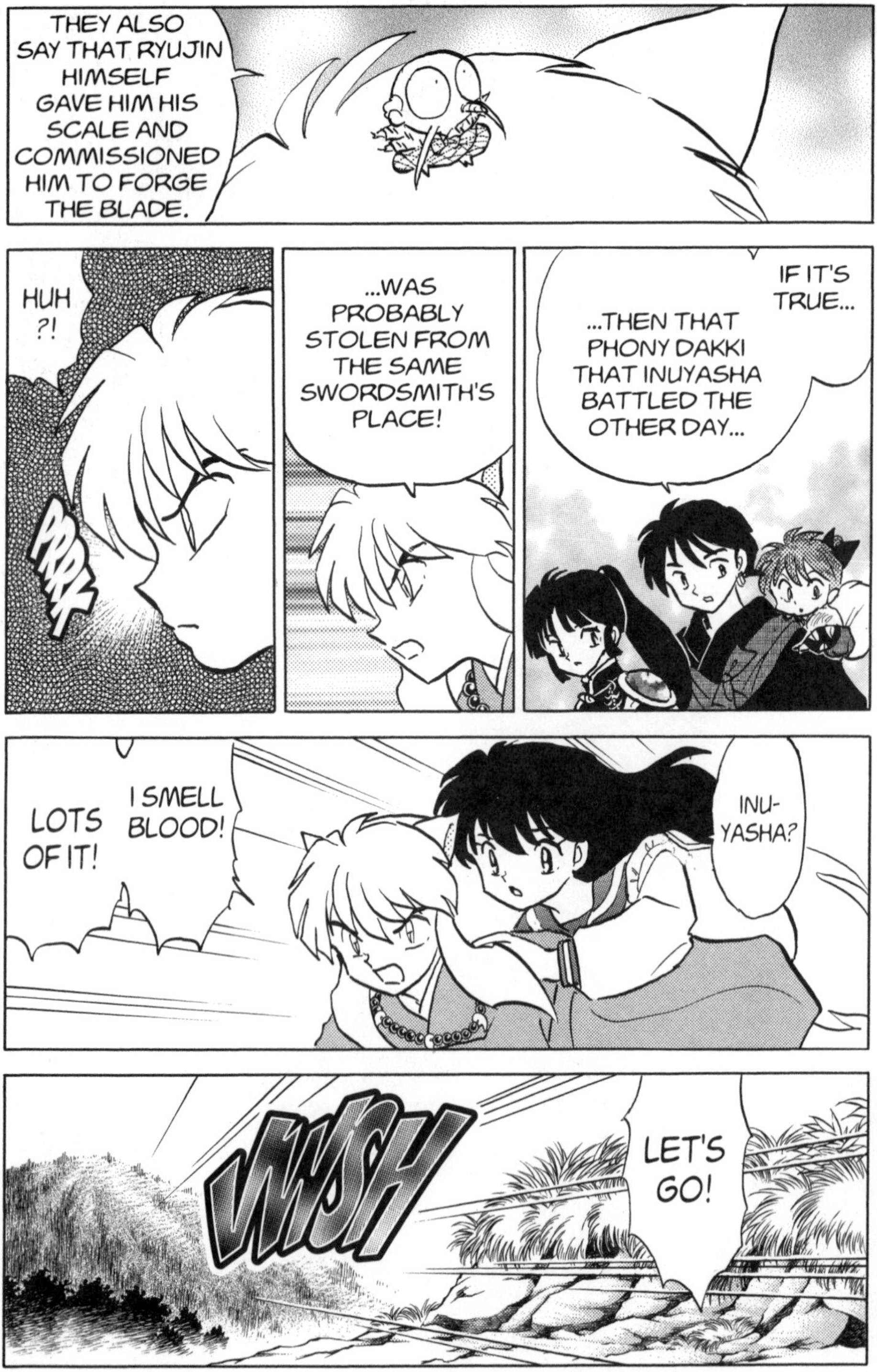
THEY ALSO SAY THAT RYUJIN HIMSELF GAVE HIM HIS SCALE AND COMMISSIONED HIM TO FORGE THE BLADE.
IF IT'S TRUE...
...THEN THAT PHONY DAKKI THAT INUYASHA BATTLED THE OTHER DAY...
...WAS PROBABLY STOLEN FROM THE SAME SWORDSMITH'S PLACE!
HUH ?!
PRRK
INU-YASHA?
I SMELL BLOOD!
LOTS OF IT!
LET'S GO!
WHSH

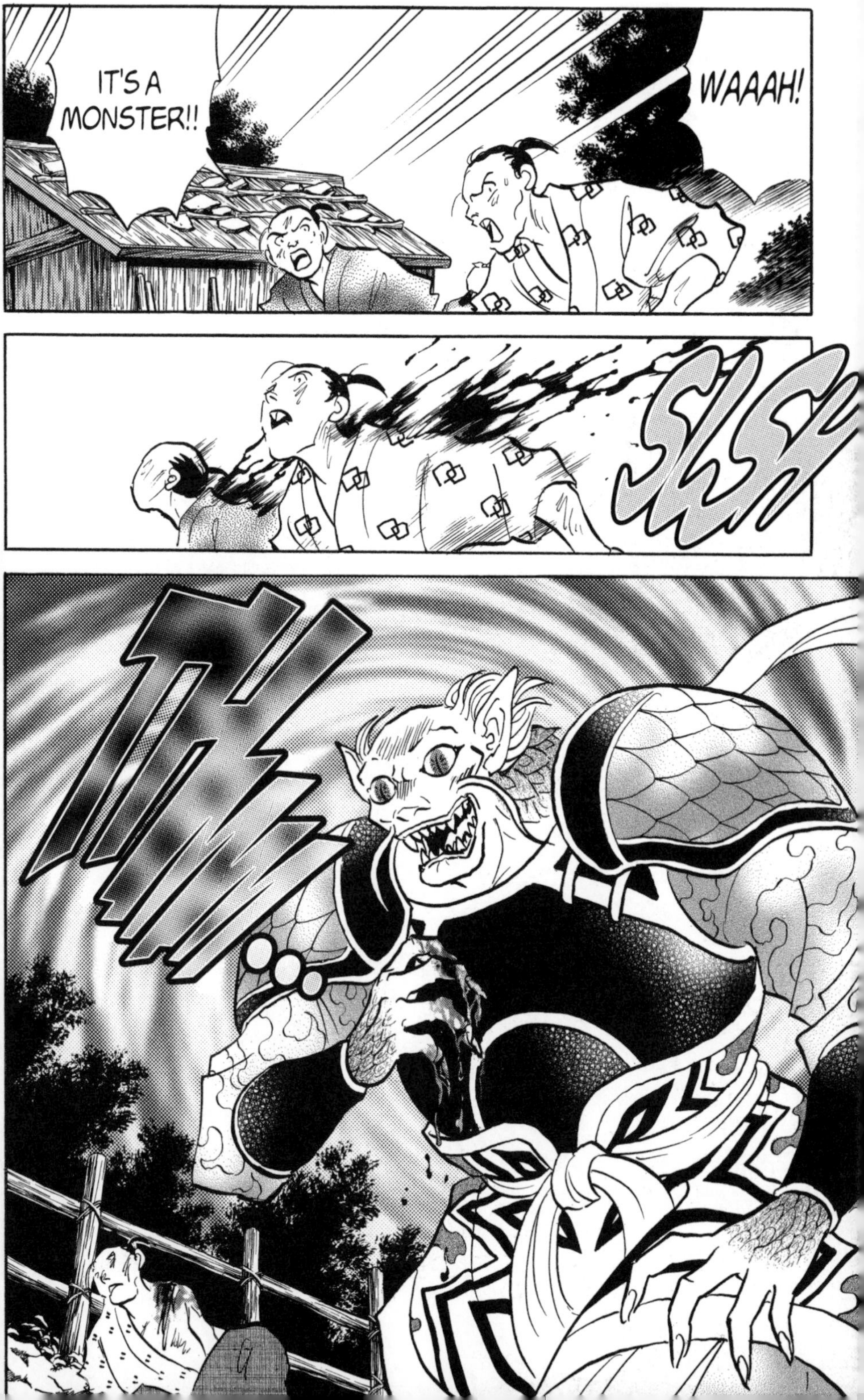
WAAAH!
IT'S A MONSTER!!

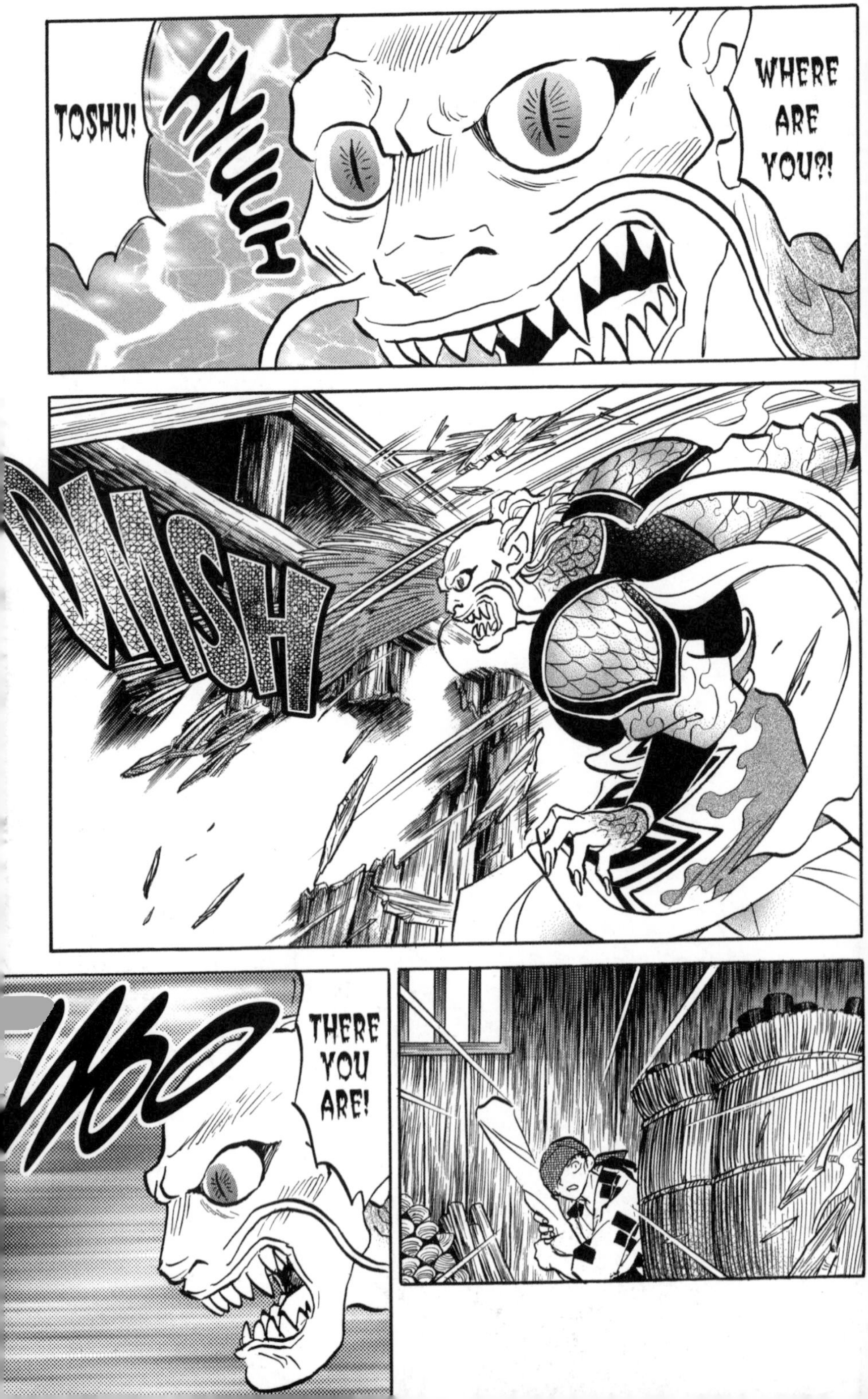
WHERE ARE YOU?!
HNUUH
TOSHU!
THERE YOU ARE!

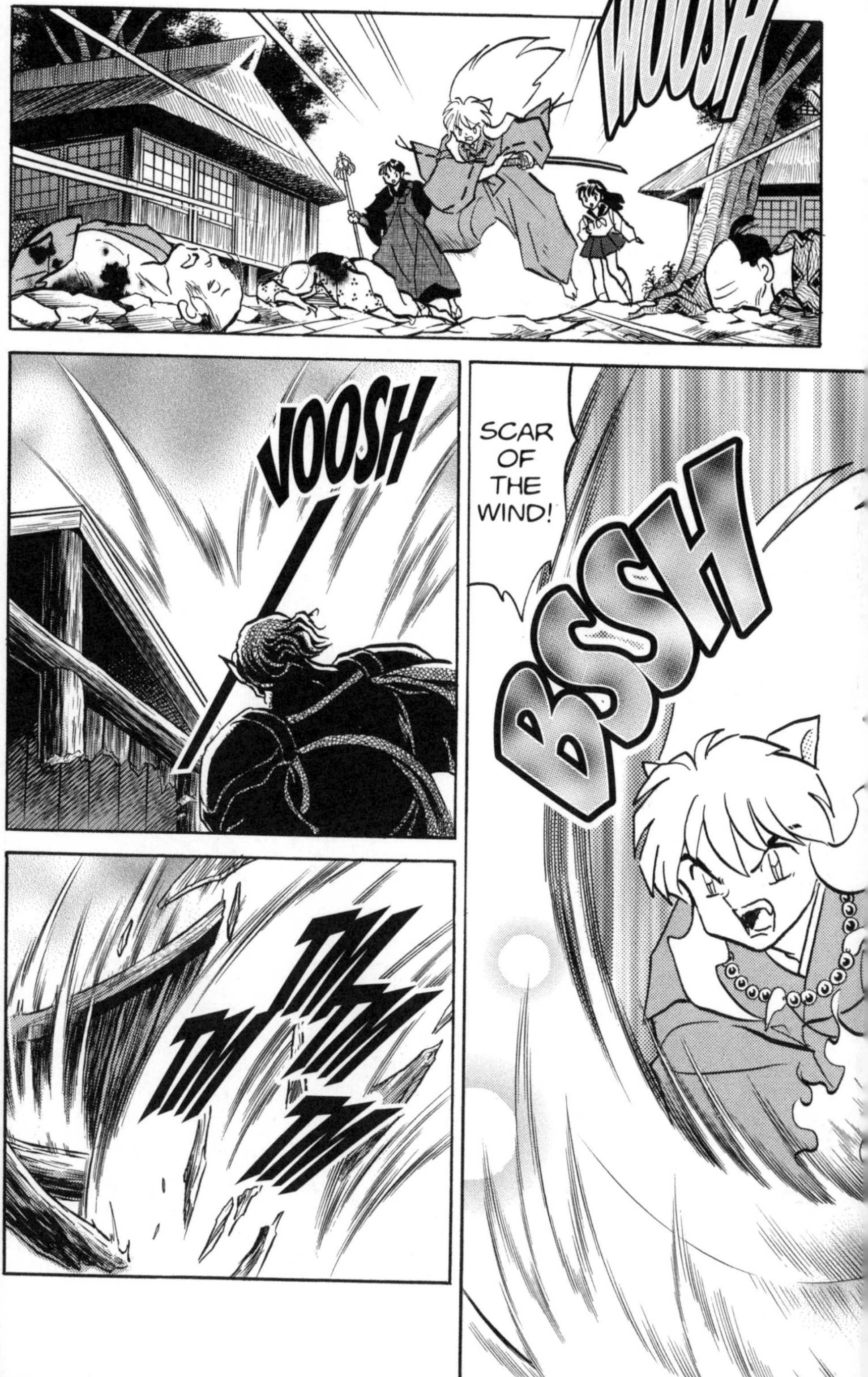
WOOSH
SCAR OF THE WIND!
BSSH
VOOSH

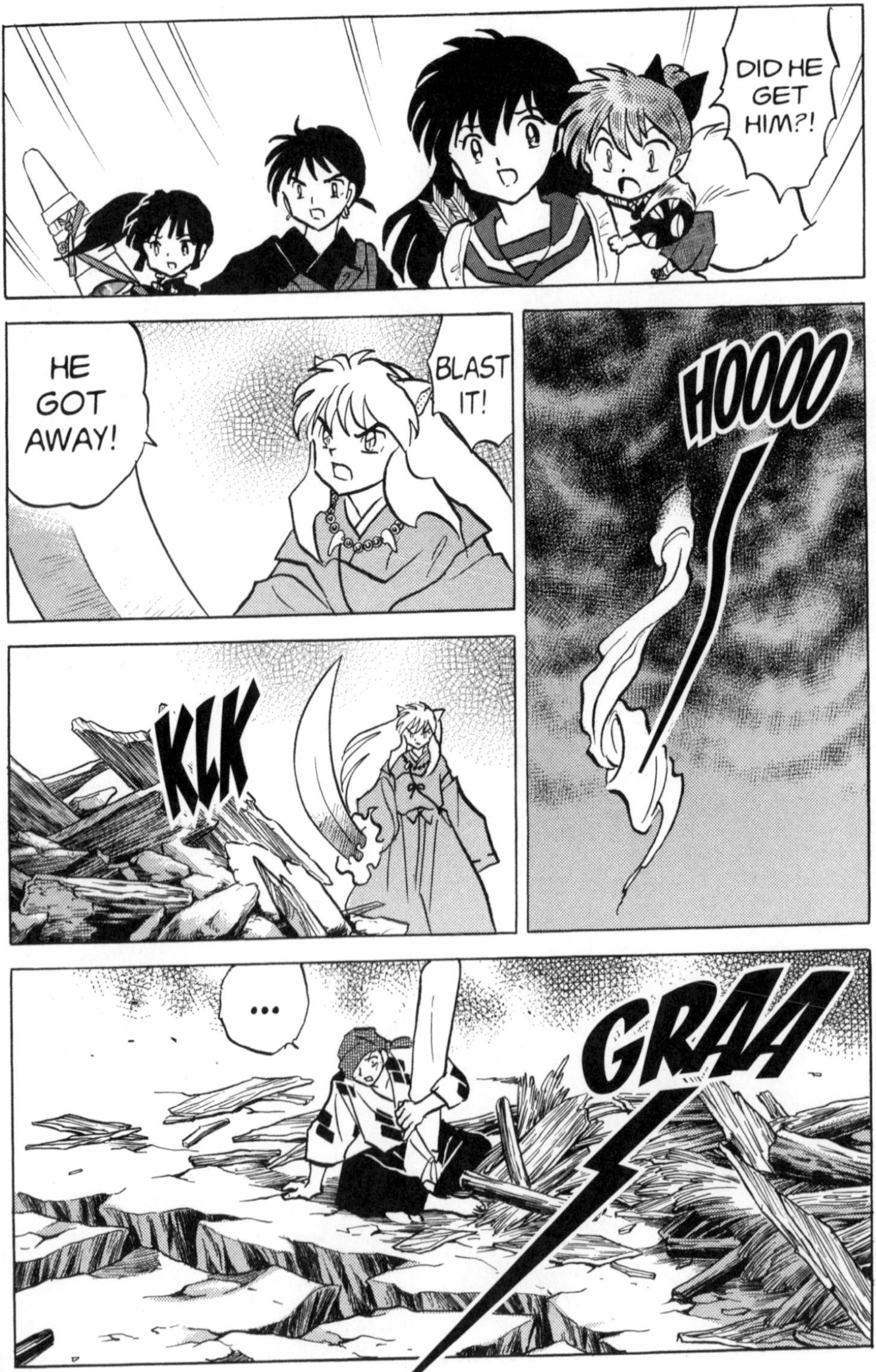
DID HE GET HIM?!
HOOOO
BLAST IT!
HE GOT AWAY!
KLK
GRAA
...

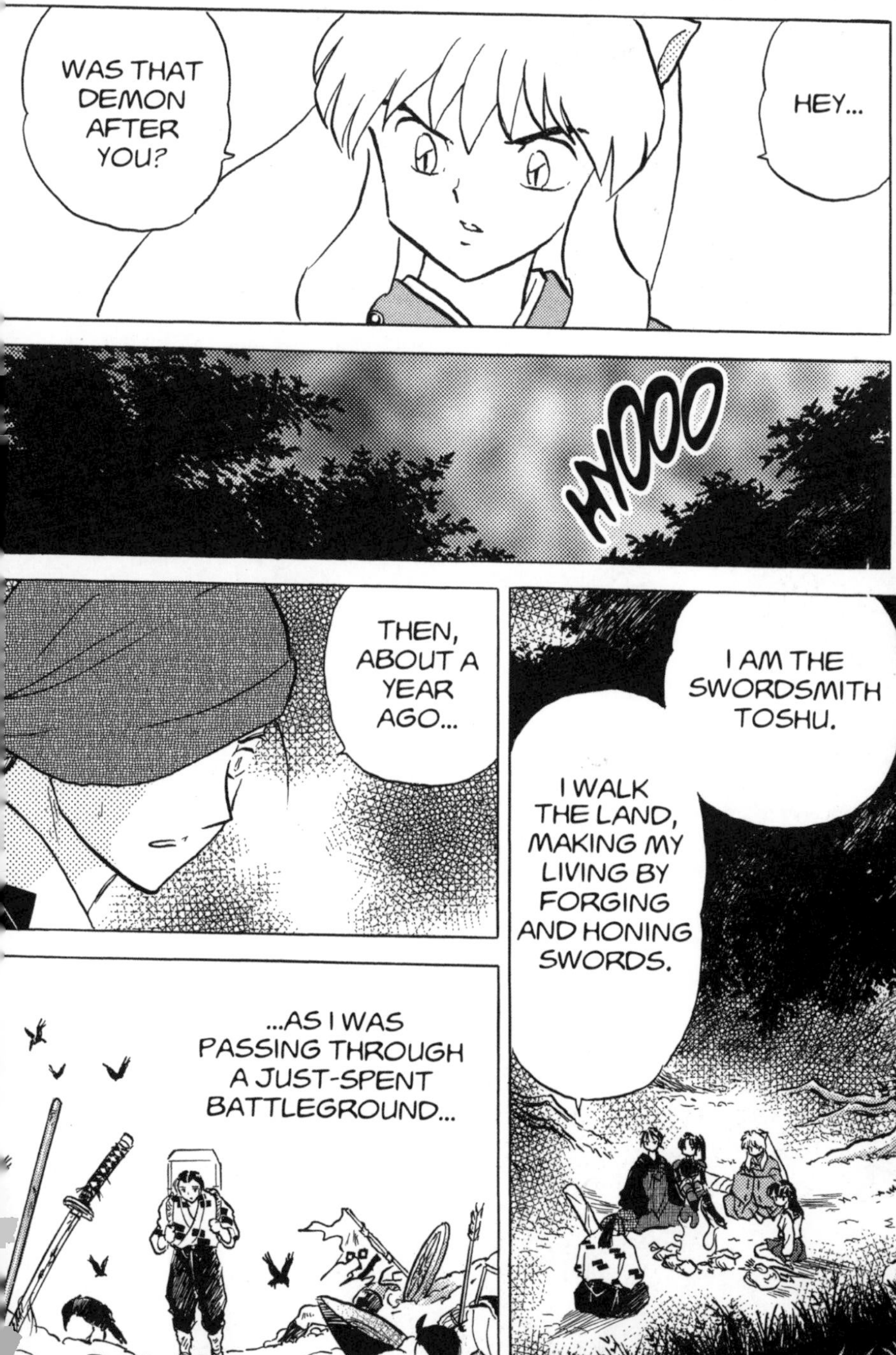
HEY...
WAS THAT DEMON AFTER YOU?
HYOOO
I AM THE SWORDSMITH TOSHU.
I WALK THE LAND, MAKING MY LIVING BY FORGING AND HONING SWORDS.
THEN, ABOUT A YEAR AGO...
...AS I WAS PASSING THROUGH A JUST-SPENT BATTLEGROUND...

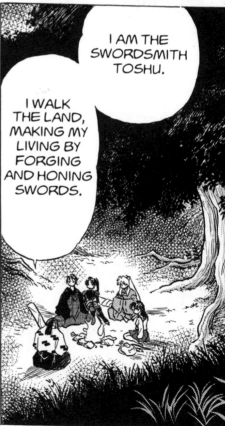

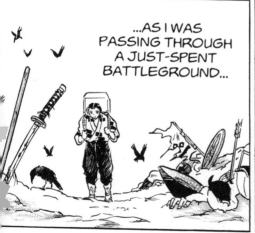

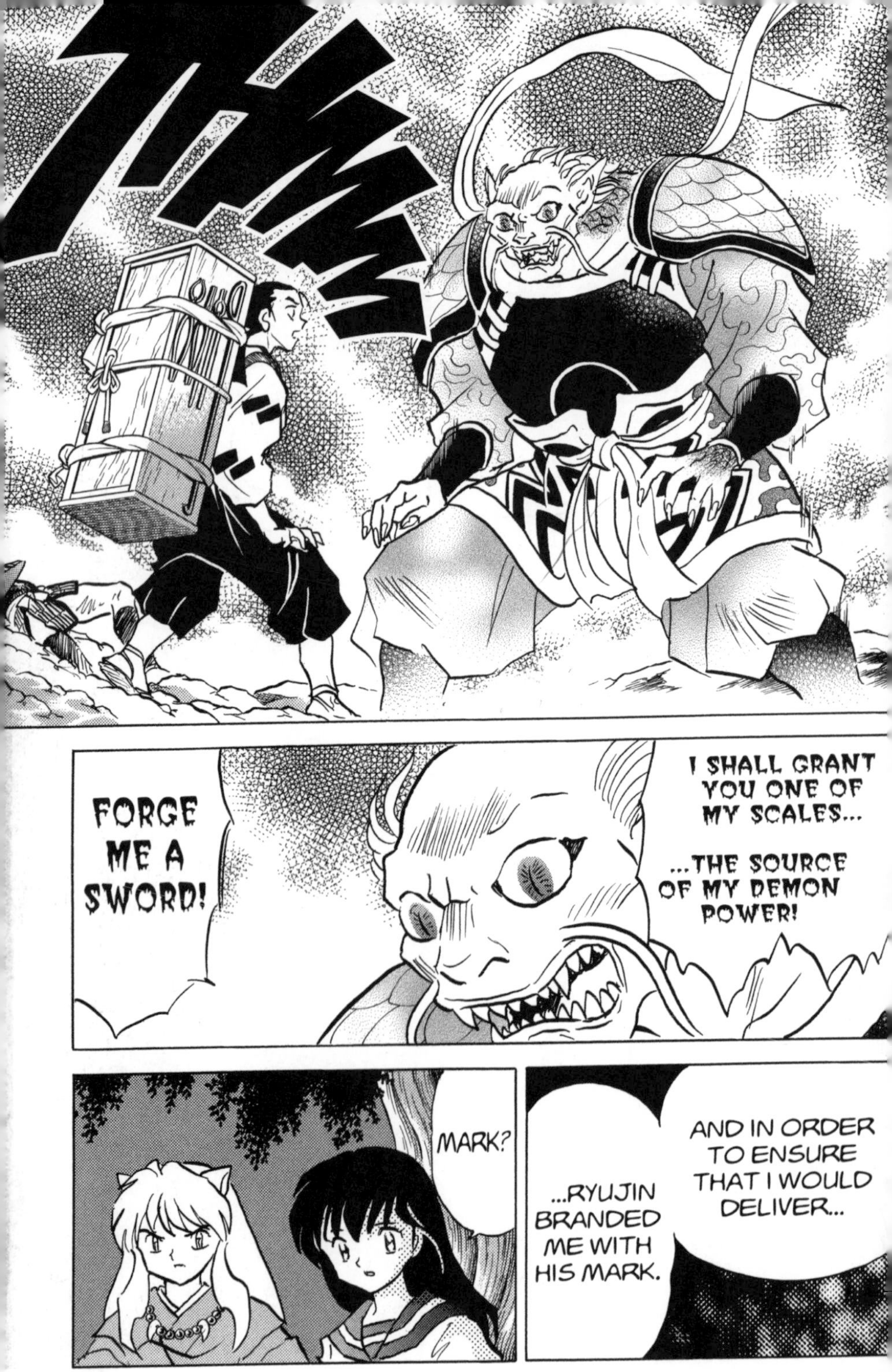
I SHALL GRANT YOU ONE OF MY SCALES...
...THE SOURCE OF MY DEMON POWER!
FORGE ME A SWORD!
AND IN ORDER TO ENSURE THAT I WOULD DELIVER...
...RYUJIN BRANDED ME WITH HIS MARK.
MARK?

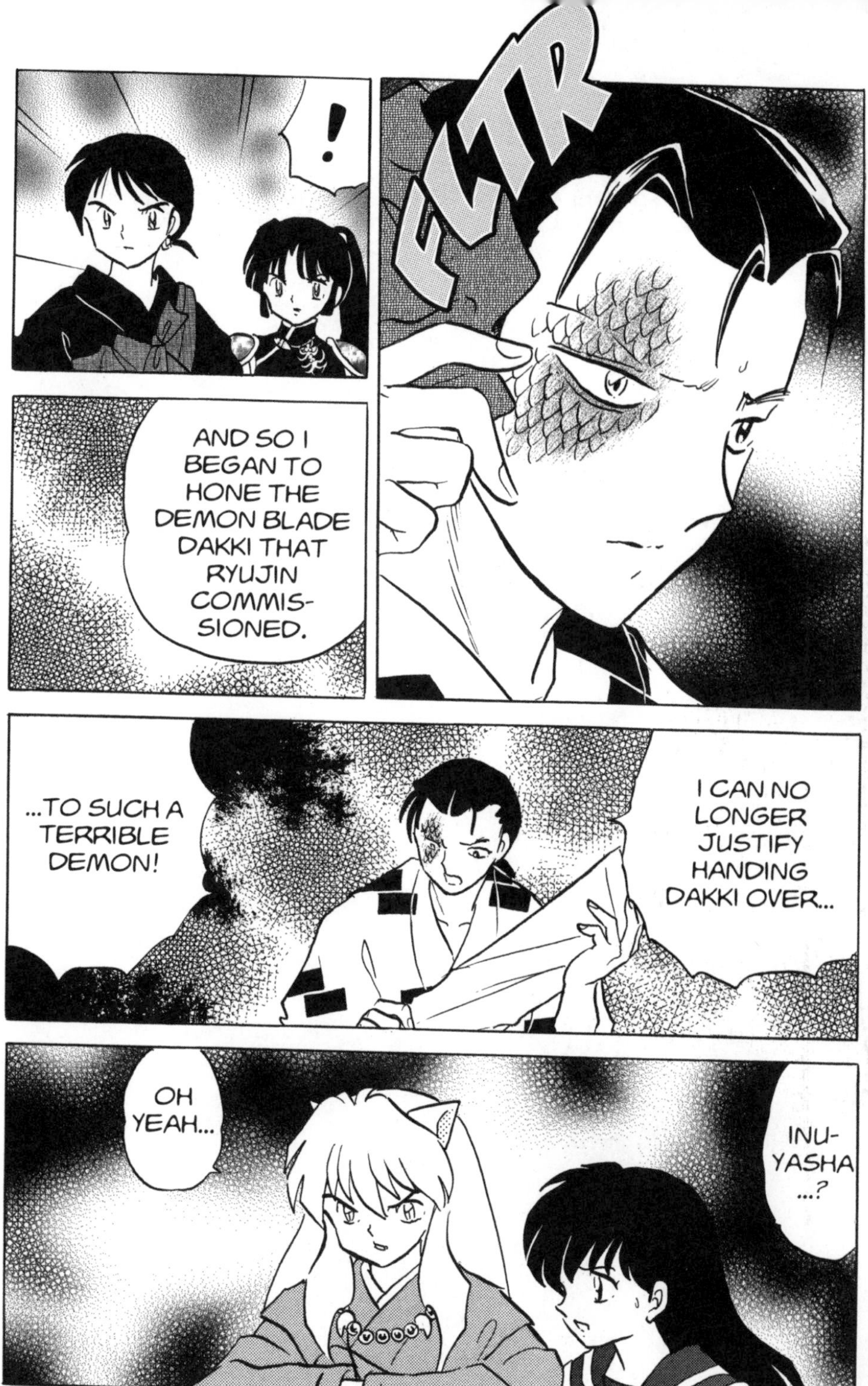
FLTR
!
AND SO I BEGAN TO HONE THE DEMON BLADE DAKKI THAT RYUJIN COMMIS-SIONED.
I CAN NO LONGER JUSTIFY HANDING DAKKI OVER...
...TO SUCH A TERRIBLE DEMON!
INU-YASHA ...?
OH YEAH...

SCROLL NINE
RYUJIN'S SHIELD

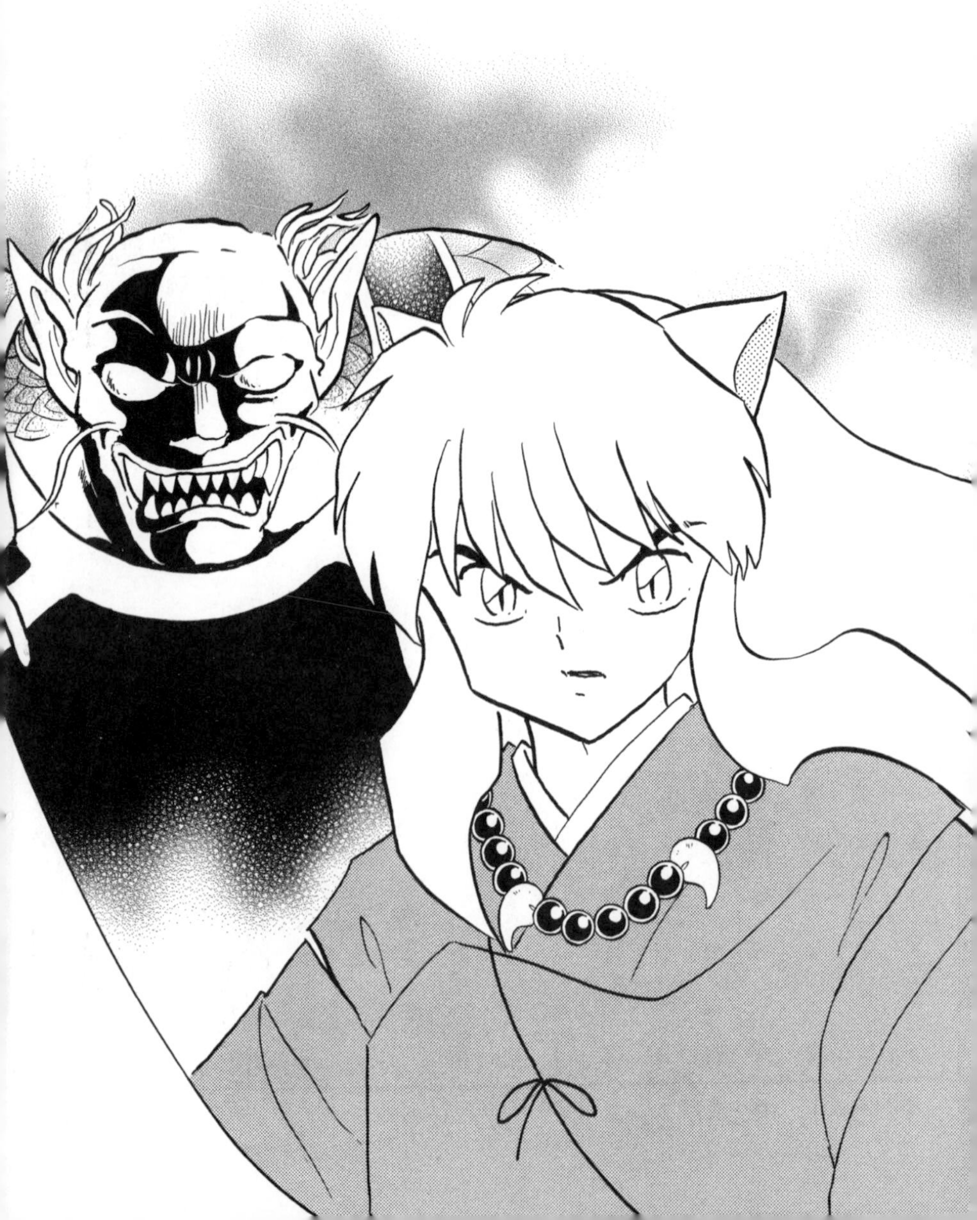

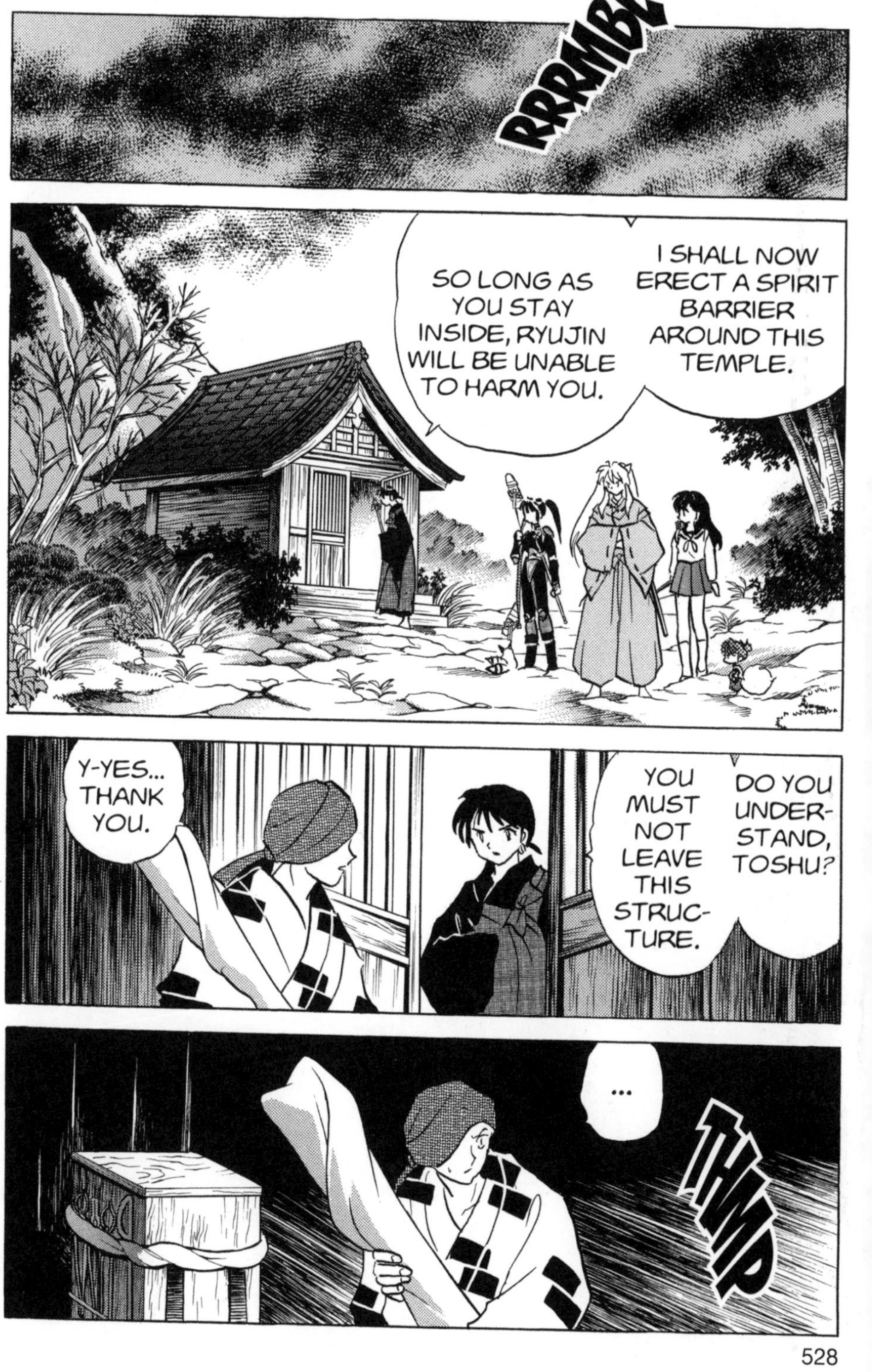
RRRMBL
I SHALL NOW ERECT A SPIRIT BARRIER AROUND THIS TEMPLE.
SO LONG AS YOU STAY INSIDE, RYUJIN WILL BE UNABLE TO HARM YOU.
DO YOU UNDER-STAND, TOSHU?
YOU MUST NOT LEAVE THIS STRUC-TURE.
Y-YES... THANK YOU.
...
THMP

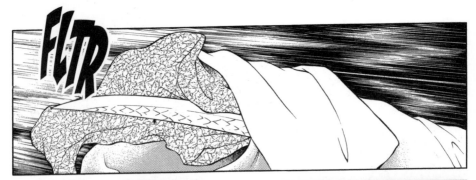

FLTR
BZZZ
DAKKI IS... AGITATED...
ARE YOU SURE ABOUT THIS, LORD INUYASHA?
ABOUT WHAT, OLD MAN?
THE DEMON-BLADE DAKKI IS RIGHT IN FRONT OF YOU!

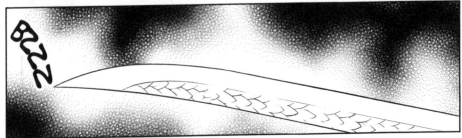

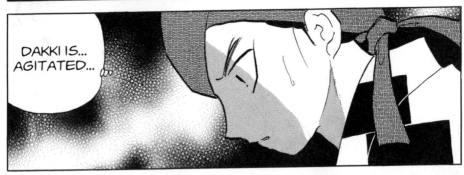

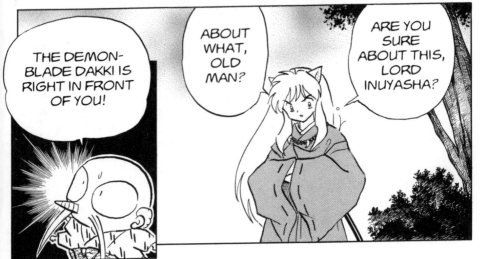

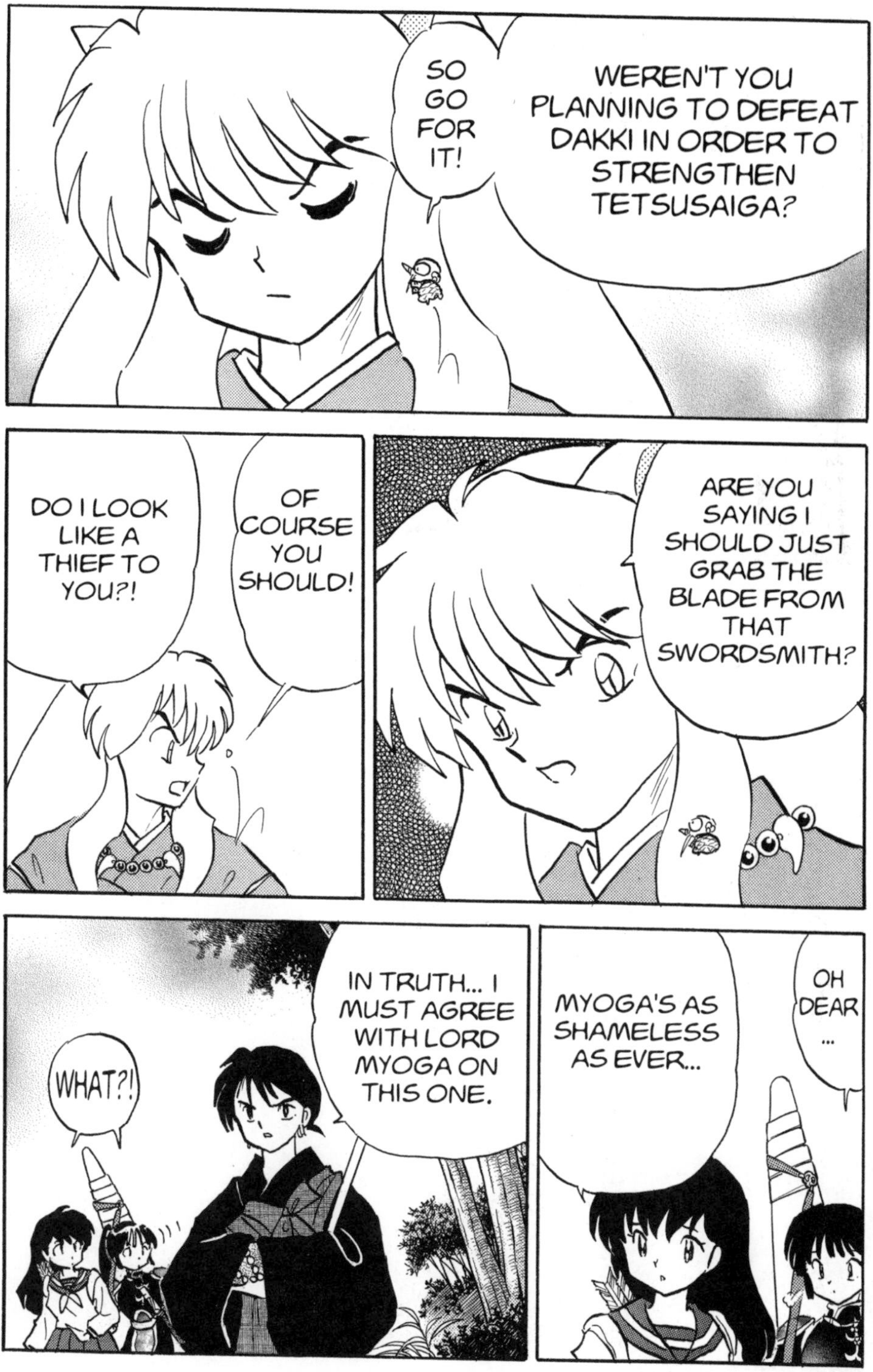
WEREN'T YOU PLANNING TO DEFEAT DAKKI IN ORDER TO STRENGTHEN TETSUSAIGA?
SO GO FOR IT!
ARE YOU SAYING I SHOULD JUST GRAB THE BLADE FROM THAT SWORDSMITH?
OF COURSE YOU SHOULD!
DO I LOOK LIKE A THIEF TO YOU?!
OH DEAR ...
MYOGA'S AS SHAMELESS AS EVER...
IN TRUTH... I MUST AGREE WITH LORD MYOGA ON THIS ONE.
WHAT?!

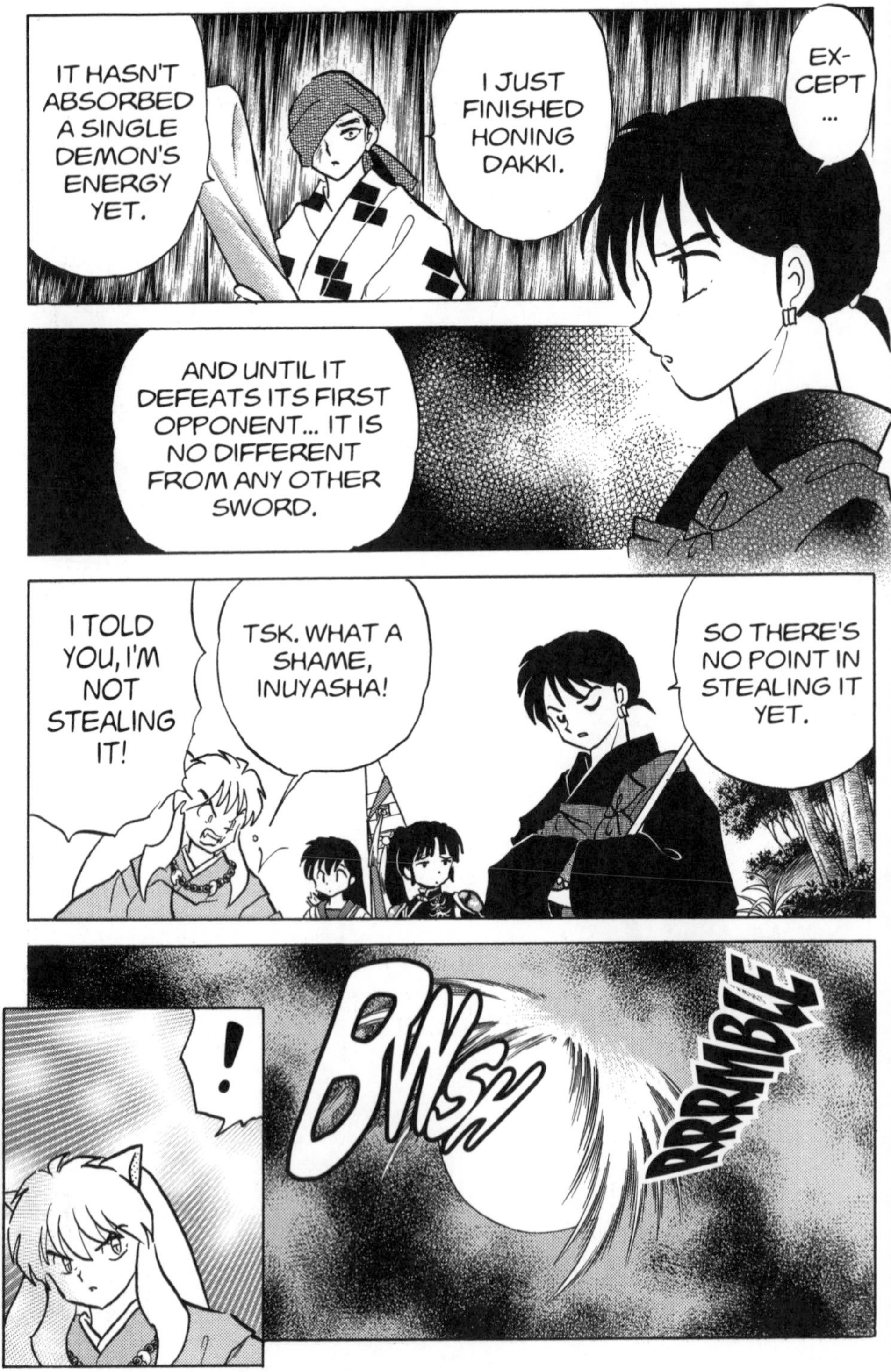
I JUST FINISHED HONING DAKKI.
IT HASN'T ABSORBED A SINGLE DEMON'S ENERGY YET.
EX-CEPT ...
AND UNTIL IT DEFEATS ITS FIRST OPPONENT... IT IS NO DIFFERENT FROM ANY OTHER SWORD.
SO THERE'S NO POINT IN STEALING IT YET.
TSK. WHAT A SHAME, INUYASHA!
I TOLD YOU, I'M NOT STEALING IT!
BWSH
RRRMBLE
!

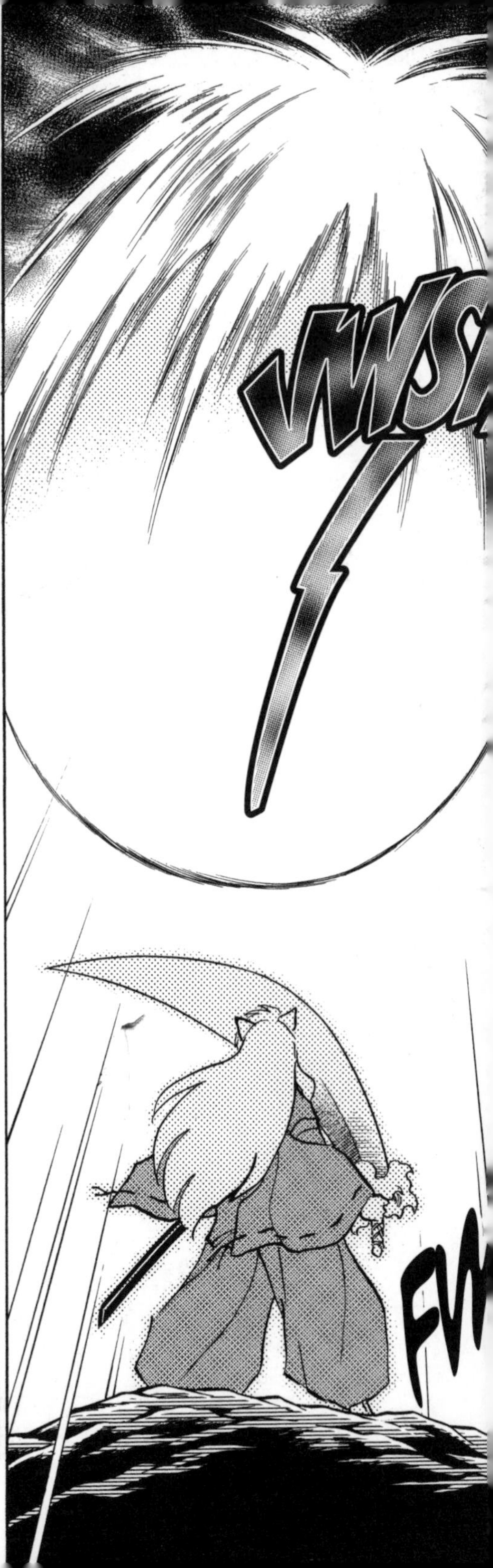

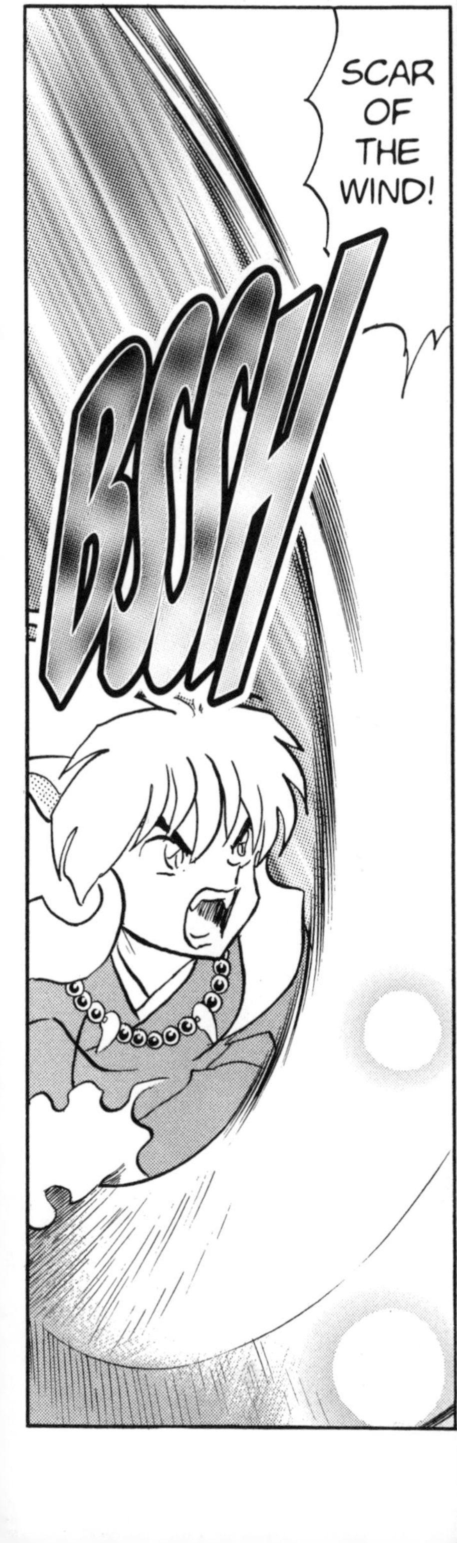
SCAR OF THE WIND!

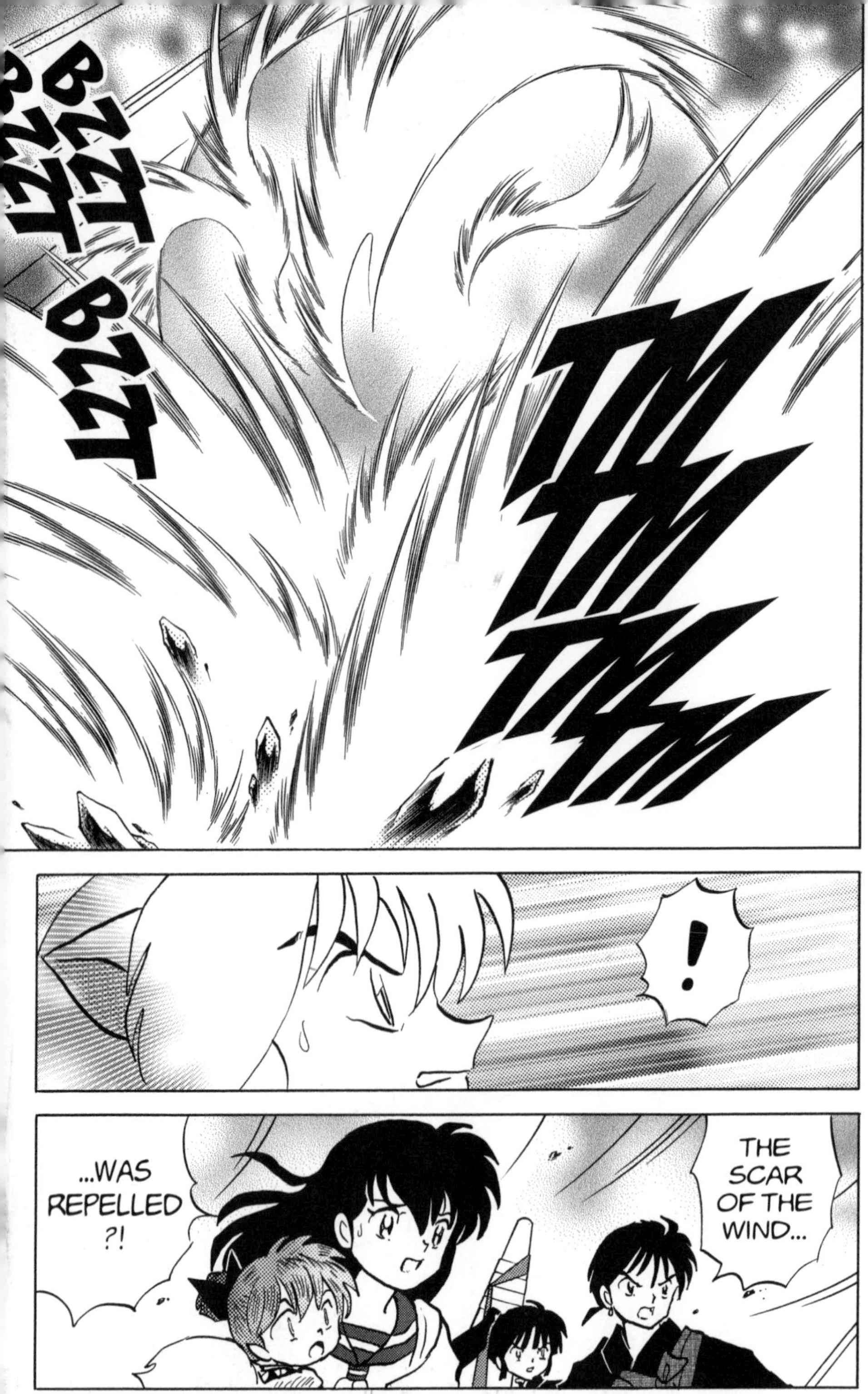
BZZT
BZZT BZZT
!
THE SCAR OF THE WIND...
...WAS REPELLED ?!

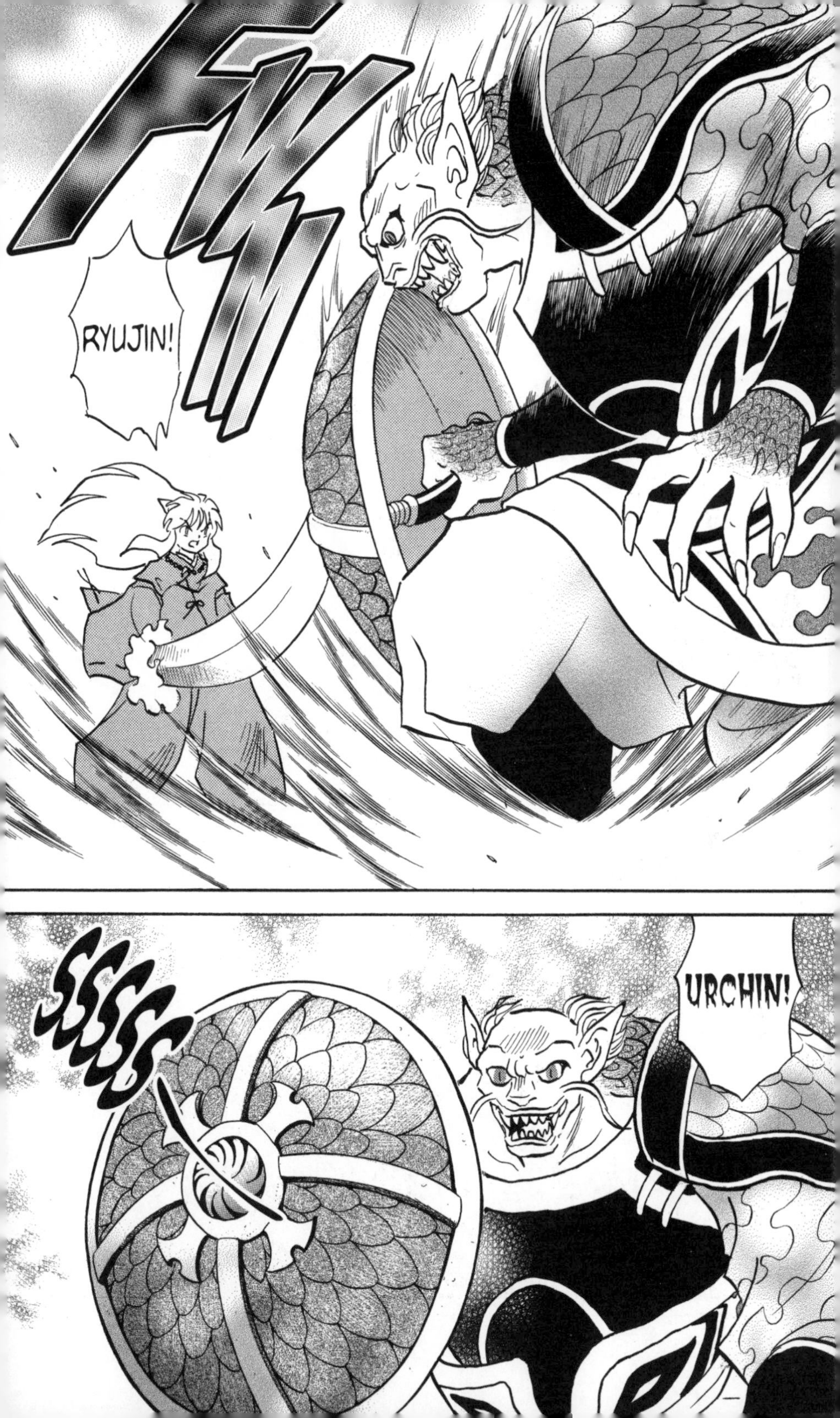
RYUJIN!
URCHIN!
SSSS

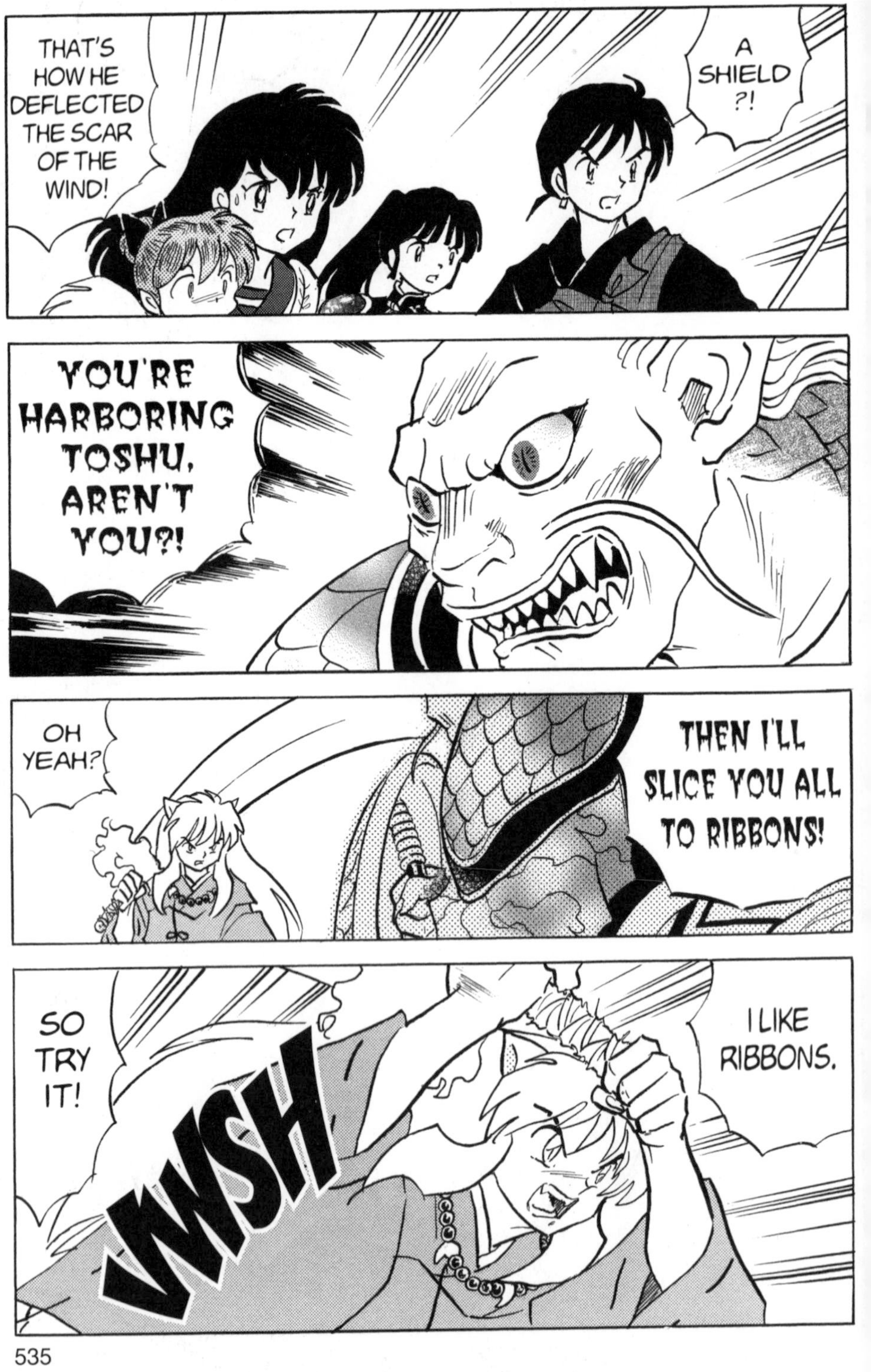
A SHIELD ?!
THAT'S HOW HE DEFLECTED THE SCAR OF THE WIND!
YOU'RE HARBORING TOSHU, AREN'T YOU?!
THEN I'LL SLICE YOU ALL TO RIBBONS!
OH YEAH?
I LIKE RIBBONS.
SO TRY IT!
VWSH

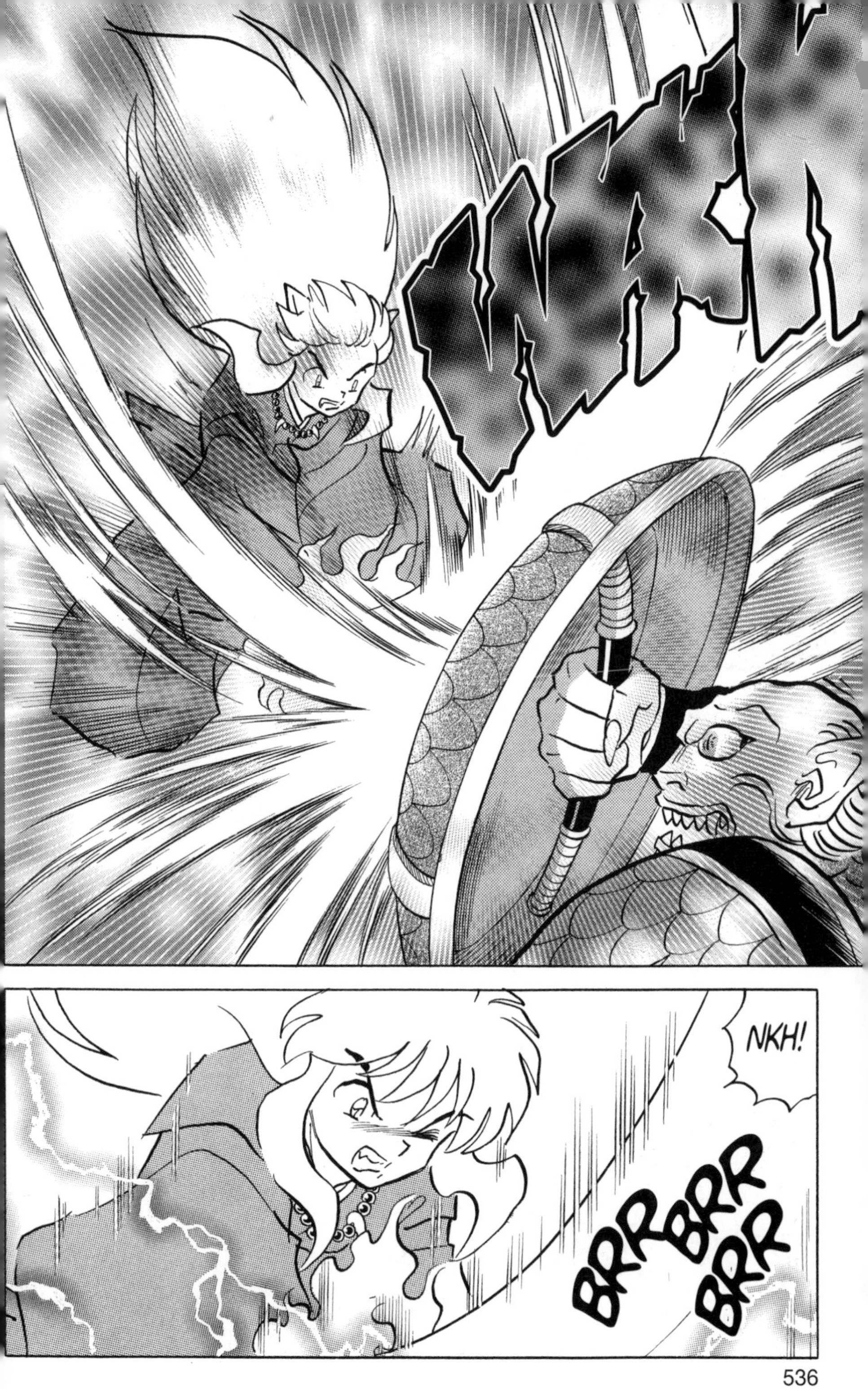
WHAM
NKH!
BRRBRR
BRR

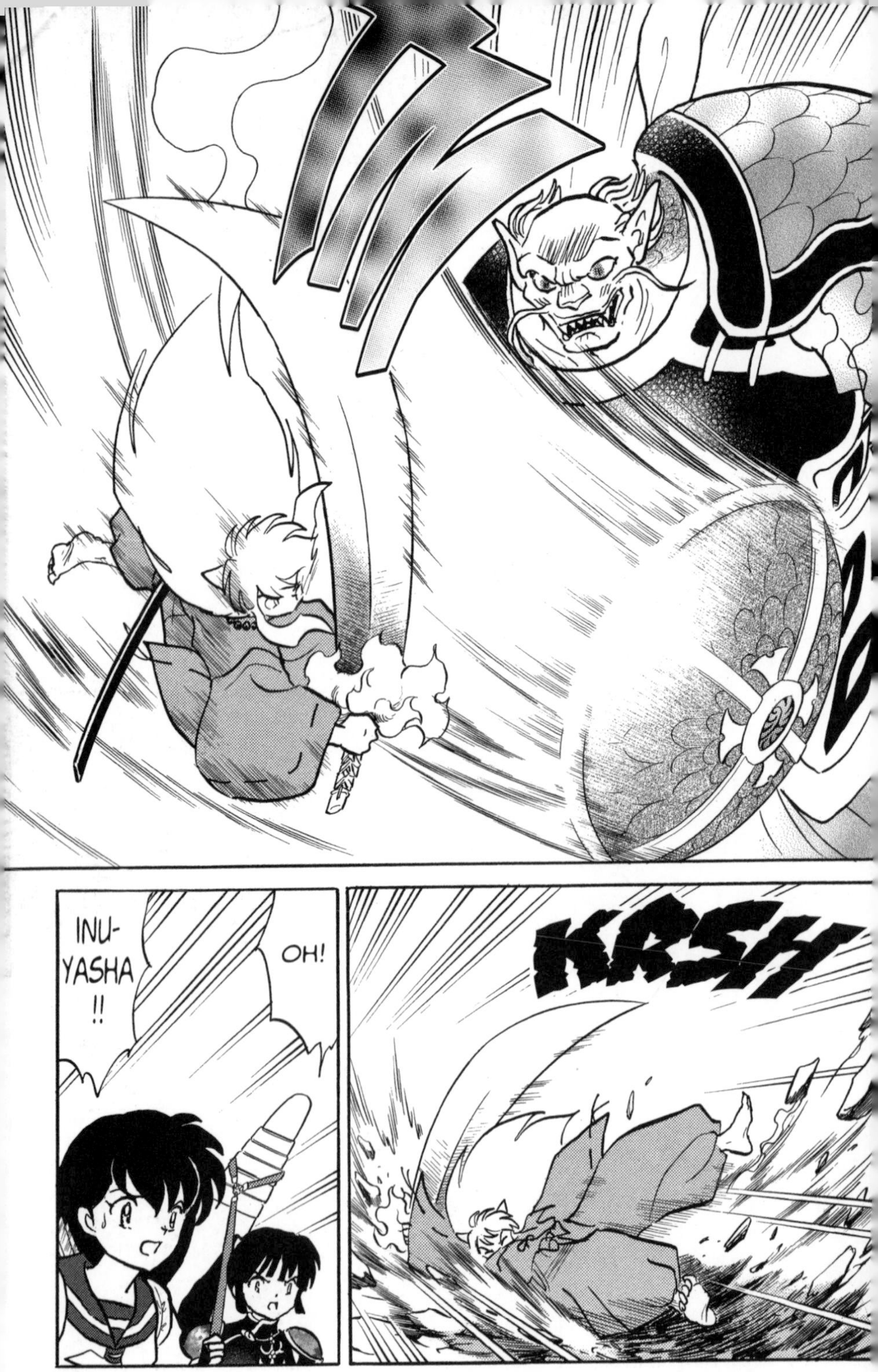
KRSH
OH!
INU-YASHA!!

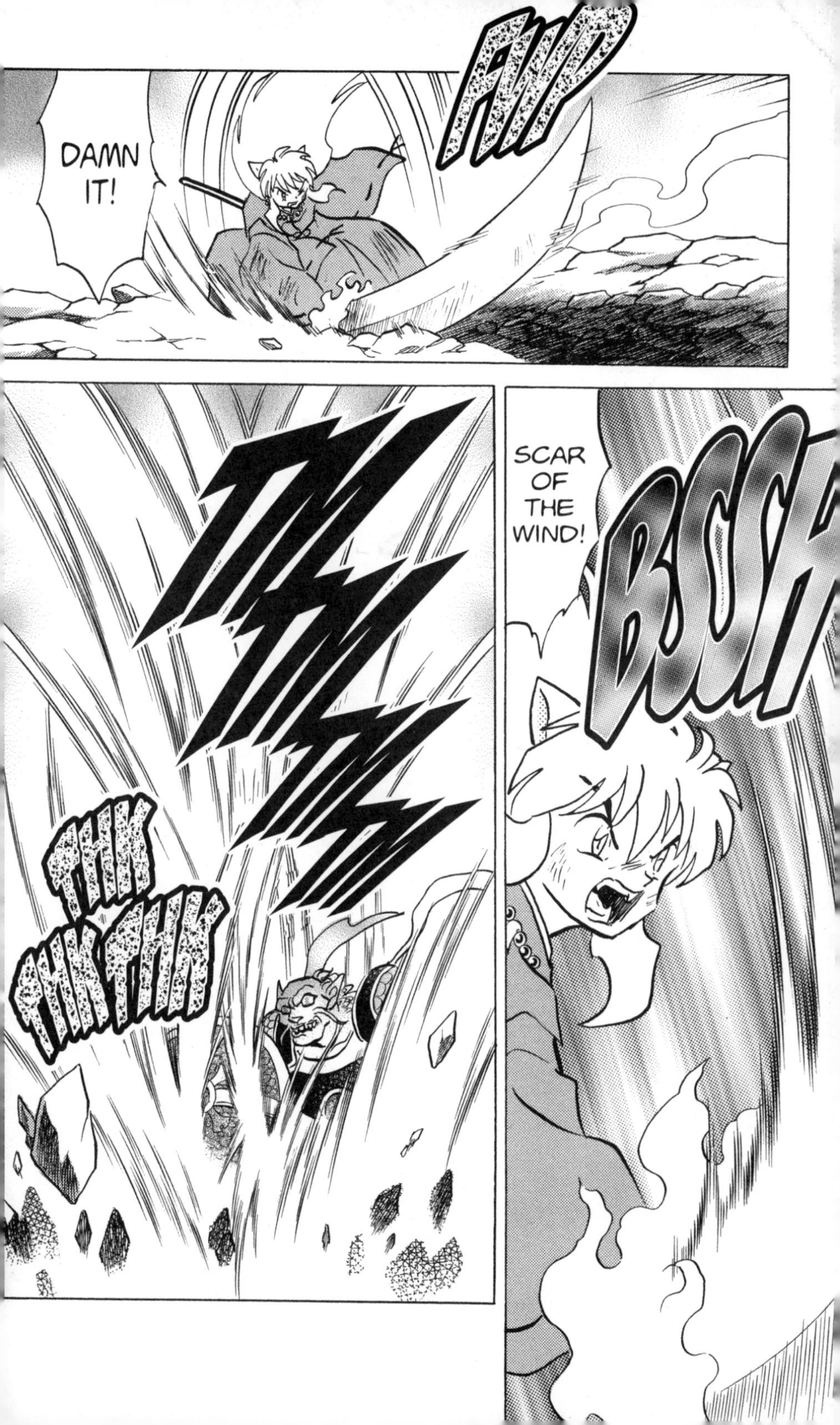
FWP
DAMN IT!
SCAR OF THE WIND!
BOO
THK THK THK

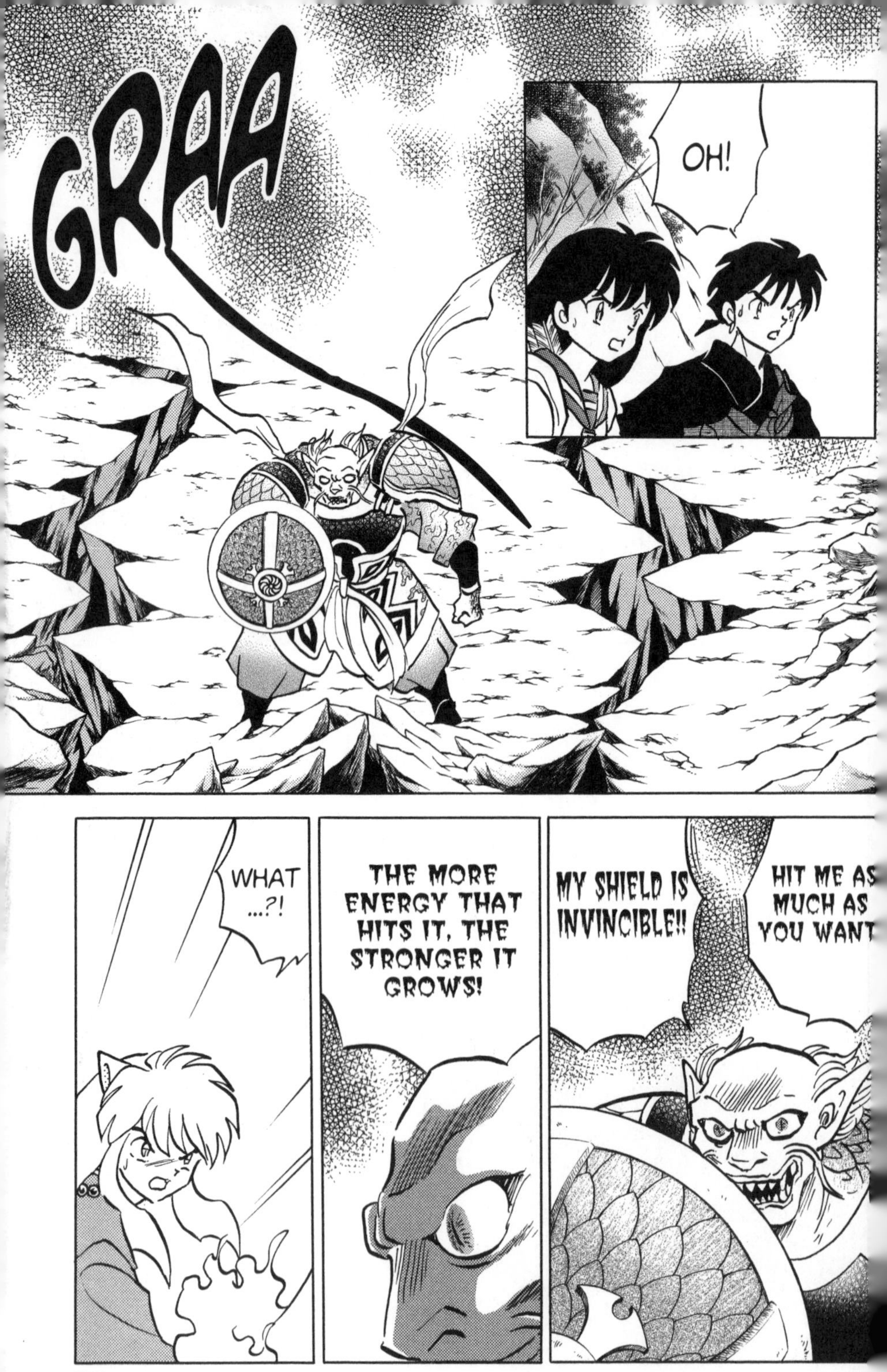
OH!
GRAA
HIT ME AS MUCH AS YOU WANT
MY SHIELD IS INVINCIBLE!!
THE MORE ENERGY THAT HITS IT, THE STRONGER IT GROWS!
WHAT ...?!

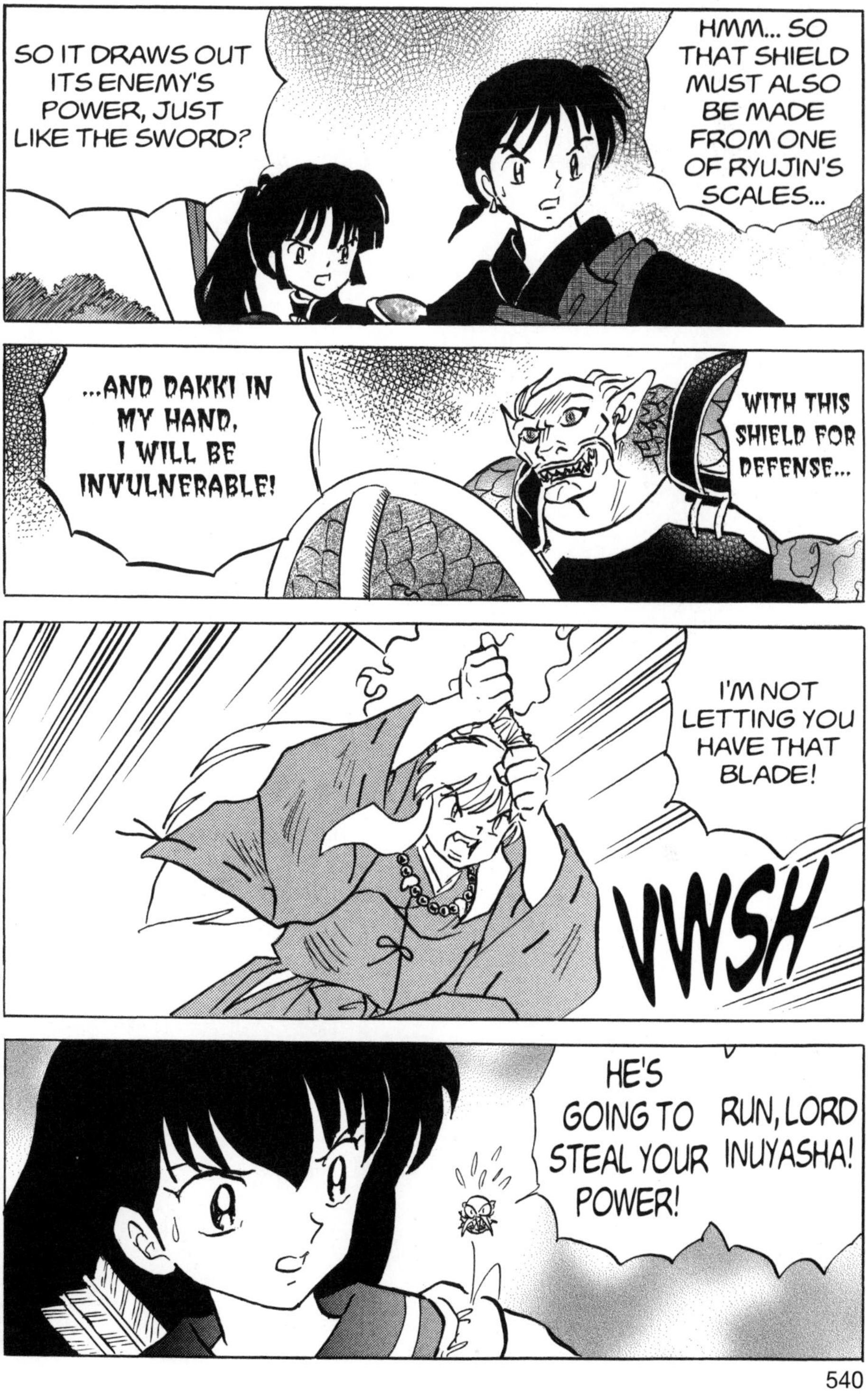
HMM... SO THAT SHIELD MUST ALSO BE MADE FROM ONE OF RYUJIN'S SCALES...
SO IT DRAWS OUT ITS ENEMY'S POWER, JUST LIKE THE SWORD?
WITH THIS SHIELD FOR DEFENSE...
...AND DAKKI IN MY HAND, I WILL BE INVULNERABLE!
I'M NOT LETTING YOU HAVE THAT BLADE!
VVNSH
RUN, LORD INUYASHA!
HE'S GOING TO STEAL YOUR POWER!

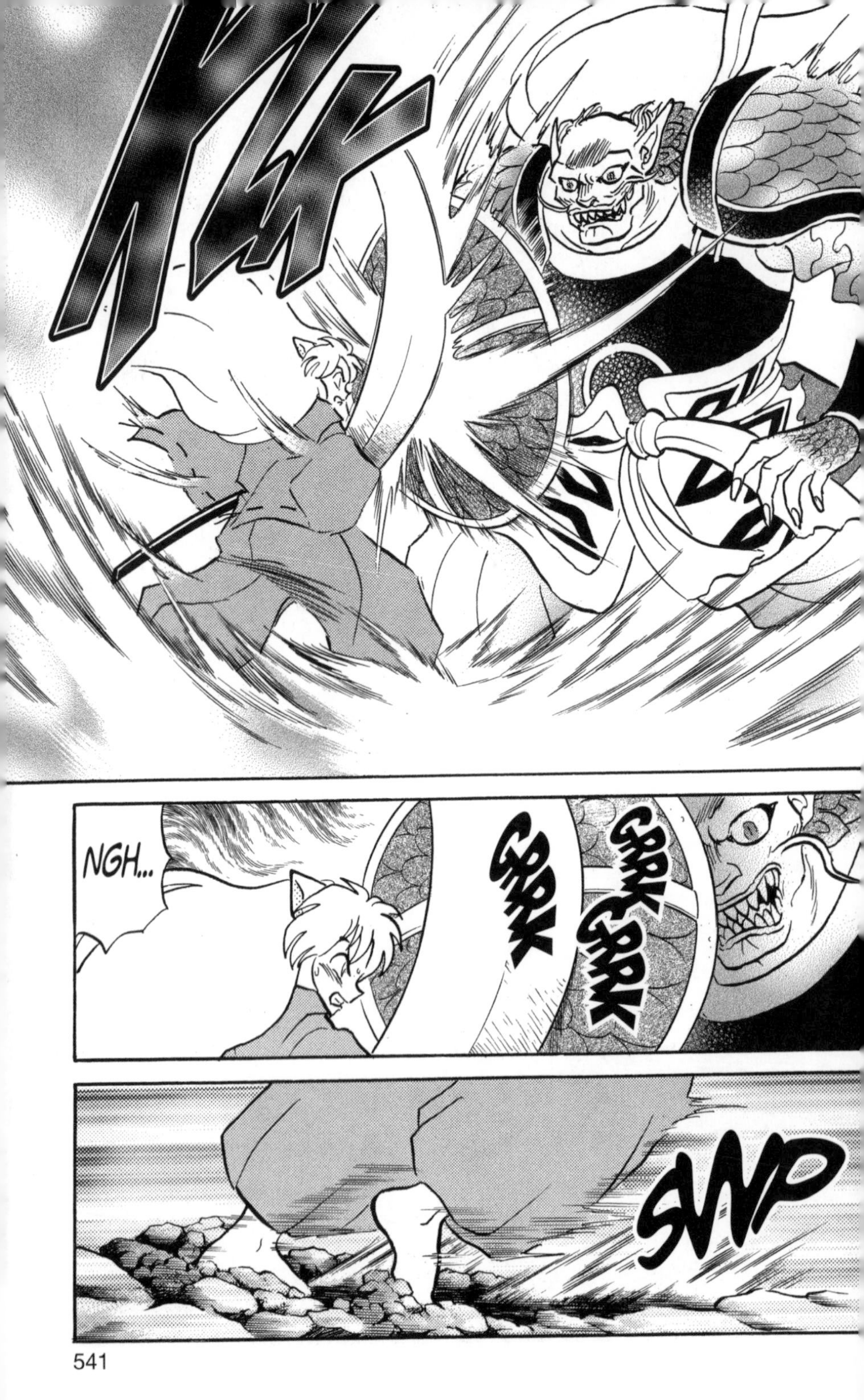
GRRK GRRK GRRK
NGH...

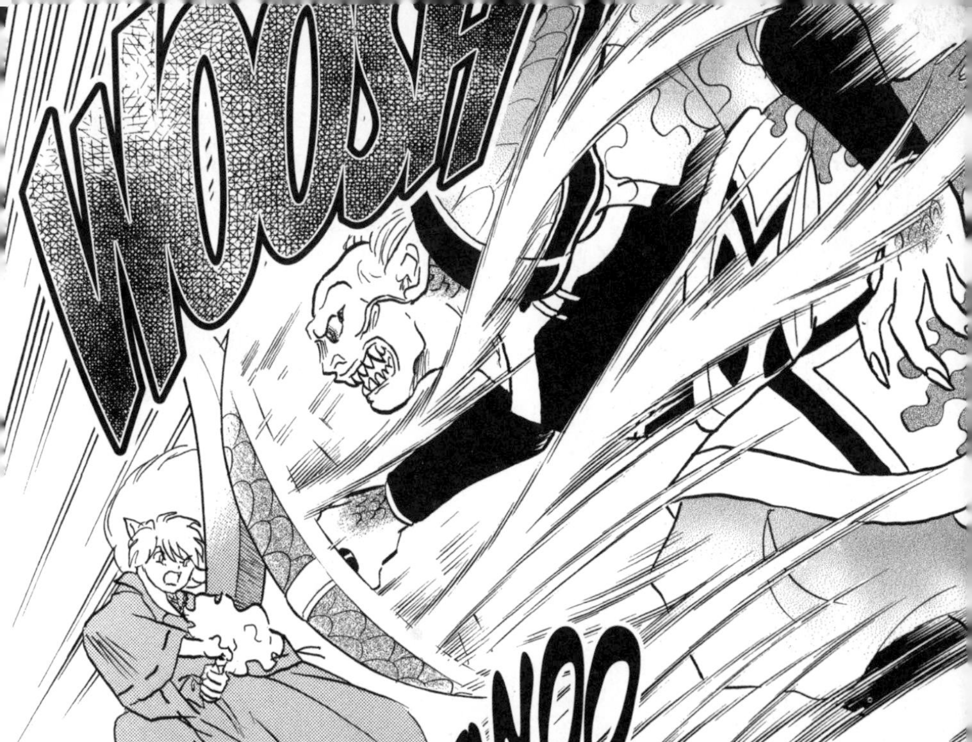
WOOSH
FWOO

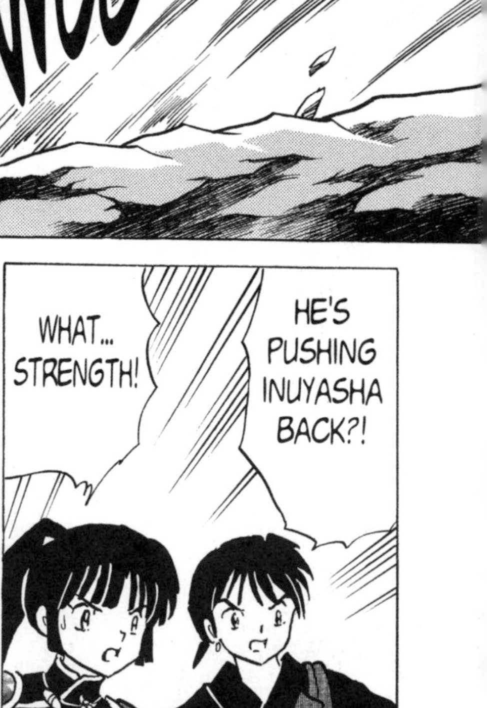
HE'S PUSHING INUYASHA BACK?!
WHAT... STRENGTH!

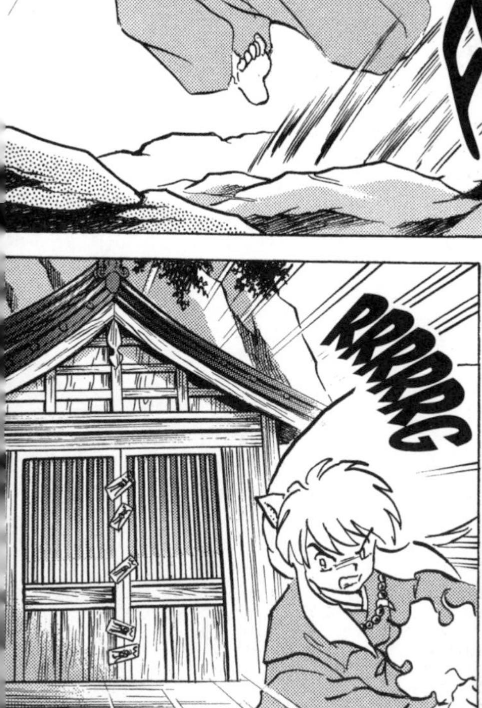
RRRRRG

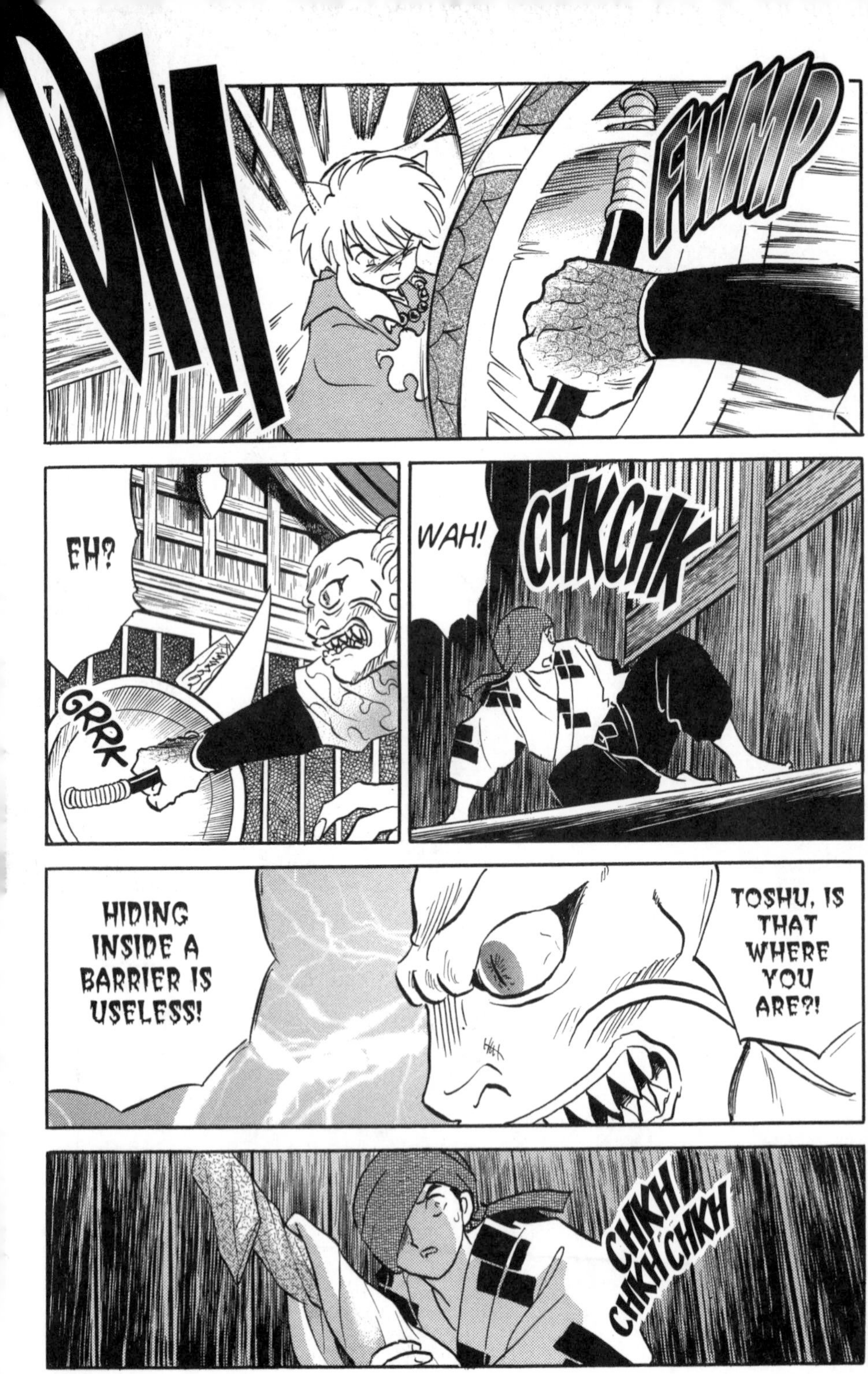
FWMP
WAH!
CHKCHK
EH?
GRRK
TOSHU, IS THAT WHERE YOU ARE?!
HIDING INSIDE A BARRIER IS USELESS!
CHKH CHKH CHKH

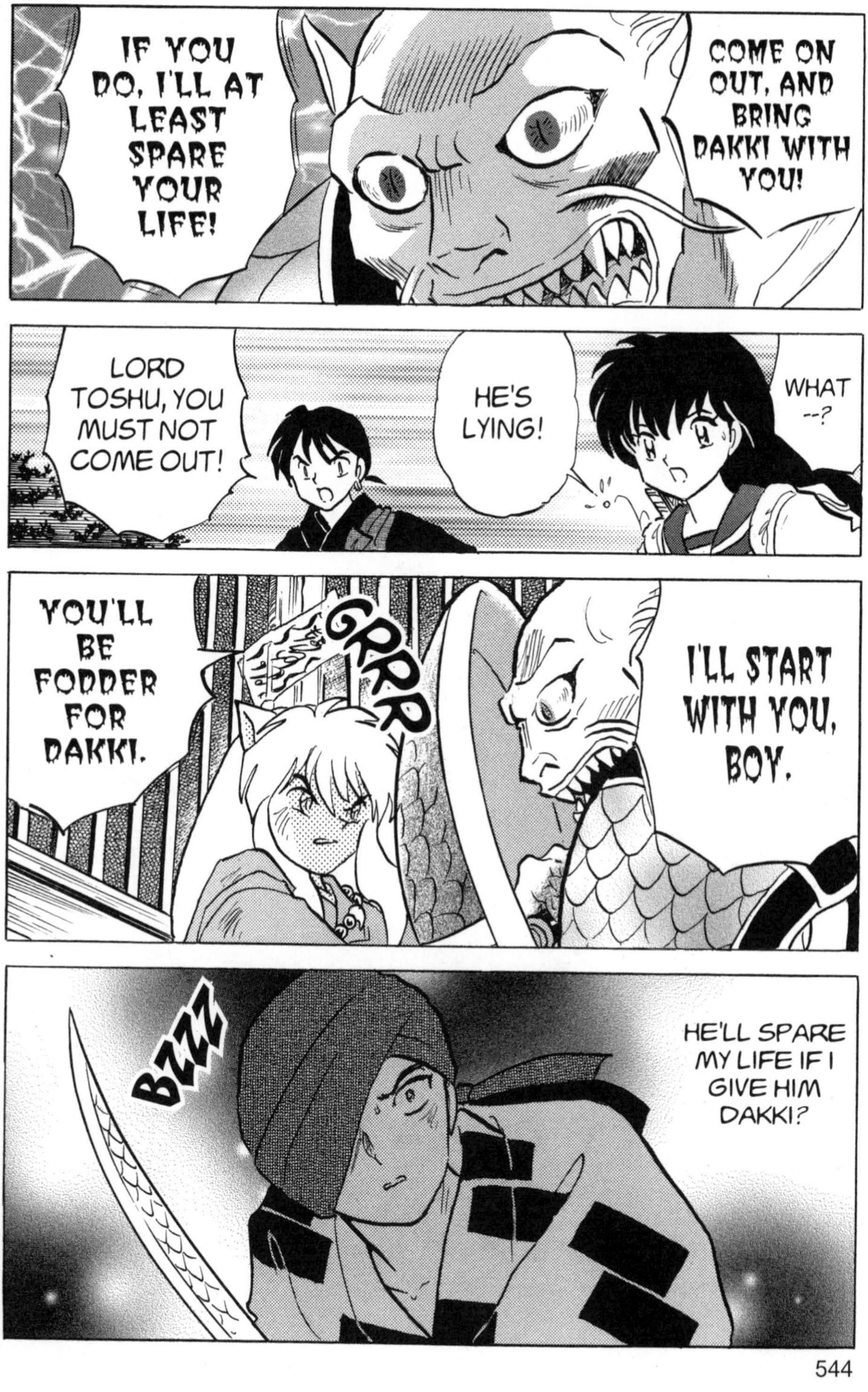
COME ON OUT, AND BRING DAKKI WITH YOU!
IF YOU DO, I'LL AT LEAST SPARE YOUR LIFE!
WHAT --?
HE'S LYING!
LORD TOSHU, YOU MUST NOT COME OUT!
I'LL START WITH YOU, BOY.
GRRR
YOU'LL BE FODDER FOR DAKKI.
HE'LL SPARE MY LIFE IF I GIVE HIM DAKKI?
BZZZ

SCROLL TEN
THE WIELDER OF DAKKI

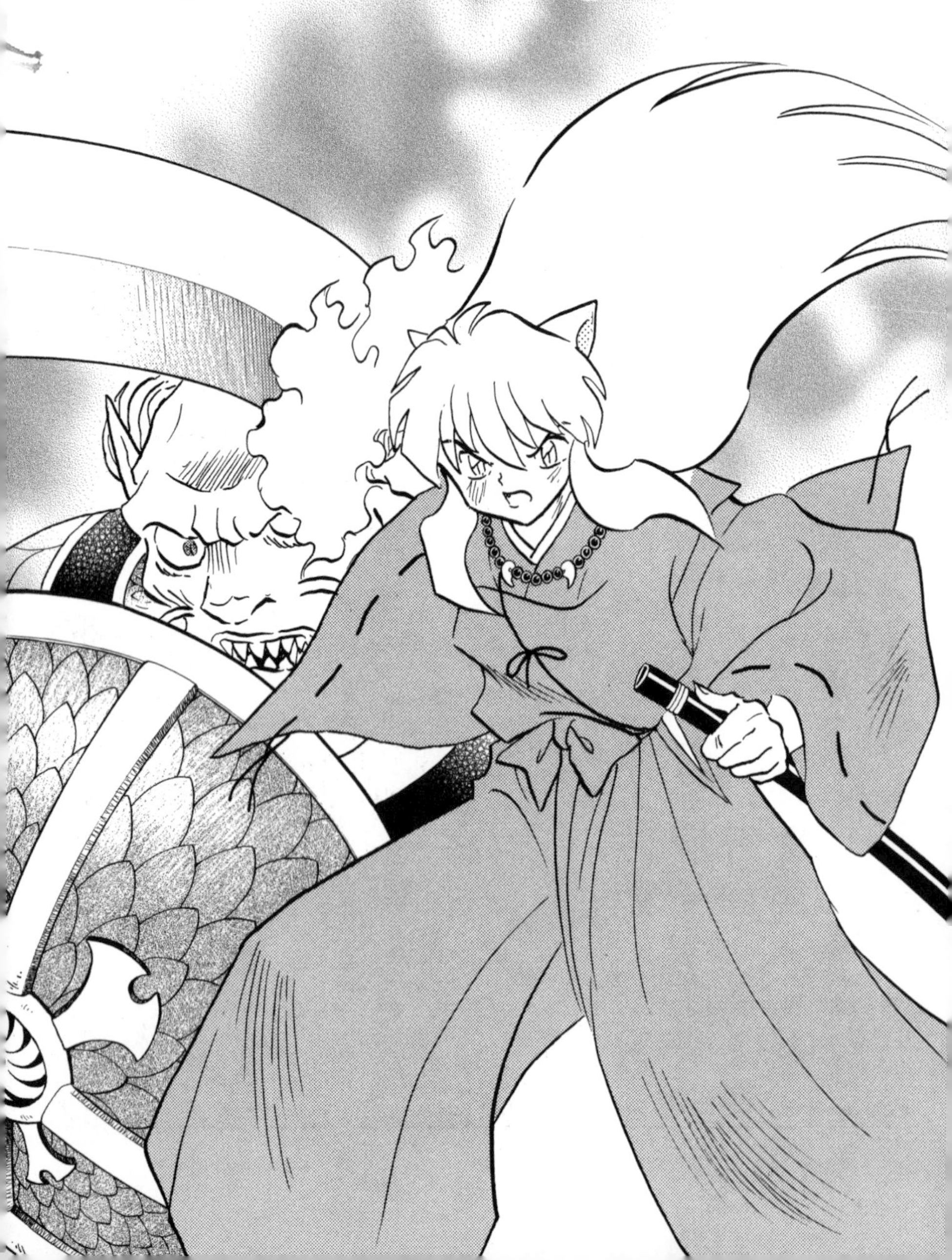

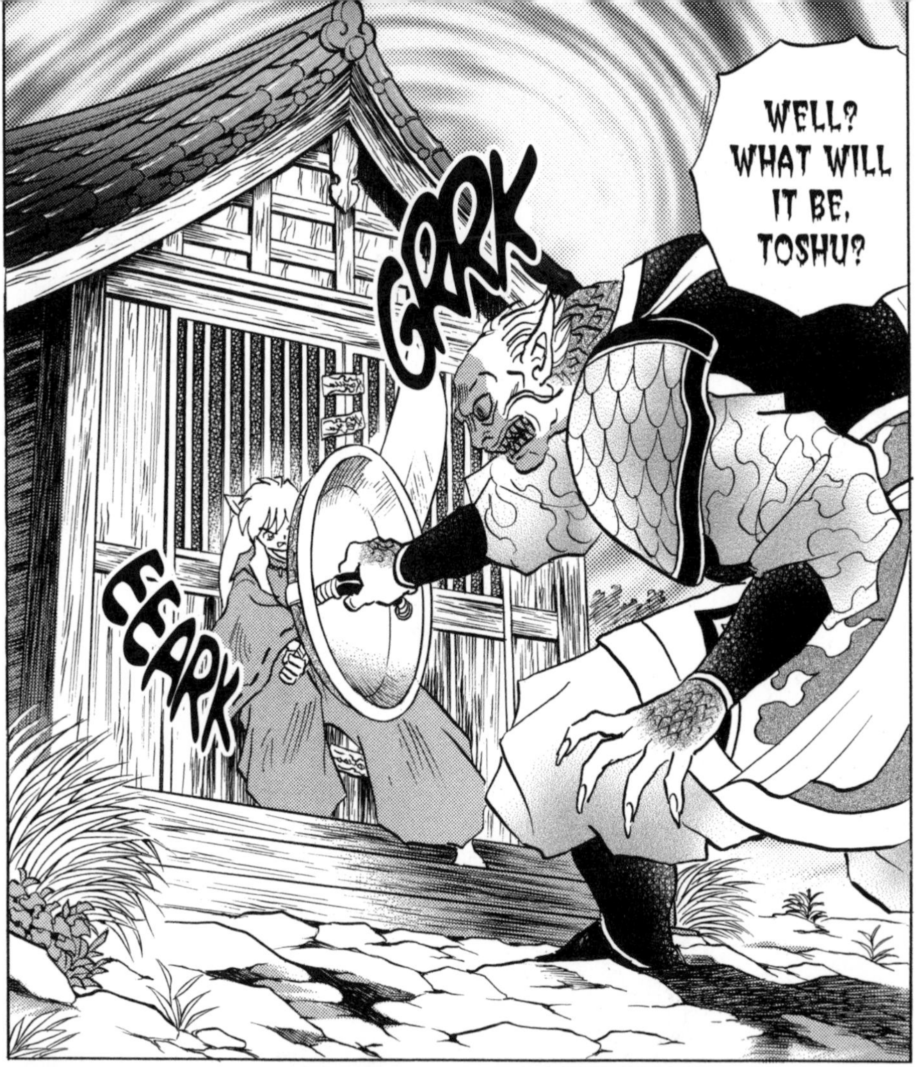
WELL? WHAT WILL IT BE, TOSHU?
GRRK
EEARK

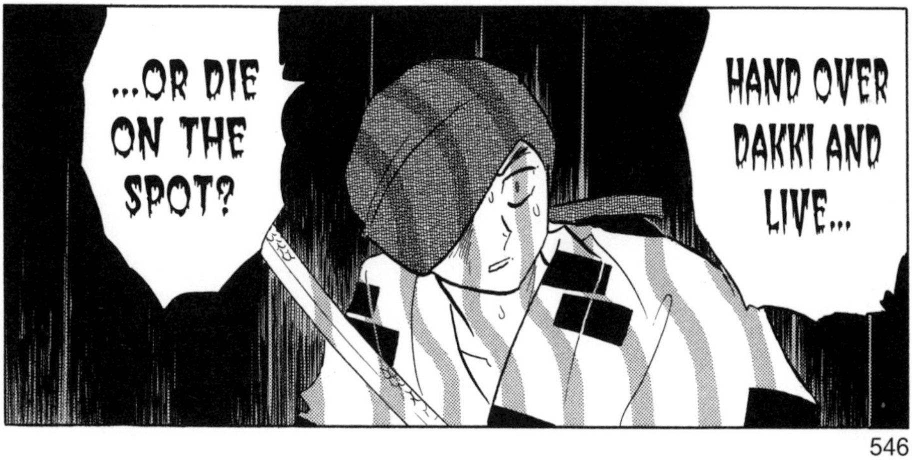
HAND OVER DAKKI AND LIVE...
...OR DIE ON THE SPOT?

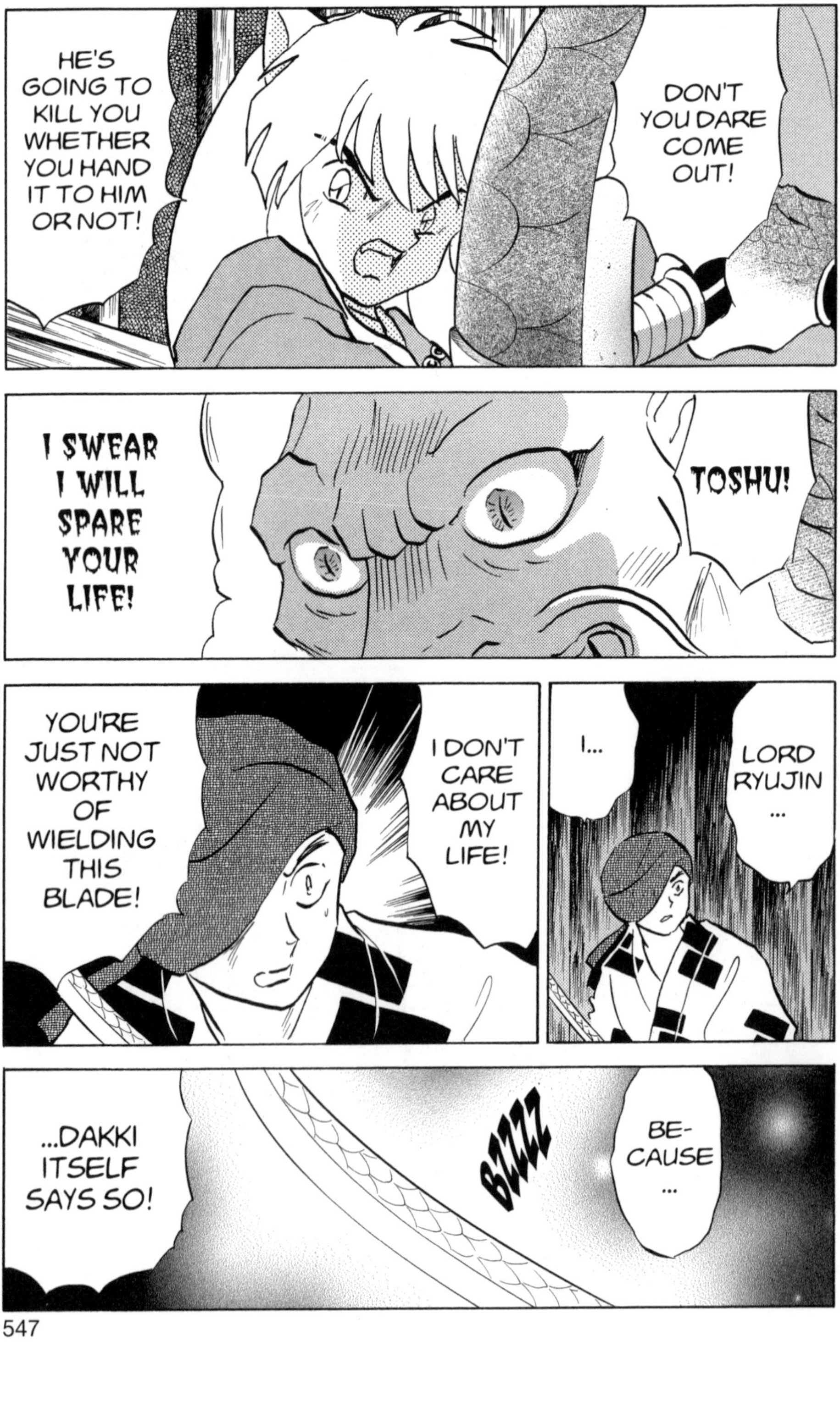
DON'T YOU DARE COME OUT!
HE'S GOING TO KILL YOU WHETHER YOU HAND IT TO HIM OR NOT!
TOSHU!
I SWEAR I WILL SPARE YOUR LIFE!
LORD RYUJIN ...
I...
I DON'T CARE ABOUT MY LIFE!
YOU'RE JUST NOT WORTHY OF WIELDING THIS BLADE!
BE- CAUSE ...
BZZZZ
...DAKKI ITSELF SAYS SO!

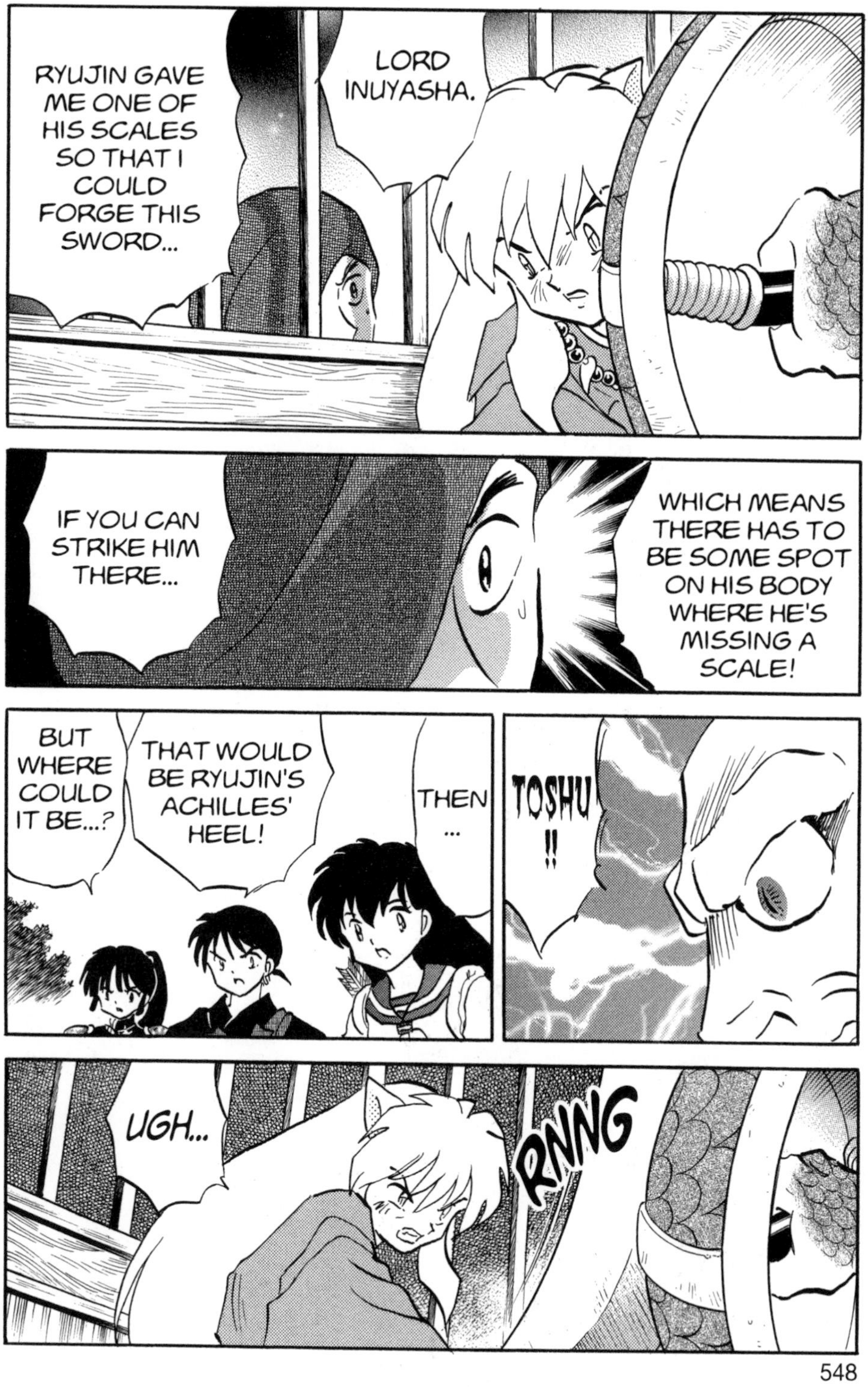
LORD INUYASHA.
RYUJIN GAVE ME ONE OF HIS SCALES SO THAT I COULD FORGE THIS SWORD...
WHICH MEANS THERE HAS TO BE SOME SPOT ON HIS BODY WHERE HE'S MISSING A SCALE!
IF YOU CAN STRIKE HIM THERE...
TOSHU!!
THEN...
THAT WOULD BE RYUJIN'S ACHILLES' HEEL!
BUT WHERE COULD IT BE...?
RNNG
UGH...

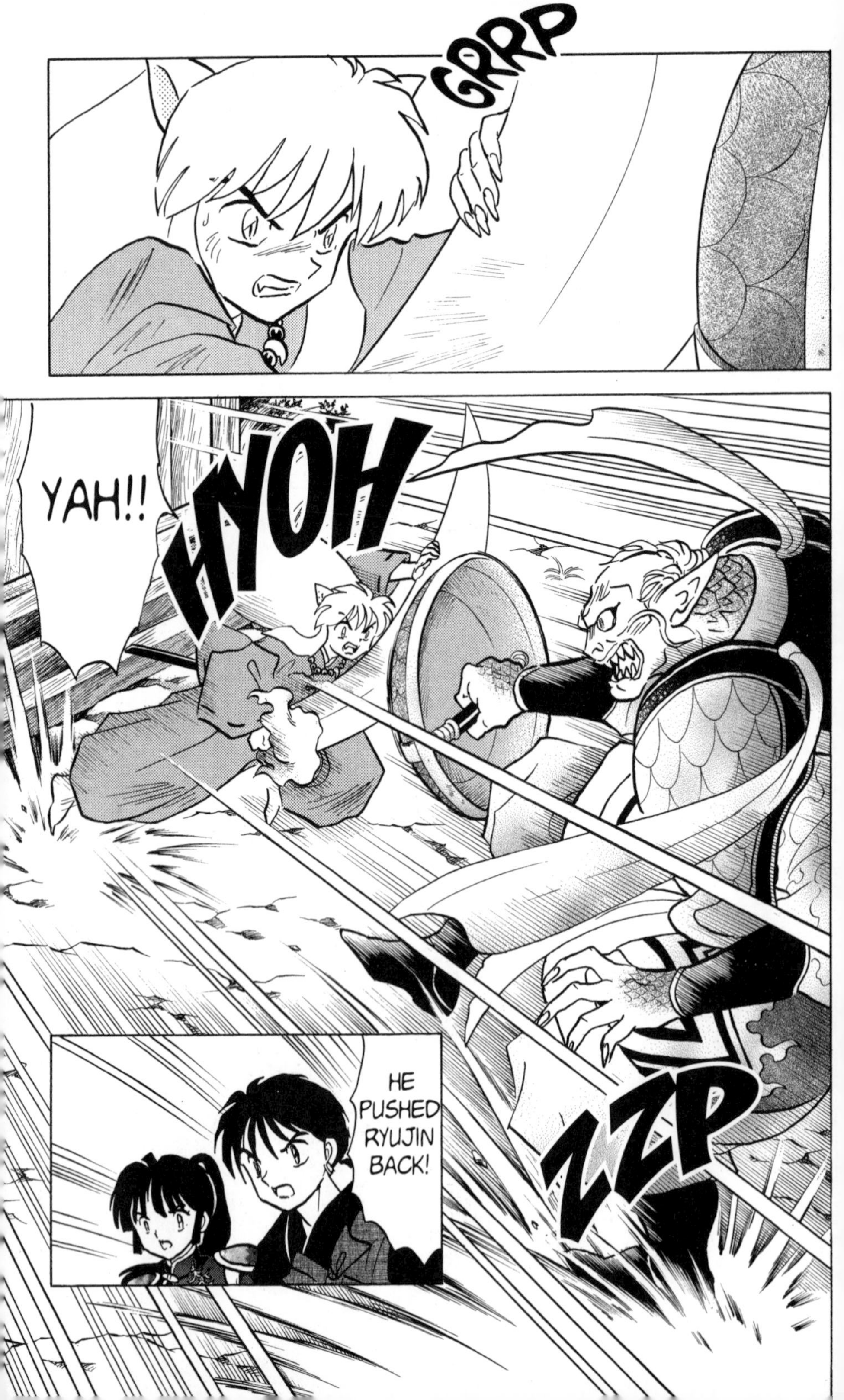
GRRP
YAH!!
HYOH
ZZZP
HE PUSHED RYUJIN BACK!

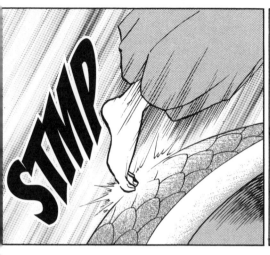

STMP

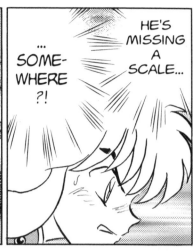

HE'S MISSING A SCALE...

...SOME- WHERE ?!

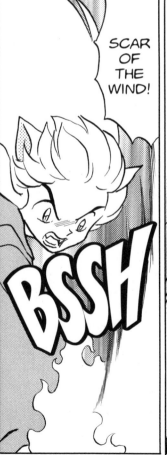

SCAR OF THE WIND!

BSSH

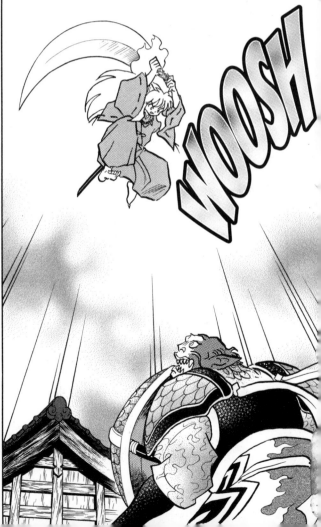

WOOSH

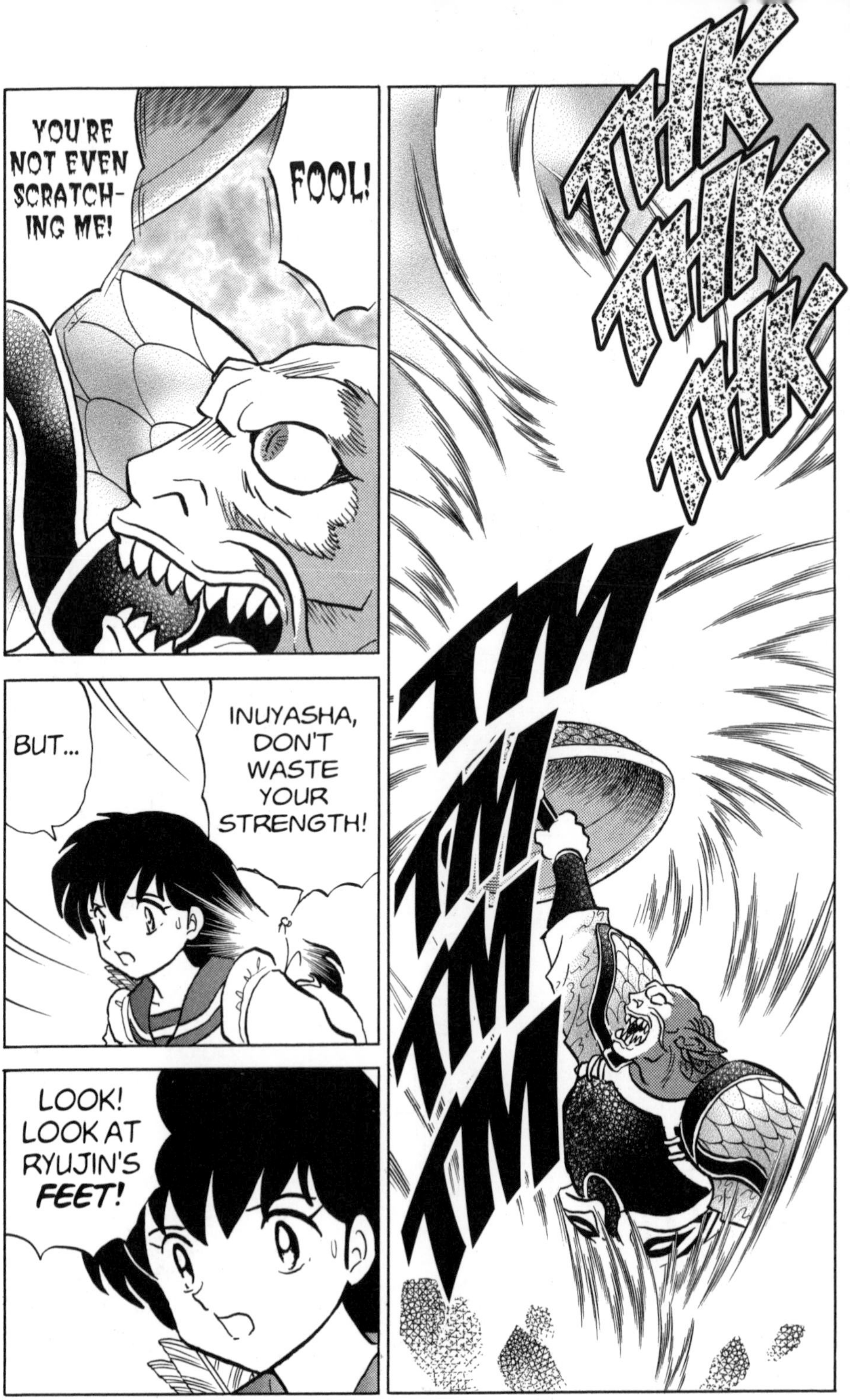
THIK THIK THIK
TIM TIM TIM TIM
FOOL!
YOU'RE NOT EVEN SCRATCHING ME!
INUYASHA, DON'T WASTE YOUR STRENGTH!
BUT...
LOOK! LOOK AT RYUJIN'S FEET!

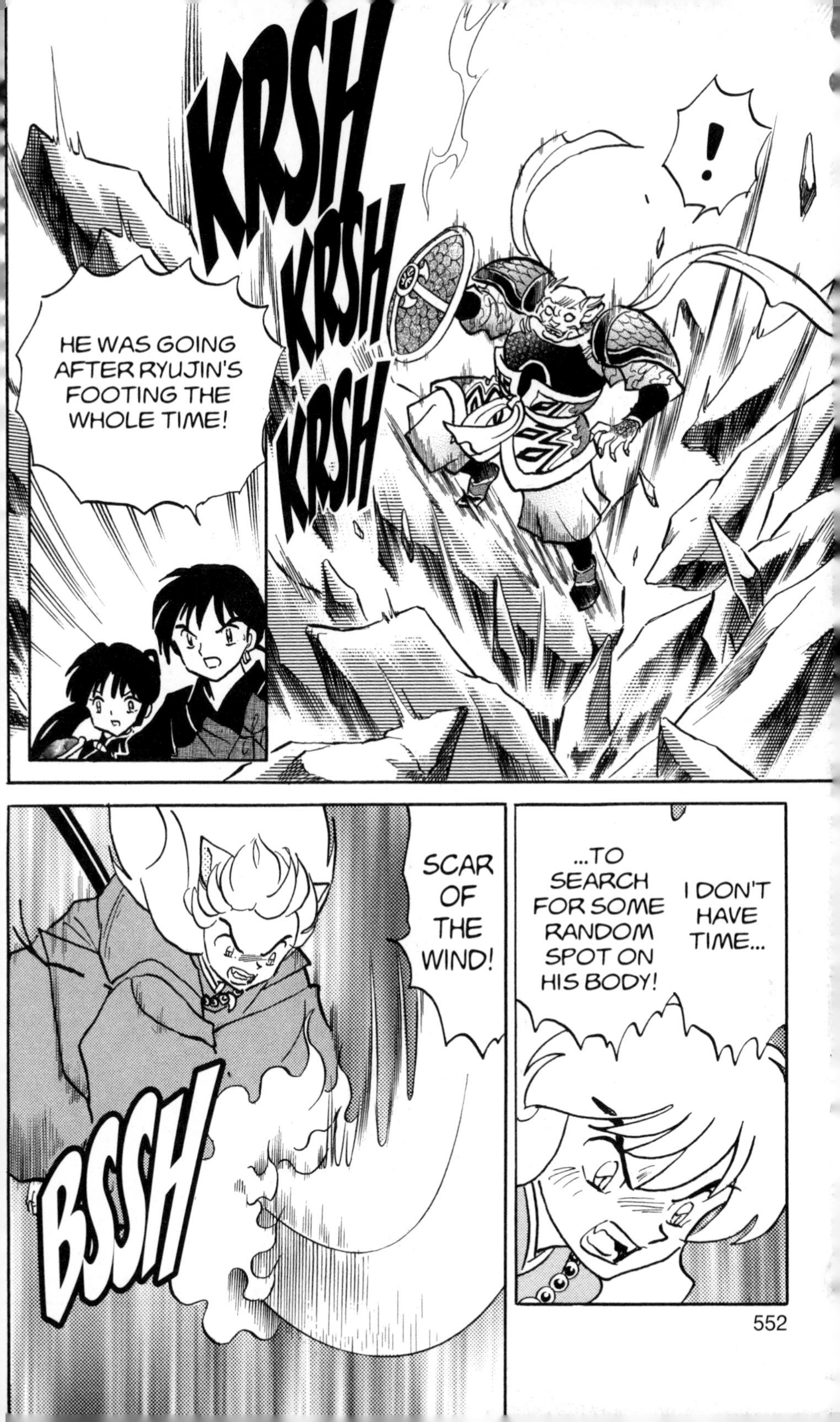
!
KRSH KRSH KRSH
HE WAS GOING AFTER RYUJIN'S FOOTING THE WHOLE TIME!
I DON'T HAVE TIME...
...TO SEARCH FOR SOME RANDOM SPOT ON HIS BODY!
SCAR OF THE WIND!
BSSH

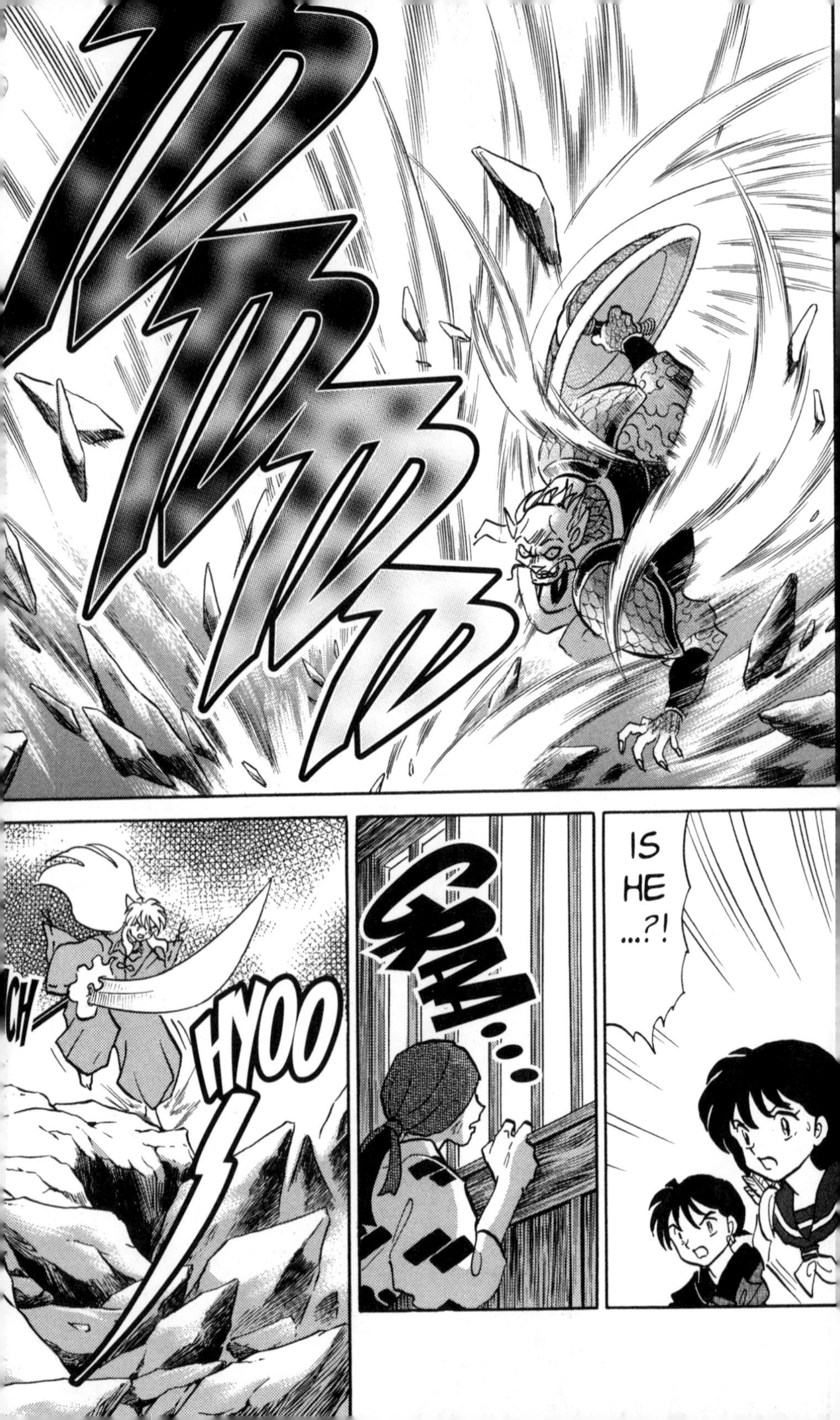
IS HE ...?!
GRAA...
HYOO

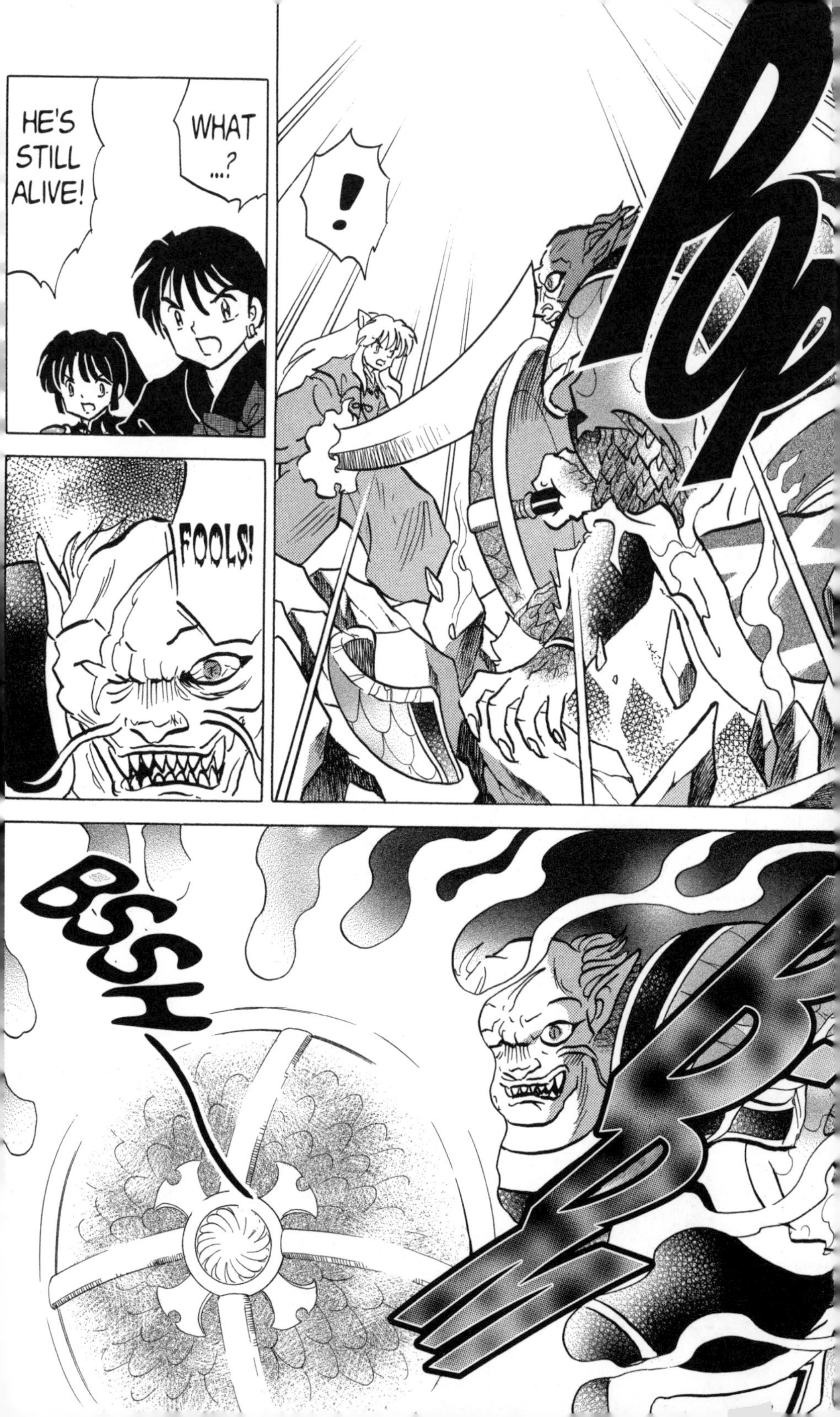
!
WHAT ...?
HE'S STILL ALIVE!
FOOLS!
BSSH

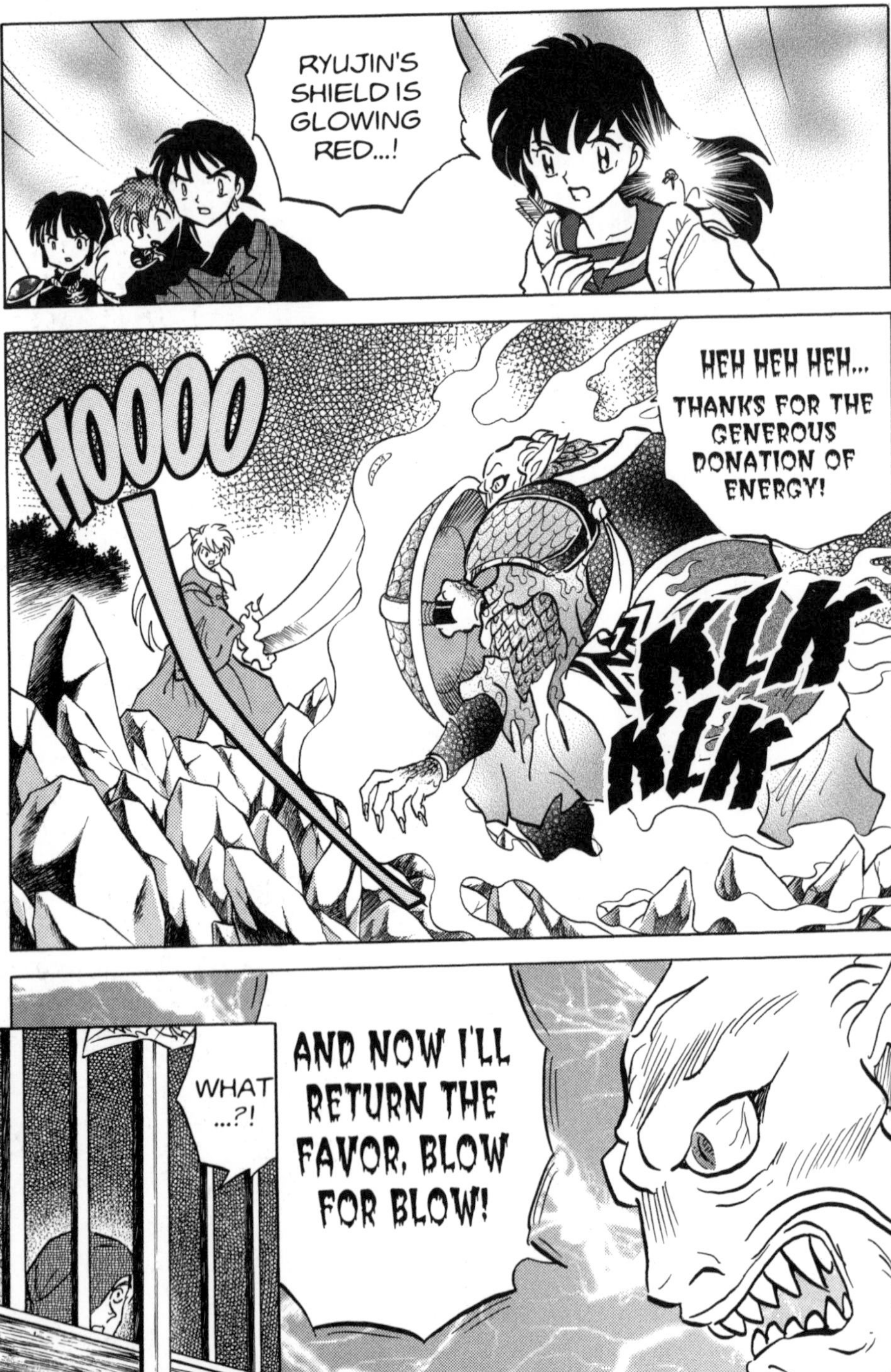
RYUJIN'S SHIELD IS GLOWING RED...!
HEH HEH HEH... THANKS FOR THE GENEROUS DONATION OF ENERGY!
HOOOO
KLIK KLIK
AND NOW I'LL RETURN THE FAVOR, BLOW FOR BLOW!
WHAT ...?!

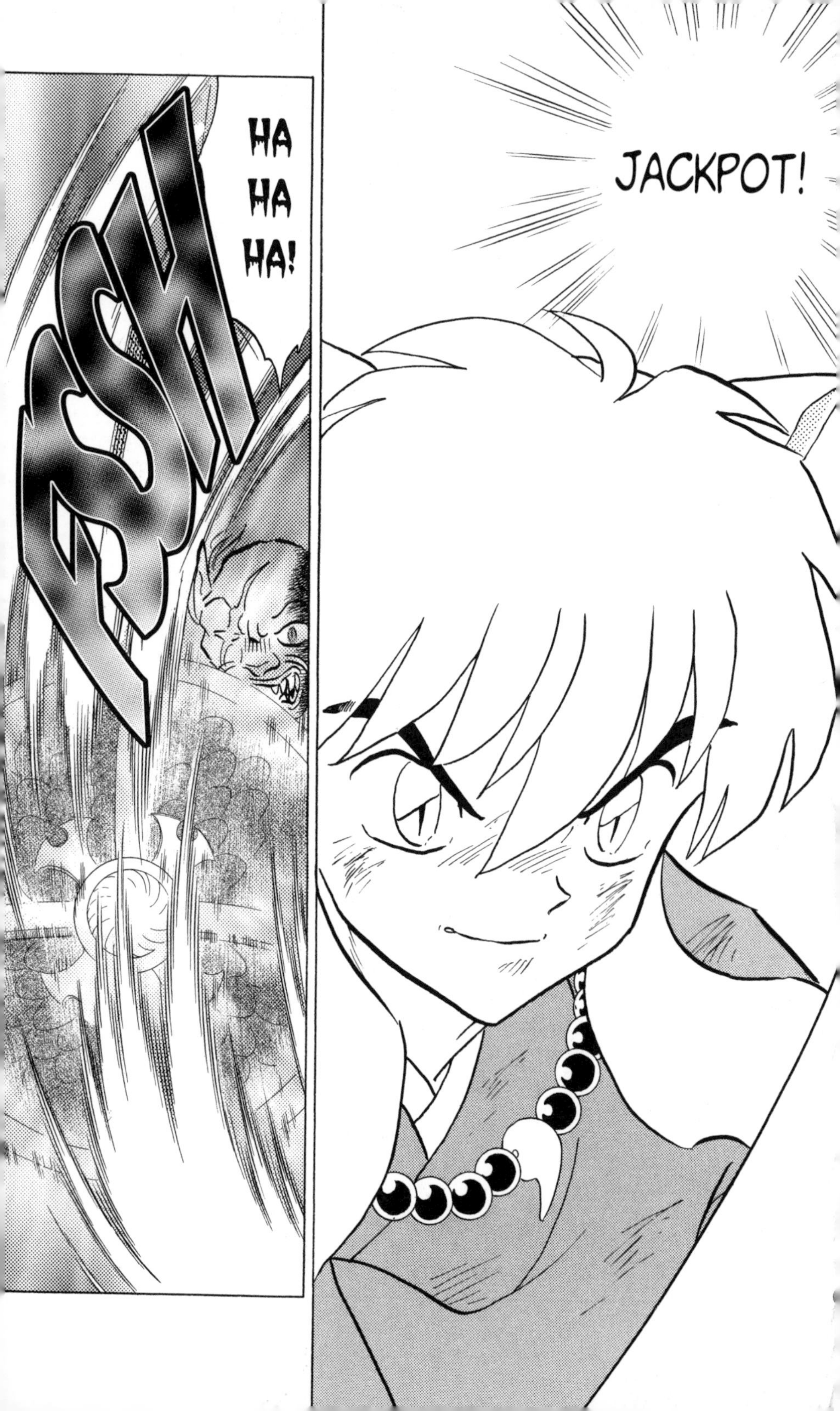
JACKPOT!
HA HA HA!
FSSH

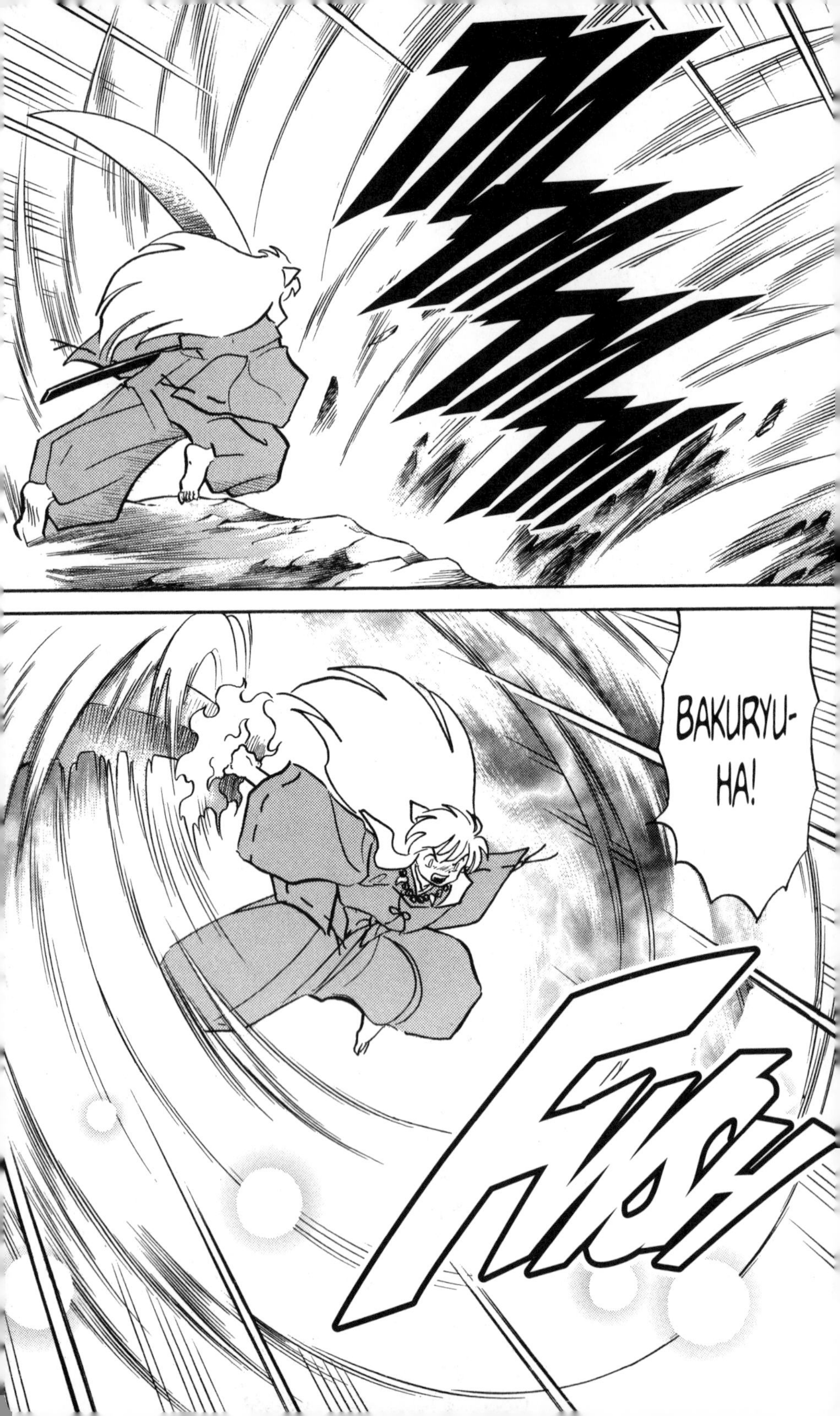
BAKURYU-
HA!

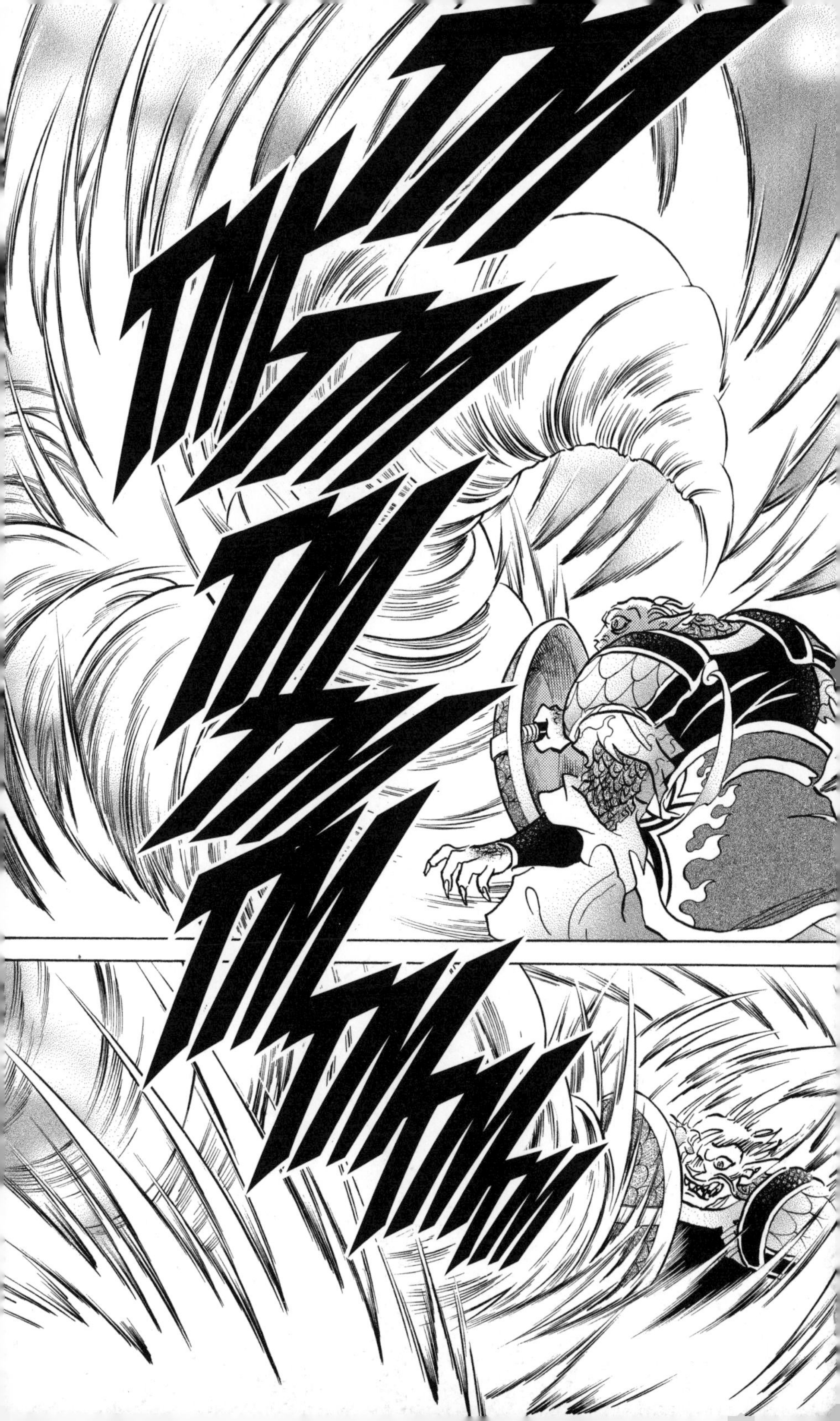

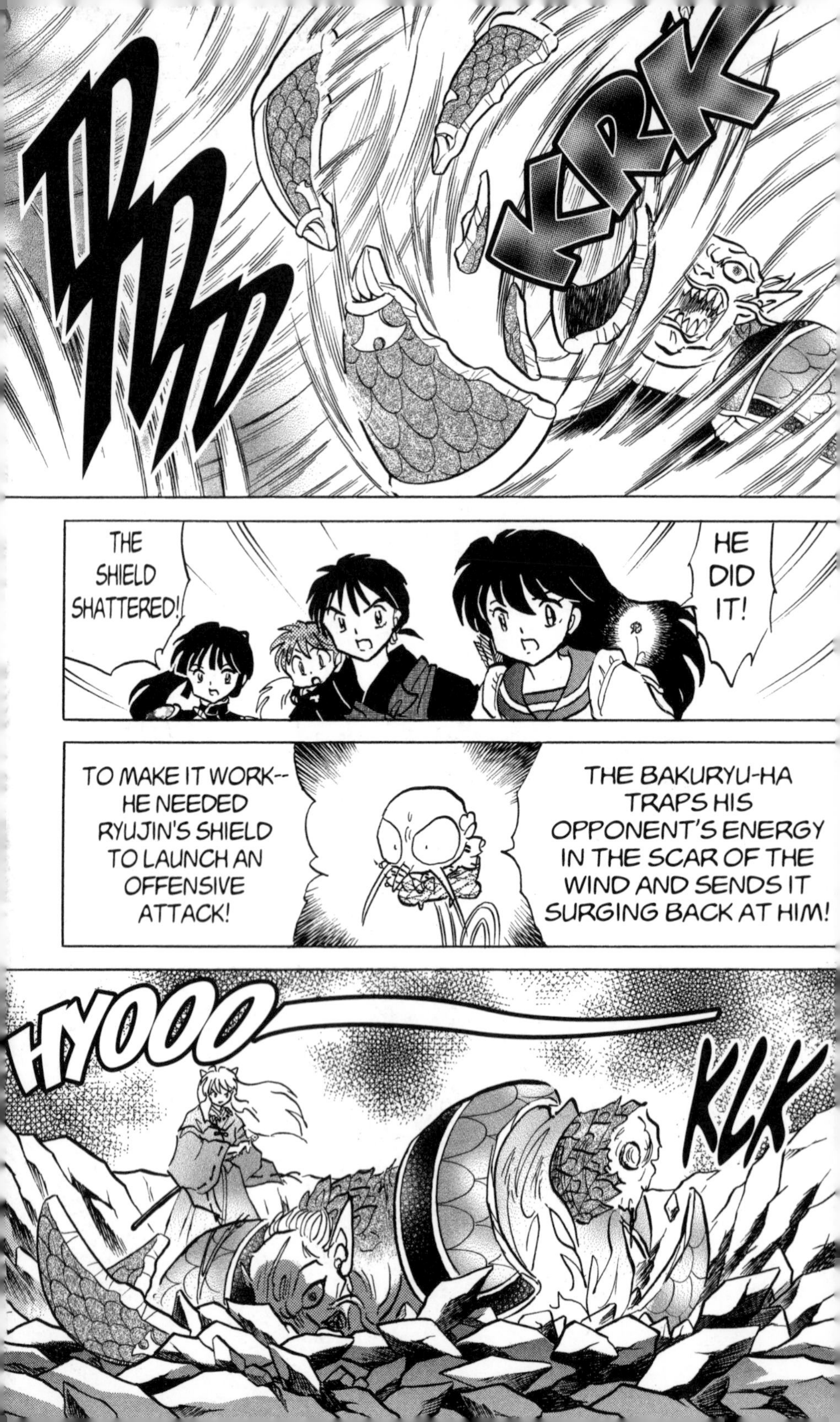
KRK
HE DID IT!
THE SHIELD SHATTERED!
THE BAKURYU-HA TRAPS HIS OPPONENT'S ENERGY IN THE SCAR OF THE WIND AND SENDS IT SURGING BACK AT HIM!
TO MAKE IT WORK-- HE NEEDED RYUJIN'S SHIELD TO LAUNCH AN OFFENSIVE ATTACK!
KLK
HYOOO

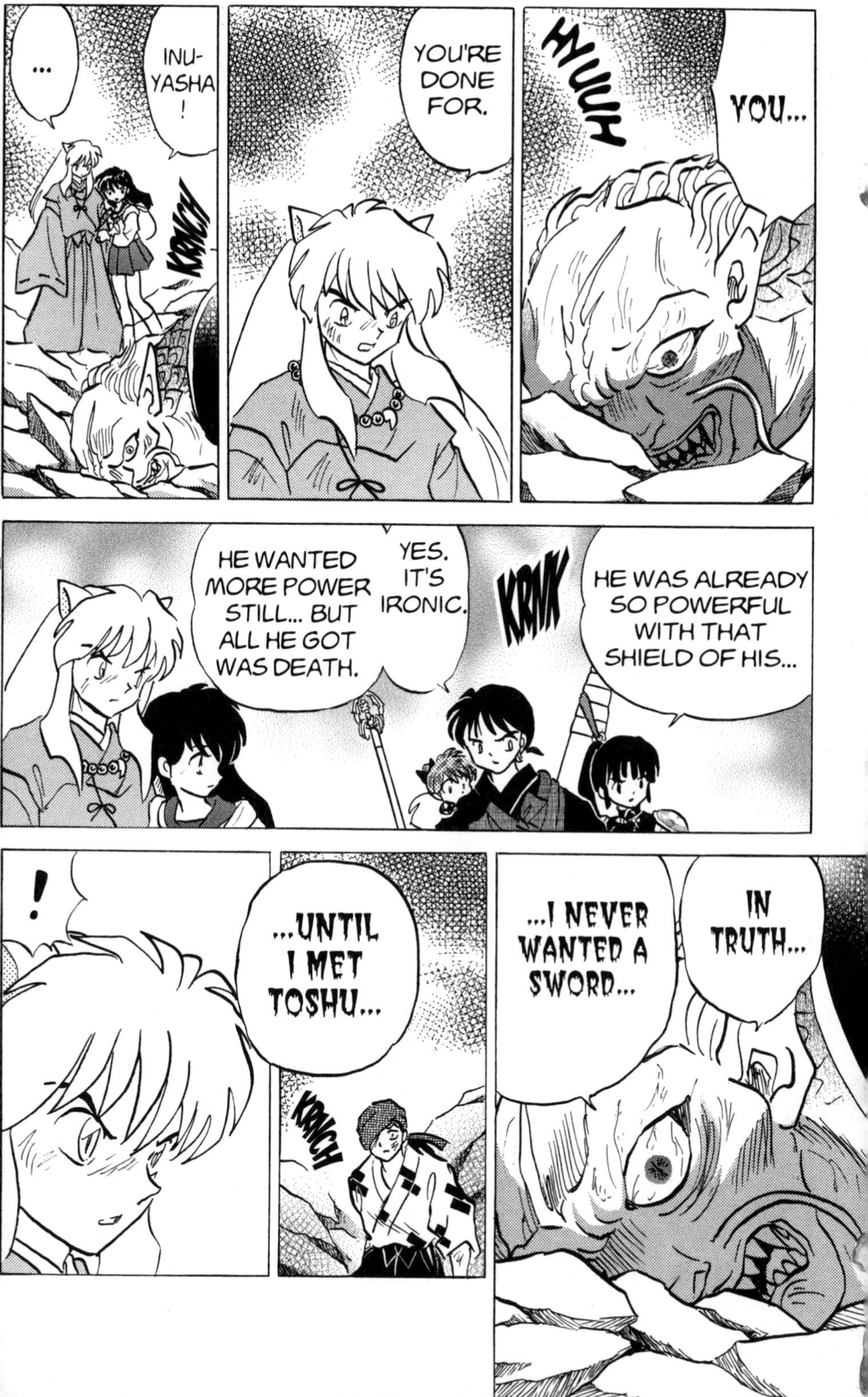
HNUUH
YOU...
YOU'RE DONE FOR.
INU-YASHA!
...
KRNCH
HE WAS ALREADY SO POWERFUL WITH THAT SHIELD OF HIS...
KRNK
YES. IT'S IRONIC.
HE WANTED MORE POWER STILL... BUT ALL HE GOT WAS DEATH.
IN TRUTH...
...I NEVER WANTED A SWORD...
...UNTIL I MET TOSHU...
KRNCH
!

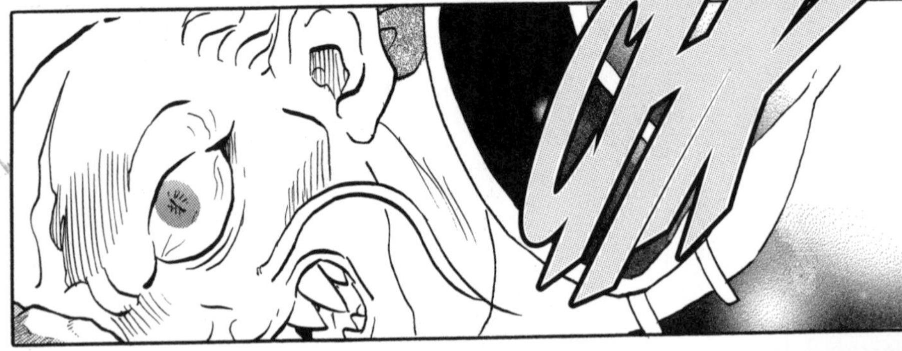

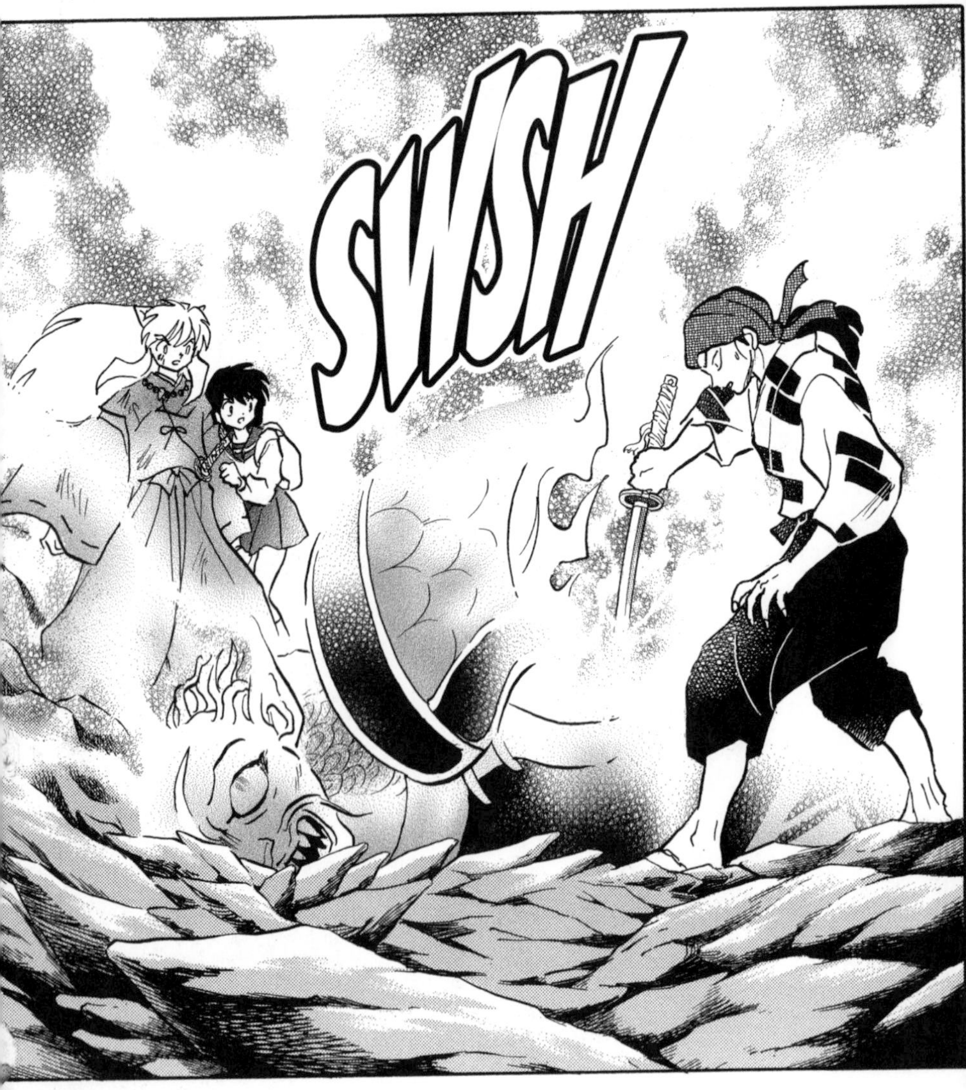
SWISH

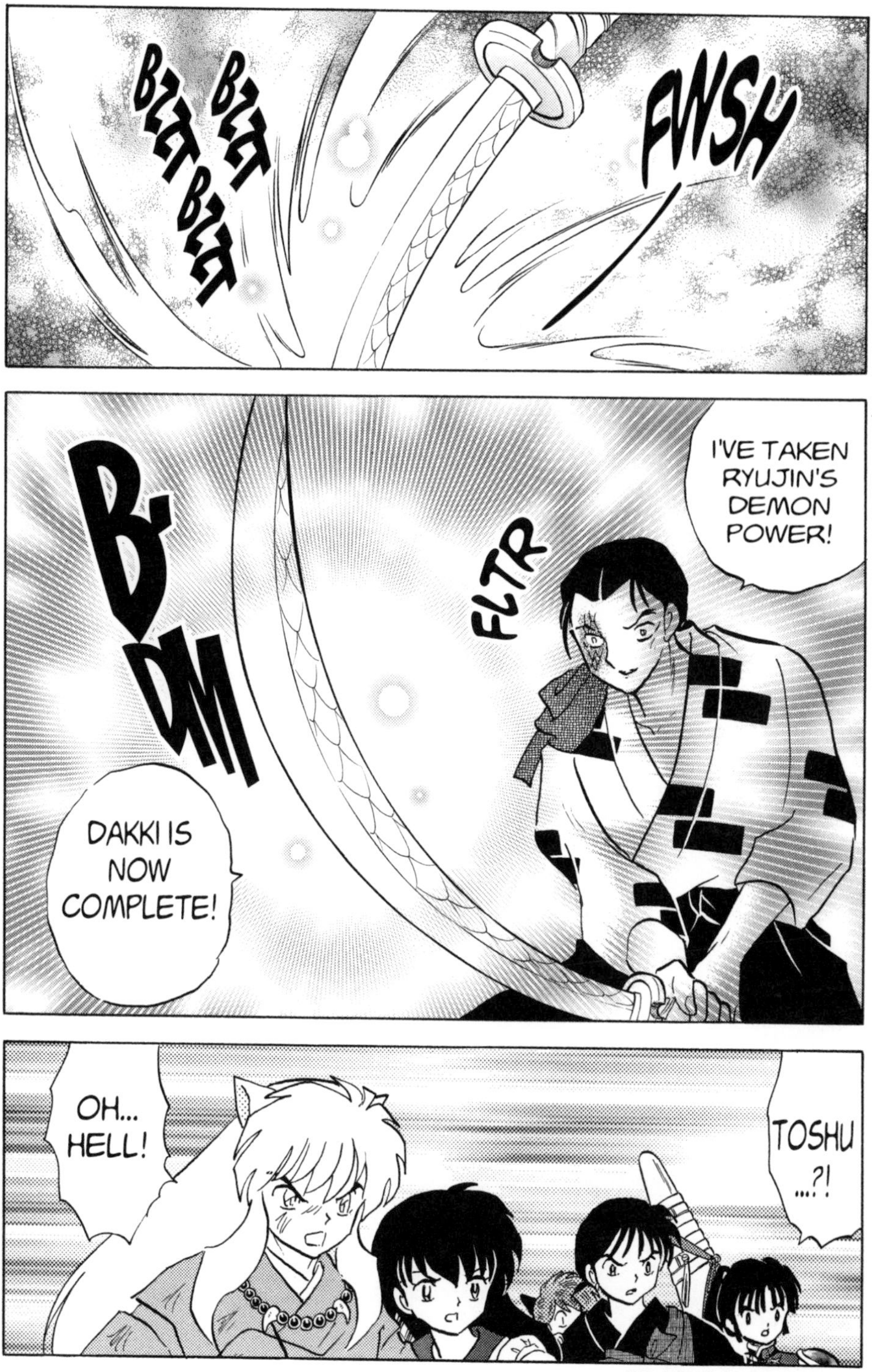
FWSH
BZZT BZZT
BZZT
I'VE TAKEN RYUJIN'S DEMON POWER!
FLTR
B'DMM
DAKKI IS NOW COMPLETE!
TOSHU ...?!
OH... HELL!

TO BE CONTINUED...

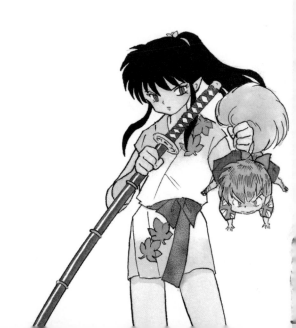

Original Cover Art Gallery

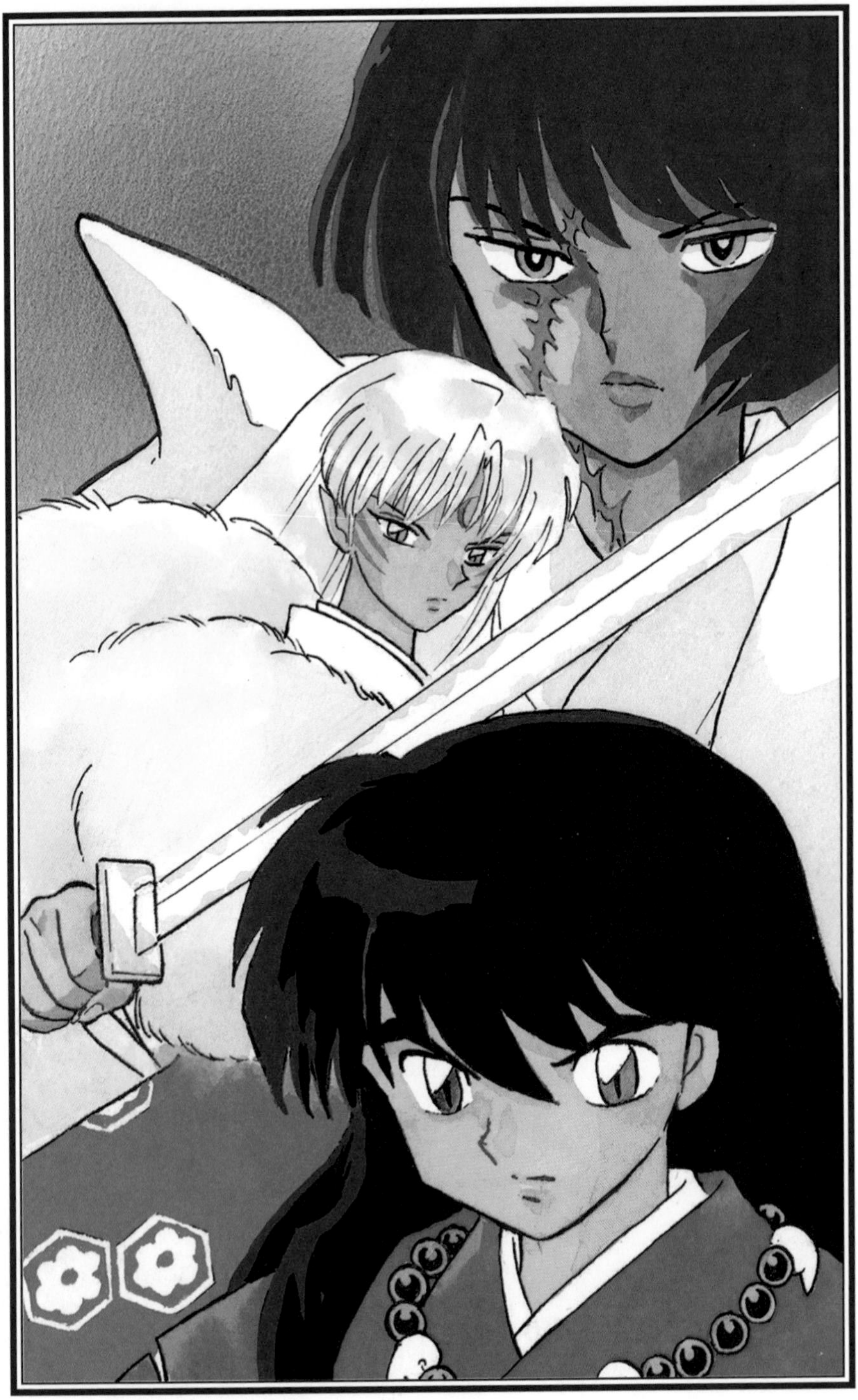

Original cover art from volume 37, published 2009

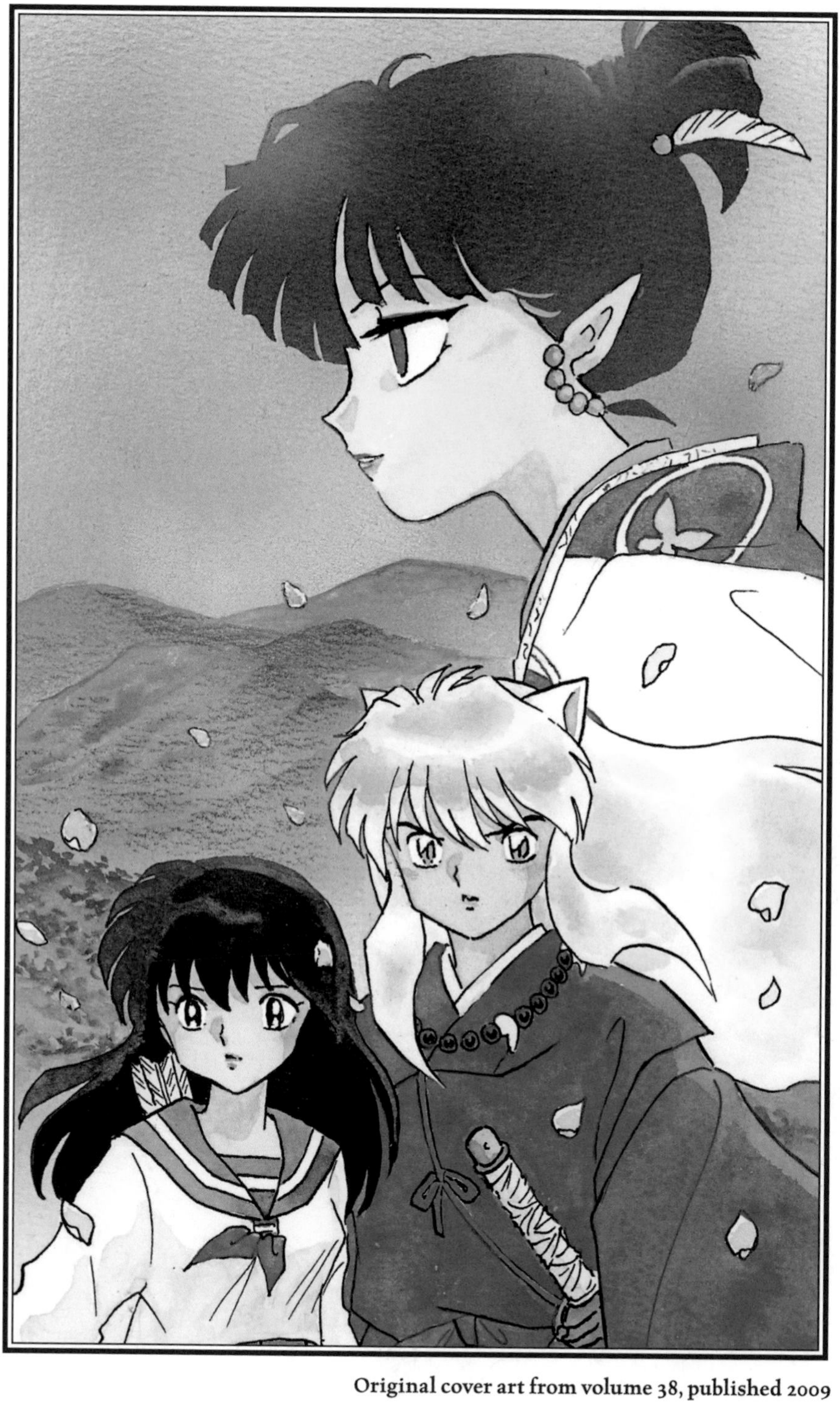

Original cover art from volume 38, published 2009

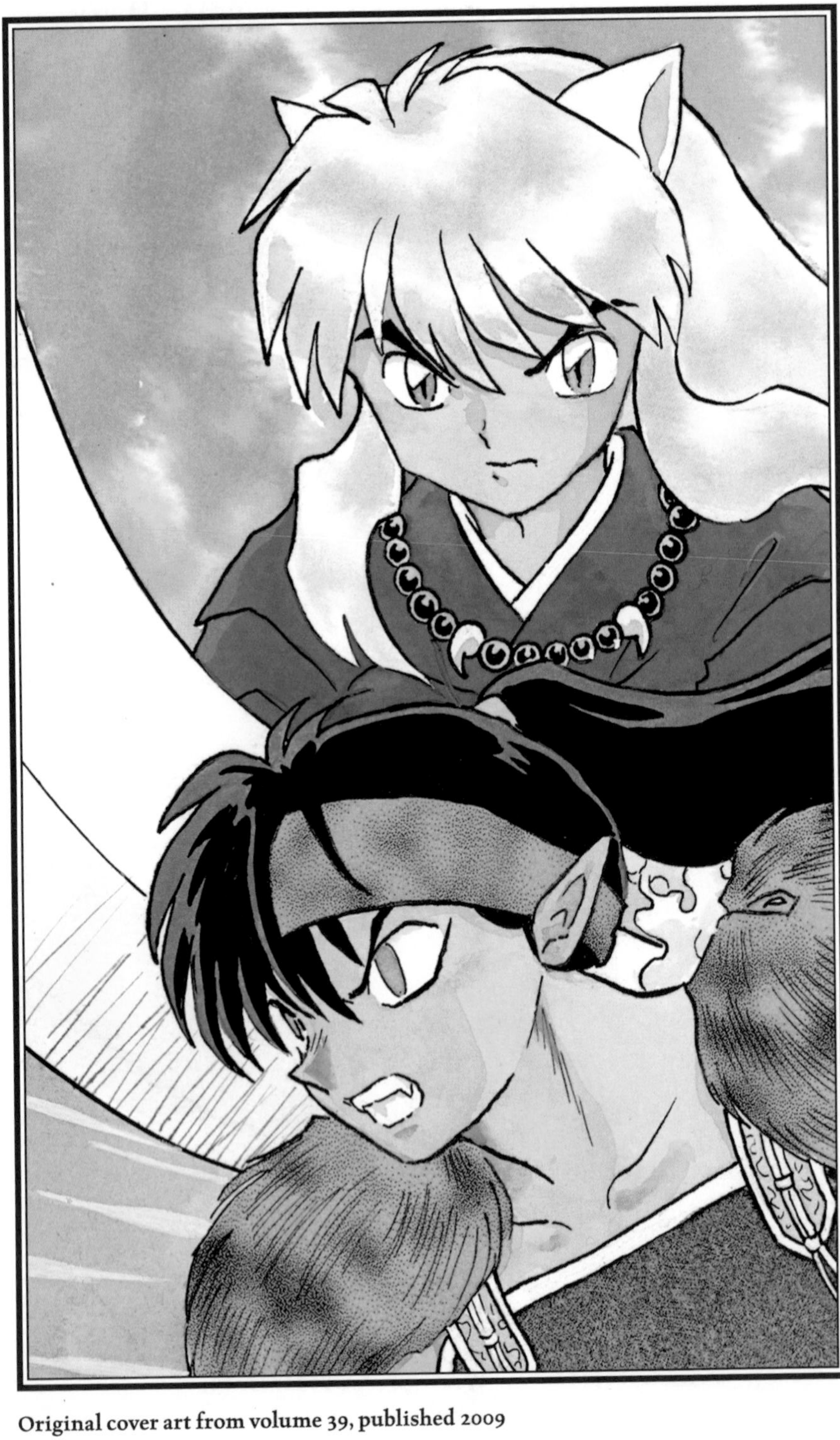

Original cover art from volume 39, published 2009

Coming Next Volume

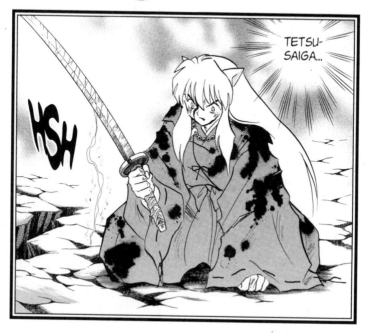

Inuyasha is attacked by a corrupted human wielding a mysterious sword known as "Dakki." If our hero loses this battle, he will lose his mighty sword Tetsusaiga as well! Then, the corpse of the turtle demon Meioju is revived by a piece of Moryomaru's flesh. Meioju's shell is said to be the toughest of any armored demon... Even with the aid of Sesshomaru, does Inuyasha stand a chance of penetrating Meioju's armor?! Finally, a battle with a treacherous tree demon leaves our friends...puzzled. What devious twisted plan is Naraku concocting now...?

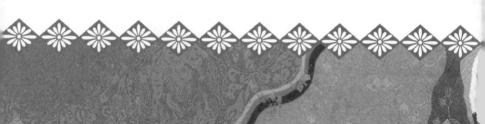

INUYASHA

Volume 13
VIZBIG Edition

Story and Art by RUMIKO TAKAHASHI

© 1997 Rumiko TAKAHASHI/Shogakukan
All rights reserved.
Original Japanese edition "INUYASHA"
published by SHOGAKUKAN Inc.

English Adaptation/Gerard Jones
Translation/Mari Morimoto
Transcription/David Smith
Touch-up Art & Lettering/Steve Dutro, Leonard Clark, Primary Graphix
VIZ Media Series Design/Yuki Ameda
VIZBIG Edition Design/Sam Elzway
VIZ Media Series Editors (VIZ Media/Action Edition)/
Ian Robertson, Shaenon K. Garrity
VIZBIG Edition Editor/Annette Roman

The stories, characters and incidents mentioned in
this publication are entirely fictional.

No portion of this book may be reproduced or transmitted in any form or
by any means without written permission from the copyright holders.

Printed in China

Published by VIZ Media, LLC
P.O. Box 77010
San Francisco, CA 94107

10 9 8 7 6 5 4 3 2 1
First printing, November 2012

PARENTAL ADVISORY
INUYASHA is rated T+ for Older Teen and is
recommended for ages 16 and up. This volume
contains fantasy violence and partial nudity.
ratings.viz.com

www.viz.com

WWW.SHONENSUNDAY.COM

P9-ARX-679

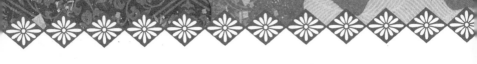

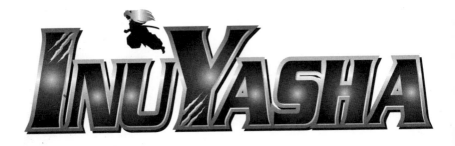

INUYASHA

Story & Art by
Rumiko Takahashi

WITHDRAWN

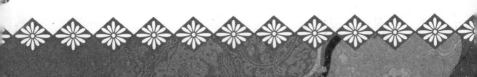